12-07

William Edward Burghardt Du Bois

AFRICANA

The Encyclopedia of the African and African American Experience

The Concise Desk Reference

Praise for the original *Africana*:

"Attractive and well-designed. . . . It is the first reference work I have encountered that is attractive enough and accessible enough to simply pick up, open to any page and start reading. . . . A major achievement."

—The Los Angeles Times Book Review

"For this accessible, fascinating volume, [Gates and Appiah] have commissioned and condensed more than 3000 articles by more than 400 scholars . . . Bursting with information and enhanced by contributions from its illustrious advisory board . . . this book belongs on every family's reference shelf. Du Bois himself could not have done better."

—Starred Publisher's Weekly Review

"A landmark achievement."

—Publisher's Weekly Best Books 99

"An informational jewel."

—Emerge

"The editors have admirably fulfilled the dream of African American scholar and leader W.E.B. Du Bois, who worked for much of his life to create such a monument. Highly recommended reading for all."

—Library Journal

"The best one-volume reference book on Africa and the African diaspora now available . . . Excellent articles . . . remarkably up to date."

—The Philadelphia Inquirer

"*Africana* holds a unique place among reference works by bridging the Atlantic in numerous ways . . . the strength of *Africana's* unique linkage of the African and African-American becomes evident in comparison to other reference works treating one or the other half of that whole . . . *Africana* includes unique entries not found in the African American Almanac (Gale, 1997), An African Biographical Dictionary (ABC-CLIO, 1994), Encyclopedia of African American Culture & History (Macmillan 1996) to cite but a few prominent examples."

—Booklist

"Imposing in its sheer mass, *Africana* . . . is a 2,096-page, single volume 'encyclopedia of the black world.' This is no overstatement, as the range of entries ably demonstrates."

—Vibe

"Complete, balanced, informative, and addictively fun to browse."

—*Boston Magazine*

"A source of information that would surely make Du Bois proud."

—*The Tampa Tribune*

"Editors Henry Louis Gates and Kwame Anthony Appiah fulfilled W.E.B. Du Bois' vision on an encyclopedia of African-based culture throughout the world. The scholarship is unassailable [and] the text is accessible and understandable."

—*The Seattle Times*

"An invaluable resource of the historical, social, and cultural lushness of a scattered and varied people . . . Deserve[s] a place in every library, in every heart."

—*The Miami Herald*

"Belongs in every student's library and school . . . A monumental record of the black experience."

—*The Baltimore Sun*

"As the second millennium ends and a third begins, a new landmark volume brings together the richness and history of African and African-American culture."

—*Beyond the Cover*

"A monumental reference work, brings the richness of African and African American culture out of the shadows and into the living rooms of families across America . . . Destined to have a major effect by filling a cultural void . . . *Africana* presents exacting scholarship in an accessible, entertaining and visually animated style . . . conveys the richness, variety, and sweep of the African and African American experience as no other project before it . . . A reference work of both range and depth that symbolically will reunite the richly varied strands of the African Diaspora."

—*The Portland Skanner*

"A long-awaited overview of the history of the peoples of Africa and the African diaspora."

—*Wall Street Journal*

"*Africana* will be a very useful tool, and may even set new standards and change attitudes about the African and African-American experience."

—*The New York Times Book Review*

AFRICANA

*The Encyclopedia of the African
and African American Experience*

The Concise Desk Reference

Editors

Kwame Anthony Appiah, *Princeton University*
Henry Louise Gates, Jr., *Harvard University*

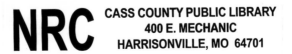
RUNNING PRESS
PHILADELPHIA · LONDON

Copyright © 2003 by Kwame Anthony Appiah and Henry Louis Gates, Jr.

All rights reserved under the Pan-American and International Copyright Conventions
Printed in the United States

*This book may not be reproduced in whole or in part, in any form or by any means, electronic or
mechanical, including photocopying, recording, or by any information storage and retrieval system
now known or hereafter invented, without written permission from the publisher.*

9   8   7   6   5   4   3   2
Digit on the right indicates the number of this printing

Library of Congress Control Number: 2003105522

ISBN-13 978-0-7624-1642-4
ISBN-10 0-7624-1642-4

Cover design by Bill Jones, adapted from the design for the original *Africana* by Bruce W. Bond.
Interior design by Bob Anderson
Edited by Veronica Mixon, Carole Verona, and Deborah Grandinetti
Typography: 9.5/11.5 Berling Roman

An expanded version of the entries in *Africana: The Concise Desk Reference* originally appeared in
Basic Civitas Books' *Africana: The Encyclopedia of the African and the African American Experience*
© 1999 Kwame Anthony Appiah and Henry Louis Gates, Jr.

This book may be ordered by mail from the publisher.
Please include $2.50 for postage and handling.
But try your bookstore first!

Running Press Book Publishers
125 South Twenty-second Street
Philadelphia, Pennsylvania 19103-4399

Visit us on the web!
www.runningpress.com

*To the memory of William Edward Burghardt Du Bois
and in honor of Nelson Rolihlahla Mandela*

Advisory Board

Table of Contents

Introduction

Editor's Note on this Edition: *Africana: The Concise Desk Reference* was abridged from *Africana: The Encyclopedia of the African and African American Experience*. Some of the entries are accompanied by all new photographs. Credit goes to Veronica Mixon for distilling the very best of the original *Africana* into this more portable, compact desk reference. While all of the charts and graphs were published in the original edition, there are some new photographs in this edition.

The history of how the original *Africana* came to be is a poignant story of faith, politics, and persistence despite what seemed, at times, like an insurmountable struggle. Kwame Anthony Appiah, and Henry Louis Gates, Jr., editors of that original edition, told the story in its introduction. We've chosen to reprint that introduction in this edition, to help you appreciate the struggle that gave birth to *Africana* and the editorial decisions that shaped it.

May the story hearten you as you advance toward your own dreams.

How the original *Africana* Came to Be

Between 1909 and his death in 1963, W. E. B. Du Bois, the Harvard-trained historian, sociologist, journalist, and political activist, dreamed of editing an "Encyclopedia Africana." He envisioned a comprehensive compendium of 'scientific' knowledge about the history, cultures, and social institutions of people of African descent: of Africans in the Old World, African Americans in the New World, and persons of African descent who had risen to prominence in Europe, the Middle East, and Asia. Du Bois sought to publish nothing less than the equivalent of a black *Encyclopedia Britannica*, believing that such a broad assemblage of biography, interpretive essays, facts, and figures would do for the much denigrated black world of the twentieth century what *Britannica* and Denis Diderot's *Encyclopédie* had done for the European world of the eighteenth century.

These publications, which consolidated the scholarly knowledge accumulated by academics and intellectuals in the Age of Reason, served both as a tangible sign of the enlightened skepticism that characterized that era of scholarship, and as a basis upon which further scholarship could be constructed. These encyclopedias became monuments to "scientific" inquiry, bulwarks against superstition, myth, and what their authors viewed as the false solace of religious faith. An encyclopedia of the African diaspora in Du Bois's view would achieve these things for persons of African descent.

But a black encyclopedia would have an additional function. Its publication would, at least symbolically, unite the fragmented world of the African diaspora, a diaspora created by the European slave trade and the turn-of-the-century "scramble for Africa." Moreover, for Du Bois, marshalling the tools of "scientific knowledge," as he would put it in his landmark essay, "The Need for an Encyclopedia of the Negro" (1945), could also serve as a weapon in the war against racism: "There is need for young pupils and for mature students of a statement of the present condition of our knowledge concerning the darker races and especially concerning Negroes, which would make available our present scientific knowledge and set aside the vast accumulation of tradition and prejudice which makes such knowledge difficult now for the layman to obtain: A Vade mecum for American schools, editors, libraries, for Europeans inquiring into the race status here, for South Americans, and Africans."

The publication of such an encyclopedia, Du Bois continued, would establish "a base for further advance and further study" of "questions affecting the Negro race." An encyclopedia of the Negro, he reasoned, would establish both social policy and "social thought and discussion . . . upon a basis of accepted scientific conclusion."

Du Bois first announced his desire to edit an "Encyclopedia Africana" in a letter to Edward Wilmot Blyden, the Pan-Africanist intellectual, in Sierra Leone in 1909: "I am venturing to address you on the subject of a Negro Encyclopædia. In celebration of the 50th anniversary of the Emancipation of the American Negro, I am proposing to bring out an Encyclopedia Africana covering the chief points in the history and condition of the Negro race." Du Bois sent a similar letter to dozens of other scholars, white and black, including William James, Hugo Munsterberg, George Santayana, Albert Bushnell Hart (his professors at Harvard), President Charles William Eliot of Harvard, Sir Harry Johnston, Sir Flinders Petrie, Giuseppe Sergi, Franz Boas, J. E. Casely-Hayford, John Hope, Kelly Miller, Benjamin Brawley, Anna Jones, Richard Greener, Henry Ossawa Tanner, and several others, all of whom—with the sole exception of President Eliot—agreed to serve on his editorial board. Du Bois sought to create a board of "One Hundred Negro Americans, African and West Indian Scholars," as he put it in a letter, and a second board of white advisors. Du Bois, in other words, sought the collaboration of the very best scholars of what we would call today African Studies and African American Studies, as well as prominent American and European intellectuals such as James and Boas.

Nevertheless, as he put it to Blyden, "the real work I want done by Negroes." Du Bois, admitting that this plan was "still in embryo," created official stationery that projected a publication date of the first volume in 1913—"the Jubilee of Emancipation in America and the Tercentenary of the Landing of the Negro." The remaining four volumes would be published between 1913 and 1919.

Despite the nearly unanimous enthusiasm that greeted Du Bois's call for participation, he could not secure the necessary funding to mount the massive effort necessary to edit an encyclopedia of the black world. But he never abandoned the idea. At the height of the Great Depression, the idea would surface once again.

Anson Phelps Stokes, head of the Phelps-Stokes Association, a foundation dedicated to ameliorating race relations in America, called a meeting of 20 scholars and public figures at Howard University on November 7, 1931, to edit an "Encyclopedia of the Negro," a Pan-African encyclopedia similar to Du Bois's 1909 project. Incredibly, neither Du Bois nor Alain Locke, a Harvard trained Ph.D. in philosophy and the dean of the Harlem Renaissance, nor Carter G. Woodson (like Du Bois, a Harvard Ph.D. in history and the founder of the Association for the Study of Negro Life and History) was invited to attend. Du Bois protested, angrily, to Phelps Stokes. A second meeting was convened on January 9, 1932, at which Du Bois was unanimously elected editor-in-chief. Between 1932 and 1946, Du Bois would serve as "Editor-in-Chief" of the second incarnation of his project, now named "The Encyclopædia of the Negro," and housed at 200 West 135th Street in New York City.

Du Bois planned a four-volume encyclopedia, each volume comprising 500,000 words. Just as he had done in 1909, he secured the cooperation of an impressive array of scholars, including Charles Beard, Franz Boas, John R. Connors, Edith Abbott, Felix Frankfurter, Otto Klineburg, Carl Van Doren, H. L. Mencken, Roscoe Pound, Robert E. Park, Sidney Hook, Harold Laski, Broadus Mitchell, "and scores of others," as Du Bois put it in a letter to the historian Charles Wesley. Du Bois's "Encyclopedia of the Negro" would require a budget of $225,000. It would be written by a staff of between "25 and 100 persons" hired to be "research aides," to be located in editorial offices to be established in New York, Chicago, Atlanta, and New Orleans. They would prepare bibliographies, collect books and manuscripts, and gather and write "special data" and shorter entries. Black and white scholars, primarily located in Europe, America, and Africa, would write longer interpretive entries.

Du Bois tells us that his project was interrupted by the Depression for three years. But by 1935, he was actively engaged in its planning full-time, time made available by his forced resignation from his position as editor of *The Crisis* magazine, the official organ of the National Association for the Advancement of Colored People, which Du Bois had held since its first publication in 1910. Du Bois had written an editorial advocating the development of independent Negro social and economic institutions, since the goal posts of the Civil Rights Movement appeared to be receding. The NAACP's board of directors was outraged and demanded his resignation. Du Bois obliged. Du Bois sought funding virtually everywhere, including the Works Progress Administration and the Federal Writers' Project, to no avail, despite the fact that Phelps Stokes had pledged, on a matching basis, half of the needed funds. He continued to write to hundreds of scholars, soliciting their cooperation. E. Franklin Frazier, the great black sociologist, declined Du Bois's overture, citing in a letter dated November 7, 1936, the presence of too many "politicians," "statesmen," "big Negroes," and "whites of good will" on Du Bois's editorial board. Throw out the table of contents, fire the board of editors, replace them with scholars, Frazier wrote, and he would consider joining the project.

A few months before this exchange, Du Bois was viciously attacked by Carter G. Woodson in the black newspaper the *Baltimore Afro-American.* On May 30, 1936, a page-one headline blared the news that Woodson "Calls Du Bois a Traitor if He Accepts Post," with a subtitle adding for good measure: "He Told Ofays, We'd Write Own History." Woodson charged that Du Bois had stolen the idea of *The Encyclopedia of the Negro* from him and that his project was doomed to failure because Du Bois was financed by, and his editorial board included, white people. Du Bois was embarrassed and sought to defend himself in letters to potential contributors and board members. Between his enemies at the NAACP and his intellectual rivals such as Woodson and Frazier, Du Bois faced an enormous amount of opposition to his encyclopedia project. In this swirl of controversy, in the midst of the Depression, funding appeared increasingly elusive.

Du Bois's assistant editor, Rayford Logan, like Du Bois, Woodson, and Charles Wesley a Harvard-trained Ph.D. in history, told a poignant story about the failure of this project to receive funding. By 1937, Du Bois had secured a pledge of $125,000 from the Phelps-Stokes Fund to proceed with his project—half of the funds needed to complete it. He applied to the Carnegie Corporation for the remaining half of his budget, with the strong endorsement of Phelps Stokes and the president of the General Education Board, a group of four or five private foundations that included the Rocke-feller Foundation. So convinced was Du Bois that his project would finally be funded, that he invited Logan to wait with him for the telephone call that he had been promised immediately following the Carnegie board meeting. A bottle of vintage champagne sat chilling on Du Bois's desk in a silver bucket, two cut crystal champagne flutes resting nearby.

The phone never rang. Persuaded that Du Bois was far too "radical" to serve as a model of disinterested scholarship, and lobbied by Du Bois's intellectual enemies, such as the anthropologist Melville J. Herskovits, the Carnegie Corporation rejected the project.

Nevertheless, Du Bois stubbornly persisted, even publishing two puta-tive "entries" from the *Encyclopædia* in *Phylon* magazine in 1940, one on Robert Russa Moton, the principal of Tuskegee Institute between 1915 and 1935, the other on Alexander Pushkin. He even was able to publish two editions, in 1945 and 1946, of a *Preparatory Volume with Reference Lists and Reports of the Encyclopædia of the Negro.* But the project itself never could secure adequate backing.

David Levering Lewis, Du Bois's biographer, tells us what happened to Du Bois's promised funding. The executive committee of the General Edu-cation Board rejected the proposal early in May 1937. "In his conference a few days later with Carnegie Corporation president Frederick Keppel, GEB's Jackson Davis paradoxically pleaded for favorable Carnegie consider-ation of the project. 'Dr. Du Bois is the most influential Negro in the United States,' Davis reminded Keppel. 'This project would keep him busy for the rest of his life.' Predictably, Carnegie declined. Within a remarkably short time, the study of the Negro (generously underwritten by the

Carnegie Corporation) found a quite different direction under a Swedish scholar then unknown in the field of race relations, one whose understanding of American race problems was to be distinctly more psychological and less economic than was Du Bois's. . . . When the president of the Phelps Stokes Fund wrote Du Bois in 1944 at the time of the publication of *An American Dilemma: [The Negro Problem and Modern Democracy]* that 'there has been no one who has been quite so often quoted by [Gunnar] Myrdal than yourself,' Du Bois must have savored the irony."

Adding insult to injury, in 1948 the General Education Board, along with the Dodd Mead publishing company, approached Frederick Patterson, the president of Tuskegee Institute, to edit a new incarnation of the project, to be entitled *The Negro: An Encyclopedia.* Then in 1950, the historian Charles Wesley wrote to Du Bois, informing him that in the wake of Carter Woodson's death, the Association for the Study of Negro Life and History had decided to resurrect *The Encyclopedia Africana* project, reminding him of Woodson's claims to have conceived of it in 1921. Du Bois wished him well, but cautioned him in a postscript that "there is no such thing as a cheap encyclopedia." Everyone, it seemed, wanted to claim title to the encyclopedia, but no one wanted Du Bois to serve as its editor. For black scholars, Africana had become the Grail. Its publication, as Du Bois put it "would mark an epoch."

Long after Du Bois had abandoned all hope of realizing his great ambition, an offer of assistance would come quite unexpectedly from Africa. On September 26, 1960, Du Bois announced that Kwame Nkrumah, the president of the newly independent Republic of Ghana, had invited him to repatriate to Ghana, where he would serve as the editor-in-chief of *The Encyclopædia Africana.* Du Bois accepted, moving in 1961. On December 15, 1962, in his last public speech before his death on the eve of the March on Washington in August 1963, Du Bois addressed a conference assembled expressly to launch—at last—his great project.

He wanted to edit "an Encyclopædia Africana based in Africa and compiled by Africans," he announced, an encyclopedia that is "long overdue," referring no doubt to his previously frustrated attempts. "Yet," he continued with a certain grim satisfaction, "it is logical that such a work had to wait for independent Africans to carry it out [because] the encyclopedia is concerned with Africa as a whole." Citing his own introductory essay in the *Preparatory Volume* of 1945, Du Bois justified this project by railing against "present thought and action" that "are all too often guided by old and discarded theories of race and heredity, by misleading emphasis and silence of former histories." After all of these centuries of slavery and colonialism, on the eve of the independence of the Continent, "it is African scholars themselves who will create the ultimate *Encyclopædia Africana.*" Eight months later Du Bois would be dead, and with him died his 54-year-old dream of shepherding a great black encyclopedia into print. Nevertheless, the Secretariat of the *Encyclopædia Africana*, based in Accra, Ghana, which Du Bois founded, eventually published three volumes of biographical dictionaries, in the late seventies and early eighties, and has recently announced plans to publish an encyclopedia about the African continent in 2009, which is welcome news.

We first became enamored of this project as students at the University of Cambridge. One of us, Henry Louis Gates, Jr., was a student of Wole Soyinka, the great playwright who in 1986 became the first African to receive the Nobel Prize for Literature. The other, Kwame Anthony Appiah, was an undergraduate studying philosophy. Though we came from very different backgrounds—rural West Virginia and urban Asante, in Ghana— we both already had, like Soyinka, a sense of the worlds of Africa and her diaspora as profoundly interconnected, even if, as we learned ourselves, there were risks of misunderstanding that arose from our different origins and experiences. The three of us represented three different places in the black world, and we vowed in 1973 to edit a Pan-African encyclopedia of the African diaspora, inspired by Du Bois's original objective formulated in 1909. Du Bois's later conception of the project was, we felt, too narrow in its scope, and too parochial in its stated desire to exclude the scholarly work of those who had not had the good fortune, by accident of birth, to have been born on the African continent. (Du Bois himself, had this rule been literally applied, would have been excluded from his own project!) Instead, we sought to edit a project that would produce a genuine compendium of "Africana."

Our own attempts to secure the necessary support were in vain too until four years ago when, first, Quincy Jones and Martin Payson, and then Sonny Mehta and Alberto Vitale at Random House, agreed to fund the preparation of a prototype of a CD-ROM encyclopedia of the African diaspora, to be edited by us, with Soyinka serving as the chair of an international and multiethnic board of editors. Two years later we secured the support for a 2-million-word encyclopedia from Frank Pearl, the CEO of a new publisher called Perseus Books, and from the Microsoft Corporation. Modifying the editorial structure that Du Bois planned to use to complete *The Encyclopædia of the Negro*, we deployed a staff of some three dozen writers and editors, and we solicited about 400 scholars to write longer, interpretive articles.

Du Bois's own idea, although he did not admit this, probably arose at least in part out of the publication of the *Encyclopædia Judaica* in 1907, as well as black encyclopedia antecedents such as James T. Holly, who published *The Afro-American Encyclopedia* in 1895, Alexander W. Wayman's *Cyclopedia of African Methodism* (1882), Charles O. Boothe's *The Cyclopedia of the Colored Baptists of Alabama* (1895), and Revels Adams's *Cyclopedia of African Methodism in Mississippi* (1902). Other unpublished projects patterned after Du Bois's 1909 proposal included Daniel Murray's monumental "Historical and Biographical Encyclopædia of the Colored Race Throughout the World," which was to have been published in 1912 in six volumes and, later, Edward Garrett's self-written "A Negro Encyclopedia," consisting of 4000 entries, and completed on the eve of World War II. Both encyclopedias exist in manuscript form, but tragically were never published. All told, more than two dozen black encyclopedias have been published in the past century with limited distribution, but none has explored in a single compass both the African continent and the triumphs and the tragedies of Africa's people and their descendants around the globe.

That continent is where human prehistory begins. It was in Africa, as biologists now believe, that our species evolved, and so, in a literal sense, every modern human being is of African descent. Indeed, it was probably only about 100,000 years ago that the first members of our species left Africa, traveled across the Suez Peninsula, and set out on an adventure that would lead to the peopling of the whole earth.

It is important to emphasize that Africa has never been separate from the rest of the human world. There have been long periods and many cultures that knew nothing of life in Africa. For much of African history, even in Africa, most Africans were unaware of other peoples in their own continent, unaware, in fact, that they shared a continent at all (just as most people in Europe, Asia, Australasia, and the Americas would have been astonished to learn that they were Europeans, Asians, Australasians, or Americans!). But the Straits of Gibraltar and the Suez Peninsula were always bridges more than obstacles to travel; the Mediterranean was already a system of trade long before the founding of Rome; the Sahara Desert, which so many people imagine as an impenetrable barrier, has a network of trade routes older than the Roman Empire. Starting some 2,000 or so years ago, in the area of modern day Cameroon, Bantu-speaking migrants fanned out south and east into tropical Africa, taking with them the knowledge of iron smelting and new forms of agriculture. And so, when Greek and Arab travelers explored the East Coast of Africa in the first millennium C.E., or European explorers began to travel down the West African coast toward the equator in the fifteenth century, they were making direct contact with cultures with which their ancestors had very often been in remote and indirect contact all along.

The first European scholars to write about Africa in the modern period, which begins with the European Age of Discovery, knew very little of Africa's history. They did not know that their ancestors thousands of generations ago had also lived in Africa. If they had read Herodotus, they might have noticed his brief discussion of the civilizations of the upper Nile, and so they might have realized that Egypt was in touch with other African societies. However, it would probably not have occurred to them that, since those societies were also in touch with still others, Egypt was in touch with Central Africa as well. So they thought of much of Africa as being outside the human historical narrative they already knew.

These first scholars were also obviously struck by the physical differences between Africans and themselves—especially of skin color and hair—and by the differences between the customs back home and the ones the European explorers found on the Guinea coast. And so they thought of Africans as different in kind from themselves, wondering, sometimes, whether they were really also descendants of Adam and Eve.

Attitudes like these had already distorted Western understandings of

Africa from the fifteenth century on. Worse yet, as the transatlantic slave trade developed, so did an increasingly negative set of ideas about African peoples and their capacities. It became normal to think of black Africans as inferior to Europeans, and many Europeans found in that inferiority a rationalization for the enslavement of Africans. As a result, much of the writing about Africans and about people of African descent in the New World was frankly derogatory. Because modern Africans were educated in European colonies, they too inherited a distorted and dismissive attitude toward Africa's past and African capacities, and one of the first tasks of modern African intellectuals has been to try to frame a sense of the world and our place in it that is freed from these sad legacies.

There have been many skirmishes in the battle to find a just representation of Africa and her peoples. But in the course of this century—and more especially in the last 30 or 40 years—a more objective knowledge of Africa has gradually emerged, both in Africa and elsewhere. Anthropologists began to describe the rich religious, artistic, and social life of African peoples. African historians have learned to interpret oral histories, passed down in Africa's many traditions, cross-checking them against archæological and documentary evidence to produce a rich picture of the African past. Economists and political scientists, literary critics and philosophers, scholars of almost every discipline in the social sciences and the humanities have contributed to this new knowledge, as have scholars on every continent, Africans prominent among them. Work in African American Studies has led to new understandings of the culture of slaves and of the role of people of African descent in shaping the New World's language, religion, agriculture, architecture, music, and art. As a result, it is now possible to comb through a great library of material on African history and on the peoples of Africa and her diaspora, and to offer, in a single volume, a compendium of facts and interpretations.

An encyclopedia cannot include everything that is known about its subject matter, even everything that is important. So we have had to make choices. (And, alas, some of the most interesting questions are as yet unanswered.) But we have sought to provide a broad range of information and so to represent the full range of Africa and her diaspora. About two-fifths of the text of the encyclopedia has to do exclusively, or almost so, with the African continent: the history of each of the modern nations of Africa and what happened within their territories before those nations developed; the names of ethnic groups, including some that were formerly empires and nations, and their histories; biographies of eminent African men and women; major cities and geographical features: rivers, mountains, lakes, deserts; forms of culture: art, literature, music, religion; and some of Africa's diverse plant and animal life. Another third deals mostly with Latin America and the Caribbean, focusing on the influence of African cultures and people of African descent in shaping those portions of the New World. Slightly less than a third of the material deals with North America in the same way. And the rest is material of cross-cultural significance or has to do with the African presence in Europe, Asia, or the rest of the world.

Our main focus has been on history—political and social—and on literature and the arts, including music, to which African and African American contributions have been especially notable in modern times. Our aim has been to give a sense of the wide diversity of peoples, cultures, and traditions that we know about in Africa in historical times, a feel for the environment in which that history was lived, and a broad outline of the contributions of people of African descent, especially in the Americas, but, more generally, around the world.

It is natural, faced with a compendium of this sort, to go looking first for what we know already and to be especially pleased with ourselves if we find something missing! But in setting out to make an encyclopedia in a single volume, we had to make choices all the time about what to include, and we did so in the light of our own best judgments, in consultation with many scholars from around the world. It has been one of the great satisfactions of compiling a work with so many colleagues with so many different specialized areas of knowledge, that we have been able to fill in some of our own many areas of ignorance. That, we believe, is the great pleasure of this new encyclopedia: it not only answers many questions that you knew you wanted to ask, it invites you to ask questions that you had not dreamed of asking. We hope you will find, as we have, that the answers to these unfamiliar questions are as amazing and as varied as Africa, her peoples, and their descendants all around the globe.

We mentioned earlier some of the many encyclopedias of various aspects of African and African American life that have been published in the past. The publication of *Africana: The Encyclopedia of the African and African American Experience* as a one-volume print edition aspires to belong in the grand tradition of encyclopedia editing by scholars interested in the black world on both sides of the Atlantic. It also relies upon the work of thousands of scholars who have sought to gather and to analyze, according to the highest scholarly standards, the lives and the worlds of black people everywhere. We acknowledge our indebtedness to these traditions of scholarly endeavor—more than a century old—to which we are heirs, by dedicating our encyclopedia to the monumental contribution of W. E. B. Du Bois.

Kwame Anthony Appiah
Henry Louis Gates, Jr.

Acknowledgments

Building an encyclopedia requires the labor and support of hundreds of individuals and many institutions. In addition to the contributors, who are acknowledged elsewhere in this book, the editors wish to express their profound gratitude to the following persons:

Sharon Adams, Rachel Antell, Bennett Ashley, Robbie Bach, Tim Bartlett, Craig Bartholomew, John Blassingame, William G. Bowen, Peggy Cooper Cafritz, Elizabeth Carduff, Albert Carnesale, Jamie Carter, Sheldon Cheek, Chin-lien Chen, Coureton C. Dalton, Karen C. C. Dalton, the late Charles T. Davis, Rafael de la Dehesa, John Donatich, David Du Bois, Joseph Duffy, Olawale Edun, Richard Ekman, Lynn Faitelson, Amy Finch, Henry Finder, Lisa Finder, Kerry Fishback, Susanne Freidberg, Elaine Froehlich, Tony Gleaton, Peter Glenshaw, Lisa Goldberg, Matthew Goldberg, Jaman Greene, Holly Hartman, Pete Higgins, Jessica Hochman, Chihiro Hosoe, Pat Jalbert, Mary Janisch, Quincy Jones, Paul Kahn, Leyla Keough, Jeremy Knowles, Joanne Kendall, Harry Lasker, Todd Lee, Krzysztof Lenk, Erroll McDonald, Jack McKeown, Della R. Mancuso, Nancy Maull, Sonny Mehta, Joel W. Motley III, Richard Newman, Peter Norton, Mark O'Malley, Jennifer Oppenheimer, Francisco Ortega, Martin Payson, Frank Pearl, Ben Penglase, Kevin Rabener, Toni Rosenberg, Daryl Roth, Michael Roy, Neil Rudenstine, Kelefa Sanneh, Carrie Seglin, Keith Senzel, Bill Smith, Wole Soyinka, Patti Stonesifer, Patricia Sullivan, Carol Thompson, Larry Thompson, Lucy Tinkcombe, Kate Tuttle, Charles Van Doren, Robert Vare, Michael Vazquez, Alberto Vitale, Sarah Von Dreele, Philippe Wamba, Carrie Mae Weems, and X Bonnie Woods.

Contributors to the original *AFRICANA: The Encyclopedia of the African and African American Experience*

Rosanne Adderley, *Tulane University*
Marian Aguiar, *Amherst, Massachusetts*
Emmanuel Akyeampong, *Harvard University*
Suzanne Albulak, *Cambridge, Massachusetts*
Samir Amin, *Director of the Forum Tiers Monde, Dakar, Senegal*
George Reid Andrews, *University of Pittsburgh*
Abdullahi Ahmed An-Na'im, *Emory University*
Rachel Antell, *San Francisco, California*
Kwame Anthony Appiah, *Princeton University*
Jorge Arce, *Boston Conservatory of Music*
Alberto Arenas, *University of California at Berkeley*
Paul Austerlitz, *Brown University*
Karen Backstein, *City University of New York, College of Staten Island*
Anthony Badger, *University of Cambridge*
Lawrie Balfour, *Babson College*
Marlyse Baptista, *University of Georgia*
Robert Baum, *Iowa State University*
Stephen Behrendt, *Harvard University*
Patrick Bellegarde-Smith, *University of Wisconsin at Milwaukee*
Eric Bennett, *Iowa City, Iowa*
Suzanne Preston Blier, *Harvard University*
Juan Botero, *Former Executive Director, Instituto de Ciencia Politica, Bogota, Colombia*
Keith Boykin, *Washington, D.C.*
Esperanza Brizvela-Garcia, *London, England*
Diana DeG. Brown, *Bard College*
Eva Stahl Brown, *University of Texas at Austin*
Barbara Browning, *New York University*
Eric Brosch, *Cambridge, Massachusetts*
John Burdick, *Syracuse University*
Andrew Burton, *London, England*
Alida Cagidemetrio, *University of Udine, Italy*
Chloe Campbell, *London, England*
Sophia Cantave, *Tufts University*
Yvonne Captain, *George Washington University*
Judy Carney, *University of California at Los Angeles*
Vincent Carretta, *University of Maryland at College Park*
Clayborne Carson, *Editor, Martin Luther King, Jr., Papers Project, Stanford University*

Odile Cazenave, *University of Tennessee*
Alistair Chisholm, *London, England*
Jace Clayton, *Cambridge, Massachusetts*
Patricia Collins, *University of Cincinnati*
Nicola Cooney, *Harvard University*
Belinda Cooper, *New School for Social Research*
Frederick Cooper, *University of Michigan at Ann Arbor*
Juan Giusti Cordero, *Universidad de Puerto Rico*
Thomas Cripps, *Morgan State University*
Selwyn R. Cudjoe, *Wellesley College*
Carlos Dalmau, *San Juan, Puerto Rico*
Darién J. Davis, *Middlebury College*
James Davis, *Howard University*
Martha Swearington Davis, *University of California at Santa Barbara*
Cristobal Diaz-Ayala, *Independent Scholar*
Rafael Diaz-Diaz, *Pontificia Universidad Javeriana, Bogota, Colombia*
Quinton Dixie, *Indiana University*
Andrew Du Bois, *Cambridge, Massachusetts*
Christopher Dunn, *Tulane University*
Anani Dzidzienyo, *Brown University*
Jonathan Edwards, *Belmont, Massachusetts*
Roanne Edwards, *Arlington, Massachusetts*
Joy Elizondo, *Cambridge, Massachusetts*
Robert Fay, *Medford, Massachusetts*
Martine Fernández, *Berkeley, California*
Paul Finkelman, *Harvard Law School*
Victor Figueroa, *Harvard University*
Gerdes Fleurant, *University of California at Santa Barbara*
Juan Flores, *Hunter College and City College of New York Graduate Center*
Paul Foster, *Chicago, Illinois*
Baltasar Fra-Molinero, *Bates College*
Gregory Freeland, *California Lutheran University*
Susanne Freidberg, *Dartmouth College*
Nina Friedemann, *Pontifica Universidad Javeriana, Bogota, Colombia*
Rob Garrison, *Boston, Massachusetts*
Henry Louis Gates, Jr., *Harvard University*
John Gennari, *University of Virginia*
Danielle Georges, *New York, New York*
Peter Gerhard, *Independent Scholar*
Mark Gevisser, *Editor of Defiant Desire: Gay and Lesbian Lives in South Africa*
Patric V. Giesler, *Gustavus Adolphus College*
Peter Glenshaw, *Belmont, Massachusetts*
Matthew Goff, *Chicago, Illinois*
Flora González, *Emerson College*
Mayda Grano de Oro, *San Juan, Puerto Rico*
Sue Grant Lewis, *Harvard University*

Roderick Grierson, *Independent Scholar*
Barbara Grosh, *New York, New York*
Gerard Gryski, *Auburn University*
Betty Gubert, *Former Head of Reference, Schomburg Center for Research in Black Culture, New York Public Library*
Michelle Gueraldi, *San José, Costa Rica*
Stuart Hall, *The Open University, London*
Michael Hanchard, *Northwestern University*
Julia Harrington, *Banjul, The Gambia*
Elizabeth Heath, *San Francisco, California*
Andrew Hermann, *Former Literary Associate, Denver Center Theatre Company*
Evelyn Brooks Higginbotham, *Harvard University*
Jessica Hochman, *New York, New York*
Cynthia Hoehler-Fatton, *University of Virginia*
Peter Hudson, *Toronto, Canada*
Michelle Hunter, *Cambridge, Massachusetts*
Abiola Irele, *Ohio State University*
David P. Johnson, *Jr., Boston, Massachusetts*
Bill Johnson-González, *Cambridge, Massachusetts*
André Juste, *New York, New York*
Chuck Kapelke, *Boston, Massachusetts*
Ketu Katrak,University of California at Irvine
Robin Kelley, *New York University*
R. K. Kent, *University of California at Berkeley*
Leyla Keough, *Cambridge, Massachusetts*
Muhonjia Khaminwa, *Boston, Massachusetts*
David Kim, *Cambridge, Massachusetts*
Martha King, *New York, New York*
Franklin W. Knight, *Johns Hopkins University*
Peter Kolchin, *University of Delaware*
Corinne Kratz, *Emory University*
Modupe Labode, *Iowa State University*
Peter Lau, *New Brunswick, New Jersey*
Claudia Leal, *Former Assistant Director, Socioeconomic Area of the Biopacific Project, Bogota, Colombia*
René Lemarchand,University of Florida
W. T. Lhamon, *Jr., Florida State University*
Margit Liander, *Belmont, Massachusetts*
David Levering Lewis, *Rutgers University*
Marvin Lewis, *University of Missouri at Columbia*
Lorraine Anastasia Lezama, *Boston, Massachusetts*
Kevin MacDonald, *University of London*
Marcos Chor Maio, *Rio de Janeiro, Brazil*
Mahmood Mamdani, *University of Cape Town*
Lawrence Mamiya, *Vassar College*
Patrick Manning, *Northeastern University*

Peter Manuel, *John Jay College of Criminal Justice*
Dellita Martin-Ogunsola, *University of Alabama at Birmingham*
Waldo Martin, *University of California at Berkeley*
J. Lorand Matory, *Harvard University*
Felix V. Matos Rodriguez, *Northeastern University*
Marc Mazique, *Seattle, Washington*
José Mazzotti, *Harvard University*
Elizabeth McHenry, *New York University*
Jim Mendelsohn, *New York, New York*
Gabriel Mendes, *Annandale, New York*
Claudine Michel, *Wellesley College*
Georges Michel, *Military Academy of Haiti, Port-au-Prince, Haiti*
Gwendolyn Mikell, *Georgetown University*
Zebulon Miletsky, *Boston, Massachusetts*
Irene Monroe, *Harvard Divinity School*
Sally Falk Moore, *Harvard University*
Judith Morrison, *Inter-American Foundation at Arlington, Virginia*
Gerardo Mosquera, *Independent Scholar*
Luis Mott, *Federal University of Bahia, Brazil*
Salikoko S. Mufwene, *University of Chicago*
Edward Mullen, *University of Missouri at Columbia*
Kurt Mullen, *Seattle, Washington*
Stuart Munro-Hay, *Independent Scholar*
Aaron Myers, *Cambridge, Massachusetts*
Abdias do Nascimento, *Former Senator, Brazilian National Congress, Brasilia*
Ari Nave, *New York, New York*
Marcos Natali, *University of Chicago*
Okey Ndibe, *Connecticut College*
Nick Nesbitt, *Miami University (Ohio)*
Richard Newman, *W. E. B. Du Bois Institute for Afro-American Research, Harvard University*
Liliana Obregón, *Harvard Law School*
Kathleen O'Connor, *Cambridge, Massachusetts*
Tejumola Olaniyan, *University of Virginia*
Mark O'Malley, *Cambridge, Massachusetts*
Yaa Pokua Afriyie Oppong, *London, England*
Carmen Oquendo-Villar, *Cambridge, Massachusetts*
Kenneth O'Reilly, *University of Alaska at Anchorage*
Carlos L. Orihuela, *University of Alabama at Birmingham*
Francisco Ortega, *Harvard University*
Juan Otero-Garabis, *Universidad de Puerto Rico*
Deborah Pacini Hernandez, *Brown University*
Carlos Parra, *Harvard University*
Ben Penglase, *Cambridge, Massachusetts*
Pedro Pérez-Sarduy, *London, England and Havana, Cuba*
Julio Cesar Pino, *Kent State University*
Donald Pollock, *State University of New York at Buffalo*

Angelina Pollak-Eltz, *Univesidad Catolice A. Bella*
Paulette Poujol-Oriol, *Port-au-Prince, Haiti*
Richard J. Powell, *Duke University*
Jean Muteba Rahier, *Florida International University*
João José Reis, *Federal University of Bahia, Brazil*
Carolyn Richardson Durham, *Texas Christian University*
Alonford James Robinson, Jr., *Washington, D.C.*
Lisa Clayton Robinson, *Washington, D.C.*
Sonia Labrador Rodrigués, *University of Texas at Austin*
Gordon Root, *Cambridge, Massachusetts*
Aninydo Roy, *Colby College*
Sarah Russell, *Cambridge, England*
Marveta Ryan, *Indiana University (Pennsylvania)*
Ali Osman Mohammad Salih, *University of Khartoum*
Lamine Sanneh, *Yale University*
Jalane Schmidt, *Cambridge, Massachusetts*
Charles Schmitz, *Sonoma State University*
Brooke Grundfest Schoepf, *Harvard University*
LaVerne M. Seales-Soley, *Canisius College*
James Clyde Sellman, *University of Massachussetts at Boston*
Thomas Skidmore, *Brown University*
James Smethurst, *University of North Florida*
Paulette Smith, *Tufts University*
Suzanne Smith, *George Mason University*
Barbara Solow, *Associate of the W. E. B. Du Bois Institute for Afro-American
    Research, Harvard University*
Doris Sommer, *Harvard University*
Thomas Stephens, *State University of New Jersey*
Jean Stubbs, *London, England and Havana, Cuba*
Patricia Sullivan, *Harvard University*
Carol Swain, *Princeton University*
Katherine Tate, *Univerity of California at Irvine*
Richard Taub, *University of Chicago*
April Taylor, *Boston, Massachusetts*
Christopher Tiné, *Cambridge, Massachusetts*
Richard Turits, *Princeton University*
Kate Tuttle, *Cambridge, Massachusetts*
Timothy Tyson, *University of Wisconsin*
Charles Van Doren, *Former Vice President/Editorial, Encyclopædia
    Britannica Inc.*
Alexandra Vega-Merino, *Harvard University*
Joëlle Vitiello, *Macalester College*
Peter Wade, *University of Manchester*
James W. St. G. Walker, *University of Waterloo*
Phillipe Wamba, *Cambridge, Massachusetts*
William E. Ward, *Harvard University*
Salim Washington, *Boston, Massachusetts*

Christopher Alan Waterman, *University of California at Los Angeles*
Richard Watts, *Tulane University*
Harold Weaver, *Independent Scholar*
Norman Weinstein, *State University of New York at New Paltz*
Amelia Weir, *New York, New York*
Tim Weiskel, *Harvard University*
Alan West, *Northern Illinois University*
Cornel West, *Princeton University*
Norman Whitten, *University of Illinois at Urbana*
Andre Willis, *Cambridge, Massachusetts*
Deborah Willis, *Center for African American History and Culture, Smithsonian Institution*
William Julius Wilson, *Harvard University*
Barbara Worley, *Cambridge, Massachusetts*
Eric Young, *Washington, D.C.*
Gary Zuk, *Auburn University*

Charts, Maps, and Tables

Maps: Thematic

Tables

Articles

Aaron, Henry Louis (Hank)

(b. February 5, 1934, Mobile, Ala.), African American baseball player, broke Babe Ruth's record for career home runs in 1974.

His first experience with professional baseball came in the Negro Leagues, as he moved up through the ranks with the Pritchett Athletics, the Mobile Black Bears, and the Indianapolis Clowns. In 1952 Aaron received his first opportunity to play in the newly integrated major leagues as a short-stop with the Milwaukee Braves' farm team. Moving from Eau Claire, Wisconsin, to Jacksonville, Florida, Aaron made it to the major leagues in 1954, playing for the Milwaukee Braves (now the Atlanta Braves).

Aaron is considered by some the best baseball player in history. Over his 23-year Major League baseball career, Aaron compiled more batting records than any other player in baseball history. He holds the record for runs batted in with 2297, and was a Gold Glove Winner in 1958, 1959, and 1960. Aaron's most acclaimed accomplishment came on April 8, 1974. At the age of 40, he hit a 385-foot home run against the Los Angeles Dodgers, thus surpassing Babe Ruth's record of 714 career home runs. He ended his career with 755 home runs. He was inducted into the Baseball Hall of Fame in 1982.

Abbott, Robert Sengstacke

(b. November 28, 1868, Frederica, Ga.; d. February 22, 1940, Chicago, Ill.), African American founder, editor, and publisher of the *Chicago Defender*.

Abbott founded the *Chicago Defender*, a weekly newspaper, on May 6, 1905. He started the paper with $25, and at first operated it out of his

kitchen. Under his direction, the *Defender* became the most widely circulated African American newspaper of its time and a leading voice in the
fight against racism. Abbott cultivated a controversial, aggressive style,
reporting on such issues as violence against blacks and police brutality. The
Defender raised eyebrows with its anti-lynching slogan, "If you must die,
take at least one with you" and its condemnation of Marcus Garvey's Universal Negro Improvement Association (UNIA). Through the *Defender*,
Abbott also played a major role in the Great Migration of many African
Americans from the South to Chicago.

Abbott developed tuberculosis in 1932 and died in Chicago of Bright's
disease. The *Defender* continued under the control of Abbott's nephew,
John H. Sengstacke, who began publishing it as a daily in 1956.

Africa

Abd al-Qadir

(b. May 26, 1807; d. 1883), Algerian religious and military leader credited with
unifying Algerian territory into a state through his campaign against French
colonization.

Considered a hero of anticolonial resistance by many contemporary
Algerians, Abd al-Qadir created an Arab-Berber alliance to oppose
French expansion in the 1830s and 1840s. He also organized an Islamic
state that, at one point, controlled the western two-thirds of Algeria's
inhabited land. His legacy remained an inspiration through the War of
Independence (1954–1962). In 1968 the newly independent nation
erected a monument to Abd al-Qadir in the place where a French monument to General Bugeaud had stood, and took up his green and white
standard as its flag.

North America

Abdul-Jabbar, Kareem

(b. April 16, 1947, Harlem, N.Y.), African American basketball player, widely
considered to be one of the greatest National Basketball Association (NBA)
players in history.

Kareem Abdul-Jabbar, the highest scorer in NBA history, was born Ferdinand Lewis Alcindor Jr. in Harlem, New York. Raised in a middle-class
household and educated at Catholic schools in Manhattan, he was introduced to basketball at age nine and played competitively throughout elementary and high school. He was 6 ft, 8 in (2.05 m) tall by the time he was
14. He continued his dominant play at the University of California Los

Angeles (UCLA), where the team won three National Collegiate Athletic Association championships. An outspoken political activist who was influenced by the Black Power movement, he changed his name from Alcindor to Kareem Abdul-Jabbar in 1971 after converting to Islam. A popular NBA star from 1969 to 1989, he thwarted opponents with his "skyhook" shot and became professional basketball's most imposing offensive threat. In his 20-year professional career, Abdul-Jabbar played on 18 All Star teams and claimed six championships, six most valuable player awards, and numerous other NBA records.

North America

Abernathy, Ralph David

(b. March 11, 1926, Linden, Ala.; d. April 17, 1990, Atlanta, Ga.), American minister and civil rights leader who organized nonviolent resistance to segregation and succeeded Martin Luther King Jr. as president of the Southern Christian Leadership Conference (SCLC).

Ralph Abernathy was born on March 11, 1926, in Linden, Alabama. He and Martin Luther King Jr. led the successful boycott of the Montgomery bus system in 1955, protesting segregated public transportation. In 1957 Abernathy helped King found the Southern Christian Leadership Council (SCLC) to coordinate nonviolent resistance to segregation. After King's assassination in 1968, Abernathy served as SCLC president until he resigned in 1977.

Africa

Abrahams, Peter

(b. March 19, 1919, Vrededorp, South Africa), expatriate South African novelist.

The son of an Ethiopian father and a mother of French and African descent, Peter Abrahams was considered "Coloured" in the South African racial classification scheme. He grew up outside Johannesburg and began working at the age of nine, never having attended school. He later enrolled, however, after he was inspired by hearing *Othello* read to him by a co-worker. Abrahams wrote six of his seven novels about his home country. *Song of the City* (1945) and *Mine Boy* (1946) explore the racial injustices of a rapidly industrializing and urbanizing South Africa. Abrahams also wrote a historical novel about South Africa's Afrikaners, *Wild Conquest* (1950), and another about African-Indian solidarity, *A Night of Their Own* (1965). An assignment in Jamaica led him to move his family there in 1956. *This Island Now* (1966) deals with political struggles in a fictional Caribbean setting.

Latin America and the Caribbean

Acea, Isidro

(b.?; d. November 12, 1912, Güira de Melena, Cuba), Afro-Cuban hero of the independence war of 1895–1898.

Isidro Acea was greatly respected for his bravery and unceremonious nature. Acea lived during a period of Cuban history when the society was highly politicized around the issue of race, particularly after the independence war. Afro-Cubans were frustrated by the Cuban administration, United States military occupation, and Spanish migration, all of which exacerbated social inequity for people of African descent in the nation. Acea, like some other Afro-Cuban veterans, attempted to connect with the community and gain support by entering the political arena on a pro-black platform in the early 1900s. The platform lacked patronage particularly because of U.S.-imposed restrictions on male suffrage that required literacy and ownership of property, thus limiting access by Afro-Cuban voters. Information regarding the life, as well as the death, of Isidro Acea is not well documented and requires further investigation.

Africa

Achebe, Chinua

(b. November 16, 1930, Ogidi, Nigeria), Nigerian author whose novel *Things Fall Apart* (1958) is one of the most widely read and discussed works of African fiction.

Chinua Achebe once described his writing as an attempt to set the historical record straight by showing "that African people did not hear of culture for the first time from Europeans; that their societies were not mindless but frequently had a philosophy of great depth and value and beauty; that they had poetry and, above all, they had dignity." Achebe's works portray Nigeria's communities as they pass through the trauma of colonization into a troubled nationhood. In bringing together the political and the literary, he neither romanticizes the culture of the indigenous nor apologizes for the colonial.

In his first novel, *Things Fall Apart*, Achebe retold the history of colonization from the point of view of the colonized. Immediately successful, the novel secured Achebe's position both in Nigeria and in the West as a preeminent voice among Africans writing in English. Achebe subsequently wrote several novels: *No Longer at Ease* (1960), *Arrow of God* (1964) and *A Man of the People* (1966)—a work Achebe has characterized as "an indictment of independent Africa"—which is set in the context of the emerging African nation state. Achebe's critical political commentary continues in *Anthills of the Savannah* (1987).

Achebe's nonfiction works address such topics as the role of the writer in the postcolonial African nation, literary depictions of Africa, and the debate over language choice by African writers.

North America

Adderley, Julian Edwin ("Cannonball")

(b. September 15, 1928, Tampa, Fla.; d. August 8, 1975, Gary, Ind.), African American alto saxophonist who explored bebop, modal, and soul-fusion styles.

Adderley was introduced to music by his father, a cornetist, and was performing in bands by the time he was 14. He immediately found success on the New York jazz scene, joining the bands of Oscar Pettiford and, later, Miles Davis. The recordings Adderley made with Davis—which included John Coltrane on tenor saxophone, Paul Chambers on bass, and Wynton Kelly on piano—are some of the most celebrated of the 1950s. In 1959 Adderley and his brother, Nat, formed their own quintet and built on the influence of Davis and Charlie Parker. During its 15 years, the quintet played soul jazz style, fusion, and mainstream post-bop, earning critical and popular acclaim and a reputation for drawing heavily on blues and gospel. Some critics hailed Adderley as the "new Bird," noting his style's debt to Parker. At times, Adderley doubled on soprano saxophone. An important innovator on his horn, Adderley also taught and lectured on jazz. Some of his finest performances appear on *Something Else Cannonball and Coltrane*, Miles Davis's *Kind of Blue*, and the popular Adderley quintet album *Mercy, Mercy, Mercy! Live at "the Club"* (1966).

Julian Adderley earned the nickname "Cannonball," a corruption of "cannibal," for his huge appetite. He died of a stroke while onstage in 1975.

Africa

Addis Ababa, Ethiopia,

the capital and largest city in Ethiopia.

Addis Ababa is Ethiopia's political, commercial, manufacturing, and cultural center. Located at the approximate geographical center of Ethiopia, it is the hub of the country's highway network and contains its international airport and the inland terminus of its only railroad. Its manufacturing sector produces consumer goods and building materials. In addition, the city houses Addis Ababa University and other cultural institutions. Addis Ababa is also the headquarters of the Organization of African Unity and the United Nations Economic Commission for Africa, both of which are located in Africa Hall.

Ade, King Sunny

(b. September 22, 1946, Ondo, Nigeria), popular Nigerian vocalist and guitarist, innovator of *juju* music.

Sunday Anthony Ishola Adeniyi Adegeye, known internationally to African music fans as King Sunny Ade, was raised in a home where Christian and Yoruba religious and cultural perspectives were thoroughly intermingled. Ade attended missionary schools, then dropped out of college in the 1960s to pursue a career as a drummer in *juju* bands. *Juju* is a form of Nigerian pop music first developed by Yoruba musicians in the 1920s. Ade's chief musical inspiration was I. K. Dairo, though Ade's later song lyrics drew more inspiration from his Christian education.

The early 1970s marked the birth of Ade's reputation as an African superstar with an international audience. Ade deviates from the Dairo legacy through a series of innovations. He expands the *juju* band lineup from a single electric guitarist to as many as six, played with at least that number of drummers, and introduces both the pedal steel guitar (previously identified with American country music) and the synthesizer. Ade's recordings—over 110 currently—break new ground in two other arenas. *Juju* music lyrics before Ade relied almost entirely upon Yoruba folkloric sayings. Ade's first hit recording in Nigeria, by way of contrast, was a newsy account of soccer. Although vocals, guitar lines, and drum patterns are still based on traditional Yoruba speech, proverbs, and metaphors, Ade's song topics have included local and world politics, the dishonest nature of the music industry, and a Christian interpretation of the world's end. Ade's other innovation involves song length. He expands the length of songs to a half-hour or more, turning them into intricately layered drum and guitar jams. Ade gained renown with international music fans primarily through a single album, *Juju Music* (1982), released on the Island label.

Affirmative Action,

policies used in the United States to increase opportunities for minorities by favoring them in hiring and promotion, college admissions, and the awarding of government contracts. Depending on the situation, "minorities" might include any underrepresented group, especially one defined by race, ethnicity, or gender. Generally, affirmative action has been undertaken by governments, businesses, or educational institutions to remedy the effects of past discrimination against a group, whether by a specific entity, such as a corporation, or by society as a whole.

Until the mid-1960s legal barriers prevented blacks and other racial minorities in the United States from entering many jobs and educational institutions. While women were rarely legally barred from jobs or education, many universities would not admit them and many employers would not hire them. The Civil Rights Act of 1964 prohibited discrimination in public accommodations and employment. A section of the act known as Title VII, which specifically banned discrimination in employment, laid the groundwork for the subsequent development of affirmative action. The Equal Employment Opportunity Commission (EEOC), created by the Civil Rights Act of 1964, and the Office of Federal Contract Compliance became important enforcement agencies for affirmative action.

The term *affirmative action* was first used by President Lyndon B. Johnson in a 1965 executive order. This order declared that federal contractors should "take affirmative action" to ensure that job applicants and employees "are treated without regard to their race, color, religion, sex, or national origin." While the original goal of the Civil Rights Movement had been "color blind" laws, simply ending a long-standing policy of discrimination did not go far enough for many people. President Richard Nixon was the first to implement federal policies designed to guarantee minority hiring. Responding to continuing racial inequalities in the work force, in 1969 the Nixon administration developed the Philadelphia Plan, requiring that contractors on federally assisted projects set specific goals for hiring minorities. Federal courts upheld this plan in 1970 and 1971.

Controversy

From its beginnings in the United States in the mid-1960s, affirmative action has been highly controversial. Critics charge that affirmative action policies, which give preferential treatment to people based on their membership in a group, violate the principle that all individuals are equal under the law. These critics argue that it is unfair to discriminate against members of one group today to compensate for discrimination against other groups in the past. They regard affirmative action as a form of reverse discrimination that unfairly prevents whites and men from being hired and promoted.

Advocates of affirmative action respond that discrimination is, by definition, unfair treatment of people because they belong to a certain group. Therefore, effective remedies must systematically aid groups that have suffered from discrimination. Supporters contend that affirmative action policies are the only way to ensure an integrated society in which all segments of the population have an equal opportunity to share in jobs, education, and other benefits. They argue that numerical goals for hiring, promotions, and college admissions are necessary to integrate fields traditionally closed to women and minorities because of discrimination.

Legislation and Supreme Court Rulings

The scope and limitations of affirmative action policy have been defined through a series of legislative initiatives and decisions by the Supreme Court of the United States. In *Griggs v. Duke Power* (1971) the Supreme Court held that Title VII bans "not only overt discrimination but also practices that are fair in form but discriminatory in operation." In order to avoid discrimination lawsuits under Title VII, public and private employers began to adopt hiring policies designed to recruit more minorities. The Equal Opportunity Act of 1972 expanded Title VII protections to educational institutions, leading to the extension of affirmative action to colleges and universities.

In later cases the Supreme Court upheld the constitutionality of affirmative action but placed some restrictions on its implementation. The Supreme Court's ruling in *Regents of the University of California v. Bakke* (1978) declared that it was unconstitutional for the medical school of the University of California at Davis to establish a rigid quota system by reserving a certain number of places in each class for minorities. However, the ruling upheld the right of schools to consider a variety of factors when evaluating applicants, including race, ethnicity, gender, and economic status. The majority of the justices believed that the Congress of the United States has special powers to remedy past and ongoing discrimination in the awarding of federal contracts.

Conservative justices appointed to the Supreme Court by Republican presidents in the 1980s and 1990s attempted to limit the scope of affirmative action. Although sharply divided on the issue, the Court has struck down a number of affirmative action programs as unfair or too broad in their application. In *Wygant v. Jackson Board of Education* (1986) the Supreme Court struck down a plan to protect minority teachers from layoffs at the expense of white teachers with greater seniority. In *Richmond v. J. A. Croson Co.* (1989) the Court rejected a local set-aside program for minority contractors, ruling that local governments do not have the same power as Congress to enact such programs. These rulings did not signal the end of affirmative action. In *Metro Broadcasting v. Federal Communications Commission* (1990) the Court upheld federal laws designed to increase the number of minority-owned radio and television stations. Meanwhile, Congress responded to a number of conservative rulings by the Supreme Court by passing the Civil Rights Act of 1991, which strengthened antidiscrimination laws and largely reversed the *Ward's Cove* decision.

Recent Developments

In the 1990s affirmative action became a highly charged legal and political issue. In *Adarand Constructors v. Peña* (1995) the Supreme Court examined a federal statute that reserved "not less than 10 percent" of funds provided for highway construction for small businesses owned by "socially and economically disadvantaged individuals." The Court's majority opinion, written by Sandra Day O'Connor, overturned the statute and declared that even federal affirmative action programs are constitutional only when they are "narrowly tailored" to serve a "compelling government interest." In April 1998 a federal appeals court eliminated a Federal Communications Commission program designed to increase opportunities for minorities in broadcasting.

Affirmative action has been controversial in local politics as well. Under pressure from Governor Pete Wilson, the regents of the University of California voted in 1995 to end all affirmative action in hiring and admissions for the entire state university system. In 1996 the Fifth U.S. Circuit Court barred the University of Texas Law School from "any consideration of race or ethnicity" in its admissions decisions. Since these rulings have been enacted, both institutions have seen a dramatic drop not only in the admissions of black and Hispanic students but also in the number of minority applicants.

In 1996 voters in California endorsed Proposition 209, called the Civil Rights Initiative by its supporters, ending all state-sponsored affirmative action programs. At that time, commentators predicted a wave of similar state rulings barring race and gender preferences. However, efforts failed in Ohio, Colorado, and Florida to collect signatures for a similar ballot initiative. Bills modeled on Proposition 209 have been introduced in 13 state legislatures and none has been successful. In November 1997 Houston, Texas, voters defeated a ballot measure that would have repealed the city's race- and gender-based hiring programs. With legislatures, the public, and the courts divided over the issue, the status of affirmative action remains uncertain.

Africa

Afonso I (also known as Alfonso I)

(b. ?; d. 1543, São Salvador, present-day Democratic Republic of the Congo), king of the Kongo kingdom, the first Kongo king to embrace Catholicism and European trade relations.

Born Nzinga Mbemba, Afonso I ascended the throne in 1506 after the death of his father, Nzinga a Nkuwu. Unlike his father, who had rejected Catholicism and limited contact with the Portuguese explorers, Afonso immediately proclaimed Catholicism the state religion and established a strong trade alliance with the Portuguese Crown.

Eager to acquire European goods and to educate and Christianize his people, Afonso asked King Manuel of Portugal to send him priests, craftsmen, and military supplies. In return, Afonso supplied the monarch with ivory and slaves, two things for which the Portuguese seemed to have an unlimited appetite. This demand ultimately strained relations between the Portuguese and Kongo. He could do little to stop the Portuguese, who were now determined to procure not only slaves but also the kingdom's alleged mineral wealth. Even after the Portuguese attempt to assassinate the Kongo king in 1540, he maintained relations with the Europeans in the hope that they would eventually send more missionaries. At the time of his death in 1545, however, no missionaries had arrived. Although some Kongolese later claimed that Afonso's contacts with the Portuguese ultimately led to the breakup of the kingdom, others, such as the famous prophetess Dona Beatrice, looked back at Afonso's reign as the golden age of the Kongo.

Latin America and the Caribbean

Afoxés/Blocos Afros,

black Carnival organizations in Salvador, Bahia, Brazil that parade annually with costumes, music, and songs, using African and Afro-Brazilian themes; they also function as community service organizations.

During the 1960s and 1970s, influenced by the Civil Rights and Black Power movements in the United States and nationalist movements in Africa, Afro-Brazilians experienced a surge in black pride. This heightened black consciousness was also prompted by denouncements of racism and praises to "Mother Africa" heard in Jamaican reggae, increasingly popular in Brazil during the 1970s. As a result, black Brazilians, especially those in cities such as Rio de Janeiro, São Paulo, and Salvador, reaffirmed their connection with Africa and became more vocal about problems facing their community, particularly racial discrimination. This process was accelerated by the *abertura* (opening)—the gradual return to democratic rule that began in 1979 and loosened restrictions on free speech. In Salvador, this newfound black pride reinvigorated the old and waning afoxés and gave birth to a new type of black Carnival organization, the bloco Afro.

Afoxés emerged in the late nineteenth century. The prominent rhythm of the afoxés is called *ijexá*. It is a slow, hypnotic rhythm that is derived from the ceremonial music of Candomblé. Afoxés are the predecessors of the blocos Afros, which appeared during the mid-1970s. In part, blocos Afros were a black response to the *trios elétricos*, predominantly white musical ensembles riding on large trucks equipped with numerous amplifiers. In contrast to afoxés, blocos Afros have reached out to the black community in Salvador by establishing schools and creating community uplift programs. They have also influenced contemporary popular music in Bahia. As a result of the growing popularity of the afoxés and blocos Afros, words in African languages, especially Yoruban, and numerous references to Africa have become more common in Brazilian music. Today, afoxés and blocos Afros are the most distinguishing elements of Salvador's Carnival, annually involving over 100,000 people.

Africa

African Cup of Nations,

a biennial tournament among African national football (soccer) teams.

The African Cup of Nations was founded to be not only a sporting event, but also a means of promoting African sovereignty and unity. Despite religious and linguistic differences among member nations and periods of political instability, both the number and quality of competitors in the African Cup have steadily increased since its founding over 40 years ago. The history of the African Cup of Nations has been marred by political conflict on several occasions, the African Cup is still considered by its supporters to be the continent's premier sporting event and a showcase for its increasingly talented football players. Numerous scouts from European professional leagues make a biennial pilgrimage to the tournament, hoping to discover the latest African talent.

North America

African Free School,

(1787–1834), a primary school in New York City that preceded the establishment of public education for African Americans.

The African Free School (AFS) was founded in 1787 in a private home in New York City by the Anglican and Quaker New York Manumission Society. The school was opened after the abolition of slavery in several Northern states. The AFS became an essential vehicle for the primary education of African Americans in New York City for almost 50 years. As in other schools, the curriculum of the AFS stressed reading, writing, and arithmetic, but it also provided specialized training in navigation to encourage seafaring as potential employment for blacks. In addition to teaching students basic skills, the black faculty of the AFS provided moral and religious instruction to its students, some of whom became prominent in the black community. Among this influential group were James McCune Smith, Ira Aldridge, Peter Williams Jr., and Alexander Crummell. In 1830 Samuel Cornish, editor of *Freedom's Journal*, doubled the school's enrollment, and two years later he opened four more schools to accommodate the growing student body. In 1834 the New York State Public School Society assumed control of the AFS.

North America

African Methodist Episcopal Church,

independent African American Methodist organization dedicated to black self-improvement and Pan-Africanist ideals.

In response to discrimination, African American Methodists in Baltimore, Maryland, and Philadelphia, Pennsylvania, began holding separate prayer meetings as early as 1786. By 1794 Philadelphia's black Methodists had raised enough money to build their own church, which a majority of the congregation voted to align with the Episcopalians rather than the Methodists. They named it the St. Thomas African Episcopal Church. Richard Allen, however, believing that "no religious sect or denomination would suit the capacity of the colored people as well as the Methodists," purchased that year a blacksmith shop with his own money and converted it into a storefront church. Methodist bishop Frances Asbury named it the Bethel African Methodist Episcopal (AME) Church.

By 1816 black Methodists, still facing persistent discrimination, had come to believe that separate churches were not enough. In April, 16 representatives from five congregations met at Bethel, Philadelphia, to discuss their legal independence from the main body of the Methodist church. Voting to organize under the name the African Methodist Episcopal Church, they then successfully sued for independence before the Supreme Court of Pennsylvania. Allen became the first AME bishop after the elected bishop Daniel Coker declined the position.

The new AME Church was not greatly different from the original Methodist Church. But cultural practices distinct to African Americans assumed greater importance. The AME Church was also distinguished by social activism in the United States and throughout the African diaspora. It followed the precedent set by the uplift projects of the Free African Society, and was influenced by the emergent philosophies of Black Nationalism and Pan-Africanism. During the twentieth century, the AME Church was active in the Civil Rights Movement and in attending to the needs of African Americans dislocated in the northern exodus of the Great Migration. Through a pragmatic, activist gospel, the church addressed housing, welfare, and unionization issues for new immigrants to northern cities. At mid-century, AME pastors filed suits against public school segregation, which culminated in the *Brown v. Board of Education of Topeka, Kansas* (1954) decision.

Although women were not ordained until 1960, unordained women had worked as church activists and evangelists since Richard Allen approved Jarena Lee to work as an adviser in 1819.

Africa

African National Congress,

South African antiapartheid organization, now the country's leading political party.

In the history of South Africa, no group is more identified with the struggle against apartheid than the African National Congress (ANC). It was the ANC's Nelson Mandela who, through negotiations with the ruling National Party, finally brought about apartheid's demise. And in South Africa's first free elections in 1994, it was the ANC that won the majority of legislative seats and the presidency.

Since its founding in 1912 by middle-class, college-educated black South Africans, the ANC has changed with the times. After Great Britain's colonies and the Afrikaner republics were brought together in the Union of

South Africa in 1910, the "color bar" was further institutionalized by a wide range of restrictive race-based policies. In response, a group of mostly for-eign-educated Africans, including Pixley ka Izaka Seme, Sol Plaatje, and John Dube, formed the South African Native National Congress (renamed the African National Congress in 1923). The ANC initially fought the color bar through legal and constitutional means—mostly petitions, speeches, and publicity drives. These efforts accomplished relatively little, but for several years the ANC membership resisted a more radical approach.

In 1943 young ANC members, including Nelson Mandela, Oliver Tambo, Walter Sisulu, and Anton Lembede, formed the ANC Youth League (ANC-YL). Their passion and political savvy drove the ANC for the next 50 years. In 1949, a year after the newly elected National Party government began implementing its apartheid policies, the ANC-YL took over the ANC leadership. Influenced by the principles of nonviolent action and passive resistance pioneered by Indian nationalist leader Mohandas K. Gandhi, in 1952 the ANC drafted the "Defiance Campaign against Unjust Laws." The campaign's acts of civil disobedience did not result in any legislative reforms, but they did help swell the ANC. In addition, the campaign ush-ered in a new era of cooperation with antiapartheid groups representing other racial constituencies, such as the Coloured People's Congress, the South African Indian Congress, and the white Congress of Democrats.

These groups, together with the ANC, formed the Congress Alliance, which convened a large "Congress of the People" that adopted the Freedom Charter on June 26, 1955. The charter called for multiracialism, economic equality, and full democratic rights for all South Africans, and was adopted by the ANC as its official program in 1956. Even as the ANC's membership and alliances grew, however, the organization faced new challenges. Increased harassment by the government resulted in treason charges against 156 members and helped provoke the defection of several ANC leaders, who subsequently founded the more militant Pan-Africanist Congress (PAC) in 1959.

The struggle against apartheid intensified after March 21, 1960, when police opened fire on a group of unarmed protesters at a PAC anti-pass demonstration in Sharpeville, a black township south of Johannesburg. Sixty-nine people were killed, shot in the back as they fled. Riots ensued, and the government banned both the PAC and the ANC. In May 1961, operating underground, Mandela and other ANC leaders concluded that the time had come to meet government violence with armed resistance. Mandela, Tambo, and longtime ANC associate and Communist Party leader Joe Slovo informed ANC president Albert Luthuli of their plan to form a separate paramilitary organization. *Umkhonto we Sizwe*, "the spear of the nation," was launched in December 1961.

Although *Umkhonto* primarily committed acts of sabotage against sym-bols of apartheid, such as the Bantu Administration Offices, and against South African industry and infrastructure, in 1962 its leaders began plan-ning a guerrilla war, hoping to inspire a popular uprising that would topple the apartheid government. These plans were foiled when police raided

Umkhonto's South African headquarters at Rivonia. Evidence found there was used to convict Mandela and others of treason. Mandela, already in prison for inciting strikes, was given a life sentence and sent to Robben Island. Slovo, out of the country at the time of the raid, went into exile.

With most of its leaders either exiled or imprisoned, in the 1960s the ANC entered a period of internal turmoil. Factions disputed the role of economic versus political liberation. Beginning in the 1970s, however, the ANC, now led by Oliver Tambo, was reenergized by both the student-led Black Consciousness movement and South Africa's increasingly militant labor unions. The Soweto uprising of June 1976, sparked by a police massacre of protesting students, helped unite disparate antiapartheid elements and heal the generational rifts that had dogged the ANC. At the same time, the defeat of white-ruled regimes in Angola and Mozambique brought new hope that the battle against apartheid could be won.

The government responded to the ANC's growing strength with harassment, detentions, torture, and assassination. But the crackdown only solidified the ANC's standing as the most viable alternative to apartheid rule. As international pressure grew in the 1980s, the South African government began secretly negotiating with Mandela and others. When F. W. De Klerk succeeded P. W. Botha as president in 1990, he freed Mandela from his 27-year imprisonment and lifted the ban on the ANC.

Three years later, talks among more than 20 organizations—but dominated by the ANC and the ruling National Party—led to a transitional government, new constitution, and plans for the country's first democratic election in April 1994. The electoral power of black South Africans, exercised for the first time, swept the ANC into a commanding legislative majority, and Nelson Mandela into the presidency.

Since becoming the nation's ruling party, the ANC has faced the challenge of retaining and broadening its appeal with considerable success. Under the leadership of Nelson Mandela, the ANC has crafted an image of pragmatism over militancy that attracts liberal capitalists and continues to be popular with labor, socialists, and women's groups. Even potentially damaging testimony about *Umkhonto* activities before the Truth and Reconciliation Commission, which investigated South Africa's apartheid-era crimes, did not significantly erode the ANC's popularity. In the 1999 elections Thabo Mbeki, who assumed ANC leadership in December 1997, was the ANC candidate and the winner.

Africa

Afwerki, Isaias

(b. February 2, 1946, Asmara, Eritrea), leader of Eritrean fight for independence from Ethiopia and president of Eritrea since 1993.

As leader of the largest rebel force in Eritrea's independence struggle, Isaias Afwerki strove to unify peoples of diverse cultures and religious beliefs.

Since assuming office, he has been widely praised for his pragmatism and modesty, and for maintaining a regime free of corruption. Like Rwanda's Paul Kagame, Uganda's Yoweri Museveni, and Ethiopia's Meles Zenawi, Afwerki belongs to what has been called Africa's "new generation" of leaders, all of whom are known for their military backgrounds and for their tactical rather than ideological approach to leadership.

Isaias Afwerki was born at a time when the fate of the former Italian colony of Eritrea was in limbo. By the time he graduated from the elite Prince Makonnen Secondary School in Asmara in 1965, Ethiopia had annexed Eritrea. After only a year, however, he was gripped by the revolutionary fervor sweeping through the Eritrean student body, and he quit school to join the Eritrean Liberation Front (ELF). Afwerki rose through the ranks to become a deputy division commander for the ELF but soon clashed with the organization's Muslim-dominated leadership. A few years later he helped found the Eritrean People's Liberation Front (EPLF). The EPLF described itself as a Marxist organization, and Afwerki was among those who went to China for training in guerrilla warfare. By the time the Ethiopian regime fell in 1991, the EPLF had moderated its previous positions, and Afwerki was the clear choice to become independent Eritrea's first leader. He served as acting president until the country gained official independence on May 24, 1993, and was formally elected president by the National Assembly shortly thereafter. Since then he has generally enjoyed broad popular support.

Latin America and the Caribbean

Aguirre Beltrán, Gonzalo

(b. Veracruz, Mexico, 1918; d. Veracruz, Mexico, 1995), one of Mexico's most influential historians and anthropologists, who almost single-handedly revived interest in the history and contemporary lives of Afro-Mexicans.

Gonzalo Aguirre Beltrán received his primary and secondary schooling in Veracruz, where there was a strong African influence, before studying medicine in Mexico City. Although Africans had played a vital role in early Mexico, and although hundreds of thousands of modern Mexicans are descended from Africans—most of whom were brought to Mexico as slaves—modern Mexico largely denied the existence of both historic and contemporary Afro-Mexicans before Aguirre Beltrán published his groundbreaking work. In *La población negra de México*, published in 1946, Aguirre Beltrán undertook an exhaustive study of black ethnicity and history that detailed the origins in Africa of Mexico's blacks, the routes they traveled to Mexico, their settlement patterns once there, and their treatment by Spanish colonists. Aguirre Beltrán convincingly established that early Afro-Mexicans far out-numbered Spanish colonists. He was also one of the first historians to shed light on the rigid caste system that the Spanish church and state created and maintained in Mexico. This system stigmatized blacks, who received better treatment if they could claim they were *mestizo*, or biracial. Aguirre Beltrán argued that centuries of intermarriage among blacks, Indians, and whites, combined with the caste stigma, led to the gradual disappearance of full-blooded Afro-Mexicans and the decline of Afro-Mexican culture. His conclusions drew praise from those who valued his "re-discovery" of black Mexicans and hostility from those who continued to see Mexico's black heritage as a stain. Half a century after Aguirre Beltrán's pioneering study, however, Mexico's government officially acknowledged this black "third root" as a part of the country's heritage no less integral than Mexico's Indian and European roots.

Africa

Aidoo, Ama Ata

(b. 1942?, Abeadzi Kyiakor, Ghana), writer whose plays, novels, and poetry examine the traditional roles assigned to African women.

Aidoo's first play, *The Dilemma of a Ghost* (1965), was staged in 1964 by the Student's Theatre at the University of Ghana. With this play, Aidoo earned her lasting reputation as a writer who examines the traditional African roles of wife and mother. The play, like many of her later works, also demonstrated her willingness to grapple with complex and controversial issues. *No Sweetness Here* (1970) was a collection of short stories that undertook a number of complicated themes, including the divide between men and women and between rural and urban societies. In these stories, Aidoo brought a sense of the oral to the written word through the use of elements such as African idioms. In 1982 Aidoo was appointed Ghana's minister of education. She left the country a year later for Zimbabwe, where she continued to teach as well as write poems, published in the collection *Someone Talking to Sometime* (1985), and two children's books. The 1991 novel, *Changes*, explores the possibilities of self-determination for contemporary women. The story narrates a woman's experience of a polygamous marriage, and her ultimate decision to leave her husband. For Aidoo, who once proclaimed that, given the seriousness of Africa's political problems, she could not imagine herself writing something so frivolous as an African love story, the novel was a realization that "love or the workings of love is also political."

North America

Ailey, Alvin

(b. January 5, 1931, Rogers, Texas; d. December 1, 1989, New York, N.Y.), African American dancer and choreographer who founded the Alvin Ailey American Dance Theater (AAADT) and incorporated African American styles and themes into dance performance.

Ailey's dancing career began in 1949 when a high school friend, Carmen DeLavallade, introduced him to Lester Horton, his first dance instructor at the Lester Horton Dance Theater. When Horton died in 1953, Ailey became the director of the company. The following year Ailey moved to New York City, where he joined DeLavallade in the Broadway dance production *House of Flowers*. While appearing in other stage performances, Ailey continued his studies under Martha Graham, Charles Weidman, and Karel Shook. In 1958 Ailey assembled his own dance company, the Alvin Ailey American Dance Theater. Ailey himself stopped dancing in 1965 and reduced his choreographic assignments during the 1970s in order to seek more funding for his growing dance enterprise. The Alvin Ailey Dance Center School, founded in 1969, is dedicated to educating dance students in the history and art of both modern dance and ballet. The school's curriculum includes courses in choreography, dance technique, music for dancers, and theatrical design. Ailey's own works, whose style is founded on the techniques of modern dance, ballet, and jazz dance, draw upon African American themes, many of which are rooted in his boyhood experiences. Two of his major pieces, *Blues Suite* (1958) and *Revelations* (1960), for example, were inspired by a bar in Texas named the Dewdrop Inn, and the Mount Olive Baptist Church he attended as a boy. *Revelations*, the AAADT's most celebrated number, explores the different facets of black religious worship and is performed to a series of spirituals and gospel music selections. His 1971 ballet *Cry*, a tribute to African American women, is dedicated to his mother. The company toured the United States and the world so extensively that by 1989, the year that Ailey died, they had performed in 48 states and 45 countries on six continents.

Latin America and the Caribbean

Albizu Campos, Pedro

(b. June 29, 1893, Ponce, Puerto Rico; d. April 21, 1965, San Juan, Puerto Rico), Afro-Puerto Rican nationalist leader of African descent, considered by many to be the foremost advocate of Puerto Rico's independence and one of the most controversial figures in political and social struggles of the twentieth century.

A passionate speaker and outspoken critic of United States imperialism and the 1898 invasion and occupation of Puerto Rico, Pedro Albizu Campos spent many years in prison for his role in the pro-independence nationalist movement, during the turbulent years of the 1930s through the 1950s. He opposed Puerto Rico's association with the United States, which started when the island was ceded by the Spanish after the Spanish-Cuban-American War. For Albizu, Puerto Ricans—ethnically mixed and culturally different—were not, and should not be, Americans. Independence was the only legitimate and anti-imperialist solution to the island's status.

Albizu's uncompromising quest for independence is for some Puerto Ricans the highest possible example of dignity and courage. For them, "Don

Afro-Puerto Rican nationalist leader Albizu Campos talks to reporters following his unsuccessful "Revolt of 50," an insurrection that took place in different parts of Puerto Rico in October 1950. CORBIS/Bettmann

Pedro" is one of the fathers of Puerto Rican national identity. For others, he was plainly wrong in trying to achieve independence for the island. Despite the controversy, Pedro Albizu Campos remains one of the towering figures of Puerto Rican history.

North America

Aldridge, Ira

(b. 1807, New York, N.Y.; d. 1867, Lodz, Poland), the most highly esteemed African American actor of the nineteenth century.

Ira Aldridge earned international recognition as one of his era's finest actors for his moving theatrical performances throughout England, Scotland,

Ireland, Europe, and the United States. Though born free in New York City, the son of a slave turned Calvinist preacher, Aldridge saw limited theatrical opportunities in the United States and, after training at the African Free School in New York City, left the United States for England in 1824.

Debuting onstage at the Royal Coburg in London in 1825, Aldridge won widespread praise for his portrayal of *Othello*, a role that became his trademark. After this success, he performed in the Theater Royal in Brighton and then went on to tour England, Scotland, and Ireland for the next six years. In 1867, at the height of his career, he died of respiratory failure while on tour in Lodz, Poland, and was buried in that city. Aldridge not only left a rich legacy of drama, voice, and rhetoric, but he marked the beginning of the tradition of polished African American artists who would do most of their work outside the United States because of American racism.

Latin America and the Caribbean

Alexis, Jacques Stéphen

(b. April 22, 1922, Gonaives, Haiti; d. 1961, Haiti), Haitian novelist whose politically committed works made a profound impact on Haitian letters.

Jacques Stéphen Alexis was born into one of Haiti's literary families. His father, Stéphen Alexis, was the author of *Le Nègre masqué* (1933) and wrote a work on the history of Haiti. Jacques Stéphen Alexis's first two novels, *Compère Général Soleil* (1955) and *Les arbres musiciens* (1957) cover the tumultuous period from 1934 to 1942 (the United States occupied Haiti from 1934 to 1957) and paint a complex picture of the psychological, social, and political life of the people of the island. The third novel, *L'Espace d'un cillement* (1959), moves away from the heroic narratives of the first two. Still, his importance lies in his vibrant evocation of the island's past and in his hope for a brighter future for its people.

Africa

Algeria,

republic of western North Africa; bounded on the north by the Mediterranean Sea; on the east by Tunisia and Libya; on the south by Niger, Mali, and Mauritania; and on the west by Morocco.

To many outside observers, Algeria has been a preeminent symbol of post-colonial independence, a nation that waged a highly visible war against a European colonial power, France, in the mid-twentieth century, and won an independent secular state. The electoral success during the early 1990s of the Islamic Salvation Front (FIS), considered by many to be an Islamic fundamentalist group, was all the more startling. This apparent inconsistency

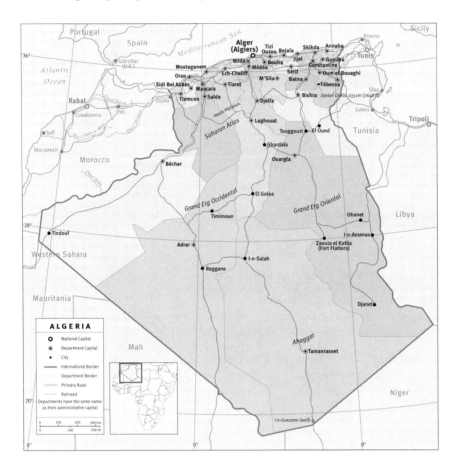

revealed a complexity that stems from the fact that Algeria spans the traditions of the Berber, Arab, and European worlds. For the people of Algeria,
Islam has been central to the culture since the seventh century. Within its
history are many other strands as well, including the uneasy integration of
Berber-dominated territories, the experience of women at the forefront of
the independence struggle, the socialist strategies of the newly independent
state, and the capitalist vision of economic development that supplanted it.

Africa

Algeria (Ready Reference)

Official Name: Democratic and Popular Republic of Algeria

Area: 2,381,741 sq km (919,595 sq mi)

Location: Northern Africa; bordering the Mediterranean Sea, Morocco,
Tunisia, Libya, Mali, Mauritania, Niger, and the Western Sahara

Capital: Algiers (population 1,687,579 [1987 estimate])

Other Major Cities: Oran (population 916,000), Constantine (662,330 [1987 estimate])

Population: 29,852,000 (1998 estimate)

Population Density: 12 persons per sq km (about 31 persons per sq mi)

Population Below Age 15: 38 percent (male 5,923,087; female 5,709,814 [1998 estimate])

Population Growth Rate: 2.14 percent (1998 estimate)

Total Fertility Rate: 3.38 children born per woman (1998 estimate)

Life Expectancy at Birth: Total population: 68.93 years (male 67.78 years; female 70.12 years [1998 estimate])

Infant Mortality Rate: 45.44 deaths per 1000 live births (1998 estimate)

Literacy Rate (age 15 and over who can read and write): Total population: 61.6 percent (male 73.9 percent; female 49 percent [1995 estimate])

Education: Primary education is free and compulsory for all children between the ages of six and 15. In the early 1990s some 4.6 million pupils attended primary schools, 2.3 million were enrolled in secondary schools, and another 147,418 attended vocational schools. By the mid-1990s nearly 300,000 were pursuing higher education.

Languages: Arabic is the official language and is spoken by about 83 percent of the population; most of the remainder speak Berber. French, the colonial language, is still widely read and spoken by many educated Algerians.

Ethnic Groups: Arabs, Berbers, or people of mixed Arab-Berber ancestry make up 99 percent of the population; Europeans constitute less than 1 percent.

Religions: Sunni Islam is the state religion and is practiced by 99 percent of the population; 1 percent of the population are Christians or Jews.

Climate: The Tell region in the north has warm, dry summers and mild, rainy winters, with an annual rainfall of between 400 and 1000 mm (16 to 39 in). During the summer an exceedingly hot, dry dust and sand-filled wind, the *sirocco* (known locally as the Chehili), blows north from the Sahara. To the south the climate becomes increasingly dry, with an annual rainfall in the High Plateau and Saharan Atlas from about 200 to 400 mm (about 8 to 16 in). The Sahara is a region of daily temperature extremes, wind, and great aridity; annual rainfall is less than 130 mm (5 in) in all places.

Land, Plants, and Animals: The Tell region, between the northern Mediterranean coast and the mountainous Tell Atlas area, contains most of Algeria's arable land. The country's principal river, the Chelif (725 km/450 mi long), flows from the Tell Atlas to the Mediterranean Sea. Lying to the south and southwest is the High Plateau, a level, sparsely vegetated highland region. During rainy periods, basins collect water, forming large, shallow lakes that become salt flats, called *chotts*, or *shotts*, during dry seasons. The mountains

The mosque and university at al-Karawiyyin, a complex of Islamic worship and learning that was begun in 859 by Fatima al-Fihri, the daughter of a wealthy merchant. Expansions throughout the next five centuries made al-Karawiyyin the largest mosque in North Africa, capable of accommodating 22,000 worshipers. *CORBIS/The Purcell Team*

of the Saharan Atlas lie south of this region. More than 90 percent of the country's total area lies in the Algerian Sahara, covered mostly by gravel with vast regions of sand dunes. Rising above the desert to the south are the Ahaggar Mountains, with Mount Tahat (3003 m/9852 ft), the highest peak in Algeria.

Remnants of forests exist in a few areas of the higher Tell and Saharan Atlas. Scattered plant life in the Sahara consists of drought-resistant grasses, acacia, and jujube trees. Wildlife includes scavengers, such as jackals, hyenas, and vultures, as well as antelope, hares, gazelles, and reptiles.

Natural Resources: Petroleum, natural gas, iron ore, phosphates, uranium, lead, zinc

Currency: The Algerian dinar

Gross Domestic Product (GDP): $15.38 billion (1994 estimate)

GDP per Capita: $4000 (1997 estimate)

GDP Real Growth Rate: 2.5 percent (1997 estimate)

Primary Economic Activities: Mineral production (primarily crude petroleum and natural gas), agriculture, fishing. Since the late 1960s the government has instituted major industrialization programs.

Primary Crops: Wheat, barley, potatoes, tomatoes, melons, grapes, dates, olives, tobacco

Industries: Petroleum, light industries, natural gas, mining, electricity production, petrochemical, food processing

Primary Exports: Petroleum and natural gas make up 97 percent of export revenues. Other exports include iron ore, vegetables, tobacco, phosphates, fruit, cork, and hides.

Primary Imports: Machinery, textiles, sugar, cereals, iron and steel, coal, gasoline

Primary Trade Partners: Italy, France, United States, Germany, Spain, Japan

Government: Under the constitution adopted in February 1989, Algeria is a socialist republic, and a president is elected to a five-year term by universal adult suffrage. A unicameral National People's Assembly of 295 members was elected in 1987. In January 1992, the assembly was suspended to prevent the Islamic Salvation Front (FIS), a Muslim fundamentalist party, from gaining a legislative majority. Since then, Algeria has been governed by the High Council of State, headed by President Liamine Zeroual, with Prime Minister Ahmed Ouyahia appointed by the president.

North America

Ali, Muhammad

(b. January 17, 1942, Louisville, Ky.), African American heavyweight prize-fighter, convert to Islam, antiwar protester, and international ambassador of goodwill.

Muhammad Ali was born Cassius Marcellus Clay. As the dominant heavyweight boxer of the 1960s and 1970s, Muhammad Ali won an Olympic

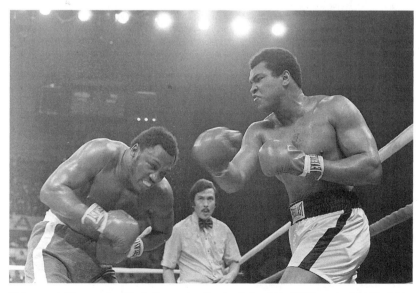

Muhammad Ali connects with challenger Joe Frazier during their 1975 heavyweight title fight in Manila, Philippines. *CORBIS/Bettmann*

gold medal, captured the professional world heavyweight championship on three separate occasions, and successfully defended his title 19 times. Ali's extroverted, colorful style, both in and out of the ring, heralded a new mode of media-conscious athletic celebrity. Through his bold assertions of black pride, his conversion to the Muslim faith, and his outspoken opposition to the Vietnam War, Ali became a highly controversial symbol of the turbulent 1960s.

Ali's 1981 retirement from boxing did not diminish his status in international public culture. Despite suffering from Parkinson's disease, he remained on the world stage as an adherent of the Nation of Islam, an advocate of children and war victims, and a proponent of international understanding. Ali has been described as "the most recognizable human being on earth."

Africa

Amin, Idi

(b. 1925, Koboko, Uganda), president of Uganda from 1971 to 1979.

Idi Amin made a name for himself as one of the most despotic and brutal rulers in postcolonial Africa. He served in Somalia, Uganda, and Kenya during the suppression of the Mau Mau and earned a reputation as a skilled and eager soldier. But early in his career his excessive tendencies were already apparent. When Uganda achieved independence in 1962, Amin was one of only two African officers in the Ugandan armed forces. Amin had been an early political supporter of Milton Obote, the first prime minister of independent Uganda. Amin ousted Obote while the president was in Singapore. Ugandans, disillusioned with the corrupt Obote, initially welcomed Amin, as did the international community. But the new president's brutality quickly dampened his popularity within Uganda.

Among Amin's first targets were the ethnic Acholi and Lango, who dominated the Ugandan army. Amin dealt a severe blow to the Ugandan economy. In 1972 he declared an "Economic War" on the country's large Asian population, which dominated the trade and manufacturing sectors and also played an essential role in the civil service. After giving the 70,000 holders of British passports three months to leave the country, Amin nationalized all British holdings in the country after the former colonial power severed diplomatic ties.

Paranoid and volatile, Amin frequently reorganized his army and security forces as well as his diplomatic alliances. After initially close ties with Israel, he later turned to Libya and the USSR for political and military support. In 1978 Amin's megalomanic ambitions finally led to his fall from power. In October of that year he attempted to annex the Kagera Salient, a part of Tanzania. The Tanzanian president, Julius Nyerere, responded by sending troops into Uganda. The Tanzanian army, supported by rebel

Ugandan forces, captured Kampala in April 1979 whereupon Amin fled to Libya. Shortly afterward, he slipped into Saudi Arabia and has remained exiled there ever since.

Amistad Mutiny,

(July 1839, off the northern coast of Cuba), rebellion of Africans held captive aboard the slave ship *La Amistad*.

Although England and Spain had signed a treaty in 1817 prohibiting the slave trade, a group of African Mende were captured in an area near Sierra Leone in April 1839 and forced onto a Portuguese slave ship bound for Havana. To avoid prosecution for breaking international law, the captives were smuggled onto the island at night when the ship reached Cuba. While in Havana, 53 Africans (49 adult males, 3 girls, and 1 boy) were sold to two Spaniards, José Ruiz and Pedro Montes, who intended to use them as slaves on Cuban plantations. On June 28, 1839, the Africans were loaded aboard the Spanish schooner *La Amistad* as it set sail along the Cuban coast for Puerto Príncipe.

On the *Amistad*'s fourth day at sea, a few of the captives were allowed to come on deck for exercise. One of them, Joseph Cinque, found a nail and smuggled it back below with him. Using the nail to force open their chains and shackles, Cinque and his comrades seized cane knives and initiated the rebellion. Along with the ship's captain and cook, ten Africans were killed. Ruiz and Montes were captured, and, with translation provided by a slave cabin boy named Antonio, were instructed to sail the ship back to Africa. Cinque and the others were able to use the rising sun to ensure that the ship headed eastward during the day. However, unable to navigate by the stars, the Africans were tricked by Ruiz and Montes into sailing northwest at night.

The *Amistad* zigzagged through the waters for two months, finally landing near Culloden Point, Long Island, New York, on August 24, 1839. When Cinque sent a group to find water and food on shore, Lt. Thomas R. Gedney of the United States Navy seized the ship and arrested the Africans for murder and piracy. Three New York abolitionists, Lewis Tappan, Joshua Leavitt, and Simeon Jocelyn, formed a committee called Friends of the *Amistad* to help defend the African captives. On March 9, 1841, the U.S. Supreme Court ruled that President Martin Van Buren did not have the right to return the Africans to Cuba, and that the Africans were never slaves under international law and should be granted their freedom. Despite their victory in court, only 35 of the original 53 Africans survived to board the ship *Gentleman* that set sail for Africa on November 27, 1841. Arriving in Sierra Leone in January 1842, three years from the start of their voyage, these Africans regained their freedom.

Amo, Anton Wilhelm

(b. 1703?, Akonu, Gold Coast [present-day Ghana]; d. 1754?, Gold Coast),
scholar and state councilor, one of the first prominent blacks in Germany.

Anton Wilhelm Amo, brother of a slave, was brought to Germany from the
Gold Coast in 1707 as a gift from the Dutch West India Company to the
dukes August Wilhelm and Ludwig Rudolf von Wolfenbüttel. Although it
was the fashion at the time in Europe to make blacks servants or clowns,
the dukes raised and educated Amo as a nobleman. They then sent him to
the university in Halle, where he became acquainted with Enlightenment
thinkers such as Christian Wolff, Christian Thomasius, John Locke, and
René Descartes. His first work, published in 1729 and now lost, concerned
the rights of Africans in Europe. Amo received his doctorate in 1734 with a
thesis on the duality of body and soul and made his mark as a lecturer in
philosophy at the universities in Halle, Wittenberg, and Jena. At a time
when many Europeans believed that Africans were racially inferior, Amo
proved that they could be the equals of Europeans in abilities and achievements. He was also appointed a Prussian government councilor in Berlin.
He returned to the Gold Coast in 1747, apparently disenchanted by the
racism that he had experienced in Germany. He worked as a goldsmith in
Africa, where he died in 1754. In 1965 the University of Halle, in the
former East Germany, erected a statue in his honor.

Amsterdam News,

New York City's largest black-owned newspaper and the oldest black-owned
newspaper in the United States.

Founded by entrepreneur James H. Anderson in 1909, the New York
Amsterdam News presents news and events by and for the African American
community, which historically have been underreported by the mainstream
white press. The *Amsterdam News* has featured the writing of many important black journalists and leaders, including Cyril V. Briggs, T. Thomas
Fortune, Adam Clayton Powell Jr., W. E. B. Du Bois, and Roy Wilkins.
During World War II, the paper was criticized for its coverage of sensational
subjects such as murder and gambling rings, but it also protested segregation
in the armed forces, sought to ally blacks with Jews, and argued for racial
equality.

Although the *Amsterdam News* struggled financially during World War
II, it flourished in the postwar era with a weekly circulation of 100,000. But
increased competition from mainstream newspapers, which in the 1960s
began to cover black-oriented stories, eroded its base, and by 1996 its circu-

lation had fallen to 27,938. Wilbert Tatum, the paper's principal stock-holder since 1984, returned the paper to profitability but was criticized for his controversial stances and for what critics described as his willingness to forsake journalistic objectivity for "black boosterism." In December 1997 Tatum promoted his daughter Elinor to the position of publisher and editor-in-chief. She endeavored to keep the paper a vital voice in New York's African American community.

North America

Anderson, Eddie ("Rochester")

(b. September 18, 1905, Oakland, Calif.; d. February 28, 1977, Los Angeles, Calif.), American actor best known for his comic portrayal of the character Rochester on the Jack Benny radio show.

The humor and energy between Jack Benny and Eddie Anderson led to the development of a 20-year collaboration that delighted radio, television, and film audiences. The relationship between Anderson and Benny, for all of its sarcasm, wit, and camaraderie, was typical of the "Uncle Tomism" of the era (Anderson's trademark line to Benny became "What's that, Boss?"), yet blacks not only appreciated the comedy, but were also pleased that the character was played by a black actor instead of a white actor attempting to imitate black expression. After appearing in his first film, *Green Pastures* (1936), Anderson was invited to play the role of Rochester, a Pullman porter on the Jack Benny radio show. Though it was only intended to be a one-show deal, Anderson struck such a chord with audiences that he was offered a permanent spot in the cast.

In addition to teaming up with Benny in the classic films *Man About Town* (1939), *Buck Benny Rides Again* (1940), and *Love Thy Neighbor* (1940), Anderson also acted in numerous films without Benny, including *Jezebel* (1938), *Gone With the Wind* (1939), *Birth of the Blues* (1941), and the "race" films *Stormy Weather* (1943) and *Cabin in the Sky* (1943).

North America

Anderson, Marian

(b. 1900?, Philadelphia, Pa.; d. 1993), American singer and first African American to perform at the Metropolitan Opera.

Marian Anderson was born in Philadelphia, Pennsylvania, around 1900 and began singing professionally and touring during high school to earn money for her family. In 1925 she won the opportunity to appear at Lewisohn

After the Daughters of the American Revolution refused to allow her to perform in Constitution Hall in Washington, D.C., Marian Anderson was invited by Secretary of the Interior Harold Ickes, Jr., to sing at the Lincoln Memorial. Her performance drew 75,000 people. *CORBIS*

Stadium with the New York Philharmonic Orchestra. Between 1925 and 1935, Anderson studied and toured in Europe, and her career began to develop. Her repertoire expanded to comprise over 100 songs in various languages.

In 1939 the Daughters of the American Revolution (DAR) denied Anderson's request to perform at its Constitution Hall in Washington, D.C., because she was African American. Eleanor Roosevelt, wife of President Franklin D. Roosevelt, resigned from the DAR in protest. Reacting to the outrage the DAR inspired, the secretary of the interior, Harold Ickes, arranged an open-air concert at the Lincoln Memorial on Easter Sunday, which was attended by 75,000 people. Anderson performed once more from the steps of the Lincoln Memorial, as part of the March on Washington in 1963, a key event in the Civil Rights Movement. In 1955 Anderson became the first African American to perform at the Metropolitan Opera, singing the role of Ulrica in Verdi's *Un Ballo in Maschera*. In 1958 President Dwight D. Eisenhower appointed her to the United States delegation to the United Nations and she sang at President Eisenhower's inauguration. In 1977, President Jimmy Carter presented her with a Congressional gold medal bearing her profile.

Latin America and the Caribbean

Andrada e Silva, José Bonifácio de

(b. June 13, 1763, Santos, São Paulo, Brazil; d. April 6, 1838, Niterói, Brazil), the first prime minister of independent Brazil, an early advocate of the abolition of the slave trade and the gradual emancipation of slaves.

José Bonifácio de Andrada e Silva is best known for helping Brazil achieve independence in 1822. It is less often recognized that the year after independence he authored a plan for "the slow emancipation of the blacks." Andrada e Silva's abolition project was intended to become part of independent Brazil's new constitution. It would have granted slaves the right to purchase themselves at market price, provided free persons of color with land grants, and regulated slave work conditions. But before these articles could be debated, Emperor Pedro I dissolved the Congress. Notoriously impatient, Andrada e Silva turned against the throne and was exiled from Brazil. He returned to Brazil in 1829 and regained the support of Pedro II, but soon fell from favor. Despite this, Andrada e Silva was celebrated by Brazilian abolitionists of the 1880s, who built upon many of his arguments.

North America

Angelou, Maya

(b. April 4, 1928, St. Louis, Mo.), American writer and actress who was the featured poet at President Bill Clinton's 1993 inauguration.

Maya Angelou was born Marguerite Johnson and she was sent to Stamps, Arkansas, to be raised by her paternal grandmother. When Angelou was seven, she was raped by her mother's boyfriend. The trauma of this experience rendered Angelou mute for five years, and it was during this period that she began to read extensively. She gave birth at age 16 to her only child, Guy Johnson. To support herself and her son she took a variety of jobs, working as a cook, a waitress, and a madam to two prostitutes. She became a professional dancer and made a 1954 tour of Europe and Africa in *Porgy and Bess*. After her return to the United States, Angelou joined the Harlem Writers Guild. James Baldwin's editor at Random House was impressed by her poetry and her life story and asked her to consider writing an autobiography. The result was *I Know Why the Caged Bird Sings*, which was published in 1970 and became a best-seller.

In 1971 Angelou's first published book of poetry, *Just Give Me a Cool Drink of Water 'fore I Diiie*, was nominated for a Pulitzer Prize. Since then she has published five other volumes of poetry. The other volumes of her prose autobiography are *Gather Together in My Name* (1974), *Singin' and Swingin' and Gettin' Merry Like Christmas* (1976), *The Heart of a Woman* (1981), and *All God's Children Need Traveling Shoes* (1986). In 1993 she published a collection of essays, *Wouldn't Take Nothing for My Journey Now*, and *On the Pulse of Morning*, the poem she read at President Bill Clinton's 1993 inauguration.

Angelou has had a distinguished career in film and television as well. Throughout her diverse career, Angelou has often broken new ground. Maya Angelou's willingness to share herself in her work have earned her widespread admiration, respect, and love.

Africa

Angola,

a country on the southwest coast of Africa.

Few African countries have seen their natural and human potential as underutilized and thoroughly ravaged by violence as Angola. In precolonial southern Africa the area was home to some of the continent's richest kingdoms, which welcomed European merchants and missionaries in the fifteenth century, only to be corrupted and ultimately destroyed by the transatlantic slave trade in the sixteenth century. The abolition of the trade—a politically and economically destabilizing event—was followed by the repressive taxation and forced labor regimes of Portuguese colonialism.

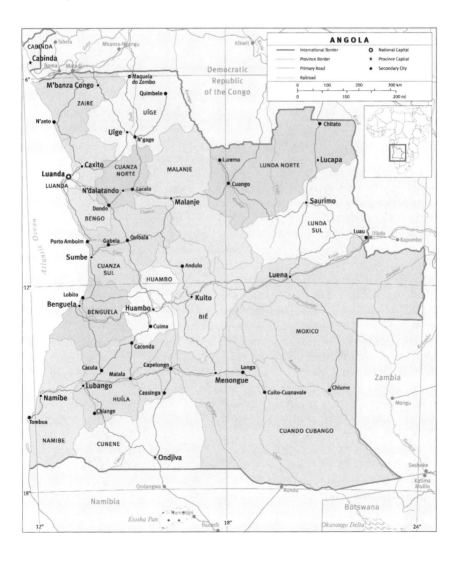

According to the United Nations, Angola has among the highest percentage of amputees in the world, the result of landmines used in the country's long and bitter civil war. *CORBIS/Baci*

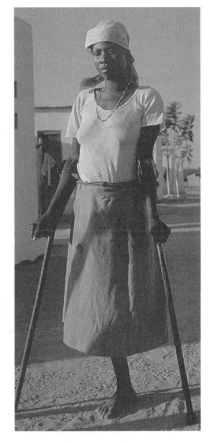

Although much of the rest of the continent underwent rapid decolonization in the 1960s, the armed struggle for independence in Angola took nearly 15 years and perpetuated internal divisions that turned into a two-decades-long civil war fed by cold war superpower rivalries. Only recently has fighting ceased. Although Angola's vast natural resources hold great promise, immense obstacles to development remain, particularly landmines and a shattered infrastructure.

Africa

Angola (Ready Reference)

Official Name: Republic of Angola

Former Name: People's Republic of Angola

Area: 1,246,700 sq km (498,680 sq mi)

Location: Southern Africa, bordering the South Atlantic Ocean, between Namibia and the Democratic Republic of the Congo

Capital: Luanda (population 1.2 million [1988 estimate])

Other Major Cities: Huambo (population 203,000), Benguela (155,000), Lobito (150,000), Lubango (105,000 [1983 estimate])

Population: 10,864,512 (1998 estimate)

Population Density: 9 persons per sq km (about 23 persons per sq mi)

Population Below Age 15: 45 percent (male 2,393,009; female 2,327,186 [1997 estimate])

Population Growth Rate: 2.84 percent (1998 estimate)

Total Fertility Rate: 6.2 children born per woman (1998 estimate)

Life Expectancy at Birth: Total population: 47.86 years (male 45.6 years; female 50.23 years [1998 estimate])

Infant Mortality Rate: 132.44 deaths per 1000 live births (1998 estimate)

Literacy Rate (age 15 and over who can read and write): 42 percent (male 56 percent; female 28 percent [1998 estimate])

Masks and masquerades are important elements in many African ceremonies. On the border between Angola and Zambia, three men prepare to play the roles of an old man, an old woman, and a sorcerer in an initiation ritual. *CORBIS/Charles Lenars*

Education: Officially compulsory for children age 7 to 15, but the majority of the population is rural and poor. Educational reforms enacted in the 1990s have produced an increase in primary school enrollment to 1.3 million students in 1993. Angola's only university is Agostinho Neto University, founded in 1976 in Luanda.

Languages: Portuguese is the official language. More than 90 percent of the population speaks Bantu languages. The most commonly spoken include Kimbundu, Umbundu, and Kikongo.

Ethnic Groups: Ovimbundu 37 percent, Kimbundu 25 percent, Bakongo 13 percent, *mestiço* (of indigenous and European descent) 2 percent, European 1 percent, other 22 percent

Religions: Indigenous beliefs 47 percent, Roman Catholic 38 percent, Protestant 15 percent

Climate: Angola is a tropical country. It is semi-arid in the south and along coast to Luanda; the north has cool, dry season (May to October) and hot, rainy season (November to April). Annual rainfall ranges from 50 mm (about 2 in) near the Namibe desert to 1500 mm (about 60 in) in the central plateau.

Land, Plants, and Animals: Angola is the seventh largest country in Africa. The majority of the land comprises meadows, pastures, forests, and woodlands. Less than 3 percent of the land is arable. The primary rivers, the Cuanza and Cunene, drain to the Atlantic Ocean. Angola has no major lakes.

Natural Resources: Petroleum, diamonds, iron ore, phosphates, copper, feldspar, gold, bauxite, uranium, manganese

Currency: The new kwanza

Gross Domestic Product (GDP): $8.2 billion (1996 estimate)

GDP per Capita: $800 (1996 estimate)

GDP Real Growth Rate: 9 percent (1996 estimate)

Primary Economic Activities: Subsistence agriculture provides the main livelihood for 80 to 90 percent of the population but accounts for less than 15 percent of the GDP. Oil production and the supporting activities are vital to the economy, contributing about 50 percent to the GDP.

Primary Crops: Coffee, cassava, bananas, sugar cane, sisal, corn, cotton, manioc (tapioca), tobacco

Industries: Mining of petroleum, diamonds, iron ore, phosphates, feldspar, bauxite, uranium, gold; fish processing; food processing; brewing; tobacco processing; sugar; textiles; cement; basic metal products

Primary Exports: Oil, diamonds, refined petroleum products, gas, coffee, sisal, fish and fish products, timber, cotton

Primary Imports: Capital equipment (machinery and electrical equipment), food, vehicles and spare parts, textiles and clothing, medicines, substantial military deliveries

Primary Trade Partners: United States, European Union (Portugal especially), Brazil

Government: Angola currently has a transitional government and is nominally a multi-party democracy with a strong presidential system. Universal suffrage begins at age 18. The legislative branch is unicameral, and the National Assembly (Assembleia Nacional) seats 223. The president appoints the judges of the Supreme Court (Tribunal da Relação) and the Council of Ministers. Major political parties include the Popular Movement for the Liberation of Angola (MPLA) and the National Union for the Total Independence of Angola (UNITA). National independence was achieved on November 11, 1975 (from Portugal). President Jose Eduardo Dos Santos (since September 21, 1979) was originally elected without opposition under a one-party system and stood for election in Angola's first multiparty elections on September 29-30, 1992. He received 49.6 percent of the total vote, making a runoff election necessary between him and second-place Jonas Savimbi; the runoff was not held and Savimbi's UNITA party disputed the results of the first election; the civil war was resumed. As of mid-1998, a fragile ceasefire prevailed.

Latin America and the Caribbean

Anguilla,

a British dependent territory located in the Caribbean at the northern end of the Leeward Islands.

Anguillan tradition holds that Christopher Columbus himself named the narrow island Anguilla—which is Spanish for "eel"—during one of his early trips to the Caribbean at the end of the fifteenth century. English colonists established the first settlement in 1650. Despite attempted attacks by the French, the Irish, and Carib Amerindians from nearby Dominica, Anguilla was one of the only Caribbean islands that remained under the control of a single power throughout the colonial period.

Today, Anguilla is slowly developing a reputation as a tourist destination, but the government is making efforts to ensure that the island remains underdeveloped to retain most of its natural beauty. The traditional Caribbean Carnival, popular boat races, and the Anguilla Cultural Festival are just a few of the shared celebrations that Anguillans take part in throughout the year. In the words of one locally published history of the island, Anguillans regard themselves as contentedly holding on to their own piece of "English heaven."

In 1997 Kofi Annan became the first person from sub-Saharan Africa to serve as secretary general of the United Nations. *CORBIS/AFP*

Africa

Annan, Kofi

(b. April 8, 1938, Kumasi, Gold Coast [present-day Ghana]), secretary general of the United Nations (UN).

The first person from sub-Saharan Africa to head the United Nations, Kofi Annan is also the first Secretary General to have risen through the ranks of that organization. A lifelong diplomat, Annan assumed the UN's top post in January 1997 to serve a term ending December 31, 2001. Annan impressed the international diplomatic community while serving as undersecretary general for peacekeeping, a job in which he coordinated efforts to help such tortured areas as

Rwanda, Somalia, and the former Yugoslavia. He began his term as Secretary General under pressure to reform the large and economically troubled UN bureaucracy. Following his appointment, Annan pledged to improve the effectiveness of UN programs in poor countries, saying, "Economic development is not merely a matter of projects and statistics. It is, above all, a matter of people—real people with basic needs: food, clothing, shelter, and medical care."

Latin America and the Caribbean

Antigua and Barbuda,

a country comprising three islands that lie in the eastern arc of the Lesser Antilles, approximately 650 km (404 mi) southeast of Puerto Rico, between the Atlantic Ocean and the Caribbean Sea.

In 1988 writer Jamaica Kincaid published an acclaimed but honest and critical history of her childhood home, Antigua, entitled *A Small Place.* Antigua—a country consisting of the Antigua, Barbuda, and the tiny uninhabited Redonda islands—is indeed a small place. But its strategic location at the edge of the Caribbean Islands, its high rates of sugar production, and its tourist appeal have made it a valuable country. As Kincaid pointed out, however, this economic value—with profits concentrated in the hands of a few and labor spread out over the backs of many—has not enriched most Antiguans' lives. In recent decades Antigua's challenge has been to take advantage of its natural beauty and resources without continuing to do so at the expense of its people.

Africa

Apartheid,

social and political policy of racial segregation and discrimination enforced by white minority governments in South Africa from 1948 to 1994.

The term apartheid (from the Afrikaans word for "apartness") was coined in the 1930s and used as a political slogan of the National Party in the early 1940s, but the policy itself extends back to the beginning of white settlement in South Africa in 1652. After the primarily Afrikaner Nationalists came to power in 1948, the social custom of apartheid was systematized under law.

The implementation of the policy, later referred to as "separate development," was made possible by the Population Registration Act of 1950, which put all South Africans into three racial categories: Bantu (black African), white, or Coloured (of mixed race). A fourth category, Asian

Nelson Mandela stares out the window from his former cell in Robben Island prison. Convicted of sabotage for actions taken against apartheid, Mandela spent 18 of his 27 years in prison on the island. *CORBIS/David Turnley*

(Indians and Pakistanis), was added later. The system of apartheid was enforced by a series of laws passed in the 1950s: the Group Areas Act of 1950 assigned races to different residential and business sections in urban areas, and the Land Acts of 1954 and 1955 restricted nonwhite residence to specific areas. These laws further restricted the already limited right of black Africans to own land, entrenching the white minority's control of over 80 percent of South African land. In addition, other laws prohibited most social contacts between the races; enforced the segregation of public facilities and the separation of educational standards; created race-specific job categories; restricted the powers of nonwhite unions; and curbed non-white participation in government.

In 1961 South Africa was forced to withdraw from the British Commonwealth by member states who were critical of the apartheid system, and in 1985 the governments of the United States and Great Britain imposed selective economic sanctions on South Africa in protest of its racial policy. As anti-apartheid pressure mounted within and outside South Africa, the South African government, led by President F. W. de Klerk, began to dismantle the apartheid system in the early 1990s. The year 1990 brought a National Party government dedicated to reform and also saw the legalization of formerly banned black congresses and the release of imprisoned black leaders. In 1994 the country's constitution was rewritten and free general elections were held for the first time in its history, and with Nelson Mandela's election as South Africa's first black president, the last vestiges of the apartheid system were finally outlawed.

North America

Apollo Theater,
the most influential African American popular theater.

The Apollo Theatre, located at 253 West 125th Street in central Harlem, was the most important venue in black show business from the 1930s through the 1970s, when waning popularity caused it financial problems. With live broadcasts that featured the Duke Ellington and Count Basie orchestras, the Apollo became a mecca for jazz bands in the 1930s and 1940s. By the 1950s the theater was the nation's top stage for established black artists. Its famous Amateur Night, in which unknown performers had their talent assessed by the notoriously raucous Harlem audience, had become a springboard for numerous careers. Ella Fitzgerald, Sarah Vaughan, and Pearl Bailey, for example, were all early Amateur Night winners, and later acts like the Jackson 5 and Stevie Wonder also enjoyed their first major exposure at the Apollo. As musical styles changed, the theater evolved with the times, booking rhythm and blues, gospel, funk, soul and hip hop acts, and hosting landmark performances by artists like James Brown. Its declaration as a national historic landmark in 1983 secured the building's survival.

Latin America and the Caribbean

Argentina,
second largest country in South America after Brazil, forming the southern tip of the South American continent; Argentina enjoys a great many natural resources, including the *pampas* (fertile plains) made famous by *gauchos* (cowboys) who are immortalized in the national literature.

Bordered by Bolivia, Brazil, Chile, Paraguay, Uruguay, and the Atlantic Ocean, Argentina comprises 35.8 million people, over 85 percent of whom are of white European descent. Another 15 percent of the population is of indigenous or *mestizo* (European and indigenous) origin. Though traditionally known for its early Spanish and nineteenth-century Italian and German heritage, Argentina had a large black population during much of the colonial and independence periods. Today the Afro-Argentine population is estimated at a few thousand and is often remembered as part of the country's folklore: Afro-Argentines have been incorporated in independence celebrations as soldiers, or in traditional dances called *candombes*. Scholarly research about this group has been limited to the colonial period and the slave trade, or to songs, portraits, and folklore studies from the 1950s. Though the Indian has become a mythical symbol incorporated by nationalistic discourse in *indigenismo* (a literary and artistic movement that appropriated indigenous culture and images) and *mestizaje* (racial mixing), black contributions to Argentina's history have attracted little interest until fairly recently.

Latin America and the Caribbean

Aristide, Jean-Bertrand

(b. July 15, 1953, Port-Salut, Haiti), president of Haiti from February 1991 to September 1991 and from October 1994 to February 1996.

Jean-Bertrand Aristide rose from the role of country priest to the presidency of Haiti. He was born in a rural area far removed from the modern amenities of the city. In 1974, following graduation from the seminary, Aristide left Haiti to spend a year in the Dominican Republic. Returning to Port-au-Prince, he enrolled at National University in 1979, where he completed a degree in psychology. In September 1985 he was appointed master of studies at the National School for Arts and Crafts in St. Jean Bosco, a parish on the edge of a large slum in Port-au-Prince known for helping the poorest youth.

This is when Aristide's political activities became well known, particularly his staunch support of democracy and his devotion to improving the lives of Haiti's poor. Shortly after arriving at his new post, he organized thousands of young people in the *Solidarité Ant Jen* (or "Solidarity Among Youth") committee to press for democracy, the end of Haitian dictator Jean-Claude Duvalier's rule, and better conditions for Haiti's poor. By the end of 1985 St. Jean Bosco had a reputation as a center for political organizing. As a result, Aristide also attracted the government's hatred, On January 31, 1986, Aristide survived the first of several assassination attempts.

As Aristide became known for his personal bravery and his commitment to Haiti's poor, both his popularity and his congregation grew. At the same time popular resistance to the rule of Duvalier led to his resignation on February 7, 1986. Duvalier's exit did not put a halt to Aristide's political cause or religious conviction. The harassment carried out against Aristide during the Duvalier regime continued. Opposition from the Roman Catholic Church continued as well. The Vatican had supported or ignored liberation theology and its practitioners in the 1960s and 1970s, but it was now an active critic. Also, because of his activism, Aristide was seen as a threat by the United States government, which referred to him in diplomatic cables as a "radical firebrand." More important, Aristide survived two more assassination attempts.

Despite tremendous odds and harassment, on December 16, 1990, Aristide won the presidency of Haiti in a landslide with 67 percent of the vote. His overwhelming support astonished many outside observers. Aristide was sworn in on February 7, 1991. However, Aristide's policies, tinged with socialism and liberation theology, met with severe criticism, especially within the military. During his first seven months in office he proposed raising the minimum wage, dismantling the repressive rural section chief system, and instituting literacy campaigns. The human rights situation in Haiti also improved dramatically. But on September 30, 1991, Aristide was toppled from office by a military coup led by Brig. Gen. Raoul Cedras. Aristide went initially to Venezuela, then spent most of the years 1992 to 1994 in the United States, where he wrote and gave speeches before numerous groups.

Calls for Aristide's reinstatement as the Haitian president gathered significant support both in the United States and internationally. But the period of Aristide's ouster saw severe political turbulence in Haiti. Two of Aristide's top supporters —Justice Minister Guy Malary and Father Jean-Marie Vincent—were killed. Finally, in September 1994, after intense pressure by the United States and the United Nations, and negotiations spearheaded by former president Jimmy Carter, Gen. Colin Powell, and Sen. Sam Nunn, the Haitian military agreed to step down. On September 19, U.S. military forces began a virtual occupation of Haiti, eventually coming to number more than 20,000. At the culmination of this effort, Aristide resumed his presidency on October 15, 1994. Returning to Haiti with U.S. Secretary of State Warren Christopher, Rev. Jesse Jackson, and members of the Congressional Black Caucus, Aristide vowed to restore democracy and urged reconciliation and forgiveness for supporters of the military regime. His return was met with countrywide celebrations. The agreement that restored him to office stipulated that he serve only two years, and in the next election René Préval was sworn in as Haiti's new president on February 7, 1996. Aristide now lives as an ex-president, but his popularity continues to be strong among the people.

Africa

Armah, Ayi Kwei

(b. 1939), Ghanaian novelist and journalist.

Born in the western region of Ghana, Ayi Kyei Armah is known for his novels, short stories, and poems. Armah is famed for his venomous attacks on the leaders of Ghana, particularly Prime Minister and later first president Kwame Nkrumah, for what Armah saw as Nkrumah's corrupt and abusive practices. He is also known for the force and sweep of his prose, a sturdy complement to the power of his polemic. Best known for his three novels, The *Beautyful Ones Are Not Yet Born* (1968), *Fragments* (1970), and *Why*

Are We So Blest? (1971), Armah critically examines the political and social consequences of colonialism in Ghana, leaving readers with little optimism about future change. Armah's later novels, *Two Thousand Seasons* (1973) and *The Healers* (1978), are much more allegorical and less dependent on realistic detail, a shift from his earlier work.

North America

Armstrong, Louis ("Satchmo")

(b. August 4, 1901, New Orleans, La.; d. July 6, 1971, New York, N.Y.), African American trumpet player and vocalist; commonly regarded to be the most significant soloist in the history of jazz.

More than anyone else, Louis Armstrong was responsible for legitimizing and popularizing jazz for a wider public. A much-admired jazz trumpeter and gravel-voiced vocalist, Armstrong was also a consummate entertainer, steadily expanding his career from instrumentalist to popular singer, to film and television personality, and, ultimately, to cultural icon. He acquired many nicknames throughout his life, including Dippermouth, Pops, and Satchelmouth—the latter often contracted to Satchmo. As Satchmo, he was instantly identifiable around the world, decades before Prince, Madonna, or Sting. The international appeal of his music in effect made Armstrong the American Goodwill Ambassador to the world.

Armstrong transformed jazz in two profoundly important ways. Early jazz was characterized by freewheeling group improvisation, but Armstrong, by his virtuosity and lyricism, almost single-handedly elevated the individual soloist to preeminence. In addition, his relaxed phrasing catalyzed a shift away from the staccato and jerky rhythms of early jazz to the even, four-beat swing that still characterizes most jazz today.

Armstrong was, above all, a soloist, in much the same sense as tenor saxophonist Coleman Hawkins and alto saxophonist Charlie Parker. Unlike Duke Ellington, the other great jazz figure to emerge in the 1920s, Armstrong revealed little distinction as a composer, arranger, or bandleader. Armstrong's most successful ensembles were small. His Hot Five and Hot Seven, for example, were strictly studio bands that never made regular public appearances. As was apparent in his big-band recordings of the early 1930s, Armstrong had an astonishing ability to transcend the limits of mediocre and sloppy accompaniment, which was a sign not only of his self-sustaining inspiration, but also of his casual attitude toward the quality of his sidemen.

For much of his career, he offered no direct challenge to racial discrimination other than the indictment that was implicit in his own vast talent. Otherwise, he made his peace with the status quo. In light of the harsh racial environment of the early decades of the twentieth century, his attitude made practical sense. But it is worth remembering that not all black musicians of that era chose, as Armstrong did, to project a smiling acquiescence in the midst of racism.

Unfortunately, Armstrong's happy-go-lucky disposition and good humor provided a convenient reinforcement for the racial prejudices of many white listeners. Jazz musicians of the bop generation, who came to maturity in the 1940s and early 1950s, including trumpeters Dizzy Gillespie and Miles Davis, later condemned Armstrong for "Tomming"—in other words, for being an Uncle Tom, the uncomplaining "good" slave character in Harriet Beecher Stowe's *Uncle Tom's Cabin* (1852). Gillespie criticized his "plantation image," that "public image of him, handkerchief over his head, grinning in the face of white racism." Such comments suggest the vast difference between Armstrong's experiences and those of a younger generation of black musicians. Despite such criticisms, however, Armstrong clearly demonstrated his ability to take a stand during the late 1950s and the 1960s. For much of his career, however, he revealed few political convictions.

Latin America and the Caribbean

Aruba,

an island in the Caribbean Sea 32 km (19 mi) north of Venezuela.

Aruba is one of the few Caribbean Islands whose people are still largely descended from an original indigenous population. This is partly because Aruba was never the site of plantation slavery and so was never home to the

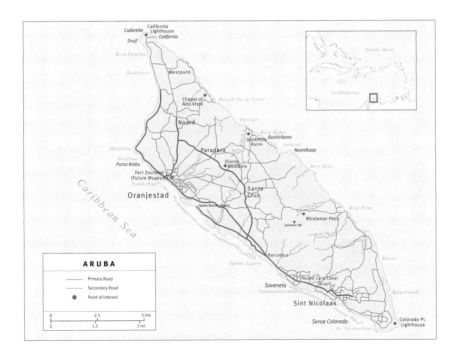

large numbers of African slaves who are the ancestors of most other contemporary Caribbean islanders. Over 85 percent of Arubans are of mixed Arawak Indian and European ancestry (see Indigenous Cultures in the Caribbean). A majority of the remaining 15 percent are black immigrants from other Caribbean Islands who have come to Aruba to fill some of the many available jobs in thriving tourist and oil industries.

North America

Ashe, Arthur Robert, Jr.

(b. July 10, 1943, Richmond, Va.; d. February 6, 1993, New York, N.Y.), African American tennis player, number one ranked player in the world in 1975, vocal critic of racial intolerance and historian of African American sports.

Arthur Robert Ashe Jr. was born July 10, 1943, in Richmond, Virginia, to Mattie and Arthur Robert Ashe Sr. He began playing tennis at the age of ten under the guidance of Dr. Robert Walter Johnson, a prominent coach of African American youth from Charlottesville, Virginia. Under Johnson, Ashe won three American Tennis Association (ATA) Boys' Championships, becoming the first African American junior to be ranked by the United States Lawn Tennis Association (USLTA).

Between 1960 and 1963, Ashe won three ATA Men's Singles titles, became the first African American on the United States Junior Davis Cup team, and the first African American to win a USLTA national title in the South. His achievements earned him a full scholarship to the University of California at Los Angeles, where he received a bachelor's degree in business administration in 1966. While in college Ashe won the U.S. intercollegiate singles championship, leading UCLA to the National Collegiate Athletic Association (NCAA) team championship. He won the 1968 U.S. Open in the first year that amateurs were allowed to compete. He turned professional in 1969. Over his 11-year career, Ashe played in 304 tournaments, winning 51, including the 1970 Australian Open and Wimbledon in 1975. He was the number one ranked player in the world in 1975. Although a life-threatening heart condition forced him to retire in 1980, Ashe continued to serve as the nonplaying captain of that year's U.S. Davis Cup team. In 1985 he became the second African American inducted into the International Tennis Hall of Fame. The first was Althea Gibson in 1971.

After his career in tennis, Ashe became an eloquent spokesperson against racial intolerance. He was a critic of South Africa's racist system of apartheid, and in the United States he created tennis programs to benefit inner-city youth. He wrote a three-volume history of the African American athlete titled *A Hard Road to Glory* (1988).

In 1992 Ashe announced that he had contracted human immunodeficiency virus (HIV) from a blood transfusion during one of his two heart bypass operations. After his announcement, he became an active leader in the fight to raise awareness of acquired immune deficiency syndrome (AIDS) and to increase funding for AIDS research. Suffering complications from AIDS, Ashe died in New York on February 6, 1993.

North America

Ashford, Evelyn

(b. April 15, 1957, Shreveport, La.), African American sprinter, four-time winner of Olympic gold medal.

Born in Shreveport, Louisiana, Evelyn Ashford grew up in Roseville, California. She attended the University of California at Los Angeles (UCLA) on a scholarship. She participated in four Olympic Games (1976, 1984, 1988, 1992), winning a total of four gold medals and one silver medal. In 1979 she set a world record in the 200-meter dash. Ten years later she received the Flo Hyman Award from the Women's Sports Foundation. In 1992 the United States Olympic team asked Ashford to carry the U.S. flag during the opening ceremonies in Barcelona. She retired in 1993 at the age of 36.

North America

Atkins, Cholly

(b. September 30, 1913, Birmingham, Ala.), African American choreographer, dancer, and dance coach best known for his team tap dancing with the great Charles "Honi" Coles.

Cholly Atkins began performing at the age of ten, when he won a Charleston contest, and he learned basic jazz and soft shoe steps while in high school. He began his formal career as a singing waiter in 1929 and soon teamed up with William Porter, a dancing waiter, to form the Rhythm Pals, a vaudeville song and dance team. After ten years with Porter, Atkins left the Rhythm Pals to begin dancing and choreographing for the Cotton Club Boys, a tap troupe that toured with Cab Calloway's band and performed with Bill "Bojangles" Robinson in a swing musical, *The Hot Mikado*, at the World's Fair in New York City. A partnership with Dotty Saulters followed but was interrupted when Atkins was drafted into the army in 1943.

After serving in the military, Atkins joined forces with Charles "Honi" Coles, and they soon became one of the best known black tap duos of the late 1940s. From 1946 to 1950, they toured Europe and the United States (headlining at venues like Harlem's Apollo Theater) and often performed with the bands of Billy Eckstine, Count Basie, the Mills Brothers, and Louis Armstrong. They also appeared on Broadway in *Gentlemen Prefer Blondes* (1949–1952). In 1952 Atkins took a brief respite from live performing and began teaching tap at the Katherine Dunham School of Arts and Research in New York City. With interest in tap waning, Atkins gave up performance in favor of choreography, creating dance routines for the Supremes, the Temptations, Gladys Knight and the Pips, and the O'Jays as a staff choreographer for Motown Records from 1965 to 1971. He also applied his talents to Broadway musicals, winning a Tony Award for his choreography work on *Black and Blue* in 1989.

Atlanta Compromise,

(September 18, 1895, Atlanta, Ga.), speech by Booker T. Washington advocating black self-help and accommodation to segregation and disenfranchisement.

The period in American history known as Reconstruction (1863–1877) gave emancipated slaves the opportunity to participate in American society in an unprecedented fashion. Opportunities were opened in education, race relations, public facilities, and employment. Perhaps most important, African American men were given the right to vote and hold public office. By 1877, during the period referred to as Retrenchment, Southern whites had begun to wipe away many of these newfound freedoms, including the franchise. By 1895, 32 years after Emancipation, African Americans were faced with virtual elimination of their freedoms along with new challenges in the struggle for justice and equality.

In this context Booker T. Washington, the founder of Tuskegee Institute (now Tuskegee University), addressed the Atlanta Exposition in 1895. Formerly known as the Cotton States and International Exposition, the Atlanta Exposition provided Washington the opportunity to address one of the most urgent dilemmas facing the nation. Washington's remarks received widespread approval among white Americans, who then saw him as the leading spokesperson for the African American community.

Speaking with regard to the conflict between the white demand for segregation and African American insistence on civil and political equality, Washington offered a compromise. He urged African Americans to replace the quest for civil and political equality with black economic empowerment, claiming that "the agitation of questions of social equality is the extremist folly."

The Atlanta Compromise formed the basis of what became Washington's ideology of black self-reliance. He urged African Americans to abandon the struggle for civil rights, and instead, to work for economic power. It was an argument for African Americans to help themselves and to stop looking for help from white Americans. Critics called the compromise accommodationist, but supporters saw it as empowering. One of Washington's most severe critics, W. E. B. Du Bois, later challenged the self-help philosophy in his essay on Washington in *Souls of Black Folk* (1903). Where Washington advocated the right of African Americans to build schools to promote segregated developments in agriculture and industry, Du Bois pointed to the inability of African Americans to participate in the very institutions that made America a "democracy." This debate was essential to the development of African American civil rights strategy and placed Booker T. Washington at the forefront of the debate on American race relations.

North America

Atlanta, Georgia

Before the Civil War, the African American presence in Atlanta was smaller than in other Southern cities. Its population was overwhelmingly made up of slaves who arrived between 1850 and 1860. Dispersed throughout Atlanta, they lacked a substantial community.

A postwar migration transformed the city. By 1870 African Americans composed 46 percent of 21,700 residents, a proportion they maintained for the remainder of the nineteenth century. The community lacked political strength, however. In 1870, when the "Radical" forces of Reconstruction were at their peak in Atlanta, only two city councilmen were African Americans—William Finch and George Graham, from the predominantly black third and fourth wards. One year later, the Georgia State legislature effectively ended black political representation when it changed city elections in Georgia from a ward to an at-large selection process. After 1875 white hostility in Atlanta reached levels that many considered the greatest in the South.

The African American community turned inward, establishing its own institutions and cultural life. In the 1870s and 1880s it founded lodges of the Colored Odd Fellows, a library, and three black newspapers. As Atlanta grew, a black middle class developed around prominent black churches. The Summer Hill subdivision in south Atlanta and the Green's Ferry Street neighborhood were two such "respectable black communities." On the western side of the city, an unparalleled center of black colleges and universities developed with the founding of Atlanta University (where W. E. B. Du Bois taught from 1897 to 1910), Atlanta Baptist College (Morehouse), Clark University, Spelman Seminary for Women, and Morris Brown College—all between 1865 and 1881.

Despite these developments, as of the 1890s most African Americans were not well off. In Atlanta, archetype of the "New South," 90 percent of the unskilled labor force were African Americans, and 92 percent of all working black women were in domestic service. An 1892 law decreed that only white males could vote in primary elections, and by the turn of the century segregation extended into public transportation. Booker T. Washington's response to black discontent and white hostility in the South formed the basis of his Atlanta Compromise speech of 1895.

In 1906 a race riot engulfed Atlanta. Provoked by sensational news stories of black men menacing white women, 10,000 white men attacked African Americans in the downtown area and invaded black neighborhoods. The riot led to a modest effort at racial cooperation but a greater commitment from white politicians to exclude blacks from the political process. In 1915 the Ku Klux Klan was reborn, with Atlanta as its headquarters. The Klan's membership in Atlanta reached 15,000 by 1923. Hostility and restrictive housing codes condensed the African American community into neighborhoods on the near eastern and western sides of the city while many black businesses moved east from integrated Peachtree Street to form a black business district on Auburn Avenue.

Modest improvements in race relations followed World War I. The Commission on Interracial Cooperation was created in 1919, and the first city-funded, all-black high school was established on the booming west side. Meanwhile, the Auburn Avenue business and cultural district became very prosperous, increasing the influence of the black business and church elite in Atlanta. African American political strength grew after World War II.

Just as the war ended, the state legislature repealed the poll tax and the federal courts outlawed the all-white Democratic primary. African Americans registered 18,000 new voters to participate in the 1946 primary elections, and formed the bipartisan Atlanta Negro Voters League. The effects of this larger black electorate appeared in the early 1950s, when African American leaders were able to bargain peacefully for increased land, low-income housing, and the gradual elimination of all Jim Crow laws.

Atlanta remained substantially segregated, however. By 1959 African Americans represented 30 percent of the population but occupied 16 percent of the land. Four white high schools integrated in 1961, but restaurants, department stores, and many other businesses remained segregated. Organizing sit-ins and boycotts, black university students became more confrontational, which placed them in conflict with the older black leaders of Atlanta. A generational shift in black activism was under way, which eventually forced Martin Luther King Jr.—often a leader of non-violent demonstrations—to mediate between students and a black elite, which included his father.

In 1962 the city tried to prevent African Americans from further integrating a neighborhood in southwest Atlanta. The "Peyton Road barricades" received national attention, galvanized local black activism and, at least officially, ended segregation in housing. A profound demographic change followed. Whites in south and east Atlanta moved to the suburbs, while blacks migrated to the city. By 1970 African Americans composed a majority of the city population; three years later, Maynard Jackson was elected the first African American mayor. Since then, Atlanta has elected two more black mayors, Andrew Young and Bill Campbell, who was elected to a second term in 1997. While there remains a significant interracial presence in the city, greater Atlanta continues to be effectively segregated into white suburbs and a black city.

North America

Attucks, Crispus

(b. 1723?; d. March 5, 1770, Boston, Mass.), American patriot and the first martyr of the American Revolution.

Information on the birth and early childhood of Crispus Attucks is inconclusive, but historians believe that he was part African and part Native American and was once the slave of William Brown of Framingham,

A lithograph by American patriot and engraver Paul Revere shows British troops firing on and killing five unarmed colonists in the 1770 event that became known as the Boston Massacre. Among those killed was African American Crispus Attucks, a protest leader.
CORBIS/Bettmann

Massachusetts. In November 1750, Attucks escaped. For the next 20 years, he worked on whaling ships docked in ports throughout New England.

His fame is attributable largely to a single fateful day in Boston, March 5, 1770, when anticolonial patriot Samuel Adams urged dockworkers and seamen in Boston to protest the presence of British troops guarding the customs commissioners. Attucks was among an estimated 50 men who gathered that night to confront the British, and is alleged to have rallied his comrades by declaring, "Don't be afraid" as he led the ranks. When British soldiers fired on the protesters, Attucks was the first of five men killed in what became known as the Boston Massacre.

The colonial protesters carried Attucks's body to Faneuil Hall in downtown Boston, where it rested for three days before he and the other four victims were given a public funeral attended by an estimated 10,000 people. At an ensuing trial, Attucks was blamed by the defense for inciting the riot, and the British troops who fired into the crowd were acquitted. Nonetheless, American patriots hailed Attucks's heroism in the skirmish, and perceived it as thez incident that sparked the American Revolution.

For more than a century, March 5 was celebrated as Crispus Attucks Day by blacks living in Boston. A monument commemorating the historic night and honoring Attucks and the other four martyrs was erected in Boston Common in 1888. Attucks's symbolic importance is exemplified by the many schools and institutions throughout the country that bear his name. African American leaders throughout the century have unsuccessfully lobbied the government to create a national holiday on March 5.

Africa

Augustine, Saint

(b. November 13, 354, Thagste, Numidia; d. August 28, 430, Hippo Regius), Catholic saint from North Africa whose doctrinal innovations influenced much subsequent Christian theology.

One of the most famous theologians of his time, Augustine was raised in a mixed household: his mother was Christian but his father, an official of the Roman empire, was pagan. He spent his early years in what is today called Souk-Ahras, in Algeria. Despite the piety of his mother, Augustine abandoned Christianity at an early age, attracted instead by Manichaeism, a system of material dualism that claimed the human soul was like light imprisoned by darkness. A precocious learner, Augustine considered Christian Scripture intellectually crude. Inspired by Hortensius, a now-lost text by Cicero, he mastered rhetoric and, while still in his teens, held a professional chair of rhetoric in Carthage.

Ever questioning the nature of things, Augustine discarded Manichaeism for Academic Skepticism, and, later, Neoplatonism. At the age of 28, he left Carthage for the Roman capital of Milan in search of better-disciplined students. In Milan, Augustine was profoundly impressed by Saint Ambrose, the preeminent Roman churchman of the time, and converted to Christianity. Saint Ambrose baptized Augustine, who thereafter returned to Africa and passed the remainder of his life deep in Christian thought. In contrast to his youthful agnosticism, the repentant Augustine decided that faith was the first and most essential step toward wisdom. He was ordained as an assistant priest in Hippo Regius in 391, and became the bishop of Roman Africa five years later.

Augustine's famous autobiography, *Confessions*, showcases the tormented self-deprecation that not only underpins Augustine's theology but also flavors 1500 years of Christian faith. Augustine's most influential works include his philosophy of creation and of time, his philosophy of history, and his theory of salvation. Although his work affected Western Europe more than it did Africa, Augustine was part of an imperial order that suppressed the Donatists, African Christians who often contested the Catholic establishment for economic and social as well as religious reasons.

Augustine died on August 28, 430, as Vandals were besieging the city of Hippo; August 28 has since become the day on which Catholics honor him.

B

Bahamas,

a country comprising an archipelago of about 700 flat, low-lying islands, 30 of them inhabited, in the western Atlantic Ocean, extending for 1250 km (750 mi) between a point southeast of Palm Beach, Florida, and a point off the eastern tip of Cuba.

The Bahamas may be best known as the setting for one of the most charged events in history: the "discovery" of the New World by the Old. The exact place that Columbus first landed in the Americas has long been debated. Many sources have long believed it to be Long Bay; other possible sites may be San Salvador Island, Cat Island, Samana Cay, or one of several other Bahama islands. But historians agree that Columbus and his crew were in the waters of the Bahamas when they came ashore at 7:00 in the morning on Friday, October 12, 1492. In this way, the Bahamas became the backdrop for the cultural encounter that would eventually bring Europeans, Africans, and Asians to inhabit the Americas and the Caribbean.

Latin America and the Caribbean

Bahia,

a state in northeastern Brazil, considered the cradle of Afro-Brazilian culture.

Of all the states in Brazil, Bahia has maintained the strongest ties with Africa and African culture. During the first two centuries of the colonial era, Bahia absorbed most of the slaves who were imported to Brazil. At this time, the slaves came to constitute a majority of Bahia's population and exerted a proportional effect on the developing character of the state. Today, Bahia's traditions and customs are living testimony to the enormous influence of Africans and their descendants.

Slaves were sold and publicly punished in the Largo do Pelourinho neighborhood in Salvador, capital of the Brazilian state of Bahia. The state is considered the center of Afro-Brazilian culture.
Alex Braga/Contexto

Bailey, Pearl

(b. March 29, 1918, Newport News, Va.; d. August 17, 1990, Philadelphia, Pa.),
African American singer, actress, and entertainer known for her comedic timing
and charm, honored for her service to American troops, and named as special
delegate to the United Nations.

Pearl Bailey made her stage singing debut when she was 15 years old. She
won a contest at Harlem's famous Apollo Theater, and she decided to
pursue a career in entertainment. In 1941, during World War II, she toured
the country with the United Service Organizations (USO), performing for
American troops. Her solo successes as a nightclub performer were followed
by acts with such entertainers as Cab Calloway. In 1946 Bailey made her
Broadway debut in *St. Louis Woman* and won the Donaldson Award for
most promising newcomer of the year. As an actress, she was known for her
mix of charm and comedic timing. She went on to appear onstage in *Arms
and the Girl* (1950), *Bless You All* (1954) and in 1947 Bailey made her film
debut in *The Variety Girl*. She followed that screen appearance with larger
roles in Carmen Jones (1955), *Saint Louis Blues* (1958) and *Porgy and Bess*
(1959). She also appeared regularly on television variety shows, such as the
Ed Sullivan and Perry Como shows.

In 1967, Bailey returned to Broadway with the title role in an all-black
production of *Hello Dolly*! She won a Tony Award for that role in 1968
and that same year, President Richard Nixon named her the Ambassador
of Love. She was also named a special delegate to the United Nations
under the Ford, Reagan, and Bush administrations. Through all of these
honors, Bailey continued to perform. While in her sixties, Bailey decided
to complete her education, and in 1985 she received a B.A. in Theology
from Georgetown University. In 1988 President Reagan awarded her
the Presidential Medal of Freedom. Pearl Bailey died in Philadelphia on
August 17, 1990.

Baker, Ella J.

(b. December 13, 1903, Norfolk, Va.; d. December 13, 1986, New York, N.Y.),
social justice activist who was instrumental in the founding of the Student
Nonviolent Coordinating Committee.

The granddaughter of slaves, Ella Baker began her career as an activist early.
As a student at Shaw University in Raleigh, North Carolina, Baker chal-
lenged school policies that she found demeaning. In 1956 Baker, Bayard
Rustin, and Stanley Levison established In Friendship, an organization
dedicated to raising money to support the Southern struggle. She moved to
Atlanta the following year to organize Martin Luther King Jr.'s newly

formed Southern Christian Leadership Conference (SCLC) and to run the Crusade for Citizenship, a voter registration campaign. Baker stayed at SCLC for two years, but she never accepted its policy of favoring strong central leadership over local, grassroots politics.

When a group of students in Greensboro, North Carolina, touched off a sit-in campaign, Baker left SCLC. Determined to assist the fledgling student movement, she took a job at the Young Women's Christian Association (YWCA). She invited sit-in leaders to attend a conference at Shaw University in April 1960. From that conference, the Student Nonviolent Coordinating Committee (SNCC) was born the following October. Unlike older civil rights groups, SNCC was a decentralized organization that stressed direct-action tactics and encouraged women, the young, and the poor to take leadership positions. Among SNCC's achievements was its role in founding the Mississippi Freedom Democratic Party. Baker was a key player in the party's attempt to replace the all-white delegation from Mississippi at the 1964 Democratic party convention.

North America

Baker, Josephine

(b. June 3, 1906, St. Louis, Mo.; d. April 12, 1975, Paris, France), African American expatriate dancer, singer, and entertainer.

For many people, Josephine Baker's name will always evoke a familiar, controversial image: the "black Venus" naked onstage, except for a string of bananas around her waist, dancing to African drums before her white Parisian audiences. It was this image that first made Baker a star, one whose international fame lasted for five decades. Her first break came when she was featured in *Shuffle Along*, Broadway's first black musical, in 1921. Originally rejected from the show for being too young, too thin, and too dark, she eventually won the role of the comic "end girl" in the chorus line and wound up stealing the show. Four years later she was offered the opportunity to go to Paris and perform in *La Revue Nègre*.

In the midst of all this adulation, however, American audiences were still cool. Baker returned to the United States to appear with the Ziegfeld Follies in 1936 and white America did not

Josephine Baker opens her first Broadway engagement in 15 years, at the Strand Theater in New York City in 1951. *CORBIS/Bettmann*

seem ready to see a sophisticated black star on stage. During World War II she served as an intelligence liaison and an ambulance driver for the French Resistance and was awarded the Medal of the Resistance and the Legion of Honor. She won respect and praise from African Americans for her support of the Civil Rights Movement. She also participated in the 1963 March on Washington, and later that year gave a benefit concert at Carnegie Hall for the NAACP, the Student Nonviolent Coordinating Committee, and the Congress of Racial Equality.

North America

Baldwin, James

(b. August 2, 1924, Harlem, N.Y.; d. December 1, 1987, St.-Paul-de-Vence, France), African American novelist, essayist, playwright, and poet known especially for his astute commentary on American race relations.

James Baldwin was continually conscious of the hypocrisies and injustices in the world around him, and as a writer, he strove to make his audiences aware of the possibility that people could do, and be, better. An expatriate most of his adult life, Baldwin nevertheless wrote tirelessly about the contradictions inherent in American identity, and especially about the state of American race relations. He came to be respected as one of the sagest intellectuals in the Civil Rights Movement and as a leading figure in the African American literary tradition.

Baldwin was born in Harlem in 1924 and his troubled relationship with his strict, domineering stepfather, David Baldwin, a factory worker and Pentecostal minister, colored much of his childhood and he turned to reading as a means of escape. At Frederick Douglass Junior High School Baldwin edited the school paper and belonged to the literary club, whose adviser was poet Countee Cullen. At 14, his literary career was temporarily challenged by a new vocation when he became a junior minister at a Harlem storefront church,

James Baldwin, novelist and essayist, who has been elected a member of the National Institute of Arts and Letters, the nation's highest honor society of the arts. *Bettmann/CORBIS* drawing crowds bigger than his stepfather's. Three years later he decided to leave the church and Christianity.

During the winter of 1944–1945 he met the celebrated black writer Richard Wright, who became a mentor and father figure to him and in 1946 he published his first essay in the *Nation*. He soon became well known as an essayist. In 1948 Baldwin was awarded a Rosenwald Fellowship and used the prize money to buy a one-way ticket to Paris.

As an openly gay African American, Baldwin had long felt stifled by the prevailing racial and sexual prejudices in the United States. The 1948 trip marked the beginning of his career as an expatriate writer. Baldwin's 1949 essay *Everybody's Protest Novel* and 1951 essay *Many Thousands Gone,"* however, both of which criticized Wright's *Native Son*, created a lasting break in that friendship. But by then Baldwin was well on his way to establishing his own identity as a writer. Baldwin finished his long-awaited first book, *Go Tell it on the Mountain*, and published it in 1953. The novel, a largely autobiographical account of his teenage years, received critical acclaim, but his next two novels caused controversy. *Giovanni's Room* (1956) and *Another Country* (1962) featured characters struggling to define sexual, racial, and national identities, and the matter-of-fact depictions of gay relationships in both books surprised many readers. During the same period, however, Baldwin also published three collections of essays, and it was the nonfiction books—*Notes of a Native Son* (1955), *Nobody Knows My Name* (1961), and *The Fire Next Time* (1963)—that secured his reputation as an important American writer and social critic.

Africa

Balewa, Abubakar Tafawa

(b. 1912, Bauchi State, Nigeria; d. January 15, 1966), first prime minister of independent Nigeria.

Unlike other members of the northern Nigerian elite that he was to join, Alhaji Abubakar Tafawa Balewa was born into a low-status, non-Fulani family. In September 1957 Balewa became the prime minister of Nigeria under British control, a position he held until 1959. In 1960 he was knighted in England. When Nigeria gained independence in 1960, Balewa served a second term as prime minister. Although he could act independently, Balewa's power depended on the support of a stronger politician, Ahmadu Bello, a traditional leader of northern Nigeria in Sokoto. Presiding over a new, volatile, and deeply divided political landscape, Balewa espoused moderate positions that probably saved Nigeria from disintegration during its early years. Despite his diligence and integrity, Balewa was assassinated on January 15, 1966 during a coup.

Bâ, Mariama

(b. 1929, Dakar, Senegal; d. 1981), Senegalese writer whose work highlighted the social inequities facing women.

Mariama Bâ was born into a highly educated Muslim family, the daughter of Senegal's first minister of health. Bâ's father had a strong belief in the value of education and, ignoring traditional prohibitions, insisted that his daughter pursue higher education. An active participant in women's organizations, the young Bâ found her voice as a spokesperson for African women facing new troubles in the traditional institution of marriage. Later, as a mother of nine, Bâ would confront these difficulties in her own life, when her marriage to a Senegalese politician ended in divorce.

Bâ's first and best-known novel, *Une si longue lettre* (1980; So Long a Letter), articulates the social inequities facing women in contemporary Senegalese society, particularly the practice of polygamy. The Noma Prize-winning novel takes the form of a letter from Ramatoulaye, whose husband has just died, to her friend Aïssatou. Both women have suffered from their marriages, and the fact that they are highly educated and married for love does not protect them from the oppression experienced by their mothers.

Bambara, Toni Cade

(b. March 25, 1939, New York, N.Y.; d. December 9, 1995, Philadelphia, Pa.), African American novelist, short story writer, and social activist whose work emphasizes the importance of community, history, and social engagement.

Toni Cade was born in New York City in 1939. When Cade discovered "Bambara" as a signature in her grandmother's sketchbook, she added it to her name. In 1970 Bambara edited the anthology *The Black Woman*. This work was partially a response to the civil rights and women's movements, and included works by Nikki Giovanni, Audre Lorde, Paule Marshall, and Alice Walker. In 1971 she edited a second anthology, *Tales and Stories for Black Folks*. Bambara's first collection of short stories, *Gorilla, My Love*, was published in 1972, and her second, *The Sea Birds Are Still Alive*, in 1977. Her novel *The Salt Eaters* was published in 1980 and won the American Book Award in 1981. She began writing and editing documentary films in the 1980s, and in 1986 won the Best Documentary Academy Award for Louis Massiah's *The Bombing of Osage Avenue*. Bambara stated often that art needed to reflect social commitment, and her fiction emphasized the importance of community and social activism.

Banks, Ernest (Ernie)

(b. January 31, 1931, Dallas, Tex.), American professional baseball player who established a major league record in 1955 by hitting five grand-slam home runs in a single season.

Ernie Banks was the first player in the National League (NL) to be named most valuable player two years in a row (1958, 1959). The shortstop and first baseman played all of his 19 major league seasons (1953–1971) with the Chicago Cubs and earned the nickname "Mr. Cub."

As a child, Banks excelled in high school baseball, basketball, and track and field. He pursued baseball, signing with the Kansas City Monarchs of the Negro American League in 1950. After a stint in the army from 1951 to 1953, Banks finished the 1953 season with the Monarchs. He then signed a contract with the Chicago Cubs, making him that team's first black player. In Chicago Banks became a favorite among fans when he hit 44 home runs in 1955, a major-league record for a shortstop. Three years later he broke his own record by hitting 47 home runs. For four consecutive years (1957–1960) he hit more than 40 home runs, ending his career with a total of 512.

A popular figure among fans, Banks possessed an infectious enthusiasm for the game and was known for his favorite saying, "Let's play two today!" He was elected to the Baseball Hall of Fame in 1977.

Banneker, Benjamin

(b. November 9, 1731, Baltimore County, Md.; d. October 9, 1806, Baltimore, Md.), African American self-taught astronomer and mathematician who built a clock out of wood, planned the survey for the establishment of Washington, D.C., and published important almanacs.

Benjamin Banneker was one of several children born to Robert, a freed slave from Guinea, and Mary Banneker. Mary's mother, Molly Welsh, came to the American colonies as an indentured servant from England and later married one of her slaves, an African of royal descent named Bannaka or Banneky. Banneker and his sisters were born free and grew up on a self-sufficient 100-acre tobacco farm. Banneker received the equivalent of an eighth-grade education at a local integrated school and also was tutored by his grandmother. In his early years, he spent much of his free time devising and solving mathematical puzzles. He took over the farm after his father's death in 1759.

Baraka, Amiri

(b. October 7, 1934, Newark, N.J.), African American writer, playwright, and political activist.

Amiri Baraka is a prolific writer who has worked across a range of genres: poetry, drama, the novel, jazz operas, and nonfiction. He also played a crucial role as an organizer, editor, and promoter of the avant-garde movements of the New American Literature in the 1950s and early 1960s and the Black Arts Movement in the late 1960s and early 1970s.

Born Everett Leroy (later LeRoi) Jones, Baraka attended Newark public schools and studied chemistry at Howard University before turning to literature and philosophy. Baraka moved to Greenwich Village in New York City and established relationships with members of the avant-garde Beat, Black Mountain, and New York School movements. He published his acclaimed book of poetry, *Preface to a Twenty Volume Suicide Note* (1961), and co-edited the poetry journals *Yugen* and *Floating Bear* with his then-wife Hettie Jones and poet Diane Di Prima, respectively.

Baraka began distancing himself from the bohemian literary scene after a trip to Cuba. Influenced by the artists of the newly revolutionary country, and by the Civil Rights Movement and black political figures such as Malcolm X, his work became more politically and socially committed. His plays *Dutchman* and *The Slave* (both 1964) combined the nonrealistic staging of early-1960s experimentalist theater with militant and often violent assertions of black pride. The poems collected in *The Dead Lecturer* (1964) are similar; their violent imagery and fragmentary style and syntax provide a vivid record of the black intellectual and artist in torment and transformation.

Baraka was also influenced by musicians such as Ornette Coleman, John Coltrane, Cecil Taylor, and Sun Ra—New Jazz players of the late 1950s and early 1960s who demonstrated that it was possible for black artists to produce avant-garde art rooted in African American cultural traditions. A series of shorter essays that helped introduce the New Jazz to a wider audience was collected in *Black Music* (1968). His history of jazz, *Blues People* (1963), was one of the first books to trace the social and political development of African American music.

While Baraka became increasingly involved with militant political organizations in the mid-1960s, it was the assassination of Malcolm X in 1965 that led to his final break with the predominantly white bohemian world. Shortly thereafter, Baraka abandoned his family and moved to Harlem where he was instrumental in creating the Black Arts Repertory Theatre, the major impetus in creating a well-defined black aesthetic. Though short-lived, it provided the blueprint for similar theaters across the country and helped develop the cultural corollary to black nationalism, the Black Arts Movement.

Though Baraka left Harlem after a year for his native Newark, he continued to serve as a Black Arts Movement and Black Power leader. Heavily influenced by the cultural nationalist Maulana Karenga (from whom he received the name Amiri Baraka), Baraka was an advocate of an Afrocentric doctrine of separatism, self-determination, and communual African American cultural and economic self-development. *The Motion of History* (1978) and *The Autobiography of LeRoi Jones* (1984) were published during this time.

Barbados,

a former British colony that was given the nickname "Little England" because British culture is highly visible throughout the island. Barbados is located between the Caribbean Sea and the North Atlantic Ocean, northeast of Venezuela in an island chain known as the Windward Islands of the Lesser Antilles.

Blacks in Barbados speak with a British accent, play the traditionally British sport of cricket, and adhere to British custom in their legal and political affairs. Great Britain has indeed been an important force in the nation's

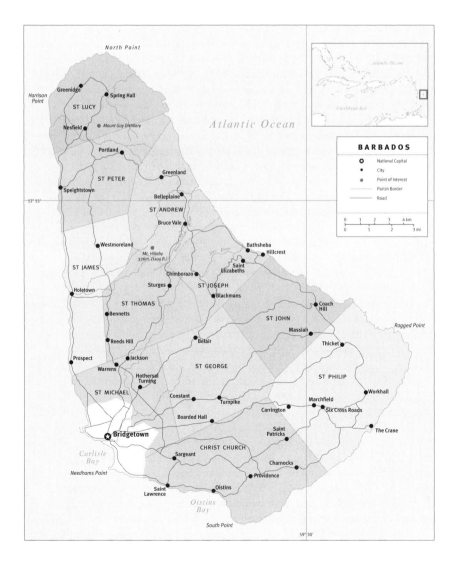

development. But standard accounts of the history of Barbados have often focused on its British character at the expense of its African heritage. Some historians have emphasized the British role in creating the institutions that govern Barbados today. Similarly, its educational system, sports industry, and economy have all been tied to Great Britain. However, British culture has not necessarily played the most important role in the historical emergence of Barbados as a free and democratic society.

Many historians now acknowledge that slavery was perhaps the defining institution in Barbados and that African slaves are essential players in the island's history. In fact, the African roots of contemporary Barbadian society are evident in its music, literature, and poetry. On an equally compelling note, the history of this island country offers a fitting introduction to the rise and fall of European colonialism. Slavery and the sugar plantation were first perfected in the seventeenth century by British planters in Barbados.

The economic role that Barbados played in the development of European capitalism is vital to an understanding of both the history of slavery and its demise in the Western world. Barbados was a colony founded entirely on slave labor. As early as the seventeenth century black slaves outnumbered whites by nearly four to one, culminating in the creation of legal and political institutions that dominated and subjugated the island's black majority for more than 300 years. The authoritarian style with which the white minority ruled Barbados was admired and emulated by white colonists throughout the Caribbean. By the mid-seventeenth century Barbados was the prototype for European colonialism, and the demise of that system on the island bears vivid testimony to the ability of African slaves to overcome enormous obstacles on the road to freedom.

Latin America and the Caribbean

Barbosa, José Celso

(b. 1857, Bayamón, Puerto Rico; d. 1921, Santurce, Puerto Rico), Afro-Puerto Rican doctor, politician, and legislator who struggled for the island's autonomy from Spain and defended the annexation to the United States after the Spanish-Cuban-American War in 1898. He played a key role in the politics of this transitional period, denouncing the Creoles' political aspirations. He also represented the complexities and contradictions confronted by black Puerto Ricans of his time regarding race issues.

José Celso Barbosa's achievements were not typical of blacks in Puerto Rico at the turn of the century. He represented the self-made man who came from humble origins. He had the opportunity to study at the only institution of secondary education in the island, thanks to the determination of his aunt. He completed his studies in the Jesuit seminary before going to the

University of Michigan Medical School in Ann Arbor, where he graduated in 1880. His experience in the United States made him an admirer of republican democratic ideals for social equality and justice.

The Spanish-Cuban-American war of 1898 marked a turning point in the island's history when Spain ceded Puerto Rico to the United States. Barbosa, who first believed that Puerto Rico had to be independent from Spanish colonial rule, then defended the idea that the island should become a state. In 1900 he founded the Puerto Rican chapter of the United States Republican Party and was appointed as a member of the executive council by U.S. president William McKinley.

His ideals were often questioned because he was black and defended the island's annexation to an openly racist country. Many considered him a traitor to his race. This juxtaposition is emblematic of the contradictions concerning race definitions and relations in Puerto Rico.

Latin America and the Caribbean

Barnet, Miguel

(b. 1940), Cuban writer and ethnologist; author of *Biografia de un cimarrón* (Autobiography of a Runaway Slave, 1966), which recounts Esteban Montejo's accounts of his life as a runaway slave in Cuba and as a soldier in the Spanish-Cuban-American War (1895-1898). Other works by Barnet include *Canción de Raquel* (Rachel's Song, 1969), *Mapa del tiempo* (Map of Time, 1989); and *Oficio de angel* (Angel's Craft, 1989).

North America

Barnett, Claude Albert

(b. 1889, Sanford, Fla.; d. August 2, 1967, Chicago, Ill.), founder of the Associated Negro Press (ANP), which distributed news to black newspapers for half a century.

Claude Albert Barnett discovered that the newspapers, too poor to afford news wire services, were hungry for national news. In 1919, the ANP began operation. The ANP, like its model the Associated Press, was a cooperative: newspapers paid a fee to join and in turn contributed articles about important local events. Barnett oversaw a small staff in Chicago who collected, edited, and two or three times weekly mailed articles to the ANP's subscribers. Most of the articles focused on news affecting blacks, often stories that the white press had overlooked. After several years of steady growth, the ANP maintained a few of its own reporters in major American cities and foreign countries.

During World War II Barnett and other blacks pressured the federal government to accredit black journalists as war correspondents, partly to cover the war but also to cover race relations in the armed services. After the war, the ANP expanded its distribution service to Africa, where it offered articles in both French and English.

Influenced by his years at Tuskegee, Barnett also worked to improve the condition of black tenant farmers and sharecroppers in the South. In the early 1940s he offered to serve, and was accepted, as a consultant to the United States Department of Agriculture (USDA). His efforts, however, did little to improve the condition of Southern farmers and in 1953, with the inauguration of Republican president Dwight Eisenhower, Barnett was dismissed.

As the power of black newspapers waned in the 1960s, so too did the ANP. By the time Barnett died of a cerebral hemorrhage in 1967, the ANP's subscribers had dwindled to about 100, and the organization ceased altogether shortly after his death.

Latin America and the Caribbean

Barreto, Ray

(b. 1929), percussionist and bandleader, renowned for his contributions to Latin jazz and salsa. Born in New York of Puerto Rican heritage, Barreto joined Tito Puente's big band in the 1950s. In the 1960s he established the Ray Barreto Orchestra, which recorded under the Fania label. In 1992 he established the jazz band New World Spirit.

North America

Barthé, Richmond

(b. January 28, 1901, Bay Saint Louis, Miss.; d. March 6, 1989, Altadena, Calif.), a sculptor of the Harlem Renaissance era whose sculptures and busts defied universal negative representations of African Americans and other individuals of African descent. Barthé introduced such themes as balance, rhythm, grace, and beauty to the image of his subjects.

Richmond Barthé grew up in Bay Saint Louis, Mississippi, and New Orleans, Louisiana. He graduated from the Chicago Art Institute in February 1929 and moved to New York City that same year. The time after his relocation to New York proved to be prosperous for him; his work was widely honored and exhibited. For example, in 1932 he sculpted *Blackberry Woman*, and *African Dancer* in 1933. The Whitney Museum of American Art purchased these two pieces in 1935. The Caz Delbo Galleries granted Barthé his first solo show in 1934, and he also gained greater recognition after his 1939 exhibit at the Arden Galleries in New York. As a result, he was nominated for and accepted a Guggenheim Fellowship in 1940 and 1941.

He captured the complexities of movement in *The Boxer* (1943), and in 1946 he commemorated such African American achievers as George Washington Carver and Booker T. Washington. The bust of Booker T. Washington was created for the Hall of Fame of New York University. Barthé also modeled a portrait of Othello after the actor Paul Robeson for the Actors Equity. His other commissions included a bas-relief of Arthur Brisbane for New York's Central Park. He designed a large frieze, *Green Pastures: The Walls of Jericho*, for the Harlem River Housing Project, and the *General Toussant L'Ouventure* Monument for Port-au-Prince, Haiti.

Richmond Barthé's career spanned more than 60 years. The art world consistently responded to his work with acclaim. It recognized him for his impressive bronzes and immense statues by electing him to the National Academy of Arts and Letters in 1915; he was the first black sculptor to receive this honor. His work has also been incorporated into the collections of the Metropolitan Museum of Art, the Pennsylvania Museum of Art, the Virginia Museum of Fine Arts, and the Museum of the Art Institute of Chicago.

North America

Basie, William James ("Count")
(b. August 21, 1904, Red Bank, N.J.; d. April 26, 1984, Hollywood, Calif.), African American piano player and big-band leader from the mid-1930s to the 1980s whose band made hard-swinging Kansas City jazz popular across the United States.

Though white clarinetist Benny Goodman was proclaimed the "King of Swing," by all rights the title belonged to Count Basie. For nearly half a century, with the exception of a brief interruption between 1949 and 1952, Basie headed one of the finest big bands in jazz, one that has enjoyed an unrivaled longevity. No other jazz orchestra has continued so long under the same leadership.

Latin America and the Caribbean

Basora, Santiago
Afro-Dominican military leader of the African Batallion; Basora was born in Africa.

Santiago Basora served as a captain in the African Battalion during the Haitian occupation of Santo Domingo (present-day Dominican Republic), which lasted from 1822 to 1844. In February 1844, the Santo Domingo Independentistas, led by Juan Pablo Duarte and the group of conspirators known as La Trinitaria, declared independence from Haiti. Shortly after the declaration of independence, Afro-Dominicans in Monte Grande, led by Basora, revolted, demanding guarantees that slavery not be reinstituted and that Basora be integrated into the government. In response to their demands, on July 17, 1844, the new Dominican government published a law that outlawed slave trafficking of any kind and declared that enslaved individuals entering the Dominican Republic would immediately gain their freedom.

North America

Basquiat, Jean-Michel

(b. December 22, 1960, Brooklyn, N.Y.; d. August 12, 1988, Brooklyn, N.Y.), American painter, initially a street artist, whose graffiti-inspired work won international acclaim during the 1980s.

Born to a Haitian father and a first-generation Puerto Rican-American mother, Jean-Michel Basquiat grew up in Brooklyn. His early interest in art was nurtured by his mother, who often took him to local art museums. In May 1968, Basquiat was hit by a car. He suffered a broken arm and his spleen had to be removed. While he was hospitalized, his mother gave him a copy of Gray's Anatomy, a book that inspired many of his later works.

Basquiat's career as an artist began in 1977 when he began to spray-paint New York City streets and subways with one of his high school classmates, Al Diaz. The works were signed SAMO, an acronym for "same old shit," and consisted of short poetic phrases such as "Plush safe he think; SAMO." They strategically placed these street texts in SoHo and the East Village, where they were more likely to be seen by people in influential artistic circles.

Basquiat's art was publicly exhibited for the first time in the 1980 Times Square Show. Basquiat was also featured in the 1983 Biennial Exhibition at the Whitney Museum of American Art in New York, becoming the youngest artist ever to be included. Within the span of eight years, Jean-Michel Basquiat went from being an anonymous tag-writer to an internationally celebrated artist. His large, colorful works combine graffiti art with abstract expressionism. Some of Basquiat's paintings celebrate African American jazz musicians and boxers, while others address issues such as mortality, racism, and commercialism. The three-pointed crown and the circled c of the copyright symbol are recurrent images in his paintings. Basquiat's work is characterized by the inclusion and canceling out of words, which he explained by saying, "I cross out words so you will see them more; the fact that they are obscured makes you want to read them." Basquiat's rhythmic juxtaposition of words and images constitutes one of his most distinctive contributions to twentieth-century painting.

North America

Bates, Daisy Lee Gatson

(b. 1920, Huttig, Ark.), African American civil rights activist who coordinated the integration of Central High School in Little Rock, Arkansas.

It was as president of the Arkansas state conference of the National Association for the Advancement of Colored People that Daisy Lee Gatson Bates coordinated the efforts to integrate Little Rock's public schools after the Supreme Court's Brown v. Board of Education decision outlawed segregated public schools in 1954. Nine African American students, the "Little Rock Nine," were admitted to Little Rock's Central High School for the 1957–1958 school year. Violent white reaction to integration forced President Dwight D. Eisenhower to order 1000 army paratroopers to Little Rock to restore order and protect the children. Bates was the students' leading advocate, escorting them safely to school until the crisis was resolved. She continued to serve the children, intervening with school officials during conflicts and accompanying parents to school meetings. In 1962 Bates published her memoir of the Little Rock crisis, *The Long Shadow of Little Rock*.

Latin America and the Caribbean

Batista, Fulgencio

(b. January 16, 1901, Oriente Province, Cuba; d. August 6, 1973, Guadalmira, Spain), Afro-Cuban dictator and president ousted by Fidel Castro.

Fulgencio Batista y Zaldivar was a controversial Cuban leader who dominated much of the country's politics for three decades. Batista ruled through a series of puppet presidents and was himself elected in 1940, defeating his rival, Grau. As president from 1940 to 1944, Batista passed a number of reforms governing the areas of health, welfare, and labor. He also legalized the Communist Party. Constitutionally prohibited from running a consecutive term as president, Batista moved to Florida, returning to Cuba in 1948. He ran for his second presidential term and was elected in 1952. In 1954 he won again in a rigged election. In the 1950s Cuba was relatively prosperous among Latin American countries, ranking second in *per capita* gross domestic product, fourth in literacy, and first in the number of televisions and radios *per capita*. Nonetheless, Cuban society was tremendously inequitable. Afro-Cubans, in particular, were socially and economically marginalized, excluded from private beaches and social venues and discriminated against in employment and education. It was these social tensions as well as Batista's refusal to abdicate power that led to his overthrow by Fidel Castro in 1959. After the Cuban Revolution, Batista lived in exile in Europe. He died in 1973 in Spain.

North America

Battey, Cornelius M.

(b. 1873, Augusta, Ga.; d. 1927), African American photographer known for his portraiture technique; established the photography department at Tuskegee Institute.

By the age of 27, Cornelius Battey was well known for his photographic portraiture in New York City and Cleveland. At his popular portrait studio on New York's Mott Street, he photographed such celebrities as Frederick Douglass and President Calvin Coolidge. In 1914 he set up a photography department at Tuskegee Institute and headed it from 1914 until his death in 1927. As an artist he created picture postcards of major African American figures, which were sold nationwide. Between 1915 and 1927 his photographs were featured on the covers of the *Crisis*, *Messenger*, and *Opportunity* magazines.

North America

Battle, Kathleen

(b. August 13, 1948, Portsmouth, Ohio), African American soprano in international opera.

Kathleen Battle began singing in church as a child and received bachelor's and master's degrees in music from the University of Cincinnati College Conservatory of Music. She made her professional debut as an opera singer at the 1972 Spoleto Festival in Italy.

Battle debuted at New York's Metropolitan Opera in 1977 and became internationally known within a few years. In addition to singing soprano roles in opera houses and with symphony orchestras, her repertoire has expanded to include spirituals and the work of George Gershwin and Duke Ellington. Battle has received many honors for her work, including five Grammy Awards and a Candace Award from the National Coalition of 100 Black Women. She is the recipient of six honorary doctorates from American universities, and in 1999 was inducted into the NAACP Image Hall of Fame.

Latin America and the Caribbean

Batuque,

a religion practiced in Belém, a city in Brazil, which combines elements of rural "caboclo" religions with the more African-derived Tambor de Mina religion. Batuque is also commonly used as a generic term for any type of Afro-Brazilian religion or religious ritual.

Bauza, Mario

(b. April 28, 1911, Havana, Cuba; d. July 11, 1993, New York, N.Y.), Afro-Cuban trumpet player, bandleader, and arranger who had a key role in the creation of Afro-Cuban jazz.

Mario Bauza was a talented multi-instrumentalist whose greatest musical achievement lay in his prominent role in the founding of Afro-Latin jazz. Prior to his 1930 departure for New York City, Bauza had concentrated on classical music, playing oboe and clarinet in the Havana Philharmonic. But in the United States he found his true calling as a jazz musician. In 1932, while working in Noble Sissle's band, Bauza began to perform on trumpet, and he went on to serve as a trumpet player and the musical director for Chick Webb's big band (1933–1938). While working with Webb, Bauza helped convince the initially skeptical bandleader of Ella Fitzgerald's great potential as a vocalist. Later Bauza played trumpet with bandleaders Don Redman (1938–1939) and Cab Calloway (1939–1941). Bauza played a major role in convincing Calloway to hire the brash young trumpeter Dizzy Gillespie, whom Bauza had met two years earlier during his stint with Webb. Particularly impressed by the surging polyrhythms of Cuban conga drummers, Gillespie resolved that if he ever organized his own band, he would make sure to include a conga drummer.

At that time Gillespie's notion was a radical one. Although most big bands had at least one so-called Latin number in their books, swing-era jazz remained closed off from authentic Afro-Latin music. At last, in the 1980s, Bauza organized his own big band, the Afro-Cuban Orchestra. The band released three albums of Bauza's compositions and arrangements, the last of which was recorded just two months before his death. These albums gained him a measure of well-deserved critical and popular acclaim.

Bearden, Romare

(b. September 2, 1912, Charlotte, N.C.; d. March 12, 1988, New York, N.Y.), African American artist famous for his collages, which capture the daily rhythms of black life.

Romare Bearden was inspired by the work of such European artists as Pablo Picasso, Henri Matisse, and Joan Miró, who, in the early twentieth century, championed a collage aesthetic. These artists painted or pasted onto canvas elements from various sources, creating images with stylistic and spatial distortions. Bearden was also inspired by the Civil Rights Movement, and he assembled a group of African American artists in the early 1960s to create artwork in celebration of the movement. When they rejected his suggestion that collage be the official medium of the group, Bearden began to create collages on his own.

Bearden became famous for his collage work of the 1960s. The works from this period combine acrylic or oil paints, or both, with images from magazines, newspapers, and photographs. Bearden drew on these various pictorial sources to construct African American people and their surroundings. Most of Bearden's collages are informed by his childhood memories from Pittsburgh, Charlotte, and Harlem in the 1920s. His collages depict African Americans engaged in everyday activities in both street and interior settings. *Evening 9:10, 431 Lenox Avenue* (1964), for example, shows an apartment in which three people are involved in a card game. One of Bearden's outdoor scenes is *Watching the Trains Go By* (1964), in which one of the people waiting for a train strums a guitar to pass the time.

Bearden's collages are uniquely African American. He occasionally juxtaposed African masks with contemporary black American figures in his compositions. Art critic Hilton Kramer interpreted this juxtaposition as the "morphology of certain forms that derive originally from African art, then passed into modern art by way of cubism, and are now being employed to evoke a mode of African American experience." The African American character of these collages also derives from their connection with jazz music.

North America
_____

Beasley, Delilah Isontium

(b. September 9, 1872, Cincinnati, Ohio; d. August 18, 1934, San Leandro, Calif.), African American journalist and historian, campaigned to stop the use of derogatory racial terms in newspapers and chronicled the presence of African Americans in California history.

Delilah Beasley was born on September 9, 1872, in Cincinnati, Ohio. Beasley wrote a weekly column for the Sunday *Oakland Tribune* called "Activities among Negroes" for 20 years. She spoke out against racial stereotyping and discrimination throughout her career. One of her most significant contributions to journalism was her campaign to stop the use in mainstream newspapers of such derogatory terms as "darky" and "nigger" to refer to African Americans.

Beasley also studied history informally at the University of California at Berkeley and by searching research archives and collecting oral histories across the state. In 1919 she published *The Negro Trail-Blazers of California*, which chronicled the presence of African Americans in California history.

Africa
Beatrice, Dona

(b. 1682?, Kongo Kingdom [present-day Democratic Republic of the Congo, or Congo-Kinshasa]; d. July 2, 1706, São Salvador, present-day Congo-Kinshasa), seventeenth-century Kongo prophet who preached the reunification of the Kongo Kingdom.

During a period of instability and fragmentation within the Kongo Kingdom, a young woman named Kimpa Vita (later baptized Beatrice and known as Dona Beatrice) led a religious movement to restore the empire to its former glory. Beatrice began her movement, later called *Antonianism*, in 1704, when she claimed to have had a near-death vision of Saint Anthony. She said the popular Portuguese saint appeared to her as an African, after which she died and came back to life as the saint. Soon afterward she began preaching a religious message that combined an anti-Catholic Christianity with Kongo culture, through which she hoped to reunite the Kongo Kingdom.

North America
Beavers, Louise

(b. March 18, 1902, Cincinnati, Ohio; d. 1962), African American film actor best known for her 1934 portrayal of the mother in *Imitation of Life*.

Born in Cincinnati, Ohio, on March 18, 1902, and raised in Los Angeles, Louise Beavers began her career in the silent film *Uncle Tom's Cabin* (1927). She appeared in over 120 motion pictures, always typecast as a Southern mammy or a source of comic relief. Although her portrayal of the mother in *Imitation of Life* (1934) was called the finest film performance of 1934 and established her career, her acting potential was never allowed to develop. Her notable roles included Pearl, Mae West's sassy maid in *She Done Him Wrong* (1933), Robinson's mother in *The Jackie Robinson Story* (1950), and the title role in the popular ABC television series *Beulah* (1952–1953).

North America
Bechet, Sidney Joseph

(b. May 14, 1897, New Orleans, La.; d. May 14, 1959, Paris), African American clarinet and soprano saxophone player who was, along with Louis Armstrong, one of the greatest jazz soloists of the 1920s.

Although well known to jazz listeners and critics, Sidney Bechet has never enjoyed the reputation of his only peer, cornet and trumpet player Louis Armstrong. Yet in recent years Bechet has gained greater recognition, at least from jazz scholars and critics. For example, Barry Singer, in a 1997 *New York Times* article, described him as an "intrepid musical pioneer who was not merely Louis Armstrong's contemporary but in every way his creative equal."

In many respects, the two men shared much: they were near contemporaries, born and raised in New Orleans, and both were virtuosos on their chosen instruments. Both were known above all as improvisers, as soloists rather than bandleaders, composers, or arrangers. At heart, however, the divergent reputations of the two men reflect profound differences in personality and background. Throughout his long career, from the pinched social world of the Jim Crow South to international acclaim, Armstrong always projected a happy-go-lucky demeanor. Bechet, on the other hand, fought to contain a powerful temper and seething rage toward racial injustice.

Africa

Bedouin,

Arabs who live in the deserts of the Middle East and North Africa and who have traditionally practiced nomadic pastoralism.

The Bedouin are Arab nomads who traditionally controlled caravan trade routes through the Arabian and Saharan deserts and played a substantial role in the politics and economy of the Middle East and North Africa. Proud of their strict ethical codes and their nomadic lifestyle, the Bedouin helped introduce Islam to Africa.

North America

Belafonte, Harold George (Harry)

(b. March 1, 1927, New York, N.Y.), African American singer, actor, producer, and activist who has used his position as an entertainer to promote human rights worldwide.

Harry Belafonte may be best known to American audiences as the singer of the "Banana Boat Song" (known popularly as "Day-O"), but it is his commitment to political causes that inspired scholar Henry Louis Gates Jr.'s comment that "Harry Belafonte was radical long before it was chic and remained so long after it wasn't."

Harold George Belafonte was born in Harlem, New York, to West Indian parents. Belafonte's performance as the only black member of the cast of John Murray Anderson's *Almanac* earned him a Tony award in 1953. A year later he starred with Dorothy Dandridge in *Carmen Jones*, a movie remake of Bizet's opera that brought widespread attention to Belafonte's sensual good looks. His other early films include *Island in the Sun* (1957) and *The World, the Flesh, and the Devil* (1959). In addition, for his work in *Tonight with Belafonte* in 1960 he became the first African American to receive an Emmy Award. As Belafonte began to achieve success as an actor,

Harry Belafonte waves to Martin Luther King Jr. after walking in the 1965 Selma-to-Montgomery civil rights march. Actor Tony Perkins, behind Belafonte, was another of the celebrities who participated in the march. *UPI/CORBIS-Bettmann*

he stumbled into the singing career that made him one of the most popular entertainers of the late 1950s. In 1949 a performance at an amateur night at the Royal Roost nightclub in New York led to an RCA recording contract. Belafonte's 1956 album *Calypso* became the first record to sell more than a million copies and started a craze for his husky voice and for the infectious rhythm of such songs as "Matilda," "Brown Skin Girl," and "Jamaica Farewell."

Belafonte's appeal to white audiences did not, however, protect him from racial segregation. As a result, he refused to perform in the South from 1954 until 1961, and he became deeply involved in the Civil Rights Movement. In 1956 Belafonte met Martin Luther King Jr. in Montgomery, Alabama, and they quickly became close friends. Belafonte was also a friend of Attorney General Robert F. Kennedy and frequently served as a liaison between King and policymakers in Washington, D.C. Belafonte's idea for the hit song "We Are the World" generated more than 70 million dollars to fight famine in Ethiopia in 1985. Two years later he became the second American to be named UNICEF Goodwill Ambassador. A long-time antiapartheid activist, Belafonte recorded an album of South African music, *Paradise in Gazankulu*, in 1988 and chaired the welcoming committee for Nelson Mandela's visit to the United States in 1990.

Latin America and the Caribbean

Belize,

country in northeastern Central America, bounded on the north and northwest by Mexico, on the east by the Caribbean Sea, and on the south and west by Guatemala. Known until 1973 as British Honduras, Belize became independent in 1981 and is a member of the Commonwealth of Nations.

In a region dominated by the Spanish Empire, Belize was conquered by England and has long been an unusual country in the context of Central America. It is the only country in the region in which blacks have consti- tuted a majority of the population for most of the twentieth century, in which English is the official language, and in which Caribbean culture predominates. In 1981 it became the last country in Central America to achieve independence from its European colonizer. For all these reasons and more, few of the generalizations that apply to other Afro-Central American histories and cultures apply to Belize.

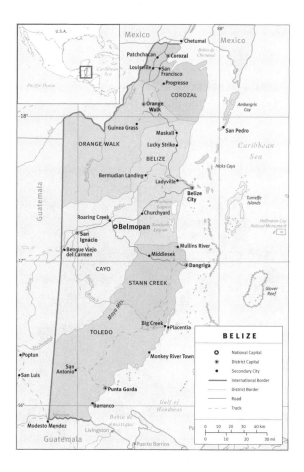

Benin,

West African country bordered by Togo, Burkina Faso, Niger, Nigeria, and the Atlantic Ocean.

Benin, formerly Dahomey, is a country better known by its past than its present. Along its narrow tropical coast, pre-colonial kingdoms grew wealthy through participation in the transatlantic slave trade. Developing rich religious traditions, such as Vodou, they also built formidable armies, which for years resisted French conquest. But during the colonial era Dahomey, a small palm oil exporter known for frequent uprisings, found itself on the periphery of France's West African empire. In the years that followed independence in 1960, Dahomey maintained its reputation for political volitility while doing little to invigorate an economy still heavily dependent on palm oil exports. Since democratic reforms in the early 1990s, however, Benin's political climate and economy have both improved considerably. Observers are now waiting to see if this progress continues after the 1996 re-election of former dictator Mathieu Kérékou.

Benin (Ready Reference)

Official Name: Republic of Benin
Former Name: Dahomey
Area: 112,620 sq km (43,483 sq mi)

Villagers pole skiffs past houses on stilts in a Benin fishing village. *CORBIS/Caroline Penn*

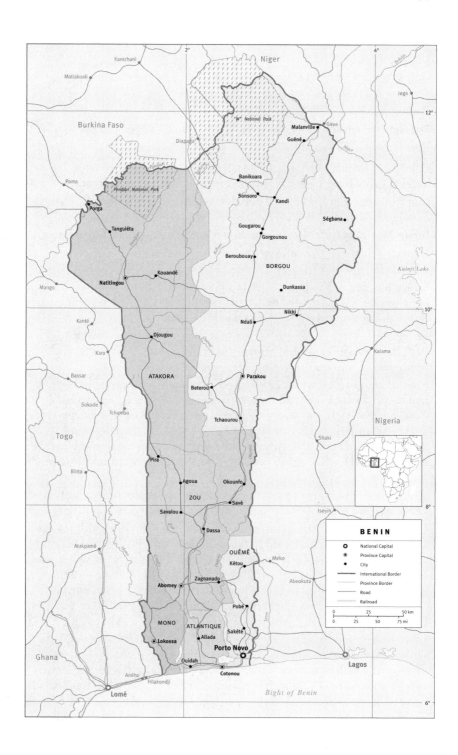

Location: West Africa, bordering the Atlantic Ocean, Burkina Faso, Nigeria, Niger, and Togo.

Capital: Porto-Novo (population 164,000 [1984 estimate])

Other Major Cities: Cotonou (population 533,212 [1992 census]) and Parakou (92,000 [1984 estimate])

Population: 6,100,799 (1998 estimate)

Population Density: 52 persons per sq km (about 136 persons per sq mi)

Population Below Age 15: 48 percent (1998 estimate)

Population Growth Rate: 3.31 percent (1998 estimate)

Total Fertility Rate: 6.48 children born per woman (1998 estimate)

Life Expectancy at Birth: Total population: 53.61 years (male 51.56 years; female 55.72 years [1998 estimate])

Infant Mortality Rate: 100.22 deaths per 1000 live births (1998 estimate)

Literacy Rate (age 15 and over who can read and write): Total population 37 percent (male 48.7 percent; female 25.8 percent [1995 estimate])

Education: In 1975 Benin made education free and compulsory. However, literacy rates have increased only to 37 percent, and only 61 percent of all primary-school-age children are enrolled in schools.

Languages: French is the official language, but most people speak an African language. Yoruba and Fon are the most common languages in the south, and at least six major languages are spoken in the north.

Ethnic Groups: At least 42 different ethnic groups are represented in Benin's population. The Fon, or the Dahomeans, and the closely related Adja group account for at least 59 percent of the total population, and they are the major ethnic groups in the south. In the north the Bariba and Somba (together about 15 percent of total population) are the largest ethnic groups. The Yoruba (9 percent of total population) predominate in the southeast.

Religions: About 70 percent of the population adhere to indigenous beliefs. Christians and Muslims each account for 15 percent of the population.

Climate: Tropical in the south, semi-arid in the north. The south receives about 1300 mm (about 51 in) of rainfall a year, mostly between March and July and between October and November. The average temperatures in the south range from 20°C (68°F) to 34°C (93°F). The temperatures in the north are nearly the same. In the north the rainy season occurs between May and September and annual rainfall averages 890 mm (about 35 in).

Land, Plants, and Animals: Benin is mostly flat to undulating plains, with some hills and low mountains. At one time dense tropical forest covered much of the land near Benin's coast. Most of this forest has been cleared, except near the rivers. Palm trees now dominate the south. Central Benin is covered by woodlands, and northern Benin is savanna. Animals found in Benin include elephants, buffalo, antelope, panthers, monkeys, crocodiles, and wild ducks.

Natural Resources: Offshore oil deposits, limestone, marble, and timber

Currency: The CFA franc

Gross Domestic Product (GDP): $11.3 billion (1997 estimate)

GDP Per Capita: $1900 (1997 estimate)

GDP Real Growth Rate: 5.8 percent (1997 estimate)

Primary Economic Activities: Agriculture employs 60 percent of the labor force. The remainder are engaged mostly in small-scale trade and manufacturing.

Primary Crops: Corn, sorghum, cassava (tapioca), yams, beans, rice, cotton, palm oil, peanuts, and livestock

Industries: Textiles, cigarettes, beverages, food, construction materials, and petroleum.

Primary Exports: Cotton, crude oil, palm products, and cocoa

Primary Imports: Foodstuffs, beverages, tobacco, petroleum products, capital goods, and light consumer goods

Primary Trade Partners: France, Thailand, the Netherlands, the United States, and China

Government: Benin is a republic under multiparty democratic rule. The executive branch is led by President Mathieu Kérékou and the Executive Council, which he appoints. The legislative branch is the elected 83-member National Assembly.

Latin America and the Caribbean

Bermuda,

a British dependent territory that consists of an archipelago of about 150 islands in the Atlantic Ocean, 117 km (70 mi) off the coast of South Carolina (United States).

Bermuda's reputation as a tropical paradise leads many outsiders to mistakenly identify it as part of the Caribbean Islands. In fact, Bermuda is closer to New York and New England than to Florida and the Caribbean, and as far from the Caribbean as Washington, D.C., is from Dallas, Texas. As a dependent territory of Great Britain, it shares a common legacy of colonialism and slavery with countries in the British Caribbean. But Bermuda was actually part of British North America, and its history is connected to the early British colonies in Virginia.

The name "Bermuda" is used in the singular to describe a country of nearly 150 islands. The principal island is St. George's. Most Bermudans live on one of seven islands; the other islands are uninhabited. Bermuda was first discovered by the Spanish sailor Juan de Bermudez in 1503.

Africa

Bikila, Abebe

(b. August 7, 1932, Mout, Ethiopia; d. October 25, 1973, Addis Ababa, Ethiopia), Ethiopian two-time Olympic gold medalist in the marathon.

Before competing as a runner, Abebe Bikila was a member of the imperial bodyguard of Haile Selassie I, the Ethiopian emperor. The marathon at the 1960 Olympic Games in Rome, Italy, was only Bikila's third race at this distance, but he set a new world best time of 2 hours, 15 minutes, 16.2 seconds, and also attracted attention by running barefoot. (The designation world best is used instead of record because marathon courses differ greatly and comparison of finish times is difficult.)

At the 1964 Olympic Games in Tokyo, Japan, Bikila, no longer competing barefoot, became the first runner to win the Olympic marathon twice, finishing with a new world best time of 2 hours, 12 minutes, 11.2 seconds (his previous mark had been broken several times between the Olympic Games). During his career Bikila won 12 of the 15 marathons he entered, an outstanding accomplishment. Since then, many Ethiopian distance runners have followed in his record-breaking footsteps, including Fatima Roba, who in 1996 became the first Ethiopian woman to win an Olympic gold medal in the Olympic marathon. Bikila's career marked the beginning of a period of excellence by Ethiopian runners at longer distances.

Africa

Biko, Stephen

(b. December 18, 1946, Tarkastad, South Africa; d. September 12, 1977, Port Elizabeth, South Africa), founder of the South African Students' Organisation and leader of the Black Consciousness Movement.

Steve Biko's death at the age of 30 robbed South Africa of one of its most popular and effective antiapartheid activists and gave the movement its most famous martyr. Memorialized in the 1987 film *Cry Freedom*, Biko became an international symbol of the brutal repression facing those who fought racial injustice in South Africa.

Resolving that it was time to reject the help of white liberals and form an all-black antiapartheid organization, Biko and other members of the National Union of South African Students (NUSAS) and the University Christian Movement (UCM) founded the South African Students' Organisation (SASO) in 1968. As SASO's first president, Biko traveled throughout South Africa training students to lead their own SASO chapters. In his SASO newsletter column "I Write What I Like," he expressed his views on Black Consciousness, the belief that black South Africans could overcome injustice only by first defeating the mentality of oppression. Even after stepping down as president in 1970-SASO's bylaws provided for a new president every year he continued to function as the organisation's heart and soul. His studies suffered, and in 1972 he left the university without receiving his medical degree.

He was detained twice under the Terrorist Act, and then on August 18, 1977, he was once again taken into police custody, where he was stripped naked and beaten for refusing to cooperate. Less than a month later, his naked, manacled body was found in a Pretoria jail cell. An official investigation into Biko's death cleared the police, and in October 1977 the government banned all Black Consciousness Movement organizations. In 1997 testimony before the Truth and Reconciliation Commission and the public, including Biko's widow, Nontsikelelo, the officers involved finally admitted to having tortured and murdered Biko 20 years earlier. Biko, who was eulogized by then Bishop Desmond Tutu, left behind three young children.

North America

Birth of a Nation, The,

American director D. W. Griffith's silent film about the rise of the Ku Klux Klan, one of the most controversial films of all time because of its demeaning portrayal of blacks.

First released on February 8, 1915, *The Birth of a Nation*'s depictions of blacks as idling and brutish sparked a massive wave of protests from thousands of African Americans. The explosive controversy set off by the film revealed Hollywood's power to reflect and shape public attitudes about race, while setting the stage for what would be a decades-long struggle to improve the portrayal of blacks on film.

North America

Black Aestheic, The,

an expression of the Black Power Movement's principles and aspirations in literature, in which its proponents challenged artists and writers to establish new standards of beauty and judgment based on African American values in opposition to Western aesthetic ideals, and to forge a sense of black cultural pride and nationalism.

The term *black aesthetic* was used informally during the 1960s and adopted as a theoretical concept in 1971 with the publication of Addison Gayle's *The Black Aesthetic*, a collection of essays on the characteristics of the black aesthetic in literature and music. The black aesthetic encompasses a body of oral and written nonfiction and fiction that asserts the equality, uniqueness, and sometimes the superiority of African American modes of perception and expression; a set of political principles opposing inequality; and ethical and artistic criteria outlining what is valid and invalid writing by black Americans. One of the main expectations for a black aesthetic work is that it be politically engaged and socially uplifting.

Black Consciousness in the United States,

One of the most important aspects of the Civil Rights (1945-1965) and Black Power (1966-1975) Movements, or simply put, The Movement, was the increasing awareness among contemporary Negroes of the centrality of a positive racial identity. Black Consciousness here refers to how and with what consequences peoples of African descent in the United States have defined themselves as a people.

Since the creation of the American nation, and especially since emancipation in the Civil War and Reconstruction years, each generation of Negroes has consistently endeavored to build upon the struggles of its forebears. Black Consciousness crystallizes this enduring sensibility of struggle—both failure and achievement. Consequently, it includes how they have collectively viewed their history and culture. Black Consciousness also reflects the relationship between Africans in Africa and those spread throughout the African diaspora, in this case African Americans in the United States. *Black* succeeded *Negro* as the major term of self-definition during the Black Power years. In the late 1980s, in the aftermath of a smaller cultural nationalist moment, African American superseded black as a preferred term of self-reference. On the cusp of the twenty-first century, black and African American are often used synonymously.

Black Nationalism in the United States,

the set of beliefs or the political theory that African Americans should maintain social, economic, and political institutions separate and distinct from those of whites.

Black Nationalism, also known as black separatism, is a complex set of beliefs emphasizing the need for the cultural, political, and economic separation of African Americans from white society. Comparatively few African Americans have embraced thoroughgoing separatist philosophies. In his classic study *Negro Thought in America, 1880-1915*, August Meier noted that the general black attitude has been one of "essential ambivalence." On the other hand, nationalist assumptions inform the daily actions and choices of many African Americans.

Over the course of the nineteenth and twentieth centuries, Black

Nationalists have agreed on two defining principles: black pride and racial separatism. Black Nationalism calls for black pride and seeks a unity that is racially based rather than one grounded in a specific African culture or ethnicity. Thus the basic outlook of Black Nationalism is premised upon Pan-Africanism.

North America

Black Panther Party,

a militant black political organization originally known as the Black Panther Party for Self-Defense.

The Black Panther Party (BPP) was founded in Oakland, California, by Huey Newton and Bobby Seale in October 1966. Newton became the party's defense minister and Seale its chairman. The BPP advocated black self-defense and restructuring American society to make it more politically, economically, and socially equal.

Newton and Seale articulated their goals in a ten-point platform that demanded, among other items, full employment, exemption of black men from military service, and an end to police brutality. Both Newton and Seale were influenced by the black Muslim leader Malcolm X, who called on black people to defend themselves. They also supported the Black Power

Black Panther Party members at the Alameda County Courthouse in July 1968, as the murder trial of Panther leader Huey Newton begins. Newton was accused of killing an Oakland, California, policeman. *UPI/CORBIS-Bettmann*

Movement, which stressed racial dignity and self-reliance. The BPP established patrols in black communities in order to monitor police activities and protect the residents from police brutality. The BPP affirmed the right of blacks to use violence to defend themselves and thus became an alternative to more moderate civil rights groups. Their militancy quickly attracted the support of many black residents of Oakland. Newton, who had studied law, objected strongly when police engaged in brutality, conducted illegal searches, and otherwise violated the civil rights of black citizens.

The BPP combined elements of socialism and Black Nationalism, insisting that if businesses and the government did not provide for full employment, the community should take over the means of production. It promoted the development of strong, black-controlled institutions, calling for blacks to work together to protect their rights and to improve their economic and social conditions. The BPP also emphasized class unity, criticizing the black middle class for acting against the interests of other, less fortunate blacks. The BPP welcomed alliances with white activists, such as the Students for a Democratic Society (SDS) and later the Weather Underground, because they believed that all revolutionaries who wanted to change United States society should unite across racial lines. This position differed from the views of many black organizations of the late 1960s, such as the Student Non-violent Coordinating Committee (SNCC), which excluded white members after 1966.

The party first attracted attention in May 1967 when it protested a bill to outlaw carrying loaded weapons in public. Reporters quickly gathered around the contingent of protesters, who had marched on the California state capital in Sacramento armed with weapons and wearing the party's distinctive black leather jackets and black berets. After Seale read a statement, police arrested him and 30 others. News coverage of the incident attracted new recruits and led to the formation of chapters outside the San Francisco Bay Area. The BPP grew throughout the late 1960s and eventually had chapters all around the country.

Among those arrested in Sacramento was Eldridge Cleaver, a former convict who had recently published a book of essays called *Soul on Ice* (1967). Cleaver's influence in the party increased when Newton was arrested in October 1967 and charged with murder in the death of an Oakland police officer. Cleaver was a powerful speaker who took the lead in building the Free Huey Movement to defend Newton.

As part of this effort, Cleaver and Seale contacted Stokely Carmichael, the former chairman of SNCC and a nationally known proponent of Black Power. Carmichael agreed to become prime minister of the party and speak at Free Huey rallies during February 1968. The Free Huey movement allowed the BPP to expand its following nationally, particularly after it recruited well-known figures such as Carmichael and other SNCC members. The campaign on behalf of Newton saved him from the death penalty, but in September 1968 he was convicted of voluntary manslaughter and sentenced to 2 to 15 years in prison. This conviction was appealed and was overturned in 1970 due to procedural errors.

The SNCC-Panther alliance began to disintegrate in the summer of 1968. As racial tension increased around the country, the Federal Bureau of Investigation (FBI) blamed the Black Panthers for riots and other incidents of violence. The bureau launched a program called COINTELPRO (short for counterintelligence program) designed to disrupt efforts to unify black militant groups such as SNCC, BPP, and US. FBI agents sent anonymous threatening letters to Panthers, infiltrated the group with informers, and worked with local police to weaken the party. In December 1969 two Chicago leaders of the party, Fred Hampton and Mark Clark, were killed in a police raid. By the end of the decade, according to the party's attorney, 28 Panthers had been killed and many other members were either in jail or had been forced to leave the United States in order to avoid arrest. In 1970 Connecticut authorities began an unsuccessful effort to convict Seale and other Panthers of the murder of a Panther who was believed to have been a police informant. In New York, 21 Panthers were charged with plotting to assassinate police officers and blow up buildings. Chief of staff David Hilliard awaited trial on charges of threatening the life of President Richard Nixon. Cleaver left the United States for exile in Cuba to avoid returning to prison for parole violations.

After Newton's conviction was reversed, he sought to revive the party and reestablish his control by discouraging further police confrontations, calling instead for the development of survival programs in black communities to build support for the BPP. These programs provided free breakfasts for children, established free medical clinics, helped the homeless find housing, and gave away free clothing and food. This attempt to shift the direction of the party did not prevent further external attacks and internal conflicts, and the party continued to decline as a political force.

North America

Black Power,

political movement expressing a new racial consciousness among blacks in the United States in the late 1960s. Black Power represented both a conclusion to the decade's Civil Rights Movement and a reaction against the racism that persisted despite the efforts of black activists during the early 1960s.

The meaning of Black Power was debated vigorously while the movement was in progress. To some it represented blacks' insistence on racial dignity and self-reliance, which was usually interpreted as economic and political independence, as well as freedom from white authority.

These themes had been advanced most forcefully in the early 1960s by Malcolm X, the articulate and controversial black Muslim leader. He argued that blacks should focus on improving their own communities rather than striving for complete integration, and that blacks had the right to retaliate against violent assaults. Other interpreters of Black Power emphasized the cultural heritage of blacks, especially the African roots of black identity. This view encouraged study and celebration of black history and culture. In the late 1960s black college students requested curricula in black studies that explored their distinctive culture and history. Led by the cultural critic Harold Cruse and the poet Amiri Baraka, some black intellectuals called for a cultural-nationalist perspective on literature, art, and history in the belief that blacks had separate values and ways of living. Blacks often expressed a sense of cultural nationalism by wearing loose, bright-colored African garments, called *dashikis*, and the natural "Afro" hairstyle.

Still another view of Black Power called for a revolutionary political struggle to reject racism and imperialism in the United States, as well as throughout the world. This interpretation encouraged the unity of nonwhites, including Hispanics and Asians, against their perceived oppressors. Revolutionary nationalists like Stokely Carmichael, later known as Kwame Turé, first advocated a worldwide Marxist revolution but later emphasized Pan-Africanism, the political and cultural unity of all people of African origins.

Black Power as a political idea originated with the Student Nonviolent Coordinating Committee (SNCC) in the mid-1960s. By 1965 many SNCC workers, frustrated at Southern whites' continued resistance to black civil rights, believed that any future progress could come only through independent black political power. When that faction took over the organization in 1966, with Carmichael leading the way, whites were ejected from SNCC membership.

Widespread use of the term *Black Power* started in June of 1966 during a protest march through Mississippi begun by James Meredith, who had been the first black to attend the University of Mississippi. Meredith was wounded by a sniper during the march and had to be hospitalized. Leaders of several civil rights organizations, including Carmichael and Martin Luther King Jr., took up the march. Along the route, Carmichael and SNCC activists exhorted marchers by demanding, "What do you want?" and then leading the response, "Black Power!"

From 1966 to 1969 SNCC and the Congress of Racial Equality (CORE), a New York-based civil rights organization, were dominated by Black Power. In 1966 and 1967 Carmichael and his successor as chairman of SNCC, H. Rap Brown, became well known as national spokespeople for Black Power. Brown once said, "Violence is as American as apple pie." Such statements were condemned by many whites and some blacks as efforts to instigate racial division and violence.

Although Black Power as a movement largely disappeared after 1970, the idea remained a powerful one in the consciousness of black Americans.

North America

Blaxploitation Films,

popular film genre of the 1970s that depicted African American heroes defying an oppressive system.

The term *blaxploitation* was first coined to describe Gordon Parks Jr.'s *Superfly* (1972). Two earlier films are frequently cited as forerunners of the genre: Melvin Van Peebles's *Sweet Sweetback's Baadasssss Song* (1971), and Gordon Parks Sr.'s *Shaft* (1971). Throughout the 1970s it is estimated that some 150 films were made within the blaxploitation genre.

Drawing upon both the mainstream marketability of action films and the growing Black Power Movement, blaxploitation films were popularly well received, if not always critically acclaimed. In these films, the black hero fought back and won, often against overwhelming odds. Filled with fast-paced action, the plot usually involved a male hero, or antihero, who found it necessary to renounce the system and resort to violence. These films portrayed a virile black male sexuality that had been missing in both mainstream and African American cinema up to that point. A few films, such as *Coffy* (1973) with Pam Grier, featured female protagonists.

Blaxploitation films drew criticism for resorting to formulas and portraying unrealistic scenarios, and were actively opposed by a coalition that included the National Association for the Advancement of Colored People (NAACP). Many critics felt that the films were too simplistic to offer any kind of viable model for African American resistance to an oppressive system. Others noted that the character development, particularly of women, was limited. Some, such as black psychiatrist Alvin Poussaint, saw the films as dangerous for their glorification of criminal life and *machismo*, and as ultimately destructive to the black community.

For director Melvin Van Peebles, however, this was not the point. The blaxploitation film's attraction was that "the black audience finally gets a chance to see some of their own fantasies acted out—it's about rising out of the mud and kicking ass."

North America

Blues, The,

an African American music originating in the late nineteenth century that connoted both an emotional state and a musical format. During the twentieth century the blues became the most familiar musical form in the world through its role in rhythm and blues (R&B) and early rock 'n' roll.

The blues is a uniquely African American music and reflects the particular

With "Memphis Blues" (1912), arguably the first blues song to be published in sheet music form, composer William Christopher "W.C." Handy (1873–1958) began his long career as a popularizer of African American music. *CORBIS/Robert Dowling*

William Hudson Ledbetter (1885-1949), best known as Leadbelly, inspired a generation of black bluesmen and also helped bring the Blues to a white audience. *CORBIS/Bettmann*

history and culture of black America. It emerged during the troubled times of the post-Reconstruction South, when Southern blacks experienced political disfranchisement, economic subordination, and systematic physical violence. During the twentieth century the blues moved from South to North, accompanying the Great Migration. The music itself shifted from simple rural blues to rhythmic and rollicking urban blues; it also became an important influence in jazz.

As African Americans rose to prominence in popular culture, the blues reshaped the vernacular music of the United States and the entire world. During the late 1940s the blues became an important element in the black popular music known as rhythm and blues (R&B). In the following decades it provided the musical structure—though not the emotional depth or state of mind—for much rock 'n' roll. In addition, bop, hard bop, and free jazz musicians introduced new musical complexities to the blues. Today the blues can be heard all over the world—in Norway and England, Japan and Taiwan, Brazil and Africa. But America is its true home.

North America

Bluford, Guion Stewart (Guy), Jr.
(b. November 22, 1942, Philadelphia, Pa.), American astronaut; first African American in space.

The eighth launching of the *Challenger* by the National Aeronautics and Space Administration (NASA) was a momentous occasion for the African American community. NASA brought more than 250 famous black educators and professionals to Houston, Texas, to witness Guy Bluford's historic venture into space. The launch, which took place at 2 A.M. on August 30, 1983, illuminated the dark skies for miles around, temporarily turning night into day. Bluford recalled how the blastoff was like riding in a high-speed elevator through a great bonfire.

Guy Bluford broke the color line in space exploration. Five months after his historic flight, another African American, Ronald E. McNair, traveled into outer space. Bluford himself would fly once more aboard the *Challenger*, in October 1985, and twice aboard the orbiter *Discovery*, in April 1991 and December 1992. The Air Force, NASA, and numerous African American organizations have recognized Bluford's accomplishments with various awards.

Latin America and the Caribbean

Bolivia,

landlocked country in central South America; bordered on the north and east by Brazil, on the south by Argentina, and on the west by Chile and Peru.

To those who think of the Andes region and conjure up images of indigenous populations such as Aymara- and Quechua-speaking peoples, it is surprising to realize that black people also live in Bolivia. Even within

the country itself, there are citizens who are unaware of this fact. Many Bolivians, not aware of their country's historic involvement in the trans-Atlantic slave trade, think that blacks are migrants from Brazil or other nearby countries. The scarcity of Afro-Bolivians in the country (about 2 percent of the population) may partially explain the superstition held by some citizens that pinching someone when they see a black person will bring good luck. Whatever the origin of this belief may be, the objectification of black people that it represents illustrates the subtle forms of racism that Afro-Bolivians find offensive.

Reputed to be the most Indian of the American republics because of its large Aymara- and Quechua-speaking population, Bolivia accords little if any recognition to other ethnic groups that reside within its territory. Afro-Bolivians are one such ignored group. It is currently impossible to know the number of blacks in Bolivia because the national census classifies populations only by language, not by race or ethnicity. Unlike indigenous people, blacks are not officially considered a separate ethnic group, since they speak Spanish and do not exhibit marked cultural traits that would distinguish them from the rest of Bolivia's populations. In mainstream society, Afro-Bolivians are pejoratively referred to as *negritos* (little black people) and are seen as part of Bolivia's history, not its present.

Currently, at a time when ethnic groups are receiving recognition and support from governmental and international sources, Afro-Bolivians are moving into the spotlight by showcasing their culture to demonstrate their contribution to Bolivian society. Hoping to distinguish themselves as a unique ethnic group, Afro-Bolivians attempt to rectify the marginalization caused by slavery and its aftermath. The reconstruction of dance, song, and music that were on the verge of extinction is part of this effort. An Afro-Bolivian movement has been established with the goal of effecting social change and promoting cultural awareness.

North America

Bond, Julian

(b. January 14, 1940, Nashville, Tenn.), African American civil rights leader, politician, and educator.

In 1965 Bond won a seat in the Georgia House of Representatives in a newly created black district in Atlanta. However, his statements against the war in Vietnam led the House to bar him from his seat. In December 1966 the Supreme Court ruled in his favor and he was seated in 1967. In 1968 he led a separate delegation to the Democratic National Convention in Chicago to protest the exclusionary practices of the Georgia delegation. He brokered a deal to receive a partial vote and became the first African American placed in nomination for the vice presidency.

After leaving Georgia's House of Representatives in 1975, Bond was a

Georgia state senator from 1975 to 1986, when he ran unsuccessfully for the United States House of Representatives. Since then he has served as regional president of the National Association for the Advancement of Colored People (NAACP), and as president of the Southern Poverty Law Center. He has taught at several universities, including American University in Washington, D.C., and the University of Virginia. In February 1998, Bond was elected chairman of the NAACP.

Africa

Botswana,

a landlocked country in southern Africa bordered by Namibia to the north and west, Zambia and Zimbabwe to the northeast, and South Africa to the southeast.

In many ways, Botswana challenges stereotypical notions about African nations. Since 1970 this former British protectorate has boasted one of the fastest-growing economies in the world. Spurred by the discovery of vast diamond deposits in the late 1960s, Botswana has swiftly transformed itself from an agrarian society, whose chief export was beef, into an efficiently managed, mineral-based economy. Botswana's economic success has been instrumental in ensuring its equally remarkable political stability; since independence in 1966, the Botswana Democratic Party (BDP) has kept its majority in the National Assembly, the country's chief legislative body, despite an open electoral process and the presence of numerous opposition parties.

In recent years, however, economic disparities have sparked growing popular discontent. Botswana's mining- and cattle-based economy has produced an ever-widening gap between a wealthy class of ruling Tswana families and urban elites and a poor, ethnically diverse, and mostly rural population. For the present, however, Botswana appears poised to continue along its path of rapid economic development and political stability.

Africa

Botswana (Ready Reference)

Official Name: Republic of Botswana

Former Name: Bechuanaland

Area: 600,372 sq km (231,805 sq mi)

Location: Southern Africa, north of South Africa

Capital: Gaborone (population 133,791 [1991 estimate])

Other Major Cities: Francistown (population 65,026), Selebi-Pikwe (39,769), Molepolole (36,928), Kanye (31,341), Serowe (30,706 [1991 estimate])

Population: 1,478,454 (1998 estimate)

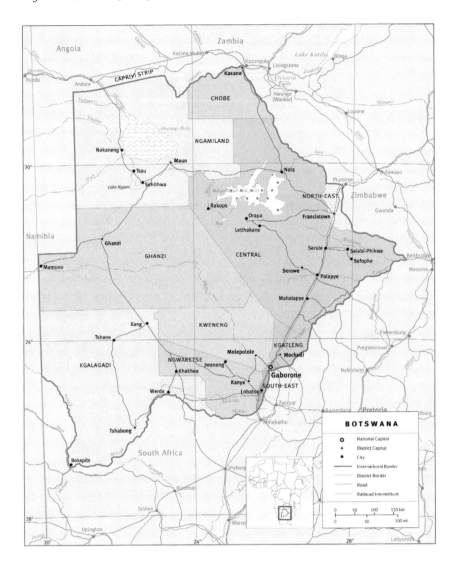

Population Density: 2 persons per sq km (about 6 persons per sq mi)

Population Below Age 15: 42 percent (male 317,254; female 309,617)

Population Growth Rate: 1.11 percent (1998 estimate)

Total Fertility Rate: 4.03 children born per woman (1998 estimate)

Life Expectancy at Birth: Total population: 40.09 years (male 39.46 years; female 40.75 years [1998 estimate])

Infant Mortality Rate: 59.29 deaths per 1000 live births (1998 estimate)

Literacy Rate (age 15 and over who can read and write): Total population: 69.8 percent (male 80.5 percent; female 59.9 percent [1995 estimate])

Education: Most primary schools are supervised by district councils and township authorities, and are financed from local government revenues assisted by grants-in-aid from the central government. In the mid-1990s, Botswana's primary schools had an annual enrollment of about 301,400, and secondary schools about 99,600; about 4500 students were enrolled in the University of Botswana in Gaborone.

Languages: English is the official language, but most people speak Setswana, a Bantu language.

Ethnic Groups: The Tswana are the largest ethnic group in Botswana. There are also significant populations of Kalanga and San.

Religions: About half the population practices indigenous beliefs; the remainder are Christians.

Climate: The climate of Botswana is semi-arid and subtropical, with warm winters and hot summers. The average annual rainfall varies from about 640 mm (about 25 in) in the north to less than 230 mm (less than 9 in) in the Kalahari Desert.

Land, Plants, and Animals: Most of Botswana is a flat to gently rolling tableland; the Kalahari Desert lies in the southwest. Savanna vegetation predominates in most parts of the country. Principal species include acacia, bloodwood, and Rhodesian teak. Wild-life is abundant and includes lions, giraffes, leopards, antelope, elephants, crocodiles, and ostriches.

Natural Resources: Diamonds, copper, nickel, salt, soda ash, potash, asbestos, coal, iron ore, silver

Currency: The pula

Gross Domestic Product (GDP): $7 billion (1997 estimate)

GDP per Capita: $3300 (1997 estimate)

GDP Real Growth Rate: 6 percent (1997 estimate)

Primary Economic Activities: The economy has historically been based on cattle raising and crops. Agriculture today provides a livelihood for more than 80 percent of the population but supplies only about 50 percent of food needs and accounts for only 5 percent of GDP. Subsistence farming and cattle raising predominate. Erratic rainfall and poor soils plague the sector. The driving force behind the rapid economic growth of the 1970s and 1980s has been the mining industry. This sector, mostly on the strength of

Gwi children sing and clap to a playful song in the Ghanzi district of Botswana. *CORBIS/Peter Johnson* diamonds, has gone from generating 25 percent of GDP in 1980 to 39 percent in 1994.

Primary Crops: Sorghum, maize, millet, pulses, groundnuts (peanuts), beans, cowpeas, sunflower seeds

Industries: Diamonds, copper, nickel, coal, salt, soda ash, potash; livestock processing

Primary Exports: Diamonds, copper, nickel, meat

Primary Imports: Foodstuffs, vehicles and transport equipment, textiles, petroleum products

Primary Trade Partners: Switzerland, Southern African Customs Union (SACU), United Kingdom, United States

Government: Botswana is a parliamentary republic. Universal suffrage begins at age 21. The president is elected for a five-year term by the National Assembly, one of the two houses of Botswana's legislature. The president appoints a 10-member cabinet. Botswana's legislative branch consists of the 44-member National Assembly and the 15-member House of Chiefs. The House of Chiefs is a largely advisory body made up of the chiefs of the 8 principal tribes, 4 elected sub-chiefs, and 3 members selected by the other 12. Major political parties in Botswana include the Botswana Democratic Party (BDP), Botswana National Front (BNF), Botswana People's Party (BPP), and Botswana Independence Party (BIP).

Africa

Boutros-Ghali, Boutros

(b. November 14, 1922, Cairo, Egypt), lawyer, professor, journalist, and diplomat; the first Arab and first African to serve as Secretary General of the United Nations.

Boutros Boutros-Ghali was born to a prominent Coptic Christian family in Egypt. He also held teaching posts at Princeton University in the United States and at universities in India, Poland, and Tanzania. In October 1977 Boutros-Ghali left his teaching post to serve in the government of Egyptian president Anwar al-Sadat as a minister of state for foreign affairs. The following month, after Egypt's foreign minister resigned to protest Sadat's intention to hold peace talks with Israel, Boutros-Ghali served as interim foreign minister. He accompanied Sadat on a visit to Jerusalem and later headed the negotiating team that crafted the Camp David Accords with Israel. Boutros-Ghali never became foreign minister, however, because it was a position traditionally reserved for Muslims.

Boutros-Ghali went on to build a career as an international statesman. An expert on development issues, he authored studies and articles on the disparity in wealth between rich and poor countries. He also negotiated agreements in several African conflicts, and his efforts helped win the prison release of South African leader Nelson Mandela. Boutros-Ghali was elected to the position of secretary-general of the United Nations (UN) in November 1991, based on many qualifications: his reputation as a negotiator; his first-name relationship with government officials in the East and the West; his fluency in Arabic, French, and English; and UN members' strong desire for an African in that position.

Boutros-Ghali faced a difficult tenure as head of the UN. His term in office began in 1992, when the world was reorganizing politically in the wake of the cold war. Boutros-Ghali attempted to negotiate several post-cold war conflicts with limited success. He supported sending UN peace-keeping troops to trouble spots around the globe, including the former Yugoslavia, Somalia, and Rwanda. He was outspoken and independent, and these traits did not sit well with some member countries, most importantly the United States.

Latin America and the Caribbean

Brazil,

largest country of South America, with a total area of 8,511,965 sq km (3,286,488 sq mi). It shares a border to the north with French Guiana, Suriname, Guyana, and Venezuela; to the west, with Colombia and Peru; and to the southwest, with Bolivia, Paraguay, Argentina, and Uruguay. Its Atlantic coastline stretches 7491 km (4655 mi).

Many people associate Brazil with the seductive rhythms of samba, the annual Carnival celebration, soccer, and beautiful beaches. Few realize that Brazil's population includes the largest number of people of African descent in the Western Hemisphere. Only Nigeria, with some 115 million people, claims a larger black population. The contribution of Africa to the population and development of Brazil has been prodigious and pervasive, and few, if any, aspects of Brazilian society and civilization have remained untouched by its influence.

The strong show of Afro-Brazilian culture during Carnival brings together Brazilians of all colors, helping to create the impression that Brazil is a racial democracy where people of diverse heritages live together happily and share in equal opportunities. While white Brazilians tend to embrace this notion, black leaders say it is a myth. Despite the prestige they enjoy during the four days of Carnival, Afro-Brazilians as a group lack political and economic power. Even the firmest believers in racial democracy cannot deny that Afro-Brazilians lag in education, employment, health, housing, and a host of other social indicators. In Brazil, where slavery lasted longer than in any other country in the New World, the Afro-Brazilian struggle for complete freedom, initiated by rebel slaves such as Zumbi, continues today.

BRAZIL

⊙	National Capital
⊛	State Capital
•	Secondary City
	International Border
	State Border
	Primary Road
	Railroad

0   250   500   750 km
0   250   500 mi

Europe

Brixton Riots of 1981,

the most publicized of the London 1980-1981 race riots, which showed the extent of social injustice and racial tension in Great Britain.

The riots in London's Brixton district during the weekend of April 10, 1981, were the first large-scale racial confrontations between black British youth and white British police officers. Aggressive and likely racist behavior by the white officers contributed to these and subsequent disturbances. Violence between blacks and whites had erupted in Bristol in 1980 when the police raided a local café patronized mostly by blacks. Similar circumstances led to rioting in Liverpool and London; most notorious of the London disturbances were the Brixton Riots of 1981.

Since World War II the area of Brixton had been in a decline characterized by a falling population, homelessness, and high unemployment.

Though several redevelopment plans had been proposed for this area in London since the 1960s, none was implemented. At the time of the 1981 riots less than half of Brixton's population were people of color. Most of these people of color were of West Indian descent, but some were of African, East Indian, or other cultural backgrounds. Nonwhites made up approximately 4 percent of the total population of Great Britain; almost half of these nonwhites were born in Great Britain. According to experts, many of these people faced educational and employment discrimination that fostered a sense of frustration and deprivation.

On Friday, April 10, 1981, a three-day streak of violent looting and rioting against the police in Brixton was started by both black and white youths. The worst violence, on Saturday, April 11, lasted for over eight hours and covered a large geographical area. On Sunday over 1000 police were deployed to quell the riots, but by this time the disorders were not as violent; by Monday the violence had subsided. About 150 shops suffered losses, 28 properties were burned down, and other buildings were structurally damaged or entirely demolished. Only two people—both policemen—were injured and hospitalized. The police arrested a total of 282 people, most of whom were black.

North America

Brown, Hubert G. ("H. Rap")

(b. October 4, 1943, Baton Rouge, La.), American writer and activist also known as Jamil al-Amin; outspoken advocate of Black Power, elected national chairman of the Student Nonviolent Coordinating Committee in 1967.

Hubert "H. Rap" Brown was born October 4, 1943 in Baton Rouge, Louisiana. In 1962 he dropped out of Southern University to join the Nonviolent Action Group (NAG) at Howard University. In 1965 he became chairman of the NAG. Labeled an "extremist" by the media for his nationalist views, he was an outspoken advocate of Black Power. In May 1967, when Stokely Carmichael stepped down, he was elected national chairman of the Student Nonviolent Coordinating Committee (SNCC).

That same year, Brown was charged by the states of Maryland and Ohio with inciting violence. He was harassed by the police and targeted by the Counterintelligence Program of the Federal Bureau of Investigation (FBI). While under indictment, he was arrested for transporting weapons across state lines. He resigned as SNCC chairman in 1968 and later that year was sentenced to five years in prison on federal weapons charges.

Fearing for his life, Brown refused to appear at his trial in Maryland, and in 1970 was placed on the FBI's Ten Most Wanted List. He was captured in 1972 and spent the next four years in prison. While incarcerated, Brown converted to Islam, taking the name Jamil ("servant of Allah") al-Amin ("the trustworthy"). After his release, Brown moved to Atlanta, Georgia, where he is in charge of the Community Grocery Store and serves as imam (spiritual leader) to Muslim families in and around Atlanta.

North America

Brown v. Board of Education,

the 1954 United States Supreme Court decision that overturned the "separate but equal" doctrine that, since 1896, had made racial segregation legal in public facilities.

On May 17, 1954, in the case of *Brown v. Board of Education of Topeka*, the U.S. Supreme Court ended federally sanctioned racial segregation in the public schools by ruling unanimously that "separate educational facilities are inherently unequal." A groundbreaking case, *Brown* not only overturned the precedent of *Plessy v. Ferguson* (1896), which had declared "separate but equal facilities" constitutional, but also provided the legal foundation of the

Nettie Hunt hugs her daughter, Nikie, 3, on the steps of the Supreme Court building after the court announced its decision in *Brown* v. *Board of Education. CORBIS/Bettmann*

Civil Rights Movement of the 1960s. Although widely perceived as a revolutionary decision, *Brown* was in fact the culmination of changes both in the Court and in the strategies of integration's most powerful legal champion, the National Association for the Advancement of Colored People (NAACP).

The cases came from Kansas, South Carolina, Virginia, and Delaware, with a related case from the District of Columbia. Each was a class-action lawsuit involving state-imposed school segregation.

Beginning in 1949, NAACP lawyers presented cases before federal tribunals in their respective districts. Among the evidence they presented was that of academic experts like social psychologist Kenneth B. Clark, known as the "doll man," whose work with children demonstrated the damaging psychological effects of segregation. As expected, the tribunals relied on Supreme Court precedent—*Plessy*—and ruled with the defendants. But the opinions gave hope to Thurgood Marshall, NAACP chief counsel. Now consolidated under the name *Brown v. Board of Education*, the five cases came before the Supreme Court in December 1952. The NAACP followed the same strategy that had brought success in *Sweatt (v. Painter)* and *McLaurin (v. Oklahoma State Regents)*. Marshall and his colleagues wrote that states had no valid reason to impose segregation, that racial separation—no matter how equal the facilities—caused psychological damage to black children, and that "restrictions or distinctions based upon race or color" violated the equal protection clause of the Fourteenth Amendment. Lawyers for the states argued that *Plessy* was correct: as long as accommodations were "equal," segregation itself hurt no one. They predicted dire consequences for integrated education, particularly in a South accustomed to segregation.

Though a majority of the justices already favored the NAACP's clients, some feared issuing a ruling that might have to be implemented by force. They decided to have the cases reargued the following term. In the intervening time, Chief Justice Fred Vinson died and President Eisenhower replaced him with California governor Earl Warren, who used his political skills to negotiate a unanimous Court verdict for desegregation.

The opinion, written by Warren and read on May 17, 1954, was short and straightforward. It echoed Marshall's expert witnesses, stating that for African American schoolchildren, segregation "generates a feeling of inferiority as to their status in the community that may affect their hearts and minds in a way unlikely to ever be undone." Critics decried such emphasis on psychological and sociological evidence, but Chief Justice Warren later argued for the importance of contradicting *Plessy*, which had stated that African Americans themselves had imagined any "badge of inferiority" conferred by segregation. The decision went on to say that segregation had no valid purpose, was imposed to give blacks lower status, and was therefore unconstitutional based on the Fourteenth Amendment.

Despite victory in the nation's highest court, desegregation was not immediate, easy, or complete. A separate decision, known as *Brown II* (1955), set guidelines for dismantling segregation. But without deadlines— the opinion contained the infamous phrase "with all deliberate speed"—

desegregation came slowly. Throughout the South, whites reacted violently to school integration. Crowds threw rocks at black grade-schoolers in Little Rock, Arkansas, in 1957, and in 1962, Alabama governor George Wallace blocked the door when the first African American students attempted to enter the state university. Throughout the 1960s and 1970s urban schools increasingly experienced de facto segregation as middle-class whites fled to the suburbs. New strategies to achieve integration, like busing, sparked renewed frustration, anger, and resentment on all sides.

At present, many urban American schools are nearly all-black while many suburban schools are all-white. In some cases, these schools are as unequal as those before *Brown*. Despite such setbacks, however, the case, considered by many legal scholars to be the most significant of the twentieth century, brought racial integration to thousands of American schools and inspired the Civil Rights Movement of the 1960s.

North America

Bunche, Ralph Johnson

(b. August 7, 1904, Detroit, Mich.; d. December 9, 1971, New York, N.Y.), American diplomat and political scientist who won the Nobel Peace Prize in 1950, the first black American so honored.

While still a graduate student, Ralph Bunche established himself as a professor and an activist for civil rights. In 1928 he joined the faculty of Howard University in Washington, D.C., where he founded and chaired the political science department. Bunche expressed his commitment to racial integration and to economic improvement for workers during his years at Howard by participating in civil rights protests and in the establishment of the National Negro Congress in 1936. From 1938 to 1940, Bunche collaborated with Swedish sociologist Gunnar Myrdal on the research for Myrdal's massive study of American race relations, *An American Dilemma: The Negro Problem and Modern Democracy* (1944).

After years as a scholar of international politics, Bunche assumed a more active role during World War II. In 1941 he left Howard and joined the Office of Strategic Services (the predecessor of the Central Intelligence Agency), where he specialized in African affairs. He moved to the State Department in 1944, and, as the first African American to run a departmental division of the federal government, continued to work on Africa and on colonial issues.

Bunche's association with the United Nations (UN) also began in 1944. Bunche first made his name as a peace-maker in 1949, when, defying all expectations, he negotiated the truce that ended the first Arab-Israeli War. Originally sent to Jerusalem in 1948 as the assistant to UN mediator Count Folke Bernadotte, Bunche stepped in when Bernadotte was assassinated and worked almost single-handedly to bring Israel and the Arab states to an agreement. For his efforts Bunche was awarded the Nobel Prize for Peace in 1950.

In 1955 Bunche was appointed UN undersecretary for special political affairs. In that capacity he oversaw UN peacekeeping operations in some of the most heated conflicts around the world. As director of UN activities in the Middle East during and after the Suez Crisis of 1956, he broadened the organization's peacekeeping role by creating the United Nations Emergency Force. He represented the UN during crises in the Republic of the Congo, Cyprus, India, Pakistan, and Yemen. His successor, Sir Brian Urquhart, described Bunche as "the original principal architect" of the concept of international peacekeeping.

Africa

Burkina Faso,

landlocked West African country bordered by Côte d'Ivoire, Mali, Niger, Benin, Togo, and Ghana.

In 1984 the leaders of Upper Volta changed the name of this former French colony to Burkina Faso, a name that combines two of the country's many languages and means "land of upright people." As one of the world's poorest nations, Burkina Faso counts people among its most important resources; remittances from migrant laborers working in the more affluent Côte d'Ivoire

Burkina Faso's Sanou Wilfred competes for possession of the ball during his team's trip to the semifinals of the Sub-17 World Cup. Soccer tournaments such as this are among Africa's most popular pastimes and often draw thousands of spectators.
AFP/CORBIS

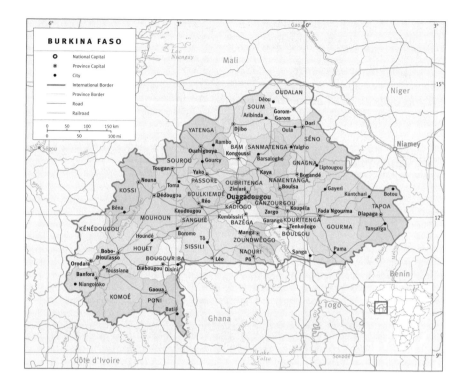

sustain the households of many of the approximately 10 million citizens in Burkina Faso, over 80 percent of whom live in rural areas. The tradition of southward migration became firmly established during the colonial era, when France incorporated the Volta region into its West African empire precisely in order to turn the drought-prone but relatively populous Mossi plateau into a labor reserve. As the French colonial administration invested little in developing Upper Volta itself, *de jure* independence in 1960 heralded a new era of *de facto* dependence on foreign donors, especially France. But steady infusions of aid failed to prevent either the onset of two famines or the overthrow of six governments. In 1983 flight commander Thomas Sankara came to power promising an end to both neo-colonialism and rural suffering. Although the Burkinabè revolution was cut short by Sankara's assassination in 1987, it did initiate improvements in rural literacy, health, and food security as well as women's rights. The current regime of President Blaise Compaoré has deregulated the economy, mended relations with the West, and pledged a commitment (viewed skeptically by many Burkinabè) to democracy. Burkina Faso is still extremely poor but enjoys a reputation for religious and ethnic tolerance as well as for its rich performing arts traditions.

Burkina Faso (Ready Reference)

Official Name: Burkina Faso

Former Name: Upper Volta

Area: 274,200 sq km (about 105,869 sq mi)

Location: Inland West Africa, bordered by Mali, Niger, Benin, Togo, Ghana, and Côte d'Ivoire

Capital: Ouagadougou, population 500,000 (1990 estimate)

Other Major Cities: Bobo-Dioulasso, population 250,000, Koudougou, population 70,000 (1990 estimate)

Population: 11,266,393 (July 1998 estimate)

Population Density: 38 persons per sq km (about 98 persons per sq mi)

Population Below Age 15: 44.9 percent

Population Growth Rate: 2.72 percent (1998 estimate)

Total Fertility Rate: 6.64 children born per woman (1998 estimate)

Life Expectancy at Birth: Total population: 46.1 years (male 45.38 years; female 46.85 years [1998 estimate])

Infant Mortality Rate: 109.15 deaths per 1000 live births (1998 estimate)

Literacy Rate (age 15 and over who can read and write): Total population: 19 percent (male 29.5 percent; female 9.2 percent [1995 estimate])

Education: Officially compulsory for children aged 7 to 13, but less than one-third of all children aged 6 to 11 attended school in the early 1990s, and only 7 percent of those aged 12 to 17. Far fewer girls than boys attend school. In the mid-1990s Burkina Faso's primary schools had an annual enrollment of about 650,195, secondary schools about 116,033, and vocational schools about 8808; about 9452 students were enrolled at the university level.

Languages: French is the official language but is not widely spoken outside of cities. More than half the population speaks Moore; the remainder speak a variety of Mande languages.

Ethnic Groups: Most people belong to two major West African cultural groups, the Voltaic and the Mande. The Voltaic are the most numerous and include the Mossi, who constitute about 60 percent of the population. Other principal ethnic groups are the Fulani, Lobi, Bobo, Sénufo, Gourounsi, Bissa, and Gourmantche.

Religions: About 65 percent of the population adhere to indigenous beliefs. About 25 percent are Muslim and 10 percent Christian (mainly Roman Catholic).

Climate: Semi-arid; the weather is cool and dry from November through March, hot and dry from April through May, and warm and rainy from June through October. Average annual rainfall ranges from 1000 mm (more than 40 in) in the southwest to less than 250 mm (less than 10 in) in the north. Average temperatures in Ouagadougou vary from 24° C (76° F) in January to 28° C (83° F) in July.

Land, Plants, and Animals: Burkina Faso is located on a plateau sloping generally to the south and situated from about 200 to 700 m (about 650 to 2300 ft) in elevation. The plateau is drained to the south by the Black Volta (Mouhoun), Red Volta (Nazinon), and White Volta (Nakanbe) rivers and to the east by small rivers connecting with the Niger; none is navigable. Most of the country is covered with savanna grasses and small trees. Animals include elephants, hippopotamuses, buffalo, antelope, and crocodiles.

Natural Resources: Mineral resources include manganese and gold as well as small deposits of copper, nickel, bauxite, lead, silver, iron ore, cassiterite (tin ore), and phosphates. Except in the southwest of the country, water is scarce and most of the soils are relatively poor.

Currency: The CFA franc

Gross Domestic Product (GDP): $10.3 billion (1997 estimate)

GDP per Capita: $950 (1997 estimate)

GDP Real Growth Rate: 6 percent (1997 estimate)

Primary Economic Activities: Agriculture (32 percent of GDP, 80 percent of employment), livestock, small-scale commerce, gold mining, and migrant labor (approximately 20 percent of the male labor force migrates annually to neighboring countries).

Primary Crops: Millet, sorghum, corn, rice, peanuts, shea nuts, sesame, cotton, and livestock

Industries: Cotton lint, beverages, agricultural processing, soap, cigarettes, and textiles

Primary Exports: Cotton, livestock products, and gold

Primary Imports: Foodstuffs, petroleum, textiles, iron, steel, metal products, vehicles, electrical equipment, and machinery

Primary Trade Partners: European Union (especially France), Côte d'Ivoire, Taiwan, and Thailand

Government: Parliamentary; nominally a constitutional multiparty democracy. The executive branch is led by President Blaise Compaoré and an appointed 29-member cabinet, which includes Prime Minister Roche Kabore. The legislative branch is the elected 107-member National Assembly, currently dominated by President Compaoré's party, the Organization for Popular Democracy-Labor Movement (ODP-MT).

Africa

Burundi,

a small country located between East and Central Africa, bordered by Rwanda, the Democratic Republic of the Congo, and Tanzania.

Nineteenth-century European travelers described the kingdom of Burundi as "a land of almost ideal beauty." Today, the national borders of Burundi, one of Africa's most densely populated countries, remain virtually

1. Travailler ensemble,
2. Travailler avec courage,
3. Le travail avance rapidement.
4. Le travail est bien fait.
5. Travailler avec amour.
6. Travail en paix
7. Travail avec beaucoup de joie.

A teacher at a peace education class in Burundi instructs Hutu and Tutsi students in principles for working together, including working with love, peace, and joy. *CORBIS/Howard Davies*

unchanged, but political turmoil has disfigured its idyllic landscape. Formerly ruled by traditional monarchies, Burundi was colonized by Germany in the late nineteenth century and was under German and then Belgian administration until its independence in 1962. Just ten years after independence, an abortive coup d'état in 1972 provoked brutal massacres, claiming the lives of more than 100,000 people. Tens of thousands more have since died, particularly in 1988 and 1993, in what is usually referred to as "ethnic conflict" between the country's Hutu majority, composing approximately 85 percent of its 6 million inhabitants, and the 15 percent Tutsi minority. But this explanation for Burundi's violence overlooks the long history of cohabitation and intermarriage between these two groups. More fundamentally, it does not do justice to the extraordinarily complex social, economic, and political meanings of ethnic identity in Burundi.

Africa
Burundi (Ready Reference)
Official Name: Burundi
Area: 27,834 sq km (10,750 sq mi)
Location: Central Africa, bordered by Rwanda, Tanzania, the Democratic Republic of the Congo (formerly Zaire), and Lake Tanganyika
Capital: Bujumbura (population 300,000 [1993 estimate])
Other Major City: Gitega (population 95,000 [1987 estimate])
Population: 5,537,387 (July 1998 estimate)

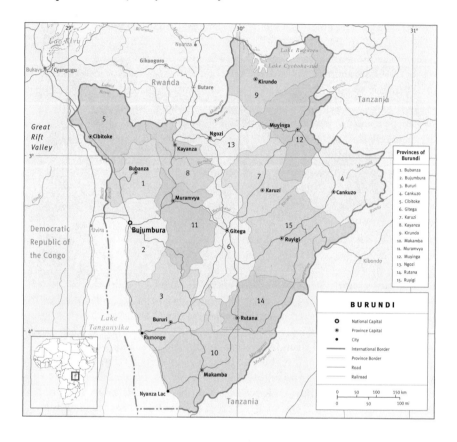

Population Density: 228 persons per sq km (about 590 persons per sq mi)

Population Below Age 14: 47 percent

Population Growth Rate: 3.51 percent (1998 estimate)

Total Fertility Rate: 6.4 children born per woman (1998 estimate)

Life Expectancy at Birth: Total population: 45.56 years (male 43.79 years; female 47.38 years [1998 estimate])

Infant Mortality Rate: 101.19 deaths per 1000 live births (1998 estimate)

Literacy Rates (age 15 and over who can read and write): Total population: 35 percent (male: 49.3 percent; female: 22.5 percent [1995 estimate])

Education: Schooling is free and officially compulsory for children aged 7 through 12. In the early 1990s about 631,039 students annually attended primary schools and about 46,500 attended secondary schools. The University of Burundi (founded in 1960), located in Bujumbura, is the leading institution of higher education; it had an enrollment of about 3800 in the early 1990s.

Languages: Kirundi and French are the official languages. Swahili is spoken along Lake Tanganyika and in the Bujumbura area.

Ethnic Groups: The chief ethnic groups are the Hutu, a Bantu-speaking people making up about 85 percent of the population, and the Tutsi, a Nilotic-speaking people forming about 14 percent of the total. Since October 1993, hundreds of thousands of refugees have fled Burundi and crossed into Rwanda, Tanzania, and the Democratic Republic of the Congo because of ethnic violence between Hutu and Tutsi factions.

Religions: About 67 percent are Christian (62 percent are Catholic, 5 percent are Protestant), 32 percent practice indigenous beliefs, and Muslims constitute 1 percent of the population.

Climate: Tropical, moderated in most places by altitude. The average annual temperature is 20° C (68° F) on the plateau and 23° C (73° F) in the Great Rift Valley. Dry seasons are from May to August and from January to February.

Land, Plants, and Animals: Burundi is mostly a hilly plateau region, with an elevation ranging between 1400 and 1800 m (between 4600 and 5900 ft). Elevations decrease gradually to the east and southeast. The narrow western margin of the country, bordering the Rusizi River and Lake Tanganyika, lies in the trough of the Great Rift Valley. The main rivers are the Rusizi, the Malagarasi, and the Ruvuvu. Savanna vegetation, a grassland interspersed with trees, predominates in most of the country. Eucalyptus, acacia, and oil palm are the most common trees. Wildlife is diverse: the elephant, hippopotamus, crocodile, wild boar, leopard, antelope, and flying lemur are common, as are the guinea hen, partridge, duck, goose, quail, and snipe.

Natural Resources: Mineral resources include nickel, uranium, rare earth oxides, peat, cobalt, copper, platinum (which has not yet been exploited), and vanadium. Current environmental issues facing Burundi include soil erosion because of overgrazing and the expansion of agriculture into marginal lands; deforestation (little forested land remains because of uncontrolled cutting of trees for fuel); and loss of habitat, which threatens wildlife populations.

Currency: The Burundi franc

Gross Domestic Product (GDP): $4 billion (1997 estimate)

GDP per Capita : $660 (1997 estimate)

GDP Real Growth Rate: 4.4 percent (1997 estimate)

Primary Economic Activities: subsistence agriculture (54.1 percent of GDP, 93 percent of employment); industry (mining) (16.8 percent of GDP, 1.5 percent of employment); service industries (29.1 percent of GDP, 4 percent of employment)

Primary Crops: Coffee, cotton, tea, corn, sorghum, sweet potatoes, bananas, manioc, meat, milk, and hides

Industries: Light consumer goods such as blankets, shoes, and soap

Primary Exports: Coffee, cotton, hides, tea

Primary Imports: Textiles, motor vehicles, flour, and petroleum products

Primary Trade Partners: European Union, United States, and Asia

Government: Republic; a constitutional multiparty democracy. The executive branch has been led by president Pierre Buyoya since September 27, 1996. The government is headed by Prime Minister Pascal-Firmin Ndimira (since July 31, 1996) and the Council of Ministers, who are appointed by the prime minister. The Assemblée Nationale (National Assembly) is a unicameral legislative branch, most of which (71 percent) is represented by the Burundi Democratic Front (FRODEBU), with most of the remaining seats (21 percent) filled by representatives of the Unity for National Progress (UPRONA) party.

Cabrera, Lydia

(b. May 20, 1900, Havana, Cuba; d. September 19, 1991, Miami, Fla.), Cuban writer and cultural anthropologist who played a central role in documenting and promoting an appreciation of Afro-Cuban culture.

Born in Cuba, Lydia Cabrera moved to Paris in 1927 and during the next decade traveled back and forth between Europe and Cuba. She returned to Cuba in 1938 and sought exile in Miami, Florida, following the Cuban Revolution of 1959.

Cabrera is widely considered one of the two most important twentieth-century researchers and writers on Afro-Cuban culture; the other is Fernando Ortíz. Cabrera wrote more than a dozen volumes of investigative work on the subject, including her pioneering *El monte* (1954), subtitled *Notes on the Religion, the Magic, the Superstitions, and the Folklore of Creole Negroes and the Cuban People* and *Reglas de congo* (1980), a book on Bantu (known as congo in Cuba) rituals. According to Ana María Simo, author of *Lydia Cabrera: An Intimate Portrait*, Cabrera's "is the most important and complete body of work on Afro-Cuban religions" of its time. Cabrera also wrote four volumes of short stories inspired by Afro-Cuban legends and beliefs. Her fiction is rich in metaphor and symbolism and has been compared stylistically with the writings of Spanish poet and playwright Federico García Lorca.

Some literary scholars have compared Cabrera's early fiction with that of the Negrista writers, in particular those who had a tendency to exoticize black culture and perpetuate ethnic stereotypes. In 1954 she established herself as a major intellectual figure with the publication of her book *El monte*, a meticulously researched study of Afro-Cuban religious beliefs, practices, deities, and folk medicine. Between 1970 and her death in 1991, she produced nine additional anthropological works as well as three collections of short stories, including *Ayapá—cuentos de Jicotea* (1971), considered by Simo to be perhaps the most 'African' of her books.

Cairo, Egypt,

the capital of Egypt and one of the largest cities in Africa

Cairo is the industrial, commercial, cultural, and administrative center of Egypt and the Arab League headquarters. Home to a number of universities and many Arabic-language publishing houses, Cairo is considered by many people to be the cultural capital of the Arabic-speaking world. It occupies approximately 453 sq km (about 175 sq mi) on both banks of the Nile River, and includes several of the river's islands. Its architecture, a mixture of the ancient and the modern, reflects its long and rich history. Although Cairo proper was founded in 969 C.E., the area has been a center of civilization for roughly 5000 years. The ancient Egyptian capital of Memphis was founded in the fourth millennium B.C.E., approximately 25 km (about 14 mi) south of modern Cairo. The invasion of Egypt by Islamic Arabs in 641 C.E. sparked the foundation of the city that has become Cairo. The Arab city, known as al-Fustat (roughly, "tent city"), grew from the collection of tents pitched by the Arab army that was besieging Babylon-in-Egypt. Until the Arab invasion, Alexandria had served as Egypt's capital, but the Arabs established their capital at al-Fustat. In 969 the Fatimids, an Islamic dynasty from modern Tunisia, founded a new capital, al-Qahirah (Cairo).

Meanwhile, Cairo had become the center of Egyptian economic, political, and cultural life. In the thirteenth century, the city became the capital of the Mamluks. During their rule the city achieved its greatest prosperity. Indeed, Cairo's grandeur exceeded that of any other city in Africa, Europe, or western Asia. The city became the center of the lucrative East-West spice trade, and was the home of the renowned al-Azhar University. The city began to decline after the bubonic plague devastated its population in 1348. Its central economic role disappeared when Portuguese explorer Vasco da Gama opened the route from Europe to the Indian Ocean ending Cairo's spice trade monopoly. The Turks of the Ottoman empire seized the weakened Cairo in 1517 and made the city a provincial capital in its vast empire. Ottoman rule lasted until Napoleon briefly took the city for France in 1798. The Turks returned three years later and in 1805 appointed Muhammad Ali as the pasha. Muhammad Ali founded a dynasty that ruled Egypt, albeit under increasing British colonial domination. The British occupied Egypt beginning in the 1880s and declared it a protectorate in 1919. Ali's descendants ruled as puppets under British occupation until 1952, when a coup led by Gamal Abdel Nasser established the Egyptian republic, with Cairo as its capital.

Today Cairo remains the commercial and industrial center of Egypt. The city has numerous historical and cultural sites to which tourists have been drawn for centuries, including the Blue Mosque, the Museum of Islamic Arts, the Egyptian Museum (including the Tutankhamen collection), the Coptic Museum, the Al Gawhara Palace Museum, and—at nearby Giza—the Great Pyramids and Sphinx. The Citadel, begun by emperor Saladin in 1176, lies in east Cairo, also the site of the Muhammad Ali Mosque.

Calloway, Cabell (Cab)

(b. December 25, 1907, Rochester, N.Y.; d. November 18, 1994, Hosckessin, Del.), African American singer and bandleader famed for his showmanship and skill at jive.

It was at the Cotton Club that Calloway wrote and introduced *Minnie the Moocher* (1931), a song that would be forever linked to him. The song combined scat-singing with nonsense syllables and lyrics freighted with the argot of drug use, recounting how Minnie and her cocaine-using lover, Smokey Joe, went to Chinatown, where "he showed her how to kick the gong around"—slang for opium smoking. Calloway became known as a master of jive, the term then applied to African American slang (particularly that used by blacks in the entertainment industry). He wrote *The Hepster's Dictionary* (1938), which sold 2 million copies and became the New York Public Library's standard reference work on the subject.

Calypso,

the Carnival music of Trinidad that first appeared in the early twentieth century; characterized by simple melodies, infectious rhythms, and topical lyrics and often played by Trinidad's distinctive steel-drum bands.

Most calypso music is created for Trinidad's extended Carnival. Carnival season commences soon after Christmas and reaches its climax on Carnival Tuesday, the day before Ash Wednesday and the beginning of Lent. During the nineteenth century, calypso music evolved out of earlier musical forms that reflect the island's complex cultural heritage.

During the late nineteenth century, Trinidad's middle class took an increased interest in Carnival. Their involvement brought various changes, the most important of which, in musical terms, was to substitute English for French Creole. During the 1920s singing contests were held in "calypso tents"; these contests eventually became national competitions to crown a calypso monarch. Carnival ensembles varied widely in the early twentieth century. During the 1920s Venezuelan-style string bands came into fashion among the well-to-do. In the following decade American jazz band instrumentation—with trumpets, saxophones, and trombones —became popular. In 1934 two major calypsonians, Atilla the Hun (Raymond Quevedo) and the Roaring Lion (Hubert Charles, now known as Raphael do Leon), journeyed to New York City to record for the American record labels Decca and American Recording Company. These and subsequent recordings before World War II inspired a Depression-era calypso boom in the United States.

In the 1970s Lord Shorty was responsible for the development of soca, which transformed calypso into modern dance music through the use of new rhythms and electronic instruments. Soca deemphasizes the role of lyrics, and though this is a development that many established calypsonians deplore, it has attracted a young audience that had displayed little interest in traditional calypso music.

Africa
***

Cameroon,

African country on the Gulf of Guinea, bordered by Nigeria, Chad, Central African Republic, Republic of the Congo, Gabon, and Equatorial Guinea.

Cameroon, the country where Central and West Africa meet, is in many ways a microcosm of the continent. Resource-rich and ecologically diverse, the mountainous country is home to more than 250 ethnic groups. For centuries, the peoples of Cameroon experienced particularly regional histories, shaped in the south by the transatlantic slave trade and the Christian missionary presence, and in the north by the trans-Saharan slave trade, Islam,

A woman cleans fish at Rey Bouba, Cameroon. *CORBIS/Michael & Patricia Fogden*

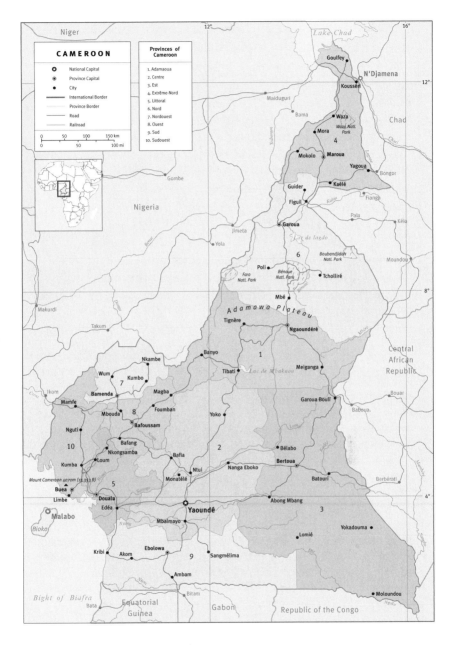

and neighboring savanna empires. During most of the colonial period, two different European powers controlled the country's east and west. Yet unlike much of the rest of postcolonial Africa, Cameroon has forged a strong sense of nationhood while maintaining relative economic and political stability. Still, Cameroon's state remains far from democratic, and its future stability is far from certain.

Cameroon (Ready Reference)

Former Name: French Cameroun and British Cameroon

Area: 475,440 sq km (183,568 sq mi)

Location: Coastal West Africa, bordered by Nigeria, Chad, Central African Republic, Republic of the Congo, Gabon, and Equatorial Guinea

Capital: Yaoundé (population 800,000 [1992 estimate])

Other Major Cities: Douala (population 1,200,000), Garoua (population 160,000), Maroua (population 140,000 [1992 estimate])

Population: 15,029,433 (1998 estimate)

Population Density: 28 persons per sq km (about 72 per sq mi)

Population Below Age 15: 46 percent (male 3,295,924; female 3,266,429 [1997 estimate])

Population Growth Rate: 2.9 percent (1996 estimate)

Total Fertility Rate: 5.9 children born per woman (1996 estimate)

Life Expectancy at Birth: Total population: 52.6 years (male 51.55 years; female 53.68 years [1996 estimate])

Infant Mortality Rate: 78.7 deaths per 1000 live births (1996 estimate)

Literacy Rate (age 15 and over who can read and write): Total population: 63.4 percent (male 75 percent; female 52.1 percent [1995 estimate])

Education: High rate of school attendance; about 2.1 million children attended primary and preprimary schools in the early 1990s; in secondary schools, about 410,000. The University of Yaoundé, established in 1962, has faculties of law, arts, and science. More than 64,500 students are enrolled in institutions of higher education.

Languages: French and English are both official languages, but French is more widely used; 24 major African languages are represented in Cameroon.

Ethnic Groups: Nearly one-third of the population are Cameroon Highlanders (31 percent), one-fifth are Equatorial Bantu (19 percent); some 200 ethnic groups are represented in the population, of which 11 percent are Kirdi, 10 percent Fulani, 8 percent North-western Bantu, 7 percent Eastern Nigritic, and less than 1 percent non-African. The remaining 13 percent are from other African ethnic groups.

Religions: About half the population adheres to indigenous beliefs (51 percent), about one-third are Christian (33 percent), and the remainder are Muslim (16 percent).

Climate: Tropical near the coast, dry inland. Average annual rainfall is about 4060 mm (about 160 in) along the coast; precipitation in the western mountains is year round, as much as 10,160 mm (400 in) annually; in the north, which has a dry season from October to April, yearly rainfall averages 380 mm (about 15 in). Average temperature along the coast is

25° C (77° F), on the central plateau 21° C (70° F), and in the dry north 32° C (90° F).

Land, Plants, and Animals: Cameroon has a dense rain forest along its coastal plain, with mountains in the west, including an active volcano, Mount Cameroon (4095 m/ 14,435 ft), the highest peak in western Africa. In the center is the Adamawa Plateau, becoming savanna plains in the north. Rivers flowing through Cameroon include the Nyong, Sanaga, Mbéré, Logone, and the Benue, linking up with the Niger River system. Animals include elephants, lions, monkeys, chimpanzees, gorillas, and antelope.

Natural Resources: Timber, petroleum, bauxite, and iron ore

Currency: The CFA franc

Gross Domestic Product (GDP): $30.9 billion (1997 estimate)

GDP per Capita: $2100 (1997 estimate)

GDP Real Growth Rate: 5 percent (1997 estimate)

Primary Economic Activities: Agriculture (29 percent of GDP, 74.4 percent of employment), industry, transport, and other services

Primary Crops: Cacao, coffee, tobacco, cotton, bananas, rubber, palm products, sugar cane, plantains, sweet potatoes, cassava, millet, and corn. Livestock raised in the Adamawa Plateau region include cattle, goats, sheep, and pigs.

Industries: Lumber, petroleum production and refining, textiles, food processing, and light consumer goods

Primary Exports: Petroleum, coffee, cocoa, lumber, aluminum, and cotton

Primary Imports: Machines and electrical equipment, food, consumer goods, transport equipment, and petroleum products

Primary Trade Partners: European Union (France and Germany), African countries (especially Nigeria), Japan, and the United States

Government: Cameroon is a unitary republic, under a constitution established in 1972. It has a multiparty regime currently dominated by the government-controlled Cameroon People's Democratic Movement (CPDM). The executive branch is led by President Paul Biya, who appoints the head of government (currently Prime Minister Simon Aachid Achu), a cabinet of federal ministers, and the governors of ten provinces. The legislative branch is the elected unicameral National Assembly.

North America

Campanella, Roy

(b. November 19, 1921, Philadelphia, Pa.; d. June 26, 1993, Los Angeles, Calif.), one of the first African American stars in major league baseball.

Roy Campanella began playing semiprofessional baseball with Philadelphia's Bacharach Giants when he was 16 years old. After playing briefly with the Giants, Campanella joined the Baltimore Elites of the Negro National

League (NNL). He starred in the NNL until 1946, when he signed a minor league contract with the Brooklyn Dodgers. Campanella played for Dodgers farm clubs until 1948—the year after Jackie Robinson broke baseball's color barrier—when he became the Dodgers' starting catcher.

An excellent all-around player, "Campy" starred from 1948 to 1957, helping the Dodgers capture five National League (NL) Pennants. He won the NL most valuable player (MVP) award three times, in 1951, 1953, and 1955. In 1951 Campanella hit .325 with 33 home runs and 108 runs batted in (RBI). His best season was in 1953, when he hit 41 home runs and 142 RBI, both major league records for a catcher. He also set a defensive record that year with 807 putouts. Campanella had a career average of .276, 242 home runs, and 856 RBI, totals that would have been greater had the major leagues not prohibited African American players until 1947. He was inducted into the Baseball Hall of Fame in 1969.

Africa
_____

Cape Verde,

a small West African country comprising ten volcanic islands and five islets off the coast of Senegal.

For more than 400 years, Portugal claimed the rocky, arid islands of Cape Verde. This long history of colonial rule permanently affected Cape Verdean culture, making the small country seem distinct from other African

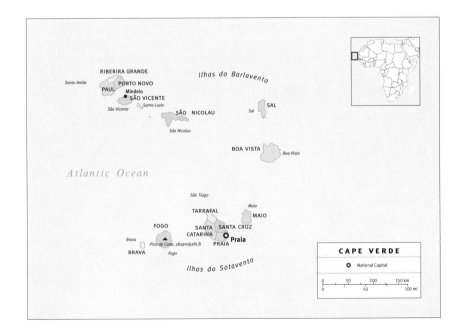

Cape Verde men play music at home in Mindelo, on São Vicente island. *CORBIS/Robert van der Hilst*

nations—"more European." But such a view ignores the shared ancestries and political struggles that link the islands to the mainland. Cape Verde is home to a population descended from free people and West African slaves as well as a diverse mix of peoples: Fula, Wolof, Papeis, Balanta, Bijago, Jalofa, Fulupe, Mandingo, Manjaco, Portuguese, Moroccan, Sephardic Jewish, Lebanese, Dutch, Genoese, Chinese, French, English, American, and Brazilian. The children of these settlers and passers-by forged a hybrid culture and language known as Crioulo (Portuguese for Creole), drawing upon the legacies brought to the islands by slavery and colonialism.

Africa

Cape Verde (Ready Reference)

Official Name: Republic of Cape Verde

Area: 4033 sq km (1557 sq mi)

Location: Cape Verde is an archipelago, consisting of ten islands and five islets, in the Atlantic Ocean, due west of the western-most point of Africa, near Mauritania and Senegal. The windward, or Barlavento, group of islands on the north includes Santo Antão, São Vicente, São Nicolau, Santa Luzia, Sal, and Boa Vista; the leeward, or Sotavento, group on the south includes São Tiago, Brava, Fogo, and Maio.

Capital: Praia, São Tiago (population 61,644 [1990 estimate])

Other Major Cities: Mindelo, São Vicente (47,109 [1990 estimate])

Population: 399,857 (1998 estimate)

Population Density: 111 people per sq km (about 288 per sq mi)

Population Below Age 15: 46 percent (male 91,409; female 89,810 [1997 estimate])

Population Growth Rate: 2.9 percent (1996 estimate)

Total Fertility Rate: 5.2 children born per woman (1997 estimate)

Life Expectancy at Birth: Total population 63.4 years (male 61.5 years; female 65.4 years [1996 estimate])

Infant Mortality Rate: 54.3 deaths per 1000 live births (1996 estimate)

Literacy Rate (age 15 and over who can read and write): 71.6 percent (male 81.4 percent; female 63.8 percent [1995 estimate])

Education: Six years of primary school are compulsory.

Languages: Portuguese is the official language; the national language, however, is Crioulo, a Creole based on archaic Portuguese incorporating many African elements.

Ethnic Groups: More than two-thirds of the people of Cape Verde are either mulatto (of mixed African and European descent) and are known as Creoles, or mestiços (of indigenous and European descent). Nearly all of the remainder are of African ancestry.

Religions: Roman Catholicism is the dominant religion, but is often fused with indigenous beliefs.

Climate: Tropical and dry, showing little variation throughout the year. The average temperature in Praia, the capital, ranges from 20° to 25° C (68° to 77° F) in January and 24° to 28° C (75° to 83° F) in July. Winds are frequent, occasionally carrying clouds of sand from the Sahara in Africa to the east. Precipitation is slight and irregular, and the islands are subject to drought. Average precipitation in Praia is 260 mm (10 in), nearly all of which falls from August through September.

Land, Plants, and Animals: The islands are volcanic in origin, and all but three—Sal, Boa Vista, and Maio—are mountainous. The highest point, Pico do Cano (2829 m/9281 ft) on Fogo, is also the group's only active volcano. Vegetation is sparse and consists of various shrubs, aloes, and other drought-resistant species. Wildlife is limited and includes lizards, monkeys, wild goats, and a variety of bird life.

Natural Resources: Cape Verde is located in the midst of rich fishing grounds, although the industry has yet to develop to its potential. Mineral resources are meager and primarily include *pozzolana* (a volcanic rock used in making cement) and salt. Salt is mined on Sal, Boa Vista, and Maio, with annual production of about 7000 metric tons.

Currency: The Cape Verdean escudo

Gross Domestic Product (GDP): $538 million (1997 estimate)

GDP per Capita: $1370 (1997 estimate)

GDP Real Growth Rate: 4.5 percent (1997 estimate)

Primary Economic Activities: 60 percent of the GDP comes from service-oriented industries, including commerce, transport, and public services. Despite scarce arable land and regular drought, 70 percent of the population lives in rural areas, and agriculture is the nation's principal economic activity. Fish-processing facilities have been constructed in Mindelo, and the government has initiated programs to modernize the fishing fleet. Cape Verde is attempting to capitalize on its strategic location at the crossroads of mid-Atlantic air and sea lanes by expanding airports and port facilities.

Primary Crops: Staple crops are maize and beans, sweet potatoes, coconuts, potatoes, cassava, and dates. Some bananas are grown for export, and sugar cane is raised for the making of rum. Fishing yields yellow fin tuna, skipjack, wahoo (a type of large mackerel), and lobsters.

Industries: Fish processing, salt mining, garments, ship repair, food, and beverages

Primary Exports: Fish and bananas

Primary Imports: Foodstuffs, consumer goods, industrial products, and transport equipment

Primary Trade Partners: Portugal, Spain, Netherlands, Brazil, the United States, and Japan

Government: A new constitution declared in 1992 affirmed Cape Verde as a multiparty democracy, expanding on reforms begun in 1990 that introduced free and popular elections for president and parliament. Legislative power is held by the 79-member National Assembly; members are elected by the voters to five-year terms. The head of state is the president, currently Antonio Mascarenhas Monteiro, also elected to a five-year term. A prime minister, currently Carlos Alberto Wahnon de Carvalho Veiga, is nominated by the assembly and appointed by the president.

Latin America and the Caribbean

Carew, Rod

(b. October 1, 1945, Gatun, Panama), Hall of Fame baseball player who played 19 major league seasons and became one of the most successful hitters of baseball's modern era.

Rod Carew started playing baseball at an early age in Panama. At age 17 he moved with his mother to New York City, where he played ball in sandlots. In his major league debut in 1967, he played second base for the Twins, hitting .292 in 137 games and winning the American League Rookie of the Year Award. In 1976 he was moved to first base, in part because of a serious knee injury suffered in 1970. In 1979, after announcing that he would become a free agent, Carew was traded to the California Angels. He hit .305 or better in each of the next five seasons before dropping below .300 for the first time since 1968. His playing career ended in the spring of 1986. He later became the batting coach for the Angels.

Carew, who threw right-handed and batted left-handed, won seven batting titles (1969, 1972–1975, 1977–1978) and had a lifetime batting average of .328. In 1969 he stole home seven times, setting a league record. In 1977 he won the American League's Most Valuable Player award after hitting .388, a career best, with 239 hits and 128 runs scored. In the 1985 season he became the 16th player in major league history to reach 3000 hits. He was inducted into the Baseball Hall of Fame in Cooperstown, New York, in 1991. Throughout his career in the United States, Carew retained his citizenship and ties to Panama, where he is now a national hero.

North America

Carmichael, Stokely

(b. July 29, 1941, Port-of-Spain, Trinidad; d. November 15, 1998, Conakry, Guinea), activist and writer who inaugurated the Black Power Movement of the 1960s.

Stokely Carmichael was not the first to use the phrase "Black Power," but he made it famous. Critical of Martin Luther King Jr's. peaceful approach, Carmichael advanced a militant stand on civil rights as chairperson of the Student Nonviolent Coordinating Committee (SNCC) in the 1960s.

A native of Trinidad, Carmichael moved with his family to a mostly white neighborhood in the Bronx, New York, when he was 11. Carmichael became involved in civil rights protests during his years at Howard. He participated in demonstrations staged by the Congress of Racial Equality, the Nonviolent Action Committee, and SNCC. He was arrested as a Freedom Rider in 1961 and served seven weeks in Parchman Penitentiary for violating Mississippi's segregation laws. Carmichael returned to the South after college and devoted himself to the organization of SNCC's black voter registration project in Lowndes County, Alabama. There, he also founded an independent political party called the Lowndes County Freedom Organization, which used the black panther as its symbol.

Carmichael became chairman of SNCC in 1966. He catapulted into the national spotlight in August of that year, when he ended a speech with a call for Black Power. Black Power became a rallying cry for black protests during the 1960s and 1970s, and it created a wedge between SNCC and more moderate civil rights groups. Although it is defined in many ways, Black Power emphasizes independent political and economic development by blacks as a necessary element of social change. Carmichael and political scientist Charles Hamilton elaborate on the concept in their book, *Black Power* (1967).

A 1967 world tour to publicize the black struggle in the United States brought Carmichael more controversy in Washington, D.C. His passport was revoked for visiting Cuba and, when he returned to the United States, he faced indictment for sedition; however, he was never prosecuted. The following year, he became prime minister of the Black Panther Party.

In 1969 Carmichael began to focus his political activity on Africa. Having left the Black Panthers, he went to work for the All-African People's Revolutionary Party in Ghana. In that same year, he and his wife, the South African singer Miriam Makeba, went to live in the African nation of Guinea. In 1978 Carmichael took the first name of his mentor, Kwame Nkrumah of Ghana and the last name of Ahmed Sékou Touré of Guinea to become Kwame Turé. He continued to travel and to lecture on U.S. imperialism, Pan-Africanism, and socialism until his death from cancer in November 1998.

North America

Carroll, Diahann

(b. July 17, 1935, New York, N.Y.), African American singer and actor who starred in the first television series with a black woman as its main character.

Born Carol Diahann Johnson, she took her professional name at age 16 when she appeared on Arthur Godfrey's Talent Search, a television showcase for aspiring performers. Despite her parents' wish that she attend Howard University—she had earned money for college by modeling for *Ebony* magazine—she stayed in New York. She left college after one semester at New York University to accept a long-term nightclub engagement. Soon after she went on the road, singing at resorts in the Catskill Mountains and elsewhere, honing her demure, elegant image, a persona that caused one critic to describe her as "Doris Day in blackface."

At age 19 she won her first film role, co-starring with Dorothy Dandridge, Harry Belafonte, and Pearl Bailey in *Carmen Jones* (1954). Returning to New York, Carroll next appeared in Truman Capote's *House of Flowers* on Broadway, a part that brought her a Tony Award nomination. In 1956 she married Monte Kay, a white casting director. On the set of her next movie, *Porgy and Bess* (1959), she met and fell in love with costar Sidney Poitier; their affair lasted nine years. During a brief reconciliation in 1961, Carroll and Kay had a daughter, Suzanne. Later that year, Carroll appeared again with Poitier in the film *Paris Blues* (1961).

Over the next decade Carroll had a series of successful roles, although she never escaped the racial discrimination that pervaded the entertainment industry. On the day after winning another Tony nomination for *No Strings* (1962), she learned that her role would be played in the movie version by a Eurasian actress. Between acting roles she continued to sing, appearing often in Las Vegas. Starring in *Julia*, a television series launched in 1968, Carroll played a widow who was raising her child alone. Despite the show's success, Carroll was stung by criticism of both the character's single motherhood and her unrealistically affluent lifestyle. In addition, the white press seemed to expect Carroll to act as a spokesperson for black America, an impossible task in a politically fractured era. Carroll quit the show in 1971.

Turning down offers for similar television roles, Carroll could not find anything in film to interest her until *Claudine* (1975), a realistic, gritty survivor's story in which she costarred with James Earl Jones. It was not until 1982 that she had another significant acting role, this time on Broadway in *Agnes of God*. Carroll then returned to the small screen to play "television's first black bitch" on the hit series *Dynasty* She has also appeared on *A Different World*, a comedy about students at a historically black university.

North America

Carter, Betty

(b. May 16, 1930, Flint, Mich.; d. September 26, 1998, New York, N.Y.), African American jazz singer credited with integrating bebop into swing jazz style.

Betty Carter, born Lillie Mae Jones, began working as a singer in Detroit clubs when she was in high school. In 1948 she began touring with Lionel Hampton, who gave her the nickname Betty Bebop. She settled in New York City in 1951, where she sang at the Apollo Theater, the Village Vanguard, and the Blue Note. She toured with Miles Davis (1958–1959) and Sonny Rollins (1963, Japan) and formed her own record company, Bet-Car Productions, in 1971. Carter's work includes *Baby It's Cold Outside* (1966, with Ray Charles) and *Look What I Got* (1988), for which she received a Grammy Award. In 1997 *Newsday* described her as the "best jazz singer alive;" the same year, she was awarded the National Medal of Arts by President Bill Clinton.

North America

Carver, George Washington

(b. 1864, Diamond, Mo.; d. January 4, 1943, Tuskegee, Ala.), African American agriculturist, inventor, and educator known for the development of peanut products.

In 1896 George Washington Carver, a recent graduate of Iowa State College of Agriculture and Mechanical Arts (now Iowa State University), accepted an invitation from Booker T. Washington to head the agricultural department at Tuskegee Normal and Industrial Institute for Negroes (now Tuskegee University). During a tenure of nearly 50 years, Carver elevated the scientific study of farming, improved the health and agricultural output of Southern farmers, and developed hundreds of uses for their crops.

As word of Carver's work at Tuskegee spread across the world, he received many invitations to work or teach at better-equipped, higher-paying institutions. Yet he decided to remain at Tuskegee, where he could be of greatest service to his fellow African Americans in the South. Carver epitomized Booker T. Washington's philosophy of black solidarity and self-reliance. He worked hard among his own people, lived modestly, and avoided confronting racial issues.

Latin America and the Caribbean

Cayman Islands,

a dependent territory of Great Britain consisting of three islands in the Caribbean Sea, 300 km (180 mi) northwest of Jamaica and 333 km (200 mi) south of Cuba.

When the Spanish explorer Christopher Columbus first saw the Cayman Islands during his fourth visit to the Caribbean in 1503, he named them Las Tortugas, Spanish for "the turtles," after the large number of turtles that inhabited the island. By 1530, however, other Europeans were calling the islands Caymanas, the Carib Amerindian name for crocodile, this time probably to describe the iguanas who shared the islands with the turtles. The islands were not inhabited by people when Columbus saw them, and though he claimed them for the Spanish Crown, Spain made no attempt to settle them. Instead, they were a popular stop for sailors from other European countries, who stayed just long enough to stock up on fresh water and turtle meat before continuing to other European islands.

It was these British settlers who brought African slaves to the Cayman Islands. Because the islands are not well suited for agriculture, they were never considered a good site for establishing plantation slavery. Instead, the slaves in the Caymans were employed primarily in turtle fishing, subsistence farming, and domestic tasks.

When change eventually did come, the first wave was political. Jamaicans were among the first of the British colonies to push for independence from the British Crown, and they were granted that status in 1962. At that point the Cayman Islands could no longer be considered a dependency of Jamaica, so instead they became direct colonies of Britain. The new arrangement was accompanied by a new constitution that gave the islanders more power over their internal government, but otherwise very little changed; Cayman Islanders were for the most part content with their continued colonial status. But two developments in the second half of the century shook the status quo more noticeably and brought the Caymans increased prominence and prosperity: the rise of tourism and off-shore banking.

The development of the islands' tourist industry was part of an increased emphasis on tourism throughout the Caribbean. The Cayman Islands established a tourist board in 1966, and since then have been extremely successful in attracting visitors to the territory. Their emphasis has been on the luxury North American market, and in 1994 over 1 million tourists visited the islands, 70 percent of them from the United States.

Banking provided the islands' second boon. The Cayman Islands have enjoyed tax-free status for over 200 years, and legend has it that King George III first granted the status to Cayman Islanders after several of them helped rescue members of the royal family from a dramatic shipwreck in 1788. But in the mid-1960s, legislators passed new laws to take advantage of that status by encouraging offshore banking, trust-company formation, and company registration in their islands. As a result, over 500 banks and thousands of companies are now registered in the islands, bringing revenue into the country. Also, 27 percent of the resident population are now foreign nationals who are often wealthy individuals taking advantage of the tax haven, and they add yet more money to the islands' strong economy.

Africa

Central African Republic,

a country in the center of Africa bordered by the Sudan, the Democratic Republic of the Congo, the Republic of the Congo, Cameroon, and Chad.

Located in the middle of the continent, the Central African Republic (CAR) has the potential to be one of Africa's richest countries; during the colonial era, it was known as the Cinderella of the French Empire. The soil is highly fertile and the country possesses vast mineral wealth, valuable forests, and an abundance of wildlife for tourism. Although it has a diverse population, the CAR has experienced little ethnic or religious strife. Yet a tragic history has kept the country from fulfilling its potential. The slave trade and French colonialism devastated its population. Since independence, it has suffered a series of repressive and sometimes brutal regimes, and has remained economically and militarily dependent on France. And in recent years, despite efforts toward democratic reform, a number of attempted coups and rebellions have shaken the country. This ongoing violence and unrest make it unlikely that the CAR will soon realize the promise of its natural riches.

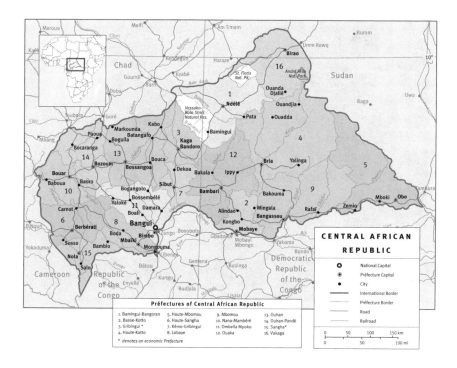

Préfectures of Central African Republic

1. Bamingui-Bangoran	5. Haute-Mbomou	9. Mbomou	13. Ouhan
2. Basse-Kotto	6. Haute-Sangha	10. Nana-Mambéré	14. Ouhan-Pandé
3. Gribingui *	7. Kémo-Gribingui	11. Ombella Mpoko	15. Sangha*
4. Haute-Kotto	8. Lobaye	12. Ouaka	16. Vakaga

* denotes an economic Prefecture

Africa

Central African Republic (Ready Reference)

Former Name: Central African Empire

Area: 622,436 sq km (about 240,323 sq mi)

Location: Central Africa, north of Democratic Republic of the Congo (formerly Zaire), bordered by Cameroon, Chad, Republic of the Congo, and Sudan, and the Democratic Republic of the Congo

Capital: Bangui (population 451,690 [1988 estimate])

Population: 3,375,771 (1998 estimate)

Population Below Age 15: 44 percent (male 738,623; female 731,163 [1997 estimate])

Population Growth Rate: 2.1 percent (1996 estimate)

Total Fertility Rate: 5.4 children born per woman (1996 estimate)

Life Expectancy at Birth: Total population: 45.24 years (male 44.4 years; female 46.1 years [1997 estimate])

Infant Mortality Rate: 111.7 deaths per 1000 live births (1996 estimate)

Literacy Rate (age 15 and over who can read and write): Total population: 60 percent (male 68.5 percent; female 52.4 percent [1995 estimate])

Education: Officially compulsory; however, only about half of the eligible children of the Central African Republic receive primary education.

A bicycle wheel becomes festive headgear during celebrations of the coronation of Central African Republic emperor Bokassa I in 1977. *CORBIS/Yann Aarthus-Bertrand*

Secondary and higher education facilities are limited. In the early 1990s about 308,400 pupils annually attended primary schools, and about 47,200 students were enrolled in secondary and technical institutions.

Languages: French is the official language, but Sango, an African language, is the most commonly spoken. Many other African languages are also spoken.

Ethnic Groups: The main ethnic groups of the Central African Republic are the Baya, Banda, Sara, Mandjia, Mboum, and M'Baka.

Religions: Approximately 24 percent of the total population follow African religions, 25 percent are Protestant, 25 percent are Roman Catholic, 11 percent are other, and 5 percent are Muslim.

Climate: Hot and humid; the average annual temperature is about 26° C (about 79° F). Annual rainfall varies from about 1800 mm (about 70 in) in the Ubangi River valley to about 200 mm (about 8 in) in the semi-arid north.

Land, Plants, and Animals: The Central African Republic is situated on the northern edge of the Zaire (Congo) River Basin. Most of the land is a plateau that ranges in elevation from about 610 to 790 m (about 2000 to 2600 ft). Savanna vegetation covers most of the country except for a dense rain forest in the southwest. Open grassland is found in the extreme north, and a dense rain forest covers a major part of the southwestern area. The country is drained by several major rivers, the Bamingui and Ouham rivers in the north, and the Ubangi, a tributary of the Zaire, in the south.

Commercially valuable trees include the sapele mahogany and the obeche. Many species of wildlife are found in the country.

Natural Resources: Although relatively undeveloped, mineral resources include diamonds, uranium, iron ore, gold, lime, zinc, copper, and tin.

Currency: Communauté Financière Africaine franc

Gross Domestic Product (GDP): $3.3 billion (1997 estimate)

GDP per Capita: $1000 (1997 estimate)

GDP Real Growth Rate: 4.1 percent (1995 estimate)

Primary Economic Activities: Agriculture (50 percent of GDP, 85 percent of employment), forestry, and mining

Primary Crops: Cotton, coffee, tobacco, manioc (tapioca), yams, millet, corn, bananas, and timber

Industries: Diamond mining, sawmills, breweries, textiles, footwear, assembly of bicycles and motorcycles

Primary Exports: Diamonds, timber, cotton, coffee, and tobacco

Primary Imports: Food, textiles, petroleum products, machinery, electrical equipment, motor vehicles, chemicals, pharmaceuticals, and consumer goods

Primary Trade Partners: European Union, Japan, Algeria, Cameroon, Namibia, United States, and Iran

Government: The Central African Republic is a multiparty republic. The executive branch is headed by a president (Ange Patassé since October 22, 1993) and the Council of Ministers, which the president directs. The president is popularly elected to a six-year term. Legislative authority is held by the National Assembly, made up of 85 members who are popularly elected to five-year terms. The Central African Democratic Rally is the leading political party. The president's party is The Movement for the Liberation of the Central African People.

Latin America and the Caribbean

Central America,

isthmus connecting North and South America, comprising the countries of Belize, Costa Rica, El Salvador, Guatemala, Honduras, Nicaragua, and Panama. The region is home to a small number of Afro-Central Americans, descended either from slaves shipped to Central America from Africa or the Caribbean (sixteenth to nineteenth century) or from West Indian workers of the United Fruit Company (late nineteenth to early twentieth century).

In the decades after 1513, when the Spanish explorer Vasco Núñez de Balboa crossed Panama and claimed the Pacific Ocean for Spain, slaves from Africa began to trickle into Central America. Spanish settlements were

fewer in Central America than in other regions of the New World, in large part because few of the mines in the region yielded large loads and most agriculture was on a small scale. Lacking these economic engines, there was neither need nor money to pay for numerous slaves, especially since large Amerindian populations continued to be available in what are now Guatemala and Honduras.

Africa

Chad,

a landlocked country bordered by Libya, Sudan, Central African Republic, Cameroon, Nigeria, and Niger.

Chad's contemporary poverty and ethnic discord have deep historical roots. Beginning in the late first millennium, powerful kingdoms and empires arose in the central Sahel region. Their power derived in part from their control over the trans-Saharan trade carried by the Toubou and Arab pastoralists of the northern desert. The peoples of both the desert and Sahel regions adopted Islam during the Middle Ages. Until the late nineteenth century, the Sahel kingdoms carried out slave raids on the peoples of the south, who lacked states and complex social hierarchies and who maintained traditional religious practices.

French colonialism reversed the traditional dominance of the Islamic northern and central regions. The French concentrated development in southern Chad because of its greater agricultural capacity, while they disrupted the trans-Saharan trade that had made the northern and central regions powerful and wealthy. As a consequence, southerners, especially the Sara people, rose through the colonial civil service and dominated Chad's government after independence. Their indifference or hostility toward the peoples of the central and northern regions sparked resentment and, eventually, more than two decades of intermittent civil war. During the 1990s

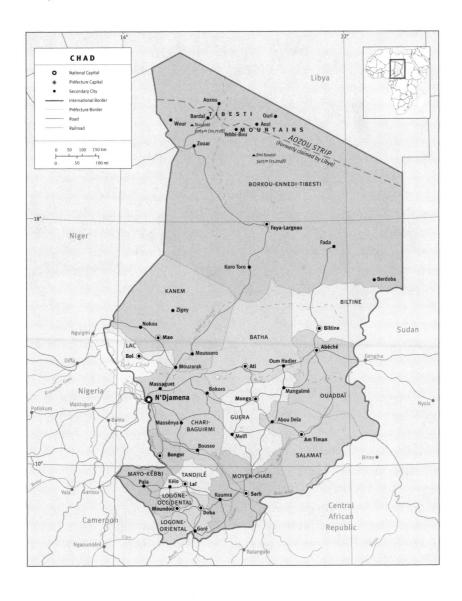

In a Chad market a young woman sits in the midst of decorated, hollowed gourds that contain the milk she is selling. *CORBIS/Paul Amasy*

relative peace slowly returned to Chad, as democratic elections took place and the country's war-torn economy gradually recovered. However, the country remains one of the poorest in the world, and low-level ethnic conflicts continue, particularly in the south.

Africa

Chad (Ready Reference)

Area: 1,284,000 sq km (495,753 sq mi)

Location: Central Africa, south of Libya

Capital: N'Djamena (population 500,000 [1992 estimate])

Other Major Cities: Sarh (population 113,400), Moundou (102,000) (1988 estimate)

Population: 7,359,512 (1998 estimate)

Population Density: 5 persons per sq km (about 14 per sq mi)

Population Below Age 15: 44 percent (male 1,586,873; female 1,579,086 [1997 estimate])

Population Growth Rate: 2.7 percent (1996 estimate)

Total Fertility Rate: 5.8 children born per woman (1996 estimate)

Life Expectancy at Birth: Total population: 47.6 years (male 45.2 years; female 50 years [1996 estimate])

Infant Mortality Rate: 120.4 deaths per 1000 live births (1996 estimate)

Literacy Rate (age 15 and over who can read and write in French or Arabic): Total population: 48.1 percent (male 62.1 percent; female 34.7 percent [1995 estimate])

Education: In the 1990s there were 591,417 primary and 72,641 secondary students, attending approximately 2500 schools. In the late 1980s there were 3000 students enrolled at institutions of higher education, including the University of Chad.

Languages: French and Arabic are the official languages. Hausa is spoken in the Lake Chad region; Sara and Sango are spoken in the south. More than 100 different languages and dialects are spoken in all.

Ethnic Groups: The north is inhabited mainly by Muslim peoples, including Arabs, Toubou, Hadjerai, Fulbé, Kotoko, Kanembou, Baguirmi, Boulala, Zaghawa, and Maba. Mostly non-Muslims live in the south: Sara, Ngambaye, Mbaye, Goulaye, Moundang, Moussei, Massa; of the 150,000 non-indigenous inhabitants, 1000 are French.

Religions: Half the population is Muslim, one-fourth is Christian, and one-fourth of the people adhere to traditional beliefs.

Climate: The Saharan north is hot, dusty, and dry throughout the year. South of the desert there is a hot, dry season from March to July; a rainy season from July to October, with average rainfall 250 to 750 mm (about 10 to 30 in); and a cool, dry season during the remaining months. Rainfall is higher in the south, averaging 1145 mm (about 45 in).

Land, Plants, and Animals: Chad's land-locked terrain is dominated by the low-lying Chad Basin (elevation about 250 m/820 ft), which rises gradually to mountains and plateaus on the north, east, and south. The greatest elevations are reached in the Tibesti massif in the north, with a maximum height of 3415 m (11,204 ft) at Emi Koussi. The northern half of the republic lies in the Sahara. The only important rivers, the Logone and Chari (Shari), are located in the southwest and flow into Lake Chad. The lake doubles in size during the rainy season.

Natural Resources: Petroleum (currently being developed), uranium, natron, kaolin, and fish

Currency: The CFAF (Communauté Financière Africaine franc)

Gross Domestic Product (GDP): $4.3 billion (1997 estimate)

GDP per Capita: $600 (1997 estimate)

GDP Real Growth Rate: 5.5 percent (1997 estimate)

Primary Economic Activities: agriculture (49 percent of GDP; 85 percent of employment), industry, and services

Primary Crops: Cotton, sorghum, millet, peanuts, rice, potatoes, and manioc (tapioca); cattle, sheep, goats, and camels

Industries: Cotton textiles, meat packing, beer brewing, natron (sodium carbonate), soap, cigarettes, and construction materials

Primary Exports: Cotton, cattle, textiles, and fish

Primary Imports: Machinery and transportation equipment, industrial goods, petroleum products, foodstuffs; textiles, and military equipment

Primary Trade Partners: United States, France, Nigeria, Cameroon, Italy, and Germany

Government: Chad is nominally a republic. It is a constitutional multiparty democracy, led by President Lt. Gen. Idriss Deby and Prime Minister Djimasta Koibla. Under the constitution passed in 1996, the legislature consists of the 125-member unicameral National Assembly, first elected in 1997.

North America
Chamberlain, Wilton Norman (Wilt)

(b. August 21, 1936, Philadelphia, Pa.), African American basketball player who won seven consecutive National Basketball Association (NBA) scoring titles from 1960 to 1966 and who is the NBA's second all-time leading scorer after Kareem Abdul-Jabbar.

Wilt Chamberlain revolutionized the game of basketball, inspiring rule changes and creating a premium role for the big scoring and rebounding center. Over 14 seasons in the National Basketball Association, "Wilt the Stilt" —or, as he preferred to be called, "the Big Dipper"—averaged 30.1 points a game, second only to Michael Jordan. In the 1961–1962 season, playing for the Philadelphia Warriors, Chamberlain averaged 50.4 points a game. He scored 100 points in a single game against the New York Knickerbockers, played on March 2, 1963, in Hershey, Pennsylvania.

North America
Charles, Ray (Ray Charles Robinson)

(b. September 23, 1930, Albany, Ga.), African American rhythm and blues (R&B) pianist and singer, known as the Father of Soul.

During the 1950s and 1960s Ray Charles was a key figure in the development of rhythm and blues, an African American style that transformed American popular music. Charles and other black R&B musicians gave popular music a broader expressive range and a powerful rhythmic drive, laying the groundwork for rock 'n' roll. In particular, Charles was a leader in incorporating the gospel music of the black church into secular music, investing his compositions with propulsive energy and emotional power.

During the 1960s Charles branched out into other musical styles, including country and western, such as *Your Cheatin' Heart* (1962), and middle-of-the-road pop music, such as *You Are My Sunshine* (1962); he even released a rendition of the Beatles' *Eleanor Rigby*(1968). During the 1980s Charles achieved the status of popular-culture icon. In 1986 he was one of the first inductees in the Rock and Roll Hall of Fame. Two years later, he provided the voice-over for a television commercial for the California Raisin Advisory Board, and in 1990 he appeared in a series of Diet Coke commercials that won accolades from the advertising industry and an enthusiastic response from the American public. Charles currently records for Quincy Jones's Qwest Records.

North America

Checker, Chubby

(b. October 3, 1941, South Carolina), singer best known for his hit song *The Twist.*

Born Ernest Evans, Chubby Checker got a break when Hank Ballard failed to appear for the American Bandstand session and Checker played Ballard's song *The Twist*. The song quickly reached number one on the pop charts, and sold over 3 million records. This television appearance started a nation-wide dance craze. Checker went on to record 20 Top 40 hits by 1964, including *Pony Time, Slow Twisting,* and *Limbo Rock* His song *Let's Twist Again* was also a hit in Great Britain and sold even more copies there than the original.

North America

Chicago Defender,

the largest black-owned daily newspaper in the United States and a catalyst for the Great Migration.

Chicago Defender founder Robert Sengstacke Abbott took from his father the notion that " . . . a good newspaper was one of the best instruments of service and one of the strongest weapons ever to be used in defense of a race which was deprived of its citizenship rights." In fact, Abbott named the paper the *Defender* because he intended to use its pages to fight discrimination, segregation, and disfranchisement.

The *Chicago Defender* differed from other black publications of the time; Abbott courted a popular audience rather than only the well-educated black readership. The newspaper combined muckraking and political reporting with sensational stories involving scandals, prostitution and gambling rings, and murder. But the *Chicago Defender* had its biggest influence in its role as African Americans' advocate and adviser in the South. The paper's Northern location meant that it could safely report stories that Southern black papers, for fear of white retribution, could not. The *Chicago Defender* exposed the daily horrors that characterized the racist South, including police brutality, lynchings, and white economic exploitation of the disfranchised black population. In response to the lynching of blacks by white mobs, the *Defender* once advised: "When the Mob Comes and You Must Die Take at Least One With You."

Such defiant statements earned the paper intense loyalty among African Americans and antipathy among white Southerners who sought to prohibit its sale and distribution throughout the South. By 1916 the *Chicago Defender* had become the best-selling black newspaper in the United States, and had begun urging African Americans to leave the South for the prospects of economic advancement and relative freedom that the wartime economy made possible in the North. African Americans responded. In large part because of the newspaper's encouragement, hundreds of thousands of blacks migrated North—substantially increasing Chicago's population and changing the character of the city—in a population shift that became known as the Great Migration. Many blacks turned to the *Chicago Defender* for assistance in making the trip North and then adjusting to urban life. The paper reacted by organizing clubs that provided lower cost rail fares for migrants and directed new arrivals to jobs, housing, and social service agencies.

Latin America and the Caribbean

Chile,

country of South America bordered on the west by the Pacific Ocean, on the north by Peru, on the northeast by Bolivia, and on the east by Argentina.

Chilean society prides itself on its racially mixed past, as expressed in the mythic belief in *la raza chilena*, a special race produced by noble Spaniards and the original inhabitants of the land, the Araucanian indigenous people. What this myth omits is the contribution that Africans brought to the racial mix. Not only are blacks ignored in the standard contemporary vision of Chilean society, but their role in the country's history is generally overlooked as well. While a fleeting look at the population of modern Chile might reveal a marginal presence of people of African descent, the Afro-Chilean contribution becomes clear upon closer examination. Blacks made their greatest impact in colonial Chile as exploited slave labor and honored soldiers, helping to forge a nation on the frontier. Once the new republic

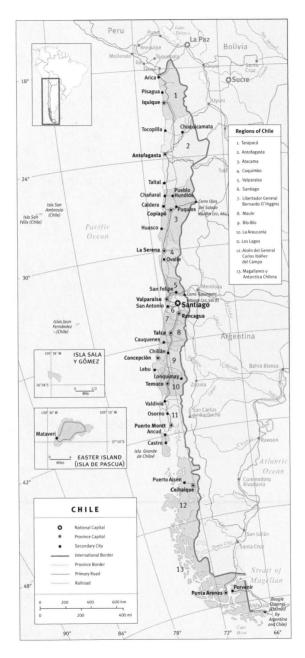

Regions of Chile

1. Tarapacá
2. Antofagasta
3. Atacama
4. Coquimbo
5. Valparaíso
6. Santiago
7. Libertador General Bernardo O'Higgins
8. Maule
9. Bío-Bío
10. La Araucanía
11. Los Lagos
12. Aisén del General Carlos Ibáñez del Campo
13. Magallanes y Antarctica Chilena

CHILE

- ⊙ National Capital
- ◉ Province Capital
- • Secondary City
- ▬ International Border
- ┈ Province Border
- ┅ Primary Road
- ─ Railroad

| 0 | 200 | 400 | 600 km |
| 0 | | 200 | 400 mi |

was established in 1818, Afro-Chileans seem to have all but vanished. There may be various reasons for their alleged disappearance, but we are likely never to know because of insufficient national research, which reflects clear disinterest in this group by Chilean society as a whole.

Cinque, Joseph

(b. 1813, Sierra Leone; d. 1879, Sierra Leone), an African man abducted into slavery who led a rebellion aboard the Spanish slave ship Amistad.

Although Sengbe—pronounced "Sin'gway," and later Anglicized as Joseph Cinque—lived for approximately 66 years, he is best known for his role in a drama that lasted a little more than three years. Scholars believe that Cinque, who belonged to the Mende ethnic group, was a married father before his abduction. When he was about about 26, slave raiders kidnapped him and sold him to Portuguese slave traders, who took him to Havana, Cuba. There Cinque and other abductees, were resold and put aboard the Amistad.

Shortly after the ship left Havana harbor, in June 1839, Cinque led a group of 53 slaves who freed themselves and killed all but two crew members. The rebels ordered these two to help them sail back to Africa, but the crew members tricked them into sailing north. About two months later the ship reached Long Island, New York, where United States naval officers arrested the Africans for murder and piracy.

Their case made a national celebrity of Cinque. He attracted both praise and condemnation. Former president John Quincy Adams defended Cinque and the others in court, and the U.S. Supreme Court eventually ruled in favor of the Africans and freed them to return to Africa. In November 1841, the 35 surviving Africans sailed for Sierra Leone, where they landed in January 1842, more than three years after they had been abducted. Little is known of what Cinque did after his return. Some reports state that he became a slave trader himself, but there is no known documentation of this claim. In 1997 American filmmaker Steven Spielberg recreated the dramatic but little-known events that Cinque and his fellow rebels survived in a film titled *Amistad*.

Cissé, Souleymane

(b. April 21, 1940, Bamako, Mali), Malian filmmaker; one of the most popular filmmakers in Africa.

Souleymane Cissé became a film devotee as a young child, when his brothers took him to the open air cinemas of Bamako. After seeing a film on Patrice Lumumba, former leader of the Democratic Republic of the Congo, in 1962, Cissé decided to become a filmmaker and won a scholarship to the State Institute of Cinema in Moscow in 1963.

After graduating in 1969, Cissé returned to Mali, where he was hired to make news-reels and documentaries for the Ministry of Information. Three years later he completed his first fiction film, *Cinq jours d'une vie* (1972). This, like all of his subsequent feature films—*Den muse* (1975), *Baara* (1978), *Finyé* (1982), and *Yeleen* (1987)—won acclaim at international film festivals. Although Cissé's style has been influenced by Italian neorealism and by Soviet social realism, his working conditions have been shaped by the socioeconomic realities familiar to most African filmmakers.

Baara and *Finyé* have been two of the most commercially successful African movies to be seen on both continents. In addition to working on his own films, Cissé has been an active member of the Fédération Panafricaine des Cinéastes (FEPACI) and has been leading the effort to increase African film distribution and help new African filmmakers overcome the technical and economic obstacles to their work.

North America

Civil Rights Movement

The Civil Rights Movement had its roots in the Constitutional amendments enacted during the Reconstruction era. The Thirteenth Amendment abolished slavery, the Fourteenth Amendment expanded the guarantees of federally pro-tected citizenship rights, and the Fifteenth Amendment barred voting restric-tions based on race. The Reconstruction amendments were, as civil rights lawyer Oliver Hill observed, "a second Bill of Rights" for black Americans.

The enactment of the Civil Rights Act of 1964 and the Voting Rights Act of 1965 reinforced the guarantees of full citizenship provided for in the Reconstruction amendments nearly a century earlier, and marked the end of

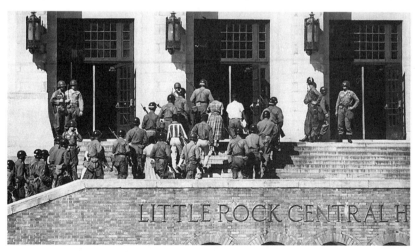

Escorted by United States troops, nine black students walk up the stairs to the main entrance of Central High School, Little Rock, Arkansas, on the first full day of integration, September 25, 1957. *CORBIS/Bettmann*

SOUTHERN STREETCAR BOYCOTTS

- Negro-run transit companies formed in 1905-1906
- Boycotts during Reconstruction (dates unspecified: between 1865 and 1890)
- Boycotts between 1891 and 1906
- State Capital

0   250 km
0   250 mi

The above is probably underlisted. There were protests in all former Confederate states, all major cities in TN and VA, and most major cities in GA.

the Jim Crow system in the South. The desegregation of public facilities was swiftly implemented, and the rapid increase in black voting had far-reaching consequences for politics in the South and the nation. With the enforcement powers of the federal government greatly enhanced, the desegregation of public schools proceeded steadily.

The fall of Jim Crow in the South removed the most extreme manifestation of racial discrimination and inequality, only to reveal deeply entrenched patterns of racial discrimination. For African Americans segregated in Northern cities and locked into poverty, the gains of the Southern movement had little direct relevance. Five days after President Johnson signed

A black student sits at a lunch counter in Nashville, Tennessee, in 1960. The "sit-in" movement began in February 1960 after four black college students in Greensboro, North Carolina, sat at a whites-only lunch counter to protest racial segregation in restaurants and other public accommodations. *CORBIS/Bettmann* the Voting Rights Act, black frustration erupted into nearly a week of rioting in the Watts section of Los Angeles; urban disturbances and rebellions followed in other cities over the next three years. In 1968 the National Committee on Civil Disorders (also known as the Kerner Commission), appointed by the president, described "a nation moving towards two societies—one black, one white, separate and unequal."

The Civil Rights Movement vastly expanded the parameters of American democracy and the guarantees of citizenship, while also raising new challenges. Martin Luther King Jr. carried his efforts forward in very different settings: supporting challenges to residential discrimination in Chicago; protesting America's involvement in Vietnam; aiding striking garbage workers in Memphis; and developing plans for a Poor People's March on Washington. The call for Black Power focused renewed attention on black political and economic empowerment, while heightened black consciousness and racial pride found expression in the cultural renaissance of the Black Arts Movement of the late 1960s and the 1970s.

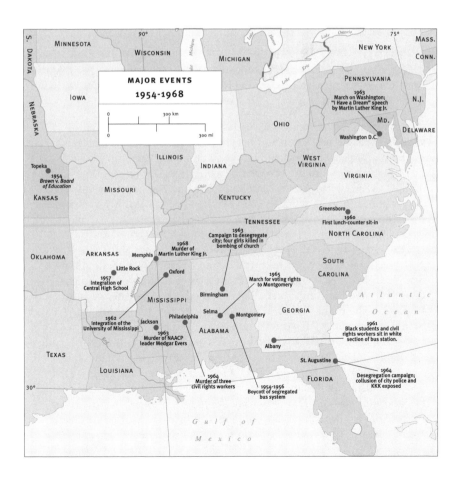

Clarke, John Henrik

(b. January 1, 1915, Union Springs, Ala.; d. July 16, 1998, New York, N.Y.),
African American writer, educator, and Pan-African nationalist.

John Henrik Clarke was a central figure in late-twentieth-century vernacular
American Black Nationalism. As a teacher, writer, and popular public
speaker, he emphasized black pride, African heritage—especially commu-
nalism—and black solidarity. From the rural South he rode a freight train to
New York, where he actively participated in the literary and political life of
Harlem in the 1930s. Arthur Schomburg, the black bibliophile, was a major
intellectual influence. Largely self-educated, Clarke became professor of
Africana and Puerto Rican Studies at New York's Hunter College and president of Sankofa University, an on-line Internet school.

Cleaver, Eldridge Leroy

(b. August 31, 1935, Wabbaseka, Ark.; d. May 1, 1998, Pomona, Calif.), African
American writer, political activist, and former minister of information for the
Black Panther Party.

After growing up in Wabbaseka, Arkansas, and Los Angeles, California,
Eldridge Cleaver spent much of his young adulthood in the California state
penitentiary system. Convicted on drug and rape charges in 1953 and 1958,
he used his prison time to broaden his education During this time, Cleaver
studied the teachings of the Nation of Islam and became a devoted supporter of Malcolm X. With the assassination of Malcolm X in 1965, Cleaver
broke his ties to the Nation of Islam and sought to carry on the mission of
Malcolm X's Organization of Afro-American Unity.

   Paroled in 1966, Cleaver went to work as an editor and writer for *Ram-
parts* magazine. Soon after his introduction to Huey Newton and Bobby
Seale, cofounders of the Black Panther Party, in Oakland, California,
Cleaver joined the Panthers and became the party's minister of information.
In this role, he called on black men to "pick up the gun" against the United
States government. The year 1968 was one of turning points for Cleaver.
He established himself as a gifted essayist and cultural critic with the publi-
cation of *Soul on Ice*, a collection of prison writings that earned him the
Martin Luther King Memorial Prize in 1970. A varied and prolific writer,
Cleaver authored numerous political pamphlets, short stories, and poetry.
His books *Elridge Cleaver: Post-Prison Writings and Speeches* and *Elridge
Cleaver's Black Papers* both appeared in 1969. *The Black Panther Leaders
Speak: Huey P. Newton, Bobby Seale, Elridge Cleaver, and Company Speak*

Out Through the Black Panther Party's Official Newspaper was published seven years later.

Clemente, Roberto

(b. August 18, 1934, Carolina, Puerto Rico; d. December 31, 1972, Puerto Rico), Puerto Rican baseball player and the first Latin American to be inducted into the Hall of Fame in 1973.

As a youth Roberto Clemente achieved such skill at Puerto Rico's favorite sport that at age 14 he played in exhibition games against major league and Negro League players. After debuting with a local Puerto Rican team in 1952, he was signed by the Brooklyn Dodgers for a $10,000 bonus. In 1955 Clemente joined the Pittsburgh Pirates.

Clemente stayed with the Pirates for the rest of his career, for a total of 18 seasons. He won National League batting titles in 1961, 1964, 1965, and 1967, the National League Most Valuable Player award in 1966, and the Babe Ruth Award for his memorable performance in the 1971 World Series. He left the game with a batting average of .317 and 4000 hits. He also won 12 consecutive Gold Gloves and is considered by many experts the best defensive right fielder in the history of the game. Clemente is also remembered for his humanitarianism. He died in a plane crash on December 31, 1972, while en route from Puerto Rico to Nicaragua on a relief mission to help victims of an earthquake. During his professional career he protested the discrimination that Latino and black players encountered in the United States. The building of a Sport City, Clemente's project to help underprivileged Puerto Rican children in San Juan, was completed after his death. In 1973 the Baseball Hall of Fame inducted Roberto Clemente, waiving the customary five-year waiting period. In 1984 he became the second baseball player to be honored on a U.S. postage stamp.

Cliff, Jimmy

(b. James Chambers) (b. April 1, 1948, Somerton, Jamaica), Jamaican musician whose film career introduced many Americans and Europeans to reggae.

Like many Jamaicans, Jimmy Cliff migrated from the countryside to Kingston, the country's capital, during the political upheaval that accompanied Jamaica's independence in 1962. At the time of the move, Cliff was 14 and already had been singing and playing music for years. He sought opportunity and adventure in Kingston, finding both when his improvised rendition of *Dearest Beverly* inspired a partnership between himself and a Chinese storeowner, Leslie Kong, who agreed to record and produce his music. By the age of 15 Cliff had become a Kingston celebrity. In the early 1960s he toured with a ska band, appeared in the promotional video *This is Ska* and recorded early hits such as *Hurricane Hattie, King of Kings,* and *Miss Jamaica.*

Cliff appeared in a semi-autobiographical film, *The Harder They Come* in 1970. Released in the United States in 1973, the movie introduced many Americans to Jamaica's new music.

Coleman, Ornette

(b. March 9, 1930, Fort Worth, Tex.), African American alto saxophonist, composer, and free jazz innovator.

Nearly 40 years after he appeared on the jazz scene, Ornette Coleman remains a controversial and innovative musician. Along with John Coltrane, Eric Dolphy, and Cecil Taylor, he is one of the major figures of the 1960s jazz avant-garde. Indeed, only Coltrane has had a greater influence on the recent development of jazz. During the 1960s Coleman was central to the rise of free jazz, which represented the first significant break with the conventions of bebop or modern jazz that crystallized in the 1940s. In the mid-1970s he formed the group Prime Time, which combined free jazz-improvisation and heavy funk-based rhythms to create a new subgenre of "free funk."

Cole, Nat ("King")

(b. March 17, 1919, Montgomery, Ala., as Nathaniel Adams Cole; d. February 15, 1965, Santa Monica, Calif.), African American pianist and singer.

Nat King Cole began his career as a pianist in 1936 when he joined Eubie Blake's traveling revue *Shuffle Along.*

In 1937 Cole settled in Los Angeles and formed a trio with guitarist Oscar Moore and bassist Wesley Prince. The group achieved its first major success in 1944 with "Straighten Up and Fly Right" which featured a stellar three-part vocal arrangement. In 1946 his version of Mel Tormé's "The Christmas Song" became Cole's first mainstream hit. In this and many subsequent recordings, Cole showcased his sultry voice, singing highly orchestrated pop ballads. In 1948 he sold a million records with "Nature Boy"; other hits included "Route 66" (1946), "Unforgettable" (1950), and "Mona Lisa" (1950). Although Cole continued to record jazz, he shifted his focus from piano to voice, and his pop ballads soon wooed white as well as black audiences. In the late 1940s Cole's combo became the first black group to have its own radio program.

Latin America and the Caribbean

Colombia

In Colombia mixing among Native Americans, Africans, and Europeans, has occurred for centuries and with greater frequency than in North America. "Black" and "white," instead, "black," "white," and "Indian" are polar points of reference within which many categories of racial mixture are recognized. In addition, there are the native inhabitants of the islands

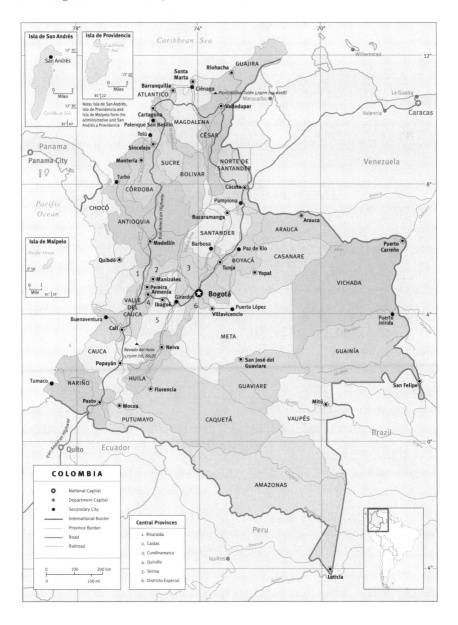

of San Andrés, Providencia, and Santa Catalina, islands off Nicaragua's Caribbean coast. These people belong historically and culturally to a West Indian cultural complex formed under British colonial influence, but since the 1950s they have been subject to formal incorporation within the Colombian nation.

Black Colombians have made an important contribution to the nation's cultural life. Notable writers include Manuel Zapata Olivella (also a black history and folklore scholar and current ambassador to Trinidad and Tobago), Carlos Truque, and Arnoldo Palacios; influential poets include Candelario Obeso and Jorge Artel. The lawyer and scholar Diego Luis Córdoba was an important politician and champion of black rights. Popular music in Colombia has been strongly influenced by blacks, and the dance music that became popular in the twentieth century (*porro, cumbia, vallenato*) originated in the Caribbean coastal region, where black cultural influence has been strong and musicians such as Alejo Durán and Totó la Momposina have become nationally popular.

Colón, Willie

(b. April 28, 1950, the Bronx, N.Y.), one of salsa music's pioneers, who started his recording career at age 16.

Willie Colón's first album, *El Malo* (The Bad Guy, 1967), gave him the image by which he was known for the first decade of his career. This image made fun of the negative stereotype of violence attributed to Puerto Rican communities in New York City, especially those perpetuated by Hollywood movies. With some of his lyrics, this Mafia-style image helped develop the identification of the Puerto Rican community in New York with *salsa* music.

Colon introduced the *jíbaro* sound into salsa. Jíbaro comes from the Spanish heritage of Puerto Rico, while salsa is based on Afro-Cuban rhythms.

Colón has recorded and produced more than 30 records and has been nominated for five Grammy Awards in Latin music. He started his career as a trombone player and later also became the lead singer on his recordings. His recordings with Rubén Blades, *Metiendo mano and Siembra*, are among the best-selling records in salsa history. He also has recorded with Celia Cruz, Fania All Stars, Mon Rivera, and Ismael Miranda, among other great salsa singers and groups. His most outstanding records include *Cosa nuestra* (Our Thing, 1971), *El juicio* (The Trial, 1972), *Asalto navideño* (Christmas Assault, 1971), *El Baquiné de angelitos negros* (The Wake of the Little Black Angels, 1976), and *Solo* (1980).

Coltrane, John William

(b. September 23, 1926, Hamlet, N.C.; d. July 17, 1967, Long Island, N.Y.), African American jazz saxophonist, composer, band leader, and stylistic and compositional innovator, widely recognized as the leader of the New Thing or Free Jazz avant-garde movement of the 1960s.

By the late 1940s Coltrane had developed into a first-class rhythm and blues saxophonist. He switched from alto to tenor saxophone while working with Earl Bostic, who played the alto. On the alto Coltrane was heavily influenced by the playing style of Charlie Parker. On the tenor Coltrane had more varied influences from the start, as he was listening especially attentively to Dexter Gordon, Edward "Sonny" Stitt, Theodore "Sonny" Rollins, and Stan Getz. Though still relatively unknown to the public, Coltrane was admired by musicians and by the early 1950s he had served apprenticeship with many big name R&B and jazz artists, including King Kolax, Big Maybelle, Bull Moose Jackson, Dasie Mae and the Hep Cats, Earl Bostic, Eddie "Cleanhead" Vinson, Jimmy Smith, Johnny Hodges (his earliest model on the alto), and Dizzy Gillespie.

The year 1955 was a momentous one for Coltrane both personally and professionally: he married Juanita Grubbs (Naima) and joined the Miles Davis quintet. Coltrane's tenure with Davis lasted off and on through 1960, when he left Davis to form his own quartet. During these years, Coltrane's playing became more personal. He introduced a hard tone that struck some listeners as "hauntingly beautiful" and others as "harsh." Coltrane became a favorite among recording musicians; with Sonny Rollins he was now one of the leading hard bop voices on tenor saxophone.

In Davis's band, Coltrane's playing reached the limelight through club and concert appearances throughout the country, a few television appearances, and commercial recordings. Coltrane began to attract critical attention through such recordings as 'Round About Midnight (on the Columbia label), Steamin', Relaxin', Cookin', and Workin' (all on the Prestige label). In 1957 he was fired from Davis's band and traded places with Sonny Rollins, who left Thelonious Monk's quartet. Monk hired Coltrane for his famous Five Spot Café engagement, which lasted for several months. This engagement is legendary in jazz history for three reasons: first, it launched the Five Spot as the premiere club in New York for experimental jazz (other artists who similarly served the Five Spot were Cecil Taylor and Ornette Coleman); second, it marked the "rediscovery" of Thelonious Monk, who had been barred from playing in New York clubs through alleged police harassment; and third, during this engagement Coltrane came into maturity as a musician.

In 1961 he formed what became known as his classic quartet, featuring himself on tenor and soprano saxophones, McCoy Tyner on piano, either Jimmy Garrison or Reggie Workman on bass, and Elvin Jones on drums. Eric Dolphy also performed with the group periodically until his death in

1964.The music made with his classic quartet is widely considered the high point of Coltrane's *oeuvre*. The quartet toured throughout the United States and Europe. Starting in 1961 Coltrane won the Down Beat Poll in at least one category every year. He was inducted in the Down Beat Hall of Fame in 1965 as Jazz Man of the Year when his recording, *A Love Supreme*, was declared Record of the Year. Coltrane's work with the quartet was daringly innovative and has made him, after Charlie Parker, the most imitated saxophonist in jazz history.

Africa

Comoros,
an Indian Ocean island nation off southeast Africa.

The Comoro Islands is an archipelago country known for its perfumed crops—vanilla, ylang-ylang, and cloves —and a celebrated past awash in legends of early Jewish settlers and famous buccaneers. More recently,

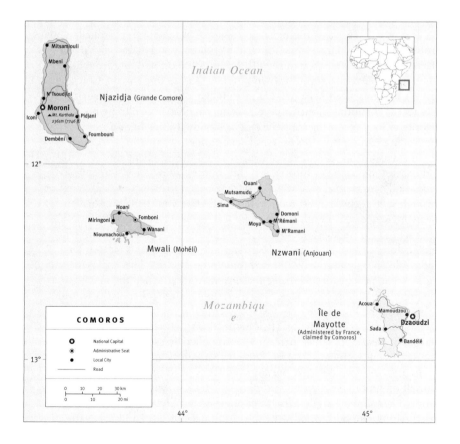

Comoros has earned a degree of notoriety as a home for mercenaries. On the four Comoro Islands—Njazidja, Nzwani, Mwali (formerly known as Grande Comore, Anjouan, Mohéli, respectively), and Mayotte—Islam is the predominant religion, but the influences of Arabic, African, Malagasy, and European cultures are apparent both in the language and in daily life. Although the islands are a popular destination for European and South African tourists, they continue to struggle with problems they have faced since independence: low economic growth, scarce land and other resources, and chronic political instability.

Africa

Comoros (Ready Reference)

Official Name: Federal Islamic Republic of the Comoros

Area: 2170 sq km (838 sq mi)

Location: A group of three islands, Njazidja, Mwali and Nzwani (formerly known as Grande Comore, Mohéli, and Anjouan, respectively), off the coast of southern Africa in the Mozambique Channel, approximately two-thirds of the way between northern Madagascar and northern Mozambique. These three islands broke from French rule in 1975, while a fourth island, Mayotte, remained a French dependency.

Capital: Moroni (population 25,600 [1993 estimate])

Other Major Cities: Mutsamudu (population 14,700) on Nzwani, Fomboni (8200) on Mwali

Population: 545,528 (1998 estimate)

Population Density: 500 persons per sq km (1300 per sq mi)

Population Below Age 15: 48 percent (male 137,235; female 136,207 [1996 estimate])

Population Growth Rate: 3.6 percent (1996 estimate)

Total Fertility Rate: 6.7 children per women (1996 estimate)

Life Expectancy at Birth: Total population: 58.7 years (male 56.4 years; female 61 years [1996 estimate])

Infant Mortality Rate: 75.3 deaths per 1000 live births (1996 estimate)

Literacy Rate (age 15 and over who can read and write): Total population: 57.3 percent (male 64.2 percent; female 50.4 percent [1995 estimate])

Education: Many children attend Islamic schools and state education is officially compulsory from age 7 to 16. Although 75 percent of the school-age group attend primary school, only 17 percent (20 percent of males, 15 percent of females) complete secondary schooling.

Languages: French and Arabic are the official languages, but most people use one of the island dialects, collectively called Shimasiwa. Shimasiwa dialects are related to Swahili.

Ethnic Groups: The population was formed by successive settlements over at least 1000 years, including migrations from Madagascar. Residents trace lineage back to Kilwa, Zanzibar, islands off the coast of Tanzania, and even Arabia and the Persian Gulf region. Some citizens descended from slaves from Mozambique. Today no strong ethnic conflicts divide the population; rivalries between the islands are more important than ethnic differences.

Religions: Sunni Muslims compose 86 percent of the population, and Roman Catholics form the only significant religious minority.

Climate: The islands, which lie within the region of the Indian Ocean monsoons, experience the dry season between April and October, with heavy rains and cyclones the rest of the year. Daily temperatures seldom rise above 30° C (85° F), and 5080 mm (200 in) of rain per year fall on the slopes of Karthala, the site of the heaviest rainfall in Comoros. Despite heavy rainfall, Njazdja retains no water, due to the porous nature of its volcanic rock. Islanders build cisterns to store rainwater for the dry season. In Nzwani, however, streams flow from the mountains throughout the year.

Land, Plants, and Animals: All three islands are of volcanic origin and are mountainous. The island shores are rocky, with offshore islets and a steeply sloping seabed. Njazidja has virtually no topsoil, but the volcanic rocks nevertheless support a dense rain forest. The other islands have soils that are rich in minerals and very fertile, providing ideal conditions for the growth of sugar cane, ylang-ylang trees (the blossoms of which are used to make a perfume), vanilla, cloves, and a wide variety of tropical fruits and flowers. A variety of flycatcher called Humblot's flycatcher breeds only on Njazidja. The seas off the Comoros are the home of the famous coelacanth, a fish that was thought to have been extinct for millions of years until 1938, when one was caught live.

Natural Resources: Flowers and spices constitute the basic commercial crops and grow readily in the fertile soil of Mwali and Nzwani.

Currency: The Comorian franc

Gross Domestic Product (GDP): $400 million (1997 estimate)

GDP Real Growth Rate: 3.5 percent (1997 estimate)

GDP per Capita: $685 (1997 estimate)

Primary Economic Activities: Agriculture, horticulture, fishing, hunting, forestry, and tourism

Primary Crops: Vanilla, ylang-ylang, cloves, perfume oil, copra, and cassava (tapioca)

Industries: Tourism, perfume distillation, textiles, furniture, jewelry, construction materials, and soft drinks

Primary Exports: Vanilla, ylang-ylang, cloves, perfume oil, and copra

Primary Imports: Rice and other foodstuffs, petroleum products, cement, and consumer goods

Primary Trade Partners: France, South Africa, Kenya, and Japan

Government: After gaining independence from France in 1975, Comorans suffered a tumultuous 21 years of nationalist regimes, mercenary coups, and French intervention. In March 1996 Mohamed Taki Abdulkarim was elected president, in the first democratic elections of Comoros. The latest constitution was established in 1992. The president is elected for five years and can serve only two terms of office. The federal constitution allows each island to have autonomy in internal matters and to elect its own governor. The legislative branch of government comprises two multiparty houses, a federal assembly and a senate.

In 1997 Nzwani and Mwali attempted to secede from the Comorian government, possibly with the help of mercenaries. Citing corruption in the local government, secessionists sought to reunite with France. Although the revolt was put down and the French claimed no part in the affair, the future of Nzwani and Mwali is unclear.

Africa

Congo, Democratic Republic of the,

the largest country in Central Africa, bordering nine other countries and the Atlantic Ocean.

One of the largest and most ethnically diverse African countries, the Democratic Republic of the Congo (henceforth Congo) is extremely rich in natural resources, including diamonds, copper, and gold, as well as the enormous hydro-electric potential of the Congo River. Historically, however, these resources have benefited only the political and commercial elite. Subject to one of the most oppressive regimes in all of colonial Africa, then to the 32-year rule of Mobutu Sese Seko, Congo is now impoverished and unstable. In 1996 rebel leader Laurent-Désiré Kabila rode to power on promises to revitalize and democratize the country. As Kabila settles into the presidency, the Congolese population and the international community wait to determine whether he can, in fact, govern this vast, diverse nation.

Maj. Gen. Joseph Mobutu (later Mobutu Sese Seko), commander in chief of the Congolese armed forces, talks with President John F. Kennedy during a 1963 visit to the White House in Washington, D.C. *CORBIS/Hulton-Deutsch Collection*

Africa

Congo, Democratic Republic of the (Ready Reference)

Former Name: Republic of Zaire

Area: 2,344,885 sq km (905,365 sq mi)

Location: Central Africa, bordered by Sudan, Angola, Burundi, Central African Republic, Republic of the Congo, Rwanda, Uganda, and Zambia

Capital: Kinshasa (population 3,804,000 [1991 estimate])

Other Major Cities: Lubumbashi (formerly Elisabethville; population 739,082), Kisangani (formerly Stanleyville; population 373,397 [1995 estimates])

Population: 49,000,511 (1998 estimate)

Population Density: 19 persons per sq km (about 48 per sq mi [1995 estimate])

Population Below Age 15: 43 percent (male 5,201,585; female 5,003,503 [1997 estimate])

Population Growth Rate: 1.7 percent (1996 estimate)

Total Fertility Rate: 6.6 children born per woman (1996 estimate)

Life Expectancy at Birth: Total population: 46.7 years (1996 estimate)

Infant Mortality Rate: 108 deaths per 1000 live births (1996 estimate)

Literacy (age 15 and over who can read and write in French, Lingala, Kingwana, or Tshiluba): Total population: 77.3 percent (male 86.6 percent; female 67.7 percent [1995 estimate])

A Congolese woman watches two United Nations soldiers as they patrol in Leopoldville in 1960.
CORBIS/BETTMANN-UPI

Education: About 60 percent of Congolese children between the ages of 6 and 11 attend primary school; attendance at secondary school has risen rapidly since the early 1960s. In the late 1980s about 4.4 million pupils annually attended primary schools; about 508,000 attended secondary schools; and about 558,000 attended vocational and teacher-training schools.

Languages: Although over 200 languages are spoken, French is the official language and the principal business and social language. Four African languages are also widely spoken: Swahili in the east, Kikongo in the area between Kinshasa and the coast, Tshiluba in the south, and Lingala along the Zaire River.

Ethnic Groups: More than 200 ethnic groups live in the Democratic Republic of the Congo, about 80 percent of which are Bantu-speaking peoples. Sudanese peoples live in the north, and small numbers of Nilotic, Pygmy, and other peoples are present in various areas. The largest single groups are the Kuba, Bakongo (Kongo), and Mongo (all Bantu), and the Mangbetu-Azande (Hamitic). A small number of Europeans live in the Democratic Republic of the Congo.

Religions: About 50 percent of the people of the Democratic Republic of the Congo are Roman Catholic, while 20 percent are Protestant and 10 percent are Muslim. Most of the rest adhere to traditional animist beliefs, although Syncretic sects, such as Kimbanguism, which combines Christian and traditional elements, likewise have a significant number of followers.

Climate: Extremely hot and humid except in the upland regions. The average annual temperature is about 27° C (about 80° F) in the low central area, with extremes consider-ably higher in February, the hottest month. In areas with altitudes above about 1500 m (about 5000 ft), the average annual temperature is about 19° C (about 66° F). Average annual rainfall is about 1520 mm (about 60 in) in the north and 1270 mm (50 in) in the south.

Land, Plants, and Animals: The dominant physical feature of the country is the Zaire (Congo) River basin. This region, constituting the entire central area, is a vast depression that slopes upward on all sides into plateaus and mountain ranges. The highest mountain group in this area is the Mitumba Range, on the country's eastern border. The Ubangi River, chief northern tributary of the Zaire (Congo), rises on the northwestern slopes of this range. In the southeast the basin is fringed by rugged mountain country, sometimes called the Katanga, or Shaba, Plateau. This region, about 1220 m (about 4000 ft) above sea level, contains rich copper fields, uranium, and other mineral deposits.

In the southwest of the Democratic Republic of the Congo the mountain chains are collectively designated the Kwango-Kwilu Plateau. Virtually impenetrable equatorial forests occupy the eastern and northeastern portions of the country. The largest, known variously as the Ituri, Great Congo,

Pygmy, and Stanley Forest, extends east from the confluence of the Aruwimi and Zaire (Congo) rivers nearly to Lake Albert, covering some 65,000 sq km (some 25,000 sq mi). In this area, on the Ugandan border, is the Ruwenzori Range, containing the country's highest point, Margherita Peak (5109 m/16,762 ft). Large regions of the Congo Basin consist of savanna land.

Vegetation consists of rubber trees of various species, oil palms, coffee and cotton, banana, coconut palm, and plantain, teak, ebony, African cedar, mahogany, iroko, and redwood trees. Animals include the elephant, lion, leopard, chimpanzee, gorilla, giraffe, hippopotamus, okapi, zebra, wolf, buffalo, mamba, python, crocodile, parrot, pelican, flamingo, cuckoo, sunbird, heron, and spur-winged plover. Insects include ants, termites, and mosquitoes, including the Anopheles mosquito, host of the malaria parasite. Another disease-bearing insect, prevalent in the lowlands, is the South African tsetse fly, disseminator of sleeping sickness.

Natural Resources: Cobalt, copper, gold, cadmium, petroleum, industrial and gem diamonds, silver, zinc, manganese, tin, germanium, uranium, radium, bauxite, iron ore, coal, and hydropower potential

Currency: The zaire

Gross Domestic Product (GDP): $18 billion (1996 estimate)

GDP per Capita: $400 (1996 estimate)

GDP Real Growth Rate: 1.5 percent (1996 estimate)

Primary Economic Activities: Agriculture accounts for 65 percent of the labor force, while 16 percent are employed in industry; services account for another 19 percent of the labor force (1991 estimate).

Primary Crops: Coffee, sugar, palm oil, rubber, tea, quinine, cassava (tapioca), palm oil, bananas, root crops, corn, and fruits; wood products

Industries: Mining, mineral processing, consumer products (including textiles, foot-wear, cigarettes, processed foods, and beverages), cement, and diamonds

Primary Exports: Copper, coffee, diamonds, cobalt, and crude oil

Primary Imports: Consumer goods, foodstuffs, mining and other machinery, transport equipment, and fuels

Primary Trade Partners: United States, Belgium, France, Germany, Italy, United Kingdom, Japan, and South Africa

Government: Since the takeover of the government by rebel leader Laurent-Désiré Kabila in May 1997, the government has been in a state of flux. On May 28, 1997, Kabila, who assumed the presidency, issued a 15-point proclamation, which nominally established three branches of government. True power resides with Kabila, however. In addition to his role as commander-in-chief, Kabila can also rule by decree and hire and fire government employees at will. The democratic presidential and legislative elections that Kabila promised for April 1999 did not take place.

Africa

Congo, Republic of the,

a highly urbanized, oil-rich country in Central Africa, bordered by the
Democratic Republic of the Congo, the Central African Republic, Cameroon,
Gabon, and the Atlantic Ocean.

In the Republic of the Congo (henceforth Congo), regional shifts in population and power have long shaped the country's history. In precolonial times
migrations, state formation, and slave trading concentrated population along
the coastline and in the river valleys of the south, leaving northern peoples
relatively isolated. French colonialism widened regional differences by
pouring resources into urbanization and infrastructural development in the

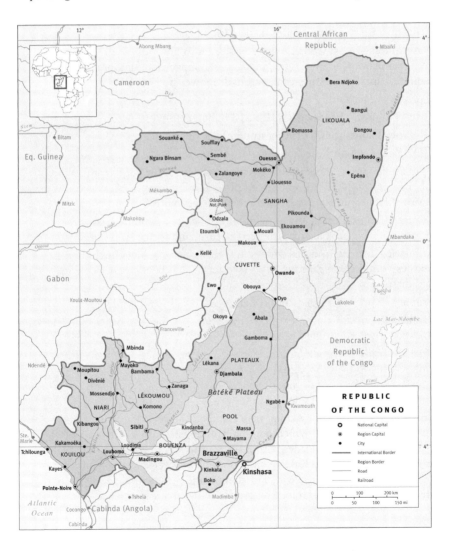

south while drawing military recruits from the less-developed north. In the early years of Congo's independence, Communist rhetoric flourished in the south's burgeoning cities —home to vocal intellectuals, students, and workers—but power was held by a military elite from the north. Some of the country's leaders have since attempted to address the uneven development between north and south, city and countryside. However, progress has been slowed by economic crises and by the highly militarized nature of national politics. Short-lived political liberalization in the 1990s was brought to an abrupt halt in 1997 by civil war, fought on the streets of the capital, Brazzaville.

Africa

Congo, Republic of the (Ready Reference)

Area: 342,002 sq km (132,047 sq mi)

Location: Western Africa, bordering the South Atlantic Ocean, Gabon, Cameroon, Central African Republic, and the Democratic Republic of the Congo (formerly Zaire)

Capital: Brazzaville (population 760,300 [1990 estimate])

Other Major Cities: Pointe-Noire (population 387,774 [1990 estimate])

Population: 2,658,123 (1998 estimate)

Population Density: 8 persons per sq km (about 20 per sq mi) (1995 estimate)

Population Below Age 15: 43 percent (male 557,996; female 552,022 [1997 estimate])

Population Growth Rate: 2.2 percent (1996 estimate)

Total Fertility Rate: 5.15 children born per woman (1996 estimate)

Life Expectancy at Birth: Total population: 45.8 years (male 44.2; female 47.3 [1996 estimate])

Infant Mortality Rate: 108.1 deaths per 1000 live births (1996 estimate)

Literacy (age 15 and over who can read and write): Total population: 74.9 percent (male 83.1 percent; female 67.2 percent [1995 estimate])

Education: Free and compulsory for children ages 6 to 16. In the early 1990s about 502,900 pupils annually attended primary schools, and more than 183,000 attended secondary schools, including technical and teacher-training schools.

Languages: French is the official language; Lingala and Kikingo are the most widely spoken African languages.

Ethnic Groups: There are four major ethnic groups: the Bakongo (the major group, accounting for about 50 percent of the total population), the Mboshi, the Sanga, and the Téké, who live in the central region. There are 75 subgroups of these four major groups. About 12,000 Pygmies live in the Republic of the Congo, as do 8500 Europeans.

Religions: About half the population follows traditional religious beliefs. Most of the remainder are Christian, primarily members of the Catholic Church. Fewer than 1 percent are Muslim.

Climate: Tropical, with mostly high heat and humidity. While the Mayumbe Mountains experience a long dry season, parts of the Congo Basin receive more than 2500 mm (more than 100 in) of rainfall annually. Average temperatures in Brazzaville are 26° C (78° F) in January and 23° C (73° F) in July, with an annual rainfall of about 1500 mm (about 60 in). Temperatures along the coast are slightly cooler.

Land, Plants, and Animals: Along the Atlantic coast is a low, treeless plain, which rises inland to the Mayumbe Mountains, an almost completely forested region with an average elevation of about 550 m (about 1800 ft). In the south central region is the fertile valley of the Niari River. To the north lies the central highlands region, the Batéké Plateau. The plateau is cut by numerous tributaries of the Zaire (Congo) and Ubangi rivers. Dense tropical rain forests cover approximately half of the country and constitute a major natural resource. The principal commercial species are okoumé (a mahogany) and limba (a hardwood). Savanna vegetation is found in the northeast and the higher plateau areas. Wildlife is diverse and abundant, including antelope, giraffe, cheetah, crocodile, and numerous birds and snakes.

Natural Resources: Offshore petroleum potash, gold, iron ore, lead, and copper

Currency: Communauté Financière Africaine (CFA) franc

Gross Domestic Product (GDP): $5.25 billion (1996 estimate)

GDP per Capita: $2000 (1996 estimate)

GDP Real Growth Rate: 4 percent (1996 estimate)

Primary Economic Activities: Agriculture, handicrafts, oil production, and forestry

Primary Crops: Cassava, sugar, rice, corn, peanuts, vegetables, coffee, cocoa, and forest products

Industries: Petroleum extraction, cement kilning, lumbering, brewing, sugar milling, palm oil, soap, and cigarette making

Primary Exports: Crude oil (90 percent of export revenue), lumber, plywood, sugar, cocoa, coffee, and diamonds

Primary Imports: Intermediate manufactures, capital equipment, construction materials, foodstuffs, and petroleum products

Primary Trading Partners: European Union, United States, Taiwan, Japan, and Thailand

Government: A multiparty republican system with a directly elected president (Pascal Lissouba since August 1992) who is elected to a five-year term. The president appoints the Council of Ministers, including the prime minister (Jacques Joachim Yhombi-Opango since 1993) and a bicameral legislature, the 125-seat National Assembly, and the 60-seat Senate. Presidential elections scheduled for July 1997 were postponed because of a civil conflict between President Lissouba's forces and militiamen employed by the former head of state, Gen. Denis Sassou-Nguesso.

North America

Congressional Black Caucus,

the coalition of black members of the United States Congress committed to promoting and protecting policies favorable to the African American community.

The South African human rights activist Bishop Desmond Tutu once said, "Politics is the art of the possible." In 1969 the nine blacks then in Congress were isolated and powerless, unable to prevent passage of legislation detrimental to African Americans and other minorities. That year, Rep. Charles Diggs, a black Democrat from Michigan, formed the Democratic Select Committee, in the belief that a unified black voice could exert a measure of political influence in Congress. The committee investigated the murders of several Black Panther Party members in Chicago, Illinois, and defeated the nomination of conservative judge Clement Haynesworth to the Supreme Court. The potential strength of a collective black voice was immediately evident, and on June 18, 1971, at its first annual dinner, the Democratic Select Committee was reorganized as the Congressional Black Caucus (CBC), with Representative Diggs as its first chairperson. Despite the opposition, the CBC gained national attention in 1971 when its members presented President Richard Nixon with a list of 60 recommendations concerning foreign and domestic issues. In 1972 the caucus was one of the sponsors of the National Black Political Convention held in Gary, Indiana. That year, at the Democratic Party's national convention, the caucus drafted the Black Declaration of Independence, which urged the Democratic Party to commit itself to effecting complete racial equality. It also drafted the Black Bill of Rights, demanding, among other things, full employment and an end to subversive American military activity in Africa. The caucus established the Congressional Black Caucus Foundation, a "nonprofit public policy, research, and educational institute," in 1976. Later that year, it formed the Congressional Black Caucus Graduate Intern Program to increase the number of African American professionals working for congressional committees.

North America

Congress of Racial Equality,

American civil rights organization that pioneered the strategy of nonviolent direct action, especially the tactics of sit-ins, jail-ins, and freedom rides.

The Congress of Racial Equality (CORE) was founded in 1942 as the Committee of Racial Equality by an interracial group of students in

Chicago. Many of these students were members of the Chicago branch of the Fellowship of Reconciliation (FOR), a pacifist organization seeking to change racist attitudes. The founders of CORE were deeply influenced by Mahatma Gandhi's teachings of non-violent resistance.

CORE started as a nonhierarchical, decentralized organization funded entirely by the voluntary contributions of its members. The organization was initially co-led by white University of Chicago student George Houser and black student James Farmer. In 1942 CORE began protests against segregation in public accommodations by organizing sit-ins. It was also in 1942 that CORE expanded nationally. James Farmer traveled the country with Bayard Rustin, a field secretary with FOR, and recruited activists at FOR meetings. CORE's early growth consisted almost entirely of white middle-class college students from the Midwest.

From the beginning of its expansion, CORE experienced tension between local control and national leadership. James Farmer became the first national director of CORE in 1943. In the aftermath of the 1954 *Brown v. Board of Education* decision, CORE was revived from several years of stagnation and decline. CORE provided the 1955 Montgomery Bus Boycott with its philosophical commitment to nonviolent direct action. As the Civil Rights Movement took hold, CORE focused its energy in the South.

While middle-class college students predominated in the early years of the organization, increasingly the membership was made up of poorer and less educated blacks. CORE provided guidance for action in the aftermath of the 1960 sit-in of four college students (who were not CORE members) at a Greensboro, North Carolina, lunch counter and subsequently became a nationally recognized civil rights organization. As a pioneer of the sit-in tactic, the organization offered support in Greensboro and organized sit-ins throughout the South. CORE members then developed the strategy of the jail-in, serving out their sentences for sit-ins rather than paying bail. In May 1961 CORE organized the Freedom Rides, modeled after their earlier Journey of Reconciliation. Near Birmingham, Alabama, a bus was firebombed and riders were beaten by a white mob. After this event CORE ended the rides; however, the Student Nonviolent Coordinating Committee (SNCC) resumed the rides in Mississippi.

By 1963 CORE had already shifted attention to segregation in the North and West, where two-thirds of the organization's chapters were located. In an effort to build CORE's credibility as a black-protest organization, leadership in these Northern chapters had become almost entirely black. Many new members advocated militancy and believed that nonviolent methods of protest should be used only if they proved successful. As the tactics were being questioned, so was the role of white members. In 1966 CORE endorsed the term Black Power, and by 1967 the word "multiracial" was no longer in the CORE constitution. Finally, in 1968, Roy Innis replaced Farmer as the national director, and Innis soon denied whites active membership in CORE and advocated Black Separatism.

Córdoba, Diego Luis

(b. 1907, Quibdó, Chocó Province, Colombia; d. 1964), Afro-Colombian politician and an important figure in promoting black participation in electoral politics in Colombia.

Diego Luis Córdoba was born near Quibdó, Chocó Province, and studied in Quibdó, later moving to Medellín and Bogotá to study law. He was politically ambitious during a time when Chocó's 90 percent black population was ruled by a small white elite. Córdoba was one of a growing number of educated blacks who were dissatisfied with this situation. He achieved national status as a radical student leader and stood as a Liberal candidate for the position of representative to Congress in 1933 but was not nominated.

Córdoba then started his own party, Acción Democrática (AD), later labeled Cordobismo, which gained the support of many local blacks. AD candidates were elected to the city council and found favor with some of the white elite. Córdoba was elected to Congress as an independent representative and AD gained local power.

Cosby, Bill

(b. July 12, 1937, Philadelphia, Pa.), African American comedian whose multifarious talent, friendliness, and commitment to positive values led him to become a preeminent television celebrity in the 1980s and a performer admired by both whites and blacks.

Born in a poor section of Philadelphia, Pennsylvania, Bill Cosby left home for a stint in the United States Navy that lasted from 1956 to 1960. He studied at Temple University but dropped out to devote his time to stand-up comedy. After establishing his name on the night-club circuit in 1963, he auditioned successfully to fill a guest spot on Johnny Carson's Tonight Show. An instant success, Cosby became the first African American to host the program regularly. In 1965 he became the first black person to have a starring role on a predominantly white television drama, appearing with Robert Culp on the program *I Spy*. Because of his Emmy Award–winning success on *I Spy*, many fans considered Cosby "the Jackie Robinson of television."

In the mid-1970s Cosby returned to school, earning a doctorate in education at the University of Massachusetts in Amherst. In the 1980s Cosby combined his paternal interests with the sophisticated humor of his prime-time career on the hit program *The Cosby Show* (1984–1992). *The Cosby Show* ranked third in Nielsen ratings its first season and held the number-one slot for three years. It created a glowing embodiment of the American middle-class dream and drew the attention of 38 million people. Cosby's vision of

Dr. Cliff Huxtable, his beautiful lawyer wife, and their five handsome, successful children included jokes and conflicts that transcended race. While some critics claimed that *The Cosby Show* failed to address the reality of black America—or, worse, depicted successful blacks as assimilated blacks —others lauded its positive presentation of family values.While *The Cosby Show* debunked racial stereotypes on screen, Cosby fought discrimination within the television industry. He took advantage of the show's tremendous success, demanding a large role in its production. He hired black writers and directors and invited black celebrities, such as Dizzy Gillespie and Judith Jamison, to make guest appearances; he contracted Professor Alvin Poussaint, an African American professor of psychiatry from Harvard University, as an adviser; and he hung the artwork of black artist Varnette Honeywood on the walls of the set. Cosby's commitment to education has been persistent. In the 1980s he and his wife made frequent donations to African American colleges. In 1989 they gave their biggest gift, $20 million, to Spelman College. Cosby's philanthropy has benefited many other African American organizations, including the National Association for the Advancement of Colored People, the United Negro College Fund, the National Sickle-Cell Foundation, and the National Council of Negro Women.

Latin America and the Caribbean

Costa Rica,

republic in southern Central America, bounded on the north by Nicaragua, on the east by the Caribbean Sea, on the southeast by Panama, and on the southwest and west by the Pacific Ocean. The uninhabited and densely wooded tropical Cocos Island, about 480 km (about 300 mi) to the southwest in the Pacific Ocean, is under Costa Rican sovereignty. The total area of Costa Rica is 51,060 sq km (19,714 sq mi). The country's capital is San José.

Africa

Côte d'Ivoire,

a country in West Africa bordered by Liberia, Guinea, Mali, Burkina Faso, Ghana, and the Atlantic Ocean.

The recent history of Côte d'Ivoire is rife with contradictions. The country that offered some of the most sustained resistance to French colonialism has in the post-colonial era become one of France's most loyal clients. Economic growth and prosperity for elites and foreign investors have come at the price of poverty for large segments of the population. Finally, though many have praised Côte d'Ivoire as a model of political stability, its autocratic regime has maintained power by repressing democratic opposition. Côte d'Ivoire has had only two leaders since 1960: Félix Houphouët-Boigny, who led the country from colonial rule through three decades of independence, and his successor, Henri-Konan Bédié. Both helped build a nation of political

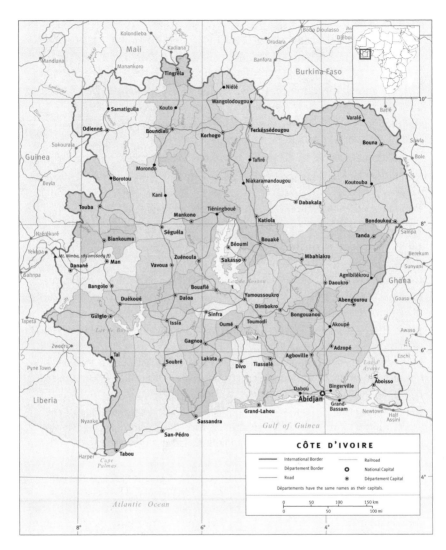

stability and limited economic prosperity known as the Ivoirian Miracle. At the same time, both have maintained a neocolonial dependence on France and have blocked effective democratic reforms.

Africa

Côte d'Ivoire (Ready Reference)

Official Name: Republic of Côte d'Ivoire

Former Name: Ivory Coast

Area: 322,462 sq km (122,503 sq mi)

Location: Western Africa; borders the North Atlantic Ocean, Ghana, Burkina Faso, Mali, Guinea, and Liberia

Capital: Yamoussoukro (population 106,786 [1988 estimate]) has been the official capital since 1983; however, Abidjan (population 2,700,000 [1990 estimate]) is the de facto capital and contains the administrative center. It is also where most foreign governments maintain their official presence.

Other Major Cities: Bouaké (population 329,850), Daloa (121,842 [1988 estimate]), Gagnoa (population 59,500 [1986 estimate])

Population: 15,446,231 (1998 estimate, including at least 3 million immigrant workers and their families)

Population Density: 45 persons per sq km (about 116 persons per sq mi)

Population Below Age 15: 47 percent (male 3,537,190; female 3,496,749 [1997 estimate])

Population Growth Rate: 2.9 percent (1996 estimate)

Total Fertility Rate: 6.2 children born per woman (1996 estimate)

Life Expectancy at Birth: Total population: 44.8 years (male 43.6 years; female 46 years [1997 estimate])

Infant Mortality Rate: 82.4 deaths per 1000 live births (1996 estimate)

Literacy Rate (age 15 and over who can read and write): Total population: 40.1 percent (male 49.9 percent; female 30 percent [1995 estimate])

Education: Education is free, and primary education is compulsory. A vast television education program was established in the early 1970s that has helped to improve literacy rates. In the early 1990s about 1.5 million students annually attended primary schools and about 423,000 attended secondary and vocational schools.

Languages: French is the official language and a large percentage of the population uses it, especially for written communication. There are, however, over 60 other languages spoken in Côte d'Ivoire; of these, Dioula is the most widely used.

Ethnic Groups: The population of Côte d'Ivoire contains over 60 ethnic groups. The largest groups are Baule, 23 percent; Bété, 18 percent; and Senufo, 15 percent. Other groups include Malinke, Agni, Kru, Voltaic, and Mande peoples. There is a significant Lebanese community. A large number of immigrants come from Liberia, Burkina Faso, and Mali.

Religions: About 60 percent of the population adhere to indigenous beliefs. About 20 percent are Christians (mostly Roman Catholic) and 20 percent are Muslims.

Climate: Tropical along the coast, semi-arid in the far north, and varying at the center between forest and savanna. In the southern region temperatures vary between 22° C (72° F) and 32° C (90° F) and there are two rainy seasons, April to July and October to November. In the central part of the country, the temperatures are more extreme, ranging from 12° C (54° F) and 40° C (104° F). Annual rainfall average is 2100 mm (83 in) in coastal Abidjan and 1200 mm (about 48 in) in Bouaké, on the central plain.

Land, Plants, and Animals: Côte d'Ivoire is flat with some undulating plains, except for mountains in the northwest region. The north central region has savanna. From the coast to the southern central region there is dense forest containing *obeche*, mahogany, and *iroko*. Animals include the jackal, hyena, panther, elephant, chimpanzee, crocodile, and various lizards and venomous snakes.

Natural Resources: Rich, arable soil and forests containing commercially valuable hardwoods. Côte d'Ivoire has mineral deposits of gold, iron ore, manganese ore, diamonds, and petroleum. Hydroelectric plants on the Bia and Bandama rivers provide a significant amount of electricity.

Currency: The Communauté Financière Africaine (CFA) franc

Gross Domestic Product (GDP): $25.8 billion (1997 estimate)

GDP per Capita: $1700 (1997 estimate)

GDP Real Growth Rate: 6.5 percent (1997 estimate)

Primary Economic Activities: Agriculture (85 percent of population), industry, and commerce

Primary Crops: Coffee, cocoa, bananas, corn, rice, manioc, sweet potatoes, sugar, cotton, rubber, and timber

Industries: Foodstuffs, beverages, wood products, oil refining, automobile assembly, textiles, fertilizer, construction materials, and electricity

Primary Exports: Cocoa, coffee, tropical woods, petroleum, cotton, bananas, palm oil, pineapples, cotton, and fish

Primary Imports: Food, capital goods, consumer goods, and fuel

Primary Trade Partners: France, Nigeria, Japan, Netherlands, United States, and Italy

Government: Côte d'Ivoire is a constitutional republic with a multiparty presidential regime. The executive branch is led by President Henri-Konan Bédié and Prime Minister Daniel Kablan Duncan, who was appointed by the president. The legislative branch is the elected 175-member National Assembly, which is currently dominated by President Bédié's party, the Democratic Party of the Côte d'Ivoire.

North America

Cotton Club,

a prestigious white-owned Harlem nightclub of the 1920s and 1930s that featured prominent African American musicians, singers, and dancers performing for a white clientele.

The Cotton Club was one of Harlem's premier nightclubs, renowned for its superb jazz music and the exotic routines of its female dancers. The club was also a constant reminder of the reality of segregation in the North as well as the South. Although its performers and waiters were all black and it was located for many years in the heart of Harlem in New York City, the Cotton Club had a whites-only policy, and it only hired female dancers who were light-skinned and who emulated white standards of beauty.

The Cotton Club had its beginnings in 1920, when the controversial African American boxing champion Jack Johnson opened the Club Deluxe on Lenox Avenue and 142nd Street in Harlem. Johnson sold the club to white gangster Owney Madden, who reopened it in the fall of 1923 as the Cotton Club. Under Madden, the Cotton Club's floor shows and decoration highlighted black primitivism and sensuality. Decorated inside and out in the style of a log cabin and featuring pseudo-jungle décor, the club's appearance starkly revealed prevailing white stereotypes of African Americans.

Madden's timing was fortuitous, for during the 1920s New York City's elite displayed a sudden interest in black life and culture. The smart set considered it fashionable to journey into Harlem to visit the Cotton Club. "Join the crowds after theater," a 1929 advertisement declared. "All Broadway comes to Harlem." The club's entertainment was certainly first-rate. Perhaps the most significant musician connected with the Cotton Club was Duke Ellington, whose orchestra played there from 1927 to 1931. Singer Cab Calloway first performed at the club in 1930, and in the following year his orchestra took over from Ellington's as the club's house band. During Ellington's tenure, the club was wired for radio broadcasts, which helped Ellington build a national audience for his music. Among the club's featured entertainers were singers Ethel Waters and Billie Holiday and dancers Bill "Bojangles" Robinson and Earl "Snake Hips" Tucker; in the chorus line was young Lena Horne. The 1929 stock market crash and the onset of the Great Depression put a damper on the Cotton Club's free-wheeling entertainment, but the club did not shut down. The Harlem Riot of 1935 had a more serious impact. In the aftermath of the riots, Madden moved the club out of Harlem, reopening in 1936 in a supposedly safer downtown location on Broadway and 48th Street. The club continued in operation until 1940.

Latin America and the Caribbean

Cruz, Celia

(b. October 21, c. 1929, Havana, Cuba), Cuban-born, African American vocalist, one of the most recognizable singers of the popular Latin dance music known as *salsa*.

Nicknamed the Queen of Salsa, Celia Cruz has recorded more than 50 albums, collaborating with many of the leading figures of Latin popular music. During a career that has spanned more than four decades, Cruz has gained a reputation for her tireless work, warm personality, and emotive style of singing. In performance she is known for her skillful improvisation of lyrics. She is one of a few successful female vocalists in a genre dominated by men.

Born in a poor section of Havana, Cruz demonstrated her singing talents at a very young age, but she studied to be an elementary school teacher because her father did not consider singing to be a suitable career for a woman. Encouraged by her mother and a teacher, however, she nevertheless pursued a singing career. In 1950 she became lead vocalist for Sonora Matancera, one of the most popular *conjuntos* (ensembles) in Cuba. Although the group was criticized for hiring a black singer, Cruz's hard work and talent eventually won her popular acclaim. In 1960, following the Cuban Revolution, Cruz left Cuba for Mexico. A year later she moved to the United States and married Pedro Knight, a trumpeter for Sonora Matancera, who subsequently became her manager. Cruz made a series of recordings for popular bandleader Ernesto "Tito" Puente from 1966 through 1972. Band-leader Johnny Pacheco and Fania Records owner Jerry Masucci took an interest in her, leading to her portrayal of Gracia Divina in the concert production and musical recording of *Hommy*, A Latin Opera (1973). In the mid- and late 1970s she collaborated with many of the best-known salsa performers, including Pacheco, Ray Barretto, Willie Colón, Bobby Valentín, and the Fania All Stars. Cruz continued to perform actively through the 1980s and appeared in several celebrated reunion concerts with Sonora Matancera. In 1990 she shared a Grammy Award with Ray Barretto for their 1988 recording *Ritmo en el Corazón*. She was also recognized with an honorary doctorate from Yale University and, in 1994, with a National Medal of the Arts from President Bill Clinton. Cruz has appeared in several motion pictures, most notably the 1992 film *The Mambo Kings*.

Latin America and the Caribbean

Cuba,

an archipelago comprising the island of Cuba, the Isle of Youth, and a number of smaller keys and islets. It is located at the entrance to the Gulf of Mexico, with the Atlantic Ocean to the north and the Caribbean Sea to the south. It lies south of the Florida Straits and east of the Yucatan Peninsula. It is the largest island of the Greater Antilles.

Many associate Cuba's history before the 1959 revolution with the resorts and casinos of the 1940s and 1950s that made it a favorite stopping point for American tourists; since the revolution, it has been associated with cold war tensions and the singular figure of Fidel Castro.

The early black presence is reflected in the first major literary work in seventeenth-century Cuba, a poem titled *El espejo de paciencia* (The Mirror of Patience), by Silvestre de Balboa de Troya y Quesada. It describes the

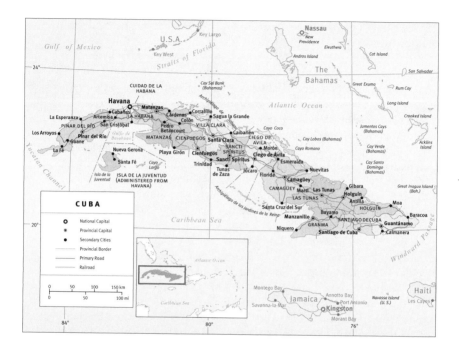

kidnapping of Bishop Fray Juan de las Cabezas Altamirano by the French pirate Gilberto Girón. A bold and brave black man, Salvador Galomón, kills the kidnapper and saves the eastern town of Holguín from danger. This early literary representation of the black juxtaposes the injustice of enslavement and the heroism of the black protagonist.

These two themes were to be repeated through history. The Indian and slave rebellions of the early colonization period might be regarded as forerunners to the rebellions that accompanied the huge influx of African slaves in the nineteenth century.

Da Costa, Mathieu

(b. ?; d. 1606?, Montreal, Quebec), first known person of African descent to visit Canada.

The history of black people in Canada can be dated back to the early seventeenth-century New World expeditions of the French explorer Pierre du Gua, Sieur de Monts. With du Gua was an African man, Mathieu de Costa, who worked as an interpreter between the French and the indigenous Mic Mac Indians. Little is known of de Costa, or of how he gained his surprising fluency in the language of the Mic Macs. Historians speculate that he may have visited Canada earlier as a crew member of a Portuguese vessel, fishing off the coast of Newfoundland.

Dahomey,

Early Kingdom of, pre-colonial West African kingdom located in what is now southern Benin.

Dahomey reached the height of its power and prestige during the heyday of the Atlantic slave trade in the eighteenth and nineteenth centuries. Abomey, future capital of Dahomey, was founded around 1620 by Dogbari, who had fled Allada after a power struggle among his brothers for control of that kingdom. Under Dogbari's grandson, Wegbaja (c. 1645–1685), Abomey was expanded through military conquest and consolidated into a powerful state. Wegbaja's grandson, Agaja, conquered both Allada and Whydah in the 1720s, founding the kingdom of Dahomey with its capital at Abomey. Its government was an absolute monarchy with a well-established centralized state and bureaucracy. Dahomey became heavily involved in the

European slave trade, which had begun in earnest a century previous with the arrival of the Dutch.

The rule of Gezu (1818–1858), who overthrew King Adandozan, marked the pinnacle of Dahomey's power and influence. Military victories enabled Dahomey to stop paying its annual tribute to the Oyo Empire of what is now Nigeria. Still, the end of the slave trade in the mid-nineteenth century greatly affected the economic fortunes of Dahomey, forcing it to provide primary products for newly important colonial markets. Palm oil, its main export, was never able to generate the same kinds of revenues that the slave trade had yielded. After the French gained control of Porto-Novo, commerce declined. Under the leadership of Glele (1858–1889), Dahomean troops resisted the French occupation; in 1889 the entire French merchant community on the coast was forced to flee into British territory.

Benhazin (1889–1894), Glele's successor, was willing to trade with the French, but only if they agreed to grant Dahomey unconditional independence. In 1892 the French launched a full-scale offensive against Dahomey. Benhazin surrendered in 1894 and was exiled to Martinique, and the kingdom became the French colony of Dahomey.

Africa

Dakar, Senegal,

a major West African port and the capital and largest city of Senegal.

Cosmopolitan, hedonistic Dakar has been called the Paris of West Africa. Once the capital of French West Africa, Dakar no longer dominates West Africa economically or politically, but it remains an important cultural center. It lies on Cape Verde, near the westernmost point in Africa. Scholars have suggested two origins for the name Dakar. Fugitives from the tyrannical pre-colonial states of the interior called the Cape Verde Peninsula Deuk Raw ("land of refuge"), which might have evolved into Dakar. The name could also derive from the Wolof word for tamarind tree, Dakhar.

Latin America and the Caribbean

Dancehall,

currently the most popular form of reggae in Jamaica, featuring DJs toasting over raw rhythms with sparse melodic accompaniment.

Dancehall grew out of the roots reggae scene of the mid-1970s. Beginning in the 1980s reggae tracks grew increasingly stripped down. Insistent percussion and sparse melodies took a back seat to the vocal acrobatics of DJs, vocalists who would chat, rhyme, and "toast" over the instrumental tracks.

Starting with Count Machuki in the 1950s, there emerged a long tradition of talk-over DJs, but the form didn't become widely popular until the 1980s. DJs such as Yellowman started releasing albums recorded live in the Jamaican dance halls, and within a few years *dancehall* denoted this raw new form of reggae. Current *dancehall* features an occasional hip hop collaboration due to strong West Indian communities in the New York City neighborhoods of Brooklyn and the Bronx, where hip hop first developed.

Dancehall is primarily heard in Jamaica and foreign cities with sizable West Indian populations. Racially mixed working-class communities in London developed British *dancehall* culture into various cross-cultural fusions. In the early 1990s black London DJs incorporated *dancehall* toasting, dubbed reggae bass lines, and speeded-up hip hop breakbeats to form a new musical form known as *jungle*. Early *jungle* sounds like a frenzied *dancehall* song, complete with simulated gunfire, elemental bass, and a DJ improvising crowd-moving lyrics. *Dancehall* toasters such as General Levy and Super Cat have scored hit singles in both genres. Around the same time, London's Southeast Asian community looked to West Indian dancehall for inspiration. The resulting synthesis was termed *bhangramuffin*, and combined equal elements of Indian *bhangra* and Jamaican *raggamuffin* (or *dancehall*) rhythms. British-Indian vocalist Apache Indian sings in Punjabi, English, and Jamaican patois, highlighting the multicultural nature of *dancehall* in Great Britain.

North America

Dance Theater of Harlem,

multiracial American dance troupe that was the world's first professional all-black classical ballet company.

Established just months after the assassination of Dr. Martin Luther King Jr., the Dance Theater of Harlem (DTH) has evolved into one of the world's most respected dance companies and a treasured artistic resource in the black community. As its founder and long-time director Arthur Mitchell has said, the group's goal is not only to present dynamic classical dance performances but also "to ignite some sort of passion in young people." To that end, in addition to its professional troupe of more than 30 dancers, the DTH sponsors a dance school in its New York home as well as *Dancing Through Barriers*, a program designed to nurture young artists in several other cities, including Detroit, Michigan, and Washington, D.C. Another aspect of the DTH's mission is to disprove the once-popular notion that black people are anatomically unable to dance ballet. (No longer exclusively African American, the DTH retains its commitment to dancers of all skin tones by dyeing costumes and shoes in varying shades of brown and beige.)

Dandridge, Dorothy

(b. November 9, 1922, Cleveland, Ohio; d. September 8, 1965, Hollywood, Calif.), actress who was the first African American woman to receive an Academy Award nomination.

The daughter of a minister and an aspiring actress, Dorothy Dandridge began her career as a singer in 1951, performing at the Cotton Club in New York with the Dandridge Sisters (1951) and as a soloist with the Desi Arnaz Band. As a child, Dandridge appeared in bit parts in several films. She moved quickly from playing small roles in films such as *Flamingo* (1947) to lead roles in a number of low-budget films, including *Tarzan's Perils* (1951), *The Harlem Globetrotters* (1951), and *Jungle Queen* (1951). Her breakthrough role was *Carmen Jones* (1954), for which she became the first black woman to receive an Academy Award nomination for Best Actress. Her next film, *Island in the Sun* (1957), which was the first mainstream film to portray an interracial romance, was not received as well. In 1959 she regained critical recognition for her role as Bess in *Porgy and Bess* (1959).

Danticat, Edwidge

(b. January 19, 1969, Port-au-Prince, Haiti), premier Haitian American writer in the United States.

Edwidge Danticat's three major publications, *Breath, Eyes, Memory* (1994), *Krik? Krak!* (1995), and *The Farming of Bones* (1998), extend the Haitian literary border to encompass the English language and United States geography as central elements in Haiti's unfolding narrative at the start of the twenty-first century. For her the United States becomes the site of abrupt and unavoidable change, and of struggles for cultural continuity; the sea becomes yet another "passage of death for modern-day Haitians." Haiti in Danticat's work is a complex place full of love, violence, pride, and pain.

Dash, Julie

(b. October 22, 1952, Long Island City, N.Y.), American filmmaker best known for *Daughters of the Dust*, the first full-length general release film by an African American woman.

Born and raised in the Queensbridge Housing Projects in Long Island City, Julie Dash stumbled into filmmaking at age 17, enrolling with a friend in a workshop at the Studio Museum in Harlem. By 19 she had made her first film, shot with a Super 8 camera using pictures from Jet magazine attached to pipe cleaners.

Dash moved to Los Angeles after graduation, gaining experience working on many film crews. In Los Angeles, she became the youngest fellow ever at the Center for Advanced Film Studies. During her two-year fellowship, Dash adapted an Alice Walker short story, *Diary of an African Nun* (1977). An experimental dance film that she conceived and directed, *Four Women*, won the Gold Medal for Women in Film at the 1978 Miami International Film Festival.

In 1981 Dash received a Guggenheim grant to study the Gullah culture of the South Carolina coast, which resulted in *Daughters of the Dust* (1992), making her the first African American woman to create a full-length general release film.

North America

Davenport, Willie D.

(b. 1943, Troy, Ala.), African American track and field athlete who won the Gold Medal in the 110-meter high hurdles event at the 1968 Olympic Games in Mexico City.

Willie D. Davenport was educated at Southern University. His specialty was the indoor 60-yard high hurdles race, which is not an Olympic event. In the 60-yard hurdles, he won the United States national title five times (1966, 1967, 1969–1971).

He won the 120-yard hurdles event at the U.S. national track and field championships for the next three years (1965–1967), and he earned a Gold Medal in the 110-meter hurdles at the 1968 Olympic Games. At the 1980 Winter Olympic Games, Davenport became one of the few athletes to appear in both the summer and winter Olympic Games, competing as a member of the U.S. four-man bobsledding team. He was inducted into the National Track and Field Hall of Fame in 1982 and into the U.S. Olympic Hall of Fame in 1991.

North America

Davis, Angela Yvonne

(b. Jan. 26, 1944, Birmingham, Ala.), African American political activist, philosopher, and educator whose imprisonment for murder generated worldwide protest.

Angela Davis was, in several ways, born into the heart of the civil rights struggle. Her family lived in the middle-class section of Birmingham, Alabama, that came to be known as Dynamite Hill because there were so

WANTED BY THE **FBI**

INTERSTATE FLIGHT - MURDER, KIDNAPING

ANGELA YVONNE DAVIS

FBI No. 867,615 G

Photograph taken 1969   Photograph taken 1970

Alias: "Tamu"

DESCRIPTION

Age: 26, born January 26, 1944, Birmingham, Alabama
Height: 5'8"
Weight: 145 pounds
Build: Slender
Hair: Black
Occupation: Teacher
Scars and Marks: Small scars on both knees

Eyes: Brown
Complexion: Light brown
Race: Negro
Nationality: American

Fingerprint Classification: 4 M 5 Ua 6
                            I 17 U

CAUTION

ANGELA DAVIS IS WANTED ON KIDNAPING AND MURDER CHARGES GROWING OUT OF AN ABDUCTION AND SHOOTING IN MARIN COUNTY, CALIFORNIA, ON AUGUST 7, 1970. SHE ALLEGEDLY HAS PURCHASED SEVERAL GUNS IN THE PAST. CONSIDER POSSIBLY ARMED

An FBI poster lists Angela Davis among its ten most wanted fugitives after she went underground in 1970 to escape prosecution. Davis was eventually acquitted of all charges.
CORBIS/Bettmann

many Ku Klux Klan bombings. Davis attended segregated schools where children were taught black history but at the same time were denied adequate school supplies and facilities. From 1961 to 1965 Davis attended Brandeis University in Waltham, Massachusetts, and graduated with honors. She spent her junior year in Paris, where her contact with Algerian students provided her with a global perspective on the struggle against colonialism and oppression. Her political commitments intensified in 1963, when four girls whom Davis had known were killed in the 16th Street Baptist Church bombing in Birmingham.

While in graduate school Davis became increasingly politically active. At a workshop sponsored by the Student Nonviolent Coordinating Committee (SNCC), Davis met Frank and Kendra Alexander, both active members of SNCC, the Black Panthers, and the Communist party. Davis moved to Los Angeles to join the Alexanders in their work and in 1968 joined the Communist Party.

Davis's political activities earned her international attention in 1970. Through the Black Panthers, Davis became an advocate for black political prisoners and spoke out in defense of the inmates known as the Soledad Brothers. After the killing of inmate George Jackson by guards at Soledad Prison, his younger brother, Jonathan, attempted to free another prisoner from a Marin County, California, courthouse by taking hostages. Four people were killed in the shoot-out that followed. The guns Jackson used belonged to Davis. Even though she was not at all near the courthouse at the time, she was charged with kidnapping, conspiracy, and murder. When Davis defied the arrest warrant and went into hiding, she was placed on the FBI's ten-most-wanted list. Her capture in a New York motel room and subsequent imprisonment inspired "Free Angela" rallies around the world. Davis spent 16 months in jail before being released on bail in 1972; she was later acquitted of all charges.

Davis is the author of several books, including *If They Come in the Morning* (1971), *Angela Davis: An Autobiography* (1974), *Women, Race and Class* (1983) and *Women, Culture and Politics* (1989).

Davis, Anthony

(b. Paterson, N.J., February 20, 1951), African American composer and pianist whose innovations in modern classical music conflate jazz styles and global rhythms.

The son of the first African American professor at Princeton University, Anthony Davis studied classical music as a child in New York, and as an undergraduate at Yale University he played free-jazz with Anthony Braxton. After earning his B.A. at Yale in 1975, Davis moved to New York City, where he supported himself as a jazz pianist. As he developed musically, his compositions deviated from traditional jazz. He often abandoned improvisation and drew elements from Western classical music and African and South Asian rhythms. His recordings from this period include *Hidden Voices* (1979) and *Lady of the Mirrors* (1981). In 1981 he formed an eight-piece ensemble, *Episteme*, whose repertoire included a combination of improvised and scored music, blurring the distinction between jazz and classical music.

Davis has taught at Yale and Columbia Universities, composed scores for numerous dance companies, and written music for several films. His symphonic works have been performed by the New York Philharmonic, the Brooklyn Philharmonic, and the San Francisco Symphony. He won a Pulitzer Prize for his piano concerto Wayang no. 5 (1984).

Davis, Benjamin O., Jr.

(b. December 18, 1912, Washington, D.C.), first African American general of the United States Air Force.

Benjamin Oliver Davis Jr. was the son of Elnora and Benjamin Oliver Davis Sr., the first black general of the U.S. Army. After living on a number of military bases during his childhood, Davis entered a predominantly white high school in Cleveland, Ohio. He hoped to enroll in the U.S. Military Academy at West Point. At the time, the academy actively discouraged blacks from applying. With the help of black Chicago congressman Oscar DePriest, however, Davis took the entrance examinations and entered the academy in 1932. At West Point, because he was black, Davis was subjected to four years of a campaign called silencing: no one ate with him, roomed with him, answered his questions, or spoke to him unless issuing an order. He nonetheless graduated in the top 15 percent of his class and became West Point's first African American graduate since Reconstruction. Because of his high class ranking, he should have been allowed to choose which branch of service to enter; however, when he requested the air corps (then a branch of the army), he was told that there were no black squadrons and that the government had no intention of assigning a black lieutenant to a white squadron.

In the early 1940s President Franklin D. Roosevelt, seeking wider support among African Americans, approved several changes that gave blacks greater roles in the armed services. One such change was the promotion of Benjamin Davis Sr. as the first black army general. Another was allowing African Americans into the Air Corps on an experimental basis. A training program for black pilots was established at the historically-black Tuskegee Institute and Benjamin Davis Jr. was ordered to attend the first class. Completing the training in 1942, Davis was given charge of the Ninety-ninth Pursuit Squadron, the first black air unit, and was sent the following year to North Africa to serve in World War II. During the Korean War, he commanded a racially integrated flying unit and was afterward promoted to brigadier general, the first black to reach that rank in the air force. In 1965 he became the first African American in any military branch to reach the rank of lieutenant general. In 1970, after commanding the Thirteenth Air Force in the Vietnam War, he retired.

North America

Davis, Miles Dewey, III

(b. May 25, 1926, Alton, Ill.; d. September 25, 1991, Santa Monica, Calif.), African American trumpet player and band leader who contributed significantly to bebop, cool jazz, modal jazz, and fusion or jazz-rock.

The role of Miles Davis is unparalleled in the history of jazz. Many great jazz musicians—including Louis Armstrong, Coleman Hawkins, Charlie Parker, and Dizzy Gillespie—gained renown for their technical mastery and their distinctive approaches to improvisation. Others, such as Duke Ellington, Count Basie, Thelonious Monk, Charles Mingus, and Ornette Coleman, achieved greatness less through instrumental prowess than through compositions and performances in a distinctive style. Davis is unique in having made his mark through neither technical mastery nor a single identifiable style, but rather through his constant evolution and stylistic innovation. Jazz scholar Joachim Berendt has observed that Davis three times altered the history of jazz, by introducing cool jazz, modal jazz, and fusion. Since his death, his influence has continued to be greater than that of any other jazz musician, including tenor saxophonist John Coltrane. The son of a prosperous dentist, Davis grew up in a middleclass home in East St. Louis, Illinois. His mother, Cleota Henry Davis, who was a classically trained musician, gave Davis his first trumpet at age 13. By his mid-teens he was playing in the St. Louis area—in the process befriending St. Louis jazz trumpeter Clark Terry. Shortly after graduating from high school in 1944, Davis substituted for a sick third trumpet player in Billy Eckstine's orchestra during its two-week gig in St. Louis.

The Eckstine band was then the most innovative group in jazz. It featured a number of the young lions of bebop, most notably Dizzy Gillespie on trumpet and Charlie Parker—Bird—on alto sax, but also vocalists Eckstine and Sarah Vaughan. Davis attended Juilliard School of Music but never graduated; he gained far more of his musical education in the jazz clubs of 52nd Street. He quickly established himself in the jazz community, playing with tenor saxophonist Coleman Hawkins, pianist and composer Tadd Dameron, and pianists Bud Powell and Thelonious Monk. He became a regular member of the Eckstine band.

Over the course of 45 years, Davis's playing fell into five distinct, sometimes overlapping phases: bebop (1945–1948), cool jazz (1948–1958), hard bop (1952–1963), modal (1959, 1964–1968), and electric or fusion (1969–1991).

North America

Davis, Ossie

(b. December 18, 1917, Cogdell, Ga.), widely acclaimed African American actor, playwright, producer, and director who has long been an activist and leader within the black community.

The son of a railway engineer, Ossie Davis grew up in Waycross, Georgia. The harassment of his parents by the Ku Klux Klan impelled him early on to become a writer so that he could "truthfully portray the black man's experience." At Howard University, under the tutelage of drama critic Alain Locke, Davis developed his theatrical talent, performing in a 1941 production of *Joy Exceeding Glory* with Harlem's Rose McClendon Players. Following his theater debut, however, he received few job offers and for nearly a year found himself living on the street. Davis never lost his sense of purpose. In 1948 he married fellow performer Ruby Dee, who became his lifelong collaborator on stage, on screen, and as a political activist.

Davis is best known for his roles in Lorraine Hansberry's award-winning Broadway play *A Raisin in the Sun* (1959) and its 1961 film version, as well as for his own satirical play *Purlie Victorious* (1961). He has since written and directed *numerous films, including Cotton Comes to Harlem (1970) and Countdown at Kusini* (co-produced with Dee, 1976), the first American feature film to be shot entirely in Africa by black professionals. Davis has also starred in numerous films that address issues critical to African Americans, such as Spike Lee's *Do the Right Thing* (1989), *Jungle Fever* (1991), and *Malcolm X* (1994). Among the many awards Davis has received are the Hall of Fame Award for outstanding artistic achievement in 1989 and the U.S. National Medal for the Arts in 1995.

Sammy Davis Jr. talks with President Richard M. Nixon at the 1972 Republican National Convention.
CORBIS/Bettmann

Davis, Sammy, Jr.

(b. December 8, 1925, New York, N.Y.; d. May 16, 1990, Los Angeles, Calif.), African American singer, dancer, and actor who starred on the vaudeville stage, Broadway, television, and in motion pictures.

Sammy Davis Jr., the son of vaudeville performers Elvera Sanchez Davis and Sammy Davis Sr., began a life-long career of entertaining at the age of three, appearing in the vaudeville group in which his parents danced, Will Mastin's *Holiday in Dixieland*. Two years later, after his parents' divorce, he stayed with his father and officially joined the group. Davis made his movie debut with Ethel Waters in *Rufus Jones for President* (1933), and then filmed *Season's Greetings*. Throughout the 1930s he toured with the Will Mastin Trio, becoming the central figure in the group, singing, dancing, and playing several instruments.

Davis's recording career began to take off in 1946, when he signed with Capitol Records. The song "The Way you Look Tonight" was selected by Metronome as record of the year and Davis was chosen as Most Outstanding New Personality. Decca Records signed him in 1954 and released *Starring Sammy Davis Jr.*, which reached number one on the charts. In 1956 he made his Broadway debut, starring in *Mr. Wonderful*. He moved back to film with *The Benny Goodman Story* (1956), *Anna Lucasta* (1958), and *Porgy and Bess* (1959).

In the 1960s Davis socialized and made films with the Rat Pack, a Hollywood group led by Frank Sinatra and Dean Martin. These films included *Oceans Eleven* (1960), *Sergeants Three* (1962), and *Robin and the Seven Hoods* (1964). Also during the 1960s Davis starred on Broadway in *Golden Boy*, which ran for 568 performances. His 1965 autobiography, *Yes I Can*, earned him the Spingarn Medal from the National Association for the Advancement of Colored People.

Deadwood Dick

(b. June, 1854, Davidson County, Tenn.; d. 1921?, Los Angeles, Calif.), African American cowboy.

Deadwood Dick was born Nat Love, a slave in a log cabin, the youngest of three children. A lucky raffle ticket brought him the money to seek greater opportunities, so he started on foot for the West in 1869. On his arrival in Dodge City, Kansas, he found work as a cowboy. He immediately earned admiration for his ability to ride a bucking bronco that his new companions had furnished him for his initiation. Because of this feat, the "tenderfoot" was accepted by the Duval outfit at $30 a month.

At a Fourth of July celebration in 1876, he found himself in competition with the best cowboys in the West. He won the contest to rope, throw, tie, bridle, saddle, and mount an untamed bronco, a feat he accomplished in 9 minutes, a record, and won the shooting contests with a rifle at 100 and 250 yards and with the Colt 45 at 150 yards. He was given the name Deadwood Dick by his admiring fans.

In 1890, with the passing of the great era of the cowboy, Deadwood Dick became a Pullman porter. Despite the slavery-era statutes that outlawed black literacy, he had learned to read and write at his father's knee, and in 1907 he wrote an autobiography titled *The Life and Adventures of Nat Love: Better Known in the Cattle Country as "Deadwood Dick."*

North America

Declaration of Independence,

American document of July 4, 1776, declaring the separation of 13 British colonies in North America from Great Britain; although the final document held that "all men are created equal," the Continental Congress deleted earlier passages that condemned slavery.

Africa

Decolonization in Africa: An Interpretation

The most difficult problem in writing the history of decolonization is the temptation to write it backwards. We know that almost all African colonies eventually became independent states, hence a tendency to relate the triumph of nationalism—of an African conquest of the colonial state. We know now that the fruits of independence have often turned bitter, hence a temptation to write the history of disappointment—of the continued subordination of Africa to Western powers. Neither the triumphalist history nor the story of frustrated aspirations is sufficient.

If instead of writing history from the present to the past we watch it run forward, the history of Africa from the 1940s onward opens up to a much wider range of actions, aspirations, and possibilities. We see political movements directed not just at taking over the nation-state, but at revitalizing local belief systems or forging connections among people of African descent all around the world. We see African workers organizing to demand wages equal to those of whites, merchants seeking access to markets alongside European firms, peasants trying to restore harmony to the land. People act

Kenyan prime minister Jomo Kenyatta, *right,* waves to a crowd of supporters as he enters the East African Heads of Government Conference in Nairobi, Kenya, in 1964. With Kenyatta are, *left,* Julius Nyerere of Tanzania and, *center,* Milton Obote of Uganda. *CORBIS/Bettmann*

together as members of an Islamic brotherhood or as migrants from a particular rural area. Such collectivities are important not simply as they contributed to anti-colonial or nationalist movements—even though many of them did—but because they helped reshape people's lives.

A number of scholars would dispense with the concept of decoloniza-

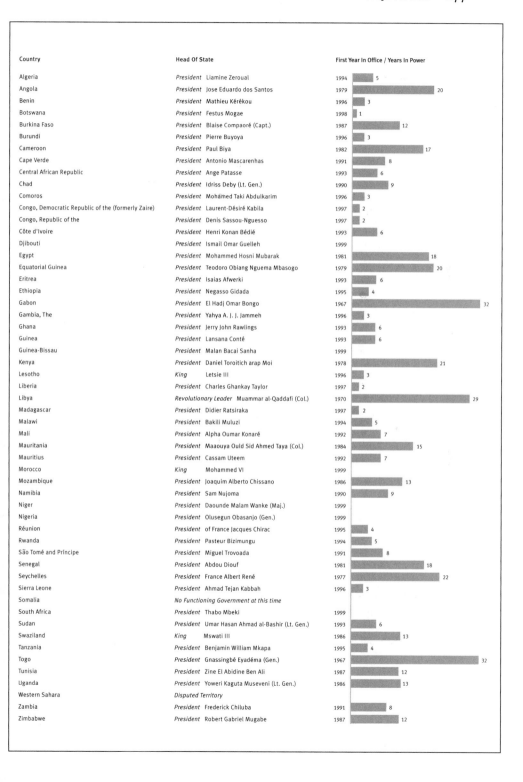

Country	Head Of State		First Year In Office / Years In Power	
Algeria	*President*	Liamine Zeroual	1994	5
Angola	*President*	Jose Eduardo dos Santos	1979	20
Benin	*President*	Mathieu Kérékou	1996	3
Botswana	*President*	Festus Mogae	1998	1
Burkina Faso	*President*	Blaise Compaoré (Capt.)	1987	12
Burundi	*President*	Pierre Buyoya	1996	3
Cameroon	*President*	Paul Biya	1982	17
Cape Verde	*President*	Antonio Mascarenhas	1991	8
Central African Republic	*President*	Ange Patasse	1993	6
Chad	*President*	Idriss Deby (Lt. Gen.)	1990	9
Comoros	*President*	Mohámed Taki Abdulkarim	1996	3
Congo, Democratic Republic of the (formerly Zaire)	*President*	Laurent-Désiré Kabila	1997	2
Congo, Republic of the	*President*	Denis Sassou-Nguesso	1997	2
Côte d'Ivoire	*President*	Henri Konan Bédié	1993	6
Djibouti	*President*	Ismail Omar Guelleh	1999	
Egypt	*President*	Mohammed Hosni Mubarak	1981	18
Equatorial Guinea	*President*	Teodoro Obiang Nguema Mbasogo	1979	20
Eritrea	*President*	Isaias Afwerki	1993	6
Ethiopia	*President*	Negasso Gidada	1995	4
Gabon	*President*	El Hadj Omar Bongo	1967	32
Gambia, The	*President*	Yahya A. J. J. Jammeh	1996	3
Ghana	*President*	Jerry John Rawlings	1993	6
Guinea	*President*	Lansana Conté	1993	6
Guinea-Bissau	*President*	Malan Bacai Sanha	1999	
Kenya	*President*	Daniel Toroitich arap Moi	1978	21
Lesotho	*King*	Letsie III	1996	3
Liberia	*President*	Charles Ghankay Taylor	1997	2
Libya	*Revolutionary Leader*	Muammar al-Qaddafi (Col.)	1970	29
Madagascar	*President*	Didier Ratsiraka	1997	2
Malawi	*President*	Bakili Muluzi	1994	5
Mali	*President*	Alpha Oumar Konaré	1992	7
Mauritania	*President*	Maaouya Ould Sid Ahmed Taya (Col.)	1984	15
Mauritius	*President*	Cassam Uteem	1992	7
Morocco	*King*	Mohammed VI	1999	
Mozambique	*President*	Joaquim Alberto Chissano	1986	13
Namibia	*President*	Sam Nujoma	1990	9
Niger	*President*	Daounde Malam Wanke (Maj.)	1999	
Nigeria	*President*	Olusegun Obasanjo (Gen.)	1999	
Réunion	*President* of France	Jacques Chirac	1995	4
Rwanda	*President*	Pasteur Bizimungu	1994	5
São Tomé and Príncipe	*President*	Miguel Trovoada	1991	8
Senegal	*President*	Abdou Diouf	1981	18
Seychelles	*President*	France Albert René	1977	22
Sierra Leone	*President*	Ahmad Tejan Kabbah	1996	3
Somalia	*No Functioning Government at this time*			
South Africa	*President*	Thabo Mbeki	1999	
Sudan	*President*	Umar Hasan Ahmad al-Bashir (Lt. Gen.)	1993	6
Swaziland	*King*	Mswati III	1986	13
Tanzania	*President*	Benjamin William Mkapa	1995	4
Togo	*President*	Gnassingbé Eyadéma (Gen.)	1967	32
Tunisia	*President*	Zine El Abidine Ben Ali	1987	12
Uganda	*President*	Yoweri Kaguta Museveni (Lt. Gen.)	1986	13
Western Sahara	*Disputed Territory*			
Zambia	*President*	Frederick Chiluba	1991	8
Zimbabwe	*President*	Robert Gabriel Mugabe	1987	12

tion altogether, for some because it never really happened—because Africa remains subordinated to Europe—for others because the term suggests that colonial rule marched along to its own end, rather than being overthrown by people striving to liberate themselves. The term is still useful, as long as one does not read more into it than it deserves. Colonialism may be distinguished from other systems in which a few people ruled over many by the institutions colonial regimes created that explicitly reproduced social difference and inequality. Colonial states drew and redrew distinctions among people under its rule, defining some as "natives" (in turn divided into "tribes") and others as "citizens" or "Europeans," with different rights and obligations, administered through different agencies. Although states often used similar techniques at home and overseas to command obedience, the ruling fiction in the colonies was difference, while the ruling fiction at home in Europe, at least since the nineteenth century, was the legal and political equivalence of citizens. Colonial rulers passed laws against intermarriage and tried to prevent whites from "going native," or "educated natives" from thinking too highly of themselves.

These distinctions became increasingly difficult—and then impossible—to sustain in the period after World War II. Decolonization entailed the transition from empires in which distinction was emphasized to a global system of states in which all states were formally equivalent and in which each regarded its own citizens as formally equivalent to one another.

The word "formal" is crucial. The world and its individual states have always been and remain driven by distinctions. Sovereignty allowed African leaders to make certain kinds of claims on world resources, and many became adept at appealing, using a vocabulary of "nation-building" and " development," to rich states' interests in having a world order of states participating in global institutions and markets. Internally, sovereignty also had its uses: sovereign power could be used to reward friends and punish enemies, to forge symbols of national solidarity. The politics of running a state, in short, are not the politics of running a colony.

The Crisis of Colonialism

In 1945 the idea that most of Africa would be divided into independent states within 20 years would have struck most Europeans—and possibly most Africans—as unimaginable. By 1965 it was a fact. Part of understanding this transition is figuring out how the transfer of power became imaginable—in Paris, in Accra, in villages in rural Tanganyika (present-day Tanzania).

Another of the temptations the historian faces is that of making colonialism into more than it was—a solid and unchanging edifice of power. Colonists wanted to believe this, as did anti-colonial movements, for it defined their own heroism. Colonialism, in fact, came apart at its cracks, even as colonial regimes tried to remake themselves.

What conquering powers could do best was concentrate forces—to smash African political units one by one, to punish rebellion brutally, and to round up labor or seize resources at certain moments. What they could do

(continued on page 182)

AFRICAN INDEPENDENCE
Chronology of African Independence

State	Date of Independence	Colonial Power	Notes
Ethiopia	Ancient		Italian occupation 1936-1941.
Liberia	July 26, 1847		Private colony 1822-1847. Home for freed American slaves.
South Africa	May 31, 1910	Britian	(Suid Afrika) Union of four colonies, Cape Colony, Natal, Orange River Colony (Oranje Vrij Staat) and Transvaal (Zuid Afrikaansche Republiek), the last two of whichl had been independent Boer republics to May 31,1902. The Union became republic outside British Commonwealth May 31, 1961.
			White minority rule. Unrecognized 'independent' homelands:
			Transkei October 26, 1976
			Bophuthatswana December 6, 1977
			Venda September 13, 1979
			Ciskei December 4, 1981
Egypt	February 28, 1922	Britian	Joined with Syria as United Arab Republic (UAR) from February 1, 1958 to September 28, 1961. Federated with Kingdom of (North) Yemen from March 8, 1958 to December 26, 1961. Name UAR retained by Egypt to September 2, 1961.
Libya	December 24, 1951	Italy	British (Tripolitania and Cyrenaica) and French (Fezzan) administration 1943-1951.
Ethiopia (Ogaden)	February 28, 1955		Italian occupation 1936-1941. British administration 1941-1955
Sudan	January 1, 1956	Britain & Egypt	Anglo-Egyptian condominium.
Morocco	March 2, 1956	France	(Marcoc)
Tunisia	March 20, 1956	France	(Tunisie)
Morocco (part)	October 29, 1956		International zone (Tangiers).
Ghana	March 6, 1957	Britain	(Gold Coast) including British Togoland (UN Trust), part of former German colony of Togo.
Morocco (part)	April 27, 1958	Spain	(Marruecos) Spanish southern zone.
Guinea	October 2, 1958	France	(Guinée Française)
Cameroon	January 1, 1960	France	(Cameroun) UN Trust. Larger part of former German colony of Kamerun.
Togo	April 27, 1960	France	UN Trust. Larger part of former German colony of Togo.
Senegal	June 20, 1960 (August 20, 1960)	France	First independent as 'Federation of Mali' with Mali (former French Soudan). Federation dissolved after two months. Joined Gambia in Confederation of Senegambia, January 1, 1982 to October 6, 1989.
Mali	June 20, 1960 (September 22, 1960)	France	(Soudan Française) Independent initially as 'Federation of Mali' with Senegal. Federation dissolved after two months.
Madagascar	June 26, 1960	France	(Malagasy, Republique Malagache)
Zaire	June 30, 1960	Belgium	Congo Free State (Etat Indépendant du Congo) May 2, 1885 to November 11, 1908 when it became the Belgian Congo (Congo Belge, Belgisch Congo). Name changed from Congo October 27, 1974.

AFRICAN INDEPENDENCE
Chronology of African Independence

State	Date of Independence	Colonial Power	Notes
Somalia	July 1, 1960	Italy & Britain	UN Trust. Union of two colonies, Italian and British Somaliland. British Somaliland independent prior to union on June 26, 1960.
Benin	August 1, 1960	France	Name changed from Dahomey November 30, 1975.
Niger	August 3, 1960	France	
Burkina Faso	August 5, 1960	France	Name changed from Upper Volta (Haute Volta) August 4, 1984.
Ivory Coast	August 7, 1960	France	(Côte d'Ivoire)
Chad	August 11, 1960	France	(Tchad)
Central African Republic (CAR)	August 13, 1960	France	(Oubangui-Chari, Republique Centrafricaine) Central African Empire from December 4, 1976 to September 20, 1979.
Congo (Brazzaville)	August 15, 1960	France	(Moyen Congo)
Gabon	August 17, 1960	France	
Nigeria	October 1, 1960	Britain	
Mauritania	November 28, 1960	France	(Mauritanie)
Sierra Leone	April 24, 1961	Britain	
Nigeria (British North Cameroon)	June 1, 1961	Britain	UN Trust. Part of former German colony of Kamerun. Plebiscite February 11-12, 1961.
Cameroon (British South Cameroon)	October 1, 1961	Britain	UN Trust. Part of former German colony of Kamerun. Plebiscite February 11-12, 1961. Union with Cameroon as United Republic of Cameroon.
Tanzania	December 9, 1961	Britain	(Tanganyika) UN Trust. Greater part of former German colony of Deutsche Ostafrika. Name changed to Tanzania following union with Zanzibar April 27, 1964.
Burundi	July 1, 1962	Belgium	UN Trust. Ruanda-Urundi, divided at independence, was smaller part of former German. colony of Deutsche Ostafrika.
Rwanda	July 1, 1962	Belgium	UN Trust. Ruanda-Urundi, divided at independence, was smaller part of former German. colony of Deutsche Ostafrika.
Algeria	July 3, 1962	France	(Algérie)
Uganda	October 9, 1962	Britain	
Tanzania (Zanzibar)	December 10, 1963	Britain	Union with Tanganyika as Tanzania April 27, 1964.
Kenya	December 12, 1963	Britain	
Malawi	July 6, 1974	Britain	(Nyasaland) Federated with Rhodesia October 1, 1953 to December 31, 1963.
Zambia	October 25, 1964	Britain	(Northern Rhodesia) Federated with Nyasaland and Southern RhodesiaOctober 1, 1953 to December 31, 1963.
Gambia	February 18, 1965	Britain	Joined with Senegal as Confederation of Senegambia, January 1, 1982 toOctober 6, 1989.
Botswana	September 30, 1966	Britain	(Bechuanaland)

AFRICAN INDEPENDENCE
Chronology of African Independence

State	Date of Independence	Colonial Power	Notes
Lesotho	October 4, 1966	Britain	(Basutoland)
Mauritius	March 12, 1968	Britain	
Swaziland	September 6, 1968	Britain	
Equatorial Guinea	October 12, 1968	Spain	Comprises Rio Muni and Macias Nguema Biyogo (Fernando Poo)
Morocco (Ifni)	June 30, 1969	Spain	(Territorio de Ifni)
Guinea-Bissau	September 10, 1974	Portugal	Guine-Bissau formerly Guine-Portuguesa.
Mozambique	June 25, 1975	Portugal	(Mocambique)
Cape Verde	July 5, 1975	Portugal	(Cabo Verde)
Comoros	July 6, 1975	France	Archipel des Comores. Excluding island of Mayotte which remains a French Overseas Territory (Territoire d'Outre-Mer).
São Tomé and Príncipe	July 12, 1975	Portugal	(St. Thomas and Prince Islands)
Angola	November 11, 1975	Portugal	Includes detached enclave of Cabinda.
Western Sahara	February 28, 1976	Spain	(Rio de Oro and Sequit el Hamra) On Spanish withdrawal seized by Morocco. Occupation disrupted POLISARIO, formed May 10, 1973.
Seychelles	June 26, 1976	Britain	
Djibouti	June 27, 1977	France	(Territoire Française des Afars et des Issas formerly Côte Française des Somalis
Zimbabwe	April 18, 1980	Britain	(Rhodesia, formerly Southern Rhodesia) Unilateral Declaration of Independence (UDI) in effect from November 11, 1965 to December 12, 1979. Federated with Northern Rhodesia and Nyasaland October 1, 1953 to December 31, 1963.
Namibia	March 21, 1990	South Africa	(South West Africa) UN Trust. Former German colony of Deutsche Sudwestafrika.
Eritrea	May 24, 1993	Italy Ethiopia	British administration 1941-1952. Federated with Ethiopia September 11, 1952. Union with Ethiopia November 14, 1962.

African Territories and Islands Not Independent

State	Colonial Power	Notes
Spanish North Africa	Spain	Plazas de Soberania: Ceuta, Islas Chafarinas Melilla, Penon de Velez de la Gomera, Penon de Alhucemas. Small enclaves and islands on the north coast of Morocco.
Madeira	Portugal	(Arquipelago da Madeira)
Canary Islands	Spain	(Islas Canarias)
St Helena with Ascension and Tristan da Cunha	Britain	British Crown Colony.
Socotra	Yemen	
Mayotte	France	Island of Comoros Group. Territoire Française d'Outre-Mer.
Reunion	France	Ile de la Réunion, Département d'Outre-Mer (from 1946).
French Indian Ocean Islands	France	Ile Europa, Ille Juan de Nova, Bassas da India, Iles Glorieuses, Tromelin (all near Madagascar).

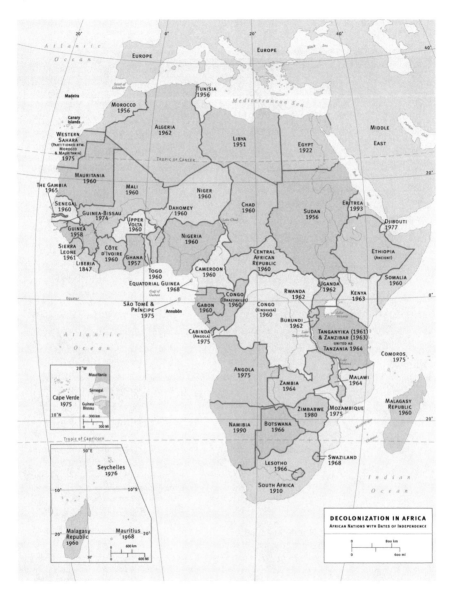

least well, try as they did, was to insinuate themselves into the routine exercise of power. In South Africa, Algeria, Southern Rhodesia (present-day Zimbabwe), and parts of other colonies, white settlers both forced indigenous people off their land and provided a surveillance and control over agricultural and mineral production that was impossible elsewhere. When two decades into the colonial period British rulers proclaimed themselves advocates of "indirect rule," they were accepting their incapacity either to make Africans into replicas of Europeans or else to turn Africans into the servants of European will. They insisted that keeping African societies in their allegedly timeless integrity had been British policy all along. Actually, this "ethnicization" of Africa—French Africa as well as British—came at a time shortly after World War I when educated Africans were building associations and political organizations and acting disturbingly like "citizens."

At the very time, in the 1920s, when European powers were pretending that Africans were living within tribal cages, many were deeply involved in boundary-crossing activities: as farmers, opening up new territories; as merchants, exchanging goods from different ecological zones; and as workers, seeking as best they could to obtain cash wages without losing access to land and community. Religious movements were shaping affinities that crossed or expanded lines of language and culture. African intellectuals forged connections throughout the African Diaspora and with intellectuals from other colonized regions (see Pan-Africanism), while working-class Africans entered into Diasporic relations when black sailors and dock workers from Africa and the Americas met on ships or in ports, and eventually contributed to the rise of the Garvey movement.

The colonialism that collapsed in the 1950s was not the stagnant colonialism of the 1920s or 1930s, but colonialism at its most arrogantly interventionist, its most self-consciously reformist. In the 1920s and 1930s France and Great Britain rejected efforts from within the colonial establishment for a more vigorous "development" of African resources. A crisis came with recovery from the 1930s depression, as African workers returned to employers slow to raise wages recently cut, to cities with virtually no social services. The result was a wave of strikes beginning in the British Copperbelt (in present-day Zambia) in 1935, where it spread beyond the mines to engulf entire towns, extending to railroads in the Gold Coast and ports in Kenya, Tanganyika, and elsewhere. The wave struck the British West Indies as well. In London this was seen as an empire-wide threat. More important, it revealed that pretending to keep colonized people in their tribal cages was a failure. The British government decided it had to reclaim the initiative with the Colonial Development and Welfare Act of 1940. This recognized that resources would have to be put into colonies—not just extracted from them—if social peace and colonial initiative were to be restored.

Then came the war—to which Africans contributed their bodies and their labor, and for which they received little. Another strike wave hit British Africa, and this time officials focused specifically on the labor question, partially giving in to wage demands and at last acknowledging the "worker" as something more than the "detribalized

Patrice Lumumba, leader of the movement for independence in the then Belgian Congo, is greeted by supporters as he arrives in Brussels for a conference in 1960. *CORBIS/Hulton-Deutsch Collection*

African." In French Africa, parallel developments occurred after the war—in the shadow of major strikes and urban conflicts between 1945 and 1948—and also resulted in a new development initiative.

Development in the Service of Empire

The international situation had also changed. On the one hand, Europe needed African minerals and crops more than ever. On the other hand, empire became more vulnerable politically. Hitler gave racist ideologies a bad name, and imperial leaders were at pains to explain why "self-determination" was a useful cry against Nazi conquests but not against imperial domination. Would Africa simply become a zone of heightened extraction, or could imperial powers reconcile expanding production with containing protest and re-legitimizing empire internationally? For France and Great Britain, the development idea seemed for a time to offer an answer: their capital and knowledge would both increase output and raise the standard of living of Africans. Development would be the salvation of empire.

In Portuguese Africa production was expanded within a highly authoritarian system of rule and a highly coercive system of labor recruitment. In Belgian Africa, development meant more power for the already powerful mining companies, which provided services to "stabilize" workers in their employment. Belgium boasted of health and other services, but it did little to train an elite and less to allow expression, suppressing numerous peasant uprisings, religious movements, strikes, and mutinies.

Modernizing colonialism sharply raised the stakes: the old empire on the cheap was becoming economically and politically impossible, while the expensive empire of the postwar era had yet to prove itself. In fact, the development drive did more to foster demands and disorder than to contain them. And meanwhile, the attempt to legitimize the colonial order was opening cracks in the structure of power, which African political movements quickly pried wider open.

Political Mobilization in Africa

If one can sense the vulnerability of European powers, one needs to understand the multiple ways in which Africans mobilized, and the diverse objectives that they sought. It is too easy to project backwards the struggle for the nation-state, but important to note the way in which African political parties brokered quite diverse movements and aspirations—well enough to create plausible political organizations, not well enough to deepen those connections into a sense of common purpose.

There were struggles to group together chiefdoms into larger units with more influence in the colonial capital, attempts to install younger or more "progressive" chiefs in place of reactionary ones, efforts of urban migrants to strengthen and expand their communities of origin, and attempts to combat spiritual threats to the health of local communities. These movements used local languages and religious beliefs, and they often involved people literate in English or French who might enhance oral tradition by compiling it in written form. There were Muslim brotherhoods with networks of Koranic schools and leadership hierarchies across West and North Africa as well as Christian communities and breakaway, sometimes millennial, religious organizations—all bringing people together in other ways. Pan-Africanism in its various forms confronted imperialism on a world scale, insisting that the oppression of people of color demanded a global liberation. South Africans had organized effective labor and strike movements from the 1920s, while Algerian workers—more of whom had jobs in France than in Algerian cities—built a powerful organization of North African workers in France, linked to currents of proletarian internationalism in Europe. It would soon catalyze radical nationalism in Algeria itself.

What was really new after World War II was the possibility of articulating these concepts not simply among people of African descent literate in French and English, but between the elite and wider groupings of people within their respective territories.

Before the war, political parties and other political organizations existed within a number of colonial territories, but most importantly across them— the National Congress of British West Africa and later the West African Students Union notable among these. In North Africa, where European colonization had never eclipsed the merchant or administrative elite of the previous Ottoman Empire, elite movements such as the Young Algerians or Young Tunisians (see Tunisia) claimed meaningful forms of citizenship. In Egypt a relatively brief period of formal British rule gave way in 1922 to a restored Egyptian monarchy, besieged by students, commercial elite, and other "modernizers," and increasingly by mobilization among workers and peasants, all demanding that the state be truly independent, be truly national, and respond to their needs. Throughout North Africa, Islamic reform movements sought to purify social life and link the region to a broader Islamic world. In the 1940s these movements focused more clearly on demands for political autonomy, but with considerable disagreement over whether this should take place in relation to France or Great Britain, under a monarchy poised between traditionalist and modernizing political movements, or in an explicitly national form.

In South Africa from 1912, the African National Congress (ANC) drew on Anglo-American traditions of peaceful petition and protest to insist that democracy made sense in Africa too. By World War II, the young educated elite throughout Africa were adding a new militancy, linkages to labor movements, and connections to radical anti-imperialists in European and colonial capitals. In French Africa, the Rassemblement Démocratique Africain organized a wide political movement in 1946, and territorial political parties came under its umbrella.

Social action was necessarily political, and political action invariably had social implications. Yet a labor union was, first of all, a labor union, struggling for better wages and working conditions. In the 1945–1950 strike wave, unions in French Africa turned the government's idea of a single, transoceanic "France" into demands that all workers within that unit receive the same pay and benefits. Although political leaders saw workers as a constituency, and unions saw political action as useful to their cause, a tension between the idea of solidarity among workers and unity among Africans grew. Similarly, the wide variety of movements among peasants—against the intrusiveness of colonial agricultural projects, over land issues, against below-market prices paid to farmers by colonial crop marketing boards—must be seen in all their specificity, though every success any movement had contributed to a broader sense of empowerment.

It was the genius of men such as Kwame Nkrumah and Léopold Senghor that they could bring together diverse movements and tendencies. They were machine politicians in the best sense of the word. They drew together the poor peasant hemmed in by colonial agricultural policies, the well-off merchant feeling the heavy hand of the European import-export houses, the railway worker facing barriers to advancement, the literate clerk trapped in the racial hierarchy of a bureaucracy, the lawyer espousing constitutional justice into what—for a time at least— was a coherent movement against the injustices of colonial states. Studies of politics in different territories stress that political parties *both* were constrained by regional and ethnic differences *and* cut across them, and in any case the affiliations that defined an "ethnic group" changed in the course of political mobilizations.

The institutions that colonial powers created failed to contain political mobilization, but they often channeled it in certain directions. After World War II, France and Great Britain—but not Portugal and Belgium—sought to open up electoral institutions that would co-opt elite Africans and justify the argument that colonial stewardship was preparing Africans for a democratic, modern future. Limited as these initially were, colonial political institutions defined a game with clear rules. Politics was encouraged when it took the form of electoral campaigns for the legislative body created for each colony, for the local councils, and in the French case the territorial units that elected representatives to the Paris legislature, where they would constitute a numerically small voice in the sovereign body. In Nigeria or Senegal, businessmen, teachers, and trade unionists became the building blocks of early parties. However, in French Equatorial Africa—where a particularly brutal and exploitative form of colonization had been practiced— the electoral system created by the French after 1945 constituted its own political reality, in which politicians turned categories such as urban youth into political units and redrew the boundaries of ethnic affiliations to fit the constituencies they were organizing.

Meanwhile, other forms of political connection—from Pan-Africanism to Muslim brotherhoods—received no such representation, no such encouragement. Indeed, from Sétif (Algeria) in 1945 to Madagascar in 1947 to Central Kenya in 1952 or Cameroon in 1956 and most notoriously Algeria after 1954, colonial repression was brutal toward move-

ments that strayed beyond quite unclear limits. Yet the interest of
Great Britain and France in stopping "extremism" gave the "moderates"
more room to maneuver. Nkrumah and later Jomo Kenyatta successfully
combined enough mass support with enough demonstrated respect for
existing economic and political institutions to shed the label of dangerous
demagogue for that of responsible moderate. Whether "modern national
mass movements"—as political scientists in the 1960s called them—
were all that modern, all that national, or all that mass is a complicated
question; the languages and networks of mobilization were indeed diverse
and contradictory.

Abandoning an Empire: The French and British Cases

For all their searching for the moderates with whom to negotiate the evolution of the colonial relationship, Great Britain and France soon became
trapped in an expanding spiral of demands: for broadening the franchise, for
giving more power to elected legislatures, for making good on promises of
equivalent salaries for African workers and agricultural opportunities in
rural areas. By insisting that European society and the European standard of
living were models for the world, France and Great Britain in fact legiti-
mated a wide range of claims on European budgets.

As early as 1951 or 1952, officials in France and Great Britain were
complaining about the results of the development drive: that heavy public
expenditure was failing to stimulate private investment, that the inadequate infrastructure was choking on the new supplies coming in, that the
lack of trained personnel (African and European) and the strength of
African trade unions in ports, mines, and railways were driving up labor
costs, and that African societies were stubbornly resisting colonial aspirations to change the way they produced and lived. Ironically, this was the
great era of expansion of African exports—the most impressive of the
colonial era—when exports of copper, cocoa, and coffee soared. But the
act of imagination that had made "development" the watchword of colonialism created its own standards: officials began with an imagined end
point—industrialization, European social relations, legislative institutions—rather than with the nature and dynamics of African societies
themselves. Nor was the development project doing the political work
expected of it: development efforts created more new points of conflict
than they resolved. More intensive agriculture by white or black farmers
forced tenants off the land—a major cause of the rebellion in Kenya
known as Mau Mau—and heavy-handed soil conservation or land consolidation projects led to peasant movements against this disruption of the
harmony of relations with nature. Even the heroes of economic growth—
prosperous cocoa farmers or owners of transportation fleets—often used
their gains to challenge European-owned firms or support political activity
that was critical of colonial rule.

By 1956 or 1957 British and French governments and part of the press were doing something they had not done before: coldly calculating the costs and benefits of empire. Old images that had once justified colonization now appeared in conservative arguments for letting go: Africa as vast, untamed space, inhabited by backward people, remote from the notions of "the citizen" or of "economic man" that the European elite associated with themselves. The two governments began to think about extricating themselves, a process that was as much an abdication of responsibility for the consequences of their own actions as the devolution of power.

Part of the postwar thinking about development and modernization eased the imaginative transition: development (unlike civilization) was a universal possibility, so that the European elite could expect that Africans would follow a foreordained path that would keep them in close relationship to Europe. But there was an element of cynicism too: an awareness growing out of the experiences of 1945–1955 of the conflict and uncertainty surrounding political and social change, and a desire that African governments, not European ones, be blamed for whatever went wrong.

African politicians had built their power bases within territories defined by the colonial powers. These boundaries and the institutions of state provided the basis for negotiated decolonization, marginalizing other kinds of affinities and aspirations. The recalculation was eased in Ghana by Nkrumah's espousal of his own variant of development, linking him economically to the very forces he criticized as neo-imperialist; it was eased in Morocco and Tunisia by relatively coherent political movements willing to open the conservative elite to a measure of nationalism, but not too much. In Egypt, however, Gamal Nasser's coup of 1952 threw awry the neocolonial arrangements Great Britain had with the former regime and put in place a symbol of nationalism who influenced other decolonization struggles.

Great Britain and France had more trouble in colonies with white settlers, both because of the settlers' ability to play racial politics (and to threaten or effect a whites-only form of decolonization) and because of the intensity of social conflicts. It was most difficult of all for France to rethink its empire in Algeria. In this case, a divided French polity was caught between the Right's support of an "Algérie française" that denied Muslims full citizenship in their own country and the Left's attachment to "developing" Algeria, while Algerian nationalists themselves fought over strategies and objectives. A brutal colonial war from 1954 to 1962 called into question France's own republican principles. After 1962, newly liberated Algeria was torn by fighting and coups.

Decolonization in Portuguese Africa

The Portuguese Empire does not fit the timing outlined above. As a weak European power it lacked the confidence that its market power, capital, and technology could shape African evolution when it acted even slightly less "colonial." Moreover, Portugal itself was ruled by a dictatorship, and the legitimacy crisis that beset France and England after the war did not apply. Portugal set out to "develop" Mozambique, Angola, and Guinea-Bissau, but it was a thoroughly authoritarian version, entailing new waves of white emigration to Africa to take the leading roles in the "modern" sectors. But Portuguese Africa could not escape the ferment and opportunities around it—or the contradictions within. By the mid-1960s in Guinea-Bissau, Angola, and Mozambique, political movements, well aware of the liberation around them, had turned toward armed struggle, using bases in neighboring countries and a wide range of networks and affiliations, although the Portuguese limited their success by manipulating regional rivalries.

The Portuguese government had its own regional connections—with the white regimes of South Africa and, after 1965, Rhodesia (present-day Zimbabwe), which helped with military support as well as economic interaction. The region was caught up in cold war politics: Soviet support played an important role for nationalist movements such as the Front for the Liberation of Mozambique (FRELIMO), Popular Movement for the Liberation of Angola (MPLA), and PAIGC (as well as for the ANC in South Africa, and ZANU and ZAPU in Rhodesia), and the United States quietly helped the South African and Portuguese militaries and some of the "anticommunist" guerrilla movements they sponsored, even while claiming to oppose racist governments. Portugal's entanglement with its African colonies and the effects of prolonged war came home to Portugal itself. A military coup d'état ended the dictatorship in 1974, and the decision of army and civilian moderates (some of whom knew African leaders from anti-government networks) brought to an end over 400 years of colonization, in favor of an effort to "Europeanize" Portugal itself. As with the earlier decolonizations, this one involved an abdication of responsibility for the sins of colonial rule and for the viciousness of the final struggle itself, from the land mines and assassinations to the hasty pullout of Portuguese civil servants and professionals, seeking their European future.

White Rule in Southern Africa

The persistence of white rule in Rhodesia—to 1979—and South Africa—to 1994—has much to do with the ambiguity of the colonial situation there. For most Africans, these were the most colonial of colonial regimes, with a settled white population big enough to staff an effective military and bureaucracy, closely integrated into farms and industries that took control of African labor to ground (or below ground) level. But for many whites, particularly Afrikaans speakers, the sense of possessing the land in which they lived—and of having no "home" to go back to—was deep and the willingness to fight to stay strong. But their identification with Africa was not complete. Racial domination was also rooted in a sense of being "Western." And social life, especially as white society became relatively prosperous, implied belonging to a global bourgeoisie—of having access to the same commodities, sports events, and travel possibilities as Europeans and North Americans.

Here is where these regimes lost the battle of civilization, Christianity, progress, and democracy, a battle that had begun in the early twentieth century, when the first African national movements began to appropriate the vocabulary of democracy and rule of law. As much as liberation movements in Rhodesia and South Africa drew on affinities and a language of solidarity rooted in the daily lives of different African communities, they also built global networks via churches, labor unions, human rights and antiracist groups, and Pan-Africanist organizations—building on ideologies of self-determination and antiracism—to attack the legitimacy and sustainability of racist rule. In the end, the ruling regimes could not maintain unity and ideological coherence, even if for a time they could repress (but not eliminate) armed struggle. The last decolonization, 342 years after the original Dutch intrusion into South Africa, was, remarkably, a negotiated one.

The Consequences of Decolonization

What ended with the decolonizations of 1957–1965, of 1974, of 1979, and of 1994 were the very categories of empire and colony, of white rule. These had been considered normal for centuries; they ceased to be imaginable politically. Decolonization did not end social or political inequality, or the uneven power to determine what kinds of policies are discussible. The International Monetary Fund (IMF) is much better able to make the alleged mismanagement of exchange rates by an African government into an issue demanding correction than an African government is able to make the unavailability of clean water into a question requiring global action.

It would be a mistake either to see colonialism as a phenomenon that could be turned off like a television set—with all problems instantly turned into "African" problems—or to define a colonial "legacy" that determined what African polities could do, without considering the openings and closures that occurred during the process of struggle. The anxieties—and the brittle repression—of new African rulers reflected as much their appreciation and fear of the diverse movements they had ridden to power as their inability to confront the divisions in society that colonial regimes had encouraged. Colonial regimes and their successors were gatekeeper states, facing great difficulty making routine the exercise of power domestically outside of capital cities and commercial or mining centers, and best able to manipulate the interface between their country and the outside world. Their taxation power relied heavily on import-export controls, their patronage on insisting that outside resources pass through them. Their great fear was that social movements would draw on connections independent of the regime. Postcolonial gatekeeper states were more knowledgeable than colonial ones, better able to forge relations of clientelism within their boundaries, but without coercive power coming from without they were extremely vulnerable to any attempt to contest access to the gate itself. Hence the cycles of coups and military governments that beset Africa shortly after decolonization, and also the hostility of many governments to the political, intellectual, and cultural autonomy of their citizens.

Great Britain, France, and Belgium and later Portugal never learned how they could adapt state power to working with African societies as they actually were, not as they were imagined to be. In abdicating responsibility for the consequences of their own actions, the decolonizing powers assumed the easier task of judging how Africans carried out the tasks of "governance" that they themselves had been unable to perform. Such judgments need not be left unchallenged. The history of Africa from the 1940s reveals that many futures have been and can be imagined, that political mobilizations have taken place and can take place on a variety of lines, and that such mobilizations can turn what seemed impossible into an everyday fact. Such an observation applies as much to Africa's future as to its past.

North America

Dee, Ruby

(b. October 27, 1924, Cleveland, Ohio) African American actress, writer, and social activist; the first black woman to play major parts in the American Shakespeare Festival at Stratford, Connecticut; and a major American film and television performer.

Ruby Dee's work has run the gamut of entertainment media; she has acted on stage and in film, television, and radio, and she has recorded poetry. Her Broadway debut, a walk-on part in *South Pacific* (a play about World War II that appeared before the Rogers and Hammerstein musical) came in 1943, while she was still at college. Only three years later, she appeared on Broadway in *Jeb* (1946), opposite her husband-to-be, Ossie Davis. They married in 1948, and have collaborated closely ever since. She achieved national recognition in the title role of *Anna Lucasta* (tour, 1946–1947) and went on to principal roles in *A Raisin in the Sun* (1959); *Purlie Victorious* (1961), subsequently filmed in 1963; and Athol Fugard's *Boesman and Lena* (1970), with James Earl Jones, for which she won an Obie in 1971.

Dee has appeared in over 20 films, most importantly as the baseball player's wife in *The Jackie Robinson Story* (1950), with Sidney Poitier in *Edge of the City* (1957), and in Spike Lee's *Do the Right Thing* (1989). Her television work is more extensive, including many guest appearances, the series *With Ossie and Ruby* (PBS, 1981), and dramas such as *Long Day's Journey into Night* (PBS, 1983). She has received numerous awards, including an Emmy for *Decoration Day* (NBC) in 1991, and a Literary

Guild Award (1989) in recognition of her plays, poems and children's stories. She has been inducted into both the Black Filmmakers Hall of Fame (1975) and the Theater Hall of Fame (1988).

A well-known social activist and a member of the National Association for the Advancement of Colored People (NAACP) and the Southern Christian Leadership Conference, Dee speaks at many high-profile benefits. Having experienced firsthand the difficulties encountered by minorities in her profession, she established the Ruby Dee Scholarship in Dramatic Art for talented young black women.

North America

Delaney, Beauford

(b. 1902, Knoxville, Tenn.; d. March 26, 1979, Paris, France), African American artist admired for his exquisite use of light and who painted portraits of many of the great figures of jazz.

Even as a young child growing up in Tennessee, Beauford Delaney was preoccupied with art, according to his younger brother, painter Joseph Delaney. Beauford Delaney received his first formal art training from Lloyd Branson, a white artist living in Knoxville. With Branson's encouragement, in 1924 Delaney went to Boston, where he studied painting at the Massachusetts Normal School, the South Boston School of Art, and the Copley Society.

In 1929 Delaney moved to New York City and held a variety of jobs while he established himself as a painter. Twelve of his portraits were displayed in a 1930 group show at the Whitney Studio Galleries (later the Whitney Museum of American Art). In exchange for working at the Whitney as a guard, telephone operator, and gallery attendant Delaney received studio space and a place to live. He had his first one-man exhibition in 1932 at the 135th Street Branch of the New York Public Library.

A music lover throughout his life, Delaney met and painted many of the great figures of jazz. W. C. Handy, Louis Armstrong, Duke Ellington, and Ethel Waters were among the musicians and singers who went to Delaney for their portraits. Additionally, he developed friendships with a wide range of writers and other artists in New York in the 1930s and 1940s. One of Delaney's closest friends was the novelist James Baldwin, who first visited Delaney's Greene Street studio (in the area now known as SoHo) when he was a teenager and always gave Delaney credit for showing him that a black American could make a living as an artist.

Delaney is also remembered for his paintings of street scenes. Critics admired his use of color in these paintings and his efforts to convey the variations of light through more abstract paintings. "I learned about light from Beauford Delaney," Baldwin wrote in a 1965 issue of *Transition* magazine. In 1978 the Studio Museum in Harlem dedicated the first show of its *Black Masters* series to Delaney's work.

Delaney, Joseph

(b. September 13, 1904, Knoxville, Tenn.; d. November 20, 1991, Knoxville, Tenn.), African American artist known for his paintings of people, in individual portraits and in groups.

His older brother, Beauford Delaney, was also a painter, but their styles differed greatly; Beauford painted abstract works, while Joseph painted representations of people, in portraits and in crowd scenes. Delaney began studying at the Art Students League in New York in 1930 with the artist and teacher Thomas Hart Benton, whose call for American scenes depicting people had a great influence on Delaney and his fellow students, including artists Jackson Pollock and George Bridgman. Delaney continued painting at the league until 1985. During the Great Depression he worked as a model, waiter, and window washer, but he also received some portrait commissions from society women. In that period he also taught drawing and participated in the creation of the Index to American Design.

Returning to Knoxville in 1985, Delaney became an artist-in-residence at the University of Tennessee, where he worked until the time of his death in 1991. His paintings are in private collections and in several public collections, including the Knoxville Art Museum, the National Museum of American Art, Clark-Atlanta University, and the University of Arizona Museum of Art.

Delany, Martin Robison

(b. May 6, 1812, Charles Town, Va. [present-day Charleston, W. Va.]; d. June 24, 1885, Wilberforce, Ohio), African American abolitionist, black nationalist, and author; the highest ranking African American officer during the Civil War.

During the nineteenth century Martin Robison Delany was a prominent African American leader, but his repeated political shifts undermined his standing and obscured his legacy. In contrast to Frederick Douglass, whose outlook was integrationist, Delany stressed the importance of blacks' African heritage and the need for black self-reliance.

During the 1840s Delany wrote antislavery pamphlets, helped escaping slaves on their way to freedom, and staunchly opposed the efforts of the American Colonization Society to colonize blacks in Africa or assist them in emigrating elsewhere, which he viewed as a form of forced exile.

During the tumultuous 1850s, however, Delany changed his views. He began advocating emigration from the United States. During the 1850s Delany concentrated his prodigious energies on emigration and colonization ventures. He played a leading role in African American emigration conferences held in 1854, 1856, and 1858. Late in 1858 he set sail for West

Africa. In 1859, after visiting Alexander Crummell in Liberia, Delany signed a treaty with Alake of Abeokuta, in present-day Nigeria, to allow African American settlement and the development of cotton production using free West African workers. But the coming of the Civil War disrupted those plans. In his final years, Delany published *Principia of Ethnology: The Origin of Races with an Archaeological Compendium of Ethiopian and Egyptian Civilization* (1879) and was active in the ill-fated Liberian Exodus Joint-Stock Steamship Company.

North America

Denmark Vesey Conspiracy,

an extensively organized but thwarted plan to end slavery in South Carolina.

During the summer of 1822 an ex-slave named Denmark Vesey, who had purchased his freedom by winning a lottery 23 years earlier, gathered more than 9000 South Carolina slaves for an insurrection. The plan was to seize weapons and travel throughout the state to kill white slaveholders and liberate their slaves. Like past slave uprisings, the Denmark Vesey conspiracy was proof that slaves would go to great lengths to attain their freedom.

Despite the efforts at secrecy, the plan was betrayed on May 30. Denmark tried to push the insurrection forward to June 16, but to no avail. White officials offered black informants modest cash awards and immediately arrested the conspirators. On July 2, Vesey was captured. He refused to confess and was executed along with 34 other blacks. Thirty-seven men were deported to unknown locations.

Latin America and the Caribbean

Deschamps Chapeaux, Pedro

(b. 1913), Cuban historian who has written extensively on the history of Afro-Cubans. His works include *El Negro en el Periodismo Cubano en el Siglo XIX* (1963, The Black in Nineteenth-Century Cuban Journalism); *El Negro en la Economía Habanera del Siglo XIX* (1970, The Black in the Nineteenth Century Havana Economy); and *Batallones de Pardos y Morenos* (1976, Battalions of Free Coloreds and Blacks) (see Cuba).

Latin America and the Caribbean

Dessalines, Jean-Jacques

(b. 1758, Grande-Rivière du Nord, Haiti; d. October 17, 1806, Pont-Rouge, Haiti), one of the leaders, with Toussaint L'Ouverture, of the Haitian Revolution; first emperor of Haiti.

Jean-Jacques Dessalines was born to Congolese parents on the Cormiers plantation in Saint-Domingue (as Haiti was known prior to independence). He was given the name of the plantation owner, Duclos, before assuming the name of the freed black landowner who purchased his services as a slave, Dessalines. Unlike his future comrade-in-arms, Toussaint L'Ouverture, Dessalines was treated harshly as a slave and joined the ranks of maroons (runaway slaves) at a young age. In 1792 he became a partisan of the slave uprising led by Boukman, a slave of Jamaican origin, and impressed his compatriots with his courage in fighting. Yet Dessalines acts of cruelty that frightened some in the rebellion.

Following the abolition of slavery in Saint-Domingue in 1793, Toussaint L'Ouverture allied himself with the French. Dessalines joined him, eventually becoming Toussaint's second in command. Dessalines was instrumental in keeping British and Spanish forces at bay and helped Toussaint consolidate control of the island by putting down the mulatto rebellion led by André Rigaud, reportedly killing between 5000 and 10,000 of Rigaud's supporters. In return, Toussaint promoted Dessalines to general and made him governor of the south of the island. When Toussaint promulgated a constitution in 1801 that effectively proclaimed Saint-Domingue's independence, Dessalines defended Toussaint from the troops led by the French general Charles Leclerc, whom Napoleon Bonaparte had sent to reclaim the island.

Although he was loyal to Toussaint until the latter's capture and deportation to France in 1802, Dessalines had learned enough from his mentor to realize that he had to return once again to the French fold or suffer the same fate as Toussaint. But this alliance would not last long. After spending only a short time on the island, the French troops were decimated by yellow fever. Leclerc himself succumbed to the disease on November 2, 1802. Shortly thereafter, Dessalines initiated a new rebellion that would conclude successfully on January 1, 1804, the day on which Dessalines declared Saint-Domingue independent from France. He renamed the country Haiti (an Arawak Indian word) and had himself appointed, as Toussaint had done in 1801, governor for life (see Haitian Revolution).

It was at this point that Haiti's ongoing cycle of violence and retribution began in earnest. Dessalines ordered the execution of most of the whites who remained on the island, as well as anyone who questioned his authority. In a sign of the new regime's growing instability, several of Dessalines's officers—including two future leaders of the country, Henri Christophe and Alexandre Pétion—did not carry out these orders. To give his authority more symbolic resonance, Dessalines proclaimed himself Emperor Jacques I of Haiti on September 2, 1804, following the lead of Bonaparte, who, a few months earlier, had pronounced himself Emperor Napoleon I of France. Dessalines did not bother creating a noble class, since, as he put it, only he was noble. Whereas the Haitian people revered Toussaint and his ability to govern, they simply feared Dessalines. Citizens of Haiti were divided into two categories of forced labor: agricultural and military. As public anger spread regarding these policies and others, some of

Dessalines's lieutenants hatched a plot to wrest power from their tyrannical leader. They ambushed Dessalines on October 17, 1806, dismembering the body of the man many say served as an example for the brutal twentieth-century regime of François Duvalier.

North America

Diddley, Bo

(b. December 30, 1928, McComb, Miss.), African American singer, guitarist, and songwriter; member of the Rock and Roll Hall of Fame.

Bo Diddley, born Otha Elias Bates, was sent as a baby by his family to live with cousins in Chicago, Illinois, where he took the name McDaniel. He learned to play the guitar in his teens. At 23, he took a regular job at the 708 Club in Chicago, playing blues and rhythm and blues. He toured the Midwest with rhythm and blues groups and as a solo artist.

As rock 'n' roll began its rise to popularity in the mid-1950s, he began to write songs in the new style. He came to the attention of Chess Records in Chicago and took the name Bo Diddley in his first recordings for the label. Sources differ on the name's origin. It may have been a childhood nickname for a mischievous boy, a slang term for a witty storyteller, or the name under which he had boxed in his youth.

He gave his first single the same name. The song "Bo Diddley" became a nationwide hit in 1955. Diddley produced more Top 10 singles during the next five years. He established himself as a major concert attraction, known for his distinctive cigar-box shaped guitar as well as his vital performances.

Diddley's music owed much to the blues. Songs like "I'm a Man" and "Who Do You Love" emphasized his persona of powerful independence and manhood. The distinctive stuttering rhythm of many of his compositions became a hallmark of early rock 'n' roll.

Diddley continued to tour and record in the four decades that followed his early fame. He was inducted into the Rock and Roll Hall of Fame in 1987.

Latin America and the Caribbean

Diegues, Carlos

(b. May 19, 1940, Alagoas, Brazil), Brazilian filmmaker and one of the pioneers of Cinema Novo, a modern, socially committed cinema that arose in the late 1950s and 1960s in response to changing conceptions of Brazilian national identity.

Carlos Diegues is one of the most prolific and controversial film directors of the Cinema Novo generation. Like other filmmakers of New Brazilian cinema, he aimed "to study in depth the social relations of each city and region as a way of critically exposing, as if in miniature, the sociological structure of the country as a whole." Of particular interest to Diegues were the social and historical dimensions of Afro-Brazilian culture. While some critics have accused Diegues of perpetuating racial and sexual stereotypes, others contend that some of his films countered the notion—expounded by the sociologist Gilberto Freyre—that Brazil is a racial democracy and that slavery in Brazil was less brutal than in the United States.

During the early 1960s Cinema Novo filmmakers, influenced by the populist agenda of President João Goulart, focused their films on the country's impoverished rural communities. Diegues's first professional film, *Escola de Samba, Alegriade Viver* (1962, Samba School, Joy of Living), portrays the samba schools organized by black favela (or squatter settlement) dwellers as a part of the preparations for Carnival. Like many films of the time, it is flawed by a didactic approach to the country's poor communities. As film scholar Randal Johnson notes, *Escola de Samba . . .* provides "a view from the outside looking in, and rejects popular culture in favor of a paternalistic . . . view of the people."

Rejecting his early didacticism, Diegues produced his first feature film, *Ganga Zumba* (1963), with a predominantly black cast. Based on João Felício dos Santos's novel *Ganga Zumba*, the film focuses on the lives of three fugitive slaves who eventually make their way to Palmares, the seventeenth-century maroon republic that survived nearly a century, despite repeated attacks by the Dutch and Portuguese. As film scholar Robert Stam confirms, "*Ganga Zumba* deserves praise for its uncompromising portrait of Brazilian slavery. . . . An ode to black liberation, [it] assumes a black perspective throughout, showing blacks not as mere victims but as active historical agents." Due to a lack of funds, Diegues was not able to reconstruct the second half of dos Santos's novel until 1984, with the film *Quilombo*—a representation of the history of Palmares that employs aspects of Afro-Brazilian popular culture, such as Carnival and Candomblé.

Although Diegues believed that Cinema Novo should be socially committed, he defended cinematic pluralism and the filmmaker's freedom of expression. "In this sense," as Johnson notes, Diegues "opposed authoritarianism of both the Right and the Left, and for this he has been harshly criticized by both sides." Diegues's intensely personal approach to filmmaking is exemplified in *Xica da Silva* (1976), the true story of an eighteenth-century black woman, who, through a 43-year liaison with a rich public official, becomes the "power behind the throne." Detractors found fault in the very conception of the film as a comedy about slavery; they also criticized the film's lack of historical accuracy and its portrayal of Xica's sexual power. Popular critics, on the other hand, received the film enthusiastically, as did the Brazilian public. Indeed, fellow Cinema Novo filmmaker Glauber Rocha praised *Xica da Silva* as an "Afro-feminist, pan-sexualist, libertarian, nationalist, radical and humanist . . . tropical baroque." In 1996 *Xica da Silva* became a popular television miniseries.

Dinkins, David Norman

(b. July 10, 1927, Trenton, N.J.), first black mayor of New York City (1989–1993).

In his inaugural address on January 1, 1990, New York mayor David Dinkins invoked the theme of racial progress on which he had successfully campaigned. "I stand before you today," he said, "as the elected leader of the greatest city of a great nation, to which my ancestors were brought, chained and whipped in the hold of a slave ship. We have not finished the journey toward liberty and justice, but surely we have come a long way." When he defeated three-time mayor Edward Koch, Dinkins, a Democrat, became the city's first black mayor. A contrast to the outspoken and pugnacious Koch, Dinkins's dignified civility seemed likely to soothe a racially tense city.

Diop, Alioune

(b. January 20, 1910, Saint-Louis, Senegal; d. May 2, 1980, Paris, France), Senegalese writer and editor who became a central figure in the Négritude movement.

Alioune Diop was born in Saint-Louis, Senegal, whose inhabitants enjoyed automatic French citizenship during the colonial period. He obtained his secondary education at the Lycée Faidherbe in Saint-Louis, then studied in Algeria and at the Sorbonne in Paris. He took a position as professor of classical literature in Paris and represented Senegal in the French senate after World War II. In 1947 Diop founded *Présence Africaine*, perhaps the most influential intellectual journal of its time on anti-colonial and emancipatory culture and politics among Africans and peoples of African descent. With frequent contributions from his friend and associate Léopold Sédar Senghor, Diop's journal helped foster the Négritude movement, which aimed to promote an African cultural identity and the liberation of the people of Africa and the African Diaspora.

Djavan (Djavan Caetano Viana)

(b. 1949, Maceió, Alagoas, Brazil), contemporary Afro-Brazilian pop music composer and performer.

Djavan was born and raised in the northeastern state of Alagoas, Brazil, where he played guitar in various pop bands before moving to Rio de Janeiro in 1973 and beginning his professional career. In 1975, at the age of 27, he encountered his first national success, taking second place in the

Abertura Festival for his composition "Fato Consumado." From that point on, his career has steadily expanded, and some 14 albums later, he is one of the most acclaimed artists of Brazilian pop music.

Djebar, Assia

(b. August 4, 1936, Cherchell, Algeria), Algerian writer and motion picture director, known for her works about women in the Islamic societies of North Africa. She is one of a generation of female writers offering a view of history that gives women a central role.

Assia Djebar was born Fatima-Zohra Imalayen in Cherchell, a small coastal town west of Algiers, to a schoolteacher father and a mother who died while Djebar was a child. She finished her early studies in Algeria, then became the first Algerian student to be admitted to the prestigious L'Ecole Normale Supérieure de Sèvres in France.

Djebar's first novel, *La soif* (1957; translated as The Mischief, 1958), received both critical and popular attention. It was followed by *Les impatients* (The Impatient Ones) a year later, which drew criticism for its eroticism and bourgeois (middle-class) values. Two more novels followed: *Les enfants du nouveau monde* (1962, The Children of the New World) and *Les alouettes naïves* 1962, The Innocent Larks). She also worked in theater, coproducing the play *Rouge l'aube* (1960, Red Dawn), and wrote poetry, collected in *Poemes pour l'Algérie heureuse* (1969, Poems for a Happy Algeria).

Djebar then stopped writing for several years, citing discomfort from writing about subjects too close to her own life—especially in a traditional society where women did not speak of the self. During this period she concentrated on filmmaking, creating *Walid Garn* (1977), which deals with women's responses to liberation struggles. She then made a controversial feminist film, *La nouba des femmes de Mont Chenoua* (1979, The Festival of the Women of Mount Chenoua), for Algerian state television. The film weaves together what Djebar called "a polyphony of women's voices." In her next film, *La Zerda et les chants de l'oubli* (1982, Zerda or the Songs of Forgetting), Djebar superimposed Algerian women's songs over French news reels of World War I (1914–1918) to document women's participation in the war.

Djibouti,

a small coastal country in the Horn of Africa bordering Eritrea, Ethiopia, and Somalia.

Djibouti's strategic location on the Strait of Mandeb, where the Red Sea meets the Indian Ocean, has shaped its history. For centuries, the region was

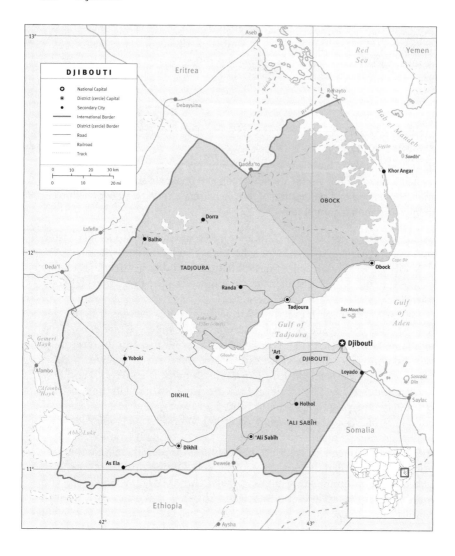

a crossroads where the peoples of Africa and the Middle East mingled and traded. In modern times, Djibouti, devoid of significant natural resources, has depended economically on its role as an outlet to the European and Indian Ocean trade for landlocked Ethiopia. While Djibouti's arid countryside supports a population of nomadic pastoralists, the country produces only 3 percent of its required food. Most of the population lives in the capital of the virtual city-state, Djibouti City, whose rail connections and free port provide most of the country's income. Because of the economic and military vulnerability of the country, the population moved slowly to sever ties with France, and Djibouti was one of the last African colonies to declare independence. Though Djibouti has a strong commercial sector and one of Africa's best telecommunications infrastructures, much of the population remains impoverished. And while the country has avoided the warfare that has devastated its neighbors, long-standing ethnic antagonisms continue to divide its population.

Djibouti (Ready Reference)

Official Name: Republic of Djibouti

Former Name: French Territory of the Afars and Issas; French Somaliland

Area: 22,000 sq km (13,675 sq mi)

Location: Eastern Africa; borders the Gulf of Aden, the Red Sea, Eritrea, and Somalia

Capital: Djibouti (population 348,000 [1993 estimate])

Other Major Cities: Roseau (population 20,755 [1991 estimate])

Population: 440,727 (1998 estimate); population swelled in 1992 due to the influx of 20,000 Somali refugees.

Population Density: 43.1 persons per sq km (69 persons per sq mi [1998 estimate])

Population Below Age 15: 43 percent (male 92,920; female 92,584 [1997 estimate])

Pedestrians cross an open plaza in Djibouti City, capital and important port of Djibouti.
CORBIS/Wolfgang Kaehler

Population Growth Rate: 1.5 percent (1998 estimate)

Total Fertility Rate: 6 children born per woman (1998 estimate)

Life Expectancy at Birth: Total population: 51 years (male 49.1 years; female: 53.1 years [1998 estimate])

Infant Mortality Rate: 102.4 deaths per 1000 live births (1998 estimate)

Literacy Rate (age 15 and over who can read and write): Total population 46.2 percent (male 60.3 percent; female 32.7 percent [1995 estimate])

Education: Primary and secondary schools are mostly taught in French, though Islamic teaching has recently been emphasized, due to Saudi Arabia's expressed willingness to subsidize such efforts. In 1995–1996, there were 591,784 primary school students; 10,008 secondary school students; 104 teacher-training school students; 1,748 vocational school students; and 130 students enrolled at institutions of higher education.

Languages: Arabic and French are the official languages; Somali and Afar are also widely spoken.

Ethnic Groups: About 20 percent of the population are Afar, 35 percent Issa, 20 percent non-Issa Somali, 5 percent Arab, 5 percent French; other foreigners make up the remaining 15 percent.

Religions: 94 percent of the population are Muslim, while the remaining 6 percent are Christian.

Climate: Torrid and dry, although humidity is high in the monsoon season from June to August. The average annual rainfall varies from 210 mm (about 8 in) in December to 400 mm (about 16 in) in June.

Land, Plants, and Animals: Djibouti's landscape is extremely varied, ranging from low desert plains in the west and south to mountains in the north. Most of the country is volcanic desert and still geologically active. As rainfall is infrequent, vegetation is minimal. Wildlife includes antelopes, gazelles, hyenas, jackals, and ostriches. Offshore in Djibouti's waters marine life includes tuna, barracuda, and grouper.

Natural Resources: Minerals (including gypsum, mica, amethyst, sulfur); geothermal energy, natural gas; livestock, fish

Currency: Djiboutian franc

Gross Domestic Product (GDP): $520 million (1997 estimate)

GDP per Capita: $1200 (1997 estimate)

GDP Real Growth Rate: .5 percent (1997 estimate)

Primary Economic Activities: The economy is based on the services Djibouti, a strategic port, provides as both a transit port for the region and as an international shipment and refueling center, and to a lesser extent on the railroad to Addis Ababa. As it has few natural resources and little industry, the country depends heavily on foreign aid, particularly from France. Due to scant rainfall, most food must be imported. During the last six years, due to recession, civil war, and a high population growth rate (including immigrants and refugees), economic growth has evaded Djibouti.

Primary Crops: Fruits, vegetables; goats, sheep, and camels

Industries: Small-scale dairy products and mineral-water bottling

Primary Exports: Hides and skins, coffee

Primary Imports: Foods, beverages, transport equipment, chemicals, petroleum products

Primary Trade Partners: Somalia, Ethiopia, Thailand, France, Yemen, and Saudi Arabia

Government: Djibouti became a constitutional republic with a multi-party system by referendum on September 4, 1992. Guerrilla warfare erupted in 1991 due to ethnic tensions between the Afars in the north and the Issa majority in the south. The president, currently Ismail Omar Guellah, is elected by popular vote to a six-year term. A Council of Ministers is responsible to the president. The head of government is currently Prime Minister Barkat Gourad Hamadou. Djibouti's legislative branch is a 65-seat unicameral Chamber of Deputies whose members are elected to serve five-year terms. The dominant political party is the president's party, the People's Progress Assembly (RPP). Other parties include the Democratic Renewal Party (PRD) and the Democratic National Party (PND).

Latin America and the Caribbean

Dominica,

island country between the Caribbean Sea and the North Atlantic Ocean, about half the distance between Puerto Rico and Trinidad and Tobago.

Dominica is nicknamed the Caribbean's "nature island" because of the lush foliage, green mountains, and abundant farms that cover the country. These natural resources are now touted as a tourist attraction, but in the centuries following European colonization, they also provided a fortunate haven for many indigenous and enslaved Dominicans. The rugged terrain made it difficult for white colonists to establish permanent settlements on the island, and then difficult for them to cultivate large plantations there. The mountains and forests even made Dominica a refuge for slaves from other islands who knew its terrain could provide a safe hiding space. Even today, Dominica is one of the least overdeveloped islands in the Caribbean. In recent years, Dominica began to advertise its resources as ideal for hikers and naturalists who enjoy visiting untouched spaces. Dominica is home to one of the last remaining indigenous communities in the Caribbean, and it is among the few islands where most of the land is owned and worked by individual farmers.

Latin America and the Caribbean

Dominican Republic,

a country in the Caribbean that is located on the eastern two-thirds of the island of La Hispaniola, with Haiti occupying the western part of the island; bounded on the south by the Caribbean Sea, on the north by the Atlantic Ocean, on the east by the Mona Passage, which separates it from Puerto Rico, and on the west by Haiti.

In 1492 Christopher Columbus became the first European to arrive on the island of La Hispaniola. Spain fought with France for control of the island until 1697, when it was divided into two territories by the Peace of Ryswick: French Saint-Domingue, which occupied the westernmost third and became the Republic of Haiti in 1804, and Spanish Santo Domingo, which occupied the eastern two-thirds and became the Dominican Re-public in 1844 after having been controlled by Haiti for 20 years. The population of the Dominican Republic, which fought for independence from Spain in 1865 and against the United States occupation in 1916, has always been composed mainly of blacks and mulattos.

The nation's African heritage is evident in every aspect of Dominican life: music and dance, cuisine, language, the Dominican Vodoun religion, and the Gagá cult. But this heritage has been marginalized by the widespread belief that Dominicans are mostly Hispanic, or even Taíno Indian, rather than black. Nevertheless, Dominicans generally recognize their African heritage as part of their ethnicity, though they do not necessarily see blackness as central to their identity. For Afro-Dominicans the process of defining racial identity has been complicated by the fact that the Dominican nation emerged from the black Republic of Haiti. The anti-black and anti-Haitian ideology of the Dominican Republic's dominant classes has existed alongside the awareness of the Dominicans' African heritage.

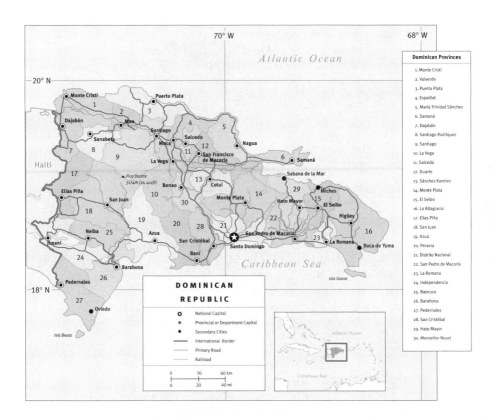

Domino, Antoine ("Fats"), Jr.

(b. February 26, 1928, New Orleans, La.), African American singer, pianist, and songwriter whose songs topped both rhythm and blues and rock 'n' roll charts during the 1950s.

Fats Domino was one of the few black musicians of the 1950s to success-fully span rhythm and blues (R&B) and rock 'n' roll, appealing to young white audiences while maintaining his popularity with black audiences. His formula for success was a driving, boogie-woogie style of piano playing and a New Orleans Creole style of singing.

After signing a contract with New Orleans-based Imperial Records, Domino collaborated with Dave Bartholomew to record "The Fat Man" (1950), his first R&B hit. His "Goin' Home" reached the number one slot on the R&B charts in 1952.

Domino's songs began to storm Billboard's rock 'n' roll charts in the mid-1950s. "Ain't That a Shame" (1955) marked the beginning of a string of hits in 1956 that included "I'm in Love Again," "My Blue Heaven" and "Blueberry Hill." Domino continued to record hits with Bartholomew, who served as his arranger, conductor, and producer, and even made some movie appearances before leaving Imperial Records in 1962.

Even though some of his songs were stolen and quickly marketed by such white artists as Pat Boone and Ricky Nelson, Domino put more than a dozen songs in the Top 10 and sold more than 65 million records between 1950 and 1962. With the exception of Elvis Presley, no other artist was more popular than Fats Domino during the 1950s. In 1986 he was inducted into the Rock and Roll Hall of Fame.

Dorsey, Thomas Andrew

(b. July 1, 1899, Villa Rica, Ga.; d. January 23, 1993, Chicago, Ill.), African Amer-ican pianist, arranger, and composer, known as the "Father of Gospel Music."

Thomas A. Dorsey's name is synonymous with modern gospel music. Dorsey composed over 1000 songs in his lifetime, half of which were pub-lished. With creative genius and business savvy, Dorsey popularized songs that combined the rhythm and tonality of blues with lyrics about personal spiritual salvation. Countless gospel performers achieved their first success singing Dorsey's music. His most famous song, "Precious Lord, Take My Hand" is one of the most popular gospel songs in America.

Douglas, Aaron

(b. May 26, 1899, Topeka, Kans.; d. February 2, 1979, Nashville, Tenn.), African American artist closely associated with the Harlem Renaissance; Douglas synthesized formal and symbolic elements of African art with a modern European aesthetic.

Aaron Douglas came to Harlem from Topeka, Kansas, in 1925, the year in which the cultural critic and philosopher Alain Locke launched the "New Negro" Movement. This movement expressed African Americans' new pride in their African heritage, which manifested itself in literature, song, dance, and, most significantly for Douglas, art.

Douglas developed a unique aesthetic that linked black Americans with their African past by using imagery derived from African sculptural and ancestral art to express aspects of the black experience in the United States. The two principal types of works he executed were drawings and murals. His drawings were characterized by bold, sharply delineated designs in black and white. On the other hand, softer outlines, superimposed forms, and a subdued color scheme in the red-green range characterized his murals. His murals focus on African American history and religious practices.

Though he had been instructed in the academic mode of painting at the University of Nebraska, Douglas rejected realism in favor of a geometric painting style that he developed while studying under Winold Reiss during the late 1920s. Douglas reduced forms to their fundamental shapes, such as circles, triangles, and rectangles. He tended to represent both objects and black people as silhouettes. Most of these forms are hard-edged and angular, reminiscent of the art deco designs popular in the United States during the early twentieth century.

He burst onto the art scene in 1925 with a cover illustration for *Opportunity* magazine and a first-place award from the *Crisis* magazine for his drawing *The African Chieftain*. Douglas became a regular contributor to each of these publications. In that same year, he collaborated with Reiss to illustrate Locke's *The New Negro*, a landmark anthology of black writers.

North America

Douglass, Frederick

(b. February 1818?, Talbot County, Md.; d. February 20, 1895, Washington, D.C.), the principal nineteenth-century African American spokesperson, abolitionist, reformer, author, and orator.

The Historical Significance of Frederick Douglass

Frederick Douglass was more than a great African American leader. Douglass had a prominent role in nineteenth-century reform, not only through his abolitionism but also in his support for women's rights and black suffrage. Unlike many of his contemporaries, he stayed true to his principles, remaining steadfast in his commitment to integration and civil rights. Douglass was militant but never a separatist. He rejected the nationalist rhetoric and latter-day conservatism of black abolitionist Martin R. Delany as well as the accommodation of Booker T. Washington.

Douglass was also a literary figure. Aside from drafting countless speeches and essays, he excelled at autobiography. His three memoirs—*The Narrative of the Life of Frederick Douglass* (1845), *My Bondage and My Freedom* (1855), and *Life and Times of Frederick Douglass* (1881, revised 1892)—represent his greatest literary achievement. Although born into slavery and self-educated, Douglass was a superb stylist who avoided the florid tendencies typical of his era.

North America

Dred Scott v. Sanford,

1857 case in which the United States Supreme Court ruled that U.S. territories could not prohibit slavery and that neither free nor enslaved blacks had constitutional rights.

Scott's Case

Dred Scott was born a slave in Virginia around 1795, His original name was Sam Blow. Peter Blow, his owner, moved him first to Alabama in 1818, then to St. Louis in 1830. After Blow died, his son sold Sam to John Emerson, a surgeon in the U.S. Army. In 1834 Emerson was transferred to Fort Armstrong, Illinois, where slavery was prohibited by the Northwest Ordinance of 1787. The ordinance had allowed then territories in the West to become states with the condition that they forbid slavery. Like many other slave-owning army officers, Emerson did not believe that his postings in free states subjected him to anti-slavery laws, so he brought Sam with him.

In 1843 Emerson died and left his property—including slaves—in trust to his wife. In 1846, with the help of friends, Scott sued Mrs. Emerson in local court for his family's freedom. His lawyers argued that the Scotts' stay in free territory had emancipated them, citing several precedents in Missouri case law, the most important of which was Rachael v. Walker (1837). The Scotts lost the case, moved for the verdict to be set aside, and at a new trial in 1850 won their freedom.

CHIEF JUSTICE TANEY.

Chief Justice Roger Taney crafted the Supreme Court's decision in the 1857 Dred Scott v. *Sanford* case. CORBIS/Bettmann

Mrs. Emerson appealed to the Missouri Supreme Court, which issued a 2-to-1 decision in 1852 returning the Scotts to slavery. While the state court case was being processed, Mrs. Emerson's brother, John Sanford of New York, had taken over the affairs of her estate. In 1853 Scott filed suit against Sanford, this time in federal court. Scott argued that because he and Sanford lived in different states, their case required a federal trial. Sanford argued that Scott was still a slave and even if he were free, a black descendant of slaves was not entitled to bring suit. The federal court in St. Louis rejected Sanford's argument that free blacks could not bring suit, but concluded that Scott was still a slave. Scott appealed, and in 1856 the U.S. Supreme Court heard his case.

Not wanting to affect the presidential elections of 1856, the Court postponed its ruling in Scott v. Sanford until two days after President James Buchanan's inauguration. On March 6, 1857, a mostly Southern 7-to-2 majority found that Scott was still a slave. The Court therefore needed only to agree with the lower court, remand parts of the decision that needed clarification, and be done with the case. However, several recent events conspired to put pressure on the Court to make additional rulings that would settle the question of slavery. Chief among these events was Congress's 1850 passage of the Fugitive Slave Act, which placed severe penalties on Northerners who helped runaway slaves.

Against this backdrop, Chief Justice Roger B. Taney decided to use Scott v. Sanford to address the constitutionality of slavery. Writing for the court, he gave an extremely narrow interpretation of the Constitution's view of blacks. Taney began by arguing that the Constitution did not allow Congress to regulate slavery—or anything else—in the territories. Rather, the Constitution's statements about regulating territories applied only to those territories in the states' possession in 1789, when the Constitution was ratified. Since the United States acquired the Louisiana Territory through the Louisiana Purchase in 1803, Congress had no power to regulate Purchase territories until they became states. The ruling effectively made the Missouri Compromise unconstitutional—only the second time that the Supreme Court had declared a statute of Congress unconstitutional.

Taney also interpreted the Constitution's Fifth Amendment, which prohibits the taking of property without due process of law, to apply to slaves. He argued that since slaves were property, they could not be taken from their owners, regardless of whether they had crossed into a free state or territory. He further asserted the Constitution never intended blacks—even free blacks in free states—to be citizens. Therefore, even if Scott were free, he was not entitled to bring a suit in a federal court. Taney based this decision largely on a clause of the Constitution that he interpreted as denying blacks some of the rights and duties of citizenship, such as serving in militias.

Soon after the Supreme Court issued its decision, Dred Scott and his family were sold to a son of Peter Blow, Scott's original owner, who freed them instantly. Scott did not live long enough to see the many changes his case brought about. In September 1858 he died of tuberculosis in St. Louis.

North America

Drew, Charles Richard

(b. June 3, 1904, Washington, D.C.; d. April 1, 1950, Burlington, N.C.), African American surgeon and hematologist who made pioneering discoveries about blood plasma and set up blood banks in the 1930s and 1940s.

Charles Richard Drew became interested in studying blood as a student at McGill University in Montreal, Canada, during the late 1920s and early 1930s. At that time, medical science had not yet determined how to preserve blood, a dilemma that became Drew's mission. Later, while interning at Presbyterian Hospital in New York City and pursuing a doctorate at Columbia University, Drew discovered that unlike whole blood, which deteriorates after a few days in storage, blood plasma—the liquid portion of the blood without cells—can be preserved for long periods of time and substituted for whole blood in transfusions.

In the late 1930s Drew set up an experimental blood bank at Presbyterian Hospital and wrote a thesis titled *Banked Blood: A Study in Blood Preservation* which earned him a doctor of science in medicine from Columbia University in 1940. His medical breakthrough helped save thousands of lives by making more blood available to the many people in need of transfusions.

After the success of his blood preservation and transfusion efforts in Europe, Drew was enlisted by the American Red Cross in 1941 to establish a blood bank program in the United States. Drew protested the segregation of blood and, as a result, was forced to resign his position as director of the Red Cross Blood Bank Program. He argued, "The blood of individual human beings may differ by blood groupings, but there is absolutely no scientific basis to indicate any differences according to race." Not until 1949 did the U.S. military end the segregation of banked blood.

North America

Du Bois, William Edward Burghardt (W. E. B.)

(b. February 23, 1868, Great Barrington, Mass.; d. August 27, 1963, Accra, Ghana), writer, social scientist, critic, and public intellectual; cofounder of the Niagara Movement, the National Association for the Advancement of Colored People (NAACP), and the Pan-African Congress; editor of the NAACP magazine the *Crisis*.

Along with Frederick Douglass and Booker T. Washington, historians consider W. E. B. Du Bois one of the most influential African Americans before the Civil Rights Movement of the 1960s. Born only six years after emancipation, he was active well into his nineties. He died in 1963, on the eve of the March on Washington.

Despite near-constant criticism for his often contradictory social and political opinions—he was accused, at various times, of elitism, communism, and black separatism—Du Bois remained throughout his long life black America's leading public intellectual.

Born in a small western Massachusetts town, Du Bois and his mother—his father had left the family when he was young—were among the few African American residents. Of his heritage, Du Bois wrote that it included "a flood of Negro blood, a strain of French, a bit of Dutch, but, Thank God! No 'Anglo-Saxon'. . . . " After an integrated grammar-school education, Du Bois attended the historically black Fisk University in Nashville, Tennessee, then Harvard University, from which he received a bachelor's degree in 1890. That fall Du Bois began graduate work in history at Harvard under the legendary professors George Santayana, William James, and Josiah Royce. Du Bois was especially influenced by Albert Bushnell Hart, one of the fathers of the new science of sociology. After two years at the University of Berlin (1892–1894), he received a Ph.D. from Harvard in 1895. His dissertation, *The Supression of the African Slave Trade to the United States of America, 1638–1870* was published in 1896 as the first volume in the Harvard Historical Studies series.

Despite exceptional credentials, discrimination left Du Bois with no options other than a job at Wilberforce College, a small black school in Ohio. Arriving in 1895, Du Bois left a year later with his wife, his former student Nina Gomer. They went to Philadelphia, where the University of Pennsylvania had invited Du Bois to conduct a sociological study of that city's black neighborhoods. The work led to *The Philadelphia Negro* (1899), which provided the model for a series of monographs he wrote while at Atlanta University, whose faculty he joined in 1897.

As a young sociologist, he sought to "study [social problems] in the light of the best scientific research." But the persistence of segregation, discrimination, and lynching led Du Bois to feel increasingly that "one could not be a calm, cool, and detached scientist while Negroes were lynched, murdered, and starved. . . . "

In 1903 Du Bois published his first collection of essays, *The Souls of Black Folk*, which many have called the most important book ever written by an African American. In it he identified "the color line" as the twentieth century's central problem, and dismissed the accommodationism advocated by Booker T. Washington.

Du Bois helped found the most influential civil rights organization of the twentieth century: the National Association for the Advancement of Colored People (NAACP).

Unlike the Niagara Movement, the NAACP was an interracial organization from the start. Its leadership was largely white; as director of publications and research, Du Bois was the only African American among its early officers. In 1910 Du Bois left Atlanta for the NAACP's New York City headquarters, where he founded the *Crisis*, the association's magazine. As editor he published the work of Langston Hughes, Countee Cullen, and other Harlem Renaissance literary lights as well as his own wide-ranging and provocative opinions. From 1910 until his resignation as editor in 1934, Du Bois's editorials revealed the continuing evolution of his political thought. Early calls for integration and an end to lynching hewed the NAACP line.

In 1915 he wrote *The Negro*, a sociological examination of the African Diaspora. In 1919 he helped organize the second Pan-African Congress.

Visiting Africa in the 1920s, he wrote that his chief question was whether "Negroes are to lead in the rise of Africa or whether they must always and everywhere follow the guidance of white folk."

Along with anti-imperialism, Du Bois also expressed interest in socialism, possibly in response to the disproportionate effect that the Great Depression was having on African Americans, as well as his favorable impressions of a visit to the Soviet Union in 1926. Meanwhile, starting with a new essay collection, *Darkwater: Voices from Within the Veil* (1920), Du Bois's writing became more militant and controversial, and conflicts with NAACP secretary Walter F. White led to Du Bois's resignation as editor of the *Crisis* in 1934.

Returning to Atlanta University, Du Bois continued to write weekly opinion columns in black newspapers, as well as books such as *Black Reconstruction in America* (1934); *Black Folk: Then and Now* (1939); and *Dusk of Dawn: An Autobiography of a Concept of Race* (1940). In 1939 he founded *Phylon*, a journal devoted to race and cultural issues, and whose radical nature may have contributed to his forced resignation from Atlanta University in 1944. Then in his mid-seventies, Du Bois did not retire but instead rejoined the NAACP staff (although he did not resume editorship of the *Crisis*).

Declaring that he would spend "the remaining years of [his] active life" in the fight against imperialism, Du Bois helped reorganize the Pan-African Congress, which in 1945 elected him its international president. In that same year he published *Color and Democracy: Colonies and Peace*, and in 1947 produced *The World and Africa*. Du Bois's outspoken criticism of American foreign policy and his involvement with the 1948 presidential campaign of Progressive Party candidate Henry Wallace led to his dismissal from the NAACP in the fall of 1948.

During the 1950s Du Bois's continuing work with the international peace movement and open expressions of sympathy for the Soviet Union drew the censure of the United States government and further isolated Du Bois from the civil rights mainstream. In 1960 Du Bois attended his friend Kwame Nkrumah's inauguration as the first president of Ghana; in the following year the Du Boises accepted Nkrumah's invitation to move there and work on the *Encyclopaedia Africana*, a project that was never completed. Du Bois died at the age of 95, six months after becoming a Ghanaian citizen.

Europe

Dumas, Alexandre, Père

(b. July 24, 1802, Villers-Cotterêts, France; d. December 5, 1870, Puys, France), French novelist, dramatist, and essayist of African descent, a central figure in nineteenth-century French Romantic literature.

Dumas's career as a novelist began between 1837 and 1843. During this period, after some disappointing reactions to some of his plays, he sought a new audience among the readers of romans-feuilletons (serial novels published in newspapers and journals). In 1838 he published four novels, including two romans-feuilletons, but it was not until the publication of *Le chevalier d'Harmental* in 1842 that he became established as a novelist. During the next 13 years, he produced a wealth of novels. His most important (close up) historically-inspired works are the *D'Artagnan* trilogy, which includes his most famous work, *Les trois mousquetaires* (The Three Musketeers); the Valois cycle, which includes La reine Margot (Marguerite de Valois) and draws on the bloody religious wars in France in the 1570s and 1580s; and the five Marie-Antoinette romances, which span the reign of Louis XVI and the French Revolution. His *Le comte de Monte Cristo* (1846, The Count of Monte-Cristo), enjoyed instantaneous and enduring success.

Dumas's nonfiction works—travel writings and a 3000-page memoir—present a portrait of an energetic and curious adventurer. Indeed, Dumas often found himself personally caught up in the political upheavals of mid-nineteenth century Europe.

North America

Dunbar, Paul Laurence

(b. June 27, 1872, Dayton, Ohio; d. February 9, 1906, Dayton, Ohio), African American poet, often remembered for his Dialect Poetry.

Dunbar was the most famous African American poet and one of the most famous American poets of his time. His career brought him international fame and by any measure was a tremendous success. Although Dunbar felt his best work was his poetry in standard English, he was celebrated almost exclusively for his folk poetry about African Americans written in dialect— the "jingle in a broken tongue." This identification of Dunbar with dialect poetry disappointed him during his lifetime and alienated some later African American readers. But Dunbar's poetry has also been praised by readers from W. E. B. Du Bois to Nikki Giovanni, who recognized the challenges Dunbar faced as a turn-of-the-century black poet trying to sound the "deeper note."

Dunbar's parents had both been slaves on plantations in Kentucky. Although Dunbar was born in Ohio during Reconstruction, his parents' stories about slavery were the basis for some of his folk poetry. He attended Dayton public schools and was the only student of color at Dayton High School, where he was class president, editor of the school paper, president of the literary society, and class poet. After graduating in 1891 Dunbar tried to pursue a career in journalism; when he could not find a writing job because of his race, he became an elevator operator. He earned the nickname "the elevator boy poet," however, when he continued writing.

North America

Dunham, Katherine

(b. June 22, 1909, Glen Ellyn, Ill.), African American dancer, choreographer, and anthropologist who incorporated African-based cultural forms into dance.

Born to Fanny June Taylor, a French Canadian and Native American, and Albert Dunham, Katherine Dunham attended school in Chicago and began to dance at a young age.

In order to explore the cultural and social dimensions of African-based dance forms, Dunham obtained a Guggenheim Award from the Julius Rosenwald Foundation for travel to the Caribbean. In Jamaica, she was accepted into a community of maroons, who allowed her to view their sacred war dance, the Koromantee. Similarly, in Haiti, she was initiated into Vodou and subsequently permitted to participate in secret ritual dances. Throughout her life, Dunham has maintained a special relationship with Haiti through continued association with Haitian arts, politics, and society.

Dunham wrote several books, including *Journey to Accompong* (1946), *A Touch of Innocence* (1959), *Kasamance* (1967), and *Islands Possessed* (1969). She presented lectures and demonstrations at Yale University, Case Western Reserve, Southern Illinois University, and the University of Chicago. She also served as a committee member of the Illinois Project of the Federal Writers' Project from 1935 to 1940.

Dunham communicated her knowledge of cultures primarily through choreography and dance performance. In 1940 she formed the Katherine Dunham Dance Company, which toured the world performing dances she choreographed. These include *L'An' Ya* (1938), *Le Jazz Hot* (1939), *Tropics* (1939), *Bal Nègre* (1943), *Tropical Revue* (1943), and *Shango* (1945). Dunham choreographed and performed in several shows and films, such as the Broadway musical *Cabin in the Sky* (1940) and the motion picture *Star Spangled Rhythm* (1942). In 1943 she established the Dunham School of Arts and Research in New York City, which offered classes in dance, theater, and world cultures. Dunham became the first black woman to choreograph an opera, *Aida*, for the New York City Metropolitan Opera, in its 1963–1964 season.

Durand, Oswald

(b. September 17, 1840, Cap-Haïtien, Haiti; d. April 22, 1906, Haiti), Haitian poet and politician.

In 1842 at age 2, Charles Alexis Oswald Durand became an orphan when an earthquake destroyed the city of Cap-Haïtien in northern Haiti, on the Atlantic Ocean. He then went with his grandmother to the frontier town of Ouanaminthe. Little is known of his first years of studies, but at age 16 he was already working for his living as a tinsmith. While making pots and pans in the tiny village of St.-Louis du Nord, he read and wrote his first verses. He was later offered a job as a primary school teacher.

Demesvar Delorme, already a renowned politician and writer, assisted Durand in publishing his first books of poetry. Durand was elected to the Chamber of Deputies in 1885, where he served several terms. He was elected president of Parliament in 1888.

In 1888 Durand was invited to France as a guest of honor of the famous Société des Gens de Lettres. His "godfather" in French literary circles was the celebrated poet and playwright François Coppée, the favorite author of Sarah Bernhardt, then the world's most renowned actress.

Durand's reputation as a poet grew, particularly after the publication of *Choucoune* in 1883, which recounts the seduction of the narrator's beautiful black mistress by a white foreigner. Much of his poetry calls up images of Haitian women and the Haitian landscape. Durand's love poems are widely known in Haiti, and he is considered by many to be Haiti's greatest poet. When he died suddenly on April 22, 1906, Haiti mourned for its national bard. Other works include *Quatre nouveaux poèmes* (1896) and *Rires et pleurs* (1899).

E

Ebony,

published by the Johnson Publishing Company, *Ebony* is the largest circulation African American magazine.

In 1945 John H. Johnson founded *Ebony* magazine. Already publisher of the successful *Negro Digest*, Johnson aimed to create a monthly magazine that told about black life and achievements in words and photographs, similar to *Life* magazine, the popular weekly. It was an instant success. While circulation grew rapidly, Johnson at first had a difficult time securing advertising from white firms. Johnson's persistence, along with *Ebony*'s appeal as a dependable vehicle for tapping into a national market of black consumers, finally attracted major advertising dollars, securing the magazine's great financial success.

Echemendía, Ambrosio

(b. 1843 Trinidad, Cuba; d. circa 1880s), Afro-Cuban poet born a slave in Trinidad, Cuba (a municipality near the city of Cienfuegos).

Ambrosio Echemendía was one of the remarkable cases of slaves in Cuba who wrote poetry to attain his manumission with the profits from his publications. An exceptional poet, he has not been as studied as other nineteenth-century black Cuban intellectual figures such as Plácido, Manzano, or Morúa Delgado.

His only published book, *Murmurios del Táyaba* (1865, Murmurs of the Táyaba), is a collection of poetry in which he used the pseudonym Máximo Hero de Neiba. Shortly thereafter, his master took him to the nearby city of Cienfuegos, east of Havana, where the proceeds from the sale of his book, along with a general collection taken among the city's elite, allowed him to purchase his freedom.Little is known of Echemendía's life after his manumission; few of his poems were published after 1865, and the date of his death is uncertain. However, the success of his publishing effort inspired other Afro-Cuban enslaved poets, such as Manuel Roblejo, Juan Antonio Frías, and Néstor Cepeda, to campaign for their freedom by writing and publishing poetry.

North America

Eckstine, William Clarence (Billy)

(b. July 8, 1914, Pittsburgh, Pa.; d. March 8, 1993, Pittsburgh, Pa.), African American jazz singer and bandleader.

Billy Eckstine (born Eckstein) became famous in the 1950s as the smooth-voiced baritone singer of such hits as "Fools Rush In" and "Skylark," but music critics and serious jazz fans know him as the man whose big band launched such renowned performers as Dizzy Gillespie, Miles Davis, Charlie Parker, Dexter Gordon, and Sarah Vaughan. After attending Howard University, he began singing with various groups, touring in the Midwest before settling in Chicago in 1939, where he joined the band led by Earl "Fatha" Hines.

It was with Hines that Eckstine had his first hit, the blues song "Jelly Jelly," which he wrote and sang. In 1944 he formed his own big band. Always a favorite with other musicians, the band helped pioneer the then-new bebop sound. Its avant-garde musicianship often overshadowed Eckstine's more traditional vocals, and the band suffered from being badly recorded. Though it left behind no notable recordings, music historians consider it one of the most influential big bands of its era. Eckstine's solo career took off after the band dissolved in 1947. With his deep, romantic voice, elegant presence, and good looks, he became a popular performer. Often referred to as "Mr. B," he garnered several film roles in the following decades, and many have called him the first black sex symbol.

Latin America and the Caribbean

Ecuador,

country on the northwest coast of South America, bordered by Peru to the south and east, Colombia to the north, and the Pacific Ocean to the west.

Ecuador shares with Colombia and Panama a region comprising the Pacific Lowlands Black Culture. This unique Afro-Hispanic culture stretches from Ecuador's Esmeraldas Province through the San Juan River of the Valle del Cauca Department and the Chocó region of Colombia to Panama's Darién Province. It developed through Afro-Hispanic migration and intermixing

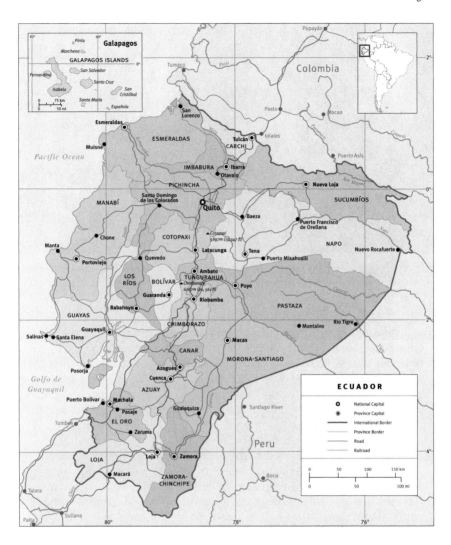

beginning in the colonial period. Blacks in Ecuador settled in the three main geographic regions of the country (the highlands, the coast, and the tropical lowlands of the Amazon region in the east), often displacing or mixing with indigenous populations to create the ethnic diversity that exists today.

During colonial times, the Spanish minority imposed a social system of formally stratified ethnic castes that discriminated against the racially mixed majority. Remnants of that system persist in Ecuadorian society, reflected in a broader ideology of racial and cultural whitening (*blanquemiento*), held up as an ideal achievable through the process of *mestizaje* (racial and cultural mixing, generally implying assimilation into a dominant culture). The belief in racial and cultural blending toward whiteness is overwhelmingly strong in Ecuador, even among black communities. It is in part responsible for the

Adrià Sánchez Galquez painted this 1599 work titled *Mulatto Ambassadors to Province Esmeraldas*, showing Afro-Indian ambassadors from Esmeraldas (Ecuador). This is the earliest signed and dated painting from South America. *CORBIS/Archivo Iconografico, S.A.*

socioeconomic rifts that deeply divide Ecuadorians. The widespread acceptance of the ideology of whitening is evident in the use of *negro* (black), a term that can be offensive to Ecuadorians because it implies lower-class status and other negative stereotypes. Dissociation from this term and its connotations has led to the use of various labels to define Ecuadorian people of African descent. Most of these labels have political and historical implications, often reflecting class boundaries. *Negro fino* ("refined black"), for instance, is used to differentiate blacks with higher levels of education and white-collar jobs from the rest of the community. *Gente morena* (dark people), *morena* (brown-skinned), *gente negra* (black people), and *zambo* (of African and Indian descent) all describe degrees of racial mixture and may carry pejorative connotations or implications about social status, depending on the context and the user. Afro-Ecuadorians self-identify in various ways, making political unity difficult; despite their differences, they have mobilized to effect change. To this end, relatively small circles of intellectuals and political activists have adopted the terms Afro-latino-americano and Afro-ecuatoriano, which emphasize the unity of all people of African descent.

North America

Edelman, Marian Wright

(b. June 6, 1939, Bennettsville, S.C.), founder and president of the Children's Defense Fund, America's leading advocacy group for children.

Marian Wright Edelman was the youngest of Arthur and Maggie Wright's five children. When blacks in her hometown of Bennetsville, South Carolina, were forbidden to enter city parks, her father, a Baptist minister, built a park for black children behind his church. Edelman would later credit him with instilling in her an obligation to right wrongs. By 1964 she was working as a lawyer in Mississippi, where volunteers for the Civil Rights Movement were jailed and often beaten on fabricated charges. In the course of representing them for the National Association for the Advancement of Colored People (NAACP), she became the first black woman to pass the bar in Mississippi. She also became a nationally recognized advocate for Head Start, a pre-kindergarten education program. Relocated to Washington, D.C., Edelman started the Washington Research Project (WRP), which sought to discover how existing and proposed laws affected the poor. Over the next several years, the project evolved into the Children's Defense Fund (CDF). Meanwhile, Edelman directed Harvard University's Center for Law and Education in Cambridge, Massachusetts, and became the first black woman to serve on the board of directors of Yale University. When the CDF was incorporated in 1973, Edelman became its president. She returned to Washington in 1979 to direct the day-to-day operations of this increasingly influential advocacy group. Edelman was aware that with more than half of black children being born out of wedlock, many of them to teenagers, future generations of blacks were assured of living in poverty. She also realized that because teenage pregnancy affected both whites and blacks, a campaign against it could attract broad support. In the early 1980s the CDF sponsored thousands of television, radio, and billboard advertisements counseling teenagers about the risks and costs of pregnancy. Edelman had gained a national reputation as "the children's crusader."

Africa

Egypt,
the nation in the northeastern corner of Africa, where a land bridge connects the continent with Asia; it borders the Mediterranean Sea to the north, Israel to the northeast, the Red Sea to the east, Sudan to the south, and Libya to the west.

Since ancient times, Egypt's cultural and political significance has extended far beyond its borders. Ancient Egypt, whose pharaohs first came to power nearly 5000 years ago, pioneered one of the world's earliest advanced civilizations. Ancient Egypt served as a crossroads between the Middle East and sub-Saharan Africa, and its culture and people included elements from both neighboring regions. During the twenty-fifth dynasty (about 767-671 B.C.E.), black pharaohs from the neighboring kingdom of Kush ruled Egypt, and links of trade and migration have linked Egypt with East and Central Africa since prehistoric times. The ancient Egyptians' distinctive culture, which developed in the fertile Nile Valley and Delta, surrounded by hostile deserts, provided a model for surrounding peoples, including the Greeks.

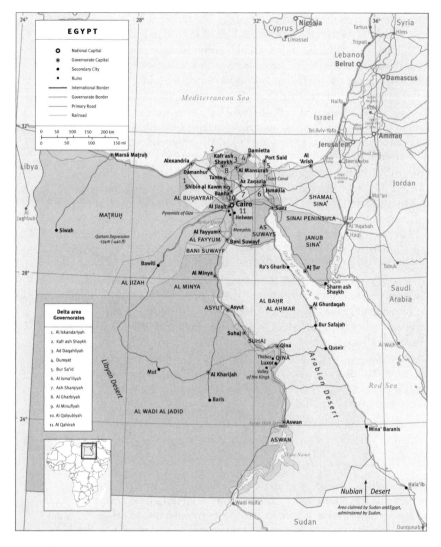

By the fourth century B.C.E. the tide had turned, and Greek-speaking Macedonian invaders conquered Egypt. Repeatedly over the centuries, Egypt has undergone foreign domination and exploitation only to reemerge as a powerful cultural and political center across wide areas of Africa and the Middle East. After three centuries as the center of the powerful Ptolemaic Empire, Egypt was conquered by the Romans, who made it a province of their own empire and appropriated its agricultural surplus to feed Roman soldiers and citizens.

Conquered by Muslim Arab armies during the seventh century, Egypt became the center of the powerful Mamluk state during the thirteenth. Subdued by the Ottoman Turks during the sixteenth century, Egypt went

Buyers and sellers bargain over camels at the Imbaba market in Cairo. *CORBIS/K.M. Westermann*

on to conquer large parts of present-day Sudan and the Arabian Peninsula under Muhammad Ali after 1805. Virtually a colony of Great Britain by 1900, Egypt emerged as a champion of Arab nationalism under Gamal Abdel Nasser in 1952. Today Egypt's significance revolves around its cultural and political leadership in the Arab world and its important role in Middle Eastern geopolitics.

Africa

Egypt (Ready Reference)

Former Name: United Arab Republic (with Syria)

Official Name: Arab Republic of Egypt

Area: 1,001,450 sq km (about 386,662 sq mi)

Location: North Africa, on the Mediterranean Sea, bordered by the Gaza Strip, the Red Sea, Sudan, and Libya

A fisherman pulls in his net as he fishes the Damietta arm of the Nile River in Egypt. *CORBIS/Kevin Fleming*

bottom: The mausoleum of Barquq stands in the foreground of this view of Cairo. *CORBIS/ K.M. Westermann*

Capital: Cairo (population 6,800,000 [1995 estimate])

Other Major Cities: Alexandria (population 2,917,300), Giza (3,700,100), Port Said (399,800), Suez (326,800) (1986 estimates)

Population: 66,050,004 (1998 estimate)

Population Density: 64 persons per sq km (164 per sq mi)

Population Below Age 15: Total population: 36 percent (male 12,173,882; female 11,637,239 [1998 estimate])

Population Growth Rate: 1.86 percent (1998 estimate)

Total Fertility Rate: 3.4 children born per woman (1998 estimate)

Life Expectancy at Birth: Total population: 62.07 years (male 60.09 years; female 64.14 years [1998 estimate])

Infant Mortality Rate: 69.23 deaths per 1000 live births (1998 estimate)

Literacy Rate (age 15 and over who can read and write): Total population: 51.4 percent (male 63.6 percent; female 38.8 percent [1995 estimate])

Education: Compulsory for children between the ages of 6 and 11; 89 percent of primary school-age children were enrolled in school in the mid-1990s. Secondary school enrollment was 65 percent, including vocational and teacher training schools. Seventeen percent of college-age Egyptians attended universities or other institutions of higher education during this time. Egypt has 13 state universities, as well as numerous technical colleges and institutes of art and music.

Languages: Arabic is the official language; English and French are also used by educated classes.

Ethnic Groups: Egyptians, Bedouins, and Berbers of Hamitic descent make up 99 percent of the population, while Greek, Nubian, Armenian, and other European groups (mostly Italian and French) make up the remaining 1 percent.

Religions: Muslim, 94 percent; Coptic Christian and other, 6 percent

Climate: Hot, dry, and dusty over most of the country; the hot season is from May to September and the cool season from November to March. In the coastal region, average annual temperatures range from a maximum of 37° C (99° F) to a minimum of 14° C (57° F). Wide variations of temperature occur in the deserts, ranging from a maximum of 46° C (114° F) during daylight hours to a minimum of 6° C (42° F) after sunset. During the winter season desert temperatures often drop to 0° C (32° F). The most humid area is along the Mediterranean coast, where the average annual rainfall is about 200 mm (8 in). Precipitation decreases rapidly to the south;

A woman addresses a crowd on one of the prinicipal streets of Cairo. This incident, which took place in 1919, marked the first time Egyptian women entered public political debate.
CORBIS/Bettmann

Cairo receives on average only about 29 mm (1.1 in) of rain a year, and in many desert locations it may rain only once in several years.

Land, Plants, and Animals: Egypt is situated on a desert plateau bisected by the Nile River. Less than one-tenth of the country is settled or under cultivation, principally along the valley and delta of the Nile, in desert oases, and around the Suez Canal. Over 90 percent of the country is in the desert, including the Libyan Desert west of the Nile, the Arabian Desert in the east, and the Nubian Desert in the south. The Sinai Peninsula consists of sandy desert in the north and rugged mountains in the south. The vegetation of Egypt is confined largely to the Nile delta, the Nile Valley, and the oases. Wild animals include the gazelle, desert fox, hyena, jackal, wild ass, boar, jerboa, ichneumon, lizard, poisonous snakes, crocodile, hippopotamus, and numerous species of birds and insects.

Natural Resources: Petroleum, natural gas, iron ore, phosphates, manganese, limestone, gypsum, talc, asbestos, lead, and zinc

Currency: The Egyptian pound

Gross Domestic Product (GDP): $267.1 billion (1997 estimate)

GDP per Capita: $4400 (1997 estimate)

GDP Real Growth Rate: 5.2 percent (1997 estimate)

Primary Economic Activities: Agriculture (40 percent of employment), fishing, oil production, manufacturing, tourism, and other services

Primary Crops: Cotton, rice, corn, wheat, beans, fruits, vegetables; cattle, water buffalo, sheep, goats, and fish

Industries: Textiles, food processing, chemicals, petroleum, construction, cement, and metals

Primary Exports: Crude oil and petroleum products, cotton yarn, raw cotton, textiles, metal products, chemicals, fruits, and vegetables

Primary Imports: Machinery and equipment, food grains, fertilizers, wood products, durable consumer goods, and capital goods

Primary Trade Partners: United States, European Union, and Japan

Government: Constitutional republic. The executive branch is led by President Mohammed Hosni Mubarak, nominated by the 454-member People's Assembly (elected in late 1995) and validated by a national, popular referendum. The prime minister (currently Kamal Ahmed al-Ganzouri) and the Cabinet are appointed by the president. The legislature comprises the 454-seat People's Assembly, currently dominated by Mubarak's National Democratic, and the 264-seat Advisory Council, which plays only a consultative role.

Africa

Ekwensi, Cyprian

(b. Sept. 26, 1921, Minna, Nigeria), Nigerian novelist, short-story writer, and children's author who has portrayed the moral and material problems besetting rural West Africans as they migrate to the city.

Born Cyprian Duaka Odiatu Ekwensi in Minna, Nigeria, he began his secondary education at Government College in Ibadan and completed it at Achimota College in present-day Ghana (then the Gold Coast) in 1943. In the early 1950s he studied pharmacy at the Chelsea School of Pharmacy in London, England. While working at various jobs—forestry official, teacher, journalist, and broadcasting executive—Ekwensi pursued his writing career. He got his start as a writer by reading his work on a West African radio program. His first published success came with the novella *When Love Whispers* (1948). *People of the City* (1954), a collection of short stories tied together almost as a novel, chronicles the frantic pace of life in modern Lagos, Nigeria's commercial capital. The book introduced the critical view of urban existence that won Ekwensi national as well as international attention.

From 1957 to 1961 Ekwensi was head of features at the Nigerian Broadcasting Company, and from 1961 to 1967 he was federal director of Information Services. During this period he wrote his most successful novel, *Jagua Nana* (1961), the story of a vibrant middle-aged prostitute who moves between the corrupt, pleasure-seeking life of the city and the pastoral life of her rural origins. He continued exploring the contrast between the appeal of city life and its corruption in his collection *Lokotown and Other Stories* (1966). During the Nigerian Civil War (1967–1970) Ekwensi was director of the Broadcasting Corporation of Biafra, and in 1968 he won the Dag Hammarskjöld International Prize for Literary Merit. After the war Ekwensi continued his career as a writer, reflecting on the war and its aftermath in the novels *Survive the Peace* (1976) and *Divided We Stand* (1980). In 1986 he published a sequel to *Jagua Nana* called *Jagua Nana's Daughter*. His children's books include *The Passport of Mallam Ilia* (1960), *The Drummer Boy* (1960), and *Juju Rock* (1966).

North America

Elders, M. Joycelyn Jones

(b. August 13, 1933, Schaal, Ark.), surgeon general of the United States (1993–1994) whose outspokenness led to her dismissal.

Jocelyn Elders was born Minnie Joycelyn Jones in a poor, remote farming village of southwestern Arkansas. In 1993 Clinton, as U.S. president, nominated Elders for the post of U.S. surgeon general. Her support for sex education, distribution of condoms, abortion rights, and the use of marijuana for medical purposes brought her predictable and stern opposition from conservatives in Congress and around the country. Elders did little to ease their fears. During her brief tenure she tried to increase medical services in rural and poor communities by promoting the training of nurse-practitioners, physician assistants, and certified nurse midwives. In December 1994 she was asked whether masturbation should be encouraged as a way to discourage minors from having sex. She responded that masturbation "is part of human sexuality and a part of something that perhaps should be taught." The next day President Clinton asked for and received her resignation. Soon thereafter, Elders returned to her teaching position at the University of Arkansas Medical Center.

North America

Ellington, Edward Kennedy ("Duke")

(b. April 29, 1899, Washington, D.C.; d. May 24, 1974, New York, N.Y.), African American jazz pianist and bandleader, and widely held to be the greatest composer in the history of jazz.

For nearly half a century Duke Ellington led the premier American big band, and through his compositions and performances he brought artistic credibility to African American jazz. Ellington played the piano, but his orchestra was his true instrument. In the late 1920s he perfected an exotic style that was later termed *jungle music*. During the 1930s Ellington developed a lush approach to orchestration that introduced new complexity to the simplistic conventions of swing-era jazz. Through out the 1930s and 1940s he struggled against the limitations of the three-minute 78 rpm recording and the general adherence to 12- and 32-bar song forms, in the process vastly extending the scope of jazz. Personally and politically, he preferred to avoid direct confrontation; yet he was active as far back as the early 1940s in the cause of racial equality.

Ellington took what had begun as a vernacular dance music and created

American composer, bandleader, and pianist Duke Ellington poses in 1931 with members of his band Nuf Said. *CORBIS/Bettmann*

larger and more artistically challenging musical forms, exemplified in his three-movement composition *Black, Brown, and Beige* (1943). Due to his fame as a bandleader, Ellington-the-pianist is often overlooked. Yet particularly during the 1960s some of his most creative playing took place in small groups and demonstrated his willingness to engage such younger musicians as tenor saxophonist John Coltrane.

Ellington's Musical Beginnings and His Move to New York City

Ellington was born to a middle-class black family in Washington, D.C., at a time when Washington was the nation's preeminent black community. He began studying piano at age seven and quickly exhibited a gift for music. He began playing professionally as a teenager in a style derived from ragtime, which had a particularly strong influence in the vicinity of Baltimore and Washington. By 1919 he had emerged as a leader of small groups that played for local parties and dances. Although ragtime pianists led most of these bands, the other musicians were mainly reading musicians who played in a sweet style and did not improvise.

In 1922 Ellington moved to New York City, which was then emerging as the nation's jazz capital. He played with various theater orchestras and with jazz-oriented bands like the one led by Elmer Snowden (1900–1973). He also made his first foray into musical theater, writing the music for an ill-fated Broadway comedy, *Chocolate Kiddies* of 1924. In 1924 he took over the Snowden band, and that six-man group became the nucleus of the Ellington Orchestra. By 1926 the group had grown to 11 members; the most important additions were cornetist Bubber Miley and trombonist "Tricky Sam" Nanton (1904–1946). Through their influence the orchestra moved away from its sweet style and embraced a bluesy and improvisational jazz.

Like many jazz pianists of the day, Ellington came under the sway of the Harlem "stride" piano style, exemplified in the playing of James P. Johnson (1894–1955) and Willie "the Lion" Smith. The stride style essentially divides the piano keyboard into three ranges. The pianist's left hand covers the two lower ranges, alternating single bass notes at the bottom with chord clusters struck higher up. The style takes its name from the characteristic, bouncing "oom-pah, oom-pah" produced by the pianist's striding left hand. The pianist's left hand thus establishes a propulsive beat and outlines the tune's harmonic structure; the right hand plays melody, adds ornamentation, and improvises solo lines. Ellington evolved from this rather florid piano style, in part, by simplifying it and by adding harmonic complexities and dissonance that at times foreshadowed the playing of bop pioneer Thelonious Monk and free-jazz pianist Cecil Taylor (b. 1929).

Ellington at the Cotton Club, 1927–1931

In the fall of 1927 the Ellington Orchestra secured a long-term gig at the Cotton Club, New York City's most prestigious nightclub, which was wired to permit "live" remote radio broadcasts that gave Ellington nationwide recognition. The demanding stint at the Cotton Club also gave him a crash course in composing and arranging. Many of his early orchestrations involved little more than transposing note for note what he composed at the piano to the instruments of the band. While at the Cotton Club he became more adventuresome in his harmonies and voicings, and he began to experiment with changes in tempo and meter. By 1928 his orchestra had emerged as the nation's foremost jazz ensemble, surpassing the bands of Fletcher Henderson and King Oliver. During 1927–1928 Ellington made a series of recordings that epitomized the orchestra's first classic style. They featured the growling, plunger-muted solos of Miley and Nanton, who virtually defined the orchestra's "jungle" style. Miley also composed or co-wrote several key songs, including the masterpieces "East St. Louis Toodle-Oo" (1926) and "Black and Tan Fantasie" (1927). These songs and Ellington's lyrical "Black Beauty" (1928) were staples in the band's repertoire for years to come.

Moving Beyond the Boundaries of Dance Music

Ellington gained further exposure during the 1930s. The orchestra was featured in RKO's popular Amos 'n' Andy film *Check and Double Check* (1930). In 1931 Ellington wrote his first extended work, "Creole Rhapsody." The Victor version of the song, recorded in June 1931, filled two sides of a 12-inch 78 rpm record and was eight and a half minutes long. In the mid-1930s Ellington wrote the score for a nine-minute musical film, *Symphony in Black* (1935), which featured young Billie Holiday and foreshadowed *Black, Brown, and Beige*. Devastated by the death of his mother in 1935, Ellington wrote *Reminiscing in Tempo* (1935) as his tribute to her. His most ambitious work to date, it was a unified composition that filled four album sides. None of Ellington's contemporaries in jazz had attempted such large-scale works. Among his important shorter compositions of this period were "Mood Indigo" (1930), "It Don't Mean a Thing If It Ain't Got That Swing" (1932), "Sophisticated Lady" (1933), and the haunting ballad "In a Sentimental Mood" (1935). During the mid-1930s new swing bands—under the leadership of Count Basie, Jimmie Lunceford, and such white bandleaders as Benny Goodman and Artie Shaw—threatened to eclipse the Ellington Orchestra. Although Ellington's "In a Sentimental Mood" never became a hit, Goodman's simplified 1936 rendition did. Moreover, the personnel of the Ellington Orchestra, normally quite stable, underwent considerable turnover during the mid-1930s.

Despite these difficulties, the Ellington Orchestra had many strengths, in particular its many talented soloists. Most swing big bands got by with two or three prominent soloists. During the mid-1930s Ellington's Orchestra featured nine significant solo talents: alto saxophonist Johnny Hodges; clarinetist Barney Bigard (1906–1980); baritone saxophonist Harry Carney (1910–1974); trumpeter Cootie Williams (1910–1985); cornetist Rex Stewart (1907–1967); trombonists Nanton and Lawrence

Brown (1907–1988); vocalist Ivie Anderson (1905–1949); and Ellington himself on piano. Despite setbacks, the Ellington Orchestra toured constantly during the Great Depression and made successful visits to Europe in 1933 and 1939.

The Great Ellington Band: The Early 1940s

By 1940 Ellington and his orchestra had overcome the difficulties of the mid-1930s. In 1938 Billy Strayhorn began his nearly 30-year stint as Ellington's closest collaborator; he composed such memorable works as the orchestra's longtime theme, "Take the A Train" (1941). Ellington himself had a burst of creativity during which he produced some of his most enduring compositions. He benefited from an outstanding group of musicians, including two vital new additions—tenor saxophonist Ben Webster (1909–1973) and virtuoso bassist Jimmy Blanton (1918–1942). Among the orchestra's most important recordings of this period were "Ko-Ko" (1940), "Cotton Tail" (1940), and "I Got It Bad and That Ain't Good" (1941). In 1943 Ellington appeared at New York City's prestigious Carnegie Hall. The first African American bandleader to be so honored, he responded with the 44-minute-long *Black, Brown, and Beige: A Tone Parallel to the History of the American Negro*, a path-breaking work in twentieth-century American music. Unfortunately, the ambitious piece broke the conventions of both jazz and classical music, satisfying neither audience. The critical response deeply disappointed Ellington; following his Carnegie Hall appearance (and an earlier run-through in Boston), he never performed the work in its entirety again.

Later Large-Scale Works and Ellington's Social Activism

Neither Ellington nor Strayhorn was dissuaded from creating other large-scale jazz suites, including the *Liberian Suite* (1947); *Harlem* (1951); the *Festival Suite* (1956); *Such Sweet Thunder* (1957), a musical tribute to Shakespear; *Suite Thursday* (1960), which paid tribute to author John Steinbeck; and the *Far East Suite* (1966). Ellington also composed film scores for *Anatomy of a Murder* (1959) and *Paris Blues* (1961). In 1965 Ellington broke new ground with his [first] *Sacred Concert*, commissioned by San Francisco's Grace Episcopal Church. In the concert the Ellington Orchestra was joined by the Grace Cathedral Choir; the Herman McCoy Choir; singers Jon Hendricks (b. 1921), Esther Marrow, and Jimmy McPhail; and tap dancer Bunny Briggs. "In the Beginning, God" Ellington's opening movement, won a 1966 Grammy Award for best original jazz composition. In 1968 Ellington composed the *Second Sacred Concert*. At the time of his death he was preparing a third.

From the early 1940s Ellington was active in the emergent Civil Rights Movement, although his role has largely been overlooked. In 1941 he wrote the score for the groundbreaking musical *Jump for Joy*, which challenged the demeaning stereotypes of African Americans in Hollywood films and throughout American popular culture. *Jump for Joy* had a buoyant sense of optimism that is suggested in such numbers as "Uncle Tom's Cabin is a Drive-In Now." Ellington's speaking voice, like his musical one, was eloquent and complex. He disliked head-on confrontation. As Ellington biographer John Edward Hasse has observed, in Ellington's 1973 autobiography *Music Is My Mistress*, there is "hardly a negative word," passing in silence over various personal conflicts and his negative encounters with Jim Crow segregation. This indirection was equally evident in his political activism. During the Carnegie Hall premiere of *Black, Brown, and Beige*, Ellington looked out on the formally attired ranks of New York's elite and declared: "[W]e find ourselves today struggling for solidarity, but just as we are about to get our teeth into it, our country is at war, [so, of course], we . . . find the black, brown, and beige right in there for the red, white, and blue." Though stressing African American patriotism, Ellington—in his distinctly oblique way—voiced black aspirations for racial equality and integration. In 1951 Ellington premiered *Harlem*, which he regarded as his most successful extended work, at a benefit concert for the National Association for the Advancement of Colored People (NAACP). Two months before the concert he wrote to President Harry S. Truman, stating that concert proceeds would "help fight for your civil rights program—to stamp out segregation, discrimination, [and] bigotry." He suggested that Truman's daughter, Margaret Truman, serve as honorary chair for the event. Ellington biographer Hasse notes that Truman or someone on his staff wrote on the letter "an emphatic 'NO!' in inch-high letters, underlined twice."

Ellington's Later Career

During the 1950s and 1960s Ellington and his orchestra led a split existence. They debuted substantial extended works in concerts and recordings, but they also endured a grueling schedule of one-night stands in which the orchestra reprised old hits with what bordered on formulaic playing. An inspiring performance at the 1956 Newport Jazz Festival helped draw the orchestra out of a creative slump. Ellington also found inspiration in a series of small-group recordings, such as *Money Jungle* (1962), featuring bassist Charles Mingus and drummer Max Roach, and *Duke Ellington and John Coltrane* (1962), a classic collaboration between two of the seminal figures in jazz.

In these years Ellington faced the loss of several long-term orchestra members, including the irreplaceable Johnny Hodges, who died in 1970. But the greatest loss was that of Billy Strayhorn, who died of throat cancer in 1967. In *And His Mother Called Him Bill* (1967), Ellington paid tribute to his long-time collaborator with a set of Strayhorn compositions; the emotional recording sessions yielded one of the orchestra's last great albums.

In 1969 President Richard Nixon presented Ellington with the Medal of Freedom at a gala 70th birthday party. Ellington gave little sign of slowing down in the early 1970s, but in 1973 he learned that he had lung cancer.

Even after he was hospitalized in the spring of 1974, he continued to work on new compositions. Following his death, some 65,000 people came to view his body, and more than 10,000 turned out for his funeral. In subsequent years Ellington's reputation has continued to grow. He is rightly acclaimed as one of America's greatest composers.

North America

Ellison, Ralph

(b. March 1, 1914, Oklahoma City, Okla.; d. April 16, 1994, New York, N.Y.), African American writer; author of Invisible Man (1952), one of the most famous twentieth-century American novels.

The great irony of the career of Ralph Ellison, one of the most acclaimed and influential of all American novelists, may be that when he died at the age of 80, he had only published one novel. His second, on which he had been working for almost 40 years, was still unfinished. But with that extraordinary first work, *Invisible Man*, Ellison changed the standards for the American novel. As the *Norton Anthology of African American Literature* says, with *Invisible Man* Ellison simultaneously "defined the historic moment of mid-twentieth century America" and "single-handedly re[wrote] the American novel as an African American adventure in fiction."

Ellison was born in 1914 in Oklahoma City. His parents had migrated to Oklahoma from the South because they hoped the West might offer better opportunities for African Americans. Ellison's father, an avid reader, named his son Ralph Waldo after the nineteenth-century white American writer Ralph Waldo Emerson. His father died when Ellison was only three, and his mother worked at a variety of jobs to raise Ralph and his brother. Ellison attended segregated public schools in Oklahoma City and excelled in music. When he graduated, local officials—afraid he would try to integrate a white Oklahoma college—gave him a scholarship to Tuskegee Institute in Alabama, and he arrived there by hitching a ride on a freight train in 1933.

Ellison had been encouraged to read widely since childhood, but a sophomore English class introduced him to a new variety of authors. He was especially captivated by the way he felt T. S. Eliot's poem *The Waste Land* captured the rhythms of jazz. Ellison later said that discovery of the potential connections between music and literature was what led him to consider writing instead of music as a career. In 1936, when his scholarship ran out, he took what he thought would be a short break in New York, planning to save enough money to return in the fall. Instead, Ellison met the great writers Langston Hughes and Arna Bontemps, who in turn introduced him to novelist Richard Wright. Once he had been exposed to the black New York literary scene, he essentially remained in it, and in New York, for the rest of his life.

Ellison took a series of odd jobs to support himself and studied writers Ernest Hemingway, James Joyce, and Fyodor Dostoyevsky. In 1938 he took a position with the Federal Writers' Project collecting black folklore and oral histories through interviews with older African Americans, which provided him with stories and insights that ultimately found their way into his later writings. Meanwhile, Wright, who was already known in New York as a writer and a Communist Party activist, became Ellison's mentor. Ellison's first published work was a 1937 book review in *New Challenge*, a radical journal that Wright edited. More reviews and essays in similar journals followed over the next few years. Ellison's first short stories, *Slick Gonna Learn* (1939) and *The Birthmark* (1940), explored the political and social constraints on black life in a narrative mode similar to the novel Wright was working on, *Native Son* (1940). When even Wright criticized Ellison's style for being too derivative of his own, their relationship deteriorated. Ellison gradually rejected Wright's aesthetics and his politics, and matured into a style that was indisputably his own.

In 1940 and 1941 Ellison published two essays that praised the use of African American folklore in African American fiction. Black folklore, language, and customs figured prominently in several of his subsequent stories, including *Flying Home* (1944), which most closely prefigured *Invisible Man*. *Flying Home* was initially meant to be part of a novel about a black American World War II pilot captured by the Nazis. But in 1945, while still at work on that project, Ellison wrote a single sentence on a piece of paper: "I am an invisible man." He later recalled that at the time, he had no idea what that line meant, but he became consumed by trying to imagine what kind of character would say such a thing. Over the next seven years the line turned into a story of its own, and became the opening sentence of *Invisible Man*.

Invisible Man follows its unnamed black protagonist from South to North, from youth to adulthood, and from innocence and naiveté to experience and awareness. At the novel's beginning, the protagonist is just about to graduate from high school with a scholarship to attend a prestigious Southern black college. He is ambitious and optimistic that the world will be full of promise for a smart black boy who works hard. But shortly before leaving home he has a dream in which his dead grandfather appears to him and, in a parody of a high school graduation, presents him an engraved plaque that reads "To Whom It May Concern: Keep This Nigger Boy Running."

The protagonist is kept running for the rest of the novel—by the patronizing white trustees and accommodationist black founder of his college; by the white men he hopes will hire him when he is forced to leave school and seek work in New York; by the boss at the paint factory where he does find a job; and by the leaders of the Brotherhood, an organization much like the Communist Party, who recruit and train him to be a leader but reject him when he becomes more powerful than they would like. At the novel's end, the protagonist finally realizes that he has suffered because he has allowed his identity to be defined by others who do not really know him, who see him as indistinguishable from other black people, who do not value his individuality. He has been defined by people to whom he is invisible.

Invisible Man was immediately celebrated not only as a key exploration of the contemporary African American psyche, but also for its very modern depiction of the fragmentation, invisibility, and lack of self-knowledge many people experienced in the larger American society. In 1965 a poll of 200 critics called *Invisible Man* "the most distinguished American novel written since World War II." Ellison followed the book with two successful collections of his essays, interviews, and speeches on the African American experience, *Shadow and Act* (1964) and *Going to the Territory* (1987). In the late 1950s he began work on his much-awaited second novel.

During the 1960s many black writers were critical of Ellison's belief that African Americans are fundamentally American, shaped by the United States more than by Africa. But within several years, public opinion had swayed to affirm Ellison's point of view, and readers once again held high hopes for the next novel, which Ellison hinted would be a multi-volume magnum opus. He apparently kept going even after a fire at his summer home destroyed a year's worth of manuscript, but he died of cancer in 1994 without having completed it. Several of Ellison's unpublished short stories were posthumously collected along with his earlier stories in the 1996 volume *Flying Home*. In 1999 Random House published *Juneteenth*, a 400-page novel that Ellison's literary executor crafted from the thousands of pages Ellison left when he died.

In his creation of a new style that embraced black folk tradition and emphasized the importance of self-knowledge and self-awareness for African Americans, Ellison broke new ground for the generation of black authors who followed him. And his sharp observations on the problem of black "invisibility" in white culture gave new insights on the American racial scene to a generation of black and white readers.

Latin America and the Caribbean

El Salvador,
a country in Central America.

Africa

Emecheta, Buchi
(b. July 21, 1944, Yaba, Nigeria), Nigerian writer whose novels have focused on the lives of women.

Florence Onye Buchi Emecheta was born near the city of Lagos, Nigeria. At a young age, she lost her mother as well as her father, who was killed while serving the British army in Burma. After completing a degree at the Methodist girls' high school in Lagos, she married Sylvester Onwordi at age 16. The couple moved to London, and during the next six years, Emecheta bore five children while supporting the family financially. She began to write during this time, but, as she later said in an interview, "The first book I wrote, my husband burnt, and then I found I couldn't write with him around."

Emecheta left her husband in 1966, supporting herself for the next few years by working at the library in the British Museum. She enrolled at the University of London, where she received a sociology degree in 1974. In her first literary works she represented her own experiences of poverty, racism, and motherhood, "the cumulative oppression resulting from being alien, black and female," as she described it. These reflective, semi-fictional accounts were first published in *New Statesman* and later collected into her first novel *In the Ditch* (1972). She followed this with *Second-Class Citizen* (1974), which drew on the earlier years of her life and her experience of immigration. Both *In the Ditch* and *Second-Class Citizen* dealt with the socioeconomic problems of Africans in both Africa and the Diaspora, and particularly highlighted the multiple oppressions of women.

Emecheta's next novel, *The Bride Price* (1976), was set in Nigeria in the early 1950s. She told the story of a young Ibo woman who defies tradition by running away with a man descended from a slave caste. The novel portrays a woman constrained by Ibo social hierarchies and beliefs, including the belief that if the bride price is not paid, the bride will die in childbirth. The story ends without resolution: Emecheta leaves the reader to imagine whether the traditional prophecy is fulfilled. In *The Slave Girl* (1977), set in early twentieth-century Nigeria, a young girl is forced into domestic slavery by her brother, then bought from her master by a suitor. Emecheta uses the narrative to illustrate a parallel between slavery and marriage.

Emecheta published her best-known work, *The Joys of Motherhood*, in 1979. This story, depicting the migrant rural Ibo community in Lagos, spans the time in Nigeria between the 1930s and independence in 1960. Emecheta focuses on the lives of women who can achieve status only through motherhood—specifically, their ability to bear sons. Emecheta's early portrayals of oppressive gender relations created a great deal of controversy, especially among her African readership. Some critics accused her of portraying African men unfairly. Others, especially in the West, held her up as one of Africa's most eloquent feminists. Yet Emecheta herself has consistently rejected the title "feminist." In an interview, she clarified her position: "I do believe in the African kind of feminism. They call it womanism, because, you see, you Europeans don't worry about water, you don't worry about schooling, you are so well off. Now, I buy land, and I say, 'OK, I can't build on it, I have no money, so I give it to some women to start planting.' That is my brand of feminism." In her later novels, Emecheta addressed a range of sociopolitical issues. *Destination Biafra* (1982) was, in the words of Emecheta, a novel that "needed to be written" about the civil war that wracked Nigeria from 1967 to 1970. *Double Yoke* (1982) dealt with the moral deterioration of postcolonial Nigeria. *The Rape of Shavi* (1983), an experimental departure from Emecheta's realist style, was a slightly disguised tale of colonization.

Emecheta returned to the theme of the immigrant experience with the novel *Gwendolen* (1989) (published in the United States as *The Family*, about a Caribbean immigrant girl who experiences rape and incest. Throughout much of her writing career, Emecheta has taught at various universities. In addition, she founded the publishing company Ogwugwu Afor, which specializes in African literature. She has also published an autobiography, two children's books, and several books for young adults, amassing an impressive total of 16 works published in 14 years.

Latin America and the Caribbean

Engenho Velho,

one of the oldest *terreiros*, or temples, of the Afro-Brazilian religion of Candomblé. Located in the northeastern state of Bahia, it is thought to have been established by three freed African women in the 1830s and may have existed long before then.

Africa

Equatorial Guinea,

a small country on the coast of Central Africa including both the Bioko Island, just south of Nigeria, and the mainland province of Mbini, lying between Cameroon and Gabon.

Equatorial Guinea is an anomaly in Africa. Due to early migration patterns, a multiethnic society, dominated by the Fang, resides on the mainland, while a single ethnic group, the Bubi, live on Bioko Island. Early European imperialism and the transatlantic slave trade exaggerated the differences between the island and mainland. The only Spanish colony in sub-Saharan Africa, Equatorial Guinea was run by a dictatorial colonial regime, primarily devoted to exploiting the small territory's rich natural resources. The leadership since independence has proven equally undemocratic: for three decades two men from the same family have ruled Equatorial Guinea, making use of clan patronage and widespread repression to maintain their rule and their control over the country's wealth. Increasing oil exports in recent years have brought extraordinarily high rates of economic growth (67 percent in 1997). But most of the country's 350,000 citizens have seen little, if any, of the profits.

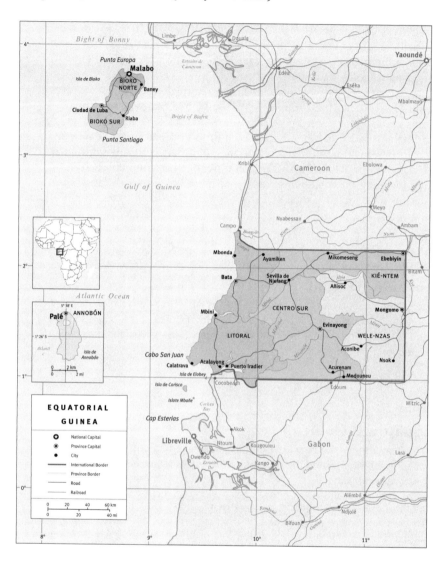

Africa

Equatorial Guinea (Ready Reference)

Official Name: Republic of Equatorial Guinea

Former Name: Spanish Guinea

Area: 28,051 sq km (about 10,831 sq mi)

Location: Western Africa, bordering the North Atlantic, between Gabon to the south and east and Cameroon to the north. Equatorial Guinea also includes islands off the coast, the largest of which is Bioko.

Capital: Malabo, on Bioko (population 38,000 [1989 estimate])

Population: 454,000 (1998 estimate); many thousands more are believed to be living abroad, due to the nation's tumultuous political climate.

Population Density: 14 people per sq km (37 per sq mi)

Population Below Age 15: 43 percent (male 97,993; female 97,470 [1998 estimate])

Population Growth Rate: 2.56 percent (1998 estimate)

Total Fertility Rate: 5.1 children born per woman (1998 estimate)

Life Expectancy at Birth: Total population: 53.93 years (male 51.61 years; female 56.31 years [1998 estimate])

Infant Mortality Rate: 93.45 deaths per 1000 live births (1998 estimate)

Literacy Rate (age 15 and over who can read and write): Total population: 78.5 percent (male 89.6 percent; female 68.1 percent [1995 estimate])

Education: Free and compulsory for children between the ages of 6 and 14. Still, an estimated 30 percent of school-age children do not attend primary school, and even fewer advance to secondary school. The Spanish National University of Distant Education operates centers for higher education at Malabo and Bata. Some Equatorial Guineans also go abroad (mostly to Spain and France) for a college education. In 1990 there were 578 college and university students.

Languages: Spanish is the official language, but Fang, a Bantu language, is most widely spoken.

Ethnic Groups: Ethnic lines correspond to geographic boundaries, with Bubi and Fernandinos populations on Bioko and a Fang population in Río Muni.

Religions: About 90 percent of the people are affiliated with the Roman Catholic church, although traditional beliefs are widely practiced.

Climate: Tropical; the average annual temperature in Malabo is about 25° C (77° F) and on average more than 2000 mm (80 in) of rain falls a year. The wettest season is December through February.

Land, Plants and Animals: On the mainland the terrain rolls gently and is heavily forested. The Mbini (formerly Benito) River drains about 60 percent of the land. Bioko has fertile volcanic soil watered by several large streams.

Natural Resources: The rich volcanic soil supports extensive agriculture.

Currency: The Communauté Financière Africaine franc

Gross Domestic Product (GDP): $660 million (1997 estimate)

GDP per Capita: $1500 (1997 estimate)

GDP Real Growth Rate: 10 percent (1995 estimate)

Primary Economic Activities: Agriculture and forestry

Primary Crops: Coffee, tropical hardwood timber, cassava, and sweet potatoes

Industries: Oil, soap, cocoa, yucca, coffee, and seafood processing

Primary Exports: Coffee, cocoa beans; timber

Primary Imports: Petroleum, food, beverages, clothing, machinery

Primary Trade Partners: Cameroon, France, Italy, Netherlands, Spain, and United States

Government: Under the 1982 constitution, Equatorial Guinea was a single-party state. This governmental party was named the Democratic Party of Equatorial Guinea in 1987. A new multiparty constitution was approved by public referendum in 1991. It established an 80-member House of Representatives to replace the existing 41-member legislature. Under the constitution, the voters elect a president to a seven-year term and legislators to five-year terms. Obiango Macías Nguema Mbasogo has been president since 1979 and was last re-elected in 1996.

Africa

Equiano, Olaudah

(b. 1745, Nigeria; d. April 31, 1797, England), African ex-slave and abolitionist who wrote the first autobiographical slave narrative.

First published in Great Britain in 1789, *The Interesting Narrative of the Life of Olaudah Equiano, or Gustavus Vassa the African*, written by himself, became a bestseller within Olaudah Equiano's lifetime, with nine English editions and one American as well as translations in Dutch, German, and Russian. *The Interesting Narrative* is considered the first autobiography of an African slave written entirely by his own hand. This makes Equiano the founder of the slave narrative, a form central to African American literature.

Equiano describes his abduction in Africa, his enslavement in the West Indies, and his manumission in Britain, as well as the legal insecurity and terror faced by both enslaved and free West Indian blacks. His autobiography greatly influenced the rhetorical strategies, content, and presentation of later nineteenth-century slave narratives, such as Frederick Douglass's *The Life and Times of Frederick Douglass* (1845).

Africa

Eritrea,

nation in the Horn of Africa, bordering the Red Sea, Sudan, Ethiopia, and Djibouti.

Eritrea is one of the world's newest nations and one of its poorest. Small and drought-prone, it boasts few natural resources. But Eritrea's Red Sea

A young Eritrean woman loads donkeys with casks of water. *CORBIS/Caroline Penn*

location has a rich cultural history, produced over centuries of migrations and trade, as well as a long history of warfare, fueled largely by the strategic interests of its neighbors and other foreign powers. Compared to other African countries, Eritrea has some of the oldest traditions of Islam and Christianity and one of the shortest experiences of European colonialism: less than 50 years under Italian rule. The region's colonial borders, however, took on new significance as soon as Italy was removed from power and Eritrea was handed over to Ethiopia.

In the face of Emperor Haile Selassie I's despotism, Eritrean nationalism developed quickly and endured through roughly a 30-year war for independence, ending when Eritrea became Africa's newest nation in 1993. Since then, the country has enjoyed a remarkable political consensus, and most agree that it is a society where ethnic distinctions matter less than differences in religion and lifestyle between the Christian agricultural highlands and the Islamic pastoral lowlands. Although during the war Eritrean freedom fighters never received much outside support, independent Eritrea soon became the darling of the international aid community, lauded for its honest government and economic pragmatism. In mid-1998, however, renewed tensions with Ethiopia threw into doubt Eritrea's future recovery.

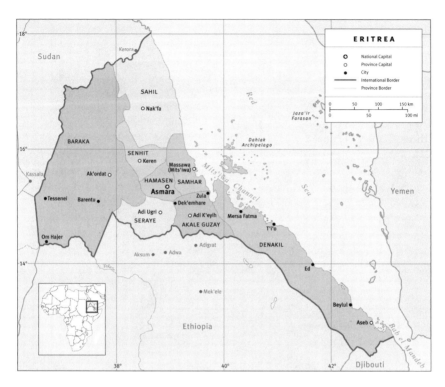

Africa

Eritrea (Ready Reference)

Official Name: State of Eritrea

Former Name: Eritrea Autonomous Region in Ethiopia

Area: 121,144 sq km (46,774 sq mi)

Location: Northeastern Africa; borders the Red Sea, Djibouti, Ethiopia, and the Sudan and includes the Dahlak Archipelago in the Red Sea

Capital: Asmara (population 400,000 [1993 estimate])

Population: 3,842,436 (1998 estimate)

Population Density: 28 per sq km (73 per sq mi); approximately 80 percent of Eritrea's population lives in rural areas.

Population Below Age 15: 43 percent (male 826,686; female 818,323 [1998 estimate])

Population Growth Rate: 3.39 percent (1998 estimate)

Total Fertility Rate: 5.9 children born per woman (1998 estimate)

Life Expectancy at Birth: 55.31 years (male 53.19 years; female 57.51 years [1998 estimate])

Infant Mortality Rate: 78.51 deaths per 1000 live births (1998 estimate)

Literacy Rate (age 15 and over who can read and write): Total population: 20 percent (1993 estimate)

Education: Few schools functioned during the war of independence that ended in 1993. Officially, seven years of primary education are now compulsory, with lower grades taught in African languages and higher grades in Arabic or English.

Languages: The main language groups are Tigrinya, Tigre, Kunama, Hedareb, Afar, Bilien, Saho, Nara and Rashaida. Arabic is also widely spoken, but English is used in secondary schools and universities.

Ethnic Groups: Ethnic Tigrinya, 50 percent; Tigre and Kunama, 40 percent; Afar, 4 percent; Saho (Red Sea coast dwellers), 3 percent; other, 3 percent

Religions: Muslim, Monophysite creed of the Ethiopian Orthodox church, Roman Catholic, and Protestant

Climate: The narrow coastal plain receives little rainfall and is extremely hot, with a mean annual temperature of 30° C (86° F). The mean annual temperature in Asmara, located in the plateau highlands, is 16° C (61° F). The plateau receives 400-500 mm (16-20 in) rainfall per year, while the hill country north and west of the core plateau generally receives less. The Denakil depression in the southeast has been the site of some of the highest temperatures recorded on earth, and receives practically no rain.

Land, Plants, and Animals: Eritrea's topography consists of four types of land surface. The Red Sea coastal plain widens to include the Denakil Desert in the south. The south central plateau highland is the most agriculturally fertile and densely populated part of the country. To the north of the highlands lies hill country, and to the west lie broad plains. These plains lie to the west of the Baraka River and north of the Setit River. The Mereb (or Gash), the Baraka, and the Anseba flow from the plateau west into Sudan, while the Falkat, Laba, and Alighede flow from the northern highlands to the Red Sea. Off the coast, more than a hundred small islands make up the Dahlak Archipelago.

Natural Resources: Eritrea's resources have supported a largely agricultural way of life. The nation possesses potentially valuable potash deposits and possibly gold, iron, and petroleum, but exploration and exploitation of its mineral resources were severely hindered by three decades of war. The Red Sea is rich in fish, but commercial fishing in Eritrea is also relatively underdeveloped.

Currency: The nafka

Gross Domestic Product (GDP): $2.2 billion (1996 estimate)

GDP per Capita: $600 (1996 estimate)

GDP Real Growth Rate: 6.8 percent (1996 estimate)

Primary Economic Activities: More than 80 percent of the population engage in agriculture that nonetheless produces only a quarter of the total gross domestic product. The country's small industrial sector is recovering from the war. Migrant labor is also an important source of income.

Primary Crops: Sorghum, lentils, vegetables, maize, cotton, tobacco, coffee, and sisal (for making rope); livestock includes goats; fish

Industries: Food processing, beverages, clothing, and textiles

Primary Exports: Livestock, sorghum, and textiles

Primary Imports: Processed goods, machinery, and petroleum products

Primary Trade Partners: Ethiopia, Italy, Saudi Arabia, United Kingdom, United States, and Yemen

Government: A May 1993 decree set up a National Assembly, a president, and a Council of Ministers. Isaias Afwerki was elected by the National Assembly and currently serves as president. The country's nine provinces are under the control of administrators appointed by the president. In addition to the People's Front for Democracy and Justice (formerly the Eritrean People's Liberation Front), other political organizations include the Democratic Movement for the Liberation of Eritrea and the Eritrean Liberation Front (ELF).

Latin America and the Caribbean

Esmeraldas,

province on the northern Ecuadorian coast with a large Afro-Ecuadorian population; site of an Afro-Ecuadorian maroon community.

The province of Esmeraldas, on the northern coast of Ecuador, constitutes the southern extremity of a vast black cultural area called the Pacific Lowlands, which includes the Pacific coasts of Colombia and of the province of Darién in Panama. Mangroves abound on the seashore and in the dense rain forest inland. Around 70 percent of the province's population is of African descent. The rest of the population is composed of Amerindians (the Cayapas or Chachis) and *mestizos* (persons with both European and Native American ancestry). The mestizos migrated principally from the Ecuadorian Andes, from the province of Manabí, and from southern Colombia. For the most part, they constitute the Esmeraldian elite.

North America

Essence,

African American women's magazine, founded in 1970, focusing on health, self-improvement, beauty, fashion, fiction, and issues of interest to contemporary, upscale black women.

In 1970 Clarence Smith and Edward Lewis published 50,000 copies of *Essence*, the first issue of a monthly magazine aimed at black women in the post-civil rights era. It was designed to build self-esteem, encourage a more powerful self-concept, and provide a platform for African American women to express themselves during a time when the black middle class was expanding rapidly. Much of the magazine's success is attributable to

Essence's affirmative portrayal of black women, and to its carefully crafted artwork and photographs.

Estebanico

(also known as Estevanico, Esteban, Estevanico the Moor, Esteban de Dorantes, Black Stephen) (b. 1503?, Azemmour, Morocco; d. 1539?, Hawikuh, N. Mex.), an Arab slave who became an explorer and guide in New Spain (Florida, Texas, and northern Mexico), he is allegedly the first black man to have set foot on the territory of the present-day United States.

Estebanico may have been captured by Portuguese slave traders in North Africa between 1513 and 1521, and later sold in Europe. He was bought by a Spanish explorer named Andrés de Dorantes, whom he accompanied on a 1528 expedition, led by conquistador Pánfilo de Narváez, to settle unknown territory in northern America. When they arrived in Florida, Narváez's group of some 300 men encountered many obstacles and were forced to split up in order to survive.

The legendary explorer Alvar Nuñez Cabeza de Vaca headed the group that included Estebanico. They traveled around the area now known as the Florida Panhandle and the Mississippi River, and harsh climatic conditions caused them to suffer shipwreck on what is now Galveston Island in Texas. Eventually, almost all of the expedition's members died from hunger, thirst, exhaustion, or disease, or in clashes with native tribes. In his account of the expedition, Cabeza de Vaca relates that there were only four survivors: himself, Alonso del Castillo Maldonado, Andrés de Dorantes, and Estebanico.

Estupiñán Bass, Nelson

(b. 1912, Esmeraldas, Ecuador), Afro-Ecuadorian poet and novelist; alongside Adalberto Ortiz and Antonio Preciado Bedoya, he is one of the prominent black writers of this South American country.

Primarily a novelist, Estupiñán Bass also wrote, particularly at the beginning of his career, collections of poems, including *Audición para el negro* and *Canto negro por la luz*, as well as a few plays.

Beyond his importance as a figure in Afro-Esmeraldian literature, Estupiñán Bass is garnering increasing recognition as a major Ecuadorian author. Among other national literary prizes, he received the prestigious Premio Eugenio Espejo from the Casa de la Cultura Ecuatoriana in 1993.

His first novel, *Cuando los guayancanes florecían* (When the Guayacans Were in Bloom), is the best known of the nine novels he has written to date. The narratives of his novels are characterized by a thematic tension between two different, and in some ways opposed, aims: on the one hand he strives to celebrate blackness, Afro-Esmeraldian identity, and the respectability of Afro-Esmeraldian cultural traditions in particular. On the other hand he downplays race, making it secondary to class.

Africa

Ethiopia,

a country in the Horn of Africa bordering Eritrea, Djibouti, Kenya, Somalia, and Sudan.

The land we now know as Ethiopia witnessed the birth of modern humanity more than 100,000 years ago, and it was home to some of Africa's most ancient and advanced civilizations. Indeed, Ethiopia is one of the oldest nations on earth. For centuries the people of Ethiopia's highlands have maintained a rich cultural legacy, including a literary tradition dating from more than 2000 years ago and a form of Christianity dating from the time of the Roman Empire. Over the centuries many of the country's people came to practice Islam, and by the twentieth century, Ethiopia incorporated one of the most ethnically and culturally diverse populations in Africa. From the 1960s to the early 1990s Ethiopia suffered a long economic decline, famine, and civil warfare, first under an autocratic emperor and later under a brutal socialist military government. In the late 1990s Ethiopia faced the challenge of overcoming ethnic strife and years of economic mismanagement to recover the prosperity and cultural richness it once enjoyed.

Africa

Ethiopia (Ready Reference)

Official Name: Federal Democratic Republic of Ethiopia

Area: 1,130,000 sq km (436,300 sq mi)

Location: Eastern Africa; bounded by Eritrea, Djibouti, Somalia, Kenya, and the Sudan

Capital: Addis Ababa (population 2,200,186 [1993 estimate])

Population: 58,390,351 (1998 estimate)

Population Density: 51 persons per sq km (133 persons per sq mi)

Population Below Age 15: 46 percent (male 13,468,783; female 13,398,500 [1998 estimate])

Population Growth Rate: 2.2 percent (1998 estimate)

Total Fertility Rate: 6.88 children born per woman (1998 estimate)

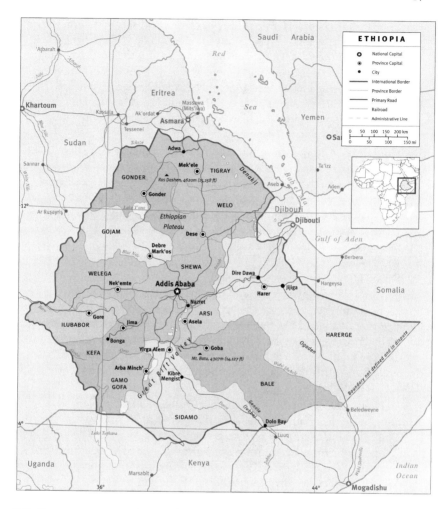

Life Expectancy at Birth: Total population: 40.8 years (male 39.7 years; female 42 years [1998 estimate])

Infant Mortality Rate: 125.6 deaths per 1000 live births (1998 estimate)

Literacy Rate (age 15 and over who can read and write): Total population: 35.5 percent (male 45.5 percent; female 25.3 percent [1995 estimate])

Education: Free education exists from primary school through the college level, but regular school facilities are available to only about one-third of the children of school age. In the early 1990s about 2.8 million students attended primary and secondary schools run by the government and religious groups. Addis Ababa University (1950) has branches in several locations.

Languages: Amharic is the official language; Tigrinya, Orominga, Guaraginga, Somali, Arabic, and English are also spoken.

Ethnic Groups: The Amhara, a highland people partly of Semitic origin, and the related Tigreans constitute about 32 percent of the total population. The Oromo people, living mainly in central and southwestern Ethiopia, constitute about 40 percent of the population. The Shangalla, a people found in the western part of the country from the border of Eritrea to Lake Turkana, constitute about 6 percent of the population. The Somali, who live in the east and southeast, notably in the Ogaden region, are approximately equal in number to the Shangalla. The Denakil inhabit the semidesert plains east of the highlands. The non-indigenous population includes Yemenis, Indians, Armenians, and Greeks.

Religions: About 40 percent of the people of Ethiopia are Christians, many from the Ethiopian Orthodox Union Church, an autonomous Christian sect headed by a patriarch and closely related to the Coptic church of Egypt. Christianity is predominant in the north; all the southern regions have Muslim majorities, who represent about 45 percent of the country's population. The south also contains large numbers of animists. The Falashas, who practice a type of Judaism that probably dates back to contact with early Arabian Jews, were airlifted to Israel in 1991 during Ethiopia's civil war.

Climate: The principal rainy season occurs between mid-June and September, followed by a dry season that may be interrupted in February or March by a short rainy season. The tropical zone has an average annual temperature of about 27° C (about 80° F) and receives less than about 510 mm (about 20 in) of rain annually. The subtropical zone, which includes most of the highland plateau, has an average temperature of about 22° C (about 72° F) with an annual rainfall ranging from about 510 to 1530 mm (about 20 to 60 in).

Land, Plants, and Animals: The Ethiopian Plateau, a high table land covering more than half the total area of the country, is split by the Great Rift Valley. In the north, the plateau is cut by many rivers and deep valleys, and capped by mountains in the region surrounding Lake T'ana (the lake in which the Blue Nile rises). The northeastern edges of the plateau are marked by steep escarpments, which drop to the sun-baked coastal plain and the Denakil Desert. Along the western fringe the plateau descends gradually to the desert of Sudan. Along the southern and southwestern limits, the plateau lowers toward Lake Turkana (formerly called Lake Rudolf). The lower areas of the tropical zone have sparse vegetation, but in the valleys and ravines almost every form of African vegetation grows profusely. Afro-alpine vegetation is found on the highest slopes. The giraffe, leopard, hippopotamus, lion, elephant, antelope, and rhinoceros are native to most parts of the country. The lynx, jackal, hyena, and various species of monkey are also common. Birds of prey include the eagle, hawk, and vulture. Heron, parrot, and such game birds as the snipe, partridge, teal, pigeon, and bustard are found in abundance. Among the many varieties of insects are the locust and tsetse fly.

Natural Resources: The resources of Ethiopia are primarily agricultural. The plateau area is fertile and largely undeveloped. The wide range of soils, climate, and elevations permits the production of a diversified range of agricultural commodities. A variety of mineral deposits exist and have been commercially exploited.

Currency: The birr

Gross Domestic Product (GDP): $29 billion (1997 estimate)

GDP per Capita: $530 (1997 estimate)

GDP Real Growth Rate: 5 percent (1997 estimate)

Primary Economic Activities: The economy of Ethiopia remains heavily dependent on the earnings of the agricultural sector. Participation by most of the people in the monetary economy is limited; much trading is conducted by barter in local markets. Traditional agriculture, including livestock raising, is the most characteristic form of Ethiopian economic activity. Commercial estates, which are run by the government, supply coffee, cotton, sugar, fruit, and vegetables to the nation's processing industries and for export. Coffee is Ethiopia's most important commodity.

Primary Crops: Coffee, cotton, sugar, fruit, vegetables, pulses (chickpeas, lentils, haricot beans), oilseeds, and cereal grains; livestock includes cattle, sheep, goats, poultry, horses, mules, donkeys, and camels.

Industries: Food processing, beverages, textiles, chemicals, metal processing, and cement

Primary Exports: Coffee, leather products, and gold

Primary Imports: Capital goods, consumer goods, and fuel

Primary Trade Partners: Germany, Japan, Saudi Arabia, France, Italy, and United States

Government: Ethiopia is a federal republic. According to the 1994 constitution, the head of state is the president, currently Negasso Gidada, who is nominated by the legislative body, the Council of People's Representatives. A president may not serve more than two six-year terms. The council also nominates a prime minister from among its members, a position currently held by Meles Zenawi, who is the chief executive and heads a Council of Ministers made up of representatives from a coalition of parties constituting a majority in the legislature. The Council of People's Representatives consists of a maximum of 550 directly elected members; at least 20 of these representatives must be members of minority ethnic groups.

Latin America and the Caribbean

Etienne, Franck (Franketienne)

(b. April 12, 1936, Port-au-Prince, Haiti), poet, playwright, novelist, teacher, and politician whose strikingly original works in both Creole and French mark him as a key figure in contemporary Haitian literature.

Born to a black mother and a white father, Franketienne (this is the Creolized spelling of his name that he adopted in 1972) grew up in one of Port-au-Prince's poorer neighborhoods. At school, he was called *blanc manant* (white peasant), a derogatory nickname he later embraced.

Franketienne's work reflects his in-between status in Haitian society.

He writes about the black bourgeoisie in the novel *Mur à crever* (1968), but also represents rural life in Haiti, as in *Dézafi* (1975), one of the first novels ever written in Creole. His poetry also bears the mark of his desire to exist in two worlds simultaneously. In his writing as well as in his painting, inspired in part by the work of Hieronymus Bosch, images of putrefaction abound. One of the few Haitian writers who did not go into exile during the reign of the Duvaliers, Franketienne expressed his horror at Haiti's self-destruction through the metaphorical description of the island as a body plagued by leprosy, wasting away in its own filth. This imagery appears most strikingly in the nightmarish *Fleurs d' insommnie* (1986), published just after Jean-Claude Duvalier's removal from office. Although he is considered a poetic innovator, Franketienne's importance lies perhaps more in his uncompromising resistance to the Duvaliers and in his willingness to be a voice of the Haitian people when they had none.

Africa

Euba, Akin

(b. April 28, 1935, Lagos, Nigeria), Nigerian composer whose classical works combine elements of European and Yoruba music.

In 1972 Akin Euba's *Dirges* was premiered at the Munich Olympic Games, a tribute to his achievement in synthesizing Western and African musical traditions. Throughout his career Euba has striven to create African classical music that is accessible to Africans and non-Africans alike.

Europe

Europe,

a subcontinent lying directly across the Mediterranean Sea from Africa where Africans and people of African descent have had a presence since ancient times.

Many blacks did land on the shores of Europe, particularly after the rise of the trans-Atlantic slave trade in the sixteenth century. Though most blacks in Europe worked as slaves or paid servants during the early modern period, a few blacks and people of African descent achieved renown as artists and scholars. During the early twentieth century Europe was the site of a remarkable intellectual, political, and artistic ferment among Africans and people of African descent that prompted such movements as Pan-Africanism and Négritude. Since the 1950s a wave of black immigration has transformed many European nations and given rise to a new population of Afro-Europeans.

Three young African-French children stand before a wall in Paris. France's black population grew quickly in the 1980s and 1990s as immigrants from Africa and the West Indies joined hundreds of thousands of people of African descent who had lived there for generations. CORBIS/OWEN FRANKEN

At a ceremony held in 1965 in the Basilica of St. Peter in Rome, Pope Paul VI, assisted by African and European clergy, officiates at the beatification of new African saints. CORBIS/David Lees

Evans, Mari E.

(b. July 16, 1923, Toledo, Ohio), African American poet and teacher.

Mari Evans lost her mother at age seven and was raised by her father, an uphol-sterer, whom she credits with nurturing her love of writing. She attended the University of Toledo. Langston Hughes's works influenced her considerably from an early age, and Hughes himself later became a friend and mentor.

A "blues philosopher" who believes that a poet must be politically engaged, Evans became a respected figure in the Black Arts Movement. Her work focuses on such wide-ranging themes as black enslavement and poverty in the United States, the oppression blacks share with other Third World peoples, and failed relationships between black men and women. In addition, it celebrates blackness, Africa, and the struggles of the Civil Rights Movement. Her work has been published in more than 200 anthologies, and among her best-known works are *I Am a Black Woman* (1970) and an edition of collected essays, *Black Women Writers* (1950–1980): *A Critical Evaluation* (1984). She has also authored several works for children.

From 1968 to 1973 Evans created and hosted a weekly television pro-gram, *The Black Experience*, in Indianapolis. She also adapted Zora Neale Hurston's *Their Eyes Were Watching God* as a musical, *Eyes* (1979). Evans has held numerous teaching posts at universities, including Purdue, Northwestern, Cornell, and Indiana. Among many honors and awards, she received an honorary doctorate in 1979 from Marian College and won a National Endowment for the Arts Creative Writing Award in 1981. Evans is divorced and has two sons, and lives in Indianapolis.

Evers, Medgar Wylie

(b. July 2, 1925, Decatur, Miss.; d. June 12, 1963, Jackson, Miss.), African American civil rights leader whose assassination for his work as field secretary for the National Association for the Advancement of Colored People (NAACP) in Mississippi galvanized the Civil Rights Movement.

As a representative of the NAACP, Medgar Evers worked for the most estab-lished and in some ways most conservative African American membership organization. He was, by all accounts, a hardworking, thoughtful, and some-what quiet man. Yet the work he did was groundbreaking, even radical, in that he risked and eventually lost his life bringing news of his state's violent white supremacy to nationwide attention. When Evers was assassinated in his front yard by Byron de la Beckwith, a white racist, he became a symbol of the brutality with which the old South resisted the Civil Rights Movement.

Raised in a small central Mississippi town, Evers absorbed his parents' work ethic and strong religious values early. Friends, including his brother, Charles, remember him as a serious child with an air of maturity about him. At age 17 he left school to serve in the army during World War II, where, according to writer Adam Nossiter, his experience fighting the supremely racist Nazis made a lasting impression on him. After the war, Evers got his high school diploma and immediately entered Alcorn A&M College, where he played football, ran track, edited the campus newspaper, and sang in the choir.

Upon graduation Evers took a job with Magnolia Mutual Insurance, one of Mississippi's few black-owned businesses. Through his employer, he became involved with the NAACP, selling memberships at the same time that he was selling insurance policies. Despite its moderate, systematic approach, the NAACP was still considered a radical organization by many in Mississippi; it was a state in which, as Nossiter writes, the organization had essentially given up hope. Too likely to be victims of harassment, assault, or murder for any kind of political action, blacks in Mississippi's Delta region were often afraid even to talk about the NAACP.

In 1954, when the national organization decided to hire field secretaries in the Deep South, Evers moved to Jackson, the state capital, and went to work full-time for the NAACP. He had two main roles—to recruit and enroll new members, and to investigate and publicize the racist terrorism experienced by African Americans. It was a dangerous job. Evers was followed, mocked, threatened, and beaten while he traveled throughout Mississippi—the state that had seen more lynchings than any other in the country. Organizations like the White Citizens' Councils and the State Sovereignty Committee spied on him. In May 1963, a month before Evers was murdered, someone threw a bomb into his garage.

Not only did Evers continue the NAACP's long-standing research on lynching, he also worked on the legal front, filing petitions and organizing protests against the Jim Crow segregation that still made it impossible for African Americans to go to movie theaters, eat in restaurants, or make use of public libraries, parks, and pools. Throughout the spring of 1963 he was the leader of a series of boycotts, meetings, and public appearances that were designed to bring Mississippi out of its racist past.

Just before midnight on June 11, 1963, when Evers was arriving home, Beckwith shot him in the back; Evers died a few minutes later. In two separate trials in 1963 and 1964, all-white juries could not decide Beckwith's fate. Free for more than 30 years after committing murder, Beckwith was finally convicted and jailed for the crime in 1994.

North America

Evers-Williams, Myrlie

(b. 1933, Vicksburg, Miss.), African American civil rights activist, first woman chair person of the National Association for the Advancement of Colored People (NAACP).

Myrlie Evers-Williams was raised by her grandmother, McCain Beasley, and her aunt, Myrlie Beasley Polk. She married civil rights activist Medgar Evers in 1951, and together they worked for the NAACP to end discrimination and segregation in Mississippi. Medgar Evers was assassinated in 1963 by the white supremacist Byron de la Beckwith.

After her husband's death, Evers-Williams moved her family to California, where she continued to work for the NAACP by speaking publicly about her struggles for black equality. In 1987 she became the first black woman to serve as commissioner on the Los Angeles Board of Public Works. She was elected vice-chairperson of the NAACP in 1994, and in 1995 became the first woman chairperson. In 1998 Julian Bond succeeded Evers-Williams as chair of the NAACP. With William Peters, she co-authored *For Us, the Living* (1967).

Africa

Evora, Cesaria

(b. 1941, Mindelo, Cape Verde), internationally renowned Cape Verdean singer.

One of seven children, Cesaria Evora was born into a musical family, including not only her violinist father, who died when she was a child, but also her uncle Francisco Xavier da Cruz, a songwriter whose songs she has recorded. Evora herself was singing in bars in Mindelo by age 16.

Evora sings in Criuolo, a Creole derived from Portuguese and African languages. She is most famous for singing *morna*, which roughly translates to "songs of mourning." As with many other kinds of folk music, *morna* songs are handed down from generation to generation, and trace dominant themes in a people's history. Many *morna* songs, for example, lament Cape Verdeans' losses to the slave trade and emigration. Often accompanied by acoustic guitars, violins, accordions, and *cavaquinho*, a four-string guitar or ukulele, Evora's vocals have been described as a cross between Edith Piaf and American jazz singer Billie Holiday.

Evora's career grew after she made a recording for national radio at age 20. She received offers from bars and nightclubs throughout the ten Cape Verdean Islands, and soon became known as the "queen of *morna*." Although several tapes of her music traveled to Portugal and the Netherlands, she never performed outside Cape Verde. Evora once recalled, "I used to sing for tourists and for the ships when they would come here. That's why I always thought that maybe if I made it, people from different countries would love my music." By the 1970s, however, she quit recording and performing, claiming that she was not "making any money."

Evora emerged from retirement in 1985 to contribute two songs to an album of Cape Verdean women's music. Soon after, the Cape Verdean concert promoter Jose da Silva convinced her to come to France to record. There she became known as the "barefoot diva," because she regularly performs shoeless. Whether Evora's habit is a symbol of her empathy for Cape Verde's poor women and children (as has been claimed) or simply a personal preference, the nickname became the title of her first album, *La Diva aux Pieds Nus* (1988). After *Distino di Belita* (1990) and *Mar Azul* (1991), Evora made her first international hit at age 51 with *Miss Perfumado* (1992), which sold 200,000 copies.

Evora undertook a tour of the United States in 1995 in support of that year's release, *Cesaria Evora*, which was a gold record in France and reached number seven on Portugal's charts. Her popular success has been reinforced by critical and peer recognition. In 1996 *Cesaria Evora* was nominated for a Grammy Award in the United States as best world music album. In addition, at the 1997 KORA All Africa Music Awards, Evora received the Judges Merit Award, Best Artist from West Africa Award, and Best African Album. A regular performer at world music festivals, Evora has opened for such pop acts as Natalie Merchant and counts pop star Madonna as a fan.

Even after reaching global stardom, Evora has chosen to remain in Cape Verde with her mother and her children and grandchildren (thrice divorced, she has vowed never to marry again). "I wasn't astonished by Europe," she has said, "and I was never that impressed by the speed and grandeur of modern America. I only regret my success has taken so long to achieve."

North America

Ewing, Patrick

(b. August 5, 1962, Kingston, Jamaica), African American professional basketball player who became a center for the New York Knicks in 1985 and who was a member of the United States men's basketball team that won a Gold Medal at the 1992 Summer Olympic Games.

Patrick Ewing played cricket and soccer as a youngster in Jamaica before moving in 1975 to Cambridge, Massachusetts, where he first played basketball. His first organized games took place at the Achievement School, a remedial center for junior high students where Ewing worked on his language skills. At Rindge and Latin High School, where Ewing reached his full height of seven feet, he starred as the basketball team's center, leading the team to three consecutive state championships. By his senior year Ewing's basketball record had rendered him the most sought-after college recruit in the country. He chose to attend Georgetown University in part because of the notable reputation of its basketball coach, John Thompson.

In his freshman year Ewing led Georgetown to the 1982 National Collegiate Athletic Association (NCAA) championship game. In the 1983–1984 season the team won the NCAA championship for the first time, and Ewing was named the tournament's Most Valuable Player. That summer he played on the U.S. Olympic basketball team, which won the Gold Medal. The following year, when Georgetown again reached the NCAA finals, the National Association of Basketball Coaches named Ewing the college player of the year.

In the NBA draft of college players in 1985, Ewing was the first player chosen. He signed a contract with the New York Knicks for $1.7 million, at the time the highest salary ever paid to an NBA rookie. Although injuries forced Ewing to miss 51 games in his first two years with the Knicks, he was named rookie of the year in 1986 and led all first-year players in scoring and rebounding. In 1988–1989 the Knicks won the NBA's Atlantic Division for the first time in 18 years. In 1991–1992 Ewing was named to the second team of the NBA's All-League and All-Defensive Teams. In 1992 Ewing earned a Gold Medal at the Summer Olympic Games as a member of the first U.S. Olympic basketball team to allow NBA players.

North America

Exodusters,

African Americans who fled the post-Reconstruction South for the promise of freedom in Kansas.

Throughout the spring of 1879, the banks of the Mississippi River were crowded with hundreds of black families awaiting the steam ships that would take them north to St. Louis, Missouri. Many had seen posters promising free transportation to the farmland of Kansas, where they could escape the South's poverty and terrorism. The Exodusters—so-called for their participation in the Kansas Fever Exodus of 1879—were refugees resolved to make a better life for themselves.

The South the Exodusters left behind was increasingly treacherous. Following emancipation in 1865, the Reconstruction period increased African Americans' political and economic power. But white Southerners fought back with a campaign they called "redemption," attempting to overturn the pro-black liberal Republican legislation of the Reconstruction era. Racist groups such as the White League and the Ku Klux Klan mounted a campaign of murder and terrorism designed to destroy black political activism. Democrats stole elections through blatant ballot stuffing and by intimidating or assaulting blacks who attempted to vote. Former slave owners—who still controlled the land, tools, livestock, cotton gins, and markets—kept nearly all black tenant farmers in an unending state of severe poverty. Faced with these conditions, many African Americans considered migration out of the South. For years, a steady stream of blacks from the border states of Tennessee, Kentucky, and Missouri had formed their own colonies in Kansas, attracted by the state's abundant land, fertile soil, and abolitionist history. By the time the 1879 Louisiana Constitutional Convention declared that the issue of suffrage should be one of "states' rights"—effectively denying blacks the vote—thousands of African Americans had had enough. Fearful of a return to slavery, some 6000 people gathered their belongings and fled in a matter of weeks.

At St. Louis, it became clear that the rumors of free passage to Kansas were false. The Exodusters were stranded. Though ridiculed for their credulity, the Exodusters resisted returning to the South. "I'd sooner starve here," one woman told a reporter. As historian Nell Painter points out, it was "terrorism and poverty," not swindlers and pipe dreams, that drove the Kansas Fever Exodus. Many Exodusters saw themselves as modern versions of the Israelites, leaving persecution behind as they headed for a promised land. Some called Kansas "the Negro Canaan."

They were aided in their migration by a group of clergymen from the black churches of St. Louis, along with various Eastern philanthropists, who had formed an organization called the Colored Relief Board soon after the refugees began arriving. With the Kansas Freedmen's Aid Society, the board helped more than 5000 Exodusters reach Kansas from St. Louis. Around 4000 arrived later from Texas. Altogether, nearly 15,000 African Americans came to Kansas throughout 1879 and 1880. Although most remained impoverished, they fared better economically than they would have in the South. About three-quarters of the families came to own their own homes. "All in all," Painter writes, "the Exodus to Kansas was a qualified but real success."

Explorers in Africa Before 1500:

foreigners who traveled to sub-Saharan Africa before 1500 to investigate its geography and peoples.

Outsiders have remained in contact with the peoples of Africa since the first modern humans began trickling out of the continent. Desert nomads have crossed the Sahara and coastal traders have crossed the narrow Strait of Mandeb for thousands of years. From the beginnings of history, the Mediterranean Sea facilitated continuous contact between North Africa and the peoples of Europe and the Middle East. Certainly trade connections existed between Egypt and the peoples of sub-Saharan Africa by the second millennium B.C.E., and Carthaginians and Asian peoples may have been trading along the coasts of Africa more than 2000 years ago. However, none of these ancient traders or explorers left written accounts that survive today, so we know little about them and nothing of what they saw during their travels.

Our earliest surviving accounts of sub-Saharan Africa come from ancient Greek authors. Herodotus of Halicarnassus wrote extensively about Africa. It was during his travels to Egypt and Libya in the middle of the fifth century B.C.E., that Herodotus learned about Africa. He was highly knowledgeable about the Nile as far south as Gondokoro. Some of his work was based on the travels of the Egyptian pharaoh Necho II, who ruled from about 610 to 594 B.C.E.

Early European knowledge of East Africa came from two sources: the *Periplus of the Erythraean Sea*, written during the first century C.E. by an

This European map of Africa was made in 1679. *CORBIS/Anthony Bannister; ABPL*

anonymous Greek trader who lived in Egypt, and *Ptolemy's Geography*, probably written in the second century C.E.

Between 1000 and 1500 C.E., Berber Ibadi traders of North Africa traveled south across the Sahara. Other Arabs and North Africans traveled south of the Sahara on a religious mission to convert sub-Saharan Africans to Islam. Traders from the Arabian Peninsula also made regular journeys to coastal East Africa. Many of these traders settled in coastal communities, where they contributed to the emerging Swahili culture.

In the fourteenth century, Ibn Battutah, a North African who explored out of curiosity, traveled extensively throughout North Africa, Egypt, and East Africa, and crossed the Sahara to the West African kingdom of Mali, including the city of Tombouctou (Timbuktu). Descriptions of his journeys were published in the *Rihlah* (Travels), which greatly expanded knowledge of African geography in the Muslim and Western worlds.

Chinese explorers also traveled to Africa at an early date. Chinese writings include information on East Africa, mainly gathered from Muslim traders, as early as the eighth century C.E. Chinese rulers began sending trading expeditions across the Indian Ocean during the fifteenth century, and two of these expeditions reached the Horn of Africa, one in 1417–1419, the other in 1421–1422. Fei Hsin, an officer who participated in these voyages, wrote an account of his observations that survives today.

Scottish explorer and medical missionary David Livingstone reads the Bible to some of his African workers in an engraving dating from 1875.
CORBIS/Bettmann

By the middle of the fifteenth century, Chinese knowledge of Africa exceeded that of Europeans.

Beginning in the fifteenth century, Portugal became the first European nation to undertake an extensive investigation of Africa. Prince Henry (later known as Prince Henry the Navigator) spearheaded the explorations. Shortly after 1419, Henry established a research institute to gather information about Africa. Besides his desire for increased trade and for exploration, he was motivated by a dream of forming a Christian union with the legendary Prester John of Africa. In addition, he intended to divert the Muslim-dominated overland gold trade by sending Portuguese ships to the west coast of Africa. By the 1480s Africa's west coast was well known to the Portuguese.

The Portuguese also sought a greater share of the spice trade, which reached Europe via the Indian Ocean and the Mediterranean Sea. Pedro da Covilhã explored the east coast of Africa during the late 1480s. The knowledge he gathered may have aided the voyage of Vasco da Gama, who in 1497–1498 became the first known European to sail around the Cape of Good Hope to the Indian Ocean. Though Portuguese government officials remained predominantly on the coast, Portuguese clergy, especially the Jesuits, traveled inland to seek converts to Catholicism. Portuguese missionaries reached as far as Angola, the kingdom of Monomotapa (also known as Munhumutapa) in present-day Zimbabwe, and Ethiopia.

These Portuguese explorers connected the African coast with Europe and the rest of the world. Their explorations changed the course of African history and paved the way for later explorers. They also paved the way for the continent's exploitation and the beginnings of the brutal slave trade.

Africa

Explorers in Africa, 1500 to 1800:

foreigners who traveled to sub-Saharan Africa between 1500 and 1800 to investigate its geography and peoples.

Earlier explorers had essentially finished mapping the African coast by 1514. The interior posed a far more formidable obstacle, however. During the period between 1500 and 1800, Europeans accumulated knowledge intermittently and established few outposts beyond coastal areas.

One of the first Europeans to explore inland Africa was Leo Africanus, who was born in Granada, Spain, and lived there until 1492, when Spain expelled all Muslims. He then traveled with his parents to Morocco. In about 1507 he began traveling around North and Central Africa, where he served as a diplomat. He visited Tombouctou (Timbuktu) twice. After his second visit there, he traveled to Egypt via the Bornu Kingdom and Lake Chad. He also visited present-day Sudan twice between 1509 and 1513, and his observations provided the basis for European knowledge of the region until well into the nineteenth century. After his African travels, Leo Africanus settled for a time in Rome, Italy, where he published *Navigationi et viaggi* (1550), subsequently translated into English as *A Geographic History of Africa* (1600).

The Portuguese exploration of Africa, which began in the fifteenth century, continued in the sixteenth. But their inland explorations remained modest in comparison to their earlier coastal discoveries. The Portuguese Antonio Fernandes explored present-day southern Zimbabwe, where he visited the gold mines of Monomatapa (or Munhumutapa) between 1511 and 1514. In 1616 Gaspar Bocarro traveled as far as Tete on the Zambezi River. During the late eighteenth century, the Portuguese established bases on the Zambezi, first at Sena, then at Tete, hoping to control trade from these locations. In 1793 Alexandre da Silva Teixeira reached the Luval people of present-day Zambia. In 1798 Francisco José de Lacerda journeyed from Tete to the court of the Kazembe on Lake Mweru on the southeastern border of present-day Congo-Kinshasa.

The Portuguese also gained considerable knowledge about Ethiopia, a Christian empire that they initially believed to be the legacy of the legendary Prester John. Francisco Alvarez, a member of a Portuguese embassy to the court of Ethiopian emperor Lebna Dengel, provided descriptions of Ethiopia that greatly increased European knowledge of that country, as did Jesuits such as Pedro Páez (who also discovered the source of the Blue Nile) and António Fernandes. In addition, the Frenchman Charles Poncet visited the Ethiopian court at Gonder in about 1699.

The travels and discoveries of the Portuguese generated interest in other European nations, which began to send their own expeditions to Africa. Portuguese power gradually declined during the sixteenth and seventeenth centuries, and after 1600, British, Dutch, and French traders began to seize control of Portuguese trading coasts, particularly in West Africa. In 1652 the Dutch established the first permanent European post at the Cape of Good Hope in present-day South Africa. By the early 1700s Dutch colonists had begun to explore the region's interior. In West Africa, British traders had traveled as far as the Barracuda Falls by 1651, and by 1659 Cornelius Hoges had reached Bambuk in present-day eastern Senegal. During the seventeenth century, the French sailed up the Senegal River as far as Malam. In 1700 the French established a fort in the region.

The British adventurer James Bruce published *Travels to Discover the Source of the Nile* (1790), which added insight to European knowledge of Africa and also sparked interest in Africa among Europeans, especially in London and Paris. This popularity led to the establishment in London in 1788 of the Association for Promoting the Discovery of the Interior Parts of Africa, also called the African Association. It was this organization that supported James Watt and Matthew Winterbottom in their travels to Fouta Djallon and the Rio Nunez in present-day Guinea. In 1796 Mungo Park traveled up the Niger River and arrived at Ségou in present-day Mali.

In the final 25 years of the eighteenth century, travel books dealing with Africa attracted an enthusiastic audience. The nature of exploration would change, however, in the nineteenth century. Although many nineteenth-century explorers came as Christian missionaries, the information they gained on their travels contributed to the colonization of Africa.

Africa
_____

Explorers in Africa Since 1800,

foreigners who traveled to sub-Saharan Africa after 1800 to investigate its geography and peoples.

Building on the work of earlier explorers, European explorers of Africa after 1800 provided information used by European powers to carry out their colonization of the continent. By crisscrossing the vast continent's interior, nineteenth-century explorers, many of them Christian missionaries, contributed far more to Western knowledge of Africa and its peoples than earlier explorers had. These Europeans discovered that beyond the African coast lay a continent much more hospitable than their legends and myths of the "dark continent" had suggested.

European exploration of Africa during the nineteenth century had three main goals: (1) the elimination of the slave trade, (2) the imposition of "legitimate" commerce, and (3) the spread of Christianity among Africans. This new phase of exploration began at the end of the eighteenth century. The Association for Promoting the Discovery of the Interior Parts of Africa—founded in 1788 by a small group of wealthy Englishmen and popularly called the African Association—first supported the exploration of North and West Africa. The association funded the efforts by Scotsman Mungo Park to travel to the upper Niger River during the 1790s. Park discovered that the river flowed eastward, not westward as Leo Africanus had incorrectly asserted.

Some of the African Association's members convinced the British government that the exploration of Africa was an endeavor worthy of government support, and it was in the employ of the British that Park undertook another—but fatal—expedition in 1805 to chart the course of

French explorer Pierre Savorgnan de Brazza founded the colony of Moyen-Congo, present-day Republic of Congo, in 1880. *CORBIS/Leonard de Selva*

the Niger. The British government also funded famed explorers Maj. Dixon Denham and his two fellow travelers, Lieut. Hugh Clapperton and surgeon Walter Oudney, who crossed the Sahara after visiting Bornu and Hausaland from 1823 to 1825. The brothers John and Richard Lander, who charted the course of the lower Niger in 1830, were funded by the British, as was the German Heinrich Barth, who charted the central and western Sudan from 1850 to 1855.

The quintessential Christian missionary explorer was perhaps David Livingstone, who in 1841 traveled to South Africa as a member of the London Missionary Society. In 1853 Livingstone traveled from the south to Victoria

Falls and from there west to Luanda. He then turned to the east and found the mouth of the Zambezi River. Livingstone's subsequent book, *Missionary Travels and Researches*, went through nine editions in England and transformed public opinion of the continent.

Britain's Royal Geographical Society, formed in 1830, took the place of the African Association. Unlike its predecessor, it received government funding. Its officers had access to high-placed government officials, and in 1858, it arranged for Livingstone to undertake an expedition up the Zambezi as British consul in charge. After his expedition stalled at the Quebrabasa Falls, Livingstone traveled up the Shire River, attempting to reach the African interior, again without success. He may have taken consolation in the discovery of Lake Malawi. Livingstone continued his exploration at his own expense (his travel books had made him a fortune), and he spent his final years, from 1867 to 1873, in the upper reaches of the Congo.

Early in the nineteenth century, France—which had been active in the slave trade and had sent explorers up the Senegal in the eighteenth century—contributed little to the exploration of Africa. The only journey of note was undertaken by René Caillié, who went from Rio Nunez to Tombouctou (Timbuktu) and across the Sahara to Tangier. In contrast to the French, Germans and German speakers contributed much to European knowledge of Africa, many working with British support.

German missionaries combed East Africa in their search for converts. Missionaries Johannes Rebmann, Johann Ludwig Krapf, and J. J. Erhardt were the first Europeans to see Mount Kilimanjaro and Mount Kenya. Gerhard Rohlfs traveled extensively in the Sahara. Gustav Nachtigal built on the work of Rohlfs. Between 1870 and 1874, Nachtigal explored present-day Sudan and Chad. During the scramble for Africa, Nachtigal played a key role in establishing German colonies. Through threats and manipulation, he secured treaties in 1884 with Mlapa III, the chief of Togoville, Togo, and with the Duala people of Cameroon, that provided the basis for German colonial claims to those regions. Later that year, Nachtigal signed a treaty establishing an additional colony in what is currently Namibia.

As European colonial powers completed their conquest of most of the continent during the 1890s and the early twentieth century, their scouts and agents surveyed the territory to be subdued. Mary Kingsley, one the few European women to explore the continent, toured the interior of present-day Gabon during the 1890s. By about 1914 virtually the entire continent had been surveyed by the representatives of European governments.

It is also important to remember that most, if not all, European explorers relied on Africans as soldiers, guides, translators, porters, cooks, and personal servants. Given the possible hazards in Africa—such as hostile animals, Africans seeking to defend themselves against intruders, rough terrain, and disabling diseases—the success of a European explorer's journey depended on the ability and skill of his African employees. Although they faced the same difficulties as their famous employers, their names, sadly, are largely lost to us today.

Exú

(known as Exú in Brazil, and as Elegbara or Elegguá in Cuba and the United States), one of the major *orisha*, or Yoruba deities.

Exú, or Elegguá, is regarded differently in the Cuban tradition than he is in Brazil. The trickster deity of the crossroads, in Cuba, Elegguá is regarded as temperamental, but helpfully benign if properly propitiated with candies, toys, and children's parties. In Brazil, Exú is regarded as extremely dangerous, and special propitiatory ceremonies are held several hours before major rituals to send him away so that he will not disrupt the ritual.

Eyadéma, Gnassingbé

(b. 1936, in Pya, Togo), president of Togo (1967-).

In power for 32 years, General Eyadéma has outlasted all other African leaders. He owes his longevity both to a system of patronage that earned the support of important segments of Togolese society and to personal control over the country's military, which has consistently and often violently repressed political opposition.

According to official sources, Eyadéma was born on December 27, 1936, as Étienne Gnassingbé, to Kabré peasants. He completed six years of school before enlisting in the French army in 1953, like other poor young Kabré. He served in Dahomey, Indochina, Algeria, and Niger. Upon his discharge in 1962 he returned to Togo, as did over 600 other mostly Kabré French veterans.

When Togo's then president, Sylvanus Olympio, refused to enlarge Togo's 150-man army to accommodate these veterans, a number of them, including Gnassingbé, staged West Africa's first military coup in January 1963, during which Olympio was killed. After the killing, Gnassingbé took Eyadéma, a Kabré word implying courage, as his surname. He claims that Olympio was firing a gun while seeking refuge at the gates of the U.S. embassy, but other accounts suggest that Eyadéma murdered a defenseless Olympio.

Under Nicolas Grunitzky, chosen by the coup's instigators as Olympio's successor, Eyadéma assumed leadership of an expanded military. When

Olympio's political heirs threatened to unseat Grunitzky and bring Olympio's murderers to justice, a military junta seized power in early 1967. Later that year, Eyadéma dismissed the junta, named himself president, and had himself promoted to the rank of general.

Togo was just beginning large-scale phosphate exports when Eyadéma assumed power. Phosphate revenues funded a program of political patronage, infrastructural development, and free trade that earned Eyadéma support throughout Togo, and particularly among Lomé's powerful market women. Following the example of his idol, Zaire's president Mobutu Sese Seko, Eyadéma institutionalized his rule by establishing Togo as a one-party state. He built a personality cult around himself and had larger-than-life images of himself installed throughout the country. According to an official legend of invincibility, his survival of a mysterious plane crash and coup attempts imply divine intervention on his behalf.

However, the patronage gradually degenerated into fiscal irresponsibility and debilitating cronyism. When phosphate revenues declined in the late 1970s, a severe debt crisis brought on by an economically unviable industrialization program forced Eyadéma to cut spending and implement austerity measures mandated by the International Monetary Fund. An increasingly paranoid Eyadéma withdrew into a circle of sycophants and undermined or eliminated potential rivals. The military, overwhelmingly Kabré and led by recruits Eyadéma handpicked from his home village of Pya, has perpetuated Eyadéma's grip on power, subjecting his political opponents to repeated imprisonment, torture, and murder.

During the 1990s internal and international pressures forced Eyadéma to allow a more open political process.

North America

Eyes on the Prize,

award-winning PBS television series documenting the Civil Rights Movement from 1954 to 1965.

Following its release in 1987, *Eyes on the Prize* became the most celebrated documentary series in the history of public television. Many reviewers hailed the documentary as the finest depiction to date of the civil rights era. Carolyn Fluehr-Lobban of *American Anthropologist* wrote that what distinguishes the series from its predecessors "is not only its comprehensive grasp of the civil rights period, but its fair and equal representation of all of the signal events and the heroes and heroines of the Civil Rights Movement." The series won more than 20 awards, including the Peabody Award and the

DuPont-Columbia Award, and has become a standard reference source in American libraries and schools.

Produced by African American Henry Hampton of Blackside, Inc., *Eyes on the Prize* comprises six one-hour television programs. It covers the 11 years between the landmark 1954 Supreme Court ruling to desegregate schools and the 1965 march from Selma to Montgomery and passage of the Voting Rights Act. Narrated by civil rights activist Julian Bond, the series combines archival films, newsreels, photographs, and interviews with those involved in the events. To accompany the series, Viking/Penguin published two guides for instructional use: *Eyes on the Prize: Americas' Civil Rights Years* and *A Reader and Guide: Eyes on the Prize* edited by Clayborne Carson.

In 1990 Hampton produced *Eyes on the Prize II*, which chronicles the continuing civil rights struggles of African Americans from 1965 to 1985.

Latin America and the Caribbean

Ezeiza, Gabino

(b. February 3, 1858, Buenos Aires, Argentina; d. October 12, 1916, Buenos Aires, Argentina), Afro-Argentine poet, editor, journalist, and one of the most famous of the *payador* (dueling singers) of his time.

The son of an ex-slave, Gabino Ezeiza first picked up a guitar at age 15. Drawing from a rich oral tradition of earlier *payadores*, he gradually attracted an impressive following by taking his improvisational virtuosity on the road. The *payada*, a duel-like exchange in which singer-guitarists spontaneously compose formulaic refrains, is derived from both Spanish versification and African traditions of musical contests. In Argentina, it is considered "popular literature," inextricably tied to the most symbolic of national figures: the "*gaucho* of the *pampas*" (roughly equivalent to cowboys on the range). While still a teenager, Ezeiza began writing for *La Juventud*, a Buenos Aires newspaper for and by members of the black community. From 1876 to 1878, while still building a reputation as a *payador*, publishing poetry, and writing news, he became the editor of *La Juventud*.

Before the twentieth century and the disappearance of the Afro-Argentine (see Argentina) community, *payadores*, whether *gaucho* or not, were typically rural blacks who traveled the countryside performing at private ranches and *pulperías* pulperías (local bars). Ezeiza brought *payadas* into the spotlight, moving them from the backwater milieu to circuses and theaters in the heart of Buenos Aires. He produced nearly 500 compositions, many of which were known throughout the country, including *Salve* (Hail), *Libertador* (Liberator), *Heroica* (Heroic), *Paysandú*, and *El remate* (The Conclusion). During his years as a *payador* he engaged the best of his opponents, including Higinio D. Cazón (1830–1914) and Luis García

(1875–1961). One *payada* with rival Pablo Vásquez took place in Teatro Florida in 1891 and lasted for three nights straight.

In 1892 Ezeiza won a sizable amount in the lottery and purchased a circus called Pabellón Argentina. He continued performing, attracting fans of some notoriety, including president-to-be Hipolito Yrigoyen, whose middle-class party, the Radical Civic Union, Ezeiza actively supported. Though his lyrical themes shied away from politics or overt black consciousness, he deftly managed to one-up frustrated opponents who made race-based attacks.

Fania Records,

generally regarded as the most important *salsa* music record company.

Founded in 1964 by the Dominican band leader Johnny Pacheco and the Italian-American lawyer Jerry Massuci, Fania is responsible for spreading the term *salsa*, a label used to name the Afro-Cuban and Afro-Caribbean music produced in New York City. This company is responsible for that deep change in the Afro-Cuban music played in New York City in the 1950s and 1960s. Its main contribution has been to match small groups and new interpreters with recognized musicians and band leaders, facilitating the introduction of a new New York-based sound into Afro-Cuban music. This musical style combined strong Afro-Cuban roots with other Afro-Caribbean rhythms, such as calypso, cumbia, bomba, and plena, and with sounds and styles from African American musical forms, such as soul and rock 'n' roll. This gave the Afro-Caribbean rhythms the taste of New York City's life.

Fania popularized New York Latin music among the Latin communities in the United States and among Spanish-Caribbean countries with the recordings of its band, the Fania All Stars. Especially significant were the records *Fania All Stars Live at Cheeta* and *Fania All Stars Live at Yankee Stadium*, and the promotional movies *Our Latin Thing* and *Salsa*. Among the most important bands and musicians that recorded for Fania in the late 1960s and early 1970s were Pacheco, Ray Barretto, Larry Harlow, Willie Colón, Bobby Valentín, and Roberto Roena and his Apollo Sound. Later, Fania included other *salsa* big names like Celia Cruz, Eddie Palmieri, Ismael Rivera, and Rubén Blades. But because of the emphasis on commercial success, Fania, which started as the company that allowed the free combination of rhythms and musical sounds that developed into *salsa*, became part of the mainstream industry. It thus controlled this musical production, reducing experimentation and promoting a more homogeneous sound that facilitates its consumption.

Fanon, Frantz

(b. July 20, 1925, Fort-de-France, Martinique; d. December 6, 1961, Washington, D.C.), political philosopher, essayist, psychologist, and revolutionary who, in his short but full life, developed and acted upon theories for the decolonization of Africa.

Born into a conventional, bourgeois family, Frantz Fanon grew up with assimilationist values that encouraged him to reject his African heritage. This influence was countered by one of Fanon's high school teachers, Aimé Césaire, who introduced Fanon to the philosophy of Négritude and taught him to embrace the aspects of self that the colonizer had previously forced him to reject. The encounter with Césaire proved to be a turning point in Fanon's intellectual development.

In 1940, following France's capitulation to the Germans in World War II, the part of the French Navy that had declared its allegiance to the collaborationist Vichy regime began the occupation of Martinique. It was in this context that Fanon first experienced the full force of white racism. He experienced similar racial alienation after joining De Gaulle's Free French forces in 1943 and serving with them in Algeria. The experiences of the war left Fanon deeply cynical about France's commitment to humanist ideals when it came to its black population.

Upon his return to Martinique, Fanon became involved in politics, helping Césaire win a seat in the French parliament. In 1947, after the death of his father, he went to France to pursue an advanced degree, enrolling in medical school at Lyon University in 1948. While obtaining his degree (he specialized in psychiatry), Fanon continued to read the thinkers to whom Césaire had introduced him: Hegel, Marx, Lenin and, in particular, Sartre. He also formed a student journal, *Tam-Tam*, that attracted the attention of the editors of *Présence Africaine*. It was through his connection to this journal that he was able to meet Sartre, who remained Fanon's friend for life. It was also during this time that he began writing *Peau noire, masques blancs* (1952; translated as Black Skin, White Masks, 1967), a work that took its inspiration from Césaire's protest poetry but brought a psychiatrist's eye to the question of the intellectual and cultural alienation of blacks in a world dominated by whites and white values.

Peau noire, masques blancs describes the untenable position of the black bourgeoisie in Martinique who, disdainful of their own race, realize with regret that they cannot become white. Still, Fanon separates himself in this work from the philosophy of Négritude by rejecting the idea of an immutable black essence and by seeking a solution to the problems he describes in a non-racist humanism.

In 1953 Fanon began the African chapter of his life. He assumed the post of chief of staff at the psychiatric hospital in Blida, Algeria, where during the day he treated French soldiers who were suffering the effects of inflicting torture on the local population, and at night surreptitiously treated the Algerian victims of that torture. Fanon came to the conclusion that there was no cure for his patients in such a barbaric context. He resigned from the hospital and, after participating in a strike of doctors sympathetic to the Front de Libération Nationale (FLN, the group waging war against the French colonizer), was expelled from Algeria.

Fanon left for Tunisia in 1957 to work full time for the FLN, writing for its official organ, *El Moudjahid*. But Fanon's seemingly boundless enthusiasm for the cause of Algerian and, more generally, African liberation was tempered in late 1960 when he learned that he was suffering from leukemia. He was sent to the Soviet Union for treatment, but once there he was encouraged to go to a center for the treatment of leukemia at the National Institute of Health in Bethesda, Maryland. Fanon could not bring himself to travel to the "nation of lynchers," as he put it, and returned to Accra, where he immersed himself in the work of completing *Les damnés de la terre* (1961; translated as *The Wretched of the Earth*, 1967).

Shortly prior to the publication of this work (with a preface by Sartre), Fanon had a relapse of his leukemia and was forced to seek treatment in the United Sates. According to the American journalist Joseph Alsop, the Central Intelligence Agency (CIA) arranged for Fanon to be brought to Washington, D.C., where he was kept in a hotel room for eight days prior to being hospitalized. It is impossible to know what transpired during that time, but Fanon's wife has denied that he gave any information to the CIA. Fanon died in a Washington, D.C., hospital while reading the proofs of *The Wretched of the Earth*. A collection of essays by Fanon on the decolonization of Africa, *Pour la révolution africaine* (1964; *Toward the African Revolution*, 1969), was published posthumously.

Africa

Farah, Nuruddin
(b. 1945, Baidoa, Somalia), a contemporary Somali writer.

As the son of Aleeli Faduma, a woman considered a master of Somali oral poetry, Nuruddin Farah was born into an artistic tradition of language. Unlike his mother, however, he found his own expression in the foreign tongue of English, on the written page, and in a location far from his home country. With a nonlinear, complicated prose style influenced by Western modernist and contemporary Indian writing as well as by Somali oral tradition, Farah has developed a distinct voice in contemporary English-language African literature.

Farah's education brought him first to the capital city of Mogadishu, then to England, and finally to Punjab University in Chandigarh, India, where he received his B.A. in 1970. By this time he had already published the novella *Why Die So Soon?* (1965) and written his first novel, *From a Crooked Rib* (1970). Centering on the journey of a woman from her small village to Mogadishu, the novel depicts the different worlds that exist within the nation of Somalia. With his complex treatment of gender, particularly his perceptive representation of female characters, Farah initiated an exploration of female and male identities that would characterize his fictional work.

Meanwhile, events in Somalia prompted a shift in Farah's focus. In 1969 Muhammad Siad Barre staged a coup d'état and established a military dictatorship. In Farah's next novel, *A Naked Needle* (1976), he grappled with the subject of revolution. In 1972 Farah started a fictional series in the newly scripted Somali language, but censorship once again stood in his way. By this time it was clear that Farah presented a threat to the Barre's regime. While traveling abroad, Farah learned that he would be in danger if he returned to Somalia. He began a life of exile, living at times in other parts of Africa, including Nigeria, as well as in Europe and the United States. During this time he taught at several universities and worked as a playwright.

In perhaps his best-known work, *Maps* (1986), Farah returned to the issue of national identity as he traced a young man's path from his village to the city. A sophisticated work that experimented with shifting narrative voice, *Maps* sifted through layers of selfhood and identity. The second novel in a planned trilogy, *Gifts* (1992), considered the theme of dependency, juxtaposing a love relationship with the politicized context of African economic dependency.

North America

Fard, Wallace D.

(b. ?; d. ?), primary founder of the Nation of Islam.

Wallace D. Fard entered public life in Detroit, Michigan, in the summer of 1930. Hailing from obscure origins, perhaps Egyptian or Hawaiian, he peddled "notions"—trinkets, silks, and raincoats—to residents of Paradise Valley, a predominantly African American neighborhood of Detroit. Fard claimed to have come from Africa, identified his goods as the wares of African peoples, and satisfied his customers—many of whom were uprooted Southerners—by providing them with a sense of cultural identity and stories of a common heritage. At first he moved from house to house, talking of his travels, but soon popular interest in his anecdotes encouraged him to move his storytelling to a hall.

Although Fard initially proscribed foods and moral codes, he began to address deeper theological concerns as his popularity grew. He cited the Bible, not to teach Christianity but to debunk it, espousing instead the Islamic faith. Fard called white people "blue-eyed devils," scorned their "tricknology"—which facilitated the exploitation of blacks—and taught that human culture began in Africa. He advocated an independent republic of African Americans in the United States and instituted the practice of dropping Western European surnames. By assuming, instead, the last name "X," followers of Fard rejected the names given to them in slavery.

What began as an impassioned travelogue grew into a multi-tiered organization, 8000 members strong. Under the auspices of the Lost Found Nation of Islam, Fard founded the University of Islam in Detroit (a school for elementary and high school students) and the Muslim Girls Training Corps, as well as the Fruit of Islam, a paramilitary organization that trained men in the use of firearms. Fard appointed and trained both a Minister of Islam and a retinue of underlings to preside over the Nation, enabling him to relinquish his duties and withdraw from the public eye. Elijah Poole, a former member of the Moorish Science Temple of America, succeeded Fard, adopting the name Elijah Muhammad.

In 1934 Fard disappeared as mysteriously as he had arrived, and every speculation about his disappearance remains unsubstantiated. Elijah Muhammad capitalized on this mystery, transforming Fard's disappearance into a serviceable mythology upon which he based the Nation's religious authority. By 1942 the Nation had assigned Fard divine status as an embodiment of Allah; through the end of the twentieth century Fard provided the spiritual foundation of the Nation's life.

North America

Farmer, James

(b. January 12, 1920, Marshall, Tex.; d. July 9, 1999, Fredericksburg, Va.), educator, administrator, and founder of the Congress of Racial Equality (CORE).

Raised in an environment that valued education and religious faith, James Farmer was an outstanding student. After skipping several grades in elementary school, at age 14 he entered Wiley College in Marshall, Texas (where his father, one of the few African American Ph.D.s in the South, had taught). Graduating in 1938, Farmer went on to Howard University's School of Religion. He graduated from Howard in 1941. Farmer opposed war in general, and more specifically objected to serving in the segregated armed forces. When the United States entered World War II later that year, he applied for conscientious objector status but found that he was deferred from the draft because he had a divinity degree.

Rather than become an ordained Methodist minister, Farmer, who told his father he would rather fight that church's policy of segregated congregations, chose to go to work for the Fellowship of Reconciliation (FOR). Farmer was FOR's secretary for race relations, helping the Quaker, pacifist organization craft its responses to such social ills as war, violence, bigotry, and poverty. It was a job that left Farmer, who was then living in Chicago, Illinois, enough time to begin forming his own approach to these issues— one based less on FOR's religious pacifism than on the principle of nonviolent resistance.

Founded in 1942, Farmer's new group, CORE, was at first called the Committee on Racial Equality; the name was later changed to the Congress of Racial Equality. Using pacifist techniques borrowed from the Indian nationalist leader Mohandas K. Gandhi, CORE members sought to end racial segregation and discrimination by putting their bodies on the line. Some of CORE's first actions included restaurant sit-ins, in which African American and mixed-race groups tried to be served at various Chicago restaurants, where, despite civil rights statutes on the books in Illinois, many of the establishments still refused to serve black customers. CORE's sit-ins were so successful that they greatly influenced student activists nearly 20 years later.

In addition to sit-ins, stand-ins, and boycotts, CORE pioneered the technique called Freedom Rides. Starting in the late 1940s and most famously used in 1961, Freedom Rides tested the legality of segregation on interstate transportation in the South. Always risking violent retaliation and often enduring jail for their efforts, CORE members were specially trained to maintain a peaceful, nonviolent demeanor. Their work led to the desegregation of more than 100 Southern bus terminals.

CORE also worked with other civil rights groups on issues such as school desegregation, voter registration, and job training (most notably during 1964, known as Freedom Summer, when CORE collaborated with the Student Nonviolent Coordinating Committee [SNCC]). By the late 1960s, however, Farmer, seeing CORE drift away from its Gandhian roots, left the organization he had founded and had led for more than 20 years. Always an active writer and speaker, he continued to lecture publicly on civil rights and eventually took a teaching position at Lincoln University in Pennsylvania. In 1968 Farmer ran for the United States Congress on the Liberal Party ticket and was defeated by Shirley Chisholm, an African American running as a Democrat. He went to work for Republican president Richard M. Nixon's administration as assistant secretary of health, education, and welfare shortly thereafter.

In the years following retirement from politics (1971), Farmer served on many organizational boards, including the Coalition of American Public Employees. He also continued to teach and lecture widely. In 1985 he published his autobiography, titled *Lay Bare the Heart*, and in 1998 President Bill Clinton awarded him the Congressional Medal of Freedom. Farmer died a year later.

North America

Farrakhan, Louis Abdul

(Louis Eugene Walcott; b. May 17, 1933, Bronx, N.Y.), African American religious leader, head of the Nation of Islam, a black religious organization in the United States that combines some of the practices and beliefs of Islam with a philosophy of black separatism.

Louis Farrakhan preaches the virtues of personal responsibility, especially for black men, and advocates black self-sufficiency. His message has appealed primarily to urban blacks, and draws on a long history of black nationalists who have called for black self-reliance in the face of economic injustice and white racism. His more inflammatory remarks have caused critics to claim that he has appealed to black racism and anti-Semitism to promote his views.

Born Louis Eugene Walcott in New York City, Farrakhan grew up in Boston, Massachusetts. In 1955 Malcolm X, a minister for the Nation of Islam, convinced Walcott to join the organization. Walcott dropped his last name and became known as Minister Louis X. The practice of dropping surnames is common among black Muslims, who often view them as names that were imposed on slaves and handed down over the years by white society. He later adopted the name Abdul Haleem Farrakhan and came to be known as Louis Farrakhan.

Farrakhan's speaking and singing abilities helped him to rise to prominence within the Nation of Islam, and he led the group's mosque in Boston, Massachusetts. In 1963 a split developed between Malcolm X and Elijah Muhammad, the leader of the Nation of Islam, and Malcolm X was suspended as a minister. Malcolm X had become increasingly dissatisfied with the group's failure to participate in the growing Civil Rights Movement, and Muhammad seemed threatened by the growing popularity of Malcolm X. Farrakhan sided with Muhammad in this dispute. In 1964 Malcolm X left the Nation of Islam and formed a new group, the Organization of Afro-American Unity (OAAU). Farrakhan publicly criticized Malcolm X for his break with the Nation of Islam. In 1965 Malcolm X was assassinated while addressing an OAAU rally in New York City. Three black Muslims were eventually convicted and jailed for the killing. While Farrakhan denied any connection with the shooting and never faced any charges related to Malcolm X's death, he later conceded that he had helped to create an atmosphere that may have induced others to carry out the assassination.

After the death of Malcolm X, Farrakhan became the head of a large mosque in Harlem, a neighborhood in New York City, and was the principal spokesperson for Muhammad. Farrakhan held high office in the Nation of Islam until Muhammad died in 1975. Muhammad's son, Wallace Muhammad, succeeded his father and asked Farrakhan to move to Chicago to assume a new national position. Wallace Muhammad downplayed Black Nationalism, admitted non-black members, and stressed strict Islamic beliefs and practices. Under Wallace Muhammad, the group's name changed to the World Community of Islam in the West, and later, to the American Muslim Mission.

In the late 1970s Farrakhan led a dissident faction within the organization that opposed any changes in the major beliefs and programs that had been instituted by Elijah Muhammad. In 1978 Farrakhan left Wallace Muhammad's organization and formed a new organization that assumed the original name, the Nation of Islam, and reasserted the principles of black separatism.

Farrakhan's public profile rose throughout the 1980s as he established new mosques, used radio appearances to increase his following in black communities, and was the featured speaker at events that often drew large crowds. His message of black self-reliance and mistrust of whites struck a responsive chord among young urban blacks, many of whom viewed Farrakhan as a courageous leader willing to confront a racist society. His followers praised his insistence that blacks assume moral and economic responsibility for themselves—that they avoid drugs and crime; that they provide for their children; that they stay in school and become involved in their communities.

Controversy surrounding the Nation of Islam also grew, primarily because Farrakhan attacked white society and voiced the anti-Semitism growing among some blacks in the inner cities. He was once quoted as calling Judaism a "gutter religion" and referred to German dictator Adolf Hitler, who was responsible for killing millions of Jews, as a great man. Farrakhan's controversial remarks on the radio and at press conferences were widely condemned by other black leaders.

In the 1990s Farrakhan continued his call for poor blacks to make stronger commitments to education and to their families. He also called on blacks to end black-on-black crime and to be less dependent on government welfare. In October 1995 Farrakhan organized the Million Man March in Washington, D.C. At the march, hundreds of thousands of black men vowed to renew their commitments to family, community, and personal responsibility. Although the march renewed criticism of Farrakhan's anti-Semitic statements and some black leaders refused to participate, it was widely regarded as a successful display of black solidarity.

North America

Fauset, Jessie Redmon

(b. April 27, 1882, Camden County, N.J.; d. April 30, 1961, Philadelphia, Pa.), influential African American novelist and editor during the Harlem Renaissance.

Poet Langston Hughes referred to Jessie Fauset as one of "the three people who mid-wifed the so-called New Negro literature into being," a statement that reveals how influential Fauset was as an editor during the Harlem Renaissance of the 1920s and 1930s. But Fauset was also the era's most prolific black novelist, publishing four books between 1924 and 1933. In both capacities, Fauset helped shape one of the most important movements in African American literature.

Fauset was born in what is now Lawnside, New Jersey, and grew up in Philadelphia. She hoped to attend Bryn Mawr College, but instead of admitting a black student, Bryn Mawr arranged for Fauset to receive a scholarship to Cornell University. There, Fauset became the first black woman in the country to be elected to Phi Beta Kappa, the academic honorary society. She also began corresponding with the noted black intellectual W. E. B. Du Bois, whose work she admired, forming an association that would become the cornerstone of her literary career.

After graduation Fauset moved to Washington, D.C., where she taught at the prestigious all-black M Street (later Dunbar) High School from 1905 to 1919 while taking courses toward a master's degree in French from the University of Pennsylvania. But beginning in 1912, Fauset was also a literary contributor to *Crisis*, the journal of the National Association for the Advancement of Colored People (NAACP), which Du Bois edited. When the *Crisis* created the position of literary editor at its New York office in 1919, Du Bois offered it to Fauset, and she accepted.

It was at the *Crisis* that Fauset cultivated the talents of many younger Harlem Renaissance writers, including Langston Hughes, Jean Toomer, Countee Cullen, and Claude McKay. Under her tenure, *Crisis* became one of the major publishing outlets for black writers at the time. But Fauset also published short stories, essays, reviews, and poems of her own in both *Crisis* and its short-lived children's magazine, *The Brownie's Book*. In 1924 she published her first novel, *There Is Confusion*. Many of her stories and all four of her novels feature light-skinned, middle-class black protagonists. Fauset left her position at the *Crisis* in 1926—perhaps because of a falling out with Du Bois—and took another teaching job, this time in New York. Although *There Is Confusion* had been well received by black critics, she still had difficulty securing publishers for her later novels—perhaps because she was a novelist at a time when black poets were in vogue. But she continued to write, publishing *Plum Bun* in 1929, *The Chinaberry Tree* in 1931, and *Comedy: American Style* in 1933.

Latin America and the Caribbean

Favelas,

squatter settlements or shantytowns that provide shelter to millions of Brazil's poor, among them a large percentage of Afro-Brazilians.

Favelas represent the plight and promise of the urban poor in Brazil. Although they can be found throughout the country, *favelas* are most numerous in Rio de Janeiro, once the nation's federal district (1889–1960) and still its second largest city. Shantytowns such as Rocinha and Jacarez-

Rio de Janeiro's *favelas* (squatter settlements) are the largest and most populous in Brazil. Favelas inhabitants are predominantly people of African descent. *CORBIS/Dave G. Houser*

inho have become an indelible part of the landscape of the Cidade Maravil-
hosa (Marvelous City). Other Brazilian metropolises—São Paulo, Salvador,
Recife—have their own *favela*s, with populations numbering in the hundreds of thousands, but these settlements have not attained the political
prominence or journalistic notoriety of the ones in Rio.

The *favela* is fundamentally different from inner-city slums and tene-
ments, the types of poor people's housing prevalent in the developed world.
The latter are usually rundown buildings owned by a landlord where the
occupants pay rent. Squatter settlements, by contrast, are units of self-
constructed housing built on terrain seized and occupied illegally, most often
located in the urban periphery. Residences are built without license, usually
on lands belonging to third parties. Inside the *favela* there is a near total
absence of numbered streets, sanitation networks, electricity, telephones, or
plumbing. This is not to say that the *favela* lacks organization. Popularly
elected residents' councils maintain order; religious institutions, social clubs,
and political parties forge bonds among *favelados* (squatters) and connect
them to the outside world. Yet *favela* living is a rational choice for many of
the poor. Shantytowns offer proximity to the workplace, saving the laborer
costly transportation fare and hours of travel. There is a political advantage to
favela residency as well; so long as they stay within city limits, squatters can
claim the right to public services like education and health care.

Africa

Faye, Safi
**(b. 1943, near Dakar, Senegal), Senegalese film director, one of the few
independent women filmmakers in Africa.**

Safi Faye is not only one of the few independent African women film
directors, but also one of the few making ethnographic films. The daughter
of a village chief and businessman of Serer origin, Faye moved to Dakar at
age 19 to become a teacher. While in Dakar she became interested in the
educational and ethnographic uses of film and upon meeting Jean Rouch,
the French filmmaker and ethnologist, she embarked on a film career.

Faye acted in Rouch's *Petit à petit ou Les Lettres persanes* (1968). She
also learned about Rouch's style of cinéma-vérité, characterized by an unob-
trusive camera and spontaneous nonprofessional acting, which would later
influence her own film work. With Rouch's encouragement she moved to
Paris in 1972 and enrolled in the Ecole Pratique des Hautes Etudes to study
ethnology, and the Louis Lumière Film School to study film. She completed
film school in 1974, and began using film as a way to publish her ongoing
research on the Serer. By the time she received her Ph.D. she had produced
three films—*Kaddu beykat* (1975); *Fad'jal* (1979); and *Goob na nu* (1979).
Although much of her work focuses on the Serer, she has also produced

documentaries for the United Nations and German and French television stations, filmed in both Europe and Africa.

Federal Writers' Project,

a project funded by the United States government during the 1930s to collect American history through oral narratives, including the testimonies of ex-slaves.

Although their accuracy and usefulness have been debated, the slave narratives collected through the Federal Writers' Project (FWP) represent a significant addition to the study of American slavery. The FWP began in 1935 as part of President Franklin D. Roosevelt's Works Progress Administration, which created new jobs for Americans suffering during the Great Depression. The Writers' Project hired unemployed writers to collect folklore and histories from each state for a series of books called *Guide to America*, and President Roosevelt's Black Cabinet—African American advisers John Davis, William Hastie, and Robert Weaver—persuaded the administration to include oral testimonies of former slaves and other African Americans as part of this program.

As a result thousands of African Americans were interviewed between 1935 and 1939 through the FWP's Office of Negro Affairs. The FWP produced more than a dozen collections of rural and urban black studies. Its largest contribution to black history and literature is the slave narrative collection. More than 2000 ex-slaves in 18 states, an estimated 2 percent of the surviving ex-slave population, were interviewed. The topics discussed in the conversations included the type of work the interviewees had done as slaves, what they ate and what they wore, and what their families and homes were like. Published collections of their narratives include Benjamin Botkins's anthology *Lay My Burden Down: A Folk History of Slavery* (1945) and George P. Rawlins's comprehensive 41-volume *The American Slave: A Composite Autobiography* (1972, 1977, 1979).

The FWP employed several prominent African American writers. Sterling A. Brown was the FWP Negro Affairs director, and Zora Neale Hurston briefly directed the Florida office. Richard Wright, Arna Bontemps, and Margaret Walker worked in the office, and Wright, Claude McKay, and Ralph Ellison all worked in New York. The position gave many of these writers extra time for their own writing—Hurston, for example, finished three novels during her fieldwork, and Wright wrote *Twelve Million Black Voices* as part of the project and *Native Son* during his free time.

But while the FWP was an excellent opportunity for these black authors, the program failed to employ large numbers of African Americans—in 1937, only 106 out of the 4500 writers were black. Several state offices simply refused to hire black workers for the project. Many historians have argued that the racial inequality on the staff undermined the value of the endeavor, because black interviewees tended to censor themselves when they were responding to white questioners. This has become one of the major criticisms of the project.

Fedon, Julien,

a mixed-race landowner in Grenada who, inspired by the French Revolution, led a rebellion against British colonial rule that lasted from March 1795 to June 1796.

Feliciano, José "Cheo"

(b. 1935), Afro-Puerto Rican singer of *salsa* and *boleros.* Born in Ponce, he moved to New York, where he launched his singing career. In the 1950s he sang on occasion with the Tito Rodriguez big band. Between 1957 and 1967, he attained considerable success singing with the Joe Cuba Sextette. In the 1970s he sang with the Fania All Stars.

Fernandes, Florestan

(b. 1920, São Paulo, Brazil), a Brazilian social scientist who had a powerful influence on the study of race relations in Brazil, documenting the importance of race in Brazilian society and the existence of racial discrimination.

Florestan Fernandes was one of a group of social scientists who challenged the Brazilian myth of racial democracy, which held that racism was not a significant factor in Brazilian society. Fernandes criticized what he termed the Brazilian "prejudice of having no prejudice." Together with other Brazilian and foreign social scientists, partly inspired and funded by the Race Relations Project of the United Nations Educational, Scientific, and Cultural Organization (UNESCO), Fernandes revolutionized the study of race, though his conclusions would later be the subject of much debate. According to fellow social scientist Carlos Hasenbalg, Fernandes "substantiated the significance of racism and racial discrimination in industrial and capitalist Brazil, but saw them as an archaic survival from the seignorial, pre-capitalist and pre-industrial past."

Fernández Robaina, Tomás

(b. 1941), Cuban librarian and bibliographer. His works include *Bibliografía de estudios afro-americanos* (1969, Bibliography of Afro-American Studies), *La prosa de Guillén en defensa del negro cubano* (1982, The Prose of Guillén in Defense of the Black Cuban), *Bibliografía grafía de temas afrocubanos* (1986, Bibliography of Afro-Cuban Themes), and *Bibliografía de autores de raza de color* (1988, Bibliography of Authors of the Colored Race).

Fetchit, Stepin

(b. May 30, 1902, Key West, Fla.; d. November 19, 1985, Woodland Hills, Calif.), American actor known for his film portrayal of stereotypical African American minstrel characters.

Born Lincoln Theodore Monroe Perry, "Stepin Fetchit" became an almost mythical figure in African American popular culture. After attending a Catholic boarding school until he was 12, Perry joined the vaudeville circuit accompanied by comic Ed Lee performing a minstrel act called *Step 'n' Fetchit: Two Dancing Fools from Dixie*. In the early 1920s Perry went solo and retained Stepin Fetchit as his stage name. As Stepin Fetchit, he became quite popular on the Theater Owners Booking Association (TOBA) performance circuit. After moving to Hollywood, Perry appeared in more than 40 films between 1927 and 1976, including *In Old Kentucky* (1927), *Judge Priest* (1934), and *The Steamboat Round the Bend* (1935).

Fierro, Francisco "Pancho"

(1810–1879), self-taught mulatto artist who became one of Peru's most famous *costumbrista* painters.

Fifteenth Amendment to the United States Constitution,

amendment ratified on March 30, 1870, that guaranteed African American men the right to vote.

The Fifteenth Amendment states that "the right of citizens of the United States to vote shall not be denied or abridged by the United States or by a State on account of race, color, or previous condition of servitude." The text also gives Congress the power to enforce the amendment. Although African

This 1870 lithograph celebrating the passage of the Fifteenth Amendment shows recently emancipated African Americans engaged in education, work, and political life. *CORBIS*

Americans had been freed from slavery and made citizens after the Civil War by the Thirteenth and Fourteenth Amendments, Southern states used a variety of tactics, including violence, to keep blacks from voting, and even some Northern states had not given blacks the franchise. Radical Republicans in Congress proposed the Fifteenth Amendment to rectify this problem.

Most people, blacks and whites alike, believed that the franchise was the best assurance of progress and success for the freed people. Most whites felt that the right to participate in the political process was, in fact, all the nation owed the former slaves. But debate immediately arose over how strongly worded the amendment should be. Many Republicans feared that if the language were not strong, the South would keep blacks from voting through such indirect means as poll taxes and violence. Other Republicans, however, believed that all states—Northern and Southern—should have the right to keep illiterate citizens from voting. (Many Northerners feared the growing influence of foreign immigrants and wanted the literacy test to limit their power.) The resulting compromise was the Fourteenth Amendment, which was ratified with the help of Reconstruction governments in the South, but which soon proved incapable of guaranteeing the franchise for blacks.

For a brief period during Reconstruction many African Americans voted, and some were elected to public office. In the late 1870s, however, enthusiasm for ensuring black equality waned in both the North and the Republican Party, and by 1877, when federal troops were withdrawn from the South, blacks were left to the power of whites committed to "redeeming" the South—that is, to restoring white supremacy. To quash the black vote, Southern states employed the poll tax, which poor blacks (and whites) were hard-pressed to pay; the literacy test, which uneducated blacks were ill-equipped to pass; confusing election procedures, which were not explained to blacks; and the grandfather clause, which allowed anyone whose father or grandfather had been registered to vote before the Fifteenth Amendment—in other words, almost any white man—to continue voting even if he could not pay the poll tax or pass the literacy test.

Where these methods failed, Southerners established whites-only voting in party primaries (which guaranteed election as the South became over-whelmingly Democratic) or gerrymandered electoral districts, thus diluting the strength of black voters. Most effective were intimidation and violence.

Not until the twentieth century would the Supreme Court invoke the Fifteenth Amendment in striking down state grandfather clauses and white primaries. But such changes had little effect on black voting: during World War II, only 5 percent of Southern blacks were registered to vote. Not until the Voting Rights Act of 1965 did discrimination in voting begin to end and did courts enforce the Fifteenth Amendment.

North America

Fifty-fourth Regiment of Massachusetts Volunteer Infantry,

one of the first black Union regiments of the American Civil War (1861–1865).

At the beginning of the American Civil War, thousands of blacks throughout the North volunteered for service in the Union army but were turned away. President Abraham Lincoln believed that the war would be short-lived and feared that enlisting black volunteers would unnecessarily antagonize the South. He was also afraid of losing the support of the four slave-owning border states that remained tenuously loyal to the Union, as well as alienating the North's large number of pro-slavery (or at least non-abolitionist) Democrats. Both the border states and Democrats, it was assumed, would have seen the enlistment of black troops as a sign that the North meant to abolish slavery, which was not an original aim of the war.

As the war widened, however, it became clear that the Union Army needed more manpower. Not only were Northern blacks not contributing, but freed Southern slaves in Union-occupied lands were either returned to their owners or used by the army, if at all, for labor. Moreover, slaves in the Confederacy contributed mightily to the wartime economy, freeing white Southerners to fight. In the summer of 1862 Congress authorized

Union troops to confiscate Southern property, including slaves, who could then be used in military-support roles. Congress hoped the act would give slaves an incentive to flee toward advancing Union troops. In September Lincoln issued a preliminary Emancipation Proclamation freeing slaves and allowing the entry of both newly freed slaves and Northern blacks into the armed services.

John A. Andrew, the abolitionist governor of Massachusetts, authorized the formation in his state of a black regiment to be led by white officers. In early 1863 Col. Robert Gould Shaw, the 25-year-old son of a prominent Boston antislavery family, was given command of the Fifty-fourth Massachusetts Volunteer Infantry. Blacks, some from elite families (two sons of Frederick Douglass were among the troops), came from throughout the North to serve in the regiment. The officers were drawn from New England's white elite, mostly from families with abolitionist views.

Although the Fifty-fourth Massachusetts was among the best known of the black regiments, it was not the first. In 1862 several Union commanders fighting in the lower Mississippi Valley, on the Kansas-Missouri border, and in the South Carolina Sea Islands had quietly organized black troops and sent them into combat. Although these early black soldiers fought with distinction, their actions were little publicized. Many Northerners remained dubious as to whether blacks would make good soldiers, and the new black troops were relegated largely to support roles.

The Fifty-fourth completed its training in May 1863 and in July was sent from Boston to the South Carolina Sea Islands, at the mouth of Charleston Harbor. Confederate troops were stationed on several of the harbor's protective islands, including a well-guarded garrison at Fort Wagner on Morris Island. Fort Wagner was buffered on one side by ocean and on the other by swamp, leaving only a narrow neck of thick-sanded beach for a land approach. On the evening of July 18, several Union regiments were ordered to attack the fort by land, and the Fifty-fourth, numbering about 650 men, was placed at the front of the charge.

The fort was believed to be weakened by earlier shelling from the Union Navy. But as the Fifty-fourth soon discovered, the Confederate base was largely untouched, allowing its occupants to rain shells and gunfire on the Union troops. Suffering devastating casualties, the Fifty-fourth nonetheless advanced to the fort's walls, breaching its defenses. Colonel Shaw was killed on the rampart. William H. Carney, the Fifty-fourth's standard bearer, was shot in both legs, the chest, and one arm but dragged himself to safety with the colors aloft. He became the first black recipient of the Congressional Medal of Honor. Finally overwhelmed, the Fifty-fourth and other Union regiments retreated; almost half of the Fifty-fourth's officers and enlisted men were killed or wounded.

A correspondent from the *New York Tribune* gave a vivid report of the battle for Northern readers. Thereafter, the ability of the black soldier largely ceased to be an issue of debate, and the idea of freeing Southern slaves also became much more popular. These events helped Lincoln change the war from a fight exclusively to end a rebellion against the United States government to a moral fight to end slavery. The events also hastened the enlistment of black troops—186,000 of whom were mustered in the next three years.

The Fifty-fourth Massachusetts also played an important role in gaining equal pay for black soldiers. In 1862 the federal government authorized payment to black soldiers but at a lower wage than to white soldiers. The Fifty-fourth refused to accept any pay until it was the same as whites'. Following the battle at Fort Wagner, the movement to equalize pay grew in strength, and in the summer of 1864, Lincoln's attorney general ruled that all soldiers were entitled to the same pay. Congress passed an act making it so, and in late 1864 the soldiers of the Fifty-fourth received back wages.

With the death of Shaw, Col. Edward N. Hallowell, who was seriously wounded at Wagner, took command of the regiment. Several months passed while the unit filled with new recruits. In early 1864 the replenished regiment was part of a force that occupied Jacksonville, Florida, without resistance. A wing of the Union forces, including the Fifty-fourth, continued inland from Jacksonville; at Olustee, they were met by a large and well-supplied Confederate force. Ill-supplied and poorly prepared, the forward Union regiments were routed until the Fifty-fourth Massachusetts and another black regiment reinforced them from the rear—saving them from complete devastation at the cost of heavy casualties to themselves.

Near the end of the war the Fifty-fourth fought in several campaigns in Georgia and South Carolina, and was among the first of Northern troops to occupy Charleston. Throughout their tour of duty, the Fifty-fourth and other black regiments fought with the knowledge that they might be enslaved or executed if taken prisoner. The Fifty-fourth Massachusetts was mustered out in August 1865. The movie *Glory* (1989), which told the story of the Fifty-fourth, created popular interest in the black regiments of the Civil War.

North America

Fisk Jubilee Singers,

choral group from Fisk University that introduced African American spirituals to a worldwide audience in the 1870s and helped preserve the work songs of the slaves.

The Fisk Jubilee Singers was founded in 1867 by George L. White, the treasurer and vocal-music teacher at Fisk University in Nashville, Tennessee. The university had been established two years earlier to educate newly freed black slaves. Since few students could afford the tuition, the school needed other sources of revenue, and White came up with the idea of a performing choir as a way to raise money.

After several successful local appearances, the reputation of the 11-member choir began to spread, and in 1871 the Jubilee Singers embarked on a tour of the Northeast, performing mainly in churches before all-white audiences. Their repertoire included anthems, popular ballads, and operatic excerpts, but their most popular pieces proved to be African American spirituals and work songs, which many in their audiences were hearing for the first time. With the money they raised, Fisk University was able to complete construction in 1875 of its first permanent building, called Jubilee Hall. Thanks to the work of the Fisk Jubilee Singers and other groups like them, these songs did not die, and are now celebrated as an indigenous American music.

North America

Fisk University,

one of the first and most respected African American liberal arts institutions.

Like many other new schools for African Americans at the end of the Civil War, Fisk University was founded and largely supported by white benefactors. But it differed significantly from other black schools, such as Tuskegee and Hampton Institutes, in its emphasis on liberal arts education rather than vocational training. Its founders saw Fisk as a school that would measure itself by "the highest standards, not of Negro education, but of American education at its best."

Fisk was established in Nashville, Tennessee, in October 1865 by Erastus Milo Cravath and the Reverend Edward P. Smith, both members of the American Missionary Association, and John Ogden, superintendent of the Tennessee Freedmen's Bureau's Department of Education. It began as an elementary school to meet the basic educational needs of the newly freed slaves, and its first students ranged in age from 7 to 70. In 1867 Tennessee passed a new law that mandated free elementary schools for all races. Since this meant that many of its elementary students would be able to receive a public education, Fisk was able to focus on postgraduate and college courses. In August 1867 Fisk was incorporated as a private, coeducational university providing higher education for men and women of all races.

North America

Fitzgerald, Ella

(b. April 25, 1917, Newport News, Va.; d. June 15, 1996, Beverly Hills, Calif.), African American singer; one of the greatest jazz vocalists of all time, she was known as the First Lady of Song.

Ella Fitzgerald was quite possibly the greatest vocalist in the history of jazz. Only Billie Holiday and Sarah Vaughan offer her any serious competition. Both Vaughan and Fitzgerald were blessed with pure voices and exceptionally clear enunciation. But only Fitzgerald melded the headlong swing of the 1930s with the adventurous harmonies of modern jazz.

Jazz vocalist Ella Fitzgerald performs in the 1950s, a decade during which she made classic recordings in her mature style. *CORBIS/Hulton-Deutsch Collection*

During the bebop or bop era of the mid-1940s and early 1950s, Fitzgerald honed her jazz abilities and emerged as one of the foremost exponents of scat singing, in which the singer's voice mimics a soloing horn, using nonsense syllables in place of words or song lyrics. During 1946 she toured with Dizzy Gillespie's big band and in the late 1940s recorded exciting scat versions of "Oh, Lady Be Good" and "How High the Moon." In 1948 *Downbeat*, the jazz magazine, proclaimed her "as great a master of bop as she has been of swing." Fitzgerald later recalled, "I thought bebop was 'it,' and that all I had to do was go someplace and sing bop." But when many listeners rejected the complex harmonies and challenging angularity of modern jazz, she decided to modify her style. What she achieved in the 1950s was a remarkable synthesis of accessibility and sophistication. A year after appearing in the film *Pete Kelly's Blues* (1955), Fitzgerald signed with Norman Granz's Verve Records and made some of the greatest recordings of her career.

North America

Foreman, George Edward

(b. January 10, 1949, Marshall, Tex.), African American two-time heavyweight boxing champion whose long career has included evangelical preaching and sitcom acting.

George Foreman grew up in Houston, Texas, and led a rough early life, dropping out of high school, drinking heavily, and committing petty larcenies. In 1965 he turned his life around by joining the Job Corps, where he was introduced to boxing. Showing exceptional natural aptitude, Foreman won his first official amateur fight in 1967 with a first-round knockout. His talent developed quickly and by 1968 he had won a Gold Medal for the United States at the Summer Olympic Games in Mexico City.

In 1969 Foreman launched a record-breaking professional career. By 1973 he had knocked out 36 consecutive opponents and won the title of heavyweight champion from Joe Frazier. Foreman defended his title until 1974, when underdog Muhammad Ali knocked him out in Kinshasa, Zaire.

After a fight in Puerto Rico in 1977, Foreman experienced a religious epiphany that prompted him to retire from boxing and become a self-ordained evangelical Christian minister. Returning to Houston, he founded the George Foreman Youth and Community Center, to which he devoted most of his time. During the 1980s he became a television personality by promoting products, and in 1993 his amicability earned him his own situation comedy, *George*.

Ostensibly to raise funds for his social programs, Foreman returned to professional boxing in 1987. His comeback astonished the boxing world, especially as it culminated in his defeat of heavyweight champion Michael Moorer in 1994. Foreman regained his title at the unprecedented age of 45.

North America

Forman, James

(b. October 4, 1928, Chicago, Ill.), civil rights activist who is credited with giving the Student Nonviolent Coordinating Committee (SNCC) a firm organizational base.

While reporting for the *Chicago Defender* in 1960, James Forman learned of black farmers in Tennessee who had been evicted by their white landlords for registering to vote. In support, Forman joined a program sponsored by the Congress of Racial Equality (CORE) that provided relief services to the displaced farmers. Later that year, he participated in Freedom Rides, in which blacks rode in buses throughout the South testing court-ordered integration of public transportation. Forman then joined SNCC and began working for black civil rights full time.

Having served in the air force during the Korean War, Forman possessed more maturity and experience than most of the young members of SNCC. His organizational skills thrust him into a leadership role at the organizationally weak SNCC, where he directed fundraising and supervised staff. In 1964 he became SNCC's executive secretary, a post he held until 1966. In addition, Forman participated in many of SNCC's direct-action protests and helped organize voter registration drives in Alabama and Mississippi.

North America

Forty Acres and a Mule,

a phrase whose meaning has evolved since its Civil War beginnings. It is also currently the name of filmmaker Spike Lee's film company.

The phrase "40 acres and a mule" probably stems from a field order given in 1865 to former slaves in the Savannah area of Georgia. On January 16,

1865, Gen. William T. Sherman of the Union Army issued Special Field Order 15. This order reserved the Sea Islands and areas of coastal South Carolina, Florida, and Georgia for freed people to own. Each person or family was to receive a 40-acre plot of agriculturally-fit land. With Sherman's permission, the army could also loan mules to former slaves. These former slaves settled 400,000 acres of land (called Sherman Land) within six months. In March 1865 Congress authorized the Freedmen's Bureau to rent 40-acre plots of confiscated and abandoned lands to freed people. But radical land redistribution never took place. "Forty acres and a mule" became a symbol not only of the limitations of Reconstruction but of African Americans' unfulfilled reparations, expectations, and hopes.

Fourteenth Amendment to the United States Constitution,

amendment ratified on July 28, 1868, that was intended to guarantee the civil rights of African Americans.

During the Civil War the Thirteenth Amendment freed Southern slaves, but after the war most blacks in the segregated South were able to realize little of their new freedom. President Andrew Johnson, who wanted to accommodate the defeated Confederate states, was reluctant to press the South for black equality. As a result, Radical Republicans in Congress drafted and secured passage of the Fourteenth Amendment. Their intent was partly to guarantee black freedom as granted by the Thirteenth Amendment and partly to limit the power of the reconstructed South.

The Fourteenth Amendment contains five sections, the heart of which is Section 1 (discussed below). Section 2 guarantees that if black men (or other male citizens) are denied the right to vote, their state's representation in Congress will be reduced proportionately. Section 2 was motivated by Republicans' fears that although blacks were now considered fully in the apportionment of representation to Congress (previously black men counted for only three-fifths of a person for congressional apportionment), because they were too intimidated to vote, the white South might gain more representation in Congress as a result of freeing the slaves. In fact, the North's fears proved correct, but Section 2 was never enforced. Section 3 forbids former Confederate soldiers to hold political office, but enforcement of this ban also turned out to be short-lived. Section 4 absolves the United States government of responsibility for the war debt of the Confederate. Section 5 gives Congress the power to enforce the amendment.

Section 1, historically the most important of the sections, is divided into four main clauses. The first clause, known as the citizenship clause, grants state and federal citizenship to "all persons born or naturalized in the United States" with the exception of Native Americans. The citizenship clause was intended to undo Supreme Court rulings such as *Dred Scott v. Sanford* (1857), in which the court held that neither slaves nor their descendants were citizens of the United States.

The second clause, known as the privileges and immunities clause, holds that no state shall "abridge the privileges or immunities" of citizens. This was an attempt to keep Southern states from passing racially discriminatory laws. The full potential of the clause was never realized, however, because the Supreme Court ruled in 1873 that only the rights of federal citizenship were protected by the clause. States, said the court, were free to restrict the rights of state citizenship as they saw fit. Because most matters of everyday life were governed by states, the practical effect of the ruling was that schooling, housing, employment, and other immediate concerns were ruled by discriminatory state laws; federal law protected mostly uncommon circumstances, such as life on the high seas.

The third clause of Section 1, the due process clause, holds that states shall not "deprive any person of life, liberty, or property without due process of the law." A restatement of a similar clause in the Fifth Amendment, it soon opened a debate among scholars and judges about whether the clause was meant to "incorporate" the Bill of Rights into the Fourteenth Amendment. In other words, was the clause an attempt to apply the protections of the Bill of Rights to the states instead of just to the federal government? (In *Barron v. Baltimore* [1833], the Supreme Court had ruled that the Bill of Rights did not apply to state laws.) The debate over the due process clause has never been resolved, but judges in the 1960s and 1970s used it to secure some rights for blacks and other minorities, including several rights related to desegregation.

A fourth and final clause, the equal protection clause, provided the framework for many anti-discrimination rulings. The clause holds that no state shall "deny to any person within its jurisdiction the equal protection of the laws." In the late nineteenth century the equal protection clause was routinely ignored by states and finally rendered useless by the Supreme Court in *Plessy v. Ferguson* (1896). In *Plessy* the court established its doctrine that facilities could be "separate but equal"—that segregation alone did not violate the equal protection clause. More than half a century later, however, the court relied on the equal protection clause to reverse *Plessy*. In *Brown v. Board of Education* (1954) the court argued that segregation was "inherently unequal" and therefore a violation of the Fourteenth Amendment. Thus rehabilitated, the equal protection clause provided the basis for desegregation of schools and housing as well as reapportionment of unfairly drawn congressional districts. The equal protection clause has also been used to guarantee the right to birth control devices and abortions.

Europe

France,

a country in Western Europe where blacks have had a presence for centuries.

The French historian Henri Blet claimed: "Frenchmen have never adopted racial doctrines affirming the superiority of whites over men of color." It is true that the French Revolution, with its pioneering slogan of liberty, equality, and fraternity, inaugurated a still vigorous French intellectual tradi-

TOP: A Tunisian baker working in Roubaix, France. *CORBIS/Marc Garanger*
BOTTOM: Many Algerians fleeing civil war lived in shantytowns like this one near Nanterre on the outskirts of Paris, France, in 1961. *CORBIS/Hulton-Deutsch collection*

Teenagers stand in line outside a Paris movie theatre. In 1998 more than 350,000 people of West African descent lived in France; an estimated 400,000 West Indians lived in Paris alone. *CORBIS/Owen Franken*

tion of rationalism, tolerance for difference, and resistance to authority. It is also true that many twentieth-century black musicians, writers, and artists have experienced France as a haven of racial tolerance. Yet France, like other European powers, was an active participant in the transatlantic slave trade and developed a colonial empire that systematically subordinated blacks to

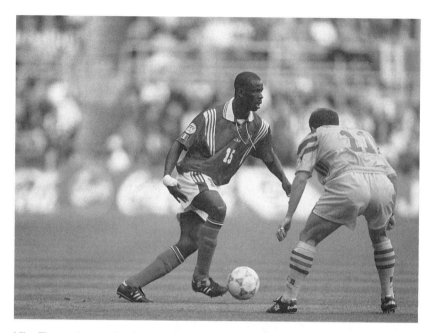

Lilian Thuram, born on Guadeloupe, joined the French national soccer team in 1996 and soon was considered one of the best defenders in international play. *CORBIS/Christian Liewig; TempSport*

The great French writer André Gide was a champion of civil rights for blacks. *CORBIS/Bettmann*

whites. France has also been a major contributor to European racist ideologies over the centuries, including late nineteenth-century "scientific" racism and the current views of the National Front. Moreover, while many more blacks live in France today than ever before, they are largely relegated to the least desirable positions in society.

North America

Franklin, Aretha Louise

(b. March 25, 1942, Memphis, Tenn.), the preeminent black female vocalist of the 1960s and 1970s, who earned, through her secular and gospel masterpieces, the title Queen of Soul.

As a daughter of the renowned Baptist preacher C. L. Franklin and his wife, Barbara Siggers Franklin—whose singing won the laurels of Mahalia Jackson—Aretha Franklin was born into gospel. As a child she began to sing in her father's New Bethel Baptist Church in Detroit, Michigan. From Franklin's earliest days, something more than pure vocal bravura ignited her performances. Profound emotion infused her singing.

Franklin's friendship with gospel-gone-soul singer Sam Cooke inspired her to leave the church for a professional career in music. At age 18 Franklin went to New York, cut demos, took voice lessons, and signed a five-year recording contract with Columbia Records. Supervised by John Hammond—who had "discovered" such musicians as Count Basie, Charlie Christian, Lionel Hampton, and Billie Holiday—Franklin recorded pop standards, Broadway tunes, and jazz ballads. Due to overwrought, often saccharine arrangements, Franklin's recordings with Columbia met with limited success. They terminated her contract, but Jerry Wexler of Atlantic Records swiftly signed her to his company. He encouraged Franklin to drop her Columbia sound, thereby initiating her career in soul. Wexler claims that he "urged Aretha to be Aretha"—and indeed her Atlantic recordings of the late 1960s pulsed with an authenticity that attracted millions of fans. Although Franklin was not known as an innovator, she expressed a level of sincerity unprecedented in pop music.

Franklin's first release with Atlantic, "I Never Loved a Man (The Way I Love You)" sold a million copies and was followed by four other million-selling records that same year. Between 1967 and 1969 she won four Grammy Awards. Her cover of "Respect" by Otis Redding transformed the song into an anthem of black feminist pride. Franklin also became associated with the Civil Rights Movement by singing at the funeral of Martin Luther King Jr., a friend and colleague of her father. Her popular recognition is as the Queen of Soul.

North America

Fraunces Tavern,

a historic New York City landmark whose founder is thought by many to have been black.

Fraunces Tavern, located in lower Manhattan and still operating as a restaurant, was opened in 1762 by Samuel Fraunces (1722?–1795), a West Indian immigrant who built his business by catering to those with a taste for English cooking, especially elegant desserts. As well as being a successful entrepreneur and chef, Fraunces was deeply involved in the American Revolution and set up the tavern and its adjoining inn as a meeting place for the independence movement. Known by his contemporaries as "Black Sam," he was an avid supporter and close confidant of George Washington. His involvement in the revolution included giving aid to American prisoners of war, but the high point followed the war, when Washington bade farewell to his troops at a commemorative feast at Fraunces Tavern.

Samuel Fraunces's racial origins have long been a matter of debate. Recent research suggests that he may have been the son of white plantation owners, and he is listed as white in a 1790 census. There are those, however, who maintain that Fraunces's nickname and birthplace make it likely that he was black and perhaps passed for white. As of yet, there is no conclusive evidence about his race. On January 25, 1975, Fraunces Tavern made the political spotlight when it was bombed by members of the Fuerzas Armadas de Liberación Nacional (FALN), a Puerto Rican independence movement. Four people died in the explosion. It has never been clearly established why Fraunces Tavern was a chosen target; members of FALN later claimed that they set off the blast in retaliation for a "CIA-ordered" bombing in Puerto Rico 14 days earlier.

North America

Frazier, Edward Franklin

(b. September 24, 1894, Baltimore, Md.; d. May 17, 1962, Washington, D.C.), sociologist and activist famed for his pioneering studies of black families and his critique of the black middle class.

Taught from an early age that education was the key to both personal success and social justice, E. Franklin Frazier used his learning as a weapon during his lifelong battle against racial inequality. In a tribute to Frazier, the *Journal of Negro Education* called him "a non-confomist, a protester, a gadfly." He attacked the pretension of the black middle class, went to jail for picketing D. W. Griffith's film *The Birth of a Nation*, and publicly defended W. E. B. Du Bois and Paul Robeson, even though doing so meant risking being branded a communist.

Frazier grew up in Baltimore, Maryland, and attended Howard University on scholarship. Shortly after graduating from Howard with honors in 1916, he began his career as a professor. From 1929 until 1934 he taught at Fisk University in Nashville, Tennessee. In 1934 he was hired as the chair of the sociology department at Howard, where he remained until his retirement in 1959.

The Negro Family in the United States (1939), Frazier's first influential book, discredited the idea that problems such as illegitimacy, divorce, and desertion could be traced to biological or cultural defects. Instead, Frazier demonstrated that problems within black communities mirrored the shortcomings of American society as a whole. In 1949 he published *The Negro in the United States*, the first comprehensive textbook on black experiences.

Frazier's most controversial book, *Black Bourgeoisie*, appeared in 1957. This study concluded that the black middle class had earned "status without substance" and criticized affluent blacks for abandoning the cause of social equality in the hope of becoming part of the American elite. Despite charges of racial disloyalty, Frazier continued to write about class differences within black communities in an effort to provide a systematic account of American race relations. His other books include *The Free Negro Family* (1932), *Race and Culture Contacts in the Modern World* (1957), *The Negro Church in America* (1963), and *On Race Relations: Selected Writings* (1968). Frazier's research extended beyond the United States to include studies of race and culture in Brazil and the West Indies. Additionally, he was instrumental in the development of African studies in the United States.

North America

Frazier, Joseph William (Joe)

(b. January 12, 1944, Beaufort, S.C.), African American boxer, 1964 Olympic Gold Medalist, and world professional heavyweight champion whose bouts with Muhammad Ali were among the greatest in boxing history.

Known as "Smokin' Joe" and "Joltin' Joe," Frazier launched his professional career with a string of knockouts. His first 11 opponents went down within six rounds. Frazier became the heavyweight champion on February 16, 1970, after knocking out Jimmy Ellis in five rounds. The following year, on March 8, Frazier clashed with Muhammad Ali in one of the most anticipated and most highly publicized contests in the history of the sport. The fight was Ali's first bout since 1967, the year he was stripped of his heavyweight title for refusing to fight in the Vietnam War. Frazier responded to Ali's prefight public banter by saying, "The arm is still mightier than the mouth." Frazier won the 15-round contest by a unanimous decision.

Frazier successfully defended his title twice after the Ali bout, bringing his victory count to 31. Then, in a January 22, 1973, title bout in Kingston, Jamaica, George Foreman knocked out Frazier in the second round. This loss signaled the demise of Frazier's boxing career. In a 12-round exhibition rematch in 1974, Ali defeated Frazier. In their third bout, the 1975 "Thrilla in Manila" (Philippines), Ali defeated Frazier in the fifteenth round. Frazier retired in 1976 after George Foreman knocked him out in the fifth round of their rematch. He was inducted into the Ring's Boxing Hall of Fame in 1980 and into the International Boxing Hall of Fame in 1990.

Africa

Fredricks, Frankie

(b. October 2, 1967, Namibia), Namibian sprinter.

Although he was a talented athlete as a youth, Frank Fredricks never expected to be in the Olympic Games. His country, Namibia, was a colony until 1990 belonging to South Africa, which was banned from Olympic competition because of the South African policy of apartheid. Yet Fredricks, who has become one of the world's premiere sprinters, has brought four Olympic medals home to Namibia.

An only child, Fredricks was raised by his mother in Katutura township, just outside the Namibian capital, Windhoek. In high school he started running track, specializing in sprinting. He won both the 100- and 200-meter races in the South African school championships his senior year. After graduating, he passed up several college scholarship offers to accept a management training position with the Rossing Uranium Mine Company, which sponsored his education at Brigham Young University in the United States, where he enrolled in 1987.

At Brigham Young, Fredricks not only earned degrees in computer science and business administration, but also became the national collegiate champion in his two sprint events in 1991. When Namibia gained its independence in 1990, the ban on its international competition was lifted, and Fredricks carried the flag for the Namibian team in the 1992 Olympic Games in Barcelona, Spain. He won silver medals in the 100- and 200-meter events.

In international competition leading up to the 1996 Olympic Games Fredricks not only ended Michael Johnson's two-year unbeaten streak with a personal best 19.82 seconds in the 200-meter, but he also came within one one-hundredth of a second of breaking the world record in the 100-meter. Fredricks added two more silver medals in the Atlanta games, coming in second behind Donovan Bailey in the 100-meter and Johnson in the 200-meter.

North America

Free Blacks in the United States,

1619 to 1863, those African Americans who were not enslaved.

In 1966 black author James Baldwin wrote: "To be born in a free society and not be born free is to be born into a lie." A century after the Emancipation Proclamation, Baldwin's words conveyed the pain and the passion that characterized the lives of free blacks in America between 1619 and 1860. Many scholars suggest that during this period, free blacks in America were "more black than free." As historian Leonard Curry explains, "Their educational attainment was limited, their social development was thwarted, occupations were closed to them, housing was denied to them, personal safety eluded them, and basic human dignity was begrudged them." "Because they were black," Curry adds, "freedom was always and everywhere for them cruelly incomplete."

These free Negroes, as they were called at that time, were scattered throughout three distinct regions: the North, the Upper South, and the Lower South. Each region had its own flavor. Many of slavery's most vociferous critics lived in the Northern region, which comprised

Pennsylvania, New York, New Jersey, and the states of New England. The Upper South featured large tobacco plantations and included Virginia, Maryland, North Carolina, Tennessee, Kentucky, and Washington, D.C. The Lower South, often referred to as the Deep South, supported rice and cotton plantations and comprised South Carolina, Florida, Georgia, Alabama, Mississippi, and Louisiana.

Free blacks in America were first documented in Northampton County, Virginia, in 1662. By 1776, 60,000 African Americans—approximately 8 percent of the national black population—were free. The free black population continued to rise steadily, which intimidated many pro-slavery whites. Between 1800 and 1810 the free black population nearly doubled, from 108,395 to 186,446. By 1810, 4 percent of all African Americans in the Deep South, 10 percent in the Upper South, and 75 percent in the North were free. Most free blacks in the North were concentrated in urban cities such as Boston, New York, and Philadelphia. Between 1800 and 1850 the free black population in the nation's 15 largest cities increased ix-fold, compared to a threefold increase for the entire white population. By 1860 there were close to 500,000 free blacks in the United States, approximately 9 percent of the entire black population. It can be said with confidence that on the eve of the Civil War there were, at least, half a million stories of freedom.

Attaining Freedom

Freedom did not come easily. Thousands of runaway slaves were captured, returned to slavery, or executed by white posses. Thousands more refused even to entertain the notion of freedom, some out of fear, others out of apathy. Harriet Tubman, famed black conductor of the Underground Railroad, said, "I freed thousands of slaves. I could have freed thousands more, if they had known they were slaves." Most slaves, however, were not apathetic about freedom.

The most common route to emancipation came through manumission, which entailed the formal release of a slave. A slave could be manumitted privately by an individual or officially by a state law. Vermont became the first state to guarantee immediate manumission when it outlawed slavery in its 1777 constitution. After the American Revolution, many states followed Vermont's lead and changed their own laws regarding manumission. Several other Northern states, including New York, New Jersey, and Pensylvania, adopted a policy of gradual manumission, which meant that the children of all current slaves would automatically be free once they reached a certain age, generally 21 or 25. In the South no states changed their laws to require mandatory manumission, but several did make manumission easier, including Delaware, Maryland, and Virginia. In fact, in Delaware private manumission was so pervasive that 75 percent of all blacks in the state were free by 1810. But in most states private manumission was rare and restricted. Most slaveholders were encouraged to free their slaves only in their wills, if at all.

Not all free blacks were formally manumitted. Thousands "voted with their feet for freedom." It is estimated that between 1776 and 1860 close to 1000 slaves each year ran away. Many of those were forced to leave family members behind as they traveled cautiously along the Underground Railroad—a clandestine network comprising people (black and white) who guided runaway slaves to freedom in the North. Former slaves from the Caribbean also "voted with their feet" when thousands immigrated to America after the Haitian Revolution.

North America

Freedman's Bank,

a financial institution established after the Civil War to aid economic development among African Americans; its unexpected bankruptcy, combined with the federal government's unwillingness to intervene, left thousands of African Americans and African American institutions penniless.

The Freedman's Bank (officially called the Freedman's Savings and Trust Company) was chartered in 1865 as a nonprofit, philanthropic organization whose aim was to benefit the black community after the Civil War by encouraging thrift among African Americans. Although it was not affiliated with the Freedmen's Bureau (see Bureau of Refugees, Freedmen and Abandoned Lands), both organizations were chartered at the same time, and directors at the Freedmen's Bureau also served on the board of directors at the Freedman's Bank. Blacks believed that the bank was government-backed, a notion that the predominately white directors encouraged by using Abraham Lincoln's likeness in bank advertisements. To further inspire black confidence, the directors hired black politicians, ministers, and businessmen to serve as cashiers and advisory board members at local banks.

African Americans responded. In addition to individual deposits, African American organizations such as churches and benevolent societies invested in the Freedman's Bank. Most of the deposits were small, below $50. By 1874 more than 72,000 African Americans had deposited more than $3 million in the bank, which had established branches in all Southern states, as well as in Philadelphia, New York City, and Washington, D.C.

The bank's original charter stipulated a conservative approach, focusing on interest payments to its investors and stable investments such as government securities. Based on initial success, the directors, hoping to increase the return to investors, amended the bank's charter in 1870, allowing the bank to invest in speculative enterprises and to issue loans. Most of these investments centered on white businesses, however, and individual blacks were often unable to acquire loans, which led to black protest. In addition, many of the loans were large and unsecured. When these businesses began to fail in the early 1870s, the bank became insolvent. Most of the bank's white directors resigned during the Panic of 1873. The remaining directors attempted to keep the institution solvent, and named Frederick Douglass bank president in 1874; however, the bank closed a few months later.

Bills introduced in Congress would have provided for the government to provide a full refund of the depositors' investments, but the legislation was never passed. The bank had to sell its assets to begin reimbursing its depositors, but only about half of the bank's investors received reimbursements—and then, only approximately 20 percent of their deposits. The federal government's unwillingness to assume any responsibility for reimbursing the freed people alienated many African Americans.

North America

Freedmen's Hospital,

established by the federal government during the Civil War to offer health services to former slaves, black soldiers, and the indigent; provided treatment and medical training for several generations of African Americans.

Freedmen's Hospital was founded in 1862 to serve former slaves and Union soldiers in the Civil War. At that time—and, indeed, until the Civil Rights Movement—many hospitals and medical colleges were segregated, leaving black patients with few health care options and aspiring black physicians and nurses with limited choice about where to study and practice medicine. The Freedmen's Hospital not only provided service to poor whites and blacks in Washington, D.C., but through its close association with Howard University Medical College (the two joined in 1868 to form a teaching hospital), it came to offer medical training to African Americans.

Africa

Freedom Charter,

the document written in 1955 by the African National Congress and other anti-apartheid groups to express their goals for a free South Africa.

After South Africa's National Party won its second term in power in 1953, Z. K. Matthews, a regional leader of the African National Congress (ANC), proposed a symbolic act of opposition to the National Party's apartheid regime. Like many within the ANC, Matthews was uncomfortable with the more militant actions of the ANC's Congress Youth League and its founders, Nelson Mandela, Oliver Tambo, and others. With government harassment threatening to force the ANC underground, Matthews hoped to reprise the organization's role as the public, national voice opposing apartheid. He called for a national convention "representing all the people of this country irrespective of race or color, to draw up a Freedom Charter for the democratic South Africa of the future."

On June 25, 1955, more than 3000 delegates, representing about 200 organizations, met at Kliptown, a multiracial village outside Johannesburg. The intervening two years had been spent planning for the Congress of the People, as it was called, by soliciting the ideas and opinions of average South Africans. Thousands of fliers asking "If you could make the laws, what would you do?" had been distributed. Armed with the people's wishes, the congress delegates—most of whom were members of the ANC, the South African Coloured People's Association, the South African Indian Congress, and a white antiapartheid group called the Congress of Democrats—drafted the Freedom Charter.

The charter affirmed in its preamble that "South Africa belongs to all who live in it, black and white," then set forth ten main propositions, including "The People Shall Govern," "All Shall Be Equal before the Law," and "There Shall Be Peace and Freedom." The charter also called for equality in education, freedom in land ownership, and equal access to jobs and housing. Although it was criticized by some for its apparent advocacy of socialist economic principles, the Freedom Charter was adopted as the ANC's official platform in 1956. Nearly 30 years later, Nelson Mandela hailed it as "a revolutionary document," one that represented "the people's demands to end the oppression."

North America

Freedom's Journal,
the first African American newspaper in the United States.

Begun in 1827 as a rebuttal to often racist journalism in the mainstream white press, *Freedom's Journal* was the first in what would become a long line of African American newspapers. Its editors, Samuel Cornish and John Brown Russwurm, proposed in their first editorial that their paper, a weekly, would provide an opportunity for black people to speak for themselves rather than be represented by whites. As the first black-owned and edited newspaper in the country, *Freedom's Journal* was a strong proponent of the abolition of slavery, and Cornish and Russwurm often employed black abolitionists.

Despite the newspaper's wide popularity not only in its New York base but elsewhere—some subscribers were from as far away as Haiti—its publication history was brief. From the beginning there had been conflict between Cornish and Russwurm, mostly regarding whether African Americans ought to emigrate to Africa. Cornish, a staunch integrationist, resigned from *Freedom's Journal* in the fall of 1827, leaving Russwurm increasingly to use the paper as a pulpit for his views in favor of African recolonization by free blacks. By 1829 Russwurm had accepted a position as superintendent of education in Liberia, the African nation founded by the American Colonization Society for repatriated blacks, and soon thereafter *Freedom's Journal* ended publications.

Freedom Summer,

a highly publicized campaign in the Deep South to register blacks to vote during the summer of 1964.

During the summer of 1964, thousands of civil rights activists, many of them white college students from the North, descended on Mississippi and other Southern states to try to end the long-time political disfranchisement of African Americans in the region. Although black men had won the right to vote in 1870, thanks to the Fifteenth Amendment, many were unable to exercise that right for the next 100 years.. White local and state officials systematically kept blacks from voting through formal methods, such as poll taxes and literacy tests, and through cruder methods of fear and intimidation, which included beatings and lynchings. The inability to vote was only one of many problems blacks encountered in the racist society around them, but the civil rights officials who decided to zero in on voter registration understood its crucial significance as well as the white supremacists did. An African American voting bloc would be able to effect social and political change.

Freedom Summer marked the climax of intensive voter-registration activities in the South that had started in 1961. Organizers chose to focus their efforts on Mississippi because of the state's particularly dismal voting-rights record: in 1962 only 6.7 percent of African Americans in the state were registered to vote, the lowest percentage in the country. The Freedom Summer campaign was organized by a coalition called the Mississippi Council of Federated Organizations, which included the Congress of Racial Equality (CORE), the National Association for the Advancement of Colored People (NAACP), and the Student Nonviolent Coordinating Committee (SNCC). SNCC volunteers, led by Robert Moses, played the largest role, providing 90 to 95 percent of the funding and 95 percent of the headquarters staff. By mobilizing volunteer white college students from the North to join them, the coalition scored a major public relations coup as hundreds of reporters came to Mississippi from around the country to cover the voter-registration campaign.

The organization of the Mississippi Freedom Democratic Party (MFDP) was a major focus of the summer program. More than 80,000 Mississippians joined the new party, which elected a slate of 68 delegates to the national Democratic Party convention in Atlantic City. The MFDP delegation challenged the seating of the delegates representing Mississippi's all-white Democratic Party. While the effort failed, it drew national attention, particularly through the dramatic televised appeal of MFDP delegate Fannie Lou Hamer. The MFDP challenge also led to a ban on racially discriminatory delegations at future conventions.

Freedom Summer officials established 30 "Freedom Schools" in towns throughout Mississippi to address the racial inequalities in Mississippi's educational system. Mississippi's black schools were invariably poorly funded, and teachers had to use hand-me-down textbooks that offered a racist slant on American history. Many of the white college students were assigned to teach in these schools, whose curriculum included black history, the philosophy of the Civil Rights Movement, and leadership development in addition to remedial instruction in reading and arithmetic. The Freedom Schools had hoped to draw at least 1000 students that first summer and ended up with 3000. The schools became a model for future social programs like Head Start and for alternative educational institutions.

Freedom Summer activists faced threats and harassment throughout the campaign, not only from white supremacist groups, but from local residents and police. Freedom School buildings and the volunteers' homes were frequent targets; 37 black churches and 30 black homes and businesses were firebombed or burned during that summer, and the cases often went unsolved. More than 1000 black and white volunteers were arrested, and at least 80 were beaten by white mobs or racist police officers. But the summer's most infamous act of violence was the murder of three young civil rights workers, a black volunteer, James Chaney, and his white co-workers, Andrew Goodman and Michael Schwerner. On June 21, Chaney, Goodman, and Schwerner set out to investigate a church bombing near Philadelphia, Mississippi, but were arrested that afternoon and held for several hours on alleged traffic violations. Their release from jail was the last time they were seen alive before their badly decomposed bodies were discovered under a nearby dam six weeks later. Goodman and Schwerner had died from single gunshot wounds to the chest, and Chaney from a savage beating.

The murders made headlines all over the country and provoked an outpouring of national support for the Civil Rights Movement. But many black volunteers realized that because two of the victims were white, these murders were attracting much more attention than previous attacks in which the victims had all been black, and this added to the growing resentment they had already begun to feel toward the white volunteers. There was growing dissension within SNCC's ranks over charges of white paternalism and elitism. Black volunteers complained that the whites seemed to think they had a natural claim on leadership roles, and that they treated the rural blacks as though they were ignorant. There was also increasing hostility from both black and white workers over the interracial romances that developed during the summer. Meanwhile, women volunteers of both races were charging both the black and white men with sexist behavior. These conflicts led to lasting divisions within SNCC, especially over the role of white volunteers. Some African American officials, such as Stokely

Carmichael, reacted by gravitating toward the all-black Black Power Movement, while many white volunteers returned to their college campuses and became involved in other forms of social activism, such as the antiwar and women's movements.

Despite the internal divisions, Freedom Summer left a positive legacy. The well-publicized voter registration drives brought national attention to the subject of black disfranchisement, and this eventually led to the 1965 Voting Rights Act, federal legislation that among other things outlawed the tactics that Southern states had used to prevent blacks from voting. Freedom Summer also instilled among African Americans a new consciousness and a new confidence in political action. As Fannie Lou Hamer later said, "Before the 1964 project there were people that wanted change, but they hadn't dared to come out. After 1964 people began moving. To me it's one of the greatest things that ever happened in Mississippi."

North America

Freeman, Morgan

(b. June 1, 1937, Memphis, Tenn.), African American stage, television, and motion-picture actor best known for his critically acclaimed character roles.

Morgan Freeman began acting as a child, enlisted in the United States Air Force at 18, and later returned to acting while enrolled at Los Angeles City College. He then moved to New York City, where he perfected his craft in minor stage plays and appeared on the television soap opera *Another World*. He made his Broadway debut in 1968 in an all-black production of *Hello Dolly!* and went on to win a Tony Award nomination for his performance in *The Mighty Gents* (1978) and Obie Awards (given for off-Broadway work) for his roles in *Coriolanus* (1979), *Mother Courage and Her Children* (1980), and *The Gospel at Colonus* (1983).

Freeman's film debut, in the low-budget children's feature *Who Says I Can't Ride a Rainbow?* (1971), led to a recurring role on the educational television series *The Electric Company* broadcast by the Public Broadcasting Service from 1971 to 1977. In his first Hollywood movie, *Brubaker* (1980), a prison reform drama directed by Robert Redford, Freeman made a strong impression in a small but important part as a death-row inmate. His breakthrough came in 1987, when his chilling performance as a pimp in *Street Smart* earned Best Supporting Actor Awards from the New York Film Critics Circle, the Los Angeles Film Critics Association, and the National Society of Film Critics, in addition to an Academy Award nomination for Best Supporting Actor.

Freeman was nominated for Academy Awards as Best Actor for his performances as a long-suffering chauffeur in the sentimental drama *Driving Miss Daisy* (1989) and as a prison inmate in *The Shawshank Redemption* (1994). In 1993 he made his directing debut with *Bopha!*, a drama set in

South Africa under the country's policy of strict racial segregation known as apartheid. His performance in the 1995 thriller *Seven* won wide critical praise. Freeman's other films include *Clean and Sober* (1988), *Glory* (1989), *Unforgiven* (1992), *Kiss the Girls* (1997), and *Amistad* (1997).

French Guiana,

a former French colony and present-day overseas department of France on the northeastern coast of South America, with the Atlantic Ocean to the north, Suriname to the west, and Brazil to the south and east.

French Guiana's original inhabitants were Indians known as Carib and Arawaks, whose numbers probably did not exceed 25,000. Their first contact with Europeans occurred when Christopher Columbus landed there in 1498 during the course of his third voyage to the New World. Columbus was moved by the region's beauty; in his travelogue he compared the Oyapock River to the river that flows out of the Garden of Eden, as described in the Bible. As a result of this account, subsequent explorers assumed that hidden in Guiana's interior was the legendary lost city of gold, Eldorado (referred to in Genesis 2:10 as lying at the end of a branch of the same river). The search for this city and its treasure was foremost in the minds of Spanish and Portuguese explorers from the sixteenth century. Their lack of success did not dissuade the French, who made their first appearance in Guiana in 1604, from undertaking the same quest. However, France's search for gold in Guiana was accompanied by colonial ambitions.

Although France did not officially possess Guiana until 1667 and only consolidated control of the territory in 1817, the French brought slaves from Africa to Guiana as early as 1652. In contrast to the Caribbean Islands, the slave population in Guiana grew very slowly, mostly as a result of the small number of colonizers. Slave ships preferred to avoid this less lucrative trading spot, stopping there solely when circumstances forced them to do so. The slave population was only 5728 in 1765 and reached a high point of just 19,261 in 1830. Furthermore, many of these African slaves, like a number of their colonial masters, were felled by tropical diseases shortly after their arrival in Guiana. Other slaves fled to the interior of the country, reproducing in certain instances the hunter-gatherer existence they had known in Africa. As a result of these factors, and the sheer difficulty of engaging in agriculture in such a heavily wooded land, the plantation colonialism that was so successful for the French in Martinique and Guadeloupe was a failure in Guiana.

The French persisted in their efforts to develop Guiana. When the colony's principal industries, sugar and timber, collapsed following the abolition of slavery in 1848, France decided to transform Guiana into a penal colony. The colonial administrators defended the idea in these terms: France would be rid of its worst element, and the prisoners—who, according to the system of doublage (doubling), had to remain in the colony following their

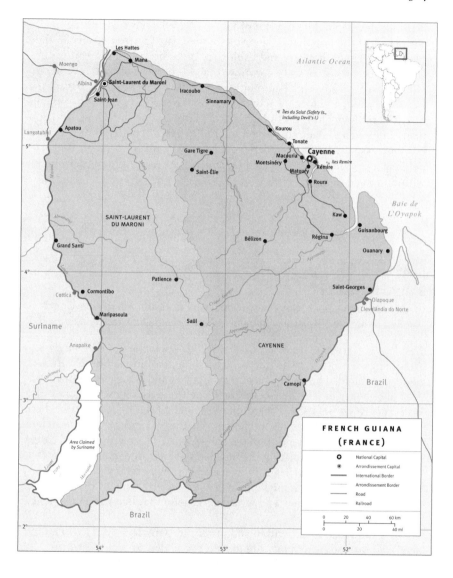

initial sentence for an equal amount of time—would eventually form a stable colonizing population. Seventy thousand convicted criminals were sent to Guiana from 1852 to 1939, including Alfred Dreyfus and Henri Charrière, whose attempt to escape Devil's Island was celebrated in Charrière's novel *Papillon* (1969). However, 90 percent of these prisoners died of malaria or yellow fever. The prisons were shut down in 1946. A more successful venture for developing Guiana was the European Space Agency's establishment of a satellite launching pad in Kourou in 1968. However, most of the jobs provided by this project have gone to expatriates, and the benefit to the local economy has been negligible.

Today, French Guiana is still perceived as a land of unfulfilled potential.

Plans for developing the interior of Guiana have largely been abandoned, with most of the population living along the coast (50 percent live in the capital, Cayenne). Forestry and fishing are now the largest industries, with fish exports accounting for more than 60 percent of total revenue in 1992. There is also a small amount of agriculture (rice, cassava, bananas, and sugar cane) and logging activity, but not enough to sustain the population. Unemployment is quite high, particularly among the young, and many in French Guiana survive on unemployment benefits from France. For this reason, there is no independence movement to speak of. What political agitation exists in French Guiana is the result of border disputes with Suriname.

Africa

Fugard, Athol

(b. June 11, 1932, near Middleburg, South Africa), South African playwright whose dramatic works deal with the personal wounds inflicted by apartheid.

Best known for his plays *Blood Knot* and *Master Harold . . . and the Boys*, Athol Fugard brought to a wide audience images of life in South Africa under apartheid. The child of an English father and Afrikaner mother, Fugard grew up in Port Elizabeth, the Cape Province city where most of his plays are set. In 1956, Fugard married Sheila Meiring, an actress whom he credits for developing his interest in theater. In 1958 he became a clerk for the Fordsburg Native Commissioner's Court. The court handled cases of people accused of violating the pass laws, which were among the many laws restricting Africans' right to live and work where they pleased. Fugard called the job "the ugliest thing I have ever been part of," but it also inspired the intimate view of apartheid's cruelty that became an element in his work.

By 1959 Fugard had written and produced two plays, *No-Good Friday* and *Nongogo*, and he and his wife moved to London to gain theatrical experience. They stayed only a year, returning to South Africa after the Sharpeville massacre in 1960. Fugard's next play, *The Blood Knot*, opened in 1961 with Fugard and an African actor, Zakes Mokae, playing two mixed-race half-brothers confronting the psychic toll of institutionalized racism. At the same time Fugard began protesting the official segregation of theater audiences.

In 1967 the South African government seized Fugard's passport and placed him under surveillance. But the harassment did not stop Fugard from collaborating in 1972 with black actor-playwrights John Kani and Winston Ntshona on *Sizwe Banzi Is Dead* and *The Island*, each of which was nominated for three Tony Awards.

Fugitive Slave Laws,

laws passed by the United States Congress in 1793 and 1850 providing for the return of runaway slaves to their owners.

Early Fugitive Laws

Before the American colonies won independence from Great Britain, several Southern legislatures passed laws providing for the return of runaway slaves. Under some of these laws, slaves who resisted arrest could be killed and their owners reimbursed by the government. Under others, penalties were levied against people who protected runaways and rewards given to those who caught them. The laws, however, had little effect outside the colonies that passed them, leaving Northerners free to harbor escaped slaves.

In 1787 the Confederated Congress passed the Northwest Ordinance, which banned slavery from the Northwest Territory but allowed slaves who fled to the territory to be caught and returned to their owners. The ordinance did not, however, require governments or settlers to cooperate in the capture and return of runaways. Two years later the U.S. Constitution took effect, with a clause in Article IV, Section 2, that said runaway slaves and indentured servants "shall be delivered" to their masters when requested. The Constitution did not specifically require governments to help in the return of fugitives.

Fugitive Slave Act of 1793

Congress intended the Fugitive Slave Act of 1793 to resolve these ambiguities. Slave catchers were permitted to capture a runaway slave in any state or territory and needed only to prove orally to a federal or state judge that the person was an escaped slave. The slave was not guaranteed a trial by jury, and the judge's decision was final. Anyone sheltering an escaped slave could be fined $500, a stiff penalty at the time.

Fuller, Meta Vaux Warrick

(b. June 9, 1877, Philadelphia, Pa.; d. March 18, 1968, Framingham, Mass.), African American sculptor, one of the earliest studio artists to depict black themes.

Meta Vaux Warrick Fuller was born in Philadelphia in 1877, the daughter of two successful entrepreneurs. Her father owned a catering business and a barber shop, and her mother was a hairdresser. She grew up in a privileged home, receiving lessons in art, music, dance, and horseback riding. When one of her high school projects at the J. Liberty Tadd Industrial Art School was selected to be part of Tadd's exhibit at the 1893 World's Columbian Exposition in Chicago, her public career as an artist began.

In 1894 Fuller received a three-year scholarship to the Pennsylvania School of Industrial Art, followed by a one-year postgraduate fellowship in 1897. As a student she received several awards and prizes for her sculpture. Her work had a signature bold, sensational style that her instructors felt would be especially successful overseas, so in September 1899, Fuller sailed for Paris. During the next four years she studied at the Académie Colarossi and the Ecole des Beaux-Arts and received private guidance from such prominent sculptors as Auguste Rodin and Augustus Saint-Gaudens. Rodin was an especially significant early supporter, and after he praised her 1901 sculpture *Secret Sorrow (Man Eating His Heart)*, her work was exhibited at several important galleries.

In Paris Fuller drew inspiration for her sculptures from Greek myths, French literature, and the Bible as well as various European traditions. Her works often portrayed dramatic and even grotesque figures—other titles included *Medusa*, *The Wretched*, and *Man Carrying a Dead Comrade*—and were praised for their force and power; the French press called Fuller "the delicate sculptor of horrors." But even as she was developing a reputation based on this genre of work, new influences began to present themselves.

One of her earliest friends in Paris was the African American painter Henry O. Tanner. In 1900, during a trip to Paris, W. E. B. Du Bois saw Fuller's work at the Paris Universal Exposition, and both Tanner and Du Bois began encouraging her to explore African American subjects. Fuller initially resisted these suggestions, content with the images that had made her a success in Paris. But when she decided to return to the United S tates in October 1902, she found the art world in her hometown unwilling to accept her. After the cold reception she received from mainstream Philadelphia critics and dealers, Fuller began constructing new pieces that appealed to the black Philadelphia audience. In the process, she became one of the first African American studio artists to depict African American faces and themes.

In 1907 Fuller became the first black woman artist to receive a federal commission for her work when she was asked to contribute a set of tableaux on African American history for the Jamestown Tercentennial Exposition. The finished work was awarded a gold medal and brought her national attention.

Funk,

a musical style pioneered by James Brown and Sly and the Family Stone during the late 1960s and 1970s; funk evolved from soul music, deepening its rhythms and incorporating psychedelic elements inspired by late 1960s rock 'n' roll.

Funk evolved from soul music during the late 1960s, much as Black Power grew out of the Civil Rights Movement. During the 1960s rhythm and blues (R&B) performers drew upon the harmonies and vocal style of gospel music to create the distinctive style that became known as soul music. Soul music voiced the pride and optimism that many blacks shared during the Civil Rights Movement. By the late 1960s, the political climate had deteriorated. The Vietnam War displaced President Lyndon Johnson's War on Poverty, and between 1965 and 1968 violence erupted in many black urban neighborhoods. The civil rights coalition was increasingly divided as the Black Power Movement brought a new militancy to African American politics.

Popular music could not help reflecting such influences, and for African Americans the result was funk. Funk was a heavily rhythmic, dance-oriented music with lyrics that mostly focused on sex, drugs, and partying. Surprisingly often, however, funk lyrics spoke to contemporary black pride and anger. In "Say It Loud (I'm Black and I'm Proud)" (1968), James Brown sang, "We'd rather die on our feet, than be livin' on our knees." Sly and the Family Stone recorded equally militant lyrics in such songs as "Don't Call Me Nigger, Whitey" (1969) and on the album *There's a Riot Going On* (1971). Parliament's "Chocolate City" (1975) envisioned the possibilities of an all-black American government.

Ultimately, funk music was not about political commentary; it was about the beat. More than any other musician, George Clinton has kept funk music alive. Through the 1970s and 1980s Clinton and his related and overlapping groups Parliament and Funkadelic, which during the 1970s began performing together as P-Funk, kept the funk beat alive during an era dominated by disco and punk rock. Other popular funk bands included Earth, Wind, and Fire; the Ohio Players; the Commodores; and the Bar-Kays.

G

Gabon,

coastal country in Central Africa, bordered by Equatorial Guinea, Cameroon, and Republic of the Congo.

Densely forested and rich in natural resources, Gabon has one of Africa's strongest economies. Gabon suffered less from the slave trade than other areas along Africa's Atlantic coast. However, French settlers, commercial enterprises, and colonial administrators irreversibly transformed its economy and society in the nineteenth century. The French created a two-tiered society, with a small elite loyal to French political and commercial interests and a poor, disfranchised majority. The leaders of independent Gabon have preserved and maintained this division. At the head of Gabon's elite is President Omar Bongo, who has maintained a firm monopoly on power since 1967. Although Bongo's government has made investments in transportation and social services, the country's large oil wealth has benefited primarily Bongo and his clients, and the vast majority of the population remains impoverished.

Gabon (Ready Reference)

Official Name: Gabonese Republic
Area: 267,667 sq km (103,347 sq mi)
Location: Bounded on the northwest by Equatorial Guinea, on the north by Cameroon, on the east and south by the Republic of the Congo, and on the west by the Atlantic Ocean
Capital: Libreville (population 365,650 [1993 estimate])

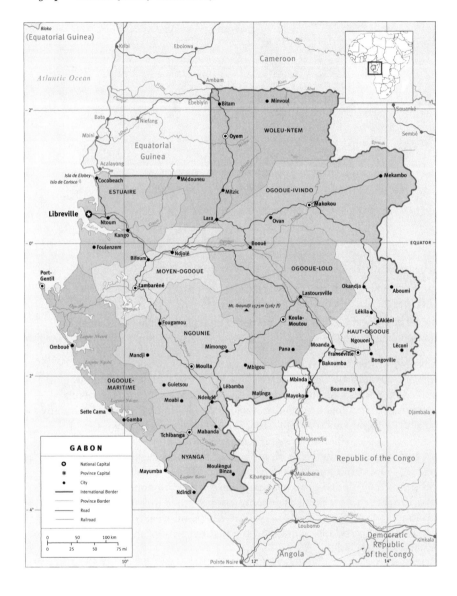

Other Major Cities: Port-Gentil (population 164,000), Franceville (75,000) (1988 estimate)

Population: 1,207,844 (1998 estimate)

Population Density: 5 persons per sq km (about 13 persons per sq mi); over half the population lives in cities, and much of the interior is uninhabited.

Population Below Age 15: 33 percent (male 202,364; female 202,249 [1998 estimate])

Population Growth Rate: 1.48 percent (1998 estimate)

Total Fertility Rate: 3.81 children born per woman (1998 estimate)

Life Expectancy at Birth: Total population: 56.51 years (male 53.55 years; female 59.56 years [1998 estimate])

Infant Mortality Rate: 85.43 deaths per 1000 live births (1998 estimate)

Literacy Rate (age 15 and over who can read and write): Total population 63.2 percent (male 73.7 percent; female 53.3 percent [1995 estimate])

Education: Schooling is compulsory in Gabon for all children between ages 6 and 16, though not all children in that age group actually attend school. In the early 1990s about 210,000 pupils were annually attending primary

A Gabonese father holds his infant daughter. *CORBIS/The Purcell Team*

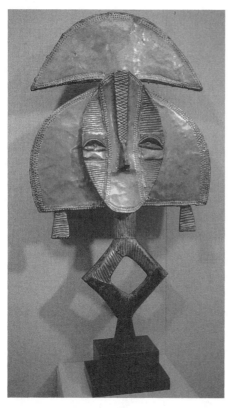

This Kota figure is made of wood overlaid with copper and brass. The function of such sculptures was to keep watch over the bones of important ancestors. *CORBIS/Charles & Josette Lenars*

schools, and about 56,700 students were enrolled in secondary schools. The country has technical institutions and teachers colleges, as well as a university, the Université Omar Bongo (founded in 1970).

Languages: The official language is French, but many Gabonese speak Bantu languages.

Ethnic Groups: The ethnic makeup of the Gabonese is diverse. Of the country's approximately 40 ethnic groups, most belong to the Fang, Pounou, Nzeiby, or Téké groupings. Europeans, mostly French, form a small but prominent minority. Pygmies are believed to have been the original inhabitants of the country, but only a few thousand remain.

Religions: About 60 percent of the population is Christian, primarily Roman Catholic. Most of the remainder, except for a small Islamic community, follow traditional beliefs.

Climate: Gabon has a hot and humid climate. The temperature varies only slightly throughout the year, hovering around 27° C (80° F). The dry seasons stretch from February to April and October to November. In Libreville the annual rainfall often exceeds 2500 mm (100 in).

Land, Plants, and Animals: Coastal lowlands gird the western shores of Gabon. The interior contains a plateau zone that extends over the entire northern and eastern sections of Gabon and part of the south. The Cristal and Chaillu mountains cut across the interior, sending numerous rivers down to the Atlantic. Dense equatorial rain forest covers three-quarters of the country.

Natural Resources: Gabon is rich in mineral resources. Deposits of uranium, manganese, and petroleum dot the country, all of which are being exploited. Large deposits of iron ore, considered among the richest in the world, have also been discovered. Other Gabonese resources include lead and silver ore. Stands of *okoume*, mahogany, *kevazing* and ebony make the forests of Gabon valuable.

Currency: The Communauté Financière Africaine franc

Gross Domestic Product (GDP): $6 billion (1996 estimate)

GDP per Capita: $5000 (1996 estimate)

GDP Real Growth Rate: 3.0 percent (1996 estimate)

Primary Economic Activities: Agriculture, forestry, fishing, and mining

Primary Crops: Cassava, plantains, sugar cane, yams, and taro

Industries: Food and beverage, textile, lumbering and plywood, cement, petroleum extraction and refining, manganese, uranium, and gold mining

Primary Exports: Crude oil, timber, manganese, and uranium

Primary Imports: Foodstuffs, chemical products, petroleum products, construction materials, and machinery

Primary Trade Partners: France, African countries, United States, Japan, and the Netherlands

Government: Under a constitution adopted in 1991, the voting population elects the president directly for a term of five years, as well as a 120-member National Assembly. The current president is El Hadj Omar Bongo; Bongo has appointed Paulin Obame Macías Nguema as prime minister.

North America

Gabriel Prosser Conspiracy,
one of the first attempted American slave rebellions.

The Gabriel Prosser Conspiracy of 1800 was one of the earliest and most extensively planned slave insurrections in American history. The plan, which was drawn up by a slave named Gabriel Prosser, called for slaves to seize weapons, kill their white masters, and free thousands of fellow slaves throughout Virginia. If a tumultuous thunderstorm and an act of betrayal had not undermined the plot, many historians believe the rebellion would have been successful.

The word "conspiracy," which has come to have almost exclusively negative connotations, was the description used by whites at that time. The word conveyed the unwillingness of most slaveholding whites to recognize the widespread discontent in the slave community. The word also suggests the fear of slave uprisings that gripped antebellum white Southerners.

Prosser and 26 other slaves were convicted of insurrection and executed. Many others faced long prison sentences. A crackdown immediately followed the foiled insurrection. Shaken by the rebellion, Virginia officials formed a state militia to monitor slave gatherings and prevent future uprisings. Throughout the South, laws restricting African American literacy were strengthened, and the freedom of slave artisans to contract out their labor was curtailed. Although Prosser's conspiracy failed, it inspired similar failed plots in North Carolina in 1802 and in South Carolina in 1822.

Gaines, Ernest J.

(b. January 15, 1933, Oscar, La.), African American novelist and short story writer best known for his 1971 novel *The Autobiography of Miss Jane Pittman*.

Although Ernest Gaines has spent much of his adult life in the San Francisco Bay Area, all of his work returns to the setting of his southern Louisiana childhood, with its complicated intersections of African American, Creole, Cajun, and white culture. In college Gaines began to read voraciously and write his own stories. He was never exposed to black writers. His literary models were such white American writers as Ernest Hemingway and William Faulkner and European writers such as Russian novelist Leo Tolstoy. He decided early, however, to focus his own writing on what he knew—which meant portraying African American culture and language. Gaines published his first short stories in a college literary magazine, where they were noticed by the white literary agent Dorothea Oppenheimer. Oppenheimer helped Gaines obtain a fellowship to Stanford University to study creative writing and a contract with Dial Press that led to his first novel, *Catherine Carmier* (1964). But it was *The Autobiography of Miss Jane Pittman* (1971) that brought Gaines widespread recognition.

In this novel the eponymous 108-year-old heroine tells her life story in her own words—a life story that follows Miss Jane and her community through slavery, Reconstruction, Jim Crow, and the Civil Rights Movement. The compelling narrative that resulted became a best-selling book and a successful made-for-television movie.

Gairy, Eric

(b. 1922; d. 1997), former prime minister of Grenada. Gairy entered public life as a union leader in Grenada. In 1951 he founded the country's first political party, the pro-union, pro-independence Grenada United Labour Party (GULP). Gairy went on to become the country's first black elected leader. He led the assembly from 1951 to 1957, 1961 to 1962, and again from 1967 until 1974 when he became the country's first prime minister. Gairy was removed from power in a military coup in 1979 (see Grenada).

Gama, José Basílio da

(b. July 22, 1740, São José do Rio das Mortes (later São José del Rei, now Tiradentes), Minas Gerais, Brazil; d. July 31, 1795, Lisbon, Portugal), mulatto poet and significant contributor to Brazil's school of Arcadian literature.

Gama, Luís Gonzaga Pinto da

(b. June 21, 1830, Salvador, Bahia, Brazil; d. August 24, 1882, São Paulo, Brazil), a founding member of the abolitionist movement in Brazil; a mulatto journalist, poet, and legal activist who worked to free Africans who had been enslaved after the ban on the international slave trade.

Gama, Vasco da

(b. 1469, Sines, Alemtejo; d. 1524, Cochin, India), Portuguese explorer who established the colony of Mozambique.

Vasco da Gama was en route to India when he became the second European to sail around the Cape of Good Hope in 1497. During the two-year voyage commissioned by King Manuel of Portugal, da Gama stopped at various points along the East Africa coast, including present-day Mozambique, Mombasa, Malindi, and Zanzibar. In 1502 da Gama was again commissioned by the king to round the Cape of Good Hope, this time to establish economic and political sovereignty over areas of East Africa. Da Gama founded the Portuguese colonies of *Mozambique* and Sofala (now part of Mozambique) and imposed Portuguese rule on the coastal islands of Zanzibar and Kilwa. The Portuguese maintained control of the coastal islands until 1729, when a group of Omani Arabs took over the islands.

Gambia River,

one of the longest navigable rivers in West Africa, flowing 1170 km (700 mi) from the highlands of Fouta Djallon in Guinea, north into Senegal, and westward through the Gambia to the Atlantic Ocean.

Gambia, The,

a small country on the far west coast of Africa.

Only a small strip of Atlantic coastline keeps the Republic of the Gambia from being completely surrounded by its larger neighbor, Senegal. Never more than 50 km (30 mi) wide, the Gambia stretches for more than 500 km (300 mi), along both banks of the Gambia River and into the center of Senegal. The Gambia owes its creation to British economic interests, first

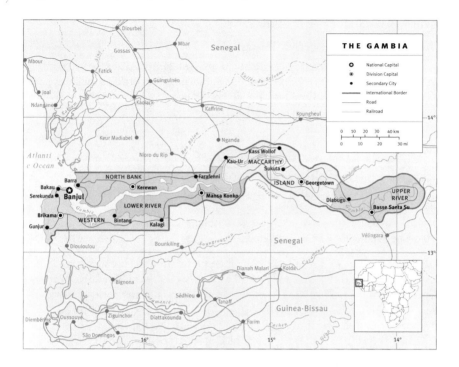

in the transatlantic slave trade, then in the coastal trade in agricultural and manufactured commodities. But the British zone of control ended where their boats encountered the Gambia River waterfalls, never reaching into the river basin's natural hinterland. This severely constrained the Gambia's economic growth and ultimately shaped its national character. Most ethnic groups of the Gambia are found in larger numbers within Senegal, and the small nation still struggles to forge a national identity, apart from a shared experience of British colonial rule. The Gambia's peculiar geography illustrates the irrationality of Africa's colonial boundaries, and the difficulty of using them as the basis for the creation of nation-states in the postcolonial era.

Africa

Gambia, The (Ready Reference)

Official Name: Republic of the Gambia

Area: 11,295 sq km (4,361 sq mi)

Location: Western Africa; borders the North Atlantic and Senegal

Capital: Banjul (formerly called Bathurst) (population 44,188 [1983 estimate])

Population: 1,291,858 (1998 estimate)

Population Density: 87 persons per sq km (about 225 persons per sq mi)

Population Below Age 15: Total population: 46 percent (male 296,108; female 295,136 [1998 estimate])

Population Growth Rate: 3.42 percent (1998 estimate)

Total Fertility Rate: 5.9 children born per woman (1998 estimate)

Life Expectancy at Birth: Total population: 53.9 years (male 51.5 years; female 56.3 years [1998 estimate])

Infant Mortality Rate: 77.1 deaths per 1000 live births (1998 estimate)

Literacy Rate (age 15 and over who can read and write): Total population: 38.6 percent (male 52.8 percent; female 24.9 percent [1995 estimate])

Education: Primary education in the Gambia is free but not compulsory. In the early 1990s nearly 52 percent of all eligible primary-school-aged children attended school, but only 15 percent of all children between the ages of 14 and 20 attended school.

Languages: English is the official language, but each ethnic group uses its own language. The most common languages are Mandinka, Wolof, and Fulani.

Ethnic Groups: The population comprises the Mandinka, accounting for 42 percent of the population; the Fulani, who predominate in the eastern part of the country and account for 18 percent of the population; the Wolof, who live mainly in Banjul and the western part of the country; the Jola, who live in the west; the Serahuli; and a small Aku community.

A district nurse holds a newborn baby in the Gambia. *CORBIS/Liba Taylor*

Women carry firewood on their heads as they walk along a street in Banjul, the capital and largest city of the Republic of the Gambia. *CORBIS/Nik Wheeler*

Religions: About 90 percent of the population is Muslim. About 9 percent is Christian, and 1 percent adheres to indigenous beliefs.

Climate: Subtropical with distinct hot and cool seasons. The temperatures range from 16° C (about 60° F) in the cool season, which lasts from November to May, to 43° C (110° F) in the summer. The rainy season lasts from June to November and the average annual rainfall is about 1020 mm (about 40 in).

Land, Plants, and Animals: Almost all of Gambia borders on the Gambia River. The country's land varies between sand and swamp land. Mangroves, oil palm, rubber vine, cedars, and mahogany trees thrive in this environment. Animals include the leopard, wild boar, crocodile, hippopotamus, and several species of antelope. Some game birds, such as the guinea fowl and the sand grouse, are also plentiful.

Natural Resources: Natural resources include the Gambia River, one of Africa's best navigable waterways; fish; and soil suited to growing peanuts.

Currency: The dalasi

Gross Domestic Product (GDP): $1.23 billion (1997 estimate)

GDP per Capita: $1000 (1997 estimate)

GDP Real Growth Rate: 21 percent (1997 estimate)

Primary Economic Activities: Agriculture (75 percent of the population), tourism, commerce, and services

Primary Crops: Peanuts, millet, sorghum, rice, corn, cassava (tapioca), palm kernels, and livestock

Industries: Peanut processing, fish and hides, beverages, agricultural machinery assembly, woodworking, metalworking, and clothing

Primary Exports: Peanuts and peanut products, fish, cotton lint, and palm kernels

Primary Imports: Foodstuffs, manufactures, raw materials, fuel, machinery, and transport equipment

Primary Trade Partners: Great Britain, China, France, Germany, Russia, and the United States

Government: The Gambia is a republic under multiparty democratic rule. Following a coup d'état in July 1994, Yahya Jammeh named himself

Gambian village women wear traditional dress. *CORBIS/Liba Taylor*

chairman of the Armed Forces Provisional Ruling Council. Bowing to external and internal pressure, Jammeh held elections in September 1996, and was elected to a five-year term with 55.5 percent of the vote. The unicameral National Assembly has 49 seats, of which 45 are elected and 4 are presidential appointees.

Latin America and the Caribbean

Ganga Zumba,

African king who led the maroon settlement Quilombo dos Palmares, in Brazil. Ganga Zumba died in 1685.

Latin America and the Caribbean

Gantois, Mãe Menininha do

(b. February 10, 1894, Salvador, Bahia, Brazil; d. August 13, 1986), one of the most famous and revered priestesses of Brazil's African-derived Candomblé religion; also known as Maria Escolástica da Conceição Nazaré.

Mãe Menininha do Gantois was born to Afro-Brazilian parents of Nigerian descent. A resident of the city of Salvador in Bahia, Mãe Menininha was one of the most respected Brazilian *mães-de-santo* or *ialorixás* (Candomblé priestesses) of her time. She was widely consulted and revered throughout Brazil. She was the head of the Terreiro do Gantois, a temple founded by her aunt and godmother Pulquéria da Conceição, also an *iaolorixá*. Mãe Pulquéria nicknamed her goddaughter Menininha, which means "little girl" in Portuguese (mãe means mother, and is a title often given to Candomblé priestesses). Mãe Menininha was a devotee, or "daughter," of Oxum, one of the *orixás* (deities) of Candomblé's pantheon.

Mãe Menininha dedicated her life to Candomblé during a time when African religions were still repressed in Brazil. She suffered imprisonment and violent persecution by the police due to her involvement with Candomblé. Her resistance to these discriminatory governmental policies against Afro-Brazilian religious practices was essential for the survival of Candomblé as an important part of Brazilian culture. Along with other prominent Candomblé priestesses such as Stella do Oxóssi, Mãe Menininha also asserted the Africanness of Candomblé, emphasizing that the religion was not the same as Roman Catholicism.

When Mãe Menininha died at age 92, the governor of the state of Bahia declared three days of mourning. Pierre Verger, an expert on Candomblé, said "With her a whole generation is gone." The Terreiro do Gantois, located in the neighborhood of Federação, was set aside as a national public historic landmark.

Latin America and the Caribbean

Garifuna,

**people of mixed Amerindian and African descent, whose unique culture origi-
nally developed in the eastern Caribbean islands; they later resettled along the
coast of southern Central America, where they continue to live today.**

The origins of the Garifuna are not entirely clear, but their Arawak-speaking
Indian ancestors almost certainly hailed from tropical forests in South
America. Between 5000 B.C.E. and 1400 C.E. these peoples migrated in successive waves to the islands of the Lesser Antilles, where European naviga-
tors later encountered them.

While some experts argue that Caribs and Arawaks indeed had distinctive traits, others believe that Europeans simply grouped native peoples by
whether they were hostile or friendly.

By the sixteenth century England and Spain had enslaved most of these
native peoples for work on Caribbean plantations or the natives had died as
a result of disease or war. The few who retained their freedom sometimes
retaliated by raiding European plantations, often carrying off black slaves
who had been imported from Africa. Other African slaves fled from their
masters to the sanctuary of the free Indian islanders.

One particular center of Carib resistance to European rule were the
islands of Dominica and St. Vincent. In 1635 two Spanish slave ships were
shipwrecked off the coast of St. Vincent, and the Caribs welcomed the
newly freed slaves into their communities. Over the decades the Africans
and Amerindians intermarried, developing a hybrid culture, and in time
became a single group now known as Garifuna or Garinagu. To Europeans,
they were known as Black Caribs, to distinguish them from Yellow or Red
Caribs. Though many state that the Garifuna are phenotypically black, culturally they retain many elements of their Carib heritage, such as their own
Arawak language and native patterns of subsistence, political organization,
and kinship.

North America

Garnet, Henry Highland

**(b. 1815, New Market, Md.; d. February 12, 1882, Monrovia, Liberia), minister
and abolitionist whose advocacy of an uprising to free the slaves made him
one of the most controversial African American leaders of the nineteenth
century.**

Henry Highland Garnet was born a slave on a plantation in Kent County,
Maryland, where his grandfather, a former chieftain in Africa, was a leader
of the slave community. In 1824 Garnet's father escaped, taking the rest of
his family with him to New York City. While the father became an active

leader of the African Methodist Episcopal Church, Garnet was enrolled in the African Free School. He spent several years afterward as a sailor and a farmer's apprentice before returning to school.

Garnet completed his studies by 1840. Settling in Troy, New York, Garnet attached himself to a black congregation and transformed the area into an important center for abolitionism. His church soon became a stop on the Underground Railroad and he published several short-lived abolitionist periodicals. In 1842 he married Julia Williams. The following year he became an ordained Presbyterian minister and made his stormy debut in national politics with his speech at a convention for African Americans.

Titled *"Address to the Slaves of the United States of America"* Garnet's real audience was the assemblage of African American leaders, whom he urged to fulfill God's will by ending slavery. At the time, invoking Christianity to call for what was essentially a slave insurrection was quite radical. Garnet's remarks brought him into direct conflict with Frederick Douglass, who favored the more gradualist approach to abolition—advocated by William Lloyd Garrison—that involved appeals to morality. Douglass called on the conventioneers to defeat a resolution for distribution of Garnet's speech. A heated debate followed and Douglass's motion narrowly carried the day. Garnet's address nonetheless gained him national notoriety, and at later conventions he introduced the speech again.

When the Civil War broke out, Garnet joined with other African Americans in pushing the reluctant Abraham Lincoln to use the opportunity the war provided to abolish slavery. He also urged Lincoln to allow blacks to serve in the Union Army, a request to which Lincoln eventually yielded. Garnet paid a price for his outspokenness. In the New York City Draft Riot of 1863, his life was endangered, his church badly damaged, and many blacks killed. He nonetheless continued his advocacy and recruitment of black troops.

In 1864 he moved his ministry to Washington, D.C., where, on the anniversary of the ratification of the Thirteenth Amendment, he became the first African American to speak before Congress.

In 1881 the government asked Garnet to serve as minister to Liberia. He had been in poor health for some time, but having long entertained the dream of redeeming Africa, he accepted the offer. He left in 1881 and died the following February.

Latin America and the Caribbean

Garrido, Juan: A Black Conquistador in Mexico

Although most blacks who came to America in early years were slaves, records of the *Casa de Contratación* show that a good many black freedpeople from Seville and elsewhere found passage on westward-bound ships. Some of them settled in the Caribbean region, and others followed the tide of conquest to Mexico and Peru, identifying themselves no doubt as Catholic subjects of a Spanish king, with much the same privileges and ambitions as white Spaniards.

There is record of an African who apparently crossed the Atlantic as a freedman, participated in the siege of Tenochtitlán and, in subsequent conquests and explorations, tried his hand as an entrepreneur (with both black and Indian slaves of his own) in the early search for gold, and took his place as a citizen in the Spanish quarter of Mexico City. His name was Juan Garrido, and he was still alive in the late 1540s when he wrote or dictated a short résumé of his services to the Crown: "Juan Garrido, black in color . . . says that he, of his own free will, became a Christian in Lisbon, [then] was in Castile for seven years, and crossed to Santo Domingo where he remained an equal length of time. From there he visited other islands, and then went to San Juan de Puerto Rico, where he spent much time, after which he came to New Spain. He was present at the taking of the city of Mexico and in other conquests, and later [went] to the island with the marquis. He was the first to plant and harvest wheat in this land, the source of all that there now is, and he brought many vegetable seeds to New Spain. He is married and has three children, and is very poor with nothing to maintain himself."

The early chronology of this statement is vague, but working backward from the fall of Tenochtitlán (1521), one can assume that Garrido arrived in America about 1510. While his role in the Tenochtitlán episode remains obscure, Garrido took part in at least one of the expeditions sent out by Cortés after the conquest of the Triple Alliance to secure control and investigate the economic potential of outlying areas.

North America

Garvey, Marcus Mosiah

(b. August 7, 1887, St. Ann's Bay, Jamaica; d. June 10, 1940, London, England), founder and leader of the Universal Negro Improvement Association, the largest organization dedicated to black economic self-determination and racial pride.

Photographs exist of Marcus Garvey in the full regal uniform that he wore during marches and rallies. These photographs are still sold on the streets of Harlem, where the Universal Negro Improvement Association (UNIA) had its headquarters in the years during and after World War I. Garvey, called a "black Moses" during his lifetime, created the largest African American organization, with hundreds of chapters across the world at its height. While Garvey is predominantly remembered as a back-to-Africa proponent, it is clear that the scope of his ideas and the UNIA's actions go beyond that characterization.

Marcus Garvey was born in St. Ann's Bay, Jamaica. In 1914 Garvey

Marcus Garvey, dressed in the uniform he adopted after the first UNIA convention elected him provisional president of Africa, rides in a parade. *CORBIS/Underwood & Underwood*

began the UNIA in Kingston. Admittedly influenced by Booker T. Washington and his autobiographical *Up from Slavery*, Garvey wanted to create an industrial training school, much like Tuskegee. Garvey envisioned an organization dedicated to racial uplift, one that would "embrace the purpose of all black humanity." Disappointed with his limited success, Garvey went to New York on March 23, 1916, planning to raise funds and lecture throughout the country. After delivering speeches around Canada and the United States, he returned to Harlem in 1917, where he became known for his street speeches. The UNIA headquarters, Liberty Hall, was reestablished in Harlem in May 1917.

The massive migration of black Southerners to Northern cities, triggered by the industrial demands of World War I, energized black urban life and stimulated racial consciousness, providing a vital outlet for the growth of Garvey's organization. At the same time, black participation in World War I, the war "to make the world safe for democracy," enticed black political aspirations. Wartime hopes, however, were quickly eclipsed by the racial violence and lynching that followed in the summer of 1919, underscoring the incongruity of America's democratic ideals and the determination of whites to maintain white supremacy.

Garvey's ideas particularly resonated with African Americans during the postwar period. At the core of Garvey's program was an emphasis on black economic self-reliance, black people's rights to political self-determination, and the founding of a black nation on the continent of Africa. Garvey's charismatic style, and the magnificent UNIA parades of uniformed corps of UNIA Black Cross nurses, legions, and other divisions, celebrated blackness and racial pride. Garvey urged black people to take control of their destiny:

The UNIA movement won broad support in New York's black community, and Garvey quickly gained national and international prominence. Within a year UNIA chapters were created throughout the United States and in Central and South America, the West Indies, West Africa, England, and Canada. The UNIA created the Negro Factories Corporation in 1918, which supported the development of black-owned businesses, including a black doll factory, which employed more than a thousand African Americans. The UNIA also began publishing the *Negro World Weekly*, which became the most widely distributed African diasporic publication.

Perhaps the largest endeavor of the UNIA was the Black Star Steamship Line, an enterprise intended to provide a means for African Americans to return to Africa while also enabling black people around the Atlantic to exchange goods and services. The company's three ships (one called the SS Frederick Douglass) were owned and operated by black people and made travel and trade possible between their United States, Caribbean, Central American, and African stops. The economically independent Black Star Line was a symbol of pride for blacks and seemed to attract more members to the UNIA.

In August 1920, 25,000 people attended the first UNIA convention in New York's Madison Square Garden. There, Garvey was elected president-general of the organization, and the Declaration of Rights of the Negro Peoples of the World was written. The convention produced an anthem—the *Universal Ethiopian Anthem*—and red, black, and green became the colors of African peoples. Around this time, a UNIA leader was sent to Liberia to develop further Garvey's idea for a colony there.

As a result of large financial obligations and managerial errors, the Black Star Line failed in 1921 and ended operations. Constant criticism from the National Association for the Advancement of Colored People (NAACP) (most visibly from member W. E. B. Du Bois) and United States government opposition took its toll on the UNIA. Early in 1922 Garvey was indicted on mail fraud charges regarding the Black Star Line's stock sale. He was convicted and given a maximum prison sentence of five years by Judge Julian Mack, also an NAACP member. Garvey appealed and was defeated; he entered the Atlanta federal penitentiary.

Garvey's second wife, Amy Jacques Garvey, led a national campaign for Garvey's release. The petition drive succeeded in winning Garvey's release after he had served nearly three years of his sentence. He was immediately deported to Jamaica and barred from entering the United States again. In Jamaica, Garvey held two more UNIA conventions. He also started two publications: *Black Man*, a monthly magazine, and the *New Jamaican*. But controlling and leading the different international branches from Jamaica proved difficult. A core group in the United States continued to support Garvey; they published the *Negro World* into the 1930s. Garvey, however, turned to Jamaican politics. He lost a race for a colonial legislative council seat in 1930. He did, however, sit on the municipal council of Jamaica's capital. Garvey moved to London in 1935. For the next few years he held annual conventions in Canada and continued to publish *Black Man*. After suffering a second stroke on June 10, 1940, Garvey died.

In the United States Garveyism was central to the development of the black consciousness and pride at the core of the twentieth-century freedom movement. The Jamaican Rastafarian movement and the United States Nation of Islam both grew out of and have been influenced by the UNIA. Jamaica named Garvey its first national hero.

North America
Gaye, Marvin

(b. April 2, 1939, Washington, D.C.; d. April 1, 1984, Los Angeles, Calif.), African American singer and songwriter, a recording artist for Motown Records, and one of the most popular and influential singers of rhythm and blues (R&B) music in the 1960s and 1970s, whose songs were notable for their brooding, introspective qualities.

Marvin Gaye began singing in church as a child. The son of a poor Pentecostal minister, he grew up listening to the music of American blues singer Ray Charles, which became a major influence on his work. In 1958 Gaye joined an R&B vocal group called the Moonglows. Three years later he signed a recording contract with Tamla, one of the Motown record companies, serving as a drummer for studio sessions and, later, as a singer. Influenced by American singers Frank Sinatra and Nat "King" Cole, Gaye had hoped to sing in the popular style known as crooning, but after his first album—a series of jazz standards—received little attention, Motown had him record up-tempo soul music material. The result was a series of songs that became classics, beginning with "Stubborn Kind of Fellow" (1963) and culminating in "I Heard It Through the Grapevine" (1968).

Gaye's other popular records from this 1960s Motown era include "Can I Get a Witness" (1963), a song with traits of gospel music and a strong influence on British rock groups such as the Rolling Stones (the group recorded the song in 1964); "How Sweet It Is" (1964), a song with jazz influences; and "Ain't That Peculiar" and "I'll Be Doggone" (both 1965), pensive songs written and produced by American Motown artist Smokey Robinson. Later in the decade Gaye recorded a series of romantic duets with Motown singer Tammi Terrell, including "Ain't No Mountain High Enough" (1967), "If This World Were Mine" (1967), "You're All I Need to Get By" (1968), and "What You Gave Me" (1969).

Shortly after Terrell's death in 1970, Gaye established a new style of soul music with the album *What's Going On* (1971), a deeply personal and spiritual reflection on family and social issues and particularly on the Vietnam War (1959–1975). A work that blended styles of soul, jazz, and rock music, the album marked one of the first times Motown had given an artist nearly complete creative control.

During the next ten years Gaye recorded and produced a series of brooding, erotic songs, including "Trouble Man" (1972), "Let's Get It On" (1973), and "I Want You" (1976). By the end of the 1970s his career was in decline and his personal problems were mounting. He retreated to Europe, where he recorded the hit song "Sexual Healing" (1982). He then returned to the United States and, after a disappointing musical tour, moved in with his parents. In 1984, in the midst of a heated quarrel, he was shot to death by his father.

In 1982 Gaye won two Grammy Awards for "Sexual Healing." In 1987 he was inducted into the Rock and Roll Hall of Fame.

Africa

Gebrselassie, Haile

(b. April 18, 1973, Arssi, Ethiopia), Ethiopian track and field star.

When Haile Gebrselassie was a child, he ran 25 km (15 mi) round trip to school each day—barefoot—good training for his future career as one of the world's elite runners. Like his brother before him, he began running competitively as a teenager. In 1992 he won both the 5000- and 10,000-meter races at the World Junior Championships. The next year, competing against adults for the first time, he won the 10,000-meter and finished second in the 5000-meter in the World Championships. In 1996 Gebrselassie not only won the 5000-meter event in the World Indoor Championships, he also set an indoor world record, the first Ethiopian to do so. He followed that feat by winning a Gold Medal in the 10,000-meter at the 1996 Olympic Games in Atlanta, Georgia, setting a new Olympic record.

Treated to a victory parade in Addis Ababa that was attended by nearly a million people, Gebrselassie became a national hero. In 1997 he set three more world records: in the 5000-meter, 10,000-meter, and 2-mile races.

In addition, he has won the 3000-meter event in worldwide competition, and reportedly plans to begin training for marathons. Gebrselassie splits his time between Addis Ababa, where he has a job with the police department, and the Netherlands, where he lives with one of his brothers and continues training.

Africa
___

Gedi,

East African coastal town founded in the thirteenth century, the ruins of which are now an important historic site in Kenya.

Located 16.7 km (10 mi) south of Malindi, Gedi is something of a mystery. Built on a coral spur, its outer wall encompassed 45 acres. The opulent town proper resided within an inner wall, containing a palace, three pillar tombs, and a great mosque as well as several smaller mosques and private houses. Lying 6.7 km (4 mi) inland and 3.3 km (2 mi) from a navigable creek, Gedi was undoubtedly influenced by Swahili culture but probably did not participate directly in the trade that linked towns along the Swahili Coast. Gedi was never mentioned by the Portuguese, who occupied Malindi from 1512 to 1593, nor in any other written record from around the time it was inhabited. Yet the ruins of Gedi show clear evidence of a highly developed and wealthy African civilization.

Archaeological excavations have determined that Gedi was founded in the thirteenth century and was probably rebuilt during the fifteenth century, the height of its prosperity. Gedi was abandoned in the sixteenth century, reoccupied for a short time, and then permanently abandoned in the early seventeenth century.

Archaeologists puzzle over why Gedi's residents abandoned it but can offer no definitive answers. Possible reasons for its downfall include a Portuguese or Galla attack, a decrease in water tables that eliminated the water supply, or some sort of epidemic. The ruins were declared a historic monument in 1927 and are open to the public.

Africa
___

Gerima, Haile

(b. March 4, 1946, Gondar, Ethiopia), Ethiopian film director, critic, and professor.

As a child, Haile Gerima acted in his father's troupe, performing across Ethiopia. In 1967 he moved to the United States and two years later enrolled in the University of California at Los Angeles (UCLA) drama school. There he became familiar with the ideas of Malcolm X and wrote plays about slavery and black militancy. After reading the revolutionary theory of *Third Cinema*, however, Gerima began to experiment with film.

Gerima returned to Ethiopia in 1974 to film *Harvest: 3,000 Years*, his first full-length film and the only one of his works to be shot in Africa. Although famine and the recent military overthrow of Emperor Haile Selassie placed severe restrictions on the film crew, the final result was a sophisticated examination, through the story of a village that finally overthrows its feudal landlord, of the centuries-old oppression of the Ethiopian peasantry. The film was well received on the international film circuit and won the 1976 Oscar Micheaux Award for Best Feature Film from the Black Filmmakers Hall of Fame.

Since *Harvest*, most of Gerima's film projects have examined problems facing African Americans. Although he is Ethiopia's best-known film director, he has spent most of his career in the United States. In 1976 he released *Bush Mama*, a black-and-white film about the political awakening of a black welfare mother. That same year, he joined the faculty of Howard University. In 1977 he released a documentary on the case of the Wilmington 10, *Wilmington 10-USA 10,000*, which he made with the help of students at Howard University and volunteers from the local community. In 1982 he finished *Ashes and Embers*, a story about African American Vietnam veterans, and in 1985 released *After Winter: Sterling Brown*, a documentary about Sterling Brown, also made with student cooperation. His recent works include *Sankofa* (1994) and the forthcoming *The Death of Tarzan, Donald Duck, and Shirley Temple* (working title), a documentary on the history of film in Africa, and *In the Eye of the Storm* (working title), about European colonialism in Africa.

Although Gerima has worked and lived in the United States since 1969, he maintains close ties with other African film directors. An active member of the Fédération Panafricaine des Cinéastes and the Comité Africain des Cinéastes, he has coordinated several colloquiums and meetings of African film directors in the United States. His own studio, Mypheduh Films, Inc., is one of the leading distributors of films by Africans and African Americans in the United States.

Europe

Germany,

a country of northern Europe where blacks have had a presence for centuries.

Although there is thought to have been a black presence in the area that would become Germany since the time of Julius Caesar (whose Italian troops conquered parts of the Rhineland, 58-50 B.C.E.), blacks first began to appear in larger numbers in the Middle Ages and the Renaissance. Contacts came, at first, through trade with Africa, and Africans began to appear in art (portraits of Africans living in Germany) and literature (the courtly epic *Parzival*, written in the twelfth and thirteenth centuries) early on. Germans also engaged in the slave trade. Traders brought Africans back in order to prove they had visited the continent and made "presents" of Africans to royal courts; Hofmohren, "court Moors," were not uncommon. Often, such court Moors were treated as servants or buffoons. An exception was Anton Wilhelm Amo (from the area known today as Ghana), who was given to the Duke von Wolfenbüttel by the Dutch West India Company in 1707. Amo studied at the universities in Halle and Wittenberg and went on to become a leading German Enlightenment scholar.

Germany came late to its colonial empire, acquiring Togo, Cameroon, German East Africa (present-day Tanzania), and German Southwest Africa (present-day Namibia) by 1885 in the scramble for Africa. The Berlin Conference, called in 1884 by German chancellor Otto von Bismarck, established African colonial boundaries. This empire would last only 35 years, until the end of World War I (1914–1918). But the acquisition of African colonies, German emigration there, and German missionary activities increased encounters with blacks and led to a spate of travel literature that provided Germans with a largely stereotypical picture of Africa. German attitudes toward their colonial subjects were paternalistic and, of course, racist: Germans came more and more to see blacks as inferior and exotic—part "noble savage," part primitive barbarian.

German colonial policy was extremely brutal. A series of revolts in its colonies in the early part of the century, such as that of the Herero in present-day Namibia, were put down with great cruelty and loss of life. Mixed-race children born in the colonies were not recognized as Germans. Germany, unlike France or England, did not grant citizenship to its colonial subjects, and to this day German citizenship depends on blood descent, a fact that continues to shape German attitudes toward race. Still, colonial Africans did develop bonds with Germany; even today, in fact, the Herero of Namibia wear German dress. Africans from the colonies came to Germany to study, and some remained.

Africa
Ghana,

a coastal West African country that borders Togo to the east, Burkina Faso to the north, and Côte d'Ivoire to the west.

Known as the Gold Coast until it achieved independence in 1957, the area that is now Ghana was one of the richest in Africa before its conquest by the British. By the early 1800s the wealthy and powerful Asante Empire controlled most of the country's modern territory. During the colonial period, Ghanaians led the struggle against British colonialism. As the first

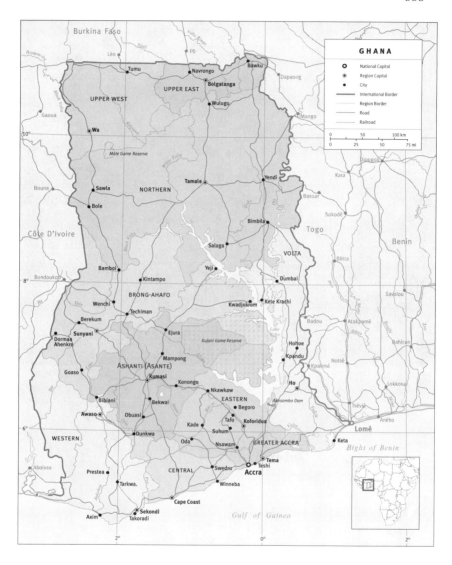

European colony south of the Sahara to gain independence, Ghana inspired nationalist movements throughout Africa and the world. Yet despite its wealth and proud traditions, Ghana, like other African countries, has struggled with persistent poverty, mounting debt, and political instability and repression. The African socialism espoused by its independence leader, Kwame Nkrumah, brought political and economic disaster. In recent years the country has seen economic recovery and democratization, but a dependence on foreign capital still keeps Ghana from reclaiming its former power and prosperity.

A Ghanaian fisherwoman dries sardines on a rack. *CORBIS/Liba Taylor*

Africa

Ghana (Ready Reference)

Official Name: Republic of Ghana

Former Name: Gold Coast

Area: 238,537 sq km (92,099 sq mi)

Location: Western Africa; borders Togo, Burkina Faso, Côte d'Ivoire, and the Atlantic Ocean

Capital: Accra (population 953,500 [1990 estimate])

Other Major Cities: Kumasi (population 399,300), Sekondi (116,500) (1990 estimate)

Population: 18,497,206 (1998 estimate)

Population Density: 73 persons per sq km (about 190 per sq mi)

Population Below Age 15: 43 percent (male 3,985,219; female 3,947,640 [1998 estimate])

Population Growth Rate: 2.13 percent (1998 estimate)

Total Fertility Rate: 4.5 children born per woman (1996 estimate)

Life Expectancy at Birth: Total population: 56.82 years (male 54.77 years; female 58.92 years [1997 estimate])

Infant Mortality Rate: 77.5 deaths per 1000 live births (1998 estimate)

Literacy Rate (age 15 and over who can read and write): Total population: 64.5 percent (male: 75.9 percent; female: 53.5 percent [1995 estimate])

Education: Primary school and the first three years of secondary school are free and officially compulsory. In the late 1980s nearly 2.3 million children were enrolled in primary schools, and almost 770,000 were enrolled in secondary schools.

Languages: English is the official language of Ghana and is used in schools. There are at least nine other languages used in Ghana, including Akaupem-Twi, Asante-Twi, Dagbani, Dangbe, Ewe, Fanti, Ga, Kasem, and Nzima, which are also used in schools.

Kwame Nkrumah, president of Ghana from 1960 to 1966, was a crusader against colonialism and for African solidarity. *CORBIS/Bettmann*

Ethnic Groups: There are at least seven major ethnic groups in Ghana, including the Fante, Asante, Nzima, Ahanta, Ga, Moshi-Dagomba, and Gonja peoples.

Religions: About 62 percent of the population are Christian. About 22 percent adhere to indigenous beliefs and about 16 percent are Muslim.

Climate: The climate of Ghana is tropical, but temperatures vary with season and elevation. In most areas there are two rainy seasons, from April to July and September to November. In the north, however, one rainy season lasts from April to November. Annual rainfall is 1100 mm (43 in) in the southern areas and 2100 mm (83 in) in the north. The *harmattan*, a dry desert wind, is felt in the north from December to March and in the south in January. The average annual temperature is 26° C (79° F).

Land, Plants, and Animals: Ghana is mostly lowland with a small range of hills on the eastern border. Eastern Ghana also has one of the largest artificial lakes in the world, Lake Volta, which was created from the Volta River by the Akosombo Dam. The vegetation varies from savanna in the northern two-thirds of the country to a tropical forest zone in the south; much of the natural vegetation in central Ghana has been destroyed by land clearing for agriculture. The southern forests include the giant silk cotton, African mahogany, and cedar trees. Animals include the leopard, hyena, buffalo, elephant, wildhog, antelope, and monkey. Ghana has many species of reptiles, including the cobra, python, puff adder, and horned adder.

Natural Resources: Mineral resources include gold, diamonds, manganese ore, and bauxite. Ghana has small deposits of petroleum and natural gas. Forests and access to the ocean are also valuable resources.

Currency: The Cedi

Gross Domestic Product (GDP): $36.2 billion (1997 estimate)

GDP per Capita: $2000 (1997 estimate)

GDP Real Growth Rate: 3 percent (1997 estimate)

Primary Economic Activities: Agriculture (55 percent of employment), manufacturing, and services

Primary Crops: Cocoa, rice, coffee, cassava (tapioca), peanuts, corn, shea nuts, bananas, and timber

Industries: Mining, lumbering, light manufacturing, aluminum, and food processing

Primary Exports: Cocoa, gold, timber, tuna, bauxite, aluminum, manganese ore, and diamonds

Primary Imports: Petroleum, consumer goods, foods, and capital equipment

Primary Trade Partners: United States, United Kingdom, Germany, Netherlands, and Japan

Government: Ghana is a Constitutional democracy. The executive branch is led by President Jerry John Rawlings. The legislative branch is the elected 200-seat National Assembly, currently dominated by the Every Ghanian Living Everywhere Party.

North America

Gibson, Althea

(b. August 25, 1927, Silver, S.C.), African American athlete, and first African American to win major tennis tournaments.

Althea Gibson, who moved with her family to Harlem at the age of three, was from an early age involved in many competitive sports. She began to play tennis in Police Athletic League paddle tennis games. In 1945 she won the girls' singles championship of the all-black American Tennis Association (ATA), and from 1947 to 1956 she held the title for the ATA women's singles. In 1946 she moved to North Carolina to live with Dr. Hubert Eaton, who, along with Dr. R. Walter Johnson, took an interest in her career. Under their tutelage, Gibson's game matured, and she developed her fast footwork and signature big server.

During the 1950s she began to challenge racial segregation in tennis by playing at tournaments sponsored by the United States Lawn Tennis Association (later renamed United States Tennis Association), which had previously been restricted to white players. In 1950 Gibson became the first black competitor at the National Championships (later renamed the U.S. Open) in Forest Hills, New York. She was invited to compete only after Alice Marble, a four-time singles winner at Forest Hills, expressed her disgust at the efforts to stop Gibson from playing because of her race. In 1951 Gibson was the first black person to play tennis at the Lawn Tennis Championships at the All-England Club in Wimbledon, England.

Gibson's game slowed down in the early 1950s, at which point she worked as a physical education teacher in Missouri for two years. However, her game was revitalized by a tennis tour of Southeast Asia organized by the United States State Department in 1955. In 1956 she won the women's singles championship at the French Open Tournament and then went on to win both the women's singles and doubles championships at Wimbledon and the U.S. National Championships at Forest Hills in 1957. In the same year, the Associated Press honored her with the Female Athlete of the Year Award. In 1958 she repeated her victories in the women's singles at both Wimbledon and Forest Hills.

Latin America and the Caribbean

Gil de Castro, José
(b. 1785; d. 1841), Afro-Peruvian painter, also known as "El Mulato Gil," celebrated for his meticulous portaits of Peru's heroes who fought for independence from Spain.

Latin America and the Caribbean

Gil, Gilberto
(b. June 29, 1942, Salvador, Bahia, Brazil), a brilliant Afro-Brazilian musician-composer who combines local concerns with a cosmopolitan, global sensibility; since the mid-1960s, Gil has also intermittently engaged in struggles for social and racial equality, democratization, and environmental preservation.

Gilberto Gil gained national recognition in 1967 at the Third Festival of Brazilian Popular Music aired by São Paulo's TV Record. He performed "Domingo no Parque" which fused Afro-Brazilian capoeira music with the sounds of a psychedelic rock band, Os Mutantes. His performance was an inaugural moment of Tropicália, a radical cultural movement that revitalized Brazilian arts. Although his partner, Caetano Veloso, is regarded as the primary intellectual author of Tropicália, Veloso himself has claimed that he was merely the apostle of Gil, the real prophet of the movement. In any case, the tropicalist movement radically transformed the conception, production, and consumption of popular music in Brazil. During the tropicalist period, Gil composed and recorded several key songs, such as "Geléia Geral" (lyrics by Torquato Neto), an ironic critique of Brazilian culture; and

"Batmacumba" whose lyrics are visually structured as a concrete poem forming a bat in flight.

In late 1968 Gil and Veloso were arrested by military authorities, who were suspicious of their subversive cultural activities; the musicians were eventually exiled to London. By that time, Gil had already begun to use elements of African American soul, which anticipated subsequent experiments with reggae, funk, rap, and other musical forms of the African diaspora. During the 1980s Gil became increasingly involved in the civic and political life of Brazil. After an unsuccessful bid for the mayor's office in 1988, he was elected to the municipal council, where he focused on protecting the environment and promoting Afro-Brazilian culture. He retreated from party politics in the 1990s to focus on music and nongovernmental activism. He maintains an expansive web site that updates his activities as a musician and public intellectual.

North America

Gillespie, John Birks ("Dizzy")

(b. October 21, 1917, Cheraw, S.C.; d. January 7, 1993, Englewood, N.J.), African American trumpet player, the co-creator with alto saxophonist Charlie Parker of bebop or modern jazz, and an Afro-Cuban jazz innovator.

John Birks "Dizzy" Gillespie may have been the greatest trumpeter in the history of jazz. His bravura trumpet playing featured a brilliant but sensitive tone, a wide range, and mind-boggling speed and articulation. To the wider public, Gillespie's name also conjured up images of his distinctive trumpet with its upswept bell, the way his cheeks bulged out when he played, and his penchant for clowning that included a seriocomic campaign for president in 1964. But Gillespie was extremely serious about his music and was a leader in two major developments in jazz. Beginning in the 1940s he played a key role in bringing Afro-Cuban music into American jazz. More significant, during the mid-1940s Gillespie was a primary force, along with alto saxophonist Charlie Parker, in the development of bebop or modern jazz.

Although Gillespie's role in this movement is well known, he has generally received less attention than Parker, in part because Gillespie did not fit the stereotype of the ill-fated and misunderstood musician. Jazz has a long tradition of mythologizing its troubled geniuses. Gillespie was in many respects closer to being the counterpart in modern jazz of Louis Armstrong in traditional jazz. As Armstrong had done in the 1920s, Gillespie redirected the course of jazz and expanded its improvisational possibilities. Both men played with a technical facility that astonished their peers. And like Armstrong, Gillespie had a winning personality and a gift for comedy.

Giral, Sergio

(b. 1937, Havana, Cuba), Cuban director and journalist who, like Sara Gómez, belongs to the second generation of Cuban Film Institute (Instituto Cubano de Arte e Industria Cinematográficas, ICAIC) filmmakers who worked under the tutelage of Tomás Gutiérrez Alea, the best-known Cuban director. Giral has directed over 20 documentaries and several major films, many of which deal with issues of slavery, race, and his Afro-Cuban cultural heritage.

Born to a Cuban father and a North American mother, Sergio Giral has lived in Cuba and the United States. After finishing high school in Cuba, he spent two years studying painting at the Art Students League in New York. Following the triumph of the 1959 Cuban Revolution he returned to live in Havana. There he began engineering studies but then joined the Cuban Film Institute in 1961. His films include a slave trilogy—comprising *El otro Francisco* (1974, The Other Francisco), *El Rancheador* (1976, The Slave Hunter), and *Maluala* (1979)—and a film on contemporary Cuban issues, *Techo de vidrio* (Glass Ceiling; 1982). In 1986 Giral directed *Plácido*, about the nineteenth-century black Cuban poet and patriot Plácido Valdés; in 1990 he directed *María Antonia*, dealing with the world of prostitution, gambling, and drugs in 1950s Havana. Since the 1990s Giral has resided in Miami, where he works as a freelance writer.

In Giral's two most important full-length films, *El otra Francisco* and *María Antonia*, the director seeks to give voice to Afro-Cuban culture. *El otra Francisco* is a response to the nineteenth-century Cuban antislavery novel *Francisco* by Anselmo Suárez y Romero, which the film criticizes for its representation of the black slave from the white abolitionist's point of view.

Glover, Danny

(b. July 22, 1947, San Francisco, Calif.), African American actor whose career has spanned television, theater, and film.

Danny Glover was born in San Francisco to politically active parents, and as a youth participated in the student activism of the Haight-Ashbury district, a center of 1960s counterculture activity. Glover distinguished himself as an actor of great promise in the early 1980s when he appeared in two plays by South African playwright Athol Fugard in New York: with *The Blood Knot* (1980) Glover made his off-Broadway debut, and for his performance in *Master Harold . . . and the Boys* (1982) he garnered high acclaim. He also appeared in *The Island, Sizwe Banzi Is Dead, Macbeth,* and *Suicide in B Flat*.

Impressed by Glover's performance in *Master Harold*, Hollywood director Robert Benson cast him as a sharecropper in *Places in the Heart* (1984), Glover's first leading role in a big-budget production. Glover's watershed came in 1985, however, when he appeared in three of the year's most successful movies: *Silverado, Witness,* and *The Color Purple.* Thereafter, lead roles in numerous top-grossing films, including *Lethal Weapon*1987), its two sequels, and other action films, indicated Glover's mainstream acceptance.

North America

Goldberg, Whoopi
(b. November 13, 1954, Chelsea, N.Y.), comedian, film star, and the first African American woman to win an Oscar (1990) since Hattie McDaniel (1939).

Whoopi Goldberg was born in New York City, where she exhibited early talent as a performer.

In 1974 Goldberg moved to California and worked a variety of jobs as she tried to launch her acting career. She helped found the San Diego Repertory Theater and began performing one-woman shows, including *Moms*, which showcased the life of black comedian Jackie "Moms" Mabley. Goldberg's satiric bite, as well as her talent for playing numerous character types, attracted the attention of producer Mike Nichols, who helped her stage an eponymous show of skits on Broadway.

Goldberg's success in New York caught the attention of Hollywood, and in 1985 Steven Spielberg cast her in his adaptation of Alice Walker's *The Color Purple,*which won her an Academy Award nomination for her portrayal of Celie, a poor young black woman who overcomes the limitations of her life in the segregated South; her status as a film actor was thereby ensured. Since 1985 she has appeared in over two dozen movies, including *Sister Act* (1992), *The Lion King* (1994), *Boys on the Side* (1995), and *Ghost* (1990), for which she won an Oscar as Best Supporting Actor.

In 1992 she cofounded Comic Relief, an annual fundraiser to help the homeless.

Latin America and the Caribbean

Gómez, Sara
(b. 1943, Cuba; d. 1974, Cuba), Afro-Cuban film director internationally known for her film *De cierta manera* (One Way or Another), which presents a feminist perspective on racial and gender tensions in revolutionary Cuban society.

Sara Gómez grew up in Cuba and initially worked as a journalist. In the 1960s she decided to change her profession and began studying film at the Instituto Cubano del Arte e Industria Cinematográficos, or ICAIC (Cuban

Institute for the Arts and Film Industry). Gómez is best known for her black-and-white film *De Cierta manera* (1975), in which she examines the problems of being both black and female in post-revolution Cuba. The movie presents the lives of a mulatto factory worker and a white schoolteacher who are subjected to the gender, class, and racial prejudices that still linger in their society. Gómez used her experience in directing documentaries and her feminist views to present a critique of gender roles from within the Cuban Revolution. Her film is a collage that juxtaposes the African, European, and nationalist elements present in Cuban identity, showing how both gender and race relations need to be radically transformed in the post-revolution era.

North America

Gooden, Dwight

(b. November 16, 1964, Tampa, Fla.), African American professional baseball player who led the New York Mets to victory in the World Series in 1986.

Africa

Gordimer, Nadine

(b. November 20, 1923, Springs, South Africa), South African novelist and Nobel Prize winner who was a vocal opponent of the system of apartheid.

A new world opened to Gordimer in 1949 when she began taking courses in Johannesburg at the University of Witwatersrand. There she mixed with musicians, journalists, and writers, crossing for the first time the color line that segregated blacks from whites. As she read the philosophies of Marxism, nationalism, and existentialism, she began to question the social structure of apartheid. She also became involved in the political and cultural movement of the Sophiatown renaissance, which produced the literary journal *Drum*.

During the same year in which she started classes in Johannesburg, Gordimer published her first book of short stories, *Face to Face*. Her first novel, *The Lying Days* (1953), was a loosely autobiographical coming-of-age story. She gained international recognition when her stories were published in the *New Yorker* magazine during the 1950s. A prominent critic of apartheid and an open supporter of the African National Congress, she continued to live in South Africa under apartheid despite the repeated banning of her books. The remarkably prolific Gordimer has published 12 novels and 13 short story collections. Her international reputation, particularly after she won the Nobel Prize for literature in 1991, has protected her from some of the reprisals that faced other South African radicals.

Gorée Island,

Senegal, island off the coast of Senegal, used as a slave port throughout the transatlantic slave trade.

Settled by southbound Portuguese explorers in the mid-fifteenth century, Gorée Island was first called Palma and served as a port of call for Portuguese ships sailing along the west coast of Africa. Though small, barren, and lacking fresh water, the island was of strategic importance to the Portuguese because it was sheltered by the tip of the Cape Verde Peninsula and had excellent anchorage for large ships. Explorers on their way to Asia around the southern tip of Africa, including Vasco da Gama and Fernando Po, frequently stopped on the island to pick up supplies and conduct repairs, and as contacts with the mainland developed, the island became a key European outpost to Africa.

Through Gorée, Senegambia became one of the most important outlets of the slave trade, supplying at least a third of the captives exported before 1600. By the sixteenth century Gorée had become a bustling port where slaves from the entire region were assembled, examined, and branded before being sent to the Americas. As one of the principal slave ports of the transatlantic slave trade, Gorée was the site of great cruelty, brutality, and violence for nearly three centuries. After the end of the slave trade in the mid-nineteenth century, economic activity shifted to the mainland and Gorée declined steadily. It is now a historic tourist attraction administered by the Senegalese government.

Gospel Music,

a style of African American sacred music that arose in the twentieth century, incorporating improvisation, blues harmonies, and a strong feeling of swing; gospel music builds upon long-standing traditions of black religious expression and stands as one of the most significant African American musical creations.

Gospel music is one of the four most significant musical creations that emerged out of African American culture during the twentieth century. Yet it has received far less attention than have jazz, blues, or rap music, the other main black musical innovations. Jazz, blues, and rap attained greater recognition in part because they offer secular music in an increasingly secular age; they were also at various times perceived as controversial or subversive. Gospel music has been less visible—to white society, in particular—because it conveys religious affirmation rather than an aura of social rebellion. Yet gospel music reflects the core of African American culture and gospel music is at heart an African American phenomenon.

Gospel music mirrors the larger contours of twentieth-century black

Mahalia Jackson (1911-1972) is generally known as the world's greatest gospel music performer. *CORBIS/Bettmann*

history. To give the music its due requires setting it in its proper context. That context is complex. First, gospel music is part of a larger transformation in black Christianity that took place during the late nineteenth and t he twentieth centuries, above all, as a result of the Great Migration. Second, gospel music cannot fully be understood apart from African American worship practices and spirituality.

Great Britain,

an island nation off the northwestern coast of Europe where blacks have had a presence for centuries.

Although it is commonly believed that blacks first entered Great Britain after World War II, a black presence there can be traced back to 200 C.E. As a result of British participation in the slave trade during the sixteenth century, a black community developed that by the eighteenth century numbered 15,000 in London alone. An irony that marked the African-British relationship is that although the British took pride in the freedom of their own land, they institutionalized slavery and colonialism abroad. Even after abolition, decolonization, and the influx of a large number of blacks after World War II, another contradiction remains: despite the fact that people of African descent have lived in Great Britain for centuries, many white British have refused to accept that their black neighbors, too, are British. But this is slowly changing, as blacks increasingly become involved in local and national politics and gain recognition for their contributions to British culture.

Black activist Bernie Grant became one of the first black members of the British Parliament.
CORBIS/Zen Icknow

Born as a neighborhood party in 1966, the Notting Hill Carnival, now held every year in August, has grown into a massive celebration of Caribbean and West Indian culture.
CORBIS/David Cummings; Eye Ubiquitous

North America

Great Migration, The,

mass movement by black Americans in the early twentieth century from the predominantly rural, segregated South to the urban North and West, where they sought greater economic, social, and political freedom.

At the end of the Civil War (1861–1865) and the abolition of slavery, 91 percent of America's 5 million African Americans lived in the Southern states, roughly the same percentage as in 1790. Blacks made up 36 percent of the total Southern population (as compared with 3 percent of the total Northern population) and worked mostly as sharecroppers, tenant farmers, and domestic servants. Very few owned property. Most black farmers were heavily in debt and struggled to pay rents. Other forms of labor open to blacks were similarly low-paying and exploitative.

Several events early in the second decade of the twentieth century coalesced to change black patterns of settlement. From 1913 to 1915 falling cotton prices brought on an economic depression that seriously hurt Southern farmers, both black and white. Just as they began to recover, they were struck by an overwhelming infestation of boll weevils, insects that destroyed much of the cotton crop between 1914 and 1917. In the Mississippi Valley, farmers suffered an additional plague: severe floods in 1915 ruined crops and homes, especially of blacks, who lived in disproportionate numbers in the

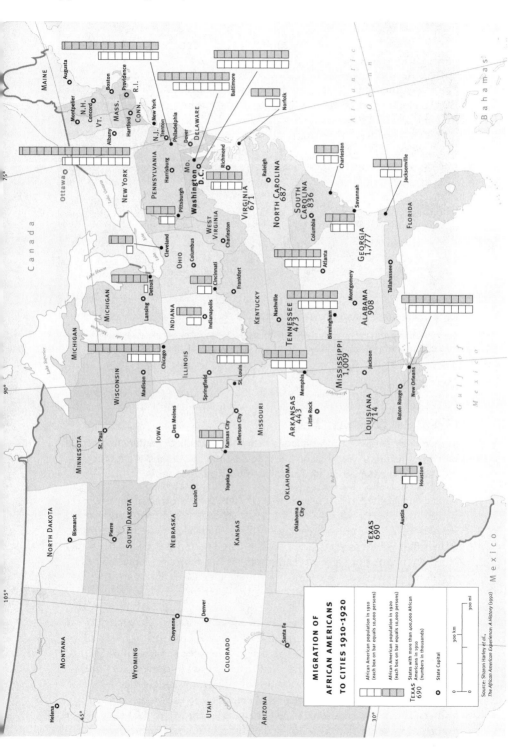

MIGRATION OF
AFRICAN AMERICANS
TO CITIES 1910–1920

African American population in 1910
(each box on bar equals 10,000 persons)

African American population in 1920
(each box on bar equals 10,000 persons)

States with more than 400,000 African
Americans in 1910
(numbers in thousands)

TEXAS
690

⊕ State Capital

0   300 km
0   300 mi

Source: Sharon Harley et al.,
The African American Experience: A History (1992)

valley's bottomlands. The few Southern blacks who had owned their own farms before 1910 were now largely reduced to sharecropping and tenant farming; most sharecroppers and tenant farmers, meanwhile, slid deeper into debt.

At the same time Northern industries were undergoing an economic boom, fueled in part by the start of World War I in Europe (1914–1918). The North and West were also experiencing a labor shortage: following several years of cheap labor from unlimited foreign immigration, Congress had now restricted the number of new immigrants. The labor shortage became even more acute as the United States entered the war in 1917. While wages in the South ranged from 50 cents to $2 a day, wages in the industrial North, expanded because of the war effort, ranged from $2 to $5 a day.

Southern blacks responded to these forces by filling Northern jobs by the hundreds of thousands. Between 1915 and 1920, from 500,000 to 1 million African Americans left the rural South for the urban North; several thousands more moved to the West. Others remained in the South but moved from the country to the city. On their arrival in the North, migrants found not just better wages but the freedom to vote, less exposure to white violence, and, sometimes, better schools for their children. Racism remained persistent, however. Discriminatory real estate practices forced blacks into ill-maintained and segregated housing, contributing to the rise of the urban black ghetto. Blacks were routinely excluded from labor unions, and many migrants were forced into menial jobs as butlers, waiters, and the like, or served as replacement workers ("scabs") during strikes by white unions.

The increased competition among blacks and whites for jobs and housing sparked race riots in dozens of Northern cities, including major white-on-black riots in East St. Louis in 1917 and Chicago in 1919. For blacks, the riots were an enduring reminder that white violence was not restricted to the states of Jim Crow. For the nation, the tensions caused by black migration made many people aware of what blacks had known for some time: the problems of race were an American, not only a Southern, phenomenon.

North America

Gregory, Richard Claxton "Dick"

(b. October 12, 1932, St. Louis, Mo.), African American comedian and civil rights activist whose social satire changed the way white Americans perceived African American comedians.

Dick Gregory entered the national comedy scene in 1961 when Chicago's Playboy Club booked him as a replacement for white comedian "Professor" Irwin Corey. Until then Gregory had worked mostly at small clubs with predominantly black audiences. His tenure as a replacement for Corey was so successful—at one performance he won over an audience that included Southern white convention goers—that the Playboy Club offered him a contract extension from several weeks to three years. By 1962 Gregory had become a nationally known headline performer, selling out nightclubs, making numerous national television appearances, and recording popular comedy albums.

Gregory began performing comedy in the mid-1950s while serving in the army. In the hopes of performing comedy professionally, he moved to Chicago, where he became part of a new generation of black comedians that included Nipsey Russell, Bill Cosby, and Godfrey Cambridge. These comedians broke with the minstrel tradition, which presented stereotypical black characters. Gregory, whose style was detached, ironic, and satirical, drew on current events, especially racial issues, for much of his material: "Segregation is not all bad. Have you ever heard of a collision where the people in the back of the bus got hurt?"

From an early age Gregory demonstrated a strong sense of social justice. While a student at Sumner High School in St. Louis he led a march protesting segregated schools. Later, inspired by the work of leaders such as Dr. Martin Luther King Jr. and organizations such as the Student Non-violent Coordinating Committee (SNCC), Gregory took part in the Civil Rights Movement and used his celebrity status to draw attention to such issues as segregation and disfranchisement. When local Mississippi governments stopped distributing federal food surpluses to poor blacks in areas where SNCC was encouraging voter registration, Gregory chartered a plane to bring in seven tons of food. He participated in SNCC's voter registration drives and in sit-ins to protest segregation, most notably at a restaurant franchise in downtown Atlanta, Georgia. Only later did Gregory disclose that he held stock in the chain.

Through the 1960s Gregory spent more time on social issues and less time on performing. He participated in marches and parades to support a range of causes, including opposition to the Vietnam War, world hunger, and drug abuse. In addition he fasted in protest more than 60 times, once in Iran, where he fasted and prayed in an effort to urge the Ayatollah Khomeini to release American embassy staff who had been taken hostage. The Iranian refusal to release the hostages did not decrease the depth of Gregory's commitment; he weighed only 97 lbs. when he left Iran.

Latin America and the Caribbean

Grenada,

country consisting of several islands in the Caribbean Sea north of Trinidad and Tobago and Venezuela; one of the largest islands of that area of the Caribbean.

Grenada's first inhabitants were Arawak Amerindians, who probably migrated north from Venezuela via Trinidad and Tobago between 1 and 500 C.E. But between 700 and 1000 C.E. in the island's first takeover, the Arawaks were wiped out by the Carib Amerindians (Caribs). By the time Spanish explorer Christopher Columbus and his crew became the first

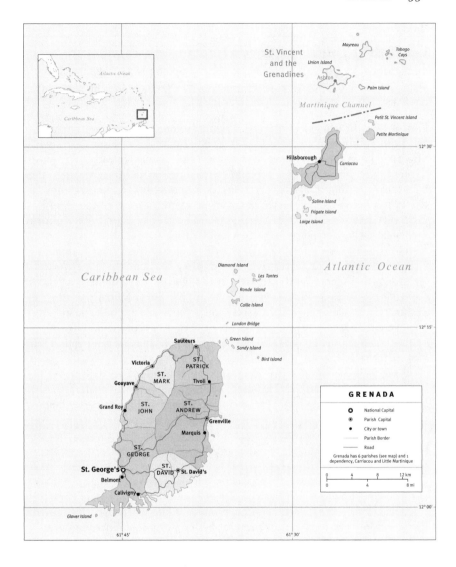

Europeans to see Grenada in 1498, the island, whose Amerindian name was
Camerhogne, was covered with well-established Carib settlements.

Columbus did not stop on the island, but he did rename it Concepción.
Over the next few decades other passing Spanish sailors gave it the name
Granada, recognizing the similarity of the country's landscape to the lush
green hills of Granada, Spain. In later years the name was modified again—
the French changed it to Grenade, and the British finally changed it to
Grenada. The fact that the Spanish, French, and British all had a hand in
naming the island gives some indication of the progression of European
powers that struggled to control the island during the colonial period.

Griffith-Joyner, Florence Delorez

(b. December 21, 1959, Los Angeles, Calif.; d. September 21, 1998, Mission Viejo, Calif.), African American track athlete who won three Gold Medals and one Silver Medal at the 1988 Olympic Games.

Florence Griffith-Joyner came out of semiretirement in track to dominate the 1988 Summer Olympic Games in Seoul, South Korea after capturing a Silver Medal in the 200-meter dash at the 1984 Games. In early 1987 she decided to return to competition and enlisted her former track coach at the University of California at Los Angeles, Bob Kersee, to help her train for the 1988 Olympic Games. Her husband, Al Joyner, winner of the 1984 Olympic Gold Medal in the triple jump and brother of heptathlon record-holder Jackie Joyner-Kersee, also coached Griffith-Joyner.

Griffith-Joyner's record-breaking performance at the 1988 Olympic Games was motivated in part by a second-place finish at the 1987 World Championship Games in Rome, Italy. Although she was a member of the Gold Medal-winning 1600-meter relay team, her Silver Medal finish in the 200-meter dash led her to say, "When you've been second best for so long, you can either accept it or try to become the best." At the 1988 Olympic Games, she won Gold Medals in the 100- and 200-meter dashes and in the 400-meter relay.

Griffith-Joyner set new world records, clocking 10.49 seconds in the 100-meter quarterfinal and 21.34 seconds in the 200-meter final. She also surpassed Wilma Rudolph's 1960 record of three Gold Medals after helping the 1600-meter relay team capture the Silver Medal. For these accomplishments in 1988, she received the Jesse Owens Award, given to the year's top track and field athlete, and the Sullivan Award, given to the year's most outstanding amateur athlete.

Griffith-Joyner earned the nickname "Flo-Jo" for her blazing speed. She also became known for her flashy one-legged uniforms and long, painted fingernails. She wore colorful combinations of bikini briefs over one-legged tights and low-cut tops in part because she found most standard uniforms uncomfortable. She retired from track in 1989.

Guadeloupe,

a Caribbean island located at the northern end of the Windward Islands, which was colonized by France in the 1600s and has been a French overseas department (Département d'Outre Mer) since 1946.

Guadeloupe, which was first colonized by the French in 1635, has produced sugar cane and its derivatives for France for nearly three centuries, thanks to the labor of African slaves and their descendants. Since the abolition of slavery in 1848, and the incorporation of the island and its dependencies into France in 1946, the predominantly black population of Guadeloupe has had to negotiate the double cultural inheritance at the root of its Creole civilization. At once African and French—with lesser proportions of Amerindian, East Indian, and Chinese cultures—Guadeloupe has striven for the economic, cultural, and psychological autonomy denied it by the structural dependencies instituted via the forces of French centralization, and, indeed, ongoing colonization.

In turn, this emphasis on Guadeloupe's ties with France has long led to a denial of an African heritage, whose recuperation and revindication began following the Martinican poet-statesman Aimé Césaire's elaboration of the concept of *Négritude* in the 1930s. The particular characteristics of this social and existential paradox are unique, among African diasporic communities, to the French overseas departments of Guadeloupe, Martinique, and French Guiana. This unresolved conflict, like the one that W. E. B. Du Bois identified among African Americans of the United States, has nonetheless proved highly productive. The tiny island of Guadeloupe (with a population of 390,000 in 1990) has produced a number of renowned writers, including Maryse Condé, Simone Schwarz-Bart, and Gisele Pineau.

Latin America and the Caribbean

Guillén, Nicolás

(b. July 10, 1902, Camagüey, Cuba; d. July 16, 1989?, Havana, Cuba), Afro-Cuban poet, writer, journalist, and social activist, one of the Caribbean's foremost *Négritude* poets, who placed the historical and social sufferings of blacks at the center of his poetic universe.

Nicolás Guillén is widely considered Cuba's preeminent poet, on a par with such Latin American literary masters as Jorge Luis Borges, Pablo Neruda, and César Vallejo. According to literary scholar Josaphat B. Kubayanda, "Guillén's poetry was the first successful development in Cuba of a vital and original aesthetic based upon the black and African elements on Caribbean soil." He was also a committed Communist, and his poems and journalism powerfully reflect his political and national concerns. Like the black American singer and antifascist activist Paul Robeson, Guillén devoted much of his life to the pursuit of peace, both in racially torn, pre-revolutionary Cuba and abroad. He traveled extensively throughout the world and in 1954 received the Lenin International Peace Prize.

Guillén is equally a part of the community of black poets exemplified by Harlem Renaissance writers Claude McKay, Sterling Brown, and Langston Hughes. In 1929, after Hughes told Guillén in an interview that it was his "greatest ambition to be the poet of the Blacks," Guillén noted, "Yes, I certainly understood; and I feel that the poem which opens this man's book of poetry springs from the depths of my own soul: 'I am a Negro / Black as the night is Black / Black like the depths of my Africa.'" Indeed, it was Guillén's powerful core of black-inspired poetry that inaugurated a sophisticated Afrocubanismo in literature and effectively contributed to freeing Cuban letters from the hegemony of Spanish culture.

Africa

Guinea,

a coastal West African country bordered by Guinea-Bissau, Senegal, Mali, Côte d'Ivoire, Liberia, and Sierra Leone.

Although today Guinea struggles with persistent poverty, the country possesses agricultural and mineral riches and an equally rich history. In precolonial days the area now known as Guinea was homeland to several distinct ethnic groups—principally the Mandinka (or Malinke), Fulani, and Susa. The region was also the site one of Africa's longest lasting,

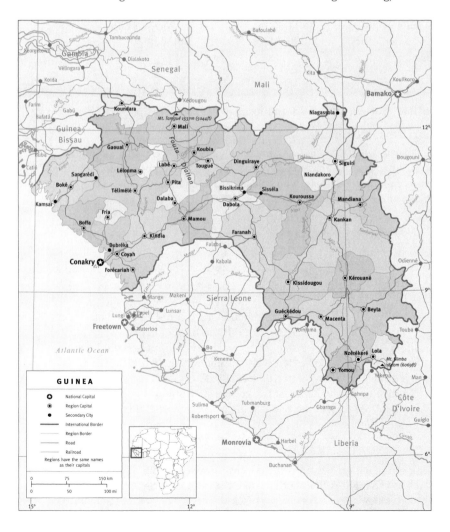

Guinean President Sékou Touré speaks before the United Nations in 1962, protesting the lack of African representation on the security council. *CORBIS/Bettmann*

autonomous Islamic theocracies, known as Fouta Djallon. Under French colonial rule, Guinea was one of the most productive of West African colonies. Its lucrative exports included rubber and bananas. However, French investors and merchants retained most of the wealth those exports produced.

Guinea achieved renown as the first of the French colonies to claim independence, and it served as an example to other African nations seeking autonomy. Guineans voted in 1958 to break ties with France. In the words of Guinea's first president, Sékou Touré, Guinea chose "poverty in freedom to opulence in slavery." In fact, poverty has haunted Guinea since independence. Hunger and disease are widespread; literacy levels are low, even by African standards; and the infant mortality rate is among the highest in the world.

Africa

Guinea (Ready Reference)

Official Name: Republic of Guinea

Former Name: French Guinea

Area: 245,857 sq km (94,925 sq mi)

Location: Guinea is bounded on the north by Guinea-Bissau, Senegal, and Mali, on the east and southeast by Côte d'Ivoire, on the south by Liberia and Sierra Leone, and on the west by the Atlantic Ocean.

Capital: Conakry (population 705,000 [1989 estimate])

Other Major Cities: Kankan (population 278,000 [1989 estimate])

Population: 7,477,110 (1998 estimate)

Population Density: 30 persons per sq km (78 people per sq mi)

Population Below Age 15: 44 percent (male 1,634,344; female 1,644,863 [1998 estimate])

Population Growth Rate: .83 percent (1998 estimate)

Total Fertility Rate: 5.59 children born per woman (1998 estimate)

Life Expectancy at Birth (total): Total population: 46.0 years (male 43.5 years; female 48.5 years [1998 estimate])

Infant Mortality Rate: 128.9 deaths per 1000 live births (1998 estimate)

Literacy Rate (age 15 and over who can read and write): Total population: 35.9 percent (male 49.9 percent; female 21.9 percent [1995 estimate])

Education: Education is free and officially compulsory for all children between the ages of 7 and 12, but in the early 1990s only about 37 percent of eligible children actually attended school. Private schools were nationalized by 1962. The universities at Conakry and Kankan, along with 21 other institutions, provide higher education.

Languages: While French is the official language, almost every Guinean speaks one of eight national languages: Malinke, Soso, Fulani, Kissi, Basari, Loma, Koniagi, or Kpelle.

Ethnic Groups: Fulani constitute 35 percent of the population, the largest group. Most other Guineans are from the Mande group, either Malinke, in northeastern Guinea, or Soso, in the coastal areas.

Religions: About 85 percent of the population practices Islam. Most of the remainder adhere to traditional beliefs. Christians form a small portion of the total population.

Climate: The dominant factor in the consideration of climatic variation is altitude. Rainfall varies most and temperature varies least in lower Guinea. Rainfall in Conakry averages 4300 mm (about 170 in) in a year, while temperature averages 27° C (81° F). In the mountainous plateau region, less rain falls and the mean temperature is 7° C (13° F) degrees lower. The climate in the highlands is equatorial, with no clearly distinguishable seasons. The rainy season in the remainder of the country occurs from April or May to October or November. In terms of heat, April is the cruelest month; July and August are the wettest.

Land, Plants, and Animals: Guinea divides into four major topographic regions. Lower Guinea, the coastal plain, extends in from the coastline. Beyond the plain is middle Guinea, the Fouta Djallon, a mountainous plateau region with an average elevation of 910 m (about 3000 ft). The savannas of Upper Guinea undulate gently, breaking occasionally into rocky outcroppings of some elevation. In the extreme southeast are forested highlands. The vegetation of Guinea includes dense man grove forests along the coast, sedge in the Fouta Djallon, savanna woodland in upper Guinea, and rain forest in the highlands. Animal life abounds. Snakes and crocodiles are common, as are tropical birds, including parrots. Mammals include leopards, hippopotamuses, wild boars, antelopes, and civets.

Natural Resources: Bauxite ore, iron ore, diamonds, gold, petroleum, uranium, cobalt, nickel, and platinum

Currency: The Guinea franc

Gross Domestic Product (GDP): $8.3 billion (1997 estimate)

GDP per Capita: $1,100 (1997 estimate)

GDP Real Growth Rate: 4.8 percent (1997 estimate)

Primary Economic Activities: Agriculture and mining

Primary Crops: Rice, cassava, plantains, vegetables, and citrus fruits

Industries: Bauxite, gold, diamonds; alumina refining; light manufacturing; and agricultural processing industries

Primary Exports: Bauxite, alumina, diamonds, gold, coffee, pineapples, bananas, and palm kernels

Primary Imports: Petroleum products, metals, machinery, transport equipment, textiles, and grain

Primary Trade Partners: France, Côte d'Ivoire, China, and Germany

Government: Since 1990 Guinea has made a transition from a one-party, military regime to a multiparty, constitutional civilian system. The new system has a unicameral legislature of 114 seats and universal adult suffrage. Presidential elections were held late in 1993 and again in December 1998; Lansana Conté is the current president. Legislative elections took place in 1995 after being postponed several times.

Africa

Guinea-Bissau,

a small country on the West African coast that lies north of Guinea and south of Senegal.

Guinea-Bissau is one of the poorest countries in the world. Its poverty derives from a long history of slave trading, Portuguese colonial neglect, an 11-year war for independence, post-independence economic mismanagement, and a lack of natural resources. The small, lineage-based communities of Guinea-Bissau have resisted domination by a series of overlords, including the precolonial kingdom of Kaabu, European slave traders, European Fulani marauders, Portuguese colonialists, and finally the Cape Verdean elite of the nationalist movement. This strong tradition of resistance has been a unifying theme in Guinea-Bissau's history.

Early History

Archaeologists believe that small groups of hunters, gatherers, and fishing

These girls on the Bijagós Islands off Guinea-Bissau play traditional drums and wear a combination of mass-produced and handcrafted clothing. *CORBIS/Dave B. Houser*

people occupied the region by 9000 B.C.E. A more pronounced migration toward the coast came around 900 C.E., when wars, poverty, and climatic shifts pushed new groups into the region from points farther east. They were primarily agriculturists and hunters, though some raised cattle on the eastern savanna. The low alluvial plains and mangrove swamps along the coast and rivers sustained salt extraction and tidal agriculture. Over time chiefdoms proliferated. Lineages held land communally and worshiped local gods in addition to their own ancestors.

The Mandinka was one of the last groups to arrive in the region. Their kingdom of Kaabu, the region's first real kingdom, emerged in present-day northeastern Guinea-Bissau around 1250, originally as a tributary of the Mali Empire. Kaabu remained powerful for the next six centuries, as it conquered small chiefdoms throughout the region and enslaved their inhabitants. Many groups fled south and west from Kaabu to the coastal lowlands. Others, such as the Balanta, literally "those who refuse," and the Bijagó of the islands, resisted Kaabu ascendancy and Mandinka dominance. Even when the Balanta were forced to pay tribute to the Mandinka, their adherence to traditional patrilineal succession limited the ability of the Mandinka Empire to incorporate them. Kaabu expanded during the

late fifteenth and the sixteenth centuries, when Songhai assaults on the
Mali Empire and trade with the Portuguese enabled Kaabu to exercise
greater autonomy.

The Slave Trade and Foreign Domination

In 1446 the Portuguese explorer Nuño Tristão sailed into the Bijagós
Archipelago and up some of the rivers, though he died on his return trip. It
was not until ten years later that Diogo Gomes returned to Portugal to tell
of the "Rivers of Guinea." The estuaries facilitated trade, and the coastal
market town of Cacheu was the commercial center of the region from
the late fifteenth to the nineteenth century. At first, the small Portuguese
population remained confined to a few coastal settlements, where they paid
tribute to local chiefs or kings for the right to stay.

Portuguese and *mesticos*, or those of indigenous and European descent,

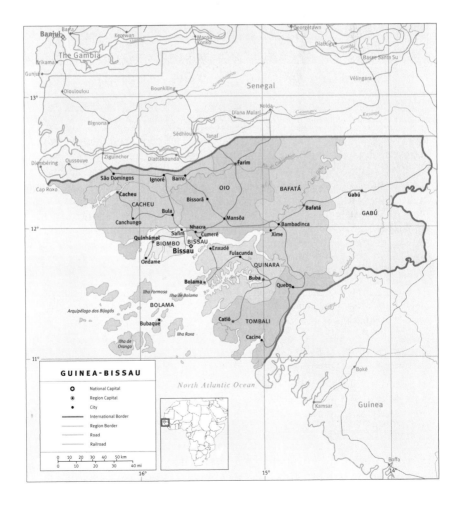

A man in Guinea-Bissau harvests peanuts, one of the country's few cash crops. *CORBIS/Dave B. Houser*

traded alcohol, horses, manufactured goods, textiles, and weapons for copra (coconut flesh, containing the oil), gold, ivory, palm oil, and, increasingly, slaves. Kaabu and other chiefdoms and kingdoms had long been involved in the Arab trans-Saharan slave trade, and they simply shifted some of this trade to the Portuguese on the coast. Some groups, such as the Balanta, Nalu, Felupe, Manjaco, and others, resisted these slave raiding parties. Nevertheless, scholars estimate that from the coming of the Portuguese to the end of the eighteenth century around 600,000 people were sent down the rivers of Guinea to the international slave market. The Portuguese sent slaves to their Cape Verde Island territory, where they were put to work on sugar plantations or shipped to the Americas.

As the transatlantic slave trade shifted farther south during the eighteenth century, Portuguese immigrants, *mesticos*, and Cape Verdeans began establishing larger agricultural estates, or *feitoras*, along the rivers, and growing peanuts, coffee, sugar cane, and cotton. In the interior, Kaabu, socially stratified and intimately involved in the slave trade, had reached its height, with 44 provinces providing troops and tribute. When Portugal outlawed the slave trade in 1837, competition in the illicit slave trade increased. Kaabu provincial governors contended for power and control of the trade in intra-dynastic feuds.

The Islamic Fulani people, who had been subject to heavy Kaabu taxation for generations, eroded the power of the war-torn kingdom through religious conversion and *jihad*, or holy wars. Often supplied with firearms by the Portuguese, Fulani from the area presently known as Guinea began pushing north in the mid-1800s. The wars between the splintering Kaabu Kingdom and the Fulani culminated in 1867 when soldiers loyal to the Fulani *marabout* (religious leader) Timbo Adbul Khudus forced the surrender of Kaabu, though internal rivalries kept the Fulani from consolidating their rule. However, the fall of Kaabu enabled Portugal to divide the peoples of the region and to rule them through pliable chiefs. In the 1870s and 1880s, Fulani slaves, uncompensated by their Fulani masters for fighting against the Mandinka, revolted. The Portuguese granted the rebellious slaves sanctuary, and in return many of them assisted in Portugal's "pacification" campaigns to subdue the indigenous population.

Portuguese Colonialism and African Resistance

When Portugal declared Portuguese Guinea a province in 1879, the Portuguese presence in the region was limited and the Africans, although divided, increasingly resisted. Suffering from tropical diseases and laboring under a lack of funding from colonial authorities on the Cape Verde Islands, the military had thus far failed in its efforts to "pacify" the region. The change in colonial status enabled the Lisbon government to allocate military resources directly to Guinea, which it declared a military district in 1892.

Portuguese pacification campaigns from the 1880s to the 1910s generally remained unsuccessful. The Africans had firearms clandestinely supplied by traders. In addition to these weapons, the Africans used their intimate knowledge of the territories along the rivers to hold off the Portuguese military campaigns with ease. In 1908 nearly the whole Portuguese population was forced into the fort at Bissau. In the next decade the new republican government in Portugal placed a greater emphasis on crushing African resistance, and the colonial administration succeeded in conquering most of the land, through manipulation and force, and in gaining the support of the Fulani.

Under a fascist dictatorship from the 1920s until 1974, Portugal centralized administrative control over the territory and instituted a harsh system of forced labor and heavy taxation. The Portuguese controlled the administration, and *mestico* and Cape Verdeans held more than 70 percent of the administrative posts. Appointed *regulos*, or chiefs, almost all of whom were Fulani, implemented forced labor on oil palm, rice, and peanut plantations. The lack of capital investment under the Portuguese limited the productivity of these ventures and created the basis for the country's persistent poverty. If they were not on forced-labor plantations, many Africans worked on state-run agricultural estates for wages to pay the high taxes demanded by the colonial state. Other Africans worked as subsistence farmers, producing enough surplus to pay taxes. Through education, employment, land ownership, or military service, Africans could attain the privilege of *assimilado* status, or Portuguese citizenship with full rights, but few did so. Discriminatory policies as well as attempts to separate ethnic groups and place them under the control of pliable *regulos*

regulos proved ineffective, because many Africans remained outside the colonial state. For example, the Balanta and the Bijagó resisted colonial authority until 1936.

In 1956 Amílcar Cabral founded the Partido Africano da Independência de Guiné e Cabo Verde (PAIGC). Originally established to advocate peacefully for independence, the party led the nationalist struggle for the next 18 years. In 1962, three years after Portuguese soldiers killed 50 striking dockworkers in Bissau, the PAIGC launched a "people's war" for independence. The southern mangrove swamps and northern forests proved favorable ground for PAIGC guerrillas. Armed with military supplies from Eastern bloc countries, the party effectively controlled two-thirds of the country by 1968, far more than their counterparts the Front for the Liberation of Mozambique (FRELIMO) and the Popular Movement for the Liberation of Angola (MPLA) would ever control in Mozambique or Angola. Even with nearly 50,000 troops, Portugal's counterinsurgency efforts failed. The population, who hated the abuses of Portuguese colonial rule and perceived its weakness, supported the nationalists.

After Cabral's assassination in 1973 by a political opponent, the Cape Verdean Aristides Pereira took over the party's leadership. The PAIGC regrouped and was so successful that it made a unilateral declaration of independence in September 1973. One year later, after a coup d'état in Portugal, Lisbon recognized Guinea-Bissau's independence, and the PAIGC took control with Luís Cabral, Amílcar Cabral's half-brother, as president.

Independence

The PAIGC, the only legitimate nationalist organization during the independence struggle, was divided between the Cape Verdean-dominated senior ranks and the young soldiers of various ethnic groups from the mainland, especially the Balanta. The party also imposed harsh discipline on soldiers and peasants alike. When Cape Verde became independent in 1975, leaders of both countries anticipated unification, but mainland resentment of *mestico* and Cape Verdean domination stood in the way. Meanwhile, the relocation of the party leadership to the capital in Bissau widened the gap between the rural population and party officials, who acquired urban lifestyles and relied on ex-colonial civil servants for technical know-how. As the sole legal party, the PAIGC kept a tight hold on power, and bureaucratic inefficiencies multiplied.

The government tried to revitalize the war-ruined economy through an expansion of state-run agricultural projects and state trading cartels, as it had attempted to do while fighting the independence war, but this was unsuccessful. At the PAIGC's Third Congress in 1977, the state outlined its goal of agricultural and industrial development. The state allowed individuals to own land privately, but state-run trading monopolies would conduct the trade in their agricultural goods. Furthermore, the central government would control all taxation, large-scale fishing projects, mining, forestry, and industrial development. By 1983 the government realized that state-led development schemes were failing due to corruption, inadequate technical training, and a lack of necessary foreign capital. Guinea-Bissau's dependence on the export of a few cash crops (cashew nuts, peanuts, palm oil) compounded these difficulties, since prices for these crops fluctuated widely a nd tended to remain low. With the failure of the government's heavy-handed, state-centered approach to economic development, the informal economy flourished.

The simmering Cape Verdean-Guinean ethnic differences came to a boil after independence, when the government proved authoritarian and inefficient. In 1980 these differences and the marginalization of the mainlander-dominated military led the former vice president and respected guerrilla commander João "Nino" Vieira to overthrow Cabral. In the short term, the influence of Cape Verdeans and *mesticos* declined and the government abandoned its attempt to control the economy; but the government remained authoritarian, and the economic and ethnic problems persisted. In the early 1980s the government demoted prominent Cape Verdeans and *mesticos* as the Balanta in the military agitated for a greater political role. Historically the Balanta, the largest ethnic group, with about 32 percent of the population, were the primary cultivators of Guinea-Bissau's staple crop of rice, but their tradition of dispersed social organization hindered their incorporation into the central government. Balanta discontentment reached its peak in the mid-1980s in the form of a messianic cult and a coup attempt.

The PAIGC sought to consolidate its control through single-party elections in 1984 and 1989. It expanded executive powers so that Vieira could squelch the opposition. Corruption pervaded the government. A 1987 structural adjustment program, sponsored by the International Monetary Fund (IMF), moved the country away from its centrally planned economy and trade with Eastern bloc countries. Divisions over the program arose within the government, as ministries feared their reduction.

Illegal opposition political parties advocating for democratic reform-many of which were led by émigrés in Portugal or neighboring Guinea-never offered a viable alternative to the supremacy of Vieira and the PAIGC. It was only international pressure and the debate concerning the implementation of the structural adjustment program that led dissenting members of the political elite to convince Vieira in 1990 to move toward political liberalization. In 1991 the PAIGC abolished its political monopoly in Guinea-Bissau; political parties soon proliferated. Nevertheless, in the first multiparty election ever held in Guinea-Bissau, in 1994, Vieira narrowly won the presidency and the PAIGC won 62 of 92 seats in the National Assembly. After being re-elected in 1997, Vieira was overthrown by a military faction in May 1999. Head of Parliament Malan Bacai Sanha was appointed interim president, pending elections in November 1999.

Guinea-Bissau has remained economically stable but poor. In the late 1990s its inflation stabilized at around 15 percent. It has strictly adhered to its structural adjustment program, including cuts in public spending, accelerated privatization, and a restrictive monetary policy, and it has begun negotiations to enter the West African monetary system and adopt the CFA franc. These steps aim to alleviate the severe poverty of Guinea-Bissau. Today, primary education is free and compulsory, but there are few secondary schools and no institutions of higher learning, and the illiteracy rate stands at 46 percent. Most of the country's 1.2 million people live in the countryside as subsistence farmers. The main economic activities are small-scale agriculture, forestry, and fishing, though over 50 percent of the country's export earnings come from cashew nuts.

Guinea-Bissau's unexploited reserves of oil have so far caused more problems than benefits. During the mid-1980s the country's relations with Guinea to the south over offshore oil reserves had to be resolved at the World Court. Beginning in 1989 relations between Guinea-Bissau and Senegal also became strained over fishing and oil rights. After Guinea-Bissau agreed to only 15 percent of the oil rights, this disagreement was settled in 1993. The country's bauxite and phosphate reserves offer better prospects for generating revenue.

Guinea-Bissau has served as a refuge for dissidents, refugees, and pilgrims from neighboring countries. Complicating the dispute between Guinea-Bissau and Senegal over offshore natural resources was the fact that Casamance separatists from Senegal had been using Guinea-Bissau as a sanctuary. In 1993 nearly 20,000 Senegalese fled to Guinea-Bissau to avoid the violence in the Casamance region. In 1998 some units of Guinea-Bissau's armed forces rebelled against the government after President Vieira dis-missed army chief Gen. Ansumane Mane on corruption charges. Rebelling officers were accused of smuggling arms to the Casamance separatists. The Senegalese government sent troops to help Vieira end the insurrection.

Indigenous African religions remain prominent in Guinea-Bissau, and pilgrims from Muslim-dominated Senegal and Guinea visit the country's many oracles and shrines. Around two-thirds of the population retain indigenous African religions and one-third follow Islam; a negligible Christian population is growing slowly. Adherence to indigenous African religions is yet another form of the resistance that has characterized the history of Guinea-Bissau's people.

Africa

Guinea-Bissau (Ready Reference)

Official Name: Republic of Guinea-Bissau
Former Name: Portuguese Guinea
Area: 36,120 sq km (about 13,945 sq mi)
Location: Western Africa; borders the North Atlantic Ocean, between Senegal and Guinea

Capital: Bissau (population 200,000 [1994 estimate])

Population: 1,206,311 (1998 estimate)

Population Density: 32 persons per sq km (about 83 persons per sq mi)

Population Below Age 15: 42 percent (male 256,315; female 255,208 [1998 estimate])

Population Growth Rate: 2.32 percent (1998 estimate)

Total Fertility Rate: 5.1 children born per woman (1998 estimate)

Life Expectancy at Birth: Total population: 49.1 years (male 47.4 years; female 50.8 years [1998 estimate])

Infant Mortality Rate: 111.6 deaths per 1000 live births (1998 estimate)

Literacy Rate (age 15 and over who can read and write): Total population: 53.9 percent (male 67.1 percent; female 40.7 percent [1996 estimate])

Education: In the late 1980s about 650 primary and secondary schools had a combined annual enrollment of more than 86,100 students. The country has several teacher training colleges. The government has undertaken a successful program to lower the high adult illiteracy rate, which stood at 81 percent in 1980.

Languages: The official language is Portuguese, but many people speak Crioulo, which combines Portuguese with African elements.

Ethnic Groups: The Balanta, Fulani, Malinke, Mandyako, and Pepel constitute the major ethnic groups, while Cape Verdeans form a small but significant minority.

Religions: A little over one half of the population follows traditional beliefs; 38 percent are Muslim and 8 percent are Christian.

Climate: The climate is tropical, with a mean annual temperature of 25° C (77° F). The rainy season lasts from June to November, bringing an average of 1950 mm (about 77 in) of rainfall.

Land, Plants, and Animals: Vegetation consists of mangrove and rain forest on the coastal plain and a savanna woodland on the interior plateau.

Natural Resources: Tropical hardwoods, bauxite, phosphate, and petroleum

Currency: The Communauté Financière Africaine franc

Gross Domestic Product (GDP): $1.15 billion (1997 estimate)

GDP per Capita: $975 (1997 estimate)

GDP Real Growth Rate: 5 percent (1997 estimate)

Primary Economic Activities: Agriculture and fishing

Primary Crops: Cashew nuts, peanuts, rice, corn, beans, cassava (tapioca), and palm kernels

Industries: Agricultural processing and beverages

Primary Exports: Cashew nuts, palm kernels, peanuts, and fish

Primary Imports: Foodstuffs, machinery, petroleum products, and transport equipment

Primary Trade Partners: China, Germany, Netherlands, Portugal, and

Senegal

Government: A constitution enacted in 1984 vests legislative power in the 150-member National People's Assembly, the members of which are chosen from directly elected regional councils. The legislature elects the five-member Council of State and its president, who heads the government. A political liberalization program approved in 1991 ended one-party dominance in Guinea-Bissau. By 1994, 12 political parties had been recognized and the first multiparty presidential and legislative elections were held. João Bernardo Vieira was re-elected president in 1997 only to face a crisis in June 1998 when a military faction revolted and accused him of corrution. When, according to a peace agreement reached in November 1998 in Abuja, Nigeria, the presidential guard refused to disarm, the military faction attacked on May 8, 1999, toppled Vieira's government, and appointed the head of Parliament, Malan Bacai Sanha, as interim president. Francisco Fadual was named interim prime minister.

North America

Gullah,

an African American culture and language strongly influenced by West Africa.

The descendants of slaves (see Transatlantic Slave Trade) who originated in West Africa, Gullah people have occupied the Sea Islands off the South Carolina and Georgia coasts since the late seventeenth century. After the Civil War they remained, the relative isolation provided by the islands preserving their cultural conditions. Although mainstream American culture has encroached on them during modern times, Gullah communities still existed during the late twentieth century (their numbers were estimated at 100,000 in 1979) in small farming and fishing villages, practicing many of the customs of their ancestors.

West African slaves were brought to the Sea Islands because of their knowledge of rice-growing, which greatly influenced rice-growing practices in South Carolina. The harsh conditions of the islands kept white settlement low and, by the late eighteenth century, more than 70 percent of the islands' inhabitants were black.

Gullah is the name not only of a people but also of their language (called Geechee in Georgia). A Creole form of English, it is a pidgin that has become the native language for its speakers. Gullah merges elements of several West African languages. Its vocabulary is predominantly English, but the syntax and grammar are more reflective of African languages.

The numbers of Gullah remaining on the Sea Islands began to dwindle during the twentieth century. In the 1920s mainland authorities constructed bridges to many of the islands. The economic opportunities associated with the war industries during World War II drew many Gullah away. In addition, in the 1950s and 1960s, developers began to purchase land on the island, developing the properties for tourism. Most vacationers know Hilton Head only as a resort, not as the home to a unique culture.

North America

Guy, Rosa Cuthbert

(b. September 1, 1925, Trinidad, West Indies), Caribbean American author and cofounder of the Harlem Writers Guild, known especially for her young adult fiction.

Over the last five decades, Rosa Guy has written books for children, teenagers, and adults, but she is best known for her novels for young adult readers. Guy places great importance on the power of communicating to teenagers through literature.

Although busy as a young working wife and mother, Guy began to study writing and drama in her free time. In the early 1940s she became part of the American Negro Theatre, a community theater group based in Harlem. A few years later she, John O. Killens, and two other black authors formed the writers' collaborative that became the Harlem Writers Guild. The guild provided an informal setting for aspiring Harlem writers to critique one another's work, and as its membership grew and its reputation spread, it became the most influential black literary organization of its time.

Her first novel, *Bird at My Window*, was published in 1966. But Guy was inspired to write for teenagers after the assassinations of Malcolm X and Martin Luther King Jr., which left her concerned about how the violence and racism in American society affected young people's lives. As a young adult writer, she is especially known for two award-winning trilogies. The first, which was published in the 1970s and begins with *The Friends* (1973), charts the friendship between a Caribbean American and an African American girl as they come of age. Guy has also received acclaim for two adult novels, *A Measure of Time* (1983), set in Harlem during the Harlem Renaissance, and *My Love, My Love; or the Peasant Girl* (1985), which was made into the 1990 Broadway musical *Once on This Island*. Her other books include several for younger children.

Latin America and the Caribbean

Guyana (formerly British Guiana),

an English-speaking nation on the northeastern coast of South America, bordered by the Atlantic Ocean, Brazil, Suriname, and Venezuela; colonized by both the Dutch and the British.

The Cooperative Republic of Guyana is one of the most diverse nations in

South America. Ninety-four percent of Guyana's estimated 864,000 residents are East Indian (Indo-Guyanese), black (Afro-Guyanese), or mulatto (of African and European descent). Guyana is also one of the poorest nations in the Western Hemisphere, and many of its most impoverished citizens are Afro-Guyanese. Less than 40 percent of the country's population lives in urban areas, and those who do are concentrated on a coastal stretch of land that spans just 8 km (5 mi). Guyana has been plagued by political violence fueled by racial conflict.

The country's largest racial group, the Indo-Guyanese, comprise 51 percent of the national population and are disproportionately represented in the nation's oldest political party, the People's Progressive Party (PPP). Afro-Guyanese compose the second largest group and have traditionally supported the nation's second oldest political party, the People's National Congress (PNC). The PPP and PNC were the two most dominant political parties for the last half of the twentieth century.

Although the Indo-Guyanese represent the largest group in the country, African culture and African traditions predominate in Guyanese society. From the time the first African slaves were sold to Dutch sugar planters in 1657 to the period of authoritarian rule by Afro-Guyanese politicians after independence in 1966, blacks have played a major role in the development of modern Guyana. Forbes Burnham, a British-educated Afro-Guyanese, was head of state for 17 years (1968–1985). Walter Rodney, an Afro-Guyanese scholar and founder of the Working People's Alliance (WPA), was a popular intellectual before he was assassinated in 1980 as a result of his participation in the Guyanese democratic movement. Other prominent Guyanese include two internationally acclaimed artists, Edward K. Brathwaite, an Afro-Guyanese writer, and Philip Moore, an Afro-Guyanese wood sculptor.

In spite of historical racial tensions in Guyana, the country has managed to create a rich and vibrant national culture. English is the official language and Christianity is the leading religion. But Guyana is a multicultural, multireligious country. Ninety-eight percent of the Guyanese population is literate. Cricket is the national pastime, but soccer and rugby are also popular activities. In addition to sports, theater is a leading cultural component of Guyanese society. For more than 20 years the Guyana Theater Guild has produced critically acclaimed plays. Obeah, a traditional African religion, is practiced widely in Guyana, and African music and dance are vibrant aspects of Guyanese culture. In contrast, Amerindian culture occupies a limited role in Guyana, maintained in small villages in the interior. Many Amerindians are poor and uneducated and have struggled to keep pace with the rapid changes in Guyanese society.

H

Hagler, Marvelous Marvin

(b. May 24, 1954, Newark, N.J.), African American boxer, middleweight champion of the world in 1980.

Hagler, the eldest of seven children, was born on May 24, 1954, in Newark, New Jersey. His family moved to Brockton, Massachusetts, when he was 17. He won 57 amateur bouts, including the Amateur Athletic Union middleweight title in 1973. At five feet nine and a half inches tall, Hagler was a powerful 160-pound left-hander. He turned professional in 1973, winning his first 26 fights by knockout, and becoming middleweight champion of the world in 1980 by defeating Alan Minter. Hagler defended his title 12 times until his defeat by Sugar Ray Leonard in 1987. He retired in June 1988.

Haile Selassie I

(b. July 23, 1892, Ejarsa Goro, Ethiopia; d. August 27, 1975, Addis Ababa, Ethiopia), last emperor of Ethiopia.

Haile Selassie I was born Lij Tafari Makonnen to Ras (Prince) Makonnen—the governor of Harer Province and a cousin, close friend, and advisor to Emperor Menilek II—and Yishimabet Ali. Young Tafari received a traditional religious education from Ethiopian Orthodox priests, who also taught him French.

Tafari proved his ability and responsibility in 1905 at age 13 when his father appointed him governor of one of the regions of Harer Province. Upon his father's death the following year, Tafari was summoned to the court of Emperor Menilek, who appointed him the governor of a small province. Tafari set out to modernize the government by instituting a paid civil service, lowering taxes, and creating a court system that recognized the rights of peasants. Menilek rewarded Tafari's success by giving him a larger province to govern in 1908.

Upon Menilek's death in 1913, his grandson Lij Yasu became emperor. Yasu, however, was considered too sympathetic toward Islam, which offended the dominant Amhara Christians. They began to see Tafari as their champion. In 1916 he and his supporters deposed Yasu and installed Menilek's daughter, Zawditu, reputedly Ethiopia's first empress. Tafari assumed the title of *ras* and served as her regent and heir apparent.

Tafari brought his modernization plan to the national level. In 1919 he created a centralized bureaucracy; two years later he installed the first courts of law. In 1923 he engineered a foreign affairs coup by securing Ethiopia's entry into the League of Nations. By 1928 his support was so strong that Tafari was able to pressure the empress to name him *negus* (king). Upon Zawditu's death in 1930, Tafari assumed the throne under his baptismal name, Haile Selassie I (Power of the Trinity). The coronation of Tafari, whose dynasty claimed descent through Lebna Dengel from the biblical King Solomon, inspired Jamaican followers of Marcus Garvey to found a new religion, known as Rastafarianism, that idolized the emperor.

In 1931 Selassie introduced Ethiopia's first constitution, which proclaimed all Ethiopians equal under the law and the emperor, and established a parliament with a popularly elected lower house. The emperor still retained the power to overturn any decision that the parliament made.

In 1935, however, Italian forces invaded Ethiopia and in 1936 Selassie fled to exile in Great Britain. During World War II Selassie helped the British liberate Ethiopia, and in 1941 a joint force of British soldiers and Ethiopian exiles restored Selassie to the throne. He spent much of the next decade rebuilding the country. He expanded Western education, in part by founding the country's first university, improved health care, and expanded the transportation network. However, Selassie left Ethiopian society—and most notably the feudal agricultural system—intact. This fact encouraged class distinctions and left many Ethiopians in poverty.

In 1952 Selassie's government annexed the province of Eritrea to provide Ethiopia with an outlet to the sea. In 1960 a group seeking democratic reforms led by students and Selassie's imperial guard staged a coup while the leader was in Brazil. Selassie quickly returned and the coup was put down by Loyalist troops. After the coup attempt, Selassie, who had spent his life attempting to modernize Ethiopia, adopted a more conservative course. In addition he now focused on foreign policy.

Selassie commanded great respect throughout Africa as an elder statesman, embraced Pan-Africanism, and sought African unity. To that end, he was instrumental in establishing the Organization of African Unity (OAU), which was later headquartered in Addis Ababa. Troubles at home demanded Selassie's attention, however. In 1962 the province of Eritrea sought independence from Ethiopia and Eritrean rebels took up armed struggle. Continuing economic problems, high unemployment, and famine caused by prolonged drought led Ethiopians to demonstrate for higher wages and against the continuing economic woes. A military contingent led by junior officers deposed Selassie on September 12, 1974, after a gradual, bloodless coup. Selassie stepped down and was held under house arrest until his death on August 27, 1975.

Latin America and the Caribbean

Haiti,

independent republic in the Caribbean, occupying the western third of the island of Hispaniola. Haiti is bounded on the north by the Atlantic Ocean, on the east by the Dominican Republic, on the south by the Caribbean Sea, and on the west by the Windward Passage, which separates it from Cuba.

By the time The Haitian Revolution ended in 1804, Haiti had become the first black republic in the world, the second independent country in the Western Hemisphere, and the first country in the Western Hemisphere to

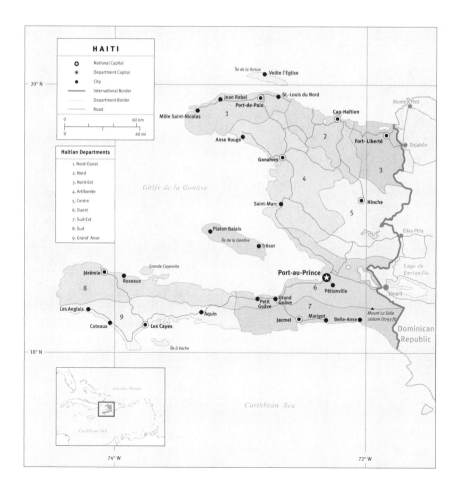

Seven years after helping to win Haiti's independence, in 1811 Henri Christophe (1767-1820) built an empire in the northern section of the country. Despite some progressive social and educational policies, Christophe's rule was brief, ending with his suicide in 1820. *CORBIS/Bettmann*

abolish slavery and grant full citizenship to nonwhites. Haiti's former slaves became an inspiration for people of African descent across the world, particularly those who remained in slavery.

The Arawaks, the original inhabitants of the island Haiti shares with the Dominican Republic, called the island *Ayti*, meaning "land of mountains."

When Christopher Columbus arrived in 1492 he named the island La Isla Española (the Spanish Island) in honor of his Spanish sponsors. The name later evolved into the present-day name Hispaniola. After an early settlement near Cap-Haïtien was destroyed by Native Americans, the Spanish settled the eastern half of the island and left the west unsettled.

French pirates operating from the island of Tortue hunted wild boar and other animals in Hispaniola to sell as food to passing ships. During their visits, the French recognized Hispaniola's potential as an agricultural center, and like the Spanish before them, they began importing African slaves to serve as forced labor. By 1697, when Spain formally ceded the western third of Hispaniola—the portion that later became Haiti—to France, the French had established a flourishing slave-plantation system throughout the colony. By the end of the next century Saint-Domingue (the French colonial term for Haiti) was the world's richest colony. By 1791 "the Pearl of the Antilles," as it was called, produced 60 percent of the world's coffee and 40 percent of its sugar.

Haiti's most serious social problems also stem from the disproportionate distribution of wealth, and some racial divisions continue between the small mulatto elite and the larger black population. Many mixed-raced Haitians still identify more strongly with the wealthy classes of other countries, especially France, than with poor Haitians. Under-developed social, economic, and political institutions—chiefly education—mean that there are still few mechanisms within the country to promote upward social mobility. Another problem preventing social cohesion is the physical isolation of rural communities; about 79 percent of Haitians have little contact with Port-au-Prince or other centers of cultural change.

But Haitians have also begun to find more common ground in celebration of their country's vibrant culture, which bridges races and fuses African, French, and West Indian elements. Haiti's prominent writers include historian Jean-Price Mars, novelists such as Jacques Roumain and Jacques Stéphen Alexis, and poets such as René Depestre, Ida Faubert, and Marie Chauvet. Most Haitian literature has traditionally been written in French, but Creole, which was once considered a social divider, was recognized as an official language in 1987. It is now being used in literature, drama, music, dance, and some schools and governmental functions. New writers in English are also emerging, such as Haitian-American novelist Edwidge Danticat, who has been called the next Toni Morrison.

Prominent musicians and musical groups include Boukman Eksperyans, Jean-Bapiste Nemours and Wéber Sicot, and Manno Charlemagne. They have contributed to developing Haiti's own vital and dynamic culture, as have artists such as Hector Hyppolite, Wilson Bigaud, and all those associated with the so-called Haitian primitivist movement. The country has several outstanding libraries and museums. The collection of the Brothers of Saint Louis de Gonzague (1912), the National Archives (1860), and the Bibliothèque Nationale (1940), all located in Port-au-Prince, contain rare works that date from the colonial period, and the National Museum (1983), located in Port-au-Prince, is devoted to Haitian history.

Haiti's rich cultural treasures are an appropriate extension of its history as one of the most influential nations in the world, particularly among people of African descent. Its legacy as the first country in which Africans were able to overthrow the system of race-based slavery remains a source of pride, and Haitians are optimistic about a more prosperous future that will fittingly reflect their remarkable past.

Latin America and the Caribbean

Haitian Revolution,

uprising in 1791 by black slaves on the Caribbean island of Hispaniola. It began as a rebellion against slavery and French plantation owners, but became a political revolution that lasted for 13 years and resulted in independence from France. By 1804 the revolution had destroyed the dominant white population, the plantation system, and the institution of slavery in the most prosperous colony of the Western Hemisphere. The colony then became the first independent black republic in the world, the Republic of Haiti.

North America

Haley, Alexander Palmer (Alex)

(b. August 11, 1921, Ithaca, N.Y.; d. February 10, 1992, Seattle, Wash.), African American writer and journalist who authored two of the most influential books in the history of African American scholarship.

Alex Haley grew up in Henning, Tennessee and settled in Greenwich Village, New York, determined to make his name as a journalist. After a period of hard work and obscurity, he broke into mainstream publications such as *Readers' Digest*, *Harper's*, and the *New York Times Magazine*. In 1962 he sold a Miles Davis interview to *Playboy* that began the magazine's famous interview series. Later that year *Playboy* commissioned Haley to interview Malcolm X, an assignment that led to Haley's first book, his ghost-written *Autobiography of Malcolm X* (1965).

The Autobiography of Malcolm X sold more than 5 million copies and changed the nation's opinion of the black nationalist leader. The book, which concludes with Malcolm X's reevaluation of the Nation of Islam, highlights the complexity, compassion, and humanity of a figure whose public image might otherwise have remained monolithic and negative. The assassination of Malcolm X in 1965 increased public interest, and Haley's book became required reading in many college courses.

Soon after the publication of *The Autobiography of Malcolm X*, Haley began research for a second contribution to African American literature. The half-fictive, half-factual epic *Roots* (1977), which traces Haley's own maternal lineage back to an enslaved West African named Kunta Kinte, captured the attention of the nation. Haley took 12 years to write and research *Roots*, consulting relatives, archives, and libraries as well as a tribal historian from Kunta Kinte's village.

Roots sold more than 8.5 million copies, was translated into 26 1 anguages, and won 271 different awards. The Pulitzer Prize and National Book Award committees honored its contribution to American history, and ABC turned it into an eight-part television series, of which 130 million Americans watched at least one episode. *Roots* not only touched blacks whose histories resembled Haley's but also whites who were confronted by America's tragic past.

North America

Hamer, Fannie Lou

(b. October 6, 1917, Montgomery County, Miss.; d. March 14, 1977, Ruleville, Miss.), African American civil rights activist who worked with the Student Nonviolent Coordinating Committee (SNCC) to secure voting rights for blacks and helped form the Mississippi Freedom Democratic Party.

The youngest of 20 children born to sharecroppers Ella and Jim Townsend, Fannie Lou Hamer began helping her family pick cotton at age six, and left school to work full-time in the fields only six years later.

In the summer of 1962 Hamer went to a mass meeting organized by the Student Non-violent Coordinating Committee, which had recently begun organizing in the Mississippi Delta, where poor blacks lived in some of the worst conditions anywhere in the United States. SNCC and other civil rights groups hoped to register and educate many of the more than 400,000 African Americans in Mississippi who were being denied their constitutional right to vote by a variety of means, including voter registration tests, poll taxes, and violent reprisals for political activity. Following the meeting, Hamer went along with 17 others to attempt to register to vote in Indianola, the county seat. Facing the registration test, which was administered in such a way as to ensure that black people never passed, Hamer and the others failed.

Returning home, Hamer refused to promise her white boss that she would stop trying to vote; he fired her and threw her off the plantation where she had lived and worked for 18 years. "They kicked me off the plantation," she later told friends, "they set me free. It's the best thing that could happen. Now I can work for my people." Hamer joined SNCC as a fieldworker, where she was soon seen by SNCC leader Robert Moses as a valuable asset because of her brilliant oratory and powerful singing. Hamer also became a living symbol of the dangers faced by civil rights workers after she was unfairly jailed and severely beaten in Winona, Mississippi (June 1963), while returning from citizenship classes. Eventually, due to the intervention of the FBI and the Justice Department, the jailers were tried for assaulting Hamer, but an all-white local jury later found the jailers not guilty.

In 1963 Hamer began working with the Council of Federated Organizations—a coalition of SNCC, the Congress of Racial Equality (CORE), and the National Association for the Advancement of Colored People (NAACP)—on what was called the Freedom Vote. The first statewide voting rights effort, Freedom Vote provided Mississippi's unregistered black citizens with "freedom ballots," with which 80,000 of the citizens cast votes. During the next year, in addition to her SNCC work during Freedom Summer (when thousands of college students came South to assist in voter education and registration), Hamer and others founded the Mississippi Freedom Democratic Party (MFDP) in an attempt to force the state's traditionally all-white, racist Democratic party to integrate.

North America

Hampton University,

a private coeducational institution of higher learning established during Reconstruction to train African American teachers.

Between 1863, the year President Abraham Lincoln issued the *Emancipation Proclamation*, thus freeing slaves in the South, and 1868, the year Hampton Normal and Agricultural Institute opened its doors in Hampton, Virginia, thousands of African Americans had settled on the Virginia Peninsula. With the financial support of Northern philanthropists and religious groups, Samuel Chapman Armstrong, a white Brevet Brigadier General who commanded the United States Eighth and Ninth black troops during the Civil War, founded Hampton to help former slaves achieve self-sufficiency. Under Armstrong's guidance Hampton developed a system of industrial education that became the model for African American education in the post-Civil War era.

Armstrong's educational philosophy, known as the Hampton Idea, emphasized the cultivation of practical skills, a moral character, and a strong work ethic. Students were required to spend two full days of the week working on the school's farm and trade shops, where they applied their classroom knowledge of botany and arithmetic. Students also received social instruction in Christian morality, personal hygiene, and social etiquette. In the aftermath of slavery, these lessons were intended to help African American students become functioning members of society. From 1878 to 1923 Hampton also educated numerous Native Americans.

In the early twentieth century such African American leaders as W. E. B. Du Bois criticized Hampton because of its exclusively industrial curriculum. Du Bois claimed that black Americans needed higher education in order to progress beyond manual labor positions. An educational reform movement in the 1920s led to the elimination of elementary- and secondary-level courses and the implementation of college-level courses at Hampton. Between 1929 and 1930 Hampton raised its admission standards by requiring applicants to have a high school education, and changed its name to Hampton Institute. In 1932 Hampton became an accredited four-year institution, and in 1956 it organized a Division of Graduate Studies. In 1984 the school changed its name to Hampton University. Today Hampton has an enrollment of more than 5500 students pursuing degrees in some 50 areas of study.

Handy, William Christopher (W.C.)

(b. November 16, 1873, Florence, Ala.; d. March 28, 1958, New York, N.Y.), composer, cornet and trumpet player, bandleader, and self-described "father of the blues."

Although personally soft-spoken and unprepossessing, W. C. Handy titled his autobiography with a bold phrase that had long been associated with him, *Father of the Blues* (1941). But as Handy well knew, the blues, an African American musical genre of incalculable significance, was in no sense the creation of any one individual. More accurately, Handy's importance lay in his success as a promoter of African American music: popularizing the blues was his greatest accomplishment.

Handy took a loosely structured folk idiom performed by unschooled musicians and formalized it, in particular regularizing its most common 12-bar form. Handy explained that he took a music "already used by Negro roustabouts, honky-tonk piano players, wanderers, and others . . . from Missouri to the Gulf [of Mexico]. . . . [and] introduce[d] this, the 'blues' form, to the general public."

His *Memphis Blues*, published in 1912, is commonly regarded as the first blues to appear in sheet music.

Hansberry, Lorraine

(b. May 19, 1930, Chicago, Ill.; d. January 12, 1965, New York, N.Y.), playwright whose award-winning play, *A Raisin in the Sun*, was the first by an African American woman to be produced on Broadway.

Hansberry set *A Raisin in the Sun*, her most famous play, in familiar territory—the terrible living conditions produced for blacks by restricted covenants. It opened at the Ethel Barrymore Theatre on Broadway on

March 11, 1959. Directed by Lloyd Richards and starring Sidney Poitier and Ruby Dee, it ran for 583 performances. *A Raisin in the Sun* was the first Broadway play directed by a black person in 50 years, and the first written by a black woman. Hansberry was the first black woman to receive the New York Drama Critics Circle Award (beating out Tennessee Williams, Eugene O'Neill, and Archibald MacLeish), and the youngest ever recipient. When it became a Columbia movie in 1961, the film received a nomination for Best Screenplay of the Year from the Screenwriters Guild and a special award at the Cannes Film Festival (1961); the musical, *Raisin* (1973), won a Tony Award. The play is widely anthologized and often revived.

Hansberry was prolific: *The Movement: Documentary of a Struggle for Equality*; *To Be Young, Gifted and Black: Lorraine Hansberry in Her Own Words*; and articles in the *Village Voice*, *Freedomways*, the *National Guardian*, and the *Black Scholar* are among her published work. In addition to the protests that her work embodied, she was a committed activist for black and gay rights, involved in the Student Nonviolent Coordinating Committee (SNCC), and a critic of the House Un-American Activities Committee.

North America

Harlem, New York,

political and cultural center of black America in the twentieth century, best known as the major site of the literary and artistic "renaissance" of the 1920s and 1930s.

The evolution of Harlem into the political and cultural capital of black America is a twentieth-century phenomenon. Housing in Harlem, which was once a wealthy suburb of New York City, soared in value at the turn of the century, only to collapse beneath excessive real estate speculation in 1904 and 1905. Those years coincided with the completion of the Lenox Avenue subway line to lower Manhattan, facilitating the settlement of African Americans migrating from the South and the Caribbean in Harlem. Philip Payton's Afro-Am Realty Company leased large numbers of Harlem apartment houses from white owners and rented them to black tenants in neighborhoods that began at 135th Street east of Eighth Avenue and over the decades expanded east-west from Park to Amsterdam avenues and north-south from 155th Street to Central Park.

By 1930 the black population of New York had more than tripled, to 328,000 persons, 180,000 of whom lived in Harlem—two-thirds of all African Americans in New York City and 12 percent of the entire population. Between 1920 and 1930 the black population of Harlem increased by nearly 100,000 persons, developing middle- and upper-middle-class neighborhoods such as Striver's Row on West 139th Street.

Not only the cultural and intellectual center of black life in the United States, Harlem has also served as a safe haven, a black community with strong connections among its inhabitants. *CORBIS/Bettmann*

The migration led to a political, cultural, and social community that was unprecedented in scope. The African Methodist Episcopal Zion Church, St. Philips' Protestant Episcopal Church, and Abyssinian Baptist Church moved north to Harlem. The *Amsterdam News* was founded in Harlem in 1919. The community also supported a vital literary and political life: by 1920 the trade union newspaper the *Messenger*, edited by A. Philip Randolph and Chandler Owen, was published in Harlem, as were the National Association for the Advancement of Colored People's (NAACP's) magazine the *Crisis*, edited by W. E. B. Du Bois and Jessie Fauset, and the National Urban League's magazine *Opportunity*, edited by Charles S. Johnson. Incipient political movements followed the establishment of a branch of the NAACP in 1910 and Marcus Garvey's Universal Negro Improvement Association in 1916. Flamboyant and charismatic, Garvey promoted both a back-to-Africa drive and the first popular Black Nationalist Movement. Harlem also nurtured a socialist movement led by H. H. Harrison, W. A. Domingo, and A. Philip Randolph.

Especially in the 1920s Harlem fostered pioneering black intellectual

From Marcus Garvey's Universal Negro Improvement Association to the National Memorial African Bookstore, pictured here in 1964, Harlem has long served as home to movements and ideas stressing African American self-reliance and self-esteem. *UPI/CORBIS-Bettmann*

and popular movements as well as a dynamic nightlife centered on nightclubs, impromptu apartment "buffet parties," and speakeasies. Many of Harlem's cultural venues developed at this time, ranging from the Lincoln and Apollo theaters to the Cotton Club, Smalls Paradise, and Savoy Ballroom. In popular dance Florence Mills was one of the most celebrated entertainers of the 1920s, while in tap, Bill "Bojangles"

Robinson was called "the Mayor of Harlem." In vaudeville Bert Williams broke the color line. In drama Paul Robeson was an honored figure for both his acting and singing.

In 1925 Alain Locke filled an issue of *Survey Graphic* magazine with black literature, folklore, and art, declaring a "New Negro" renaissance to be guided by "forces and motives of [cultural] self determination." The renaissance was led by writers such as Jean Toomer, Langston Hughes, Countee Cullen, Claude McKay, Nella Larsen, and Zora Neale Hurston, and Harlem became its symbol. In art Aaron Douglas, Richmond Barthé, and (later) Jacob Lawrence launched their careers.

In music Harlem pianists such as Fats Waller and Willie "the Lion" Smith began one of the most storied traditions of jazz in the world. In the 1920s it included big bands led by Fletcher Henderson, Duke Ellington, and Chick Webb and individual virtuosos such as Eubie Blake. Later, it included Charlie Parker, Bud Powell, Ornette Coleman, Thelonious Monk, and Miles Davis.

In the 1920s Harlem gained some political power and institutions. Arthur Schomburg's renowned collection of black literature and historical documents became a branch of the New York Public Library (see Schomburg). Three years later Charles Fillmore was elected the first black district leader in New York City, and black physicians were admitted to the permanent staff of Harlem Hospital.

But such advances were modest. Harlem blacks owned less than 20 percent of Harlem's businesses in 1929, and the onset of the Depression quadrupled relief applications within two years. Blacks continued to be excluded from jobs, even in Harlem.

During World War II migration from the South and the Caribbean increased enormously, the direct result of the opening of defense industry jobs to blacks, for which the 1941 March on Washington—organized by A. Philip Randolph—was instrumental (See Great Migration, The). But racism persisted, and an incident of police brutality in 1943 precipitated a riot. In 1944, on the heels of widespread efforts to improve race relations, Adam Clayton Powell Jr. was elected to the United States Congress and Benjamin Davis replaced him on the City Council.

The 1940s and 1950s brought further political cohesion and literary expression. Hulan Jack was elected the first black borough president in 1953. Through the 1970s Harlem was home to heralded writers such as novelist Ralph Ellison, essayist James Baldwin, playwright Lorraine Hansberry, and poets Audre Lorde and Maya Angelou—many of them associated with the Harlem Writers Guild. Yet by 1960 middle-class flight from Harlem produced a ghetto in large sections of the community. Half of all housing units were unsound, and the infant mortality rate was nearly double that in the rest of the city.

Under the leadership of Harlem Youth Opportunities Unlimited (HARYOU), organized by Kenneth B. Clark, Harlem tried to draw federal funding into the area to rebuild the community and create jobs. The effort

HARLEM

MAJOR SITES OF BLACK CULTURE
IN THE 1920S

was largely unsuccessful, and in 1964, when an off-duty police officer shot a
black youth, a riot ensued.

In the 1950s Malcolm X arrived to head the Harlem Mosque and soon
created an independent religious and Black Nationalist Movement that
declared itself ready to fight—"by any means necessary"—against white
racism and violence toward African Americans. In 1965, however, Malcolm
X was assassinated. His death made him a martyr for Black Nationalists
even as his religious movement dissipated.

By the late 1970s, however, deindustrialization and inflation led to
widespread unemployment, while poverty, drugs, crime, and a deteriorating
school system plagued the community for the next decade. When, in 1989,
Harlem's David Dinkins was elected mayor of New York, racial divisions
briefly lessened and some parts of Harlem were revitalized. But Dinkins's
defeat in the 1993 election cut short those efforts. In the more mercantilist
environment of the late 1990s Harlem turned to private development
efforts by African Americans, such as the mall for 125th Street, as a means
for rehabilitating an impoverished community.

Harrington, Oliver Wendell (Ollie)

(b. February 14, 1912, Valhalla, N.Y.; d. November 7, 1995, Berlin, Germany), African American cartoonist and expatriate best known for creating the character Bootsie.

Oliver Harrington graduated from high school in 1929 and moved to New York City during the Harlem Renaissance.

Harrington attended the National Academy of Design, where he studied painting and drawing. By 1932 his comic strips were being featured in black newspapers, including the *Pittsburgh Courier, New York Amsterdam News,* and *Baltimore Afro-American.* Bootsie, a cartoon character who mimicked the styles and trends in the urban black community, and who would become Harrington's most famous creation, first appeared in a comic strip called "Dark Laughter." In 1958 a collection of Bootsie comic strips was published as *Bootsie and Others.*

Harris, Patricia Roberts

(b. May 31, 1924, Mattoon, Ill.; d. March 23, 1985, Washington, D.C.), first black American woman to serve as an ambassador, a cabinet secretary, and a law school dean.

Patricia Roberts Harris was born and raised in a working-class suburb of Chicago. She accepted a scholarship from Howard University in Washington, D.C., where in 1943 she participated in one of the country's first student sit-ins, at a whites-only cafeteria in a black neighborhood. She later attended law school at Washington's George Washington University, from which she graduated first in her class. In 1961 she joined the faculty of Howard Law School.

A lifelong Democrat, Harris served on several federal commissions concerned with minority rights. In 1965, largely on the strength of this work, President Johnson appointed her U.S. ambassador to Luxembourg. After a brief and noncontroversial posting, she returned to Howard in 1967 and in 1969 was named dean of the law school. Immediately after her appointment, students protested for greater power in university decisions. Harris took a strong stand against them and, when she felt she was not supported by the school's president, resigned. She had served as dean for one month. For the next eight years she practiced law in a Washington firm and continued her national party activities.

In 1977 President Jimmy Carter nominated Harris secretary of the Department of Housing and Urban Development (HUD). Her confirmation hearings were contentious, mostly because liberals feared her close connection to "the establishment" would make her unsympathetic to HUD's poor constituency. In a well-publicized reply to such fears, Harris told the Senate, "You do not seem to understand who I am. I'm a black woman, the daughter of a dining car waiter. . . . I am a black woman who could not buy a house eight years ago in parts of the District of Columbia." She was confirmed, the first black woman to direct a federal department. During her tenure, she secured greater funding for HUD, which she used to increase dramatically the number of new subsidized homes and to rehabilitate rather than destroy old homes. She also promoted grants to attract businesses to blighted areas and vouchers to give poor people greater choice in housing.

In 1979 Carter appointed Harris secretary of the Department of Health, Education, and Welfare (HEW), later the Department of Health and Human Services (HHS). At HEW her main task was protecting social programs from the budget cuts of the late 1970s. Her tenure was cut short by the election of Ronald Reagan in 1980.

In 1982 Harris ran for mayor of Washington against incumbent Marion Barry. In a bitter campaign, Barry depicted her as the elitist candidate of the middle and upper classes who had lost touch with Washington's large population of poor blacks. Harris was soundly defeated in the primary. For the next two years she taught law at George Washington University. She died of breast cancer a few months after the death of her husband.

North America

Hawkins, Coleman Randolph

(b. November 21, 1904?, St. Joseph, Mo.; d. May 19, 1969, New York, N.Y.), jazz musician, called the "father of the tenor saxophone," whose career spanned the years from early swing to post-bop jazz.

Famous for his landmark 1939 recording "Body and Soul" and as sideman in the big bands of Mamie Smith and Fletcher Henderson, Coleman Hawkins is credited with bringing the tenor saxophone into the jazz ensemble. When he began his long musical career in the early 1920s, the saxophone was, according to jazz historian Joachim Berendt, in "the category of strange noise makers." No previous player had explored the instrument's potential for carrying a song's melody, for mimicking the human voice, or for use in tonal experimentation.

Hawkins, known to his contemporaries as "Hawk" or "Bean," changed all that. Born in St. Joseph, Missouri, to a musically talented mother, Hawkins began piano lessons when he was five, studied cello at age seven, and started playing the saxophone by the time he was nine. His formal training also included classes at Washburn College in Topeka, Kansas. Hawkins played at weekend dances in Kansas City, Missouri, as a young teenager, and at 17 joined the big band fronted by blues singer Mamie Smith. Two years later, in 1923, he followed her to New York City.

Hawkins left Smith to join the city's premier big band, led by Fletcher Henderson, the legendary bandleader considered by many to be the leading architect of the swing era in jazz. From 1923 to 1934 Hawkins played with Henderson's band, during which time he pioneered the saxophone as a solo instrument within the jazz ensemble. Especially on romantic ballads, his solos influenced scores of other musicians. "When I heard Hawk," the trumpeter Miles Davis once said, "I learned to play ballads." In addition to playing with Henderson, Hawkins recorded with fellow saxophonist Benny Webster in a smaller ensemble called the Chocolate Dandies.

In 1934 Hawkins left Henderson and New York for an extended European tour. He stayed for five years, playing throughout England, France, and the Netherlands. Only when World War II loomed in 1939 did he come back to the United States. Shortly after his return he recorded what would become his trademark song, "Body and Soul," a standard in which Hawkins's solo established him as the preeminent saxophonist of jazz. It was a best-selling record, his first in 20 years as a musician. From 1939 to 1940 Hawkins briefly fronted his own big band, but for the rest of his career he mostly worked solo, backed up by house musicians or playing in impromptu groups.

A lifelong innovator, Hawkins worked with musicians who were pioneering the new style known as bebop. He recorded "Woody 'n' You" in 1944 with Dizzy Gillespie and Max Roach, and later played with both Thelonious Monk and Miles Davis. In the last two decades of his life Hawkins recorded prolifically, toured Europe often, and continued to play in and around New York. He died in 1969 of liver disease. More than 500 people, including numerous jazz luminaries, attended his funeral.

North America

Hayes, Roland Willsie

(b. June 3, 1887, Curryville, Ga.; d. December 31, 1976, Boston, Mass.), African American tenor whose pioneering recitals of German *lieder* and other classical music opened the concert stage for black singers (see Opera).

Hayes was, he claimed, "born again" one evening when he heard recordings of opera singer Enrico Caruso and other classical artists.

Hayes attended Fisk University and was working as a waiter in Louisville, Kentucky, when the president of Fisk invited him to join the famous Fisk Jubilee Singers on a concert tour to Boston, Massachusetts. In Boston a benefactor arranged for voice lessons, and Hayes began studying with Arthur Hubbard in 1911. Hayes worked as a messenger for the John Hancock Insurance Company and sang in black churches. In 1920 he toured Europe, where he received positive reviews.

On December 2, 1923, Hayes presented a self-financed concert at Boston's Symphony Hall that won favorable attention and established him in a successful life-long career as an international recital artist. He sang French, Italian, and German songs around the world and was considered a master of German *leider*. Hayes had deep affection for African American folk music, and he introduced Negro spirituals to much of the world. He received many honors and awards, including the prestigious Spingarn Medal, the highest recognition of the National Association for the Advancement of Colored People (NAACP).

North America

Hemings, Sally

(b. 1773, Bermuda Hundred, Va.; d. 1836), African American slave who may have been the mistress of Thomas Jefferson.

A woman at the center of controversy for the past two centuries, Sally Hemings was born the daughter of a mulatto slave woman, Elizabeth Hemings, and a free white man, John Wayles. Wayles was also the father of Martha Wayles, President Thomas Jefferson's wife, who died in 1782. Two years later Hemings, a slave in the Jefferson estate, accompanied the widowed Jefferson to France, where he served as ambassador and she tended his daughter, Martha. Although she could have claimed her freedom in Paris, Hemings returned with Jefferson to Virginia in 1789, remaining with him until his death in 1826. Jefferson's daughter, Martha, freed Hemings after her father's death, but she continued to work at Monicello until she died ten years later.

One of Jefferson's political enemies first aired public allegations that the two were sexually involved in 1802, starting what would become nearly 200 years of dispute over the relationship between Jefferson and Hemings. While Jefferson himself never denied the accusations during his lifetime, in the years since his death some of Jefferson's white descendants, and others to whom the idea of his relationship with Hemings is distasteful, have fought against the rumors. Lacking definitive scientific proof, the question of whether or not Hemings and Jefferson were lovers was for years open to interpretation and argument.

In 1998 speculation about the paternity of Heming's children, a subject of disagreement among scholars, prompted scientists to apply newly available DNA testing to the controversy. While it is impossible to claim with absolute certainty that Jefferson fathered Hemings's children, the results convinced scientists that it is extremely likely.

North America

Hendrix, Jimi

(b. November 27, 1942, Seattle, Wash.; d. September 18, 1970, London, England), African American musician, rock 'n' roll singer, and guitar virtuoso.

Jimi Hendrix taught himself guitar by listening to Muddy Waters, B. B. King, and Chuck Berry. After serving as a paratrooper in the army, he began his music career. Under the name Jimmy James, he played as a backup guitarist for many top rock 'n' roll and rhythm and blues artists, including Little Richard, Sam Cooke, B. B. King, Wilson Pickett, Ike and Tina Turner, and the Isley Brothers. Between 1962 and 1964 Hendrix began to captivate audiences with such guitar tricks as playing with his teeth, behind his back, and between his legs.

Aspiring to move out of the background, Hendrix formed a band called Jimmy James and the Blue Flames in 1965, and played coffeehouses in New York's Greenwich Village, where he was influenced by Bob Dylan. Chas Chandler, bassist for the popular group the Animals, discovered Hendrix in New York. In 1966, Chandler, who would later become Hendrix's manager, convinced him to accompany him to London by promising to introduce Hendrix to Eric Clapton. In London, Hendrix formed a band, a power trio called the Jimi Hendrix Experience, with drummer Mitch Mitchell and bassist Noel Redding.

The London rock world, hungry for a new trend, was consumed by Hendrix. His style of playing fascinated even such elite guitarists as Pete Townsend and Eric Clapton, who placed Hendrix's musicianship on a level above their own. Considered a true virtuoso, the left-handed Hendrix played a right-handed Fender Stratocaster strung upside down. He used new techniques, including distortion, "wah-wah," and feedback to add an electrifying sonic architecture to already accomplished songs. The Experience was one of the first integrated big-time rock bands that was led by an African American.

In 1967 the Experience released its first album, *Are You Experienced?*, which contained the hits "Hey Joe" and "Purple Haze," and featured Hendrix's famously expansive lyrics ("Scuze me while I kiss the sky"). In June 1967 the Experience made a dramatic debut in the American music scene at the Monterey Pop Festival. Because Hendrix and the Experience had not yet released *Are You Experienced?* in the United States, festival promoters were unwilling to book them until Paul McCartney of the Beatles persuaded them to do so. During their performance, Hendrix tore through a set of original compositions and eclectic covers, and closed the set by setting fire to his guitar.

On the strength of the Monterey performance Hendrix became a superstar. He began spending more and more time recording and founded his own studio, Electric Ladyland, in New York, where he associated with fellow musicians, including admirer Miles Davis. The Experience slowly unraveled as Hendrix pursued side projects. In 1969 he appeared at Woodstock, performing an unorthodox, distortion-filled guitar version of "The Star-Spangled Banner" that had fans raving and had "middle America," which saw his version as blasphemous, enraged. Following Woodstock, Hendrix formed the Band of Gypsies, an all-black band with Buddy Miles, a friend from the army, on drums and Billy Cox on bass. They released one album, a self-titled recording of a live performance. At age 27, Hendrix died in London of complications following barbiturate intoxication.

North America

Henson, Matthew Alexander

(b. August 8, 1866, Charles County, Md.; d. March 9, 1955, New York, N.Y.),
African American explorer, member of the 1909 expedition with American
explorer Robert Peary that is generally credited with discovering the North Pole.

Matthew Henson's travels began when he was just a teen. He ran away
from home after his parents' death and sailed around the world for six years
as a hand aboard the merchant vessel *Katie Hines*.

Henson was working as a hat store clerk in Washington, D.C., in 1897
when Robert Peary hired him as a valet. He traveled with Peary on a survey
expedition to Nicaragua in 1897 and accompanied him on seven polar
expeditions. Henson quickly proved indispensable to Peary as a navigator in
the Arctic and as a translator among the Inuit (also known as Eskimos).

On April 6, 1909, an expedition made up of Peary, Henson, and four
Inuit claimed to be the first to reach the North Pole. Henson, who usually
broke trail while pulling a sled, may have reached the Pole 45 minutes before
Peary, although discovery of the North Pole is usually credited to Peary. In
recent years, however, most scholars have concluded that the point the
expedition reached was actually at least a few miles from the North Pole.

In 1912 Henson wrote *A Black Explorer at the North Pole*. In 1913 President Taft personally recommended Henson's appointment to the United
States Customs House in New York City in recognition of his exploits in
the Arctic. In 1944 Henson received a joint medal from the Congress of the
United States, honoring the Peary expedition to the North Pole. He was also
honored by President Truman in 1950 and admitted to the Explorer's Club,
but he passed away in relative obscurity five years later. In 1986 Henson
was commemorated on a postage stamp. Two years later he was reburied in
Arlington National Cemetery in Virginia with full honors.

North America

Herriman, George

(b. August 22, 1880, New Orleans, La.; d. April 24, 1944, Los Angeles, Calif.),
African American cartoonist whose strip *Krazy Kat* has been lauded by many
as the greatest American cartoon.

George Herriman was born in New Orleans in 1880, but his family soon
moved to California, perhaps because his light-skinned Creole parents
hoped to pass as white and start life anew. Indeed, Herriman himself
obscured his African descent all his life, earning the nick-name "the Greek"
from speculating coworkers. As a teenager Herriman contributed drawings
to local newspapers. In his early twenties he moved to New York City and
freelanced until white newspaper mogul William Randolph Hearst saw his
cartoons and hired him for the New York Evening Journal.

During the first decade of the twentieth century, Herriman explored a
number of characters and settings before developing *Krazy Kat*. The strip's
main characters emerged from a cat and mouse he drew in the margins of

his first success, *The Family Upstairs*. *Krazy Kat* gained independence on October 28, 1913, and ran until Herriman died in 1944.

Krazy Kat's title character, an androgynous cat, loves Ignatz, a married male mouse. Ignatz despises Krazy's affection and hurls bricks at him/her to make him/her go away. Krazy, however, has descended from Kleopatra Kat—an Egyptian for whom bricks were missives of love—and finds encouragement in the violence of Ignatz. Officer B. Pupp, a diligent and well-meaning dog who loves Krazy, attempts to curtail Ignatz's brick-throwing, but seldom succeeds.

The drama transpires in Coconino County, Arizona, a shifting, surreal desert landscape that was inspired by Herriman's own trip to Monument Valley. In addition to Krazy, Ignatz, and Pupp, Herriman introduced Mr. Wough Wuph Wuff, Don Kiyote, Osker Wildcat, Uncle Tomm Katt, and numerous other cleverly named characters.

Krazy Kat never achieved wide popularity among newspaper readers, though it attracted a highbrow following, including Pablo Picasso, Charlie Chaplin, Walt Disney, F. Scott Fitzgerald, Frank Capra, H. L. Mencken, and Ernest Hemingway. *Krazy Kat*'s lengthy tenure owed much to Hearst's personal love of the strip. Acceptance by the cultural mainstream grew after Herriman's death, as Krazy appeared in an animated series by Paramount Studios, in the tattoos and lyrics of rock 'n' roll stars, in a *Star Trek* episode, on T-shirts and postage stamps, in gallery shows and stage productions, and even in a novel. Throughout the twentieth century, cartoonists have considered *Krazy Kat* the founding father (or mother) of sophisticated comic strips.

North America

Hip Hop in the United States,

an umbrella term for the youth culture that originated in the South Bronx, New York, in the 1970s.

Although hip hop includes graffiti art, breakdancing, and rap music, the name connotes more than the sum of these parts. Hip hop is a means of creative expression that gives voice to young, ethnic, urban populations. Says historian Tricia Rose, "Hip hop is a cultural form that attempts to negotiate the experiences of marginalization, brutally truncated opportunity, and oppression within the cultural imperatives of African American and Caribbean history, identity, and community."

In 1959 the city of New York began to construct the Cross Bronx Expressway. Designed to connect New Jersey and Long Island with Manhattan, the freeway project reflected the needs of white suburban commuters. By causing the destruction of numerous Bronx businesses and apartment complexes, the expressway project finished what the decline of federal assistance programs had begun, catapulting the Bronx into destitution. Long-time white residents fled to the suburbs, and slumlords bought up the devalued apartments that flanked the dusty and noisy construction sites.

A power outage in New York in 1977 and the looting and disorder that followed turned public attention toward the Bronx, and the borough became a national symbol of the inner city crisis. Bronx residents, primarily African and Caribbean Americans, received little external support as they attempted to live amid an economic wasteland. Hip hop culture emerged as a new, creative, and flexible value system in a landscape stripped of value. Although neighborhoods were ugly and neglected, fashion and art could embody pride, beauty, and self-respect.

Teenagers improvised. Black and Hispanic youths who had no dance halls and community spaces began dancing in the streets—first to disco, then to Jamaican-influenced DJ remixes, then to rap. DJs tapped into street lights to drive their booming sound systems. Young musicians, whose under-funded schools could provide no instruments, used stereo technology to make new sounds. Young artists painted on walls and subway cars instead of canvases. Breakdancing, rap, and graffiti art were all, in a sense, need-in-duced innovations, and each enriched the others. Graffiti artists designed posters, stage sets, and fashions for local DJs and rap musicians; break-dancers followed the rhythms of rap.

Many of hip hop's progenitors were trained in skills such as printing and radio repair, which quickly became obsolete in postindustrial New York. Unable to secure the kinds of jobs that had abounded ten years before, these craftspersons found artistic outlets for their workplace skills; graffiti replaced letterpress printing, rap replaced radio repair. Hip hop helped to ameliorate the archaic conditions of the inner city as the world approached the computer age.

Hip hop culture emphasized the new social allegiances of "crews" or "posses." Often interethnic, always panfamilial, crews and posses resembled gangs. Although a premium was placed on musical and artistic activities, gang-like rivalries characterized intergroup relations. Dancers and rappers held showdowns, competing against opponent performers, and graffiti artists sometimes defaced the murals of rivals. Hip hop culture included ongoing battles for local status, and creative conflicts often erupted into physical fights.

In the early 1980s hip hop culture exploded into the American main-stream. Breakdancing and rap gained nationwide popularity through movies, documentaries, music videos, and albums. The rampant merchandising that followed led some observers to suggest that the social and political power of hip hop died with commercialization.

From the beginning, however, hip hop artists maintained an often ambivalent relationship to consumer culture. Rap musicians both flouted and celebrated popular commodities. Although graffiti artists painted com-mercial icons such as the Smurfs and Kodak film boxes, they often subordi-nated such images to their own massive, dynamic signatures. Breakdancers imitated Hollywood robots. Hip hop fashion mocked luxury companies such as Gucci, yet sometimes celebrated conspicuous consumption. Members of hip hop culture neither panned nor unconditionally embraced white consumer society, though often they called attention to its artifice.

As rap artists accrued wealth and notoriety, the political impact of the hip hop ethos increased. Some rappers, such as Public Enemy and NWA (Niggaz with Attitude), penetrated public consciousness with aggressive dissent that unnerved many members of the white establishment. Writer Kristal Brent Zook suggests that "there are persistent elements of Black Nationalist ideology which underlie and inform both rap music and a larger 'hip hop' culture. These elements include a desire for cultural pride, economic self-sufficiency, racial solidarity, and collective survival."

At the end of the twentieth century hip hop continues to represent the cultural movement that originally developed in the Bronx. Hip hop sensibilities, however, prevail across the nation and around the globe, comprising social conscience as well as artistic innovation.

North America

Holiday, Billie

(b. April 17, 1915, Baltimore, Md.; d. July 17, 1959, New York, N.Y.), African American jazz singer who influenced the course of American popular singing.

Billie Holiday lived two irreconcilably different lives: one as a consummate jazz artist, one as an emotionally traumatized victim of abuse. Her singing has inspired generations of musicians, and she is one of a few women— along with Bessie Smith, Ella Fitzgerald, and Sarah Vaughan—to have attained the status of jazz legend. Jazz scholars treat her no less seriously than they do Louis Armstrong or Duke Ellington. Although Holiday had limited popular appeal during her lifetime, her impact on other singers was profound. In 1958 Frank Sinatra cited Holiday as "the greatest single musical influence on me" and "the most important influence on American popular singing in the last 20 years." On the other hand, Holiday's life story partakes of myth, for example, in the inaccuracies and exaggerations of her autobiography, *Lady Sings the Blues* (1959).

Holiday was also a profoundly tragic figure. Abandoned by her father, raised in poverty, and abused as a child, she claimed that she had become a prostitute by age 11. Throughout her life she remained barely literate, and she lacked self-esteem. Many of the men in her life victimized her and, when she was in her mid-twenties, one—trumpeter Joe Guy—introduced her to heroin. Holiday became addicted, and in 1947 she was imprisoned on narcotics charges.

In attempting to explain the power of Holiday's singing, musicologist Gunther Schuller bordered on the mystical. Her art, he wrote, "transcends the usual categorizations of style, content, and technique" and reaches "a realm that is not only beyond criticism but in the deepest sense inexplicable." Schuller underscored her "uncanny ability to go . . . beyond the song material [and to] . . . characterize it in whatever mood she happened to be in." Holiday linked her life and her singing. She said that it was easy to sing songs like "The Man I Love" or "Porgy" because, in her own words, "I've lived songs like that." Yet this sort of observation reinforces an unfortunate stereotype of jazz musicians as intuitive performers whose music simply mirrors their lives. Such an image—and the related theme of jazz artists as tortured and tragic figures—discounts the hard work and creative choices that go into jazz.

Although Holiday had no formal musical training, she pursued a far more demanding course of study in the late 1920s and early 1930s in such Harlem speakeasies as the Log Cabin, the Yeah Man, and the Hotcha. She worked hard to perfect her singing. Her 1933 recording debut—a novelty number titled "Your Mother's Son-in-law"—reveals a vocalist still not in command of her art, but two years later she secured a long-term contract with Columbia Records.

Between 1935 and 1942 Holiday recorded her greatest work, including "I Must Have That Man," "I Cried for You," and "I'll Get By." She also recorded her best-known original, "God Bless the Child." Swing-era stars such as pianist Teddy Wilson and alto saxophonists Benny Carter and Johnny Hodges supported her performances, but her key collaborators were Teddy Wilson and tenor saxophonist Lester Young. Wilson's elegant style contributes to the classic quality of these recordings, and Young was Holiday's musical soul mate. He was renowned for his lyrical improvisations, and together the two achieved a rare musical intimacy. Young gave Billie Holiday her nickname, Lady Day, and she dubbed him Prez, the president of the tenor saxophone.

Holiday gained a reputation as a racial activist, although she never sought that role. In 1938 she joined clarinetist Artie Shaw's white big band for several months, which placed her in the forefront of those who were challenging racial segregation in popular music. Her most political act was singing the anti-lynching ballad "Strange Fruit" (1939), which became her signature piece. Columbia Records refused to record the song because the company feared alienating white record buyers, but at last permitted her to record it for tiny Commodore Records.

Holiday's style was simple and finely crafted. It was partly dictated by the nature of her voice. She had a limited range, and she compressed her singing into little more than an octave. Unlike Bessie Smith, she could not fill a hall with her voice, so she perfected the art of singing with a microphone. Her small voice conveyed an intimacy that more powerful singers could rarely approach. She was also highly improvisational. Even in stating a theme, Holiday reinvented and simplified the song's melody. Unlike most singers of the day, she used very little vibrato, but she employed other vocal embellishments—shifts in rhythm, especially singing behind the beat, and variations in pitch, including dips, scoops, and fall-offs.

During her lifetime these qualities worked against her. She rarely got to record the most popular songs of the day. She sang with a subtlety that did not win her great popularity, and record companies reserved the best material for their best-selling singers. In addition, music publishers and successful songwriters opposed having her record their best songs because she changed the written melodies.

Throughout her life Holiday resented the limitations of the "blues singer" label, and she was greatly disappointed when Doubleday published her autobiography under the title *Lady Sings the Blues*. She had wanted to name it *Bitter Crop*, from the final words of "Strange Fruit." Holiday—like her musical alter ego Lester Young—faced serious difficulties during the 1950s. Although she and Young did not collaborate regularly in these years, their lives remained linked. Personal problems hampered their performing abilities, and Holiday's voice, in particular, revealed the ravages of her personal life. In 1957—on *The Sound of Jazz*, a television special—the two performed together in a moving rendition of "Fine and Mellow" that perfectly captured their vulnerability and their profound musical empathy. Holiday and Young died within four months of each other in 1959.

Latin America and the Caribbean

Honduras,

republic in Central America, bounded on the north and east by the Caribbean Sea, on the south by Nicaragua, on the southwest by the Pacific Ocean and El Salvador, and on the west by Guatemala. Honduras is one of the largest Central American republics, with an area of 111,888 sq km (43,199 sq mi). The capital and largest city is Tegucigalpa (see Central America).

North America

Hooker, John Lee

(b. August 22, 1917, Clarksdale, Miss.), African American blues singer and guitarist.

John Lee Hooker's long blues career began at home, where he was influenced by his stepfather, a friend of such legendary bluesmen as Blind Lemon Jefferson and Charley Patton. Born in Mississippi, Hooker was playing and singing in Memphis nightclubs by the time he was a teenager.

In 1943 Hooker moved to Detroit, Michigan, where he worked in a factory and continued performing in clubs. Throughout the 1940s he made dozens of pseudonymous recordings for various small record labels. Influenced by the passionately expressive vocalists of the Mississippi Delta blues style, he integrated moans, groans, and howls into his more driving, electrified, urban blues sound.

Always a popular performer, Hooker sold a million records with "Boogie Chillun" (1948), and in the 1950s began working with a band, a departure from the traditional blues structure of one person with a guitar. In 1961 his song "Boom Boom" became a hit among teenagers—black and white—and helped bring a new audience to Hooker's urban blues. As the music historian Charles Kiel points out, Hooker helped popularize the blues by playing in settings—college campuses, jazz and folk festivals, and overseas venues—that were not usually frequented by bluesmen. As a result of his popularity and influence, Hooker was inducted into the Rock and Roll Hall of Fame in 1991.

Hooks, Benjamin Lawrence

(b. January 31, 1925, Memphis, Tenn.), lawyer, minister, civil rights activist, and executive director of the National Association for the Advancement of Colored People (NAACP).

After graduating from Howard University in 1944 and from DePaul University with a law degree in 1948, Benjamin Hooks worked as a public defender and a Baptist minister, serving from 1956 into the mid-1990s as a pastor of Memphis's Middle Baptist Church.

Through his legal and ministerial work Hooks became a prominent figure in the Civil Rights Movement and sat on the board of directors of the Southern Christian Leadership Conference from its founding in 1957 until 1977. In 1965 he became the first African American to become a criminal court judge in Tennessee. He was also the first black to sit on the Federal Communications Commission.

In 1977 he became executive director of the National Association for the Advancement of Colored People (NAACP) and became chairman of the Leadership Council on Civil Rights (LCCR) as well. A nationally recognized leader and the first African American to address both the Republican and Democratic national conventions, Hooks turned the attention of the NAACP to issues including national health insurance, welfare, urban problems, and the environment. He left the NAACP in 1992 and the LCCR in 1994 to return to Middle Street Church as a full-time pastor.

Horne, Lena

(b. June 17, 1917, Brooklyn, N.Y.), African American singer and actress whose refusal to be cast in stereotypical roles helped transform the popular image of black women.

Lena Horne's father left home when she was only three, and her mother departed to pursue an acting career, leaving the child in the care of her paternal grandmother, a civil rights activist and suffragist in Brooklyn.

Horne's mother did return to take her daughter on tour with her. Eventually, her mother remarried and the family returned to New York, where Horne attended high school. But financial difficulties forced her to quit school and obtain a position as a chorus dancer at the Cotton Club in Harlem, New York. She was hired for her beauty, but she worked diligently to improve her singing by taking lessons, and she became known for her sultry voice. Horne then accepted a role on Broadway in *Dance with Your Gods* (1934) and afterward left the Cotton Club to sing with Noble Sissle's Society Orchestra in Philadelphia.

In Philadelphia she was reunited with her father, who subsequently played an important role in her life and career until his death in 1970. It was through her father that Horne met Louis Jones, whom she married in 1937. The couple had two children, Gail and Teddy, but divorced in 1941. Horne performed on Broadway in *Blackbirds* of 1939 and became lead singer in Charlie Barnett's band in 1940. In 1941 she was a featured performer at the Café Society Downtown, where she became acquainted with both the singer and civil rights activist Paul Robeson and Walter White, an important figure in the National Association for the Advancement of Colored People (NAACP).

Horne left New York to perform at the Trocadero Club in California. Within a short time, she signed a Hollywood movie contract with Metro-Goldwyn-Mayer. She insisted her contract stipulate that she would not be cast in stereotypical black roles, and with her elegance and glamour, she became known for transforming the image of the black woman in film. Her first role in 1942, like many that followed, was only a guest spot number in *Panama Hattie*, but the same year she played a leading part in *Cabin in the Sky*. In 1943 she was in three films: *I Dood It, Thousands Cheer,* and *Stormy Weather*, the title song of which became her trademark. It was on the set of *Stormy Weather* that Horne met Lennie Hayton. Though the couple married in 1947, the controversial interracial marriage was not publicly announced until 1950. She appeared in *Two Girls and a Sailor* (1944), *Broadway Rhythm* (1944), Ziegfeld Follies of 1945 and 1946, *The Duchess of Idaho* (1950) and *Meet Me in Las Vegas* (1956), her first speaking part. She also starred in the Broadway show *Jamaica* (1957) and appeared on several television shows in the 1950s.

Horne has won many honors for her performances. She won a Grammy for the album based on her award-winning show *Lena Horne: The Lady and Her Music*, which began in 1981 and became the longest running one-woman show in Broadway history. In addition to the Kennedy Center Award for Lifetime Achievement in the Arts (1984), Horne received an honorary doctorate from Howard University as well as an Image Award and Spingarn Medal from the NAACP.

North America

Horse, John (also known as John Cavallo, Juan Cavallo, Cohia, Gopher John)

(b. 1812, Florida; d. 1882, Mexico City, Mexico), nineteenth-century Afro-Native American leader.

John Horse was born in 1812 in Florida to Charles Cavallo, a Seminole tribesman, and a black woman living among the Seminole people of the then-Spanish territory. The Seminoles were an American Indian nation made up of Creek refugees and both free blacks (including numerous runaway slaves) and black slaves. While many Seminoles owned slaves— Charles Cavallo presumably owned Horse's mother—modern scholars describe the Seminole practice as more feudally based, with slaves enjoying relative liberty and self-determination (families, homes, and property) for giving a percentage of their harvest to their masters. Blacks even set up independent maroon communities, and Seminoles and blacks intermarried.

Little is known of Horse's early years. In 1818 he and his mother fled their home in the village of Sewanee to escape the advance of United States troops commanded by Gen. Andrew Jackson at the conclusion of the First Seminole War. Jackson's four-month-long march through central Florida was the culmination of almost seven years of hostilities between the Seminoles and U.S. forces—both military and armed settlers—precipitated by U.S. efforts to recapture escaped slaves and seize Florida from Spain. The invasion led Spain to cede the territory to the United States in 1819, and subsequently, the Seminoles were forcibly settled on reservations near newly erected military outposts.

By 1826 Horse himself was living in a village near Camp Brooke outside Tampa Bay. A trilingual speaker (Hitchiti, a Seminole language, Spanish, and English), he frequented the military camp throughout his teens and early twenties, selling the officers wild game, running errands for them, and serving as a guide on hunting trips. He married and began accumulating property and livestock.

Although life on the reservation was harsh—frequent kidnappings by slave hunters, drought, and low government rations—it was not until President Jackson signed the 1830 Indian Removal Act, calling for the removal of all Indian peoples to the west of the Mississippi in Indian Territory (present-day Oklahoma), that the call for armed resistance arose again. A number of Seminoles, including a fiery and charismatic chief named Osceola, John Horse, King Philip, and Wild Cat, refused to leave their village, and the Second Seminole War exploded in 1835. During the war Horse served as a subchief, leading warriors and undertaking negotiations between the United States and the Seminole nation. Captured in 1838, he finally agreed to "emigrate," taking his family and more than 300 Indian and Black Seminoles. They arrived at Fort Gibson in Indian Territory in late June 1838.

Horse and the Seminole emigrants found their new "home" little better than the war-torn one they had left behind: land allotments for various relocated Indian groups were still in dispute; they were surrounded by proslavery whites and other hostile Indian nations; food was scarce; and the land was difficult to cultivate. However, in 1839, Horse traveled back to Florida to persuade the remaining Seminole resisters to relocate (perhaps seeing it as inevitable). Until 1842, when the war officially ended, he served the United States as a guide and negotiator.

When Horse returned to Indian Territory in 1843, he found his people still homeless and besieged by slave hunters, and the land gripped by drought. He made two separate trips to Washington, D.C., in 1843 and 1845 to petition for better land and recognition of Black Seminoles' freedom (one of the most contested issues in relocation negotiations), meeting with no success. In 1848 the U.S. attorney general declared the Black Seminoles not freedpeople, and therefore, Black Seminoles who had escaped from slavery were fair game for reenslavement. Although not personally threatened—his government service and father's will both rendered him free—Horse decided to defy orders to return many Black Seminoles to their former owners. In October 1849 he and his friend Wild Cat gathered up about 300 Indian and Black Seminoles and made a mass exodus to Mexico, finally crossing the Rio Grande near El Moral in Coahuila State in July 1850.

Upon arriving, Horse petitioned Mexican authorities for land, provisions, and tools. His request was granted, ironically, in exchange for assistance in Mexican efforts against Indian bands along the border. However, slave-hunting raids from Texas forced the Seminoles in Mexico farther and farther inland; they finally settled in Naciemento and Laguna das Parras. Horse himself was seized in 1852 in a Texas border town and released only after being ransomed by Wild Cat.

In the mid-1860s, when political unrest in Mexico and emancipation in the United States compelled some Mexican Seminoles to move back across the border to Indian Territory and Texas, Horse remained in Laguna. However, in 1873 he traveled to Washington again, lobbying both for land in either Indian Territory or Florida for the Seminoles in Mexico and on behalf of the Texas Seminoles, struggling because promised land and rations never materialized. He was visiting the Texas Seminoles living near Fort Clark in 1876 when he and another Black Seminole, Titus Payne, were attacked by unknown assailants. Payne died, but the elderly Horse recovered, traveling back to Naciemento the following year.

In the late 1870s ownership of the land containing the Seminoles' Naciemento settlement was disputed by an original owner's heir. At age 70 Horse rode to Mexico City to appeal to the Mexican government for formal recognition and protection of the Seminoles' land grant. His request was granted, and whenever the lands have been threatened, similar petitions have repeatedly been ratified by successive governments to the present. Soon after, Horse, the "father of his people," succumbed to pneumonia, dying in the capital on August 10, 1882. He was mourned from Indian Territory to Laguna.

North America

Howard University,

predominantly black university located in Washington, D.C., that has the largest concentration of African American students and faculty of any university in the world.

Like many of the present 117 historically black colleges and universities (HBCUs), Howard was founded by whites. In 1866 ten members of the First Congregational Society of Washington, D.C., established the Howard Normal and Theological Institute for Education of Teachers and Preachers.

The seminary, named in honor of the commissioner of the Freedmen's Bureau, Maj. Gen. Oliver Otis Howard, received its university charter from President Andrew Johnson in March 1867. Two months later the board of trustees shortened its name to Howard University and opened its doors to four young white girls—the daughters of some of the university's trustees and faculty.

Although Frederick Douglass and Booker T. Washington were appointed to the university's private board of trustees in 1871 and 1907, respectively, very few African Americans were involved in either the administration or governance of the university during its early years. In addition, early financial support came from white sources: during the institution's first five years, it received most of its financial support from the Freedmen's Bureau. After the Bureau closed in 1872, the United States Congress agreed in 1879 to make an annual appropriation to the university.

Receiving money from Congress proved to be a mixed blessing. Congressional subsidies enabled the university to flourish, but often at the expense of freedom of thought and freedom of expression. Congress pressured university officials to monitor the activities and teachings of professors who were suspected of being communists or socialists. In the early 1940s several Howard faculty members, including English scholar Alphaeus Hunton, were investigated by the House Un-American Activities Committee. Although vindication eventually came for those faculty members who were investigated, serious questions were raised about the university's lack of autonomy.

Mordecai Johnson, appointed Howard's first black president in 1926, transformed the university into a major institution of higher learning. When Johnson first arrived at Howard, the university was composed of eight unaccredited schools and colleges, with a total enrollment of 1700 and a budget of $700,000. At his retirement 34 years later, Howard had ten nationally accredited schools and colleges, 6000 students, and an $8 million budget. The reputation of Howard's faculty grew during this time, when the university included scholars such as biologist Ernest E. Just, historian Kelly Miller, writer Alain Locke, sociologist E. Franklin Frazier, and economist Abram Harris Jr.

In 1960 Dr. James M. Nabrit, a leading constitutional lawyer and former dean of the Howard Law School, succeeded Johnson as president. Nabrit is credited with establishing the first systematic civil rights course at an American law school. Between 1969 and 1988 Howard continued to grow under the leadership of James E. Cheek and Carlton P. Alexis. In 1989 Franklyn G. Jenifer became the first Howard alumnus to serve as president.

Students at Howard also have been active participants in shaping both the university's curriculum and its direction. In the late 1960s student demonstrators demanded and won an African American Studies Department. In 1989 hundreds of student protesters forced Lee Atwater, chairman of the Republican Party, to resign from the university's board of trustees. Student activists were also successful in forcing the university's financial divestment from South Africa. In 1994 controversy erupted when a student group invited Khalid Abdul Muhammad, an outspoken official of the Nation of Islam, to speak on campus.

Since its beginnings Howard has educated more than 68,000 students, including diplomat Ralph Bunche, surgeon Charles Drew, author Zora Neale Hurston, U.S. Supreme Court Justice Thurgood Marshall, and Nobel laureate Toni Morrison. Today more than 12,000 Howard students, from all 50 states and more than 100 foreign countries, choose courses among 18 fully accredited schools and colleges. There are more than 70 major buildings located throughout the university's four campuses, including WHUR-FM and WHMM-TV, the first radio and television stations to be owned and operated by a black university in the United States. The university also features the Moorland-Spingarn Research Center, one of the largest and most comprehensive black research collections in the world.

North America

Howlin' Wolf (Chester Arthur Burnett)

(b. June 10, 1910, near West Point, Miss.; d. January 10, 1976, Hines, Ill.), blues musician who helped to import the rural music of the Mississippi River Delta to Chicago in the 1950s, thus making possible the creation of the new Chicago blues sound.

Howlin' Wolf was born Chester Arthur Burnett to plantation workers in Mississippi and as a youth worked in the fields himself. Throughout his childhood he was exposed to music from the Baptist church but did not take up the guitar until his teenage years. When Wolf was 18 he met bluesman Charley Patton, who instructed him in the rudiments of the genre. Another blues musician, Sonny Boy Williamson, whom Wolf knew as the husband of his half-sister, completed Wolf's education by teaching him to play the harmonica. During the 1920s and 1930s Wolf traveled the South, sometimes performing with blues veterans such as Robert Johnson, sometimes farming to support himself.

During World War II Wolf was drafted by the United States Army. When he returned from the service in 1945, he settled in West Memphis, Arkansas, where he started a band and secured work with local radio station KWEM. Wolf established himself as a charismatic disc jockey as well as a burgeoning blues star and caught the attention of promoter and musician Ike Turner, who encouraged producer Sam Phillips (later the owner of Sun Records) to record him. Phillips did, and sold the recordings to two different labels, Chicago-based Chess Records and the Bihari Brothers in California. The tremendous popularity of these recordings set the two companies at odds, and after legal negotiations, Wolf signed with Chess and moved to Chicago in 1953.

At Chess Records Wolf met bluesman and songwriter Willie Dixon, who composed many of Wolf's hits, including "Back Door Man," "Little Red

Rooster," and "I Ain't Superstitious." Dixon meanwhile provided material for bluesman Muddy Waters, also of Chess Records, who became Wolf's local rival. Waters and Wolf—with the help of Dixon—at this time defined the Chicago Blues sound, each trying to outdo the other with rawness, intensity, and electric bravura. Wolf's performance style, which had always emulated Charley Patton's dramatic approach, became fully realized. He sang a harsh blend of gravelly bellows and falsetto howls, writhing on stage in the spirit of his music. In addition to Dixon's songs, Wolf popularized a number of his own compositions, including "Smokestack Lightning" and "Killing Floor."

Wolf's great popularity sustained him through the blues industry's lull during the late 1950s, and when British rock 'n' rollers such as the Rolling Stones and the Yardbirds began to popularize blues music among white listeners, Wolf experienced a resurgence of fame. He appeared with the Rolling Stones on the television show *Shindig*, and toured Europe and America with the white groups who had appropriated his music. In the late 1960s he recorded *The London Howlin' Wolf Sessions*, joined by white guitarist Eric Clapton as well as members of the Rolling Stones and Ringo Starr of the Beatles.

In the 1970s Wolf scaled down his demanding tour schedule due to poor health. In the early 1970s he survived a heart attack and a car accident but kidney damage from the latter killed him in 1976. Wolf gave his last performance with bluesman B. B. King in November 1975. He was inducted into the Blues Foundation's Hall of Fame in 1980 and the Rock and Roll Hall of Fame in 1991.

North America

Hughes, Langston
(b. February 1, 1902, Joplin, Mo.; d. May 22, 1967, New York, N.Y.), African American writer known especially for his poetry and for his use of Black Vernacular English, black cultural references, and black musical rhythms in his writing.

As a poet, playwright, fiction writer, autobiographer, and anthologist, Hughes captured the moods and rhythms of the black communities he knew and loved—and translated those rhythms to the printed page. Hughes has been called "the literary explicator and interpreter of the social, cultural, spiritual, and emotional experiences of Black America," and this grand description is accurate for the role his writings have played in twentieth-century American literature.

Hughes was born in Joplin, Missouri, in 1902. His father, a lawyer frustrated by American racism, emigrated to Mexico when Hughes was a year old, and Hughes spent most of his childhood at his maternal grandmother's home in Lawrence, Kansas. His grandmother had been an activist for decades. Her first husband had been killed in the slave rebellion at Harpers Ferry; her second, Hughes's grandfather, was the brother of abolitionist John

Mercer Langston and a participant in Kansas politics during Reconstruction. In his grandmother's home, Hughes was part of a close-knit black community, and he was always encouraged to read.

As a teenager Hughes lived with his mother in Lincoln, Illinois, and Cleveland, Ohio. In Cleveland he contributed to his high school literary magazine, was elected class poet his senior year, and graduated from high school in 1920. Hughes then spent a year in Mexico with his father. A poem he wrote on the train ride there, *The Negro Speaks of Rivers*, was published in the June 1921 issue of *Crisis*, the official publication of the National Association for the Advancement of Colored People (NAACP). It is still perhaps his best-known poem, and it instantly confirmed his potential as a serious writer.

At his father's wish Hughes enrolled at Columbia University in New York in the fall of 1927, but he stayed only one year and spent most of his time in Harlem, in upper Manhattan. He took a series of jobs that included traveling down the west coast of Africa and then to Europe as a crew member on a merchant steamer. Hughes continued writing poetry during his travels, publishing much of it back home in black journals such as *Crisis* and the National Urban League's *Opportunity*. By the time he returned to the United States in 1924, his reputation was already established. He won first prize in *Opportunity*'s 1925 poetry contest for his poem *The Weary Blues*, and the following year Alfred A. Knopf published *The Weary Blues*, Hughes's first volume of poetry.

By this time Hughes was recognized as one of the leading figures in the constellation of black writers, artists, and musicians in New York who created the Harlem Renaissance. Hughes's poetry was greatly influenced by the people and culture around him. He admired the narrative style of poets Carl Sandburg and Walt Whitman, but was also influenced by Paul Laurence Dunbar's poems written in black dialect, and he incorporated the rhythms of black speech into many of his poems. Above all, Hughes was influenced by black music, especially jazz and blues.

Hughes's poems are often "lyrical" in the musical sense of the word—many of them could easily be set to a rhythmic beat. They also incorporate some of the same subject matter found in many blues lyrics, and portray nuances of black life—including sexuality—missing in earlier black literature. In a 1926 essay titled "The Negro Artist and the Racial Mountain," Hughes eloquently defended the honest representations of black culture and the use of jazz, dialect, and other influences from the black vernacular that had become a trademark in the work of many Harlem Renaissance writers. As Hughes put it, "We younger Negro artists who create now intend to express our individual dark-skinned selves without fear or shame."

Hughes enrolled in Lincoln University in Lincoln, Pennsylvania, in 1927, and graduated in 1929. The next year he published his first novel, *Not Without Laughter*. After an argument with a white patron who had been supporting him financially, Hughes spent time traveling, making extended visits to Haiti, Russia, and Carmel, California. He had begun publishing in the Communist Party-sponsored journal *New Masses* even before he left the United States and wrote some of his most politically radical poetry while in Russia.

In Carmel Hughes wrote his first collection of short stories, *The Ways of White Folks* (1934). He finished the decade with several successful plays, including *Mulatto*, loosely based on his grandfather's family, which opened on Broadway in 1935 and became the longest running Broadway play by an African American until Lorraine Hansberry's *A Raisin in the Sun* 25 years later.

In 1940 Hughes published his first autobiography, *The Big Sea*. In it he discusses his childhood, his estrangement from his father, and other personal topics, but readers especially value its insider's portrayal of the Harlem Renaissance. Two years later he began writing a weekly column for the *Chicago Defender* that unexpectedly spawned his most popular literary c haracter, Jesse B. Semple. "Simple," as he was called, was a fictional Harlem resident who had little education but many street-smart opinions on everything from World War II to American race relations. Simple became a representative for the black *Everyman*, and over the next 20 years, in addition to his column, Hughes published five books and an off-Broadway play that featured Simple, who has been called "one of the more original comic creations in American journalism."

Hughes also published more poetry and plays in the 1940s, and as lyricist for the 1947 Broadway musical *Street Scene* he earned enough money to buy the Harlem home where he lived for the rest of his life. In 1951 Hughes published one of his most important poetry collections, *Montage of a Dream Deferred*, which contained such well-known works as "Harlem" and "Dream Boogie." During the 1950s Hughes published two more collections of short stories, another novel, several nonfiction works of children's literature, and his second autobiography, *I Wonder as I Wander* (1956).

In the 1960s Hughes wrote several successful Gospel plays, including *Black Nativity* (1961), which remains a holiday tradition in several cities, and *Jericho-Jim Crow* (1964), based on the Civil Rights Movement. He also published anthologies of poetry, short stories, and humor, and the book-length poem *Ask Your Mama* (1962). When he died on May 22, 1967, he was at work on a new collection of poetry celebrating the Civil Rights and Black Power movements, which was published later that year as *The Panther and the Lash*.

As a writer Hughes was prolific both in the genres he covered and the amount he produced, and he became the first African American author able to support himself completely by his writing. But his work was remarkable for much more than its quantity; Hughes's writing captured the essence of black America in a way black Americans felt it had not been captured before. As his biographer Arnold Rampersad said, "From the start, Hughes's art was responsive to the needs and emotions of the black world. . . . Arguably, Langston Hughes was black America's most original poet. Certainly he was black America's most representative writer and a significant figure in world literature in the twentieth century."

Hunter, Alberta

(b. April 1, 1895, Memphis, Tenn.; d. October 17, 1984, New York, N.Y.), African American blues and cabaret singer, an early and enduring black recording star.

Alberta Hunter adapted her large and supple voice to a variety of musical styles and had one of the longest careers of any of the early female blues singers. She ran away from Memphis at age 11 to Chicago, hoping to work as a singer and send money to her mother. She became an immediate success, and as her reputation grew she appeared in nightclubs with such American jazz musicians as cornetist King Oliver and trumpet player Louis Armstrong. She also performed on Broadway, and in 1921 she made her first record. Hunter's best-known song was "Down-hearted Blues" (1922), which she wrote. In 1923 African American blues singer Bessie Smith recorded the song, which then became widely known.

In 1927 Hunter traveled to London, where she sang opposite African American singer Paul Robeson in the British premiere of the musical *Showboat*, by American composer Jerome Kern. Hunter subsequently sang in Holland, Denmark, and France, becoming the first singer to perform American blues music in Europe. During World War II (1939–1945) and the Korean War (1950–1953), she toured the world in military entertainment shows. In 1955, when her mother died, she retired from singing. She studied to be a nurse and later worked in hospitals in New York City. In 1977 Hunter's singing talent was rediscovered, and at age 82 she renewed her singing career and became famous once again.

Hunter, Clementine Clemence Rubin

(b. December 1886, Clourtierville, La.; d. January 1, 1988, Melrose, La.), African American folk artist celebrated as the "Black Grandma Moses."

Clementine Hunter was born on a cotton plantation to Mary Antoinette Adams, a woman of Virginia slave ancestry, and Janvier (John) Reuben, a man of Native American and Irish descent. She moved with her family from Hidden Hill to Melrose Plantation (formerly Yucca), near Natchitoches, Louisiana, while she was in her early teens. She remained at Melrose, first as a cotton picker, then as the plantation cook until 1970.

Hunter had two children, Joseph and Cora, with Charles Dupree. Dupree died in 1914, and Hunter married Emanuel Hunter in 1924. She bore five more children: Mary, Agnes, King, and two who died at birth. A widow by 1944, Hunter died at age 101 a few miles from Melrose, having outlived all of her children.

Hunter became a folk artist celebrated for her paintings of familiar scenes of Southern life when she was already well into her fifties. Although she received very little formal education and remained illiterate throughout her life, she became known as the "Black Grandma Moses" for her depiction of black rural Southern life, specifically that of Cane River Settlement on Isle Breville, Louisiana. Her art, quilts, and paintings depicted religious themes, scenes of plantation work and relaxation, wildlife, and abstracts. Hunter was prolific up until her death, having completed approximately 5000 paintings.

Hunter's first artistic medium was quiltmaking. Her earliest piece is a quilt from 1938 depicting the rigors of plantation life. Her first painting dates from 1939. Her work began to draw positive attention in the late 1940s and greater admiration still in the 1950s. In 1955 she became the first African American artist to have a solo exhibition at the Delgado Museum (now the New Orleans Museum of Art). By 1973 her work was being shown at the Museum of American Folk Art in New York, and by the time of her death, she was considered one of the century's leading folk artists.

North America

Hunter-Gault, Charlayne

(b. February 27, 1942, Due West, S.C.), African American journalist.

Charlayne Hunter-Gault first came to national attention in 1961, when she and Hamilton Holmes became the first black students to attend the University of Georgia, after a two-year-long court fight. Hunter-Gault received her B.A. in journalism in 1963.

After graduation, she took a job with the *New Yorker* magazine. In 1967 she received a Russell Sage Fellowship to study social science at Washington University, St. Louis, where she was an editor at *Trans-Action* magazine. She also became a reporter and anchorwoman for WRC-TV. In 1968 she joined the *New York Times*, where she created and managed a Harlem bureau. She spent several years as codirector of the Michele Clark Fellowship program for minority students in journalism at Columbia University. In 1971 she married Ronald Gault, with whom she has a son; she has a daughter from a previous marriage.

In 1978 Hunter-Gault began to work as a correspondent for The MacNeil/Lehrer Report on the Public Broadcasting Service (PBS); she became national correspondent for the show in 1983. Hunter-Gault's accomplishments have been widely recognized by her peers. In 1986 she received the George Foster Peabody Award for Excellence in Broadcast Journalism and the Journalist of the Year Award from the National Association of Black Journalists. She has also won the National Urban Coalition Award for Distinguished Urban Reporting and two national news and documentary Emmy Awards. Hunter-Gault published her autobiography in 1992, and in 1997 left PBS and moved to Johannesburg, South Africa. National Public Radio frequently broadcasts Hunter-Gault's reports on current events in various African countries.

Hurley, Ruby

(b. November 7, 1909, Washington, D.C.; d. August 9, 1980, Atlanta, Ga.), civil rights leader who was the only full-time civil rights activist working in the Deep South in the 1950s.

Ruby Hurley began working in 1939 with the Washington chapter of the National Association for the Advancement of Colored People (NAACP). She became the National Youth Secretary of the NAACP in 1943, and during her tenure the number of youth councils and college chapters grew from 86 to more than 380.

Hurley transferred to Birmingham, Alabama, as regional secretary in 1951 in order to organize new NAACP branches throughout the South. One year later she became regional director. Hers was the NAACP's first full-time office in the Deep South. In 1955 she investigated the murders of Rev. George W. Lee and Lamar Smith, who were killed for participating in black voter registration drives in Mississippi. In the same year, with Medgar Evers, she investigated the murder of 14-year-old Emmett Till, traveling at personal risk, in disguise, to locate witnesses. She also helped register Autherine Lucy Foster, the first black student admitted at the University of Alabama.

When the NAACP was banned from operating in Alabama in 1956, Hurley relocated to Atlanta. There she became involved in disputes between the NAACP and the newer Student Nonviolent Coordinating Committee (SNCC) and the Southern Christian Leadership Conference (SCLC). She dedicated herself to defending the strategies of her generation of civil rights workers to the new generation of activists.

Hurston, Zora Neale

(b. January 7, 1891, Notasulga, Ala.; d. January 28, 1960, Fort Pierce, Fla.), African American writer and folklorist; author of *Their Eyes Were Watching God*, considered the first black feminist novel.

"I do not belong to the sobbing school of Negrohood who hold that nature somehow has given them a lowdown dirty deal and whose feelings are all hurt about it. Even in the helter-skelter skirmish that is my life, I have seen that the world is to the strong regardless of a little pigmentation more or less. No, I do not weep at the world—I am too busy sharpening my oyster knife."

This quotation from her essay "How It Feels to Be Colored Me" (1928) portrays Hurston's joyfully contrary view of herself in a world where being black was often perceived as a "problem" and portrayed that way even by black writers. Hurston considered her own blackness a gift and an opportunity. As an anthropologist and writer, she savored the richness of black

Folklorist, anthropologist, and writer Zora Neale Hurston (1891-1960) is perhaps best known for her book *Their Eyes Were Watching God* (1938). *CORBIS*

culture and made a career out of writing about that culture in all its color and fullness. In the process she became a vibrant figure in the Harlem Renaissance and is now considered one of the defining authors of the African American literary tradition.

Hurston claimed to have been born in Eatonville, Florida, in either 1901 or 1910, but recent scholarship indicates that she was probably born in Alabama in 1891. She did, however, grow up in Eatonville, the first incorporated black town in the United States. Unlike many Southern towns, where African Americans lived under the constant specter of racial harassment or discrimination from their white neighbors, in Eatonville whites only passed through on the road to Orlando. Growing up in a town where she was surrounded by black culture and self-sufficient black people was fundamental to Hurston's work. It was to this organic African American community that she kept returning as an adult—literally, for her anthropological research on black folklore, and figuratively, in her novels and stories.

In her 1942 autobiography, *Dust Tracks on a Road*, Hurston recalled that in her family, her mother, who died when Hurston was 13, was the one who encouraged her to "jump at de sun." After her mother's death Hurston left home and school to work as a maid for a traveling theater company. Her further education came slowly and sporadically, and embarrassment over this probably led her to lie about her age. Hurston received a high school degree from Morgan Academy in Baltimore in 1918 and then took courses at Howard University intermittently until 1924. What was most likely her first published story, "John Redding Goes to Sea," appeared in *Stylus*, Howard's literary magazine, in 1921.

In 1925 Hurston moved to New York and soon became part of the convergence of African American writers, artists, and musicians in Harlem known as the Harlem Renaissance. She was an immediate success in Harlem literary circles: Alain Locke chose her short story "Spunk" for inclusion in his landmark 1925 anthology, *The New Negro*, and two of her pieces received awards from *Opportunity* magazine in May 1925.

Hurston received a scholarship to study anthropology at Barnard College, under then well-known Columbia University scholar Franz Boas.

The only black student at Barnard, she received a B.A. in 1928 for research that focused on black folklore. She continued to write fiction, but in 1929 she also began a series of fieldwork trips to the American South, Haiti, and Jamaica to collect black folklore that formed the basis for much of her later writing. Hurston received Rosenwald and Guggenheim fellowships and private funding from a white patron to support her research. She wrote at least three books that focused exclusively on her findings: *Mules and Men* (1935), the first collection of black folklore by a black American; *Tell My Horse* (1938), materials on the religion Vodou gathered during travels to the Caribbean; and *The Florida Negro* (1938), which was funded by the Federal Writers' Project but never published.

Hurston's interest in black culture was also reflected in her fiction, which was often set in all-black communities and attempted to capture dialect and local life. She published four novels between 1934 and 1948, including what became her most famous work, *Their Eyes Were Watching God* (1938). But in the 1930s and 1940s Hurston's works were often considered anachronistic or offensive even by black audiences. Author Richard Wright accused her of portraying a "minstrel image" of African Americans—in contrast to more politically oriented books like his own *Native Son*.

Hurston also came under criticism from the African American community for some of her political beliefs. For example, her own positive experience within all-black communities made her an outspoken critic of integration. Many other African Americans have since come to agree with that view, but during Hurston's lifetime, black segregationists ran against the grain. And when she portrayed black characters not as victims of society, but as individuals who were as capable of succeeding and living and loving as anyone else, she was accused of being naïve and ignoring social realities.

By the 1940s Hurston's style was considered passé in the current literary scene, and she was no longer able to support herself as a writer. Largely forgotten, she returned to the South, and during the 1950s took a series of menial jobs while trying fruitlessly to find a publisher for several new works that she hoped to produce. On January 28, 1960, she died of a stroke in a Florida welfare home. She was buried in an unmarked grave.

In the 1970s Hurston's works underwent a dramatic literary renaissance, based largely on the power of *Their Eyes Were Watching God*. The story follows a black woman, Janie, through several black communities and several love relationships. Over the course of the novel, Janie comes to recognize and embrace her own identity. In the early 1970s Alice Walker published a widely read essay about Hurston and her work. *Their Eyes* was reprinted at the height of the women's movement, and black and white scholars alike embraced it as the first black feminist novel.

Since its rediscovery, *Their Eyes* has become one of the most frequently assigned novels on college campuses and one of the best-known works of African American literature. Moreover, Hurston's other books have been reprinted; scholar Robert Hemenway has written her biography; and Walker and other contemporary black women novelists freely acknowledge her influence on their work. A new generation of readers has been exposed to a writer who celebrated black culture and refused to portray blacks as victims; who saw the world as her oyster, and sharpened her knife.

North America

Hutson, Jean Blackwell

(b. September 7, 1914, Summerfield, Fla.; d. February 3, 1998, New York, N.Y.), African American librarian who developed the Schomburg Center for Research in Black Culture into the world's largest collection of materials by and about people of African descent.

Born into a middle-class family, Jean Blackwell Hutson was the second African American (following Zora Neale Hurston) to graduate from Barnard College, and the first to receive a master's degree from Columbia University's School of Library Service. She was married to Andy Razaf, the song lyricist who collaborated with Thomas "Fats" Waller, and then to John Hutson, a library security guard. Their adopted daughter, Jean Jr., died in 1992.

Hutson joined the staff of the New York Public Library in 1936 and 12 years later was appointed head of its black collection, originally the private library of Afro-Puerto Rican bibliophile Arthur A. Schomburg, on 135th Street and Lenox Avenue in Harlem. Under her leadership, the library's holdings grew from 15,000 books to its present collection of more than 5 million separately catalogued items, including manuscripts, music, art, photographs, and clipping files. Hutson at first presided over a decaying Carnegie library building where the collection was housed, but through a personal campaign secured public money to construct a new facility after library officials had ignored her pleas for support.

Kwame Nkrumah invited Hutson to establish an Africana collection at the University of Ghana, which she did in 1964–1965. A friend of African American luminaries and a colleague of nearly everyone conducting research in black studies, Hutson not only transformed a small branch library into the research center of Harlem, but built an institution considered the world's finest in its field.

Latin America and the Caribbean

Hyppolite, Hector

(b. September 16, 1894, Saint-Marc, Haiti; d. June 9, 1948, Port-au-Prince, Haiti), one of Haiti's most famous artists, once called "the greatest of Haitian primitive painters," whose work contains deep religious, cultural, and political symbolism and drew an international audience to Haitian art.

Hector Hyppolite's paintings drew international attention when art historian DeWitt Peters established the first art center in Haiti, which served as a catalyst for talented but unrecognized "naive" painters. Shortly after the center opened, Peters received a mysterious canvas from Philomé Obin depicting the arrival of United States president Franklin Roosevelt in Cap-Haïtien to lift the American occupation. This event led Peters to realize fully the museum's mission and the importance of Haitian painting as a vehicle for cultural and historical dissemination. Peters searched out Hyppolite and was startled by a sign he had painted on the door of a bar in Mont Rouis proclaiming "La Renaissance."

In his birthplace of Saint-Marc, Hyppolite practiced the profession of *houngan*, or priest (see Vodou) and lived on the meager sums he earned as a house painter. Upon moving to Port-au-Prince he set aside house painting and established a painting studio, which he advertised with the sign "Painting Depot Here." From 1945 to 1948 he produced some 70 important paintings a year. His success was due to the intriguing way in which he conveyed the subconscious through imagery. His brush strokes do not demonstrate the concern for aesthetic perfection shown by other Haitian artists such as his faithful companion, Rigaud Benoit, or Castera Bazile and Philome Obin. But the inventiveness of his work, its heterogeneity and its predominantly pink tinge, translate the Haitian spirit in a dreamy, poetic landscape that joins a subtle play of shades of light with a decided taste for the eclectic.

Much of Hyppolite's imagery came from his real and imagined travels: he claimed to have journeyed by foot from Dahomey in western Africa to Ethiopia, on the other end of the continent, and to the ancestral lands of Senegal and Abyssinia, earning his living by painting floral designs on chamber pots of local inns. From these travels and self-training emerged his imaginative artistic production.

Upon returning to France from Port-au-Prince with prized possessions purchased from the artist, André Breton exclaimed that Hyppolite's art would "revolutionize modern painting." Hyppolite's richness of design and boldness of expression fulfilled André Breton's prediction, as the surrealists found their utopian ideals embodied in Hyppolite's liberal display of his marvelous and heightened sense of the sublime.

Hyppolite drew inspiration from both the magical and spiritual realms, and his fascination with Vodou and the supernatural is unquestionably the source and sustenance of his aesthetic form. In *The Crucifixion*, for example, he blends the invisible realm of the spirits with a visible Christ who proclaims the redemption of the world. This painting, like his *Saint Francis and Christ Child* and *Jacob's Dream*, worked as much on subconscious as on conscious perception. His painting *Dream of an Angel* is a remarkable blend of Christian chromolithography and *vévés* (geometric designs evoking particular *loa*, or gods in Vodou).

In two of his paintings, Hyppolite's imagery embodies the sharp social distinctions of the Haitian caste system. *Portrait of a Habitant Woman* depicts a woman in stark peasant clothes; in the pensive *Seated Woman*, a figure is garbed in the sumptuous robe of an aristocrat, and the viewer's eye is drawn to her hand, which gestures toward her head.

In *Erzulie* or *Sirène*, Hyppolite takes the viewer back in Haitian history to the repressive plantation system, in which all representation of African deities was considered superstitious and potentially threatening and was strictly forbidden. The painting depicts Erzulie, a Vodou deity, in her aquatic aspect. Drawing upon a syncretistic logic, Hyppolite appropriated elements of Christian iconography—particularly symbols traditionally linked to the Virgin Mary—yet displaced this iconography by portraying a nude black deity. He thereby restored to Erzulie a dignity equal to that of her Roman Catholic counterpart.

Hyppolite's reputation eventually was on a par with that of the most renowned European artists. It is said that he acquired a remarkable celebrity in the great capitals of the occidental world and particularly with the subsequent special Expositions in Prague, New York, and Paris. Through his pioneering work, so-called naive art has been recognized as a serious genre, and one that conveys the culture and history of Haiti's people.

I

Ibadan, Nigeria,

the capital of the Oyo state in southwestern Nigeria and the nation's second largest city.

Ibadan's development predates written history, though its modern composition traces back to wars between the Yoruba kingdoms during the 1820s, after which victorious armies of the Oyo, Ife, and Ijebu settled on the site. Scholars and traders brought Islam to the city in the mid-nineteenth century, and missionaries brought Christianity a few decades later. In 1893 Ibadan fell under British colonial rule, and by 1912 railroads linked the city both to Lagos in the south and Kano in the north.

Local industries include the manufacture of furniture and automobiles, brewing, canning, publishing, and tobacco processing. Yoruba handicrafts such as blacksmithing and ceramics, as well as weaving, spinning, and dyeing, retain important roles in the economy. These wares, along with locally produced food, are sold in Ibadan's numerous markets. As in many other Yoruba towns, most of the city's residents have traditionally made a living from farming. Today this is less common; farmers usually supplement their agricultural income with trade or artisanal work.

Ibadan University, founded in 1948, was Nigeria's first institution of higher learning. Although national economic troubles have undermined the university's world-class reputation, it continues to earn Ibadan the status of Nigeria's intellectual center. The Agodi Gardens, the Ibadan University Zoo, two stadiums, a technical institute, three institutes of agricultural research, and a branch of the National Archives all bolster Ibadan's reputation as cultural hub of the nation.

Today Ibadan is second in size only to Lagos, Nigeria's former capital. In 1995 the city's population reached 1,295,000.

Africa

Ibn Battutah

(b. February 24, 1304, Tangiers, Morocco; d. 1368, Morocco), medieval North African jurist whose Saharan travels resulted in one of the most valuable early commentaries on African cultures.

Like most North Africans, Ibn Battutah (whose full name was Abu 'Abd Allah Muhammad ibn 'Abd Allah al-Lawati at-Tanji ibn Battutah) was ethnic Berber, and his family traced its ancestry to the nomadic Luwata tribe originating in Cyrenaica west of the Nile Delta. Born into the Muslim religious elite, he would have received a classical literary education in addition to rigorous studies in Islam.

Ibn Battutah wrote poetry in addition to traveling across Africa, Arabia, Asia Minor, India, and China. Most important of his works are his descriptions of the life and culture of peoples of the Niger Basin and Central Sahara, among the earliest and by far the most detailed. After Ibn Battutah returned from his voyages he recounted his observations to Ibn Juzayy, who recorded and edited them at Fès, in Morocco.

At age 21, Ibn Battutah set out on a pilgrimage across North Africa to Mecca, an obligation expected of all Muslims who can afford it. En route he visited Damascus and traveled throughout Syria to the borders of Asia Minor before joining the Muslim pilgrim caravan heading to Mecca, where he spent three years. He then made a visit to trading towns along the coast of East Africa, and returned to Mecca, after which he decided to go to India.

The Islamic brotherhood provided support for Ibn Battutah in his travels, supplying food and lodging as he moved from city to city throughout Asia Minor. He traveled across the Black Sea, visited Constantinople, and journeyed across the steppes of Central Asia. Wherever he traveled, rulers and wealthy people bestowed gifts on him, including many horses. He became quite rich and had many admirers. In India, the sultan was so fond of Ibn Battutah that he appointed him judge, a Malachite qadi, in Delhi, and later asked him to lead a royal envoy to the powerful Mongol emperor of China. A series of mishaps, however, left him separated from his ships and destitute for many months on the coast of Malabar. From there he sailed to the Maldive Islands, where he was again appointed judge. But after only a year there Ibn Battutah's curiosity took him in 1345 to see the "footprint of Adam" in Ceylon, where he climbed Adam's Peak.

After further journeys in Southeast Asia, Ibn Battutah finally visited China. He made the long journey home, after many years away from Morocco, returning through Sumatra, Malabar, Oman, Baghdad, Cairo, and Tunis, reaching Fès in 1349. He briefly contemplated taking part in the Crusades, and traveled to Grenada, Spain, in Andalusia.

It was toward the end of Ibn Battutah's travels that he undertook what was probably his most adventurous journey, across the Sahara to visit the peoples living along the bend of the Niger River. For three years, from 1352 to 1354, Ibn Battutah traveled by camel on ancient caravan routes from oasis to oasis, and through major market towns. He stayed for months at a time with rulers in the kingdoms of Mali and Songhai, as well as with Tuareg pastoralists living in the Niger River basin.

Ibn Battutah's description of the sultan of Mali at court is an excellent example of his keen eye for detail. "On certain days the sultan holds audiences in the palace yard, where there is a platform under a tree. . . . It is carpeted with silk and has cushions placed on it. . . . The sultan comes out of a door in a corner of the palace, carrying a bow in his hand and a quiver on his back. On his head he has a golden skullcap. . . . His usual dress is a velvety red tunic. . . . The sultan is preceded by his musicians, who carry gold and silver *guimbris* [two stringed guitars]. . . . "

Ibn Battutah is the only traveler known to have visited all the Muslim-ruled lands of medieval times. He is estimated to have traveled up to 125,000 km (75,000 mi) in all, and his observations are renowned for their detail, credibility, and color.

Africa

Ibrahim, Abdullah (Dollar Brand or Adolphus Johannes Brand)

(b. 1934, Cape Town, South Africa), prominent South African jazz pianist.

Adolphus Brand started studying piano as a young child. As a teenager in Cape Town he earned the nickname "Dollar" because he always carried United States currency to purchase the latest jazz albums from American sailors. His formidable musical talent landed him a spot in the Shantytown Sextet, a band strongly influenced by the American mainstream jazz trend toward leaner groups with the demise of the big-band sound. The Shantytown Sextet played in a style called bebop *mbaqanga*. In 1959 Brand, together with Hugh Masekela and Kippie Moeketsi, formed the Jazz Epistles, a group that won the jazz competition at the first Castle Lager Festival, held in Johannesburg in 1961.

In 1962, shortly after marrying the singer Sathima Bea Benjamin, Dollar Brand and the other members of the Jazz Epistles fled the oppressive apartheid policies of South Africa to settle in Zurich, Switzerland. There he caught the eye of Duke Ellington, who was on tour. Ellington introduced Brand to the American jazz scene, arranging for the South African musician to record an album and to play at the Newport Jazz Festival.

In 1968 Brand converted to Islam, changed his name to Abdullah Ibrahim, and returned to South Africa a world-famous musician. Of the more than 40 albums he recorded, his 1974 album *Mannenburg* is considered his best work, drawing on both the slow-tempo *marabi* South African style and American jazz elements. In 1976 Ibrahim fled apartheid oppression once again and settled in New York, where he formed the band Ekaya. With the erosion of apartheid in the early 1990s, Ibrahim returned to play music in South Africa. He remained one of the most respected jazz musicians during the 1990s, voted top jazz pianist by *Downbeat* magazine for three consecutive years.

Ice Cube (O'Shea Jackson)

(b. June 1969, Los Angeles, Calif.), African American rap artist, actor, and music producer.

Musical artist Ice Cube was born and raised in South Central Los Angeles, one of the nation's toughest inner-city neighborhoods; both of his parents held jobs at the University of California at Los Angeles. Cube, as he is known, composed his first rap, or metered, rhyming lyrics, in ninth-grade typing class, and found that his music, which combined violent fantasies and bawdy humor, was well received by peers. Within a few years he was rapping with a group, CIA, that performed at parties around South Central Los Angeles. In the mid-1980s, along with fellow rappers Eazy E., Dr. Dre, M.C. Ren, and DJ Yella, Cube formed the now-legendary group N.W.A. (usually spelled out as Niggaz with Attitude), whose gritty messages of anger and violence set them apart from the more politically minded East Coast hip hop artists.

Cube left N.W.A. in 1987 to pursue a degree in architectural drafting at the Phoenix Institute of Technology. After completing the one-year program, he returned to help with the production of N.W.A.'s seminal album, *Straight Outta Compton*, which marked the explosive emergence of "gangsta" rap, in which themes drew from life on the streets. After a bitter falling-out with band manager Jerry Heller, Cube left the group, this time heading to New York to collaborate with the Bomb Squad, producers for Public Enemy.

The resulting album, AmeriKKKa's Most Wanted (1990), established Cube as a menacing solo force. His lyrics, although more articulate and intelligent than those of many rappers, were loaded with misogyny and nihilism, and the album was sharply criticized by the press. Despite limited radio and video play, the record went gold within its first two weeks of release. Cube used profits from his first album to form a multimedia corporation, through which he began producing records for other artists. In the same year, he received critical acclaim for his acting debut as a South Central gang leader in John Singleton's film *Boyz N the Hood*.

Cube's next album, *Death Certificate* (1991), expressed even more of his venomous rage, earning him the reputation of "America's angriest black man." His song "No Vaseline" lashed out against N.W.A.'s manager Heller as Cube defended himself against the group's accusations that he had betrayed them; the song was regarded as anti-Semitic. Another track, "Black Korea" was interpreted as a call to Los Angeles blacks to burn Korean-owned grocery stores. In an unprecedented criticism, *Billboard Magazine* suggested that music stores "protest the sentiments" of the album. *Death Certificate* went platinum, and a year later, in the wake of the 1992 Los Angeles riots (in which many Korean-owned grocery stores were burned), Cube claimed to have delivered a prophetic message.

Following his conversion to the Nation of Islam, Cube released his most popular album, *The Predator* (1992), in which he aimed his lilting, aggressive rhymes at crumbling school systems and corrupt police. His next album, *Lethal Injection* (1993), was less popular, and he took a break from rapping to produce debut recordings by Da Lench Mob and Kam. In 1995 he reemerged, forming the group the Westside Connection.

Cube continued his acting career, appearing in 1995 in Singleton's *Higher Learning.* He also starred in the 1997 blockbuster thriller *Anaconda,* and he wrote, produced, and starred in *Friday,* a lighthearted look at two men spending a day in South Central Los Angeles.

North America

Ice-T (Tracey Morrow)

(b. February 16, 1958, Newark, N.J.), African American rap singer, music producer, and actor.

One of the nation's most prolific and outspoken rap artists, Ice-T helped t o pioneer the "gangsta" musical style, in which the turmoil of urban street life is exposed through blunt, explicit lyrics and a bass-heavy, fluid musical style.

Following the death of his parents in a car accident in 1968, Ice-T moved to South Central Los Angeles, where he attended high school. During this time he reportedly stole cars and wrote rhyming slogans for local street gangs. Ice-T took his name from Iceberg Slim, a local pimp who wrote novels and poetry and with whom Ice-T was personally acquainted. After high school Ice-T joined the army but returned to Los Angeles four years later, at which point he recorded "The Coldest Rap" on a local label to launch his musical career.

In 1984 Ice-T's first recording on a major label appeared, on the soundtracks for the low-budget hip hop films *Breakin'* and *Breakin' 2: Electric Boogaloo,* in which he also acted. A year later he formed his own record company, Rhyme Syndicate Productions, before signing with Warner Brothers in 1986. Ice-T wrote and performed the title song for the film *Colors* (1987), which ensured his long-term popularity. Ice-T's next album, *Power* (1988), included themes about death and street life, and thus anticipated the emergence of "gangsta" rap.

The following year, he released the album *The Iceberg/Freedom of Speech . . . Just Watch What You Say* as a political commentary on hip hop censorship. In 1992 Ice-T released *Body Count,* recorded with his heavy-metal band of the same name. It featured the song "Cop Killer" which was cited by President George Bush and Vice President Dan Quayle as an incendiary threat to law-enforcement officials. While no police were harmed as a result of the song, Ice-T voluntarily pulled "Cop Killer" from the album.

Despite these sporadic "bad boy" episodes, Ice-T has become a major spokesperson for rap music. He has worked to change the problems he sings about: in 1988 he released an anti-gang video, and he later testified before a United States Congressional Committee about the gang problem in South Central Los Angeles. He has toured the nation's college campuses speaking about censorship and promoting anti-drug and anti-violence campaigns.

Other highlights from Ice-T's musical career include his collaboration with Quincy Jones on the album *Back on the Block* (1990), which earned him a Grammy Award; and the release of *OG: Original Gangster* (1991), which is frequently hailed as his finest album. In addition to his music career, Ice-T has appeared in several films, including *New York City* (1991), *Ricochet* (1991), *Trespass* (1993), and *Tank Girl* (1995). He has also written a book, *The Ice Opinion* (1994), in which he expresses his views on music, love, religion, and politics.

Africa
Idris I (Sidi Muhammad Idris as-Sanusi)
(b. 1890, al-Joghboub, Libya; d. May 25, 1983, Egypt), emir (king) of independent Libya and a leader in the struggle for decolonization from Italy.

Muhammad Idris was the son of Sayyid al-Mahdi, leader of the Sanusi, a powerful Islamic religious order. As heir to his father's position, Idris became the de facto ruler of the Libyan region of Cyrenaica, where the Sanusi order was based. Soon after he assumed leadership at age 22, Idris began negotiations with Italy for recognition of an emirate in Cyrenaica. In 1920, in return for a promise that Cyrenaicans would lay down their arms, Italy acknowledged Idris as the autonomous Sanusi emir of several oases. Many nation-alists from both Tripolitania and Cyrenaica subsequently regarded Idris as the leader of the independence movement.

During World War II Idris risked reprisal from Italy by allying with Great Britain. Following the Allied victory he was installed as emir of Cyrenaica. Libyan support for the monarchy was in no way complete— some nationalists in Tripolitania sought a republic or simply opposed a Cyrenaican-dominated state, and some Cyrenaicans wanted autonomy. Nevertheless, under the constitution of October 1951, Idris was declared emir of Libya. Due to continuing disagreement over the choice of a capital city, Idris was forced to establish two royal cities in two regions.

After the discovery of oil in Libya, Idris continued to cultivate strong trade and military ties with the West, and authorized the construction of a giant oil pipeline. By the late 1960s Idris faced growing unrest over his alliances and priorities from a movement of young pan-Arab republicans, led by Muammar al-Qaddafi. Perhaps sensing the changing tide, Idris left the country in June 1969 for a long medical stay in Turkey. On September 1, 1969, a group of soldiers deposed the emir in his absence. Although Idris ultimately accepted the coup and handed over power peacefully, he was later tried in absentia and sentenced to death. Idris continued to live in exile in Egypt until his death in 1983.

Latin America and the Caribbean

Iemanjá

(known as Iemajá in Brazil, also called Yemayá or Yemoyá in Cuba and the United States), the mother of many of the *orisha*, or Yoruba deities. Iemanjá is the *orisha* of the ocean. Her colors are blue and crystal, and she is propitiated with red roses. In Brazil she is honored on New Year's Eve in Rio de Janeiro, and on February 2 in Bahia, when gifts of huge baskets full of flowers, perfume, and champagne are taken out to sea and put in the water for her.

Africa

Igbo,

one of the major ethnic groups in Nigeria, with roughly 17 to 20 million members concentrated in the southeastern part of the country.

Scholars believe that the Igbo language, which belongs to the Kwa subgroup of the Niger-Congo linguistic family, separated from related languages such as Yoruba, Igala, Idoma, and Edo several thousand years ago. There are some 30 Igbo dialects, which vary in their mutual intelligibility; Owerri Igbo and Onitsha Igbo are the most widely understood "standard" dialects. The traditional Igbo homeland lies on both sides of the lower Niger River, though most Igbo live to the east of the Niger between the Niger Delta and the Benue Valley. Igboland is one of Africa's most densely populated regions. Although Igbo speakers fall into more than a dozen subgroups, they share a common culture and have lived in the same area for thousands of years.

The Igbo have a long history of cultural achievement. Traditionally, they have excelled at metalwork, weaving, and woodcarving. Excavations at the village of Igbo-Ukwu have unearthed sophisticated cast bronze artifacts and textiles dating from the ninth century. Since ancient times, the Igbo have traded craft goods and agricultural products. Traditional Igbo religion varied regionally, but generally included a belief in an afterlife and reincarnation, sacrifice, and ancestor and spirit worship. The Igbo performed elaborate ceremonies marking funerals and other life passages.

Unlike some of their neighbors, the Igbo never developed a centralized monarchy. Chiefs or kings with limited powers ruled the villages of a few subgroups, such as the Nri, the Onitsha Igbo, and groups to the west of the Niger. Until the colonial era, however, most Igbo lived in autonomous, fairly democratic villages, where a complex structure of kinship ties, secret societies, professional organizations, oracles, and religious leaders regulated village society. This mix of overlapping institutions gave most Igbo some decision-making power and prevented any single person from gaining too much power.

Europeans arrived in the late fifteenth century, and by the late seventeenth century the area had become a major center for the slave trade. Many Igbo, especially those living along the Niger River, became traders who sold captives from the interior, including both interior Igbo and members of other ethnic groups. The British (and their North American colonists) played a key role in this trade during the 1700s. The British wanted to encourage "legitimate trade" in products such as palm oil, needed in British manufacturing. Igboland exported large quantities of palm oil after the British suppressed the slave trade in the early 1800s. Later in the century the British sought to establish effective control over Igboland, and the decentralized Igbo could not resist British advances. In 1885 the British established the Oil Rivers Protectorate, named for Igboland's abundant palm oil. By the 1890s the British had occupied the area. They imposed indirect rule in 1900 by appointing African warrant officers, who frequently lacked any standing in the Igbo communities they were supposed to oversee.

The decentralization and cultural openness of the Igbo made them prime targets for missionaries. Today most Igbo are Christian, and they have a high literacy rate. From the colonial period onward, the Igbo produced disproportionate numbers of civil servants and military officers. Educated Igbo played a central role in the struggle for Nigerian independence. Nigeria's first president, Benjamin Nnamdi Azikiwe, was an Igbo. When the country achieved independence in 1960, thousands of Igbo moved to cities all over Nigeria to work as civil servants and administrators. Members of other groups, especially in the north, came to resent the perceived Igbo dominance.

Rising ethnic tensions followed the discovery in the mid-1960s of large oil reserves mostly in or near Igboland. Many Igbo feared that plans to redraw the boundaries of Nigeria's internal administrative divisions would reduce their political clout and deprive them of revenue by placing the main oil-producing regions in divisions outside Igbo control. In 1966, following protests that the presidential election had been rigged, a group of Igbo military officers staged a coup. A countercoup by northern officers followed, along with a massacre of Igbo living in the north. In 1967 the military governor of the eastern region, Lt. Col. Odumegwu Ojukwu, declared the independent state of Biafra, dominated by the Igbo. Nigerian forces quickly forced the Biafran troops to withdraw to a small territory in Igboland, where hundreds of thousands of Igbo starved before Biafra surrendered to Nigerian troops in 1970.

The central government was largely magnanimous in victory. They failed to take reprisals against the Igbo and allowed Ojukwu to return from exile. While ethnic tensions remain, the Igbo are again integrated into Nigerian society. They play an important role in the oil-producing economy based in the cities of the southeast, though Igbo reside in cities throughout Nigeria. Some of Nigeria's leading writers are Igbo, including Nkem Nwankwo, Chinua Achebe, and Cyprian Ekwensi.

Latin America and the Caribbean

Ignace, Jean

(b. 1770, Guadeloupe; d. May 15, 1802, Baimbridge, Guadeloupe), co-commander, with the mixed-race Martinican colonel Louis Delgrès, of the 1802 revolt in Guadeloupe against the Napoleonic troops sent to reimpose slavery in the French Caribbean colony of Guadeloupe.

Few facts are known regarding Jean Ignace's life, and much speculation has surrounded this protean figure of Afro-Guadeloupean identity. Ignace has variously been perceived as a ferocious brute, a proto-independence fighter, a noble hero of the black race, a former maroon slave and Dessaline-like figure, and a brave though strategically naïve soldier. Born in Pointe-à-Pitre, most likely a free, mixed-race carpenter prior to the French abolition of slavery in 1794, he joined the colonial army sometime after the arrival of Victor Hugues in Guadeloupe in that same year.

The historical circumstances of Ignace and Delgrès's revolt itself are, however, fairly certain. On May 5, 1802, a fleet of ships under the command of the French general Richepance arrived in Guadeloupe. Like the troops of General Leclerc, who at the same moment were engaged in an unsuccessful struggle to retain the island of Saint-Domingue (present-day Haiti) for France, Napoleon wished through them to reactivate the economic productivity of slave labor. Following the 1794 abolition, a large number of black as well as *mulâtre* (mixed-race) troops had been incorporated into the French army in Guadeloupe, among them Ignace and Delgrès. Ignace himself rose from the rank of lieutenant in March 1795 to captain in November 1798. The revolt of May 1802 was precipitated when one of the highest ranking of Ignace's fellow *mulâtre* officers was denied promotion.

The revolt itself occurred only after it became clear to the black troops and their mixed-race leaders that Richepance intended to restore to power General Lacrosse. Ignace, then an officer with the rank of grenadier captain, had sent the once popular Lacrosse into exile the previous October when it appeared that Lacrosse was favorable to the reimposition of slavery. When Richepance failed to show the signs of respect demanded by protocol to the black troops who welcomed him, and when he then attempted to disarm them, Ignace and Delgrès fled with as many of their troops as they could gather. A series of battles ensued in which the badly outnumbered Guadeloupean soldiers attempted to stave off defeat and assert their refusal to reenter the bonds of slavery. A proclamation was issued by Delgrès (it was written by an aide) defending their cause, attacking Lacrosse, and stating their preference of death to the reimposition of servitude. Finally, Ignace and Delgrès split their troops. Delgrès remained on the western half of the island, escaping at night from Fort St. Charles (today Fort Delgrès) into the surrounding foothills of the volcano Soufrière and the plantation known as Habitation Danglemont. When on May 28, 1802, it became apparent that no further resistance was possible, Delgrès's troops mined the plantation with explosives, and upon the entry of the French, obliterated the entire plantation, along with women, children, and hundreds of soldiers from both sides.

Ignace, meanwhile, had returned to the area surrounding Pointe-à-Pitre in an attempt to create a diversion for Delgrès that would disperse Richepance's forces and draw them into fast-moving combat across unfamiliar terrain. Burning the towns of Trois-Rivières, Saint-Sauveur, and Capesterre as they went, they attempted to instigate the strategy that was to have such devastating effect in the concurrent battles in Haiti. Upon arriving in Pointe-à-Pitre, however, Ignace made the fatal decision on May 25, 1802, to withdraw with his troops into Fort Baimbridge just north of the city. The fort was nearly devoid of munitions and was soon surrounded by opposing forces. In the ensuing carnage, 675 soldiers died, including Ignace, who most likely committed suicide when faced with imminent capture. Ignace's head was subsequently exposed in Pointe-à-Pitre in the slave-owning tradition as an example to any who might consider similar resistance. Of the 250 surviving prisoners, all were executed and thrown into the ocean.

Their rebellion thus ended, all remaining participants were executed, exiled, or returned to slavery. A brutal repression and period of reaction followed in which it was made illegal even to discuss the events of May 1802. For the next 46 years the island of Guadeloupe returned to prerevolutionary social relations, including the immediate reimposition of the ownership of one human by another—although the word "slavery" remained taboo.

Africa

Ihetu, Dick ("Tiger")
(b. August 14, 1929, Nigeria; d. December 14, 1971), Nigerian professional boxer.

Known as Dick Tiger, Ihetu won crowns as both a middleweight and a light heavyweight. Little is known of his childhood, but records show he began his professional career in 1952, compiling a record of 16 wins, 1 loss over the next four years. A strong counter-puncher, he was known for his left hook. In 1956 he moved to England, where his career at first faltered—he won five and lost four bouts in his first year there. But he soon re-gained his form, winning 13 out of 15 fights over the next two years and becoming the British Commonwealth middleweight title-holder along the way.

Ihetu first fought in the United States in 1959, and by 1962 had won the World Boxing Association (WBA) middleweight title by defeating the American Gene Fullmer in 15 rounds. He twice defended the title against Fullmer in 1963, fighting in Las Vegas and in Ibadan, Nigeria. In December 1963 he lost the title to Joey Giardello, an American boxer. Two years later Ihetu defeated Giardello to regain his title but lost it again in 1966. Now fighting as a light middleweight, Ihetu won the WBA title for that weight class (which comprises fighters from 73 to 80 kg [160 to 175 lb]) in December 1966, successfully defending it until May 1968, when Ihetu was knocked out for the first time in his career. He won his next three fights but retired in 1970 with a final record of 61 wins (26 by knockout), 17 losses, and three draws. He died the following year.

Latin America and the Caribbean

Ilê Aiyê

(founded 1974, Salvador, Bahia, Brazil), the original Afro, a percussion-based music and dance troupe that initiated the "re-Africanization" of the Bahian Carnival.

Dissatisfied by the options available to Afro-Brazilians during Carnival, a group of young black petroleum workers from the working-class neighborhood of Curuzu-Liberdade organized Ilê Aiyê (Yoruba for House of Life) for the 1975 Carnival. The group's founder and president, Antônio Carlos dos Santos Vovô, cited three principal sources of inspiration: local Afro-Brazilian culture rooted in the Candomblé religion; the North American Black Power and soul movements and their Brazilian spinoffs; and the liberation of former Portuguese colonies in Africa such as Angola and Mozambique.

As a response to some elite Carnival groups who informally excluded people of color, Ilê Aiyê established a blacks-only membership policy, which it still maintains. Although Ilê Aiyê was criticized in the local press for "introducing racial politics" into the Bahian Carnival, it soon received moral support from established pop stars such as Gilberto Gil, who recorded a pop version of the group's first Carnival hit, "Que bloco é esse?" on his 1977 album *Refavela*. Caetano Veloso's praise song for the group, "Um canto de axé para o bloco do Ilê" was featured on his 1982 *Cores, nomes* album and was later included on David Byrne's popular compilation *Beleza Tropical*.

By the early 1980s Ilê Aiyê had emerged as a primary reference for Afro-Brazilians committed to political, social, and cultural affirmation while creating a viable model for subsequent *blocos* Afros, like Olodum, Malê Debalê, Araketu, and Muzenza. Its annual Carnival themes have paid homage to several African nations, including Senegal, Angola, Zimbabwe, Cameroon, and South Africa. In 1993 Ilê Aiyê's theme was Black America, which celebrated the legacy of key activists such as Marcus Garvey, Malcolm X, Fannie Lou Hamer, and Martin Luther King Jr. Each year in January the group sponsors a gala event called Noite da Beleza Negra (Night of Black Beauty), in which the band showcases new songs and the Carnival queen is chosen.

Ilê Aiyê has released three albums, all of them entitled *Canto Negro* (Black Song), featuring guest vocalists such as Gilberto Gil, Caetano Veloso, Martinho da Vila, and the Brazilian reggae singer Lazzo. In the 1990s, as Araketu and Olodum transformed into electric pop bands of international fame, Ilê Aiyê maintained a heavy, percussion-based sound as well as a resolutely Afrocentric ideological and aesthetic orientation.

Latin America and the Caribbean

Illescas, Sebastián Alonso de,

former slave during the sixteenth century, leader of maroon community in Esmeraldas Province, Ecuador.

Sebastián Alonso de Illescas was a *ladino* slave (a slave who had lived for some time in Spain, who could speak Spanish, and who had been baptized). He had taken the name of his Spanish owner after his confirmation in Seville. In 1553 he and 22 other slaves were embarked with merchandise on a ship going to the Peruvian port of Callao, where colonization was burgeoning. During the trip between Panama and Callao, a strong thunderstorm wrecked the ship against the reefs off the coast of the Ecuadorian province of Esmeraldas. The slaves killed the Spanish crew, then escaped into the forest, where they developed what some historians have called the Republic of Zambos. (A *zamba[o]* is a mixed-race person from both African and Native American ancestry.)

Under the group's first leader, Anton, the maroons grew to dominate indigenous communities in the region. The maroons took indigenous wives and were already referred to by the Spaniards as mulattos by the end of the sixteenth century. In this context Sebastián Alonso de Illescas progressively affirmed himself as the new leader of the Esmeraldian *zamba* society. His rise was due to his ingenuity, his knowledge of the cultural habits of the Spaniards, and his skills as a political strategist. He knew how to use European fire-arms and learned at least one Native American language. Around 1600, after a series of confrontations between the community and soldiers of the colonial authority, the Spanish Crown designated Illescas's son as the first governor of the province of Esmeraldas. He was also named Sebastián de Illescas and had succeeded his father as leader.

"Official" Esmeraldian history is fashioned by Esmeraldian white and white-*mestizo* (of indigenous and European descent) elite. For this reason, Sebastián Alonso de Illescas and his companions are not celebrated in the province of Esmeraldas, as are white and white *mestizo* men, as heroes of the early history of the province.

Africa

Indian Ocean Slave Trade,
the forced movement of people under bondage across the Indian Ocean.

The Indian Ocean slave trade is to a certain extent a misnomer, because it subsumes two historically and geographically distinct trades that happened to cross a single body of water. For over 1000 years, Arab traders transported African slaves across the Indian Ocean to the Arabian Peninsula, the Persian Gulf, and Asia. Centuries later they were joined by European slave traders who brought large numbers of Africans to the Mascarenes and other Indian Ocean islands, as well as to the Americas. Because the early Arab traders left few surviving records, it is difficult to estimate how many Africans they took across the Indian Ocean as slaves. It is likely, however, that about 7 to 10 million Africans traversed the Indian Ocean, compared to about 12 million Africans shipped across the Atlantic, though over a much longer period of time.

The Arab Indian Ocean Slave Trade

The earliest Arab traders probably voyaged to the east coast of Africa on *dhows*, small sailing ships developed during the first millennium B.C.E. Unlike the slave traders who crossed the Atlantic centuries later, Arab slave merchants were predominantly small dealers who transported fewer than 100 slaves at a time and usually also traded in other commodities, such as ivory, spices, and leather.

The first direct evidence of a sizable Indian Ocean slave trade dates to the seventh century C.E., when large numbers of East African male slaves labored on the plantations of the Abbasid Caliphate, in Mesopotamia. Slaves exported by Arab traders to southwest Asia, India, Indonesia, and China worked mainly as soldiers, concubines, and household servants. But African slaves were engaged in diverse occupations—in Bahrein and Lingeh, for example, they dove for pearls. Although legally they were assigned the status of chattel, Muslim law accorded slaves basic human rights. Thus, many slaves attained relatively high social status as concubines and bureaucrats, while others rebelled against the harsh conditions. In the late ninth century, for example, tens of thousands of African slaves in Abbasid revolted.

The Arab Indian Ocean slave trade went into decline for several centuries, as Arab and Asian demand for slaves was eclipsed by a demand for other African commodities, such as gold and ivory. It increased again in the late seventeenth century to meet a growing demand for labor on date plantations in Oman and, later, the sugar plantations on the Mascarene Island colonies. Large slave markets developed in Zanzibar and Pemba where, at the height of the trade, as many as 15,000 to 20,000 slaves passed through annually. The slave trade became so significant that in 1840, the sultan of Oman moved his seat of power to Zanzibar. In the East African interior, peoples such as the Nyamwezi, Yao, Ngoni, and Makua raided neighboring communities and sold their captives to Arab caravans, often in exchange for firearms. In addition to the many East African slaves sent to the distant shores of Arabia and the Persian Gulf, others remained as laborers on Arab plantations in East Africa, such as the Omani clove farms on Zanzibar.

Long after European countries outlawed the transatlantic slave trade in the early nineteenth century, Arab slave *dhows* continued to disembark from Zanzibar, Mombasa, and other depots, little hindered by the British fleet that patrolled the Indian Ocean seeking to enforce the prohibition on slaving.

The European Indian Ocean Slave Trade

European slave traders began operating in the Indian Ocean during the seventeenth century, when the settlement of the Mascarene Islands increased the demand for cheap labor. Some East African slaves during this period were shipped around the Cape of Good Hope and across the Atlantic to Caribbean colonies such as Saint-Domingue (present-day Haiti). During the eighteenth and nineteenth centuries, more and more East African slaves were sent to the Indian Ocean island colonies, such as Ile de France (in Mauritius), and Réunion. Although the vast majority of slaves ultimately would labor in the sugar cane fields, initially slaves built the islands' colonial infrastructures and cleared fields of rocks.

As the British attempted to impose controls on the West African slave trade at the beginning of the nineteenth century, European slavers grew to rely on East African markets to supply their ships. Mozambican slaves were primarily destined for Brazil and Cuba. At the height of the Indian Ocean slave trade to European colonies, as many as 15,000 slaves from Mozambique alone were exported annually. Similar numbers flowed through Zanzibar as well. The Indian Ocean slave trade did not, however, consist entirely of exports from the African mainland; in addition to slaves taken from Madagascar, the Mascarene Islands also imported slaves from India and Malaysia.

Although the slave trade was formally abolished after Britain took possession of Mauritius in 1810, slavery remained an integral part of the economy until 1835. British agents signed a treaty with Radama, the Merina king of Madagascar, to eliminate Madagascar as a principal source of slaves in the Indian Ocean. But the Merina court did not have complete control over Madagascar, nor was it entirely invested in the abolition of slavery. The independent Sakalava kingdom of Madagascar continued to route East African and Comorian slaves through Madagascar before shipping them to Mauritius under a "free labour emigration scheme." Likewise, French traders shipped slaves from Mozambique to the many islands of the Seychelles, and then introduced them "legally" to Mauritius as slaves that existed before the ban on the trade and property of French estate owners. Zanzibar and Kilwa also remained active export centers until the 1870s.

Impact of the Indian Ocean Slave Trade on East African Societies

The Indian Ocean slave trade provided one route for the introduction of Islam to East Africa, and it had many other lasting social consequences as well. Particularly as the slave trade escalated from the seventeenth through the nineteenth century, large regions of eastern, southern, and Central Africa suffered social disruption and depopulation. Although slavery had existed within Africa for centuries (see Slavery in Africa), typically it was not a commercial enterprise but rather a means of extending kinship relations and increasing social status. External demand for slaves resulted in forced migrations; weaker groups fled from slave raiders pursuing the accumulation of wealth and power made possible by the new market-based trade. While raiders traded slaves for rifles and ammunition, violence spread across the East African interior, as missionary David Livingstone observed when he visited the Lake Nyasa region in the mid-nineteenth century. Not long afterward, the need to abolish slavery and "pacify" the region became one of the primary justifications for the European colonization of East Africa.

Africa
_____

Inkatha Freedom Party,
South African political party based in the KwaZulu-Natal Province.

Inkatha was originally formed as a Zulu cultural association, but for years it has been one of South Africa's most controversial political forces. Its leader, Mangosutho Gatsha Buthelezi, was at one time a member of the African National Congress (ANC), but has now become one of the ANC's most formidable rivals. Today, despite the widespread opinion that Buthelezi commands a corrupt and undemocratic—and strictly ethnocentric—organization, Inkatha remains the dominant party in KwaZulu-Natal Province.

Inkatha the political party has its roots in Inkatha Ya Ka Zulu (Zulu National Movement), a cultural organization founded in 1928. In 1974, so me 20 years after the apartheid government designated Bantustans, or "Bantu homelands," for all the nation's major African ethnic groups, Buthelezi renewed Inkatha as Inkatha ye Nkululeko Ye Sizwe (National Cultural Liberation Movement). KwaZulu, like the other homelands, was partly self-governed, but Bantustan ministers were regarded as puppets of the national government. Most observers believe that Buthelezi revived Inkatha to undermine the Zulu king Goodwill Zwelithini, his only rival for power in KwaZulu.

Buthelezi, who had spoken out openly against apartheid, nonetheless supported the Bantustan system. He also emphasized that Inkatha, unlike many black South African political organizations, was pro-capitalist. During the 1970s Buthelezi often reminded audiences of his close ties with imprisoned ANC leader Nelson Mandela, but Inkatha criticized the ANC's support of student pro-tests and presented itself as an alternative movement. Its less ideologically militant stance, stressing cooperation with the existing regime, made Inkatha palatable to South African whites as well as to Western governments. After the Soweto uprising of 1976, Buthelezi cooperated with the South African police to form antimilitant vigilante groups, thus confirming the suspicions of critics, especially within the Black Consciousness Movement, who had branded Buthelezi a government puppet.

The ANC officially broke with Inkatha in 1980, after Buthelezi leaked details of private meetings with exiled ANC leaders. The two organizations soon became bitter enemies. Never as large or as powerful as the ANC, Inkatha dropped its initially nonviolent stance, and armed Buthelezi supporters carried out strikes against ANC and United Democratic Front (UDF) supporters throughout the 1980s. Inkatha was reportedly responsible for dozens of assassinations at ANC funerals. In 1990 Inkatha became an official political party, the Inkatha Freedom Party; a year later reports emerged that it had received past support from the South African Security Police and Military Intelligence forces. Buthelezi, seeking a sovereign Zulu state, nearly forced a delay in the 1994 elections with Inkatha demonstrations and rioting. At the last minute he allowed his name to be placed on the ballot as a candidate for president in the national elections. Inkatha won 10.5 percent of the vote nationally and 43 legislative seats. Despite efforts by moderates within the party to oust Buthelezi, he remained Inkatha's leader.

North America

Ink Spots, The,

African American quartet famous for vocal harmonies that helped lay the foundations for doo-wop, rhythm and blues, and rock 'n' roll music.

Four porters at New York's Paramount Theater formed the Ink Spots in 1934. The group's career peaked in the 1940s but continued, with changes in membership, until the 1970s. The original lineup consisted of bass

Orville "Hoppy" Jones, baritone Ivory "Deek" Watson, and tenors Slim Greene and Charlie Fuqua. Greene died shortly after the group's debut and tenor Jerry Daniels replaced him. The Ink Spots' first recording, "Swingin' on the Strings" (Victor Records, 1935), featured upbeat, walking-bass, scat-rich music reminiscent of the Mills Brothers. Bill Kenny succeeded Jerry Daniels in 1939 and it was then that the Ink Spots developed their ground-breaking sound. Kenny's sterling tenor lead vocal was backed by sparse and languid arrangements. Watson added lyricless lower-register harmonies and Jones provided spoken, bassy recapitulations of the lyrics of the song. A whole lineage of popular musicians, most notably Elvis Presley, imitated this effect. Many more imitated the Ink Spots' innovation of a guitar-riff intro-duction to a song.

Success for the group started in England, and transatlantic broadcasts of their concerts in Great Britain bolstered their following back home. The Ink Spots' first big hit in the United States was their recording "If I Didn't Care." Other songs that gained wide popularity included "We Three (My Echo, My Shadow, and Me)," "Maybe," "Java Live," and "I Don't Want to Set the World on Fire." The group re-corded with Ella Fitzgerald in the mid-1940s, ap-peared in the films *The Great American Radio Broadcast* (1941) and *Pardon My Sarong* (1942), and entertained American forces at home and in Europe during World War II. In 1952 Fuqua and Kenny split, each taking the Ink Spots name for his new ensemble. A third group, led by Stanley Morgan, also adopted the name, which led to a number of protracted lawsuits.

The Ink Spots remained active as a nostalgia act for more than two decades. Kenny, the last original member, died in 1978, and the charter group was inducted into the Rock and Roll Hall of Fame in 1989.

North America

Innis, Roy

(b. June 6, 1934, St. Croix, United States Virgin Islands), civil rights activist and promoter of black nationalism and separatism.

Roy Innis moved from the U.S. Virgin Islands to New York City with his mother in 1946. He served in the army for two years during the Korean War, before returning to City College of New York as a chemistry major. In 1963 he began a 25-year involvement with the Harlem chapter of the Congress of Racial Equality (CORE), an interracial, nonviolent civil rights organization. He was first elected chairman and became the associate national director in 1968.

Innis was also the co-editor and founder of the *Manhattan Tribune*. He gained national publicity in 1973 when he participated in a televised debate with Nobel physicist William Shockley on the topic of black genetic inferi-ority. Through his work, Innis promoted Black Power as well as black nationalism and separatism, and encouraged self-defense over nonviolence.

Institute of the Black World,

research institute that focuses on education as an instrument of social change for African Americans.

The Institute of the Black World aims to foster racial equality, black self-understanding, and black self-determination. To achieve these goals, it organizes conferences, publishes articles, and distributes audiovisual resources, such as a taped lecture series. The institute trains scholars to conduct research and develop teaching materials for black children. In the 1990s, under the leadership of historian Vincent Harding, the institute created the Black Policy Studies Center to explore ways of improving African American education.

Located in Atlanta, Georgia, the Institute of the Black World was originally a part of the Martin Luther King Jr. Center for Nonviolent Social Change. In 1969 it became an independent organization and moved into a house where W. E. B. Du Bois once lived.

Interdenominational Theological Center,

an ecumenical graduate school of theology in Atlanta, Georgia.

Six African American seminaries came together to form the Interdenominational Theological Center, whose mission is "to provide quality theological education for the predominantly black Christian churches." The center was chartered in 1958 through the cooperation of four Atlanta schools: the Morehouse School of Religion, founded at Morehouse College by the Baptist Church in 1867; the Gammon Theological Seminary, founded at Clark College by the United Methodist Church in 1869; the Turner Theological Seminary, founded at Morris Brown College by the African Methodist Episcopal Church in 1885; and the Phillips School of Theology, founded by the Christian Methodist Church in 1944. Twelve years later, the Johnson C. Smith Seminary of the Presbyterian Church and the Charles H. Mason Seminary of the Church of God in Christ joined the center.

Interdenominational Theological Center is one of the first institutions established through the cooperation of independent African American seminaries. The curriculum is geared toward students planning to serve in black churches. The school offers master's degrees in divinity, Christian education, and church music, and doctoral degrees in ministry and pastoral counseling. The center is also a part of the Atlanta University Center, which includes five other historically black colleges and universities in the city—Clark Atlanta University, Morris Brown College, Morehouse College, Morehouse School of Medicine, and Spelman College.

Irakere,

a leading Cuban music ensemble, founded in the 1970s, that combines Afro-Cuban rhythms with elements of American jazz and rock music.

Since its founding in the early 1970s, Irakere has been Cuba's best-known and most popular jazz ensemble. Luis Tamargo writes that "Irakere's sound ranges seamlessly between acoustic and electronic music, combining incredible technique and wide conceptual enlightenment with ferocious groove." The group embodies the diverse styles of Cuban music, which is founded on the traditions of both Spanish and African peoples, who have inhabited the island since colonization. Cuban music has also absorbed influences from nearby countries such as Mexico, Haiti, the United States, and—perhaps most important—the influence of American jazz.

In the 1940s and 1950s celebrated American jazz trumpeter Dizzy Gillespie began to experiment with Afro-Cuban rhythms and to collaborate with numerous Cuban musicians, including trumpeter Mario Bauza, conga drummer Chano Pozo, and bandleader Machito. At the time of this cross-cultural musical fertilization, the future founder of Irakere, Jesus "Chucho" Valdés, was a boy beginning his studies in classical piano at the Havana Conservatory. Growing up, Valdés had a strong affinity for Gillespie's music, which he called "pure fire." During the 1960s he joined the government-sponsored Orquesta Cubana de Música Moderna (Cuban Modern Music Orchestra, OCMM), which was not a jazz ensemble. But around 1972 Valdés and a number of other musicians, including saxophonist Paquito D'Rivera and trumpeter Arturo Sandoval, left the OCMM to form Irakere. Together they sought a style that would be suited to the jazz sound they loved and to their aspiration to renovate Cuban popular music.

The band's name highlights the musicians' Afro-Cuban vision: Irakere is the Yoruba word for forest. As one critic explained, the Africans who brought a rich drumming tradition to Cuba were the descendants of great percussionists who lived in a forested region of Africa called Irakere. Percussion, in fact, has been central to the band's sound. Before Irakere, writes Luis Tamargo, popular Cuban music used only the country's basic percussion instruments, including the tumbadora, bongó, pailas, and guiro. Irakere also incorporated Afro-Cuban sacred instruments like the batá drums and the chequeré, as in its recording *African Mass* (1987), which powerfully mixes Yoruba and Carabalí polyrhythms.

Irakere's first hit came in 1974 with the song "Bacalo Con Pan." In 1977 Dizzy Gillespie, Stan Getz, and various other musicians, critics, and producers made their way to Havana and described Irakere's performance as "more musically exciting than any of the groups from which they have garnered their ideas." In 1978 a number of these Americans were instrumental in arranging for Irakere's appearance at the Newport Jazz Festival. The group won a Grammy Award for its self-titled debut on Columbia Records the following year. Although some members, including D'Rivera, Sandoval, and most recently Valdés, left the group to pursue solo careers, others continued to perform and record with Irakere, including bassist Carlos del Puerto and drummer Enrique Plá.

Over the course of its long career, Irakere has embraced a wide range of styles. In addition to exploring Cuba's rich and varied musical traditions, including Son, rumba, bolero, mambo, and Afro-Cuban religious music, the group has incorporated elements of funk, rock, and classical music. Although Irakere has undergone several personnel changes and experimented with many different musical styles, it continues to feature a jazz-oriented sound with polyrhythmic percussion.

Africa

Iron in Africa,

the political, economic, and demographic history of the metal's influence on the continent.

Iron, a strong and malleable metal, can be shaped into the tools used in agriculture, hunting, forest clearing, conquest, and construction. Iron, in fact, facilitated the rise of Africa's early centralized states. Early in the twentieth century, scholars painted a succinct picture of the diffusion of iron working, from North Africa across the Sahara. The arrival of iron tools was thought to explain the rapid adoption of agriculture and the subsequent rapid Bantu dispersion across sub-Saharan Africa. Recent linguistic studies, combined with new archaeological discoveries, suggest a more complex history.

History of Metal Use

Naturally occurring metals such as gold, silver, and bronze were probably used for ornamental purposes since about the eighth millennium B.C.E. Most metal is found in ores, however, and must be heated, or smelted, to remove the impurities. Iron smelting is a particularly complex process that is believed to have been discovered only a few times in the course of human history, or, perhaps, only once. Copper smelting first appeared in West Asia in the fourth millennium B.C.E. The earliest evidence of the more difficult process of iron smelting is found among the Hittites of West Asia and dates to the second millennium B.C.E.

It is generally believed that the use of metals diffused from West Asia to North Africa and that iron smelting was introduced during the seventh century B.C.E. to Egypt by Greeks and Assyrians and to Carthage by the Phoenicians. Egyptians were using naturally occurring copper by the fifth millennium B.C.E. and were smelting copper by the following millennium. Copper became an important trade item and the standard against which other objects were weighed. Bronze—copper mixed with tin—is found in

Egypt as early as the third millennium B.C.E., and iron objects, probably imported, appear around 1400 B.C.E. Two avenues of diffusion have traditionally been suggested to explain the spread of iron smelting from North Africa to sub-Saharan Africa: along the Nile from Egypt, and across the trans-Saharan trade route from Carthage.

Diffusion from Egypt

When the iron-wielding Assyrians attacked Egypt in 670 B.C.E., Egypt's rulers fled south to Nubia, establishing the city of Meroe (in present-day Sudan) as their capital. Iron-working sites discovered at Meroe have yielded dates between the sixth and third century B.C.E. Contemporaneous iron slag has also been found at Aksum (in Ethiopia). However, there is insufficient data to prove that these sites represent a diffusion of smelting practices along the Nile. Archaeological excavations in the southern Sudan have not produced evidence of iron smelting before 500 C.E.

A Trans-Saharan Diffusion

A second theory traces the diffusion of iron smelting across the Sahara Desert. Phoenicians brought iron-working technology to North Africa from the area of Lebanon when they established the city of Carthage (in present-day Tunisia) during the ninth century B.C.E. Some scholars believe that Phoenician iron-working techniques diffused across the Sahara along established trade routes, and were adopted by Bantu-speaking populations in West Africa. Archaeologists supported the theory of iron diffusion across the Sahara by pointing out the lack of an indigenous copper industry in Africa prior to the appearance of iron, as it is widely believed that the production of copper and its related alloys is a prerequisite to the production of iron. Recent findings have established the presence of annealed copper at Sekkiret and Agades, Niger, dating to the second millennium B.C.E. Equally ancient evidence of copper-working has been found at Akjouj in Mauritania. This copper industry may have been a local invention or a product of cultural diffusion.

Several findings in West Africa support the claim of diffusion across the Sahara. Furnaces or other evidence of ironworking that dates from the seventh to the fourth century B.C.E. have been found at sites in Niger, Nigeria, Cameroon, Democratic Republic of the Congo, and Gabon. Thus iron smelting appears in West Africa at about the same time that it is believed to have reached North Africa. However, a furnace from the ninth century B.C.E. found at Do Dimmi, Niger, suggests that iron-working in West Africa may have predated the arrival of the Phoenicians. But the evidence remains inconclusive, given that carbon dating, the method used to determine the age of the furnaces, provides only approximate information.

Independent Invention?

Evidence of early ironworking has also been found in East Africa. For example, smelting furnaces in northwestern Tanzania and Rwanda have been dated to the ninth century B.C.E. Most sites, such as Urwew, near Lake Victoria, date between 300 B.C.E. and 200 C.E. The scarcity of archaeological evidence, combined with the uncertainty of carbon dating during this era, makes it difficult to reconstruct with any certainty the exact origins of copper or iron smelting. The use of metals may have diffused from Egypt and North Africa or may have arisen independently, or both.

Scholars have noted that at least three distinct kinds of iron-smelting furnaces are found in Africa: bowl furnaces, low-shaft furnaces, and high-shaft furnaces. Early bowl furnaces are found throughout eastern and southern Africa. The more common low-shaft furnaces are present from West to southeastern Africa. A few later-dating high-shaft furnaces have also been found in West Africa, Lake Tanganyika, Lake Malawi, and along the Zambezi River. This distribution gives few clues to the origin and development of ironworking technologies on the continent. Several furnaces do, however, show remarkable innovations in the shafts, bellows, and *tuyeres* (nozzles) to increase the temperature, allowing the iron bloom to reach higher carbon levels, thus effectively producing steel. Although the origins of ironworking in sub-Saharan Africa remain unclear, it is known that iron smelting was firmly established among Bantu speakers in West Africa by the first half of the last millennium B.C.E.

Bantu Dispersion and Settlement

Ironworking is associated with the spread of Bantu speakers eastward and southward beginning in the first millennium B.C.E. Numerous iron furnaces, dating between the sixth and the first century B.C.E., have been found along this route. Iron-smelting furnaces dating to the third or fourth century C.E. have also been found in KwaZulu-Natal and are viewed as markers of this migration. The importance of iron tools in fueling this rapid migration is still debated.

The Culture of Metallurgy in Africa

The importance of iron is depicted in many myths and folktales, such as Yoruba stories of Ogun, the god of iron, and the widespread depictions of African blacksmith-kings. The Italian explorer Cavazzi published a book in 1687 depicting the Ngongo king laboring at a furnace while musicians play. In many societies, such as that of the Montagnard of North Cameroon, ironsmiths form distinct castes and pass on their specialized knowledge from generation to generation. Smiths are often identified with mystical powers, and the molding of the iron bloom is interpreted as a creative, transformative process, laden with symbolism and associated with rituals and taboos. Among the Barongo of Tanzania, for example, the furnace is depicted as a womb, the iron as the offspring; the slag by-product is equated with a placenta. Modern smiths continue to produce iron products, particularly for ceremonial items such as axes. Indigenous smelting has become increasingly rare since the importation of large amounts of iron products during and since colonial times. Today a number of African countries have their own iron industries, and some, such as Liberia and Mauritania, are major iron exporters.

Isis,

in Egyptian mythology, goddess of fertility and motherhood.

Isis was the daughter of the god Keb ("Earth") and the goddess Nut ("Sky"), the sister-wife of Osiris, judge of the dead, and mother of Horus, god of day. In the late fourth century B.C.E., the center of Isis worship, which was reaching its greatest peak, was on Philae, an island in the Nile, where a great temple was built to her during the Thirtieth Dynasty. Ancient stories described Isis as having great magical skill, and she was represented as human in form, frequently wearing the horns of a cow. Her personality was believed to resemble that of Hathor, the goddess of love and gaiety.

The cult of Isis spread from Alexandria throughout the Hellenistic world after the fourth century B.C.E. It appeared in Greece in combination with the cults of Horus and Serapis, the Greek name for Osiris. This tripartite cult was later introduced (86 B.C.E.) into Rome and became one of the most popular branches of Roman religion. It later received a bad reputation because of the licentiousness of some of its priestly rites, provoking efforts to suppress or limit Isis worship. The cult died out in Rome after the institution of Christianity; the last remaining Egyptian temples to Isis were closed in the middle of the sixth century C.E.

Islam and Tradition: An Interpretation

The person who laid down the principle of tradition as an important part of the Muslim heritage was al-Shá'fí (d. 820), the great Muslim lawyer of Cairo. He believed that the community was central to maintaining tradition. Community for al-Shá'fí meant a group of recognized leaders and experts who use their knowledge to agree on something that affects public and personal life. Al-Shá'fí believed that such agreements carried the weight of truth, for in his view it was impossible for the community to agree in error. Error, he said, arose from separation, not from collective decision making. For al-Shá'fí, then, a living community was responsible for maintaining sound tradition.

However, al-Shá'fí was not just interested in tradition simply for the sake of protecting community interests. Rather, he defended the community because he saw it as necessary to preserving the tradition of the Prophet Muhammad. That tradition, called the *sunnah*, or custom of the Prophet,

A Bedouin man, facing Mecca, says his midday prayers along the Red Sea coast of the Sinai Peninsula, Egypt. *CORBIS/Jeffrey L. Rotman*

forms the superstructure of Muslim law, religion, ethics, education, worship, and devotion, and al-Shá'fí was largely responsible for making it the foundation of mainstream Islam. His book on the subject, called the *Risálah*, not only brought together the knowledge of a lawyer and a collector of tradition but it also brought about a major reform by streamlining local and regional deviations in the interpretation of Scripture and law. Al-Shá'fí simply soared in his steady drive to secure the authority of tradition for a Muslim community in serious danger of breaking up. He did this by setting up clear rules to uphold the authority of the *sunnah*. We may summarize these rules as follows: "1. The Prophet enjoys a special status (*wahy*) as God's approved messenger. 2. The Prophet's *sunnah*, therefore, has lying upon it the seal of divine approval. 3. The *sunnah* of the Prophet and the Koran, as the book of revelation, are always in agreement. 4. Therefore, conflict between the *sunnah* and the Koran cannot happen. 5. The *sunnah* can replace the Koran if the Koran has nothing to say on any subject. But even if the Koran has something to say, the *sunnah* can still provide complementary explanations."

Al-Shá'fí thus established the rule that no one was allowed to ignore tradition in Islam. He gave encouragement and a sense of unity to Muslims who were scattered in many different places and observing many different customs. Now everyone could agree on what Muslims should do and why.

Yet by making tradition so important, al-Shá'fí opened the door for people to fabricate stories about the Prophet, stories that even the most careful of scholars could not control entirely. For example, one story, or *hadith*, claimed that the Prophet said, "Whatever is said and found to be beautiful, it can be attributed to me," the sort of catch-all statement that is welcomed by the scrupulous and unscrupulous alike. In response, Muslim experts tried to organize the stories so that they could be included in official handbooks and collections. However, we must stress that such collections, called hadith collections (*ahadíth*), were not simply ornamental; their words were borrowed by people to decorate an idea they liked. They were used to allow Muslims to overcome differences among themselves. It was for the sake of that sense of unity that many of the handbooks allowed sound or holy stories about the Prophet to exist alongside weak or even dubious ones. So these handbooks became an important resource for preserving Muslim unity across centuries and cultures.

Al-Shá'fí's success in establishing tradition enabled Muslims to make changes in their religious practices without losing touch with the past. In effect, al-Shá'fí created the idea of a living tradition, which allowed Islam to enter new cultures and societies outside the Arab heartland. That was how Islam came to Africa, where Muslims followed the advice of al-Shá'fí and another Muslim scholar, Imám Málik (d. 796) of Medina. Both scholars emphasized the importance of traditions about the Prophet. However, Imám Málik was more interested in what Muslims in Medina were actually practicing, while al-Shá'fí looked for rules that Muslims everywhere should follow. For example, Imám Málik would begin his account by saying something like, "This is the agreed on way of doing things among us," or "according to the way things are done among us," while al-Shá'fí surveyed the world of Muslims and pointed out contradictions in local practice and custom. Nevertheless, their approaches were complementary, and both stressed the central importance of the Prophet's *sunnah*.

Tradition: Its Supporters and Challengers

We must now consider the pressures and challenges that tradition faces in Muslim communities. It is natural that as Muslim traders and strangers entered African societies—first in North Africa, then in East and West— they would be wary of mixing freely with their non-Muslim hosts. As a result, these early Muslims lived in secluded quarters, making only occasional and necessary trading forays. The Muslim ritual code imposes restrictions of food, dress, and calendrical observance: it prohibits pork, strangled meat, and alcoholic beverages; forbids exposure of certain parts of the body at worship; and calls for observance of the Friday sabbath, the Prophet's birthday, and the two Islamic festivals of fasting and pilgrimage. In time, Muslims' observance of the ritual code left a marked impression on neighboring populations in Africa, and an attentive ruler would be quick to draw on that appeal to keep in step with his people. Some rulers converted at this stage, but only halfway—enough to explore the potential of the new religion while still enjoying the demonstrated advantages of the old. A shrewd ruler would take care not to step too far ahead of his people as a convert to an unknown or distrusted religion, nor lag behind as a resister of a growing faith. Some rulers, in order to hedge their bets, would thus pledge their children to the different religions in their realm.

Such calculations in the conversion process introduced novel ideas and practices into Islam, creating what the upholders of Muslim tradition call "a state between two states." They are referring to an indecisiveness they find objectionable, because it creates excuses for people who are ill informed or ill intentioned. But it was in this state that the once-secluded communities of traders and strangers broadened and took in the half-hearted and the compromising. Eventually scholars would object to compromises of Muslim tradition and call for reform. But by this time, enough teachers and lawyers would have been trained, and enough people would have converted to Islam, to make successful reform reasonably certain.

Those who want to uphold the Muslim tradition face the challenge of reconciling the rules of religion with the experiences of life. If they want to change and reform Muslim practice, they will have to determine if their own societies' Muslims agree with them. They just cannot take single-handed action simply because they think they know better than others what is right and wrong. So Muslim defenders of tradition have had to walk a narrow line between what the lawyers find in the rule books and what ordinary Muslims do in real life.

The African Dimension

Let us consider more concretely how Islam spread and became established in Africa, in light of the tension between the authority of tradition and the effects of practice.

When Islam first appeared in African societies, people were intrigued, curious, puzzled, perhaps even bewildered. But they were seldom hostile, in part because of the novelty, and in part because of the small numbers involved. The welcome Muslims thus received allowed them to flourish as minority communities. They usually established themselves along important trade routes, where their usefulness to their non-Muslim hosts was assured. In time these Muslim merchant communities grew in size and influence, attracting converts from the local population. Yet these converts continued to practice their old religions, because they saw no conflict with the new religion. It was only with time that Islam gently broke away from the old religions, but even then many converts continued to observe local customs.

However, as knowledge of Muslim tradition increased and practice became less lax and better informed, some Muslims began to demand reform and a genuine break with the old customs. It typically took several generations for this reform phase to emerge, if it emerged at all. Reformers called attention to rules of faith and practice and called for sanctions against those guilty of mixing Islam and African customs. These sanctions were to be found in Muslim Scripture, law, and tradition. Only occasionally did reformist movements lead to *jihad*, or holy war. Reform was normally undertaken peacefully, such as when a charismatic Koranic schoolteacher or a holy person appeared in the land, and offered the community instruction for their uninitiated children. The children, once initiated into Islam, would be better informed than the older generation, and they would raise the standards of observance and conduct. By the time the next generation arrived, knowledge of religion and rules would have been generally

Muslims approach the Great Mosque at Touba in Dakar, Senegal. *CORBIS/Nik Wheeler*

improved. Some people would then decide to go to Mecca, the pilgrimage site in Saudi Arabia Muslims visit every year. While in Mecca pilgrims are introduced to other Muslims from all over the world, and that experience helps to strengthen the Muslim tradition back home.

Eventually, important Muslim visitors would begin to visit the community. Their coming would demonstrate the worldwide nature of Islam, and upon their departure they would leave behind some religious objects, such as an illuminated manuscript of the Koran, a legal manual, handsomely bound volumes of the Prophet's *sunnah*, an embroidered turban or prayer rug, a picture of the Ka'ba (though never of the Prophet), some prayer beads, a silk gown, and so on. Eventually a ruler would emerge in the community who would undertake the pilgrimage, and return in triumph for having visited the holy city of Mecca. His personal example would inspire respect for Islam and give it a high political profile.

What is most interesting about the historical spread and consolidation of the Muslim tradition in Africa is not what happened when the rule books were first introduced nor what happened after reforms succeeded, but rather what happened in between, because it was then that African societies took Islam and adapted it to their own traditions. Islam emerged from that adaptation clearly marked by Africa, and also with clear proof that Africans had much to contribute to Islam. So Africa provided another element in the relationship between Islam and tradition.

Let us look at how this adaptation took place. Muslims, for example, are required to pray five times a day and to fast once a year during the month of Ramadan. The five daily prayers, including the congregation worship on

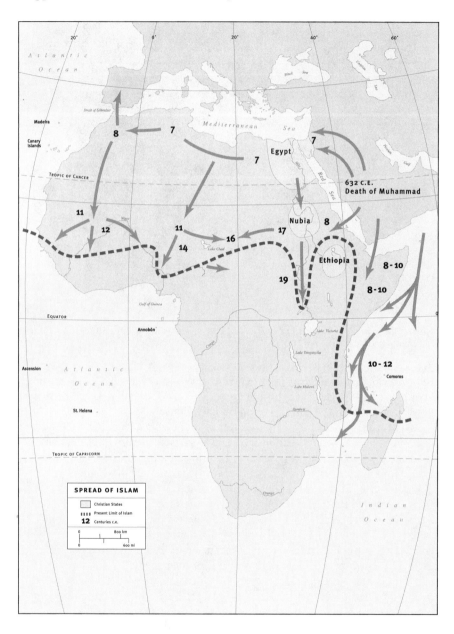

the Friday sabbath, define the Islamic week. The fast of Ramadan is determined by the Islamic annual calendar, which is a lunar calendar, and thus
approximately three weeks shorter than the solar calendar. So festivals of
the Muslim calendar occur at a different time each year. The five daily
prayers thus introduce a regular, daily habit in local Muslim observance,
while the Ramadan fast breaks with the seasonal solar cycle and its agricultural customs and ceremonies. The members of peasant communities who

converted to Islam would often find themselves absorbing Muslim feasts into a time period previously devoted to their agricultural solar festivals. They typically continued to observe these festivals but added Islamic content. For example, they would observe a new year's harvest thanksgiving at the customary time of the year but would make a tithe in compliance with the requirements of Islam.

Conversion to Islam was eased in other ways as well. For example, people would retain the local names of the old rituals marking the new year, rain, harvest, and so forth, but they would observe these occasions with prayers and rites based on the Koran and *sunnah*. If we take a long-range view, we may say that Islam undermines the old customs and will in time overthrow them. On the other hand, if we take a medium-term view, we may say that the old customs will co-opt Islam, as people adapt it in line with their own interests. Thus in Africa, dreams, dream interpretation, healing, and amulets belong as much to the Muslim religious tradition as they do to indigenous religious practice. We should not, therefore, draw too sharp a line between the two traditions.

Asserting the Primacy of Tradition

The achievement of the Muslim "founding fathers," such as al-Shá'fí and Imám Málik, has given reform-minded Muslims the incentive to safeguard the Muslim tradition from harmful compromise. In Africa one such person was the Nigerian *shaykh* Usman dan Fodio (1754–1817), who reformed Muslim practice through the strict application of Muslim law and tradition. Yet he was not opposed to using African ways to achieve reform. Accordingly he used special dream techniques, called *salát al-istikhárah*, to authorize his followers to take action. In his own account, he speaks of how, in 1794, at the significant age of 40, the need for reform ripened into a command and an obligation, with dreams and visions steadying his resolve and clarifying his goals.

"When I reached forty years, five months and some days, God drew me to him, and I found the Lord of *djinns* and men, our Lord Muhammad. . . . With him were the Companions, and the prophets, and the saints. Then they welcomed me, and sat me down in their midst. Then the Saviour of *djinns* and men, our Lord Abd al-Qadir al-Jilani, brought a green robe embroidered with the words 'There is no god but God; Muhammad is the Messenger of God' . . . and a turban embroidered with the words 'He is God, the One' . . . the Lord Abd al-Qadir al-Jilani . . . said, 'Dress him and enturban him, and name him with a name that shall be attributed exclusively to him.' He sat me down, and clothed me and enturbaned me. Then he addressed me as 'Imam of the saints' and commanded me to do what is approved of and forbade me to do what is disapproved of; and he girded me with the Sword of Truth, to unsheath it against the enemies of God. Then they commanded me . . . and at the same time gave me leave to make this litany that is written upon my ribs widely known, and promised me that whoever adhered to it, God would intercede for every one of his disciples."

The veiling of women, one of the most recognizable of Islamic customs, probably originated as a secular practice in the Persian culture from which much of Islamic tradition springs. *Reuters/CORBIS*

The authority to reform the Muslim tradition was thus obtained. As a result, Usman dan Fodio decided to confront the compromising Muslims and their corrupt political leaders. Three years later, in 1797, we find the *shakyh* firmly set on the course of reform, and preparing to arm his followers for *jihad*. He commanded that this preparation for *jihad* was a *sunnah*, an order found in the tradition of the Prophet himself. During the months of preparation, the *shakyh* used prayer to inspire his disciples. His brother, Abdalláh dan Fodio, wrote that the *shakyh* "began to pray to God that He should show him the greatness of Islam in this country of the Sudan, and he set this to verse in his vernacular ode, al-Qádiriyya ['The Qadirite Ode'], and I put it into Arabic in verses." The *shakyh* coupled this experience with a decision to emigrate from his home in the Hausa state of Gobir to Gudu. It was at that moment that he chose to launch his movement. The people of Gobir had been hostile to him and his disciples, and so he denounced them as infidels and enemies of God. Usman dan Fodio insisted on the territorial passage, the *hijrah*, as a condition of sound faith, and combined it with a call for personal sacrifice: "O brethren, it is incumbent upon you to emigrate from the lands of unbelief to the lands of Islam that you may attain Paradise and be companions of your ancestor Abraham, and your Prophet Muhammad, on account of the Prophet's saying, 'Whoever flees with his religion from one land to another, be it [merely the distance of] the span of a hand, will attain to Paradise and be the companion of Abraham and His Prophet Muhammad.'"

This denunciation of the political leaders in northern Nigeria was not a call for Muslims to retreat into prayer cells. The *shakyh* and his followers intended no flight from the world; they merely wanted to conquer it in order to change it. Religious discipline for them helped to safeguard sound tradition from compromise and error, and to warn the faithful that they should always be on guard against giving in to the world (see Sokoto Caliphate).

But Muslim African leaders have also used less harsh methods to correct falling standards. In the Fouta Djallon region of Guinea, for example, some local religious leaders in the late nineteenth century organized revival-type meetings that drew together numerous communities and taught them how to maintain proper standards. The centerpiece of these revival meetings was a form of devotion called "repeated prayer." The devotions were held in village congregations called *missidi*, and the discontented peasants, freed slaves, and poor people who attended were taught special prayers that were intended to inspire them. People came out of their prayers motivated to change the world by replacing those in power with people of their persuasion. They wanted change because they felt that the leaders of the day had abandoned the truth and followed their own ideas. However, the French colonial authorities feared these revivals might make the people revolt, and so sent troops to close down the main congregation at Diawia. That action frightened the other congregations, and people abandoned their farms and scattered. In this way the French proceeded to suppress Muslim religious activity in their colonies. They were determined that Muslims should become loyal subjects of the colonial empire, but Muslims instead became antagonized by colonial rule.

Conclusion

The leaders of the Muslim community have long recognized that the Muslim tradition will weaken unless they take steps to teach it to their children and support schools and teachers who can do that well. That is why many teachers and educators have taken responsibility for Islam, becoming active in Muslim communities as leaders of a unified, living tradition.

Africa

Islamic Fundamentalism: An Interpretation

Although they have attracted much attention since the success of the Iranian Revolution of 1979, Islamic fundamentalist movements are not new, nor have they ever been prevalent among Islamic societies. When they do emerge, these movements are more symptomatic of profound societal crises than a direct outcome of Islamic political and legal thought as such, or a common feature of all Islamic societies. But fundamentalism is not the only possible response, because societies react differently to similar crises; a history of fundamentalist response does not necessarily lead to the recurrence of the phenomenon. For example, there are more Muslims in sub-Saharan Africa than in the Middle East—twice as many if one includes North Africa. Moreover, the Sudanic belt of sub-Saharan Africa experienced strong fundamentalist movements in the eighteenth and nineteenth centuries. Yet there is little indication of fundamentalism in this part of Africa at present, except in Sudan, though the region faces similar crises to those that have prompted fundamentalist responses in North Africa and elsewhere in the Muslim world.

Islamic fundamentalism can be seen as an expression of the right of Muslim peoples to political, religious, and/or cultural self-determination.

Islamic fundamentalists claim to represent the free choice of their communities, whether in terms of demands for the strict application of *Shari'a* (Islamic law as a comprehensive way of life) by the state (when Muslims are the majority) or through voluntary compliance in social relations and personal lifestyle (when they are the minority). Much of the debate about Islamic fundamentalism tends to focus on the possibility or desirability of assertions of Islamic identity and self-determination in the abstract, with little attention to the underlying causes and dynamics of this phenomenon in the specific context of particular societies. For example, given the ideological orientation and political practice of fundamentalist groups in a variety of settings, it is pertinent to ask whether this approach is a legitimate means of realizing the right to self-determination in the modern context. A more basic question is whether fundamentalism is consistent with its own claims of exclusive representation of Islamic identity, political system, and legal order.

Defining or Identifying Islamic Fundamentalism

Like their Christian counterparts, Islamic fundamentalists see themselves as the moral guardians and saviors of their societies, which they condemn for their apostasy, godlessness, moral depravity, and social decadence. They see Islamic history as one of decline and fall, to be rectified at their hands to arrive at complete restoration and fulfillment of the divine design for all of humanity. Islamic fundamentalists share a profound mistrust of all notions of progress—gradual evolution or historical development—as antithetical to divine action and intervention in the world. As the select few, they see themselves as entrusted with discovering and implementing the will of God through the literal reading of the Koran, which they hold to be manifestly clear, unambiguous, and categorical, irrespective of the contingencies of time and place. Upholding the absolute sovereignty of God on earth, which they alone can discern and implement, Islamic fundamentalists reject the separation of Islam and state, and the sovereignty of the people. To them the state is simply an instrument for implementing the will of God, as expressed in the Koran; it does not exist for the people, as defined by secular constitutional instruments.

Fundamentalism as Self-Determination in the Modern Context

Whatever may be the potential for resurgence of Islamic fundamentalism anywhere in the world today, it is clear that the internal and external contexts within which claims of Islamic identity and self-determination are made today are radically different from the way they used to be in the precolonial era. All Islamic societies are now constituted into nation-states that are part of a global political and economic system. They are members of the United Nations and subject to international law, including universal human rights standards, some of which are binding as customary international law even if the state is not party to relevant treaties. None of these nation-states is religiously homogeneous, politically insulated, or economically independent from the non-Muslim world. Even ostensibly purely Islamic and rich countries like Saudi Arabia are in fact vulnerable to economic, security, technological, or other forms of dependency on non-Muslim parts of the world.

Therefore, it is clear that the right to self-determination cannot mean that a people are free to do as they please in their own country. Whether legally as a matter of national constitutional law or international law in relation to other states, or because of pragmatic political and economic realities, the right of one people or group to self-determination is limited by the equal right of other peoples or groups to their own self-determination as well. It is neither legally permissible nor practically possible for a group of Muslims to force non-Muslims or fellow Muslims to accept and implement a specific view of *Shari'a*, whether as a matter of state policy or informal communal practice. Any attempt to force one's own views on others in the name of self-determination is itself a negation of right as bases of the claim in the first place.

If and to the extent that Islamic fundamentalists usurp the right of other Muslims to express their views about the nature and implications of Islamic identity, or the desirability of enforcing traditional formulations of *Shari'a*, that cannot constitute legitimate exercise of the right to self-determination. Similarly, fundamentalist understandings of Islam and Shari'a that would violate the human rights of women, religious minorities, or any other individuals or groups cannot be allowed in the name of self-determination. But if fundamentalists are simply claiming the right to political participation and freedom of belief and expression and so forth, with due regard to the rights of others, then it is wrong to deny them that right simply because one strongly disagrees with their views.

North America

Isley Brothers,

an African American pop music group whose career has spanned five decades, evolving from 1960s soul to 1970s funk to 1980s pop.

As teenagers, O'Kelly, Ronald, and Rudolf Isley sang gospel music with another brother, Vernon, until he died in a car accident in 1954. In 1956 the three remaining brothers moved from their home in Cincinnati, Ohio, to New York City and struggled to establish themselves as an act. They released a series of unsuccessful singles on small New York labels before appearing at the Apollo Theater in Harlem and signing a contract with RCA Victor Records.

The Isley Brothers first reached a large audience in 1959 with "Shout," a soul music single that reflected the call-and-response style of gospel music as well as the Isleys' signature vocal style—O'Kelly and Rudolf backing Ronald's tenor lead. After an album with RCA the Isley Brothers switched to Atlantic and then Wand Records, a subsidiary of Scepter, with whom they released their second big hit, "Twist and Shout" (1962).

"Twist and Shout" was pure rhythm and blues (R&B), and for the rest of the 1960s the Isleys recorded in this vein. Under pressure from Wand Records, they released insipid rewrites of "Twist and Shout" (such as "Surf and Shout") until they started their own label, T-Neck, in 1964. At that time few African American musicians controlled the production of their own music, and in the face of the high-budget competition of white companies, the venture floundered financially. T-Neck records was precocious in another way, capturing the early guitar innovations of Jimi Hendrix, who backed the Isleys during the mid-1960s.

The Isley Brothers signed with Motown Records in 1965 and quickly sent "This Old Heart of Mine" up the R&B charts. By the end of the decade, however, they were prepared to change with the times. They replaced mole-hair suits with hipper fashions, and began writing songs that reflected the influence of James Brown and funk. The change in style was coupled with a change in roster when younger brothers Ernie and Marvin and cousin Chris Jasper joined the group. During the 1970s the Isley Brothers achieved the height of their success, combining dance rhythms with politically charged lyrics in songs such as "Fight the Power" (1975) and "Harvest for the World" (1976).

As the group's success waned in the early 1980s, the latecomers left to form their own group, Isley, Jasper, Isley. The charter members continued to record and perform until O'Kelly died of a heart attack in 1986. Thereafter, Angela Wimbush, who later married Ronald, wrote and produced most of the duo's music. The Isley Brothers continued recording into the 1990s, having influenced popular music throughout the previous four decades. In 1992 they were inducted into the Rock and Roll Hall of Fame.

Europe

Italy,

a country in southern Europe where people of African origin and descent have had a presence since ancient times.

The first recorded African migration to the Italian peninsula came in the aftermath of the conquest and destruction of Carthage (146 B.C.E.). Among the 50,000 Africans that Scipio Africanus Minor brought to Rome as slaves was probably Terence (190–159 B.C.E.), the author of such theatrical comedies as *Andria* and *Hecyra*, whose talent led to his emancipation and to lasting fame in Latin literature. Roman culture's capacity to assimilate many foreign peoples and customs makes it difficult to detect the ethnic or racial origin of people mentioned in Roman texts; the region of birth or a person's name often provides the only clue. Still, there appears to have

An Italian official rides into Addis Ababa, Ethiopia, under a banner that asks, in Italian, "Whose is the power? Ours!" and hails Italian dictator Benito Mussolini (known as *Il Duce*). *CORBIS/Hulton-Deutsch Collection*

been a constant African presence in Rome, and in southern and central Italy.

In Latin the term *Africa* referred specifically to the region centered on Carthage in present-day Tunisia and Algeria. Both North Africans and sub-Saharan Africans (known in Latin as Aethiopes) went to Italy as enslaved prisoners of war and as free men and women, counting in their ranks two Roman emperors, Septimius Severus, a native of Leptis Magna in present-day Libya, and Marcus Opellius Macrinus. There were also countless craftsmen and traders from North Africa and sub-Saharan Africa. Ivory, wood, corn, fowls, wild animals, and spices were some of the African goods carried to Rome by sea in ships often manned by Egyptians. Animal trainers, boxers and wrestlers from Ethiopia were employed in Roman circuses, and black flutists were in great demand for private and public festivities.

With the decline and fall of the Roman Empire, records of the African presence in Italy appear mainly in Muslim and Norman Sicily. Norman kings called themselves "kings of Africa," referring to the Roman province incorporating modern Tunisia and eastern Algeria.

Interest in Africa emerged in travel writing and geographic descriptions of the continent, such as Giovanni Cavazzi's account of his travels to the

A New Orleans jazz band, Italian style, welcomes trumpeter Louis Armstrong to Rome in 1949. *CORBIS/Bettmann*

Kongo kingdom and Angola. Most influential was the work of Leo Africanus, published in 1550 in Venice—included were descriptions of Tombouctou (Timbuktu) and the sub-Saharan empires of Mali and Bornu. Born al-Hassan ibn Muhammad in Granada, Spain, he was given as a slave to Pope Leo X, who baptized him and set him up as an Arabic teacher and African historian.

In Renaissance Italy Africans came as slaves, to ports such as Genoa and Naples; as scholars; and as envoys, mainly to Rome and Venice. In both Venice and Naples, African communities developed in the sixteenth century. In Naples after 1578 the Congrega dei Catecumeni was instituted; its secular and religious members helped in arranging the baptism of slaves and protected them against ill treatment. From 1605 to the next century the Jesuits established a congregation that freed African slaves and exchanged them for Christian slaves held in North Africa. Some freed slaves worked as language teachers for Jesuit missionaries. In Sicily at San Fidelfo in 1526, Benedetto il Moro, the first black African canonized by the Catholic Church (1807), was born into a family of slaves. Benedetto was granted freedom at age 10 and at 21 joined a community of hermits, among whom he led an ascetic life. He became known as a miraculous healer and was renowned for his piety and religiosity.

Near the beginning of the Renaissance, contacts between Ethiopia and Italy intensified, and an Ethiopian messenger witnessed the 1395 coronation of Giovanni Galeazzo Visconti as duke of Milan. In 1402 Ethiopian ambassadors are recorded in Venice carrying "leopards and aromatic herbs." Ethiopians appear in many Vatican documents, especially after 1481, when Pope Sixtus IV turned the church of Santo Stefano Maggiore into an Ethiopian church, Santo Stefano degli Abissini, and its convent into an asylum for Ethiopian pilgrims.

Italian Catholic institutions played their missionary role predominantly in such North African Muslim lands as Egypt, Ethiopia, and Sudan in the eighteenth and nineteenth centuries. Several Africans trained for the priesthood in Rome, notably the Ethiopian Tobia, who was consecrated bishop and translated a catechism into the Ethiopian scriptural language Geez. Within the larger movement for the emancipation from slavery, Catholic institutions such as the Collegio de Mori in Naples and the Istituto Mazza in Verona took an active role in the emancipation and education of young Africans. Ransomed children would be brought by missionaries such as Nicola Mazza, the Genoese Nicola Olivieri, or the Neapolitan Ludovico da Casoria and sent to monasteries all over Italy.

After the 1884–1885 Berlin Conference, Italy embarked on a program of colonialism, which in the next four decades led to the establishment of protectorates and colonies in Ethiopia, Eritrea, Somalia, and Libya. Italian aggression in Ethiopia represented a violent denial of black independence, as well as of the long history of a Christian state, and provoked outrage among supporters of African anti-colonial movements, bringing Africa to the center of world politics on the eve of World War II.

In the postwar era, Somalia maintained relations of cooperation with Italy, and numerous Ethiopians and Somali sought education in Italy up to the 1960s. Since the 1960s African immigrants, mainly from North Africa, have come to Italy, either to seek employment in Italy or to move on to France and Germany. This new wave of immigration has changed Italian cities, and slowly the African community in Italy has acquired a voice through the institution of unions and the formulation of a political agenda focused on the recognition of legal immigrant status and the extension of civil rights to alien residents.

Ivory Trade,

one of Africa's oldest, most lucrative, and now most controversial export trades.

Ivory is a form of dentin obtained mainly from elephant tusks. It is excellent for carving and is admired for its creamy color, smooth texture, and hardness. Long a symbol of luxury, it was used for furniture inlay, book covers, birdcages, brooches, scabbards, figurines, and boxes in ancient Egypt, Assyria (present-day Ethiopia), Crete, Greece, Italy, China, India, and Japan. Craftworkers in Benin were well known for their skill at carving masks, statuettes, caskets, jewelry, bells, and rattles. Because ivory has been highly sought, the ivory trade has historically been lucrative. In the late twentieth century, however, declining African elephant populations, attributed to poachers, brought controversy to the trade.

Ancient Egyptians from the Sixth Dynasty (2420-2258 B.C.E..) onward used ivory extensively, obtaining most of their supply from the region of present-day Sudan. The Romans in North Africa kept up a brisk trade in ivory following the demise of the Egyptian Empire. After Rome's decline, China and India became the largest importers of African ivory.

As Arab Islamic dynasties spread across North Africa in the seventh and eighth centuries, they established trade relations with peoples south of the Sahara Desert. Towns such as Koumbi Saleh, Gao, and Tombouctou (Timbuktu), became commercial centers where tusks were exchanged for salt, copper, gold, silk, and swords. European demand for ivory was sparked during the Crusades. Initially, ivory was exported to Europe primarily from North Africa, but in the late fifteenth century Portuguese merchant ships began trading European goods for ivory along the coasts of West and Central Africa.

Ivory also became an important trade commodity along East Africa's Swahili Coast, which stretches from Somalia to Mozambique. From at least the fifteenth century, Swahili merchants exported ivory to India after obtaining it from inland peoples, such as the Kamba of modern Kenya, the Nyamwezi of Tanzania, the Yao of Mozambique, and the Bisa of Zambia. In the mid-nineteenth century the Omani rulers of Zanzibar sent trading caravans into the East African interior. These merchant caravans also traded in slaves, and in fact used slave labor to carry elephant tusks from the African interior to the coast.

One of the most famous Swahili traders was Tippu Tip, a native of

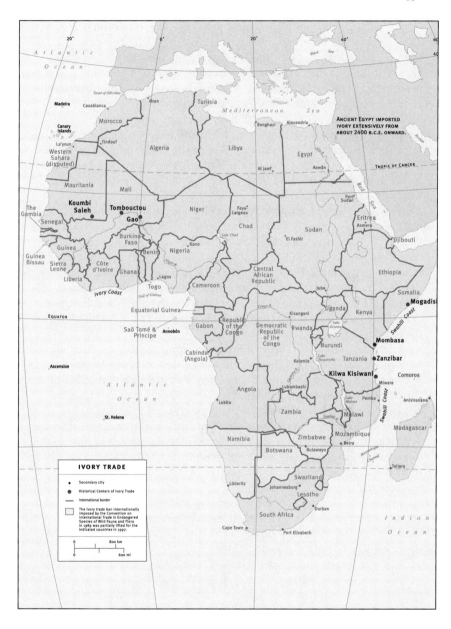

ANCIENT EGYPT IMPORTED
IVORY EXTENSIVELY FROM
ABOUT 2400 B.C.E. ONWARD.

IVORY TRADE

- Secondary city
- Historical Centers of Ivory Trade
- International border

The ivory trade ban internationally
imposed by the Convention on
International Trade in Endangered
Species of Wild Fauna and Flora
in 1989 was partially lifted for the
indicated countries in 1997.

0   800 km

0   600 mi

Zanzibar who established an inland trading empire that stretched from
Zanzibar to the Lualaba River in the modern Democratic Republic of the
Congo. In the nineteenth century the trade expanded further with the
coming of European settlers and adventurers, many of whom subsidized
their hunting expeditions by selling ivory and trophies in Europe.

At the same time, industrial revolutions in Europe and the United States drove demand for ivory to unprecedented heights, supplementing the eastern demand. By the late 1800s Great Britain and the United States imported more than 1.5 million tons of ivory per year to be used for combs, piano keys, billiard balls, and fans. This frenzy for ivory in the late nineteenth century devastated Africa's elephant populations.

European colonial-era restrictions on Africans' indigenous hunting—intended to force Africans into wage labor and preserve elephant populations for European "safari" hunters—slowed the ivory trade. By the 1930s, however, ivory exports rose again. In the 1970s booming Asian economies fueled international demand, which, because of the advent of automatic weapons, was easily met.

The African elephant population declined from approximately 1.3 million to approximately 625,000 between 1979 and 1989, and ivory had doubled in price, from around U.S.$60 per kilogram (about U.S.$132 per pound) to between U.S.$120 and U.S.$300 per kilogram (about U.S.$264 to U.S.$660 per pound). In October 1989 the nations composing the Convention on International Trade in Endangered Species of Wild Fauna and Flora (CITES), responding to pressure from United States and European environmentalist and animal welfare lobbies, agreed to a complete ban on the ivory trade.

Many disagreed with the ban, however, citing the uneven distribution of elephants in Africa. For instance, in Kenya elephant populations were as low as 19,000, mostly because of poaching, but in South Africa, Namibia, Zimbabwe, and Botswana, effective conservation programs resulted in elephant herds so large that they were damaging wild vegetation as well as farmers' fields. In these countries, elephant herds had to be culled regularly. The ivory from these culled animals represented an important potential source of income for these countries' governments. Not surprisingly, they protested the ban, arguing that they were being penalized for sound resource management.

In 1997 CITES partially lifted the ivory trade ban, allowing Botswana, Namibia, and Zimbabwe to sell their excess ivory stocks to Japan. By October 1997 critics of the lifting of the ban claimed that poaching had increased significantly throughout Africa.

Africa

Iyasu I,

known as Iyasus the Great (1682–1706), one of the great warrior emperors of Ethiopia (1682–1706).

Iyasus I was the son of Emperor Johannes I and the grandson of Emperor Fasiladas. He came to the throne at a time of decline in imperial power that had begun during his grandfather's time. Through his brilliance as a military leader, Iyasus temporarily halted the trend of decline, reestablishing control over rebellious vassals and conquering areas to the south of his domain. In addition to his military and political exploits, Iyasus was a patron of arts and letters and sponsored buildings in the city of Gonder. He also attempted to settle doctrinal differences within Ethiopia's Coptic Church, but without long-lasting success. Iyasus was deposed by his son Takla Haymanot in 1706 and later assassinated. A series of ineffectual emperors followed until the middle of the nineteenth century, leading to a decline of imperial power and loss of territory for the empire.

J

Jack and Jill of America,

an American nonprofit philanthropic organization founded in 1938 as a play group for the children of Philadelphia's African American professional elite.

Jack and Jill was born during the Great Depression and grew out of the voluntary community work of upper-class African American women in Philadelphia, Pennsylvania, who wanted their children to have cultural opportunities, develop leadership skills, and form social networks in the midst of segregation.

By 1968 Jack and Jill had become a full-fledged national organization, and the first founded by African American women. It continues to sponsor educational, health, and cultural projects in inner-city neighborhoods. Jack and Jill publishes a national journal, *Up the Hill*, and has 187 local chapters in the United States.

Jackson, George Lester

(b. September 23, 1941, Chicago, Ill.; d. August 21, 1971, San Quentin Prison, Calif.), African American anticapitalist revolutionary whose prison writings served as a manifesto for New Left activists in the 1970s.

George Jackson grew up on the West Side of Chicago, the son of Lester Jackson, a postal worker, and Georgia Jackson. Street smart and rebellious, Jackson had several run-ins with the law for petty crimes by the time he was ten. In 1956 his family moved to Los Angeles, where Jackson's troubles with the law continued, including several arrests for robbery. Paroled in June 1960, Jackson was arrested later that year for a gas station robbery that netted $71. Due to his previous convictions, he received an indeterminate sentence of one year to life. He was 19 and remained in prison for the rest of his life.

While in prison, Jackson studied the writings of Karl Marx, Frantz Fanon, Mao Zedong, Fidel Castro, and others. He developed a critique of capitalism and racism that enabled him to see his criminal activity and his imprisonment within a political context. Jackson and several others organized study groups to help raise the political consciousness of African American prisoners. Jackson, who worked as a prison organizer for the Black Panther Party, aimed to channel the anger and rebellious spirit of African Americans toward political activism. His revolutionary philosophy cohered around a program of armed struggle directed at overthrowing the racist and imperialist establishment in the United States.

Over the years Jackson was repeatedly denied parole. Prison officials said that it was because of Jackson's disruptive behavior; Jackson and his supporters argued that it was due to his political activism.

On January 16, 1970, in response to the death of three black inmates, a white guard, John Mills, was killed in Soledad Prison. Jackson and two other black men, John Clutchette and Fleeta Drumgo, were accused of the murder. The facts of their alleged involvement have never been satisfactorily established. The three accused men became known as the Soledad Brothers and attracted international attention. *Soledad Brother: The Prison Letters of George Jackson* was published during this time and became a national best-seller. Many people protested that the Soledad Brothers were being framed due to their political activities. Angela Davis played a leading role in organizing support for their defense.

The trial dissolved into complete chaos on August 7, 1970, when Jonathon Jackson, younger brother of George, attempted to take over the courthouse and free the three accused. During the melee, Jonathon was shot to death, along with the judge and two of the inmates. A little more than a year later, on August 21, 1971, prison guards killed George Jackson. The official report said that Jackson was armed, that he had participated in a revolt, killing two white prisoners and three guards, and that he was attempting to escape. Supporters have noted several inconsistencies in the report and believe that prison authorities, fearful that Jackson had grown too powerful, set him up and murdered him.

North America

Jackson, Jesse Louis

(b. October 8, 1941, Greenville, S.C.), African American minister, founder of Operation PUSH and the National Rainbow Coalition, and twice candidate for president of the United States.

One of America's best-known and most respected black leaders, Jesse Jackson appeared on the national scene following the 1968 assassination of his mentor, Martin Luther King Jr. In the years since, Jackson has continued to work for racial and economic justice, international peace, and empowerment of society's outsiders. With projects like Operation Breadbasket, Operation PUSH, and the Rainbow Coalition, as well as political action— particularly his candidacy for the Democratic nomination for president in 1984 and 1988—he has attracted fame, admiration, and criticism. He has been awarded at least 40 honorary degrees, and for ten years he has been listed among the top ten men most admired by Americans.

A football scholarship to the University of Illinois brought Jackson north in 1959, but after being denied the coveted quarterback position he returned south to the historically black North Carolina Agricultural and Technical State College. There he fulfilled his athletic and leadership potential, serving as the student body president as well as quarterback of the football team. It was also while he was at college that Jackson became involved in the Civil Rights Movement, first by protesting the whites-only local library system, then later by leading demonstrations against segregated restaurants, theaters, and hotels.

By the time Jackson graduated in 1964, he had decided to become a minister. Accepting a scholarship from the Chicago Theological Seminary, he returned to Illinois, this time with a family. At first he kept his distance from the local civil rights organizations, many of which were trying to recruit him as a potential leader. All that changed, according to Frady, when Jackson went to Selma, Alabama, in March 1965, to take part in an historic civil rights march led by Martin Luther King Jr., president of the Southern Christian Leadership Conference (SCLC). Leading a group of fellow divinity students, Jackson arrived in Selma, met King, and made himself noticed, as much for his obvious ambition as for his leadership skills.

Before long Jackson was working for SCLC. By 1966 he had left seminary to head the Chicago branch of Operation Breadbasket, an organization dedicated to improving the financial position of the black community; in 1967 he became its national chairman. Blessed with charm, energy, and a fiery oratorical style, Jackson soon found success and local fame as the man who pressured several large Chicago organizations into hiring more African Americans. Relations between Jackson and the SCLC leadership, which had been stormy at times due to competition among strong personalities, deteriorated further after King's assassination in April 1968. Jackson quickly became a national figure, assumed by some to be King's natural heir. After the SCLC board selected Ralph David Abernathy as its next president, Jackson continued with the organization, even serving as mayor of the ill-fated antipoverty demonstration Resurrection City. In 1971 he left in order to begin a new project called Operation PUSH (People United to Serve Humanity).

With PUSH and a new emphasis on voter registration drives, Jackson became a powerful voice for minorities and the poor, appearing often in the national media and speaking on behalf of political candidates. In 1983 Jackson declared himself a candidate for the presidential nomination of the Democratic Party. Emphasizing his compassion and fervor on behalf of the poor, the marginalized, and the downtrodden, he pledged to build a "rainbow coalition."

Caught between the high expectations of the black community and the fear and indifference of the white mainstream, Jackson did not win the nomination in 1984. But he did amass far more delegates than anyone had predicted. Two years later he again sought the presidency and failed to be nominated, although this time he won several major primaries and, for a while, was the frontrunner. Although nominee Michael Dukakis did not ask him to be his running mate, despite that suggestion from several polls and advisors, Jackson worked hard to support the Democratic ticket, which eventually lost to George Bush and Dan Quayle. Beyond their simple success or failure, Jackson's presidential runs were significant: through them, he galvanized black voters, millions of whom he had helped to register prior to the election; he raised important social and racial issues on the national level; and, for the first time, he introduced the possibility that an African American could win the nation's highest office.

In the decade following the 1988 election, Jackson continued in leadership roles, although he passed the political torch to his son, Jesse Jr., who is a congressman from Illinois. In 1990 he began serving as "statehood senator," a position created to lobby for statehood for the District of Columbia. Jackson also resumed the unaligned diplomacy he had begun in 1979 and that he had continued in 1983 when he had won the release of a black prisoner of war who was being detained in Syria. In 1991 Jackson's intervention was responsible for the release of hundreds of hostages being held by Iraqi president Saddam Hussein. In 1996 he returned to Chicago to resume leadership of PUSH. In 1999 Jackson succeeded in securing from Slobadan Milosevic the release of three American soldiers taken prisoner on the border between Yugoslavia and Macedonia.

North America
___

Jackson, Mahalia

(b. October 26, 1911, New Orleans, La.; d. January 27, 1972, Chicago, Ill.), African American gospel singer who fused the varied musical traditions of New Orleans to become known as the "World's Greatest Gospel Singer."

In addition to singing traditional church hymns on Sundays, Mahalia Jackson was exposed to the blues and jazz heard constantly in the streets of New Orleans. Musicians like Joseph "King" Oliver played on the bandwagons in her neighborhood and in the dance halls she frequented as a child. Although jazz bands were ever present, the two most profound influences on the young woman were blues singer Bessie Smith and the music of the sanctified church. She heard Smith's "Careless Love" and was instantly impressed by the down-home moans and shouts. Although Jackson refused to sing the blues because it was "the devil's music," Smith's contribution to Jackson's gospel style is unmistakable.

As a child Jackson lived next door to a sanctified church. She never converted to the Holiness Movement, but she was inspired by the joyous and spirited singing. The beat and bodily expression of the sanctified congregation stayed with Jackson throughout her career. In 1927 Jackson moved to Chicago to live with her aunt, Hannah Robinson. She supported herself by working as a maid and laundress but continued singing in the choir at the Greater Salem Baptist Church. Jackson also studied beauty, culture eventually opening Mahalia's Beauty Salon. This was the first of several independent business ventures, which also included a florist shop and a chain of fried chicken restaurants. It did not take long for the choir director to recognize Jackson's talent, and she soon became the church's primary soloist.

Jackson married Isaac Hackenhull in 1936. The marriage was strained from the beginning because Hackenhull, a graduate of Fisk and Tuskegee universities, wanted Jackson to take advantage of the financial opportunities available to jazz and blues singers. These conflicts led to their divorce.

By the late 1930s Jackson had begun to garner some regional popularity. In 1937 she recorded her first 78 for Decca Records, which included "God's Gonna Separate the Wheat from the Tares," an adaptation of a New Orleans funeral song; the Baptist hymn "Keep Me Every Day"; and a modern gospel piece, "God Shall Wipe All the Tears Away."

By the early 1950s Jackson began to appeal to white fans with the help of Studs Terkel, who featured her music on his radio program. In 1951 she headlined a night of gospel stars that sold out New York's Carnegie Hall. She received the French Academy Award in 1953, prompting a European tour that established her as an international musical celebrity. She also appeared on the television shows of Dinah Shore and Ed Sullivan and hosted her own show on CBS from 1954 to 1955. At the 1958 Newport Jazz Festival, she received a standing ovation from the audience of jazz enthusiasts.

During the 1960s Jackson supported Martin Luther King Jr. and the Civil Rights Movement by singing "We Shall Overcome" during her performances. After the assassinations of King and John and Robert Kennedy, Jackson no longer took part in politics. Her philanthropy continued and she established the Mahalia Jackson Scholarship Fund.

North America

Jackson, Michael, and the Jackson Family,
superstar singer and his musical siblings, who together formed the preeminent family of pop music in the 1970s, 1980s, and 1990s.

Joseph and Katherine Jackson, a working-class couple from Gary, Indiana, produced nine children, all of whom displayed considerable musical talent. Joseph encouraged his three eldest sons, Sigmund "Jackie" (b. May 4, 1951), Toriano "Tito" (b. October 15, 1953), and Jermaine (b. December 11, 1954) to practice the guitar and write songs. In the early 1960s the boys formed a trio that precocious youngsters Marlon (b. March 12, 1957) and Michael (b. August 29, 1958) joined, creating the Jackson Five. Although he was the youngest, Michael quickly became the focus of the act, deftly imitating the mannerisms of James Brown while singing with a sophistication and maturity that belied his young age.

The brothers won a talent contest in 1965 that led to a recording contract with the Indiana-based Steeltown Records. Then the Jackson Five toured regionally, opening for larger-name rhythm and blues (R&B) groups. In 1967 the brothers took first place at an amateur night at Harlem's legendary Apollo Theater, and in 1969 they signed a recording contract with Motown Records.

That year the Jackson family moved to Los Angeles, where Motown founder Berry Gordy carefully cultivated the image of the Jackson Five. Motown Records dressed the group in extravagant, hip outfits, choreographed their elaborate dance numbers, and provided them with musical material. The Jackson Five achieved success almost instantly, scoring number-one hit-singles with their first four releases: "I Want You Back" (1969), "ABC" (1970), "The Love You Save" (1970), and "I'll Be There" (1970).

In 1971, Motown launched solo careers for Michael, Jermaine, and Jackie. Michael was far and away the most successful of the three. His early solo hits include "Got to Be There" (1971) and "Rockin' Robin" (1972). Meanwhile, the Jackson Five continued recording and performing as a group, and by the mid-1970s they had forsaken Motown's songwriters to produce and record hits of their own. They also covered classic pop and R&B songs from the 1950s and abandoned their earlier soul arrangements for the harder sounds of funk. In 1975, when their contract expired with Motown, four of the five brothers switched to Epic Records. Jermaine, who had married Berry Gordy's daughter, stayed with the old label to pursue a solo career. Steven "Randy" Jackson (b. October 29, 1962) replaced Jermaine, and the new group assumed a new name, the Jacksons. In 1976 and 1977 they starred in a self-titled CBS variety show, which introduced the Jackson girls Maureen "Rebbie" (b. May 29, 1950), LaToya (b. May 29, 1956), and Janet (b. May 16, 1966) to popular audiences. In 1978 the Jacksons released the album *Destiny*, which many fans and critics consider the best of the Jackson brothers' later work.

Michael's success as a solo performer continued with his appearance as the Scarecrow in *The Wiz* (1978), an African American remake of *The Wizard of Oz*. The movie led to his partnership with Quincy Jones, who composed the soundtrack, including Jackson's duet with Diana Ross, "Ease On Down the Road." Later that year Jones and Jackson collaborated on *Off the Wall* (1979), the solo album that established Michael as a sophisticated adult pop star. *Off the Wall* sold more than 7 million copies and included four Top Ten songs. Although Michael continued to perform with his brothers, this album signaled the beginning of a solo career that eclipsed the celebrity of the other Jackson children.

In 1982 Michael released another Jones-produced album, *Thriller*, which became the best-selling pop album of all time. *Thriller* incorporated the hoary oration of Vincent Price, the hard-rock licks of Eddie Van Halen, and the cooing of Paul McCartney, as well as the R&B, soul, and disco influences of Jackson himself. More than 40 million people bought the album, whose seven chart-topping singles included the number-one hits "The Girl Is Mine," "Billie Jean," and "Beat It." Thriller was a black landmark in the white-dominated market because Jackson's videos were the first by an African American to receive regularly scheduled rotation on MTV. The success of the album was bolstered by a well-planned marketing campaign that highlighted Jackson's dancing, fashion, musicianship, and commercial endorsement of Pepsi-Cola.

Although Jackson achieved this success as a solo performer, he continued to perform with his family throughout the 1980s. He also collaborated with Lionel Richie on the humanitarian hit "We Are the World" (1985). In the late 1980s and the 1990s Michael appeared to have increasing difficulty coping with celebrity, often withdrawing from the public eye. Numerous bouts of plastic surgery, allegations of pedophilia, and a secret marriage and publicized divorce with Lisa Marie Presley all exacerbated his public image as a troubled person. Despite high-visibility appearances on the Oprah Winfrey Show in 1993 (estimated 90 million viewers) and Prime Time Live in 1995 (estimated 60 million viewers), Jackson's career was considered in decline. His poorly selling 1995 album *HIStory—Past, Present and Future, Book I*, which anthologized old hits with new material, only seemed to underscore his waning popularity.

Michael's sister Janet achieved greater celebrity as Michael lost popularity. Although she had appeared in television programs in the 1970s and released her first solo album in 1982, Janet Jackson did not win considerable public attention until her quadruple-platinum album *Control* (1986). With Janet Jackson's *Rhythm Nation 1814* (1989), she topped the charts, won a Grammy, and sold more than 8 million records. She persevered as a major name in 1990s pop, scoring hit albums with *janet* (1993) and *The Velvet Rope* (1997).

None of the other Jacksons approached Michael's or Janet's level of success, although LaToya released solo albums in the early 1980s and appeared in *Playboy* magazine, and Jermaine recorded throughout the 1980s, working with Pia Zadora as well as with Whitney Houston. Taken collectively, however, the Jackson family's career, spanning three decades, was the biggest pop-music phenomenon of the late twentieth century.

North America

Jackson, Reginald Martinez (Reggie)

(b. May 18, 1946, Wyncote, Pa.), African American baseball player, the sixth-leading home run hitter of all time (563) and the all-time career strikeout leader (2597).

Reggie Jackson (born Reginald Martinez Jackson) entered Arizona State University in 1964 and played football and baseball there before signing a baseball contract in 1966 with the Kansas City Athletics (known as the A's), who later moved to Oakland, California. Jackson joined the A's in 1967 after a brief period in the minor leagues. In 1969 he gained recognition as a power hitter when he had a career-high total of 47 home runs, with 118 runs batted in (RBI).

Jackson was traded to the Baltimore Orioles in 1976, then signed with the New York Yankees as a free agent the following season. He had his greatest success with the Yankees, leading the team to three East Division championships (1977, 1978, 1980), two American League pennants, and two World Series championships in 1977 and 1978. He hit four consecutive home runs in the fifth and sixth games of the 1977 World Series, each coming on a first pitch off four different Los Angeles Dodgers pitchers. That unprecedented performance under pressure earned Jackson the nickname "Mr. October." Jackson's brash public persona and dramatic performances on the field supported his claim that he was "the straw that stirs the drink." He retired after the 1987 season and was inducted into the Baseball Hall of Fame in 1993.

North America

Jackson State Incident,

anti-Vietnam demonstration that turned into a race riot in which two black youths were killed.

On May 13, 1970, some 150 protesters gathered on the all-black campus of Jackson State College (now Jackson State University) in Mississippi to protest the Vietnam War. The crowd was in an angry mood, their hostility fueled by the killing of four white students at Kent State University by National Guardsmen nine days earlier, and by the racially motivated murder, two days before, of six African Americans in Augusta, Georgia. While some of the young black demonstrators were content to chant slogans, others burned police barricades and threw rocks and bottles at passing white motorists. Local officials alerted the National Guard, which arrived in force on the campus when the demonstrations recurred the following day. Later that night, in the face of escalating violence, members of the Jackson police department and the Mississippi Highway Patrol fired into the crowd and killed 2 black students, wounding 12 others.

The Jackson State Incident took place at the height of the anti-Vietnam protest era, when violence and unrest gripped many American college campuses. The events at Jackson State reflected not only the national antiwar sentiment of college students but long-simmering racial conflicts. Jackson State students were protesting both President Nixon's plans to invade Cambodia and the racism of local police.

After the shootings in 1970, local politicians and law enforcement agents tried to pass the blame off on the students, claiming that a sniper had caused the deaths. Survivors and family members of the victims took the issue to court, but no local police or National Guardsman was ever indicted.

Jacobs, Harriet Ann

(b. 1813?, Edenton, N.C.; d. March 7, 1897, Washington, D.C.), African American writer known especially for her autobiography, which is the most significant African American slave narrative by a woman.

Harriet Jacobs states in the preface to her autobiography, *Incidents in the Life of a Slave Girl, Written by Herself,* published under the pseudonym Linda Brent in 1861, that she wanted her story to "arouse the women of the North to a realizing sense of the condition of millions of women at the South, still in bondage, suffering what I suffered." In this statement, which stresses her appeal to a female audience, Jacobs touches on one of her auto-biography's most important features: Jacobs is the only African American woman slave to leave a long and detailed record of the particular ways in which slavery affected women, from sexual abuse to constraints on mother-hood. For most of the twentieth century, however, scholars thought her narrative was a novel by a white author and ignored the book. It was not until the 1980s, when literary historian Jean Fagan Yellin used letters and manuscripts to prove that Jacobs had indeed written her autobiography "by herself," that readers rediscovered Jacobs as a key early African American writer.

Jacobs lived with her parents and younger brother until her mother's death, when Jacobs was six. She then was sent to live with her mother's owner, Margaret Horniblow, who treated her well and taught her to read and write. At her death, however, she willed Jacobs to her three-year-old niece, Mary Matilda Norcom, and at age 12 Jacobs was sent to live with the Norcom family. Her time with the Norcoms is a large part of her autobiography—especially the sexual harassment she received from Dr. Norcom, the evil "Dr. Flint" in her narrative. Jacobs's narrative is very frank about Norcom's frequent sexual advances and threats, and makes explicit the particular hazards slave women faced, which are often only alluded to in men's slave narratives.

In 1829 and 1833 Jacobs gave birth to Joseph and Louisa Matilda, whose father was a white neighbor. This relationship only angered Norcom, and when he began to use her children, who were legally his property, as another means of controlling her, Jacobs decided to take a chance on run-ning away. She hoped that if she were gone Norcom might sell her children to their father, and so in 1835 she ran away from the Norcom household.

Jacobs was first hidden in several Edenton homes by sympathetic black and white neighbors. But when it became apparent that it was going to be difficult for her to leave Edenton undetected, family members constructed a secret crawlspace in the house that belonged to her grandmother, who was free. The crawlspace was nine feet long, seven feet wide, and at its tallest, three feet high—but Jacobs hid in the tiny enclosure for the next seven years, a fact so harrowing that it may have been what led historians to suspect her autobiography was fictional.

In 1842 Jacobs was finally able to escape to New York. There she was reunited with her children, who had indeed been purchased by their father and sent to the North. In New York Jacobs worked as a nursemaid for a white family and became active in the antislavery movement. In 1850 her freedom was threatened when the Fugitive Slave Law stated that runaway slaves could and must be returned to their owners if apprehended in any part of the United States. The Norcom family sent agents to New York who attempted to kidnap her from her employers' home. Her employer finally secured her legal freedom by purchasing her from the Norcoms and emancipating her in 1853. That same year Jacobs began writing her autobiography, which she worked on at night after her child-care duties were done. The book was edited by white abolitionist Lydia Maria Child and received good reviews in the antislavery press when it was published in March 1861. But the outbreak of the Civil War one month later quickly stole readers' attention away. The book she wrote is now recognized as one of the most valuable testimonies on what slavery really was, especially for the black women who endured it.

Latin America and the Caribbean

Jamaica,

the third largest island in the Caribbean, located in the Caribbean Sea between Cuba and the northern coast of South America; a predominantly black nation with cultural influences from Africa, Europe, Asia, and the Middle East.

Introduction

This Caribbean island of more than 2.5 million inhabitants is perhaps best known for its beautiful beaches and majestic views. Located a little more than 160 km (100 mi) from the United States, Jamaica is a popular tourist destination. It is known around the world for its music and culture, including reggae, dub poetry, and the Jamaican *patois*. Jamaica is a stable democratic nation with an emerging economy and a long history of social activism. Jamaicans are proud of their national heroes, men and women who have made significant contributions to freedom and democracy at home and abroad. They include social activists such as Marcus Garvey, Paul Bogle, George Gordon, and the slave leader Nanny; politicians such as Michael Manley and Alexander Bustamante; and artists such as reggae musician Bob Marley and authors Claude McKay and Una Marson.

Jamaica's indigenous inhabitants predated Columbus's arrival by at least 800 years. They lived in organized, hierarchically structured, polytheistic communities. Almost immediately the Spanish settlers set out to control the island through violence and eventually succeeded in eliminating the estimated 60,000 aboriginal inhabitants on the island.

By the early sixteenth century Jamaica had become one of many islands

The third-largest island in the Caribbean, Jamaica is a popular tourist destination, in part because of its natural beauty. *CORBIS/Jan Butchofsky*

in the Caribbean to be colonized by European nations. Spain, and later England, used its military might to dominate Jamaica's indigenous community as tobacco and sugar plantations spread across the island. When the pace of plantation production outstripped the supply of indigenous labor, Spanish settlers introduced African slaves into the colonial economy. By the mid-seventeenth century, slaves were the primary source of labor in colonial Jamaica.

Experts believe that over the course of the centuries-long transatlantic slave trade, more than 2 million African slaves passed through Jamaica on their way to destinations in North America, South America, and the rest of the Caribbean. Of the slaves who remained in Jamaica, most served as chattel labor on sugar plantations. Many risked their lives either to escape bondage or to organize others for rebellion.

Spain officially transferred Jamaica to Britain in 1670 under the Treaty of Madrid. Britain moved quickly to transform Jamaica from a small-scale, cocoa-producing economy dominated by small landholders to a sugar-producing plantation society fueled by large pools of slave labor. Gone were the days when whites worked next to black slaves on small farms. England sought to solidify white control further in 1662 by granting full British citizenship to Jamaica's white settlers. As citizens of the British Crown they were able to make their own laws and establish a political system that would exclude nonwhites for more than 200 years.

Jamaica's new colonial government as well as officials back in London

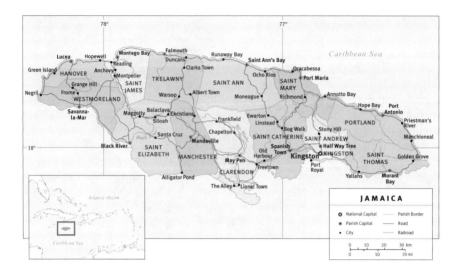

both benefited from the booming transatlantic slave trade. African slaves from the Gold Coast, the Bight of Benin, and the area that today is Nigeria were sent to the Caribbean in exchange for sugar, rum, and molasses, which were in turn sent back to Europe for mass consumption. Experts believe that more than 10 million African slaves were bought and sold in the Americas. Jamaica became a major British port in the transatlantic slave trade, serving as a respite for vessels on their way to Barbados, South Carolina, Massachusetts, and New York. Nearly 2 million African slaves were transported through Jamaican ports alone.

Plantation life was extremely hard. Although slaves shared a common physical experience, significant cultural and linguistic differences did exist among them. The largest proportion of slaves working on sugar plantations were Coromantees from the Gold Coast (Ghana) and Igbos from the Bight of Benin. In addition to the many languages and dialects spoken, slaves in Jamaica also worshiped different gods and practiced a wide array of social and religious customs. As time progressed, slave society was further complicated by a widening cultural and psychological gap between slaves who were born in Africa and then transported to Jamaica, and slaves who were born on Jamaican soil (Creoles).

Gradually, those slaves who were born in Jamaica formed a Creole language that fused both African and English dialects. The contemporary Jamaican *patois* has linguistic roots in the Creole language of the slaves. In addition to language, slaves held on to a small set of religious beliefs and customs, including a form of worship known as Obeah. The practitioner of Obeah reportedly possessed magical powers and commanded enormous fear and respect on the plantation. Obeah was so entrenched in slave culture that British officials later outlawed it. But laws could not suppress Obeah worship, and it continued to be an influential part of the underground (secret) slave society.

Slave rebellions in Jamaica involved not hundreds but thousands of slaves. A high slave-to-white ratio, a significant percentage of African-born slaves, absentee planters, and the work of black and white abolitionists all contributed to the frequency of resistance. Despite the best efforts of the colonists, thousands of slaves gained freedom by running away and hiding in the hills and mountains.

Between 1834 and 1845 more than 4000 European indentured servants immigrated to Jamaica. Many of these new workers were from Germany, Scotland, Ireland, and England. They were employed as farmers and artisans on coffee and sugar plantations and in cattle pens. These new immigrants moved into cities occupied by a small but historic community of Jewish merchants. Jews immigrated to Jamaica as indentured servants in the sixteenth century and became leading traders in the colony. Up to 10,000 African indentured servants were also recruited between 1841 and 1867. But this was stopped after critics complained that it came too close to trafficking in slaves.

The largest group of indentured servants came from India. More than 20,000 Indians immigrated to Jamaica between 1845 and the end of World War I, when the program was terminated. Life for Indian indentured servants was quite different than it was for their European counterparts. They were housed in overcrowded, unsanitary conditions on plantations. Their length of servitude was expanded over time from one year to two years, and in some cases to as long as five years. Racism made life difficult for most Indians. The Jamaican legislature passed laws prohibiting non-Christian marriages and outlawing non-Christian religions. Indians were not allowed to move into predominantly white areas, particularly in Kingston, where the white elite maintained close cultural distinctions between the city's various ethnic communities. Competition for unskilled jobs also caused increased tensions between blacks and Indians. Black workers often disparagingly called Indians "coolies," while Indians referred to blacks as *kafari*, or infidels.

Chinese indentured servants faced similar challenges. Between 1854 and 1930, 6000 Chinese workers immigrated to Jamaica from China, Hong Kong, Panama, and the United States. Hundreds of Chinese workers died on Jamaican plantations from disease, malnutrition, and exhaustion. Like their black and Indian counterparts, Chinese indentured servants worked long hours in unsanitary conditions for meager wages. Although the number of Chinese immigrants remained relatively small throughout the nineteenth and twentieth centuries, the Jamaican legislature imposed quotas on Chinese workers. On January 7, 1931, colonial officials refused to accept Chinese immigrants who were above age 14. The growing wave of immigrants placed strains on the economy and increased competition for jobs. As blacks, coloreds, Indians, Chinese, and Arabs competed for limited opportunities, they developed their own prejudices. These prejudices increased as the plantation economy collapsed.

Jamaica's black majority was strongly affected by economic and political changes but had few institutional avenues for responding. There were few colored or black representatives in the legislature. There were even fewer

registered black and colored voters. Among the exceptions was the colored
politician George Gordon, having been elected a member of the legislature
in 1840. He and black activist Paul Bogle stood at the forefront of the political consciousness that emerged in black communities throughout Jamaica
during the last decades of the nineteenth century. Property restrictions on
black voters, high property taxes, a virtually nonexistent educational system
for nonwhites, and widespread racism all contributed to the Morant Bay
Rebellion, a massive black protest orchestrated by Paul Bogle in 1865. The
rebellion began as a protest by blacks in Morant Bay who were demanding
economic and political reforms. A public demonstration on the city streets
erupted into a violent confrontation with police. The fighting spanned one
week and ended in a brutal military crackdown. Nearly 1000 black homes
were burned to the ground and more than 600 protesters were flogged.
Another 500 protesters were executed, including Bogle and Gordon, who
are now national heroes in Jamaica.

The Morant Bay Rebellion marked a new chapter in the struggle for
civil rights in Jamaica. Jamaica was designated a Crown colony in 1866—a
policy that stripped most of the formal political power from the hands of
the colony's white elite. Subsequent reforms sought to incorporate nonwhites slowly into the political process.

Economic and political reforms alleviated some of the pressures on
blacks and coloreds but did not stop thousands from migrating to the
United States, Panama, and other places in the Caribbean. Between 1888
and 1920 an estimated 146,000 Jamaicans left the country in search of
better opportunities. The Great Depression, which began in 1929, contributed to the hardship, leading to the collapse of the Jamaican sugar and
banana industries. Because of the resulting flow of migrants from Jamaica
and other parts of the developing world, the advanced industrial nations
placed strict quotas on immigration. This hampered the ability of Jamaicans
to find employment overseas, forcing them to look at home.

Throughout the 1930s the country experienced a massive migration
to urban areas such as Kingston and Saint Andrew. Urbanization soon
produced two Jamaican societies, divided by class, color, and culture.
The tensions and prejudices within Jamaica's nonwhite majority increased
as the country's white elite held on to power. It was during this period that
several black activists emerged to lead another phase of the Jamaican civil
rights movement.

Dr. Robert Love had been an early activist. Throughout the last decades
of the nineteenth century Dr. Love, a long-time Jamaican resident who
was born in the Bahamas, organized voter registration campaigns and
encouraged blacks to become active in politics. The civil rights movement
progressed slowly until black activist Marcus Garvey returned to Jamaica in
1927 after having been deported by the United States government for mail
fraud. Garvey's Universal Negro Improvement Association (UNIA) and his
Black Star shipping enterprise had made him one of the most influential
blacks in the world, and his return to his native Jamaica was hailed as a
triumph. While in Jamaica, Garvey encouraged the island's mostly poor and

A Jamaican mother takes her family to church. *CORBIS/Daniel Lainé*

black working class to challenge the racist political and economic systems that had exploited them for so long. Garvey moved to England in 1935, but before he left Jamaica, he founded a workers' association and one of the country's first political parties. Garvey's race pride also inspired the formation of other black organizations devoted to racial consciousness, including the Rastafarians, who in 1935 initiated a cultural and religious movement known as Rastafarianism.

Partially in reaction to similar anti-colonial sentiment in other Anglophone colonies, Britain gradually removed itself from the administration of Jamaica's internal affairs and passed several constitutional reforms that granted more local political control to native Jamaicans. In 1955 Michael Manley and his People's National Party (PNP) defeated Alexander Bustamante and his Jamaican Labor Party (JLP) in a general election. Jamaica moved quietly toward independence. The two-party system illustrated a democratic impulse that would carry the nation toward political freedom. On August 6, 1962, Jamaica became an independent nation but remained part of the Commonwealth of Nations.

Even though many tourists know Jamaica only as a popular vacation spot, the island's history presents a compelling story of the triumph of freedom and independence. Jamaica's history, like most former European colonies, has progressed through various stages that include slavery, independence, and civil strife. However, what makes Jamaica's history so remarkable, especially in comparison to its colonial counterparts, is the

Rastafarian bands like this one represent far more than the reggae music well known to many non-Jamaicans. Rastafarianism blends religious, political, and social philosophies to express opposition to the historic degradation of Africans in the Caribbean and worldwide.
CORBIS/Daniel Lainé

consistent involvement of hundreds of thousands of slaves and former slaves—African and Creole—in the nation's relentless trajectory toward a democratic, black-ruled nation.

Jamaica's economy is still dependent on foreign consumers, and tourism is now one of its leading industries. In order to keep attracting foreign tourists, Jamaica has been forced to build lavish resorts suitable to American and European tastes. In the process, the concerns of many of the country's poorest residents have been ignored.

North America

James, Daniel ("Chappie"), Jr.

(b. February 11, 1920, Pensacola, Fla.; d. February 25, 1978, Colorado Springs, Colo.), first African American four-star general.

Daniel James attended Tuskegee Institute, where he joined the segregated United States Army Air Corp. He served in World War II and in 1943 was commissioned a second lieutenant. He served again in Korea, leading a fighter plane squadron and devising tactics to support ground troops. During the Korean War he flew more than 100 combat missions and received the Distinguished Service Medal.

In 1957 James graduated from the Air Command and Staff College in Alabama. Nine years later, during the Vietnam War, he was promoted to deputy commander for operations of the Eighth Tactical Fighter Wing in Thailand. Speaking in favor of the war and encouraging blacks to serve made him a national figure. He was often criticized for not directly supporting the Civil Rights Movement, choosing instead to be an example of an individual overcoming barriers through persistence and service.

James became commander of the Wheelus Air Force Base in Libya in 1969. He achieved the rank of brigadier general in 1970, lieutenant general in 1973, and four-star general in 1975. In that capacity he commanded the North American Air Defense system during a critical time in the cold war. A heart condition forced his retirement in February 1978. He died later that month of a heart attack. During his career, he was awarded the Legion of Merit, the Distinguished Flying Cross, and a Presidential Unit Citation.

Latin America and the Caribbean

James, Norberto

(b. February 6, 1945, San Pedro de Macorís, Dominican Republic), Afro-Dominican writer; author of four collections of poetry, including *Sobre la marcha* (1969), *La provincia sublevada* (1972), *Vivir* (1982), and *Hago constar* (1983), none of which has been translated into English. He also wrote *Denuncia y complicidad* (1997), a book of literary criticism on two Dominican novels of the 1940s.

Norberto James was born on a sugar plantation into a community of English-speaking Afro-Caribbeans. As a youth his artistic talents led him to attend high school in the capital, Santo Domingo. There he studied music and painting, improved his Spanish, and met other artists. In 1963 a United States military intervention in the Dominican Republic overthrew then-president Juan Bosch, a novelist turned politician, in part because he attempted to renew diplomatic relations with Cuba. These circumstances both interrupted James's studies and prompted him to get involved in leftist politics. The event also convinced him to become a poet.

James cites Pablo Neruda and César Vallejo, two of the most important contemporary poets in all of Latin America, as major influences on his work. One of the principal themes of James's writing is a concern for political justice and collective well-being. Many of his poems reflect on personal experiences and on social conditions. Perhaps his best-known work is the 1969 poem *Los immigrantes*, which invites the descendants of Anglophone West Indian immigrants to embrace a Dominican national identity.

James received a bachelor's degree from the University of Havana in 1978. He later enrolled in Boston University, where he earned a master's degree in 1985 and a doctorate in 1992, both in the field of Latin American literature. He is currently an educator and a writer residing in Wellesley, Massachusetts.

North America

Jamison, Judith

(b. May 10, 1944, Philadelphia, Pa.), African American dancer and choreographer; her work typically honors black women and African American cultural heritage.

Born on May 10, 1944, in Philadelphia, Pennsylvania, Judith Jamison started dancing at age 6 at the Judimar School of Dance. At 17, she left to study psychology at Fisk University in Nashville, Tennessee. After three semesters, she returned to Philadelphia to continue her dance training at the Philadelphia Dance Company (now the University of Arts).

After a 1964 appearance with Agnes de Mille's dance troupe in New York, Jamison joined the Alvin Ailey American Dance Theatre (AAADT) in 1965. Because of this company's financial difficulties, she danced in the Harkness Ballet's 1966 season. But in 1967 she returned to AAADT to become its premier dancer, and she toured the world dancing in roles such as *Cry* (1971), her signature dance, which Ailey choreographed to honor the strength and dignity of African American women. For her performances she won a Dance Magazine award in 1972.

Jamison left AAADT to perform with Gregory Hines in the 1980 Broadway musical *Sophisticated Ladies*. With encouragement from Ailey, she also began to choreograph her own pieces honoring her African heritage, such as *Divining* (1984) and *Ancestral Rites* (1989). Because of Ailey's failing health, Jamison returned to AAADT as artistic associate in 1988. When he died in 1989, she accepted the position of artistic director of his company. She has continued the company's performance of early works choreographed by African Americans.

Africa

Jarbah, Tunisia (also known as Djerba),

an island off the southeast coast of Tunisia.

Legend has it that the island of Jarbah was the land of the lotus-eaters portrayed in Homer's *Odyssey*—a land where the sailors ate enchanted fruit and forgot everything but the beauty around them. Historians believe that the Jewish community on the island dates back to 500 B.C.E. Archaeological evidence shows that Carthaginians occupied this flat, fertile island in the Mediterranean Sea. Romans followed and named it Meninx. In 655 C.E. Arabs conquered the island, which they loosely ruled as part of the province of Ifriqiyya (present-day Tunisia and eastern Algeria).

The island became a center for the Kharijites, an Islamic sect popular among the many Berber inhabitants. By the eleventh century the Hafsid Dynasty ruled Jarbah from Tunis. The island's strategic location in the Mediterranean made it desirable to many different states. In 1284 the Spanish Aragones captured Jarbah; for the next four centuries control of

Jarbah would pass between Hafsid, Spanish, and Sicilian-Norman rule. As the Hafsid Empire waned in the sixteenth century, the struggle for control of the island revived between the Islamic and Christian forces. First the Muslim corsair Darghut took the island, but then the Spanish staged a brutal conquest in 1560, seizing the Mediterranean prize.

Only a few years later the Ottoman Empire took possession of Jarbah, initiating a rule that would last more than 300 years. Some 300 mosques still remain on the island; the Ottomans constructed most of them during this time. Residents on the island cultivated the olive and date orchards for which the island became famous. By the nineteenth century these agricultural pursuits had replaced corsair activity as the focus of the island's economy, supplemented by a fishing and artisan industry. When the French claimed Tunisia as a protectorate in 1881, they also took Jarbah. Since Tunisian independence in 1960, Jarbah has been a major tourist attraction, and the government of Tunisia has built large hotels and an international airport to cater to the European visitors who flock to the beaches. The ancient Jewish community on the island has maintained a continuous presence through centuries of different rule, and Jarbah is home to a sizable Jewish population.

North America

Jazz,

a twentieth-century African American music characterized by improvisation, a rhythmic conception termed swing, and the high value placed on each musician achieving a uniquely identifiable sound. Jazz musicians have consistently challenged musical boundaries and played leading roles in challenging racial discrimination.

Jazz is one of the crowning achievements of African American culture. It is a profoundly integrative genre, both musically and socially. Drawing on earlier traditions of New Orleans marching bands and ragtime-influenced society orchestras, jazz has continued to incorporate new musical influences, including the blues, gospel music, Latin American music, European art music, and rock 'n' roll. African Americans have accounted for every significant musical advance in jazz, but the music has been open to all, regardless of race or

Jazz trumpeter Papa Celestin plays for his young grandson on the front porch of his house in New Orleans, Louisiana. *CORBIS/Bradley Smith*

One of the greatest jazz vocalists of any era, Sarah Vaughn sings at a club in Los Angeles in 1950. *CORBIS/Joseph Schwartz Collection*

nationality. During the first half of the twentieth century—a time of pervasive racial discrimination in the United States—jazz was strikingly democratic. Although far from perfect, the jazz world was remarkably successful in challenging racial segregation.

Jazz also reflects a continuing tension between individual freedom and group structure, as seen in the shifting emphasis between the spontaneously improvising soloist, on the one hand, and composed and arranged ensemble music, on the other. Successive jazz styles—including New Orleans, swing, bop, cool, hard bop, free jazz, jazz-rock, and neo-traditionalism—have, to a considerable extent, reflected an increase in musical complexity, both in the playing of individual soloists and in the work of composers and arrangers. Jazz historians often liken the twentieth-century evolution of jazz to the changes that took place in European classical music—from eighteenth-century Bach inventions to Schönberg's 12-tone music of the twentieth century.

Widely credited as the architect of bop in the 1940s, trumpeter Dizzy Gillespie performs at the Monterery Jazz Festival in Monterey, California in the 1980s. *CORBIS/Craig Lovell*

Latin America and the Caribbean

Jazz, Afro-Latin,

a musical fusion of Latin American music and African American jazz that emerged in the 1940s, combining Latin American rhythms with jazz improvisation.

Afro-Latin jazz, as popular music writer Scott Yanow observed, "has been the most consistently popular" jazz style since the swing era of the 1930s. The new style emerged in the 1940s, in particular through the experiments of Cuban musicians in New York City. "Cuban musicians," as New York Times music critic Ben Ratliff noted in 1998, "are known for complexity of rhythm more than harmony." The Cuban and Puerto Rican musicians who created Afro-Latin jazz made use of the rhythmic variety of Latin American music while drawing on the improvisational and harmonic complexity of African American jazz.

The creation of Afro-Latin jazz involved several prior historical and musical developments. Above all, it reflected the cultural maturity of Spanish Harlem, New York City's Latin American community. Musically, it grew out of new ensembles and rhythms, mainly derived from Cuba or the United States. Afro-Latin jazz grew out of various ensembles—swing-era big bands in jazz, the rumba bands that appeared in Latin American music during the 1930s, and the Cuban *conjunto*, a medium-sized group that featured two trumpets in the front line. Directly linked with the evolution of Afro-Latin jazz were such rhythms as the mambo and, the clave beat.

North America

Jefferson, ("Blind") Lemon

(b. 1897, near Couchman, Tex.; d. 1930?, Chicago, Ill.), country bluesman who made some of the earliest blues recordings and profoundly influenced numerous subsequent blues musicians.

Blind Lemon Jefferson was born on a farm in Freestone County, Texas, where he spent his childhood. Although his mature songwriting suggests a familiarity with the visual world, Jefferson seems to have lost his sight at least by the time he was a teenager. Thereafter he devoted himself to music, a vocation that suffered little from his handicap.

Sometime around 1915 Jefferson moved to Dallas and began performing full-time in the Deep Ellum (Elm Street) neighborhood, mostly as a street musician. He commanded a broad vocal range and sometimes performed gospel songs in addition to the blues. The intricacy and staggered rhythms of his guitar accompaniments also showed his superior musical skill. A body of lore grew about Jefferson's life as a blind performer, including the claim that he could recognize the clink of pennies in his tin cup and reject them as inadequate payment. Despite his blindness, he lived a rambler's life, likely carrying a gun and bootlegging liquor. He kept company with Leadbelly (William "Huddie" Ledbetter), who also lived the rough life of his songs.

In 1925 Jefferson caught the attention of Sammy Price, a music store owner who recorded a demo for him and sent it to Paramount Records. Paramount invited Jefferson to Chicago in 1925 or 1926 and began to record his extensive repertoire of original and folk material. His first Paramount recordings were gospel songs, released under the pseudonym Deacon L. J. Bates, but soon Jefferson was a premier name in secular race records.

Jefferson created a niche for male blues artists in an industry hitherto dominated by female performers such as Ma Rainey, Ida Cox, and Bessie Smith. Although he recorded only from 1926 to his death in 1929, he cut approximately a hundred sides and left a legacy of songs that later became standards of folk and blues, including "That Black Snake Moan" (1926), "See That My Grave Is Kept Clean" (1928), "Corrina Blues" (1926), and "Match Box Blues" (1927).

The Blues Foundation Hall of Fame inducted Jefferson in 1980. His music has influenced generations of performers, including Sonny Terry, Muddy Waters, Joe Turner, T-Bone Walker, and Josh White. Even the music of performers outside the blues genre, from Bob Dylan's to Louis Armstrong's, has reflected the influence of Jefferson's singing style and repertoire.

North America

Jemison, Mae Carol

(b. October 17, 1956, Decatur, Ala.), African American astronaut, physician, and professor and the first African American woman to enter space.

Jemison joined the Peace Corps in January 1983 and worked as a medical officer in West Africa through July 1985. In 1987 she was accepted by NASA as an astronaut candidate, one of 15 who were accepted from among 2000 applicants. She completed a one-year training and evaluation program in August 1988 and became a science mission specialist, helping prepare the space shuttles for launch. She was the first black female astronaut to enter space, aboard the space shuttle *Endeavor* in September 1992. Retiring after six years with NASA, she started her own research, development, and constancy company, the Jemison Group, Inc., whose projects include ALAFIYA, a satellite-based telecommunications system to improve health care delivery in West Africa, and The Earth We Share, an international science camp for young teenagers.

The Mae C. Jemison Academy in Detroit, Michigan, teaches science and math to children in preschool through second grade. Jemison is also a professor in the Environmental Studies Program at Dartmouth College, where she heads the Jemison Institute for Advancing Technology in Developing Countries.

Jesus, Carolina Maria de

(b. 1914, Sacramento, Minas Gerais, Brazil; d. February 13, 1977, Parelheiros, São Paulo, Brazil), Afro-Brazilian writer, the first black woman from the *favelas*, or squatter settlements, to write about the everyday struggles of the Brazilian poor.

In 1960 the diary of Carolina Maria de Jesus, an impoverished black woman, was published in Brazil, an event that brought her national and international celebrity. Titled *Quarto de Despejo* (Child of the Dark), the diary sold 90,000 copies within the first six months, making it the most successful book in the history of Brazilian publishing. It was translated into more than a dozen languages and attracted worldwide attention. The book also brought Jesus financial success, allowing her to move out of the *favelas*.

Her subsequent writings, including a second diary, *Casa de Alvenaria* (1961, I'm Going to Have a Little House), were not successful, and she soon drifted into obscurity. As scholar Robert M. Levine has said, "Ill-prepared for her meteoric rise to fame after her diary was published, Carolina Maria de Jesus went from being a woman reviled for her blackness, her illegitimacy, and her poverty to a woman mocked for her supposed ingratitude and lack of docility."

Jesus, Clementina de

(b. July 7, 1902, Valença, Rio de Janeiro, Brazil; d. 1987, Rio de Janeiro, Brazil), an Afro-Brazilian singer with a low-pitched, raspy voice and deep knowledge of obscure Afro-Brazilian genres such as *jongo*, *lundu*, and *samba partido alto*.

As an adolescent, Clementina de Jesus sang in the choir of the local church in the Oswaldo Cruz neighborhood and later participated in the Portela samba school. In 1940 she married and moved to Mangueira, home to a rival samba school. For the next 20 years she worked as a maid and sang only for family and friends. In 1964 the composer and impresario Hermínio Bello de Carvalho invited her to perform with the classical guitarist Turíbio Santos. Her professional debut coincided with an emerging interest in roots music among left-wing artists and intellectuals. In the following year she participated in the highly acclaimed musical showcase *Rosa de Ouro*, which was later released on two albums.

In 1966 she represented Brazil in the First Festival of Black Arts in Dakar, Senegal. In 1968 she recorded the album *Gente da Antiga* with two early innovators of samba, Pixinguinha and João da Baiana. Two years later she finally recorded her first solo LP, *Clementina, cadê você?*, which was followed by *Clementina de Jesus-Marinheiro só*. In the Carnival of 1988, the Vila Isabel samba school commemorated the centennial year of abolition and paid homage to Clementina de Jesus in their winning theme song, "Kizomba, Festa da Raça."

Jews, Black,

groups that combine Black Nationalist and Pan-Africanist ideology with Jewish principles and symbols.

Black Jewish organizations are not affiliated with the African Americans who either converted to Judaism or were born Jewish, and although they often identify with Falasha, a group of Ethiopian Jews, they are a separate phenomenon. Also known as Black Hebrews, Black Jews refer to a range of often-militant religious groups who, through combining the philosophies of Black Nationalism and Pan-Africanism with idiosyncratic interpretations of Judaic history and teachings, identify themselves as God's chosen people.

Messianism figures prominently in their ideology; members often follow a charismatic leader who claims divine inspiration and promises eventual redemption from the material and spiritual poverty of the United States. Motifs of freedom from bondage and slavery recur, and the plight of African Americans is paralleled with the biblical story of Exodus. They proclaim that African Americans were actually Hebrews before they were enslaved and robbed of their identities. Influenced by the calls for repatriation by Marcus Garvey and other black nationalists, many Black Jews proclaimed— and often attempted—a return to homelands in Israel, Ethiopia, or other parts of Africa.

At this time the exact number of Black Jewish organizations in the United States is unknown. It seems certain, however, that as long as social and economic conditions keep African Americans disfranchised, such groups will continue to thrive.

Jim Crow,

the system of laws and customs that enforced racial segregation and discrimination throughout the United States, especially the South, from the late nineteenth century to the 1960s.

African Americans living in the South during the first half of the twentieth century saw graphic reminders of their second-class citizenship everywhere. Signs reading "Whites Only" or "Colored" hung over drinking fountains and the doors to restrooms, restaurants, movie theaters, and other public places. Along with segregation, blacks, particularly in the South, faced discrimination in jobs and housing and were often denied their constitutional right to vote. Whether by law or by custom, all these obstacles to equal status went by the name Jim Crow.

Jim Crow was the name of a character in minstrelsy (in which white performers in blackface used African American stereotypes in their songs and dances); it is not clear how the term came to describe American segregation and discrimination. Jim Crow has its origins in a variety of sources, including the Black Codes imposed upon African Americans immediately after the Civil War and prewar racial segregation of railroad cars in the North. But it was not until after Radical Reconstruction ended in 1877 that Jim Crow was born.

Jim Crow grew slowly. In the last two decades of the nineteenth century many African Americans still enjoyed the rights granted in the Thirteenth, Fourteenth, and Fifteenth amendments, along with the 1875 Civil Rights Act. But according to historian C. Vann Woodward, by the late 1890s various factors had combined to create an environment in which white supremacy prevailed. These included the reconciliation of warring political factions in the South, the acquiescence of Northern white liberals, and the United States' military conquest of nonwhite peoples in the Philippines, Hawaii, and Cuba.

Disfranchisement was often defended by invoking the mythology of Reconstruction, in which Southern whites claimed that unsophisticated black voters had been manipulated by Northern "carpetbaggers" who had moved south after the war. Jim Crow proponents also found ammunition in the incendiary propaganda of the Southern white press, which published sensational and exaggerated accounts of crimes committed by African Americans. As Woodward and other historians have pointed out, an atmosphere emerged of racist hysteria, which further fueled lynching, anti-black rioting, and the rise of the Ku Klux Klan.

Under Jim Crow etiquette, African Americans were denied all social forms of respect. Whites addressed even adult black men as "boy," and all blacks were expected to show deference to all whites. The combination of constant personal humiliation, dismal economic opportunities (sharecropping consigned most rural, Southern blacks to perpetual poverty), and inferior segregated education for their children prompted thousands of African Americans to leave the South in the Jim Crow era. Waves of exodus culminated in the Great Migration north in the 1920s, 1930s, and 1940s, but many African Americans found conditions in the North little better.

A combination of factors led to the dismantling of Jim Crow starting in the late 1940s. Attention attracted by Gunnar Myrdal's 1944 book *An American Dilemma* made Jim Crow a national embarrassment. After more than a decade of litigation, the legal work of the National Association for the Advancement of Colored People (NACCP) began to bear fruit. Supreme Court decisions in *Sweatt v. Painter* (1949) and *McLaurin v. Oklahoma* (1950) started to break down the separate but equal standard set by *Plessy* and finally outlawed state-sponsored segregation in

1954's *Brown v. Board of Education*. Violent resistance by some white Southerners was met by a growing Civil Rights Movement that used boycotts, sit-ins, marches, and other forms of nonviolent protest to achieve goals such as passage of the 1964 Civil Rights Act and 1965 Voting Rights Act. But despite victories against segregation and discrimination, African Americans continued to face unequal opportunities, and new approaches, such as the Black Power Movement, sought to repair the lasting damage of Jim Crow.

North America

Johnson, James Weldon

(b. June 17, 1871, Jacksonville, Fla.; d. June 26, 1938, Wiscasset, Maine), diplomat, poet, novelist, critic, composer, and the first African American executive secretary of the National Association for the Advancement of Colored People (NAACP).

Few leaders have combined such keen intelligence with such varied talents as did James Weldon Johnson. A leading literary and political figure, Johnson was instrumental not only in the growth of the NAACP but also in the formation and nurturing of a distinctly African American artistic community. Poetry, song lyrics, fiction, history, and editorials flowed from his pen and made him one of the great men of African American letters.

Born in Jacksonville, Florida, in 1871, Johnson grew up in a cultured household. His mother, a schoolteacher, had been born free in Nassau, Bahamas, and had spent much of her childhood in New York City. His father worked as headwaiter at a Jacksonville resort restaurant but still found time to read Plutarch; he was a self-educated man who spoke and read Spanish and enjoyed philosophical discussions.

Johnson's brother John Rosamond Johnson, who had received formal musical training in Boston, convinced Johnson to collaborate with him in writing songs. In 1900 the two wrote "Lift Ev'ry Voice and Sing," the song that became known as the Negro national anthem. Two years later Johnson accompanied Rosamond to New York, where the brothers, along with Robert Cole, became a successful songwriting team. While there Johnson studied literature at Columbia University and met other African American artists such as Paul Laurence Dunbar and Will Marion Cook. In 1904 friends from Atlanta University invited Johnson to join the Colored Republican Club in New York, where his work for presidential candidate Theodore Roosevelt earned him a consulate post; he left for Puerto Cabello, Venezuela, in 1906.

Johnson's career as a diplomat lasted eight years, during which he served in both Venezuela and Nicaragua. With his excellent Spanish and elegant social manner, he became a popular figure in the racially diverse Latin

American cities to which he was sent. Meanwhile, he continued to pursue literary work, beginning a novel that would eventually be titled *Autobiography of an Ex-Coloured Man* (published anonymously in 1912). When the Democrats regained the White House in 1914, Johnson resigned his consular duties, returned to New York, and turned his attention to literature.

He became a contributing editor at the *New York Age*, an African American weekly, writing sharp essays against racist violence, Jim Crow segregation, and the unequal treatment of blacks in the military. He also established a poetry section to showcase black literary talent.

Impressed with the multitalented young editor, the NAACP's Joel Spingarn and W. E. B. Du Bois asked Johnson to work with them. In 1916 he became the association's first field secretary, responsible for the formation of new branch offices throughout the country. While traveling in the South, Johnson recruited a young Atlantan, Walter White, who became one of the association's most important leaders. He also researched the lynchings and other racist violence that were beginning to increase in the years leading up to the Red Summer of 1919.

In 1920 Johnson became NAACP secretary, the chief executive position within the association. His ten years in office were a decade of intense legal and organizational activity for the NAACP; for Johnson himself it also heralded a period of prodigious literary output. He edited three anthologies in the 1920s: *The Book of Negro American Poetry* (1922), *The Book of Negro American Spirituals* (1925), and *The Second Book of Negro American Spirituals* (1926). In addition, he published a second collection of poetry, *God's Trombones* (1927), and oversaw the republication, this time under his own name, of *Autobiography of an Ex-Coloured Man* (1927). After retiring from the NAACP in 1930, he published a work of social history, *Black Manhattan* (1930); a memoir, *Along This Way* (1933); and a collection of essays, *Black America, What Now?* (1934).

North America

Johnson, John Arthur (Jack)

(b. March 31, 1878, Galveston, Tex.; d. June 10, 1946, Raleigh, N.C.), first African American heavyweight boxing champion and controversial symbol of racial tensions in early twentieth-century America. Jack Johnson's athletic prowess and flamboyant lifestyle challenged codes of white supremacy and racial segregation in the boxing ring and in American society at large.

Born John Arthur Johnson, Jack Johnson was the son of Tina and Henry Johnson, a porter and school janitor. He became interested in boxing while working as a janitor at a local gymnasium.

Training and fighting locally, he quickly established a reputation as the best African American boxer in Galveston. He turned professional in 1897.

In 113 fights over the next 35 years, he lost only 8. Though physically imposing and capable of unleashing a decisive knockout blow, Johnson was known for his defensive ingenuity and a compact, efficient style. He is still considered one of the great counterpunchers of all time.

A 1903 victory over "Denver Ed" Martin established Johnson as the unofficial black heavyweight champion. It was Johnson's desire, however, to prove himself against the very best competition, regardless of color. He was especially intent on undermining the reigning stereotype of African American fighters as being unable to take a punch. The leading white heavyweights, John L. Sullivan and Jim Jeffries, refused to fight Johnson, claiming that to do so would sully the sport's reputation.

Though Johnson was unable to gain a match against a white fighter in the United States, his reputation in international boxing circles mounted. On December 26, 1908, finally given the opportunity to compete for the heavyweight championship in a fight in Sydney, Australia, Johnson dethroned the reigning champion, Tommy Burns.

Johnson defended his championship against five white fighters over the next two years. Responding to the call of legions of fans anxious to restore boxing's traditional racial hierarchy, Jim Jeffries came out of retirement to challenge the African American champion.

Billed as "the Great White Hope," Jeffries fought Johnson in "the fight of the century" on July 4, 1910, in Reno, Nevada. Johnson soundly beat Jeffries. A series of race riots ensued around the country, sparked by angry whites fearful that millions of African Americans emboldened by Johnson's victory would strike out against their own subordinate status in American society.

Johnson was despised not simply for beating his white opponents, but for doing so in a manner that boldly defied white expectations of black docility and deference. He taunted, sneered, and even laughed at his opponents in the ring. In an era in which many prizefights took place in outdoor arenas, he took particular delight in having his gold front tooth gleam in the sun as he stood smiling triumphantly over a vanquished opponent. Writer Jack London spoke for many white fans when he urged Jim Jeffries to "wipe that smile off of Jack Johnson's face."

Johnson's personal life, in particular his penchant for highly publicized romantic attachments to white women, also was a flagrant violation of traditional racial norms. He married Etta Terry Duryea, a white woman, in 1911. After her suicide a year later, he married another white woman, Lucille Cameron.

In 1913 Johnson was convicted of violating the Mann Act, which forbade transporting women across state lines for immoral purposes. As a matter of course, Johnson had traveled with Duryea and Cameron across state lines; the mere fact that he had married these white women was deemed immoral. He fled the United States for France to avoid serving a prison term.

Johnson supported himself during his exile in France by conducting boxing and wrestling exhibitions. He returned to competitive boxing in

Havana, Cuba, in April 1915, losing his heavyweight title to Jess Willard. After serving a year in prison on his return to the United States in 1920, Johnson spent the rest of his life writing, appearing in boxing exhibitions, and managing a series of business enterprises.

North America

Johnson Products,
first black-owned firm to trade on the American Stock Exchange.

In 1954 the 27-year-old George E. Johnson, then a laboratory worker in a cosmetics factory, perfected a mild lye and petroleum-based hair relaxer, or straightener, for African Americans. Johnson borrowed $250 as a "vacation" loan, with which he and his wife, Joan, founded Johnson Products. They began by manufacturing and selling Ultra Wave Hair Culture for men. Johnson traveled throughout the United States to sell Ultra Wave to professional salons and hairdressers. Joan Johnson was responsible for finances and bookkeeping. Encouraged by Ultra Wave's success, Johnson Products introduced Ultra Sheen Hair products for women and sold them to haircare professionals.

By 1960 the Johnsons were confident enough to sell their products in the retail market, and within five years the company was grossing $2 million in sales annually, despite competition from less expensive brands. After the company introduced Ultra Sheen no-base cream relaxer in 1965, sales increased again, and in 1969 Johnson sold its first stock offering, of $10.2 million. In 1971 it became the first black-owned firm listed on the American Stock Exchange.

Johnson Products grossed $37.2 million in sales annually by 1975, and the company controlled 85 percent of the professional haircare market by 1975. It promoted black businesses by using black models and minority-owned advertising agencies, advertising in such publications as *Essence* and sponsoring the nationally syndicated television show *Soul Train*.

North America

Johnson Publishing Company,
the second largest black-owned company in the United States and the world's largest black-owned publisher.

The Johnson Publishing Company of Chicago, a family-owned conglomerate of media outlets and beauty products, was founded in 1945 by John H. Johnson (b. January 19, 1918, Arkansas City, Mississippi). While working for Supreme Liberty Life Insurance Company in the early 1940s, Johnson collected and prepared a digest of news affecting the African

American community for distribution among the company's upper managers. Realizing that this news digest could be marketed to African Americans, who were largely ignored by the mainstream press, he used his mother's furniture as collateral to borrow $500, with which he published the first issue of what would be called *Negro Digest*.

Similar in form to *Reader's Digest*, *Negro Digest* initially reprinted articles from other periodicals. Soon the magazine began publishing original articles and essays, notably in October 1943, with a piece written by First Lady Eleanor Roosevelt that was composed especially for *Negro Digest*. That issue doubled the magazine's usual circulation of 50,000.

The success of *Negro Digest* led Johnson to launch *Ebony* in 1945. It was modeled on the glossy picture magazine *Life* and sold well, growing steadily in circulation. *Ebony* went on to become the keystone of the Johnson Publishing Company and a familiar sight on coffee tables in African American homes nationwide; its circulation reached 2 million by 1996.

Negro Digest remained popular but its circulation stalled, hovering around 60,000. Its popularity lagged far behind that of *Ebony*. Johnson discontinued it in 1951. In its place, Johnson launched *Jet*, a pocket-size (5"x 4") weekly that offered society, entertainment, political, and sports reporting oriented to African American readers. *Jet* was an immediate success. After six issues, its circulation topped 300,000, and by 1997 *Jet*'s market covered more than 40 countries, and its weekly circulation surpassed a million.

Johnson, Robert Leroy

(b. May 8, 1911, Hazelhurst, Miss.; d. August 16, 1938, Greenwood, Miss.), African American country blues musician and Mississippi Delta legend.

The most influential bluesman in the music's history, Robert Johnson nonetheless remains an obscure figure, despite the efforts of numerous researchers to unearth more than a brief sketch of his life. Indeed, his photograph surfaced for the first time only in the late 1980s.

Johnson grew up in several different towns in the Delta and turned to music for self-expression. Charley Patton was an early influence on him, as was Son House, with whom he played as a supporting musician. Johnson became an itinerant musician after the manner of his heroes. He married at least twice and one of his wives later died in childbirth. It is presumed that like most Delta musicians, Johnson had a hard life; but his music was darker than most, with recurring references to the devil and double-dealing women.

The culmination of Johnson's career, and the basis for his posthumous reputation, were the recording sessions he did for Columbia in 1936 and

1937. He is considered to have produced one of the most important documents in American musical history. Alone with an acoustic guitar, Johnson set down a body of music characterized by richly textured lyrics and emotive guitar playing. One of his records, "Terraplane Blues," achieved modest local success, but most of the recordings were forgotten until the 1960s blues revival.

Part of the legend of Robert Johnson stems from his early death in 1938. Under mysterious circumstances, he died after playing a jook joint outside Greenwood, Mississippi. Some stories say that he was poisoned with bad whiskey, perhaps because of his penchant for married women, while others say that he was cursed by black magic and spent his final hours barking like a dog.

A lengthy catalogue of myths and rumors persists about Johnson, particularly regarding his dabblings in the supernatural. Perhaps the most famous story claims that he learned to play guitar in a deal with the devil consummated in a late-night transaction at a crossroads outside Clarksdale, Mississippi. "Crossroads" is one of Johnson's most harrowing songs, and the events it recounts have permeated the folklore of rock and roll.

North America

Jones, James Earl

(b. January 17, 1931, Arkabutla, Mississippi), African American stage, film, and television actor whose resonant bass voice is instantly recognizable.

In a long and successful career James Earl Jones has portrayed a wide range of characters in stage productions, motion pictures, and television. His beginnings were far from auspicious. Not long after his birth, his actor father Robert Earl Jones abandoned the family. Young James was adopted and raised by his maternal grandparents.

Jones's deep, resonant voice has reached countless millions of people, in particular as Darth Vader in the original *Star Wars* trilogy (1977, 1980, 1983), as father lion Mustafa in *The Lion King* (1994), and as the official voice of the telephone company Bell Atlantic. During the 1960s he had a long association with Joseph Papp's New York Shakespeare Festival. Jones also gained prominence as part of an all-black production of Jean Genet's *The Blacks*. Over the years he tackled a wide range of Shakespearean roles, including Othello, King Lear, and Oberon in *A Midsummer Night's Dream*. In 1960 he won his first leading role, in Lionel Abel's *The Pretender*.

Jones found success in motion pictures as well as on stage. In 1966 he played the fictional boxer Jack Jefferson, who is closely modeled on Jack Johnson, in Howard Sackler's *The Great White Hope*. In 1968 the play moved to Broadway, and a year later Jones's portrayal earned him a Tony Award. Reprising the role in the 1970 movie version, Jones was nominated for an Academy Award as Best Actor and won a Golden Globe for best new

Actor James Earl Jones, portraying singer and activist Paul Robeson in a one-man play, stands with a bust of Robeson. *CORBIS/Hulton-Deutsch Collection*

male talent. In 1966 he made his television debut in the daytime drama *As the World Turns*. During the 1970s he pursued a busy schedule of film and stage acting with occasional television appearances.

During 1985–1987 he won critical praise and a second Tony Award for his lead role in August Wilson's drama *Fences*. On television, he portrayed Alex Haley in: *The Roots Next Generations* (1979), the sequel to the 1977 miniseries *Roots*. Jones also appeared in such memorable films as John Sayles's *Matewan* (1987), Phil Alden Robinson's *Field of Dreams* (1989), and Darrel James Roodt's *Cry the Beloved Country* (1995).

North America

Jones, Quincy Delight, Jr.

(b. March 14, 1933, Chicago, Ill.), African American arranger, composer, and entertainment industry executive who has worked in music, film, and television.

Quincy Jones has had several careers in popular entertainment, including roles as a big-band musician, composer-arranger, record company executive, producer of films and music videos, and partner in a television production company. He has emerged as one of the most influential figures in Hollywood. As a teenager Jones played in local jazz and rhythm and blues (R&B) groups. He became acquainted with Ray Charles, an early musical influence, who moved to the Seattle area in 1950. Besides leading his own trio,

Charles wrote and arranged for the five-member R&B vocal group in which Jones sang. Before he was 16, Jones had written his first suite, *From the Four Winds*, which later earned him a scholarship to Seattle University.

Jones also found work in the big bands of Jay McShann (1949) and Lionel Hampton (1951–1953). While with Hampton, Jones played in a trumpet section that featured two superb jazz stylists, Clifford Brown and Art Farmer. Jones made his mark not by his playing but through his skilled arrangements. After leaving Hampton, he freelanced as an arranger and with his own big band led various recording dates, most memorably the sessions that produced *This Is How I Feel about Jazz* (1956). He provided arrangements for Count Basie, Billy Eckstine, Sarah Vaughan, Ella Fitzgerald, Dinah Washington, Tommy Dorsey, and others. In 1956 Jones helped organize and wrote many of the arrangements for a new big band for Dizzy Gillespie, touring Africa, Asia, and the Middle East under the auspices of the United States State Department—the first time a jazz group was chosen for such cultural diplomacy.

In the 1960s Jones moved to Los Angeles, California, and soon became one of the most successful composers and arrangers in the film industry. He followed in the footsteps of Benny Carter, the alto saxophonist, composer, and arranger who played a key role in challenging the color barrier in Hollywood during the 1940s and 1950s. According to Jones's biographer Raymond Horricks, white composer Henry Mancini aided Jones in his move into film music. Jones provided scores for many films, including *The Pawnbroker* (1965), *In the Heat of the Night* (1967), *The New Centurions* (1972), and *The Wiz* (1978). He arranged and wrote music for numerous television programs of the 1970s, including *The Bill Cosby Show*, *Ironside*, *Sanford and Son*, and the miniseries *Roots*.

During these years, Jones further extended his role in the entertainment industry. In 1980 he established his own record label, Qwest. Later in the decade he expanded into movie producing. In addition to composing the film score, Jones served as one of the co-producers for the 1985 movie version of Alice Walker's novel *The Color Purple*. He also showed his ability to master popular musical styles and media, as in the hit albums and music videos that resulted from collaborations with Michael Jackson, including *Off the Wall* (1979), *Thriller* (1982), and *Bad* (1987).

Jones became a highly visible figure in American popular culture. In the mid-1980s he was one of the driving forces behind USA for Africa, producing the *We Are the World* (1985) album and video. In the 1990s his production company developed a number of television programs, including the hit series *Fresh Prince of Bel Air*, which debuted in 1990. Jones received his first Grammy Award from the National Academy of Recording Arts and Sciences (NARAS) in 1963, and by the mid-1990s he had received nearly two dozen Grammys, making him the most honored musician in the award's history. In 1997 he produced the televised Motion Picture Academy Awards ceremony.

Joplin, Scott

(b. November 24, 1868, rural eastern Texas; d. April 1, 1917, New York, N.Y.),
African American composer and pianist properly known as the "King of
Ragtime Writers."

Scott Joplin led the black musicians who, at the turn of the twentieth century, melded African American folk music with classical and Romantic
European traditions to form ragtime, a march-based yet heavily syncopated
style of popular music. His compositions fueled the ragtime craze that led
thousands of middle-class whites to buy pianos, collect sheet music, and
enjoy, for the first time, the pulse of black vernacular culture. While Joplin's
energetic rags created a sensation in middle-class parlors, he also wrote more
conventional classical music. He composed waltzes, tangos, operas, and
ballet yet, due to his tremendous success as a sheet-music scribe—and due
to his race—he died with a reputation far smaller than the body of his work
deserved.

In 1893 Joplin emerged as a well-practiced musician at the World's
Columbian Exposition in Chicago, Illinois, where he probably played along
the Midway Plaisance. Although white management excluded African
Americans from the official program of concerts, black pianists entertained
fairgoers along the exposition's bustling periphery. These Midway performances afforded a rare opportunity for middle-class whites to experience
the lively music of African Americans. Although the ragtime craze was a
few years away, the 1893 exposition—and fairs like it—sowed the seeds.
While Joplin may have contributed some of the unofficial entertainment, he
also listened to it, absorbing the influences of such great performers as
"Plunk" Henry Johnson and Johnny Seymour.

At the same time Joplin met lifelong friend Otis Saunders, with whom
he spent the next two years traveling the Midwest in a quartet that played
many of Joplin's early compositions. By 1895 the two men were convinced
that Joplin had composed songs that the public would buy. Joplin and Saunders settled in Sedalia, Missouri. Joplin sold "Maple Leaf Rag" to white
Sedalia businessman John Stark. "Maple Leaf Rag" was an instant hit, selling
all of its 10,000-copy run and, by 1909, more than 500,000 copies. After
the success of "Maple Leaf Rag," Stark moved his business to St. Louis, and
Joplin, who had signed a contract with him, soon followed. Ironically the
success of "Maple Leaf Rag" crippled the music scene from which it was
born, as a number of influential Sedalia musicians followed Joplin to the city.

While Joplin's music deserved the enthusiasm it inspired, Stark's business savvy contributed significantly to the Joplin craze. Long before Joplin
was well known, or even very prolific, Stark dubbed him the "King of
Ragtime Writers." In the first years of the new century Joplin published
numerous rags with Stark, including "Peacherine Rag" (1901) and "The
Entertainer" (1902). Joplin also embarked on more ambitious ventures, such
as a folk ballet, *The Ragtime Dance* (1902), and his first opera, *A Guest of*

Honor (1903), the text of which does not survive. Although these works demonstrated Joplin's growing maturity as a musician, they were rarely performed. Even Stark, whose money-making priorities often slackened for Joplin, dragged his heels when it came to publishing more complex music.

In 1911 he began work on another opera, *Treemonisha*. Joplin set *Treemonisha* in rural Arkansas during Reconstruction. Its moralistic plot contrasts the evil of ignorance with the hope of education, indicting the rural superstition that Joplin remembered from his childhood. *Treemonisha* contains some of Joplin's most beautiful music, but he never did see its full production. In 1913 a theater that had promised to stage *Treemonisha* backed out on him, and in 1915 he produced the show himself without costumes, sets, or even an orchestra in the Lincoln Theater in Harlem.

In 1950, however, scholars Rudi Blesh and Harriet Janis revived public interest in Joplin with their book *They All Played Ragtime: The True Story of an American Music*. In addition, pianist Joshua Rifkin made recordings of Joplin's rags that were released in 1970, introducing many people to the music. In 1973 the Hollywood blockbuster *The Sting* featured Joplin's music on its soundtrack, launching "The Entertainer" into frequent radio play. At the same time, interest in his later work grew, and in the 1970s three different productions of *Treemonisha* were staged. In 1976 Joplin was awarded a posthumous Pulitzer Prize.

North America

Jordan, Michael Jeffrey

(b. February 17, 1963, Brooklyn, N.Y.), African American professional basket-ball player considered by many to be the best all-around player in the history of the sport.

Combining explosive athletic talent and a magnetic personality, Michael Jordan has achieved global popularity reminiscent of Muhammad Ali. After attending a summer all-star camp that showcased the nation's best high school players, Jordan was courted by numerous college coaches. He and his family chose the University of North Carolina (UNC) at Chapel Hill. In 1984 Jordan decided to forgo his senior season at UNC in order to enter the NBA draft, where he was selected as the third pick by the then-troubled Chicago Bulls. Before joining the Bulls, Jordan led the United States Olympic team to the Gold Medal in the 1984 Summer Games in Los Angeles. In his first professional season, the Bulls' record improved by 11 games and their attendance increased by 87 percent. Chosen as a starter in the midseason All-Star game, Jordan led the league in points scored with 2313 and was chosen as the NBA's Rookie of the Year.

Following his rookie season Jordan signed a contract with the Nike shoe company to create the Air Jordan sneaker. The Air Jordan sneaker became a huge popular success, fueled in part by an entertaining advertising campaign featuring Jordan and director Spike Lee. With his good looks and unassuming, natural charisma, Jordan became a highly marketable personality. He has since represented numerous companies and appeared in the feature film *Space Jam* (1996), achieving iconic status in international popular culture.

He led the league in scoring (an average of 37.1 points per game) and amassed a total of 3041 points, becoming only the second NBA player ever to score more than 3000 points in a single season. Jordan went on to win seven consecutive scoring titles, repeatedly capturing All-NBA and All-Defensive Team awards and winning the Most Valuable Player award in 1988, 1991, and 1992. He silenced critics who assailed his supposed "one-man show" style by leading the Bulls to three consecutive championships in 1991, 1992, and 1993. Jordan also played on the U.S. Olympic "Dream Team" that won the Gold Medal in Barcelona, Spain, in 1992.

Despite almost single-handedly filling the NBA void left by the retirement of marquee players Larry Bird and Earvin "Magic" Johnson, Jordan announced his retirement from basketball. Embarking on a childhood dream, Jordan signed with the Chicago White Sox to play minor league baseball. After 127 games and a .202 batting average, he returned to the Bulls with 17 games remaining in the 1995 season. He led the Bulls to the best record in NBA history, 72-10, and to another championship. In 1996 he won MVP honors in the All-Star game, in the Finals, and for the regular season, becoming the first player to garner all three awards since Willis Reed in 1970. Michael Jordan retired from basketball and the Chicago Bulls in February 1999.

North America

Jordan, Vernon Eulion, Jr.

(b. August 15, 1935, Atlanta, Ga.), African American lawyer, business executive, former president of the National Urban League and United Negro College Fund, and adviser to President Bill Clinton.

One of the most powerful, well-connected lawyers in the United States, Vernon Jordan has had a long, sometimes contradictory career. Few civil rights spokespeople of his generation have attained the kind of corporate and political influence Jordan has, an achievement enhanced by his position as a top adviser to and close friend of President Bill Clinton. Yet some critics have charged that the former National Association for the Advancement of Colored People (NAACP) field secretary and Urban League president has lost touch with his original goal: to improve the economic lives of African Americans.

Jordan's early days as a lawyer in Atlanta were devoted to the cause of civil rights. While working as a law clerk for a local black attorney, Jordan helped organize the integration of the University of Georgia, personally escorting student Charlayne Hunter (now journalist Charlayne Hunter-

Gault) past a hostile white crowd. In the following decade Jordan served as Georgia field secretary for the NAACP, director of the Voter Education Project for the Southern Regional Council, head of the United Negro College Fund, and a delegate to President Lyndon B. Johnson's White House Conference on Civil Rights.

Always more identified with mainstream groups within the Civil Rights Movement, in 1971 Jordan was named head of the National Urban League, one of the more conservative, established African American organizations. Under his leadership, the Urban League flourished. Jordan's experience in fundraising and with the business community helped him attract corporate sponsors, which allowed the organization to more than triple its budget and hire many more employees. At the same time Jordan joined the boards of many of the country's biggest corporations—including Xerox, American Express, and Dow Jones—where he was able to influence hiring policies and push for more jobs for blacks and women.

In 1981, following his recuperation from a May 29, 1980, shooting by a white supremacist, Jordan resigned from the Urban League to take a job with the Washington, D.C., office of Akin, Gump, Strauss, Hauer and Feld, an influential law and lobbying firm based in Dallas, Texas. This job, in addition to his membership in the corporate elite, and his long-standing friendship with President Bill Clinton, made Jordan one of Washington's most important power brokers. He has played a role in influencing the president's positions on foreign trade, budgetary issues, and affirmative action, as well as key decisions on personnel.

North America

Joyner-Kersee, Jacqueline

(b. March 3, 1962, East St. Louis, Ill.), African American heptathlete, one of the most successful track and field athletes of the twentieth century.

Jackie Joyner-Kersee was a starting forward on the UCLA basketball team as well as a long jumper for the track team. She was spotted by Bob Kersee, an assistant track coach, who encouraged her to pursue track and field more fully. She qualified for the 1983 world track and field championships in the heptathlon, a two-day competition in which athletes compile points in the 100-meter hurdles, high jump, shot put, and 200-meter dash on the first day, and the long jump, javelin, and 800-meter run on the second day. A pulled hamstring kept Joyner-Kersee from finishing the 1983 championships. The following year she qualified for the United States Olympic team and at the Los Angeles Olympic Games won the Silver Medal in the heptathlon. She missed the Gold Medal by only hundredths of a second in the final event, the 800-meter run.

In 1985 she set a U.S. record in the long jump with a leap of 23 feet, 9 inches. The following year she married Bob Kersee, who continued to coach her after she graduated from UCLA. At the 1986 Goodwill Games in Moscow, Joyner-Kersee set a new world record in the heptathlon, scoring 7148 points—200 more than the previous world record. She broke her own record less than a month later, in sweltering heat in Houston, with a score of 7161. At future meets often her only competition was her own record. In late 1986 she won the Sullivan Memorial Trophy, which is awarded to America's best amateur athlete. Her reputation for modesty and graciousness won her widespread popularity, and her popularity in turn made the heptathlon, previously little recognized in America, a widely watched track and field event.

Africa

Juju,

a musical genre originating among Nigerian pop musicians emphasizing speechlike layers of polyrhythmic drumming, a broad range of rhythmic and coloristic guitar patterns, and lyrics underscoring traditional Yoruba social values.

Juju music is an internationally popular musical expression growing out of a tradition of West African guitar-based popular music. The meaning of the term *juju* is unknown, though some historians have linked it to the sounds created by a tambourine. It emerged in the 1930s in southwestern Nigeria, where local Yoruba musicians began casually making music in bars (palm-wine shacks) with transient laborers and descendants of freed slaves from the Caribbean and South America. The musicians played guitars and banjos, sometimes supplemented by hand-held percussion instruments. Although early lyrics often drew on Yoruba folk sayings, *juju* songs later came to express thinly veiled anticolonial sentiments.

Kaabu, Early Kingdom of,
a historical kingdom centered in northeastern Guinea-Bissau.

Founded by Tiramakhan Traoré, a general of the Mali Empire, the Mandinka kingdom of Kaabu ruled the area that is presently known as northeastern Guinea-Bissau and southeastern Senegal from 1250 to 1867. For six centuries Kaabu dominated small chiefdoms throughout the region and enslaved their inhabitants. Initially the kingdom remained a dependency of Mali. Kaabu expanded slowly; many groups fled to the coastal lowlands, while others resisted Mandinka dominance. The kingdom was an important source of salt, gold, and slaves for Mali. It was socially stratified, with royal succession by matrilineal descent. In the late fifteenth and early sixteenth centuries Songhai assaults on Mali enabled Kaabu to assert its independence. At the same time Portuguese and other European slave traders demanded an increasing volume of slaves for the transatlantic trade. Kaabu expanded considerably through warfare that was intended to capture slaves for export. At its height the Kaabu Kingdom included 44 provinces that were providing troops and tribute.

When Portugal outlawed the slave trade in 1837, competition in the illicit slave trade increased. Kaabu provincial governors competed internally in intradynastic feuds that weakened the kingdom. The Islamic Fulani people, subject to heavy Kaabu taxation for generations, began to subvert the weakened kingdom through religious conversion and holy wars. Wars between Kaabu and the Fulani reached their apex in 1867 at the Kaabu capital, Kansala, when the Fulani Muslim religious leader Timbo Adbul Khudus and 12,000 soldiers forced Kaabu's final surrender.

Africa

Kabila, Laurent-Désiré

(b. 1939, Jadotville [now Likasi], Belgian Congo [present-day Democratic
Republic of the Congo]), African military leader and president of the
Democratic Republic of the Congo.

In 1997 international attention focused on Laurent-Désiré Kabila when he
led a seven-month rebellion in Zaire (now the Democratic Republic of the
Congo) that toppled long-time dictator Mobutu Sese Seko.

Since taking power in the Congo, Kabila has had a mixed record. At
first he was very popular among the Congolese, who applauded his
promises to rebuild and revitalize the Congo and to end the rampant
corruption that terrorized the citizenry and contributed to the country's
decay. When Kabila imposed restrictions on civil liberties and political
activity, however, he lost much of his initial popularity. Citizens complained
that they had more freedom during the last years of Mobutu's regime and
accused Kabila of nepotism and promoting only his own ethnic group, the
Luba. Kabila has also faced international criticism for not holding democratic elections, limiting free speech, and arresting and threatening opposition
groups. He has also been criticized for preventing a United Nations investigation into the disappearance of more than 100,000 Rwandan Hutu
refugees, who may have been massacred by Kabila's largely Banyamulenge
troops. Consequently, Kabila has lost millions of dollars in foreign aid that
he had once hoped would help him rebuild the Congo. In response, Kabila
has accused Western officials of hypocrisy for funding the brutal and
autocratic Mobutu but refusing to support him, despite his promise to hold
democratic elections by the year 2000.

Africa

Kabylia,

a Berber region in eastern Algeria whose inhabitants staged an important
revolt against French colonialism.

At the time of the 1871 Great Revolt against the French, the Kabylia
Berbers, who lived and farmed in the Tell mountain region in eastern
Algeria, had enjoyed centuries of local governance. Even during the more
than 250 years of Ottoman rule, Kabylia villages largely governed themselves, with decisions made by assemblies of adult men. Since the arrival of
Islam in the seventh century, Islamic law had traditionally been integrated
with customary law.

As the French moved into the region in 1850, leaders such as Bu Baghla
and, later, Lalla Fatima led the Kabylia struggle to resist conquest. Although
they were unable to stop French forces, the spirit of resistance endured,
culminating in the revolt of 1871–1872, when leader Muhammad al-Hajj

al-Muqrani proclaimed a *jihad*, or holy war, against the Christian invaders. About 150,000 Kabylias joined the rebellion, which spread toward Algiers. The French responded with military action, killing al-Muqrani and capturing his successor. Afterward, the French seized large amounts of fertile land, paving the way for colonial expansion.

The Kabylia is still known for its fierce independence. One of the most militant regions in the 1954–1962 anti-colonial war, it is now home to many of Algeria's nationalist political and cultural leaders. After independence the Kabylias revolted against the efforts of the new president Ahmed Ben Bella to centralize power. Throughout the 1980s and 1990s they were active in the national arena, opposing Arabization laws and policies and promoting Berber rights.

Africa
Kagwa, Apolo (Kagwa)
(b. 1869, Busoga; d. February 1927, Nairobi, Kenya), prime minister of Buganda (1889–1926).

Apolo Kagwa, originally a slave from Busoga, worked as a page for Kabaka Mutesa I, during a time when many Muslim and Christian missionaries were arriving in Buganda. Although Kagwa initially practiced Islam, he was later baptized in the Anglican Church.

After Mutesa I's death in 1884, religious civil war broke out in Buganda. Mutesa's successor, Mwanga II, purged many Christians from the Buganda court, but Kagwa survived. By 1887 he was commanding Buganda's royal guards. A year later Mwanga was overthrown; Kagwa fled to the neighboring Ankole Kingdom. In 1890 Kagwa returned to lead the Christian Party and help reinstate Mwanga, who in turn made Kagwa the *katikiro*, or prime minister. In this position Kagwa welcomed both the Church Missionary Society and the British East Africa Company, and signed the treaty making Buganda a British protectorate in 1894. When Mwanga rebelled against the British three years later, Kagwa helped to overthrow him. The king's infant son, Daudi Chwa, became the new *kabaka* (king), but Kagwa, as one of Chwa's three regents, effectively ruled Buganda for nearly two decades.

The British rewarded Kagwa's collaboration by promising to assure Protestant hegemony in Buganda and by granting Buganda considerable autonomy within the protectorate. Kagwa also received a vast tract of valuable land for his personal use. In 1905 the British knighted him.

After Chwa came of age in 1914, Kagwa came into increasing conflict with the new *kabaka*. His efforts to preserve Bugandan sovereignty also undermined his formerly friendly relations with the British. Ultimately, in 1926, Kagwa was forced to resign after he challenged the British colonial administration's practice of dealing directly with Ganda chiefs rather than with him. He died a year later, reportedly after a fall.

Kagwa wrote extensively in Luganda. His books on the history and culture of the Buganda kingdom are considered important early works of modern African historiography.

Kahina

(b. 575?; d. 702?), Berber priestess in the seventh century who led a campaign resisting Arab movement into North Africa.

In the seventh century the Arabs arrived in the land they called Ifriqiya, in present-day Tunisia, bringing Islam and seeking gold. The Jarawa Berbers in the Aurès mountains became the main force halting their progress through North Africa. The Jarawa were known for their military prowess, and although they offered nominal allegiance to the Byzantine Empire, they in fact ruled their own land. Their chief was Kahina, a woman who, some said, was more than 100 years old and had two sons of two fathers, one Greek and one Berber. She might have been a Christian or a Jew, and some historians have attributed her resistance to religious fervor. Or she might simply have been a strong ruler who would rather burn down her own kingdom than let it fall into the hands of an outside force. There is little historical documentation of Kahina's life, although she appears frequently in the legend and literature of the Berbers, the Arabs, and the Europeans, all groups that came to have a stake in the rich Mediterranean region.

In Arabic literature Kahina appears as an Amazon, charging fiercely into battle with her long hair streaming behind. European writers depicted her as a romantic figure who fought heroically but in vain against marauding Islamic imperialists. All the stories tell how Kahina, a traditional Berber prophetess, used divination to lead the Jarawa Berbers against the invaders. The Arab leader Hassan first reached the Aurès after defeating the Berber leader Kosaila in 686. Kahina met the Arabs on the banks of the river Meskiana, after ordering the destruction of her own capital, Baghaya, so it could not be taken. She and the Jarawa were victorious and pursued the retreating Arabs to the town of Gabès, in present-day Tunisia. There the Arabs suffered such a defeat that they halted their advance for the next five years.

While the Arabs built the city of Tunis, Kahina ruled the adjacent land in an uneasy stalemate. Stories tell of how she adopted an Arab captive during this time, a handsome man of remarkable nobility and bravery, and symbolically gave him her milk, making him her third son. She had a vision of the Arab's future triumph and of her sons being granted a place of honor among the enemy. Before Kahina faced the Arabs a final time, she sent the three sons to swear allegiance to Hassan.

Kahina then destroyed her kingdom rather than let the Arabs take it. But as she burned fields, cut down trees, and destroyed towns, she alienated her own people. When the Arabs attacked again, now bolstered by reinforcements from the East, they met a Berber force weakened by divisions. Hassan killed and took the head of the 127-year-old Kahina at the well that now bears her name, fulfilling her final prophecy of her defeat.

Africa

Kalahari Desert,

a semi-arid region in southern Africa inhabited by the Khoikhoi peoples.

Covering an area of approximately 712,250 sq km (about 275,000 sq mi), the Kalahari Desert spans southern Botswana, eastern Namibia, and northern South Africa. It stretches a maximum of 1300 km (800 mi) north to south and 1300 km (800 mi) east to west. Although it is not actually a desert (it is classified as a "thirstland"), the Kalahari is an arid region covered by grasses and brush, although tubers and bulbous plants grow there. Except for the Boteti River, the region is fed with no surface water; thus Kalahari wildlife, which includes wildebeest, zebra, eland, giraffe, and elephant, must rely on waterholes.

The Kalahari, which is largely unsuitable for agriculture, has long been inhabited only by the Khoikhoi peoples (often referred to as Bushmen), who lived by hunting, foraging, and raising livestock. Parts of the Kalahari have now been turned into national parks and game reserves. These have provided some employment for the desert's long-time residents but have also restricted access to their former hunting territory.

Africa

Kano, Nigeria,

or Kano City, a large city in northern Nigeria that serves as the capital of Kano State.

In the tenth century C.E., Bayajidda Abuyazid, said to be an exiled prince from Baghdad, is reputed to have founded seven Hausa city-states, of which Kano was one. Prehistoric stone tools discovered on the site, however, suggest that the city's actual history extends much further into the past. Scholars from the ancient Mali Empire brought Islam to Kano in the 1340s, and the city achieved great prosperity during the rule of Mohammad Rumfa (1463–1499). Walls built during that period still surround the old quarter of the city, and Rumfa's palace, located next to Nigeria's largest mosque, now serves as the emir's palace.

For centuries Kano was an important market town on trans-Saharan caravan routes. Cola and other products from the forested coastal areas of West Africa changed hands in Kano's market, as did Saharan salt, luxury goods from North Africa and Europe, and slaves. Kano's resident Hausa artisans also manufactured textiles as well as leather and metal goods for both long-distance and local commerce, while nearby villages produced most of the city's food supply. After the Fulani conquest of Hausaland in the early nineteenth century, Kano became the capital of an emirate within the Sokoto Caliphate. In the twentieth century Kano retained a vital role in the regional economy but through different means. Today the primary crop is peanuts, or groundnuts, which are consumed locally and exported. The tanning and decoration of hides and skins, however, remains a major economic activity.

Most contemporary residents still claim to be Hausa, though sizable populations of Fulani and Abagagyawa also reside in Kano. The city has six major districts: Fagge; the Syrian Quarters and adjoining Commercial Township; Sabon Gari; the Nassarawa; Bompai; and the original walled area. These districts divide further into approximately 100 small neighborhoods (*unguwa*), each of which centers on a mosque and a market. Two hills, Dalla and Goron Dutse, dominate the oldest part of Kano. At their bases, water collects in pools that provide most of the clay used in constructing homes.

Kano is still a center of old-style textile making and leather- and metalworking. But it also hosts food industries, such as meat processing, canning, bottling, and the production of peanut and vegetable oils; light manufacturing, such as modern textiles, knit fabrics, plastics, pharmaceuticals, and furniture; and heavy industries, such as steel rolling and the production of chemicals, automobiles, and asbestos. In addition, Kano remains a hub of transport. Highways converge on the city; railroads run to Nguru, Lagos, and Port Harcourt; and the airport services major international flights.

Kano is also home to numerous schools and institutes, including Kano State Institute for Higher Education, an Arabic law school, Bayero University, a state polytechnic college, a commercial school, an agricultural research institute that focuses on peanuts, two libraries, and several teacher-training institutes.

Kansas City, Missouri,

midwestern American city that was a major destination for black migrants from the South; distinguished as the birthplace of ragtime, and vibrant music scene for blues and jazz artists.

African Americans were slaves in area farm fields and on boats plying the Missouri River well before Kansas City was incorporated in 1853. While Kansas City grew around its stockyards and grain depot, a black community developed in the West Bottoms and North End. By 1880 African Americans numbered 8100 in Kansas City, or 14.5 percent of its population. By the turn of the century migration from the South and the Southwest had more than doubled that number. By then the growth of industry had forced most of the African American community to the north side of Kansas City. The black community comprised 10 to 12 percent of the city's population for the next 70 years.

Segregation had been unofficially present since the 1870s, but in the twentieth century it became overt and still more devastating. African Americans were barred outright from many hotels and theaters. At the same time a vital music scene arose in the black community. At the turn of the century James Scott and others developed ragtime. In the 1920s a prolific jazz and blues scene began developing in dozens of bars, dance halls, nightclubs, and theaters. Big Joe Turner sang the blues in the 1920s. The Bennie Moten Orchestra became one of the important jazz bands in the country, and, by 1929, it featured pianist Will "Count" Basie, who would later take over the band and define the Kansas City sound: "four heavy beats to a bar." In the 1940s Lester Young, Chauncey Downs, and bebop founder Charlie "Yardbird" Parker pioneered variations in instrumental intonation, countermelody, and rhythmic displacement.

Most African Americans in Kansas City worked as laborers and domestics because of employment discrimination. Nonetheless, Dr. J. Edward Perry organized the Perry Sanitarium in 1910, and in 1919, the *Kansas City Call* newspaper was founded by Chester A. Franklin, a crusading black journalist. In 1920 the National Negro Baseball League was started, and the Kansas City Monarchs soon became one of its great teams, featuring Satchel Paige in the 1940s.

Discrimination, however, was entrenched and rampant. At a 1942 rally, 13,000 African Americans—nearly a third of Kansas City's black population—protested job discrimination; thereafter, black hiring increased.

Kansas City began to dismantle segregation in public parks and buildings in 1951 and in schools after the 1954 *Brown v. Board of Education* Supreme Court decision. But school efforts were largely unsuccessful when many whites fled to the suburbs. By 1964 sit-ins and other protests had integrated restaurants and other facilities. Earl D. Thomas and Bruce Watkins became the first black city councilors. Nonetheless, de facto segregation of schools and the neglect of the black community by city services led to increased activism in the late 1960s. The Black Panthers organized free breakfast programs and spoke out against continued racism. When Martin Luther King Jr. was assassinated in April 1968, the refusal of city authorities to close schools sparked a riot that left six people dead.

In the 1970s and 1980s the black community in Kansas City organized politically. Freedom, Inc., led efforts to elect African Americans, and in 1982 Alan Wheat became the first black United States congressman from Kansas City. A desegregation plan went into effect in 1984; this was followed by a court-ordered plan in 1990. In 1991 Emanuel Cleaver became the city's first black mayor. Despite these gains, loss of industry has produced widespread unemployment in the black community.

Kasavubu, Joseph

(b. 1910?, near Tsehla, Belgian Congo; d. 1969?, Republic of the Congo),
first president of the Republic of the Congo and former president of the
Bakongo Alliance.

The first president of the independent Republic of the Congo, Joseph
Kasavubu became involved in politics through his desire to empower the
Kongo population. Originally trained as a Catholic priest, he dropped out of
seminary in 1940 and soon entered the colonial civil service. While a civil
servant, Kasavubu joined several Kongo cultural societies, many of which
advocated the eventual reunification of the Kongo Kingdom. In 1955 he
was elected president of the Bakongo Alliance (ABAKO), a cultural society
with political leanings, and soon transformed the group into a serious
political party advocating Kongo autonomy.

ABAKO's development coincided with the burgeoning independence
movement and, as it was one of the few organized political parties and the
dominant party in Léopoldville, Kasavubu soon became a key political
leader. In the 1957 local elections he was elected mayor of a section of
Léopoldville. Although he was arrested in 1959 after riots broke out in
Léopoldville, he was soon reinstated.

In January 1960 Kasavubu participated in the Round Table Conference on Belgian Congo independence in Brussels. Soon after the Belgians
nominated him to be president of the new Republic of the Congo and
named Patrice Lumumba prime minister. This soon proved to be an
uneasy alliance due to their vastly different political visions. Kasavubu
hoped for a federal structure that might grant the Kongo population some
autonomy, while Lumumba wanted a strong unitary state. The coalition
was further strained by the chaos that erupted after independence.
Although Kasavubu and Lumumba formally split in September 1960,
both were unseated by a military coup led by Joseph Mobutu, later called
Mobutu Sese Seko.

Kasavubu was reinstated in February 1961 and remained president
until 1965. During this time he stabilized his position by deflecting difficult
decisions to the prime minister. In 1965 Kasavubu was removed in a second
coup d'état by Joseph Mobutu, and retired from politics.

Keino, Kipchoge

(b. January 17, 1940, Kipsamo, Kenya), Kenyan long-distance runner.

Kip Keino was the first of Kenya's world-class distance runners to make his
mark on the world sports scene. He won Gold and Silver Medals at both
the 1968 and 1972 Olympic Games, set long-standing world records in

both the 5000- and 3000-meter races, and inspired a generation of Kenyan track and field athletes.

An ethnic Nandi, Keino was orphaned at age two and raised by his grandmother. His first racing success came in 1962, when he set a national record for the mile. In 1964, while working as a physical fitness instructor for a police academy, Keino participated in his first Olympic Games, where he finished fifth in the 5000-meter race. The following year he broke world records in both of his main events, the 3000- and 5000-meter races. Sports analysts see Keino's training on Kenya's mountainous terrain as one reason for his success in the next Olympic Games in 1968, which were held at Mexico City. There he won Gold in the 1500-meter race and Silver in the 5000-meter, and led a Kenyan team that garnered a total of eight Olympic medals.

In 1972 Keino repeated his two-medal performance, winning Gold in the 3000-meter steeplechase and Silver in the 1500. Soon runners worldwide were imitating his high-altitude training methods. Keino is renowned not only for his stellar track career—which he capped by serving as coach to the Kenyan national team starting in 1996—but also for his personal beneficence. Since 1964 he and his wife, Phyllis, have taken into their home as many as 100 orphans and raised them as their own children. For this humanitarian work, *Sports Illustrated* named Keino one of its Sportsmen of the Year in 1987.

Africa

Keita, Modibo

(b. 1915, Bamako, Mali; d. May 16, 1977, Bamako, Mali), president of Mali (1960–1968).

The first president of Mali, Modibo Keita is often blamed for the economic problems that have afflicted the country since independence. A descendant of the Mandinka lineage that once ruled the ancient Mali Empire, Keita originally trained to be a school teacher. After his graduation from the William Ponty School in Dakar, he taught school, but he soon abandoned teaching for politics.

Mali inherited a weak, overwhelmingly agricultural economy from French colonial rule; Keita's strict anti-colonialist and socialist policies only added to the country's economic difficulties. At first, Keita severed relations with France and pulled Mali out of the French-dominated Communauté Financière Africaine (CFA) franc zone. With the support of communist countries, Keita nationalized Mali's banks, transportation, and public services, and established village cooperatives. In addition, he imposed trade restrictions and tariffs that drove trade underground and depleted the national budget. Mali's economy rapidly deteriorated, and, against the wishes of his advisors, Keita negotiated Mali's readmission to the CFA in 1967.

Keita, however, placated his advisors with a series of political reforms styled after Mao Zedong's Cultural Revolution in China. He replaced the national legislature with a committee of radical supporters. He created a militant youth organization, the Popular Militia, to repress popular opposition. He also began purges of the government and military. In retaliation, army officers led by Lt. Moussa Traoré removed Keita in 1968 in a military coup d'état. Traoré imprisoned Keita, who died in custody on May 16, 1977.

Kenya,

East African country bordered by Ethiopia, Tanzania, Somalia, the Indian Ocean, and Uganda.

Fringed by coral beaches, crowned by Mount Kenya, and cut through by the majestic Rift Valley, Kenya's physical landscape is among the most beautiful and varied in Africa. It is a landscape made familiar to many in the West through novels, Hollywood films, and the country's well-developed tourist industry. But safari tours in Kenya's national parks provide little more than a glimpse of a country that has one of the world's longest histories of human habitation and an enormously diverse, and often divided, society.

British colonialism helped transform cultural differences into ethnic animosities, and it established enduring stratification between the land-rich and the land-poor. Rights to the fertile land in central Kenya, in fact, were at the heart of a bloody anti-colonial uprising—the so-called Mau Mau Rebellion—and after independence, export crops produced on that land contributed to the young nation's economic prosperity. But years of economic mismanagement, corruption, and political repression, especially after the coming to power of President Daniel arap Moi in 1978, have dimmed Kenya's early promise. The country is now burdened with massive foreign debt, a failing infrastructure, accusations of widespread human rights abuses, and continuing ethnic tensions.

Kenya (Ready Reference)

Official Name: Republic of Kenya

Former Name: British East Africa

Area: 582,646 sq km (224,960 sq mi)

Location: Eastern Africa, bordering the Indian Ocean, between Somalia and Tanzania; bordered by Ethiopia, Somalia, Sudan, and Tanzania

Capital: Nairobi (population 1,504,900 [1990 estimate])

Other Major Cities: Mombasa (population 442,369 [1985 estimate]), Kisumu (population 167,100 [1984 estimate]), and Nakuru (population 150,000 [1991 estimate])

With its high rise buildings and modern amenities, Nairobi is a center of trade and tourism in East Africa. *CORBIS/The Purcell Team*

Population: 28,337,071 (1998 estimate)

Population Density: 48 persons per sq km (about 123 persons per sq mi [1995 estimate])

Population Below Age 15: 44 percent (male 6,248,260; female 6,109,443 [1998 estimate])

Population Growth Rate: 1.71 percent (1998 estimate)

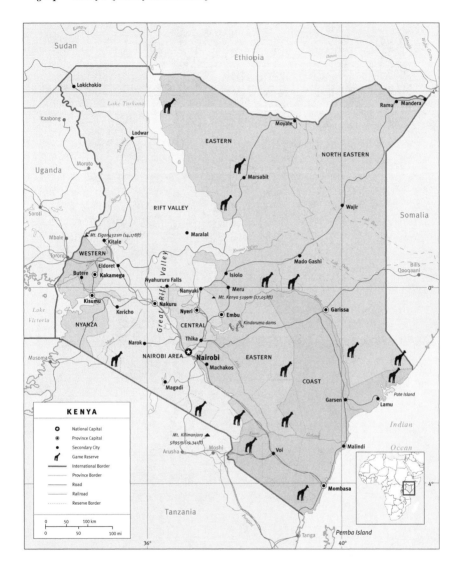

Total Fertility Rate: 4.07 children born per woman (1998 estimate)

Life Expectancy at Birth: Total population: 47.5 years (male 47; female 48.1 [1998 estimate])

Infant Mortality Rate: 59.3 deaths per 1000 live births (1998 estimate)

Literacy (age 15 and over who can read and write): Total population: 78.1 percent (male 86.3 percent; female 70 percent [1995 estimate])

Education: Though not compulsory, the first eight years of primary school are free. In the early 1990s approximately 5.4 million pupils annually attended about 14,690 elementary schools, and about 614,000 students attended the more than 2750 secondary and teacher-training schools.

Languages: Swahili is the official language, although Kikuyu, Luo, and English are also widely spoken. Nearly all Kenyan ethnic groups have distinct languages.

Ethnic Groups: Of more than 30 ethnic groups in Kenya, the largest are the Bantu-speaking Kikuyu, Luhya, and Kamba; the Nilotic-speaking Luo; and the Paranilotic-speaking Kalenjin. Small numbers of Asians, Europeans, and Arabs reside in Kenya.

Religions: About 40 percent Protestant, 30 percent Catholic, and 6 percent Muslim. The remaining 24 percent follow traditional religions.

Climate: Kenya is divided into two almost equal parts by the equator. The region north of the equator is hot and receives comparatively little rain. The southern region falls into three meteorological zones. The coast is humid with an average annual temperature ranging from about 24° C (about 76° F) in June and July to about 28° C (about 82° F) in February, March, and April; the highlands are relatively temperate; and the Lake Victoria region is tropical.

Land, Plants, and Animals: Kenya covers several well-defined topographical zones extending from the Indian Ocean coast upward to lofty mountain ranges that reach elevations of more than 3050 m (10,000 ft) above sea level. From a low coastal strip the terrain rises gradually to a broad, arid plateau that covers the largest portion of the country. The region west of the plateau contains great volcanic mountain chains, of which the principal peak is Mount Kenya (5199 m/17,058 ft). The southern and south-eastern portions of the country are heavily forested, and in the west, the immense depression of the Great Rift Valley is demarcated by a succession of steep cliffs. The chief rivers of Kenya are the Tana and Galana (known as the Athi in its upper course). Besides a small portion of Lake Victoria, Kenya contains almost all of Lake Turkana (formerly called Lake Rudolf).

Along the coast are forests containing palm, mangrove, teak, copal, and sandalwood trees. Forests of baobab, euphorbia, and acacia trees cover the lowlands to an elevation of approximately 915 m (approximately 3000 ft). Extensive tracts of savanna (grassland), interspersed with groves of acacia and papyrus, characterize the terrain from about 915 to 2745 m (about 3000 to 9000 ft). The principal species in the dense rain forest of the eastern and southeastern mountain slopes are camphor and bamboo. The alpine zone (above about 3350 m/11,000 ft) contains large senecios and lobelias. The major animal species are the giraffe, elephant, rhinoceros, zebra, lion, other large cats, birds, and reptiles.

Currency: The Kenyan shilling

Gross Domestic Product (GDP): $45.3 billion (1997 estimate)

GDP per Capita: $1600 (1997 estimate)

GDP Real Growth Rate: 2.9 percent (1997 estimate)

Primary Economic Activities: Agriculture (26 percent of the GDP), small-scale mining and manufacturing, and tourism

These men are members of the Maasai ethnic group, semi-nomadic pastoralists whose reputation as fierce warriors has sometimes led Europeans and other outsiders to romanticize them. *CORBIS/Patrick Bennett*

Primary Crops: Sugar cane, corn, cassava, pineapples, sisal, cotton, cashew nuts on the coast and in the lowlands; potatoes, coffee, tea, cotton, cereal grains, beans, peanuts, tobacco in the highlands; also stock breeding (cattle, goats, sheep, chickens) and dairy production

Industries: Small-scale mining (soda ash, salt, fluorspar, gold, garnets, limestone); large deposits of lead and silver have been discovered near Mombasa; small-scale food and raw material processing for local consumption; flour milling, cement manufacturing, oil refining, and small-scale consumer goods manufacturing

Primary Exports: Tea, coffee, petroleum products, canned pineapple, hides and skins, sisal, soda ash, and pyrethrum extract (used in insecticides)

Primary Imports: Crude petroleum, industrial machinery, motor vehicles, iron, steel, agricultural implements, pharmaceuticals, and fertilizer

Primary Trade Partners: Uganda, Great Britain, Rwanda, Pakistan, Japan, United States, United Arab Emirates, and Germany

Government: Kenya has a modified one-party parliamentary form of government. Executive authority is exercised by a president, elected for a five-year term by popular vote. Mwai Kibaki has been President of Kenya since

29 December 2002. A vice president and a cabinet are appointed by the president from members of the National Assembly, the legislative branch of government. The assembly consists of 188 directly elected members, the attorney general, the speaker, and ten members who are nominated by the president. The Kenya African National Union (KANU) was the nation's only legal political party from 1982 to 1991.

Africa

Kenyatta, Jomo

(b. 1894, Ichaweri, British East Africa [now Kenya]; d. August 22, 1978, Mombasa, Kenya), the first prime minister and first president of Kenya.

Jomo Kenyatta's life spanned almost the entire period of British colonial rule in the area that is now Kenya. Raised in the countryside near Mount Kenya and educated at a Church of Scotland mission school, Kenyatta became a leading member of the generation of African elites who rose in protest of oppressive colonial policies.

Kenyatta's political career began in 1922 when, while working as a civil servant in Nairobi, he joined the East African Association (EAA), a short-lived Kikuyu organization led by Harry Thuku that was formed to regain stolen African lands from white settlers. Pressure from the colonial adminis-tration forced the EAA to disband in 1925 and reform as the Kikuyu Cen-tral Association (KCA). In 1928 Kenyatta became general secretary of KCA, and editor of its journal, *Muiguithania* (the Reconciler). *Muiguithania* publi-cized and gathered support for the KCA's demands, which included the return of confiscated land to Africans, improved social services, African representation on Kenya's Legislative Council (Legco), the repeal of hut taxes, and noninterference in Kikuyu customs, such as polygamy. The KCA also opposed a British proposal for "closer union" among Kenya, Uganda, and Tanganyika (Tanzania).

When Kenyatta traveled to England to protest the proposal (which the British government ultimately dismissed), his speeches and publications won increased support for Kenyan reform among members of Britain's Labour Party. Kenyatta spent 1931 to 1946 away from Kenya, a time of intellectual ferment for him. In addition to his activism, he attended classes at Moscow State University and received a degree in anthropology from the London School of Economics. His thesis, *Facing Mount Kenya, a study of traditional Kikuyu customs and beliefs,* became a bestseller in England after its publication and is still considered an anthropological classic. In addition, he helped organize the 1945 Pan-African Congress in Manchester.

Kenyatta found a radically different Kenya when he returned after World War II. The colonial government had banned the KCA, and in

Kenyan leader Jomo Kenyatta, who would become the first president of an independent Kenya in 1963, speaks at a 1961 news conference. *CORBIS/Bettmann*

response, nationalist members of the KCA had formed the Kenya African Union (KAU), a multiethnic pro-independence organization, to which Kenyatta was elected president in 1947.

Growing anticolonial militancy in Kenya erupted in the 1952–1956 Mau Mau Rebellion. Mau Mau, a Kikuyu secret society that drew members from the KAU and other organizations, was committed to armed struggle to oust the British. Although excluded from Mau Mau, Kenyatta, under pressure from the colonial government, had denounced its activities, the government arrested him and some 150 other nationalists on October 21, 1952. In 1953 he was tried and convicted of "managing the Mau Mau terrorist organization" and sentenced to seven years in prison.

Although Mau Mau failed militarily, it brought international criticism to the colonial government's brutal crackdown—which cost more than 12,000 African lives—and pushed Britain to accelerate its plans for Kenyan independence. In 1960 the KAU was renamed the Kenya African National Union (KANU), and Kenyatta, still in prison, was elected its president.

After his release Kenyatta helped negotiate the terms of Kenya's independence at the London Conference in 1962. KANU won pre-independence elections in May 1963, and on independence day, December 12, 1963, Kenyatta became the country's first prime minister. The following year Kenya became a republic and Kenyatta its president, an office he held until his death in 1978.

Under his motto *Harambee* ("pulling together"), Kenyatta sought to unite Kenya and build a stable nation. He outlawed Kenya's opposition party in 1969 but also attempted to overcome ethnic divisions, appointing members of various ethnic groups to key government posts. He maintained friendly relations with Western nations, encouraged a free market economy, and promoted foreign investment and tourism, all of which helped the economy to grow five-fold between 1971 and 1981. Although most of the generated wealth was concentrated in the hands of a few—namely Kenyatta, his family, and their close associates—the president faced little opposition during his time in office.

Africa

Kérékou, Mathieu

also known as Ahmed Kérékou (1933–), president of Benin (1972–1991, 1996–).

Born in Kouarfa in what was then Dahomey (part of French West Africa), Mathieu Kérékou attended schools in Mali and Senegal before enrolling in the French army and attending Fréjus Officers School in France. In 1961 he was commissioned second lieutenant in the Dahomean army, serving as aide-de-camp (military assistant) to President Hubert Maga (1961–1963) and close adviser to Kérékou's cousin Col. Iropa Maurice Kouandete, playing an important role in Kouandete's 1967 overthrow of Christophe Soglo's military regime.

After a series of attempted military coups and mounting chaos among civilian leaders in the early 1970s, Kérékou (then a major) seized power on October 26, 1972. He dismissed most senior army officers, imprisoned all three former presidents (who were eventually released in 1984), and established a government staffed entirely by army officers under the age of 40. Kérékou proclaimed Marxism-Leninism the official ideology of the state and changed the country's name from Dahomey to Benin in 1975. In 1979 he held elections, nominally converting Benin to civilian rule, while still ensuring his own power base.

Kérékou's policies of nationalization and government expansion remained in effect until the early 1980s, when economic woes and resulting internal strife forced him to agree to reforms, including privatization and reduction of government. He abandoned Marxism-Leninism in 1989, and in March 1991, faced with international and domestic pressure, allowed free elections. Defeated by Nicéphore Soglo, he publicly apologized for the abuses of his regime and received amnesty from the new government. He remained active in politics, and after Soglo failed to revitalize Benin's economy in his first five-year term, Kérékou was reelected president in March 1996.

North America

Kerner Report,

the 1968 report of a federal government commission that investigated urban riots in the United States.

The Kerner Report was released after seven months of investigation by the National Advisory Commission on Civil Disorders and took its name from the commission chairman, Illinois governor Otto Kerner. President Lyndon B. Johnson appointed the commission on July 28, 1967, while rioting was still underway in Detroit, Michigan. The long, hot summers since 1965 had brought riots in the black sections of many major cities, including Los Angeles (1965), Chicago (1966), and Newark (1967). Johnson charged the commission with analyzing the specific triggers for the riots, the deeper causes of the worsening racial climate of the time, and potential remedies.

The commission presented its findings in 1968, concluding that urban violence reflected the profound frustration of inner-city blacks a nd that racism was deeply embedded in American society. The report's most famous passage warned that the United States was "moving toward two societies, one black, one white—separate and unequal." The commission marshaled evidence on an array of problems that fell with particular severity on African Americans, including not only overt discrimination but also chronic poverty, high unemployment, poor schools, inadequate housing, lack of access to health care, and systematic police bias and brutality.

The report recommended sweeping federal initiatives directed at improving educational and employment opportunities, housing, and public services in black urban neighborhoods and called for a "national system of income supplementation." Reverend Martin Luther King Jr. pronounced the report a "physician's warning of approaching death, with a prescription for life." By 1968, however, Richard M. Nixon had gained the presidency through a conservative white backlash that ensured that the Kerner Report's recommendations would be largely ignored.

Khaldun, Ibn

(b. May 27, 1332, Tunis, Tunisia; d. March 17, 1406, Cairo, Egypt),
fourteenth-century North African scholar, considered to be one of the greatest
Arab historians.

Ibn Khaldun wrote a monumental history of North Africa, the *Kitab al-Ibar*.
But his most significant contribution, in the eyes of many contemporary
scholars, is the *Muqaddimah*, perhaps the first systematic philosophical
study of history and society.

Ibn Khaldun was born in Tunis to a family that for centuries had played
a prominent political role in Andalusia, or southern Spain, before fleeing
to North Africa to escape the Christian Reconquest. As a young man he
received a formal education in the Koran, Arabic poetry, and Islamic law,
preparing him for a life among the ruling class of North Africa. In 1349
both his mother and father died as the black plague ravaged Tunis.

As a young married man Ibn Khaldun joined the royal court in Tunis
and later in Fès, Morocco. After a rebellion upset the court, he was accused
of treason and imprisoned. This was the first of several times Ibn Khaldun
would be ensnared in the intrigues of fourteenth-century court life, where
dynasties rose and fell and intellectuals competed for royal favor. He was
released after the sultan's death and went into exile in Muslim-held
Granada, where he worked as a diplomat. He also developed a close but
contentious relationship with Granada's prime minister and scholar, Ibn
al-Khatib. The two men's eventual falling-out, followed by another accusation of treason, forced Ibn Khaldun to flee once again.

After years of negotiating the treacherous waters of dynastic service in
the Maghreb, mostly as a diplomat and tax collector among the Berber
confederacies, around 1375 Ibn Khaldun sought refuge at a Sufi shrine. He
resigned from his royal duties and moved with his family into seclusion in a
small town in Algeria. For the next four years he wrote *Muqaddimah*,
which not only recounted the history of the region's Berbers and Arabs, but
also outlined a method for the historical study of society. Many historians
consider the work a masterpiece as well as the first study of its kind. It
foreshadowed contemporary sociology by arguing that societies are held
together by *asabiyah*, or "social cohesion," a characteristic that exists in
everything from kinship relations to dynasties, and that may be amplified
by the unifying force of religion.

While he was working on *Muqaddimah*, Ibn Khaldun began his history of
North Africa, *Kitab al-Ibar* (Universal History). He continued writing after he
returned to Tunis, but soon afterward he fell out of favor with the powerful
imam, or religious leader, of the city's mosque. In 1382 he began a pilgrimage
to Mecca. He stopped in the city of Cairo and remained there under the
patronage of Egypt's Mamluk ruler. Tragically, his family died in a shipwreck
en route to join him. While in Cairo Ibn Khaldun continued writing his mas-

sive history, taught at the famous Islamic university al-Azhar, became a grand Maliki judge, and once again became embroiled in dynastic politics.

In his remaining years Ibn Khaldun traveled farther through the Arab world, whose history he recorded for posterity. Finally he made his way to Mecca. In 1400 he traveled with Cairo's new sultan to the besieged city of Damascus, where the armies of the Tatar ruler Tamerlane had taken possession. Ibn Khaldun's reputation preceded him, and he enjoyed a hospitality not afforded to the conquered masses outside the camp's gates. After presenting the conqueror with a written history of North Africa, Ibn Khaldun returned to Cairo, where he lived until his death six years later.

Africa

Khaled Hadj Brahim

(b. February 29, 1960, Oran, Algeria), Algerian singer considered to be the most prominent star of the contemporary North African music style Rai.

Khaled Hadj Brahim grew up in Oran, a cosmopolitan port city with a rich musical tradition. By age ten he was playing the harmonica, bass, guitar, and accordion, and with his first single, "La route du lycée" (1974, The Road to School), recorded at age 14, he emerged as an underground sensation on the Algerian pop scene. He took the name Cheb, or "young," Khaled, to mark himself as part of a youth culture ready to change Algeria.

During the late 1970s and the 1980s Khaled reworked Rai, an improvisational folk music that emerged from the bordellos and bars of Oran during the 1920s. Holding on to the sounds of the traditional instruments and the outspoken, often sexually provocative lyrics, Khaled added the Western sounds of drum machines, synthesizers, and electric guitars. The new Rai, which means "opinion" in Arabic, appealed to youths disenchanted with traditional romantic lyrics that had little to do with their lives. Rai spread through-out North Africa, where more than 60 percent of the war-ravaged population is under 25, and the fame of Khaled, "the King of Rai," spread with it.

Khaled's music was censored in Algeria until 1983, when the government relaxed controls on popular culture in an effort to undermine growing support for Islamic fundamentalism. Conservative Islamic leaders saw Khaled's music as corrupting and declared a *fatwa*, or death sentence, against him. In 1990 he bargained the profits for his record "Kutche" for a visa and fled to France.

Since his move, Khaled has again updated the sound of Rai, now incorporating African American jazz saxophone improvisations and hip hop "scratching," as well as other transcultural sounds, including Asian string arrangements, found in "world beat" music. His lyrics have also evolved and now include the experiences of the North African diaspora.

By the mid-1990s Khaled was a well-known pop figure in North Africa, the Middle East, South Asia, and Europe: his single "Aicha" sold more than

1.5 million copies and went gold in Europe. With his songs featured in the popular American films *Killing Zoe* and *The Fifth Element*, he began to win recognition in North America.

Khama III

(b. 1837?, Mushu, Bechuanaland [present-day Botswana]; d. February 21, 1923, Serowe, Bechuanaland), chief of the Bamangwato (Ngwato) tribe of the Tswana people (1875–1923) in Bechuanaland, who ensured that his people came under the protection of the British rather than the Boers (Afrikaners).

Known as Knainas "Khama the Good," Khama was baptized a Christian in 1860. In 1872 he attempted to seize the chieftainship from his father, Sekgoma I, because Sekgoma opposed Christianity, but he was forced into exile. Three years later he overthrew his father and became chief of the Bamangwato with his capital at Shoshong. He was a reformer who embraced the European values that were spreading through the region at this time. He abolished a number of old tribal customs, including circumcision, rainmaking, and bride-wealth (payment made by the groom to the bride's family), which he saw as anti-Christian, and allowed the London Missionary Society to establish a mission on his territory. He was opposed to Afrikaner attempts to expand into Bechuanaland from the independent Boer state of the Transvaal and in 1876 asked for British protection.

In 1885 Khama welcomed British general Charles Warren, who established the Bechuanaland Protectorate. In 1890 he assisted British colonialist Cecil Rhodes when Rhodes took a group of pioneer settlers north into what became Southern Rhodesia (present-day Zimbabwe). When the *Ndebele* under King Lobengula rose against the white settlers in 1893, Khama led his own troops against them in support of the settlers. However, he opposed Rhodes's plan to have Bechuanaland taken over by his own British South Africa Company. In 1895, accompanied by senior Tswana chiefs, Khama went to London and successfully petitioned for Bechuanaland to remain a British protectorate and not come under the control of the settlers. Although he retained substantial powers for himself, he was obliged to surrender a strip of his land for the construction of a railway.

Khama, Seretse

(b. July 1, 1921, Serowe, Bechuanaland [now Botswana]; d. July 13, 1980, Gaborone, Botswana), first president of Botswana (1966–1980).

Born in Serowe of royal parents, Seretse Khama inherited the title of chief of the Ngwato (Bamangwato) people, who make up more than one-third of Botswana's population. When he violated the color bar by marrying a white woman in 1948, British authorities banished him from the country (1950) and deposed him as chief (1952). Allowed to return in 1956, he founded the Botswana Democratic party in 1962. Three years later, campaigning on a multiracial platform, the party was swept to power and Khama became prime minister. He was elected president in 1966 and was knighted the same year. Khama died in office.

Khartoum, Sudan,

the capital city and commercial center of Sudan, located at the confluence of the White Nile and the Blue Nile rivers.

A city of close to half a million inhabitants in 1983, Khartoum is the center of Sudan's largest urban agglomeration, including the larger city and Islamic center of Omdurman and the slightly smaller industrial city of Khartoum North. Since the resumption of the Sudanese civil war in 1983 this urban region has absorbed approximately 1.8 million refugees; the urban region's population is now more than 3 million.

In the 1820s, when Uthman Bey led an Egyptian army to occupy the region on behalf of the Ottoman regime in Egypt (known in Sudan as the Turkiyya), Khartoum was a small farming village. Recognizing its strategic importance at the most important river junction in northeast Africa, Uthman built a fort there and made it his administrative center. In 1829 Muhammad Ali, viceroy of Egypt, designated it as the capital of the Egyptian Sudan. After the opening of the White Nile to riverine commerce, Khartoum became an important center for the slave and ivory trades. In 1885 the Mahdi's defeat of the Egyptian forces and the death of General Gordon at the Battle of Khartoum marked the end of the Turkiyya administration of the Sudan. The Mahdi destroyed the city and moved the capital across the river to Omdurman, which remained the capital until 1898.

When Horatio Kitchener led a British and Egyptian army to overthrow the Mahdist state in 1898, he rebuilt Khartoum and made it the capital of Anglo-Egyptian Sudan. Upon independence in 1956, Khartoum became capital of the Republic of the Sudan. Under colonial rule, Gordon College, the first institution of higher education in Sudan, was established at Khartoum. During the 1950s it became part of the University of Khartoum. Khartoum sits at the hub of Sudan's road and rail network and, together with Omdurman and Khartoum North, serves as the cultural, financial, and industrial center of the country.

In August 1998 the United States bombed a pharmaceutical plant in Khartoum. The United States government claimed that the plant manufactured chemical weapons, but neutral observers questioned these claims.

Kidjo, Angélique

(b. July 14, 1960, Cotonou, Benin), Beninese singer and bandleader.

With music that blends African and Western influences, Angélique Kidjo has become not only a crossover star, winning worldwide popularity, but a role model for women and girls in her native Benin as well. As one of nine children in a musical family, she remembers her older siblings singing folkloric Beninese songs as part of the Kidjo Brothers Band, in addition to songs by American rock 'n' roll stars. When Kidjo began making her own music, she was influenced both by the West African rhythms of her homeland and by the American soul and pop music she heard on the radio. As a solo singer she had developed a local following by the late 1970s.

But rather than stay in Benin, where she faced pressures to perform propaganda for the communist government, in 1983 Kidjo moved to Paris and studied jazz and opera. She quickly became involved in a Parisian musical scene bursting with expatriate Africans. The cross-cultural influences of jazz, gospel, funk, hip-hop, and Western pop music are evident in *Logozo* (1991), Kidjo's first hit album. Two earlier albums, *Pretty* and *Parakou*, had limited success; *Logozo* was followed with *Ayé* (1994) and *Fifa* (1996). "Agolo," a song from *Ayé*, was nominated for a Grammy Award. With lyrics in Fon, Mina, Yoruba, and Swahili as well as French and English, Kidjo sings about love, motherhood (she has a daughter, Naima), religion, and social issues.

Kidjo is a strong, charismatic performer, and she disputes the notion that, as an African woman, she should restrict herself to African material or project an "exotic" character. Yet her cultural roots run deep, from the influence of her childhood religion, Vodou, to her frequent trips home to Benin, which, as she says, she visits to "breathe the air of the country, to see my people, my mother, and pay respect to my ancestors."

Kilimanjaro,

the highest mountain in Africa.

Called *Kilema Kyaro* ("that which makes the journey impossible") by the local Chagga people, Mount Kilimanjaro is located in northeastern Tanzania, near the border with Kenya. Kilimanjaro is a dormant volcano, its two peaks standing about 11 km (about 7 mi) apart, connected by a broad ridge. Kibo, the higher peak, rises to 5895 m (19,340 feet) above sea level, and the summit of Mawensi is 5149 m (16,892 feet) above sea level. Although Kilimanjaro lies 3° south of the equator, an ice cap covers the crater of Kibo year-round.

Kilimanjaro has a number of different vegetation zones on its steep slopes, ascending through tropical rain forests at its base and including moorlands, alpine meadows, and alpine desert. Chagga farmers grow coffee and plantains on the lower slopes of the mountain. In 1889 Kilimanjaro was scaled for the first time by German geographer Hans Meyer and Austrian mountain climber Ludwig Purtscheller. Kilimanjaro has become a highly popular destination for recreational hikers and mountain climbers and an important source of revenue for the Tanzanian government.

North America

King, Coretta Scott

(b. April 27, 1927, Marion, Ala.), widow of the slain civil rights leader Martin Luther King Jr. who is world renowned for her devotion to furthering his ideals.

Long active in the fight for civil and human rights, Coretta Scott King has become an international icon for her efforts to promote nonviolent social change.

The second of three children of Obadiah and Bernice (McMurry) Scott, King grew up in rural Alabama, where she helped her family harvest cotton and tend to their farm. Her father hauled lumber for a white sawmill owner, a job that enabled him to purchase and operate his own sawmill. The local white community resented her father's success: vandals allegedly burned his sawmill, and the Scotts's house, to the ground. King was deeply shaken by her family's trials. She dreamed of moving to the North and diligently focused on her education, enrolling in a local private high school, where she pursued her talent for music. In 1945 she won a scholarship to Antioch College in Yellow Springs, Ohio. She studied music and elementary education and in 1948 debuted as a vocalist at the Second Baptist Church. Also while at Antioch, she performed in a program with Paul Robeson, the renowned African American singer and civil rights activist, who encouraged her to pursue advanced musical training.

In 1951 King entered the New England Conservatory of Music in Boston on a scholarship. She struggled to support herself, living and working at a Beacon Hill boardinghouse. In 1953 she married Martin Luther King Jr., then a doctoral student in theology at Boston University. Her marriage to King was a pivotal point in her life: upon graduating from the conservatory, she returned with him to Montgomery, Alabama, where he worked as a pastor at Dexter Avenue Baptist Church. During the following years she reared their four children and stood by her husband at the forefront of the Civil Rights Movement. In 1962, following the King family's move to Atlanta, she taught voice lessons at Morris Brown College while continuing her civil rights work. Steadfastly loyal to her husband, she joined him in civil rights demonstrations throughout the South, led marches, spoke at rallies, and organized fundraising events at which she lectured and performed.

After the assassination of her husband in 1968, King continued to lead major demonstrations in support of striking workers and the poor, and organized marches to promote Dr. King's principles, such as the 20th anniversary March on Washington in 1983. In 1969, as a memorial to Dr. King, she founded the Atlanta-based Martin Luther King Jr. Center for Nonviolent Social Change, a center principally devoted to training people, especially students, in nonviolent social protest. Serving as the center's president and chief executive officer, she has maintained a high public profile both in the United States and abroad, and traveled through southern Africa to protest apartheid. In 1986 she prevailed in her campaign to establish a national holiday honoring Dr. King.

Since then she has continued to campaign worldwide for human rights, social justice, and urban renewal programs for disadvantaged communities.

North America

King, Don

(b. August 20, 1931, Cleveland, Ohio), controversial African American promoter of America's leading prizefighters.

Don King has emerged as the most powerful and controversial figure in American boxing. By the late 1970s he had come to dominate the boxing industry, traditionally controlled by white brokers, and since then has raised millions of dollars for such prizefighters as Muhammad Ali, Larry Holmes, Julio Cesar Chavez, and Mike Tyson. He is a flamboyant public figure whose visibility has extended far beyond the field of boxing, and some commentators have likened him to the infamous gangster Al Capone. In 1997 *Sports Illustrated* noted, "King, who has beaten tax evasion charges and countless allegations of contract fraud over the years, is nothing if not resourceful."

Released from prison in 1971 after serving a four-year term for manslaughter, King began his career as a boxing promoter. His career took off in 1974 when he successfully arranged the famous "Rumble in the Jungle" match between star boxers Muhammad Ali and George Foreman in Kinshasa, Zaire (present-day Democratic Republic of the Congo). Since then he has negotiated contracts for some of the most celebrated boxing champions and title fights in the history of modern boxing.

In July 1997 the National Association for the Advancement of Colored People (NAACP) honored King with its President's Award for his role as a "philanthropist and sports pioneer who paved the way for minority athletes to make millions of dollars."

King, Martin Luther, Jr.

(b. January 15, 1929, Atlanta, Ga.; d. April 4, 1968, Memphis, Tenn.), African American clergyman and Nobel Prize winner, one of the principal leaders of the American Civil Rights Movement and a prominent advocate of nonviolent protest. King's challenges to segregation and racial discrimination in the 1950s and 1960s helped convince many white Americans to support the cause of civil rights in the United States. After his assassination in 1968, King became a symbol of protest in the struggle for racial justice.

Education and Early Life

Martin Luther King Jr. was born in Atlanta, Georgia, the eldest son of Martin Luther King Sr., a Baptist minister, and Alberta Williams King. His father served as pastor of a large Atlanta church, Ebenezer Baptist, which had been founded by Martin Luther King Jr.'s maternal grandfather. King Jr. was ordained as a Baptist minister at age 18.

King attended local segregated public schools, where he excelled. He entered nearby Morehouse College at age 15 and graduated with a bachelor's degree in sociology in 1948. After graduating with honors from Crozer Theological Seminary in Pennsylvania in 1951, he went to Boston University, where he earned a doctoral degree in systematic theology in 1955.

King's public-speaking abilities—which would become renowned as his stature grew in the Civil Rights Movement—developed slowly during his collegiate years. He won a second-place prize in a speech contest while an undergraduate at Morehouse, but received Cs in two public-speaking courses in his first year at Crozer. By the end of his third year at Crozer, however, professors were praising King for the powerful impression he made in public speeches and discussions.

Throughout his education King was exposed to influences that related Christian theology to the struggles of oppressed people. At Morehouse, Crozer, and Boston University, he studied the teachings on nonviolent protest of Indian leader Mohandas Gandhi. King also read and heard the sermons of white Protestant ministers who preached against American racism. Benjamin E. Mays, president of Morehouse and a leader in the national community of racially liberal clergymen, was especially important in shaping King's theological development.

While in Boston, King met Coretta Scott, a music student and native of Alabama. They were married in 1953 and would have four children. In 1954 King accepted his first pastorate at the Dexter Avenue Baptist Church in Montgomery, Alabama, a church with a well-educated congregation that had recently been led by a minister, Vernon Johns, who had protested against segregation.

The Montgomery Bus Boycott

Montgomery's black community had long-standing grievances about the mistreatment of blacks on city buses. Many white bus drivers treated blacks

Martin Luther King Jr. (1929-1968) addresses a large crowd at a civil rights march in Washington, DC, 1963. *Hulton-Deutsch Collection/CORBIS*

rudely, often cursing and humiliating them by enforcing the city's segregation laws, which forced black riders to sit in the back of buses and give up their seats to white passengers on crowded buses. By the early 1950s Montgomery's blacks had discussed boycotting the buses in an effort to gain better treatment, but not necessarily to end segregation.

On December 1, 1955, Rosa Parks, a leading member of the local branch of the National Association for the Advancement of Colored People (NAACP), was ordered by a bus driver to give up her seat to a white passenger. When she refused, she was arrested and taken to jail. Local leaders of the NAACP, especially Edgar D. Nixon, recognized that the arrest of the popular and highly respected Parks was the event that could rally local blacks to a bus protest.

Nixon also believed that a citywide protest should be led by someone who could unify the community. Unlike Nixon and other leaders in Montgomery's black community, the recently arrived King had no enemies. Furthermore, Nixon saw King's public-speaking gift as a great asset in the battle for black civil rights in Montgomery. King was soon chosen as president of the Montgomery Improvement Association (MIA), the organization that directed the bus boycott.

The Montgomery bus boycott lasted for more than a year, demonstrating a new spirit of protest among Southern blacks. King's serious demeanor and consistent appeal to Christian brotherhood and American idealism made a positive impression on whites outside the South. Incidents of violence against black protesters, including the bombing of King's home, focused media attention on Montgomery. In February 1956 an attorney for the MIA filed a lawsuit in federal court seeking an injunction against Montgomery's segregated seating practices. The federal court ruled in favor of the MIA, ordering the city's buses to be desegregated, but the city government appealed the ruling to the United States Supreme Court. By November 1956, when the Supreme Court upheld the lower court decision, King was a national figure. His memoir of the bus boycott, *Stride Toward Freedom* (1958), gave a thoughtful account of that experience and further extended his national influence.

Civil Rights Leadership

In 1957 King helped found the Southern Christian Leadership Conference (SCLC), an organization of black ministers and churches that aimed to challenge racial segregation. As SCLC's president, King became the organization's dominant personality and its primary intellectual influence. He was responsible for much of the organization's fundraising, which he frequently conducted in conjunction with preaching engagements in Northern churches.

SCLC sought to complement the NAACP's legal efforts to dismantle segregation through the courts with King and other SCLC leaders protesting discrimination through the use of nonviolent action such as marches, boycotts, and demonstrations. The violent responses that direct action provoked from some whites eventually forced the federal government to confront the issues of injustice and racism in the South.

King made strategic alliances with Northern whites that would bolster his success in influencing public opinion in the United States. Through Bayard Rustin, a black civil rights and peace activist, King forged connections to older radical activists, many of them Jewish, who provided money and advice about strategy. King's closest advisor at times was Stanley Levison, a Jewish activist and former member of the American Communist Party. King also developed strong ties to white Protestant ministers in the North, with whom he shared theological and moral views.

In 1959 King visited India and worked out more clearly his understanding of *Satyagraha*, Gandhi's principle of nonviolent persuasion, which King had determined to use as his main instrument of social protest. The next year he gave up his pastorate in Montgomery to become co-pastor (with his father) of the Ebenezer Baptist Church in Atlanta.

SCLC Protest Campaigns

In the early 1960s King led SCLC in a series of protest campaigns that gained national attention. The first was in 1961 in Albany, Georgia, where SCLC joined local demonstrations against segregated restaurants, hotels, transit, and housing. SCLC increased the size of the demonstrations in an effort to create so much dissent and disorder that local white officials would be forced to end segregation to restore normal business relations. The strategy did not work in Albany. During months of protests, Albany's police chief jailed hundreds of demonstrators without visible police violence. Eventually the protesters' energy, as well as their bail money, ran out.

The strategy did work, however, in Birmingham, Alabama, when SCLC joined a local protest during the spring of 1963. The protest was led by SCLC member Fred Shuttlesworth, one of the ministers who had worked with King in 1957 in organizing SCLC. Shuttlesworth believed that the Birmingham police commissioner, Eugene "Bull" Connor, would meet protesters with violence. In May 1963 King and his SCLC staff escalated anti-segregation marches in Birmingham by encouraging teenagers and schoolchildren to join. Hundreds of singing children filled the streets of downtown Birmingham, angering Connor, who sent police officers with attack dogs and firefighters with high-pressure water hoses against the marchers. Scenes of young protesters being attacked by dogs and pinned against buildings by torrents of water from fire hoses were shown in newspapers and on televisions around the world.

During the demonstrations King was arrested and sent to jail. He wrote a letter from his jail cell to local clergymen who had criticized him for creating disorder in the city. His *Letter from Birmingham City Jail*, which argued that individuals had the moral right and responsibility to disobey unjust laws, was widely read at the time and added to King's standing as a moral leader.

National reaction to the Birmingham violence built support for the struggle for black civil rights. The demonstrations forced white leaders to negotiate an end to some forms of segregation in Birmingham. Even more important, the protests encouraged many Americans to support national legislation against segregation.

"I Have a Dream"

King and other black leaders organized the 1963 March on Washington, a massive protest in Washington, D.C., for jobs and civil rights. On August 28, 1963, King delivered the keynote address to an audience of more than 200,000 civil rights supporters. His *I Have a Dream* speech expressed the hopes of the Civil Rights Movement in oratory as moving as any in American history: "I have a dream that one day this nation will rise up and live out the true meaning of its creed: 'We hold these truths to be self-evident, that all men are created equal.' . . . I have a dream that my four little children will one day live in a nation where they will not be judged by the color of their skin but by the content of their character."

The speech and the march built on the Birmingham demonstrations to create the political momentum that resulted in the Civil Rights Act of 1964, which prohibited segregation in public accommodations as well as discrimination in education and employment. As a result of King's effectiveness as a leader of the American Civil Rights Movement and his highly visible moral stance, he was awarded the 1964 Nobel Prize for Peace.

Selma Marches

In 1965 SCLC joined a voting-rights protest march that was planned to go from Selma, Alabama, to the state capital of Montgomery, more than 80 km (50 mi) away. The goal of the march was to draw national attention to the struggle for black voting rights in the state. Police beat and tear-gassed the marchers just outside Selma, and televised scenes of the violence, on the day that came to be known as Bloody Sunday, resulted in an outpouring of support to continue the march. SCLC petitioned for and received a federal court order barring police from interfering with a renewed march to Montgomery. Two weeks after Bloody Sunday, more than 3000 people, including a core of 300 marchers who would make the entire trip, set out toward Montgomery. They arrived in Montgomery five days later, where King addressed a rally of more than 20,000 people in front of the capitol building.

The march created support for the Voting Rights Act of 1965, which President Lyndon Johnson signed into law in August. The act suspended (and amendments to the act later banned) the use of literacy tests and other voter qualification tests that had been used to prevent blacks from registering to vote.

After the Selma protests, King had fewer dramatic successes in his struggle for black civil rights. Many white Americans who had supported his work believed that the job was done. In many ways the nation's appetite for civil rights progress had been filled. King also lost support among white Americans when he joined the growing number of antiwar activists in 1965 and began to criticize publicly American foreign policy in Vietnam. King's outspoken opposition to the Vietnam War (1959–1975) also angered President Johnson. On the other hand, some of King's white supporters agreed with his criticisms of United States involvement in Vietnam so strongly that they shifted their activism from civil rights to the antiwar movement.

Black Power

By the mid-1960s King's role as the leader of the Civil Rights Movement was questioned by many younger blacks. Activists such as Stokely Carmichael of the Student Nonviolent Coordinating Committee (SNCC) argued that King's nonviolent protest strategies and appeals to moral idealism were useless in the face of sustained violence by whites. Some also rejected the leadership of ministers. In addition, many SNCC organizers resented King, feeling that often they had put in the hard work of planning and organizing protests only to have the charismatic King arrive later and receive much of the credit. In 1966 the Black Power Movement, advocated most forcefully by Carmichael, captured the nation's attention and suggested that King's influence among blacks was waning. Black Power advocates looked more to the beliefs of the recently assassinated black Muslim leader, Malcolm X, whose insistence on black self-reliance and the right of blacks to defend themselves against violent attacks had been embraced by many African Americans.

With internal divisions beginning to divide the Civil Rights Movement, King shifted his focus to racial injustice in the North. Realizing that the economic difficulties of blacks in Northern cities had largely been ignored, SCLC broadened its civil rights agenda by focusing on issues related to black poverty. King established a headquarters in a Chicago apartment in 1966, using that as a base to organize protests against housing and employment discrimination in the city. Black Baptist ministers who disagreed with many of SCLC's tactics, especially the confrontational act of sending black protesters into all-white neighborhoods, publicly opposed King's efforts. The protests did not lead to significant gains and were often met with violent counter-demonstrations by whites, including neo-Nazis and members of the Ku Klux Klan, a secret terrorist organization that was opposed to integration.

During 1966 and 1967 King increasingly turned the focus of his civil rights activism throughout the country to economic issues. He began to argue for redistribution of the nation's economic wealth to overcome entrenched black poverty. In 1967 he began planning a Poor People's Campaign to pressure national lawmakers to address the issue of economic justice.

Assassination

This emphasis on economic rights took King to Memphis, Tennessee, to support striking black garbage workers in the spring of 1968. He was assassinated in Memphis by a sniper on April 4. News of the assassination resulted in an outpouring of shock and anger throughout the nation and the world, prompting riots in more than 100 U.S. cities in the days following King's death. In 1969 James Earl Ray, an escaped white convict, pleaded guilty to the murder of King and was sentenced to 99 years in prison. Although over the years many investigators have suspected that Ray did not act alone, no accomplices have ever been identified.

After King's death, historians researching his life and career discovered that the Federal Bureau of Investigation (FBI) often tapped King's phone line and reported on his private life to the president and other government officials. The FBI's reason for invading his privacy was that King associated with Communists and other "radicals."

After his death, King came even more than during his lifetime to represent black courage and achievement, high moral leadership, and the ability of Americans to address and overcome racial divisions. Recollections of his criticisms of U.S. foreign policy and poverty faded, and his soaring rhetoric calling for racial justice and an integrated society became almost as familiar as the Declaration of Independence.

King's historical importance was memorialized at the Martin Luther King Jr. Center for Social Justice, a research institute in Atlanta. Also in Atlanta is the Martin Luther King Jr. National Historic Site, which includes his birthplace, the Ebenezer Church, and the King Center, where his tomb is located. Perhaps the most important memorial is the national holiday in King's honor, designated by the Congress of the United States in 1983 and observed on the third Monday in January, a day that falls on or near King's birthday of January 15.

North America

King, Riley B. ("B. B.")

(b. September 16, 1925), one of the most successful bluesmen to emerge from the Memphis scene.

B. B. King has served as the prime ambassador of American blues. Although others may exceed his talent, King did more than anyone else to popularize the genre. After distinguishing himself on the rhythm and blues (R&B) charts during the 1950s, he broke into the pop mainstream in the 1960s, touring with top-name rock bands. His success can be attributed to longevity as much as skill, something he himself admits: "I was 63 when my career hit its hottest stride." Having avoided the substance abuse and violence that took the lives of many of his peers, he continues to record and perform.

Born a sharecropper's son and raised on a plantation in Mississippi, King first found music through the church. After singing in a number of gospel groups, he left to play the blues in Memphis. He soon secured work at the famed WDIA radio station and began performing in bars and nightclubs. King the disc jockey was known as "the Blues Boy from Beale Street," then "Blues Boy," and then simply "B. B."

King's distinctive sound includes a robust vocal style and abbreviated, melodic guitar playing. In the tradition of call and response, King sings a line and follows it with a flourish of guitar. His riffs mimic patterns of speech, giving his performances an air of autonomous duet. Both his harmony, which uses abundant sixths, and his phrasing, which often subverts the beat, demonstrate the influence of jazz musicians such as Charlie Christian and Lester Young. King's lyrics depart from the popular blues themes of violence and sexual braggadocio. Instead, he emphasizes love, fidelity, security, reflecting his early days in gospel as well as his connection with soul.

After a series of hits on a Memphis record label in 1949, King attracted the attention of Ike Turner, who signed him to Los Angeles-based Modern Records. In 1952 King scored a number-one hit on the R&B charts with

"Three O'Clock Blues." For the next ten years, he toured the circuit of small black clubs. In the mid-1960s, just as his career seemed to be winding down, the sounds of "British Invasion" bands, particularly Cream and the Rolling Stones, introduced blues to young white Americans and renewed King's popularity. He began recording and touring with these musicians, inspiring a comeback that culminated in his 1970 release "The Thrill Is Gone."

In the 1970s King toured the Las Vegas and dinner-club circuits, appeared in films, lectured at universities, and received an honorary degree from Yale. King gave the Memphis blues something hitherto unheard of commercial importance. As an archetype, he paved the way for other blues musicians to become icons of mainstream culture. In 1987 he was inducted into the Rock and Roll Hall of Fame. He received NARAS' Lifetime Achievement Grammy

Photographed at a 1991 concert in the Netherlands, the blues guitarist B. B. King is pictured here with his guitar, nicknamed "Lucille." CORBIS/Derick A. Thomas; Dat's Jazz

Award in 1987 and has received honorary doctorates from Tougaloo College, Yale University, Berklee College of Music, Rhodes College of Memphsis, and Mississippi Valley State University.

Africa

Kinigi, Sylvie

(b. 1953?), prominent banker and first woman prime minister (1993–1994) of Burundi.

Sylvie Kinigi rose to prominence as a commercial banker and senior officer of Burundi's structural adjustment program. Kinigi, a Tutsi married to a Hutu, was appointed prime minister after Melchior Ndadaye, an ethnic Hutu, was elected president in June 1993. Kinigi and Agathe Uwilingiyimana, the premier of neighboring Rwanda, served at the same time as the first female prime ministers in Africa. Kinigi, a member of the former ruling Union for National Progress (UPRONA) party, was a political moderate, but her leadership was quickly eclipsed by events beyond her control.

In October 1993, after a military coup killed President Ndadaye and threw Burundi into violence, Kinigi sought asylum in the French embassy. Her appeals for international support convinced the military to return to its barracks, allowing Kinigi to recover her post. But when Ndadaye's successor was killed in a plane crash, conflict between the Tutsi-dominated military and Hutu militias flared again.

Kinigi concluded that Burundi "entered into democracy without having the means of dealing with it. The process was too rapid. There was no time to form political leaders. So parties formed on the simple criterion of ethnicity." Amid growing ethnic conflict, in February 1994 Kinigi disbanded her cabinet, left Parliament, and returned to commercial banking.

Africa

Kinshasa, Democratic Republic of the Congo,

formerly Léopoldville, capital and largest city of the Democratic Republic of the Congo.

The administrative, cultural, and economic center of the Democratic Republic of the Congo, Kinshasa is located on the southern bank of the Congo River, opposite Brazzaville, in the Kinshasa region of the Republic of the Congo. Although it is uncertain when people first settled in the area, Kinshasa was an important trading village and caravan stop, especially for the slave trade, during the height of the Kongo Kingdom in the fourteenth century. In 1881 explorer Henry Morton Stanley established a European trading center in the village and renamed it Léopoldville after Leopold II of Belgium, who shortly thereafter claimed the area as part of his private colony, the Congo Free State. After the 1898 completion of a railroad between the city and the Atlantic Ocean port of Matadi, Kinshasa became the major shipping port from and to the railroad in the Belgian Congo. By 1920 Kinshasa's importance and size prompted Belgian authorities to make it capital of the Belgian Congo.

After independence in 1966 the city was renamed Kinshasa, and it has since become the most populous city in the Congo. Although no reliable census data are available, it is estimated that Kinshasa has a population between 5 and 8 million and an annual growth rate of approximately 14 percent.

Since the colonial era, Kinshasa's economy has been supported by the shipping business between the Congo River and the railroad. It is also home to numerous factories that manufacture domestic and export goods such as textiles, beer, and cement. During Mobutu Sese Seko's reign, however, government corruption depleted most of the city's budget, and massive migration to the city overtaxed the few remaining resources. As a result there has been little effort to manage or maintain the city and almost no plan to deal with incoming populations. Unemployment is estimated at nearly 60 percent and most of the city's citizens live off commerce in the informal sector. Inadequate sanitation and housing in the city have contributed to public health problems, including major outbreaks of cholera and typhoid and wide-spread tuberculosis and malaria. In spite of these conditions, Kinshasa has developed a vibrant music scene and is known as the modern music capital of Central Africa.

In May 1997 Laurent-Désiré Kabila took control of the Democratic Republic of the Congo and promised, among other things, to eliminate corruption and revitalize the country. He ordered police officers and soldiers to stop robbing and harassing citizens, although it is uncertain that these orders were obeyed. Kinshasa's residents welcomed Kabila into the capital but later protested his restrictions on political demonstrations.

North America

Kitt, Eartha Mae

(b. January 26, 1928, North, S.C.), cabaret singer and stage and screen performer known for her seductive stage presence and her "sex kitten" style.

Born on a farm to poverty-stricken sharecroppers, William Kitt and Anna Mae Riley, Eartha Mae and her sister, Pearl, were abandoned by their mother at a young age. The two sisters were raised by a foster family until 1936, when they moved to New York City to live with their aunt. In New York Kitt attended Metropolitan High School (now the New York School of Performing Arts), and at age 16 was invited by Katherine Dunham to join her dance troupe. The group toured Europe and South America from 1946 to 1950, and while they were in Paris, Kitt was discovered by Orson Welles, who cast her in his 1951 production of Marlowe's *Dr. Faustus*. She returned to New York and performed at *La Vie en Rose* and the *Village Vanguard*, where she developed a sexy and sensual stage style. In 1952 she appeared in the Broadway show *New Faces of 1952* and in 1954 in the film version. She sang in nightclubs and cabarets from the mid-1950s through the 1960s.

During this period Kitt also worked in film, television, and the theater, as well as recording music. Her stage work included *Mrs. Patterson* (1954) and *Shinbone Alley* (1957). She appeared in the films *The Accused* (1957), *St. Louis Blues* (1958), and *Anna Lucasta* (1959). During this time she recorded two albums, *Bad But Beautiful* (1961) and *At the Plaza* (1965). In the 1960s she also had a stint as Catwoman in the TV series *Batman*.

In 1968, while at a luncheon at the White House hosted by Lady Bird Johnson, Kitt publicly criticized American involvement in the Vietnam War by saying that juvenile delinquency and street crime were direct results of the war. She subsequently experienced a major loss of popularity and underwent personal investigations by the FBI and CIA. After that she performed mostly in Europe until the late 1970s. In 1978 she returned to Broadway to perform in *Timbuktu* and made an album, *I Love Men* (1984). She produced two autobiographies, *I'm Still Here* (1989) and *Confessions of a Sex Kitten* (1991).

Kiwanuka, Joseph

(b. 1896?, Buganda; d. February 23, 1966, Rubaga, Uganda), the first African to serve as a Catholic bishop in the twentieth century and the first African doctor of canon law, who developed an African clergy and encouraged African leadership in religious and educational activities.

When Joseph Kiwanuka was a 12-year-old boy in the British colony of Uganda, a Catholic priest working as a missionary arranged for him to attend mission school, where he excelled. Kiwanuka went on to attend the seminary at Katigondo. After his ordination in 1929, he studied canon law in Rome and became the first African to earn the title doctor of canon law.

Missionaries in Africa, in effect, imposed a paternalistic and external Christianity on their African converts. During the colonial era Europeans largely considered Africans "inferior" and "backward," and they expected Africans simply to receive the Christianity that white Europeans conferred on them. However, Archbishop Streicher of the Catholic Church, perhaps sensing the changing nature of African society in the twentieth century, believed in the need to develop an indigenous and autonomous African clergy. Thus he trained Kiwanuka and others like him for leadership positions in the Catholic Church.

In 1939 Kiwanuka traveled to Rome for his consecration by Pope Pius XII. As a bishop, he was given charge of the Masaka district vicariate, a diocese staffed completely by African priests—an experiment of sorts—and he worked to help his diocese emerge from paternalistic, missionary Catholicism into an indigenous African expression of the faith. Bishop Kiwanuka encouraged lay participation in diocesan activities. He founded lay councils, to which local people were elected, as well as parents' associations for the church schools.

In 1961 Kiwanuka became Archbishop of Kampala in a ceremony that the king of Uganda attended. He participated in the Second Vatican Council from 1962 to 1965, which encouraged lay participation. He died in Rubaga in early 1966 after paving the way for the hundreds of African bishops who have followed in his footsteps.

Kong,

precolonial Dyula kingdom spanning what are now northern Côte d'Ivoire and southern Burkina Faso.

The kingdom of Kong originated as a small trading settlement in the eleventh or twelfth century C.E. It eventually became the center of a kingdom whose influence reached as far as Djenné in present-day Mali. It reached its pinnacle in the eighteenth century. Warfare between the

Malinké Empire builder Samory Touré and the French destroyed the city and its kingdom at the end of the nineteenth century.

Kong emerged as a trading center when Mande merchants began trading in the territory of the surrounding Senufo people. In the late fifteenth century a wave of Dyula traders moved to the area and brought with them their trading skills and connections. Kong became an increasingly important market for the exchange of northern desert goods such as salt and cloth and southern forest exports such as cola nuts, gold, and slaves. As Kong grew prosperous from trade, its early rulers—a group called the Tarawéré, apparently combining both Dyula and Senufo traditions—extended their authority over the surrounding region.

In 1710 Seku Wattara, a Dyula warrior, invaded the area and easily conquered the city of Kong with his cavalry. He established himself as ruler, and under his power Kong rose from a small city-state to an important regional power. During the 35 years of his reign Wattara unified the city-state with surrounding conquered regions, including the region centered on Bobo-Dioulasso. He imposed Dyula as the official language and Islam as the state religion. Wattara strove to increase his share of regional trade. Toward this end he put slaves to work in the manufacture of cloth. Wattara also used slave labor to cultivate rice, millet, sorghum, and cotton. Finally, he fostered trade by improving security along trading routes. By the end of his reign he had acquired a monopoly over a number of the southern trade routes.

Wattara died in 1745 and was succeeded by two able rulers—Koumbi Watara and Mori Maghari. Under their rule Kong continued to be a commercial center and also became a center of Islamic study. After the death of Maghari in 1800, his successors struggled with growing resistance from the kingdom's diverse ethnic and religious groups. Ultimately, however, Samory Touré destroyed the city of Kong when its rulers resisted his rule and refused to aid him in his campaign against French colonialists. Under colonial rule the Kong Kingdom was divided between two colonies—Côte d'Ivoire and Upper Volta (now Burkina Faso). The city of Kong, once the capital of the kingdom, became merely a small town after the French government routed the nearest rail line 70 km (45 mi) to the west.

Africa

Kountché, Seyni

(b. 1921, Fandou, Niger; d. November 10, 1987, Paris, France), military general and president of the Republic of Niger (1974–1987).

The son of wealthy *Djerma*, Seyni Kountché attended prestigious schools and joined the military after completing his studies in 1949. He quickly rose through the ranks. Under the presidency of Hamani Diori he won appointment to a series of powerful positions. Within months of his promotion to chief of staff, however, he led a military coup in 1974. He suspended the constitution and named himself president of the new regime.

Upon seizing control, Kountché enjoyed initial popularity. He moved to end the rampant corruption of the previous regime, whose officials had diverted food aid into private coffers during the severe famine and drought of the early 1970s. He chose to remain at the austere residence of the military chief of staff rather than occupy Diori's lavish presidential palace. Using military force to achieve humanitarian goals, Kountché immediately stopped the black market in food aid and distributed free seed to farmers. He increased revenues from Niger's uranium mines, the proceeds of which he initially allocated to the population of the drought-stricken countryside.

Kountché instituted *Samariya*, a new rural development project that attempted to teach villagers to increase food-crop production. The Société de Développement (Development Society), which followed this project in 1976, sought to increase communication between the national and local governments and to improve rural development projects. But the traditional elite soon co-opted the society, so that it offered little benefit for peasants, a failing that became increasingly common in the Kountché regime.

Kountché and his administration lost popularity within only a few years. An acerbic and authoritarian personality, Kountché lacked political charisma. His administration became increasingly enmeshed in internal military disputes, several of which culminated in coup attempts that were ruthlessly suppressed. Kountché subsequently gained a reputation as a bloodthirsty autocrat. He was accused of using spirit possession to undermine his rivals. After several attempted coups and other attacks, Kountché became increasingly suspicious; he frequently dismissed those he suspected of disloyalty. By 1980 he had a complete monopoly of political power in Niger, and his regime consisted almost entirely of his own civilian appointees, many of whom were his family members.

By the early 1980s Kountché had amassed a huge fortune from the state treasury, not unlike his predecessor Diori. The popularity of his regime dropped still further in the mid-1980s following a fall in the world price of uranium and continued drought. Niger experienced a severe economic crisis; the state froze spending and dismissed workers from many projects, including construction and mining. As the economy slowly improved after 1985, Kountché began to regain popularity. He adopted sweeping reforms such as a new, publicly ratified constitution in 1987. Stricken with illness, however, Kountché had to seek medical care in Paris, where he died of a brain tumor later that year.

North America

KRS One (Laurence Kris Parker)
(b. 1965, Brooklyn, New York), African American rap artist, self-styled "Teacher" of the hip-hop nation.

KRS One was born Laurence Kris Parker and grew up in the South Bronx section of New York City. A graffiti artist turned rapper, he founded the seminal rap group Boogie Down Productions (BDP) in 1986 with the disc jockey (DJ) Scott LaRock (Scott Sterling). Their first album, *Criminal Minded* (1987), combined LaRock's harsh, spare, reggae-influenced beats with KRS One's long-winded rhyme style on underground classics such as "9 MM Goes Bang" and "South Bronx." The album's gritty portrait of life on the streets (as well as the firearms that adorned its cover) influenced the "gangsta" rap movement that began in earnest two years later.

LaRock was fatally shot soon after *Criminal Minded* was released, but KRS One recruited a new production team for the second BDP album, *By All Means Necessary* (1988). The album retained some of the thuggish imagery of *Criminal Minded* but also explored the black radicalism suggested by its title, a riff on the words of Malcolm X: "by any means necessary." In tracks like "My Philosophy," "Stop the Violence," and "Illegal Business," KRS One affirmed his new persona —"The Teacher"—with scathing diatribes against institutionalized racism and black-on-black crime. Soon after, KRS One joined other rap-pers to form the Stop the Violence Movement, which addressed many of the same issues. *By All Means Necessary* stands as the most convincing political hip hop album to date.

In 1989 BDP's third album, *Ghetto Music: Blueprint of Hip Hop*, was released, and KRS One expressed his increasing Afrocentrism on a lecture tour of colleges and universities. BDP's fourth effort, *Edutainment* (1990), contained the hit "Love's Gonna Get 'Cha" (Material Love), but some critics complained that the group was running low on inspiration. After two more albums, KRS One dissolved BDP and embarked on a solo career, beginning with the highly acclaimed *Return of the Boom Bap* (1995). Since then, KRS One has maintained his status as hip hop's most committed voice. He has continued to release fairly successful solo albums, and in 1996 he founded the world's first school for hip-hop culture, the Temple of Hip Hop.

Africa

Kush, Early Kingdom of,

Egyptian name for ancient Nubia, site of highly advanced, ancient black African civilizations that rivaled ancient Egypt in wealth, power, and cultural development.

Although the world is familiar with the material, architectural, and cultural achievements of ancient Egypt, few know of the neighboring kingdoms of Kush, civilizations centered to the south of Egypt in the area called Nubia (in present-day Sudan). Over the course of ancient history, two great civilizations rose and fell in the region the Egyptians knew as Kush. Today the older of the two is better known by the name of a modern town in Sudan, Karmah (or Kerma), where the ruins of its capital stand. The more recent Nubian civilization is the kingdom usually known as Kush.

Before the late 1970s scholars saw Karmah and Kush as little more than Egyptian colonial outposts. Racist beliefs that black Africans were incapable of establishing advanced cultures and civilizations contributed to the misconception. Modern archaeologists have restored Karmah and Kush to their proper places among the great cultures in world history. Today scholars agree that Karmah and Kush were no mere copies of Egypt. Although at times during their history they borrowed, sometimes heavily, from Egyptian culture, they were indigenous, black African societies comparable to Egypt in importance, power, material wealth, and cultural development.

The civilizations of Karmah and Kush occupied the Nile Valley between present-day Khartoum (in Sudan) and Aswan (in Egypt). These areas were rich in natural resources such as gold, copper, diorite (a semiprecious stone), and the hard stone necessary for Egyptian building projects. They lay along trade routes connecting Egypt with West and Central Africa, and both civilizations grew wealthy from this trade.

Karmah

Even before the first pharaohs united Egypt around 3000 B.C.E., the black Africans of Nubia had developed one of the world's most advanced cultures. Recent archaeological finds have revealed that the region's people were producing sophisticated ceramics by 8000 B.C.E., even earlier than the people of Egypt. Indeed, it seems likely that Nubia contributed as much to ancient Egypt's development as Egypt did to Nubia's.

During Egypt's Old Kingdom (2575–2130 B.C.E.), Karmah Kingdom extended its rule over much of Nubia. Archaeologists divide Karmah's history into three periods: Early Karmah, 2400–2000 B.C.E.; Middle Karmah, 2000–1668 B.C.E.; Classic Karmah, 1668–1570 B.C.E. Each period can be distinguished by unique styles of pottery, tomb building, and burial practices. By 1700 B.C.E. the kingdom's capital had grown to a population of about 10,000. This complex society had several economic and social classes, with a king at the top, a priestly class, and an aristocracy. A firm agrarian base permitted the development of specialized occupations, including skilled artisans and an army. The town's eastern cemetery grew to about 30,000 graves.

Graves of the Early Karmah period were small and grew in size and complexity over time, suggesting that a distinct ruling class gradually accumulated wealth and power. An abundance of Egyptian articles in the graves indicates a greater contact between the two civilizations in the Middle Karmah period. The Classic Karmah period was the most prosperous for Karmah, which traded extensively with both the Egyptians at Thebes and the Hyksos people who dominated much of Egypt at the time.

Egypt had long viewed Karmah, which it called Kush, as a threat, particularly to its economic interests in Lower Nubia. Egypt controlled the area of Lower Nubia in times of political stability and withdrew from it during times of political or social upheaval. Egypt experienced such a period of upheaval beginning around 1700 B.C.E., when the Hyksos (most likely from present-day Syria) conquered lower, or northern, Egypt. The weakened armies of Upper, or southern, Egypt withdrew from Lower Nubia, which

Karmah took over. Soldiers from Karmah fought on both sides in the warfare between the Hyksos and the Egyptians.

By 1570 B.C.E. the Egyptians began a national war of liberation, first against Karmah. During the war the pharaoh Kamose intercepted a message from the Hyksos ruler to the new king of Karmah inviting Karmah to join forces with Hyksos in a conquest of Egypt so that the two powers could share the spoils. To prevent such an alliance, Egypt reconquered Lower Nubia and then drove the Hyksos from Egypt. It then waged a series of attacks against Karmah until around 1450 B.C.E., when Egypt destroyed the kingdom and its capital. Egypt then occupied Nubia for approximately 500 years, and the Nubians (or Kushites) absorbed Egyptian culture.

Kush

Around 1075 B.C.E., when Egypt entered a period of instability, the governors of Kush attempted to assert their independence from Egypt. Egypt responded by invading and re-occupying Nubia in 1070 B.C.E. By the ninth century B.C.E, however, Egypt had disintegrated into several competing states, and Nubia regained its independence. Around 850 B.C.E. a kingdom arose to dominate Nubia from Napata, the former Egyptian colonial capital.

In about 750 B.C.E., King Piye of Kush invaded Egypt, then splintered into more than 11 independent principalities. Piye and his brother Shabaka conquered and united Egypt. Shabaka founded what is known as Egypt's Twenty-fifth Dynasty. For almost 100 years Egypt was ruled by a succession of Kushites, generally considered fair and benevolent rulers. This period represented the height of Kushite power, when Kush controlled an empire stretching from present-day Khartoum to the Mediterranean Sea.

Kush had absorbed much of Egypt's culture. Kushites worshiped many of the Egyptian gods, most importantly Amon. The Kushites believed that the *ka* (spirit or soul) of Amon resided at Jebel Barkal, just outside Napata. They constructed a temple to Amon there, around which developed a priestly class with great power. Kush's rulers considered themselves the true pharaohs of Egypt and maintained the ancient pharaonic traditions. Many Egyptians, however, considered the pharaohs of the Twenty-fifth Dynasty to be foreigners and rejected their legitimacy. In 674 B.C.E., during the rule of the Kushite pharaoh Taharqa, the Assyrians, whose empire was based in present-day Iraq, invaded Egypt and defeated Taharqa's army. Taharqa fled to Napata. Even though he attempted to retake Egypt, Taharqa and his successors failed. By about 663 B.C.E., Kush had permanently lost control of Egypt.

Subsequently, Egypt ousted the Assyrians and reestablished its forts in lower Nubia. Around 590 B.C.E. the Egyptian ruler Psamtik II invaded Upper Nubia, decisively defeating the Kushite army and possibly briefly taking Napata. The kings of Kush fled to the town of Meroë in about 590 B.C.E., although Napata remained an important religious center. Each king, until around 300 B.C.E., returned there to be crowned and to be buried.

The move to Meroë marked a cultural and political change in Kush. No longer preoccupied with the Egyptian borderlands, Kush began to face south and return to its Nubian roots. Meroitic replaced Egyptian as the official language, as did a unique form of writing, which scholars have yet to decipher. The god Apedemak, depicted as a man with a lion's head, supplanted Amon as the national deity. Meroë developed ironworking technology, which was new to Africa at that time. Today large and numerous slag heaps testify to the large-scale production of iron.

The first century B.C.E. was the high point of Meroitic culture and politics; after this Meroë began a slow decline. Several factors may have caused the decline: a re-routing of the trade between Egypt and West and Central Africa to bypass Meroë; soil erosion caused by cattle overgrazing; declining agricultural yields; and deforestation (probably due to the vast amounts of timber needed to fuel iron furnaces). The last known king of Kush, Yesbokheamani, ruled from approximately 283 to 300 C.E. After his death Kush's history remains unknown. The final reference to it comes from King Ezana of Aksum (in present-day Ethiopia), who claimed to have sacked Meroë in 350 C.E.

Africa

Kuti, Fela

(b. October 15, 1938, Abeokuta, Nigeria; d. August 3, 1997, Lagos, Nigeria), Nigerian singer, saxophonist, bandleader, and composer.

One of Africa's best-known and most outspoken cultural figures for nearly 30 years was born Fela Ransome-Kuti, the son of a minister and his wife. After studying jazz and classical music in Great Britain, Fela—as he was popularly known—worked briefly for the Nigerian Broadcasting Corporation. In the late 1960s, while living in Ghana, Fela visited the United States, where he sampled various musical and political movements. He was particularly influenced by seeing James Brown in concert and meeting members of the Black Panther Party.

Returning to Nigeria in 1973, Fela—who had formed his band, *Nigeria 70*, three years earlier—began writing more overtly political songs. He attacked government corruption and took on wider social issues as well. One of his first hit songs, "Shakara/African Woman," criticized the use of white Western standards of feminine beauty in Africa. His signature sound—a blend of soul, jazz, highlife, and African percussion—was dubbed Afrobeat by Fela and spawned dozens of imitators. In the mid-1970s he opened a Lagos nightclub, the Shrine, where he presided over all-night dance parties for the next 25 years. Joined onstage by as many as 30 or 40 musicians and dancers at a time, Fela sang in a mostly English patois, his lyrics taking jabs at "all dem oppressors."

Long an irritant to authority figures, Fela's outspokenness brought him frequent harassment from the Nigerian government. In 1977 the army burned down his house, and his mother later died from beatings incurred during the same attack. After her death Fela announced the formation of his own party, the Movement of the People, and urged young Nigerians to get involved in public affairs. During an abandoned run for Nigeria's presidency, Fela announced that, if elected, he would make every Nigerian a police officer. That way, he said, "before a policeman could slap you he would have to think twice because you're a policeman too."

Fela's flamboyant ways also attracted attention. He often performed and conducted interviews wearing only his underwear. Although he avoided hard drugs, he was an enthusiastic user and proponent of marijuana, which led to several arrests during his lifetime. In 1978, already married though separated from his wife, he took 27 new brides, mostly singers and dancers with his band. In 1986, after serving 20 months in prison on drug charges, he divorced them all, saying he no longer believed in the institution of marriage.

By the 1990s, having both achieved international fame and produced dozens of hit albums, Fela turned to religion. Probably already ill with acquired immune deficiency syndrome (AIDS), the disease that would kill him, he disappointed some fans and friends by not speaking out against the excesses of Nigeria's military government, which had recently imprisoned his brother, a pro-democracy activist.

When he died in 1997, his family announced the cause of death, a rare admission in a country where AIDS is not often discussed publicly. In obituaries and editorials after his death, Fela was remembered as a giant, a genius, a hero, and an honest man.

North America

Kwanzaa,

a holiday that African Americans celebrate during the final week of the year to reaffirm their African roots.

Kwanzaa, Swahili for "first fruits," is a secular holiday. Maulana Karenga, current chairman of the Black Studies Department at California State University at Long Beach, introduced this holiday in 1966 at the height of the Black Power Movement in the United States. At that time he was a graduate student and the head of US (United Slaves), a Los Angeles-based Black Nationalist group committed to learning about African history and teaching it to African Americans. After formulating the holiday, Karenga and members of US traveled around the country to promote it. Since then, the number of African Americans who observe the holiday has dramatically increased. In 1996, 13 million African Americans in the United States and 5 million people of African descent in other parts of the world were estimated to have celebrated Kwanzaa. Although Karenga designed the holiday to "give a Black alternative to the existing holiday," many African Americans who celebrate Kwanzaa also celebrate Christmas.

An elaborate and symbolic table setting is a central part of the Kwanzaa celebration. First, African Americans place on a table one of two items—a mat made of straw or a Kente-patterned textile—which represents the African American heritage in the materials of traditional African culture. Celebrants then put a seven-pronged candleholder in the center of the mat. The candleholder contains one central black candle that is flanked by three red and three green candles. Each candle stands for one of the seven principles Kwanzaa commemorates. Near the base of the candleholder, observers place a cup, which symbolizes the unity of all African peoples. Around these two centerpieces, vegetables, fruits, and nuts are arranged, which represent the yield of the first harvest.

The philosophical foundation of Kwanzaa is the seven principles collectively known as the *Nguzo Saba*. They include *umoja* (unity); *kujichagulia* (self-determination); *ujima* (collective work and responsibility); *ujamaa* (cooperative economics); *nia* (purpose); *kuumba* (creativity); and *imani* (faith). After researching cultures throughout the African continent, Karenga selected these Swahili-named principles because of their predominance in African history. The *Nguzo Saba*, according to Karenga, are the core principles "by which black people must live in order to begin to rescue and reconstruct [their] history and lives."

Each day before dinner celebrants light a candle and interpret its corresponding principle. In addition to explaining the principle and illustrating it through parables, African Americans discuss how to live according to the principle. After dinner, they blow out the candle. On the following day they light an additional candle along with the candle(s) from the preceding day(s), until the seventh day when all seven candles burn together.

While Kwanzaa's candle-lighting ritual tends to be solemn, the rest of the celebration is upbeat and festive. On each evening of the celebration, family and friends gather to eat and drink. A typical Kwanzaa feast may feature spicy oven-fried catfish or Creole chicken accompanied by a bean or rice dish, such as Hopping John or Jollof Rice, and completed by desserts such as fried candied sweet potatoes or sweet and tart lemon cake. All celebrants drink from the unity cup in reverence of their predecessors. They tell stories about their African ancestors, sing, and dance.

As part of the celebration family members exchange gifts of cultural significance, such as dashikis (African tunics). Another popular gift is a *Nia Umoja* figurine, also known as Kente Claus, which represents an ancient African storyteller. He wears a Kente cloth robe and has a neatly trimmed gray beard.

When he introduced Kwanzaa, Karenga urged that gifts as well as all decorations for the holiday be homemade, but in recent years there has been a proliferation of Kwanzaa merchandise. Since 1990 New York City has hosted an annual Kwanzaa Holiday Expo, which has attracted an increasing number of vendors. They sell publications such as cookbooks, how-to manuals, children's stories, and paraphernalia such as factory-made mats, mass-produced unity cups, and Taiwanese-made candleholders. Hallmark, which introduced a line of Kwanzaa greeting cards in 1992, is one of several major American corporations that market Kwanzaa-related merchandise.

Some African Americans have criticized the commercialization of Kwanzaa on the grounds that black-owned businesses are not the benefactors. Karenga argued that "We [African Americans] should be producing our own items for our own practice of the holiday." Other social critics have interpreted the commercialization of Kwanzaa as society's acknowledgment of the holiday's significance and the rising economic status of blacks. Even with this commercialization, Kwanzaa continues to be a cultural mainstay in the homes of many African Americans.

L

Ladysmith Black Mambazo,
a renowned South African musical group.

By improvising on traditional Zulu singing styles, the all-male a cappella choir Ladysmith Black Mambazo became an international sensation after a series of critically acclaimed albums in the 1980s and 1990s. Choral singer Joseph Shabalala formed the ten-member group with friends and relatives in 1962. With Shabalala as lead singer and composer, Mambazo includes seven bass singers, one alto, and one tenor. Since its formation, Mambazo has recorded some 40 albums, with songs in both Zulu and English.

The group's name reflects the Zulu roots of its members. "Ladysmith" is the Shabalala family's hometown in KwaZulu-Natal Province. "Black" refers to black oxen, the strongest animals on the farm, while *mambazo* is the Zulu word for ax, implying that the group could chop down rivals during singing competitions. Their artistic roots lie in a type of performance called *iscathamiya*—Zulu for "walking like a cat"—that combines dancing and call-and-response singing. Iscathamiya originated in the mines, where workers learned to "walk like a cat" and not bother the guards. At home on Saturdays, men would sing and dance late into the evening. Today teams of roughly ten men perform iscathamiya without instrumental accompaniment in competitions before judges.

In 1988 Mambazo won the Grammy Award for Best World Music Recording with *Shaka Zulu*. Five other Mambazo albums have received Grammy nominations, including *How the Leopard Got His Spots* (1989), a collaboration with Danny Glover; *Gift of the Tortoise* (1993); *Liph' Iqiniso* (1994); and *Thuthukani Ngoxolo* (1996).

Mambazo has appeared in several films, including two 1990 documentaries, *Spike Lee & Company—Do It A Cappella* and *Mandela in America*. They were also featured in *Waati*, a 1995 political drama. The group recorded soundtracks for various other movies, including *Moonwalker, A Dry White Season, Coming to America,* and *Cry the Beloved Country.*

In 1991 Mambazo began collaborating with Chicago's Steppenwolf Theatre Company in the production of two musicals, *Song of Jacob Zulu,* which opened on Broadway in 1993 and received six Tony Award nominations, and *Nomathemba,* based on Shabalala's first composition. Mambazo sang at the ceremony when Nelson Mandela and F. W. De Klerk, then president of South Africa, won the Nobel Peace Prize in 1993; at Mandela's inauguration as South African president in 1994; and before Queen Elizabeth during Mandela's 1996 state visit. Their 1997 album, *Heavenly,* broke new ground with gospel and rhythm and blues numbers, as well as collaborations with Lou Rawls, Dolly Parton, and Bonnie Raitt.

North America
___

Lafayette Theatre,

pioneering African American theater in Harlem that staged both serious drama and light entertainment.

Like many Harlem theaters, the Lafayette Theatre originally opened in 1912 for all-white audiences. A few years later black drama critic Lester Walton leased the theater and created a black stock company to bring meaningful dramatic theater to New York's black audiences. By 1916 the Lafayette Players, led by Anita Bush, had successfully produced plays by Shakespeare, Dumas, and Molière.

Eventually, the Lafayette adapted to its audience's taste for musical comedies and more lighthearted theater. The theater remained a center for black entertainment through the 1930s, when the Federal Theater Project brought more serious works back to the Lafayette stage. In 1967, at the height of the Black Arts Movement, the New Lafayette Theatre opened in Harlem, honoring its namesake's commitment to producing theater with African American performers for African American audiences.

Africa
___

Lamu, Kenya,

an Indian Ocean island with a Swahili port town of the same name.

Lamu was one of several coastal trading communities in Kenya where the blending of African and Arab cultures gave rise to the Swahili language and culture. Although its origins are unclear, many believe that Lamu Town was founded in the fourteenth century C.E. as a trading post for Arab merchants, who later intermarried with Africans. The town saw its golden age between the seventeenth and nineteenth century, when it was an important depot for the export of gold, ivory, and, to a much lesser degree, slaves headed for Asia and the Middle East. During this time Lamu Town produced many fine examples of Swahili art and literature, including famous wood carvings and poems, some of which remain in Lamu's museum.

Such abundance was not without cost, as rival leaders of neighboring Swahili communities, including Pate Island and Mombasa, sought to control Lamu. *The Pate Chronicle* tells of a long-running conflict between 1650 and 1812 that culminated in a joint attack waged by the Mazrui clan of Mombasa and a Pate force against Lamu. The Lamuites repelled the invasion.

Ironically, the victory marked the end of Lamu's independence; shortly afterward, Lamuites requested protection from the Omani Dynasty of Zanzibar, which subsequently controlled Lamu until the late nineteenth century, when the British imposed colonial rule. Lamuites continued to identify themselves as Arabs, and when Kenya achieved independence in 1963, many lobbied for autonomy from the *Mwafrika*, or up-country Africans, fearing that the ethnic Kikuyu in particular would dominate postcolonial business and government. Today, however, because Arabs are typically considered foreigners, Lamu's residents are more likely to call themselves Swahili.

Modern Lamu's economy runs on tourism. The island has become renowned for its slow pace, tranquil beaches, traditional Swahili architecture, and tolerance for bohemian lifestyles. Despite the constant influx of foreign visitors, donkeys and cows remain the primary modes of transportation on the island, as the streets are too narrow to accommodate automobile traffic.

Latin America and the Caribbean

Lam, Wifredo

(b. December 8, 1902, Sagua la Grande Provincia de Las Villas, Cuba; d. September 1, 1982, Paris, France), Cuban modern artist and the first internationally acclaimed Afro-Cuban painter and sculptor.

Throughout his career Wifredo Lam was active in major art movements, including surrealism and modernism, and was associated with many of the best-known figures in the art world of his day, including Pablo Picasso and André Breton. Lam's surrealist compositions make use of his Afro-Chinese and Cuban ancestry, and his most famous paintings, including *The Eternal Presence* (1945) and *The Jungle* (1943), present his mythic, erotic, and syncretic inheritances in a supernatural and symbolic way. He is arguably one of the most distinguished talents of the twentieth century.

Lam left Cuba in 1923 at age 21 to study at the Madrid School of Fine Arts. While he was in Europe, his painting was influenced by the experimental mode of the era, and his compositions became increasingly abstract. After visiting Picasso's studio in 1930, he established a relationship with the artist, apparently because Picasso himself was already involved in the so-called primitivist movement and had begun to incorporate African masks and design motifs into his own painting. This was a visual vernacular with which Lam was already familiar as a result of his Cuban roots. Picasso sponsored an exhibition of Lam's work in 1938 in Paris that began to establish Lam's reputation.

In 1941, during World War II, he returned to Cuba for the first time in nearly 20 years. There he rooted his work in the specificity of his own (and the island's) historical transculturation, or cultural mixing, drawing on Chinese, African, and indigenous influences to produce the most acclaimed work of his career. Lam was also closely associated with the artists of the Négritude Movement in the French-speaking Caribbean, and with such literary figures as Aimé Césaire, all of whom wanted to plumb the depth of African heritage, spirituality, and liveliness in the Caribbean and oppose their findings to what they considered the moribund and stagnant intellectual life of Europe.

Although Cuba left its mark on his artistic work, Lam never remained in one place. He continued to live mostly in Cuba but also traveled frequently to other metropolitan centers of art in the West. In 1965 he moved to Albisola, Italy, where he remained for 17 years until his death.

North America

Larsen, Nella

(b. April 13, 1891, Chicago, Ill.; d. March 30, 1964, New York, N.Y.), African American novelist of the Harlem Renaissance; landmark figure in the black women's literary tradition.

Nella Larsen's celebrity has followed an unusual trajectory. She was one of the most celebrated black novelists during the Harlem Renaissance and received several major awards for her writing, including the first Guggenheim Fellowship ever given to a black woman. She and her husband were also notable members of the Harlem social scene, and she was friends with most of the prominent Harlem writers of her time. After a public accusation of plagiarism and an equally public divorce, Larsen removed herself from the public eye and was effectively forgotten by acquaintances and audiences until after her death. But renewed interest in both the Harlem Renaissance and black women writers has brought her back to prominence, and Larsen is again celebrated as a key figure in the African American literary tradition.

Larsen was born Nellie Walker to a Danish mother and a West Indian father in Chicago. Larsen's two novels, *Quicksand* and *Passing*, were published by the mainstream publisher Alfred A. Knopf in 1928 and 1929. Both novels deal with upper-class, mixed-race black women protagonists, reflecting the world Larsen found herself in, but they go beyond simply painting that world. Instead, they are complicated explorations of the ways in which race, gender, class, and sexuality all constrict the women's lives to varying degrees. Contemporary critics now regard her as one of the most sophisticated and modern novelists to emerge from the Harlem Renaissance, and her two books are regarded as landmark examples of black women's attempts to explain their complex identities—and the complicated forces circumscribing them—in fiction.

Latin America and the Caribbean

Las Casas, Bartolomé de

(b. 1484, Seville, Spain; d. July 18, 1566, Madrid, Spain), Spanish bishop of the Dominican Order; recognized as one of the most significant chroniclers of the Spanish Conquest, he is famous for his defense of Amerindians and his initial promotion of African slavery. He is also read as a theologian, jurist, ethnographer, humanist, historian, politician, prophet, and biographer.

Bartolomé de Las Casas is a controversial figure whose prolific and complex writings continue to raise questions after five centuries of study and debate. Though known as the most unrelenting advocate of Amerindian interests before the Spanish Crown, he endorsed the colonial system and played a role in the slave trade. Throughout his life he denounced the violence and abuse that were inherent in Spanish policies toward Amerindians while he proposed more benevolent forms of colonization. As a strategic reformist, and in the hope of saving indigenous lives, he initially advocated that imported African slaves be used in place of Amerindian forced laborers. However, toward the end of his life Las Casas regretted his promotion of black slavery and was deeply troubled for having condoned any form of human bondage. Ironically, through his repentance, he became the first colonist of the sixteenth century to denounce the injustice of African slavery.

North America

Last Poets, The,

American musical group whose style was a precursor to rap music.

Despite their name, many critics have argued that the Last Poets' innovative style made them the first rap group. The Last Poets grew out of the Black Arts Movement, a wave of socially and politically aware African American literature and art in the 1960s. Gylan Kain, Abiodun Oyewole, David Nelson, and conga player Nilija formed the Last Poets at a Harlem memorial gathering for Malcolm X in May 1968. From the beginning their lyrics represented the type of radical poetry that flourished during the Black Arts Movement, and their music emphasized both the spoken word and African-inspired drumming. Author Darius James remembered the original Last

Poets recordings this way: "The rhetoric made you mad. The drums made you pop your fingers. And the poetry made you sail. . . . Most importantly, they made you think and kept you 'correct' on a revolutionary level."

Latimer, Lewis Howard

(b. September 4, 1848, Chelsea, Mass.; d. December 11, 1928, Flushing, N.Y.), African American inventor and innovator in the electric lighting industry.

Lewis H. Latimer's father was an escaped slave from Virginia whom Frederick Douglass and William Lloyd Garrison defended when his former owner tried to have him extradited. As a boy Latimer worked in his father's barbershop and peddled Garrison's newspaper, the *Liberator*.

Latimer joined the Union Navy during the Civil War, serving on the U.S.S. Massasoit on the James River in Virginia. After an honorable discharge in 1865, he found work with Crosby & Gould, a firm of patent lawyers. Although Latimer was hired as an office boy, he cultivated drafting skills in his spare time until he was qualified for blueprint work. In addition to drawing plans for other people's inventions, Latimer brainstormed his own, patenting in 1874 a "pivot bottom" for water closets on trains. His high-caliber draftsmanship impressed Alexander Graham Bell, whose 1876 telephone blueprints were drawn up by Latimer.

In 1880 Latimer left Crosby & Gould to work for the inventor Hiram Maxim, who ran the United States Electric Lighting Company in Bridge-port, Connecticut. The previous year Thomas A. Edison had invented the light bulb, and Maxim was one of Edison's prime competitors in the institutionalization of electric light. Under Maxim, Latimer supervised the installation of electric light in New York, Philadelphia, London, and Montreal. He also developed other inventions of his own, copatenting an electric lamp with Joseph V. Nichols in 1881, and, most important, refining light-bulb technology in 1882. Although Edison had invented electric light, Latimer made it more economically feasible by developing longer- and brighter-burning filaments, specifically ones derived from bamboo slivers and the cellulose of cotton thread.

In 1884 Latimer left Maxim, possibly due to racial discrimination, and worked for two other companies before joining Edison Electric Light (later General Electric). Latimer first served Edison as an engineer but eventually became Edison's expert witness in patent dispute lawsuits. His association with the legal side of the electricity industry continued in the early twentieth century, when he worked for the law firm of Hammer & Schwartz in New York. Latimer remained involved in the technical aspects of the industry, however, publishing *Incandescent Electric Lighting* in 1896, a definitive textbook on Edison's developments.

In 1918 Latimer helped form the Edison Pioneers, an honorary group of engineers who had worked for Edison, among whom Latimer was the only African American.

Lawrence, Jacob Armstead

(b. September 7, 1917, Atlantic City, N.J.), the most acclaimed African American artist at the end of the twentieth century.

Jacob Lawrence has painted figurative and narrative pictures of the black community and black history for more than 60 years in a consistent modernist style, using expressive, strong design and flat areas of color. His parents, Jacob Armstead Lawrence of South Carolina and Rose Lee of Virginia, were part of the Great Migration, the movement of African Americans from the South to the promise of jobs in Northern industry during the two decades following the onset of World War I.

During Lawrence's youth in Harlem his mother enrolled him in after-school arts and crafts classes held at the 135th Street Branch of the New York Public Library. Charles Alston, who taught art there, later moved to the Utopia Neighborhood Center, where Lawrence also enrolled. Using a variety of techniques, including collage and papier-mâché, the young Lawrence made colorful masks and cityscapes on the insides of cardboard shoe-boxes. He was introduced to African American history in his classes, and he visited the exhibition of African sculpture held at the Museum of Modern Art in 1935.

Lawrence took classes at the Harlem Art Center and the American Artists School from 1936 through 1938, and in 1936 he also worked briefly for the Civilian Conservation Corps (CCC), one of the relief agencies set up by the Roosevelt administration to create employment for youth during the Great Depression. Among the older artists, Augusta Savage was probably the most influential on Lawrence's work. A dynamic sculptor, she believed her mission was to teach art to children and young people in Harlem, and she spearheaded the establishment of the Harlem Community Art Center in 1937, financed by the Federal Art Project (FAP) of the national Works Progress Administration (WPA). She arranged to have Lawrence hired as a professional artist in 1938 in the easel section of the FAP.

Lawrence was painting scenes of Harlem interiors and street life, using the flat style that was to become his lifelong trademark. During the next year he began his first narrative series with texts: 41 panels on the life of Toussaint L'Ouverture, the liberator of Haiti. Some of Lawrence's Harlem scenes were included in a 1937 group exhibition of the Harlem Artists Guild and then featured in his first solo exhibition, which was held in the next year at the Harlem YMCA. After a New York showing at the De Porres Interracial Center, his Toussaint series traveled to the Baltimore Museum of Art in 1939 for the exhibition *Contemporary Negro Art*.

During the late 1930s and the 1940s Lawrence worked on two other narrative series: *Frederick Douglass* (1938–1939), comprising 32 paintings, and *Harriet Tubman* (1939–1949), comprising 31 paintings. For both he received support from the Harmon Foundation. There was support from the Julius Rosenwald Fund for *Migration* (1940–1941), a series of 60 paintings; and *John Brown* (1941–1942), a series of 22 paintings. Alain Locke, who had included Lawrence in his influential book *The Negro in Art* (1940), brought him to the attention of Edith Halpert, the prominent New York art dealer, who agreed to give Lawrence a show at her Downtown Gallery.

Halpert alerted publisher Henry Luce, who reproduced 26 pictures from the *Migration* Series in the November 1941 issue of *Fortune* magazine. The 60 panels were subsequently divided between the Phillips Collection in Washington, D.C., and the Museum of Modern Art in New York City. In 1942 Lawrence received another grant from the Rosenwald Fund to create a *Harlem* series of 30 genre paintings.

During the Civil Rights Movement of the mid-1950s, he turned again to black history and painted 30 panels of a projected 60-panel series entitled *Struggle: From the History of the American People*, which highlighted the contributions of African Americans.

He designed two *Time* magazine covers, one of Jesse Jackson and one of Colonel Ojukwu, military governor of Biafra. He did a poster for the 1972 Olympic Games, and he completed the *George Washington Bush* series for the state of Washington in 1973. During the 1970s he began making paintings with the theme of building and carpenters, which to Lawrence symbolized the goal of constructing strong, integrated communities.

Major retrospective exhibitions of Lawrence's paintings have had national tours organized by the American Federation of Art in 1960, the Whitney Museum of American Art in 1974, and the Seattle Art Museum in 1986. The 60-panel *Migration* Series, organized by the Phillips Collection, circulated between 1993 and 1995. Murals on the themes of sports and work were on the walls of Kingdome Stadium, which was razed March 26, 2000, and in the New York City subway system. Lawrence was honored by President Jimmy Carter in 1980, and he was inducted into the American Academy of Arts and Letters in 1994. In 1990 he received the National Medal of Arts from President George Bush.

North America

Lawson, James Morris

(b. September 22, 1928, Uniontown, Pa.), African American minister and civil rights leader who trained early civil rights activists in nonviolent resistance tactics.

Although he served as a low-profile leader of the Civil Rights Movement, James Lawson's influence was profound and lasting. He first made his mark on the civil rights struggle by teaching Indian activist Mohandas Gandhi's nonviolent civil disobedience techniques during the Nashville, Tennessee, sit-in demonstrations of 1960. Lawson, an ordained minister and pacifist who in the early 1950s had gone to prison rather than fight in the Korean War, had traveled to India as a missionary after his release and studied Gandhi's tactics firsthand.

Though not as visible as other civil rights leaders, Lawson was involved with many of the well-known civil rights organizations and demonstrations of the Freedom Movement. He was an adviser to the Student Nonviolent Coordinating Committee (SNCC) and authored the organization's statement of purpose while attending its initial conference in April 1960. He led the direct action projects of the Southern Christian Leadership Conference (SCLC), and he participated in the Freedom Rides, which were first sponsored by the Congress of Racial Equality (CORE). In 1968, while serving as a pastor in Memphis, Tennessee, he helped coordinate the garbage workers' strike, by which he hoped to highlight the lasting and adverse economic effects of segregation.

Africa

Laye, Camara

(b. January 1, 1928, Kouroussa, French Guinea [now Guinea]; d. February 4, 1980, Senegal), Guinean novelist considered a pioneer of modern West African literature.

With the 1953 publication of his autobiography *L'Enfant noir* (published in America as *The Dark Child* in 1954), Camara Laye was hailed as having "brought French African narrative prose finally into its own." Although he published only three more books, he is widely considered one of the most important African novelists to have written in French.

Away from his country for the first time and separated from his family and community, Laye began writing the memoir that became *L'Enfant noir*. The book recounts Laye's experiences in the village, at school, and in Conakry and ends as he boards the airplane that will take him to France. The success of his first book permitted Laye to quit his job as a mechanic and write full-time. His first novel, *Le regard du roi*, appeared in 1954 and was translated as *The Radiance of the King* in 1956.

After returning to Guinea in 1956 and marrying his high-school sweetheart, Marie, Laye worked as an engineer and later for the Ministry of Information. But Guinea's independence from France in 1958 and the subsequent rule of its first president, Sékou Touré, brought disturbing changes to Laye's home country. His 1966 book, *A Dream of Africa* (*Dramouss* in French editions), openly attacked what its hero, Fatoman, called "a regime based on violence." Condemning both colonial rule and the regime that replaced it, Laye earned the hatred of Sékou Touré, and he and his family were forced into exile in neighboring Senegal soon after the book's publication.

Laye continued to write short stories, several of which were published in the literary magazines *Black Orpheus* and *Présence Africaine.*

Africa

Leakey, Louis

(b. August 7, 1903, Kabete, Kenya; d. October 1, 1972, London, England), British paleoanthropologist noted for his discoveries of fossil remains that greatly advanced the study of human evolution.

Even before he received his doctorate in anthropology from the University of Cambridge, Louis Leakey, the son of British missionaries to colonial Kenya, was convinced that human evolution began in Africa, not in Asia, as was commonly believed among his contemporaries. To prove his theory, Leakey focused his archaeological research on expeditions to Olduvai, a river gorge in Tanganyika (now Tanzania). Though he found important fossils and Stone Age tools, Leakey had not found definitive evidence that Africa was the cradle of human evolution.

That changed on an expedition to Olduvai in 1959, when his wife, Mary Leakey, with whom he had worked since 1933, discovered the partial remains of a 1.75-million-year-old fossil hominid, which Louis Leakey classified as *Zinjanthropus* (later classified as *Australopithecus boisei*). From 1960 to 1963 the Leakeys unearthed other important discoveries, including the remains of another fossil hominid, which they classified as *Homo habilis* (Latin for "handy man"), claiming it was both the first member of the true human genus and the first true toolmaker. While the exact interpretation of the Leakeys' fossil finds is still debated, their significance to the field of physical anthropology is universally acknowledged and they are considered the best evidence yet that Africa was in fact the starting point for human evolution.

In his later years Leakey became increasingly interested in studying primate behavior as a way of understanding the behavior of human ances-tors. He helped to engineer the funding and recruitment of groundbreaking researchers, including Jane Goodall, who worked with chimpanzees in Gombe, Tanzania; Dian Fossey, who studied mountain gorillas in Rwanda; and Birute Galdikas Brindamour, who researched orangutans in the Sarawak region of Indonesia. His books include *Stone Age Africa* (1936) and *Olduvai Gorge, 1951–1961* (1965).

North America

Ledbetter, Hudson William ("Leadbelly")

(b. January 21, 1885, near Mooringsport, La.; d. December 6, 1949, New York, N.Y.), African American itinerant musician who played from a wide repertoire that centered on blues but included folk ballads, popular songs, and music from the American West.

As a child Leadbelly picked cotton with his parents, first as a sharecropper in Louisiana and then on land that his parents bought in Leigh, Texas. During his youth in Leigh, he demonstrated substantial musical talent. He played the accordion, mastered the 12-string guitar, and soon frequented the red-light district of neighboring Shreveport as a musician.

Folklorist John Lomax and his son, Alan, compiled folk recordings for the Library of Congress, traveling the south with new technology to capture America's oral traditions. In Leadbelly they found an immense repository of folk and original music, which they recorded and promoted in the East. John Lomax transformed Leadbelly's life, hiring him as a chauffeur and introducing him to white audiences.

Leadbelly cut commercial recordings and released "race records" but achieved his largest following on college campuses, at political rallies, and in the folk scene of Greenwich Village in the early 1940s. He collaborated with both white and black members of this crowd, including Woody Guthrie, Brownie McGhee, Sonny Terry, and Big Bill Broonzy. Like these musicians, Leadbelly became associated with left-wing politics and wrote such overtly political tunes as "Scottsboro Boys" (1938) and "Bourgeois Blues" (1938). In the 1940s he achieved greater celebrity by appearing on radio and in film. In 1949 he toured in Europe but returned to New York, where he died later that year.

His work as a musician yielded approximately 70 original or highly reworked compositions in addition to scores of children's songs, Southern ballads, blues tunes, field hollers, and popular songs. In Europe Leadbelly influenced the skiffle bands that later culminated in the Beatles and the Rolling Stones. In the United States he inspired a generation of black bluesmen as well as white folk singers such as Joan Baez and Bob Dylan. In 1976 Gordon Parks Sr. made a biographical film about his life. In 1988 Leadbelly was inducted into the Rock and Roll Hall of Fame.

North America

Lee, Canada

(b. May 3, 1907, New York, N.Y.; d. May 10, 1952, England), African American prizefighter and actor noted for performing strong, nonstereotypical roles in the 1930s and 1940s.

As an African American actor, Canada Lee played nonstereotypical roles during the late 1930s and 1940s, when black actors and actresses were relegated to demeaning roles. Originally a boxer, he entered theater after being blinded in one eye in a fight in 1933. He began his acting career when he was cast in the role of Banquo in a black production of *Macbeth* funded by the Works Progress Administration (WPA) Negro Federal Theatre Project in 1936. The play was directed by Orson Welles and marked the beginning of Lee's casting in nontraditional roles.

Although *Macbeth* received some negative reviews (due more to the fact that a black cast was performing Shakespeare than to the acting), it gave

Lee the needed exposure to continue in such roles. Through the WPA Negro Federal Theatre Project, he continued to experiment with the non-traditional, performing in Eugene O'Neill's *One Act Plays of the Sea* (a collection of four plays) in 1937 and *Haiti*, by W. E. B. Du Bois, in 1938. Due to the "communist leanings" of the play *Haiti* and *Big White Fog* in 1940, the Negro Federal Theatre Project was halted by the House Committee on Un-American Activities (HUAC).

Nevertheless, Lee had gained enough exposure to be cast in the part of Drayton in *Mamba's Daughters* on Broadway in 1939. Further, the experience he gained with the Negro Federal Theatre Project led to his role as Bigger Thomas in *Native Son* in 1940 and 1941. Critics cite his portrayal of Bigger as the best role of his career. Because the play had an interracial cast, it became highly controversial.

Lee's visibility as a black actor doing unconventional roles inspired him to speak out against the limited casting of black actors and actresses in Hollywood and Broadway. Determined not to take stereotypical "handkerchief head roles," he decided to produce *On Whitman Avenue* to achieve that end. In 1947 the HUAC cited Lee's play as "left-wing."

Lee garnered even greater visibility when he portrayed Stephen Kumalo, a father whose son kills a white man, in the play *Cry, the Beloved Country*, produced by Zoltan Korda. Despite worldwide attention for his acting, Lee could not escape being blacklisted and pursued by HUAC as well as by the Federal Bureau of Investigation for speaking out against stereotyping.

North America

Lee, Shelton Jackson ("Spike")

(b. March 20, 1957, Atlanta, Ga.), African American film director, writer, and actor.

Starting with the phenomenal popularity of *She's Gotta Have It*, Spike Lee has emerged as one of America's most successful filmmakers, garnering both good reviews and healthy box-office receipts for his movies. He has also attracted criticism; detractors have called him arrogant and paranoid and his movies incendiary, even racist. But controversy has not kept Lee from becoming a media icon, famous for his acting, fashion sense, and provocative public pronouncements on a variety of subjects.

Raised in the Fort Greene neighborhood of Brooklyn, New York, Lee is the eldest of five children born to Bill Lee, a jazz musician and composer, and Jacquelyn Lee, a schoolteacher. In 1986, following the collapse of his plans for a movie about a bike messenger, Lee released his first feature film, *She's Gotta Have It*, a romantic comedy about a single black woman dating three men simultaneously. Critics praised the movie's style, intelligence, humor, and realistic portrayal of African Americans—something seldom seen in Hollywood productions—and it received the coveted New Film Award at the Cannes Film Festival.

It was Lee's third feature that received the most attention. *Do the Right Thing* (1989), set in the Bedford-Stuyvesant and Bensonhurst sections of

Brooklyn, came in the wake of a series of racially motivated attacks against African Americans. The movie, widely considered Lee's best film artistically, was a box-office success. Attention from *Do the Right Thing*, combined with Lee's popular commercials for Nike and other products, made him a recognizable celebrity by 1990. With the increased exposure, Lee's comments on race relations, politics, other filmmakers, and even basketball sparked heated responses from many quarters. Despite the occasionally negative press, many credit Lee's visibility and the success of his first three films with inspiring a wave of African American filmmakers. In 1992 he released his most ambitious film, *Malcolm X*, a sweeping biography of the slain civil rights leader. *Malcolm X* attracted at least as much controversy as *Do the Right Thing*, particularly within the black community, some of whom saw Lee as co-opting the Black Muslim hero's image. Lee, who had used security personnel from the Nation of Islam to guard the sets on previous films, responded with typical bravado. The film, starring Denzel Washington, received mostly favorable reviews but was criticized for its length and simplistic political message.

After *Malcolm X*, Lee made a number of movies—*Crooklyn* (1994), *Clockers* (1995), *Girl 6* (1996), *Get on the Bus* (1996), and *He Got Game* (1998)—that did not attract the critical or commercial attention that his earlier work did. Lee also continued to film commercials and music videos and command a film studio 40 Acres & A Mule.

Africa

Leo Africanus (al-Hassan ibn Muhammad al-Wizzaa al-Fasi, also known as Giovanni Leoni)

(b. 1485?, Granada, present-day Spain; d. 1554?, Tunis, present-day Tunisia), a Moorish explorer who published an influential account of the western and central Sudan.

The son of a wealthy family, Leo Africanus was originally named al-Hassan ibn Muhammad al-Wizzaa al-Fasi. He was born in Spain but moved to Fès, Morocco, as a child. There he was educated and was later employed by his uncle as a clerk. The first trip of Africanus to the western Sudan, around 1512, was part of a diplomatic and commercial mission to the Songhai Empire led by his uncle on behalf of the rulers of Fès. During this trip Africanus traveled extensively throughout the region and visited its major trading cities, including Tombouctou (Timbuktu), Djenné, Gao, and Sijilmasa. He recorded his observations on all of the region's major states: the Songhai and Mali empires, the Hausa states and Bornu, as well as the Bulala state occupying the former Kanem Empire. This trip provided much of the research for his later publications.

Between 1516 and 1518 Africanus made several trips to Egypt and possibly a trip to Constantinople. In 1518, during his return home from Egypt, Christian pirates captured the ship in which he was traveling near Tunis and

Published in 1584, this hand-colored map of Africa reflects information that travelers such as Leo Africanus brought to Europe. *CORBIS/Historical Picture Archive*

took him as a hostage. The extent of his knowledge so impressed his captors that they presented him as a slave to Pope Leo X. The pope subsequently freed the Moor, who converted to Christianity and was baptized Leo Africanus. In addition, the pope encouraged Africanus to finish *The History and Description of Africa and the Notable Things Therein Contained*, a book the traveler had begun during his journeys in Africa. Africanus finished the book in 1526; it was eventually published in Italian in 1550. At the time this book was the most important account of West Africa published since Ibn Battutah's book in 1350.

Africanus remained in Italy for approximately 20 years. In that time he occasionally taught Arabic at Bologna University and also wrote on the lives of great Arab philosophers and physicians. Late in his life he returned to North Africa, where he may have reconverted to Islam. He died in Tunis between 1552 and 1560.

Latin America and the Caribbean

León, Tania J.

(b. May 14, 1943, Havana, Cuba), Afro-Cuban composer, conductor, and pianist, one of the first women to achieve international success as an orchestral conductor of classical music.

Tania León is an internationally acclaimed composer and conductor, and a leading exponent of contemporary classical music. Her musical style is versatile and innovative: she incorporates elements of jazz and gospel into her compositions as well as the rhythms and color of Afro-Cuban music. She debuted as a conductor at the *Festival of Two Worlds* in Spoleto, Italy, in 1971—a time when there were few professional women conductors of classical music.

León grew up in Havana, Cuba, where she studied piano, violin, and composition at the Carlos Alfredo Peyrellado Conservatory. After graduation she spent several years performing as a pianist in Cuba and in 1967 emigrated to New York City. In 1969 Arthur Mitchell invited her to be the pianist for his dance troupe, Dance Theater of Harlem, an offer that led to her appointment as the troupe's music director. She wrote several ballet compositions for the troupe, including *Tones* (with Mitchell, 1970), *Beloved* (1972), and *Dougla* (with Geoffrey Holder, 1974)—all regularly performed by European dance companies. At the same time she earned a bachelor's degree in music (1971) and a master's degree in composition (1973) from New York University, and studied conducting with Leonard Bernstein and Seiji Ozawa at the Berkshire Music Center at Tanglewood.

In 1977 León founded the Brooklyn Philharmonic *Community Concert Series*, which she conducted for more than ten years. After leaving the Dance Theater of Harlem in 1980, she began touring the United States, Puerto Rico, and Europe as a guest conductor. Discovering a wealth of material, she has since aspired to bring more Latin American music into Western concert halls. In 1994 she co-organized the American Composers Orchestra's *Sonidos de las Americas* (Sounds of the Americas) festival in New York City—a series of concerts, symposia, and master classes that featured the works of Mexican composers.

León has composed and recorded a wide variety of works for orchestra, chamber groups, and solo instruments. She has also written an award-winning opera, *Scourge of Hyacinths* (1994), based on a radio play by the Nigerian dramatist Wole Soyinka.

Africa

Leopold II
(b. 1835, Brussels, Belgium; d. 1909, Brussels, Belgium), king of Belgium and infamous founder of the Congo Free State, later the Belgian Congo.

Son of Leopold I, the first king of independent Belgium, Leopold II ascended to the throne in 1865 intent on finding opportunities abroad to increase his power and personal wealth. Looking at first to the Far East, he was soon enticed by the stories of Henry Morton Stanley, an Anglo-American explorer, and the potential for wealth in the Congo basin of Central Africa. In 1876 Leopold organized an association to develop Central Africa and hired Stanley to lead an expedition to the Congo River and establish contacts with the peoples around the river. By 1884 Stanley had made 450 treaties with local chieftains on behalf of Leopold and had also constructed roads and railroads in the basin. As a result, Leopold was recognized as sovereign of the Congo Free State by the Berlin West Africa Conference (1884–1885). Leopold promised other European powers that his "exclusive mission . . . [was] to introduce civilization and trade into the Center of Africa."

Leopold claimed the Congo Free State as his personal empire, where he sold enormous concessions of land to companies for mining, rubber tapping, and speculation. During Leopold's reign the indigenous population of the Congo Free State was subject to land confiscation, forced labor, and the brutality of his military. Reports from Europeans, such as André Gide, who visited the Free States, eventually provoked international protest, and in 1906 Leopold was forced to institute modest reforms. Failing health and rising debts forced Leopold to turn the Congo Free State over to the Belgian government in 1908. He died in 1909.

Africa

Lesotho,

a small landlocked country in southern Africa, surrounded by the Republic of South Africa.

Lesotho is a mountainous, landlocked country with few natural resources apart from its water supply. It is extremely dependent on its only immediate neighbor, South Africa, for everything from food to energy to employment for hundreds of thousands of its citizens. It resisted incorporation into South Africa during its tenure as a British colony, thanks largely to a fierce nationalism that dates back to the formation of the Basutoland Kingdom in the early nineteenth century. Since achieving independence in 1966, Lesotho has suffered from political instability and oppression. Its relations with South Africa were strained during much of the late apartheid era, but the two countries' current governments are now on friendly terms. Their fates became even more closely linked in 1998 with the opening of Lesotho's Katse Dam, phase one of a massive hydroelectric project intended to bolster Lesotho's ailing economy both by making the country self-sufficient in electrical power and by generating revenue from water sales to South Africa.

Africa

Lesotho (Ready Reference)

Official Name: Kingdom of Lesotho
Former Name: Basutoland
Area: 30,350 sq km (12,140 sq mi)
Location: Southern Africa; completely encircled by South Africa
Capital: Maseru (population 109,382 [1986 estimate])

A young man saddles a horse in the mountains of Lesotho. *CORBIS/Earl Kowall*

Population: 1,970,781 (1996 estimate)

Population Density: 65 persons per sq km (about 169 persons per sq mi)

Population Below Age 15: 40 percent (male 420,526; female 419,059 [1998 estimate])

Population Growth Rate: 1.9 percent (1998 estimate)

Total Fertility Rate: 4.13 children born per woman (1998 estimate)

Life Expectancy at Birth: Total population: 53.97 years (male 52.18 years; female 55.81 years [1998 estimate])

Infant Mortality Rate: 78.3 deaths per 1000 live births (1998 estimate)

Literacy Rate (age 15 and over who can read and write): Total population: 71.3 percent (male 81.1 percent; female 62.3 percent [1995 estimate])

Education: Education is compulsory between ages 6 and 13. Nearly all of Lesotho's school-age children attend primary school. Christian missions under the direction of the Minister of Education operate most schools, which are free at the primary level. In the early 1990s nearly 362,700 pupils annually attended some 1200 primary schools, and about 53,500 pupils attended secondary and vocational schools. The National University of Lesotho (1966), in Roma, is attended yearly by about 1400 students and has a teaching staff of more than 200. The Lesotho Agricultural College (1955) is in Maseru. Lesotho has one of the highest literacy rates in Africa.

Languages: English is the official language, but Sesotho (southern Sotho), Zulu, and Xhosa are widely spoken.

Ethnic Groups: The vast majority of the population is ethnic Sotho; there is a tiny minority of approximately 1600 Europeans and 800 Asians.

Religions: Christian 80 percent; indigenous beliefs 20 percent

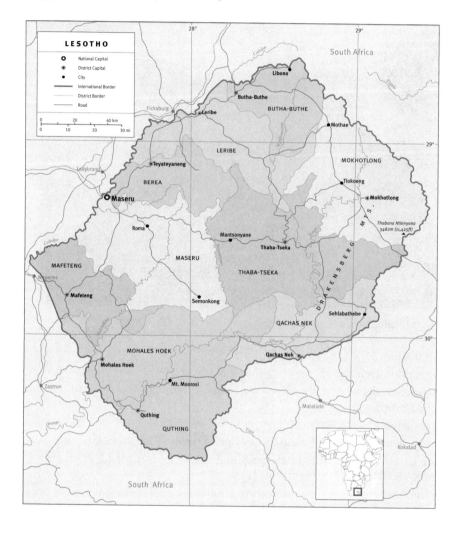

Climate: The climate is mild, with hot summer days in the lowlands relieved by cool nights. Winter can be cold, particularly in the mountains, and heavy snows occasionally occur. Precipitation falls mostly from October through April. In Maseru, located in the lowlands, average temperatures range from 14° to 28° C (57° to 82° F) in January and from -1° to 16° C (30° to 61° F) in July. The city averages 690 mm (27 in) of precipitation annually.

Lands, Plants, and Animals: Mostly highland with plateaus, hills, and mountains. Sixty-six percent of the land comprises meadows and pastures; less than 10 percent is arable.

Natural Resources: Water, agricultural and grazing land, some diamonds and other minerals

Currency: The loti

Gross Domestic Product (GDP): $5.1 billion (1997 estimate)

GDP per Capita: $2500 (1997 estimate)

GDP Real Growth Rate: 9 percent (1997 estimate)

Primary Economic Activities: Most of the labor force works in the service and industrial sectors; 86.2 percent of the resident population are engaged in subsistence agriculture, and roughly 60 percent of the active male wage earners work in South Africa. Manufacturing depends largely on farm products that support the milling, canning, leather, and jute industries.

Primary Crops: Corn, wheat, pulses, sorghum, barley; livestock

Industries: Food, beverages, textiles, handicrafts; construction, and tourism

Primary Exports: Clothing, furniture, footwear, and wool

Primary Imports: Corn, building materials, clothing, vehicles, machinery, medicines, and petroleum products

Lesotho women carry bundles of wood on their heads. *CORBIS/Nazima Kowall*

Primary Trade Partners: South Africa, Asia, the European Union, and South American countries

Government: Lesotho is a modified constitutional monarchy. Lesotho's king since 1996 (Letsie David Mohato, or Letsie III) is a hereditary monarch. But, under the terms of the constitution that came into effect after the March 1993 election, he has no executive or legislative powers. Under traditional law, the king can be elected or deposed by a majority vote of the College of Chiefs. Executive power is held by the prime minister. The legislative branch is a bicameral Parliament. The Senate consists of 33 members (the 22 principal chiefs and 11 other members appointed by the ruling party), and the 65 members of the National Assembly are elected by popular vote. Lesotho has universal suffrage beginning at age 21.

Latin America and the Caribbean

Lewis, Arthur

(b. January 23, 1915, Castries, St. Lucia, West Indies; d. June 15, 1991, Bridgeport, Barbados), West Indian economist, scholar, lecturer, writer, and government adviser who shared the 1979 Nobel Prize for Economics with the American Theodore Schultz for their pioneering research in economic development, with particular consideration of the problems of developing countries.

Arthur Lewis was the first black person to receive the Nobel Prize in a category other than peace. He once described his intellectual career as consisting of three phases: the history of world economics and development; industrial economics; and the economic problems of underdeveloped nations. In his Nobel lecture he suggested that the least developed countries should concentrate on increasing their regional trade rather than being heavily dependent on the continued growth of the most developed countries. He believed that in this way, underdeveloped nations could eventually accelerate their own economies even as growth in the more technologically advantaged nations slackened.

Lewis wanted to study engineering but decided it would be pointless since, at that time, neither the government nor white firms would hire a black engineer. A brilliant student, he received a bachelor of commerce degree with honors from Saint Mary's College in St. Lucia (1929) when he was 14 years old. He later received a scholarship for graduate study at the London School of Economics (Ph.D., 1937) and remained there as a professor from 1938 to 1947. In 1955, when he was a professor at the University of Manchester, Lewis published one of the first academic works in the area of applied developmental economics, *The Theory of Economic Growth*. During his life he was to write 11 books and more than 80 monographs and scholarly articles. His success as a scholar was recognized by the British government, who knighted him Sir Arthur William Lewis in 1963.

Lewis was a much sought after academic and economic advisor. He was professor emeritus at Princeton University in the United States from 1983 until his death.

Lewis, Edmonia

(b. 1845?; d. ?), believed to be the first woman sculptor of African American and Native American heritage.

Edmonia Lewis often drew upon her dual ancestry for inspiration. Her best-known work, *Forever Free* (1867, Howard University Gallery of Art, Washington, D.C.), was inspired by the Emancipation Proclamation. Created in marble, *Forever Free* depicts a man and a woman who have learned of their freedom. In an expression of gratitude, the woman kneels with her hands clasped; the man rests his foot on the ball that held them in bondage, raising his arm to display the broken shackle and chain on his wrist.

Little is known about Lewis's early life. Sources give differing birth dates—1843 and 1845—and birthplaces—Ohio, New York, and New Jersey. Her father was an African American, and her mother was a member of the Ojibwa community. In 1859 Lewis entered Oberlin College in Oberlin, Ohio, where she excelled at drawing. Known as Wildfire in the Ojibwa community, Lewis changed her name to Mary Edmonia during her time at Oberlin; she generally signed her sculptures and her correspondence with the name Edmonia. When a teacher at Oberlin missed some paintbrushes, Lewis was accused of the theft; she was also accused of attempted murder when two girls fell ill after drinking mulled wine, which Lewis allegedly served them. Although acquitted of both charges, she was not permitted to graduate.

In 1863 Lewis moved to Boston, where the abolitionist William Lloyd Garrison introduced her to sculptor Edward Brackett, who became her first mentor. Lewis's earliest sculptures were medallions with portraits of white antislavery leaders and Civil War heroes, which she modeled in clay and cast in plaster. Her *Bust of Colonel Robert Gould Shaw* (1865, Museum of Afro-American History, Boston, Massachusetts) depicted the young Bostonian who led an all-black battalion, the Fifty-fourth Massachusetts Volunteer Regiment, in battle against Confederate forces. Sales of replicas of the bust enabled Lewis to travel to Italy in 1865, where she established a studio in Rome.

The high point of Lewis's career was the completion of *The Death of Cleopatra* (1876, National Museum of American Art, Washington, D.C.), which created a sensation at the Philadelphia Centennial Exposition of 1876. Other sculptors generally depicted Cleopatra contemplating death; Lewis showed Cleopatra seated on her throne after death, her head thrown

back. In her right hand Cleopatra holds the poisonous snake that has bitten
her, while her left arm hangs lifelessly. This realistic portrayal ran contrary
to the sentimentality about death that was prevalent at the time.

Lewis was reported as still living in Rome in 1911, but the date and
location of her death are not known.

North America

Lewis, John

(b. February 21, 1940, Troy, Ala.), African American civil rights leader and
member of the United States House of Representatives.

John Lewis was one of ten children born to sharecroppers in Pike County,
Alabama. While a seminary student, Lewis participated in nonviolence
workshops taught by civil rights activist James Lawson. Lawson was a
member of the Fellowship of Reconciliation (FOR), an organization committed to pacifism, and he made Lewis a field secretary. Working with
Septima Clark, director of the interracial adult education center Highlander
Folk School, Lewis became a leader in the Nashville Student Movement.
He participated in sit-ins at segregated lunch counters, became a founding
member of the Student Nonviolent Coordinating Committee (SNCC) in
1960, and helped organize the Mississippi Freedom Summer in 1964 (see
Civil Rights Movement).

During his tenure as national
chairman of SNCC, Lewis delivered a powerful speech at the
1963 Civil Rights March on
Washington, criticizing the federal
government for its failure to
protect the rights of African
Americans. Two years later he
marched with Dr. Martin Luther
King Jr. from Selma to Montgomery, Alabama, in an effort to
secure voting rights for African
Americans. During the march a
confrontation with police occurred, and Lewis was one of
many beaten in what became
known as Bloody Sunday.

Lewis's commitment to nonviolence strained his relationship
with SNCC when the organization
grew more militant under the
leadership of Stokely Carmichael.

John Lewis, chairman of the Student Nonviolent
Coordinating Committee, and Hosea Williams of
the Southern Christian Leadership Conference
announce plans for demonstrations in Georgia in
1965. *CORBIS/Bettmann*

Lewis resigned from SNCC in 1966 to become director of the Atlanta-based Voter Education Project (VEP). Under Lewis's leadership the organization led voter registration drives and helped elect black politicians throughout the South. In 1976 President Jimmy Carter appointed Lewis to the staff of ACTION, a government agency responsible for coordinating volunteer activities.

After Carter's defeat in 1980, Lewis returned to Atlanta and won a seat on the Atlanta City Council. He served in this capacity until 1986, when he defeated his friend and fellow civil rights activist Julian Bond in the Democratic primary for Georgia's Fifth Congressional District seat, a position Lewis assumed when he defeated his Republican opponent later that year. In Congress, Lewis has served on the Committee on Interior and Insular Affairs, the Committee on Public Works and Transportation, and the House Ways and Means Committee.

North America

Lewis, Reginald F.

(b. December 7, 1942, Baltimore, Md.; d. January 19, 1993, New York, N.Y.), African American lawyer and businessman who managed the largest black-owned firm in the United States.

He entered Harvard Law School, graduating in 1968. After law school he worked with a number of New York law firms before opening the venture capital firm Lewis and Clarkson. In 1983 Lewis started the TLC Group as a means to pursue greater business opportunities. In 1983 TLC acquired McCall Pattern Company for $22.5 million. McCall, an ailing business that had operated for more than a century, was at the time debt-ridden. Through cost-cutting measures, Lewis helped resuscitate McCall, and in 1987 he resold the company for $90 million. Although he disliked the sobriquet, Reginald Lewis was often called the "Jackie Robinson of Wall Street" and was considered "the man who broke the color barrier in large-scale mergers and acquisitions and leveraged buyouts." With his firm, TLC, Lewis in 1987 orchestrated the largest offshore leveraged buyout in business history, paying $985 million for Beatrice International Foods. With subsidiaries in almost every continent, the renamed TLC-Beatrice International became the largest black-owned firm in the United States.

Also a philanthropist, Lewis gave generously to many charities. His gift of $3 million to Harvard Law School in 1992 was the largest single gift the law school had received and was used to found the Reginald F. Lewis Fund for International Study and Research. The Reginald F. Lewis Center at Harvard was the first facility named for an African American. He also donated $1 million to Howard University in Washington, D.C., as well as significant amounts to his alma mater Virginia State University.

Liberator, The,

publication of the American Anti-Slavery Society from 1831 to 1865; edited by William Lloyd Garrison, it was considered the most radical antislavery newspaper of the nineteenth century.

On January 1, 1831, famed white antislavery activist William Lloyd Garrison launched the first issue of the *Liberator*, a radical antislavery weekly newspaper that stood at the pinnacle of American antislavery activism for 35 years. Widely considered the most militant and most passionate antislavery publication of the nineteenth century, it served more than 2000 subscribers, many of them African American, before it stopped printing in 1865.

It featured the writings of abolitionists such as Wendell Phillips, Oliver Johnson, and British activist George Thompson. During its tenure the newspaper called for the immediate and unconditional end to slavery, rejected the efforts of the American Colonization Society to resettle free blacks in Liberia, and urged Americans to boycott goods produced with slave labor.

In 1842 Garrison wrote that the United States Constitution was "a Covenant with Death and an Agreement with Hell." This served as the newspaper's motto until 1861, when he modified it to read, "Proclaim liberty throughout the land, to all the inhabitants thereof." The newspaper supported President Abraham Lincoln during the Civil War, urging him to free America's 4 million slaves.

The *Liberator* celebrated the end of slavery and the beginning of Reconstruction with its final issue on December 29, 1865. The Emancipation Proclamation and passage of the Thirteenth Amendment, which abolished slavery, persuaded Garrison to write in 1865, "Great and marvelous are thy works, Lord God Almighty!"

Liberia,

a small West African country located on the Atlantic coast, bordered by Sierra Leone, the Republic of Guinea, and Côte d'Ivoire.

Liberia, the oldest republic in Africa, was once regarded by the West as the continent's most stable, prosperous, and peaceful country. One of only two African countries never colonized by a European power (Ethiopia is the other), Liberia's modern political foundation was built by free blacks who sailed there from the United States in the early nineteenth century. Since then, relations between Liberia's indigenous peoples and the African American settlers have rarely been easy. After more than 130 years of Americo-Liberian-dominated single-party rule, the First Republic was ended by a military coup in 1980, after which an unstable government faced a series of insurrections. Following a second revolt in 1989, throughout the early

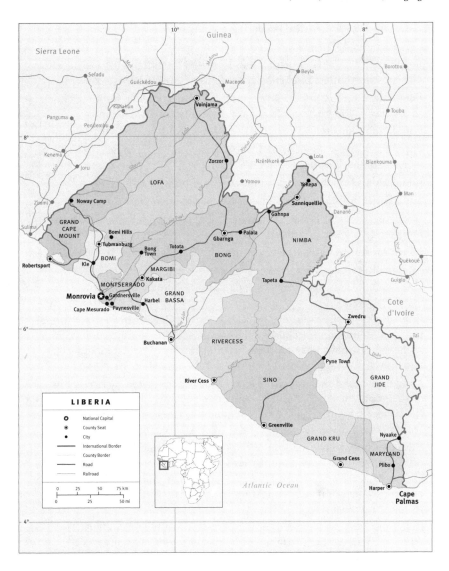

1990s Liberia suffered from political chaos, civil unrest, famine, and violence. Some experts estimate that about 10 percent of Liberia's population died during that period while another 80 percent was dislocated.

Africa

Liberia (Ready Reference)

Official Name: Republic of Liberia
Area: 99,067 sq km (38,250 sq mi)

Location: Western Africa, bordering the North Atlantic Ocean, Côte d'Ivoire and Sierra Leone

Capital: Monrovia (population 421,058 [1984 estimate])

Other Major Cities: Buchanan (population 24,000 [1984 estimate])

Population: 2,771,901 (1998 estimate); due to civil war, hundreds of thousands of Liberians are living as refugees outside the country.

Population Density: 31 persons per sq km (about 79 persons per sq mi)

Population Below Age 15: 45 percent (male 622,797; female 616,902 [1998 estimate])

Population Growth Rate: 5.76 percent (1998 estimate)

Total Fertility Rate: 6.09 children born per woman (1998 estimate)

Life Expectancy at Birth: Total population: 59.45 years (male 56.81 years; female 62.16 years [1998 estimate])

Infant Mortality Rate: 103.13 deaths per 1000 live births (1998 estimate)

Literacy Rate (age 15 and over who can read and write): Total population: 38.3 percent (male 53.9 percent; female 22.4 percent [1995 estimate])

Education: The Compulsory Education Act of 1912 provides for compulsory, free education for children. However, government attempts to implement this law have been hindered by the scarcity of educational facilities and only a small minority of children receive education.

Languages: English is the official language but is spoken by barely one-fifth of the population. Most of the population speaks at least one language from the Niger-Congo language group of about 20 languages. Some of the more widely spoken languages are Mande, West Atlantic, and Kwa.

Ethnic Groups: The majority of the population comes from one of 13 different ethnic groups. These groups include the Kpelle, Bassa, Gio, Kru, Grebo, Mano, Krahn, Gola, Gbandi, Loma, Kissi, Vai, and Bella. About 5 percent of the population are Americo-Liberians who descended from former American slaves.

Religions: About 70 percent of the population adhere to indigenous beliefs. About 20 percent are Muslim and 10 percent are Christians.

Climate: The climate is tropical and humid, particularly during the rainy seasons of June to July and October to November. Annual rainfall varies from 2240 mm (88 in) in the interior to 5200 mm (205 in) along the coast. The average temperature in Monrovia is about 26° C (79° F) in January and 24° C (76° F) in July.

Land, Plants, and Animals: Liberia is mostly flat with some hills and low mountains in the northeast that reach elevations of about 900 to 1200 m (3000 to 4000 ft). The interior is heavily forested with cotton, fig, mahogany, ironwood, palms, and rubber trees. Animals include pygmy hippopotamus, chimpanzees, elephants, buffalo, and monkeys.

Natural Resources: Minerals, such as iron ore, and forest products, such as wood and rubber. Liberia also has hydroelectric power plants on the Saint Paul River that provide a significant amount of hydroelectric power.

Currency: The Liberian dollar

Gross Domestic Product (GDP): $2.6 billion (1998 estimate)

GDP per Capita: $1000 (1997 estimate)

GDP Real Growth Rate: NA (1997 estimate)

Primary Economic Activities: Agriculture (70 percent of the population), services, industry, and commerce

Primary Crops: Rubber, coffee, cocoa, rice, cassava (tapioca), palm oil, sugar cane, bananas, and livestock

Industries: Rubber processing, food processing, construction materials, furniture, palm oil processing, iron ore, and diamonds

Primary Exports: Iron ore, rubber, timber, and coffee

Primary Imports: Mineral fuels, chemicals, machinery, transportation equipment, manufactured goods, rice, and other foodstuffs

Primary Trade Partners: United States, European Union, Japan, China, and South Korea

Government: Liberia is a constitutional republic in name; however, years of civil war have severely disrupted the government. In 1997 elections, Charles Ghankay Taylor was elected president for a term of 6 years.. Despite promises to establish a representative government, after taking office Taylor replaced much of the Liberian army and cabinet with loyalists. Fueled by conflict with opposition groups, Taylor's government underwent some instability, but now enjoys largely unopposed control.

Africa

Libya,

a large North African country bordered by Tunisia, Algeria, Niger, Chad, Sudan, Egypt, and the Mediterranean Sea.

In 1997 South African president Nelson Mandela visited the country of Libya and praised its leader, Col. Muammar al-Qaddafi, for his unceasing support during South Africa's struggle against apartheid. The international community was startled by this meeting of two of Africa's most prominent leaders, one a Nobel Peace Prize winner and the other, one of the West's most vilified enemies. But Mandela's visit only revealed to the West a picture of Libya already familiar elsewhere on the continent: that of a country as much African as Islamic. Often considered part of the Arab world, Libya is in fact one of Africa's largest and wealthiest nations, and for centuries its peoples have cultivated relations both across North Africa and south of the

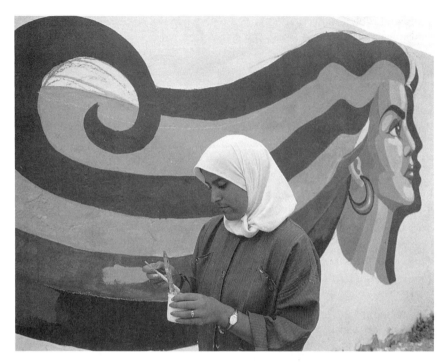

A female art student paints a mural celebrating the twentieth anniversary of Libya's revolution.
CORBIS/Caroline Penn

Sahara. Since coming to power in 1970, Qaddafi has provided both verbal and material support to a variety of African national movements as well as to governments ranging from Idi Amin's dictatorship in Uganda to Thomas Sankara's populist socialist state in Burkina Faso. In 1997 Qaddafi initiated a plan for a Sahelian-Saharan economic treaty with at least nine African nations. Although many in the West view Libya's influence in Africa with concern, many poorer African nations have welcomed the oil-rich country's largesse.

The identity of Libya as an African nation was inscribed well before Qaddafi's tenure. Trade routes and political federations had long connected parts of Libya to Egypt, to the western Islamic political entity of the Maghreb, and to sub-Saharan Africa. The concept of Libya as a distinct territory is fairly recent, arguably dating back only to the Italian colonial period. In fact, the contemporary nation comprises three historically distinct regions: Tripolitania, the cosmopolitan Mediterranean center of trade; Cyrenaica, historically linked to Egypt and the home of the powerful Islamic Sanusi sect; and Fezzan, the tribally ruled interior, linked by desert trade routes to sub-Saharan Africa. The identities of these regions shaped their individual relationships to both of the powers that occupied their land during the last two centuries—the Ottoman Empire and Italy.

Africa

Libya (Ready Reference)

Official Name: Socialist People's Libyan Arab Jamahiriya

Area: 1,759,540 sq km (679,358 sq mi)

Location: Northern Africa; borders Mediterranean Sea, Egypt, Tunisia, Republic of Sudan, Chad, Niger, and Algeria

Capital: Tripoli (population 1,500,000 [1994 estimate])

Other Major Cities: Banghazi (population 800,000 [1994 estimate])

Population: 5,690,727 (1998 estimate)

Population Density: 3 persons per sq km (about 8 persons per sq mi); more than 85 percent of the people live in urban areas.

Population Below Age 15: Total population: 48 percent (male 1,399,354; female 1,351,442 [1998 estimate])

Population Growth Rate: 3.68 percent (1998 estimate)

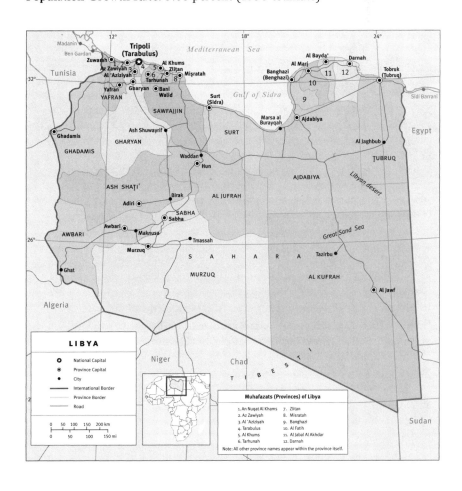

Men seated by a table of watermelons in Tripoli, the capital of Libya, a city whose history blends Mediterranean, Ottoman, and Egyptian influences. *CORBIS/Roger Wood*

Total Fertility Rate: 6.18 children born per woman (1998 estimate)

Life Expectancy at Birth: Total population: 65.44 years (male 63.21 years; female 67.78 years [1998 estimate])

Infant Mortality Rate: 59.5 deaths per 1000 live births (1996 estimate)

Literacy Rate (age 15 and over who can read and write): Total population: 76.2 percent (male 87.9 percent; female 63 percent [1997 estimate])

Education: Primary education in Libya is free and compulsory. In the early 1990s some 1,239,000 pupils were enrolled annually in primary schools, and about 215,500 students attended secondary, vocational, and teacher-training schools. Libya has five universities.

Languages: Arabic is the official language, although Berber is sometimes spoken and English and Italian are used in trade.

Ethnic Groups: The indigenous population of Libya is mostly Berber and Arab in origin; about 17 percent of the population consists of foreign workers and their families from the Mediterranean region and South Asia.

Religions: Islam is the state religion, and about 97 percent of all Libyans are Sunni Muslim. A small number are Roman Catholic.

Climate: Climatic conditions in Libya are characterized by extreme heat and aridity. Desert and sub-desert regions have little precipitation. On the coast the annual rainfall rarely exceeds 400 mm (16 in).

Land, Plants, and Animals: About 90 percent of Libya is made up of barren, rock-strewn plains and sand sea, with two small areas of hills rising to about 900 m (about 3000 ft) in the northwest and northeast. In the south the land rises to the Tibesti massif along the Chad border. Most of Libya is either devoid of vegetation or supports only sparse growth. Date palms and olive and orange trees grow in the scattered oases, and junipers and mastic trees are found in the higher elevations. Wildlife includes desert rodents, hyena, gazelle, and wildcat. Eagles, hawks, and vultures are common.

Natural Resources: The principal resource of Libya is petroleum. Others include natural gas, gypsum, limestone, marine salt, potash, and natron.

Currency: The Libyan dinar

Gross Domestic Product (GDP): $38 billion (1997 estimate)

GDP per Capita: $6700 (1997 estimate)

GDP Real Growth Rate: 0.5 percent (1997 estimate)

Primary Economic Activities: The economy depends on revenues from the oil sector, which makes up about one-third of GDP. Libya was traditionally an agricultural country, although farming was restricted primarily to the coastal regions; livestock raising has also been important.

Primary Crops: Tomatoes, wheat, potatoes, barley, citrus

Libyan leader Muammar al-Qaddafi answers questions during a new conference at the presidential palace in Cairo. Qaddafi hailed the conditional Iraqi withdrawl from Kuwait during the Gulf War. *Reuters NewMedia Inc./CORBIS*

fruits, dates, and olives; livestock includes sheep, goats, cattle, camels, and poultry.

Industries: Petroleum, food processing, textiles, handicrafts, and cement

Primary Exports: Crude oil, refined petroleum products, and natural gas

Primary Imports: Machinery, transport equipment, food, and manufactured goods

Primary Trade Partners: Italy, Germany, Spain, France, United Kingdom, Greece, Egypt, Turkey, Tunisia, and Eastern European countries

Government: Libya is governed under a constitution adopted in 1977 by the General People's Congress (GPC). Power is delegated to the head of state, or Revolutionary Leader, currently Col. Muammar Abu Minyar al-Qaddafi; five members of the General Secretariat of the GPC; and 16 members of the General People's Committee, led by a secretary (premier), currently Abd al Majid al-Qa'ud. Libya is organized into 46 municipal and 186 Basic People's Congress administrative units.

North America
_____

Lincoln University (Pennsylvania),
the oldest black institution of higher learning in the United States, located in Oxford, Pennsylvania.

Even though slavery was still legal when Lincoln University was founded, its motto has always been "If the Son shall make you free, ye shall be free indeed." Lincoln was founded in 1854 by John Miller Dickey, the white pastor of the Oxford Presbyterian Church in Oxford, Pennsylvania. Two years earlier Dickey had tried to help a black student, James Amos, gain admission to Princeton Theological Seminary and a Philadelphia Presbyterian seminary. When Amos was rejected from both schools because of race, Dickey decided that the solution was to create an institution for black men.

His school became the first in the United States dedicated to providing post-secondary instruction for African American students. It was originally named Ashmun Institute, in honor of the first governor of Liberia, but after the American Civil War it was renamed in honor of President Abraham Lincoln. Lincoln's first classes were in liberal arts, law, medicine, and theology, and the school awarded its first baccalaureate degree in 1868.

During the first 100 years of the university's existence, Lincoln alumni comprised 20 percent of the black physicians and more than 10 percent of the black lawyers in the United States. Poet Langston Hughes and Supreme Court Justice Thurgood Marshall were both Lincoln graduates. Lincoln alumni have become United States ambassadors, mayors, federal judges, college and university presidents, and pastors of prominent churches. In the twentieth century Lincoln has also gained a strong reputation for training African leaders. Nnamdi Azikiwe, Nigeria's first president, graduated in

Mary McLeod Bethune and W. E. B. Du Bois speak with Lincoln University president Horace Mann Bond after receiving the university's Alpha Medallion in 1950. *CORBIS/Bettmann*

1930, and Kwame Nkrumah, Ghana's first prime minister, graduated in 1939. Namibia's first independence government cabinet had six Lincoln University graduates. Many African students continue to come to the United States to study at Lincoln.

Horace Mann Bond, a Lincoln alumnus, became the university's first black president in 1945. In 1953 Lincoln became coeducational, and its current president, Niara Sudarkasa, is the first African American woman to lead the university.

North America

Little Richard (Richard Wayne Penniman)

(b. December 25, 1932 or 1935, Macon, Ga.), African American musician; rock and roll pioneer.

Born Richard Penniman, Little Richard was one of 12 children in a family divided by the religious concerns of some—many were Seventh Day Adventist preachers—and the more secular interests of others: his father was a bootlegger. Richard was kicked out of the house at age 13 for reasons that remain unclear but that probably relate to his precocious and adven-

Little Richard in concert at Wembley Arena in London, 1995 *Matthew Polak /CORBIS SYGMA*

turous sexuality. He was taken in by a white family who owned the Tick Tock Club in Macon, where he began his musical career.

After several years of playing around the South and recording in Atlanta and Houston, Little Richard sent a demonstration tape in 1955 to Specialty Records, a rhythm and blues label based in Los Angeles. Specialty found the tapes promising and arranged a recording session in New Orleans. This turned out to be one of the germinal sessions of rock and roll. Little Richard's explosive vocal energy heralded a new style, far removed from the conventional jump blues he had been playing.

Most of these songs were filled with barely concealed sexual imagery (even after cleaning up the lyrics), made more outrageous by Little Richard's falsetto squeals. One of them was "Tutti Frutti," featuring the immortal introduction: "A-wop-bop-a-lu-bop, a-wop-bam-boom." Other hits quickly followed, including "Long Tall Sally," "Rip It Up," "Lucille," and "Good Golly Miss Molly." Little Richard became a sensation, touring nationally and appearing in Hollywood movies about rock and roll, of which the most popular was *The Girl Can't Help It* (1956), named after one of his compositions.

In retrospect, Little Richard's popularity is startling. He may have modeled his outrageous stage persona in the tradition of effeminate black male entertainers wearing makeup, such as Billy Wright. While the sight of an African American man wearing makeup and singing about barnyard sex unnerved some, both black and white teenagers loved it. Almost as soon as Little Richard created a new hit, Pat Boone would produce a less soulful cover rendition of it. But American youth preferred and respected the Originator, as Little Richard sometimes calls himself.

In 1957, while performing successfully at the top of the American music industry, Little Richard quit rock and roll after a trip to Australia, following a religious conversion that he believed alerted him to the immorality of rock 'n' roll. After becoming an ordained Seventh Day Adventist minister, he toiled away in obscurity for several years. Little Richard returned to rock 'n' roll in the mid-sixties and toured in Europe with the Beatles and the Rolling Stones, who were among the artists directly influenced by his work. Since that time, he has moved back and forth between his church life and preaching and the world of rock 'n' roll.

In 1986, Little Richard was inducted into the Rock and Roll Hall of Fame; that same year he appeared in the film *Down and Out in Beverly Hills*. He was honored with a Grammy Award for Lifetime Achievement in 1993, and in 1994 he was among the recipients of the Rhythm and Blues Foundation's Pioneer Award.

North America

Little Rock Crisis,

1957, an early crisis in the Civil Rights Movement that began in 1957 when whites in Little Rock, Arkansas, rioted in protest against the integration of Central High School; in so doing they—and Arkansas governor Orval Faubus—challenged the supremacy of the federal courts, and President Dwight D. Eisenhower reluctantly sent in United States troops to maintain order.

North America

LL Cool J (also known as James Todd Smith)

(b. January 14, 1968, Queens, New York), African American hip hop pioneer, actor, and sex symbol whose 15 years of success make him rap's longest-running superstar.

LL Cool J—short for Ladies Love Cool James—was raised in Hollis, Queens, a neighborhood that also produced the early rap masters who formed Run-DMC. *Radio*, his 1985 debut album, sported such signature songs as "Rock the Bells" and "I Can't Live Without My Radio." It sold more than 1 million copies. The kid in the sneakers, gold chains, and Kangol hat rapped over spare, programmed beats that were sometimes splashed with rock guitar. In an art form founded on cocky sparring, LL Cool J was the king of the boast. Fans admired him for his cherubic looks and smooth style as well as his lyrical skills.

While *Bigger and Deffer* (1987), LL's second release, contained one of the all-time great battle raps, "I'm Bad," it also revealed the MC's softer side in "I Need Love," the first rap love ballad. His next album, Walking with a Panther (1989), succeeded commercially but not critically; Public Enemy's black nationalist politics were then in vogue, and critics protested LL's conspicuous materialism. The next year, in a furious rebuke to naysayers, he released *Mama Said Knock You Out*. "Don't call it a comeback," he warned on the title track and added: "I've been here for years/ I'm rockin' my peers/

Puttin' suckers in fear." The album, produced by Marley Marl, continued LL's history of hits: chart successes, such as "Around the Way Girl," "Jingling Baby," the bass-heavy "Boomin' System," and the title track, pushed album sales past the 2 million mark.

LL suffered a rare commercial failure with *14 Shots to the Dome* (1993), but as his hip hop credibility started to drop, he branched out. LL Cool J performed at Bill Clinton's 1993 presidential inauguration; starred in the popular television sitcom, *In the House*; and acted in a string of feature films. In 1995 he returned to rap music with *Mr. Smith*, a multi-platinum success that garnered little critical acclaim but earned him two Grammy Awards. With *I Make My Own Rules* (1997), a best-selling autobiography, LL confirmed his status as hip hop's preeminent superstar.

North America

Locke, Alain Leroy

(b. September 13, 1885, Philadelphia, Pa.; d. June 9, 1954, Washington, D.C.), African American philosopher, intellectual, and educator; editor of *The New Negro*, the anthology credited with defining the Harlem Renaissance.

Born into Philadelphia's black elite, Locke was the only child of school-teacher parents who were both descended from established free black families. By high school he was an accomplished pianist and violinist in addition to being an excellent student. In 1904 Locke became one of the few African American undergraduates at Harvard University, where he was elected to Phi Beta Kappa and received a B.A. in philosophy magna cum laude in 1907. That same year he became the first African American to be awarded a Rhodes Scholarship, which he used to continue studying philosophy at Oxford University and the University of Berlin.

He remained the only African American Rhodes scholar until the 1960s. He took a sabbatical in 1916–1917 to complete his Ph.D. in philosophy at Harvard, and became the chair of Howard's philosophy department upon his return. As a philosopher Locke was highly respected, and he has been called one of the most important philosophical thinkers of his day. But his best-remembered accomplishments come from his scholarship on literature and art.

In 1923 Locke began contributing essays on a range of subjects to *Opportunity*, the journal of the National Urban League. These essays gained him even wider prominence as a rising black intellectual, and in 1925 he was asked to edit the March issue of the *Survey Graphic*, a national sociology magazine, which was planned as a special issue devoted entirely to race. Locke decided to turn the issue into a showpiece for the gifted young African American writers then gathering in Harlem. The resulting journal, subtitled *Harlem: Mecca of the New Negro*, included poetry, fiction, and essays by W. E. B. Du Bois, James Weldon Johnson, Langston Hughes,

Countee Cullen, Jean Toomer, and Anne Spencer—many of them writers who were touted as the new generation in African American art, the best and the brightest black America had yet produced.

The issue was an outstanding success. Locke expanded it into a book, and *The New Negro*, published eight months later, immediately became the definitive anthology of the Harlem Renaissance. In addition to writers featured in the magazine special, *The New Negro* included poetry and fiction by Claude McKay, Zora Neale Hurston, Angelina Grimké, and Jessie Fauset; essays by scholars William Stanley Braithwaite, Kelly Miller, J. A. Rogers, and E. Franklin Frazier; and striking artwork by Aaron Douglas. The book was widely interpreted as a resounding rebuttal to the argument that African Americans were not capable of great literature and art. Locke became a leading critic and collector of both African and African American art.

Africa

Loroupe, Tegla

(b. 1973, near Kapenguria, Kenya), Kenyan long-distance runner.

When Tegla Loroupe emerged from the pack to finish first in the New York City Marathon in 1994, she was the first black African woman to have won a major marathon anywhere in the world. Because she came from Kenya, a country that was renowned for its male marathoners—and, according to Loroupe and others, a country renowned for its patronizing view of women as athletes or professionals—her victory was all the sweeter.

Back home in Kapenguria, she received a hero's welcome, including a parade, with gifts of land, cattle, and sheep. She has won the praise of Kenya's women, one of whom told Loroupe that she has "made women in Kenya proud."

North America

Los Angeles Riot of 1992,

one of the first major urban insurrections since the 1960s. This riot shocked many suburban Americans who had come to believe that the days of explosive racial tensions were behind them.

Like the Los Angeles Watts Riot of 1965, the 1992 rioting was sparked by an act of antiblack police brutality. On March 3, 1991, Los Angeles police officers stopped a car driven by a 34-year-old African American named Rodney King, who, they said, was speeding. According to the officers, King emerged from his automobile in an aggressive manner that suggested he might have been high on drugs. Before handcuffing King, the police delivered some 56 blows and kicks and a number of shocks from a stun-gun to the fallen body of the suspect. A bystander captured the beating on videotape, and within two days the footage was being broadcast all over national television.

King brought charges of brutality against four of the policemen, and the officers, who claimed they had acted in self-defense, were tried before a predominantly white jury in a white middle-class suburb of Los Angeles. On April 29, 1992, all four men were acquitted. Within two and a half hours of the verdict, a crowd of furious protesters had gathered at the corner of Florence and Normandie streets in South Central Los Angeles, and through the next day and night the rioting exploded across 130 sq km (50 sq mi) of South Central. At the same time, smaller disturbances were erupting in San Francisco, Seattle, Atlanta, Pittsburgh, and other cities. The 1992 riot represented a rude awakening for many Americans who had assumed that after two relatively quiet decades, the days of large-scale urban race riots had been put behind them.

North America

Los Angeles Watts Riot of 1965,

the first major racially fueled rebellion of the 1960s, an event that foreshadowed the widespread urban violence of the latter half of the decade.

With the arrest of a 21-year-old African American, Los Angeles' South Central neighborhood of Watts erupted into violence. On August 11, 1965, a Los Angeles police officer flagged down motorist Marquette Frye, whom he suspected of being intoxicated. When a crowd of onlookers began to taunt the policeman, a second officer was called in. According to eyewitness accounts, the second officer struck crowd members with his baton, and news of the act of police brutality soon spread throughout the neighborhood. The incident, combined with escalating racial tensions, overcrowding in the neighborhood, and a summer heat wave, sparked violence on a massive scale. Despite attempts the following day aimed at quelling anti-police sentiment, residents began looting and burning local stores. In the rioting, which lasted five days, more than 34 people died, at least 1000 were wounded, and an estimated $200 million in property was destroyed. An estimated 35,000 African Americans took part in the riot, which required 16,000 National Guardsmen, county deputies, and city police to put down.

Although city officials initially blamed outside agitators for the insurrection, subsequent studies showed that most of the participants had lived in Watts all their lives. These studies also found that the protesters' anger was directed primarily at white shopkeepers in the neighborhood and at

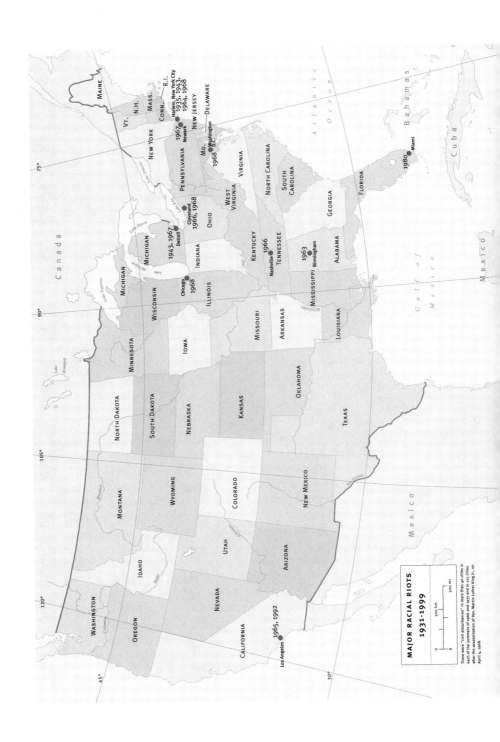

MAJOR RACIAL RIOTS
1931-1999

0   300 km
0   300 mi

There were "civil disturbances" in more than 40 cities in
each of the summers of 1966 and 1967 and in 125 cities
after the assassination of Rev. Martin Luther King Jr., on
April 4, 1968.

members of the all-white Los Angeles police force. The rioters left black churches, libraries, businesses, and private homes virtually untouched. The Watts Riot was the first major lesson for the American public on the tinderbox volatility of segregated inner-city neighborhoods.

Louis, Joe

(b. May 13, 1914, Chambers County, Ala.; d. April 12, 1981, Las Vegas, Nev.), one of the greatest boxers in modern history, widely viewed by white Americans as a symbol of racial harmony and by black Americans as a symbol of black triumph in a racist society.

Joseph Louis Barrow was born on a sharecropper's farm near Lafayette, Alabama and when Louis was ten the family followed the Great Migration north to Detroit, where his stepfather found work. He spent hours watching boxers spar at a local gym, and after leaving school at age 17, he began training on his own.

Louis lost his first amateur bout but racked up an impressive string of victories over the next three years. John Roxborough and Julian Black, two African American businessmen who were also involved in illegal gambling and running numbers, agreed to manage Louis. They encouraged him to drop Barrow from his name, thereby making it easier to remember. They also hired Jack Blackburn, a former lightweight fighter and well-regarded trainer. Discovering that Louis had little foot speed, Blackburn encouraged him to use a flat-footed shuffle. The shuffle and Louis's compact punches, became his signature traits.

Louis's managers counseled him to be a gentleman in the ring and shy with the press; he was also to avoid drinking, smoking, and being seen alone with white women in public. Publicly, Louis followed this advice, and whites, who nicknamed him The Brown Bomber, widely championed his modesty and dignity. Even white Southerners hailed him as a non-threatening black man.

Louis's professional career was nothing short of brilliant. In his first year he won more than 20 fights without a loss, typically with white opponents. Boxing was the only major sport that then allowed blacks to compete against whites, and many African Americans lived vicariously through Louis's punishing blows to whites. After a victory by Louis, entire black neighborhoods were known to burst into spontaneous celebration.

On June 19, 1936, Louis met the German fighter Max Schmeling, a former world champion, in New York's Yankee Stadium. In the 12th round, Schmeling knocked out the heavily favored Louis, dealing him his first professional defeat. Hitler cited Schmeling's victory as proof of the superiority of the Aryan race. One year to the day later, a rematch against Schmeling, with the possibility of a European war looming, the second Louis-Schmeling fight took on even more significance than the first. In the first round Louis scored a stunning knockout, making him one of the most popular athletes in America and, indeed, much of the world.

By the early 1940s, however, Louis was deeply in debt as a result of poor investments, gross financial mismanagement by his handlers, a habit of giving money away freely, and high living. In his final years he worked in Las Vegas as a greeter and companion to wealthy guests. Despite his failings, Joe Louis remained one of America's most loved sports heroes.

Europe

Lovers' Rock,

the first distinctively British variant of reggae, a fusion of soul elements and female vocalists into lush, romantic ballads.

Lovers' rock emerged in the mid-1970s as an alternative to heavy roots reggae being played in London clubs. Soundman Lloyd Coxsone anticipated lovers' rock by playing an occasional soul record in his reggae sets. The crowds enjoyed the opportunity for a close, slow dance. Coxsone teamed up with musician Dennis Bovell of the reggae band Matumbi to produce a reggae version of one of Coxsone's crowd-pleasing soul tunes. Featuring 13-year-old singer Louisa Mark, the resulting hit, "Caught in a Lie," broke new ground for British reggae. Its enormous success led Bovell to create a record label called Lovers' Rock, which would come to define the emergent sound. From the late 1970s through the early 1980s black women's lovers' rock topped British reggae charts and exerted a strong influence on reggae production in England and Jamaica.

With its easy melodies, soft soul string arrangements, and sensual reggae bass lines, lovers' rock began to outsell much of the heavier roots reggae in British markets. Female audiences were quick to embrace the form because it offered themes of love and marriage largely neglected by the male-dominated Rastafarian roots reggae lyrics. Lovers' rock allowed women to fashion a sophisticated self-image through music that was fully independent from Rastafarian preoccupations with Africa, Babylon, and mystic dread. For the first time in reggae history, female voices were given precedence over males, and this led to a sharp increase in the number of black female musicians, producers, and record-label owners.

After her 1980 hit record "Hopelessly in Love," Carroll Thompson was able to open a production company. Brown Sugar, a popular all-female group, mixed the usual romantic lyrics with "conscious" songs that dealt with black pride and cultural awareness. Singer-actress Janet Kay ushered British reggae into mainstream acceptance with a hit single that reached the number-two slot in British pop charts. Just as lovers' rock enjoyed success outside of reggae markets, several of its top performers crossed over into jazz, funk, and soul projects throughout the 1980s. Brown Sugar's Caron Wheeler went on to join the black British group Soul II Soul; Carroll Thompson moved into funk-soul while still recording lovers' rock; and many others have followed the path toward black American popular music. In Jamaica, lovers' rock was applied to any melodic, romantic reggae, such as the tales of lonely love sung by Gregory Isaacs.

Many music critics have neglected lovers' rock because of its tendency toward sentimental themes. Regardless of critical attention, significant record sales prove the genre's importance. Lovers' rock opened the doors for women in reggae further than they had been opened before. In contrast to the male-oriented lyrics or outright macho boasting of much reggae, lovers' rock explored black sexuality from the female's viewpoint. Lovers' rock made reggae relevant to the experience of black British women through a shift in themes and the addition of American soul.

Lucy Foster, Autherine

(b. October 5, 1929, Shiloh, Ala.), African American civil rights activist who sued to integrate the University of Alabama.

Autherine Lucy Foster attended public schools in Alabama and did her undergraduate work at Selma University and Miles College in Birmingham. After her graduation in 1952, she and Pollie Myers, an activist for the National Association for the Advancement of Colored People (NAACP), applied to the University of Alabama. The two women were accepted but then rejected when the university learned that they were not white. With the backing of the NAACP, they went to court and successfully charged the university with racial discrimination. While Foster was re-accepted, the university rejected Myers again, claiming that a child she had had out of wedlock rendered her an unfit student.

Foster's enrollment at the University of Alabama was met with violent anti-integration demonstrations, burning crosses, and a rioting mob that pelted Lucy with rotting food and death threats. For this, Foster was suspended "for her own safety." Again Foster sued and won, but the decision was preempted by her expulsion on the grounds that she had maligned school officials by taking them to court. Lucy and the NAACP decided to drop the case.

For many years Foster had trouble finding work as a teacher because of the controversy. She and her husband, Hugh Foster, and their five children moved throughout the South, with Foster speaking on civil rights issues. She finally was hired for a teaching position in Birmingham in 1974. In 1988 Foster's expulsion was overturned by the University of Alabama and she enrolled there, receiving an M.A. in elementary education in 1992.

Africa

Lumumba, Patrice

(b. 1925, Onalua, Belgian Congo; d. January 17, 1961, Katanga Province,
Republic of the Congo), Congolese independence leader and first prime
minister of the Democratic Republic of the Congo.

A charismatic and energetic statesman, Patrice Lumumba became politically
active as a young postal worker when he organized the Stanleyville (now
Kisangani) postal worker's union. In October 1958 he became involved
with national politics, founding the Mouvement National Congolais
(MNC), Congo's first national political party. In December Lumumba took
an MNC delegation to the All-African People's Conference in Ghana,
where he met with Pan-Africanists and African nationalists and became
friends with Kwame Nkrumah, Ghana's first African prime minister.
Influenced by the spirit of nationalism and anticolonialism that pervaded
the conference, Lumumba returned to the Republic of the Congo a militant, ready to demand independence.

Lumumba made the first public appeal for independence in January
1959. On October 31 he was arrested and held responsible for riots that
broke out after a meeting of the MNC. From jail he and his nationalist
supporters organized a boycott of the December local elections. Although
the Belgian government had proposed a five-year decolonization plan,
Lumumba and the MNC wanted immediate independence and believed a
five-year plan would give Belgium the opportunity to install a puppet
regime. In fact, Lumumba was released from jail in time to participate in
the Round Table Conference in Brussels, where the Belgians ultimately
agreed to grant independence within six months.

In May 1960 the Belgians selected Lumumba to be prime minister
under Joseph Kasavubu, who was to be president. From the beginning
relations were strained. Lumumba wanted a strong centralized state free of
outside interference and hoped to make the Republic of the Congo the
leader of a Pan-African Union of African States. Kasavubu, a federalist, took
a more moderate stance and wanted to maintain close connections with
Belgium and the West. This tension was evident from the nature of their
June 30 independence ceremony speeches; Kasavubu thanked King
Boudouin I for independence, and Lumumba reminded the king of the
atrocities of Belgian colonialism.

Shortly after independence, the government faced widespread military
revolt, and the Katanga province, supported by Belgian troops and
Western businesses, seceded. Belgium immediately sent in military troops
to restore order; Lumumba, fearing a reinstatement of colonial rule,
quickly broke diplomatic relations with Belgium. He appealed to the
United Nations (UN) for military intervention, which arrived on July 14,
1960. Lumumba, however, soon lost faith in the UN mission, which he
suspected was interested in protecting Belgian and other Western
business interests, and turned to the Soviet Union for assistance. This

action caused a complete split with Kasavubu, who dismissed Lumumba in September 1960.

Lumumba contested his removal until Kasavubu was also pushed out of office, in a military coup led by Col. Joseph Mobutu (later Mobutu Sese Sekou), who, ironically, Lumumba himself had named army chief of staff. Mobutu ordered the arrest of Lumumba. Although Lumumba, using UN protection, avoided arrest for several months, he was finally caught in January 1961 and was murdered in Katanga. It is uncertain who killed Lumumba, but there is evidence that Mobutu, working in affiliation with the United States Central Intelligence Agency (CIA) and Moise Tshombe, the leader of the Katanga secession, may have been responsible. To this day Lumumba remains one of the country's national heroes.

North America

Lunceford, James Melvin (Jimmie)

(b. June 6, 1902, Fulton, Mo.; d. July 12?, 1947, Seaside, Or.), jazz bandleader and arranger whose big band helped define the swing era of the 1930s.

Regarded as the most exciting band of its time, Jimmie Lunceford's big band was known for its precise arrangements and smoothly polished choreography. Light, swinging hits such as "My Blue Heaven" reflected the perfectionism and charm of the band and its leader. Raised in Denver, Colorado, Jimmie Lunceford graduated from Fisk University in Nashville, Tennessee, in 1926. After doing graduate work in New York City, he taught high school music and physical education in Memphis. It was there that he put together his first band, originally called the Chickasaw Syncopators.

Soon renamed the Jimmie Lunceford Orchestra, the band toured the Upper Midwest and Great Lakes region for several years before making its first New York appearance at Harlem's fabled Cotton Club. For the next decade the orchestra dominated the city's lively big-band scene. Although Lunceford's group featured talented and dynamic musicians, it became famous more for its playful sound and vibrant stage presence than for its musical virtuosity. Instead of playing any of the several instruments he had studied, Lunceford acted as the band's conductor, head arranger, and business leader, keeping the group together during more than ten years of frequent national and international touring and dozens of recordings for the Decca and Columbia labels.

Despite Lunceford's discipline and leadership, the band lost key members in the early 1940s, including arrangers Sy Oliver and Willie "the Lion" Smith, and began a decline from which it never recovered. Nevertheless, it continued working until 1947, when Lunceford died following a publicity appearance in Oregon. The band soon folded for good, but Lunceford's work has gone on to influence countless jazz ensembles.

Luthuli, Albert John

(b. 1899; d. July 21, 1967), South African leader and Nobel laureate.

Born in Southern Rhodesia (now Zimbabwe), the son of well-respected members of the Zulu ethnic group, Albert John Luthuli was educated at the mission school in which he later taught (1921–1936). In 1936 he was elected chief of the Zulu Abasemakholweni tribe in Groutville. Luthuli joined the African National Congress (ANC), a black political group, in 1946 and took an increasingly active role in campaigns to abolish apartheid, the system of racial segregation in South Africa.

In 1952 he was removed as chief by the South African government, which opposed his activities, and was forbidden to enter major South African cities and towns for one year. That same year he was elected president-general of the ANC. Because of his continued political activities, he was restricted to his farm in Groutville for two years in 1953 and again in 1959 for five years. For his nonviolent resistance to South African apartheid policies, Luthuli was awarded the 1960 Nobel Peace Prize. In 1964 the government extended its restrictions against him for another five years. His autobiography, *Let My People Go*, was published in 1962.

Lynching,

mob execution, usually by hanging and often accompanied by torture, of alleged criminals, particularly African Americans.

Apart from slavery, lynching is perhaps the most horrific chapter in the history of African Americans. Although lynching, defined as execution without the due process of law, has been used against members of many different ethnicities, the vast majority of victims have been African American men, mostly in the Southern states, during a 50-year period following Reconstruction. Despite its stated justification—that lynching is merely a response to crime—in most cases victims had not been convicted, or even charged with, a specific crime. As historian W. Fitzhugh Brundage has noted, lynching was not only "a tragic symbol of race relations in the American South" but also "a powerful tool of intimidation." A constant and unpredictable threat, lynching was used to maintain the status quo of white superiority long after any legal distinction between the races remained.

Because of its unpredictability and extra-legal nature—black men knew that they could become victims at any time, for any reason—lynching cast a shadow greater than its 3386 known black (mostly male) victims between 1882 and 1930. It is almost certain that these numbers are understated. Despite groundbreaking research into lynching by historians and sociologists, many cases were never recorded. Even those that were well documented rarely reveal the names of the perpetrators; as scholar Robert Zangrando

A crowd of white people gathers around a tree from which two black men are hanging, lynched by vigilantes in Marion, Indiana, in 1930. *CORBIS/Bettmann*

LYNCHING VICTIMS 1868-1935

Year	Blacks	Year	Blacks	Year	Blacks
1868	291	1898	101	1918	60
1869	31	1899	85	1919	76
1870	34	1900	106	1920	53
1871	53	1901	105	1921	59
1882	49	1902	85	1922	51
1883	53	1903	84	1923	29
1884	51	1904	76	1924	16
1885	74	1905	57	1925	17
1886	74	1906	62	1926	23
1887	70	1907	58	1927	16
1888	69	1908	89	1928	10
1889	94	1909	69	1929	7
1890	85	1910	67	1930	20
1891	113	1911	60	1931	12
1892	161	1912	61	1932	6
1893	118	1913	51	1933	24
1894	134	1914	51	1934	15
1895	113	1915	56	1935	18
1896	78	1916	50		
1897	123	1917	36		

points out, coroners' reports typically attributed the murder to "parties unknown," even though "lynchers' identities were seldom a secret."

More than an epidemic of racially targeted violence, lynching has become a symbol of the most disheartening aspects of American race r elations. For many African Americans, there is no more potent reminder of their history of slavery, subjugation, and pain at the hands of white society. In music—most notably jazz singer Billie Holiday's "Strange Fruit"—literature, and painting, black artists have explored this brutal and complex crime. As many scholars have pointed out, lynching was directed not only at a particular victim, but at all black people.

North America

Lynch, John Roy

(b. 1847?, Louisiana; d. November 2, 1939, Chicago, Ill.), politician and lawyer, first African American to deliver the keynote address at the Republican National Convention.

Born a slave and freed at the end of the Civil War, John Lynch became active in Republican party politics in 1867. His prominent career began with his election to the Mississippi legislature in 1869. Lynch became its Speaker in 1872.

As a United States congressman in 1873, Lynch supported the Civil Rights Bill of 1875. He lost his seat in 1876 but regained it after contesting the election; he was defeated in 1882, but two years later he gave the keynote address at the Republican National Convention. He went on to practice law and write *The Facts of Reconstruction* (1913).

M

Maasai,

an ethnic group of Kenya and Tanzania.

The Maasai have a long tradition of pastoralism, though today some are adopting settled life. They speak a language of the Eastern Nilotic Maa grouping, which also includes the languages of the Arusha and Baraguyu (or Kwafi) peoples of Tanzania.

Traditional Maasai society is governed by a series of age-based groupings, especially among males. Males between the approximate ages of 15 and 30 are junior *murran*, or warriors, whose responsibility it is to protect the herds. During this period, the *murran* live in a separate area called *manyata* and are prohibited from marrying. After age 30 they become senior warriors for approximately 15 years. During this time they live among the rest of the Maasai and serve as a sort of home guard, and have the option of marrying. Following this stage, men become junior elders. After another interval of approximately 15 years, they become senior elders, who make decisions for the group.

Land is traditionally considered communal; wealth is determined by the number of cattle owned, and families brand their cattle to differentiate them. Traditional Maasai live in temporary camps called *inkangitie* (*enkang* in the singular), composed of huts, called *kraals* or *bomas*, made of wooden poles and plastered with dung. *Kraals* include a corral for the cattle.

After Kenyan independence in 1964, significant portions of the most fertile and well-watered areas of Maasailand were taken by the government and distributed to other ethnic groups. The Maasai today face problems of overgrazing and soil erosion as they find themselves more and more constrained. The governments of both Kenya and Tanzania have encouraged them to abandon their communal land ownership practices and nomadic existence in favor of private property, either for ranching or for farming.

Madagascar,

republic in the Indian Ocean, located 390 km (242.3 mi) off the coast of Mozambique. Madagascar is made up of Madagascar Island, Africa's largest island and the fourth largest island in the world, and several small islands.

More than 1600 km (994.2 mi) long and 570 km (354.2 mi) wide, Madagascar has a total area of 587,040 sq km (226,658 sq mi). The island is both geographically and demographically complex. Some 14.8 million people of Southeast Asian, African, and Arabic descent, along with more recent Indian and Chinese immigrants, are distributed throughout the island's six microclimates. Eighteen ethnic groups are traditionally identified, each associated with a geographical area. Farmers cultivate predominately patty rice for subsistence. Coffee, cloves, and vanilla are the main cash crops.

The island of Madagascar separated from the African mainland during the Late Jurassic or Upper Cretaceous period, about 130 million years ago. The resulting isolation led to the evolution of remarkable endemic species. Most famous, perhaps, are the island's population of tarsiers, lemurs, and lorises. These primates retain many primitive features of early hominoids. Tenrecs, civets, mongooses, and bats add to the unique wildlife of the island. Five percent of the entire world's species can be found in Madagascar, 90 percent of which are endemic to the

A group of buildings in Madagascar's mountainous central plateau. *CORBIS/John Corbett; Ecoscene*

The inhabitants of Madagascar, the world's fourth largest island, share a heritage that blends African, Arabic, and Indonesian influences. *CORBIS/Chris Rainier*

island. To combat the loss of biodiversity, the World Wildlife Fund (WWF) began a debt-for-nature exchange program, setting up conservation projects. The island's unique biogeography is matched only by its colorful history, including the synthesis of a singular blend of African and Asian cultures.

Africa

Madagascar (Ready Reference)

Official Name: Republic of Madagascar

Former Name: Malagasy Republic

Area: 587,040 sq km (226,658 sq mi)

Location: Southern Africa; island in the Indian Ocean, east of Mozambique

Capital: Antananarivo (population 1,052,835 [1993 estimate])

Other Major Cities: Toamasina (population 127,441), Mahajanga (100,807), and Fianarantsoa (99,005) (1993 estimate)

Population: 14,462,509 (1998 estimate)

Population Density: 24 persons per sq km (about 62 persons per sq mi)

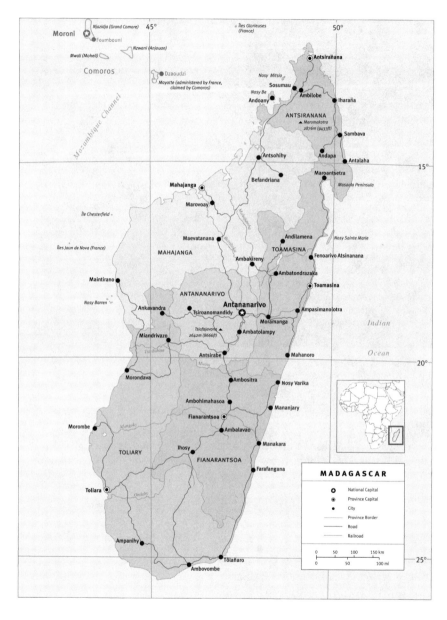

Population Below Age 15: 45 percent (male 3,272,236; female 3,196,565 [1998 estimate])

Population Growth Rate: 2.8 percent (1998 estimate)

Total Fertility Rate: 5.76 children per woman (1998 estimate)

Life Expectancy at Birth: Total population: 52.8 years (male 51.7; female 54.1 [1998 estimate])

Infant Mortality Rate: 90.5 deaths per 1000 live births (1998 estimate)

Literacy Rate (age 15 and over who can read and write): Total population: 80 percent (male 88 percent; female 73 percent [1990 estimate])

Education: Six years of primary school are compulsory. Nearly all children from 6 to 11 attend school, and 18 percent from 12 to 17 are enrolled in secondary school.

Languages: There are two official languages, Malagasy—a language of Malayo-Indonesian origin—and French.

Ethnic Groups: In the interior, around 27 percent of people belong to the Merina (Hova) group and another 12 percent belong to the related Betsileo; both groups are descendants of emigrants from Malaysia and Indonesia around 2000 years ago. The coastal areas are more diverse, with many people of mixed descent; distinct ethnic groups there include the Betsimisaraka, Tsimihety, Sakalave, and Antaisaka.

Religions: About 52 percent of the population adhere to indigenous beliefs. About 41 percent is Christian and 7 percent Muslim.

Climate: The eastern region receives abundant rainfall, in some places more than 3050 mm (120 in) annually. The interior's central plateau is drier, with the arid south and southwest receiving less than 380 mm (15 in) of annual precipitation. The coasts are tropical, with high heat year round. A temperate climate, with warm summers and cool winters, prevails inland. Average temperatures in Antananarivo, the inland capital, range from 16° to 26° C (61° to 79° F) in January to 9° to 20° C (48° to 68° F) in July.

A man from the Mahafaly ethnic group visits the tomb of his father. Although Madagascar is home to at least 18 major ethnic groups, nearly all share common Malagasy characteristics, including ancestor worship and the erection of stone monuments to the dead.
CORBIS/Chris Hellier

Farmers in Madagascar construct terraces for the rice they farm as their primary subsistence crop. Other crops include coffee, cloves, and vanilla, which are mostly raised for export.
CORBIS/Chris Hellier

Land, Plants, and Animals: Madagascar, the world's fourth largest island, rises from sea level at its coastline to altitudes of more than 2800 m (around 9400 ft) on its mountainous plateau. It is bordered by the Indian Ocean to the east and the Mozambique Channel to the west. Many rivers cross the island's interior, including the Betsiboka, Tsirivihina, Mangoky, and Onilahy. Tropical rain forests dominate eastern Madagascar, while the drier west consists of savanna woodlands and grasslands and the extreme southwest is desert. Known for its unusual and varied animal life, the island is home to lemurs, a primate family.

Natural Resources: Rich in minerals, Madagascar produces chromite, graphite, mica, bauxite, quartz, salt, coal, and semiprecious stones. The island's best soil is found along the coast and its major rivers. It also has abundant fish.

Currency: The Malagasy franc

Gross Domestic Product (GDP): $10.3 billion (1997 estimate)

GDP per Capita: $730 (1997 estimate)

GDP Real Growth Rate: 3 percent (1997 estimate)

Primary Economic Activities: Agriculture, including fishing and forestry (33 percent of GDP); industry, particularly processing of agricultural products and textile manufacturing (15 percent of GDP); some 96 percent of total labor force does not receive money wages, working mostly in subsistence agriculture.

Primary Crops: Coffee, vanilla, sugar cane, cloves, cocoa, rice, cassava, beans, bananas, and peanuts

Industries: Meat processing, soap, breweries, tanneries, sugar, textiles, glassware, automobile assembly, and petroleum refining

Primary Exports: Coffee, vanilla, cloves, shellfish, sugar, and petroleum products

Primary Imports: Petroleum, consumer goods, and food

Primary Trade Partners: France, Germany, Japan, United Kingdom, Italy, and the Netherlands

Government: Since 1993 Madagascar has been a multiparty democracy with a president, prime minister, and bicameral Parliament. President Marc Ravalomanana was elected in May 2002. The Parliament consists of a Senate and a National Assembly.

Africa

Mahfuz, Najib

(b. December 11, 1911, Cairo, Egypt), Egyptian novelist; the first Arab to win the Nobel Prize for Literature.

Upon presenting the Nobel Prize for Literature to Najib Mahfuz in 1988, the Swedish Academy of Letters announced, "Through works rich in nuance—now clearsightedly realistic, now evocatively ambiguous— [Mahfuz] has formed an Arabian narrative art that applies to all mankind." The academy stated that Mahfuz's body of writing "speaks to us all" by addressing universal themes such as injustice, the desire for freedom, and the place of the individual in society.

Critics have described Mahfuz's literary career as a journey through the history of the European novel. Over four decades he has written approximately one book a year. His best-known work, the three-volume *Cairo Trilogy* (1956–1957)—a depiction of the changes in urban society through three generations of various Cairene families from 1917 to 1944—is often compared to the social realism of Charles Dickens.

Through the realistic description of the everyday trials and tribulations of lower- and middle-class Egyptians in Cairo, Mahfuz's works offer insight into Arab society and help to bridge the cultural divide between the Western and Arab worlds. Mahfuz continues his quiet and methodical life in Cairo. He grew up in one of that city's oldest quarters, Gamaliyya, a place, like those he often portrays in his writing, full of small alleyways, monumental mosques, and tall minarets. After finishing his philosophy degree at the University of Cairo, he followed in his father's footsteps and became a civil servant. He worked in the ministry of Islamic affairs, as director of censorship in the Department of Art, and for the State Cinema organization. When Mahfuz retired in 1971, he continued to write novels, screenplays, and short stories and supplemented his income by writing for the newspaper *Al Ahram*. Writing remains a necessity in Mahfuz's life.

Africa

Malawi,

landlocked country in east southern Africa bordering Tanzania, Mozambique, and Zambia, with the third highest population density (95 people per sq km) of any African country.

Surrounded by countries rich in diamonds and gold, Malawi is known for humbler resources: fertile albeit densely populated land, a vast lake, and an abundant labor supply. Historically, the fortunes of Malawi's primarily agrarian societies have been shaped by regional patterns of trade, warfare, and conquest but also marked by the careers of ambitious if paternalistic "saviors." In precolonial times years of violent slave raids were followed by the arrival of the Scottish missionary David Livingstone, determined to rescue the region's peasants from enslavement and paganism. British colonialists followed, taking away farmland and imposing high taxes, but they were eventually pushed out by Malawian nationalists, led by the Western-educated physician Hastings Kamuzu Banda. During the three decades' rule of this self-proclaimed "paternal despot," the chasms between rich and poor, ruler and ruled, grew wider than anywhere else on the continent. Multiparty elections in 1994 finally replaced the ailing Banda; today's Malawians wait to see whether democracy and regional stability will help the country climb out of continuing poverty.

A Malawi woman rinses clothes before hanging them out to dry. *CORBIS/Gina Glover*

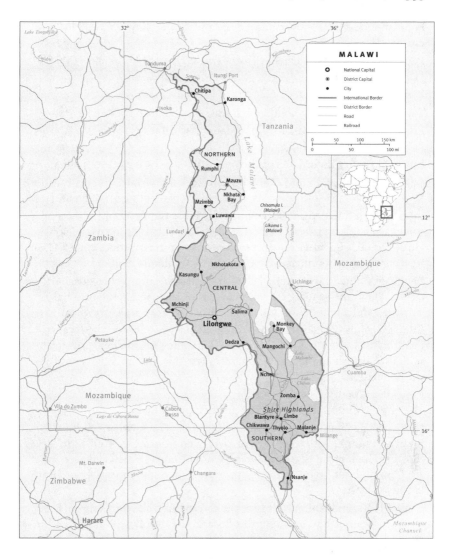

Africa

Malawi (Ready Reference)

Official Name: Republic of Malawi

Former Name: Nyasaland

Area: 118,484 sq km (45,747 sq mi)

Location: Southern Africa; borders Zambia to the west, Mozambique to the south and west, Tanzania to the northeast

Capital: Lilongwe (population 395,500 [1994 estimate])

Other Major Cities: Blantyre (population 446,800 [1994 estimate])

Population: 9,840,474 (1998 estimate)

Population Density: 95 persons per sq km (about 247 per sq mi [1995 estimate])

Population Below Age 15: 46 percent (male 2,249,108; female 2,228,934 [1998 estimate])

Population Growth Rate: 1.66 percent (1998 estimate)

Total Fertility Rate: 5.6 children born per woman (1998 estimate)

Life Expectancy at Birth: Total population: 36.59 years (male 36.64 years; female 36.54 years [1998 estimate])

Infant Mortality Rate: 133.7 deaths per 1000 live births (1998 estimate)

Literacy Rate (age 15 and over who can read and write): Total population: 56.4 percent (male 71.9 percent; female 41.8 percent [1995 estimate])

Education: In the early 1990s about 1.4 million pupils attended some 2900 primary schools and about 31,500 students attended secondary schools. However, in 1995, after the government made primary education in Malawi free, enrollment in primary schools grew to 3 million.

Languages: English is the official language and the primary language of instruction in the schools. Chichewa, a Bantu language, is the national language, and a number of other Bantu languages are widely spoken.

Ethnic Groups: Principal ethnic groups include the Chewa, the Nyanja, the Tumbuka, the Ngoni, and the Yao. Remaining inhabitants, principally settlers of British and Indian origin, form less than half of 1 percent of the population.

Religions: About 55 percent are Protestant, 20 percent Roman Catholic, 15 percent Muslim; the remainder practice traditional religions.

Climate: The climate varies with the elevation. The low-lying Shire Valley is hot and humid with temperatures averaging from 21° C (69° F) to 29° C (84° F). The highlands are more temperate. Annual rainfall averages about 2300 mm (about 90 in) in the highlands and about 800 mm (about 30 in) in the lowlands.

Land, Plants, and Animals: Part of the Great Rift Valley runs through Malawi from north to south. In this deep trough lies Lake Nyasa, the third largest lake in Africa. The Shire River flows from the southern end of the lake to the Zambezi River in Mozambique. To the east and west of the Great Rift Valley the land rises to form high plateaus. South of Lake Nyasa lie the Shire Highlands, which rise to more than 2700 m (more than 9000 ft). Thin forest covers large parts of the country. Baobab, acacia, and conifers grow in the highlands. Animals include elephants, rhinoceroses, giraffes, zebras, monkeys, antelope, hippopotamuses, snakes and other reptiles, birds, insects, and fish.

Natural Resources: The resources of Malawi are almost entirely agricultural and timber-based. Mineral wealth is slight, although some marble and limestone are produced.

Currency: The Malawian kwacha

Gross Domestic Product (GDP): $8.6 billion (1997 estimate)

GDP per Capita: $900 (1997 estimate)

GDP Real Growth Rate: 6 percent (1997 estimate)

Primary Economic Activities: Agriculture (45 percent of GDP; 43 percent of employment), industry (30 percent of GDP; 16 percent of employment in manufacturing, 7 percent of employment in construction), services (25 percent of GDP) (1995 estimate)

Primary Crops: Tobacco, sugar cane, cotton, tea, corn, potatoes, cassava (tapioca), sorghum, pulses; cattle and goats

Industries: Tea, tobacco, sugar, sawmill products, cement, and consumer goods

Primary Exports: Tobacco, tea, sugar, coffee, peanuts, and wood products

Primary Imports: Food, petroleum products, semimanufactures, consumer goods, and transportation equipment

Primary Trade Partners: United States, South Africa, Germany, Japan, United Kingdom, and Zimbabwe

Government: Malawi is a multiparty parliamentary republic, with an elected president who is both the head of government and the head of state. Bakili Maluzi was elected president on May 21, 1994 and reelected to a five-year term in 1999. Cabinet ministers are responsible to the president, who is elected to a five-year term by universal adult suffrage. The 177-member unicameral parliament, the National Assembly, is popularly elected to five-year terms. Political parties include the ruling party: United Democratic Front as well as Alliance for Democracy, Congress for the Second Republic, Malawi Congress Party, Malawi Democratic Party, People Democratic Party, and the Social Democratic Party.

North America

Malcolm X (Malcolm Little; later El-Hajj Malik El-Shabazz)

(b. May 19, 1925, Omaha, Nebr.; d. February 21, 1965, New York, N.Y.); a leading figure in the twentieth-century movement for black liberation in the United States, and arguably its most enduring symbol.

Malcolm X has been called many things: Pan-Africanist (see Pan-Africanism), father of Black Power, religious fanatic, closet conservative, incipient socialist, and a menace to society. The meaning of his public life—his politics and ideology—is contested in part because his entire body of work consists of a few dozen speeches and a collaborative autobiography whose veracity is often challenged. Gunned down three months before his fortieth birthday, Malcolm X's life was cut short just when his thinking had reached a critical juncture.

Malcolm's life is a Horatio Alger story with a twist. His is not a "rags to riches" tale, but a powerful narrative of self-transformation from petty

Malcolm X speaks to a crowd at a prointegration rally in Harlem, New York, in May 1963.
CORBIS/Bettmann

hustler to internationally known political leader. The son of Louisa and
Earl Little, who was a Baptist preacher active in Marcus Garvey's Universal
Negro Improvement Association, Malcolm and his siblings experienced
dramatic confrontations with racism from childhood. Hooded Klansmen
burned their home in Lansing, Michigan; Earl Little was killed under

mysterious circumstances; welfare agencies split up the children and eventually committed Louisa Little to a state mental institution; and Malcolm was forced to live in a detention home run by a racist white couple. By the eighth grade he left school, moved to Boston, Massachusetts, to live with his half-sister Ella, and discovered the underground world of African American hipsters.

Malcolm's entry into the masculine culture of the zoot suit, the "conked" (straightened) hair, and the lindy hop coincided with the outbreak of World War II, rising black militancy (symbolized in part by A. Philip Randolph's threatened March on Washington for racial and economic justice), and outbreaks of race riots in Detroit, Michigan, and other cities. Malcolm and his partners did not seem very "political" at the time, but they dodged the draft so as not to lose their lives over a "white man's war," and they avoided wage work whenever possible. His search for leisure and pleasure took him to Harlem, New York, where his primary sources of income derived from petty hustling, drug dealing, pimping, gambling, and viciously exploiting women. In 1946 his luck ran out; he was arrested for burglary and sentenced to ten years in prison.

Malcolm's descent took a U-turn in prison when he began studying the teachings of the Lost-Found Nation of Islam (NOI), the black Muslim group founded by Wallace D. Fard and led by Elijah Muhammad (Elijah Poole). Submitting to the discipline and guidance of the NOI, he became a voracious reader of the Koran and the Bible. He also immersed himself in works of literature and history at the prison library. Behind prison walls he quickly emerged as a powerful orator and brilliant rhetorician. He led the famous prison debating team that beat the Massachusetts Institute of Technology (M.I.T.), arguing against capital punishment by pointing out that English pickpockets often did their best work at public hangings! Upon his release in 1952 he renamed himself Malcolm X, symbolically repudiating the "white man's name."

As a devoted follower of Elijah Muhammad, Malcolm X rose quickly within the NOI ranks, serving as minister of Harlem's Temple No. 7 in 1954, and later ministering to temples in Detroit and Philadelphia, Pennsylvania. Through national speaking engagements and television appearances, and by establishing *Muhammad Speaks*—the NOI's first nationally distributed newspaper—Malcolm X put the Nation of Islam on the map. His sharp criticisms of civil rights leaders for advocating integration into white society instead of building black institutions and defending themselves from racist violence generated opposition from both conservatives and liberals. His opponents called him "violent," "fascist," and "racist." To those who claimed that the NOI undermined their efforts toward integration by preaching racial separatism, Malcolm responded, "It is not integration that Negroes in America want, it is human dignity."

Distinguishing Malcolm's early political and intellectual views from the teachings of Elijah Muhammad is not a simple matter. His role as minister was to preach the gospel of Islam according to Muhammad. He remained a staunch devotee of the Nation's strict moral codes and gender conventions.

Although his own narrative suggests that he never entirely discarded his hustler's distrust of women, he married Betty Sanders (later Betty Shabazz) in 1958 and lived by NOI rules: the man's domain is the world, the woman's is the home.

On other issues, however, Malcolm showed signs of independence from the NOI line. He was always careful to preface his remarks with "The honorable Elijah Muhammad teaches . . . " More significant, Malcolm clearly disagreed with the NOI's policy of not participating in politics. He not only believed that political mobilization was indispensable but occasionally defied the rule by supporting boycotts and other forms of protest. In 1962, before he split with the NOI, Malcolm shared the podium with black, white, and Puerto Rican labor organizers in the left-wing, multiracial hospital workers' union in New York. He also began developing an independent Pan-Africanist and, in some respects, "Third World" political perspective during the 1950s, when anti-colonial wars and decolonization were pressing public issues. Indeed, Africa remained his primary political interest outside of black America. He toured Egypt, Sudan, Nigeria, and Ghana in 1959, well before his famous trip to Africa and the Middle East in 1964.

Although Malcolm tried to conceal his differences with Elijah Muhammad, tensions between them erupted. The tensions were exacerbated by the threat that Malcolm's popularity posed to Muhammad's leadership and by Malcolm's disillusionment with Elijah upon learning that the NOI's moral and spiritual leader had fathered children by former secretaries. The tensions became publicly visible when Muhammad silenced Malcolm for remarking after the assassination of President John F. Kennedy that it was a case of the "chickens coming home to roost." (Malcolm's point was that the federal government's inaction toward racist violence in the South had come back to strike the president.) When Malcolm learned that Muhammad had planned to have him assassinated, he decided to leave the NOI.

On March 8, 1964, he announced his resignation and formed the Muslim Mosque, Inc., an Islamic movement devoted to working in the political sphere and cooperating with civil rights leaders. That same year he made his first pilgrimage to Mecca and took a second tour of several African and Arab nations. The trip was apparently transformative. Upon his return he renamed himself El-Hajj Malik El-Shabazz, adopted from Sunni Islam, and announced that he had found the "true brotherhood" of man. He publicly acknowledged that whites were no longer devils, though he still remained a Black Nationalist and staunch believer in black self-determination and self-organization.

During the summer of 1964 he formed the Organization of Afro-American Unity (OAAU). Inspired by the Organization of African Unity (OAU), made up of independent African states, the OAAU's program combined advocacy for independent black institutions (e.g., schools and cultural centers) with support for black participation in mainstream politics, including electoral campaigns. Following the example of Paul Robeson and

W. E. B. Du Bois, Malcolm planned in 1965 to submit to the United Nations a petition that documented human rights violations and acts of genocide against African Americans. His assassination at the Audubon Ballroom in New York—carried out by gunmen affiliated with the NOI—intervened, and the OAAU died soon after Malcolm was laid to rest.

Although Malcolm left no real institutional legacy, he did exert a notable impact on the Civil Rights Movement in the last year of his life. Black activists in the Congress of Racial Equality (CORE) and the Student Nonviolent Coordinating Committee (SNCC) who had heard him speak to organizers in Selma, Alabama, in February 1965 began to support some of his ideas, especially on armed self-defense, racial pride, and the creation of black-run institutions.

Ironically, Malcolm X made a bigger impact on black politics and culture dead than alive. The Watts Rebellion occurred and the Black Power Movement emerged just months after his death, and his ideas about c ommunity control, African liberation, and self-pride became widespread and influential. His autobiography, written with Alex Haley, became a movement standard. Malcolm's life story proved to the Black Panther Party, founded in 1966, that ex-criminals and hustlers could be turned into revolutionaries. And arguments in favor of armed self-defense—certainly not a new idea in African American communities—were renewed by Malcolm's narrative and the publication of his speeches. Even after the death of Martin Luther King Jr., when the civil rights leader was celebrated as an American hero by many blacks and whites, Malcolm's image loomed much larger in inner-city communities, especially among young males.

Despite the collapse or destruction of Black Nationalist organizations during the mid-1970s, Malcolm X continued to live through the folklore of submerged black urban youth cultures, making a huge comeback thanks to rap music, black-oriented bookstores, and Afrocentric street vendors. The 1980s were a ripe time for a hero like Malcolm X, as racism on college campuses increased, inner cities deteriorated, police brutality cases seemed to rise again, and young black men came to be seen as an "endangered species." Malcolm's uncompromising statements about racism, self-hatred, community empowerment, and his background as a "ghetto youth" made him the undisputed icon of the young.

Not surprisingly, the selling of Malcolm X in the 1990s generated pointed debate among African Americans. Some argued that marketing Malcolm undermined his message, while others insisted that the circulation of his image has prompted young people to search out his ideas. Some utilized his emphasis on black community development to support a new African American entrepreneurialism, while others insisted on seeing him as a radical democrat devoted to social justice. His anti-imperialism has dropped out of public memory, whereas his misogyny has been ignored by his supporters and spotlighted by his detractors. However these disputes evolve, it appears that Malcolm X's place in U.S. history, and in the collective memory of African Americans, is secure.

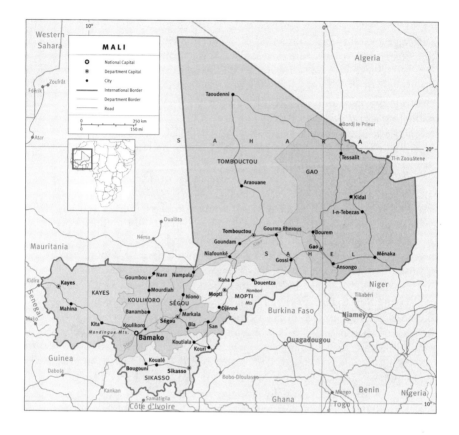

Africa

Mali,

a landlocked country in West Africa bordered by Senegal, Mauritania, Algeria, Niger, Burkina Faso, Côte d'Ivoire, and Guinea.

Mali, formerly the French Sudan, is a country best known for its ancient kingdoms and empires. Controlling the rich trans-Saharan trade in gold and slaves, kingdoms such as Ghana, Mali, and Songhai achieved prosperity and cultural advancement. During the period of colonialism, however, the French imposed an economic dependence on cash crops that left the country vulnerable to drought and the vagaries of the world market. Since independence, successive governments have attempted development strategies ranging from Marxist state-led development to market-oriented liberalism. However, the structural weakness of the country's overwhelmingly agricultural economy has left Mali one of the poorest countries in the world. In recent years economic liberalization has attracted new foreign investment to Mali. It remains to be seen whether this investment will bring renewed prosperity to modern Mali, whose history is surely one of the richest in Africa.

Mali (Ready Reference)

Official Name: Republic of Mali

Former Name: French Sudan

Area: 1,240,192 sq km (478,841 sq mi)

Location: West Africa; borders Algeria, Niger, Burkina Faso, Côte d'Ivoire, Guinea, Senegal, and Mauritania

Capital: Bamako (population 880,000 [1993 estimate])

Other Major Cities: Ségou (population 85,000), Mopti (75,000), Sikasso (73,050), Kayes (50,000), and Gao (40,000) (1993 estimate)

Population: 10,108,569 (1998 estimate)

Population Density: 9 persons per sq km (about 23 persons per sq mi)

Population Below Age 15: 47 percent (male 2,405,624; female 2,383,728 [1998 estimate])

Population Growth Rate: 3 percent (1998 estimate)

Total Fertility Rate: 7.02 children born per woman (1998 estimate)

Life Expectancy at Birth: Total population: 47.03 years (male 45.67 years; female 48.43 years [1998 estimate])

Infant Mortality Rate: 121.72 deaths per 1000 live births (1998 estimate)

Literacy Rate (age 15 and over who can read and write): Total population: 31 percent (male 39.4 percent; female 23.1 percent [1995 estimate])

Education: Annual primary school enrollment in the early 1990s was about 375,000, only about 15 percent of the eligible population. Approximately 88,600 were enrolled in secondary schools and 6700 in institutions of

Malian farmers lead their reluctant animals onto a ferry on their way to the market at Djenné.
CORBIS/Nik Wheeler

A street vendor peddles a variety of household goods in Bamako, capital and largest city of Mali.
CORBIS/Nik Wheeler

higher education in Bamako, including a teacher's college, an agricultural institute, and schools of administration, medicine, and engineering.

Languages: French is the official language; most of the population speaks Bambara; numerous other African languages are spoken, including Peul, Songhai, and Tamasheq (Tuareg Berber).

Ethnic Groups: Mali's ethnic majority is Mande. Other groups include Bambara, Boboi, Bozo, Diawara, Dioula, Dogon, Fulani, Khassonke, Malinké, Marka, Maure, Minianka, Sarakole, Senufo, Somono, Songhai, Tuareg, Tukulor, and Wassalunke.

Religions: Ninety percent of the population is Muslim, 9 percent adhere to indigenous beliefs, and 1 percent is Christian.

Climate: More than half of the country (in the Saharan north) is hot, dry, and dusty. Average temperatures range from about 24° to 32° C (about 75° to 90° F) in the south and higher in the north. Annual rainfall from June to October decreases from about 1400 mm (about 55 in) in the south to some 1120 mm (44 in) at Bamako and less than 127 mm (less than 5 in) in the north.

Land, Plants, and Animals: Most of Mali consists of low plains broken occasionally by rocky hills. In the southeast the Hombori Mountains rise to 1155 m (3789 ft), and in the southwest the Bambouk and Mandingue mountains are separated by an area of sandy lowlands north and northwest of the Niger River, which cuts an arc across Mali. The northern third of the country lies within the Sahara, while the west is a part of the Sahel, a semi-arid transitional zone. In the southern Saharan zone of Mali are found mimosa and gum trees; in the central region, thorny plants; and in the south, kapok, baobab, and shea trees. Animals include cheetah, oryx, gazelle, giraffe, warthog, lion, leopard, antelope, and jackal.

Natural Resources: Fish, gold, phosphate rock, kaolin, salt, limestone, uranium, bauxite, iron ore, manganese, tin, and copper deposits

Currency: The Communauté Financière Africaine franc

Gross Domestic Product (GDP): $6 billion (1997 estimate)

GDP per Capita: $600 (1997 estimate)

GDP Real Growth Rate: 6 percent (1997 estimate)

Primary Economic Activities: Agriculture (49 percent of GDP, 80 percent of employment); services (34 percent of GDP, 19 percent of employment); industry: 17 percent of GDP, 1 percent of employment) (1995 estimates)

Primary Crops: Cotton, millet, rice, corn, vegetables, peanuts, cattle, sheep, and goats

Industries: Light consumer goods, food processing, construction, phosphate, and gold mining

Primary Exports: Cotton, livestock, and gold

Primary Imports: Machinery and equipment, foodstuffs, construction materials, petroleum, and textiles

Primary Trade Partners: Francophone West Africa and European Union (France especially)

A Tuareg family camped outside Tombouctou, Mali, makes dinner. *CORBIS/Wolfgang Kaehler*

Government: A constitution, approved by popular referendum in January 1992, established Mali as a multiparty republic with a president directly elected to a five-year term. The president, currently Amadou Tomani Toure, appoints the prime minister, currently Ahmed Mohamed Ag Hamani, who selects the other members of the Council of Ministers. The unicameral National Assembly consists of 129 deputies elected to five-year terms.

Africa

Mandela, Nelson Rolihlahla

(b. July 18, 1918, Mvezo, South Africa), former president of South Africa, winner of the Nobel Peace Prize, and former head of the African National Congress.

The first black president of South Africa, Nelson Mandela became a worldwide symbol of resistance to the injustice of his country's apartheid system. Imprisoned for more than 27 years, and before that banned from all public activity and hounded by police for nearly a decade, Mandela led a struggle for freedom that mirrored that of his black countrymen. After his 1990 release

from the Robben Island prison, his work to end apartheid won him the 1993 Nobel Peace Prize (which he shared with South African president F. W. De Klerk) and then the presidency itself a year later.

Mandela's father, Chief Henry Mandela, was a member of the Thembu people's royal lineage; his mother was one of the chief's four wives. Mandela grew up in Qunu, a small village in the Eastern Cape. At age seven he became the first member of his family to attend school. When his father died two years later, Nelson—the Christian name he had acquired at school—was sent to live with Chief Jongintaba Dalindyebo, the regent, or supreme leader, of the Thembu people. From the regent, Mandela said, he learned that "a leader . . . is like a shepherd. He stays behind the flock, letting the most nimble go on ahead, whereupon the others follow, not realizing that all along they are being directed from behind."

South African president Nelson Mandela claps his hands to gospel music during a Sunday prayer at a church in Eldorado park in May 1999.
AFP/CORBIS

Mandela finished his secondary education at Healdtown, a missionary school where an emphasis on English traditions molded students into "Black Englishmen." Only as a student at Fort Hare University did Mandela begin to question the injustices he and all black South Africans faced. Fort Hare was considered an oasis of black scholarship; it was also a training ground for future leaders (lawyer and antiapartheid activist Oliver Tambo was Mandela's classmate, and Freedom Charter originator Z. K. Matthews taught there). But a dispute with the administration over students' rights caused Mandela to leave Fort Hare in his second year; at the same time he broke with the regent rather than accept an arranged marriage.

Jobless when he arrived in Johannesburg in 1941, Mandela found work assisting a lawyer—a job arranged by activist Walter Sisulu—while finishing his bachelor's degree by correspondence from the University of South Africa. His political education continued as well, as he met members of the Communist Party of South Africa and, more important, the African National Congress (ANC). Soon afterward Mandela and a group of fellow ANC members, including Walter Sisulu and Oliver Tambo (with whom Mandela formed South Africa's first black-run law firm), founded the ANC Youth League.

Mandela also worked as the volunteer-in-chief of ANC's Campaign for the Defiance of Unjust Laws, in which about 9000 volunteers defied selected laws and consequently were imprisoned. As a result, the National Party government banned him from all public gatherings in 1952 and again from 1953 to 1955. When, in 1960, the government banned the ANC outright in the wake of the police massacre of demonstrators in Sharpeville township, Mandela and several thousand apartheid opponents were detained. A consistent voice for nonviolence, Mandela at this point decided that "it was wrong and immoral to subject [his] people to armed attacks by the state without offering them some kind of alternative." Consequently, in 1961 he went underground and he helped create the ANC's paramilitary wing *Umkhonto we Sizwe* (Spear of the Nation), which carried out acts of sabotage against the government. Captured in August 1962, Mandela was charged with traveling outside the country without a passport and inciting workers to strike. At his trial he acted as his own lawyer, arguing not that he was innocent but rather that the South African government had used the law "to impose a state of outlawry" upon him. Several months into his five-year sentence, Mandela was charged with treason and in 1964 was sentenced to life in prison without the possibility of parole.

Until 1982 Mandela was imprisoned on Robben Island, South Africa's most notorious prison, located just offshore from Cape Town. Initially he lived in a cell measuring seven by seven feet, could write and receive only one letter every six months, and was forced to break rocks in the prison yard for hours daily. By the early 1980s South Africa's apartheid government, faced with international sanctions, began to make gestures toward Mandela, its most famous political prisoner, including moving him to Pollsmoor Prison—a much less brutal environment than Robben Island—in 1982. The negotiations unfolded gradually over the next decade. In 1985 President P. W. Botha publicly stated that he would release Mandela provided he "rejected violence as a political instrument," a deal designed to alienate Mandela from other ANC leaders. Mandela

Former South African president Nelson Mandela greets supporters of the African National Congress after a meeting with local political leaders outside Durban in May 1995. *CORBIS/AFP*

rejected the offer. In 1988 he was transferred to a private facility at Victor Verster Prison, where talks continued in secret. F. W. De Klerk succeeded P. W. Botha as president in 1989, and within a few months he lifted the 30-year-long ban on the ANC. On February 2, 1990, he announced Mandela's release from prison.

Freedom brought new challenges. During his imprisonment Mandela's wife, Winnie Madikizela-Mandela (whom he had married in 1958 following the end of his first marriage), was convicted of kidnapping and accessory to assault in the death of a Soweto teenager. The couple, who have two daughters (Mandela has three older children from his first marriage), separated in 1992.

Mandela succeeded Oliver Tambo as president of the ANC in 1992. In September 1992 he and De Klerk agreed on a framework within which to negotiate a transition to multiracial democratic rule. The Record of Understanding they signed in December 1993 provided for a new constitution and free elections to be held April 27, 1994. With black South Africans voting for the first time in their lives, the ANC won handily, and Mandela was inaugurated as president on May 10, 1994. Since assuming office he has earned a reputation as an international peacemaker, helping to mediate conflicts both in Africa and abroad. In addition, Mandela has worked to strengthen South Africa's economy by pursuing international trade agreements and foreign investment. In 1997 Mandela, who has always indicated that he would not run for reelection in 1999, stepped down as ANC leader and was succeeded by Thabo Mbeki. On his 80th birthday on July 18, 1998, Mandela married Graça Machel, the widow of Mozambican president Samora Machel. In September 1998 Mandela received the Congressional Gold Medal in a ceremony at the United States capitol. He was the first African to receive this award.

Latin America and the Caribbean

Manley, Michael

(b. December 10, 1924, St. Andrew, Jamaica; d. March 6, 1997, Kingston, Jamaica), prime minister of Jamaica (1972–1980, 1989–1992).

The son of a prominent Jamaican politician and an English sculptor, Michael Manley was born into a family of privilege. His father, Norman Washington Manley, was founder of the democratic People's National Party (PNP), prime minister of Jamaica from 1959 to 1962, and a leader in the Jamaican independence movement. The fair-skinned Michael Manley was a member of Jamaica's colored, or mixed-race, community, and he grew up around many of the most influential elites in Jamaica. He was educated at the London School of Economics and served as a freelance journalist for the British Broadcasting Corporation (BBC) upon graduation in 1949.

His privileged background notwithstanding, Manley dedicated his career to improving life for all Jamaicans. During the 1972 election for prime minister, Manley captured the hearts of many voters when he publicly acknowledged Jamaica's African roots. He often wore traditional African clothing and carried a staff reportedly given to him by Haile Selassie I, then emperor of Ethiopia. Called the Rod of Joshua, the staff symbolized African pride and moral authority.

As prime minister, Manley steered Jamaica toward socialism. He nationalized the bauxite industry, spoke out against economic dependency on foreign investment, and angered the United States government by embracing Cuba's communist president Fidel Castro. Though Manley's socialist policies improved life for many poor Jamaicans, they also weakened Jamaica's economy. By 1980 the nation stood near bankruptcy. The United States government, angered by his ties to Castro, reportedly worked secretly to remove Manley from power. He was defeated by conservative politician Edward Seaga in the violence-stricken elections of 1980.

After a nine-year hiatus, Manley was reelected prime minister in 1989. His socialist leanings tempered, Manley embraced the principles of free-market capitalism, liberalized the economy, and welcomed foreign investment. His term was cut short in 1992 when he was diagnosed with prostate cancer. He died in 1997 at his home in Kingston, leaving a wife and five children.

North America

March on Washington, 1963,

a massive public demonstration that articulated the goals of the Civil Rights Movement.

The 1963 March on Washington attracted an estimated 250,000 people for a peaceful demonstration to promote civil rights and economic equality for African Americans. Participants walked down Constitution and Independence Avenues, then—100 years after the Emancipation Proclamation was signed—gathered before the Lincoln Monument for speeches, songs, and prayer. Televised live to an audience of millions, the march provided dramatic moments, most memorably the Reverend Martin Luther King Jr.'s *I Have a Dream* speech.

Far larger than previous demonstrations for any cause, the march had an obvious impact, both on the passage of civil rights legislation and on nationwide public opinion. It proved the power of mass appeal and inspired imitators in the antiwar, feminist, and environmental movements. But the March on Washington in 1963 was more complex than the iconic images for which most Americans remember it. As the high point of the Civil Rights Movement, the march—and the integrationist, nonviolent, liberal form of protest it represented—was followed by more radical, militant, and race-conscious approaches.

The march was initiated by A. Philip Randolph, international president of the Brotherhood of Sleeping-Car Porters, president of the Negro American Labor Council, and vice president of the AFL-CIO, and was sponsored by five of the largest civil rights organizations in the United States. Planning for the event was complicated by differences among members. Known in the press as "the big six," the major players were Randolph; Whitney Young, president of the National Urban League (NUL); Roy Wilkins, president of the National Association for the Advancement of Colored People (NAACP); James Farmer, founder and president of the Congress of Racial Equality (CORE); John Lewis, president of the Student Nonviolent Coordinating Committee (SNCC); and Martin Luther King Jr., founder and president of the Southern Christian Leadership Conference (SCLC). Bayard Rustin, a close associate of Randolph's and organizer of the first Freedom Ride in 1947, orchestrated and administered the details of the march.

The rally concluded with Rustin's reading of the march's ten demands—which included not only passage of the civil rights bill but also school and housing desegregation, job training, and an increase in the minimum wage. As marchers returned to the buses that would take them home, the organizers met with President Kennedy, who encouraged them to continue with their work.

Although white racists decried it as a sentimental appeal to mainstream white America, the March on Washington was a success. It had been powerful yet peaceful and orderly beyond anyone's expectations, including those of the organizers themselves. Yet it was, according to most historians, the high tide of that phase of the Civil Rights Movement that looked to white support and government solutions. The bombing, just three weeks later, of the Sixteenth Street Baptist Church in Birmingham, Alabama, which resulted in the deaths of four young black girls, reminded African Americans of the depth and violence of segregationist America. Increasingly, young African Americans turned to the Black Power Movement or to the Nation of Islam (whose leader, Malcolm X, had criticized the march) in their search for freedom and strength.

Latin America and the Caribbean

Marley, Bob

(b. February 6, 1945, Rhoden Hall, Jamaica; d. May 11, 1981, Miami, Fla.), Jamaican singer and songwriter whose name invokes reggae music, the tenets of Rastafarianism, and, more broadly, the struggle of the economically and politically oppressed.

The first global pop star to emerge from a developing nation, Bob Marley has won fans from nations around the globe who share his vision of redemption and freedom and love his innovative blend of American and Caribbean music.

Like a number of their contemporaries, Marley and Bunny Neville O'Riley Livingston listened to radio from New Orleans; and like their peers they adopted the sounds of rhythm and blues, combined them with strains of a local musical style, *mento*, and produced a new music called *ska*. Peter

McIntosh (later Peter Tosh) joined Bunny and Marley's musical sessions, bringing with him a real guitar. In the early 1960s the three formed a harmony group, the Wailing Wailers; meanwhile, Marley recorded a few songs with producer Leslie Kong, to whom local *ska* celebrity Jimmy Cliff had introduced him. Marley's earliest recordings received little radio play but strengthened his desire to sing.

In 1967, he converted from Christianity to Rastafarianism and began the mature stage of his musical career. Marley reunited with Bunny Neville O'Riley and Peter Tosh, and together they called themselves the Wailers and began their own record label, Wail 'N' Soul. They abandoned the rude-boy ethos for the spirituality of Rastafarian beliefs and slowed their music under the new rocksteady influence. During the early 1970s the band recorded an album each year and toured extensively, slowly breaking into the European and American mainstream. They played shows with American superstars Bruce Springsteen and Sly and the Family Stone, and in 1974 British rocker Eric Clapton scored a hit with "I Shot the Sheriff," a Marley composition. In 1975 the Wailers made their first major splash in the United States with "No Woman No Cry" as well as an album of live material. At this point, Peter Tosh and Bunny left the band, which took the name Bob Marley & the Wailers.

Although Marley had melded politics and music since the early days of *Simmer Down*, as his success grew he became increasingly political. His 1976 song "War" transcribed a speech of Haile Selassie I, the Ethiopian king upon whom the Rastafarian sect was based. In addition to Rastafarian spirituality and mysticism, his lyrics probed the turmoil in Jamaica. Prior to the 1976 elections, partisanship inspired gang war in Trench Town and divided the people against themselves. By siding with Prime Minister Michael Manley—and by singing songs of a political bent—Marley angered some Jamaicans. After surviving an assassination attempt in December, he fled to London until the following year. Marley's activism extended beyond Jamaica, and people from developing nations around the world found hope in his music. In 1980 Bob Marley & the Wailers had the honor of performing at the independence ceremony when Rhodesia became Zimbabwe. The group's concerts in the late 1970s attracted enormous crowds in West Africa and Latin America as well as in Europe and the United States.

North America

Marshall, Thurgood

(b. July 2, 1908, Baltimore, Md.; d. January 24, 1993, Bethesda, Md.), first black United States Supreme Court justice, founder of the NAACP Legal Defense and Educational Fund; lawyer whose victory in *Brown v. Board of Education* (1954) outlawed segregation in American public life.

When Thurgood Marshall died in 1993, he was only the second justice to lie in state in the Supreme Court's chambers. Chief Justice Earl Warren, who had written the opinion in Marshall's most celebrated case, *Brown v.*

Representing defendant Walter Lee Irvin, *third from left,* at his second trial for rape are, *left to right,* Paul C. Perkins, Jack Greenberg, New York attorney for the National Association for the Advancement of Colored People (NAACP), and Thurgood Marshall, chief counsel for the NAACP. *CORBIS/Bettmann*

Board of Education, was the other. Marshall's tenure as chief counsel for the National Association for the Advancement of Colored People (NAACP) and founder of its Legal Defense and Educational Fund made him one of America's most influential and best-known lawyers. His 30 years of public service—first as a federal appeals court judge, then as America's first black solicitor general, and finally as the first black U.S. Supreme Court justice—came after he had already helped millions of African Americans exercise long-denied constitutional rights.

Marshall once said that his father told him, "If anyone calls you nigger, you not only have my permission to fight him, you got my orders." Both of Marshall's parents—William, who worked as a dining steward at an all-white private club, and Norma, a grade school teacher—instilled in their son racial pride and self-confidence. As a child, Marshall later recalled, he was a "hell-raiser," whose high school teacher punished him by sending him to the school's basement to read and copy passages from the United States Constitution. It was valuable training for the future lawyer, who claimed that by the time he graduated he could recite nearly the entire document by heart. From Baltimore's Douglass High School, Marshall entered Lincoln University in Oxford, Pennsylvania, where he won respect as a debater and graduated with honors in 1930.

Denied admission to the University of Maryland's all-white law school—an institution whose segregation he later challenged and defeated in *Murray v. Maryland* (1936)—Marshall entered the law school at Howard University. There he met Charles H. Houston, the school's vice dean, who became the

NAACP's first chief counsel and the first black man to win a case before the U.S. Supreme Court. Shortly after graduating magna cum laude in 1933, Marshall went to work for Houston at the NAACP, replacing him as chief counsel in 1938.

From Houston, Marshall absorbed the lesson that lawyers could be "social engineers." Marshall and the NAACP began asking whether separate could ever be equal. The case that finally ended legal segregation in America was *Brown v. Board of Education*. Drawing on psychological and sociological evidence, Marshall argued that the mere fact of racial separation, even without gross inequality, irrevocably harmed African American children. The Court unanimously agreed. In *Brown* (1954) and its companion decision, *Brown II* (1955), the Supreme Court outlawed state-imposed segregation and set guidelines for eradicating it, a process that was neither quick nor easy nor complete. But despite often violent resistance to desegregation, the constitutional impact of Marshall's victory in *Brown* was enormous and lasting.

Thurgood Marshall brought 32 cases before the Supreme Court; he won 29 of them. He had an even more impressive record as a judge for the U.S. Court of Appeals, a position to which President John F. Kennedy appointed him in 1961. Of the 112 opinions he wrote for that court, not one was overturned on appeal. In 1965 President Lyndon B. Johnson appointed Marshall solicitor general of the United States—in essence, the nation's chief counsel. Two years later Johnson nominated Marshall to fill the Supreme Court vacancy left by Justice Thomas C. Clark. The first African American to serve as solicitor general or a Supreme Court justice, Marshall said he hesitated to take on the roles, not wanting to abandon his friends in the Civil Rights Movement. But, he said, "when one has the opportunity to serve the Government, he should think twice before passing it up."

Latin America and the Caribbean

Martinique,

former French colony and present-day overseas department of France in the Caribbean, situated among the Lesser Antilles halfway between Puerto Rico and Trinidad, with St. Lucia directly to the south and Dominica directly to the north.

At the time of French colonization in the mid-1600s, Martinique's inhabitants were Indians who are known as the Carib, who had migrated into the Caribbean from South America and had displaced the Arawak, probably the earliest inhabitants of Martinique. The Carib first came into contact with Europeans when Christopher Columbus landed on Martinique on June 15, 1502, during his fourth voyage to the Americas. Unclaimed by Spain, Martinique and the surrounding islands attracted the attention of the French in the seventeenth century. In 1635 an expedition led by Pierre

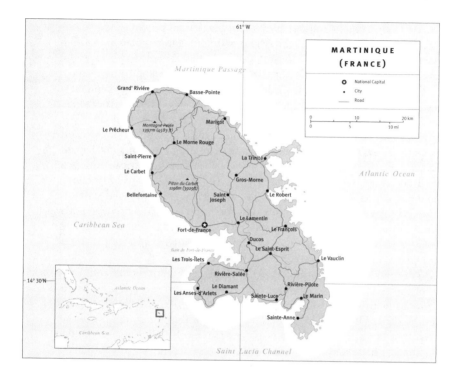

d'Esnambuc overcame Carib resistance and established a French foothold at
Saint-Pierre. (This city became and was to remain the capital of Martinique
until the volcanic eruption of Mount Pelée in 1902 destroyed the city,
killing 30,000 of its inhabitants.) Following the success of d'Esnambuc's
mission, France claimed Martinique as a colonial possession. Except for the
periods 1762–1763, 1793–1802, and 1809–1815, when the British disputed
and temporarily wrested ownership of the island from the French, the island
has remained under French control.

The twentieth century has witnessed dramatic changes in Martinique.
Politics, once the exclusive domain of *békés*, opened up to the descendants
of slaves. In 1945 Aimé Césaire, the black poet, politician, and intellectual, ran for the position of Martinican deputy to France's parliament. In
a surprising upset he won, and Césaire remained a force in Martinican
politics both as deputy and as mayor of Fort-de-France until he retired
from politics in 1993. Césaire helped stimulate Martinique's cultural
renewal with the publication of *Cahier d'un retour au pays natal* in 1939.
Although Césaire sought to promote the cultural singularity of the
Caribbean and its inhabitants in his poetry and in the Négritude ideology
he helped create and disseminate, his politics have always been assimilationist. Césaire supported Martinique's change in status on March 19,
1946, to French overseas department, effectively making the island an
integral part of France.

Since that time, Césaire has never called for Martinique's independence
from France. For this reason, he has come under fire from a younger genera-

tion of intellectuals—most notably Edouard Glissant and Raphaël Confiant—who argue that the descendants of slaves and indentured laborers in Martinique will never have a culture of their own until all official ties with France are severed. But the independence forces have had trouble convincing a populace that recognizes the extent to which it is dependent on France. Today most of Martinique's trade is with the French mainland, and Martinique receives massive subsidies from France. But as with all French departments, whether in the Caribbean or on the mainland, Martinique has gained a degree of autonomy through the decentralization of the French political system that took place in the 1980s. It remains to be seen, though, if these changes will suffice to keep the forces of independence at bay on an island whose inhabitants generally consider themselves to be more Caribbean than French.

Africa

Masekela, Hugh Ramopolo

(b. April 4, 1931, Witbank, South Africa), noted South African trumpeter.

Born in a coal-mining town near Johannesburg, trumpet player Hugh Ramopolo Masekela is one of Africa's most influential contemporary jazz musicians. His father was a health inspector and sculptor. Masekela attended mission schools. Introduced to the trumpet by anti-apartheid activist Father Trevor Huddleston, a British Anglican priest, Masekela was soon caught up by the musical innovation sweeping South Africa in the 1950s. By mixing American jazz with traditional African rhythms and melodies, he became one of the leaders in creating a new cosmopolitan style. He played with the Father Huddleston Band, the Jazz Dazzlers, and pianist Dollar Brand, now known as Abdullah Ibrahim.

By the 1960s South African jazz had become intertwined with the struggle against apartheid. Masekela went to London, where he attended the Guildhall School of Music, and then traveled to New York City, where he attended the Manhattan School of Music from 1960 to 1964. From 1964 to 1966 he was married to another South African musical exile, the legendary singer Miriam Makeba. In 1968 Masekela, then living in New York City, recorded his first commercial hit, "Grazing in the Grass." In 1987, along with the band Ladysmith Black Mambazo, he joined Paul Simon's Graceland tour, which highlighted South African music.

In the early 1990s Masekela returned to a postapartheid South Africa and began urging young South Africans to rediscover their musical roots. He was appointed codirector of the State Theatre in Pretoria in 1995. A year later he joined a gala performance in London before Queen Elizabeth II. He also bought a jazz nightclub, J & B Junction, in the trendy Johannesburg suburb of Yeoville.

Africa

Mau Mau Rebellion,

an anti-colonial rebellion that took place predominantly among the Kikuyu ethnic group in British-ruled Kenya, ultimately accelerating the process of Kenyan independence.

The British had used the term *Mau Mau* as early as 1947 to refer to the intermittent but escalating Kikuyu violence that was taking place in both rural and urban areas of colonial Kenya. Later it came to describe the anti-colonial guerrilla movement that launched a four-year revolt beginning in 1952. The movement's grievances centered on colonial land policies, which confiscated prime farmland for white settlers while relegating Africans to overcrowded "tribal reserves." Although the origins of the term *Mau Mau* are still debated, in the Gikuyu language it means "greedy eating." Many participants in the rebellion rejected the label, instead favoring such names as *Kiama Kia Muingi* (the Community's Party),

Defendants hold identification numbers in a 1953 trial of those suspected of fighting in the anticolonial Mau Mau rebellion. At its height between 1952 and 1956, the rebellion claimed the lives of more than 12,000 Africans and 100 Europeans. The British colonial government hanged an estimated 1000 Africans convicted of participation. *CORBIS/Hulton-Deutsch Collection*

Muhimu (Swahili for "important"), the African Government, and the Kenya Land Freedom Army.

Although Mau Mau's leaders and most of its members were ethnic Kikuyu, the movement also attracted small numbers of supporters from other ethnic groups. Few disagree with the basic facts surrounding the rebellion, but interpretation remains contentious, suggesting that Mau Mau was a diffuse movement with objectives that varied among members. What is certain is that the British reaction to Mau Mau was severe and bloody but largely futile, because afterward Great Britain only hastened its plans for decolonization.

By the end of the military phase of the rebellion in 1956 (the state of emergency was not lifted until 1960), Mau Mau and related events had claimed the lives of more than 12,000 Africans (approximately 1000 of whom the British hanged) and 100 Europeans. Though militarily defeated, Mau Mau had broken British resolve in Kenya and cost the government approximately £60 million. Furthermore, international criticism of its repressive tactics convinced Great Britain to accelerate its departure from Kenya rather than risk another conflict.

Debate continues over the significance of Mau Mau. Initially the British government described it as a movement by Africans who, unable to adapt to the social changes associated with modernization, reverted to their barbaric roots. This view held until the mid-1960s, when scholars declared Mau Mau a peasant liberation movement. Others cast it as a Kikuyu religious movement because of the secret membership oaths, while still others maintain that it was both a political and religious organization. Most agree that the rebellion was never as unified as the British believed, and that it was a "movement" only in the sense that the inequities of the colonial system inspired widespread resistance.

Europe

Maurice, Saint (Saint Maurice d'Agaune)

(d. 287 C.E?), Christian martyr and saint.

According to Christian legend, Maurice, the first Christian saint to be explicitly represented as an African, was a *primicerius* (a high-ranking officer) in the Roman army whose legion was massacred by the Romans in the late third century for refusing to participate in a pagan ritual.

Maurice and his legion, all baptized Christians, were recruited for military service in Thebaid, an Egyptian province on the Upper Nile (near the present-day border between Egypt and Sudan). Thebaid, with its capital at Thebes, was the southernmost region of the Roman Empire, then ruled by co-emperors Diocletian (284–305) and Maximian (240–310).

In 287 Maximian, commander of the Roman army in Gaul, led his troops, which included Maurice's legion, in a military campaign against insurgents in Gaul. On the eve of battle, the army camped at Octodurum (in what is now Martigny, Switzerland), and Maximian ordered his soldiers to participate in a sacrifice to the Roman gods to ensure their success in battle. Maurice, refusing to betray his Christian convictions, moved his legion to a camp at Agaunum (now Saint-Maurice-en-Valais) to avoid participating in the ritual. Maurice and three other Theban officers—Exuperius, Innocent, and Candidus—refused Maximian's orders to return to Octodurum, and, in retaliation, the Roman emperor decimated the Theban legion, ordering every tenth soldier killed in an attempt to force the remaining legionnaires to take part in the sacrifice. When these soldiers continued to disobey, the legion was decimated a second time. In 962 Emperor Otto the Great, who was anointed in a cathedral devoted to Saint Maurice, nominated him patron saint of the Holy Roman Empire. His saint's day is September 22.

Though often described as "the first black saint," Saint Maurice was not represented as a black man until 1240, when construction (begun in 1211) was completed on the Cathedral of Magdeburg, which houses his relics and contains a life-size stone statue of him clad in chain mail and with dark skin and unambiguously African features. Before the sculpting of this figure, and for a long time afterward, there were no other comparably explicit representations of black saints.

The shift toward representations of Saint Maurice as a black man was doubtlessly encouraged by the growing public prevalence of Moors in the entourage of the German emperor Frederick II, a leader with a special affinity for and fascination with Africa. Frederick employed African political advisers and soldiers and thus helped to expose and accustom Europeans to the physical appearance of Africans. His interest in and employment of Africans, and Maurice's role as an effective political symbol, led to more depictions of the saint as black. As the influence of the Holy Roman Empire grew, representations of Maurice as an African spread beyond Magdeburg and across the empire on into the sixteenth century.

Africa

Mauritania,

a country of northwest Africa bordered by Senegal, the Western Sahara, Mali, Algeria, and the Atlantic Ocean.

Situated between North and sub-Saharan Africa, precolonial Mauritania was a land of salt mines and caravan routes, and a meeting ground between the powerful empires of the western Sudan and the Arab and Berber dynasties of the north. During the colonial era French rule effectively divided northern and southern Mauritania. Independence reunited the country geographically, but internal racial tensions and several cross-border conflicts have contributed to political instability and drained the country's limited resources.

A boy prepares tea in Rosso, Mauritania. *CORBIS/Bernard and Catherine Desjeux*

Africa

Mauritania (Ready Reference)

Official Name: Islamic Republic of Mauritania

Area: 1,030,700 sq km (397,955 sq mi)

Location: Northern Africa; borders the North Atlantic Ocean, Senegal, Mali, Algeria, and the Western Sahara

Capital: Nouakchott (population 550,000 [1992 estimate])

Other Major Cities: Kaédi (population 74,000), Nouadhibou (70,000) (1992 estimate)

Population: 2,511,473 (1998 estimate)

Population Density: 3 persons per sq km (about 5 persons per sq mi)

Population Below Age 15: 46 percent (male 584,303; female 583,526 [1998 estimate])

Population Growth Rate: 2.52 percent (1998 estimate)

Total Fertility Rate: 6.41 children born per woman (1998 estimate)

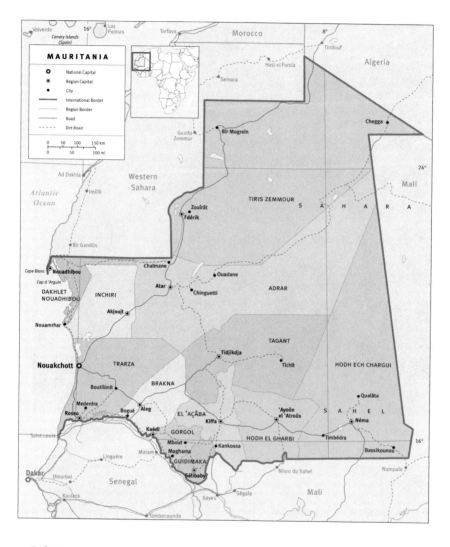

Life Expectancy at Birth: Total population: 49.9 years (male 46.95 years; female 53.11 years [1998 estimate])

Infant Mortality: 78.22 deaths per 1000 live births (1998 estimate)

Literacy Rate (age 15 and over who can read and write): Total population: 37.7 percent (male 49.6 percent; female 26.3 percent [1995 estimate])

Education: The government of Mauritania attempts to provide free primary education. These efforts, however, have been hindered by the nomadic practices of the people. In the early 1990s only 55 percent of all eligible children were attending primary school.

Languages: Hasaniya Arabic is the official language. Poular, Wolof, and Soninké are also recognized as national languages.

Ethnic Groups: The majority of the population is Moors (of mixed Arab and Berber ancestry), many of whom lead nomadic lives.

Religions: Islam, which is the state religion, is practiced by more than 99 percent of the population.

Climate: Except for a narrow strip in the south along the Senegal River, the country lies entirely within the Sahara Desert. Day-time temperatures in most of the country average near 37.8° C (100° F) during the day for more than six months of the year, but the nights are cool. Annual rainfall varies from less than 130 mm (less than 5 in) in the north to about 660 mm (26 in) in the Senegal Valley.

Land, Plants, and Animals: In Mauritania there are mostly flat Sahara plains with some hills. The elevation varies from about 150m (500 ft) in the southwest to about 460 m (about 1500 ft) in the northeast. Few animals and little plant life thrive in the northern region. Lions and monkeys inhabit the region near the Senegal River.

Natural Resources: Mauritania's natural resources include iron ore, gypsum, fish, copper, and phosphate.

Currency: The ouguiya

Gross Domestic Product (GDP): $4.1 billion (1996 estimate)

GDP per Capita: $750 (1996 estimate)

GDP Real Growth Rate: 6 percent (1996 estimate)

Primary Economic Activities: Agriculture (47 percent of population), industry, and commerce

Primary Crops: Millet, sorghum, root crops, dates, and livestock

Industries: Fish processing and mining of iron ore and gypsum

Primary Exports: Iron ore, fish, and fish products

Primary Imports: Foodstuffs, consumer goods, petroleum products, and capital goods

Primary Trade Partners: Algeria, China, United States, France, Germany, Spain, and Italy

Government: Mauritania is a constitutional republic that obtained its independence from France on November 28, 1960. The executive branch is led by President Col. Maaouya Ould Sidi Ahmed Taya and the Council of Ministers. The president is elected by popular vote for a six-year term. The legislative branch is bicameral, consisting of the 56-seat Senate, or *Majlis al-Shuyukh*, whose members serve six-year terms, and the 79-member National Assembly, or *Majlis al-Wajani*, whose members serve for five years. The judicial system is based on Islamic (*Shari'a*) courts, special courts, and state security courts; the state security courts are being phased out. Though politics often falls along tribal lines, some fledgling political parties include the Democratic and Social Republican Party, the Union of Democratic Forces-New Era, and the Assembly for Democracy and Unity.

Africa

Mauritius,

African island republic in the western Indian Ocean, located 800 km (497 mi)
east of Madagascar and 200 km (124.3 mi) northeast of Réunion. The
country includes the island of Mauritius; the island of Rodrigues to the
east; the Agalega Islands to the north; and the Cargados Carajos Shoals to
the northeast.

The small, volcanic island of Mauritius remained unsettled until the
seventeenth century. More than 1.1 million people, descendants from India,
Africa, Europe, and China, now claim the island as their home. Although
Mauritius was initially discovered by Arab seafarers, European colonialism
and mercantile economic forces later brought colonists, soldiers, slaves,
indentured laborers, and traders to the island, resulting in a remarkably
diverse mixture of people and cultures. In recent years Mauritius has
transformed itself from an obscure sugar plantation colony into a major
European tourist destination boasting a strong, rapidly expanding and
diversifying economy overseen by a stable, democratic political regime.

Women wash and rinse clothes in a narrow canal on Mauritius. *CORBIS/Wolfgang Kaehler*

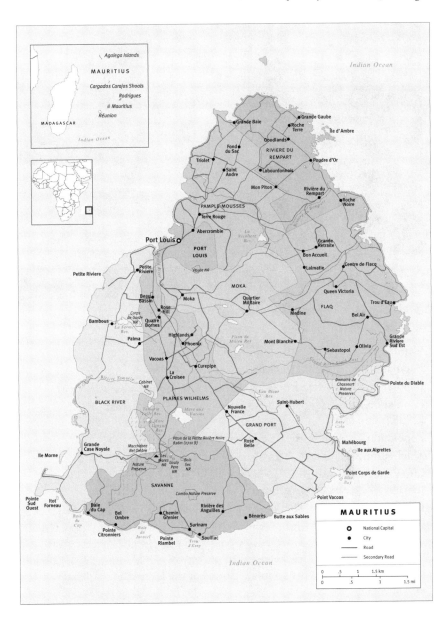

Africa

Mauritius (Ready Reference)

Official Name: Republic of Mauritius

Area: Mauritius Island, 1865 sq km (720 sq mi); includes Rodrigues and the Agalega Islands, and the Cargados Carajos Shoals, 2040 sq km (787 sq mi)

Location: Islands in the western Indian Ocean, west of Madagascar

Grass sun umbrellas line the beach at St. Geran, Mauritius. *CORBIS*

Capital: Port Louis (population 142,850 [1992 estimate])

Population: 1,168,256 (1998 estimate)

Population Density: 554 persons per sq km (1436 persons per sq mi)

Population Below Age 15: 26 percent (male 155,917; female 152,563 [1998 estimate])

Population Growth Rate: 1.2 percent (1998 estimate)

Total Fertility Rate: 2.2 children born per woman (1998 estimate)

Life Expectancy at Birth: Total population: 70.9 years (male 67.0 years; female: 74.7 years [1997 estimate])

Infant Mortality Rate: 16.5 deaths per 1000 live births (1998 estimate)

Literacy Rate (age 15 and over who can read and write): Total population: 82.9 percent (male 87.1 percent; female 78.8 percent [1995 estimate])

Education: Education has been a high priority of the Mauritius government since the early 1980s; the country has one of the highest literacy rates in Africa.

Languages: English is the official language, but French, Hindi, and Creole—a French patois—are more commonly spoken. There are also speakers of Urdu, Hakka, and Bojpoori.

Ethnic Groups: More than 60 percent of Mauritians are Indian immigrants and their descendants. Another 25 percent are Creole (of mixed African and European heritage). There is a small ethnically-Chinese population.

Religions: About 52 percent of the population is Hindu, and around 28 percent is Christian (mostly Roman Catholic). Another 16 percent is Muslim.

Climate: The climate is tropical; the weather is warm and dry during the winter months (May through October) and hot, wet, and humid in the summer (November through April). Average annual rainfall ranges from about 1000 mm (40 in) on the coast to about 5000 mm (200 in) in the central plateau. Strong cyclones occur often during the summer. The average annual temperature on the coast is 23° C (73° F).

Land, Plants, and Animals: The main island of Mauritius is volcanic in origin and rises from a narrow coastline to jagged mountains ringing the central plateau. Its highest elevation, Piton de la Petite Rivière Noire, is 826 m (2710 ft). Coral reefs circle the coastline, except at Port Louis, the capital, which has a deep-water harbor. The lushly forested interior has many lakes and small streams.

Natural Resources: Fertile, arable soil and fish

Currency: The Mauritian rupee

Gross Domestic Product (GDP): $11.7 billion (1996 estimate)

GDP per Capita: $10,300 (1996 estimate)

GDP Real Growth Rate: 5.4 percent (1996 estimate)

Primary Economic Activities: Agriculture, food processing, manufacturing, and tourism

Primary Crops: Sugar cane (grown on 90 percent of cultivated land), tea, peanuts, tobacco, and vegetables

Industries: Food processing, textiles, leather goods, chemicals, metal products, and electronic components

Primary Exports: Textiles and sugar

Primary Imports: Food, petroleum products, and chemicals

Primary Trade Partners: European Union, United States, South Africa, and Japan

Government: Though formerly a constitutional monarchy, since 1992 Mauritius has been a constitutional republic. It is headed by a president elected by a legislative body, the National Assembly, and a prime minister appointed by the president. Karl Auguste Offmann has been president since 2002. Sir Anerood Jugnauth has been prime minister since 2000. Major parties include the coalition of the Mauritius Labor Party (MLP) and the Mauritian Militant Movement (MMM), which currently dominates the National Assembly and executive branch. An opposition party, the Mauritian Socialist Movement (MSM), controls about 20 percent of the votes in the assembly.

North America
McDaniel, Hattie
(b. June 10, 1895, Wichita, Kans.; d. October 26, 1952, Woodland Hills, Calif.), African American singer, actress, and radio performer, the first black ever to win an Oscar for her role as Mammy in *Gone With the Wind*.

Hattie McDaniel appeared in more than 300 films and, despite her considerable talent, was limited to mainly housemaid roles, as were most black actresses of the 1930s and 1940s, including Louise Beavers, Ethel Waters, and Lillian Randolph. Although McDaniel's housemaid roles often exemplified the stereotypes blacks abhorred, she transformed many of these roles into sassy, independent-minded characters. In a Hollywood that enshrined white stars at the expense of black performers, she became the first black ever to win an Academy Award—as Best Supporting Actress for her "Mammy" role in the 1939 film *Gone With the Wind*.

Arriving in Los Angeles in 1931, McDaniel visited film studios looking "for work. In 1932 she won her first, uncredited film role as a Southern house servant in Fox's *The Golden West*. Numerous offers followed and in 1934 she was chosen to play the washerwoman Aunt Dilsey, a lead part in Will Rogers's film *Judge Priest*. By the late 1930s she had become a widely recognized Hollywood "Mammy" with two distinct film personae. As her biographer Carlton Jackson points out, while "she was much too servile in *The Little Colonel* for the liking of many blacks, she was much too independent in *Alice Adams* for numerous whites." Indeed, with the exception of the 1941 film *In This Our Life*, in which McDaniel's character, Minerva Clay, openly confronts racial issues, her film roles alternated between subservient and cantankerous maids. Although McDaniel relished her success, her film personae weighed heavily on her. During the 1940s she spent much time defending herself before the National Association for the Advancement of Colored People (NAACP), which claimed that she was perpetuating a stereotype. The NAACP particularly criticized her role in *Gone With the Wind*, in which Mammy spoke nostalgically about the Old South.

From 1947 to 1952 McDaniel was the host of *The Beulah Show*, a nationally broadcast radio program later transferred to television. She portrayed Beulah, an ebullient Southern maid, yet this time without using dialect and entirely on her own terms. Beulah was also the first radio program in which a black played the starring role. Praised by the NAACP and the National Urban League, The Beulah Show attracted nearly 20,000 listeners weekly and finally provided McDaniel with a role in which she could truly be herself.

Latin America and the Caribbean

McKay, Claude
(b. September 15, 1889, Sunny Ville, Jamaica; d. May 22, 1948, Chicago, Ill.), Jamaican poet, essayist, and novelist who was one of the founders of both modern African American and modern Jamaican literature.

Claude McKay's work as a poet, novelist, and essayist heralded several of the most significant moments in African American culture. His protest poetry of the second and third decades of the twentieth century was seen by may of his contemporaries as the premier example of the "New Negro" spirit. His novels were sophisticated considerations of the problems and possibilities of Pan-Africanism at the end of the colonial era, influencing writers of African descent throughout the world. His early poetry in Jamaican patois, and his fiction set in Jamaica, are now seen as crucial to the development of a national Jamaican literature.

McKay moved to the United States in 1912 to attend Tuskegee Institute. After brief stints at Tuskegee and Kansas State University, he left for Harlem. There he wrote poetry while holding several menial jobs, including working on a railroad dining car. This period of McKay's work is best remembered for his militant protest sonnets, notably *If We Must Die*, considered by such

Jamaica-born poet and novelist Claude McKay became a pivotal figure in the Harlem Renaissance. *CORBIS*

contemporaries of McKay as James Weldon Johnson and Walter White to be the beginning of the Harlem Renaissance. McKay also wrote many poems of exile, such as *Flame-Heart* and *The Tropics in New York*, in which he nostalgically invokes a tropical landscape and the desire to return to a remembered community. Even many of the protest sonnets can be considered exile poems, since a break between the poem's speaker and his original community is often at the root of the speaker's anger. Much of McKay's early poetry was collected in the book *Harlem Shadows* (1922).

In his two novels of the 1920s, *Home to Harlem* (1928) and *Banjo* (1929), McKay investigated how the concepts of race and class worked in a world dominated by capitalism and colonialism, and how cosmopolitan and rural black communities can be reconciled to each other. *Home to Harlem* was more commercially successful than any novel by an African American author to that point.

During the 1920s and early 1930s he moved further away from the communist movement, becoming at last an active anticommunist. His final books, the autobiographical *A Long Way from Home* (1937) and the sociological *Harlem: Negro Metropolis* (1940), were in large part attacks on the Communist Party of the United States of America (CPUSA). Throughout this work, McKay became increasingly isolated from the mainstream of black artists and intellectuals.

North America

Meredith, James H.

(b. June 25, 1933, Kosciusko, Miss.), African American who in 1962 became the first black student to enroll at the University of Mississippi; this landmark event and the attention surrounding his 1966 "walk against fear" were central events of the Civil Rights Movement.

While attending the all-black Jackson State University in Jackson, Mississippi, James Meredith applied to the all-white University of Mississippi. Rejected because he was black, he sued for admission, and after a series of appeals the university was ordered to admit him. Gov. Ross Barnett, with support of the state legislature, vowed to block Meredith. On September 30, 1962, federal marshals escorted Meredith to the Ole Miss campus in Oxford, Mississippi. Approximately 3000 whites rioted in protest. More than 23,000 United States troops restored order by the next morning. But two people had been killed and 160 injured. Meredith attended classes and graduated the following year.

After studying at Ibadan University in Nigeria and at the Columbia University School of Law, in 1966 Meredith returned to Mississippi to stage a 225-mile march from Memphis, Tennessee, to Jackson, Mississippi. By completing this "walk against fear," Meredith hoped to inspire blacks to vote in the upcoming primary elections. He was shot on the second day of his march and, although he was not seriously injured, was hospitalized and unable to complete the march. Major civil rights organizations started from the spot of the shooting and finished Meredith's march to Jackson. Significant was SNCC member Stokely Carmichael's use of the phrase "Black Power" during the march, which signaled a schism between moderate and militant civil rights groups.

Latin America and the Caribbean

Mexico,

republic of North America sharing a border with the United States and Guatemala and home to a significant African population since colonial times.

Mexico prides itself on being a nation of *mestizos*, people of indigenous and European descent. This intermixing is said to reflect Mexico's ethnic harmony and its so-called cosmic race. Too often, however, these homogenizing beliefs call on the nation's ethnic minorities to assimilate into a dominant culture and obscure the social and political marginalization that they continue to face. Furthermore, the existence of Afro-Mexicans is often denied by an image of the nation as principally a mixture of European and Indian. In fact, Afro-Mexicans have played an important role in Mexican history and remain a significant though often overlooked minority.

The African presence in what is today known as Mexico dates to the first of the Spanish incursions in the New World. When the conquistador Hernán Cortés came ashore in the area of Veracruz in 1519, a free black man named Juan Garrido was with him. Garrido may have participated in the conquest of the Aztec capital Tenochtitlán and was a known participant in several expeditions in other parts of New Spain after Cortés toppled Tenochtitlán. He is also said to have been the first person to farm wheat in Mexico. Free blacks, however, were uncommon in early Mexico; more common were the several African slaves who also accompanied Cortés and his invading army. Little is known about what role these slaves played.

As Spanish settlers arrived in Mexico in the mid-1500s, they relied heavily on Amerindians for labor in mines and on plantations; but even then settlers supplemented the labor base with a small but steady stream of African slaves. In the first 60 years after the fall of Tenochtitlán, between 30,000 and 40,000 slaves arrived in Mexico. Some of these were Hispanicized slaves, Africans who had been enslaved in Spain for some time before arriving in the New World. Most were imported directly from Africa. Regardless of origin, the slaves were mostly male: typically three men were imported for every woman because they were seen as better suited for work

in the mines. This ratio forced many enslaved African men to seek Amerindian mates, beginning a process of miscegenation that would continue throughout Afro-Mexican history. Such intermixing had further implications. Since under Spanish law freedom followed the mother's line, the children of an enslaved man and a free woman would be freeborn. Thus if the slave population was to grow, the Spaniards would fuel it with infusions of slaves from Africa instead of with reproduction in Mexico.

Beginning in the 1940s and 1950s interest in Afro-Mexicans slowly revived, urged largely by the pioneering studies of Gonzalo Aguirre Beltrán. Beltrán's work in turn gave impetus to recognition of Afro-Mexicans by the government, which in 1991 gave its support to a project called Nuestra Tercera Raíz (Our Third Root), intended to further the study of Afro-Mexicans. Today the largest Afro-Mexican settlements are in the Pacific region known as Costa Chica, where escaped slaves from Acapulco and Huatulco established palenques. Other black settlements are near Veracruz and, to a lesser degree, in the northern desert states of Coahuila, Zacatecas, and Sinaola and in the southern Yucatán and Quintana Roo. The Afro-Mexican population in Coahuila is supplemented by the descendants of escaped North American slaves who intermarried with Seminole Indians.

North America

Micheaux, Oscar

(b. January 2, 1884, near Murphysboro, Ill.; d. March, 25, 1951, Charlotte, N.C.), African American filmmaker, novelist, businessman, and pioneer best known for his dramatic films about African American life.

Oscar Micheaux was born in 1884, the fifth of 13 children. At age 17 he went to Chicago, where he worked as a shoeshine boy and Pullman porter. In 1904 he used his savings to buy a homestead in South Dakota on land newly opened to settlement. Micheaux's experiences as an African American settler in the rough-and-tumble environment of the South Dakota frontier provided him with material for several of his most important books and movies.

Micheaux's first creative work was the 1913 novel *The Conquest: The Story of a Negro Pioneer*. When black filmmakers George and Noble Johnson negotiated unsuccessfully with Micheaux to film *The Homesteader* in 1919, the writer's interest turned to making movies. He filmed *The Homesteader* himself, and subsequently renamed his business the Micheaux Book and Film Company. He went on to produce, write, and direct more than 30 films—the exact number remains unclear—over the next three decades. The first African American feature-length sound movie, *The Exile* (1931), was a Micheaux creation. Another Micheaux film, *Body and Soul* (1924), featured singer and actor Paul Robeson in his first American appearance on screen.

The budgets for Micheaux's many films came from the director's own entrepreneurial efforts. He personally transported prints from town to town, sometimes for a single showing, and edited his movies on the road. To raise money from theater owners, Micheaux asked his actors to give private performances of scenes from upcoming productions. At the height of his success, branch offices of Micheaux's film company opened in New York and Chicago.

Many of Micheaux's films have been lost. Those that survive today include *Within Our Gates* (1919), *Body and Soul,* and *God's Step-children* (1937). Micheaux's works dramatized individual characters' struggles against prejudice within the black community as well as in opposition to outer racism. Booker T. Washington's doctrines of industry, self-sufficiency, and accommodation to whites profoundly influenced Micheaux's world-view and art.

African American reviewers in Micheaux's own time sometimes criticized his films for their perpetuation of negative stereotypes, idealization of interracial relationships, and blindness to the problems of a black lower class. Recent scholars such as Bell Hooks (pseudonym of Gloria Watkins) and Joseph Young have defended Micheaux's portrayals of black women and a black middle class as subversive antidotes to the racial myths of Micheaux's era.

Cross Cultural

Middle East,

a region comprising the present-day countries of Israel, Jordan, Lebanon, Syria, Iraq, Iran, and the Arabian Peninsula that has imported slaves and drawn migrants from Africa since ancient times.

Because the Mediterranean Sea, the Red Sea, and the Indian Ocean have always been active trading zones between Africa and the Middle East, an African presence has existed in the Arabian Peninsula, the Persian Gulf, and other parts of the Middle East since ancient times. Even before the emergence of Islam in the seventh century C.E., Arabs had contact with the Africans of "Habash," a term used to refer to Ethiopia and the Horn of Africa. After the early Islamic jihads, or holy wars, brought them into contact with larger areas of Africa, Arabs referred to the entire region west of Ethiopia and south of the Sahara as "al-Sudan," meaning the land of the blacks. They referred to the East African coast and its people as Zanj. Poets and leaders of African descent were famous in the Middle East from pre-Islamic times, and Africans numbered among the prophet Muhammad's companions. Many Africans ended up in the Middle East as a result of the slave trade across the Red Sea and the Indian Ocean. Most of these slaves were concubines, domestics, or eunuchs, although some labored as agricultural workers. In contrast to the Americas, these slaves did not leave distinct communities of descendants. Most scholars believe that the peoples of the

Middle East gradually accepted the slaves' descendants into their communities through intermarriage. The expansion of Islam continues to bring many Muslims from Africa and the African diaspora to the Middle East in the twentieth century.

Cross Cultural

Middle Passage,

term used to describe the transatlantic slave voyages between Africa and the Americas that claimed the lives of approximately 1.8 million slaves over a period of about 350 years.

The Middle Passage was a physical and psychological nightmare for an estimated 12 million slaves who were packed like animals aboard slave vessels. This middle or second leg of the transatlantic slave trade marked the beginning of a terrifying experience. Olaudah Equiano, a former slave turned antislavery activist, captured his experience aboard a slave vessel in his autobiography: "When I looked round the ship . . . and saw . . . a multitude of black people of every description chained together, every one of their countenances expressing dejection and sorrow, I no longer doubted my fate; and, quite overpowered with horror and anguish, I fell motionless on the deck and fainted."

Typically, Equiano and others were shackled in pairs, the right arm and leg of one chained to the left leg and arm of the other. Men were separated from women, but all were confined below deck and packed into "slave quarters" throughout the ship's belly. These quarters were no more than six feet long and not high enough to allow an individual to sit upright. Conditions were miserable. Slaves were forced to lie naked on wooden planks, and many developed bruises and open sores. The unbearable heat below deck, mixed with the human waste and vomit, produced an overpowering stench. The unsanitary conditions were breeding grounds for diseases like dysentery, small-pox, and measles. Close to 5 percent of the slaves aboard these vessels died from disease, and many more died from malnutrition. Slaves were fed twice a day rations of fish, beans, or yams that were prepared in large copper vats below deck. Those who refused to eat, hoping to starve themselves to death, were force-fed.

Slaves were sometimes allowed, in small groups, to come on deck for exercise. Women and children were often permitted to roam freely, a practice that opened opportunities to the ship's crew for abuse and rape. Occasionally some slaves managed to break free from their shackles and organize mutinies. There are more than 250 documented cases of rebellion at sea, including the Amistad Mutiny, an unsuccessful revolt that was the subject of a film by director Steven Spielberg in the fall of 1997.

Resistance was not limited to mutiny. Instances of Africans in war canoes attacking slave vessels near the African coast are known. Eyewitness reports tell of slaves hanging or starving themselves to death during the Middle Passage. Some captives jumped overboard to escape slavery.

Millions of Africans were forced to endure the dehumanizing Middle Passage as they were transported into slavery in the New World. Of these millions, Toni Morrison wrote: "Nobody knows their names, and nobody thinks about them. In addition to that, they never survived in the lore; there are no songs or dances or tales of these people. The people who arrived—there is lore about them. But nothing survives about that."

North America

Million Man March,

a 1995 Washington, D.C., rally organized by Nation of Islam minister Louis Farrakhan and Benjamin Chavis to draw attention to the social conditions of African Americans and to urge black men to assume control over their lives.

The Million Man March emerged from Nation of Islam minister Louis Farrakhan's call for a Day of Atonement that would draw attention to the social and economic problems plaguing African American males. On October 16, 1995, approximately 900,000 black men congregated in Washington, D.C., to hear speeches from black luminaries such as Rosa Parks, Jesse Jackson, and Maya Angelou. Farrakhan provided the keynote address. He asked black men to assume responsibility for themselves, their families, their communities, and America as a whole instead of placing the blame for their conditions on outside forces. Primarily organized by Benjamin Chavis, former executive director of the National Association for the Advancement of Colored People (NAACP), it was the single largest gathering of African Americans in history—surpassing in size the 1963 March on Washington.

North America

Minstrelsy,

the most popular nineteenth-century American vernacular entertainment, featuring white performers mimicking blacks; it reinforced negative stereotypes of African Americans, yet preserved aspects of black humor and performance style.

During the Middle Ages minstrels were servant-performers who entertained their patrons by playing music, singing, telling stories, juggling, or performing comic antics and buffoonery. In the antebellum United States, the term referred to comic performers, almost always white, who wore blackface makeup—generally burnt cork—and mimicked African Americans.

The most popular entertainment of that century, minstrel shows had a powerful impact on American culture; in particular, they served to "codify the public image of blacks as the prototypical Fool or Sambo," as Mel Watkins observed in his *On the Real Side: Laughing, Lying, and Signifying: The Underground Tradition of African-American Humor.*

The career of Thomas D. "Daddy" Rice marked the true beginnings of American minstrelsy. In about 1828 Rice began impersonating a black man during the inter-missions in a minor drama of the period. His act featured a song and dance that became known as Jim Crow. Rice claimed that he based his sketch on a song and dance he had seen performed, in the words of Mel Watkins, by a "crippled and deformed black hostler or stable groom."

Rice dressed his Jim Crow character in the long blue coat and striped pants associated with another popular stereotype, the stage Yankee. Rice's sketch won him such acclaim that he quickly added additional blackface characters and music to his performances. Another African American source for Rice's minstrel act was the black street vendor and singer known as Signor Cornmeali, or "Old Corn Meal." Signor Cornmeali traveled about New Orleans with horse and cart, selling cornmeal and singing such songs as "Rosin Up the Bow" and his own "Fresh Corn Meal" in a rich baritone alternating with a resonant falsetto. Thomas "Daddy" Rice heard Cornmeali in 1837 and soon added a sketch titled "Corn Meal" to his minstrel act. The notion of a minstrel troupe emerged as a response to a severe depression that began in 1837, an economic downturn that continued into the early 1840s and hit theatrical performers particularly hard.

During the 1840s and 1850s the United States received its first massive influx of European immigrants. To many native-born Anglo-Americans these newcomers seemed frighteningly alien. In an atmosphere marked by political acrimony and social tension, minstrelsy had a vital unifying function for white Americans. By constructing an image of happy-go-lucky plantation slaves and irresponsible free black dandies, minstrel shows made light of slavery and emancipation as political issues and denied the human suffering that the institution exacted daily. In addition—much like their medieval counterparts—antebellum minstrels and their absurd antics served not only to entertain, but also to reassure their patrons of their own superiority. By defining blackness so ludicrously, antebellum minstrels constructed a cultural "other" over whom all whites—whether immigrant or native-born, urban or rural, working class or well-to-do—could feel superior. Thus minstrelsy provided indirect but not inconsequential grounds for white social and political unity—at the expense of African Americans.

The first influential black minstrel troupes appeared during the Reconstruction era. In 1865–1866 an African American company known as Brooker and Clayton's Georgia Minstrels toured in the Northeast, billing itself as "the Only Simon Pure Negro Troupe in the World." As black minstrel troupes proved their popularity and profitability, their ownership and management generally fell into the hands of whites. By the mid-1870s the most successful black minstrel troupes were all white-owned.

Minstrelsy provided invaluable experience for countless African American composers, comedians, and musicians. W. C. Handy, who later gained fame as the composer of "St. Louis Blues," worked for many years as a cornet player and bandleader with Mahara's Minstrels. James Bland—best remembered for composing "Carry Me Back to Old Virginny" and "Dem Golden Slippers"—was a particularly prolific minstrel composer. The talented African American minstrel and dramatic actor Sam Lucas also composed numerous minstrel songs, of which "Grandfather's Clock" remains the best known.

Numerous twentieth-century black performers also had experience with minstrelsy. Vaudeville comedians Bert Williams and Ernest Hogan got their start by serving as endmen in minstrel troupes. Blues singer Gertrude "Ma" Rainey was a featured performer with the Rabbit's Foot Minstrels, a company that also included a young dancer who would one day be recognized as the greatest of all female blues singers, Bessie Smith. New Orleans jazz musicians such as pianist Ferdinand "Jelly Roll" Morton and trumpeter Bunk Johnson did stints playing in minstrel companies. And modern jazz trumpeter John Birks "Dizzy" Gillespie made his first public performance in 1929 playing for a minstrel show put on by his elementary school.

Although black performers found opportunities in minstrelsy, they also found themselves trapped by its restrictive racial conventions. During the late nineteenth century, as racial hostilities sharpened throughout the United States, white audiences came to expect that all minstrels, black as well as white, should appear in blackface, and the practice became general among black troupes. Black minstrel companies often featured renditions, in harmony, of spirituals, jubilee songs, and sentimental ballads. The singing of such professional entertainers—along with performances by college-trained choirs, such as the Fisk Jubilee Singers—had a profound influence on subsequent vocal harmony groups, evident in secular singing no less than in gospel quartets. Professional minstrels and college choral groups offered slick versions of African American music, but they nonetheless provided an eye-opening experience for white audiences, and they inspired countless young African American singers and performers.

North America

Montgomery Bus Boycott,

the year-long protest in Montgomery, Alabama, that galvanized the American Civil Rights Movement and led to a 1956 United States Supreme Court decision declaring segregated seating on buses unconstitutional.

In December 1955, 42,000 black residents of Montgomery began a year-long boycott of city buses to protest racially segregated seating. After 381 days of taking taxis, carpooling, and walking the hostile streets of Montgomery, African Americans eventually won their fight to desegregate seating on public buses, not only in Montgomery, but throughout the United States.

An empty bus makes its rounds of the city during the Montgomery, Alabama, bus boycott in 1956. *CORBIS/Bettmann-UPI*

The protest was first organized by the Women's Political Council as a one-day boycott to coincide with the trial of Rosa Parks, who had been arrested on December 2, 1955, for refusing to give up her seat to a white man on a segregated Montgomery bus. By the next morning, the council, led by JoAnn Robinson, had printed 52,000 fliers asking Montgomery blacks to stay off public buses on December 5, the day of the trial. Meanwhile, labor activist E. D. Nixon, who had bailed Parks out of jail, notified Ralph Abernathy, minister of the First Baptist Church, and Martin Luther King Jr., the new minister at Dexter Avenue Baptist Church, of her arrest. A group of about 50 black leaders and one white minister, Robert Graetz, gathered in the basement of King's church to endorse the boycott and begin planning a massive rally for the evening of the trial. Graetz offered his support from the pulpit of his predominantly white Lutheran church. The Montgomery Chapter of the National Association for the Advancement of Colored People (NAACP), which had been looking for a test case for segregation, began preparing for the legal challenge.

The issue of segregated seating had long been a source of resentment in Montgomery's black community. African Americans were forced to pay their fares at the front, and then reboard the bus at the back. They faced systematic harassment from white drivers, who sometimes pulled away before black passengers could reboard. On the bus blacks sat behind a mobile barrier dividing the races, and as the bus filled, the barrier was pushed backward to make room for white passengers. No black person could sit in the same row as a white, and whites had priority in this middle "no-man's land."

The Montgomery Bus Boycott had implications that reached far beyond the desegregation of public buses. The protest propelled the Civil Rights Movement into national consciousness and Martin Luther King Jr. into the public eye. In the words of King: "We have gained a new sense of dignity and destiny. We have discovered a new and powerful weapon—nonviolent resistance."

Africa

Morocco,

hereditary monarchy in the northwest of Africa, bounded on the north by the Mediterranean Sea, on the east and southeast by Algeria, on the south by Western Sahara, and on the west by the Atlantic Ocean. The southeastern boundary, in the Sahara, is not precisely defined.

Morocco is a nation known by its cities. Marrakech, Rabat, Fès, Casablanca, and Tangier all played crucial roles in the nation's dynastic history, serving as political, economic, and cultural capitals of the kingdoms that mapped what is now Moroccan territory. For centuries these cities also provided

Dressed in traditional finery, a Berber man awaits his wedding. *CORBIS/Robert van der Hilst*

Moroccan horsemen brandish elaborately ornamented guns as they gallop in a Fantasia, a traditional Arabic equestrian event. *CORBIS/Robert van der Hilst*

vital centers for the commerce in goods and ideas that came from the Islamic world and Christian Europe as well as sub-Saharan Africa. In the nineteenth century, as European investment poured in, Morocco's cities held perhaps too much appeal: the gravitation of people and resources toward urban areas, especially on the coast, sapped the vitality of the rural agricultural economy on which urban prosperity had always depended. After becoming perilously indebted to Europe, Morocco fell under French control in the early twentieth century. Even as French colonial planners attempted to impose functionality and racial segregation on Morocco's cities, European and American artists, writers, and wanderers were drawn by a vision of the "exotic" beauty of Morocco. Today Morocco's economy still depends largely on agriculture, but its cities remain dynamic commercial centers as well as destinations for migrants seeking a better life and travelers in search of legends.

Africa

Morocco (Ready Reference)

Official Name: Kingdom of Morocco

Area: 446,550 sq km (about 172,413 sq mi); the southeastern boundary, in the Sahara, is contested; within Morocco are the Spanish exclaves of Ceuta and Melilla.

Location: Northern Africa; borders the Mediterranean Sea, Algeria, Western Sahara, and the Atlantic Ocean

Capital: Rabat (population 1,472,000 [1990 estimate])

Other Major Cities: Casablanca (3,210,000), the country's largest city and main seaport; Marrakech (1,517,000) and Fès (1,012,000), both important trade centers; and Tangier (554,000), a seaport on a bay of the Strait of Gibraltar (1990 estimates)

Population: 29,114,497 (1998 estimate)

Population Density: 67 persons per sq km (about 172 persons per sq mi); the population has almost an equal number of urban and rural dwellers. Most Moroccans inhabit the Atlantic coastal plain.

Population Below Age 15: 36 percent (male 5,398,592; female 5,200,660 [1998 estimate])

Population Growth Rate: 1.89 percent (1998 estimate)

Total Fertility Rate: 3.5 children born per woman (1997 estimate)

Life Expectancy at Birth: Total population: 68.51 years (male 66.49 years; female 70.64 years [1996 estimate])

Infant Mortality Rate: 52.99 deaths per 1000 live births (1998 estimate)

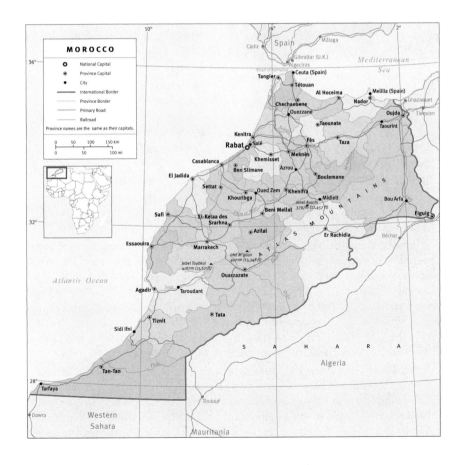

A Berber bride wears her robe and jewelry at an engagement festival in Imilchil, Morocco.
CORBIS/Nik Wheeler

Literacy Rate (age 15 and over who can read and write): Total population: 43.7 percent (male 56.6 percent; female 31 percent [1995 estimate])

Education: Schooling is compulsory in Morocco for children between ages 7 and 13, but significantly fewer girls than boys attend classes, and less than 40 percent of secondary-school-age Moroccans actually attend secondary school. Arabic is the main language of instruction, and French is also used in secondary schools. Traditional higher education is centered in Fès at al Qarawîyîn University, and modern higher education is offered at Mohammed V University, Mohammed Ben Abdellah University, Cadi Ayyad University, Hassan II University, and Mohammed I University.

Languages: Arabic is the official language. Berber languages, French, and Spanish are also spoken.

Ethnic Groups: Arab-Berber, 99.1 percent; European (mostly French), 0.7 percent; Jewish, 0.2 percent

Religions: Islam is the established state religion of Morocco. Almost the entire population is Sunni Muslim. The monarch is the supreme Muslim authority in the country. About 1 percent of the population is Christian, and less than 0.2 percent is Jewish.

Climate: Along the Mediterranean, Morocco has a subtropical climate, tempered by oceanic influences that give the coastal cities moderate temperatures averaging about 16.4° C (61.5° F) in January and 22.5° C (72.5° F) in August. Toward the interior, the mean temperature is 10° C (50° F) in January and 26.9° C (80.5° F) in August. At high altitudes temperatures of less than -17.8° C (0° F) are not uncommon. Rain falls mainly during the winter months, with precipitation heaviest in the northwest: about 955 mm (about 37.5 in) in Tangier and less than 102 mm (4 in) in the Sahara.

Land, Plants, and Animals: Morocco has an area of highlands, called *Er Rif*, that parallels the Mediterranean coast. The Atlas Mountains extend across the country in a southwestern to northeastern direction, while a region of broad coastal plains stretches along the Atlantic Ocean. South of the Atlas Mountains, plains and valleys merge with the Sahara along the southeastern borders of the country. Morocco has many rivers, including the Moulouya and the Sebou. The mountainous regions of Morocco contain extensive forests, including large stands of cork oak, evergreen oak, juniper, cedar, fir, and pine. Moroccan wildlife includes the gazelle, wild boar, panther, baboon, wild goat, fox, rabbit, otter, squirrel, and horned viper.

Natural Resources: Morocco's resources are primarily agricultural, but mineral resources are also significant. Among the latter the most important is phosphate rock; other minerals include coal, iron, lead, manganese, petroleum, silver, tin, and zinc. Cork is a major forest product of Morocco.

Currency: The Moroccan dirham

Gross Domestic Product (GDP): $107 billion (1997 estimate)

GDP per Capita: $3500 (1997 estimate)

GDP Real Growth Rate: -2.2 percent (1997 estimate)

Primary Economic Activities: Morocco is primarily an agricultural country but is also a leading producer of phosphate rock.

Primary Crops: The principal crops of Morocco are cereals, particularly wheat and barley, plus potatoes, tomatoes, melons, olives, grapes, pulses, dates, sugar cane, and sugar beets. Livestock includes sheep, goats, and cattle; fishing yields pilchard, tuna, mackerel, anchovies, and shellfish.

Industries: Phosphate rock mining and processing, food processing, leather goods, textiles, construction, and tourism

Lengths of dyed cloth billow over the Street of Dyers in the famous bazaar of Marrakech, Morocco. *CORBIS/Robert Holmes*

Primary Exports: Food and beverages, semiprocessed goods, consumer goods, and phosphates

Primary Imports: Capital goods, semiprocessed goods, raw materials, fuel and lubricants, food and beverages, and consumer goods

Primary Trade Partners: European Union, Japan, United States, Libya, India, Saudi Arabia, United Arab Emirates, and Russia

Government: Morocco is a hereditary monarchy governed by a king, currently Mohammed VI, who appoints the prime minister, currently Driss Jellou, and cabinet. Under the constitution of 1972 Morocco has a unicameral legislature called the Chamber of Representatives. Deputies for 206 seats are chosen by direct universal suffrage; deputies for the remaining 100 seats are named by local political and economic groups. The major political parties are the Istiqlal (Independence Party), the Popular Movement, the National Rally of Independents, and the Constitutional Union. The king has the power to call for a reconsideration of legislative measures and to dissolve the legislature. Morocco's provinces are administered by governors who are appointed by the king. Each province is divided into cercles, which are subdivided into circonscriptions (constituencies).

Africa

Mozambique,

republic on the eastern coast of southern Africa, bounded on the north by Tanzania; on the east by the Mozambique Channel of the Indian Ocean; on the south and southwest by South Africa and Swaziland; and on the west by Zimbabwe, Zambia, and Malawi.

Mozambique's history has been marked by strife. Conflicts that existed between the numerous indigenous societies were exacerbated by the initial expansion of regional kingdoms in the eighth century as well as by Portuguese imperialism beginning in the sixteenth century. Eventually, Mozambicans turned against the Portuguese in a long and bloody war for independence. However, Mozambique had to defend its hard-won independence from Rhodesia (now Zimbabwe), South Africa, and an indigenous insurgency movement. The government's survival came at the cost of abandoning its socialist development policies and of turning to the West for assistance. Although a

A land mine found outside Dombe in Mozambique during the war for independence from Portugal, which lasted from 1964 to 1975. *CORBIS/Gary Trotter; Eye Ubiquitous*

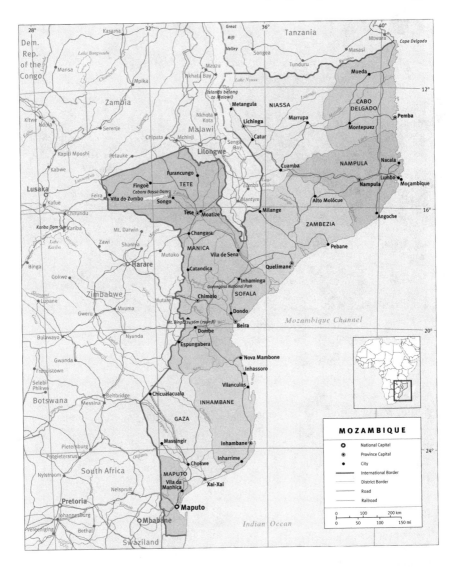

fragile peace has recently come to Mozambique, external involvement continues to be central to the country's political and economic life.

Africa

Mozambique (Ready Reference)

Official Name: Republic of Mozambique

Area: 799,380 sq km (308,641 sq mi)

Location: Southern Africa, bounded on the north by Tanzania; on the east by the Mozambique Channel of the Indian Ocean; on the south and south-

The bridge over the Zambezi River, Mozambique, indicates efforts to modernize the transportation system. *CORBIS/Jon Spaull*

west by South Africa and Swaziland; and on the west by Zimbabwe, Zambia, and Malawi

Capital: Maputo (population 1,098,000 [1991 estimate])

Other Major Cities: Beira (population 299,300 [1990 estimate]) and Nampula (202,600)

Population: 18,641,469 (1998 estimate)

Population Density: 20 persons per sq km (53 persons per sq mi)

Population Below Age 15: 45 percent (male 4,129,779; female 4,232,091 [1998 estimate])

Population Growth Rate: 2.57 percent (1998 estimate)

Life Expectancy at Birth: Total population: 45.37 years (male 44.22 years; female 46.55 years [1998 estimate])

Infant Mortality Rate: 120.26 deaths per 1000 live births (1998 estimate)

Literacy Rate (age 15 and over who can read and write): Total population: 40.1 percent (male 57.7 percent; female 23.3 percent [1995 estimate])

Education: Due to civil instability and the limited number of trained teachers, in the early 1990s only about 1.2 million pupils attended primary schools and just over 150,000 students went to secondary schools.

Languages: Portuguese is the official language, though Swahili and various Bantu languages are spoken commonly.

Ethnic Groups: Mozambique has ten major ethnic groups, including the Makua-Lomwe (which accounts for nearly 50 percent of the northern population), Tsonga, Malawi, Shona, and Yao.

Religions: Indigenous beliefs, 50 percent; Christian, 30 percent; Muslim, 20 percent

Climate: Mozambique has tropical savanna with a dry season lasting from April to October. July (winter) temperatures range from an average of 21° C (70° F) in the north to 18° C (65° F) in the south. January (summer) temperatures average about 27° C (80° F). Although rainfall can be irregular, the northern regions receive around 1500 mm (about 60 in) annually, as opposed to 750 mm (about 30 in) in the south.

Land, Plants, and Animals: Two-fifths of Mozambique is coastal lowland. Inland the land rises to the western low hills and plateaus to the far western mountains, including Mount Binga's 2436 m (7992 ft) peak. Northwest Mozambique's Angonia Plateau lies in the Great Rift Valley. Flowing from the western highlands to the Mozambique Channel are several rivers, including the Zambezi; other major rivers include the Ruvuma, Save, and Limpopo. With landscapes ranging from grassland to tropical rain forest, Mozambique is home to many species, including zebra, buffalo, rhinoceros, giraffe, lion, and elephant.

Natural Resources: Mineral resources include coal, iron, salt, tantalite, diamonds, asbestos, bauxite, copper, manganese, titanium, natural gas, and soil.

Currency: The metical (Mt)

Gross Domestic Product (GDP): $14.6 billion (1997 estimate)

GDP per Capita: $800 (1997 estimate)

GDP Real Growth Rate: 8 percent (1997 estimate)

Primary Economic Activities: Agriculture, industry, and services

Primary Crops: Cotton, cashew nuts, sugar cane, tea, cassava, corn, rice, and tropical fruits

Industries: Food, beverages, chemicals (fertilizer, soap, paints), petroleum products, textiles, cement, glass, asbestos, and tobacco

Primary Exports: Shrimp, cashews, cotton, and sugar

Primary Imports: Food, clothing, farm equipment, and petroleum

Primary Trade Partners: South Africa, United Kingdom, France, Japan, and Portugal

A child drinks from a water spout in Mozambique. Years of civil turmoil have severely damaged the country's education system. *CORBIS/Liba Taylor*

Two Mozambican soldiers guard a civilian convoy from attack by Mozambican National Resistance guerillas in 1985. *Reuters/CORBIS*

Government: Following a new constitution in 1990, a multiparty republic was instituted. In the executive branch, the prime minister, currently Pascal Mocumbi, is head of government, while the president, currently Joaquim Chissano, is chief of state. The People's Assembly, a unicameral national legislature, is directly elected. In the 1994 elections, the Front for the Liberation of Mozambique (FRELIMO) won a slight majority; the main opposition party, the Mozambique National Resistance (RENAMO), won full legal recognition only in 1992.

North America

Muhammad, Elijah (Elijah Poole)

(b. October 1897, Sandersville, Ga.; d. February 25, 1975, Chicago, Ill.), leader of the Nation of Islam; black separatist.

The sixth of seven children of William and Mariah Poole, Elijah was the favorite of his siblings, parents, and grandfather, and was perceived by them as being destined for greatness. It was his grandfather who named him after the biblical Elijah, and throughout his childhood he was teasingly referred to as "the Prophet."

Aside from sharecropping and working at a sawmill, William Poole pastored at two Baptist churches. Young Elijah was exposed to the ministry from a tender age. He took an avid interest in Christian theology, but his father's fire and brimstone sermons caused him to question what seemed like a dour intrepretation of spirituality. It was many years before he would break away from Christianity completely, and ironically it was his father who first introduced him to the Nation of Islam.

It was at this time that his father, on a spiritual quest of his own, started speaking to Elijah and his brothers about the Islamic movement. In 1931 Elijah attended his first Islamic meeting and met its leader, Wallace D. Fard. He became fully immersed in the movement, abandoning his "slave owner" surname. He was initially called Karriem, and later Muhammad. Within the year he became Fard's top assistant. As the Muslim movement grew more prominent in the black community, it became a target for government investigation, and Fard's leadership began to suffer. In 1933, in an attempt to remove himself from the negative spotlight, Fard named Muhammad Supreme Minister and gave him full administrative power.

Despite continual police hostility and subsequent relocation to Chicago, the Nation of Islam under Muhammad prospered and evolved. Rather than shunning the technology of Western culture, as Fard had encouraged, Muhammad invested in radios and modern farm equipment. In order for black separatism to succeed, he believed, total economic independence was crucial. In 1945 the Nation purchased 140 acres of farmland in Michigan. Two years later a Nation-owned grocery store, restaurant, and bakery opened in Chicago.

As the Nation's influence spread throughout various black communities around the United States, Muhammad began to live a more luxurious lifestyle that seemingly contradicted the Muslim creed of stringency and humility. He purchased cars and real estate and apparently had sexual liaisons with a number of young women in the movement. When Malcolm X was murdered after leaving the movement, there were many who believed that Muhammad's violent denunciation of his one-time protégé had instigated the assassination.

As a leader in the quest for black nationalism, Muhammad was, for a long time, considered a hostile force by the United States government. He served a jail sentence for draft evasion during World War ll and was wired by the FBI for more than two decades. Nevertheless, by the time of his death in 1975, his conservative approach made him seem moderate compared to other radical groups of the Civil Rights era. His emphasis on black self-suffiency rather than overthrow of the government made him an appealing ally to such local officials as Mayor Richard Daley, who in 1974 declared March 29 "Honorable Elijah Muhammad Day in Chicago."

NAACP Legal Defense and Educational Fund,

the major organization by which African Americans have, through law, achieved advances in civil rights in the twentieth century.

Created in 1940 by the National Association for the Advancement of Colored People (NAACP), the NAACP Legal Defense and Educational Fund (LDF) pioneered the field of public interest law, using the courts to gain and expand civil rights for African Americans when other avenues were blocked. The LDF was most visible during the 1940s, when its first director, future Supreme Court justice Thurgood Marshall, led it in the fight against legal segregation in the South. Its victories laid the groundwork for, and inspired the participants in, the Civil Rights Movement. After overcoming legalized segregation in the courts, the LDF fought against the backlash of angry Southern state governments, several of which attempted to challenge the LDF's right to practice in their states. It worked to strengthen and protect those rights through the courts, by lobbying and providing scholarships to help African Americans attend law schools.

The LDF is most famous for arguing before the Supreme Court in 1954's landmark *Brown v. Board of Education of Topeka, Kansas*, which ended legal segregation in United States public education. *Brown*, however, marked the culmination of the strategy to desegregate public education.

Nabuco, Joaquim

(b. August 19, 1849, Recife, Pernambuco, Brazil; d. January 17, 1910, Washington, D.C.), Brazilian politician, author, and abolitionist whose 1883 book, *O abolicionismo*, one of the most influential abolitionist works of its time, catalyzed Brazil's abolition movement.

Born into an aristocratic and politically active family, Joaquim Nabuco spent the first eight years of his life on his family's large sugar plantation in the northeastern province of Pernambuco. He later moved with his parents to Rio de Janeiro, then attended the prestigious law academies of São Paulo and Recife. At the former, he met Antônio de Castro Alves, the "Poet of the Slaves," and abolitionist Rui Barbosa. Between 1873 and 1876 he made several trips to Europe and the United States, where he learned about abolitionists such as William Lloyd Garrison, in the process strengthening his belief in abolition.

Nabuco had become familiar with abolitionist activities at a young age. His father, José Tomás Nabuco de Araújo, a prominent politician and advocate of gradual emancipation, was instrumental in passing the so-called Free Womb Law, which freed all children born to slave women. While in law school, Nabuco composed his own abolition treatise and, in a case in which he eloquently critiqued slavery and capital punishment, saved from the death penalty a young black man accused of murdering several people.

Following the death of his father in 1878, Nabuco was elected to the Brazilian Parliament and initiated his abolitionist campaign by introducing bills providing for a gradual end to slavery. After their rejection, in 1880 Nabuco founded the Sociedade Brasileira contra a escravidão (Brazilian Antislavery Society) and the monthly bulletin O abolicionista (The Abolitionist).

Nabuco was defeated in the 1881 parlia-mentary elections and spent the next three years in London writing his book O abolicionismo (1883), a comprehensive analysis of the slave trade, slavery, and the abolition movement in Brazil. The publication of this book renewed the antislavery movement in Brazil, sparking emancipation movements in the provinces of Amazonas and Rio Grande do Sul.

Nabuco returned to Brazil in 1884 and resumed his abolition campaign. He was elected to the Brazilian Parliament in 1885. That year he became an outspoken critic of the Saraiva-Cotegipe or Sexagenarian Law, which freed slaves aged 65 and older. Although this law liberated the oldest slave—and, not coincidentally, the least economically valuable—Nabuco feared that plantation owners would use it to abandon the old and infirm, and argued that the nation was in need of more radical reforms.

Nabuco lost the 1886 elections, but an article he had written about the death of two slaves who had been sentenced to 300 lashes inspired a bill to outlaw corporal punishment of slaves. The bill became a law later that year and, with the threat of whipping removed, slaves abandoned plantations in large numbers. The military soon complained about having to pursue runaway slaves, and was absolved of this responsibility. Responding to these and other pressures, Princess Isabela freed Brazil's slaves on May 13, 1888, by signing the Lei Aurea (Golden Law). Nabuco remained active in politics and died in 1910, after five years of service as an ambassador in the United States.

Nairobi, Kenya,

capital and largest city of Kenya.

The largest city between Cairo and Johannesburg, with an estimated 1990 population of 1.5 million, Nairobi sits at an elevation of approximately 1,660 m (about 5,450 ft) in the highlands of southern Kenya. It was founded in 1899 by the British, at the 317th-mile peg of the railroad they were constructing between the Indian Ocean port city of Mombasa and Lake Victoria. Named for a nearby Maasai watering hole, *Enkare Nairobi* ("cold water"), it became a stopping point for the railway project's 32,000 workers (many of them from India) and eventually grew into a small town. In 1905 the British declared Nairobi the capital of the British East African Protectorate, which they moved from Mombasa.

Around 1900 Indian merchants in the town established a small bazaar, which soon became the main marketplace for nearby Kikuyu farmers to sell their produce. European settlers, drawn by the fertile hinterlands and temperate climate, also came, as did big game hunters. In 1919 Nairobi was declared a municipality; it earned city status in 1954. By that time Nairobi had become the center of Kenya's growing agroprocessing industries, and had developed large working-class neighborhoods. Kikuyu migrants, many of whom had been educated at mission schools and held municipal jobs, began to organize politically in the city in the 1920s.

Although Kenya's tourist industry has suffered from the country's recent political unrest, Nairobi is still a prime destination for tourists to East Africa, who are attracted by the abundance of modern conveniences, including cafés, bars, bookstores, and museums, as well as the proximity of game parks such as Amboseli, Tsavo, and Maasai Mara. Nairobi is also Kenya's most industrialized city, and its skyscrapers house the headquarters of many foreign corporations.

Namib Desert,

the world's oldest desert and the only true African desert south of the equator.

Lying along Africa's west coast, the Namib Desert stretches from Namibe in Angola south through Namibia to the Olifants River in Cape Province, South Africa, extending some 1900 km (about 1200 mi) from north to south. The Namib reaches eastward about 130 to 160 km (about 80 to 100 mi) from the Atlantic Ocean to the foot of the Great Escarpment of southern Africa. The Benguela Current, which carries icy Atlantic water from Antarctica to the African coast, helps to cool the desert. The collision of cold water with warm air creates a dense fog that causes a hazard to ships in the area, now known as the Skeleton Coast. The current also provides moisture for the coastal region of the desert, supplementing the scant 10 mm (0.4 in) of rain it averages yearly.

Though many describe the landscape as barren, the Namib in fact supports a variety of vegetation, including Tumboa (*Welwitschia mirablisis*). Numerous forms of wildlife also inhabit the desert, including antelopes, ostriches, zebras, jackals, and large flocks of birds along the coast. Several indigenous groups practice pastoralism, including the Ovahimba and Obatjimba Herero, who herd goats between waterholes in the north, and Topnaar Nama (Khoikhoi), who graze sheep and cattle along the Kuiseb River in the central Namib region. In addition, the desert is the largest source of diamonds in the world.

Some parts of the Namib Desert are spectacularly scenic. The Sossusvlei region, located in the Namib-Naukluft National Park, is known for its huge sand dunes, some of which rise as high as 60 to 240 m (about 200 to 800 ft) and span 16 to 32 km (about 10 to 20 mi) in length. The Namib-Naukluft National Park is also home to the Naukluft Mountains and Sesriem Canyon.

Africa

Namibia,

country on the southwest coast of Africa.

The history of Namibia, one of Africa's newest independent countries, has long been shaped by its geography. For centuries few African populations inhabited its two vast deserts, the Namib and the Kalahari, while European vessels avoided its rough coastline. The region was still sparsely populated when missionaries and, later, traders finally arrived in the eighteenth century, but its inhabitants fiercely resisted German settlement and colonization, resulting in one of Africa's bloodiest colonial wars of suppression.

South Africa wrested control of the mineral-rich South-West Africa from Germany in 1915, but its occupation proved no less repressive and discriminatory than European colonialism had been. Land and labor policies that were aimed at creating a cheap migrant labor supply for the region's diamond and gold mines fostered nationalist sentiment and, ultimately, armed struggle. The war between South Africa and nationalist forces, fueled by international cold war rivalries, finally ended with Namibian independence in 1990. Today land distribution in Namibia is still highly stratified, and labor unions remain a powerful political force. In addition, the government's efforts to harness the natural resources needed to support Namibia's growing population and economy have met with protests from its neighbors and international groups.

A San man, with his bow and arrows over his shoulder and a cargo of gourds, rides his bicycle through the Namibian bush. *CORBIS/Anthony Bannister; ABPL*

Africa

Namibia (Ready Reference)

Official Name: Republic of Namibia

Former Name: South-West Africa

Area: 824,268 sq km (about 318,252 sq mi)

Location: Southwestern Africa; borders Angola, Zambia, Botswana, South Africa, and the Atlantic Ocean

Capital: Windhoek (population 125,000 [1990 estimate])

Population: 1,622,328 (1998 estimate)

Population Density: 2 persons per sq km (about 5 persons per sq mi)

Population Below Age 15: 44 percent (male 362,310; female 354,386 [1998 estimate])

Population Growth Rate: 1.6 percent (1998 estimate)

Total Fertility Rate: 4.9 children born per woman (1998 estimate)

Life Expectancy at Birth: Total population: 41.48 years (male 41.73 years; female 41.24 years [1998 estimate])

Infant Mortality Rate: 66.7 deaths per 1000 live births (1998 estimate)

Literacy Rate (age 15 and over who can read and write): Total population: 38 percent (male 45 percent; female 31 percent [1960 estimate])

Education: Compulsory for nine years; in the early 1990s about 349,200 students attended primary schools and 84,600 attended secondary schools.

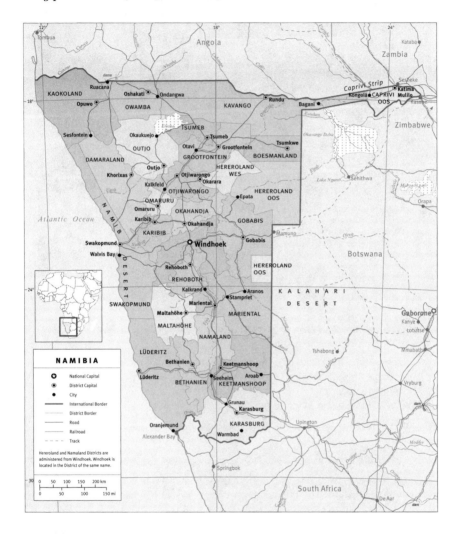

Languages: English, Afrikaans, and German are the official languages; Afrikaans is the most widely spoken. Indigenous languages include Oshivambo, Herero, and Nama.

Ethnic Groups: About 50 percent of the population belong to the Ovambo cultural group. Other principal ethnic groups include the Kavango, the Herero, the Damara, the Khoikhoi, and the San.

Religions: About 80 to 90 percent of the population are Christian (mainly Lutheran), and about 10 to 20 percent adhere to indigenous beliefs.

Climate: Namibia has a hot, dry, desert climate. Average rainfall ranges from 50 mm (about 2 in) in the Namib Desert along the coast to about 560 mm (about 22 in) in the north. Average temperatures in Windhoek vary from 17° C (63° F) in January to 6° C (43° F) in July.

Land, Plants, and Animals: Namibia is located mostly on a high plateau, with the Namib Desert along the coast and the Kalahari Desert in the east; its highest point is about 2606 m (8550 ft) in elevation. Vegetation is sparse in both deserts. A woodland savanna is found in the central plateau, and forests in the northeast. Animals include elephants, rhinoceroses, lions, giraffes, zebras, and hartebeests.

Natural Resources: Diamonds, copper, uranium, zinc, lead, gold, tin, lithium, cadmium, salt, vanadium, suspected deposits of natural gas, oil, coal, and iron ore; Namibia's waters also have over a million metric tons of fish.

Currency: The Namibian dollar

Gross Domestic Product (GDP): $6.2 billion (1996 estimate)

GDP per Capita: $3700 (1996 estimate)

GDP Real Growth Rate: 3 percent (1996 estimate)

Primary Economic Activities: Livestock raising and subsistence agriculture (60 percent of employment), mining (32 percent of GDP), industry and commerce (20 percent of employment)

Primary Crops: Millet, sorghum, peanuts, and livestock

Industries: Meat packing, fish processing, dairy products, and mining

Primary Exports: Diamonds, copper, gold, zinc, lead, uranium, cattle, processed fish, and karakul skins

Primary Imports: Food, petroleum, machinery, and equipment

Primary Trade Partners: South Africa, Germany, Switzerland, United Kingdom, and United States

Government: Namibia is a constitutional republic. The executive branch is led by President Sam Nujoma. The bicameral legislative branch consists of the 26-member National Council and the 72-member National Assembly, both currently dominated by President Nujoma's party, the South West Africa People's Organization (SWAPO).

Latin America and the Caribbean

Nascimento, Abdias do

(b. March 14, 1914, Franca, São Paulo, Brazil), Afro-Brazilian playwright, poet, educator, artist, and political activist; one of the leading figures of Brazil's black movement.

Abdias do Nascimento grew up in Franca, São Paulo. Nascimento's first major Afro-Brazilian project was the *Teatro Experimental do Negro* (TEN) (Black Experimental Theater), which he founded in 1944. For the next 24 years he worked as its director and as a playwright. He created TEN in order to redefine the role of blacks in Brazilian theater. TEN trained the first generation of Afro-Brazilian actors and actresses and won critical acclaim for its productions of Eugene O'Neill's *Emperor Jones* and *Nascimento's Sortilégio* (Black Mystery).

TEN also served as a vehicle for Nascimento's political activism. From 1949 to 1951, TEN published *Quilombo: Black Life, Problems, and Aspirations*, a journal promoting the Afro-Brazilian freedom struggle through various Afro-Brazilian-centered articles, biographies, and illustrations. In 1968, four years after a military dictatorship suspended many individual and collective rights, Nascimento sought exile in the United States.

In addition to his work as a scholar, Nascimento devoted himself to painting while in exile. Just before his departure from Brazil, he founded the Blacks Arts Museum in Rio de Janeiro in 1968 and began to create his own artwork. While in exile Nascimento also participated in and helped organize many Pan-African conferences. These included the Sixth Pan-African Congress (Dar es Salaam, Tanzania; 1974), the Encounter for African World Alternatives (Dakar, Senegal; 1976), and the Second World Festival of Black and African Arts and Culture (Lagos, Nigeria; 1977). He also played a major role in all three of the Congresses of Black Culture in the Americas (held in Cali, Colombia, in 1977; Panama in 1980; and São Paulo, Brazil, in 1982).

Nascimento has also been deeply involved in electoral politics, mainly through the Partido Democrático Trabalhista (PDT), led by Leonel Brizola. In the 1940s Nascimento, along with Brizola, cofounded the Rio de Janeiro branch of the Brazilian Labor Party (PTB), and helped create a black caucus within the party to work for Afro-Brazilian interests.

Nascimento's academic, artistic, and political experiences while in exile prepared him for increased political activism upon his return to Brazil in 1981. In 1982 Nascimento was elected to the House of Deputies and became the first federal congressman to defend systematically the civil rights of Afro-Brazilians. In a 1983 bill he encouraged the House of Deputies to create a Committee on African Brazilians. He advocated that November 20, the anniversary of the death of Zumbi—the leader of the famous quilombo Palmares—be declared National Black Consciousness Day, and proposed that racial discrimination be declared a crime against humanity. He also pressed the issue of affirmative action as compensation for centuries of persecution and discrimination. In terms of employment, Nascimento's bill proposed setting 20 percent hiring quotas for Afro-Brazilian men and women and offering incentives to private businesses to eliminate racial discrimination. The bill also called for the creation of scholarships for Afro-Brazilian students and the inclusion of African and Afro-Brazilian histories in school textbooks.

In the years leading up to the 1988 constitutional assembly, Nascimento stressed that racism and racial discrimination were not merely black communal concerns, but issues of national significance. Partly as a result of his efforts, the 1988 constitution included provisions that recognized the multiethnic character of Brazilian society, defined racism as an "imprescriptable and non-bondable crime," and determined the boundaries of lands that were formerly quilombos.

In 1990 Nascimento was elected to the Senate as a delegate from Rio de Janeiro State. Soon thereafter he became a member of the Rio de Janeiro State Council of Culture. The following year the governor of Rio de Janeiro created the Secretariat for the Defense and Promotion of Afro-Brazilian Peoples (SEAFRO), the first state agency of its sort, and appointed Nascimento as its state secretary.

In February 1997 Nascimento was reelected to represent Rio de Janeiro State in the Senate. As a congressman and senator, he has addressed not only Afro-Brazilian issues, but also international issues concerning Africans. He has addressed relations between South Africa and Brazil and defended efforts of Portuguese-speaking countries in Africa to achieve national liberation. In addition to his political accomplishments, he has written or edited more than 20 books, plays, and collections of essays on Afro-Brazilian culture and politics. Nascimento's achievements in such diverse fields have led some scholars to call him the twentieth century's most complete African intellectual.

North America

Nash, Diane Bevel

(b. May 15, 1938, Chicago, Ill.), African American civil rights activist, a founder of the Student Nonviolent Coordinating Committee (SNCC), and one of the few female leaders of the Civil Rights Movement.

Diane Nash attended Howard University and then transferred to Fisk University in Nashville, where she confronted Southern racial segregation and became active in the young Civil Rights Movement. She cofounded the Student Nonviolent Coordinating Committee (SNCC) in Raleigh, North Carolina, in April 1960. In February 1961 in Rock Hill, South Carolina, she was a member of the first group arrested for civil rights protest who refused to pay bail and remained in prison as a symbol of the plight of blacks in America.

Nash soon became SNCC's head of direct action. After marrying fellow civil rights activist James Bevel, taking his last name as her middle name, Nash moved to Georgia in 1962. There she worked with the Southern Christian Leadership Conference (SCLC), a civil rights organization led by Martin Luther King Jr., which coordinated civil rights activities. SCLC awarded Bevel and Nash the Rosa Parks Award in 1965.

North America

National Association for the Advancement of Colored People,

an interracial membership organization, founded in 1909, devoted to civil rights and racial justice.

Founded February 12, 1909, the National Association for the Advancement of Colored People (NAACP) has been instrumental in improving the legal, educational, and economic lives of African Americans. Combining the

The NAACP joined with civic and religious groups to organize the 1917 silent protest parade in Harlem. About 8000 African American men, women, and children marched down Fifth Avenue, silently bearing signs protesting the racist violence of the recent East St. Louis riot and the continuing scourge of lynching. Marchers questioned as well the bitter irony of the United States's entrance into World War I – a war meant to "make the world safe for democracy" – while the government continued to tolerate racial injustice at home.
CORBIS/Bettmann

white philanthropic support that characterized Booker T. Washington's accommodationist organizations with the call for racial justice delivered by W. E. B. Du Bois's militant Niagara Movement, the NAACP forged a middle road of interracial cooperation. Throughout its existence it has worked primarily through the American legal system to fulfill its goals of full suffrage and other civil rights and an end to segregation and racial violence. Since the end of the Civil Rights Movement of the 1960s, however, the influence of the NAACP has waned, and it has suffered declining membership and a series of internal scandals.

The NAACP was formed in response to the 1908 race riot in Springfield, the capital of Illinois and the birthplace of President Abraham Lincoln. Appalled at the violence that was committed against blacks, a group of white liberals that included Mary Ovington White and Oswald Garrison Villard, both the descendants of abolitionists, issued a call for a meeting to discuss racial justice. Some 60 people, only 7 of whom were African American (including W. E. B. Du Bois, Ida B. Wells-Barnett, and Mary Church Terrell), signed the call, which was released on the centennial of Lincoln's birth. Echoing the focus of Du Bois's militant all-black Niagara Movement, the NAACP's stated goal was to secure for all people the rights guaranteed in the Thirteenth, Fourteenth, and Fifteenth Amendments to the United States Constitution, which promised an end to slavery, the equal protection of the law, and universal adult male suffrage.

The NAACP established its national office in New York City and named a board of directors as well as a president, Moorfield Storey, a white constitutional lawyer and former president of the American Bar Association (ABA). The only African American among the organization's executives, Du Bois was made director of publications and research, and in 1910 he established the official journal of the NAACP, the *Crisis*. With a strong emphasis on local organizing, by 1913 the NAACP had established branch offices in such cities as Boston, Kansas City, Washington, D.C., Detroit, and St. Louis.

A series of early court battles—including a victory against a discriminatory Oklahoma law that regulated voting by means of a grandfather clause (*Guinn v. United States*, 1910) —helped establish the NAACP's importance as a legal advocate, a role it would play with overwhelming success. The fledgling organization also learned to harness the power of publicity in its 1915 battle against D. W. Griffith's inflammatory *Birth of a Nation*, a movie that perpetuated demeaning stereotypes of African Americans and glorified the Ku Klux Klan.

With its membership growing rapidly—from around 9000 in 1917 to around 90,000 in 1919—and with more than 300 local branches, the NAACP leadership soon included more African Americans. The writer and diplomat James Weldon Johnson became the association's first black secretary in 1920, and Louis T. Wright, a surgeon, was named the first black chairman of its board of directors in 1934; neither position was ever again held by a white person. Meanwhile, the *Crisis* became a voice of the Harlem Renaissance, as Du Bois published works by Langston Hughes, Countee Cullen, and other African American literary figures.

Throughout the 1920s the fight against lynching was among the association's top priorities. After early worries about its constitutionality, the NAACP strongly supported before the U.S. Congress the Dyer Bill, which would have punished those who participated in or failed to prosecute lynch mobs. Though Congress never passed the bill, or any other anti-lynching legislation, many credit the resulting public debate—fueled by the NAACP's report *Thirty Years of Lynching in the United States, 1889-1919*—with drastically decreasing the incidence of lynching.

When Johnson stepped down as secretary in 1930, he was succeeded by Walter F. White, who had been instrumental not only in his research on lynching (in part because, as a very fair-skinned African American, he had been able to infiltrate white groups) but also in his successful block of segregationist judge John J. Parker's nomination by President Herbert Hoover to the U.S. Supreme Court. Though some historians blame Du Bois's 1934 resignation on White, the new secretary presided over the NAACP's most productive period of legal advocacy. In 1930 the association commissioned the Margold Report, which became the basis for its successful drive to reverse the "separate but equal" doctrine that had governed public facilities since the *Plessy v. Ferguson* decision in 1896. In 1935 White recruited as NAACP chief counsel Charles H. Houston, the Howard University law school dean whose strategy on school-segregation cases paved the way for his protégé Thurgood Marshall to prevail in 1954's *Brown v. Board of Education*, the decision that overturned *Plessy*.

During the Great Depression of the 1930s, which was disproportionately disastrous for African Americans, the NAACP began to focus on economic justice. After years of tension with white labor unions, the association cooperated with the newly formed Congress of Industrial Organizations (CIO) in an effort to win jobs for black Americans. Walter White, a friend and adviser to First Lady Eleanor Roosevelt—who was sympathetic to civil rights—met with her often in attempts to convince President Franklin D. Roosevelt to outlaw job discrimination in the armed forces, defense industries (which were booming in anticipation of U.S. entry into World War II), and the agencies spawned by Roosevelt's New Deal legislation. Though this effort was not initially successful, when the NAACP backed labor leader A. Philip Randolph's March on Washington movement in 1941, Roosevelt agreed to open thousands of jobs to black workers and to set up a Fair Employment Practices Committee (FEPC) to ensure compliance.

Throughout the 1940s the NAACP saw enormous growth in its membership, claiming nearly half a million members by 1946. It continued to act as a legislative and legal advocate, pushing—albeit unsuccessfully—for a federal antilynching law and for an end to state-mandated segregation. By the 1950s the NAACP Legal Defense and Educational Fund, headed by Marshall, secured the second of these goals through *Brown v. Board of Education*, which outlawed segregation in public schools. The NAACP's Washington, D.C., bureau, led by lobbyist Clarence M. Mitchell Jr., helped advance not only integration of the armed forces in 1948 but also passage of the Civil Rights Acts of 1957, 1964, and 1968 as well as the Voting Rights Act of 1965.

Despite such dramatic courtroom and congressional victories, the implementation of civil rights was a slow, painful, and sometimes violent process. The unsolved 1951 murder of Harry T. Moore, an NAACP field secretary in Florida whose home was bombed on Christmas night, was just one of many crimes of retribution against the NAACP and its staff and members during the 1950s. Violence also met black children attempting to enter previously segregated schools in Little Rock, Arkansas, and other Southern cities, and throughout the South many African Americans were still denied the right to register and vote.

Arising out of frustration at the continuing lack of equality and justice, the Civil Rights Movement of the 1960s echoed the NAACP's moderate, integrationist goals, but leaders such as the Reverend Martin Luther King Jr.

of the Southern Christian Leadership Conference (SCLC) felt that direct action was needed to obtain them. Though the NAACP was opposed to extralegal popular actions, many of its members, such as Mississippi field secretary Medgar Evers, participated in nonviolent demonstrations such as sit-ins to protest the persistence of Jim Crow segregation throughout the South. Although it was criticized for working exclusively within the system by pursuing legislative and judicial solutions, the NAACP did provide legal representation and aid to members of more militant protest groups.

Led by Roy Wilkins, who had succeeded Walter White as secretary in 1955 the NAACP cooperated with organizers A. Philip Randolph and Bayard Rustin in planning the 1963 March on Washington. With the passage of civil rights legislation the following year, the association had finally accomplished much of its historic legislative agenda. In the following years the NAACP began to diversify its goals and, in the eyes of many, to lose its focus. Rising urban poverty and crime, de facto racial segregation, and lingering job discrimination continued to afflict millions of African Americans. With its traditional interracial, integrationist approach, the NAACP found itself attracting fewer members, as many African Americans became sympathetic to more militant, even separatist, philosophies, such as the beliefs espoused by the Black Power Movement.

Wilkins retired as executive director in 1977 and was replaced by Benjamin L. Hooks, whose tenure witnessed the *Bakke* case (1978), in which a California court outlawed several aspects of affirmative action. At around the same time tensions between the executive director and the board of directors—tensions that had existed since the association's founding—escalated into open hostility that threatened to weaken the organization. With the 1993 selection of the Reverend Benjamin F. Chavis (now Chavis Muhammad) as director, new controversies arose. In an attempt to take the NAACP in new directions, Chavis offended many liberals by reaching out to Nation of Islam leader Louis Farrakhan. After using NAACP funds to settle a sexual harassment lawsuit, Chavis was forced to resign in 1995 and subsequently joined the Nation of Islam.

Now headed by Kweisi Mfume, former congressman and head of the Congressional Black Caucus, with Julian Bond acting as chairperson of the board, the NAACP has focused in recent years on economic development and educational programs for youth, while also continuing its role as legal advocate for civil rights issues. The organization currently has more than half a million members.

Africa

Nationalism in Africa

Between 1951 and 1980 nationalist movements—efforts toward establishing national sovereignties unfettered by colonial rule—toppled European colo-

Kenya's prime minister Jomo Kenyatta pictured on the eve of independence in 1963 with former Mau Mau field marshall Mwariama. *CORBIS/Bettmann*

nial governments throughout Africa. The names of these movements' leaders are legendary: Kwame Nkrumah in Ghana; Gamal Abdel Nasser in Egypt; Jomo Kenyatta in Kenya; Léopold Sédar Senghor in Senegal; Julius Nyerere in Tanzania; Amílcar Cabral in Guinea-Bissau; and Nelson Mandela in South Africa. More recently, in 1993, Eritrea won a decades-long struggle for independence from Ethiopia, arguably showing that nationhood is still a viable goal for African regions seeking political autonomy.

African nationalism was born out of opposition to the injustices of colonial rule and thus was inseparable from the struggle for decolonization. Since race had provided European powers with a rationale for colonial domination, racial identification was one important source of anticolonial solidarity and nation building, but it was certainly not the only source. P articipants in independence struggles sought to reclaim appropriated lands, rid themselves of poverty and burdensome taxation, and gain the civil liberties enjoyed by citizens of the colonizing countries themselves— England, France, Portugal, Belgium, Italy, and (on much smaller scales) Germany and Spain.

The advantages of national sovereignty were debated among African leaders, particularly in France's colonies in West and Central Africa. There, leaders such as Senghor of Senegal and Félix Houphouët-Boigny of Côte d'Ivoire advocated not complete independence but rather "association" with France (a comparable option was not given to the English colonies). These leaders had enjoyed the privileges accorded to assimilés (French-speaking Africans whose education qualified them for French citizenship) and believed their countries would benefit both economically and strategically from continued close ties with France and neighboring Francophone territories. In 1958 French president Charles de Gaulle allowed France's African colonies to vote on their proposed membership in an international French community of semi-autonomous countries; all but Guinea voted in favor of the revised political alliance.

Although Guinea's 1958 vote was anomalous—and owed much to the charisma and organizing talents of labor activist and political leader Sékou Touré—the aspirations of the colony's people to achieve independence were not unique. The motivation for decolonization was in part economic: Touré's movement depended on convincing Guinea's peasants, market women, wage workers, and youth—all citizens who had never enjoyed opulence under colonial rule anyway—that they could only ultimately escape poverty if their colony achieved independence. But when Touré proclaimed, "We prefer poverty in freedom to opulence in slavery," he underscored the fact that it was the desire for autonomy that ultimately propelled nationalist movements throughout Africa.

Since the end of the cold war and the speedup of economic globalization, political turmoil both in Africa and elsewhere has led many to question the meaning of nationalism and the future of the nation-state. But these concepts have not lost relevance in Africa. In South Africa the African National Congress (ANC) finally achieved its long-standing goal: the transformation of the nation to one in which all races are afforded equal rights. In Central Africa, Laurent-Désiré Kabila's 1997 overthrow of Zairean dictator Mobutu Sese Seko proved that an era of cold-war-enforced balances of power in the region had definitely ended. One of Kabila's first actions as self-proclaimed president was to change the country's name from Zaire—a name associated with Mobutu, since he chose it for the former Belgian colony in 1965—to the Democratic Republic of the Congo. Whether or not Kabila had any intention of establishing a democracy soon became questionable, but by changing the name of the entire country he demonstrated that the image of national liberator was still significant in contemporary Africa. Finally, when tensions over trade and a disputed border between Eritrea and Ethiopia erupted into armed conflict in mid-1998, the two countries—whose citizenries are linked by language, religion, and even family ties—justified their actions as the defense of national sovereignty. All these events demonstrate that national movements and national identity remain dynamic concepts in contemporary Africa.

National Urban League,

an interracial social service organization that attempts to obtain full participation in American society for African Americans through lobbying, research, and direct social services.

Unlike organizations such as the National Association for the Advancement of Colored People (NAACP), which has been judged by how successfully it has fought for blacks' civil and political rights, the National Urban League (NUL) has pursued less measurable goals. Since its founding in 1911, the organization has used the tools of scientific social work to offer programs to help African Americans. The NUL originally provided direct services to African Americans who had migrated from the rural South to Northern cities. Later in the century, as social conditions changed, the organization increased its scope. It undertook sociological research that disputed commonly held misconceptions about African American inferiority; began to lobby businesses, labor unions, and the government; and embraced direct protest during the Civil Rights Movement as a means of gaining greater social and economic participation for African Americans.

At its inception the NUL modeled its social services on white charitable organizations of the day, such as settlement houses, charitable agencies, and immigrant aid societies, and adapted them to blacks' needs. As many African Americans moved north during the Great Migration, the NUL worked through local affiliates to help them adjust to urban life. The affiliates taught basic skills such as behavior, dress, sanitation, health, and homemaking. The NUL also sponsored community centers, clinics, kindergartens, day care, and summer camps. League workers provided individual care to African Americans in a range of areas, including juvenile delinquency, truancy, and marital adjustment.

The Great Migration increased demands on the NUL, and the organization soon had affiliates in nearly every industrial city in the United States. The NUL began offering vocational training to immigrants, urging businesses to hire blacks and attempting to persuade unions such as the Amer-

PERSONS LIVING BELOW THE POVERTY LEVEL 1959-1990				
Year	Total (In Millions)	Percent	Blacks (In Millions)	Percent
1959	39.5	22.4	9.9	55.1
1970	25.4	12.6	7.5	33.5
1980	29.3	13.0	8.6	32.5
1990	33.6	13.5	9.8	31.9

* Persons are classified as being above or below the poverty level using the poverty index, based on the Department of Agriculture's 1961 Economy Food Plan. Poverty thresholds are updated every year. In 1990 the weighted average poverty threshold for a family of four was $13,359.
Sources: *Encyclopedia of African-American Culture and History* (1996): "Persons Living Below the Poverty Level, 1959-1990" (Table 5.1); *Statistical Abstract*, 1992.

Vernon Jordan announces his resignation as president of the National Urban League in 1981, a year after he was wounded in an assassination attempt. *CORBIS/Bettmann*

ican Federation of Labor (AFL) to accept black members. The NUL achieved its primary aim of improving employment opportunities for blacks, but such gains were temporary: at the end of World War I returning soldiers put many blacks out of work again.

During World War II the NUL fought to desegregate wartime employment and the armed forces, supporting A. Philip Randolph's plan for a March on Washington. In exchange for Randolph's calling off the march, Roosevelt issued Executive Order (E.O.) 8802, which barred discrimination in defense industries and in federal agencies, and established the Fair Employment Practices Committee (FEPC), which was responsible for implementing E.O. 8802.

In the 1960s, under Whitney M. Young Jr., the NUL expanded its traditional social service approach by strengthening its commitment to civil rights. It embraced direct action, promoted community organization, and sponsored leadership development and voter education and registration projects. It helped organize two important events of the Civil Rights Movement: the March on Washington in 1963 and the Poor People's Campaign in 1968. Toward the end of the 1960s the NUL attempted to revitalize ghettos by calling for a domestic Marshall Plan.

Following Whitney Young's death in 1971, Vernon Jordan became president of the NUL. Jordan helped to begin programs in health, housing, education, and job training. In 1975 the NUL began to publish a journal, the *Urban League Review*, and began issuing an annual report, *The State of Black America*. In 1982 Jordan was succeeded by John Jacobs.

When the federal government cut social programs in the 1980s, the NUL responded by emphasizing self-help and seeking solutions to new and continuing problems facing African Americans, including high rates of teen pregnancy, families headed by single women, declining quality of public schools, and crime. Under Hugh Price, who became NUL president in 1994, the Urban League tackled the consequences of welfare "reform," the rollback of affirmative action programs, and the persistence of racial discrimination and exclusion in the workplace. A communications veteran, Price has been a strong national voice on behalf of economic opportunity and equality.

North America

Nation of Islam,

religious movement based on black separatism; founded around 1930 in Detroit, Michigan.

The Nation of Islam (NOI) was established in Detroit at the beginning of the Great Depression, by Wallace D. Fard, a door-to-door silk salesman. In addition to selling his wares, he spread his message of salvation and self-determination throughout Detroit's black neighborhoods. He held the first meetings in people's homes, but the movement soon grew big and Fard rented halls for his gatherings. Far from adhering to strict Islamic law, NOI under Fard was an eclectic mix of philosophy that borrowed from earlier black Muslim movements, Christian Scripture (largely to debunk Christianity), and Fard's Afrocentric interpretation of the story of Origin. The organization attracted many followers because of its angry rejection of white society.

Fard wrote two manuals, *The Secret Ritual of the Nation of Islam*, which is still used as a blueprint for oral instruction, and *Teaching for a Lost-Found Nation of Islam in a Mathematical Way*, written in a coded language that a select few are able to decipher. He also established the University of Islam, the Muslim Girls Training Corps—an instruction center that trained females to follow the tenets of proper Muslim womanhood—and the Fruit of Islam, a militaristic unit that served as Fard's bodyguard faction and enforced the Nation's laws.

Benjamin Chavis, *right*, chats with Louis Farrakhan at the African American Leadership summit in Washington, D.C., in November 1995. *CORBIS/Jacques M. Chenet*

When word reached white authorities that Fard was preaching about the Western "blue-eyed devil" whose civilization would soon perish, the Nation was deemed subversive. The hostile relationship between the movement and law enforcement (including ultimately the FBI) would continue for the next several decades.

Fard apparently had the foresight to know that his presence in the Nation would potentially lead to its demise. In 1933, months before he was told to leave Detroit or face incarceration, Fard began preparing his young right-hand man, Elijah Muhammad, for leadership. Fard's departure and his replacement by Muhammad led to internal strife within the movement. The Nation of Islam splintered, and within a couple of years Muhammad's trusted circle, including his family, moved to Chicago. The Temple of Islam No. 2 was built and later became the national headquarters of the Nation.

Under Muhammad the Nation was able to put into practice the concept of black economic self-sufficiency, a premise that Fard had envisioned but never fully realized. Because of their highly disciplined lifestyle, Muslims were hired more readily than other blacks. A good portion of their salary went into the Nation's coffers. One decade later, in 1945, members had pooled enough earnings to invest in 57 hectares (140 acres) of farmland in rural Michigan. In subsequent years more than 100 temples flourished nationwide, and Muslim-owned bakeries, grocery stores, and other small businesses were opened in African American communities.

During its early days the NOI tended to attract Southerners who had migrated north and had little formal education. The appeal of the movement was not just self-sufficiency but the structured lifestyle, with its emphasis on marriage, family, strict diet, and hygiene. In particular, the image of womanhood in the Nation of Islam was acclaimed for "purity, domesticity, and piety." Muhammad carried on Fard's program of providing female members with an education that included classes in nursing, gymnastics, cooking, sewing, child rearing, and the proper approach to gender relations. While its women seemed to be put on a pedestal, NOI has nevertheless been criticized over the years for being ambiguously caught between glorification and objectification of females.

By the 1950s NOI did begin to resemble a nation. Complete with its own national flag and anthem, militaristic marches and salutes, the movement was, in essence, a military theocracy. The structure and ritual, and the promise of salvation from the "grave"—the soulless, dog-eat-dog world outside the Nation—appealed to many poor blacks, particularly convicts in jail. One of those recruited from prison was a young man named Malcolm Little. Like all inductees into the movement, Little discarded his "slave" surname; he became known as Malcolm X. Recognized as a brilliant orator, Malcolm X quickly rose through the ranks of the Nation. He had arrived at an opportune time. The early rumblings of the Civil Rights Movement were beginning as a result of the government's failure to satisfy African American demands for equality. The Nation would soon be competing with other black movements for members. Malcolm's charisma and the advent of television brought the movement greater visibility than ever before. NOI actively began to recruit black, middle-class professionals. Not only was Muhammad interested in incorporating their skills for the betterment of the Nation, but he was also adamant that their expertise not be wasted in "the white man's world."

By the late 1950s NOI's separatist beliefs stood in contrast to the growing Civil Rights Movement, which sought integration. The primary focus of NOI was economic self-sufficiency, and by the early 1960s some, including Malcolm X, criticized the interest in financial gain and the money-and-wealth fixation among the upper ranks of the movement. In 1964, discontented with Muhammad's political philosophy and allegations that the leader had fathered several illegitimate children, Malcolm broke away from the Nation to form his own religious organization. One year later he was assassinated.

Critics of Muhammad claimed that his violent denunciation of Malcolm X in speeches and in the Nation's newspaper, *Muhammad Speaks*, incited the murder. The Nation has continued to prosper economically, but there has not been another surge in membership since the 1960s. In 1975, after Elijah Muhammad's death, his son Wallace Deen Muhammad was named supreme minister. However, two months into his leadership he declared that whites were no longer viewed as evil and would be allowed into the movement. This shift, as well as a move toward the more orthodox Sunni Islam, shocked and alienated a large group of followers. The Nation splintered into several alliances, and by 1978 national spokesman Louis

Farrakhan led a group that resurrected the original Nation of Islam teachings of Black Nationalism and separatism.

Despite his controversial persona, Farrakhan in the 1990s has been credited with reaching out to non-Muslim black religious leaders and activists in order to effect positive change in inner cities. In 1995 he successfully orchestrated the Million Man March, an event that brought together many people and organizations of opposing political viewpoints.

There is no official information on the size of NOI membership as of 1998. Various sources estimate that it numbers between 10,000 and 100,000.

Navarro, Theodore "Fats"

(b. September 24, 1923, Key West, Fla. ; d. July 7, 1950), African American jazz trumpeter who helped pioneer the genre of jazz known as bebop during the 1940s.

Theodore "Fats" Navarro was considered one of the foremost jazz trumpeters of the 1940s, helping to pioneer the new style of jazz known as bebop, which featured quick tempos and highly complex musical phrasing. Navarro, with the help of Dizzy Gillespie, toured with several famous musicians in his career, including Billy Eckstine, Lionel Hampton, and Coleman Hawkins. Navarro was a big man who at one point weighed more than 136 kg (300 lb), earning him the nickname "Fat Girl." Despite an addiction to heroin and a severe case of tuberculosis, Navarro continued to record until his 1950 death.

Nefertiti,

a queen of ancient Egypt.

Nefertiti was one of the most powerful women in the history of Egypt. Scholars generally believe that she exercised priestly powers previously reserved for the pharaoh alone. However, our knowledge of Nefertiti comes almost exclusively from the archaeological record, which allows few firm conclusions and leaves much room for speculation.

Nefertiti's origins are uncertain, although many believe she was a princess from the Middle East. She was the chief wife of the pharaoh Akhenaten, who reigned from 1353 to 1336 B.C.E. Akhenaten's rule is famous because of the religious reforms that he and Nefertiti instituted. Some scholars believe that Nefertiti was primarily responsible for these reforms. The royal couple established monotheism in Egypt by abandoning the Egyptian pantheon and instituting the worship of the sun god Aton and requiring all Egyptian people to do the same.

By all accounts Nefertiti believed devoutly in Aton, and some scholars believe that her devotion may have contributed to her loss of power. Such religious innovation was controversial in Egypt, which had a powerful priestly caste that pressured Akhenaten to revert to traditional religious beliefs. The woman with whom Akhenaten had six daughters and who, in Akhenaten's words, was "the Hereditary Princess, Great of Favor, Mistress of Happiness . . . Great and Beloved Wife of the King... Nefertiti" largely disappears from the historical record in the twelfth year of his reign. Many scholars believe she retired to the northern palace at Amarna after a confrontation with Akhenaten in which she proved unwilling to abandon exclusive worship of Aton. Nefertiti is perhaps best known from the painted limestone bust that was discovered at Tell el-Amarna, the ruins of the ancient capital, Akhetaton, from which she reigned until her fall from grace.

Cross Cultural

Négritude,

neologism coined by Martinican poet and statesman Aimé Césaire in Paris in the 1930s in discussions with fellow students Léopold Sédar Senghor and Léon-Gontran Damas.

The concept of Négritude represents an historic development in the formulation of African diasporic identity and culture in this century. The term marks a revalorization of Africa on the part of New World blacks, affirming an overwhelming pride in black heritage and culture, and asserting, in Marcus Garvey's words, that blacks are "descendants of the greatest and proudest race who ever peopled the earth." The concept finds its roots in the thought of Martin Delany, Edward Wilmot Blyden, and W. E. B. Du Bois, each of whom sought to erase the stigma attached to the black world through their intellectual and political efforts on behalf of the African diaspora. Early in this century French Caribbean politicians such as Hégésippe Légitimus, René Boisneuf, and Gratien Candace affirmed the right and necessity of blacks to enter into the global community as equals, while historians such as Oruno Lara strove to "edify a more beautiful past, drawing upon our heritage of sacrifice and probity." The inspiration for Césaire's term comes most directly, however, from the example of the Harlem Renaissance, in which writers such as Langston Hughes and Claude McKay explored and revindicated the richness of black culture. Léopold Senghor himself referred to McKay as "the true inventor of [the values of] Négritude. . . . Far from seeing in one's blackness an inferiority, one accepts it, one lays claim to it with pride, one cultivates it lovingly." Like the evolution of the term black in the United States, Négritude took a stigmatized term and turned it into a point of pride.

Negro Ensemble Company,

longest-running black theater company in the United States.

The Negro Ensemble Company was founded in New York City in 1967 by actor-director-playwright Douglas Turner Ward, actor Robert Hooks, and white manager Gerald Krone. Their intent was to provide a space where black playwrights "could communicate with an audience of other Negroes, better informed through commonly shared experience to readily understand, confirm, or reject the truth or paucity of [their] creative explorations." This was during the height of the Black Arts Movement, and many other companies shared the vision of creating theater by black people for black people. But while others were committed to theater with strong nationalistic and political messages, the Negro Ensemble Company produced a much wider spectrum of plays, including family dramas, folk musicals, and plays from African and Caribbean perspectives.

The company was criticized by more militant artists for its less political messages and for its early support from mainstream white sources such as the Ford Foundation. Its broader appeal, however, gave it staying power. In addition to producing plays, the company also offered actor training programs and playwrights' workshops. The Negro Ensemble Company's most successful productions included Joseph Walker's *The River Niger* (1972), which went to Broadway and won a Tony Award for Best Play of the Year; Charles Fuller's Pulitzer-Prize winning *A Soldier's Play* (1982); and *Samm-Art Williams's Home* (1979), which also became a Broadway success.

Negro Leagues

Baseball is said to be America's national pastime, but only since the spring of 1947 can it be said to have become truly national. That year Jack Roosevelt Robinson entered the Brooklyn Dodgers lineup, becoming the first African American to play major league baseball since Moses Fleetwood "Fleet" Walker and his brother Weldy played for Toledo in 1884. The exclusion of African Americans from major league baseball paralleled their treatment in other areas of American society. And, like other segregated African American institutions, Negro baseball leagues recognized and developed the talent of black people in their full humanity.

Early Professional Teams

During the Jim Crow period baseball became one of the most thriving institutions of African American life. Professional teams began forming in the 1880s, including the Philadelphia Orions (1882), the St. Louis Black Stock-

NEGRO BASEBALL LEAGUES

Negro National League I

Birmingham Black Barons	1925, 1927-1930	Detroit Stars	1920-1931
Chicago American Giants	1920-1931	Indianapolis ABCs	1920-1926, 1931
Chicago Giants	1920-1921	Kansas City Monarchs	1920-1931
Columbus Buckeyes	1921	Louisville White Sox	1931
Cuban Stars	1920, 1922	Memphis Red Sox	1924-1925, 1927-1930
Cleveland Browns	1924	Milwaukee Bears	1923
Cleveland Cubs	1931	Nashville Elite Giants	1930
Cleveland Elites	1926	Pittsburgh Keystone	1922
Cleveland Hornets	1927	St. Louis Giants	1920-1921
Cleveland Tate Stars	1922	Toledo Tigers	1923
Dayton Marcos	1920, 1926		

Negro National League II

Bacharach Giants (Atlantic City)	1934	Homestead (Pa.) Grays	1935-1948
Baltimore Black Sox	1933-1934	Nashville Elite Giants	1933-1934
Baltimore Elite Giants	1938-1948	Newark Dodgers	1934-1935
Brooklyn Eagles	1935	Newark Eagles	1936-1948
Cleveland Giants	1933	New York Black Yankees	1936-1948
Cleveland Red Sox	1934	New York Cubans	1935-1936, 1939-1948
Cole's American Giants (Chicago)	1933-1935	Philadelphia Stars	1934-1948
Columbus Blue Birds	1933	Pittsburgh Crawford	1933-1938
Columbus Elite Giants	1935	Washington Black Senators	11938
Detroit Stars	1933	Washington Elite Giants	1936-1937
Harrisburg-St. Louis Stars	1943		

Eastern Colored League   *(American Negro League, 1929)*

Bacharach Giants (Atlantic City)	1923-1929	Homestead (Pa.) Grays	1929
Baltimore Black Sox	1923-1929	Lincoln Giants (New York)	1923-1926, 1928-1929
Brooklyn Royal Giants	1923-1927	Newark Stars	1926
Cuban Stars East	1923-1929	Philadelphia Tigers	1928
Harrisburg (Pa.) Giants	1924-1927	Washington Potomacs	1924
Hilldale (Philadelphia)	1923-1927, 1929		

Negro Southern League

Cole's American Giants (Chicago)	1932	Memphis Red Sox	1932
Columbus Turfs (Ohio)	1932	Monroe Monarchs	1932
Indianapolis ABCs	1932	Montgomery Grey Sox	1932
Louisville Black Caps	1932	Nashville Elite Giants	1932

East-West League

Baltimore Black Sox	Spring 1932	Hilldale (Philadelphia)	Spring 1932
Cleveland Stars	Spring 1932	Homestead (Pa.) Grays	Spring 1932
Cuban Stars	Spring 1932	Newark Browns	Spring 1932

Negro-American League

Atlantic Black Crackers	1938	Indianapolis Athletics	1937
Baltimore Elite Giants	1949-1950	Indianapolis Clowns	1943-1950
Birmingham Black Barons	1937-1938, 1940-1950	Indianapolis Crawfords	1940
Chicago American Giants	1937-1950	Jacksonville Red Caps	1938, 1941-1942
Cleveland Buckeyes	1943-1948, 1950	Kansas City Monarchs	1937-1950
Cincinnati Buckeyes	1942	Louisville Buckeyes	1949
Cincinnati Tigers	1937	Memphis Red Sox	1937-1941, 1943-1950
Cleveland Bears	1939-1940	New York Cubans	1949-1950
Detroit Stars	1937	Philadelphia Stars	1949-1950
Houston Eagles	1949-1950	St. Louis Stars	1937, 1939, 1941
Indianapolis ABCs	1938-1939	Toledo Crawfords	1939

ings (1882), and the Cuban Giants (1885). Under the management of S. K. Govern, the Cuban Giants were immensely successful, spawning numerous African American teams named the Giants including the Columbia Page Fence Giants, the Chicago Leland Giants, the Brooklyn Royal Giants, and even the Cuban X Giants. The "genuine" Cuban Giants competed in the predominantly white Middle States (minor) League from 1889 to 1891, along with another African American team, the New York Gorhams (or Gothams). In 1886 and 1887 African American baseball leagues were formed but soon folded.

Barnstorming

During the height of Jim Crowism, from 1890 to 1920, successful African American baseball teams played outside formal leagues, "barnstorming" the nation. Teams such as the Indianapolis ABCs and the Lincoln Giants went to any town or city that could field an opposing team and promise financial return. The major problem for barnstormers was dependence on white booking agents who controlled the sporting activities in major cities. Games between barnstorming teams were quite lucrative, because they allowed fans to watch black teams face anyone who would play, including teams comprising white major and minor leaguers.

The Negro Leagues

At the turn of the century Andrew "Rube" Foster, a star pitcher for several African American teams, envisioned a baseball league for blacks that would rival the white Major League, eventually forcing full recognition and inclusion of African American ballplayers. With partner John Schorling, in 1911, Foster formed the Chicago American Giants and set the foundation for the creation of a Negro baseball league. In February 1920 Foster founded the Negro National League (NNL) with the owners/representatives of the Indianapolis ABCs, the Chicago Giants, the Kansas City Monarchs (owned by white promoter J. L. Wilkinson), the St. Louis Giants, the Detroit Stars, and the Cuban Stars. As the first enduring professional sports league managed by African Americans, the NNL was widely successful. With players such as sluggers Oscar Charleston, John Henry Lloyd, and the great "Smokey Joe" Williams, the new, mostly Midwestern league garnered much fanfare and popular support in African American communities. In 1923 the Eastern Colored League (ECL) was formed by white booking agent Nat Strong, leading to a feud with the NNL. Tensions were alleviated in 1924 when owners in each league agreed to a system based on the Major League, with split schedules and the two best teams meeting for a "black World Series." During the mid-1920s league teams such as the Birmingham Black Barons and the Cuban Stars enjoyed success in both league play and the ever-fruitful barnstorming circuit.

Both leagues failed, however, soon after Foster's leadership was cut short by mental illness in 1926 and his death in 1930. The ECL folded in 1928 and the NNL in 1931. In 1932 black baseball thrived mainly in the Southern

Negro League (which had been a lesser league prior to that year) and in Latin America, where great ball players were welcome regardless of race.

Demise of the Negro Leagues

The Negro National League folded in 1948, due in great part to Jackie Robinson's inte-gration of the major leagues. Although the Negro American League lasted until 1960, in its later years it failed to capture the imagination of black ticket buyers, who were now watching former Negro Leaguers in the Major Leagues including Monte Irvin (NL: Newark Eagles, ML: New York Giants); Roy Campanella (NL: Baltimore Elite Giants, ML: Brooklyn Dodgers); "Satchel" Paige (NL: Philadelphia Stars, ML: Cleveland Indians); Henry "Hank" Aaron (NL: Indianapolis Clowns, ML: Milwaukee Braves); and Willie Mays (NL: Birmingham Black Barons, ML: New York Giants).

African American baseball players have had a profound impact on major league baseball by bringing to center stage the showmanship and skill that characterized the Negro Leagues. The legacy of vision and excellence proffered by the Negro Leagues has been recognized recently by many Americans and has emerged as a source of great pride, as well as an unavoidable embarrassment to those who permitted the system of exclusion.

North America

Negro National Anthem,
the African American national hymn.

"Lift Ev'ry Voice and Sing," popularly considered the Negro national anthem, was composed in 1900 at the Colored High School in Jacksonville, Florida, by James Weldon Johnson and his brother, J. Rosamond Johnson. It is a 34-line poem that expresses the difficulty African Americans have experienced in reaching the present, exemplified in such lines as "Stony the road we trod." Despite acknowledging the pain and disappointment faced by black Americans, the song is essentially a hymn of faith in God, to whom it says, "Thou has brought us thus far on the way," and the Johnsons' lyrics express both hope for the future and American patriotism.

Latin America and the Caribbean

Nemours, Jean Baptiste and Sicot, Wéber,
musicians who contributed to the development of Haiti's first national pop music. Nemours was a Haitian bandleader during the 1950s and 1960s, a saxophonist, composer, and inventor of the Haitian musical form compas-direct. Sicot, initially in Nemours's band, went on to have a career of his own as one of Haiti's most influential musicians.

During the summer of 1955 Haitian bandleader Jean Baptiste Nemours initiated a transformation of Haitian popular music by creating a new dance rhythm that he called the compas-direct (direct beat). At first compas sounded quite similar to the Dominican merengue, which was enormously popular in Haiti at that time. Nevertheless, ethnomusicologist Gage Averill notes an important distinction between the repeated rhythmic pattern of the tambora (conga-like drum) in merengue and that of its cousin, the tanbou, in compas music. He explains that the pattern on the tanbou is shifted forward one eighth note in compas, spilling over into each following measure. This shift creates an even stronger forward propulsion in compas than is found in the Dominican merengue.

Nemours was not alone in his attempt to corner the market on Haitian music. He had many imitators and rivals, including former bandmate Wéber Sicot. Nemours and Sicot played together briefly in a band called Conjunto International, eventually splitting up in order to form their own groups. In 1958 relations between the two musicians became irreparably strained when Sicot coined a new dance rhythm that was almost indistinguishable from Nemours's compas-direct. He called his rhythm kadans ranpa (from rempart, meaning "defense" or "fortification"). From that point on, their relationship was strictly competitive, the two composers constantly striving to imitate and outdo the other. Occasionally their rivalry resulted in the outright piracy of material. Today Nemours and Sicot are both considered important figures in the development of compas, Haiti's first national pop music.

Latin America and the Caribbean

Netherlands Antilles,

a part of the kingdom of the Netherlands consisting of five islands in the Caribbean Sea. Curaçao and Bonaire, located north of Venezuela, constitute one island group, and St. Maarten, St. Eustatius, and Saba, located east of the Virgin Islands, constitute a second.

The present-day kingdom of the Netherlands consists of three separate states: the Netherlands, the Caribbean island of Aruba, and the five Caribbean islands that together compose the Netherlands Antilles. Many European nations competed to be part of the fifteenth- and sixteenth-century European invasion of the Caribbean, and most of them were hoping to establish control of islands that contained either gold or fertile soils that would facilitate plantation farming. But the Dutch had a simple, unique need that led them to establish Caribbean colonies: salt. The herring industry was an important part of the Dutch economy, and salt was required to cure the fish. This salt had traditionally come from the Spanish Iberian Peninsula, but conflicts between the Netherlands and Spain in the 1500s led Spain to outlaw that trade. The Dutch needed to find a new region of the world that could furnish a suitable salt supply. The result of their quest changed the kingdom and the six Caribbean islands that were destined to become part of it.

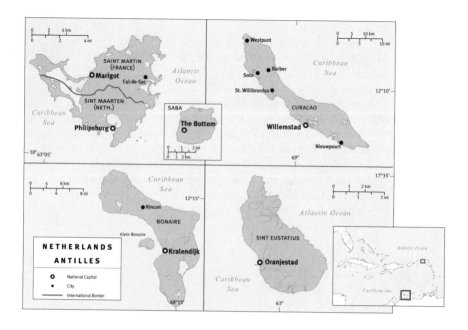

As the Netherlands Antilles enter the twenty-first century, the islands' residents are determined to maintain the unification of their country. Daily life is still very different for a refinery worker in Curaçao and a fisherman on tiny Saba, but the five islands share a common history under the Dutch flag and some aspects of a common culture that blends Dutch and African elements. Many Caribbean traditions, such as the Carnival celebration, are also a part of the Netherlands Antilles culture. The warm Papiamento phrase *bon bini* ("welcome") has been adopted as a general introduction to all of the Netherlands Antilles.

Europe

Netherlands, The,

a Western European country in which blacks have had a presence for centuries.

As early as the sixteenth century a small population of Africans and people of African descent resided in the Netherlands as servants and laborers, military servicemen, and intellectuals. Black military recruits served in the Dutch army in Suriname and Indonesia and fought for the Dutch in World War II. Black Surinamese intellectuals, who have studied in the Netherlands, have challenged racism in Dutch society, the Dutch view of its colonies, and the self-image of tolerance and pluralism that is prevalent among the Dutch.

However, a significant black presence in the Netherlands did not exist until the 1950s. With the arrival of blacks from former Dutch colonies, the

Netherlands has faced the consequences of its past involvement in the slave trade and colonialism. In the 1960s Moroccans and other North Africans entered the Netherlands to work in Dutch industry. When Suriname attained independence in 1975, many Surinamers migrated to the Netherlands to retain their Dutch citizenship. While the Netherlands is known as a country of refuge and home to one of the most comprehensive social benefits systems in Europe, the continued presence of these ethnic minorities has revealed the limits of Dutch tolerance. However, the Dutch government has attempted to accommodate these migrants by promoting multiculturalism and addressing issues of economic disparity and racial discrimination.

North America

Newton, Huey P.

(b. February 17, 1942, New Orleans, La.; d. August 22, 1989, Oakland, Calif.), cofounder of the American black nationalist organization the Black Panther Party.

Huey Newton grew up in Oakland, California, a place that would become the West Coast center of the American black nationalist movement. While attending Merritt College in Oakland, he met Bobby Seale, and the two began to work together on a project to diversify the school's curriculum. Inspired by nationalist struggles in the Third World and revolutionaries such as Fidel Castro and Mao Zedong, Newton became critical of the racist oppression of blacks in the United States and the capitalist system he saw as underpinning that exploitation.

As a response to the condition of black America, Newton and Seale founded the Black Panther Party for Self-Defense, later simply called the Black Panther Party. "We want land, bread, housing, education, clothing, justice and peace," concluded the organization's ten-point program, which Newton coauthored. Patrolling black neighborhoods with shotguns, which were deemed legal as long as they were visible, the Panthers set themselves up as monitors of the police. These "justice patrols" sought to inform African Americans of their rights and to counteract a history of police brutality against blacks. Not surprisingly, the Panthers developed a hostile relationship with the police, with Newton becoming a magnet for police antagonism.

On October 28, 1967, Newton was charged with the murder of a police officer and the wounding of another. He pleaded innocent, and the trial provoked an intensive "Free Huey" campaign, drawing thousands to Black Panther rallies and rapidly boosting Panther membership and visibility. Viewed by many as a political prisoner, Newton continued to address political issues from prison.

In 1970, after his 1968 conviction was overturned because of procedural errors, Newton left prison to return to the Black Panther Party. He found the party weakened by regional conflict, in part because of disputes about the militant programs of Eldridge Cleaver, who influenced an East Coast-based movement. Leading a West Coast faction, Newton advocated political education and programs that he believed would link the Panthers to the broader African American community.

As his prominence in the Panthers declined, conflict with the law continued to trouble Newton. In 1974 he was accused of killing a woman and fled to Cuba. Three years later he returned to face the murder charge, which after two hung juries the state eventually dropped. He was retried and convicted for the 1967 murder of the policeman, but the conviction was later overturned.

In 1980 Newton received a Ph.D. in social philosophy from the University of California at Santa Cruz; he wrote a thesis titled the *War Against the Panthers—A Study of Repression in America*. Newton's life began a downward spiral after the Panthers finally disbanded in 1982. Rumors about drug abuse surrounded him, and he was arrested in 1989 for embezzling funds from an Oakland children's nutritional program founded by the Panthers. He served six months of jail time. Later that year he was killed in what was believed to be a drug-trade related incident.

North America

New York City Draft Riot of 1863,

the Civil War's most violent urban insurrection, largely directed at black Americans.

In Northern American cities like Toledo, Cincinnati, Harrisburg, and Detroit, the economic and social disruption caused by the Civil War led to violence directed at free Northern blacks, but the New York City Draft Riot of 1863 was by far the most violent. Before the 1840s New York City's blacks held most of the city's jobs as longshoremen, hod carriers, brick makers, barbers, waiters, and domestic servants. Irish immigrants, particularly those arriving after 1846, competed with blacks for these unskilled jobs and eventually gained control of the occupations, leaving many blacks to work only as strike breakers.

The animosity between New York's whites and blacks was further intensified by the Emancipation Proclamation. Democratic politicians used it to their advantage by claiming, paradoxically, that Republicans would transport freedpeople to New York to replace white workers while lazy blacks lived on relief services provided by industrious whites. Shortly after President Abraham Lincoln issued the Emancipation Proclamation, Congress passed the Conscription Act, which had a provision allowing a draftee to decline service for a $300 fee. This financial arrangement widened class divisions.

The three-day riot began on July 13 as a protest against the Conscription Act. After the protesters, many of them Irish laborers, destroyed draft headquarters, they roamed the streets, at times razing entire city blocks, cutting telegraph lines, tearing up railroad tracks, and causing factories and shops to close. They assaulted the offices of the *New York Tribune*, trying to find the pro-Union editor Horace Greeley, and they attacked the home of the city's provost marshal.

The mob then split into groups. Some destroyed mansions; others attacked the mayor's house in a failed attempt to level it. Still others targeted New York's black residents with intense violence. They terrorized blacks, burned the Colored Orphan Asylum, and looted the Colored Seamen's Home. They raided and destroyed homes; they shot, stomped, clubbed, burned, and hanged black victims. Eleven blacks were killed by rioters. Most blacks fled the city, but a few desperately sought the sanctuary of police-station jail cells. Union army regiments—including some men returning from the Battle of Gettysburg—finally restored order.

Though New York City merchants raised $50,000 to pay black victims and rebuild the Colored Orphan Asylum, the psychic scars remained. By 1865 New York's black population had decreased by 20 percent.

North America

New York Slave Rebellion of 1712,

a rebellion against inhumane treatment that resulted in harsher slave codes in New York.

On April 6, 1712, about 25 American Indian and black slaves in colonial New York City retaliated against harsh treatment by their masters. They set fire to an outhouse, then lay in ambush, killing nine men and wounding seven others as they came to extinguish the fire. The slaves then fled to the woods. Within two days more than 40 had been arrested and 6 had committed suicide before arrest.

Twenty-seven slaves were convicted of murder and sentenced to death, although much of the evidence used to convict them was suspect; 18 were acquitted. Six, including a pregnant woman, were reprieved. Historians disagree on the exact number of people executed, but it is likely that approximately 20 people were hanged, including a pregnant woman. Three more were burned to death, one was hung in chains until he died, and one was broken on the wheel.

Shortly after the rebellion, New York's legislature toughened its slave codes. Slaves gathering in groups of three or more were subject to 40 lashes, and such crimes as burning barns, outhouses, stables, and stacks of corn or hay were all made punishable by death. Wanting to avoid similar uprisings, the Massachusetts legislature passed a law forbidding slave importation, and the Pennsylvania legislature placed an import duty on blacks that effectively ended their importation.

North America

Niagara Movement (1905–1910),

African American political action organization founded by W. E. B. Du Bois and William Monroe Trotter.

At the start of the twentieth century no African American voice carried such authority with both black and white audiences as that of Booker T. Washington. The founder of Tuskegee Institute, he presided over a network of membership organizations, including the Afro-American Council and the National Negro Business League, that worked to promote racial uplift among black Americans. Some African Americans, however, were dissatisfied with Washington's message of accommodationism, which counseled economic self-help and patience. Washington's critics demanded that black American citizens be granted the same civil rights enjoyed by whites. The militant Niagara Movement was a direct response to Washington's cautious approach to racial justice; though short-lived, it was an important step in the formation of modern African American protest movements.

Both W. E. B. Du Bois and William Monroe Trotter, the movement's organizers, had long opposed Washington's philosophy. Trotter, the editor of the Boston Guardian, an African American daily newspaper known for its militant editorials, had publicly rebuked Washington at a meeting in Boston in 1903; after the meeting, Trotter was jailed for nearly causing a riot. That same year Du Bois had published in his classic book *The Souls of Black Folk* an essay condemning Washington for his acceptance of lowered expectations for African Americans.

The Niagara Movement placed itself in direct opposition to Booker T. Washington's cautious stance. Though never naming Washington, the declaration further said, "We refuse to allow the impression to remain that the Negro-American assents to inferiority, is submissive under oppression and apologetic before insults."

Even before the Niagara members met, spies from the Washington camp had tried to infiltrate the movement, though they were stymied by the change in location. After the first meeting the black press, which typically championed Washington, kept mention of the Niagara Movement from its pages. Though the movement grew to include 170 members in 34 states, by 1906 it was already in trouble. Trotter and Du Bois clashed on the inclusion of women, which Trotter opposed, and feuds within Boston's black community further unbalanced the *Guardian's* editor. In 1907 Trotter resigned his chairmanship of the press committee. The following year neither Du Bois nor Trotter attended the annual conference. In 1908 Trotter started his own group, the Negro-American Political League, and by 1909 Du Bois was asking remaining Niagara contacts to consider joining the newly formed National Association for the Advancement of Colored People (NAACP).

Historian Stephen R. Fox cites three reasons, in addition to the tensions between Du Bois and Trotter, for the collapse of the Niagara Movement:

Washington's opposition; a persistent lack of money, stemming in part from the white philanthropic world's loyalty to Washington; and a racial message too militant for its own time. This plea for racial justice was later voiced by the NAACP and other groups, and resonated during the Civil Rights Movement of the 1960s; but in 1905 few Americans were ready to hear it.

North America

Nicholas Brothers

(Fayard, b. 1918, and Harold, b. 1924, Philadelphia, Pa.), African American tap dancers who performed in Hollywood musicals in the 1930s and 1940s.

Fayard and Harold Nicholas began dancing in Philadelphia in the 1930s. Rising to stardom as a tap-dancing duo, they appeared in the musicals *Tin Pan Alley*, *Stormy Weather*, *Down Argentine Way*, and *The Big Broadcast of 1936*. The pair performed with such contemporary stars as Josephine Baker, Lena Horne, Gene Kelly, Bill ("Bojangles") Robinson, and Cab Calloway. In the late 1940s, with tap dance's popularity waning in the United States, the Nicholas Brothers moved to Europe. They gave a royal command performance for the king of England in 1948 and performed at the inauguration of United States president Dwight D. Eisenhower in 1955.

Africa

Niger,

a West African country bordered by Burkina Faso, Benin, Nigeria, Chad, Libya, Algeria, and Mali.

Straddling the Sahara Desert and the Sahel, the fragile environment of Niger has shaped the lives of its peoples from the earliest days to the present. Niger's early societies enabled their people to sustain themselves even in times of drought through such means as shifting cultivation and participation in trans-Saharan trade networks that supplemented local production. These practices preserved the fragile Sahel and buffered against famine. During the twentieth century, however, French colonialism forced Nigeriens to abandon such centuries-old techniques in order to produce cash crops. This left Nigeriens more vulnerable to drought and dependent on unreliable global commodity markets. French colonial neglect and the demands of the global market economy have perpetuated Nigerien poverty, ecological vulnerability, and political instability since independence. As a result, Nigheriens, like other peoples of the Sahel, struggle to meet their social and ecological needs amid the pressures of the global economy.

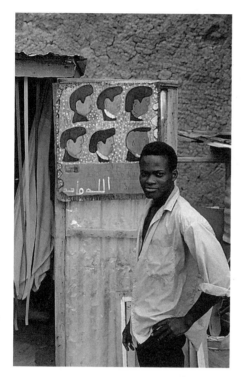

A barber stands in front of a sign advertising the kinds of haircuts he offers. *CORBIS/The Purcell Team*

Africa

Niger (Ready Reference)

Official Name: Republic of Niger

Area: 1,267,000 sq km (489,189 sq mi)

Location: Inland West Africa; borders Algeria, Libya, Chad, Nigeria, Benin, Burkina Faso, and Mali

Capital: Niamey (population 398,265 [1988 estimate])

Other Major Cities: Zinder (population 120,900), Maradi (113,000), Tahoua (51,600), and Agadez (50,200) (1988 estimate)

Population: 9,671,848 (1998 estimate)

Population Density: 7 persons per sq km (about 19 persons per sq mi); 90 percent of the population lives near the southern border.

Population Below Age 15: 48 percent (male 2,374,482; female 2,277,176 [1998 estimate])

Population Growth Rate: 2.96 percent (1998 estimate)

Total Fertility Rate: 7.3 children born per woman (1998 estimate)

Life Expectancy at Birth: Total population: 41.52 years (male 41.83 years; female 41.21 years [1998 estimate])

Infant Mortality Rate: 114.39 deaths per 1000 live births (1998 estimate)

Literacy Rate (age 15 and over who can read and write): Total population: 13.6 percent (male 20.9 percent; female 6.6 percent [1998 estimate])

Education: In the early 1990s Niger had some 368,700 pupils in primary schools, 74,300 in secondary schools, and 2400 in vocational and teacher-training schools. Only about 25 percent of primary-school-aged children receive an education. Advanced training is given at the University of Niamey.

Languages: French is the official language. Hausa, the first language of over half the population, is also used as a trade language by a large number of Nigeriens (see Hausa Language). Other spoken languages include Temasheq (Tuareg Berber), Djerma (Songhai), Fulani, and Arabic.

Ethnic Groups: More than half the population is Hausa. Other ethnic groups include the Songhai, Fulani, Tuareg, Beriberi (Kanuri), Arab, Tubu, and Gourmantche. There are about 4000 French expatriates.

Religions: 85 percent are Sunni Muslims; fewer than 1 percent are Christian; and the remainder practice traditional religions.

Climate: Rainfall (June through October) is minimal over most of Niger; the southern farming zone receives an average of 820 mm (32 in) per year. Average annual temperature at Niamey is 29.4° C (85° F).

Land, Plants, and Animals: The northern half of the country is in the Sahara Desert and has little or no vegetation; the Sahel region south of the Sahara is semi-arid brush country; the extreme south is partially forested. The Air Mountain range is located in the center of Niger, in the southern Sahara. The Niger River flows through the western part of the country, and Lake Chad lies on the southeastern border. Wildlife on protected reserves include elephants, hippopotamuses, giraffes, and lions; gazelles, hyenas, and vipers are widespread, and monkeys are found in the Air Mountains.

Natural Resources: Gold, uranium, coal, iron ore, tin, and phosphates

Currency: The Communauté Financière Africaine franc

Gross Domestic Product (GDP): $6.3 billion (1997 estimate)

GDP per Capita: $670 (1997 estimate)

The lifestyle of nomads in Niger, such as the Tuareg and the Toubou, has been threatened by both colonial and postcolonial regimes, which have attempted to suppress the nomads' movements in the Sahel. *CORBIS/Tiziana and Gianni B*

GDP Real Growth Rate: 4.5 percent (1997 estimate)

Primary Economic Activities: Agriculture (farming and animal husbandry, 38.5 percent of GDP, 90 percent of employment), industry, and other services

Primary Crops: Cowpeas, cotton, peanuts, millet, sorghum, cassava (tapioca), rice; cattle, sheep, and goats

Industries: Cement, brick, textiles, food processing, chemicals, slaughterhouses, and other small, light industries; uranium mining

Primary Exports: Uranium ore, livestock products, cowpeas, and onions

Primary Imports: Consumer goods, primary materials, machinery, vehicles and parts, petroleum, and cereals

Primary Trade Partners: France, Nigeria, Côte d'Ivoire, Italy, Germany, and Japan

Government: Niger is nominally a constitutional multiparty republic, but events in 1999 threatened that form of government. Under normal circumstances the president appoints the prime minister and his cabinet, the National Salvation Council. The unicameral 83-seat National Assembly is elected by proportional representation for five-year terms. However, in April 1999 President Ibrahim Bare Mainassara, who took power in a 1996 military coup and who was elected president later that same year, was assassinated. The army vested power in a National Reconciliation Council— slated to rule for nine months—and appointed Maj. Daouda Malam Wanke as president.

Africa

Nigeria,

country with the world's largest black population, located on the Atlantic coast of West Africa, sharing borders with Benin, Niger, Chad, and Cameroon.

The Niger River is Nigeria's most remarkable physical feature, as well as the source of its name. But Africa's most populous nation did not even have a name before the late nineteenth century, nor for that matter a national

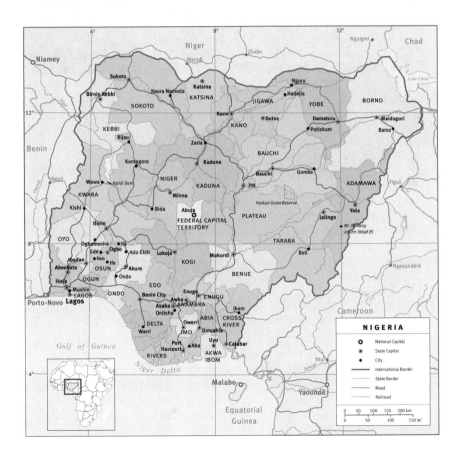

Pedestrians and vans crowd a street market in Lagos, the capital of Nigeria.
CORBIS/Daniel Lainé

identity. Rather, British colonization brought together three vast and culturally distinctive regions—north, southeast, and southwest—and at least 250 different language groups, more than any other African country.

Generously endowed as well with natural resources such as crude oil, gas, coal, iron, limestone, columbite, and tin, Nigeria in its early postcolonial years was viewed as a potential middle-level economic power. Since independence in 1960, however, corrupt military rule has conspired with religious as well as ethnic fractiousness to all but dissipate the nation's early promise.

Following independence Nigeria was rocked by political crises: disputed elections led to widespread violence, then to a coup and countercoup, then to ethnic tensions that exploded into the 30-month Biafran War (1967–1970). In the nearly three decades since the Biafran War, promised returns to democratic civilian rule have been repeatedly thwarted by military-sponsored coups, crackdowns on opposition groups, and electoral maneuverings. Many of Nigeria's most esteemed intellectuals have left the country, while others have faced severe state persecution. By the late 1990s many Nigerians viewed head of state Gen. Sani Abacha's ostensible democratic transition with great skepticism. In mid-1998 Abacha's sudden death, followed a month later by the equally unexpected death of one of his greatest rivals, the imprisoned businessman Moshood Abiola, left the country's political future even more uncertain.

Nigeria (Ready Reference)

Official Name: Federal Republic of Nigeria

Area: 923,768 sq km (356,669 sq mi)

Location: West Africa, on the Gulf of Guinea, bordered by Benin, Niger, Chad, and Cameroon

Capital: Abuja (population 107,129,469 [1997 estimate])

Other Major Cities: Lagos (official population 1,347,000 [1992 estimate], the metropolitan area has an estimated 10 million residents), Ibadan (1,295,000), Niger (2,482,000 [1991 estimate]), Bauchi (4,294,000), Sokoto (4,392,000), Kano (5,632,000), and Ondo (3,884,000)

Population: 110,532,242 (1998 estimate)

Population Density: 137 persons per sq km (356 per sq mi)

Population Below Age 15: 45 percent (male 24,871,855; female 24,661,134 [1998 estimate])

Population Growth Rate: 2.96 percent (1998 estimate)

Total Fertility Rate: 6.09 children born per woman (1998 estimate)

Life Expectancy at Birth: Total population: 53.55 years (male 52.68 years; female 54.45 years [1998 estimate])

Infant Mortality: 70.2 deaths per 1000 live births (1997 estimate)

Literacy Rate (age 15 and over who can read and write): Total population: 57.1 percent (male 67.3 percent; female 47.3 percent [1995 estimate])

Education: In the early 1990s Nigeria had 14.8 million pupils enrolled in primary schools and more than 3.6 million in secondary schools. Institutions of higher education include the University of Ibadan, Ahmadu Bello University, the Obafemi Awolowo University, the University of Lagos, and the University of Nigeria.

Languages: English is the official language. Hausa, Yoruba, Ibo, and Fulani are also spoken.

Ethnic Groups: Hausa and Fulani in the north, along with Yoruba in the southwest and Ibos in the southeast, together make up 65 percent of population. Other ethnic groups include the Edo, Ijaw, and Ibibio in the south, the Nupe and Tiv in the central part of the country, and the Kanuri in the northeast.

Religions: Muslim 50 percent; Christian 40 percent; indigenous beliefs 10 percent.

Climate: Nigeria has two distinct climatic zones: high humidity and heavy rainfall along the coast, and dry and dusty conditions in the north. The temperature varies considerably with the season, as does rainfall, of which there is far less in the north than in the south.

Land, Plants, and Animals: Along the coast the Niger delta region, mangrove forests and swamps extend inland some 100 km (some 60 mi). North of the coast is a forested belt, rising to the Jos Plateau. Farther north is a savanna region and a semidesert zone in the extreme north. Vegetation zones in Nigeria parallel the climatic zones. In the south the well-watered zone is partly covered by dense tropical forests containing hardwoods such as mahogany and obeche and abundant oil palms. In the plateau and savanna regions forests give way to grasslands and such hardy trees as the baobab and the tamarind. In the extreme northeast semidesert vegetation prevails. Crocodiles and snakes are found in the swamps and rain forest zones. Most large animals have disappeared from heavily populated areas. Some antelope, camels, and hyenas live in the north.

Natural Resources: Petroleum, tin, columbite, iron ore, coal, limestone, lead, zinc, and natural gas

Currency: The naira (N)

Gross Domestic Product (GDP): $132.7 billion (1996 estimate)

GDP per Capita: $1,300 (1996 estimate)

GDP Real Growth Rate: 3.3 percent (1996 estimate)

Primary Economic Activities: Agriculture, mining, manufacturing, and services

Primary Crops: Yams, cassava, sorghum, rice, millet, maize, sugar cane, taro, plantains, peanuts, palm oil, chiles and green peppers, tomatoes, palm kernels, cotton lint, cacao beans, livestock, and poultry

Industries: Crude oil, coal, tin, columbite, palm oil, peanuts, cotton, rubber, wood, hides and skins, textiles, cement and other construction materials, food products, footwear, chemicals, fertilizer, printing, ceramics, and steel

Primary Exports: Oil, cocoa, and rubber

Primary Imports: Machinery, transportation equipment, manufactured goods, chemicals, and food

Primary Trade Partners: United States, Europe, and Japan

Government: Nigeria has been a military government since 1983, and its 1979 constitution remained in force until May 1999. In June 1998 the country's repressive president, Gen. Sani Abacha, died suddenly. His replacement, Gen. Abdulsalam Abubakar, pledged to hold elections and transfer power to a civilian government on May 29, 1999. A former military leader, Gen. Olusegun Obasanjo, won the nationwide elections in February

1999 with 62 percent of the vote; he assumed the office of president in May 1999. The National Assembly consists of a 360-member House of Representatives and a 109-seat Senate.

Nkomo, Joshua

(b. June 19, 1917, Semokwe Reserve, Southern Rhodesia, now Zimbabwe; d. July 1, 1999, Harare, Zimbabwe), nationalist leader and politician in Zimbabwe.

From humble beginnings, Joshua Nkomo rose to become a leading nationalist figure and prominent politician in independent Zimbabwe. After attending elementary school in Southern Rhodesia, Nkomo traveled to South Africa for high school in Durban and college in Johannesburg. He returned to Rhodesia in 1947, becoming a social worker for the railways and then secretary of the Railway Worker's Association. An effective organizer, in 1952 Nkomo was elected president of the Southern Rhodesia African National Congress, or ANC, and represented African opinion in the Central African Federation.

After the ANC was banned, Nkomo, in London, was elected president of the new Rhodesian National Democratic Party, or NDP, in absentia in 1960. The NDP was also banned, reforming as the increasingly militant Zimbabwe African People's Union, or ZAPU, with Nkomo as president. Soon afterward many of his cohorts left ZAPU to form the Zimbabwe African National Union, or ZANU. From 1964 to 1974 Nkomo remained either in confinement or restricted to certain areas, rarely appearing in public. Nevertheless, his stature grew as ZAPU built a conventional army and carried out attacks on the Rhodesian establishment. After his release Nkomo worked hard to negotiate a peaceful transition to independence; fought to retain his position in ZAPU in the face of opposition from younger, more militant members; and, later, led ZAPU from Zambia in its fight against the Rhodesian regime.

In the transition to independence, Robert Mugabe and ZANU disavowed Nkomo, leading to ZAPU's electoral defeat. Nkomo became the minister of home affairs but was soon forced from office when Mugabe cracked down on opposition parties, particularly ZAPU. Outside of government he retained a huge popular following among the Ndebele people in southern and western Zimbabwe. In 1988, with the creation of the united ZANU-PF, Nkomo reentered the government as a senior minister and as one of two vice presidents. He transferred his allegiance to ZANU-PF and, although promoting development in Matabeleland, remained strongly aligned with the policies of Mugabe and ZANU. When Nkomo stepped down from his government positions in late 1997 in ill health, the question of who would succeed him as the de facto leader of the Ndebele remained unclear. Nkomo died at age 82 in July 1999.

Nkrumah, Kwame (Francis Nwia Kofi Nkrumah)

(b. September 21, 1909, Nkroful, Gold Coast [present-day Ghana]; d. April 27, 1972, Bucharest, Romania), leading nationalist and prime minister of the Gold Coast from 1952 until its independence in 1957; later prime minister (1957–1960) and president (1960–1966) of independent Ghana.

Leader of the first sub-Saharan African colony to gain independence, Kwame Nkrumah was a towering figure in the Pan-African movement and a tireless advocate of an independent African socialism. Nkrumah was born into a Nzima family in the southwestern Gold Coast. His father was a goldsmith and his mother a retail market trader. A baptized Roman Catholic, Nkrumah attended the Roman Catholic mission school in the nearby town of Half Assini and graduated from another Roman Catholic school in Sekondi. He studied teaching at Achimota College. After teaching in the early 1930s Nkrumah considered becoming a Jesuit priest, but decided to study in the United States instead. He earned degrees from Lincoln University and the University of Pennsylvania. Nkrumah's political philosophy began to develop as he studied the international socialism of Marx and Lenin, the African nationalist writings of American leader Marcus Garvey, and the nonviolence of Mohandas Gandhi. He also met W. E. B. Du Bois and George Padmore, leading advocates of Pan-Africanism.

When he moved to England in 1945 to earn a doctorate degree from the London School of Economics, Nkrumah became secretary of the West African Students Union and helped organize the fifth Pan-African Congress in Manchester. He also wrote three pamphlets on fighting colonialism and met other future leaders, including Jomo Kenyatta of Kenya and Kamuzu Banda of Malawi. In 1947 Nkrumah returned to Africa to become secretary general of United Gold Coast Convention (UGCC), a party calling for self-government in the Gold Coast, at the invitation of its leaders, including Joseph B. Danquah. Membership in the party increased as Nkrumah toured the region, urging Africans to unite. In 1948 the British colonial governor, Gerald Creasy, blamed rioting and looting on the party's activities and ordered the arrests of Danquah and Nkrumah. Police found a Communist Party membership card in Nkrumah's possession, but it was not signed and Nkrumah denied ever having joined the party, calling himself a Marxist-socialist and nondenominational Christian. Later that year he established the *Accra Evening News*. In 1949 Nkrumah broke with the UGCC because its middle-class leaders distrusted his more radical populism; he formed the Convention People's Party (CPP), which advocated mass action in the form of boycotts, strikes, and civil disobedience to gain independence.

This strategy led to Nkrumah's arrest and imprisonment on charges of "subversion" and "sedition," which won him widespread public sympathy. In February 1951 the CPP won 34 of the 38 popularly contested seats in the Legislative Assembly. Consequently, the British administration released Nkrumah from jail. On the next day, Governor Charles Arden-Clarke summoned him to Christiansborg Castle in Accra and asked him to lead the new government in cooperation with the colonial administration. He took office as prime minister in 1952 and guided the country to independence on March 6, 1957, with the name Ghana. In 1960 a new constitution made Ghana a republic, with Nkrumah as president.

At first the Nkrumah administration was widely popular. Nkrumah brought Africans into the government, offered free education, provided scholarships for study abroad, built hospitals, and paved roads. But the borrowing necessary to pay for domestic spending pushed Ghana into debt. His government abandoned its 1959 Development Plan two years later in the face of mounting financial problems. Meanwhile, Nkrumah became increasingly autocratic. He introduced laws enabling the government to jail without trial people who were labeled security risks. In 1961 Nkrumah strengthened his grip on the CPP. Later that year he introduced a law under which anyone found guilty of insulting Nkrumah faced a three-year prison term. Economic troubles, worsened by falling cocoa prices, generated labor unrest and a general strike in 1961. Following the strike Nkrumah assumed command of the armed forces and dismissed all foreign officers. In 1964 Nkrumah declared Ghana a one-party state, and his government tightened censorship. Several assassination attempts prompted Nkrumah's increasing isolation, a substantial increase in the internal security apparatus, and the number of political prisoners.

While the situation within Ghana deteriorated, Nkrumah continued to advocate Pan-Africanism internationally. From 1960 to 1963 Ghanaian troops served with United Nations forces in Congo-Kinshasa. Ghana became a charter member of the Organization of African Unity in 1963. Also that year Nkrumah published his book, *Why Africa Must Unite*. On February 24, 1966, while Nkrumah was visiting Beijing and Hanoi in an effort to end the Vietnam War, a military coup ousted him from office. He went into exile in Guinea. He wrote *Handbook for Revolutionary Warfare* (1968) and *Class Struggle in Africa* (1970). Nkrumah died in 1972 while seeking cancer treatment in Romania.

North America

Norman, Jessye

(b. September 15, 1945, Augusta, Ga.), African American opera singer.

Jessye Norman is a dramatic soprano whose rich voice is recognized for its strength, warmth and intensity, dynamic coloration, affective depth, and impressive range—from the E above high C to the E below middle C. She is one of five children from an educated and musical family. Her mother, Janie

(King), is an amateur pianist. Her father, Silas, an insurance broker, often sang in Augusta's Mount Calvary Baptist Church, the site of Norman's earliest singing performances.

Norman entered Howard University in 1963 on a full-tuition scholarship to train under voice instructor Carolyn Grant, and received her B.Mus. degree cum laude in 1967. The following year she won the International Music Competition in Munich. This showing won her a 1969 operatic debut with the *Deutsche Oper* and many subsequent performances before German and Italian audiences. The glowing reviews from these European recitals, her 1972 United States appearances, and her recordings for Philips Records attracted a sellout crowd to her January 21, 1973, New York debut in the Great Performers series at Lincoln Center.

Norman is an internationally recognized performer and is considered to have excellent stylistic and linguistic command of the French, German, and Italian compositions of the operatic canon. She has broadened her performance repertoire by reintroducing lesser-known works, including significant interpretations of theater songs and African American spirituals, to the appreciation of audiences and critics alike. In addition to performing as a recording artist, guest orchestral soloist, and recitalist, Norman directs master classes.

North America

Notorious B.I.G. ("Biggie Smalls") (Christopher Wallace)

(b. 1972, New York, N.Y.; d. March 9, 1997, Los Angeles, Calif.), African American rap artist murdered in 1997.

Notorious B.I.G.'s debut album, *Ready to Die*, appeared on Sean "Puffy" Combs's Bad Boy Entertainment music label in 1995. The record was a critical and commercial success, exhibiting the rapper's lyrical talents through a series of taut, first-person narratives chronicling life as a hustler on the streets of New York's Bedford-Stuyvesant neighborhood. The grim humor of B.I.G.'s lyrics emphasized the claustrophobia of his ghetto universe; on "Warning," he raps, "There's gonna be a lot of slow singing / and flower bringing / If my burglar alarm starts ringing." Songs like "Suicidal Thoughts" and "Things Done Changed" helped create one of gangsta rap's most sophisticated personas, a strange brew of subdued self-loathing and energetic violence. In B.I.G.'s world, the sexual boasting typical of hip hop became an occasion for self-parody, as on *#!*@ Me (Interlude)*, a skit describing a sexual encounter complicated by the rapper's prodigious girth.

Soon after the success of his debut album, B.I.G. found himself immersed in a simmering feud with Los Angeles gangsta rap label Death Row Records, in a manifestation of hip hop's growing coastal animosity. Death Row star Tupac Shakur claimed that B.I.G. and Combs were behind a 1994 robbery in which Shakur was shot five times in the chest. The violent climate turned fatal in September 1996, when Shakur was murdered in a mysterious Las Vegas drive-by shooting; some suggested that the Bad Boy Entertainment crew was involved. Soon after, in March 1997, Notorious B.I.G. was gunned down while making an appearance in Los Angeles.

B.I.G.'s posthumously released double album, *Life After Death* (1997), topped the Billboard album charts and sold more than 7 million copies, thanks to radio-friendly songs like "Mo Money Mo Problems" and "Hypnotize." Death has only enhanced B.I.G.'s legend: Sean "Puffy" Combs's "I'll Be Missing You," a tribute to his fallen friend, was one of the best-selling singles of 1997.

Ntare II (d. 1852),

considered the first monarch of present-day Burundi.

Although fifth in a line of Burundian kings, Ntare II is widely regarded as the first monarch of the nation, because it was during his reign that the kingdom expanded to the borders of present-day Burundi. Born Rugaamba, he ascended the throne upon the death of his father, Mwambutswa I, and took the name Ntare, meaning "skin of the lion."

Ntare II conquered outlying chieftainships until his own kingdom included parts of present-day Rwanda and Tanzania, establishing himself in history as one of Burundi's most powerful kings. Although the spoils of his victories went to his sons, several of them ultimately rebelled. The families of these rebellious sons became known as the Batare clan, and the family of Ntare II's successor son, Gisabo Mwezi IV, became known as the Bezi. Conflicts between the two clans influenced Burundian politics long before the conflicts between the Hutu and Tutsi. Ntare II died in 1852.

Nubia,

a historical region encompassing present-day southern Egypt and northern Sudan.

What was Nubia? This has always been a controversial question. The controversy stems from difficulties in determining the origin of the name Nubia, the time when Nubia first appeared in history, and its geographical limits. There is general agreement among most scholars that the name derives from *nob*, the Nubian word for gold, and is linked to the importance of gold to the Nubians.

However, recent research is looking into other possibilities. The modern

Nubian word *kiji* means "fertile land, dark gray mud, silt, or black land"; the sound of this word is near to the Egyptian name Kish or Kush, referring to the land south of Egypt. It is believed that the name Kush also meant "the land of dark silt" or "the black land." This was the Egyptian name for Nubia.

We know from ancient and recent analogies that peoples do not always adopt the name attributed to them by others. Therefore it is likely that the Egyptian's Kushites had their own name for their home, which must have had the same meaning as Kush: the black land. It was Nubia, the black land, the Sudan of today, which is a straightforward Arabic translation: *sud* is the plural form of *aswad*, meaning "black"; *an* means "of the"; thus, Sudan means "of the blacks." In modern Nubian, *nugud* means "black." So do *nuger*, *nugur*, and *nub*. This suggests that Kush, Nubia, and Sudan all mean the same thing—the "black land" and/or the "land of the blacks."

It is evident both historically and archaeologically that Nubia's boundaries have fluctuated through time. In other words, there were times when Nubian rule and cultural influence were limited to lower and middle Nubia, in the Sudanese-Egyptian borderlands; at other times Nubia covered all of present-day northern Sudan, while its cultural influence extended to an even vaster territory.

However, in modern times, Nubia typically refers to the region along the Nile River between the first cataract (just south of Aswan in Egypt) and present-day Ed Debba in Sudan, where Nubian speakers live today. The region borders the Nubian Desert to the east and the Libyan Desert to the west. Land suitable for farming is confined to scattered plots along the riverbanks. Modern Nubians live in the region's many irki (villages or communities), which are distributed unevenly on both sides of the Nile and on islands within the course of the river, wherever there is land suitable for cultivation.

From this description it is obvious that Nubia is not rich in resources. Why then was Nubia subject to repeated raids and domination by its neighbors, especially Egypt to the north? First, Egypt tried to expand its authority over Nubia to secure its southern frontier. Second, Egyptians greatly desired Nubian natural resources, in the form of gold, copper, diorite stones used to build royal monuments, and African animal products. Third, the Egyptians sought African slaves for many purposes.

The trade in natural resources and slaves between Egypt and the African interior, together with the fertile riverine ecology of the Nile and its banks, encouraged settlement in Nubia from early times. And despite the scarcity of land for cultivation, agricultural activities were and still are the basis of the subsistence economy of most Nubians. To compensate for the limited quantity of land, the Nubians adopted intensive rather than extensive cultivation. Moreover, in recent years the Nubian economy has increasingly relied on income from Nubians working outside their country, particularly in the Middle East.

Nubia has never been the exclusive domain of any one group of people. Foreign conquerors, alien merchants and adventurers, and both friendly and hostile nomads have always interacted with and settled among the indigenous peasant population of Nubia and have contributed significantly to its cultural development. Hence the present population is the product of a long and fairly continuous mingling of the ancient inhabitants with new-comers from a variety of places.

In the seventh century Arab tribesmen settled in Nubia and intermar-ried with the indigenous population. During the sixteenth century the Ottoman sultan Salim sent garrisons into Nubia, composed largely of sol-diers from Bosnia, Circassia, Hungary, and Kurdistan. They were stationed at Aswan, Gasr Ibrim, and Sai to protect Egypt's southern borders. Their descendants (known as al-Kushaf), born of Nubian women and speaking only the Nubian language, regarded themselves as Bosnians or Turks rather than Nubians and claimed special privileges on this basis as late as the nine-teenth century. Consequently, one can say that Nubian society now consists of a mixture of indigenous as well as Arab and Turkish elements.

Other groups of non-Nubians inhabit the area. They are small in number and made up of descendants of slaves and nomadic and seminomadic groups. Descendants of slaves who have been living with Nubians for generations and are accustomed to their ways of life can be regarded cultur-ally as Nubians. They work mainly in domestic service and farming. Other non-Nubians in the region include Arab tribes, mainly Bisharia and Gararish, who raise camels. They play an important role in the Nubian economy and society. During the nineteenth and early twentieth centuries, Arab camel drivers provided the only means of transporting heavy loads, but during the late twentieth century the Arabs have been obliged to adopt a settled life beside the Nile and have begun to cultivate small plots leased from the Nubians. They have no land rights, and although they use the Nubian language to communicate with Nubians, they are linguistically and culturally distinct from them. This ethnic diversity reflects Nubia's ancient history as a cultural crossroads.

Africa

Nwapa, Flora (full name Florence Nwanzuruahu Nkiru Nwapa)

(b. January 18, 1931, Oguta, Nigeria; d. October 16, 1993, Enugu, Nigeria), Nigerian author of children's books and novels dealing with the transformation of women's roles.

Nigeria's best-known woman writer, Flora Nwapa was also a teacher, busi-nesswoman, and government official. Her multiple careers echo the compli-cated lives of her fictional female characters: women who grow beyond the traditional ambitions of wife and motherhood to seek economic and per-sonal independence. Nwapa changed her society through business as well as art, founding Tana Press Limited and Flora Nwapa Books. She was, in fact, the first African woman to own and operate a publishing house.

Nwapa was the eldest daughter in a large and relatively wealthy Igbo family. After traveling to the United States for further study in 1965, Nwapa returned to Lagos, where, with the help of novelist Chinua Achebe, she found a publisher for her first novel, *Efuru* (1966). Nwapa, who later said that she never planned to become a writer, had begun the book while working as a teacher and quickly realized that she had "a good story to tell." Like many of her subsequent novels, *Efuru* was about a woman struggling with the traditional roles of wife and mother. Between the publication of *Efuru* and *Idu* (1970), Nwapa served as minister of Nigeria's East Central State during the turmoil of the Nigerian Civil War (also called the Biafran War). Her 1980 short story collection, *Wives at War*, describes the importance of women to the Biafran cause, both as family wage earners and as expert bargainers who negotiated with the enemy for needed supplies. She married and had her second child (the first was born while Nwapa was single). A third child was born in 1971, and shortly thereafter Nwapa, at the suggestion of writer Christopher Okigbo, began writing children's books.

Nwapa's government career continued after the war; she was appointed commissioner for health and social welfare in 1971 and later headed the Commission for Lands, Survey, and Urban Development. Her belief that Nigerian women deserved a greater role in politics was inspired by both modern feminism and Igbo political traditions, in which priestesses held great power. Establishing her own publishing house in 1977, Nwapa took control of her literary career, which many critics believe reached its peak in the 1980s.

One Is Enough (1981) attacks multiple marriage—a widespread custom in Nigeria—and features a heroine who chooses single motherhood over subservience. *Women Are Different* (1986) reasserts women's need for economic independence, as does *Wives at War* (1980), a collection of short stories that deals with the disintegration of traditional society following civil strife. Since her death in 1993, Nwapa has been hailed as a literary pioneer who gave eloquent voice to the lives of African women.

Latin America and the Caribbean

Nyabinghi,

ceremonial music of the Rastafarian faith played at ritual meetings called *groundings* or *grounations*; often refers to ceremonies held to mark special occasions.

The birth of Rastafarianism in Jamaica in the late 1930s brought with it the need for a liturgical music based on African sources, rather than the European-influenced Jamaican folk music. Dissatisfied with the Revivalist Afro-European hymns rewritten with Rastafarian lyrics, Rastas turned to the drumming of the rural Burru men for inspiration. The Burrus originally worked on plantations but relocated to urban centers as agricultural work declined. Considered disreputable by mainstream Jamaicans, the Burrus found fraternity among the equally downtrodden Rastafarians. The two groups shared proximity while living in West Kingston ghettos. Burru music was performed at Christmas time and to welcome released prisoners back into the community. Burru featured a West African rhythmic base with sung and chanted accompaniment. Rastas swiftly embraced Burru drumming as their own liturgical music. The Burrus in turn adopted Rastafarianism, and with this exchange the two groups combined into one.

Music of the neo-African Kumina cult also influenced the evolution of Rastafarian nyabinghi. Nyabinghi uses three drums: the bass (used for timekeeping), the funde (used for syncopation), and the repeater (featured in improvisational solos). Religious nyabinghi is called "churchical" and employs slow, ponderous drumming. The secular version, known as "heartical," relies on a lighter, faster sound. The term nyabinghi originally meant "death to the white oppressors and their black allies." Passage of time softened the definition into "death to evil forces." The music is played continually throughout Rastafarian grounation ceremonies, often called reasonings, where believers discuss biblical Scripture and philosophy, often sharing a "chalice" filled with *ganja*, or marijuana (considered a holy sacrament by many Rastafarians).

Nyabinghi has exerted a profound influence on reggae music. Renowned Rasta drummer Count Ossie held lengthy open jams in Kingston during the late 1940s. Roots reggae songs featuring *nyabinghi* influences surfaced regularly. Bob Marley's "Rastaman Chant" is an excellent example of the churchical style fused with reggae.

Obasanjo, Olusegun

(b. March 5, 1937, Abeokuta, in Ogun State, Nigeria), former military officer and head of state; writer, agricultural reformer, and international activist; president of Nigeria (1999–).

Olusegun Obasanjo was born to a Christian Yoruba family that lacked the means to send him to college. He excelled at the provincial Abeokuta Baptist High School, however, and when he enlisted in the army in 1958 it was partly with an eye toward further schooling. During his tenure as a soldier he studied in both India and England.

Obasanjo specialized in engineering and rose through the ranks of Nigeria's Engineering Corps. Later, while serving as head of state, he credited this military training for the systematic clarity of his thought. Between 1959 and 1976 Obasanjo advanced from second lieutenant to chief of staff, supreme headquarters. During this time he led Nigerian forces in the country's civil war (1969–1970), and he accepted the surrender of the Biafran troops in 1970.

Obasanjo was devoted to military service but appeared to have a limited appetite for power. He claimed that his ascendance to head of state after Murtala Muhammad's assassination in 1976 was "not my will." This reticence distinguished Obasanjo as the only Nigerian leader ever to relinquish power peacefully, which he did three years later.

Obasanjo's regime faced the task of preparing Nigeria for civilian rule. He oversaw the Constituent Assembly that drafted the constitution and ensured that the transition occurred according to the initial timetable. He also worked to integrate Nigeria's profusion of trade unions into the National Labor Congress. After the 1979 election Obasanjo duly handed over power to the elected government.

Obasanjo retired from the government and military service and took up farming in his home region. He made this move partly out of concern for the country's agricultural development, which suffered, in his view, from a lack of esteem for farming and farmers in Nigeria. He also continued his studies, at the University of Ibadan.

Obasanjo, though not directly active in politics, remained a steady critic of Nigerian political life. As a consequence, the repressive Nigerian military government imprisoned him in 1995 under charges of "concealing treason." He was sentenced to death, but after international protest the sentence was commuted to 15 years in prison. He was released in June 1998 after the death of Gen. Sani Abacha. Gen. Abdusalam Abubakar assumed the role of president and, following the death of a popular opposition figure, Moshood K. O. Abiola, announced a timetable for elections and a return to civilian rule. In the February 1999 elections General Obasanjo ran for the presidency against Olu Falae and won.

Africa

Obiang Nguema Mbasogo, Teodoro

(b. 1942, Acoacan, Equatorial Guinea), president of Equatorial Guinea (1996-).

Born to the Esangui (Fang) ethnic group at Acoacan in mainland Equatorial Guinea, Obiang Nguema went to secondary school in Bata and underwent military training at Saragossa Military Academy in Spain from 1963 to 1965. His uncle Francisco Macías Macías Nguema was elected Equatorial Guinea's first president in 1968, and Obiang Nguema was appointed military governor of the island of Fernando Po. In 1975 he became the tyrannical President Macías Macías Nguema's personal aide-de-camp (military assistant). Early in 1979 one of Obiang Nguema's brothers, who complained about not receiving the wages he was due, was executed on Macías Macías Nguema's orders, and Obiang Nguema began plotting the overthrow of his uncle. In August 1979 Obiang Nguema, then a lieutenant-colonel, seized power with the support of the Supreme Military Council. Obiang Nguema proclaimed an amnesty for refugees overseas and released an estimated 5000 political prisoners, but his close identification with the Macías Macías Nguema regime (even after Macías Macías Nguema's trial and execution) meant that most were still afraid to return home.

After being sworn in as president in October 1979, Obiang Nguema continued his uncle's policies of absolute personal control and extensive corruption. He took over companies he coveted, executed opponents, and ruled through a single-party state. A series of coup attempts was harshly subdued. A new constitution approved by 95 percent of the voters in 1982 provided for a return to civilian government after a seven-year transitional period, but it also gave Obiang Nguema nearly total powers as president. Although in 1985 and 1986 the United Nations Human Rights Commission complained of repeated flagrant violations of human rights in the country, Obiang was reelected in 1996.

Ogot, Grace

(b. 1930-), Kenyan author of short stories and novels; the first female writer from Kenya to win international attention. She is one of the most widely read short story writers from that country.

Born Grace Emily Akinyi in the village of Butere in western Kenya, Grace Ogot received her early education in local schools before training as a nurse in Uganda and England. After working as a nurse in the 1950s in Kenya and Uganda, Ogot's career followed several different routes, although her writing continued to draw on her nursing experience.

Ogot worked as a broadcaster and script writer for the British Broadcasting Corporation in London in 1959 and 1960 and later as an announcer on a weekly radio magazine program in the Luo and Kiswahili languages for the Voice of Kenya broadcasting company. Her career moved in a literary direction in the early 1960s, and she wrote most of her works in English. Her first novel, *The Promised Land* (1966), explores the issue of marriage in modern Kenya, especially a woman's relationship to her husband. It also considers the relation of past and present in traditional and modern medicine. In her work Ogot focuses on the preservation of family and on the sacrifices made to achieve that goal. She is also committed to showing the truths embodied in traditional law and folk wisdom. Both of these issues appear as themes in her short-story collections *Land Without Thunder* (1968) and *The Other Woman* (1976).

In 1975 and 1976 Ogot lived in New York City, first as a delegate to the General Assembly of the United Nations (UN) and then as a member of the Kenya delegation to the United Nations Educational, Scientific and Cultural Organization (UNESCO). The short story collection *The Island of Tears* (1980) reflects her UN experiences as well as her interest in the common ancestry of African Americans and Africans. Ogot later became involved in politics and served in the National Assembly, the legislative branch of Kenya's government, from 1983 to 1992. Her other works include the novella *The Graduate* (1980) and the Luo-language novel *Miaha* (1983; translated as *The Strange Bride* 1989).

Okigbo, Christopher

(b. August 16, 1932, Ojoto, Nigeria; d. August 1967, Nsukka, Nigeria), Nigerian poet.

Born in Ojoto, a small village in eastern Nigeria, Christopher Okigbo was the fourth of five children of a Catholic school teacher of Igbo heritage. He attended Catholic schools, the Umuahia Government College (secondary school), and the University of Ibadan, receiving a degree in classics in 1956. He worked as a teacher, an editor, a librarian at the University of Nsukka, and as secretary to the Nigerian minister of research and information; he was also the West African editor of the journal *Transition*. He published two volumes of poetry—*Heavensgate* (1962) and *Limits* (1964)—as well as poems in the journals *Horn*, *Black Orpheus*, and *Transition*. His work shows the influence of Igbo mythology and the American modernists as well as his training in Greek and Latin.

Offered the poetry prize at the 1966 Dakar Festival of Negro Arts, Okigbo declined it because he thought it racially exclusive to black writers. "There is no such thing as Negro art," he said. Deeply committed to political change, he resisted the 1930s neologism Négritude, a concept introduced by Aimé Césaire and Léopold Sédar Senghor that describes a particular mode of black experience and artistic expression. He also showed little interest in the opinions of critics and literary theorists. He was planning to establish a publishing house along with Nigerian writer Chinua Achebe when he was killed while fighting on the Biafran side during the Biafran war of independence from Nigeria. His collected poems were published as *Labyrinths with Path of Thunder* (1971).

Africa

Okri, Ben

(b. March 15, 1959, Minna, Nigeria), prize-winning Nigerian-British author whose work incorporates elements of magical realism and social commentary.

Ben Okri, the son of a British-educated tenants' lawyer, was born in Nigeria to parents of the Urhobo ethnic group. Through his father's work, Okri was exposed to the world of the dispossessed; through myths and folktales as well as Western classics, he discovered the landscape of the imagination. He finished school at age 14 and went on to spend the next five years writing. His first publication was an article on a rent edict, but he soon turned to writing short stories for Nigerian women's journals and evening papers.

In 1978 Okri went to England to study philosophy and English at the University of Essex. Two years later he published his first novel, *Flowers and Shadows*. In chronicling a son's discovery of his businessman father's legacy of corruption, the story depicts the moral disintegration of contemporary Nigeria. His next work, *The Landscapes Within* (1981), was a novel Okri described as a "double mirror" of two realities: the psychic world of the artist and the chaos of daily life. Although *The Landscapes Within* gives an account of what Okri has called "the violent relations" of Nigeria, it marked a shift toward his growing preoccupation with the spiritual world.

During the next six years Okri worked as a journalist for BBC Television's African department and as a poetry editor for *West Africa* magazine. His short stories and poetry received growing recognition and were published in prominent journals such as *Paris Review*, *New Statesman*, *Firebird*, and *PEN New Fiction*. In 1986 he published *Incidents at the Shrine*, a collection of short stories that won the *Paris Review* Aga Khan Prize for Fiction, and, the following year, the *Commonwealth Writers* Prize for Africa. Set in the seamy urban underworld of Nigeria and England, Shrine blurs the boundaries between the "real world" and the world of the dream. In Okri's next collection, *Stars of the New Curfew* (1988), Okri moved further into the literary realm known as magical realism.

Okri's Booker Prize-winning novel *The Famished Road* (1991) is told from the view-point of Azaro, who is an abiku, a child believed to be caught in a cycle of death and rebirth. Set in the squalor of the ghetto, the novel's experimental storyline, which Okri characterizes as "open toward infinity," mirrors the cyclical and eternal nature of the abiku cycle. Okri continued the story of Azaro in *Songs of Enchantment* (1993), setting even more of the narrative in the spiritual world.

The novel *Astonishing the Gods* (1995) recounts a man's transformative explorations of an enchanted island. Okri's most recent works are *Birds of Heaven* (1996), *Dangerous Love* (1996), and *A Way of Being Free* (1997).

Africa

Olajuwon, Hakeem

(b. January 21, 1963, Lagos, Nigeria), Nigerian-born basketball player.

One of the first African professional basketball players in the United States, Hakeem Olajuwon did not take up the game until he was 15. The third of six children, Olajuwon had been a standout high-school soccer player. The 2.06 m (6 ft, 9 in) teenager was discovered by the coach of the Nigerian national basket-ball team, and by age 17 he was receiving recruitment offers from several United States colleges. Olajuwon chose the University of Houston, which he entered in 1981. Sitting out one year to gain weight and focus on the sport's fundamentals, Olajuwon, soon nick-named "the Dream," was starting at center by his sophomore year. Twice he took his team to the final four of the National Collegiate Athletic Association (NCAA) basketball tournament. At the end of his junior year Olajuwon entered the draft of the National Basketball Association (NBA).

Now 2.13 m (7 ft) tall and weighing 107 kg (235 lb), Olajuwon was the first player chosen in the 1984 NBA draft. As a rookie for the Houston Rockets he soon established himself as one of the league's best players, averaging 20.6 points and 11.9 rebounds per game. Over the next decade Olajuwon played in 12 All-Star games and won Most Valuable Player for the league (1993–94 season) as well as for the playoff finals (1993–94, 1994–95). In 1996 he was named one of the NBA's 50 greatest players of all time. Despite his intelligent play and brilliant athleticism, Olajuwon's criticism of management has earned him a mixed reputation, and his Nigerian accent has denied him the lucrative endorsement contracts lesser NBA stars enjoy.

O'Leary, Hazel Rollins

(b. May 17, 1937, Newport News, Va.), African American public official, first female Secretary of Energy.

Hazel O'Leary was raised by her father, Russell E. Reid, a physician, and by her stepmother. She earned a B.A. from Fisk University in Nashville, Tennessee, in 1959, and a J.D. from Rutgers University Law School in 1966.

From 1974 to 1980 O'Leary worked in the Federal Energy Administration (later part of the Department of Energy), reaching the position of chief of the Economic Regulatory Administration. She worked at her own energy consulting firm from 1980 to 1989. She was president of Northern States Power Company in 1993, when President Bill Clinton appointed her Secretary of Energy.

Oliver, Joseph ("King")

(b. May 11, 1885, Donaldsville, La.; d. April 8, 1938, Savannah, Ga.), African American cornetist and bandleader; pioneering figure in New Orleans- and Chicago-style jazz.

Joseph Oliver was born in Donaldsville, Louisiana. After his family moved to New Orleans he learned to play the trombone from local street musicians. He soon switched to the cornet and trumpet, and by 1907 Oliver had begun to play professionally with various local brass bands.

From 1916 to 1919 Oliver played in Edward "Kid" Ory's band. Ory gave him the moniker "King" because he was the best cornetist in the most popular jazz band in New Orleans. In 1918 Oliver was courted by bassist/banjoist Bill Johnson to join his band in Chicago, Illinois. A year later Oliver moved to Chicago, where he became first cornetist in Johnson's Creole Jazz Band. Oliver soon assumed the leadership of the band, taking the group to California from 1920 to 1921.

Returning to Chicago, Oliver solidified the Creole Jazz Band with powerful new members, creating one of the most important ensembles in the history of jazz. From 1922 to 1924 the band included Louis Armstrong on cornet, Honore Dutrey on trombone, Johnny Dodds on clarinet, his brother Baby Dodds on drums, Lil Hardin (Armstrong) on piano, and Bill Johnson on bass and banjo. Featuring a "wa-wa" cornet sound and polyphonic four-to-the-beat rhythmic attack, such performances as "Dipper Mouth Blues," "Riverside Blues," and "Snake Rag" influenced a new generation of jazz musicians that included many aspiring white performers.

The Creole Jazz Band disbanded after Armstrong left. Oliver then recorded several duos with the great Jelly Roll Morton during 1924. From 1924 through 1927 Oliver led the Dixie Syncopators, made up of former Creole Jazz Band members along with trombonist "Kid" Ory and clarinetist and saxophonist Barney Bigard. From 1930 until 1937 he led several bands on tours of the Midwest and the South, but did not play after 1931 due to painful gum disease. Oliver retired from music in 1937.

Africa

Omotoso, Kole

(b. April 21, 1943, Akure, Western State, Nigeria), Nigerian novelist, poet, and critic who has maintained a commitment to address the common people of Africa.

Kole Omotoso was born into a Yoruba family in the Western State of Nigeria. Inspired by his uncle, the author Olaiya Fagbamigbe, and evenings spent listening to Yoruba folk-tales, after an education in local schools Omotoso published stories while at King's College in Lagos. He earned a bachelor of arts degree in French and Arabic from the University of Ibadan in 1968 and a docorate in modern Arabic literature from the Univer-sity of Edinburgh in Scotland in 1972. He returned to Nigeria to write and teach and took a post as professor at the University of Ibadan in 1976.

Influenced by the Nigerian writer Wole Soyinka, Omotoso's increasingly political writings have dealt with issues affecting Africa's future from the perspective of ordinary people. Omotoso believes in the power of the arts to bring social change. He contributes frequently to magazines and newspapers and has written novels, plays, short stories, essays, and literary criticism. Focusing on Nigeria and Africa, Omoto's works address interracial marriage, the effects of poverty on children, communism, socialism, the Nigerian civil war, and criticisms of materialism and neo-colonialism—especially the relationship of Africa's colonial past to its postcolonial economic problems and ethnic discord.

The tireless Omotoso was a founder of the Association of Nigerian Authors and served as its national secretary and its national president. He also helped found the Union of Writers of the African Peoples in Accra, Ghana, and worked as an editor of *Afriscope* and *Ch'Indaba Magazine*.

In 1991 he made a controversial decision to leave Nigeria for South Africa, which was then still a white-ruled apartheid state. He took a position as professor at the University of the Western Cape, and his writings after 1991 addressed the transition to majority rule in South Africa and the implications of the South African experience for the rest of Africa.

North America

O'Neal, Shaquille

(b. March 6, 1972, Newark, N.J.), African American basketball player, one of the greatest players of the 1990s.

Shaquille O'Neal attended high school in San Antonio, Texas, where he led the school basketball team to the state championship. O'Neal then entered

Louisiana State University (LSU) in 1989. He quickly became a dominating player in college basketball, and he averaged 21.6 points and 13.5 rebounds per game over three seasons. In his last year at LSU he led the nation in blocked shots and was second in rebounding.

In 1992 he entered the National Basketball Association (NBA) draft and was the first player chosen by the Orlando Magic, then a recent expansion team. Although his inexperience was evident in his first professional year, O'Neal's high level of play made him a nearly unanimous choice as rookie of the year for the 1992–1993 season. That year he led the season's rookies in points (23.4), rebounds (13.9), and blocked shots (3.53) per game, and he was second overall in the league in rebounds and eighth overall in scoring. During the 1993–1994 season O'Neal's play continued to improve. He led the NBA in field-goal percentage (.599) and finished second in points (29.3) and rebounds per game (13.2). In 1994 he was also a member of the United States national basketball team known as Dream Team II, which won the gold medal at the world basketball championships in Toronto, Ontario, in Canada.

In the 1994–1995 season O'Neal led the NBA in points per game (29.3) and finished second in field-goal percentage (.583) and third in rebounds per game (11.4). He also led the Magic to the NBA Finals, where the team lost to the Houston Rockets. O'Neal's success continued in the 1995–1996 season, when he was selected as an All-Star for the fourth consecutive year. After the season he played for the U.S. national basketball team at the 1996 Olympic Games in Atlanta, Georgia. In July 1996 O'Neal signed as a free agent with the Los Angeles Lakers; he powered the team to playoff appearances in the 1996–1997 and 1997–1998 seasons. O'Neal appeared in his fifth All-Star game in 1998.

O'Neal also became popular as an entertainer. In 1993 *Shaq Diesel*, a best-selling rap music album, was released. The following year he acted in the motion picture *Blue Chips*. In 1994 he issued a second rap album, *Shaq Fu—Da Return*, and an action-oriented home video game, *Shaq-Fu*, which stars O'Neal as a kung fu warrior. Further entertainment projects included the albums *You Can't Stop the Reign* (1996) and *The Best of Shaquille O'Neal* (1997) as well as a role in the 1997 movie *Steel*.

Cross Cultural

Opera,

musical theater that originated in seventeenth-century Florence, Italy; numerous African Americans have risen to prominence within the genre.

Early nineteenth-century African American opera singers and performers were crossover artists. Barred from all major American stages, they transgressed the boundaries between high and low culture by playing the marginal American concert stages and opera houses that permitted them, as well as minstrel and vaudeville shows. Careers were short lived, usually lasting only two or three years—the length of time it typically took for the novelty of seeing a black singer to wear off on white audiences. Europe often proved a more hospitable climate for African American artists.

Nonetheless, a number of black performers rose to prominence in the American opera scene. Elizabeth Taylor Greenfield—*The Black Swan*—toured North America and England with an African American troupe in the 1850s and 1860s. During the same period the multitalented Luca family included opera in their performances, as did the Hyers Sisters—renowned for their renditions of the works of Verdi and Donizetti. Sissieretta Joyner Jones was the most celebrated opera performer of the time. Known as *Black Patti* after white soprano Adelina Patti, she gave a recital at the White House for President Benjamin Harrison. Jones outlasted her contemporaries—extending her career to 15 years—by forming, in 1896, the Black Patti Troubadours, which mixed opera with musical theater and offered a vehicle to showcase her talents. Similarly, soprano Nellie Brown Mitchell's career lasted almost ten years, thanks to her creation of the Nellie Brown Mitchell Concert Company.

Until the color bar that prevented African Americans from performing on America's greatest stages was lifted, recitals were the quickest way to success for black performers. In 1955 contralto Marian Anderson, thanks to her unmatched talent and the breadth of her repertoire, became the first African American to perform at New York City's Metropolitan Opera, after years of dazzling audiences on recital stages. Anderson's performances, like those of her predecessor, the tenor recitalist Roland Hayes, opened the stages to other opera singers. Both Anderson and Hayes incorporated the concert spiritual—an indigenous African American contribution that fused European art music with black spirituals—into their recitals.

Throughout the mid-twentieth century blacks were usually cast in secondary roles, confined to playing marginal dark-skinned characters. This began to change in 1966. The era of the African American diva began when Mississippi-born soprano Leontyne Price performed at the opening of the new Metropolitan Opera House at New York City's Lincoln Center. By the 1980s the concept of the African American diva had been well established by the glamorous sopranos Jessye Norman and Kathleen Battle.

African American opera companies have developed alongside individual artists. Organizations such as the Colored American Opera Company and the Theodore Drury Opera Company staged productions in the early twentieth century. This work was followed by productions by the Imperial Company, the National Negro Opera Company, the Dra-Mu Opera Company, and the Harlem Opera Company. With the establishment of Opera/ South and the National Ebony Opera in the 1970s, black productions flourished. Their mandate was to create opportunities for professionals.

By the early 1990s mainstream American stages began to reconsider early compositions written by African Americans and to stage productions that conveyed the tragedy and triumph of the black experience. Duke

Ellington's *Queenie Pie* and Leroy Jenkins's *The Mother of Three Sons* were among the first to take part in this mainstream revival. These compositions are part of a body of African American work that includes long-neglected pieces by composers like Harry Laurence Freeman, writer of 14 grand-style operas including the *Octoroon* and the early Jazz opera, *The Flapper*, and ragtime innovator Scott Joplin, who attempted to create an indigenous African American opera in *Treemonisha*. Anthony Davis, founder of the instrumental group Episteme, is the dominant figure in late twentieth-century African American opera composition. His *X: The Life and Times of Malcolm X, Under the Double Moon*, and *Amistad* have all reached well-known United States halls, bringing a contemporary flavor to traditional opera.

Operation Breadbasket,

organization formed by the Southern Christian Leadership Conference (SCLC) and later led by Jesse Jackson that put pressure on corporations to hire blacks and support black businesses.

In 1962 Operation Breadbasket was established by the SCLC to put "bread, money, and income into the baskets of black and poor people." With the mandate of improving the economic conditions of African Americans, Operation Breadbasket organized black consumers to press for jobs and to encourage and expand black-owned businesses. In its first campaign in Atlanta, Georgia, the organization won a commitment from local companies to create 5000 jobs over the next five years.

After establishing affiliates in several Southern states, the organization expanded north. In 1966 Jesse Jackson, then a student at Chicago Theological Seminary, helped found the Chicago chapter, which directed protests at several dairy companies and supermarket chains to demand that they hire black workers and support black-owned businesses. Although the protesters were able to secure promises of employment for black workers from several major corporations, they had trouble ensuring compliance. The A&P supermarket, for example, promised 770 permanent jobs and 1200 summer jobs in May 1967, but did not deliver until another protest was launched in 1970.

As Operation Breadbasket expanded across the country in 1967, Martin Luther King Jr. appointed Jackson to be its national director. From then on the group became increasingly identified with Jackson's high-profile leadership. Under Jackson, Operation Breadbasket took on a number of projects, among them a free breakfast program and the 1968 Poor People's Campaign in Washington, D.C. The organization also became a voice in local and national politics, opposing welfare cuts and supporting electoral candidates.

Operation PUSH,

organization founded by Jesse Jackson in 1971 to promote economic
security for black workers and businesses and to provide assistance to African
American urban youth.

Jesse Jackson left Operation Breadbasket, the economic arm of the
Southern Christian Leadership Conference, in 1971 to found Operation
People United to Save Humanity (PUSH). Like Operation Breadbasket,
the new organization set its sights on strengthening the economic security
of African Americans. Under Jackson's charismatic leadership, Operation
PUSH organized boycotts for black consumers to press for minority
employment and support for black-owned businesses.

   Over the years Operation PUSH expanded its mission and focused on
national issues like education and national politics. In the late 1970s Jackson
brought national attention to the subject of minority education and raised
money for an elementary school education program called PUSH for
Excellence, or PUSH/EXCEL. Despite substantial federal and private support, the education program foundered because of poor administration.
Following accusations of shady business alliances and embezzlement, the
organization scaled down and, by the early 1980s, had reduced its agenda
to consciousness-raising.

   Operation PUSH, which was largely dependent on Jackson's powerful
personality for its success, lost momentum when he left to run in the 1984
presidential election primaries. Jackson remained a spokesperson for the
organization through the 1980s, however, keeping Operation PUSH afloat
through his fundraising efforts. Returning to a more active role in 1991,
Jackson turned the group toward the issues that had been a part of his
election campaign, including the crises of acquired immune deficiency
syndrome (AIDS) and urban violence. In 1993 Operation PUSH began a
program in Chicago to promote education and employment opportunities
for minority youth.

Orishas,

a pantheon of deities in the traditional Yoruba religion of Nigeria and in Yoruba-
derived religious traditions in the African diaspora. The name for these deities
is spelled differently in different languages and cultural areas—orisa in Yoruba,
orixá in Portuguese, and orisha in Spanish—and orishas are also often known
colloquially as *santos*, or saints.

The orishas are not equal to the sky god (Olodumaré), nor do they supplant
him. Rather they are semi-independent divinities capable of working their
own will with or without propitiation (often in the form of offerings) or

Macumba worshipers prepare food for the orishas before a ceremony inducting a novice into their temple in Rio de Janeiro. *CORBIS/Stephanie Maze*

supplication by human beings. They are believed to act in accordance with the wishes of Olodumaré, but they often appear autonomous in their behavior and in how they are worshipped and propitiated. Although their names are the same in all areas, they are spelled differently. For reasons of consistency this essay uses the most common Cuban spelling, unless otherwise indicated.

The religion based on the worship of the orishas is known by several names. In urban Brazil, especially Bahia, Rio de Janeiro, and São Paulo, one form is called Candomblé and another Umbanda. There is a significant difference between these two in that Umbanda incorporates a great deal of the spiritism, or European philosophy developed by the French writer known as Alan Kardec, with a complicated pantheon of spirits that are not orishas. Spiritism is a type of spiritual practice that originated in France in the mid-nineteenth century and combines healing, the summoning of disincarnated spirits, and the practice of charitable activities. Further, in Umbanda humans negotiate neither with God nor with the orishas, who are considered too remote, but rather with lesser spirits.

Farther north in Brazil, in Recife, the religion is known as Xangó; in Trinidad the same term is spelled Shango. Both Xangó and Shango refer to a specific orisha, *Changó*. In the United States and Cuba the orisha religion is called Santería, a colonial term imposed by the Spanish and maintained in academia and journalism. Terms more frequently used by practitioners in the United States and Cuba are *Regla de Ocha* or *Ocha* or simply, "the religion."

Divination constitutes one of two primary activities in the orisha religion. The divination system most frequently used is the 16-cowrie shell system (*dilogun*). It is through this system that the orishas speak and their will can be determined. Typically the diviner throws the cowrie shells onto a special tray. Each orisha corresponds to a specific number and sign, which is indicated by the way the cowrie shells fall. In this manner the diviner ascertains the problem or situation facing the practitioner, what is causing the problem, and which orisha will help.

Another more complicated system of divination is ifa, the tool of the high priests, the *babalawo*s. Ifa divination contains 256 signs, or *odu*, and each sign contains hundreds of verses, each potentially pertaining to the individual's destiny. Here the position of the cowrie shells, or often the position of several necklaces tossed onto a sacred tray, determines which odu is to be interpreted and applied to the particular question or problem put to the *babalawo*. Ifa divination is consulted in all major life changes, such as birth, marriage, and death. Ifa divination can be used for everyday consultations, but also for determining the destiny of the person in a ritual called *Mano de Orúnmila* (Hand of Orúnmila) for men and *Kofa* for women. Ifa divination relays the words and advice of the orisha Orúnmila, who also is in charge of the 16 cowries. Orúnmila never comes to earth, however, and speaks only through ifa divination. Apparently Orúnmila was insulted by the youngest of his 16 sons, who refused to bow to his father (denying him the appropriate greeting to a senior family member in Yoruba culture) and who believed himself as wise and talented as his elder. Orúnmila removed himself to heaven and refused to come back. After being entreated by his children to return to earth, Orúnmila sent instead 16 palm nuts, which would speak in his absence. The palm nuts became the basis of the system of divination known as Ifa.

Through further divination the diviner determines what type of offering should be given to the *orisha* to ensure his or her help. An offering is called an ebo. This cycle of divination and ebo represents the fundamental daily custom of worship in the orisha religion. Since the orishas are embodiment of the forces of nature and manifestations of energy, it is this

A woman in an elaborate ceremonial costume participates in a Camdomblé religious ritual in Belém, Pará, Brazil. *CORBIS/Barnabas Bosshart*

The African deities known as orishas have their own particular colors, symbols, and ritual garments. These two members of a Candomblé in Belém are dressed as Omolú, *left,* and Xangó. *CORBIS/Barnabas Bosshart*

energy that is harnessed through *ebo* to work on behalf of the practitioner.

The other major activity in the orisha religion is possession. The orishas visit the earth and, to do so, they must borrow the body of a devotee who has been ritually prepared and trained to receive them. Mediums can enter a trance state and begin channeling the orisha at any time, whenever the orisha wants to come, but this activity mostly occurs within the context of a party for the orisha. At these parties, called *festas* in Brazil and *tambors* in the United States and Cuba, people gather to hear drumming and singing, and specific members of the group, or "house," dance.

In Brazil festas are highly choreographed performances. The members of the house dance in a circle (*roda* or *roça*); the women wear fine traditional dress consisting of several heavily starched petticoats under a brightly colored full skirt and a lace blouse. They are then wrapped with a large cloth (*pano da costa*), which extends from chest to knees, and finally the costume is tied just under the armpits and tightly across the breasts with a long strip of cloth. The head is always covered with a scarf, often made of lace.

The dancers dance in order of length of time initiated. Songs and dances specific to the orishas are performed in a predetermined order. Interestingly, the order corresponds to that of the Cuban tradition. After the songs have been performed to each orisha, and generally not before, the dancers begin falling into trance and become possessed by their orishas. In Brazil most mediums present become possessed with their orishas.

At this point the mediums are cared for by special priestesses called *ekedes,* whose role is to take care of the belongings of the persons in trance, to bring them out of trance when necessary or at the orders of the house leader, to wipe the sweat off their faces as they dance, and to adjust their clothing. Ekedes go through an initiation process similar to that of a medium, but unlike the medium their head is not shaved, as it was determined through divination that they were not destined to become possessed. In the Cuban tradition there is no official role analogous to the ekede, but frequently a medium brings trusted assistants who essentially perform the same function with him or her.

After the orishas appear and possess their mediums, they dance a little bit and then are taken away from the scene of the dancing and are dressed in ritual clothing specific to their attributes and colors. They are subsequently brought back out to dance and to dispense advice to those present. In the United States and Cuba the orishas are allowed to remain as long as they want at a tambor, and individual supplicants seek their advice. In Brazil, however, the orishas speak much less to individual guests, and they are not free to come and go but are handled skillfully by the ekedes. Each orisha dances for a few songs only, and then leaves. In the Cuban tradition generally only one or two orishas come and take possession of a medium at a tambor, and they stay much longer, being the center of attention while they are at the tambor.

Each orisha has certain attributes corresponding to a natural phenomenon. Changó is represented by lightning and thunder; Oyá or Yansa by the wind; Oko by the farm or agriculture in Cuba and the United States and by the home in Brazil; Agayú by the volcano; Ochún by the river and sweet water; and Yemayá by the sea (in Trinidad these aspects of *Yemayá* and Ochún are reversed). Many orishas live in the forest and can be worshipped in wooded areas or urban parks. These include Osain, the herbalist and doctor, and Ochosi, the hunter. Ogun, the solitary warrior, divinity of iron and the forge, can be found wherever transportation facilities, especially train tracks and stations, are located, and in contemporary times is thought to inhabit airports. Elegguá, the trickster, is the lord of the crossroads. His offerings are frequently taken to a crossroads.

The warrior orishas include Elegguá, Ogun, and Ochosi. Members of the religion in the Cuban tradition who have not yet been initiated into the priesthood can be dedicated to, or "given to," these orishas, along with Osun, the guardian of one's destiny, in a ritual known as "giving the warriors." There does not appear to be an analogous initiation in Brazil. In fact, Elegguá in Brazil, where he is known as Exú, is treated completely differently than he is in Caribbean culture. This is one of the most interesting discrepancies in a comparative study. In the Cuban tradition Elegguá is a trickster and causes many problems, such as car trouble or other problems in travel, or inexplicable confusions. He is the orisha of choices, and he must be propitiated first, before all other orishas, so that he is kept content and so that he does not play disruptive jokes. Although considered dangerous, he is something of a childlike orisha in that he likes toys and candy. He manifests in his devotees at tambors, is taken along on vacations, and is kept close to his keepers—inside the house behind the door to guard the home, where practitioners can ask him for protection before exiting.

In Brazil, however, *Exú* is thought of as quite maleficent. There he also lives behind the door or preferably outside at the front gate. He is also propitiated first, but this is done in order to send him away so that he will not disrupt rituals and festas. He is sent away at least three hours before a festa begins: for example, the ceremony to propitiate Exú usually takes place at approximately five o'clock in the afternoon for a nine o'clock festa. In Brazil Exú is regarded with absolute respect mixed with a little terror. The idea of giving him candy and toys and keeping him nearby is met with horrified looks. Speaking to him or propitiating him by spraying rum on him prior to leaving the home is thought to cause problems by "calling" him.

The orishas all have their favorite foods, colors, and numbers. Offerings as well as material culture adhere to these specific preferences. A typical food offering for Changó might be okra cooked with cornmeal; for Oxun of Brazil one might cook a dish of black-eyed beans or for Ochun of Cuba, a pastry soaked in honey. The food and colors of Obatalá (Oxalá in Brazil) are all of the strictest purity and white, such as the whites of eggs and cocoa butter. Oyá or Yansa uses brown, and Babaluaiyé, the orisha of smallpox, uses purple and burlap in Cuba and the United States, and raffia in Brazil.

Material culture in the orisha religion is quite rich. Practitioners of Ocha, from the very earliest initiations, all wear strings of beads in the specific colors of the orishas. Generally a newcomer starts with five necklaces, called elekes, which correspond to Obatalá (white), Changó (red and white), Ochún (yellows, gold, and coral with possibly a few single green and blue beads), Elegguá (black and red), and Yemayá (blue, crystal, and silver). Bead wearing in Brazil is at once more casual and more formal: casual wearing of the beads can be observed among non-members who simply are fond of the religion from the outside, and initiates wear long, heavy strings, often of 21 strands held together at points by larger beads. The colors in the two areas are very similar; the notable exceptions are the beads for Ogun (green and black in the Cuban tradition and dark blue in Brazil). In Brazil, further, one does not wear beads for Exú.

Costumes for the orishas are very elaborate in both the Brazilian and the Cuban tradition. In the Cuban initiation the novice must have seven new white outfits consisting of a full petticoat, an overskirt, and a lace blouse. During the party for the new initiate on the third day, he or she wears a very elaborate costume in the colors of the orisha to whom the initiate is dedicated. These clothes are usually in nineteenth-century colonial style, with long full skirts, puffed sleeves, and tight waists for the women; the men wear tunics with loose pants. The preferred fabric is heavy satin; the costumes are decorated with sequins, lace, and appliqués and are often heavily and beautifully beaded. In Brazil the preferred decoration is lace, as lace making is a skill that remains fairly common, although the process is increasingly expensive, as are the fabrics. Clothing design in Brazil, as described above, is an intriguing combination of the colonial with the African: colonial skirts and blouses are worn below an African pano da costa, which is tied on top. In both traditions the legs are covered for modesty.

The orishas have Catholic saints to which they correspond as well. Changó, for example, corresponds to Saint Barbara in most areas. Other correspondences are not uniform and vary regionally, even within the same country. The linking of orishas to saints occurred from the entry of the orisha religion into the diaspora. Most slave-receiving areas were Catholic, and slaves were required to embrace the faith of their masters. Since Catholicism already had an established group of saints, it was easy for slaves to view the saints as manifestations of their orishas and worship them in this guise. The orishas, therefore, are also known from colonial times as the saints (los santos or os santos). This subterfuge has caused the religion in all areas, particularly Trinidad, often to be described in academic discourse as "syncretic," that is, a melding of two traditions.

The more research scholars do, however, the clearer it becomes that the two traditions are not melded at all but are kept very strictly apart. For example, in Ocha homes there may be an altar to the Catholic saints and family ancestors on which are placed glasses of water, crucifixes, images of saints and pictures of deceased relatives, candles, and flowers. In another space, on the floor, there may be a shrine to the egun, the ancestral African dead. For the egun there may be candles, servings of food, coffee, rum, and cigars. But the two shrines are never under any circumstances combined. Also, at *missas*, or seances in which non-orisha spirits are contacted, all manifestations of the *orisha* religion, such as the elekes, are removed.

In Brazil Candomblé ceremonies have no Catholic saints represented whatsoever, although one might see an image or a lithograph of a saint corresponding to the orisha who rules the house. Special Catholic masses figure in Candomblé and Ocha ritual festivity, but these are always held in separate spaces. Masses on the first Friday of every month are held at the Church of Nosso Senhor do Bomfim in Bahia in honor of Oxalá, who corresponds loosely to Jesus Christ. However, it is unclear that the mass is being said for Christ, since it is Oxalá who is mentioned in the homily, and fireworks are set off (a common means in Brazil to attract the attention of the orishas). In the ritual context, however, no Catholic processes or imagery appear.

Latin America and the Caribbean

Ortiz, Adalberto

(b. 1914, Ecuador), light-skinned Afro-Ecuadorian writer, painter, poet, teacher, and diplomat. Along with Manuel Zapata Olivella and Quince Duncan, he is one of the most recognized Afro-Spanish American writers.

When Adalberto Ortiz was three months old, his mother and grandmother abruptly left Esmeraldas with him for Guayaquil to escape from the civil war, La Guerra de Concha, or the "revolt of the Esmeraldian colonel Carlos Concha" against the national government in Quito. His father stayed in Esmeraldas. After the escape his mother joined a convent, and Ortiz grew up with his maternal grandmother. He discovered his father in Esmeraldas when he was 11 years old. Due to family financial constraints he had to work at a young age. An assiduous reader, he soon developed a taste for literature. In 1928 he obtained a scholarship to study in the Colegio Normal Juan Montalvo in Quito, which was one of the most exclusive schools in the country. He spent most of his academic holidays in Esmeraldas. He obtained his diploma as a schoolteacher in 1937.

During a boat trip from Guayaquil to Esmeraldas in 1937, Ortiz had the opportunity to read Emilio Ballagas's *Antología de poesía Negra* (Anthology of Black Poetry). The reading of that text marked, in his own words, the awakening of his interest in writing negrista poetry—a genre that tries to "convey the rhythm and musicality" of black speech—which he did while teaching in various schools in Esmeraldas. Ortiz was greatly influenced by and participated actively in the Grupo de Guayaquil or Generación del 30 (Group of Guayaquil or Generation of the 1930s), which was a group of innovative writers residing in Guayaquil who had a great impact on modern Ecuadorian literature.

In 1939 Ortiz moved back to Guayaquil, taught in a correctional school, and wrote his first novel, which is also his most famous: *Juyungo: Historia de un negro, una isla y otros negros* (translated as Juyungo: A Classic Afro-Hispanic Novel by Jonathan Tittler and Susan Hill, Washington D.C.: Three Continents Press, 1982). After many difficulties with Ecuadorian publishing companies, the first edition came out in Mexico in 1943.

From 1944 on, with the inauguration of the first government of José María Velasco Ibarra, Ortiz pursued a diplomatic career. He was first sent to Mexico for more than three years as the secretary of the Ecuadorian embassy there. While in Mexico he published *Tierra, son y tambor* (1944) and *Camino y puerto de la angustia* (1945), two collections of poems. His diplomatic career also took him to Panama, Paraguay, and Argentina.

Ortiz has published to date nine tales or novels and eight collections of poems. *Juyungo* has been re-edited numerous times in Spanish since 1943, and it has been translated into French, German, Russian, Croat, and English. The central themes Ortiz addresses in his work are those of black, Indian, and white interracial relations and processes of identity formation. While *Juyungo* expresses some Marxist views, over time Ortiz became less and less preoccupied with political engagement. In *El espejo y la ventana* (1967), he portrays the decadence of an Ecuadorian mulatto (of African and European descent) family that immigrated to the coastal city of Guayaquil. In this work he explores the psychological dimensions of racial identity in an Ecuadorian social context. More recent publications include *La envoltura del sueño* (1982), *Niebla encendida* (1984), and *Poemas de Adalberto Ortiz* (1985). In 1995 he received a literary prize, Premio Eugenio Espejo.

For more than 30 years Ortiz has also been a renowned painter, exhibiting his work numerous times in Guayaquil and Quito.

Ortiz, Fernando

(b. July 16, 1881, Havana, Cuba; d. April 10, 1969, Havana, Cuba), Cuban scholar, scientist, sociologist, musicologist, writer, linguist, ethnologist, social psychologist, journalist, anthropologist, legal expert, and criminologist.

Fernando Ortiz's intellectual legacy is one of astonishing breadth and erudition. Cuban scholar Juan Marinello has likened him to a third discoverer of Cuba, after Columbus and Humboldt. A Cuban-American critic has called him "Mr. Cuba." The claim is no exaggeration: he is one of a great line of Caribbean intellectual figures such as Eugenio María de Hostos, José Martí, Pedro Henríquez Ureña, Frantz Fanon, and C. L. R. James.

Along with the work of Lydia Cabrera, Ortiz's seminal works deal with the African traditions that have uniquely shaped the identity of Cuban music, religion, society, and culture. His major theoretical contribution is the concept of transculturation, a term used to describe the rich, textured, and sometimes bloody encounter between two or more cultures that mutually transforms them. It provides a refined framework for understanding the complexity and diversity of Caribbean culture, history, and identity.

While a meticulous social scientist, Ortiz created work that was unique in its creativity, expressiveness, and freedom of form. He wrote ingeniously about different themes, using a contrapunteo, or contrapuntal method, that allowed for solid research with immense literary flair. Ortiz created a discourse that blurred the boundaries among essay, history, and narrative.

Born of a Spanish father and Cuban mother, Ortiz spent most of his youth in Menorca (1882–1895), then returned to the island to study law at the University of Havana. He eventually obtained a degree in law from the University of Barcelona (1900) and a doctorate in law one year later from the University of Madrid.

In Madrid he began his first criminological investigations, observing prisoners in jail using the positivist scientific theories of Cesare Lombroso and Enrico Ferri. This marked the beginning of Ortiz's interest in the social behavior of both individuals and groups, a lifelong pursuit that over time shifted from a scientific to a historical-humanistic methodology.

Ortiz held a wide variety of professional positions over the years. In 1902 he worked in the Cuban consulate in Italy, where he met Lombroso and Ferri as well as Marxist sociologist Alfonso Asturaro. From 1906 to 1908 Ortiz was a lawyer for the district court of Havana, and from 1908 to 1917 he was a professor in the School of Public Law at the University of Havana.

During this period he wrote and edited a prolific body of work, often engaged with his political life. Beginning in 1910, along with Ramiro Guerra, Ortiz codirected (and later directed) the magazine *Revista Bimestre Cubana*, until it ceased publication in 1959. By 1915 he had joined the Liberal Party, and in 1917 he became the party's representative in the Chamber of Deputies. Five years later, disgusted with the corruption and political chaos of the country, he retired from the chamber but kept active politically. In 1924 he founded the Sociedad de Folklore Cubano, as well as the magazine *Archivos de Folklore Cubano* (1924–1929). By this time the Machado dictatorship (1925–1933) was in power. Ortiz, who fervently opposed the regime, spent from 1931 to 1933 in Washington, D.C., involved in the anti-Machado struggle, returning to the island after the dictator fled. In 1936 Ortiz founded the Institución Hispanoamericana de Cultura and edited its magazine, *Ultra* (1936–1947). A year later he founded the Sociedad de Estudios Afrocubanos, which also published a journal, *Estudios Afrocubanos* (1937–1940 and 1945–1946). Ortiz was also active during the 1940s in organizing intellectuals against fascism.

In 1942 he inaugurated an ethnographic seminar at the University of Havana and continued publishing as well as lecturing widely, penning four books in that period. In the 1950s Ortiz published eight books totaling more than 3500 pages, almost all related to the themes of Afro-Cuban music and culture; he continued to lecture internationally and was awarded honorary doctorates from many prestigious universities.

In 1961 he was designated a member of the National Commission of the Cuban Academy of Sciences and during the 1960s continued working on the third volume (*Los negros curros*) of his trilogy *Hampa afrocubana*, which remained unfinished at the time of his death.

Ortiz was influenced by positivism in the beginning of his career; he was concerned with the terrible problems that beset Cuba: poverty, unemployment, racism, crime, political corruption, and fragmentation. His intellectual formation was within a largely white and Hispanophile cultural elite, which had little interest in or appreciation of the black population of the island and was deeply influenced by the legal and criminological studies of the time.

Ortiz's first book, *Los negros brujos* (1906), revealed a certain Eurocentric and white bias as he saw blacks as "outside" of societal norms. And yet Ortiz admitted that without blacks there would be no Cuba, in the truest sense of the word. Speaking of the book some 40 years after its publication, Ortiz said it was motivated by the absolute lack of sociological research on blacks in Cuba. It was also the first major book published on the island to use the term Afro-Cuban. Ortiz's discourse on identity began a major shift in white Cuban discourse on identity and race. Furthermore, the book, as well as his subsequent research, dispelled the notion of a monolithic black culture in Cuba. While the Yoruba influence is perhaps the strongest, there are Abakuá, Arará, Carabalí, Congo, Wolof, and Bantu influences that are by no means insignificant.

Aside from some legal writings, research on the indigenous roots of Cuban culture, and a long historical tome on the seventeenth century, the bulk of Ortiz's writing focused on Cuba's African traditions. His research delved into linguistics (*Glosario de afronegrismos*), economics (*Contrapunteo cubano del tabaco y el azúcar*), racism (*El engaño de las razas*), history (*Los negros esclavos*), music (*Africanía de la música folklórica de Cuba*), and dance and theater (*Los bailes y el teatro de los negros en el folklore de Cuba*), as well as other fields of study. His best-known work is *Contrapunteo cubano del tabaco y azúcar* (1940; Cuban Counterpoint: Tobacco and Sugar, 1947, 1995), in which he elaborates the concept of transculturation, his most influential contribution. Ortiz's work was a constant reminder to whites in Cuba that the contribution of Afro-Cubans was not merely limited to the provision of cheap labor in a plantation economy but was essential to Cuba's identity in its patterns of socialization, cuisine, language, productivity, worship, and play.

But Ortiz's legacy is more than one of the devoted scholar doing meticulous research. He lectured widely, wrote about current affairs, and was very active in the fight to combat racism in Cuba. He belonged to a generation of reformist intellectuals that could be highly critical of Cuban society, including Carlos Loveira, Miguel de Carrión, Ramiro Guerra, and Medardo Vitier. The next generation would include such revolutionaries as Ruben Martínez Villena, Julio Antonio Mella, Juan Marinello, and Nicolás Guillén, all of whom had close relations with Ortiz.

Ortiz's work has also illuminated complex issues of contemporary Caribbean culture in the work of scholars such as Stuart Hall, Edouard Glissant, and Antonio Benítez-Rojo. In addition, his influence has reached beyond a geographical sphere to inflect the work of Latino writers in the United States such as Guillermo Gómez-Peña, Juan Flores, and Gloria Anzaldúa, who struggle with the issues of borders, cultures, and migration.

North America

Ory, Edward ("Kid")

(b. 1889, St. John Baptist Parish, La.; d. January 23, 1973, Hawaii), African American musician, jazz trombonist, and band leader; pioneer of New Orleans-style jazz.

Born on a farm near New Orleans, Edward "Kid" Ory arrived on the music scene of New Orleans in 1917. Joining up with cornetist Joe "King" Oliver and clarinetist Johnny Dodds, he led several prominent bands in New Orleans. He carried the tradition of New Orleans-style jazz to California in 1919, leading Kid Ory's Brownskinned Babies and Kid Ory's Original Creole Jazz Band in the Los Angeles and San Francisco Bay Area.

Ory's Sunshine Orchestra recorded such hits as "Ory's Creole Trombone" and "Society Blues" in June 1922. With these recordings, Ory's band became the first African American group to make all-instrumental jazz records. Ory moved to Chicago in 1925, where he participated in some of the most significant sound recordings of the period, alongside Louis Arm-

strong in "Muskrat Ramble" (1926), with "Jelly Roll" Morton in "Doctor
Jazz" (1926), and with King Oliver in "Every Tub" (1927).

Ory's style was distinctive: expressive and highly rhythmic, incorporating glissando runs of the early tailgate trombone style. With his recorded
compositions, including "Muskrat Ramble," he left the sounds of New
Orleans-style jazz as his legacy to music history. In 1930 Ory left the music
scene for ten years, returning to California to work on a poultry farm and
in a railroad office. He regained some prominence when he performed on
an Orson Welles radio broadcast in 1944. He toured until 1966, when he
retired to Hawaii.

Osei Tutu

(b. 1650?, present-day Ghana; d. 1717, Pra River, present day Ghana), founder
and first king of the Asante nation.

Following a model established by the earlier Akan military states, Denkyira
and Akwamu, Osei Tutu forged Asante into a powerful state that dominated most of present-day Ghana, except the coast, for 200 years. Tripling
the area under Asante control, Osei Tutu gained the Asante access to (but
not control of) the ocean, where they could trade directly with the Europeans to exchange slaves and gold for guns.

According to legend Osei Tutu was named after the shrine of Otutu,
where his mother had prayed for a child. Obiri Yeboa, ruler of Kwaman (an
Asante chiefdom) and Osei Tutu's uncle, sent the young man as his heir for
training at the court of Denkyira, the state that then ruled over the Asante.
A love affair with the Denkyira king's sister forced Osei Tutu to flee to
Akwamu, a neighboring state to the east. There he met Okomfo Anokye, an
Akwamu priest who became his lifelong friend and adviser. After observing
the political institutions of the powerful kingdoms of Denkyira and
Akwamu, Osei Tutu determined to unite the Asante into a single state.
Succeeding his uncle, he ascended to the stool of Kwaman around 1670 and
combined the various Asante chiefdoms into a military alliance under his
leadership, though the other chiefs retained rights and privileges. From
1698 to 1701 Asante crushed Denkyira. In 1701 Asante won sovereignty
over Elmina Castle, a Dutch trading post, which paid tribute to Asante and
offered the nation access to the lucrative slave trade.

To unify the new nation, Osei Tutu and Anokye created a state structure
that endured for 200 years. They made Kwaman, renamed Kumasi, the
kingdom's capital. They borrowed the Denkyira concept of a sacred stool
for the monarch: according to legend the Asante Golden Stool descended
from heaven onto Osei Tutu's knees. The stool became a revered symbol of
Asante nationhood. In addition, Osei Tutu established the Odwira (yam)
Festival, in which the bones of enemies were displayed and Asante solidarity

celebrated. He also created a bureaucracy to administer the newly conquered vassal states. Osei Tutu died in 1717 during a battle on the Pra River
in which Akyem Kotoku defeated Asante.

Ossie, Count (Oswald Williams)

(b. 1928, St. Thomas Parish, Jamaica; d. October 18, 1976, Kingston, J
amaica), Jamaican drummer and composer; leader of the Mystic Revelation
of Rastafari band, best known for recordings combining Afro-Jamaican
musical ritual rhythms.

Count Ossie, whose given name was Oswald Williams, was drawn to hand
drumming accompanied by chanting as a young child. Since his impoverished family could not afford to buy him a drum, Ossie did his first drumming on discarded tin cans. Through informal contacts with Rastafarian
drummers, Count Ossie began to gain enough proficiency on his instrument
to start his own drumming band, the Count Ossie Group, in the 1950s. He
would have been one of many obscure drummers using a "Back to Africa"
concept if not for a historic collaboration with singer/ producer Prince
Buster (Cecil Bustamante). The result was "Oh Carolina," the first Jamaican
recording to combine Rastafarian ritual music ska and reggae. Count Ossie's
drum rhythms undergirding this pop music hit on several continents greatly
influenced the evolution of ska and reggae, inspiring scores of musicians to
incorporate these African-tinged sounds. Jam sessions organized by Count
Ossie attracted major Jamaican pop and jazz musicians. Two recordings by
Count Ossie and his Mystic Revelation of Rastafari band in the 1970s,
"Grounation" and "Tales of Mozambique," combine chanting, storytelling,
spoken poetry, jazz sax improvisations, and ritual drumming, telling tales to
catalyze Afrocentric consciousness. After successfully touring the United
States, Count Ossie died in a tragic accident at the National Arena,
Kingston, at age 48.

Ouédraogo, Idrissa

(b. 1954, Banfora, Upper Volta [present-day Burkina Faso]), Burkinabé film
director.

Idrissa Ouédraogo is widely considered one of the leading members of a
new generation of African filmmakers. The son of a civil servant, Ouédraogo studied English at the University of Ouagadougou in the capital city
of Burkina Faso. But forays into playwriting soon piqued his interest in film,

and he enrolled in the Institut Africain d'Éducation Cinématographique de Ouagadougou, Burkina Faso's film institute. He later studied film at the Gorki Institute in Russia and at the Institut des Hautes Études Cinématographiques (IDHEC) in Paris. He graduated from the IDHEC in 1985 but remained in France to pursue a Ph.D. under the direction of anthropologist Jean Rouche.

As a film director Ouédraogo has produced a number of widely acclaimed films. He is one of the most technically accomplished film directors in Africa. His first film to receive international attention was *Yam Daabo*, which opened at the 1986 Cannes Film Festival in France. Other internationally recognized films by Ouédraogo include *Zan Boko* (1988), *Yaaba* (1989), *Tilai* (1990), *Samba Traoré* (1992), *Afrique mon Afrique* (1994), and *Kini and Adams* (1997). The latter film—his first in English—was the opening feature at the 1997 Festival Panafricain du Cinéma (FESPACO) in Ougadougou.

Ouédraogo's fluid style and skillful film technique have prompted critics to compare him to the French film director Jean Renoir. Ouédraogo's films have also won praise for their sensitive portrayals and astute criticisms of Burkinabé society. Although many of his films take place in rural Mossi villages, *Zan Boko* examines life in Ouagadougou, and *Kini and Adams* was shot in an industrializing region of southern Africa.

Africa
Ousmane Sembène

(b. 1923, Cassamance region, Senegal), Senegalese novelist and film director; considered one of Africa's leading film directors.

Ousmane Sembène is a pioneer and foundational figure in the history of cinema in Africa. During a career that has spanned 30 years, Ousmane Sembène has revolutionized African film through changes in film subject and cinematic language. His film style has influenced numerous film directors and has set standards for the premier organization of African film directors—La Fédération Pan-africaine des Cinéastes (FEPACI).

Born in 1923 in the Cassamance region of Senegal, Ousmane Sembène received only three years of formal education. He was dismissed from primary school after he struck the headmaster. In 1942 he enlisted in the army and was sent to fight with French troops in World War II. Ousmane Sembène's experiences in Europe made him keenly aware of the inequalities of the colonial system, and he began to participate in anticolonial movements, such as the 1947 Dakar-Niger railroad strike, after returning to Senegal. In 1948 he moved to France, where he worked as a docker. While in France, Ousmane Sembène began to experiment with writing.

Ousmane Sembène's interest in writing first began when he realized that there was a lack of literature by African writers available in Europe.

Through literature he hoped to correct some of the misperceptions that Europeans held about Africans. He published his first book, *Le Docker noir*, in 1956, and his second book, *O pays mon beau peuple*, a year later. After an injury Ousmane Sembène dedicated all of his attention to writing and returned to Africa to travel and write. During his travels Ousmane Sembène confronted the limited accessibility of literature caused by illiteracy and became interested in film. Believing that film had the potential to reach a wider audience, he enrolled in the Gorki Studio in Moscow in 1961. After he completed his training, he returned to Senegal and began work as a film director.

His first movies, *Barom Sarret* (1963) and *Niaye* (1964), were highly acclaimed by critics and received prizes at film festivals. In 1966 Ousmane Sembène finished the first feature-length film to be produced in sub-Saharan Africa: *La Noire de. . . .* He soon established his own studio and devised a balance between writing and directing his own films, and producing documentaries to provide funding for his films. While working on his early films, Ousmane Sembène also created a way to overcome distributional problems and a lack of theaters by initiating film tours that allowed him to travel to the villages in Senegal and show his movies. These techniques were lauded by FEPACI and were soon adopted by other African film directors.

The tours also helped him in his efforts to create an African cinematic language. He aspired to develop a filmic vocabulary that addressed the problems posed by multiple African languages and dialects. His developments toward an African cinematic language can be clearly seen in *Le Mandat* (1968) and *Xala* (1974). In *Le Mandat*, Ousmane Sembène attempts to integrate pictures, images, and gestures as a vital part of the story text. By supplementing the text in this way, Ousmane Sembène was able to communicate the overall plot of the movie even though he chose to have actors speak in Wolof, one of four major languages in Senegal. In *Xala*, Ousmane Sembène continued to supplement the narrative, this time with a series of symbols used in conjunction with each character to explicate the finer points of the narrative that might be lost between different languages. The filmic language developed in these films became the model for FEPACI film directors.

Since completing his landmark film, *Xala*, Ousmane Sembène has worked on larger films about historical events in Senegal. *Ceddo* (1977) examines the religious wars in Africa during the seventeenth and eighteenth centuries. His next film, *Camp de Thiaroye* (1987), explores the conditions that preceded the massacre of Senegalese infantrymen, veterans who had served in the French army in World War II, by the French army in Thiaroye. *Camp de Thiaroye* won the Jury Special Award at the Venice Film Festival in 1989.

In recent years Ousmane Sembène has concentrated on his newest, and to many film critics, his most ambitious film—*Guelwaar*. In *Guelwaar* Ousmane Sembène addresses the problem of food aid diversion by the government in postcolonial Africa, specifically in Senegal. He finished the film in 1994, but the Senegalese government has prevented Ousmane Sembène from releasing and showing Guelwaar in Senegal. The film has had only minor distribution and screening in other areas of the world.

Owens, James Cleveland ("Jesse")

(b. September 12, 1913, Oakville, Ala.; d. March 31, 1980, Tucson, Ariz.), African American sprinter, winner of four gold medals in the 1936 Olympic Games, and in his time heralded as "the world's fastest human."

James Cleveland Owens was the tenth of 11 children of Henry and Emma Fitzgerald Owens, who worked as sharecroppers. As a child Jesse Owens was chronically ill, probably because of poor diet, substandard housing, and inadequate clothing. During several winters he contracted pneumonia, which he was forced to endure since his family lacked money for a doctor or medicine. In the early 1920s the Owens family left the South as part of the Great Migration and settled in Cleveland, Ohio, where Owens's father and three brothers found work in the steel mills. For the first time in his life Owens was able to attend school regularly.

Owens set a new world record with his 8m 6cm (26ft 5in) longjump at the 1936 Olympic Games. *CORBIS/Bettmann*

Shown here at a 1937 track meet, Jesse Owens was one of the greatest athletes of all time, whose four gold medals at the 1936 Olympic Games stood as an unparalled accomplishment for nearly 50 years. *CORBIS/Bettmann*

In a racially integrated junior high school a white physical education teacher named Charles Riley noticed Owens's athletic ability and began coaching him in track and field. After Owens entered a vocational high school Riley continued to coach him. Owens's success was immediate: school records in the 220-yard and 100-yard sprints and the long jump fell to his smooth stride.

In 1932 he made an unsuccessful attempt to join the United States Olympic Team, but by 1933 his dominance of the sport was undeniable. At a high school meet in May 1933 he set a world record in the long jump with a leap of 7.41 m (24 ft 3Iin)—an improvement of more than 76.2 mm (3 in) on the old mark. A month later he helped his high school to a national track title with another world record in the long jump and a 9.4-second 100-yard dash, which tied the world record. Cleveland welcomed him home with a celebratory parade.

Owens was the first member of his family to graduate from high school. Although by most accounts his educational preparation was minimal, he was recruited aggressively by colleges around the country because of his athletic prowess. Despite the fact that he was urged by the black press to choose a less discriminatory school, Owens chose to stay near home. He entered Ohio State University in Columbus, where he was barred from

Left to right, Owens with Ralph Metcalfe, Foy Draper, and Frank Wykoff, his teammates on the gold-medal winning 400-meter relay team. German dictator Adolph Hitler left the stadium early to avoid having to congratulate the team. *CORBIS/Bettmann*

living on the whites-only campus, and where he and other black athletes were forced to ride to meets in cars separate from their white teammates.

By the spring of 1934 Owens was on academic probation, which prompted his coach to set up public speaking engagements for him—perhaps to bolster his confidence, or perhaps in the belief that an African American could not be helped academically. Whatever the motivation, the chance to develop and display his charisma and charm was fortuitous; it was a strength he would rely on the rest of his professional life. In May 1935 Owens broke five world records at a single meet, earning him the title among sports-writers of "the world's fastest human."

The 1936 Olympic Games in Berlin were embroiled in controversy long before the athletes arrived. The Amateur Athletic Union (AAU) threatened a United States boycott to protest the treatment of German Jews under Adolf Hitler, and black journalists were inflamed by Nazi claims of Aryan racial superiority. The American Olympic Committee, however, overruled the AAU and sent athletes to the games. To many American blacks Owens symbolized a rebuttal to Nazi racism, and he became a symbol that gained all the more importance after German boxer Max Schmeling delivered a surprising defeat to black American Joe Louis in early 1936.

Owens delivered an outstanding Olympic performance. He won gold medals for the 100-meter and 200-meter sprints, the 400-meter relay, and the long jump, in which he set a record that lasted 25 years. When Hitler refused to invite Owens and other black victors to shake his hand (an invitation that had been extended to several German athletes), the press seized on the snub and the International Olympic Committee rebuked the German leader.

Owens was welcomed home to a series of triumphal parades, but before long he was again confronted with American racism—forced to enter through back doors and ride at the back of buses—and he found that no jobs were open to him. As he later told an interviewer, "I wasn't invited up to shake hands with Hitler, but I wasn't invited to the White House to shake hands with the president, either." He was initially given several offers for public appearances, but most opportunities dissolved or were bogus. Failing to graduate from Ohio State, Owens relied on low-income jobs and the few personal appearances he could muster for money—including carnival races against horses.

He started a laundry business that failed, then returned to Ohio State. After four semesters, however, his grades were no better than they had been in his first effort. He withdrew. By the 1940s Owens was able to rely on public speaking for his income; he eventually opened his own public relations firm. In his later years Owens abstained from the Civil Rights Movement. His conservative response to the Black Power salute of Tommie Smith and John Carlos at the 1968 Olympic Games in Mexico City won him derision as an "Uncle Tom" by young black activists, but others continued to admire him for his entrepreneurial achievements.

Africa

Oyo, Early Kingdom of,
precolonial West African state.

Oyo was the most powerful of the Yoruba states during the peak of its power between roughly 1650 and 1750 C.E. Its capital, the town of Oyo, was situated slightly to the north of present-day Oyo in Nigeria. Legend has it that Oyo's first *alafin*, or ruler, was a son of Oduduwa, the mythical ancestor of the Yoruba people. In the sixteenth century Oyo began its ascent to power under the *alafin* Orompoto, who established a cavalry and maintained a trained army. During the first half of the eighteenth century Oyo subjugated the neighboring kingdom of Dahomey, but in 1818 Dahomey regained its independence from Oyo. Numerous internal disputes, war with Dahomey, and an invasion by the Fulani from the north contributed to the collapse of the empire soon afterward. In the mid-1830s the old town of Oyo was destroyed by a Fulani invasion, and the capital was subsequently relocated to its present site. In the treaty of 1888 after the Yoruba civil wars of the middle part of the century, Oyo, along with much of Yorubaland, was placed under British rule.

P

Pace, Harry Hubert

(b. January 6, 1884, Covington, Ga.; d. July 26, 1943, Chicago, Ill.), music publisher and founder of the first African American recording company.

Harry Pace began his printing and business career in 1903, opening a company in Memphis with former teacher W. E. B. Du Bois. Together they produced *Moon Illustrated Weekly* (1905), the first illustrated African American journal. Pace met composer W. C. Handy in 1908, and they formed one of the most enduring African American music companies, Pace and Handy Music Co. (1909). Pace went on to establish Pace Phonograph Company, issuing records by such artists as Alberta Hunter and Ethel Waters under the label of Black Swan. With the bankruptcy of the company in 1923, Pace returned to insurance work, expanding Chicago's Supreme Liberty Life Insurance Co. into the largest black-owned business in the North.

Pacheco, Johnny

(b. March 25, 1935, Santiago de los Caballeros, Dominican Republic), Afro-Dominican bandleader, composer, singer, flutist, and percussionist who played an important role in creating New York salsa music during the 1960s and 1970s; an important Latin music record producer and cofounder of Fania Records.

Johnny Pacheco made his mark during the 1960s and 1970s as part of New York City's Latin music scene. Pacheco's father, Rafael Azarías Pacheco, was a prominent clarinetist and conductor of the Orquesta Santa Cecilia, a leading Dominican orchestra. In the late 1940s the family moved to New York City. Johnny Pacheco learned to play saxophone, flute, and percussion in high school. In 1959 Pacheco joined the pianist

Charlie Palmieri (1927–1988) as the flutist in the newly formed group Charanga Duboney.

Charanga Duboney, featuring a Cuban-style charanga flute-and-violins front line, inspired an early 1960s charanga craze among Latino New Yorkers. In September 1959, Pacheco left Palmieri to organize his own charanga. With the album *Pacheco y su Charanga* (1961) he introduced the pachanga, an energetic dance style that combined elements of the charanga and the chachachá.

During the mid-1960s when the pachanga fell out of favor with the Latin music audience, Pacheco turned to the Cuban conjunto, a traditional ensemble that featured a two-trumpet front line, as a new formula for success. His group, Pacheco y su Nuevo Tumbao, was a Cuban-style conjunto that featured pianist Eddie Palmieri (b. 1936), the younger brother of Charlie Palmieri. The band renewed interest in traditional Cuban music among New York City's Latino population, spearheading what became known as the típico movement. More than a musical style, típico reflected, as John Storm Roberts wrote, a "prevailing rhetoric of roots, purity, and a concept (related to the growth of Latino political awareness) of 'community music.'"

Over the years Pacheco continued to play traditional, Cuban-influenced music. At the same time he was instrumental in broadening the Cuban musical legacy. In part, his success was a matter of historical timing. As a result of the successful revolution led by Fidel Castro and a United States embargo on trade with Cuba, there were few new musical influences coming from the island, allowing Pacheco and other Latino musicians in New York City to develop their own sound.

In 1964 Pacheco turned his attention from musical performance to the recording business. He established his own record company, Fania Records. In partnership with Gerald "Jerry" Masucci, he helped shape a Latin music style that Fania Records marketed as salsa music. At the outset the company's prospects were hardly promising. The only group signed to the label was Pacheco's own, and the two partners delivered their records to music stores out of their car trunks. Although the company started with little money and few resources, it quickly built a reputation for excellence among Latino listeners.

As Fania's musical director, Pacheco recorded many of the major talents in Latin music, including trombonist Willie Colón, percussionist Ray Barreto, singer/songwriter Rubén Blades, and vocalists Celia Cruz, Hector Lavoe, and Pete "El Conde" Rodriguez. For several years Pacheco led the Fania All Stars, before Willie Colón assumed the leadership. The Fania All Stars, with its irresistibly danceable, percussion-driven sound, epitomized salsa music. Blades, who sang with the Fania All Stars for six years before launching a solo career, brought an innovative social consciousness to his lyrics. Through the influence of Blades and other songwriters, salsa music came to reflect closely the realities of life in El Barrio, New York City's poor Latino community. During the 1970s the salsa sound gained a following throughout Latin America and with a broad range of non-Latino listeners as well.

New York Times music critic Peter Watrous noted that for more than a decade Fania Records was "extraordinarily consistent, comparable to Motown at its peak in popular music or the Blue Note label for jazz." Changing musical tastes brought hard times for the independent label, and Fania ceased operations in the 1980s. For some time Pacheco seemed to fall from sight as well. In 1992, however, the label was resurrected and reissued several albums under his leadership. Pacheco's legacy extends well beyond both his musical career and his entrepreneurial achievements. During the 1960s and 1970s his music and the albums that he produced for Fania Records expressed a growing pride in Latino identity and were an important counterpart of other contemporaneous forms of Latino empowerment.

Latin America and the Caribb\ean

Padmore, George

(b. 1902?, Tacarigua, Trinidad; d. September 23, 1959, London, England), anti-colonial activist, Communist, and Pan-Africanist whose career spanned the Americas, Europe, the Soviet Union, and Africa.

George Padmore dedicated his life to the black liberation movement in Africa. After Padmore died in 1959, Ghanaian leader Kwame Nkrumah stated that "one day the whole of Africa will surely be free and united and when the final tale is told the significance of George Padmore's work will be revealed."

Padmore was born Malcolm Ivan Meredith Nurse. He was the son of Anna Susanna Syminster and James Nurse, a senior agricultural instructor and the son of a former slave. After graduating from a Trinidadian private school in 1918 Padmore became a reporter for the *Weekly Guardian* newspaper. In 1924 he immigrated to the United States with the aim of obtaining a university medical education, and a year later he enrolled at Fisk University in Nashville, Tennessee. He did not, however, complete his degree at Fisk, possibly because of Ku Klux Klan threats, and in 1927 he transferred to Howard University Law School, where he became known as an excellent public speaker and student leader. As his professor Metz Lochard recalled, Padmore "was admired immensely by both faculty and student body. . . . He was our favorite speaker." Padmore also organized protests on campus, including a demonstration against a visit to the university by British ambassador Sir Esme Howard.

By 1928 Padmore had joined the Communist Party, adopting the name he is now known by as a cover for his political work. A year later he took up an invitation from the Moscow-based Communist International (Comintern) to visit the Soviet Union, which many black intellectuals at the time regarded as a haven of racial tolerance and a positive force for black emancipation worldwide. On receiving his tickets he discovered that they provided one-way passage only, and that the Comintern expected him to stay abroad.

Such was his enthusiasm for the Communist cause that he withdrew from Howard and immigrated to the Soviet Union. He never returned to the United States.

In 1935 Padmore moved permanently to London. Over the next 20 years, with the help of his typist and companion Dorothy Pizer, he established himself as a leading spokesman for anti-colonialist sentiment in Africa and around the world. His numerous books on Africa's struggle for independence include *How Britain Rules Africa* (1936), *Africa and World Peace* (1937), *Africa: Britain's Third Empire* (1949), and *Pan-Africanism or Communism?* (1956). Shortly before World War II he established the International African Service Bureau, which in 1939 condemned all the European colonial powers, equating the Nazi takeover of Europe with the European colonization of Africa. That same year he wrote an article humorously titled "The British Empire Is the Worst Racket Yet Invented by Man."

During the 1940s Padmore moved closer to Pan-Africanism, advocating the unification of Africa into a single country. He was instrumental in founding the Pan-African Federation (PAF), which in 1945 organized the All-Colonial Peoples' Conference in Manchester, England. Among those attending was Kwame Nkrumah, a radical Pan-Africanist leader from the British Gold Coast (present-day Ghana). Padmore and Nkrumah became close friends. As Nkrumah later recalled, "there existed between us that rare affinity for which one searches for so long but seldom finds in another human being." Nkrumah's Convention People's Party came to power in 1956 and helped Ghana achieve independence the following year, and Padmore became Nkrumah's chief advisor on African affairs. He met with considerable opposition from Ghana's elite, who objected to his special privileges as an outsider. Illness and exhaustion forced Padmore to return to Great Britain in 1959, shortly before his death.

North America

Paige, Leroy Robert ("Satchel")

(b. July 7, 1906, Mobile, Ala.; d. June 8, 1982), American baseball player, the first African American pitcher in the American League, and the first representative of the Negro Leagues to be inducted into the Baseball Hall of Fame.

Born in Mobile, Alabama, to gardener John Paige and washerwoman Lulu Paige, Leroy Paige earned his nickname as a boy, carrying satchels, or suitcases, at the Mobile train station. Accused of stealing toy rings, Paige was sent at a young age to reform school in Mount Meigs, Alabama. It was here that he began to play baseball, assuming a place on the pitcher's mound that he held for more than 40 years and becoming, according to ballplayer Dizzy Dean, the greatest pitcher of all time.

Paige began his career with the semipro Mobile Tigers in 1924. He played for several teams in the Negro Leagues, including the Birmingham

Black Barons. Paige was the most widely known African American baseball player until Jackie Robinson integrated the major leagues in the late 1940s. With a lanky 6 ft 3 in body and huge feet, Paige had a characteristic stance that was unmistakable on the mound as he uncoiled his long arms and let the ball fly. In the 1930s he drew huge crowds as he was pitted against major leaguers, including Dean. Throughout the 1930s Paige appeared regularly in the East-West "All-Star" games, and due in part to his enormous popular following, this yearly event drew unprecedented numbers of African Americans together. The "barnstorming tours" of the Negro League were exhausting, as the teams traveled sometimes as much as 30,000 miles a year to play exhibition games. Paige once commented that at times it was only when he put on his uniform that he found the spark to continue. It is little wonder that Paige suffered from exhaustion: he once pitched 29 consecutive games in 29 days.

As a free agent Paige played throughout North and South America, as well as in the Caribbean during winter seasons. He left the Pittsburgh Crawfords in 1937 to accept the invitation of President Rafael Trujillo to play for the Dominican Republic team Ciudad Trujillo. He returned to the United States several years later and pitched the Kansas Monarchs to victory in the 1942 Negro League World Series.

Paige became the first African American pitcher in the American League when he joined the Cleveland Indians in 1948. With Paige on the pitcher's mound, the Indians won the World Series in his first year on the team. By 1952 he was pitching on the American League All-Star squad. Paige, who kept fans guessing his true age, was in his forties by this time. "Don't look back," the quick-witted Paige once advised, "Some thing might be gaining on you."

By his own count, Paige threw 55 no-hitters and won more than 2000 of the 2500 games he pitched. He pitched his last game for the Indianapolis Clowns in 1967. Four years later, long after the disbanding of the Negro League, he was the first member of that league to be inducted into the Baseball Hall of Fame. Paige continued to work as a pitching coach for the Atlanta Braves of the National League. Appropriately, his autobiography is titled *Maybe I'll Pitch Forever* (1961).

Latin America and the Caribbean

Palacios, Arnoldo

(b. January 20, 1924, Certeguí, Chocó, Colombia), Afro-Colombian novelist, short story writer, and collector of cultural artifacts from the Pacific coast and the department of Chocó, a predominantly black region.

Little is known about the life of Arnoldo Palacios, an intensely private man. He grew up in his native Chocó and moved to Bogota to continue his studies at the Universidad Nacional. Later he left the country and lived in

France and Russia. His reputation was established in 1949 with publication of the critically acclaimed novel *Las estrellas son negras* (The Stars Are Black). Set on the riverbank of the Atrato River in the department of Chocó, the book portrays the brutal impact of utter poverty and social marginalization on the region's black communities. In its detached and cold depiction of the cruelest aspects of poverty, the novel recalls other classics in the genre, such as Knut Hamsun's Hunger (1890), Richard Wright's American Hunger (1977), and Carolina Maria de Jesus' Quarto de Despejo (1962, Child of the Dark).

Using a technique reminiscent of James Joyce's stream of consciousness, *Las estrellas son negras* follows the path of a man, Israel, for a whole day and records in their most minute details the hopelessness, terror, and humiliation brought about by constant pangs of hunger. Israel, or Irra (phonetically, "anger" in Spanish), as he is referred to throughout the novel, in the end realizes that his will to survive is greater than his desire for violent retaliation or self-destruction. Despite its fierce depiction of misery, the novel reaches a lyric beauty that has few precedents in black literature in Spanish America.

In 1958 in Moscow Palacios published *La selva y la lluvia* (*The Jungle and the Rain*). More recently, it has been hailed by some as a superb synthesis of the region's three cultural influences (African, Indian, and European), especially in its treatment of oral culture. Palacios has also published various books about the region's folklore and a survey of black literature in the Americas.

Latin America and the Caribbean

Palenque de San Basilio,
a Colombian community descended from an encampment of fugitive, African-born slaves.

The Palenque de San Basilio, a settlement of some 3000 inhabitants in the foothills of the Sierra de María, is 43.75 miles from Cartagena de Indias, the principal Caribbean port of the transatlantic slave trade from the sixteenth century to the beginning of the nineteenth century. In Cartagena de Indias resistance to slavery was constant. Those who were able to escape were known as cimarrones, a word that in the Americas was applied to insurgent Native Americans, wild plants and fruits, escaped domesticated animals, and later, runaway African slaves. The slaves fled from the galleys of ships, from mining operations, from ranches, and from domestic service; after their escape they often came together to form small bands. Many were able to settle in rough encampments protected by swamps and thick brush. To protect themselves from the weapons and dogs of the Spanish slave-hunting parties, these communities surrounded themselves with fences made of posts, branches, and thorns. Such encampments became known as palenques.

Armed with arrows, blunderbusses, and stones, the encamped cimarrón communities fought furiously against colonial domination and often went to battle with their faces painted red and white.

Palenque de San Basilio is the result of a series of concessions agreed to by Spaniards and palenqueros in the Sierra de María in 1713. It was established as the outcome of a dispute mediated by the bishop of Cartagena, Father Antonio María Casiani, concerning the recognition of land rights and the authority of a palenquero government that was led by a cimarrón capitán. The bishop gave the palenque the name San Basilio. In 1774 San Basilio for the first time figured in the census of the Spanish colonial government.

Latin America and the Caribbean

Palés Matos, Luis

(b. March 20, 1898, Guayama, Puerto Rico; d. February 23, 1959, San Juan, Puerto Rico), Puerto Rican poet and novelist who explored the contributions of African culture to the Americas in his writing.

Neither black nor mulatto, Luis Palés Matos is of the few non-Cuban poets from the Caribbean to have seriously represented blacks in his literary work. The Palés Matos family was very prominent in Puerto Rico, and Luis probably got his first exposure to African culture from the black servants who lived in the family mansion and who took care of him as a boy.

Palés Matos began his career writing modernist poems (his first book, *Azaleas*, was published in 1915) and acquired fame when he started publishing poems with a "Negro" theme, including "Danzarina Africana" (1918) and "Pueblo Negro" (1925). His work picked up on the contemporary cultural interest in primitivism, African arts, and folklore, with the "Negro" in Palés Matos's writing symbolizing a redemptive, primitive, sensual revitalizing force that stands in antithesis to a desiccated Western civilization.

Cross Cultural

Pan-African Congress of 1919,

major international gathering to promote worldwide black unity, held in Paris in 1919.

African American activist and writer W. E. B. Du Bois organized the Pan-African Congress in order to bring together Africans and leaders of nations involved in the African diaspora, and to promote the cause of African independence. Du Bois insisted that the conference be held in Paris in 1919 during the proceedings of the Paris Peace Conference, soon after World War I. He wanted Germany's former colonies in eastern and southern Africa internationalized as the first step in gradual African self-determination. The Paris gathering followed a previous conference held in London in 1900, organized by Henry Sylvester Williams, a London barrister born in Trinidad.

The congress received considerable publicity, partly because of the cooperation of French Prime Minister Georges Clemenceau, who accepted its resolutions. The congress delegates did not advocate immediate independence for Africa. Instead they called for greater African participation in the affairs of the colonies and for the newly created League of Nations to undertake the protection and wellbeing of the African people. Individual resolutions called on the colonial powers to allow Africans to own land and participate in government, to tax and regulate companies operating in Africa in the interests of Africans' welfare, to ban forced labor and corporal punishment, and to safeguard Africans' religious and social freedom.

Cross Cultural

Pan-Africanism,

a wide range of ideologies that are committed to common political or cultural projects for Africans and people of African descent.

In its most straightforward version Pan-Africanism is the political project calling for the unification of all Africans into a single African state to which those in the African diaspora can return. In its vaguer, more cultural forms Pan-Africanism has pursued literary and artistic projects that bring together people in Africa and her diaspora.

The Pan-Africanist Movement began in the nineteenth century among intellectuals of African descent in North America and the Caribbean who thought of themselves as members of a single, "Negro," race. In this they were merely following the mainstream of nineteenth-century thought in North America and Europe, which developed an increasingly strong focus on the idea that human beings were divided into races, each of which had its own distinctive spiritual, physical, and cultural character. As a result the earliest Pan-Africanists often limited their focus to sub-Saharan Africa: to the region, that is, whose population consists mostly of darker-skinned (or, as they would have said, "Negro") peoples. In this way they intentionally left out lighter-skinned North Africans, including the large majority who speak Arabic as their first language.

In the twentieth century this way of thinking of African identity in racial terms has been challenged. In particular, the intellectuals born in Africa who took over the movement's leadership in the period after the World War II developed a more geographical idea of African identity. The founders of the Organization of African Unity (OAU), such as Gamal Abdel Nasser of Egypt and Kwame Nkrumah of Ghana, for example, had a notion of Africa that was more straightforwardly continental. African unity for them was the unity of those who shared the African continent (though it continued to include, in some unspecified way, those whose ancestors had left the continent in the enforced exile of the slave trade).

Nevertheless, the movement's intellectual roots lie firmly in the racial understanding of Africa in the thought of the African American and Afro-Caribbean intellectuals who founded it. Because Pan-Africanism began as a movement in the New World, among the descendants of slave populations, and then spread back to Africa, it aimed to challenge anti-black racism on two fronts. On the one hand, it opposed racial domination in the diaspora; on the other, it challenged colonial domination, which almost always took a racial form, in Africa itself. The stresses and strains that have sometimes divided the movement have largely occurred where these two rather different goals have pulled it in different directions.

Africa
_____

Pan-Africanist Congress,
South African antiapartheid organization and political party.

Founded in 1959 as an offshoot of the African National Congress (ANC), the Pan-Africanist Congress (PAC) has always been the more radical of the two antiapartheid organizations. Explicitly nationalistic and racialist, less committed to nonviolence than the ANC, the PAC has played an important role in South African history while never achieving the membership or international recognition of its parent organization.

Among the PAC's founders were Robert Sobukwe, Potlako Leballo, A. P. Mda, and other former ANC members. They were disappointed by what they saw as the older organization's excessive caution and willingness to compromise in its campaign to overthrow South Africa's apartheid regime. In particular, PAC leaders opposed the ANC's multiracialism—it welcomed white and Indian members—and what was seen as the ANC's embrace of communism.

Their objections grew following the ANC's 1956 adoption of the Freedom Charter, a document calling for multiracial cooperation and communal economic principles. Arguing for "authentic African nationalism," Sobukwe and others tried to take over the local ANC leadership in the Transvaal, which some felt was the region of strongest Africanist sentiment. Failing that, and after Labello's expulsion from the ANC, Sobukwe and his fellow dissidents announced the formation in April 1959 of the Pan-Africanist Congress.

Latin America and the Caribbean
_____

Panama,
republic of Central America and home to a large black minority comprising the descendants of slaves or of West Indian workers brought to the country to build the Panama Canal.

Panama has been inhabited by aborigines, descendants of migrants who crossed from Asia to North America, for at least 10,000 years. Pre-Columbian peoples settled in Panama and the surrounding region, devel-

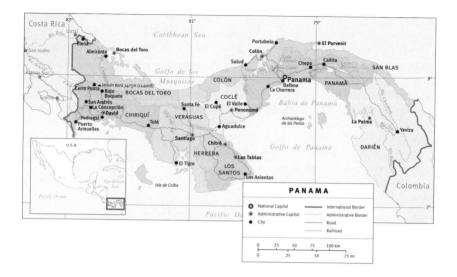

oped agriculture and stone tool making, and eventually produced elaborate gold jewelry, beads, and multicolored pottery, which have been found in their huacas (burial mounds). Later peoples flourished, but a single, powerful kingdom comparable to the Mayan, Aztec, or Incan was not in evidence at the time of European arrival. Most early inhabitants farmed, fished, traded goods among villages, and lived in thatched-roof huts like those in which many of their descendants live today.

Spaniards first arrived in Panama in 1501, and among the several hundred who arrived in the century's first decade were many African slaves. Most of the earliest settlers—European and African alike—succumbed to tropical disease and other perils. Nonetheless, when the Spanish explorer Vasco Núñez de Balboa mounted a journey across the Panamanian isthmus in 1513, African soldiers and assistants went with him. Thus as Balboa became the first European to see the Pacific Ocean, so too were his black cohorts the first Africans to reach the Pacific. The following year the new royal governor of the colony brought with him to the isthmus a group of ladino servants, Africans who had been christianized and "hispanicized" in Spain.

Panama was important to Spain because it offered the narrowest land route from the Atlantic to the Pacific—and thus an ideal place from which to launch military expeditions to Peru and the rest of South America.

As long as whites and blacks were both outnumbered by Amerindians, slaves received some degree of preference since it was important for Europeans to have reliable allies against the numerous natives. However, as the Indian population declined and the black population grew, Africans and their descendants began to be viewed by whites as the larger threat. Accordingly, racial segregation and restrictions on social mobility grew rigid. As the free black population grew (slaves were emancipated either by their masters or by buying their own freedom) and some blacks were able to acquire education and income, they were banned from many professions as well as most political offices. Free blacks thus were limited to lesser roles as artisans and petty bureaucrats. As trade increased on the isthmus and more blacks were brought to Panama, their sheer numbers, coupled with the scarcity of whites in parts of the country, assured the penetration of free blacks into at least the lower and middle echelons of government and the small shop-owning class. Through the seventeenth and eighteenth centuries the work and lifestyle of Afro-Panamanians changed little. By 1789 nearly 23,000 of the 36,000 residents in Panama were of African descent.

In the mid-1980s Gen. Manuel Antonio Noriega became the first person of African descent to rule Panama since Carlos Mendoza (a light-skinned mulatto who ruled for eight months in 1910 after the death of the former president; he did not attempt reelection). Noriega's authoritarianism was unpopular with many Panamanians, and his African heritage was often cited as an aggravating factor in his disfavor. In December 1989 the United States invaded Panama and overthrew Noriega. Among the 2000 Panamanians who died, there were many more who remain unaccounted for, and who lost their homes in the invasion. A disproportionate number lived in poor neighborhoods and were determined to be Afro-Panamanian.

Despite the destruction of 1989, Afro-Panamanians achieved a few modest gains in the 1990s. Another round of congresses was held to address the devastation following the U.S. invasion; the Center for Afro-Panamanian Studies in Panama City gained prominence as a repository of information on blacks; and the University of Panama devoted greater attention and funding to black studies. Many challenges confront Afro-Panamanians as they enter the twenty-first century. They must achieve unity between blacks from the West Indies and blacks who have long lived in Panama (currently, the former group leads most activist organizations), and they must elect political candidates who help blacks receive better education, health care, housing, and economic development. Moreover, as prominent Afro-Panamanian women like Graciela Dixon have emphasized, female activists face an extra burden in that they must overcome discrimination not only against their race but also within their race. Machismo and prejudice against women are prevalent in both the minority and majority cultures, and even fewer inroads have been made to achieve equality for black women than for black men.

Latin America and the Caribbean

Paraguay,

landlocked country of South America. It is bordered to the north by Bolivia; to the northeast and east by Brazil; and to the south and southwest by Argentina.

Paraguay has been described as the most homogeneous society in all of South America. The mixing of Guaraní Indian and Spanish created a largely mestizo (of indigenous and European ancestry) society that prides itself on its

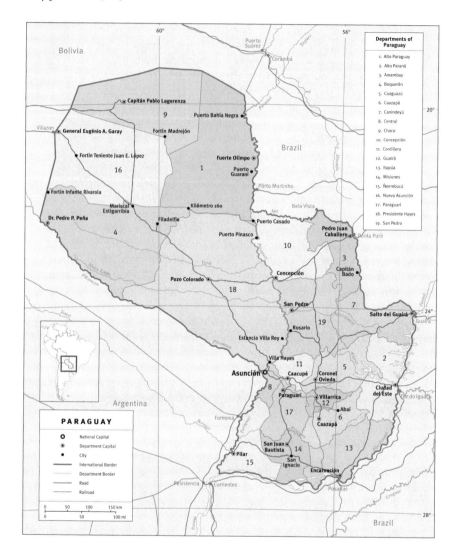

Guaraní descent. What is often overlooked is that people of African descent were also part of the racial and cultural mix since early colonial times. The country's long history of re-enslavement under the amparo system and its claim to being the last former Spanish South American territory to emancipate its slaves have gained little notice. Considering their history and their contributions to the country's development, Afro-Paraguayans deserve more than the brief mention they have traditionally received.

A small number of Africans was introduced into the region in the early 1520s, when the first explorers entered Paraguay searching for gold and other riches. Large-scale importation did not occur in Paraguay as compared to other territories in the southern region of South America because the country lacked significant exploitable resources and had a large Indian population to fulfill its labor needs. The labor that black slaves initially performed in Paraguay was no different from that of the Indians: cattle ranching, agricultural tasks, and domestic servitude. Only later would blacks be placed in more specialized fields such as iron smelting and road repair.

African slaves were imported to the region through the ports of Buenos Aires and Montevideo. Like most Africans who passed through these ports, most of these slaves were from Angola, taken from the Guinea and Congo River Stations on the western coast of Africa. Many slaves in Paraguay were of the same cultural group, but there is no indication that they formed ethnic communities once in Paraguay. The number of blacks in Paraguay increased mainly from racial intermixing, not additional importations of African slaves. Estimates of the Afro-Paraguayan population in the colonial period are incomplete as a result of inconsistent records and the misleading observations of record keepers. In 1570, for example, 3000 mulattos (persons of African and European descent) and mestizos were counted together, with no mention of other black groups.

The historical records of Afro-Paraguayans become inconsistent and incomplete in the period after Brazil enacted total emancipation. Some sources report that people of African descent were completely absorbed into the racial mix of the country and as a result lost any distinctiveness. Other sources claim that the Afro-Paraguayan population flourished in the twentieth century. By 1925 there were an estimated 10,000 to 31,500 Afro-Paraguayans in the country. In the 1990s some sources claimed that blacks constituted 3.5 percent of the nation's population, placing their number at 156,000. It is difficult to determine the accuracy of these often-contradictory sources, given the very limited amount of research that is available on the Afro-Paraguayan population.

North America
Parker, Charles Christopher ("Bird")

(b. August 29, 1920, Kansas City, Kans.; d. March 12, 1955, New York, N.Y.), masterful alto saxophonist who, along with Dizzy Gillespie, founded bebop, or modern jazz.

Together with trumpeter John Birks "Dizzy" Gillespie, Charlie Parker was the primary creator of bebop, or modern jazz. His musical innovations profoundly influenced other alto saxophonists, as is evident in the playing of Julian "Cannonball" Adderley, Eric Dolphy, Lou Donaldson, Charles McPherson, and Frank Morgan. Indeed, Parker's influence extended well beyond jazz to popular music and film and television scores. Despite his musical brilliance, however, Parker led a troubled life that included the use of heroin at an early age, an addiction that contributed materially to his death and was deeply intertwined with his musical mystique.

Parker was born in Kansas City, Kansas, across the Kaw River from the much larger Kansas City, Missouri. Between 1927 and 1931 the family moved to Kansas City, Missouri, the jazz capital of the Southwest.

Under the corrupt reign of Democratic boss Thomas Pendergast, Kansas City was a wide-open town, and its bars, honky-tonks, and nightclubs remained open until dawn, featuring live music and often no-holds-barred jam sessions. Kansas City gave birth to a freewheeling, stripped-down form of swing music that was deeply grounded in the blues and was epitomized by the Count Basie Band. Parker soon developed an interest in music.

During 1935 and 1936, when Parker was about 15, his life changed dramatically. He dropped out of school, married Rebecca Ruffin, began playing with the Deans of Swing—a band led by Lawrence Keyes—and had his first experience with heroin. Within a year he was addicted. Periodically throughout his life Parker would try to limit his heroin use, generally by substituting large quantities of alcohol, which was no less debilitating. In 1938 his first son, Francis Leon Parker, was born. Over the next few years Parker concentrated on his music and learned from older musicians in Kansas City and at resorts in the Ozarks. In 1939 Parker decided to hazard a trip to New York City, the nation's jazz center. There he took part in jam sessions, most notably at two Harlem nightspots, Clark Monroe's Uptown House and Dan Wall's Chili House.

While jamming at the Chili House one night in December 1939, Parker had a profound musical breakthrough. Although it took Parker several years to consolidate the full implications of this discovery, his achievement heralded a new era in jazz.

During the swing era big bands provided the majority of job opportunities for jazzmen, but musicians such as Parker and Dizzy Gillespie, then playing in Cab Calloway's orchestra, rankled at their lack of artistic freedom. Parker's job with Jay McShann did bring him back to New York City in late 1941 or 1942. Soon he began collaborating with Gillespie, who had independently achieved comparable harmonic breakthroughs.

The musical sparks Parker and Gillespie struck while playing together created modern jazz, initially known as bebop or simply bop. Parker clearly recognized the musical symbiosis between the two and regarded Gillespie as "the other half of my heartbeat." They worked together during 1943 and 1944 in Earl Hines's big band, an important bop incubator. But they perfected their music in jam sessions, especially at Monroe's Uptown House and Minton's. The new music offered richer harmonic textures with more varied tempos—both much faster and, on ballads, much slower than typical swing-era jazz—and a subtler rhythmic pulse.

Besides his advanced harmonic approach, Parker attained a previously unheard of rhythmic subtlety with his elliptical and fluid melodic lines. His technical mastery allowed him continuously to reinvent melodies, including rapid double-time passages, over the chord sequence of a given song. He was also at ease playing in every key, at a time when many jazz musicians were far more limited.

Parker's first significant recording sessions came in late 1944 and 1945 for Savoy and, under Gillespie's leadership, for Musicraft. The latter produced a number of particularly fine recordings, including "Salt Peanuts" and "Shaw 'Nuff." Gillespie and Parker also played an extended gig at the Three Deuces, which Gillespie later described as the "height of perfection of our music." But Parker's subsequent career was increasingly erratic. Gillespie asked Parker to join him on a trip to California to play at Billy Berg's, a Los Angeles nightclub. For Parker, the decision to go was a fateful one.

In California Parker made his first classic Dial recordings—including "Moose the Mooche," "Yardbird Suite," and "Ornithology." Yet the arrest of his drug dealer, Emery "Moose the Mooche" Byrd, resulted in Parker's having a nervous breakdown on July 29, 1946, while recording "Lover Man." Parker spent several months in Camarillo State Hospital, and Ross Russell, the owner of Dial Records, released his tortured "Lover Man." Beginning in 1947 Parker made New York City his home base. There he formed his great quintet, which included Miles Davis and Max Roach, and recorded a number of sessions for Dial, highlighted by the superb ballads "My Old Flame," "Embraceable You," and "Don't Blame Me." In 1948 Parker began recording with Norman Granz's Verve label, including groundbreaking sessions with strings. However, the greatest moments of his later career took place in concert. Two of these were recorded, a 1949 appearance at Carnegie Hall and a 1953 reunion with Gillespie at Toronto's Massey Hall. During these years Parker regularly won the annual *Downbeat* magazine readers' poll as best alto player, and his fame extended to Europe, taking him to Paris in 1949 and to Scandinavia the following year.

But Parker's personal life became increasingly troubled. Due to a drug conviction he lost his "cabaret card," required of all musicians playing in New York City nightclubs from 1951 to 1953, seriously limiting his ability to work. The physical cost of Parker's heroin and alcohol abuse was also clearly mounting and he died in 1955.

North America

Parks, Gordon, Sr.

(b. November 30, 1912, Fort Scott, Kans.), African American photographer famous for his portrait photography; first African American director of a major Hollywood film.

The youngest of 15 children, Gordon Parks, the son of a dirt farmer, left home when he was 16, shortly after his mother's death.

Working as a waiter on the Northern Pacific Railroad, Parks saw magazine photos produced by the Farm Security Administration, a federally funded project chronicling the Great Depression in rural and urban America. Later, after watching a World War II newsreel by documentary filmmaker Norman Alley, Parks resolved to become a photographer.

Based in St. Paul, Minnesota, the self-taught Parks immediately showed an original eye for his subjects, even if he lacked the technical training at the time to capture them flawlessly. Once, after finally getting the big break of a fashion shoot, he double-exposed all but one photo. Yet even the results of these mishaps captivated his viewers, and Parks soon had established himself as a much-in-demand fashion photographer in St. Paul. His work eventually was discovered by Marva Louis, the wife of boxer Joe Louis, who helped him set up shop as a fashion photographer in a bigger market, Chicago.

In his spare time Parks turned his camera from the fantasy world of fashion to the destitute streets of the South Side of Chicago. These pictures, exhibited at the South Side Community Art Center, won him a Julius Rosenwald Fellowship in 1941 and an opportunity to work at the Farm Security Administration, where he took on the assignment of showing the "face of America." Under the tutelage of Roy Stryker, the director of the staff photographers, Parks found that he could express himself more powerfully with the camera than with words.

In 1948 Parks was hired by *Life* magazine, then one of America's leading pictorial publications, and spent two years based in Paris. His work in the United States in the 1950s and early 1960s, and a highly acclaimed series on the slums of Rio de Janeiro won Parks international recognition as a photojournalist. His photographs in the United States dealt with many arenas, from politics to entertainment to the daily routines of ordinary men and women. Particularly noteworthy were his chronicles of the political activities of African Americans: the Civil Rights Movement (later collected into the 1971 anthology *Born Black*), the Black Power movement, and the growth of the Nation of Islam.

With photographs driven by a strong sense of narrative, it is no surprise that Parks found another calling in writing. In 1963 he published *The Learning Tree*, the saga of a farm family in the 1920s very much like Parks's own. *The Learning Tree* was the first in a trilogy of autobiographical novels, followed three years later by *A Choice of Weapons* and *To Smile in Autumn*, a memoir in 1979. Parks combined his literary and visual talents in a 1969 movie version of *The Learning Tree*, becoming the first African American director of a major Hollywood movie. His hit movie *Shaft*, often cited as a forerunner of the blaxploitation genre, was released in 1971, followed by *Leadbelly* (1976) and *The Odyssey of Solomon Northup* (1984), the story of a free black sold into slavery. Parks, also a poet and composer, wrote the music for a ballet about the life of Dr. Martin Luther King Jr.

Parks received the Spingarn Medal from the National Association for the Advancement of Colored People in 1972, and the National Medal for the Arts in 1986. He is the father of the late filmmaker Gordon Parks Jr., whose credits include *Superfly* (1972).

Parks, Rosa Louise McCauley

(b. February 4, 1913, Tuskegee, Ala.), African American civil rights activist, often called the "Mother of the Civil Rights Movement"; her arrest for refusing to give up her seat on a bus triggered the 1955–1956 Montgomery bus boycott and set in motion the test case for the desegregation of public transportation.

On December 1, 1955, in Montgomery, Alabama, the arrest of a black woman, Rosa Parks, for disregarding an order to surrender her bus seat to a white passenger galvanized a growing movement to desegregate public transportation, and marked a historic turning point in the African American battle for civil rights. Yet Parks was much more than an accidental symbol. It is sometimes overlooked that at the time of her arrest she was no ordinary bus rider, but an experienced activist with strong beliefs.

Parks was the granddaughter of former slaves and the daughter of James McCauley, a carpenter, and Leona McCauley, a rural schoolteacher. The future civil rights leader grew up in Montgomery, Alabama, where she attended the all-black Alabama State College. In 1932 Parks married Raymond Parks, a barber, with whom she became active in Montgomery's chapter of the National Association for the Advancement of Colored People (NAACP).

Raymond Parks' volunteer efforts went toward helping to free the defendants in the famous Scottsboro case, and Rosa Parks worked as the chapter's youth advisor. In 1943, when Rosa Parks actually joined the NAACP, her involvement with the organization became even greater as she worked with the organization's state president E. D. Nixon to mobilize a voter registration drive in Montgomery. That same year Parks also was elected secretary of the Montgomery branch.

The segregated seating policies on public buses had long been a source of resentment within the black community in Montgomery and in other cities throughout the Deep South. African Americans were required to pay their fares at the front of the bus and then reboard the bus through the back door.

On December 1, 1955, Parks took her seat in the front of the "colored section" of a Montgomery bus. When the driver asked Parks and three other black riders to relinquish their seats to whites, Parks refused (the others complied). The driver called the police, and Parks was arrested. Later that night she was released, after Nixon and Virginia and Clifford Durrs posted a $100 bond. The morning after her arrest Parks agreed to let the NAACP take on her case. Within 24 hours of Parks' defiance, the Women's Political Council had distributed more than 52,000 fliers announcing the bus boycott that was to take place the day of Parks' trial. On December 5, as buses went through their routes virtually empty, Parks was convicted by the local court. She refused to pay the fine of $14, and with the help of her lawyer, Ed D. Gray, appealed to the circuit court.

On the evening of December 5, several thousand protesters crowded into the Holt Street Baptist Church to create the Montgomery Improvement Association (MIA) and to rally behind its new president, Rev. Martin Luther King Jr., who had just moved to Montgomery as the new pastor at the Dexter Avenue Baptist Church. What was planned as a day-long bus boycott swelled to 381 days, during which time 42,000 protesters walked, carpooled, or took taxis, rather than ride the segregated city buses of Montgomery. In a move designed to reverse the segregation laws on public transportation, King and the MIA filed a separate case in United States District Court. The district court ruled for the plaintiffs, declaring segregated seating on buses unconstitutional, a decision later upheld by the U.S. Supreme Court.

Parks was widely known as "the Mother of the Civil Rights Movement," but her iconic stature afforded her little financial security. She lost her job as a seamstress at Montgomery Fair and was unable to find other work in Montgomery. Parks and her husband relocated to Detroit, Michigan, in 1957, where they struggled financially for the next eight years. Parks' fortunes improved somewhat in 1965, when Congressman John Conyers hired her as an administrative assistant, a position she held until 1987.

Parks has remained a committed activist.

Latin America and the Caribbean

Partido Independiente de Color,

black political party organized in 1908 by Afro-Cuban activists, many of whom were veterans of the War of Independence (1895–1898). Two years after it was founded, the party was banned, accused of being divisive for Cuba, where, its critics alleged, special political organizations for Afro-Cubans were unnecessary. In 1912 members of the outlawed party organized an insurrection—the Guerrita de Mayo (Little War of May)—were met with harsh state repression against party members and other Afro-Cubans, leaving more than 3000 dead.

North America

Passing in the United States,

the phenomenon of African Americans, who in physical appearance approach the "white" racial type, choosing to live and identify themselves, whether temporarily or permanently, as white.

Africa

Pass Laws,

South African legislation controlling the movements of blacks and Coloureds (people of mixed racial descent) under the system of apartheid, or racial segregation. The earliest pass controls were developed in the eighteenth century by the whites in South Africa in order to control black labor and to keep blacks and Coloureds in inferior positions.

A regulation of 1760 passed in the Cape Colony (what is now western South Africa) required slaves moving between town and country to carry passes signed by their owners authorizing their journeys. When the British purchased the Cape Colony from the Dutch in 1814, a system of passes already existed for Coloureds and blacks. Beginning in 1809 pass laws were introduced and amended frequently across South Africa. The purpose of these laws was to control the movement of blacks and to obtain their labor in both rural and urban areas. The mining industry became a major force behind demands for pass law controls.

Many demonstrations, acts of passive resistance, and uprisings were directed at the pass system. In 1930, for example, the Communist Party organized a mass burning of passes on Dingane's Day, a day celebrated in honor of the Zulu chief Dingane. A major anti-pass campaign was mounted in 1944. In March 1960 countrywide demonstrations against the pass laws culminated in the Sharpeville Massacre of March 21, when the police fired on a crowd of demonstrators, killing 69 blacks. Between 1952 and 1986, the courts punished millions of blacks for failing to carry their passes and by the early 1970s about one million blacks were arrested every year under the pass laws. The pass laws and influx control were finally abolished in 1986 when the process of dismantling the apartheid system began.

Latin America and the Caribbean

Patrocínio, José Carlos do

(b. October 8, 1853, Campos, Rio de Janeiro, Brazil; d. February 1, 1905, Rio de Janeiro, Brazil), one of Brazil's most influential abolitionists and journalists of African descent.

The son of a white Catholic priest and a free black fruit vendor, José Carlos do Patrocínio grew up on his father's plantation in Campos, Rio de Janeiro, where he was exposed to the brutalities of slavery. In 1868 he left home to begin an apprenticeship at Misericórdia Hospital in Rio de Janeiro. With the financial assistance of his father and a beneficent society, he went on to complete the pharmacy course. Unable to secure work as a pharmacist, he accepted an offer to live with and tutor the children of a wealthy realtor, whose daughter he later married.

Patrocínio first established himself as an opponent of slavery through the press. In 1877 he joined the staff of the *Gazeta de notícias*, Rio's daily newspaper. His editorials and poetry won him recognition as a leading abolitionist. In 1881, with the financial support of his father-in-law, Patrocínio bought and took over the *Gazeta de tarde*, turning it into Brazil's most influential abolitionist newspaper. In 1887 he established the equally authoritative abolitionist journal *A Cidade do Rio*. In his lifetime he published hundreds of articles opposing slavery.

Patrocínio was instrumental in persuading Princess Isabela, who was acting as regent, to sign the Lei Aurea (Golden Law), which on May 13, 1888, freed all of Brazil's slaves. After abolition Patrocínio sought to defend the princess from a growing Republican movement and facilitate her ascension to the throne by forming a black militant association called Guarda Negra (Black Guard). But a military revolt in 1889 established the Republic of Brazil, leading to Patrocínio's exile to Amazonas and the suspension of his newspaper. He eventually resumed his journalistic activities and continued writing until his death in 1905.

North America

Patterson, Floyd

(b. January 4, 1935, Waco, N.C.), African American professional boxer, an Olympic gold medalist, and the first to lose and then regain the heavyweight championship title.

Born in Waco, North Carolina, Floyd Patterson moved with his family to Brooklyn, New York, as a young boy and had a difficult childhood. He was sent to the Wiltwyck School, where he learned to box. When he returned to New York City he entered Golden Gloves competitions, winning national titles in 1951 and 1952 as a middleweight. At the 1952 Summer Olympic Games in Helsinki, Finland, he won all of his fights and the gold medal. After the games he turned professional.

In his first 36 professional fights Patterson lost only once, and in 1956 he beat Archie Moore for the heavyweight title. Patterson became the youngest heavyweight champion and the first Olympic gold medalist to hold the title. He made four successful title defenses before losing to Sweden's Ingemar Johansson in 1959. Johansson knocked Patterson down seven times before the fight was stopped. A year later Patterson knocked out Johansson in the fifth round and became the first boxer to regain the heavyweight title. Patterson defended his title successfully until losing to Sonny Liston in 1962. Patterson continued to fight but never won another title. In his last fight, in 1972, Muhammad Ali knocked him out. Patterson later became a sports official in the state of New York.

North America

Patton, Charley

(b. 1887, Edwards, Miss.; d. April 28, 1934, Indianola, Miss.), African American blues guitarist and vocalist, a key figure in the development of the Mississippi Delta blues style.

Although he possessed a strong, deep voice, Charley Patton was of small stature and too frail to perform the difficult labor on the farms of the Mississippi Delta region, where he lived his entire life. Instead, Patton—whose inability to read, rough personality, and womanizing epitomized the bluesman—learned to play the guitar and compose his own songs. By his early teenage years he began playing local gigs, performing in Jackson and Yazoo City at parties, work camps, juke joints, and picnics.

After his family's 1912 move to Will Dockery's plantation near Cleveland, Mississippi, Patton began performing with Willie Brown, Dick Bangston, and Tommy Johnson. He is considered a creator of the Delta blues, the most primitive blues genre, which is characterized by uneven rhyming, spoken—as opposed to sung—lyrics, including shouts, guttural groans and haunting moans, and a bottleneck guitar technique in which melodic phrases are often blurred and repeated. Patton's lyrics often recounted the events of his life and those of his friends. His innovative playing style included thumping, and at times talking to, his guitar, which created a musical tension and dynamism often imitated by later blues musicians.

Patton made many recordings between 1929 and 1934, including ragtime, folk songs, white rural music, adaptations of popular tunes, religious songs, and of course, blues. Through these recordings he became one of the first Delta blues performers to emerge from anonymity and achieve broader musical influence.

Latin America and the Caribbean

Pelé (Edson Arantes do Nascimento)

(b. October 23, 1940, Tres Corações, Brazil), Afro-Brazilian soccer player, considered by many to be the greatest in the history of the game, and one of the most recognized black people in the world.

Born in a small town in the state of Minas Gerais with a semiprofessional soccer player as a father, Edson Arantes do Nascimento grew up in the city of Bauru. It was at this time that he acquired the nickname "Pelé," by which he is now known throughout the world. At age 15 Pelé was transferred to Santos, a team in the much larger port city with the same name. Pelé would play for Santos for most of his career, and he would forever become associated with its white Number 10 shirt—along with the yellow shirt of the Brazilian national team.

In the 18 years that Pelé played at Santos, the club team won numerous state and national championships in Brazil and two world club championships, in 1962 and 1963. During what has been called Pelé's reign (in Brazil he is referred to as "King Pelé"), Santos frequently toured throughout the world and enormous crowds gathered wherever the team played.

In Asia, Africa, and Europe fans paid homage to this black Brazilian. Concerned that such devotion might result in offers for Pelé to play for teams in richer countries, in 1962 the Brazilian Congress declared the 22-year-old to be a "non-exportable national treasure." And in a story often recalled, a visit to Nigeria by Pelé's Santos in 1969 caused the warring factions in a civil war to agree to a temporary truce lasting the duration of the Brazilian's stay.

Pelé retired from his club team, Santos, in 1974, and it is rumored that even the president of Brazil attempted, unsuccessfully, to convince him to continue playing. In 1975, however, a multimillion-dollar offer lured him back into the game to play for the New York Cosmos as a North American league attempted to spread soccer to the United States. His second and final retirement came in October 1977.

Pelé's importance in Brazil is of such magnitude that some have claimed that he would be elected president if he ever chose to be a candidate. Yet Pelé's fame reaches far beyond the confines of Brazil and sports. He was the first black man to be on the cover of *Life* magazine, for instance, and even more than two decades after the end of his professional soccer career he is certainly among the most recognized people of African descent in the world.

Africa

Perry, Ruth

(b. 1939?, Liberia), former transitional president of Liberia; the first woman head of state in modern Africa.

Ruth Perry served as a senator from Grand Cape Mount County in northern Liberia before being named chairwoman of Liberia's transitional Council of State in September 1996. Her appointment came at the hands of the factional leaders whose fighting had thrust Liberia into a seven-year-long civil war, but Perry, a widowed grandmother of 57, dealt firmly with the rival warlords, overseeing a mostly successful disarmament and free elections in July 1997.

Perry, the mother of seven children, first became involved in politics when she finished her husband's term as senator after his death. In the 1980s she attracted attention for her public opposition to then-President Samuel K. Doe's efforts to legalize polygamy. After Charles Taylor's National Patriotic Front of Liberia began to take control of the Liberian countryside in 1989, the country's government collapsed and Perry returned to her home (where she helped shelter refugees). A series of transitional governments was appointed throughout the 1990s, but none held much real power. In 1996 at Abuja, Nigeria, the Economic Community of West African States brought together the most powerful of the factional leaders to draft a disarmament plan and name a new head of state.

Analysts reported surprise at the choice of Perry, but she quickly warned Taylor and the other warlords that she would "treat them like a mother and, if necessary, that means discipline." Lacking money and political power, Perry used her largely symbolic position to try to educate Liberians about their basic political rights. After nearly a year in office Perry oversaw the July 1997 elections, widely considered fair, in which Charles Taylor was elected president.

Peru,

country of South America bordered on the east by the Pacific Ocean, on the south by Chile, on the west by Brazil, on the southwest by Bolivia, and on the north by Ecuador and Colombia.

Peru has long been known for the powerful and sophisticated Incas, who built their cities high in the mineral-rich Andes Mountains; for the Spanish conquistadors who marched into Peru and conquered the enormous Inca Empire in a matter of months; and for the thousands upon thousands of tons of gold and silver that Spain extracted from the region now known as Peru over the next several centuries. It is less well known that the conquest, the extraction, and indeed much of contemporary Peruvian culture were the result of the labor and input of African slaves and their descendants.

When Pizarro captured and executed the Inca leader Atahualpa in 1532, and when he defeated and plundered the Inca stronghold of Cuzco in 1533, African soldiers were among his ranks. Perhaps the most notable of the early black conquistadors of Peru was a slave named Juan Valiente. The life of the early Afro-Peruvian slave revolved around the coastal capital of Lima, founded by Pizarro in 1535, and former Inca cities like Cuzco, which were being transformed into Hispanic cities. Afro-Peruvians performed much of the land clearing, road building, and construction to erect these cities. In Lima slaves were also prominent among the dockworkers and mule drivers who greased the gears of the rapidly growing export of gold and silver and import of food and other goods. Female slaves also performed highly valued domestic tasks like cooking and laundering.

By the end of the sixteenth century Peru also had a substantial number of free blacks: perhaps one-fourth to one-third of Afro-Peruvians had bought their freedom under Spanish laws, had arrived free, or had been granted their freedom for fighting in the conquest with Pizarro. Most of the free blacks, known as libertos, shunned the agricultural regions for the cities, particularly Lima, where they worked as low- to mid-wage laborers, maids, and the like. Their actions were rigidly circumscribed: in 1577, for example, the viceroy of Peru banned any black person from owning a weapon, and throughout colonial times blacks were barred as a matter of course from many of the skilled trades. Although in word Spanish law allowed any slave to buy his or her freedom, slaves' activities were closely monitored.

At the turn of the twentieth century and for decades to come, many Afro-Peruvians remained in poverty, and most lived in urban slums, pri-

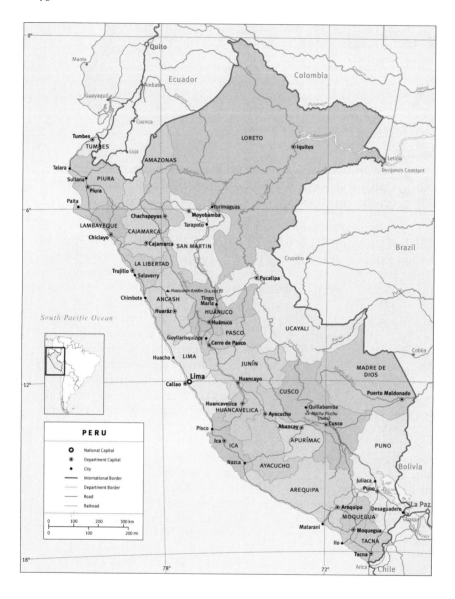

marily in Lima. Many Afro-Peruvians denied their African ancestry when they could. Afro-Peruvians commonly aspired for their children to marry lighter-skinned people. Still, the influence of Afro-Peruvian culture extended from music to cooking to sports.

After World War II Peru underwent a gradual but disruptive change from rule by a privileged oligarchy to rule by a more representative democracy, though military leaders still held power. This change yielded new opportunities in schooling and health for the poor and, simultaneously, a massive rural-to-urban migration. These two factors made Peruvian cities vibrant centers of black culture. African dance and theater groups were founded, Afro-Peruvian literature was more widely disseminated, and racial discrimination against blacks and other minorities eased somewhat by the 1950s and 1960s. Influenced by the Civil Rights Movement in the United States during this time, Afro-Peruvians formed several groups to agitate for political reforms to help blacks. Perhaps the most important of these were the Movimiento Negro Francisco Congo (Francisco Congo Black Movement) and the Asociación pro Derechos Humanos del Negro (Association for Black Human Rights).

As of the late 1990s, however, Afro-Peruvians had yet to coalesce behind one or more political parties that would promote an agenda to help blacks—thus leaving a significant challenge for Afro-Peruvians of the twenty-first century.

North America

Pickett, Bill

(b. December 5, 1870?, Williamson County, Tex.; d. April 2, 1932), cowboy and rodeo star.

Bill Pickett invented and popularized "bulldogging," a method of steer wrestling inspired by cattle dogs. To bring a bull to the ground, Pickett would leap atop its back, twist its horns with his hands, and bite its upper lip. Pickett initially adopted bulldogging while working as a ranch hand, but his steer wrestling skills soon launched him into the rodeo show business of the West.

Pickett was born near Austin, Texas. He quit school after the fifth grade and began working full-time as a cowboy, developing his talents in roping and horsemanship. As a teenager he began performing at carnivals, rodeos, and county fairs throughout the southwest. Initially promoters dressed Pickett as a Mexican bullfighter, obscuring his African American descent for commercial reasons. In 1907 Pickett signed on with the Miller Brothers 101 Ranch Wild West Show, based in Oklahoma's Cherokee Strip. Pickett adopted the name "The Dusky Demon" and soon earned top billing. Pickett and the Miller Brothers toured widely throughout the United States, playing Madison Square Garden and other top venues. They also performed in Canada, South America, and Europe, where Pickett unveiled his rodeo tricks for the likes of King George V and Queen Mary of England. Pickett went into partial retirement after 1916, but remained active both as cowboy and performer until 1932 when he died after a kick in the head from a horse.

Pickett was widely admired for his showmanship and bravery. One of his most devoted fans was the comedian Will Rogers, with whom Pickett sometimes performed. In 1971 the National Rodeo Cowboy Hall of Fame inducted Pickett as its first black honoree, and in 1994 he appeared on a commemorative postage stamp.

Pinchback, Pinckney Benton Stewart

(b. May 10, 1837, Macon, Ga.; d. December 21, 1921, Washington, D.C.),
America's first black governor. He held more major political positions than any
other African American during Reconstruction.

P. B. S. Pinchback was the freeborn son of a wealthy white planter, William
Pinchback, and his longtime mistress, an emancipated slave named Eliza
Steward. In 1862, after working as a steward on a Mississippi riverboat,
Pinchback joined the Union Army in New Orleans. He recruited and commanded a company of the Corps d'Afrique, a Louisiana cavalry unit. Pinchback remained in New Orleans after the Civil War, helping to shape
Louisiana's Republican Party and holding public offices. In 1867 he served
as a member of the state's Constitutional Convention, and a year later he
was elected to Louisiana's state senate. He served as president pro tempore
of the senate in 1871, and succeeded Oscar J. Dunn as lieutenant governor
after Dunn's death in January 1872. When the Louisiana House of Representatives began impeachment proceedings against Governor Henry Clay
Warmoth in December 1872, Pinchback became Louisiana's acting governor, serving until January 1873, when W. P. Kellogg succeeded him.

Pinchback's career suffered several political setbacks. He was elected to
the United States House of Representatives in 1872, but both Pinchback
and his opponent, George A. Sheridan, claimed victory. They contested the
seat until February 4, 1875, when the House Committee on Elections
judged Sheridan the winner. Meanwhile, in January 1873, the Louisiana
legislature elected Pinchback to the U.S. Senate, but another rival, W. L.
McMillen, also contested this mandate. Though McMillen eventually
acknowledged Pinchback's claim to the seat, senators uncovered evidence
that Pinchback had paid $10,000 to obtain it. On March 13, 1875, the
Senate denied Pinchback his seat by a vote of 32 to 29.

Pinchback succeeded in several business ventures throughout his life. He
was a cotton dealer and helped to found the Mississippi River Packet Company. He also profited from his positions in government and the information that they provided. In 1897 Pinchback and his wife, Nina Hawthorne,
moved to Washington, D.C., where he became a leading member of the
city's black social elite until his death in 1921. Among his grandchildren
was Jean Toomer, the well-known novelist of the Harlem Renaissance.

Pippin, Horace

(b. February 22, 1888, West Chester, Pa.; d. July 6, 1946, West Chester, Pa.),
African American painter who became famous for his nonacademic approach
to art and superimposition of historical events and personal experiences.

Art critic and historian Christian Brinton discovered Pippin after seeing his
"Cabin in the Cotton" on display in a barbershop window in 1936. Brinton

sought Pippin out and arranged for ten of his works to be displayed at the West Chester Community Center on June 9, 1937. Within a year four of Pippin's works were included in an exhibition of self-taught French and American painters, "Masters of Popular Painting," at the Museum of Modern Art. In 1940 artist-turned-dealer Robert Carlen mounted Pippin's first gallery show in Philadelphia, Pennsylvania. During the 1940s Pippin's paintings were purchased by several major American museums, and galleries throughout the country mounted exhibitions featuring his works.

Part of the reason Pippin began to paint was to rehabilitate his right arm following a World War I injury. Pippin had taken an interest in drawing at an early age. As a boy he won a box of crayons and a set of watercolors for his entry in an art supply company's advertising contest. Pippin used the crayons and watercolors to decorate doilies, which were sold in a Sunday school festival. During his childhood and early adulthood he spent much of his free time drawing.

Pippin's disability check was not enough to support the two of them, and he did his best with his good left arm to assist his wife at her laundry service. In 1925 he began to make pictures by burning images onto wood panels with a hot poker. This endeavor was intended to serve as therapy for his injured arm, which he rested across his knee. It also allowed him to work out the war memories that continued to trouble him.

Unlike other important self-taught artists who tended to repeat themselves, Pippin explored a variety of subjects (American history, biblical themes, winter landscapes, portraits, and scenes of everyday black communal life) on a variety of mediums (fabric, paper, and wood). In attempting to be direct and true to reality as he understood it, Pippin created works with some of modern art's fundamental characteristics—unmodulated, sharply delineated colors and flat, shadow less forms—which makes him one of the twentieth century's most remarkable artists.

North America

Plessy v. Ferguson,

1896 United States Supreme Court case that reconciled the equal protection clause of the Fourteenth Amendment with a system of state-imposed racial segregation via the formula "separate but equal."

When 30-year-old shoemaker Homer Plessy refused to leave his seat on a New Orleans train in 1892, he set in motion a battle that traveled all the way to the U.S. Supreme Court. The court's 1896 decision, *Plessy v. Ferguson*, permitted states to institute racially separate public accommodations despite the Constitution's Fourteenth Amendment, which guarantees all citizens equal protection under the law. It would take nearly 60 years for the court to reverse itself, in *Brown v. Board of Education* (1954), and overturn the judicial precedent for segregation.

Plessy's lawyer, the white activist and writer Albion Tourgée, brought the case before the U.S. Supreme Court in 1896. Tourgée's brief argued that the

Louisiana law "is obnoxious to the spirit of republican institutions, because it is a legalization of caste." He also stated that the law violated both the Thirteenth and Fourteenth Amendments in limiting "the natural rights of man."

The Court ruled seven to one (one justice did not participate) that Plessy's constitutional rights had not been violated. In a lone but strong dissent, Justice John Marshall Harlan, a Southerner, cited cases in which segregated juries had been found unconstitutional, and went on to say in plain language what Plessy's opponents would not admit: that the separate car law not only separated the races but did so to accommodate white racial prejudice. Harlan's words proved prophetic. The "separate but equal" doctrine relegated African American children to inadequate, unsafe schools, while the South's Jim Crow laws forbade black citizens from exercising their rights as citizens on an equal footing with white citizens. Not until the Supreme Court reversed itself in 1954's *Brown v. Board of Education* would African Americans be able to claim the rights promised in the U.S. Constitution.

North America

Poitier, Sidney

(b. February 20, 1927, Miami, Fla.), African American actor, director, and film-maker, leading post-World War II African American movie star.

Sidney Poitier was raised in the Bahamas and returned to the United States as a teenager. Poitier's first film role was in *No Way Out* (1950). Many leading roles followed, and in 1963 he became the first African American to win the Oscar for Best Actor for his performance in *Lilies of the Field.* Poitier's other films include *Blackboard Jungle* (1955), *The Defiant Ones* (1958), *In the Heat of the Night, To Sir with Love,* and *Guess Who's Coming to Dinner* (all 1967). He also originated the role of Walter Lee Younger in the 1959 Broadway production of Lorraine Hansberry's *A Raisin in the Sun.*

Poitier was the first African American to become a major Hollywood star with mainstream audiences. In the process, he was criticized by some members of the black community for portraying stereotypical "noble Negroes." In response, as the 1960s ended, Poitier began to play more diverse roles. He also began to produce and direct films, and directed several hit films in the 1970s and 1980s. In 1993 Poitier won the National Association for the Advancement of Colored People's first Thurgood Marshall Lifetime Achievement Award.

Latin America and the Caribbean

Porres, San Martín de

(b. December 9, 1579, Lima, Peru; d. November 3, 1639, Lima, Peru), Afro-Peruvian saint canonized in 1962.

Six officially recognized saints lived in colonial Peru during the sixteenth and seventeenth centuries, four of whom belonged to the Dominican order.

Martín de Porres is distinctive for being the first mulatto (person of African and European descent) ever to be canonized by the Roman Catholic Church.

De Porres was born in Lima on December 9, 1579, the natural son of Juan de Porres, a Spanish nobleman, and Ana Velázquez, a free black woman from Panama. At age 15, he received the habit of the Third Order of Saint Dominic and entered the Rosary convent of the Friar Priests in Lima, where he spent the next 45 years. The Dominican order prohibited black men from receiving the habit. For this reason, Martín de Porres entered the order as a donate (servant) for nine years, without being allowed to become a member. However, in 1603, after Martin showed much devotion and dedication to helping the poor and sick, the order made an exception and admitted him as a lay brother. As an official member of the community, he worked as a barber, healer, and farmer, and allegedly performed miraculous cures on sick people and animals.

Martín based his spiritual life on the strictest practices of prayer and penance, according to the ascetic models of his time. His charity reputedly had no limits either in or out of his convent. He disregarded racial remarks belittling him and tried to aid those who called on him. The future saint was instrumental in founding an orphanage and a foundling hospital in the city of Lima. He also ministered among the African slaves who were brought to Peru. Even animals received the benefit of his generosity.

Martín de Porres was beatified two centuries later by Pope Gregory XVI in 1837. In 1945 Pope Pius XII proclaimed him the patron of social justice. He was canonized in 1962 by Pope John XXIII in the context of the preparation for the Second Vatican Council. Martín's fame has transcended the boundaries of Peru and South America. For his followers in the five continents, he represents a different paradigm of holiness. As an illegitimate child and a person of color, he was subjected to social and ecclesiastical discrimination, yet he became a symbol of understanding and compassion.

Europe

Portugal,

a country in southwestern Europe in which blacks have had a presence for centuries.

Black Africans and people of African descent almost certainly came to present-day Portugal with the Romans and Carthaginians toward the end of the first millennium B.C.E., but little record remains of their presence. Likewise, the Muslim occupation (711–1250 C.E.) brought many people of African descent to the region. However, Portugal's modern expansion toward Africa dates from the end of the fourteenth century, with the partial occupation of the Canary Islands and the island of Madeira.

All sectors of Portuguese society—clergy, nobles, and commoners—owned slaves, though usually only the more affluent could afford them. The nobility used them primarily as domestic servants and as an external sign of power and prestige, but no group, with the exception of the royal government, possessed large numbers at any point during the fifteenth and sixteenth centuries. On the other side of the spectrum, some black slaves were purchased for employment in undesirable tasks, such as hospital work, then a dangerous occupation due to frequent epidemics.

During the sixteenth century the Portuguese began to bring enslaved Africans to Portugal in larger numbers. By about 1600 blacks constituted almost 10 percent of the population of Lisbon and parts of the Algarve. There is also abundant evidence of the employment of blacks as crew on ships sailing between Portugal and Africa. Ferrymen carrying passengers across the River Tagus in Lisbon were mostly black. These ferrymen were a source of worry to the authorities since their control of ferries enabled them to engage in illegal traffic, including the smuggling of escaped slaves.

Integration into the larger society was always hampered by legal constraints based on principles of limpeza de sangue, or blood purity. Free blacks, for instance, were barred from most trades and professions. The guilds of Lisbon and Oporto started passing bans against the admission of blacks, both free and enslaved, as officers in different trades, which consigned them to the trades' lower levels. Black women, on the other hand, had even fewer possibilities for gainful employment, since trade guilds were exclusively male domains. The most lucrative of all forms of self-employment for women was street vending. Black women sold mostly foodstuffs.

New arrivals of black Africans in Portugal in the twentieth century took place as a result of colonial policies. Immigration of blacks from the African colonies was severely restricted until the 1960s, when international pressure forced the Oliveira Salazar regime to grant the black population of the African colonies equal status with the whites living both in Africa and on the Portuguese mainland. The new African immigrants living in Portuguese cities faced chronic unemployment and substandard living conditions that the economic crisis of Portugal during the 1970s only worsened. Many of them migrated to other European countries, such as France, the Netherlands, and even Spain. After the 1974 revolution, provoked by the unresolved colonial war, Portugal granted independence to its African colonies. Since the 1970s Portugal has emulated the models of France and Great Britain in attempting to create a community of Portuguese-speaking peoples, including Brazil and the five new Luso-African republics. Cultural and economic ties between Portugal and its former colonies remain strong.

Migrants from the ex-colonies to Portuguese cities faced new restrictions with the change in policies after the admission of Portugal to the European Union in 1986. Meanwhile, increasing numbers of Africans from countries other than Portuguese ex-colonies migrated to the Algarve and Setubal regions, mainly seeking work as agricultural laborers under substandard living conditions. However, the Afro-Portuguese population continued to increase, and not only in the main cities such as Lisbon and Porto. The lack of economic opportunity for blacks in Portugal did not impede a high rate of educational achievement, which increased their social status.

Powell, Adam Clayton, Jr.

(b. November 29, 1908, New Haven, Conn.; d. April 4, 1972, Miami, Fla.),
African American congressman and minister, one of the most vocal and
flamboyant black campaigners for civil rights.

Adam Clayton Powell Jr. grew up in Harlem, where his father was the
minister of Abyssinian Baptist Church, one of the largest congregations
in the nation. In 1943 a new congressional district was established in
Harlem that would almost certainly produce the state's first black con-
gressperson. Powell undertook an ambitious campaign for the seat, winning the support of Democrats (on whose ticket he ran), Republicans,
and Communists. In 1945 he became the second of two black members
then serving in Congress.

In his first year in Washington, D.C., Powell denounced First Lady Bess
Truman for her affiliation with the Daughters of the American Revolution,
which then had racially discriminatory policies. President Harry S. Truman
was outraged, and Powell fell out of favor with the White House. Also
relegated to a marginal role in the legislature, Powell pressed for changes
where he could—personally demanding to be served by discriminatory
Washington businesses, ending segregation in congressional service facilities,
campaigning to have black journalists admitted to the press galleries, and
challenging congresspersons who used the word "nigger" on the House
floor. He also repeatedly tried to pass what became known as the Powell
Amendment, which would have denied funding to institutions that practiced racial discrimination.

In the 1956 presidential election Powell infuriated his party by supporting Republican Dwight D. Eisenhower, whom he saw as mildly progressive on civil rights. However, in 1960 Powell campaigned ardently for
Democrat John F. Kennedy and brought with him many of the black votes
that had gone to Eisenhower in 1956. Kennedy's narrow victory coincided
with Powell's rise to the chairmanship of the House Committee on Education and Labor; this was the first time an African American had headed
such a powerful committee. Powell was highly instrumental in passing
much of the progressive legislation enacted in the 1960s, including increases
to the minimum wage; the creation of Medicare, Medicaid, and Head Start;
and the protection of civil rights. A version of the Powell Amendment was
finally codified in the landmark Civil Rights Act of 1964.

At the same time that Powell's power was growing, his support was
being drained by accusations and scandals. The most serious of these
emerged in the early 1950s when several of his aides were convicted of
income tax evasion and rumors circulated that they had also given kickbacks
from their salaries to Powell. He also received negative publicity for his
many absences from Congress and for his personal extravagances. After
the November 1966 elections the House voted to deny to seat Powell. He
challenged the vote, and in 1969 the United States Supreme Court held

that although Congress could expel a member, it could not deny to seat someone duly elected. Powell was finally seated, after an absence of two years, but without his seniority and with his pay docked to pay for financial abuses. In 1970 Charles Rangel emerged from a field of several Democratic challengers to defeat him.

North America

Pride, Charley Frank

(b. March 18, 1938, Sledge, Miss.), first African American country music superstar.

The son of sharecroppers in rural Mississippi, Charley Pride spent his early years surrounded by blues music, but chose to pursue country music professionally. Pride began his bid to be the first black to mount the Grand Ole Opry stage (the apex of country music performance) unconventionally—as a baseball player in the late 1950s. In between innings and on the tour bus as an outfielder for several Negro League teams, Pride displayed his sinewy voice and self-taught mastery of the guitar. Eventually, his nightclub singing was noticed and encouraged by Nashville producers. He gave up baseball for music in 1963. The popularity of his first hits, "Snakes Crawl at Night" (1965) and "Just Between You and Me" (1966), earned him invitations to perform at the Opry, making him the first black country music star to appear there.

Success in music and business followed. He is a superstar singer/composer of more than 50 Top Ten hits, the winner of three Grammy Awards, Cash Box magazine's Top Male Country Singer of the Decade (1970s), and the 1971 Country Music Association Entertainer of the Year. He is second only to Elvis Presley in records sold for the RCA label. In addition to owning other businesses whose profits have made him a multi-millionaire, Pride owns First Texas Bank in Dallas, Texas.

While Pride's rise to fame was meteoric, he faced criticism from within the black community, which perceived country music to be a white arena. Also, early in his career, the Nashville music industry hid Pride's race by issuing publicity material without his photo. In order to help others avoid such discrimination, Pride has been active in a new Nashville organization, the Minority Country Music Association.

North America

Prince (♀, born Prince Rogers Nelson)

(b. June 7, 1958, Minneapolis, Minn.), virtuoso pop musician known for his provocative musical and personal style.

Born Prince Rogers Nelson, ♀ had many transformations on the journey from his childhood nickname, "Skipper," to his current name, ♀ an unpronounceable glyph that he assumed in 1993 that is representative of male and female principles. Deliberately frustrating efforts to characterize his image and his music, he announced a new persona with his 1996 album, *Emancipation*, which was a hoped-for return to his commercial and artistic success of the 1980s.

Notoriously private about his personal life, ♀ is the biracial son of jazz musicians Mattie Shaw Nelson and John Nelson. Self-taught on the guitar, piano, and drums, he received a recording contract at age 20. His first album, 1978's *For You*, blends funk, rock, pop, and jazz; like those albums that follow, it evidences the eclectic musical influences of James Brown, George Clinton, Jimi Hendrix, and the Beatles.

Like his idol, Little Richard, ♀ is flamboyant in dress and personality. After *For You*, his next few albums brought him notoriety as a result of their explicitly sexual lyrics and his own provocative androgyny. Neither black nor white, his music neither rock nor funk, ♀ appealed to all, a fact that helped him crossover onto MTV. He created a virtual cult following with the 1982 album "1999," which went triple platinum, and with 1984's "Purple Rain," which won three Grammy Awards. ♀ starred in and produced the semiautobiographical film *Purple Rain*, for which he earned an Oscar for best score.

Europe

Prince, Mary

(b. 1788, Bermuda; d. ?, Great Britain), first black woman to publish a slave narrative.

The History of Mary Prince, A West Indian Slave, Related by Herself (1831) was the earliest account that gave a firsthand description of the brutality women suffered under slavery. Prince's autobiography became very popular and stirred debate on slavery and the treatment of slaves in the West Indies. Born a slave in Bermuda around 1788, Prince was separated from family members when they were sold to different West Indian plantation owners. Prince herself worked on various estates as a domestic servant and in the fields. Not only did she experience sexual exploitation but she was left with severe scarring from beatings. Finally, while traveling in England with her masters, John Wood and his wife, Prince escaped in 1828.

Prince was determined to fight for her freedom in the English courts, Parliament, and the press. She recounted her slave narrative to a female member of the Anti-Slavery Society; it was then edited by Thomas Pringle, who took pains to keep to the original wording. Despite the publicity she received from the popularity of her book, she seems to have lost her celebrity status soon after. It is known that she remained legally a slave until 1834, when slavery was abolished in England and its colonies.

North America

Pryor, Richard Franklin Lenox Thomas

(b. December 1, 1940, Peoria, Ill.), African American comedian known for his free-flowing, uncensored brand of humor.

Considered by many to be the most influential comedian since 1970, Richard Pryor was born to Gertrude Thomas and Leroy Pryor, who met in a brothel managed by Marie Carter, Leroy's mother. Raised in the brothel primarily by Carter, Pryor gravitated to humor early on to cope with his chaotic family life. A disruptive student, Pryor left school at age 14 and joined a community drama group, which he quit two years later. After serving in the army for two years Pryor began his stand-up comedy career. He performed successfully in Peoria nightclubs, giving him the confidence to go to the more competitive nightclub scene of New York City. Pryor modeled his first performances in New York closely on the comedy of Bill Cosby and Dick Gregory.

By the late 1960s, however, Pryor had decided to present "the real side" of himself, replacing a more refined persona with a raw, unvarnished funkiness. His recognition grew as he recorded stand-up routines and appeared in several films, including *Lady Sings the Blues* and *Uptown Saturday Night*, Pryor's classic explorations of black life. In 1974 Pryor appeared on the cover of *Rolling Stone* magazine because of his gold-selling album, *That Nigger's Crazy*. Despite his overwhelming success Pryor was plagued with financial and drug problems. In 1980, at the time of the release of his first self-produced film, *Bustin' Loose*, he had a near fatal accident while free-basing cocaine. Throughout his turbulent life Pryor retained his sense of humor, as he demonstrated in his autobiographical film *Jo Jo Dancer, Your Life is Calling* (1986). Diagnosed with multiple sclerosis in 1986, Pryor continued to appear in several films, notably in *Harlem Nights* (1989).

North America

Public Enemy,

one of the premier African American rap music groups of the 1980s and 1990s. Public Enemy infused a funk- and soul-based sound with sound samples (electronic snippets of prerecorded music) and other sound fragments, such as traffic noise and police sirens. A political consciousness pervaded this multilayered sound, through rap texts and through physical appearance: group members held fake automatic weapons and wore army fatigues and boots, projecting an image of black militancy. Public Enemy's strident lyrics were highly controversial, striking responsive chords with many people while drawing critical responses from many others.

Public Enemy formed in Long Island, New York, in 1987 out of collaborations among lead rappers Chuck D. (Carlton Ridenhour) and Flavor Flav (William Drayton), disk jockey (DJ) Terminator X (Norman Rogers), and the group's so-called minister of information, Professor Griff (Richard Griffin). The group's producers, Hank Shocklee, Eric "Vietnam" Sadler, and Chuck D., were collectively known as the Bomb Squad. The group took its name from "Public Enemy Number One," a popular rap written by Chuck D. along with DJs Hank and Keith Shocklee.

Public Enemy's first release, "Yo! Bum Rush the Show" (1987), relied upon the rhythms of funk music to create an aggressive sound. The group's second release, "It Takes a Nation of Millions to Hold Us Back " (1988), was layered with additional samples to form a more complex sound. As the group perfected its production and sampling techniques, the content grew more politicized and Public Enemy grew more popular. Chuck D.'s strong vocals were countered by Flavor Flav's rasping voice, with dance steps by the militaristic quartet known as the S1W (Security of the First World). With this combination the group advocated black nationalist activism and opposed what it felt was mindless American consumerism. This worldview in combination with Public Enemy's occasional invectives against whites, women, gays, and Jews elicited strong reactions from listeners—both positive and negative.

In 1989 Public Enemy's song "Fight the Power" was part of the soundtrack for the motion picture *Do the Right Thing*, directed by African American filmmaker Spike Lee. Shortly thereafter Professor Griff made some anti-Semitic statements to the American press, and the group temporarily disbanded. It soon returned, without Griff, and released the commercially successful and critically acclaimed albums *Fear of a Black Planet* (1990) and *Apocalypse 91 . . . The Enemy Strikes Black* (1991). Other albums by Public Enemy include *Greatest Misses* (1992) and *Muse Sick-N-Hour Mess Age* (1994).

Latin America and the Caribbean

Puente, Ernesto Antonio (Tito)

(b. April 20, 1923, New York, N.Y.), bandleader, composer, multi-instrumentalist—accomplished on timbales, conga, bongos, vibraphone, piano, and saxophone—and last of the great originators of Afro-Latin jazz.

With the death of Mario Bauza in 1993, Tito Puente became the last of the early innovators of Afro-Latin jazz who continued to be musically active. Although best known as a bandleader and timbales player, Puente is a multi-instrumentalist, performing on a wide range of percussion instruments as well as on piano and saxophone. For over half a century he has been a dynamic entertainer, emerging in the 1980s as a pop-culture celebrity.

Puente was born in New York City's Spanish Harlem. He had hoped to become a dancer, but an ankle injury led him to choose a career of instrumental performance. During the late 1940s and early 1950s Puente played a key role in the merging of Latin American rhythms with contemporary jazz that produced Afro-Latin jazz. In the late 1940s he formed the Piccadilly

Tito Puente, composer, bandleader, percussionist, outstanding *timbales* player, and an originator of Afro-Latin jazz, performs at the Monterey Jazz Festival. *CORBIS/Craig Lovell*

Boys, which became the Tito Puente Orchestra. The group played a major role in promoting the mambo craze of the late 1940s. A decade later Puente helped popularize the chachachá sound. He produced swinging and danceable style by transforming the music of charanga bands, which feature violin and flute, and arranging it for a Latin jazz big band with saxes, trumpets, and trombones. In the 1970s, when salsa became popular, he gained a new and younger audience.

Since 1949 Puente has released more than 100 albums as a leader, an accomplishment rivaled by few musicians of any genre. His recording "Abaniquito" (1949) was a hit single and an early crossover success. In the 1970s Carlos Santana covered two of Puente's compositions: "Para los rumberos" (1956) and a hugely popular rendition of "Oye como va" (1963). Puente's various bands have featured many musicians who went on to prominence in Afro-Latin jazz, including percussionists Ray Barreto, Mongo Santamaría, and Willie Bobo; Fania Records founder Johnny Pacheco; and, more recently, saxophonist Mario Rivera, pianist Hilton Ruiz, trumpeter Charlie Sepúlveda, and drummer Ignacio Berroa. Outside of the world of jazz Puente has performed with various Latin music stars, including the Fania All Stars, Celia Cruz, and Carlos "Patato" Valdez.

Since the late 1970s Puente has also gained wider exposure in American popular culture. In the 1980s he appeared on "The Cosby Show" and in a stylish and well-received Coca-Cola commercial. He received Grammy Awards for" A Tribute to Benny Moré" (1979), "On Broadway" (1983), "Mambo Diablo" (1985), and "Goza mi timbal" (1989).

Latin America and the Caribbean

Puerto Rico,

the easternmost island of the Greater Antilles, bounded on the north by the
Atlantic Ocean, on the south by the Caribbean Sea, on the east by the Virgin
Passage, and on the west by the Mona Passage, which separates it from the
Dominican Republic.

Heralded as "the shining star of the Caribbean" in tourism brochures and
advertisements, Puerto Rico exemplifies the complexities of race relations
and the use of terminology and definitions to describe them. Considered by
some as "the whitest of all the Antilles," Puerto Ricans are usually described
as mostly Hispanic, a homogeneous race of mixed people. This conception
of the Puerto Rican underestimates the African component, one that has
had a significant impact on the culture and ethnic composition of Puerto
Rico. The African traditions brought to Puerto Rico were syncretized with
the Spanish, the Taíno, and, later, the Anglo-American traditions to produce
a rich cultural and ethnic amalgam. The racial mixture between blacks and
whites has shaped the conception of race in Puerto Rico. There has been a
growing scholarly interest in the Creole blacks and their importance in the
formation of the Puerto Rican society, in contrast to the traditional history
that has focused on the actions of the ruling white Creole elite.

Traditional United States conceptions of blackness (including anyone
with some African blood) and whiteness are of limited use in assessing
Puerto Rican conceptions of race. The population's seemingly genial
attitude toward race relations gives the impression of a society free from
racism and prejudice. Yet this idea is proved wrong by the social, political,
and economic status of Afro-Puerto Ricans.

In 1898, just as Puerto Rico was making strides toward autonomy, it was
ceded to the United States under the Treaty of Paris, after the Spanish-
Cuban-American War. The military led the island for a short time, followed

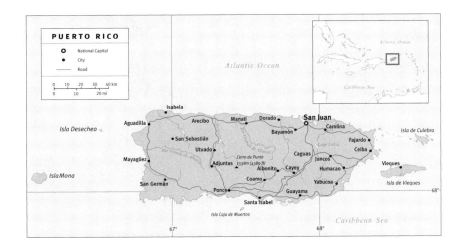

by a civil government outlined in the Foraker Act, which was approved in 1900. United States racial attitudes and race issues then began to affect Puerto Rican life, aggravating the already existing racism on the island in which the definition of a national identity privileged the Hispanic heritage over the African.

The Bill of Rights of Puerto Rico's Constitution was approved in 1952 and included a specific provision prohibiting discrimination on the basis of race, color, or social condition. In 1965 a civil rights commission was created for the purpose of investigating and educating the public and proposing legal reforms on issues of civil rights, including racial discrimination. Under the commonwealth status, the United States Constitution and civil rights laws are fully applicable to Puerto Rico, reinforcing the local laws that existed before federal protections became effective.

African heritage is an essential and undeniable part of Puerto Rican culture. It is evident in musical expressions like salsa; in the vernacular rhythms of plena and bomba, which are also dances; in the language; in the cuisine; and in popular traditions of the island. Afro-Puerto Ricans like Roberto Clemente have distinguished themselves in sports. Many political leaders of African descent, such as Pedro Albizu Campos, Ernesto Ramos Antonini, and José Celso Barbosa, have played important roles in history. In the arts, musicians like Rafael Cortijo, Ismael Rivera, Rafael Hernández, and Willie Colón; painters like José Campeche; and writers like Julia De Burgos, Luis Palés Matos, and Luis Rafel Sánchez serve as examples of the importance of Afro-Puerto Rican culture and ethnicity.

Europe

Pushkin, Alexander

(b. June 6, 1799, Moscow; d. February 10, 1837, St. Petersburg, Russia), Russian poet and author of plays, novels, and short stories, considered the founder of modern Russian literature; his maternal great-grandfather was African.

Alexander Pushkin was of high birth: his father came from a long line of Russian aristocracy, and his mother was the granddaughter of Abram Hannibal, who proclaimed himself to be an African prince. Sold into slavery in the early eighteenth century, Hannibal became an engineer and major general in the Russian army and was a favorite of Tsar Peter I (Peter the Great).

Enchanted with his African ancestry, Pushkin often employed the subject in his poetry, to the point of exaggeration and obsession, according to his critics. Pushkin was deeply influenced by the Russian folklore and stories his maternal grandmother told him as a child, and he searched out similar stories from Russian villagers throughout his life. As were many Russian aristocrats, he was also well versed in French language and literature. Educated at the Imperial Lyceum at Tsarkoye Selo, Pushkin demonstrated an early poetic genius in works such as "To My Friend the Poet" (1820), which demonstrated his allegiance to Romantic literary styles.

Pushkin diverged from this style in later works. In *Ruslan and Liudmila* (1820) he espoused a literary manner characterized by ample use of Russian folklore in the form of a narrative poem. Because this work rejected established rules and genres, he was criticized by the main literary schools of the day, classicism and sentimentalism. Still, *Ruslan and Liudmila* earned him a reputation as one of Russia's most promising poetic talents.

In 1817 Pushkin accepted a position in the Ministry of Foreign Affairs in St. Petersburg. He participated in the city's social life and belonged to an underground branch of the revolutionary group Union of Welfare. The radical fervor he expressed through his verse made him an inspiring spokesman for the revolutionaries who fought in the 1825 Decembrist uprising for a constitutional monarchy. They were violently suppressed. It was during this period that Pushkin wrote "Ode to Liberty" (1820), for which he was exiled to the Caucasus.

This undated illustration by Vasily Tropinin shows the poet Alexander Pushkin (1799-1837), whose work reflected both his love of Russian folktales and his fascination with his partially African heritage. His great-grandfather, Abram Hannibal, was a slave who had become a major general in the Russian army. *CORBIS/Bettmann*

Pushkin's works written in exile, called his "southern cycle," were clearly influenced by the English poet Lord Byron. He demonstrates the love for liberty typical of his contemporaries in the romantic narrative poems "The Prisoner of the Caucasus" (1822), "The Fountain of Bakhchisarai" (1824), and "The Gypsies" (1824). In 1823 he began *Eugene Onegin* (1831), known to be the first of the great Russian novels (although in verse). Though a Byronic love story, *Eugene Onegin* treats the Russian historical setting realistically and the characters objectively.

Pushkin was transferred to Odessa in 1823, but after a series of incidents, including an affair with a superior's wife, he was dismissed from government service in 1824. He was banished to his mother's estate near Pskov, where he wrote Boris Godunov (1931), a Russian historical tragedy in the Shakespearean tradition. In Boris Godunov, Pushkin emphasizes the moral and political importance of "the judgment of the people" toward their rulers, and proved that he could, as he felt poet-prophets should, "fire the hearts of men with his words."

In 1826 Tsar Nicholas I, recognizing Pushkin's enormous popularity, pardoned him. On his return to the capital Pushkin continued to evoke Russian nationalist themes in two long poems, *Poltava* (1828) and *The Bronze Horseman* (1833), as well as in his novel of the Pugachev rebellion, *The Captain's Daughter* (1836). He also wrote short stories including "The Queen of Spades" (1834) and a fictionalized biography of his great-grandfather, *The Negro of Peter the Great* (unfinished version published in 1837). In this biography Pushkin represented Hannibal in a completely positive manner, making the novel one of the earliest to promote the "Negro as hero" in world literature.

Qaddafi, Muammar al-

(also spelled Moammar Gadhafi, or Mu'ammar al-Qadhdafi); (b. 1942), head of state in Libya since 1970.

Muammar al-Qaddafi was born to a Bedouin family near the Libyan town of Surt. The strict Islamic Bedouin way of life profoundly influenced Qaddafi's later asceticism as well as his political philosophy. When Qaddafi was a young man, both Gamal Abdel Nasser's nationalist struggle in neighboring Egypt and the Arab struggle for Palestine drew him to Arab populist politics. In 1961 he entered the Libyan military academy in Binghazi, where he helped found a student military group called the Free Officers Movement and met the men who would eventually plot to overthrow the Libyan monarchy.

In September 1969, at a time when anti-Western, Arab nationalist sentiments were running high in Libya, the Free Officers Movement seized power in a two-hour bloodless coup. Once in power Qaddafi immediately began to overhaul Libyan government and society. He charged many of the nation's former leaders with treason, outlawed the politically influential Islamic Sanusi sect, and weakened tribal affiliations by reorganizing administrative structures. He denounced communism for its atheism, and promoted Muslim asceticism by banning liquor. In 1973 he instituted People's Committees to give citizens direct control of local and regional government. The General People's Congress took over as the national representative body from the RCC, and Qaddafi became the general secretariat of the Socialist People's Libyan Arab Jamahiriya (state of the masses)—thus remaining the nation's ultimate decision maker and military leader. Several years later he created "revolutionary committees" to guide the People's Committees, and took the title "Leader of the Revolution." He also nationalized the oil and banking industries as well as a large proportion of the retail sector. All these measures were inspired by Qaddafi's vision of populist Arab nationalism, which he described in *The Green Book (1976)*.

Not surprisingly, Qaddafi's policies provoked significant opposition. Many of the middle class fled the country. Islamic leaders resented the nationalization of Islamic properties as well as Qaddafi's theological justifications of political policy. Army officers opposed to his reforms staged an unsuccessful coup in 1975; they were subsequently arrested and executed. Qaddafi dealt severely with all his challengers and allegedly sponsored the assassination of exiled opposition leaders.

Throughout the 1970s and 1980s the United States accused him of supporting anti-Western movements. Following several diplomatic conflicts over the extradition of suspected terrorists, the United States bombed Libya in 1986. Since then tensions between the former trading partners remain high, and the United States has accused Qaddafi of manufacturing chemical weapons.

Despite the United States' and the United Nations' ongoing embargoes on trade with and international flights to the country, Libya under Qaddafi is still one of the richest countries in Africa, enjoying high levels of literacy and social services. Qaddafi has had little trouble finding European investors or trading partners, and in recent years he has stepped up efforts to cultivate political and economic ties with sub-Saharan African nations. Seemingly secure in his seat of power, Qaddafi continues to pursue ambitious projects, such as the $30 billion "Great Man-Made River," billed as the soon-to-be world's largest pipeline, intended to move subterranean water in the southern desert to the heavily populated Mediterranean coast.

North America

Quarles, Benjamin

(b. January 23, 1904, Boston, Mass.; d. November 17, 1996, Cheverly, Md.), African American historian, author, and editor, key figure in the emergence of African American history as an academic discipline.

Benjamin Quarles was the son of a subway porter. He earned a B.A. in 1931 from Shaw University, in Raleigh, North Carolina, an M.A. in 1933, and a Ph.D. in 1940, both from the University of Wisconsin. Quarles taught at Shaw, was the dean of Dillard University in New Orleans, Louisiana, and served as chair of the history department at Morgan State University in Baltimore, Maryland.

One of the focuses of Quarles's historical research and writing was race relations. His first published journal article was "The Breach Between Douglass and Garrison," which appeared in the *Journal of Negro History* in 1938. Many of his other scholarly articles and monographs developed the same theme. However, Quarles has also focused on the black contribution during two major American crises in *The Negro in the American Revolution* (1961) (see American Revolution) and *The Negro in the Civil War* (1953).

Early in Quarles's career, two popular misconceptions existed regarding African American history. The first was that African Americans could not write objective history. The second was that few documentary sources existed for research and writing in African American history. Quarles's scholarship did much to dispel these notions. He was the first African American to publish essays in the *Mississippi Valley Historical Review* (now the *Journal of American History*), in 1945 and 1959. He served as a contributing editor to the journal *Phylon* and as an associate editor of the *Journal of Negro History*. Quarles also wrote two textbooks, *The Negro in the Making of America* and *The Negro American: A Documentary History*.

North America

Queen Latifah

(b. March 18, 1970, Newark, N.J.), African American rap artist, actress, entertainment executive, and entrepreneur.

Queen Latifah, born Dana Owens in Newark, New Jersey, was nicknamed "Latifah" (which means "delicate" and "sensitive" in Arabic) at age eight by a Black Muslim cousin. Soon afterward her parents separated, and Latifah moved with her mother, Rita, and older brother, Lance Jr., into a housing project in East Newark.

In high school Latifah played Power Forward on the school's basketball team. During her sophomore year she began rapping with two friends in an all-women's group called Ladies Fresh. Encouraged by her mother, she began recording and performing, and added "Queen" to her nickname.

Latifah was attending the Borough of Manhattan Community College in Manhattan when a demo tape featuring her rap "Princess of the Posse" made its way to Tommy Boy Records, based in New York City. She was quickly signed by the label, and in 1988 she released two singles, "Wrath of My Madness" and "Dance for Me." In 1989 she toured Europe, appeared at the Apollo Theater in Harlem, and issued her first album, *All Hail the Queen*, to wide acclaim. The album earned her the Best New Artist Award for 1990 from the New Music Seminar of Manhattan, and subsequently went platinum. Its second single, "Ladies First," celebrated black women's contributions to the struggle for black liberation in America, Africa, and around the world. It became a rap classic, eventually named by the Rock and Roll Hall of Fame as one of the 500 Songs That Shaped Rock and Roll.

By the time her second album Nature of a Sista' came out in 1991, Latifah had begun investing in small businesses in her neighborhood and acting both in television and movies. These successes were marred by contract conflicts that caused her to leave Tommy Boy, and by her brother's tragic death in a motorcycle accident in 1992.

After signing with Motown in 1993, Latifah released her third album, *Black Reign*, and with her newfound clout founded Flavor Unit Records and Management, which primarily handles rap and new-style rhythm and blues groups. "U.N.I.T.Y.," the album's first single, denounced sexist attitudes and violence against women. Latifah also landed a regular spot on the highly rated television sitcom, "Living Single," which lasted five seasons. Over the next few years Latifah went on to more film roles, including the critically acclaimed portrayal of Cleo, a lesbian bank robber, in *Set It Off* (1996). In 1997 Queen Latifah was awarded the Aretha Franklin Award for Entertainer of the Year at the Soul Train Lady of Soul Awards. She released her fourth album, *Order in the Court*, in 1998.

Africa

Queen of Sheba,

legendary queen of South Arabia or Ethiopia, credited in Ethiopian tradition with marrying King Solomon of Israel and founding Ethiopia's ruling Dynasty.

According to the Book of Kings in the Bible, the Queen of Sheba learned of the wisdom of King Solomon and went to Jerusalem to test him "with hard questions." She arrived in a vast caravan, "with camels that bore spices, and very much gold, and precious stones."

Yemenis and Ethiopians both claim that the Queen of Sheba once ruled in their country. While an ancient kingdom of Saba did flourish in South Arabia (present-day Yemen) some centuries after the reign of Solomon, growing rich from the spice trade, ancient inscriptions reveal that there was also a kingdom in Ethiopia known by the dual name Daamat and Saba. The incense, or spice, that grew in South Arabia also grew on the other side of the Red Sea.

The Ethiopian claim to the Queen of Sheba is detailed in the famous epic, *Kebra Nagast* (The Glory of Kings). It is based on the visit described in the Bible but adds that the queen bore a son, Menilek, to King Solomon. When Menilek was grown he visited his father, who anointed him to rule in Africa and sent the sons of his own counselors to help Menilek as king. The young men were unhappy to leave the famous temple in Jerusalem, especially as it contained the Ark of the Covenant, in which the presence of God was believed to dwell. In secret they removed the Ark and took it with them to Ethiopia. For centuries Ethiopian tradition has maintained that it is still preserved in the cathedral at Aksum.

The Ethiopian epic seems to have been compiled and recorded in writing during the thirteenth century, but its origin is difficult to determine. It is certainly true that from the restoration of the Solomonic Dynasty around 1270 until the death of the last emperor, Haile Selassie I, in 1974, the emperors of Ethiopia claimed descent from Solomon and the Queen of Sheba. The claim was even part of the constitution proclaimed by Haile Selassie in 1955.

Querino, Manoel Raimundo

(b. July 28, 1851, Santo Amaro, Bahia, Brazil; d. February 14, 1923, Salvador, Bahia, Brazil), the first Afro-Brazilian historian to document African contributions to Brazil.

During a lifetime that spanned the abolition movement, the emancipation of the slaves, and the beginning of modernization in Brazil, Manoel Raimundo Querino distinguished himself as an artist, teacher, social activist, and above all, historian. He was born free one year after the abolition of the slave trade in Brazil. In 1855 a cholera epidemic swept Bahia, claiming the lives of some 30,000 people, including Querino's parents.

Querino's career as an artist and teacher began in 1871, when he returned to Salvador. Querino participated in the abolition movement in Brazil during the 1880s, joining the Bahian Liberation Society (established 1887) and writing a number of articles calling for the "immediate and unconditional freedom" of the slaves. Nevertheless, he did his most important work in connection with Afro-Brazilians after abolition in 1888. While remaining committed to art and the working-class struggle, Querino spent an increasing amount of time researching and writing about Afro-Brazilian culture and history. Up until the early twentieth century books on Brazilian history made little or no mention of the contributions of Africans to the country's development. Querino began documenting and analyzing the history of black Brazilians in order to revise and balance the traditional historiography on Brazil that emphasized European experiences.

Thus Querino was not only the first Afro-Brazilian historian, but also one of the first Brazilian historians of any background to research and document the importance of African culture in Brazil. In highlighting the struggles and achievements of Afro-Brazilians, Querino hoped to combat racism and to imbue Afro-Brazilians with a sense of pride in their past. In works such as "O colono prêto como fator da civilação Brasileiro" *(The African Contribution to Brazilian Civilization)*, Querino introduced readers to numerous accomplished Afro-Brazilian figures from the past and asserted that "in truth, it was the black who built Brazil."

Before Querino, no Afro-Brazilian had given his or her perspective on Brazilian history. His perspective was based not only on his own research, but also on his exchanges with the members of the predominantly black neighborhood of Matutú Grande where he lived. For this reason Arthur Ramos, a leading scholar of Afro-Brazilian history, said, "[Querino] remains one of the most solid sources of honest documentation for the Negro in Brazil."

R

Ragtime,

a late nineteenth-century African American musical genre that influenced strongly an emerging American popular music and that provided a major impetus in the development of jazz.

Although ragtime has come to connote a particular form of piano music associated with composer Scott Joplin, the term originally applied to a larger body of instrumental music and song. Emerging in the 1890s, ragtime thrived for two decades, as millions of middle-class whites bought sheet music, pianos, and piano rolls. Through its immense commercial success, ragtime gave birth to the American music industry, and through its rhythmic and melodic innovations, it signaled the end of America's dependency on Western European music. Ragtime ushered in a new style of concert music that built upon Afro-diasporic musical traditions.

Because ragtime emerged from African American folk music, its precise origins remain undocumented and obscure. Yet the roots of ragtime undoubtedly lie in the music of itinerant black pianists who played in bordellos and saloons. Ironically, ragtime's quick acceptance was due in part to the minstrel tradition that portrayed African Americans as exotic, lazy, and funny. Primed by these stereotypes as well as bastardized versions of black songs, middle-class audiences readily accepted real African American music.

The origin of the word "ragtime" also remains obscure. Some historians suspect it derives from the "ragged," or syncopated, playing style that characterized black music in the late nineteenth century. Others cite the use of "rag" as a name for a short African American folk tune. Evidence such as an early piece by Joplin, "Original Rags," suggests that ragtime piano originally anthologized folk melodies. Bordello pianists probably collected and blended familiar strains. Nevertheless, "rag" soon came to designate the larger structure instead of the fragments that composed it.

The popularity of ragtime provoked much criticism from both musical and moral conservatives. Because ragtime's new rhythms inspired lively dancing, many older people found it threatening, and some musicians trained in simple European rhythms found its syncopation cacophonous. The controversy reflected ragtime's revolutionary significance. By ushering in the jazz age and establishing African American rhythms as viable roots for classical music, ragtime challenged the old order, socially as well as musically. J. B. Priestly wrote, "Out of this ragtime came the fragmentary outlines of the menace to old Europe, the domination of America, the emergence of Africa, the end of confidence and any feeling of security, the nervous excitement, the feeling of modern times."

North America

Rainey, Gertrude Pridgett ("Ma")

(b. April 26, 1886, Columbus, Ga.; d. December 22, 1939, Columbus, Ga.), African American classic blues singer and vaudeville performer.

Born to minstrels Thomas and Ella Pridgett, Gertrude Pridgett entered show business at age 14 as a member of the traveling stage show the "Bunch of Blackberries." In 1904 she married showman William "Pa" Rainey, and the two formed a song and dance act called "Rainey and Rainey: The Assassinators of the Blues" that lasted until 1916. While touring mostly in the South during that period, and subsequently as a soloist with the Rabbit Foot Minstrels on the Theater Owners' Booking Association circuit, Ma Rainey developed her "classic blues" style of rough-edged reality moans and humorous shouts.

In 1923 Ma Rainey began a brief but prolific recording career with Chicago-based Paramount Records with "Moonshine Blues." By 1928 she had recorded 93 songs, many of which she wrote herself. As a result of the wide circulation of these records, Rainey gained enormous popularity with African Americans. Her contract was rescinded by Paramount, however, because it was felt that her style could not compete with the new male acts such as "Big Bill" Broonzy and "Leadbelly," nor with her friend Bessie Smith's growing status and stature. Rainey's once appealing raw style was believed to be out of vogue with the African American record-buying public.

Ma Rainey maintained a loyal fan base, however, and continued to perform throughout the country until 1935, when both her sister Malissa and her mother died. Returning to her home in Columbus, she owned and managed two theaters until her death four years later. Rainey's significance within African American popular culture is exemplified not only by her impact on musical heirs such as singer Koko Taylor, but also by her appearance in the writing of poet Sterling Brown ("Ma Rainey") and playwright August Wilson (*Ma Rainey's Black Bottom*). In 1990 Ma Rainey was inducted into the Rock and Roll Hall of Fame.

Randall, Dudley Felker

(b. January 14, 1914, Washington, D.C.), African American poet and publisher who was instrumental in promoting poetry of the Black Arts Movement.

Dudley Randall was the son of a teacher, Ada Viola Bradley Randall, and a Congregational minister, Arthur George Clyde Randall. In 1923 the family moved from Washington, D.C., to Detroit, Michigan, where Randall has since spent most of his life.

After completing high school, Randall worked for the Ford Motor Company and served in the army during World War II. He was unable to attend college until his early 30s. In 1949 Randall received a B.A. in English from Wayne University (now Wayne State University). He then earned a master of library science from the University of Michigan in 1951, providing him with credentials to work as a reference librarian at several colleges, including Morgan State College (now University) and the University of Detroit. In addition, he taught poetry at the University of Michigan and was poet-in-residence at the University of Detroit from 1969 to 1977.

In 1965 Randall established Broadside Press. He published his own poems and other important works by such writers as Gwendolyn Brooks, Sonia Sanchez, Haki Madhubuti (Don L. Lee), and Audre Lorde. These artists viewed African American creativity as the essence of their culture and contributed to the Black Arts Movement of the late 1960s and early 1970s. Randall's poetry collections include *Cities Burning* (1968), *Love You* (1970), and *A Litany of Friends: New and Selected Poems* (1981).

Randall's major contribution to African American literature has been to offer access to a liberating voice in print, where one had not existed on a mass scale since the Harlem Renaissance. According to poet Addison Gayle, he has "bridged the gap between poets of the 20s and those of the 60s and 70s."

Randolph, Asa Philip

(b. April 15, 1889, Crescent City, Fla.; d. May 16, 1979, New York, N.Y.), founder and president of the Brotherhood of Sleeping Car Porters (BSCP); editor of *The Messenger*; and architect of the March on Washington Movement in 1941, which led to the establishment of the Fair Employment Practices Committee (FEPC), and the 1963 March on Washington.

Although many civil rights leaders focused on voting, education, and other governmental functions, A. Philip Randolph spent his long career as a labor leader working to bring more and better jobs to African Americans. After a long, successful battle to win representation for the nation's Pullman porters, Randolph was instrumental in the formation of the FEPC, which

A. Philip Randolph stands before the Lincoln Memorial on August 28, 1963, the day of the March on Washington, an event that was the culmination of Randolph's long career as an advocate of racial and economic justice. *CORBIS/Bettmann*

protected African Americans against job discrimination in the army and defense industries. In addition, Randolph co-founded and edited *The Messenger*, the socialist black magazine.

In 1914 Randolph met Chandler Owen, whose progressive politics and interest in socialism matched his own. In 1917 the two began *The Messenger*, whose editorials strongly opposed United States entry into World War I, stating, "No intelligent Negro is willing to lay down his life for the United States as it now exists." Though the magazine was never profitable, it was influential, offering a more radical voice than that of W. E. B. Du Bois's *Crisis* or the even more conventional *New York Age. The Messenger*, with its advocacy of labor unions, was especially popular among Pullman porters—all of whom were black—who served white railroad passengers in luxurious sleeping cars. Founded just after the Civil War, the Pullman Company had by the 1920s become the nation's single largest employer of African Americans. Many of the Pullman porters were college graduates who enjoyed great respect within their communities, but at work they were subjected to unfair and discriminatory practices.

In 1925 with Randolph at the helm, the BSCP began organizing the nearly 10,000 porters. For ten years Randolph kept the members unified and inspired, often in the face of intimidation and firings, while he negotiated with the president and Congress to amend the Railway Labor Act.

Finally, in a hard-won victory hailed by African Americans and progressives nationwide, the company recognized their union in 1935.

Randolph continued to fight for racial and economic justice in the late 1930s as president of the National Negro Congress before resigning in protest over its increasing domination by Communists. In 1940 he returned to the issue of jobs, joining Walter White, secretary of the National Association for the Advancement of Colored People (NAACP), and T. Arnold Hill of the National Urban League in urging President Franklin D. Roosevelt to desegregate the military and defense industries before World War II. After an unsatisfactory resolution to a meeting with the president, Randolph began planning a march on Washington, D.C., by the BSCP and others to demand "the right to work and fight for our country." The date for at least 10,000 African Americans to demonstrate before the Lincoln Memorial was set for July 1, 1941. Despite the president's wish to avoid a mass demonstration, Randolph refused to call off the march unless Roosevelt banned discrimination in the burgeoning defense industries. Following another meeting with Randolph and White, the president at last issued Executive Order 8002, which not only outlawed such discrimination but also established the FEPC to investigate breaches of the order.

Though the FEPC operated only from 1941 to 1946, Randolph continued to push for his other goal: desegregation of the U.S. armed forces. When President Harry S. Truman instituted a peacetime draft, Randolph told him "this time Negroes will not take a Jim Crow draft lying down." In July 1948 Truman signed Executive Order 9981, finally ending the historic segregation of African American soldiers.

Throughout the 1950s Randolph worked with the NAACP and other civil rights leaders. He helped plan and spoke at Pilgrimage Day, a 1957 prayer meeting in Washington, D.C. He met with President Dwight D. Eisenhower to push for faster school integration in the wake of *Brown v. Board of Education* and planned a 1958 Youth March for Integrated Schools. He also continued his union work and became vice president of the newly consolidated AFL-CIO from 1955 to 1968.

Randolph's brainchild, the March on Washington Movement, bore new fruit in 1963 with the help of Bayard Rustin and Rev. Martin Luther King Jr., who, along with Randolph, mobilized the largest demonstration of the Civil Rights Movement. Speaking before King did, the 74-year-old Randolph exhorted the crowd of 250,000 to take part in a "revolution for jobs and freedom." The next year President Lyndon B. Johnson signed the Civil Rights Act of 1964 and awarded Randolph the Presidential Medal of Freedom. In his final years Randolph established the A. Philip Randolph Institute, a job skills and training bureau in Harlem. Upon Randolph's death in 1979, Rustin said of his late colleague, "No individual did more to help the poor, the dispossessed and the working class . . . than A. Philip Randolph."

Rap,

an urban music that emerged from the hip-hop movement of the South Bronx, New York, in the 1970s and that still thrives today.

Rap music combines rhythmic instrumental tracks created by a disc jockey, or DJ, with the spoken, rhyming bravura of a master of ceremonies, or MC. DJs often "sample" pieces of other recorded music in the creation of songs. MCs frequently rap about politics, sexual exploits, the conditions of daily life, and their own (sometimes exaggerated) personal attributes. MCs and DJs appropriate pop culture through lyrical allusions as well as rhythmic sound bites, leading many critics to consider rap the preeminent example of postmodern music. Rap gives some African Americans a powerful voice. The eager embrace of rap by young whites, however, complicates the dynamic. Rap reflects racial confusion as well as cultural innovation in an age of cable television, digital technology, and marked class stratification.

Rap lyrics descend directly from a few specific cultural figures of the twentieth century. Heavyweight champion boxer Muhammad Ali show-cased the craft of clever rhymes and cocky toasts. "H. Rap" Brown, a Black Nationalist who was active in the 1960s, gave both his name and his oratory style to rap music. In the late 1960s the Watts Prophets of Los Angeles and the Last Poets of Harlem pioneered a kind of proto-rap by setting Brown's speaking style to rhythmic, musical accompaniments. Rap originally took its rhythms from the soul and funk of James Brown, George Clinton, and others who had emerged from the rhythm and blues (R&B) tradition. As rap developed, other kinds of music were sampled and imitated. In the 1990s Wu Tang Clan borrowed orchestral excerpts and Sean "Puff Daddy" Combs achieved popularity by rapping to the rhythm track of "Every Breath You Take," a song by the British rock band The Police.

Despite the depressed economic conditions under which rap developed, early rappers seldom wrote socially conscious lyrics. As rappers attracted larger audiences in the early 1980s, however, they began to address ghetto conditions and economic inequalities of the United States under President Ronald Reagan. "The Message" (1981) by Grandmaster Flash and the Fu-rious Five marked the advent of political rap, inspiring KRS-One (short for Knowledge Reigns Supreme-Over nearly everyone), Sister Souljah, Public Enemy, and Arrested Development.

When the rap group Run-D.M.C. fused rap and hard rock on their eponymous album in 1984, rap completed its break into the mainstream. The album sold more than 500,000 copies, becoming the first rap LP to go gold. Run-D.M.C.'s label, Def Jam Records, became the most successful independent record company in the business. Def Jam released hit music by rap star LL Cool J and, in 1985, signed a major distribution agreement with Columbia Records. Run-D.M.C.'s success among white audiences as well as their contract with a white-owned label reflected the mainstream appro-priation of the new black form.

This appropriation prompted many to speculate about underlying issues of race. To some black critics, white listeners appeared to be seeking thrills from racially motivated fantasies. Writer David Samuels suggests that "the ways in which rap has been consumed and popularized speak not of cross-cultural understanding, musical or otherwise, but of a voyeurism and tolerance of racism in which blacks and whites are both complicit."

Although rap began as a predominantly male activity, a number of successful female performers punctuated its history. Hit acts included MC Lyte, the Real Roxanne, Roxanne Shante, and Yo-Yo. In the 1990s women rappers often followed the male model, however, portraying men in the same derogatory way that men portrayed women. Sister Souljah broke this limited mold by addressing drug abuse, black-on-black violence, and national politics, while Queen Latifah and Salt 'n' Pepa both addressed female self-empowerment. The successful rap arranger, writer, and producer Missy "Misdemeanor" Elliott gained fame as a performer with the 1997 release of her solo debut album, *Supa Dupa Fly*.

In the late 1980s a more brutal brand of rap developed, which described drugs, sex, and violence in detail. Tremendous white consumption of such music made the grim, lurid, and angry lyrics profitable. "Gangsta" rap, as performed by the Geto Boys, N.W.A., Ice Cube, Ice-T, and Too Short, supplied this demand. David Samuels writes that "rap's appeal to whites rested in its evocation of an age-old image of blackness: a foreign, sexually charged and criminal underworld against which the norms of white society are defined. . . . "

The glorification of misogyny and violence had ardent critics in both the black and white establishments. In 1990 a Florida district court declared the album *Nasty as They Wanna Be*, recorded by the Miami group 2 Live Crew, to be legally obscene—a ruling that outlawed the sale of the record. When Ice-T released *Cop-Killer* in 1991, policemen organized a boycott against Time Warner, the company that distributed the album. In addition, police started blaming crimes on rap songs, as criminals cited the influence of gangsta rap as part of their defense.

Many black critics declared white anger hypocritical, however, by pointing to the uncensored obscenity of popular white comedian Andrew Dice Clay as well as anti-police messages in songs by Eric Clapton, Bob Dylan, and Woody Guthrie. Events in the 1990s led critics to question the lifestyle of gangsta rappers as well as the culpability of the media in celebrity-related crime. These events included the death of rapper Eazy-E from AIDS, and the murders of East Coast-West Coast rivals Chris Wallace, a.k.a. Biggie Smalls (The Notorious B.I.G.), and Tupac Shakur, a.k.a. 2PAC.

An increasingly popular and gentrified form of rap developed concurrently with gangsta rap. In the late 1980s lighthearted songs, more in the spirit of early Bronx rap, garnered popularity. Performers such as Young MC, MC Rob Base & DJ EZ Rock, and DJ Jazzy Jeff & the Fresh Prince recorded clean hits filled with playful braggadocio. Rap-based Saturday morning cartoons appeared in the wake of such songs. In 1990 rap reached prime-time television in the form of The Fresh Prince of Bel-Air, a situation comedy. Even the more serious rappers often found themselves in the thick of popular culture. LL Cool J landed a sitcom, while Tone Loc, Ice-T, Ice Cube, and Queen Latifah appeared in Hollywood films. Will Smith, a.k.a. the Fresh Prince, went furthest in this direction, starring in two summer blockbusters, *Independence Day* (1996) and *Men In Black* (1997).

Rap had begun as a homemade music, and its commercialization did not steal it from the streets. In the late 1990s amateurs across the United States and the world continued to create innovative hip hop sounds, generating a culture far larger than that reflected by the recording industry. "Famous" rap became famous by virtue of mainstream listeners and media, while fresher sounds often remained local and undiscovered. Such new rap continues to prosper as a living art, always outdistancing its commercialized, pop-chart predecessors.

Latin America and the Caribbean

Rastafarians,

members of a social movement established in Jamaica around 1930 that combines elements of religious prophecy, specifically the idea of a black God and Messiah; the Pan-Africanist philosophy of Marcus Garvey; the ideas of Black Power Movement leader Walter Rodney; and the defiance of reggae music.

Religion has been the principal form of resistance in Jamaica since colonial times. As scholar of Rastafarianism Barry Chevannes affirms: "Whether resistance through the use of force, or resistance through symbolic forms such as language, folk-tales and proverbs . . . religion was the main driving force among the Jamaican peasants." During the early twentieth century resistance in Jamaica reached its pinnacle with the birth of Rastafarianism—as much an Afrocentric world view and form of Black Nationalism as it was a new religion, inspired by the independent, anti-colonial Christian tradition of the Ethiopian Orthodox Church. As Horace Campell notes, "Rastafari culture combines the histories of the children of slaves in different societies. Within it exist both the negative and the positive—the idealist and the ideological—responses of an exploited and racially humiliated people."

The Rastafari Movement

The roots of Rastafarianism can be traced back to Jamaica's earliest freedom fighters against colonialism. According to Leonard E. Barrett Sr., author of *The Rastafarians*, Jamaica's African population "suffered the most frustrating and oppressive slavery ever experienced in a British colony. . . . Under such complete domination two reactions were provoked: fight and flight." The Jamaican maroons—African slaves, who, following the British defeat of the Spaniards in 1655, escaped to the mountains—waged guerrilla warfare against the British colonizers. In 1738 the British were compelled to grant them a limited freedom: although the maroons were allowed their own lands and leaders, they were also required to police the plantation slaves, a duty that they accepted. Henceforth, the maroons were loyal to the Crown. Plantation slaves took up the freedom movement. Indeed, in 1831, under the leadership of the slave and Baptist religious leader Samuel Sharpe, Jamaica's slaves waged a mass rebellion against the planters. Like Sharpe, many Jamaican slaves believed that God was calling on them to fight for their freedom—a messianic vision partly influenced by Baptist and Methodist missionaries, who, during the mid-eighteenth century, established churches in Jamaica and contributed to a syncretism of Christianity and the island's African religions. Although the rebellion was violently repressed by the British, it was one of the main reasons that England emancipated the slaves in 1834.

In 1865 the Morant Bay Rebellion—another large-scale uprising of Jamaica's rural blacks against the colonial elite—forced political and economic reforms that diminished the power and privileges of Jamaica's ruling white planter class. Jamaica became a Crown Colony: the British drew up a new constitution that removed direct rule from the hands of the local elite and gave decision-making power to an appointed British governor, who presided over a legislative council. Yet the reforms only went so far: the overwhelming majority of council members, nominated by the governor himself, were white, and the gulf that existed between Jamaica's poor blacks (a significant majority of the island's population) and middle-class whites and mulattos continued to widen.

Jamaica's black population was systematically repressed until 1962; the year British colonial rule came to an end. Indeed, Jamaican blacks did not have the freedom to assemble or organize trade unions; abysmal working conditions led many to seek employment abroad. In 1914 Jamaican worker Marcus Garvey founded the Universal Negro Improvement Association (UNIA). Garvey's Pan-African philosophy, which established a sense of national identity based on race, instilled in many blacks worldwide the belief that their economic and political liberation could ultimately be found in a strong and unified Africa. After spending a decade in Great Britain and the United States, in 1927 Garvey returned to Jamaica, where he spread his political views among black workers and farmers. He told blacks to "look to Africa for the crowning of a king to know that your redemption is nigh."

In 1930 Ras Tafari Makonnen was crowned the new emperor of Ethiopia, Haile Selassie I ("Power of the Trinity," his baptismal name)—a monumental event that many blacks in Africa and the Americas saw as the fulfillment of Garvey's prophecy. Since the Middle Ages a part of Ethiopia's nobility, including the Makonnens, had perceived themselves as descendants of King Solomon of Judah and the Queen of Sheba. This was a belief stemming from biblical prophecies, including the Song of Solomon 1:5-6, which states: "I am Black, but comely, O ye daughters of Jerusalem, as the tents of Kedar, as the curtains of Solomon." As Chevannes points out, "if Solomon was Black, so was the Christ. Both were descendants of David. Redemption of the African race was therefore at hand." Emperor Haile Selassie himself, who appropriated the titles "King of Kings" and "Conquering Lion of the Tribe of Judah," further reinforcing the prophecy.

The name Rastafari is taken from Ras, meaning "prince" in the Amharic language, and Tafari, the name of the emperor of Ethiopia. The earliest preachers of the Rastafarian world view were the Jamaican workers Leonard Howell, Archibald Dunkley, and Joseph Hibbert. They asserted the idea of a black God, who physically lived on the earth; proclaimed that the African peoples shared in this divinity; and equated the liberation of blacks with their repatriation to Africa. Indeed, on three separate occasions (1934, 1956, and 1959) Jamaica's Rastafarian leaders attempted—unsuccessfully, due to a lack of governmental and organizational support—to repatriate brethren to their homeland. Howell also called for "death to Black and White oppressors," an approach that ignited considerable hostility among Jamaica's elite: both Howell and Dunkley were imprisoned on several occasions, and Howell was branded "insane."

In 1935 the Italian army invaded Ethiopia, an event that drew attention to the incompetence of the Selassie regime, which had left Ethiopia's peasantry impoverished, uneducated, and untrained in military service and thus entirely unprepared for war. Moreover, Jamaica's economic crisis continued to worsen. Black workers, plagued by malnutrition and low wages, turned to practical action instead of religion as a form of resistance. Spurred on by these developments, the Rastafarian movement became increasingly politicized: during the 1940s and 1950s leaders intensified their opposition to the colonial state by defying the police and organizing illegal street marches.

During the late 1950s, Claudius Henry, head of a Rastafarian meetinghouse in Kingston, set up a guerrilla training camp and in 1959 unsuccessfully tried to repatriate a group of Jamaican Rastas to Africa. Soon after, the police invaded Henry's headquarters, where they found a supply of arms and a letter inviting the Cuban leader Fidel Castro to take over Jamaica. Henry was arrested and tried on charges of treason. Throughout the 1960s Rastafarian demonstrations against segregation and black poverty were violently repressed by the Jamaican police and military. While several Rastafari were killed in such clashes, hundreds more were arrested and humiliated by being forced to have their dreadlocks cut off.

Philosophically opposed to a culture of violence, many Rastafari soon turned to more peaceful means of resistance—a goal considerably aided by the visit of Haile Selassie to Jamaica in 1966. As Campbell notes, "state officials had to take a back seat while the mass of the black populace thrust forward to pay homage to the Ethiopian monarch. So profound was the popular feeling expressed for Africa that the Jamaican ruling class realized that it could not simply write off Rastafari." Rastafarian culture was explored and promoted in a plethora of academic studies in Jamaica and abroad, while the Ethiopian Orthodox Church was recognized as an institution worthy of respect. Rastafarianism also gained a new measure of credibility among Jamaica's middle-class blacks and mulattos who, during the late 1960s, formed their own Rastafarian group, the Twelve Tribes of Israel.

In 1968 Walter Rodney, then a lecturer at the University of the West Indies in Kingston, started the Black Power Movement, which significantly influenced the development of Rastafarianism in the Caribbean. Black Power was a call to blacks to overthrow the capitalist order that ensured white dominion and to reconstruct their societies in the image of blacks. In Dominica, Grenada, and Trinidad, Rastafarians played a central role in r adical left-wing politics. In Jamaica, Rastafarian resistance was expressed through cultural forms, particularly reggae music. Popular reggae singers, such as Bob Marley and Peter Tosh, expressed Rastafarian ideas and social criticism in their song lyrics; during the 1970s they significantly contributed to the growth of the Rastafarian movement throughout the Caribbean, the United States, England, Canada, Europe, Australia, New Zealand, and parts of Latin America.

Rastafari Rituals, Practices, and Recent Developments

The rituals and practices central to Rastafarianism developed during the late 1930s and 1940s. Of particular importance are "reasonings" and "binghi." At reasonings, Rastafari members gather informally to offer prayers and smoke ganja, or marijuana, considered a holy weed; it is passed around in a water pipe, which some Rastafari have likened to the Christian communion cup in its symbolic significance. Binghi are all-night celebrations that feature dancing accompanied by the distinctive rhythms of Rasta drums; they are held to mark special occasions throughout the year, such as the coronation of Haile Selassie I, Marcus Garvey's birthday, and the emancipation from slavery. Other significant practices include the wearing of facial hair by adult males (Ras Tafari was pictured with a full beard) and dreadlocks, or long matted hair. According to Chevannes, dreadlocks originated among a group of Rastas known as the Youth Black Faith, who adopted the hairstyle as a symbol of their radically defiant views in a society in which blacks were made to feel ashamed of their skin color and hair texture.

Since the 1980s the Rastafarian movement has become increasingly secular: many of the movement's symbols have lost their religious and ideo-logical significance and the influence of Rastafari ideology on Jamaica's urban youth has considerably declined. The Rasta colors (red, green, and gold), in which all Rasta banners and artifacts are painted, have been largely shorn of their ideological meaning and are now worn by all. Dreadlocks too are sported as a trendy hairstyle by both blacks and whites in Jamaica and abroad. The loosening of Rastafari ideology has also led women to become increasingly outspoken within the movement. Women traditionally had been forbidden to play an important role in rituals; they were also expected to show complete deference to males. During the last decade, however, some women have begun to protest against and defy the movement's patri-archal beliefs and conventions.

The Rastafarian movement in Jamaica remains fragmented and unorganized; brethren adhere to the Rastafarian worldview through inner conviction and generally prefer autonomy to cohesive organizational structures and rules. Nonetheless, two highly organized Rastafari groups exist in Jamaica: the Bobos and the Twelve Tribes of Israel. The Bobos maintain a communal life on the fringes of Kingston, where they earn a living producing and selling brooms. The Twelve Tribes, on the other hand, is a predominantly middle-class group, led by Prophet Gad. Members of the Twelve Tribes accept the authority of designated group members, pay dues, and hold regular meetings and events. In addition, there is the House of Nyabinghi, a loosely organized assembly of Rasta elders, who settle disputes between brethren and organize events. Rastafarianism remains a culture of resistance in many parts of the world. Although the Rastafarian movement has experienced a turbulent social history in Jamaica, it retains significant moral authority there, and its influence is increasingly felt beyond Jamaica. Indeed, it was one of the first full-fledged movements to confront issues of racial identity and prejudice, and to incite Jamaica's middle-class blacks to reflect on the importance of their African heritage.

North America

Reconstruction,

the period immediately following the Civil War during which the United States sought to rebuild the South physically, politically, socially, and economically.

Reconstruction, also called the "Second American Revolution," is an often-misunderstood era of United States history. For decades historians presented Reconstruction as a time when the South was a region besieged by a punitive North. According to this view President Abraham Lincoln initially offered reasonable terms to the rebellious Southern states to speed reunion; but Radical Republicans, the liberal wing of the Republican Party, instituted a period of "Negro rule" in which blacks, incompetent to govern, mismanaged the South. In this interpretation conscientious whites "redeemed" the South by using secret patriotic organizations such as the Ku Klux Klan to depose black rule. Only during the "Second Reconstruction," the Civil Rights Movement, did most historians begin to reevaluate previous conclusions about Reconstruction. Concurring with W. E. B. Du Bois, most scholars now agree that Reconstruction was a period of progressive politics in which newly emancipated blacks, with the help of the federal government and sympathetic whites in the South, helped build a more democratic society.

The Federal Government During Reconstruction

Most historians consider Reconstruction to encompass the years between 1865 and 1877. But the course Reconstruction would take and the questions associated with it were the subjects of national debate even before the end of the Civil War. Who should be punished for inciting secession and the war? How would the Southern states be readmitted to the Union? What penalties would apply? What was the federal government's responsibility to the freed slaves? Should the government extend rights to former slaves, and, if so, which rights? How would the Southern economy replace slave labor with free labor?

Finally, and perhaps most important to the federal government, who was responsible for implementing Reconstruction policy—the president or Congress? Although Lincoln had been granted far-reaching powers during the war, Congress could not allow the president such latitude in peacetime.

By issuing the Emancipation Proclamation on January 1, 1863, Lincoln committed the United States to abolishing slavery. Because slavery had been part of the American social fabric from the nation's beginning, its abolition would fundamentally alter the nation. Combined with this drastic social and political change was the need to rebuild the war-torn South. Many Southern cities lay in ruins. In addition, the loss of farmland and animals, as well as human labor—not only black slaves but whites killed or disabled in the war—jeopardized its agrarian economy.

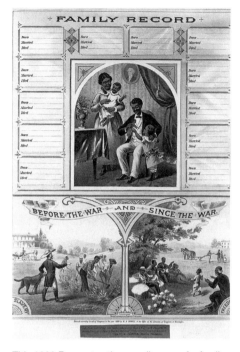

This 1880 Reconstruction-era diagram of a family tree contrasts farm life before and after the Civil War. The slave family on the left works under the watchful eye of a white master. The free family on the right enjoys leisure time together. *CORBIS*

Presidential Reconstruction

In December 1863 Lincoln introduced the first Reconstruction scheme, the Ten Percent Plan, thus beginning the period known as Presidential Reconstruction. The plan decreed that when 10 percent of a state's prewar voters had taken an oath of loyalty to the U.S. Constitution, its citizens could elect a new state government and apply for readmission to the Union. In addition, Lincoln promised to pardon all but a few high-ranking Confederates if they would take this oath and accept the fact of abolition. The plan also required that states amend their constitutions to abolish slavery. Conspicuous in this plan was the stipulation that only whites could vote or hold

The political cartoon, *Re-Construction, or "A White Man's Government,"* presents a drowning white Southerner refusing the help of a black man, who clings to an allegorical "Tree of Liberty." President Ulysses S. Grant stands onshore, urging the desperate man to accept whatever help he is offered. *CORBIS*

office. Despite the objections of Northern abolitionists, Lincoln began to implement the plan in Louisiana, which the Union army had occupied since 1862. In a private meeting at the White House a group of highly accomplished free blacks from New Orleans objected to their unequal status. Spurred by this protest, Lincoln unsuccessfully urged Louisiana's governor to allow the state's qualified free blacks to vote.

Congress, believing that Lincoln's Reconstruction plan was too permissive, took a series of steps to counteract it. Congress passed the Wade-Davis Bill in late 1864, which contained more stringent readmission policies. It required that 50 percent of a state's voters declare loyalty to the Constitution before the state could create a new government, and also that these new governments recognize freed people as equal before the law. In addition, in January 1865 Congress approved the Thirteenth Amendment, which constitutionally ended slavery. It was ratified in December of that year, and in March 1865 Congress established the Bureau of Refugees, Freedmen and Abandoned Lands, or Freedmen's Bureau, a relief agency for needy refugees. Although the agency represented both black and white refugees, it was primarily intended to aid blacks in the transition from slavery to freedom.

Lincoln indirectly vetoed Wade-Davis by leaving it unsigned until Congress adjourned in late March 1865. He considered the Ten Percent Plan experimental, however, and in his final speech indicated that at least some blacks should vote. Because of this, many historians believe he might have adapted his Ten Percent Plan had he not been assassinated. It was obvious, however, that Lincoln and Congress disagreed on the basic nature of Reconstruction policy. When the war ended and Reconstruction began in earnest, the federal government had no solid plan for its direction.

Congress had adjourned by the end of the war and did not reconvene until December. With Lincoln's assassination in early April 1865, Vice President Andrew Johnson became president, controlling Reconstruction policy at its crucial beginning. Johnson, a poor white from Tennessee, harbored disdain for both the Southern planter aristocracy and blacks. In May 1865 he began issuing proclamations that were even more lenient than Lincoln's.

Johnson pardoned all Southern whites except Confederate leaders and persons whose wealth exceeded $20,000. They would have to apply personally for Johnson's pardon. Johnson appointed provisional governors and required that to rejoin the union, the states need only abolish slavery and repudiate both secession and the Confederate war debt. After the rebellious states met these requirements they were considered "reconstructed." In addition, Johnson ordered that abandoned plantations be returned to their former owners. Though representatives from the Freedmen's Bureau initially refused to follow Johnson's directive, he ultimately sent federal troops to force the return of these lands.

Southern states, encouraged by Johnson's leniency, began to return the old elites to power. In addition, Southern state governments issued Black Codes, laws that aimed to limit black mobility and economic options, and virtually to reinstate the plantation system. Under the Black Codes interracial marriages were banned and blacks could be forced to sign yearly contracts. They could also be declared vagrants for not having a certain (typically unreasonable) amount of money on their person and be sentenced to labor on a white-owned plantation. In addition, these laws limited the types of occupations and property blacks could hold. Other laws sought forcibly to apprentice black children. As a result, freed people existed somewhere between freedom and slavery.

Hiram Rhoades Revels (1822-1901) was the son of former slaves. He became a Methodist minister, an educator, and the first African American in the United States Senate. *CORBIS*

A.R. Waud's 1867 illustration, *The First Vote*, shows recently freed African American men going to the polls for the first time in a state election in the South. *CORBIS/Bettmann*

Congress had observed these events during adjournment and, upon returning to Washington, D.C., in December 1865, sought to alter Johnson's policies. When the newly elected Southern representatives arrived and Northern congressmen discovered that many of them were former Confederate cabinet members, congressmen, and generals who had won congressional seats in the state governments restored under Johnson, Congress refused to seat them. Many congressional Republicans, especially Radical Republicans such as Thaddeus Stevens in the House and Charles Sumner in the Senate, believed that the Johnson state governments should be dissolved and Reconstruction begun again, this time based on equality under law and universal male suffrage. Moderate members of the party, however, attempted to work with Johnson and convince him to modify his policies.

In early 1866 Congress sought to advance Reconstruction by passage of the Freedmen's Bureau Act and the Civil Rights Act. The Freedmen's Bureau Act extended the agency's life for another year. The Civil Rights Act defined people born in the United States as national citizens and stated explicitly the rights to which they were entitled regardless of race. Johnson vetoed both bills, insisting that they violated states' rights. Congress quickly overrode Johnson's vetoes. Shortly thereafter, Congress approved the Fourteenth Amendment, which was ratified in 1868. Designed to protect the rights of freedpeople and to restrict the political power of former Confederates, the Fourteenth Amendment defined U.S. citizenship in much the same way as the Civil Rights Bill had and prohibited states from abridging the "privileges or immunities" of citizens without due process. Rather than prohibit states from restricting suffrage, it encouraged Southern states to allow black suffrage by reducing representation in states that disfranchised any male citizens.

Johnson's Reconstruction program became the decisive issue in the 1866 congressional elections. Although Johnson had toured the North to win support for candidates sympathetic to his program, his efforts were mostly unsuccessful. His rhetoric was more influential in the South: all of the former confederate states, except Tennessee, rejected the Fourteenth Amendment, which Johnson had publicly disavowed. By 1867 moderate and radical Republicans in Congress, tired of Johnson's obstruction to their more ambitious Reconstruction plan, began to take advantage of the president's waning power to forge an era of Congressional Reconstruction.

Congressional Reconstruction

After a series of compromises Congress decided upon a Reconstruction plan that was far more broad-ranging than Johnson's. In March 1867 Congress began by passing the Reconstruction Acts, which divided the ten unreconstructed states (except Tennessee, which had already ratified the Fourteenth Amendment) into five military districts, each headed by a commander whose responsibilities included overseeing the writing of new constitutions that provided for enfranchisement of all adult males.

Only after ratifying the new state constitution and the Fourteenth Amendment would a state be considered reconstructed and readmitted to the Union. In addition, Congress passed several laws to restrict Johnson's power to undermine congressional policy. In response, Johnson removed military officers who were enforcing the Reconstruction Act and fired his secretary of war. Shortly thereafter Congress began impeachment proceedings against Johnson, ultimately coming within one vote of conviction.

In 1869 Congress passed the Fifteenth Amendment, which broadened the Fourteenth Amendment's protection of black voting rights, stating that no citizen could be denied the vote on the basis of race, color, or "previous condition of servitude." It was ratified in 1870. In addition, Congress passed the Civil Rights Act of 1875, which barred discrimination by hotels, theaters, and railroads. The act, however, was rarely enforced.

The Supreme Court and Reconstruction

The Supreme Court, which had been largely silent during the war years, became active during this period, facilitating a retreat from Reconstruction by overturning many congressional measures. In *Bradwell v. Illinois* (1873) the Court ruled against a female attorney who claimed that in prohibiting her from practicing law because of her gender, Illinois had violated the "privileges and immunities" clause of the Fourteenth Amendment.

The following day the Court further narrowed the Fourteenth Amendment's scope in the Slaughterhouse cases (1873), rejecting the argument that the Fourteenth Amendment had transformed citizenship by making it the federal government's responsibility. In *United States v. Cruikshank* (1876), it ruled that the duty to protect citizens' rights rested with states. In *United States v. Reese* (1876), the Court ruled that the Fifteenth Amendment did not guarantee citizens the right to vote, but listed the grounds impermissible for denying the vote. Southern states now had a clear path toward the disfranchisement of black voters.

Freedpeople During Reconstruction

The first decision facing former slaves was often whether to stay on the plantation or to move. In general, the choice depended on the disposition of the former master: if a master had been mean or violent, few of his former slaves were likely to remain; if the master had been fair, however, former slaves did often stay. Southern whites exaggerated the number of black men who refused to work after emancipation as a supporting argument for black inferiority, but these numbers were in fact low. Many freedwomen, however, refused to work in the fields any longer after emancipation, choosing instead to remain at home with their children.

To some freedpeople, emancipation meant the freedom to move about, either because it had been prohibited or because they wished to search for family members who had been sold away during slavery. The Reconstruction era produced stories of ex-slaves who traveled thousands of miles, with very little information about their relatives' whereabouts, to reunite with family members. Others found no success in their searches.

Blacks, denied literacy during slavery, also sought education, often paying for it on their own. By 1877 more than 600,000 African Americans had enrolled in elementary schools throughout the South. The Freedmen's Bureau founded more than 4000 schools, including Howard University, and many benevolent organizations, black and white, offered education. The

American Missionary Association founded seven colleges, including Fisk and Atlanta universities.

Freedpeople established other black institutions, especially churches that would profoundly affect African American history. As slaves, blacks had been forced to worship in their masters' churches. After emancipation freedpeople founded their own churches or moved to black denominations, which served as social and political centers in the black community. Ministers often became community leaders, a practice that continues to this day.

Freedpeople also knew that land meant independence and that they were entitled to some of the lands of their former owners. Early in the war, as the U.S. Navy approached South Carolina, Confederates abandoned their lands on the Sea Islands. Freedpeople immediately lobbied for ownership of the land, insisting that it was rightfully theirs after generations of forced servitude. Instead, the U.S. government implemented the Port Royal Experiment, in which freedpeople labored in the abandoned Sea Island lands as wageworkers. Eventually, Gen. William T. Sherman issued Special Order No. 15, which gave the land to the freedpeople. President Johnson, however, rescinded the order, and the land reverted to its original owners. One of Reconstruction's great failings is that the U.S. government did not effectively redistribute land after the Civil War.

Most freedpeople were unable to buy land and instead rented it for farming. Freedmen's Bureau agents, many of whom wanted to change the Southern economy by introducing Northern concepts such as wage labor, needed to retain enough of the old system to ensure stability. To do this efficiently, Freedmen's Bureau agents developed work contracts, which, in the cash-poor South, would promise the slave a certain wage in exchange for crops. Although intended to mediate disputes, bureau agents often sided with the former master. The Freedmen's Bureau grew less active after 1866, leaving tenants and planters to find their own way. Thus, contracts between former slaves and masters were not enforced, and slaves often depended on the good will of their former owners.

Freedpeople also took advantage of the franchise, voting almost unanimously for Republican candidates in the 1866 congressional elections. Freedpeople also joined governments. Largely because of large black turnout and because Congress banned many former Confederates from politics, the Republican Party won control of many Southern constitutional conventions. Of the 1000 Republican delegates to constitutional conventions throughout the South, 265 were black.

Participation in government among blacks was greatest in state and local governments, where many attained high rank. Francis Cardozo was a member of South Carolina's constitutional convention and later served as state secretary of the treasury and as South Carolina's secretary of state. In Louisiana P. B. S. Pinchback became the first black governor in U.S. history. He also served as lieutenant governor and he was elected to both the U.S. Senate and the U.S. House of Representatives. Blanche K. Bruce was a U.S.

senator from Mississippi, as was Hiram Revels. In all, 16 blacks served in the U.S. Congress during Reconstruction.

Although whites who sought to disfranchise blacks justified their actions by claiming that they had been subjected to incompetent "Negro rule," blacks constituted the majority in only two state conventions, and only in South Carolina's lower house were black representatives a majority. In many ways the biracial coalitions that comprised Republican governments made progressive changes, such as creating state-funded public schools and a fairer tax system, outlawing discrimination in public transportation, and ending the death penalty.

Opposition to Reconstruction

As Reconstruction was implemented, a struggle began in the South over the new social order. On one side were the freedpeople and their allies, who wanted to participate in a free society. On the other side were white elites and their followers, who wanted to restore the old order. Many whites—even those who had not owned slaves before the Civil War— found it difficult to imagine a society in which blacks had the same rights as they.

Reconstruction inspired deep resentment among Southern whites. Former Confederates were bitter about losing the war and facing their new prospects. They believed that white Republicans were race traitors, and they objected to the high taxes that Republicans imposed to pay for Reconstruction. Many believed that Reconstruction politics and the politicians who practiced them were corrupt. Though Southerners did not have a defined course, to restore white rule meant white unity. In states with white majorities, convincing white Democrats to vote Democratic was enough to eliminate Republican rule, and by 1871 Democrats had taken back Tennessee, North Carolina, Virginia, and Georgia.

In other states, however, where Republican rule depended on interracial coalitions, white Democrats were determined to convince some people not to vote, often through the violence and intimidation of such terrorist organizations as the Ku Klux Klan, which was founded in late 1865. Often led by the most prominent whites in a community, Klan members concealed themselves in white robes and hoods and often acted at night, beating, lynching, burning, or merely threatening.

Problems existed between the elite planters, who were almost unanimously Democrats, and the Republicans, who represented three main groups: freedpeople, carpetbaggers (as Northern republicans were called, supposedly because they had come South with all their possessions in carpetbags), and scalawags, those white Southerners who supported Reconstruction. Wherever possible, white Southerners reasserted themselves and their control; forcing blacks to stop voting was their primary tool to regain control of the South. In addition, whites still exercised a great deal of economic control over blacks, as they still had to work for whites. Many blacks were told explicitly, "If you vote, don't come back to work."

Another method of increasing the dependence of blacks on whites was sharecropping, in which a farmer provided a tenant land and materials in exchange for a share of the crop. Although sharecropping began as a way to maximize land under cultivation and extend credit in a credit-poor region, it relegated many freedpeople and poor whites to a state of virtual peonage. Sometimes the conditions in which peonage and sharecropping put blacks were even worse materially than slavery.

End of Reconstruction

The country had been in an economic depression since around 1873, and white Northern attention turned from the plight of black people in the South to the national economy. State by state, Southern Democrats began to take control of local governments, working to reinstate the conditions of the antebellum South. Southern white supremacists believed, correctly, that Northern whites would no longer enforce Reconstruction policy. They began to subjugate blacks again, reinstating the Black Codes. Many Southern states began to pass segregation or Jim Crow laws.

For many, the Compromise of 1877 marks the end of Reconstruction. In the presidential election of 1876, Republican Rutherford B. Hayes and Democrat Samuel J. Tilden were virtually deadlocked. Tilden won the popular vote, but Republicans had control of South Carolina, Florida, and Louisiana, thus giving them control of the Electoral College. Because each party in those three states had competing electors, however, Congress needed to decide the election. Hayes, the incumbent, appointed an electoral commission, which, with one more Republican than Democrat, declared him the winner.

The Democrats and the Republicans had worked out a deal, however, in which the Democrats conceded the White House in exchange for "Home Rule" in the critical three states. In a meeting that, ironically, took place in the black-owned Wormly House Hotel, the Republicans agreed. The remaining military presence in the three states departed, and Republican rule crumbled: the Democrats had won back the South. Though it would take until the 1890s for them to finish the job, the white supremacists were well on their way to what Southerners referred to as "Redemption."

Historians have presented differing interpretations of the legacy of Reconstruction. Many historians now argue that Reconstruction fundamentally changed how the United States defined citizenship, as well as t he way in which U.S. citizens perceive the power and role of the federal government. The Bill of Rights, for instance, was created to prevent the federal government from infringing on the rights of the people. The Thirteenth, Fourteenth, and Fifteenth Amendments, however, placed the federal government in the role of protector of citizens' rights. This new concept of federal power and responsibility provided a framework for the Civil Rights Movement, which, a century later, realized what Reconstruction had begun.

Redding, Otis

(b. September 9, 1941, Dawson, Ga.; d. December 10, 1967, Madison, Wis.),
African American singer and songwriter who played a key role in the rise of
soul music during the 1960s, but who attained his greatest success only after
his premature death.

Otis Redding's life is the stuff of pop-music tragedy. From an early age he
clearly had musical talent, first as a drummer, then as a singer. But his
family was poor, and he had to endure a series of odd jobs and struggle to
make ends meet before he got his big break in 1963, an opportunity to
record for Memphis, Tennessee-based Stax Records. His career took off and
followed a steep upward arc, culminating with a triumphant performance at
the 1967 Monterey Pop Festival. Then—in an instant—it was over. Redding
died in December of that year when his chartered plane crashed near
Madison, Wisconsin. Since his death Redding has been hailed as perhaps
the quintessential male soul singer. But fame proved far more elusive during
his lifetime.

Redding was born to a poor Georgia family and learned to play drums in
school. On Sundays he played behind the various gospel groups that performed on local radio station WIBB. In 1957 he dropped out of high school
in order to support his family, taking a variety of menial jobs and occasional
gigs as a musician. He began to concentrate on his singing and entered a
number of local amateur contests. Redding's early singing style was in the
tradition of such rock 'n' roll shouters as Little Richard. In 1961 he made
his recording debut, on a small Macon, Georgia, label.

But his big break did not come until two years later, when he was
working in the band of guitarist Johnny Jenkins—and serving as the band's
chauffeur. During a recording session at Stax Records he had the chance to
record a featured vocal, the ballad "These Arms of Mine," which became a
rhythm and blues (R&B) hit and earned Redding a Stax recording contract.
Redding's vocals matured from his earlier shouting style to one that conveyed the emotion behind his lyrics by means of an expressive, hoarse
singing voice that was grounded in gospel sonorities.

To black listeners, Redding was one of the definitive examples of the
Memphis Soul sound. His live performances were legendary for their intensity and emotional fervor. During 1965 and 1966 Redding scored several
R&B hits—including "Mr. Pitiful," "I've Been Loving You Too Long," a version of the Rolling Stones' hit "(I Can't Get No) Satisfaction," and his now-
famous rendition of "Try a Little Tenderness"—but none "crossed over" to
the white popular-music charts. According to Norm N. Nite's *Rock On
Almanac* (1989), Redding only appeared on the American pop charts once
in his lifetime—in October 1966, with his now little remembered recording
"Fa-Fa-Fa-Fa-Fa (Sad Song)."

In 1967, however, Redding's incandescent appearance at the Monterey

Pop Festival put him on a trajectory for pop-music stardom. His musical promise is evident in many of his compositions—including "Respect," which became a much bigger hit in the hands of Aretha Franklin, and "(Sittin' on) The Dock of the Bay," which he recorded just three days before his death at age 26. Four members of the Bar-Kays, Redding's backup band, also died in the crash. With the posthumous release of "(Sittin' on) The Dock of the Bay," Redding charted his first Number One pop single.

Latin America and the Caribbean

Regla de Palo,

a Bantu-derived Cuban religion that was originally practiced by Congo slaves in Cuba's eastern Oriente province and that has gained popularity with many throughout the island.

Along with the Yoruba-derived religion of Regla de Ocha or Lucumí (more commonly known as Santería), Palo is the second most popular African-derived religious system in Cuba. Unlike Santería, which has been studied much more extensively, Palo does not feature orisha worship, an altar, or characteristic colors, clothing, or stylized dances dedicated to particular spirits. Both religions feature drumming, music, possession trance, and animal sacrifice as well as systems of divination. Palo divination is ordinarily conducted with an npaca menzo, an ox horn mounted with a mirror on its blunt end, used in conjunction with white plates and candle wax, or with chamalongos, seven pieces of dried coconut shell that are thrown on the ground. (Multiples of seven hold an important place in Palo numerology.) The word palo means "sticks" or "branches of trees," which adherents (known as Paleros) believe to hold magical powers.

The transatlantic slave trade of the sixteenth through the nineteenth century brought primarily Africans of Yoruba and Bantu origin to Cuba. These major African groups, known respectively in Cuba as the Lucumí and the Congo, have had an enormous influence on Cuban culture as a whole. The Bantu who were brought to Cuba are thought to have resided primarily in the areas of present-day Angola, Democratic Republic of the Congo, and Namibia.

Cuban Paleros believe that the power of Nzambi, a creator god, resides in all natural elements of the world (such as rocks, trees, and people) and within the spirits of the ancestors, the Nfumbi and the Npungo, who served Nzambi during their earthly lives. The Nfumbi are the spirits of recent generations of deceased ancestors, who, as a result of their more recent lives, are believed to be in closer proximity to their human descendants. The Npungo are ancestors who are thought to be united presently with the primordial forces that birthed them: namely, the forces of nature—Nzambi himself. The goal of Palo is to control events by corralling the forces of nature. This is accomplished by concentrating the powers of

Nzambi within the magical center of the religion's rituals, the nganga. The nganga is a clay pot or iron cauldron often placed in the home of the Palero. The nganga is a Cuban innovation necessitated by the conditions of slavery, which did not allow enslaved Paleros sufficient mobility: in Africa religious practitioners simply visited specific trees or stones believed to be manifestations of Nzambi. It is believed that the nganga must be "fed" with the blood of live animals, which are ritually sacrificed over the nganga by the tata nganga, a priest of Palo.

Paleros have a different relationship to their spirits than do the adherents of Santería, who must appeal to the sometimes-fickle orishas, submit to their discretion, and await their appearance and assistance, which may or may not be tendered. By contrast, it is the Paleros who are masters of the nganga, which is sometimes referred to as the Palero's "dog" or "slave." For this reason, it is often said in Cuba that if you don't mind waiting for results, consult with the Roman Catholic Church or with the orishas; if you want immediate results, go to a Palero. During palo rituals, Paleros command spirits, including Nzambi, to manifest themselves in the nganga and to perform requested deeds. A reciprocal bargaining then takes place between the Palero and the nganga: if the spirits are to follow the Palero's wishes, the Palero must "feed" the spirits (through the nganga) according to the pact that has been made between them. Without such a pact, it is believed, the spirit will not act to change events as the Palero requests.

The Palo religious community is not as central to the religion as is the "family" of Santería adherents. Although Palo has an extensive set of reglas, or rules, the religion is generally considered to be more flexible regarding the needs of its individual adherents.

North America

Reparations,

government-administered funding and social programs intended to compensate African Americans for the past injustices of slavery and discrimination.

In 1988 the United States government issued a national apology to Japanese Americans who had been placed in American internment camps during World War II and paid $20,000 to each victim. This prompted many African Americans to press for similar reparations. Cited as grounds for compensation were the unfulfilled Civil War promise that each slave would receive forty acres and a mule; the millions of dollars of German aid to Jews following the Holocaust; and the U.S. Marshall Plan, which rebuilt Europe after World War II.

Advocates of reparations have proposed packages that range from $700 billion to $4 trillion. Most favor investing the money in education and economic development for the African American community. This proposed use of reparations contrasts with that of some earlier reparation movements, which sought to found an independent black state (in Africa or in the southern United States) or secure pensions for ex-slaves and their descendants.

Some opponents of reparations believe that such payments cannot truly make up for past injustices. Although the U.S. government has not yet awarded reparations to African Americans or made a formal apology for nearly 250 years of slavery, many African Americans continue to demand that the nation officially confront and redress its past injustices.

North America

Republic of New Africa,

African American organization devoted to the establishment of an autonomous black nation in the southern United States.

At the height of the Black Power Movement in the late 1960s, members of the Republic of New Africa (RNA) called for the creation of an independent black nation spanning the states of Louisiana, Mississippi, Alabama, Georgia, and South Carolina. They advocated cooperative economics and community self-sufficiency. At the same time members of the RNA aimed to limit political rights and freedom of the press, prohibit unions, make military service mandatory, and legalize polygamy. Their manifesto demanded that the United States government cede the five proposed states to the RNA and pay $400 billion in reparations to African Americans for the injustices of slavery and segregation.

In 1968 attorney Milton Henry and his brother Richard, former acquaintances of Malcolm X who renamed themselves Gaidi Obadele and Imari Abubakari Obadele, respectively, convened a group of militant black nationalists in Detroit, Michigan, to discuss the creation of a black nation within the United States. Conference members established the RNA and declared their allegiance to the provisional government. They elected Imari Obadele as provisional president.

The RNA quickly became a target of the U.S. Federal Bureau of Investigation (FBI), which conducted raids on the group's meetings. These confrontations were violent and led to the repeated imprisonment of RNA leaders for assault and sedition. Following his 1980 release from prison, Imari Obadele attended Temple University and earned a Ph.D. in political science. While teaching at various universities, he published books and articles upholding the RNA's principles of reparations, acquisition of land, and establishment of an autonomous black nation. Based in Washington, D.C., the RNA continues to promote the formation of a black nation.

Réunion,

an island territory of France located in the Indian Ocean 760 km (407 mi) east of Madagascar.

Although most of France's overseas possessions are now independent, Réunion has remained a French Département d'Outre Mer, an overseas department intricately tied to the political economy of France. The island's demography reflects its history of colonization, slavery, and indentured labor. Creoles—people of mixed African descent—constitute the largest group, followed by people whose descent can be traced directly to France. Réunion is also home to a significant Indian population, mostly Hindu Tamils but also some Catholics and Muslims, as well as Chinese and East African communities. French culture has had a strong influence: the majority of the people speak French and/or Kreole and practice Roman Catholicism, and many combine the worship of Catholic saints with popular beliefs in magic and sorcery.

Rhythm and Blues,

an African American musical style developed after World War II that both reflected the growing confidence of urban African Americans and introduced a greater emotional depth to American popular music.

Rhythm and blues (R&B) is the general term for African American popular music since World War II. R&B melded earlier musical styles of blues, jazz, boogie woogie, and gospel music. It matured in the late 1940s and between 1954 and 1960 broke through racial barriers and achieved unprecedented visibility in white-oriented popular music. In launching R&B, however, African Americans lost control over their own musical creation as white performers, backed by major record companies and playing watered-down versions of R&B, effectively hijacked the form.

R&B thus reflects complex relationships between the races, as well as the constraints placed on black cultural expression. Yet despite these constraints, R&B transformed American popular culture. It challenged the vapidity of white pop music, and its propulsive beat and sexual overtones catalyzed rock 'n' roll. Most significant, however, R&B expressed the pride and vitality of a new urban black culture that emerged as a product of the Great Migration out of the rural South. In its heyday, R&B offered a high-spirited affirmation of black life. Most of all, it was the musical voice of a generation of African Americans who would no longer tolerate seond-class citizenship or balcony-seat tickets to the American Dream.

AFRICAN AMERICANS IN THE ROCK AND ROLL HALL OF FAME

Year	Inductee	Category
1986	Robert Johnson	Early Influences
	Jimmy Yancey	Early Influences
	Chuck Berry	Artists
	James Brown	Artists
	Ray Charles	Artists
	Sam Cooke	Artists
	Fats Domino	Artists
	Little Richard	Artists
1987	Louis Jordan	Early Influences
	T-Bone Walker	Early Influences
	Bo Diddley	Artists
	The Coasters	Artists
	Aretha Franklin	Artists
	Marvin Gaye	Artists
	B.B. King	Artists
	Clyde McPhatter	Artists
	Smokey Robinson	Artists
	Big Joe Turner	Artists
	Muddy Waters	Artists
	Jackie Wilson	Artists
1988	Berry Gordy Jr.	Nonperforming
	Leadbelly	Early Influences
	The Drifters	Artists
	The Supremes	Artists
1989	The Ink Spots	Early Influences
	Bessie Smith	Early Influences
	The Soul Stirrers	Early Influences
	Otis Redding	Artists
	The Temptations	Artists
	Stevie Wonder	Artists
1990	Lamont Dozier, Brian Holland & Eddie Holland	Nonperforming
	Louis Armstrong	Early Influences
	Hank Ballard	Artists
	The Platters	Artists
1991	Dave Bartholomew	Nonperforming
	Howlin' Wolf	Early Influences
	La Vern Baker	Artists
	John Lee Hooker	Artists
	The Impressions	Artists
	Wilson Pickett	Artists
	Jimmy Reed	Artists
	Ike and Tina Turner	Artists
1992	Elmore James	Early Influences
	Professor Longhair	Early Influences
	Bobby "Blue" Bland	Artists
	Booker T. and the MG's	Artists
	The Jimi Hendrix Experience	Artists
	The Isley Brothers	Artists
	Sam and Dave	
1993	Dinah Washington	Early Influences
	Ruth Brown	Artists
	Etta James	Artists
	Frankie Lymon & the Teenagers	Artists
	Sly & the Family Stone	Artists
1994	Willie Dixon	Early Influences
	Bob Marley	Artists

Ringgold, Faith

(b. October 8, 1934, New York, N.Y.), African American artist who has spent her artistic career breaking boundaries and clearing spaces for African American creativity, especially that of women.

Born in 1934 and raised in Harlem, Faith Ringgold's art focuses on black women and black women's issues. Diverse works—a mural in the Women's House of Detention in Riker's Island, New York (1971–1972) and a performance piece using soft cloth sculptures, "The Wake and Resurrection of the Bicentennial Negro" (1976)—focused on women's ability to heal and brought her work to a wider audience.

Since the 1970s, Ringgold has documented her local community and national events in life-size soft sculptures, representing everyone from ordinary Harlem denizens to Rev. Martin Luther King Jr. and the young victims of the Atlanta child murders (1979-80). Ringgold's latest chosen medium, fabric, is traditionally associated with women.

Ringgold's expression of black women's experience is perhaps best captured in her "storyquilts." A combination of quilting and narrative text, quilts like "Who's Afraid of Aunt Jemima?" (1982) and the series "Women on a Bridge" (1988) tell stories of pain and survival in a medium that Ringgold finds essentially female and empowering. She transformed one of her quilts into a children's book, *Tar Beach*, which won the 1992 Caldecott Honor Book Award and the Coretta Scott King award.

Robeson, Paul

(b. April 9, 1898, Princeton, N. J.; d. January 23, 1976, Philadelphia, Pa.), African American dramatic actor, singer of spirituals, civil rights activist, and political radical.

Paul Robeson was one of the most gifted men of this century. His resonant bass and commanding presence made him a world-renowned singer and actor and proved equally valuable when he spoke out against bigotry and injustice. By the 1930s Robeson was active in a wide range of causes, but his radicalism led to a long period of political harassment that culminated in his blacklisting during the McCarthy era. Although he resumed public performances in the late 1950s, this return to active life was brief. In the 1960s serious health problems sidelined him definitively.

Family Background and Education

Robeson's father, William Drew Robeson, was a North Carolina slave who escaped to freedom at age 15, graduated from college, and entered the ministry. Robeson's mother was Maria Louisa Bustill, a teacher and member of one of Philadelphia's leading black families. The youngest of five chil-

Singer, actor, and activist Paul Robeson played Othello in 1943 on Broadway. Here Robeson rehearses his part. *CORBIS/Hulton-Deutsch Collection*

dren, Robeson was only six years old when his mother died. His father set high expectations for his children and sent them to high school in the neighboring town of Somerville, New Jersey, because Princeton's segregated system offered no secondary education for blacks.

In 1915 Robeson won a scholarship to Rutgers College, where he excelled academically. Twice named an All-American in football, Robeson also lettered in baseball, basketball, and track. He graduated in 1919. Two years later, while a student at Columbia University Law School, he married Eslanda Goode.

Stage, Concert, and Film Career

While in law school Robeson had occasionally taken parts in amateur theatrical productions, leading in 1922 to his first professional roles—a lead in the short-lived Broadway play *Taboo* and as a replacement cast member in Eubie Blake and Noble Sissle's pioneering all-black musical, *Shuffle Along.* Robeson's career-making opportunity came when he was asked to join the Provincetown Players, an influential Greenwich Village theater company that included the playwright Eugene O'Neill among its three associate directors. In 1924 Robeson appeared in a revival of O'Neill's *The Emperor*

Jones and premiered in the playwright's *All God's Chillun Got Wings*. Soon Robeson was offered other roles, most notably in a 1930 London production of *Othello* opposite Peggy Ashcroft; in a 1932 Broadway revival of Oscar Hammerstein II and Jerome Kern's musical, *Showboat*, which featured Robeson's dramatic rendition of "Ol' Man River"; and in a long-running, critically acclaimed 1943 production of *Othello* on Broadway.

Equally significant were Robeson's musical contributions. Robeson and his longtime pianist and arranger Lawrence Brown played a pivotal role in bringing spirituals into the classical music repertory. Robeson's 1925 recital at the Greenwich Village Theater was the first in which a black soloist sang an entire program of spirituals. The concert garnered superlative reviews, propelling Robeson into a new career as a concert singer and inspiring similar recitals by other black artists. Robeson also signed a recording contract with the Victor Talking Machine Company, which released his first recorded spirituals later that same year. Although Robeson would sing a wide range of material—including sentimental popular tunes, work songs, political ballads, and folk music from many different lands—he made his mark as an interpreter of spirituals.

During the 1930s Robeson also emerged as a film star. His first role was in the black director Oscar Micheaux's *Body and Soul* (1925), but he was most active on the screen between 1933 and 1942, a period in which he was prominently featured in Hollywood versions of *The Emperor Jones* (1933) and *Show Boat* (1936), *Tales of Manhattan* (1942), and several British films. Robeson, however, was dissatisfied with his work in motion pictures. He came to believe that—with the exceptions of his roles in *Song of Freedom* (1936) and *The Proud Valley* (1940)—his characters reflected current racial stereotypes, or what Robeson derided as "Stepin Fetchit comics and savages with leopard skin and spear." Working in films like *Sanders of the River* (1935), which sang the praises of British imperialism, became particularly distasteful as Robeson discovered his African heritage.

His Discovery of Africa

During the 1930s Robeson made London his primary residence, and "it was there," he recalled, "that I 'discovered' Africa." In 1933 he undertook the study of several African languages at the University of London. He also took part in activities sponsored by the West African Students Union and became acquainted with future African leaders Jomo Kenyatta of Kenya and Nnamdi Azikiwe of Nigeria. Robeson began to stress the positive aspects of African life. African culture, he argued, was more spiritual and more grounded in community than that of Europe or white America.

Robeson thought it imperative that the American-born regain their own African roots. He rejected the assimilation then prevalent among the black elite. Instead he fashioned a world view that anchored cultural diversity in universal values, among which the most important was a faith in human solidarity that lay at the heart of his encounter with socialism.

Difficulties During the Cold War Era

However, as the United States entered the cold war, Robeson found himself increasingly isolated. Although he was not in fact a member of the Communist Party, he had close ties to many in the party's leadership, and he staunchly defended the Soviet Union despite the 1939 Nazi-Soviet Pact and Nikita Khrushchev's 1956 revelations about Joseph Stalin's purges. The Federal Bureau of Investigation (FBI) placed Robeson under surveillance as early as 1941 and compiled a massive dossier on his activities. Yet it seems clear that he was targeted as much for his militancy on civil rights issues as for his alleged Communism.

The real turning point for Robeson came in 1949 when the Associated Press quoted him as saying: "It is unthinkable that American Negroes would go to war on behalf of those who have oppressed us for generations against a country [the Soviet Union] which in one generation has raised our people to the full dignity of mankind."

Most Americans were outraged. The House Committee on Un-American Activities (HUAC) announced that it would hold hearings to investigate Robeson and the loyalty of black Americans. Ultimately, Robeson was silenced, but doing so required the combined efforts of the black establishment—including leaders of the fledgling Civil Rights Movement—white liberals, the entertainment industry, and the government. In 1950 the State Department rescinded Robeson's passport, preventing him from performing or traveling abroad. At home he found himself blacklisted by Broadway and Hollywood, by concert halls and record companies, radio, and television. His only opportunities to perform were at small affairs organized by a dwindling core of radicals and at a few black churches like Harlem's Mother African Methodist Episcopal Zion Church, whose pastor was Robeson's brother, Rev. Benjamin C. Robeson. Denied a public voice, Robeson struggled mightily to vindicate himself and win back his freedom of travel. In his 1956 testimony before HUAC, Robeson offered a powerful indictment of America's continuing racial injustice, but he steadfastly refused to condemn the Soviet Union, to provide the names of American Communists, or to answer whether he was a party member, a question that he viewed as a violation of his Constitutional rights. In 1957, after a seven-year delay, the State Department finally granted him a hearing on the revocation of his passport. The result was a six-hour grilling, but no change in the government's policy.

The Final Years

Robeson fought his lonely battle at great personal cost. In 1955 he began to show the first clear signs of the emotional difficulties—probably bipolar disorder, a condition once known as manic-depression—that would eventually halt his public activities. It is ironic that he should pay so dearly for his alleged Communism. In truth, what lay at the heart of Robeson's political convictions was not Marxism so much as an empathy for African culture and an identification with common people, the poor, and the oppressed.

By the end of the decade the worst years of the cold war had passed, and Robeson's troubles began to ease. In 1958 he gave his first commercial concerts in several years, appearing in Chicago, Portland, and several California cities. He published *Here I Stand*, a trenchant autobiography written with Lloyd Brown. And a Supreme Court decision once again permitted him to travel abroad. The next few years were busy ones, with American concerts and recording sessions for Vanguard; concert tours of Europe, Australia, and New Zealand; visits to the Soviet Union; and in 1959 another London production of *Othello*. But on March 27, 1961, Robeson suffered a nervous breakdown and attempted suicide. For the rest of his life he would struggle with severe depression, and his public appearances would be extremely rare. Robeson dropped out of public awareness and was largely ignored by the leadership of the Civil Rights Movement, except for the militant young leaders of the Student Nonviolent Coordinating Committee (SNCC). At a gala celebration for his 67th birthday, Robeson was deeply moved when keynote speaker John Lewis, then the chairman of SNCC, proclaimed, "We of SNCC are Paul Robeson's spiritual children. We too have rejected gradualism and moderation." Robeson's final public appearance was at a 1966 benefit dinner for SNCC.

North America

Robinson, Bill ("Bojangles")

(b. May 25, 1878, Richmond, Va.; d. November 15, 1949, New York, N.Y.), African American vaudeville performer, tap dancer, and movie star, considered the most famous African American entertainer of the early twentieth century.

Bill "Bojangles" Robinson was born Luther Robinson, the son of Maxwell Robinson, a machinist, and Maria Robinson, a singer. Robinson and his brother Bill, whose name he would later appropriate, were orphaned when their parents died in 1885. Following this the brothers lived with their paternal grandmother, Bedilia Robinson, and Robinson worked as a bootblack and danced on street corners for money. He began to use the nickname "Bojangles," which was possibly derived from "jangle," a slang term for fighting, and supposedly invented the expression "Everything's copasetic," which meant "life is great."

Robinson moved to New York in 1900, where he emerged as one of the first black stars of vaudeville. At the time black roles normally were performed by whites in blackface, but from 1902 to 1914 Robinson toured the vaudeville circuit. In 1917 Robinson performed for American serviceman ordered to Europe to fight in World War I, and in 1918 he premiered at New York's legendary Palace Theater, where he first performed his trademark "stair dance," a rapid tap dance up and down a five-step staircase, to a standing ovation. Robinson was one of the first black performers to star at the Palace, where his dancing amazed the crowds. His footwork was complex, graceful, and often improvised. Often bedecked in tails and a top hat tilted to one side, Robinson charmed audiences with his irresistible smile. His career as a vaudeville star culminated in a European tour in 1926.

Robinson became one of the first black Broadway stars, debuting as the lead in the all-black revue *Blackbirds* of 1928. Newspaper reviews hailed him as the best tap dancer ever. Robinson's other notable Broadway starring appearances include *Brown Buddies* (1930), *Blackbirds of 1933*, *The Hot Mikado* (1939), *All in Fun* (1940), and *Memphis Bound* (1945). Because of his Broadway success, Robinson was crowned the honorary "Mayor of Harlem" in 1933.

Robinson began to make Hollywood films in the 1930s, at a time when the industry offered few opportunities to blacks. His films include *Dixiana*, (1930) *Harlem is Heaven* (1933), and *Hooray for Love* (1935). His most popular films, however, were the four he made with white child star Shirley Temple: *The Littlest Colonel* (1935), *The Littlest Rebel* (1935), *Just Around the Corner* (1938), and *Rebecca of Sunnybrook Farm* (1938).

North America

Robinson, Jackie

(b. January 31, 1919, Cairo, Ga.; d. October 24, 1972, Stamford, Conn.), African American baseball player and civil rights activist; first African American to play major league baseball in modern times.

Born to sharecroppers Jerry and Mallie Robinson, Jackie Robinson was raised in Pasadena, California, primarily by his mother, who worked as a domestic after moving the family from Georgia. Taught by his mother to confront racism by showing his talent, Robinson turned to athletics as a way to compete with the white children who would shout racist epithets at him and his siblings.

Robinson left UCLA in 1941, before graduating, to become the assistant athletic director of the National Youth Administration Camp in Atascadero, California. During that year he also played semiprofessional football for the Honolulu Bears. With the onset of World War II, Robinson was drafted into the United States Army in 1942. His army experience sharpened his sense of racial injustice. Only after boxer Joe Louis intervened with officials in Washington on Robinson's behalf did Robinson become an officer at Fort Riley in Kansas. Transferred to Fort Hood in Texas after protesting the mistreatment of his fellow African American soldiers, Robinson was court-martialed for refusing to sit in the back of an army bus. He was soon reinstated but was discharged from the army in 1944.

In 1945 Jackie Robinson began his professional baseball career by joining the Kansas City Monarchs of the Negro American League with a salary of $400 per month. Robinson was not accustomed to the difficult schedule and travel of the Negro Leagues, and he was disturbed by the oppressive treatment of black ball players throughout the country. He excelled, nonetheless, during the 1945 season, batting .345 and proving himself to be an all-around talent.

It was at this time that Branch Rickey, the general manager of the Brooklyn Dodgers, quietly began to search for the best candidate to break the color barrier in major league baseball. The time was right for Rickey's

Pictured here in the uniform of his minor-league team, the Montreal Royals, Jackie Robinson went on to join the Brooklyn Dodgers in 1947 as the first African American to play in the modern-day big leagues. He finished his career with a batting average of .311 and in 1962 became the first black player elected to the Baseball Hall of Fame. *CORBIS/Bettmann*

project. In 1944 Commissioner Kenesaw Mountain Landis, who had upheld the "gentlemen's agreement" to keep the major leagues white only, died. African American sacrifices during World War II engendered hope and support for their fuller participation in all facets of American society, thus leading to a burgeoning Civil Rights Movement. In a secret vote held by new Commissioner Albert "Happy" Chandler's office, all of the major league owners rejected the idea of integrating baseball, except for Branch Rickey. On October 23, 1945, he defied the owners' vote and signed the college-educated army officer Robinson to a contract with the minor league Montreal Royals, the top team in the Dodgers' farm system.

After playing in Venezuela during the winter, Robinson joined the Royals in Florida for the 1946 spring training season. Robinson's venture into white organized baseball was opposed from the start by coaches, teammates, other teams, and many white fans. Facing racist taunts and segregated living conditions, Robinson managed to lead the Class AAA International League in batting (.349) and runs scored (113), and helped bring his team to the league championship.

In the spring of 1947 Robinson joined the Brooklyn Dodgers in Cuba for spring training. Several Dodgers circulated a petition to exclude Robinson. Dodger manager Leo Durocher told the protesters they could leave if they wanted. Nobody left, and Robinson began "baseball's great experiment" in April 1947, becoming the first African American in the major leagues since Moses Fleetwood Walker had played in 1885. He set the league on fire, earning Rookie of the Year honors with a .297 batting average and a league-leading 29 stolen bases. During his ten seasons with the Dodgers, Robinson batted .311, led the team to six pennants and one World Series Championship, won the 1949 National League Most Valuable Player award, and paved the way for African American players in all professional team sports. Robinson proved himself on and off the field to be an exemplar of character and grace. With the help of his wife Rachel, Robinson heroically upheld his promise to Rickey not to retaliate against racist insults. In 1962 he was inducted into the Baseball Hall of Fame.

After his baseball career Robinson was vocal in the struggle for integration and black self-improvement, supporting conservative means for improving the conditions of African Americans. He refused to attend games or play in "old-timers" games because of the dearth of blacks in management and coaching positions. By 1972, however, he celebrated the 25th anniversary of his debut, throwing out the first pitch in the World Series. He died nine days later, having proved the equality of African Americans in one sphere that had profound effects on the rest of American society. In posthumous tribute to Robinson's contributions and in celebration of the 50th anniversary of his debut, in April 1997 baseball commissioner Bud Selig retired Robinson's number 42 forever throughout major league baseball.

North America

Robinson, Ruby Doris Smith

(b. April 25, 1942, Atlanta, Ga.; d. October 7, 1967, Atlanta, Ga.), American civil rights activist and a founder of the Student Nonviolent Coordinating Committee (SNCC).

Ruby Doris Smith Robinson was inspired as a teenager by media images of the Montgomery bus boycott that occurred in 1955–1956. After joining the Civil Rights Movement, Robinson was arrested for the first time as part of a lunch counter desegregation sit-in in 1959 while she was a sophomore at Spelman College in Atlanta. In 1960 she became one of the founding members of the Student Nonviolent Coordinating Committee (SNCC).

Robinson was one of the original Freedom Riders, and she helped create SNCC's "jail, no bail" policy, a strategy to fill Southern jails with protesters and thus keep public attention on the movement. In 1966 Robinson became SNCC's first (and only) female executive secretary. She left SNCC in early 1967, and died of leukemia that October.

North America

Robinson, Sugar Ray

(b. May 3, 1921, Detroit, Mich.; d. April 12, 1989, Culver City, Calif.), one of the great boxers of modern history, noted for lightning speed and impressive power.

Sugar Ray Robinson was born Walker Smith Jr. He became interested in boxing early in life, idolizing heavyweight champion Joe Louis, who also came from Detroit. To compete in tournaments when he was underage, Robinson borrowed the amateur certificate of another fighter, whose name, Ray Robinson, stuck. He rode an incredible string of amateur victories in the welterweight division to Golden Gloves titles in 1939 and 1940. His style, combining graceful movement with brute power, was described by one of his handlers as "sweet as sugar."

Robinson turned professional in 1940 and won 40 straight fights—more than 20 by knockout—until Jake LaMotta beat him by decision in 1943. In World War II Robinson entered the United States Army and performed in exhibitions for soldiers on the same bill as his hero Louis. He also protested racial segregation in the armed forces, once even fighting a military policeman who harassed Louis for using a whites-only phone. After the War, in December 1946, Robinson captured the welterweight title by defeating Tommy Bell. Defending the title in 1947, he delivered fatal blows to challenger Jimmy Doyle. A reporter asked if Robinson meant to get Doyle in trouble, and Robinson is said to have replied, "Mister, it's my business to get him into trouble."

Later that year Robinson moved up to the middleweight division. In 1951 he again met LaMotta, now the world middleweight champion, in a fight reporters called the St. Valentine's Day Massacre. Robinson emerged from this savage contest the winner. Losing his title to Englishman Randy Turpin in July 1951, Robinson won it back in a rematch two months later. In 1952 Robinson went after Joey Maxim, the light heavyweight champion, at New York's Yankee Stadium. Although he out-boxed Maxim, Robinson was overwhelmed by the heat and forced to call the fight in the 13th round—this marked the only defeat by knockout in his career.

After the fight Robinson surprised the boxing world by retiring and working for two years as a tap dancer. In 1955, however, he returned, taking back his middleweight title with a second-round knockout of Bobo Olson. Twice more Robinson lost and regained the title, holding it a record five times. He permanently lost the title to Paul Pender on January 22, 1960. Although friends encouraged the 38-year-old Robinson to retire, he continued to fight until 1965, in part to maintain his income. In his later years he established the Sugar Ray Robinson Youth Foundation for children in Los Angeles.

North America

Robinson, William ("Smokey")

(b. 1940?, Detroit, Mich.), popular rhythm and blues (R&B) singer and song-writer known for his romantic lyrics and his passionate, high-reaching voice. A leading member of the Motown vocal group the Miracles from 1958 to 1971, Robinson was one of the most influential singers and songwriters in popular music during the 1960s and 1970s.

William "Smokey" Robinson was born in Detroit, Michigan. At age 18, he formed a vocal group, which later became known as the Miracles, with high school friends Ronnie White, Pete Moore, Bobby Rogers, and Rogers's sister Claudette, whom Robinson later married. The group so impressed Motown owner Berry Gordy that he signed them to a recording contract in 1960.

The Miracles' first hit record was "Shop Around" (1961), an R&B song recorded for Tamla, one of the Motown Record Company labels. It was a phenomenal success, reaching Number One on the Billboard magazine R&B charts and Number Two on the *Billboard* pop music charts, and helping to launch Gordy's fledgling music studio. In the decade that followed the Miracles produced a highly popular body of work, including the song "You Really Got a Hold on Me" (1962); hard-edged dance tunes such as "Mickey's Monkey" (1963) and "Going to Go-Go" (1965); and the dreamy songs "More Love" (1967) and "I Second That Emotion" (1967). Perhaps even more enduring are the ballads "Ooo Baby Baby" (1965), "The Tracks of My Tears" (1965), and "Baby, Baby Don't Cry" (1969). In 1967 the group became known as Smokey Robinson and the Miracles.

During the 1960s Robinson also wrote and produced classics for other Motown artists. "My Girl" was written for the vocal group the Temptations. Robinson's "You Beat Me to the Punch" (1962) and "My Guy" (1964) were written for soul singer Mary Wells, and he wrote "Ain't That Peculiar" (1965) for soul singer Marvin Gaye. Many popular musicians, including folk-rock artist Bob Dylan, admired Robinson's songwriting skills.

Robinson's songs have endured, and many were later recorded by pop artists, including British rock group the Beatles, soul singers Aretha Franklin and Luther Vandross, and popular singers Linda Ronstadt and Kim Carnes.

Robinson left the Miracles in 1972 to pursue a solo music career. He released the highly regarded album *Quiet Storm* in 1975. In the 1980s Robinson continued to release a stream of dreamy romantic songs, including "Cruisin'" (1979), written with longtime collaborator and guitarist Marv Tarplin. Robinson's other notable hits include "Being with You" (1981) and "Just to See Her" (1987; Grammy Award, 1988). Robinson won a 1990 Grammy Legends Award. He was inducted into the Rock and Roll Hall of Fame in 1987.

North America

Rosewood Case,

one of the worst race riots in American history, in which hundreds of angry whites killed an undetermined number of blacks and burned down their entire Florida community.

In 1922 Rosewood, Florida, was a small, pre-dominantly black town. During the winter of 1922 two events in the vicinity of Rosewood aggravated local race relations: the murder of a white schoolteacher in nearby Perry, which led to the murder of three blacks, and a Ku Klux Klan rally in Gainesville on New Year's Eve.

On New Year's Day of 1923, Fannie Taylor, a young white woman living in Sumner, claimed that a black man sexually assaulted her in her home. A small group of whites began searching for a recently escaped black convict named Jesse Hunter, whom they believed to be responsible. They incarcerated one suspected accomplice, Aaron Carrier, and lynched another, Sam

Carter. The men then targeted Aaron's cousin Sylvester Carrier, a fur trapper and private music instructor who was rumored to be harboring Jesse Hunter.

A group of 20 to 30 white men came to Sylvester Carrier's house to confront him. They shot his dog, and when his mother, Sarah, stepped outside to talk with the men, they shot her. Carrier killed two men and wounded four in the shootout that ensued. After the men left, the women and children, who prior to this had gathered in Carrier's house for protection, fled to the swamp where the majority of Rosewood's residents had already sought refuge.

The white men returned to Carrier's house the following evening. After a brief shootout they entered the house, found the bodies of Sarah Carrier and a black man whom they believed to be Sylvester Carrier, and set the residence on fire. The men then proceeded on a rampage through Rosewood, torching other buildings and slaughtering animals. They were joined by a mob of approximately 200 whites that converged on Rosewood after finding out that a black man had killed two whites.

That night two local white train conductors, John and William Bryce, who knew all of Rosewood's residents, picked up the black women and children and took them to Gainesville. John Wright, a white general-store owner who hid a number of black women and children in his home during the riot, planned and helped carry out this evacuation effort. The African Americans who escaped by foot headed for Gainesville or for other cities in the northern United States.

By the end of the weekend all of Rosewood, except the Wright house and general store, was leveled. Although the state of Florida claimed that only eight people died in the Rosewood riot—two whites and six blacks—survivors' testimonies suggest that more African Americans perished. No one was charged with the Rosewood murders. After the riot the town was deserted, and even blacks living in surrounding communities moved out.

It is unclear what became of Jesse Hunter. Residents of nearby Cedar Key claimed that he was captured and killed after the massacre. The descendants of the Carrier family, however, contend that Jesse Hunter was not the man who had attacked Taylor. Philomena Carrier, who had been working with her grandmother Sarah Carrier at Fannie Taylor's house at the time of the alleged sexual assault, claimed that the man responsible was a white railroad engineer. She said that the man had come to see Taylor the morning of January first after her husband left for work. After an argument between them erupted, Philomena witnessed the man exit the back door and jog down the road toward Rosewood.

The Carriers' descendants maintain that the man was a Mason who persuaded Aaron Carrier, a member of Rosewood's black Masonic lodge, to help him escape by appealing to the society's code requiring members to help one another regardless of race. Carrier in turn persuaded another black Mason, Sam Carter, one of the few men in Rosewood with a wagon, to pick up the white man at Carrier's house and drop him off in the swamp, where he disappeared without a trace.

Though the Rosewood riot received national coverage in *The New York Times* and *The Washington Post* as it unfolded, it has been neglected by historians. Survivors of Rosewood did not come forward to tell their stories because of the shame they felt for having been connected with the riot and their fear of being persecuted or killed. In 1993 the Florida Department of Law Enforcement conducted an investigation into the case, which led to the drafting of a bill to compensate the survivors of the massacre.

After an extended debate and several hearings, the Rosewood Bill, which awarded $150,000 to each of the riot's nine eligible black survivors, was passed in April 1994. In spite of the state's financial compensation, the survivors remained frightened. When asked if he would go back to Rosewood, survivor Wilson Hall said, "No, they still don't want me down there."

The director John Singleton, best known for his film *Boyz 'N the Hood*, released a fictionalized account of the massacre, called *Rosewood* which was based on survivors' testimony, in 1997.

North America

Ross, Diana

(b. March 26, 1944, Detroit, Mich.), African American singer and actress; lead vocalist of the Supremes, whose songs topped the Billboard charts throughout the 1960s, 1970s, and 1980s.

Diana Ross was born Diane Ross, the second of six children, to Fred and Ernestine Ross. She grew up in a poor district of Detroit, Michigan. As a child Ross sang with her siblings and parents in the choir at the Olivet Baptist Church and collaborated with neighborhood friends on renditions of the most popular songs of the day. She showcased her talent by performing on street corners, in school talent shows, and at dances. In 1959, while still in high school, Ross joined Mary Wilson, Florence Ballard, and Betty McGlown in a vocal group called the Primettes, the "sister act" for a group of male singers that later became the Temptations. In 1961, after both McGlown and her replacement Barbara Martin left the group, the Primettes signed a recording contract with Motown Records as a trio and changed their name to the Supremes.

The Supremes did not enjoy immediate recognition and success. Initially they sang as backup vocalists or served as "handclappers" for other Motown acts, including Mary Wells, Marvin Gaye, and the Shirelles. After three years as a group, the Supremes achieved their first number one hit in July 1964 with "Where Did Our Love Go," their ninth release. A string of number one hits followed: "Baby Love" (1964), "Come See About Me" (1964), "Stop! In the Name of Love" (1965), and "Back in My Arms Again" (1965). In 1967 Cindy Birdsong replaced Florence Ballard, and the group changed its name to Diana Ross and the Supremes. In 1970 Ross left the Supremes to pursue a solo career in singing and acting, but not before issuing one more group hit, "Someday We'll Be Together." A series of female singers assumed the lead vocals of the Supremes before the group's breakup in 1977.

Ross launched her career as a soloist with the Number One single "Ain't No Mountain High Enough" (1970). She then turned her attention to film. In 1972 Ross's portrayal of Billie Holiday in *Lady Sings the Blues,* in which she costarred with Billy Dee Williams, earned her an Academy Award nomination. Ross starred in *Mahogany* (1975), singing the hit theme song, "Do You Know Where You're Going To?," and later in *The Wiz* (1978). After recording two disco sensations, "Love Hangover" (1976) and "Upside Down" (1980), Ross collaborated with Lionel Richie on the ballad "Endless Love" (1981). Ross left Motown Records in 1981 but returned in 1989 to work as a recording artist, an equity partner, and a director of the company.

The Supremes were inducted into the Rock and Roll Hall of Fame in 1988, confirming their status as the most famous black performing group and the most famous female recording group in American music history. As the lead vocalist for the Supremes, Ross had 12 number one singles and sold more than 50 million records. Between 1970 and 1984 she recorded 31 albums and more than 50 singles, 6 of which reached the top spot on the Billboard chart. Ross is considered to be one of the most influential and versatile recording artists of the twentieth century.

North America

Run-DMC,

an early rap and influential music group from New York City. The group was known during the 1980s for its aggressive "raps" (spoken rhymes) on top of strong beats. Run-DMC further distinguished its sound by incorporating elements of rock music, specifically heavy-metal guitar, which helped popularize black rap among many white listeners. By bringing the hip hop street look to the stage, Run-DMC also changed the image of rap, wearing black leather in winter, athletic warm-up suits in summer, and always wearing their signature Adidas sneakers. The first rap group to be broadcast regularly on Music Television (MTV), Run-DMC in 1985 also became the first rap group to appear on the television program American Bandstand, hosted by media personality Dick Clark.

Run-DMC was formed in 1983 by three friends from New York City's borough of Queens. Rapper Joseph "Run" Simmons recorded as a solo artist in 1982 for his older brother, rap producer Russell "Rush" Simmons, before teaming with rapper Darryl "D.M.C." McDaniels to record two minor singles. The two then brought in disc jockey (DJ) Jason "Jam Master Jay" Mizell, and the trio soon became known as Run-DMC. The group released its first album in 1984, Run-D.M.C. On the strength of one song, "Sucker M.C.'s," the album became the best-selling rap album to that time. The album gained attention for its tough-sounding lyrics and its spare, clean sound; the group used only a drum machine and scratchy turntable noises for accompaniment. Another single from the album, "Rock Box," was one of the first rap pieces to include tracks of heavy-metal electric guitar, and was also distributed as a video.

In 1985 Run-DMC released its second album, King of Rock, and acted and performed in the motion picture *Krush Groove*, a fictionalized account of Run-DMC and the development of rap-music record label Def Jam. Also in 1985, a number of violent incidents at rap concerts caused the national media to focus on rap as a reflection of violence and drug abuse among young black males. Run-DMC and other rap groups found themselves caught between this negative image and the acceptance of rap by MTV and American Bandstand.

The group's third album, "Raising Hell" (1986), featured a remake of "Walk This Way," a song first made famous by the hard-rock group Aerosmith in 1976. The remake, which included new performances by Aerosmith members Steven Tyler and Joe Perry, was a popular success and was hailed by critics as a breakthrough that masterfully fused white rock music with black rap. In 1988 the group starred in *Tougher Than Leather*, a film produced by Def Jam's Rick Rubin. Other albums from Run-DMC include "Back from Hell" (1990) and "Down with the King" (1993). Jam Master Jay, the band's charismatic DJ, was murdered in a recording studio on October 30, 2002. The crime remains unsolved.

Europe

Russia and the Former Soviet Union,

a large country extending from eastern Europe into northern Asia, which has hosted a black population for centuries.

From the eighteenth century, when Peter the Great first recruited black servants, until the post-Soviet present, black people have been an uncommon sight in the lands that once constituted the Russian Empire and, later, the Soviet Union (or Union of Soviet Socialist Republics, USSR). Except in tiny black enclaves in the Caucasus, blacks have always been outsiders in this part of the world. As early as 1858 the celebrated black Shakespearean actor Ira Aldridge beguiled Russian audiences with the power of his performances, while his presence sparked heated discussions on racial issues in the Russian press. In the decades preceding the 1917 Bolshevik Revolution a number of American blacks went to Russia, where they pursued successful careers as businessmen and diplomats.

The heyday for blacks in Russia occurred between the 1917 revolution and the 1960s. Communist leaders, eager to display their country as a place of racial equality, gave visiting black artists, intellectuals, and political figures privileges that the average Soviet citizen could only dream of—albeit not without motives informed by Soviet ideology and international politics. Although blacks encountered racial prejudice in the former Soviet Union, the general reaction to them was one of curiosity more than hostility. Writer

Langston Hughes wrote of his 1932 experience in Russia, "What few Negroes there were in Moscow, of course, were conspicuous wherever they went, attracting friendly curiosity if very dark, and sometimes startling a peasant fresh from the country who had never seen a black face before."

North America

Russwurm, John Brown

(b. October 1, 1799, Port Antonio, Jamaica; d. June 9, 1851, Harper, Liberia), African American publisher of the first black newspaper in the United States, emigration worker, and Liberian government official.

Born John Brown to a Jamaican slave mother and a white American merchant father, he became John Russwurm when his stepmother demanded that his father acknowledge paternity by name. Sent to Quebec for schooling, Russwurm was taken by his father to Portland, Maine, in 1812. He attended Hebron Academy in Hebron, Maine, and graduated in 1826 from Bowdoin College, making Russwurm one of the first black graduates of an American college. In his graduation speech he advocated the resettlement of American blacks to Haiti.

Moving to New York City in 1827, Russwurm helped found *Freedom's Journal* with Samuel E. Cornish. It was the first black-owned and black-printed newspaper in the United States. The paper employed itinerant black abolitionists and urged an end to Southern slavery and Northern inequality. In February 1829 he stopped publishing the paper and accepted a position as the superintendent of education in Liberia. He left for Liberia having given up hope that African Americans would have any future equality or prosperity in the United States.

In Liberia, in addition to his government position, he edited the Liberia Herald and served as a Liberian agent, recruiting American blacks to return to Africa. Russwurm became the first black governor of the Maryland area of Liberia in 1836 and worked to enhance the country's economic and diplomatic position.

Africa

Rwanda,

a small Central African country bordered by Uganda, Tanzania, Burundi, and the Democratic Republic of the Congo (formerly Zaire).

Known as "the land of a thousand hills," Rwanda is one of Africa's smallest and most densely populated countries. Located in a region of fertile land and ample rainfall, pre-colonial Rwandan society was—according to early European visitors—prosperous and orderly; but it was also extremely hierarchical. A centuries-old Tutsi monarchy ruled over a bureaucracy of chiefs,

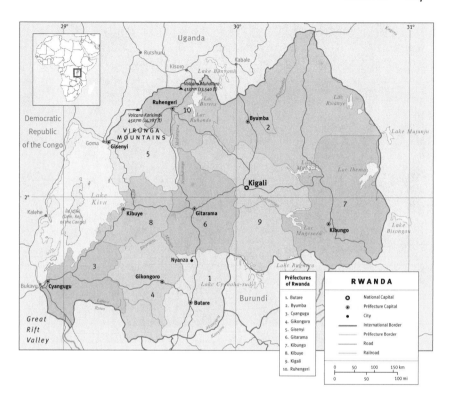

who in turn collected tribute from Hutu commoners. Under German and then Belgian colonial rule, stratification in Rwanda grew wider and more rigid, with disastrous consequences.

Even before independence in 1962 the Tutsi monarchy was overthrown by a Hutu revolution. In 1963 and 1973 civil conflict emerged, the latter episode leading to a coup d'état bringing to power Maj. Gen. Juvénal Habyarimana. In 1994, when Rwanda was coping with an invasion from Uganda, a collapsed economy, and an active democratization movement, a hard-line government seized power on the death of President Habyarimana, and proceeded to organize the calculated destruction of its Hutu opponents and all Tutsi. More than 500,000 people were killed, and over 2 million fled.

The government that took power in July 1994 pledged to bring about justice and reconciliation, but progress has been slow. Government troops under the leadership of Gen. Paul Kagame, Rwanda's most powerful political and military leader, have clashed repeatedly with Hutu militia groups, fostering ongoing insecurity in the countryside. Conflict within Rwanda has fueled—and been fueled by—conflicts elsewhere in the Great Lake Region, which also includes Burundi, Uganda, and the Democratic Republic of the Congo. Meanwhile, Rwanda faces severe land shortages, poverty, and public health problems.

Refugees returning to Rwanda after the 1994 genocide pass piles of machetes used in the slayings. *CORBIS/David Turnley*

Rwanda (Ready Reference)

Official Name: Rwandan Republic

Area: 10,169 sq mi (26,338 sq km)

Location: Central Africa; borders Burundi, Tanzania, Uganda, the Democratic Republic of the Congo (formerly Zaire)

Capital: Kigali (population 219,000 [1990 estimate])

Other Major Cities: Butare (population 21,961 [1978 estimate])

Population: 7,956,172 (1998 estimate); genocide and civil war in 1994 killed more than one million Rwandans and forced more than two million to flee to neighboring countries.

Population Density: about 819 persons per sq mi (316 persons per sq km)[1995 estimate])

Population Below Age 15: Total population: 45 percent (male 1,785,650; female 1,772,609 [1998 estimate])

Population Growth Rate: 2.5 percent (1998 estimate)

Total Fertility Rate: 5.86 children born per woman (1998 estimate)

Life Expectancy at Birth: Total population: 44.93 years (male 41.49 years; female 42.4 years [1998 estimate])

Infant Mortality Rate: 118.8 deaths per 1000 live births (1996 estimate)

Literacy Rate (age 15 and over can read and write): Total population: 60.5 percent (male 69.8 percent; female 51.6 percent [1995 estimate])

Education: Compulsory in principle for children aged seven through 15. In the early 1990s primary school enrollment in Rwanda was about 1.1 million, and secondary and technical schools had about 70,000 students.

Languages: The official languages are Kinyarwanda (a Bantu language) and French.

Ethnic Groups: Rwanda is composed of three principle ethnic groups. The Hutu constitute about 90 percent of the total population; the Tutsi, about nine percent; and the Twa, one percent. The Twa are thought to be the original inhabitants of the region.

Religions: About 65 percent of the population is Catholic, about nine percent is Muslim, and some nine percent is Protestant. Approximately 17 percent of the people follow traditional religions.

Climate: Rwanda is temperate. It has two rainy seasons (from February to April and November to January). Weather is mild in the mountains with frost and snow possible. The average yearly rainfall is 31 in (787 mm) and is heaviest in the western and northwestern mountain regions. Wide temperature variations occur because of elevation differences. The average daily temperature in the Lake Kivu area is 22.8° C (73° F). In the mountains in the northwest, frost occurs at night.

Land, Plants, and Animals: The central portion of Rwanda is dominated by a hilly plateau averaging about 5600 ft (1700 m) in elevation. On the western side of the plateau is a mountain system averaging about 2740 m (about 9000 ft), forming the watershed between the Nile and Congo river systems. The Virunga Mountains, a volcanic range that forms the northern reaches of this system, include Volcan Karisimbi (4507 m/14,787 ft), Rwanda's highest peak. Forests containing eucalyptus, acacia, and oil palms are concentrated in the western mountains and the Lake Kivu area. Wildlife includes elephants, hippopotamuses, crocodiles, wild boars, leopards, antelope, and lemurs. The Virunga Mountains in northern Rwanda are home to what is estimated to be half of the world's remaining mountain gorillas.

Natural Resources: Gold, cassiterite (tin ore), wolframite (tungsten ore), natural gas, hydropower

Currency: The Rwandan franc

Gross Domestic Product (GDP): $3 billion (1996 estimate)

GDP per Capita: $440 (1996 estimate)

GDP Real Growth Rate: 13.3 percent (1996 estimate)

Primary Economic Activities: Agriculture (52 percent of GDP, 93 percent of work force), industry (13 percent of GDP), services (35 percent of GDP) (1994 estimate)

Primary crops: Coffee, tea, pyrethrum (insecticide made from chrysanthemums), bananas, beans, sorghum, potatoes, livestock

Industries: Mining of cassiterite (tin ore) and wolframite (tungsten ore), tin, cement, agricultural processing, beverages, light consumer goods

Primary Exports: Coffee, tea, cassiterite, wolframite, pyrethrum

Primary Imports: Textiles, foodstuffs, machines and equipment, capital goods, steel, petroleum products, cement, construction material

Primary Trade Partners: Germany, Belgium, Italy, Uganda, United Kingdom, France, United States, Kenya, Japan

Government: Under a constitution approved in 1978, the sole political party in Rwanda was the National Revolutionary Movement for Development. Executive power was vested in a president, assisted by an appointed council of ministers; legislative power was exercised by an elected National Development Council. A new constitution, promulgated in 1991, provides for a multiparty democracy with a limited presidential term and independent executive, legislative, and judicial branches. In August 1994 the Tutsi-dominated Rwandan Patriotic Front placed Rwanda under martial law and suspended the 1991 constitution. Pasteur Bizimungu is president of Rwanda, but Vice President and Minister of Defense Paul Kagame is widely recognized as the most powerful government figure.

S

Sadat, Anwar al-

(b. December 25, 1918, Mit Abu al-Kum, al-Minufiyah Governate, Egypt;
d. October 6, 1981, Cairo, Egypt), president of Egypt from 1970 to 1981 and
the first Arab leader to recognize the state of Israel.

The son of a hospital clerk, Anwar Sadat was born in the Nile Delta.
Graduated from Cairo Military Academy in 1938, he was part of the first
generation of Egyptian soldiers recruited from the middle class rather than
the elite.

After Nasser was elected president of Egypt in 1956, Sadat held various
offices in the government, including two terms as vice president
(1964–1966 and 1969–1970). With Nasser's death in September 1970,
Sadat became president. Although his political opponents considered him
an interim leader, he was elected president less than a month later. Sadat
moved quickly to consolidate his support, loosening state control over the
economy and relaxing restrictions on political activity. In addition, shortly
after taking office, Sadat began to strengthen the Egyptian military, which
had been soundly defeated by Israel in the 1967 Six-Day War.

Sadat's tenure was marked by an emphasis on foreign policy. In 1972 he
expelled Soviet military advisers, signaling an end to Egypt's close ties with
the Eastern Bloc. On October 6, 1973, Egypt and Syria attacked Israel,
launching the Yom Kippur War. After Egypt's initial successes, Israel took
the offensive. Although Egypt did not win the war, it did achieve his primary goal—to improve Egypt's negotiating position with Israel. In addition,
as the first Arab military leader to reclaim land from Israel, Sadat earned
enhanced prestige in the Arab world.

Sadat's lasting legacy was his peace settlement with Israel. In November
1977 he visited Jerusalem and presented his peace plan to the Israeli
Knesset (Parliament). Despite widespread criticism from the Arab world,
Sadat held a series of diplomatic meetings with Israel, culminating in the

Camp David Accords in 1979, in which Egypt normalized relations with Israel. The fallout from the Arab world was quick and severe, however, as Egypt was soon expelled from the Arab League and denied economic support from fellow Arab nations.

On October 6, 1981, the anniversary of the Yom Kippur War, Sadat presided over a military parade in Cairo. During the parade a military vehicle stopped abruptly, and five soldiers who were later linked to an Islamic protest group leapt out and began firing machine guns and throwing hand grenades at the president. Sadat and six others were killed. The leader was succeeded by his vice president, Hosni Mubarak.

Latin America and the Caribbean

Santería,

a syncretized religion derived from African and Roman Catholic religious practices and beliefs that developed in Cuba and later spread to other countries.

Santería came into being between the sixteenth and nineteenth centuries, when the Spanish colonizers of Cuba imported hundreds of thousands of slaves from Africa to work on the island's sugar and coffee plantations. The Spanish, who established Roman Catholicism in Cuba, baptized these slaves and forbade them to practice African religions. In these circumstances slaves

Drummers play during a Santería ceremony. Each orisha, or Santería deity, has its own drum rhythm, song, and dance step. CORBIS/Françoise de Mulder

Santería, a faith that combines elements of African and Roman Catholic religious practices, developed in Cuba and spread to other countries. This photo shows a Santería altar in Havana. *CORBIS/ Robert van der Hilst*

preserved elements of their religions by identifying their deities, known as orishas, with Roman Catholic saints. This syncretism allowed slaves to worship the orishas secretly while externally paying homage to the Catholic saints. For this reason, the religion that emerged is known as Santería, "the way of the saints."

Historians have identified slaves from the Yoruba ethnic group of southwestern Nigeria as the most influential group in the forging of Santería. Yoruba slaves believed in one supreme being, Olodumare, who in Cuba became equated with the Christian concept of God, and numerous orishas, the children and servants of Olodumare, who in Cuba became correlated with the Christian saints. While the Yoruba religion includes some 400 to 500 orishas, each of which protects and is worshiped by the inhabitants of a different city, the practitioners of Santería only recognize some 16 orishas. In Cuba this smaller set of intermediary deities is sometimes termed Lucumí, the name originally used by the Spanish to refer to Yoruban slaves, in order to distinguish it from the Yoruban pantheon from which it derives.

Because practitioners of Santería regard Olodumare as a distant, inaccessible God, they focus their religious activities on the intermediary orishas. To those who worship them, the orishas are divine ancestors, immaterial in form, who control some aspect of nature and some domain of human activity. Ogun, for example, is regarded as the deity of iron and minerals, and he oversees blacksmiths and those who drive vehicles with metal parts.

A Santería high priest, or babalao, guides a devotee in a prayer before an altar.
CORBIS/Françoise de Mulder

In Santería an individual develops a reciprocal relationship with one of the orishas. In exchange for guidance and protection, the worshiper makes offerings (*ebó*) to his or her orisha. Communication with the orishas is established through various forms of divination performed by a Santería priest or priestess and through spirit possession, which takes place during drum and dance ceremonies.

Santería employs three types of divination: *obi, dilloggún,* and a combination of the *opelé* and *tablero de ifá*. In each type, a priest or priestess tosses and interprets the fall of certain objects—a quartered coconut for obi, 16 cowry shells for dilloggún, and a necklace with 8 evenly spaced disks for opelé. The tablero de ifá is a wooden tray upon which a priest sprinkles powder and draws configurations based on the heads-or-tails patterns resulting from several throwings of the opelé.

The three divination types correspond to various individuals in the Santería priesthood. The opelé and the tablero de ifá are used exclusively by *babalawos,* the male high priests of Santería. The dilloggún is used only by a *santero* or *santera,* a standard Santería priest or priestess. The obi may be used by both types of priests. Divination is used in the early stages of initiation to determine an individual's personal orisha and thereafter to determine the will of the orisha for that person. According to one scholar, divination is the process through which the orishas diagnose people's problems and recommend solutions.

Practitioners of Santería hold elaborate ceremonies called *bembés* to invoke their orishas. Each orisha has its own drum rhythm, song, and dance step. In performing the music and choreography of a particular orisha, a worshiper tries to persuade the orisha to descend upon the ceremony and possess him or her. An orisha that temporarily takes over the body of a worshiper, an act often described as "mounting," is able to participate in the festivities, accepting food offerings and giving advice. The orisha eventually takes leave of his or her human medium, who then regains consciousness without recalling the possession.

Santería has taken root beyond Cuba, especially in the United States. Hundreds of thousands of Cuban exiles have arrived in the United States since the 1959 revolution in Cuba, bringing Santería with them. Many of these Cubans settled in New York City and southern Florida. Over time the number of non-Cubans practicing Santería has increased, and the religion has become more public, but not without some resistance. Santería's use of animal sacrifice to feed symbolically the orishas triggered a controversial national debate. In 1987 the city of Hialeah, Florida, responded to this practice by banning animal sacrifice. However, a 1993 Supreme Court ruling stating that the ban represented unconstitutional infringement on freedom of religion has enabled Santería to continue to thrive in the United States.

Africa

São Tomé and Príncipe,

Africa's smallest country, comprising two islands off the coast of Gabon in the Gulf of Guinea.

The tiny island nation of São Tomé and Príncipe has had a different history than most other African countries. São Tomé and Príncipe—often referred to simply as São Tomé—comprises two separate islands. Uninhabited before Portuguese exploration in the fifteenth century, the islands were settled by both Africans and Europeans—most brought against their will. In time, a Creole people known as the *forros* emerged. Subsequent waves of involuntary migrants passed through the islands, including hundreds of thousands of African slaves on their way across the Atlantic to the markets in Brazil and Latin America. Originally a sugar-growing economy, São Tomé later produced a large share of the world's coffee and cocoa. It has never escaped the limitations of a plantation economy. Its size and a shortage of skilled workers force it to rely on imported goods and services. It achieved political independence in 1975 from Portugal, its former colonial master. Its abundant natural beauty has begun to attract tourism. However, São Tomé remains heavily dependent on foreign aid and a single plantation crop, cocoa.

Africa

São Tomé and Príncipe (Ready Reference)
Official Name: Democratic Republic of São Tomé and Príncipe
Area: 960 sq km (371 sq mi.)
Location: In the Gulf of Guinea, along the equator off the western coast of Central Africa
Capital: São Tomé (population 35,000 [1984 estimate])
Other Major Cities: Santo Antonio (population 1,000; [1984 estimate])

Population: 150,128 (1998 estimate)

Population Density: 154 persons per sq km (about 399 persons per sq mi.)

Population Below Age 15: 48 percent (male 36,127; female: 35,253 [1998 estimate])

Population Growth Rate: 3.1 percent (1998 estimate)

Total Fertility Rate: 6.19 children born per woman (1998 estimate)

Life Expectancy at Birth: Total population: 64.34 years (male 62.87 years; female 65.86 years [1998 estimate])

Infant Mortality Rate: 54.55 deaths per 1,000 live births (1998 estimate)

Literacy Rate (age 15 and over who can read and write): Total population: 73 percent (male 85 percent; female 62 percent [1991 estimate])

Education: No information available

Languages: Portuguese is the official language, but most people speak Crioulo, a language combining Portuguese and African elements.

Ethnic Groups: Because it was uninhabited before European colonization in the fifteenth century, much of São Tomé's population consists of the racially mixed descendants of Portuguese settlers and African slaves. Such mestiços are also known as *forros*, or *filhos da terra* (children of the earth). In addition, the islands are inhabited by *serviçais* (contract laborers, mostly from the Cape Verde Islands, Angola, and Mozambique), *tongas* (descendants of earlier generations of serviçais), *Angolares* (who take their name from ship-wrecked Angolan slaves, though the name now refers to all people of African descent whose livelihood depends not on the plantation economy but on fishing), and Europeans (mostly Portuguese).

Religions: Roman Catholic (about 80 percent), Evangelical Protestant, Seventh-day Adventist

Climate: Both of the islands that comprise São Tomé and Príncipe share a hot, humid, tropical climate. Temperatures range from an average of 25° C (77° F) in the lower, coastal areas to 18° C (65° F) in the higher elevations. Although there is virtually no seasonal variation in temperature, there is a rainy season from October to May. In addition, rainfall varies greatly, from 5,100 mm (about 200 in.) in the southwestern mountains to 1,020 mm (about 40 in.) in the lowlands to the northeast.

Land, Plants, and Animals: São Tomé, the larger of the two islands that make up the Democratic Republic of São Tomé and Príncipe, is home to the country's highest mountain, Pico de São Tomé, with an elevation of 2,024 m (6,640 ft.). Both islands are volcanic in origin, with rugged, mountainous interiors. Coastal areas, particularly on the southwestern and northeastern sides, are fertile lowlands. The interior mountains are forested. The islands have few native species of mammals but are home to a great variety of birds.

Natural Resources: São Tomé's most important natural resource is its rich soil, which is the basis for its plantation economy.

Currency: The dobra

Gross Domestic Product (GDP): $154 million (1996 estimate)

GDP per Capita: $1,000 (1996 estimate)

GDP Real Growth Rate: 1.5 percent (1996 estimate)

Primary Economic Activities: São Tomé's economy is almost completely dependent on its production and export of cocoa, responsible for about 60 percent of export earnings. Other crops raised include coffee, copra, oil palms, coconuts, bananas, and papayas. A small fishing industry also exists. In recent years the country has attempted to build a tourist industry capitalizing on its great natural beauty.

Primary Crops: Cocoa, coffee, palm kernels, copra, coconuts, bananas, and papayas

Industries: Food processing

Primary Exports: Cocoa, coffee, copra, and palm oil

Primary Imports: Because of its island location and agricultural specialization, São Tomé imports about 90 percent of its food and nearly all of its consumer goods.

Primary Trade Partners: Portugal, France, Netherlands, and Germany

Government: São Tomé and Príncipe has been a parliamentary republic since 1990. The country consists of two administrative districts: São Tomé and Príncipe. As of 1999, it was governed by President Miguel Trovoada and Prime Minister Raul Bragança Neto. Voters elect a unicameral National Assembly consisting of 55 legislators, which chooses the prime minister and cabinet and appoints justices to the Supreme Court. The dominant party from independence in 1975 into the late 1990s was the Movement for the Liberation of São Tomé and Príncipe (MLSTP); other parties include the Party for Democratic Reconvergence-Reflection Group (PCD-GR) and Independent Democratic Action (ADI). São Tomé has universal suffrage for those aged 18 and over.

North America

Schomburg, Arthur Alfonso

(b. January 24, 1874, San Juan, Puerto Rico; d. June 10, 1938, New York, N.Y.), Afro-Puerto Rican bibliophile and librarian who collected the literature and art of the African diaspora.

The son of a German father and a West Indian mother, Arthur Schomburg spent his childhood in Puerto Rico. After briefly attending St. Thomas College in the Virgin Islands, he came to the United States in 1891 and began working in a New York City law office. In New York, Schomburg began to collect literary works and visual art by and about people of African descent. In 1906 Schomburg began working in the mailroom at Bankers Trust Company, where he remained until 1929. He became an active Prince Hall Mason, serving as grand secretary of the Grand Lodge from 1918 to 1926.

In 1911 Schomburg and John E. Bruce founded the Negro Society for Historical Research as a base from which to publish articles on black history. In 1922 Schomburg was elected president of the American Negro Academy. Three years later his important essay "The Negro Digs Up His Past" appeared in Alain Locke's *The New Negro*. Schomburg and his collection of books, manuscripts, and artifacts was an invaluable resource and an inspiration to both historians and Harlem Renaissance artists. Through his collection of literature and art by people of African descent, Schomburg sought to disprove the pseudo-scientific racism of the day.

In 1926 the Carnegie Corporation purchased Schomburg's collection and donated it to the Negro Division of the New York Public Library, the 135th Street branch in Harlem. Schomburg was hired as curator in 1932, holding the position until his death in 1938. Two years later the library was named the Schomburg Collection of Negro Literature and History, and it has since been moved and renamed the Schomburg Center for Research in Black Culture. It is the largest, most important collection of African and African American cultural materials in the world.

North America

Scottsboro Case,

an international cause célèbre during the 1930s in which nine young black men were accused of raping two white women in Alabama.

The Scottsboro case began in 1931 when two white women falsely accused nine young African Americans of rape. Throughout the world of the 1930s the Scottsboro defendants came to symbolize the racism and injustice of the American South. In their initial trials the defendants received what critics described as a "legal lynching." But the assistance of the Communist Party of the United States of America (CPUSA) gave the young men (Clarence Norris, Olen Montgomery, Haywood Patterson, Ozie Powell, Willie Roberson, Charlie Weems, Eugene Williams, and Andrew and Leroy Wright) a second chance, and the ensuing struggle became one of the great civil rights cases of the twentieth century.

After several retrials, worldwide protests, massive publicity, and two landmark rulings by the Supreme Court of the United States, only four of the men gained their freedom, after having spent six years in jail. Full vindication did not come until 1976, when Alabama governor George Wallace pardoned all nine "Scottsboro boys." At that time only one of the defendants, Clarence Norris, was still alive to hear the news.

North America

Seale, Bobby

(b. October 22, 1936, Dallas, Tex.), political and social activist of the 1960s; cofounder of the militant Black Panther Party.

Bobby Seale, the son of George and Thelma Seale, moved to California with his family at age 10. He entered the U.S. Air Force at age 18 and served as an aircraft-sheet mechanic. Three years later he was dishonorably discharged for insubordination and absence without leave. In 1961 he was admitted to Merritt College in Oakland, California.

While at Merritt, Seale became a member of the Afro-American Association in Oakland. Through this militant organization, Seale met and befriended fellow student Huey Newton. Together, Newton and Seale formed the Soul Students Advisory Committee at Merritt. In 1966 the two created the Black Panther Party, whose political platform called for equality of opportunity for African Americans and an end to police brutality against black people.

Seale was arrested in 1968 for his participation in anti-Vietnam War demonstrations at the Democratic National Convention in Chicago, and spent two years in jail. He was arrested a second time in 1972 for the murder of suspected Black Panther informer Alex Rackley, but the charges against him were dropped. In 1973 he made an unsuccessful bid for the office of mayor of Oakland, and in 1974 he resigned as chairman of the Black Panther Party. In the 1980s Seale became involved in an organization called Youth Employment Strategies. He published two autobiographies, *Seize the Time: The Story of the Black Panther Party and Huey P. Newton* in 1970 and *A Lonely Rage* in 1978.

Africa

Senegal,

a coastal West African country bordered by Mauritania, Mali, Guinea, Guinea-Bissau, and the Atlantic Ocean and nearly surrounding the Gambia, which forms a virtual enclave within Senegal's borders.

Located in the Sahel region, where kingdoms prospered from trans-Saharan trade in pre-modern times, Senegal came to serve as the beachhead for

A man walks through the doorway of a house on Gorée Island, Senegal. The island was a major port of departure in the transatlantic slave trade. *CORBIS/Hans Georg Roth*

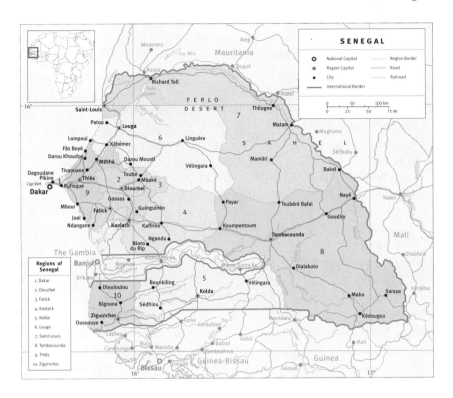

France's conquest of a colonial empire in Africa. Senegal's coastal cities were France's first colonial outposts; the country's largest city and capital, Dakar, served as the capital and the commercial center of colonial French West Africa. Citizens of Senegal were the first Africans to gain French citizenship rights, and the African nation has maintained close ties to France since independence. French-speaking Senegalese elite occupied administrative posts throughout France's African empire and contributed to the anticolonial struggles of the 1950s. Senegal's pre-colonial past, dating back to the eleventh century when the area served as point of entry for Islam south of the Sahara, is not as well known as its history under French rule. The Tukulor and Fulani peoples of interior Senegal helped spread Islam across large areas of West Africa, from Mali to Nigeria. During the 1990s the Muridiyah, an Islamic brotherhood, remained a powerful force in Senegalese society. Today Senegal faces challenges common to many African countries, including economic stagnation, large income disparities, and persistent rebellion by regional separatists in the southern Casamance region. However, Senegal's continued role as an intellectual and cultural center in French-speaking Africa, its relative stability, and its political openness offer the hope that Senegal might once again lead Africa in building a democratic and economically secure society.

Senegal (Ready Reference)

Official Name: Republic of Senegal

Area: 196,190 sq km (about 74,552 sq mi.)

Location: Western Africa; borders the North Atlantic Ocean, Guinea-Bissau, and Mauritania

Capital: Dakar (population 1,729,823 [1992 estimate])

Other Major Cities: Thiès (population 216,381), Kaolack (193,115), Ziguinchor (161,680), and Saint-Louis (132,499) (1994 estimates)

Population: 9,723,149 (1998 estimate)

Population Density: 46 persons per sq km (about 121 persons per sq mi.)

Population Below Age 15: 48 percent (male 2,331,388; female 2,343,654 [1998 estimate])

Population Growth Rate: 3.3 percent (1998 estimate)

Total Fertility Rate: 6.1 children born per woman (1998 estimate)

Life Expectancy at Birth: Total population: 57.37 years (male 54.55 years; female 60.28 years [1998 estimate])

Infant Mortality Rate: 61.2 deaths per 1,000 live births (1998 estimate)

Literacy Rate (age 15 and over who can read and write): Total population: 33.1 percent (male 43 percent; female 23.2 percent [1995 estimate])

Education: Education is officially compulsory for all children between the ages of 6 and 12, but only 48 percent of primary-school-age children attended school in the late 1980s, and only 13 percent of secondary-school-age children attended school.

Languages: French is the official language. Almost half the population also speaks Wolof, the most widely understood of the African languages, but Pulaar, Jola, and Mandingo are also spoken.

Ethnic Groups: 44 percent of the population are Wolof. Other principal ethnic groups are the Fulani, Tukulor, Serer, Jola, and Malinke.

Religions: About 92 percent of the population are Sunni Muslim. About 2 percent are Christian (mostly Roman Catholic), and 6 percent follow indigenous beliefs.

Climate: Senegal is arid desert in the north and tropical in the south. It has a transitional climate from the dry desert zone in the north to the moist tropical zone in the south. The rainy season lasts from July to October in the north. Average rainfall in the north averages about 350 mm (14 in.). In the south the rainy season lasts from June to October, with an average rainfall of about 1,525 mm (about 60 in.). Average temperatures on the coast are 22° C (72° F) in January and 28° C (82° F) in July.

Land, Plants, and Animals: The northern part of Senegal is part of the Sahel, a transition zone between the Sahara Desert on the north and the wetter regions to the south. Vegetation toward the south consists mainly of savanna grass with scattered clumps of trees and spiny shrubs. Farther south, near the Gambia River, trees are more common; in the extreme south there are mangrove swamps and dense forests of oil palms, mahogany, teak, and bamboo. Animals include elephants, lions, cheetahs, and antelope in the less populated eastern half of the country. In the rivers there are hippopotamuses and crocodiles. Senegal also has cobras and boa constrictors.

Natural Resources: Mineral resources include phosphates and iron ore. The deposits of iron ore, however, have not been exploited because of their remoteness. Senegal also has reserves of petroleum and natural gas offshore.

Currency: The Communauté Financière Africaine franc

Gross Domestic Product (GDP): $15.6 billion (1997 estimate)

GDP per Capita: $1,850 (1997 estimate)

GDP Real Growth Rate: 4.7 percent (1997 estimate)

Primary Economic Activities: Agriculture (employing 78 percent of the labor force), roundwood production, fishing, phosphate mining, and manufacturing

Primary Crops: Peanuts, millet, corn, sorghum, rice, cotton, tomatoes, green vegetables, and livestock

Industries: Agricultural and fish processing, phosphate mining, petroleum refining, and construction materials

Primary Exports: Fish, peanuts, petroleum products, phosphates, and cotton

Primary Imports: Foods and beverages, consumer goods, capital goods, and petroleum

Primary Trade Partners: European Union (France especially), Nigeria, Côte d'Ivoire, Algeria, China, and Japan

Government: Senegal is a constitutional republic under a multiparty democracy. The executive branch is led by President Abdou Diouf, who appointed Prime Minister Habib Thiam. The prime minister appoints the cabinet, called the Council of Ministers. The legislative branch is the elected, 120-member National Assembly, currently dominated by President Diouf's party, the Socialist Party.

Africa

Seychelles,

an African archipelago country located in the Indian Ocean.

Strung out along 115 islands and coral atolls in the Indian Ocean, the Seychelles is one of the smallest countries in the world, 444 sq km (171 sq mi.) of land scattered across 1.35 million sq km (500,000 sq mi.) of ocean. Most of its estimated 77,575 inhabitants live on the largest islands, Mahé, Praslin, and La Digue. Unlike other Indian Ocean island nations such as Mauritius, the Seychelles is marked by a relatively homogenous population of mixed African and European descent, except for small Indian, European and

Famous for the islands' double coconuts, known as *cocos de mer,* and their beautiful beaches, the Seychelles have stimulated their economy by developing tourism.
CORBIS/Christine Osborne

Chinese communities. Despite nearly 200 years of British rule, French cultural influences such as the Roman Catholic Church are still evident in the Seychelles, as are African religious practices. Because of the island's small size and poor soil, the inhabitants of the Seychelles have long depended on passersby to sustain their economy. Once a base for pirates and then a supply post for Indian Ocean merchant ships, the Seychelles now draws large numbers of beach-loving tourists as well as entrepreneurs attracted to its relatively open investment policies.

Africa

Seychelles (Ready Reference)

Official Name: Republic of Seychelles

Area: 455 sq km (about 174 sq mi.)

Location: Eastern Africa; a group of 115 islands scattered across the western Indian Ocean, northeast of the island of Madagascar

Capital: Victoria (population 24,324 [1987 estimate])

Population: 78,641 (1998 estimate)

Population Density: 168.2 persons per sq km (about 434 persons per sq mi.); concentrated on Mahe Island

Population Below Age 15: 30 percent (male 11,787; female 11,694 [1998 estimate])

Population Growth Rate: 0.67 percent (1998 estimate)

Total Fertility Rate: 1.98 children born per woman (1998 estimate)

Life Expectancy at Birth: Total population: 70 years (male 66.13 years; female 75.5 years [1998 estimate])

Infant Mortality Rate: 17 deaths per 1,000 live births (1998 estimate)

Literacy Rate (age 15 and over who can read and write): Total population: 58 percent (1996 estimate)

Education: Education is officially compulsory for children aged 6 to 15. In 1993 there were 9,873 primary school students, and 763 enrolled in secondary education. One year of National Youth Service is mandatory for higher education.

Languages: Creole, English, and French are all official languages.

Ethnic Groups: Most Seychellois are of mixed African and French descent; Indian and Chinese minorities are also present.

Religions: About 90 percent of the population are Roman Catholic, about 8 percent are Anglican, and about 2 percent belong to other religions.

A Seychelles baker takes freshly baked bread from the oven. *CORBIS/Zen Icknow*

Climate: The climate is tropical and humid, with a slighty cooler season during southeast monsoon (late May to September) and a slightly warmer season during northwest monsoon (March to May). For the most part, however, temperatures are roughly constant throughout the year, with average temperatures of 25° C (78° F) in both January and July. Average rainfall is 400 mm (16 in.) in January and 50 mm (2 in.) in July.

Land, Plants, and Animals: Of the 115 islands, the 32 in the Mahe Group are rocky and hilly. All of the country's principal islands belong to this group; they include Mahe Island (the largest), Praslin, Silhouette, and La Digue. The 83 coral islands are largely without water resources, and most are uninhabited. Only 18 percent of the islands' land is used for permanent crops.

Natural Resources: Guano is the only mineral product; other resources include fish, copra, and cinnamon trees.

Currency: The Seychelles rupee

Gross Domestic Product (GDP): $550 million (1997 estimate)

GDP per Capita: $7,000 (1997 estimate)

GDP Real Growth Rate: NA

Primary Economic Activities: Tourism, farming, fishing, and small-scale manufacturing

Primary Crops: Coconuts, cinnamon, vanilla, sweet potatoes, cassava (tapioca), and bananas

Industries: Tourism, coconut and vanilla processing, fishing, coir (coconut fiber) rope processing, boat building, printing, furniture, and beverage production

Primary Exports: Fish, cinnamon bark, copra, petroleum products (re-exports)

Primary Imports: Manufactured goods, food, petroleum products, tobacco, beverages, machinery, and transportation equipment

Primary Trade Partners: France, the United Kingdom, Singapore, Bahrain, and South Africa

Government: The Seychelles is a constitutional republic that gained its independence from the United Kingdom in 1976. It is divided into 23 administrative districts. The executive branch has been led by President Albert René and his appointed Council of Ministers since 1977. The legislative branch is the elected, 11-member People's Assembly (Assemblée du Peuple), currently dominated by President René's party, the Seychelles People's Progressive Front. Other political parties include the Democratic Party and United Opposition.

North America

Shakur, Tupac (2Pac)

(b. June 16, 1971, New York, N.Y.; d. September 13, 1996, Las Vegas, Nev.), African American rap star praised for his thought-provoking lyrics and criticized for his violent lifestyle; one of the most popular rap artists in the world when he was shot and killed at age 25.

Tupac Shakur was one of the most influential and controversial voices to emerge from hip hop's much maligned club of so-called gangster rappers. Criticized for their violent lyrics and misogynistic claims, gangster rappers became symbols of the best and worst of American musical creativity. Over a six-year period in the early 1990s Shakur became the voice for a generation of young, often frustrated, African Americans.

Through his music and his life Shakur embodied many of the harsh realities of "ghetto life." His raps addressed the difficulties of being young, black, and poor in the United States, and as a promising actor he captured those realities on the screen. True to the thuggish lifestyle that he rapped about, Shakur was arrested and served time in jail on more than one occasion, and often foreshadowed his own death in his songs and videos. Shakur's predictions of his violent death came true on September 13, 1996, when he was murdered shortly after attending a professional boxing match in Las Vegas, Nevada.

Shakur was born in New York City on June 16, 1971, to black activists Afeni Shakur and Billy Garland. Garland interacted infrequently with Tupac, but Shakur exposed her son to many of the activities and philosophies of the Black Panther Party. As a young teenager in Harlem, he explored his desire to act by joining the 127th Street Ensemble theater group and was cast as Travis in Lorraine Hansberry's play *A Raisin in the Sun*.

By 1988 the Shakurs had moved several times, finally settling in Marin, California. While in Marin, Shakur pursued his interest in music, leaving home in 1988 to join the rap group Strictly Dope. Three years later he left Strictly Dope and joined forces with friends from Oakland, California, who had formed the successful rap group Digital Underground. Shakur initially served as a background dancer for the group, but he was given an opportunity to rap on the group's 1991 single, "Same Son." His powerful delivery and stage charisma made an immediate impression, and friends were soon urging him to go solo.

In late 1991 Shakur released his first solo album, *2Pacalypse Now*, which sold more than 500,000 copies and featured the acclaimed hit "Brenda's Got a Baby." Heralded for its compelling portrayals of the hardships faced by single black mothers and rebuked for its vivid depictions of violence, *2Pacalypse Now* marked powerful contradictions within Shakur's music and life. These contradictions would also be manifest on the silver screen.

Shakur's portrayal of the aggressive, unbalanced character Bishop in the movie *Juice* (1992) and his role as Lucky in the film *Poetic Justice* (1993) mirrored many of the problems in his private life. In 1993 Shakur was arrested for using drugs, and he was later sentenced to ten days in jail for brutally beating another rapper with a baseball bat. In October 1993 Shakur was once again arrested, for allegedly shooting two off-duty Atlanta police officers. Although the charges were later dropped, Shakur's failure to draw a distinction between his public and private personas earned him public criticism.

By 1994 Shakur's life was a blurred reflection of his art. In March, Shakur lost his temper when he was cut from a film and was arrested when he assaulted the film's director, Allen Hughes. After Shakur spent 15 days in jail, his career received a boost when his third film, *Above the Rim*, was released. But eight months later Shakur was back in court defending himself against charges by a 19-year-old woman of sexual assault.

Shakur's troubles climaxed in 1995 when he was robbed and shot five times in the lobby of a recording studio in New York City. Like many of the characters in his movies and songs, Shakur managed to defy death. Although it is unclear who was involved in the attempt on Shakur's life, he blamed the shooting on rival rappers from New York, the Notorious B.I.G. and Sean "Puffy" Combs. At the time Shakur and B.I.G. were leading figures in a fierce rivalry between West Coast and East Coast rappers. When Shakur emerged from the hospital, a jury convicted him of sexual abuse and sentenced him to four and a half years in prison.

While in prison Shakur released his third album, *Me Against the World*, which debuted at Number One on the Billboard charts and earned him a Grammy Award nomination for Best Rap Album. *Me Against the World* went on to sell more than 2 million copies in seven months. On the album Shakur talked about his own mortality in the songs "If I Die 2Nite" and "Death Around the Corner," two of many songs that foreshadowed his violent death. Also featured on the album is the song "Dear Mama," which earned Shakur a second Grammy nomination for Best Rap Solo Performance.

After eight months in prison Shakur was released when Suge Knight, head of Death Row Records, paid his $1 million bail. Shakur joined Knight's recording label, and in 1996 he released the double album *All Eyez on Me*. The album has sold 5 million copies and contains Shakur's biggest hit to date, "California Love." While at Death Row, Shakur was part of a team that featured many of the most prominent rappers/producers on the West Coast, including Dr. Dre and Snoop Doggy Dogg. By all accounts, Shakur's future seemed very promising.

But that promise ended on September 13, 1996, when Shakur was cut down in a barrage of bullets. Shakur and Knight were in Las Vegas, Nevada, attending the championship fight of boxer Mike Tyson. After the fight Shakur and Knight were driving along the Las Vegas strip when a car pulled up next to theirs and unloaded several rounds. While attempting to flee into the car's back seat, Shakur was shot several times. Knight sustained minor injuries, but Shakur was placed in intensive care. After six days in the hospital he was pronounced dead.

Altogether, Shakur starred in six movies (three of which—*Bullet, Gridlock'd*, and *Gang-Related*—were released in 1997, after Shakur's death) and released six albums, two posthumously. He earned two Grammy Award nominations and sold millions of albums around the world. Shakur's voice echoed the concerns and the rage of many young African Americans who are left to face the challenges of the ghetto alone. But his music also spoke to young adults—many of them middle-class blacks and whites—who understood and valued Shakur's ability to bring the hardships of the marginalized to the surface of American culture.

Africa

Sierra Leone,
a country on the Atlantic coast of West Africa bordered by Liberia and Guinea.

Today war-torn and impoverished, Sierra Leone played a role in Africa's colonial history far out of proportion to its size. (It is one of the smallest West African countries and has a population of just over 4 million.) Abolitionists founded the Sierra Leone Colony at the end of the eighteenth century as a refuge for freed slaves. As Great Britain's first real colony on African soil, Sierra Leone served as a testing ground for subsequent colonial efforts elsewhere on the continent. The colony's mixed population of freed slaves, Europeans, and indigenous Africans gave rise to the unique

Regional wars and political chaos have displaced thousands of Sierra Leone natives, including these children, pictured in a displaced persons camp near Freetown in 1996. *CORBIS/Jon Spaull*

Krio culture, which blends Western and indigenous features. As the first group of Africans exposed to British cultural and administrative practices, Sierra Leoneans served in the British colonial administration throughout West Africa. During most of the twentieth century Sierra Leone provided leaders for West African nationalism. Although Sierra Leone is rich in valuable mineral deposits and agricultural potential, regional resentments and governmental corruption steadily undermined the country's economy in the years after independence and left it vulnerable to military adventurers. Intermittent warfare and civil strife since 1991 exposed Sierra Leoneans to a nightmare of violence and economic devastation. Partly as a consequence, Sierra Leone is today one of the five poorest nations on earth. However, with the return of a civilian government to power in 1998, came some hope that Sierra Leone's fortunes will improve.

Africa

Sierra Leone (Ready Reference)

Official Name: Sierra Leone

Area: 71,740 sq km (27,699 sq mi.)

Location: Western Africa; borders the North Atlantic Ocean, Guinea, and Liberia

Capital: Freetown (population 470,000 [1994 estimate])

Other Major Cities: Kenema (population 337,000) and Bo (269,000) (1994 estimates)

Population: 5,080,004 (1998 estimate)

Population Density: 66 persons per sq km (about 173 persons per sq mi.)

Population Below Age 15: 45 percent (male 1,130,728; female 1,167,084 [1998 estimate])

Population Growth Rate: 4.01 percent (1998 estimate)

Total Fertility Rate: 6.23 children born per woman (1998 estimate)

Life Expectancy at Birth: Total population: 48.57 years (male 45.56 years; female 51.66 years [1998 estimate])

Infant Mortality Rate: 129.38 deaths per 1,000 live births (1998 estimate)

Literacy Rate (age 15 and over who can read and write): Total population: 31.4 percent (male 45.4 percent; female 18.2 percent [1995 estimate])

Education: In the early 1990s annual enrollment for primary schools was about 315,000. About 79,400 were enrolled in secondary, vocational, and teacher-training schools.

Languages: English is the official language, although its regular use is

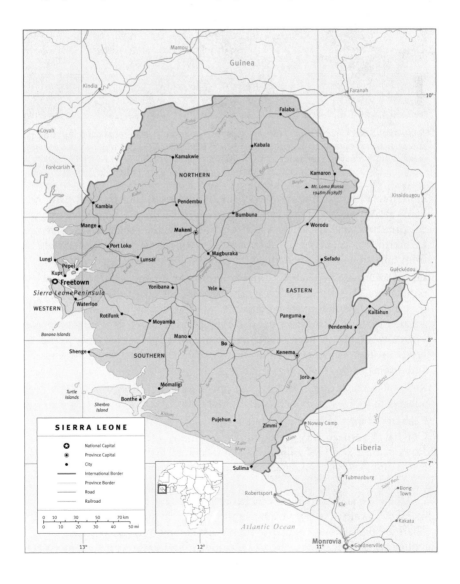

Textiles have great importance in African societies as objects of utility and beauty, as gifts, and as emblems of rank. In Gbonokobana, Sierra Leone, members of a women's cooperative make *garas*, a traditional tie-dyed cloth. *CORBIS/Caroline Penn*

limited to a literate minority (less than 20 percent of the adult population is literate). About 20 African languages are spoken in Sierra Leone. Mende is the principal language of the south, and Temne is the principal language of the north. Another common language is Krio, a Creole language derived from English and various African languages.

Ethnic Groups: There are 13 different ethnic groups in the Sierra Leone population. The largest groups are the Mende in the south, who account for nearly 30 percent of the population, and the Temne in the north, who account for nearly 30 percent of the population. Creoles, descendants of freed slaves returned from the Americas, are an important minority in the Freetown area, where small numbers of Lebanese, Indians, and Europeans also reside.

Religions: About 60 percent of the population is Muslim. About 30 percent adheres to indigenous beliefs, and 10 percent is Christian.

Climate: Tropical. Hot and humid with a rainy season between May and October. The mean temperature in Freetown is 27° C (about 80° F) in January and 26° C (78° F) in July. Annual rainfall averages more than 3,800 mm (150 in.) along the coast and 2,030 mm (about 80 in.) in the northern interior.

Land, Plants, and Animals: Sierra Leone's geography ranges from coastal mangrove swamps, grassy savanna in the north, and mountains in the east. There are dense forests in the southeast that contain varieties of palm, mahogany, and teak trees. Animals include bush pigs, chimpanzees, monkeys, and porcupines. Crocodiles and hippopotamuses are found in the rivers.

Natural Resources: Mineral resources include diamonds, bauxite, and rutile. Diamonds, however, are being produced at much lower levels than in the past due to the near exhaustion of mines, persistent smuggling, and civil insurrection in some areas.

Currency: Leones issued by the Bank of Sierra Leone.

Gross Domestic Product (GDP): $2.65 billion (1997 estimate)

GDP Real Growth Rate: -27 percent (1997 estimate)

GDP Per Capita: $540 (1997 estimate)

External Debt: $1.4 billion (year-end, 1993)

Primary Economic Activities: Agriculture (employing 65 percent of the population), industry, and services

Primary Crops: Rice, coffee, cocoa, palm kernels, palm oil, peanuts, and livestock

Industries: Mining (diamonds, bauxite, and rutile), small-scale manufacturing (textiles, beverages, cigarettes, and footwear), petroleum refining

Citizens celebrate the opening of the Sierra Leone parliament in 1996. *CORBIS/Jon Spaull*

Primary Exports: Rutile, bauxite, diamonds, coffee, cocoa, and fish

Primary Imports: Foodstuffs, machinery and equipment, fuels, and lubricants

Primary Trade Partners: United States, United Kingdom, Belgium, and Germany

Government: Constitutional multiparty democracy. The executive branch is led by President Ahmad Tejan Kabbah and the Ministers of State. The legislative branch is the elected, 105-member House of Representatives.

North America

Sit-Ins,

series of African American student protests in 1960 in which black students occupied "white-only" lunch counters and other segregated public institutions throughout the South to protest segregated seating.

On February 5, 1960, four black college students sat down at a "white-only" department store lunch counter in Greensboro, North Carolina. This Woolworth's counter was but one of the many segregated public facilities in the American South where African Americans were prohibited from such activities as eating, swimming, and drinking by whites who not only opposed equal treatment of the races, but feared any possibility of bodily contact. When the restaurant refused these students service, they remained seated until the store closed for the evening. The students returned each morning for the next five days to occupy the lunch counter, joined by a group of protesters that grew to the hundreds. Faced by a mob of angry white residents and management that refused to serve them a cup of coffee, the students maintained their protest until they forced the store to close its doors.

The protest by Joseph McNeil, Franklin McCain, Ezell Blair Jr., and David Richmand marked the beginning of a grassroots sit-in movement led by African American students against the segregated public spaces of the South. Black or racially integrated groups of students would sit down in white-only spaces and refuse to move until they were served or forcibly removed. By the end of 1960 about 70,000 black students had participated in a sit-in or marched in support of the demonstrators.

Although there had been a few sit-in protests before 1960, including two in 1943, the mass mobilization of 1960 was new. Few in the economically struggling black community of the South had been willing to undertake these types of direct-action protests, since they would be in danger of losing their jobs after an arrest. Black students generally had fewer financial responsibilities than their older counterparts, and they were interested in forcing change more immediate than that promised by the legal reform advocated by the National Association for the Advancement of Colored People (NAACP).

In 1960, as African American students entered the political arena in large numbers for the first time, the character of the civil rights protesting began to change. Influenced by the successful protests led by Mohandas K. Gandhi in India's Independence Movement, black students saw the potential for using nonviolent resistance to undermine the segregationist system and ideologies that supported it. Nonviolence was not just a strategy, although it did garner sympathy from many whites and the national press; it was a moral and revolutionary philosophy. Proponents such as James Lawson Jr. felt that nonviolence was an "invincible instrument of war," imbued with "soul force" and moral integrity, which would use the mass organization of bodies to strike at the heart of the morally unsound system of segregationism.

During 1960 sit-ins began to break down the segregation of the Upper South, and lunch counters were integrated in cities in Texas, North Carolina, and Tennessee. The reasons for integration were economic as well as moral. Boycotters, both black and white, supported the protesters, and many merchants did not want to lose the revenue of customers.

In the Deep South, however, including Louisiana, Mississippi, Alabama, Georgia, and South Carolina, white supremacy was more entrenched in the community and local government. Cities such as Montgomery, Alabama, outlawed the demonstrations, and white store owners refused to serve blacks under the rationale that they could make the rules on their own private property.

Throughout the South protesters faced not only arrest but vigilante violence as police and the Ku Klux Klan worked hand-in-hand to suppress the protests. By the end of 1960, 36,000 students had been arrested, and thousands expelled from college.

With support from Ella J. Baker of the Southern Christian Leadership Conference, students formed a permanent organization in April 1960: the Student Non-violent Coordinating Committee (SNCC). SNCC maintained the autonomy of the grassroots students' movement and facilitated training in nonviolent resistance. The strategy of occupying a place as a means of nonviolent protest gained currency in the Civil Rights Movement. Sit-ins at lunch counters inspired similar forms of protest at other types of segregated facilities, such as wade-ins at swimming places.

The efficacy of nonviolent resistance was one of the most important legacies of the 1960 sit-in protests. Segregation was seen to be a moral, as well as a legal issue, and the dignity of blacks in the face of white supremacist rage went far to win white and black support for the movement. In the words of SNCC's founding members, "By appealing to conscience and standing on the moral nature of human existence, non-violence nurtures the atmosphere in which reconciliation and justice become actual possibilities."

North America

Sixteenth Street Baptist Church (Birmingham, Ala.),

center for civil rights in Birmingham, Alabama; site of the 1963 bombing that killed four African American girls.

On September 15, 1963, four young black girls were killed and 20 other people wounded when a bomb planted by Ku Klux Klan member Robert Edward Chambliss exploded at the 16th Street Baptist Church in Birmingham, Alabama. The terrorist attack revealed the growing hostility of segregationists toward the Civil Rights Movement as it was making inroads in the Deep South. At the time of the bombing Birmingham was in a battle over the desegregation of schools; only weeks before, the National Guard had been called in to protect black students. For civil rights leaders the bombing, which followed less than three weeks after the euphoria of the 1963 March on Washington, was a reminder of the long struggle that remained.

An eyewitness reported seeing four men plant the bomb. Police arrested Chambliss after the bombing, but let him go shortly after. In 1977 Alabama Attorney General William Baxley reopened the case, and Chambliss was tried and convicted of first-degree murder.

Slave Narratives,

written autobiographies and oral testimonies by escaped or freed slaves.

Although slave narratives were written in several parts of the diaspora and in a variety of languages, the majority of published narratives by African slaves and their descendants were written in English in what is now the United States. Black literary scholar Henry Louis Gates, Jr., argues that African American slaves were unique in the history of world slavery because they were the only enslaved people to produce a body of writing that testified to their experiences.

For many of these authors, writing narratives served a dual purpose: it was a way of publicizing the horrors they had gone through and it was also a method of proving their humanity. One of the common arguments in support of race-based slavery was that blacks were simply an inferior species, incapable of thinking and feeling in the ways whites did. Through their narratives slave authors were able to display their emotions and their intellects.

Historians estimate that there are approximately 6,000 published narratives by African American slaves. This number includes both book-length autobiographies and shorter accounts published in newspapers or transcribed from interviews, and it spans 170 years' worth of testimonies from

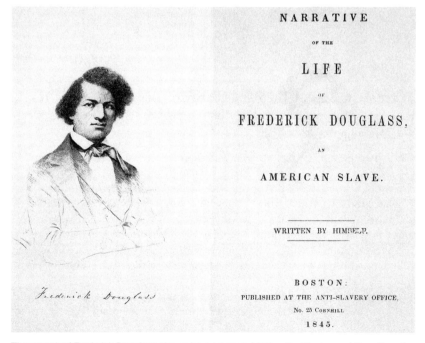

The portrait of Frederick Douglass shown here appeared facing the title page of *Narrative of the Life of Frederick Douglass, an American Slave, Written by Himself,* which was published in Boston in 1845. *CORBIS/Bettmann*

ex-slaves. Most of these narratives were published or collected after slavery was abolished in 1865, as slaves who had been emancipated looked back on their experiences. The most famous slave narratives are autobiographies by fugitive slaves that were published before 1865.

During this period ex-slaves' narratives were a powerful tool in the fight against slavery. The best-known slave narrative is Frederick Douglass's *Narrative of the Life of Frederick Douglass, an American Slave, Written by Himself* (1845). In it Douglass describes his childhood separation from his mother, his struggle to teach himself to read and write, the brutal whippings he witnessed and received, and his determination to be free—all the while stressing his own humanity and the inhumanity of the system that kept him a slave. Douglass's autobiography was an international bestseller. After its publication Douglass traveled the world as a lecturer, implicitly providing a model for just how "civilized" blacks could be, and went on to become the most famous and respected black individual of the nineteenth century. His narrative's patterns and images were repeated not only in many later slave narratives, but also in such diverse works of African American literature as Zora Neale Hurston's *Their Eyes Were Watching God* (1937) and Ralph Ellison's *Invisible Man* (1952).

In the late twentieth century the slave narratives' presence is still felt throughout African American literature in both form and function. Many authors have written contemporary retellings of slave narratives, in books as varied as Morrison's lyrical *Beloved* (1987), Octavia Butler's science fiction novel *Kindred* (1979), and Ishmael Reed's parody *Flight to Canada* (1976). Other novels, such as *Invisible Man*, use the narratives' themes and structure with very different subject matter. And throughout the history of African American literature, autobiography has remained a dominant genre. Many African Americans still identify with the need to write about themselves as a means of sharing their common humanity. Langston Hughes, Zora Neale Hurston, Richard Wright, Malcolm X, and Maya Angelou are among recent black writers who continued this tradition of using the written word to pass their stories on.

Africa

Slavery in Africa

Too often, observers have treated Africa as a region in isolation. The history of slavery, in contrast, shows the significance of Africa's socioeconomic connections to other world regions. The very distinctiveness of African society and African slavery results in large part from local responses to global connections.

The distinction between slave and master in Africa was not, as in the Americas, typically based on a distinction in race. But indicators such as name, language, scarification, dress, and manners all distinguished the identity and social status of slaves from those of their masters. Thus, while the heritage

A soldier guards a group of slaves linked together by chains in 1896.
Hulton-Deutsch Collection/Corbis

Slaves of the Pasha of Taoundenni, in Mali, stack blocks of salt in the 1950s.
CORBIS/ Hulton-Deutsch Collection

Two African slave boys in a nineteenth-century photograph. *CORBIS/Hulton-Deutsch Collection*

of slavery was kept alive in the Americas through discrimination by race, the heritage of slavery remained alive in Africa through discrimination by class. African countries, though millions of their inhabitants are descendants of slaves, have no holiday to celebrate the emancipation of slaves. The lack of a clear act of emancipation helped to propagate relations of servility into the mid- and late twentieth century.

Latin America and the Caribbean

Slavery in Latin America and the Caribbean

Slaves have existed on every populated continent since well before the opening of the Western Hemisphere to European colonization. In fact the modern word "slave" comes from the identification of slaves with Slavic peoples in the Muslim societies of the Middle East. There were still Muslim, Jewish, and Christian slaves in Europe and the Middle East in 1492. Most of these slaves were tied to their masters' households and did not produce the basic food or manufactured products in these societies. This work was usually done by free urban and peasant labor. In a few societies, however, slaves did make up the primary labor force in agriculture and industry. This type of slavery, sometimes referred to as "industrial slavery," was developed in classical Greece and Rome, and it would become the type of slavery adopted in most of the American colonies.

The end of slavery in Latin America was accomplished by a variety of means. In the continental colonies the wars of independence from 1808 to 1825 led to the freeing of large numbers of slaves by both republicans and royalists, so that even before final emancipation slaves were a reduced element among the colored population. Chile was the first to free its 4,000 slaves unconditionally in 1823, and Mexico freed the 3,000 slaves remaining there in the 1830s. Most of the other new republics did not finally liberate all remaining slaves until the 1850s, though most adopted early laws declaring freedom for all children born of slaves. In the French colonies of America some 177,500 slaves were finally liberated in 1848, but slavery continued on the islands of Cuba and Puerto Rico and in Brazil until the late 1880s. In 1871 Brazil finally adopted a law of free birth, as did Spain for Cuba and Puerto Rico in 1868. Final emancipation for all slaves came to the Spanish Caribbean islands in 1886 and to Brazil in 1888.

North America

Slavery in North America

Slavery has appeared in many forms throughout its long history. Slaves have served in capacities as diverse as concubines, warriors, servants, craftsmen, tutors, and victims of ritual sacrifice. In the New World (the Americas), however, slavery emerged as a system of forced labor designed to facilitate the production of staple crops. Depending on location, these crops included sugar,

A plaque identifies the block on a Fredericksburg, Virginia, street where slaves were sold at auction. *CORBIS/Bettmann*

coffee, tobacco, and cotton; in the southern United States, by far the most important staples were tobacco and cotton. A stark racial component distinguished this modern Western slavery from the slavery that existed in many other times and places: the vast majority of slaves consisted of Africans and their descendants, whereas the vast majority of masters consisted of Europeans and their descendants.

Slavery has played a central role in the history of the United States. It existed in all the English mainland colonies and came to dominate productive relations from Maryland south. Most of the Founding Fathers were large-scale slaveholders, as were 8 of the first 12 presidents of the United States. Debate over slavery increasingly dominated American politics, leading eventually to the nation's only civil war, which in turn finally brought slavery to an end. After emancipation, overcoming slavery's legacy remained a crucial issue in American history, from Reconstruction following the Civil War to the Civil Rights Movement a century later.

Emancipation brought many tangible rewards. Among the most obvious was the significant increase in personal freedom that came with no longer being someone else's property: whatever hardships they faced, free blacks could not be forcibly sold away from their loved ones. But emancipation did not bring full equality, and many of the most striking gains of Reconstruc-

A group of slaves stands outside their quarters on a plantation on Cockspur Island, Georgia, one of the barrier reef Sea Islands that stretch along the coasts of Florida, Georgia, and South Carolina. *CORBIS*

tion—including the substantial political power that African Americans were briefly able to exercise—were soon lost. In the decades after Reconstruction African Americans experienced continued poverty and exploitation and a rising tide of violence at the hands of whites determined to re-impose black subordination. They also experienced new forms of discrimination, spearheaded by a variety of state laws that instituted rigid racial segregation in virtually all areas of life and that (in violation of the Fourteenth and Fifteenth Amendments) effectively disfranchised black voters. The struggle to overcome the bitter legacy of slavery would be long and arduous.

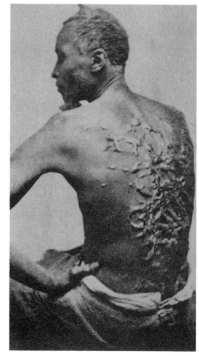

A freed slave displays his whip-scarred back in Baton Rouge, Louisiana, in 1863. The man, named Gordon, later became a corporal in the Union army. *CORBIS*

Somalia,

country on the northeastern Horn of Africa, along the Red Sea coast.

Introduction

On the surface Somalia is perhaps the most homogenous country in Africa—
most of its citizens share the same language, ethnic identity, religion, and
culture. Yet it has never achieved lasting stability as a nation; since the early
1990s its civil war has been one of the most devastating in modern African
history. Some scholars attribute this political instability to the Somali clan
system, in which retaliation for offenses committed by members of rival clans
can easily escalate into warfare. Others argue that Somalia's recent turmoil
reflects efforts by the powerful elite to manipulate clan loyalties in the hope
of increasing their own wealth. Still others contend that Somalia's homo-
geneity is in fact a myth that obscures long-standing tensions between
nomadic groups and the descendants of Bantu-speaking slaves. Finally, some
trace the roots of conflict to the colonial period, when access to power and
pastoral resources—long regulated by Somalia's many widely dispersed clan
leaders—came under the control of the centralized colonial (and then postcolonial) state.

Two boys study the Koran from a printed text. Behind them are Koran boards, on which *suras*,
or verses, of the Koran are written for the teaching of children. *CORBIS/Kevin Fleming*

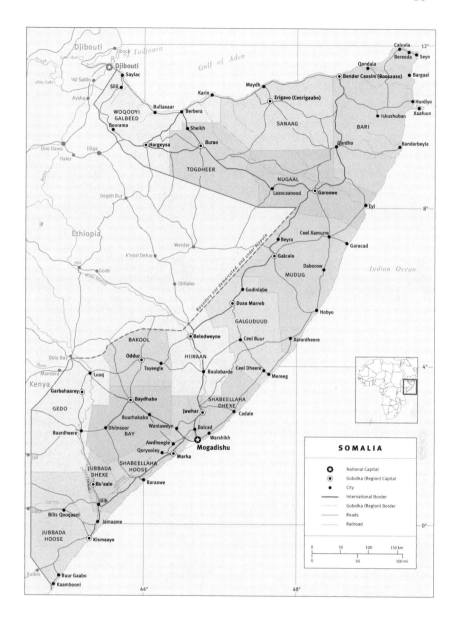

Whatever the precise reasons for violence during and since the military dictatorship of Maj. Gen. Muhammad Siad Barre, the upheaval has clearly taken its toll. The collapse of the state in the early 1990s not only undermined Somalia's ability to cope with the immediate crisis of famine, it also left the country without the government structures needed to provide education, health care, and other basic social services for the population.

Somalia (Ready Reference)

Official Name: Somalia

Area: 637,657 sq km (246,200 sq mi.)

Location: Eastern Africa; borders the Gulf of Aden, the Indian Ocean, Kenya, Ethiopia, and Djibouti

Capital: Mogadishu (population 700,000 [1985 estimate])

Other Major Cities: Hargeysa, Kismayu, and Marka

Population: 6,841,695 (July 1998 estimate)

Population Density: 15 persons per sq km (39 persons per sq mi.)

Population Below Age 15: 44 percent (male 1,512,014; female 1,511,858 [1998 estimate])

Population Growth Rate: 4.43 percent (1998 estimate)

Total Fertility Rate: 7.01 children born per woman (1998 estimate)

Life Expectancy at Birth: Total population: 46.2 years (male 44.6 years; female 47.8 years [1998 estimate])

Infant Mortality Rate: 125.8 deaths per 1,000 live births (1998 estimate)

Literacy Rate (age 15 and over who can read and write): Total population: 24 percent (male 36 percent; female 14 percent [1990 estimate])

Education: Before Somalia's government collapsed in 1991, education was free and compulsory for children between ages 6 and 14. As a result of Somalia's civil war, most schools have closed, including the Somali National University (1954–1991) in Mogadishu. In 1993 a primary school opened in Mogadishu; the only other primary schools are being operated by fundamentalist Islamic groups.

Languages: Somali is the official language. Arabic, Italian, and English are also spoken.

Ethnic Groups: Most of the population consists of Somali, a Cushitic people. A small minority of Bantu-speaking people live in the southern part of the country. Other minority groups include Arabs, Indians, Italians, and Pakistanis.

Religion: Sunni Muslim

Climate: The climate of Somalia ranges from tropical to subtropical and from arid to semi-arid. Temperatures usually average 28° C (82° F), but may be as low as 0° C (32° F) in the mountain areas and as high as 47° C (116° F) along the coast. The monsoon winds bring a dry season from September to December and a rainy season from March to May. The average annual rainfall is only about 280 mm (11 in.).

Land, Plants, and Animals: Somalia has a long coastline, but it has few natural harbors. A sandy coastal plain borders on the Gulf of Aden in the north, and a series of mountain ranges dominates the northern part of the country. To the south the interior consists of a rugged plateau. In the south a wide coastal plain, which has many sand dunes, borders on the Indian

Ocean. The country's two major rivers are found on the southern plateau, the Genale (Jubba) in the southern part and the Shabeelle in the south central section. Vegetation in Somalia consists chiefly of coarse grass and stunted thorn and acacia trees, but flora producing frankincense and myrrh are indigenous to the mountain slopes. In the south eucalyptus, euphorbia, and mahogany trees are found. Wildlife includes crocodiles, elephants, giraffes, leopards, lions, zebras, and many poisonous snakes.

Natural Resources: Livestock, agricultural crops, petroleum, copper, manganese, iron, gypsum, marble, salt, tin, and uranium

Currency: The Somali shilling

Gross Domestic Product (GDP): $8 billion (1996 estimate)

GDP per Capita: $600 (1996 estimate)

GDP Real Growth Rate: 4 percent (1996 estimate)

Primary Economic Activities: Until the civil war intensified, the economy of Somalia was based primarily on livestock raising and small-scale commerce. Crop farming was of importance only in the south.

Primary Crops: Maize, sorghum, bananas, sugar cane, cassava, and mangoes

Industries: Some small industries, including sugar refining, textiles, and petroleum refining

Primary Exports: Bananas, live animals, fish, hides

Primary Imports: Petroleum products, foodstuffs, and construction materials

Primary Trade Partners: Saudi Arabia, Germany, Italy, United States, Kenya, United Kingdom, and other gulf states

Government: Somalia has been in a state of civil war with no clear central governmental authority since the January 1991 ouster of President Muhammad Siad Barre.

Africa

South Africa,

country in Africa bordering Namibia, Botswana, Zimbabwe, Mozambique, Lesotho, and Swaziland.

Introduction

On May 9, 1994, Nelson Mandela marked his election as president of South Africa with a speech from the balcony of Cape Town's city hall, overlooking the Cape of Good Hope. Originally named by European merchant sailors, the Cape became the site of one of the earliest European colonies in sub-Saharan Africa, which would later grow to become the continent's wealthiest but also most racially oppressive independent nation. Mandela's speech, however, reclaimed the Cape as a symbol of hope for a new South Africa,

Police walk among the bodies of some of the people killed when police opened fire on demonstrators in Sharpeville, South Africa, in 1960. Of the approximately 5000 people gathered to protest pass laws, at least 69 were killed and 200 injured in the incident. *CORBIS/Bettmann*

one in which decades of struggle against the apartheid regime had finally triumphed and made possible the country's peaceful transition to a nonracial democracy. In his speech Mandela challenged South Africa's citizens to "heal the wounds of the past," a goal that later became the defining project of the Truth and Reconciliation Commission (TRC).

But upon taking office Mandela faced enormous challenges, among them high unemployment, escalating crime, and continued political violence. Militant resistance from the country's conservative white community also posed an ominous threat. Since 1994 South Africa's efforts to alleviate poverty while winning back foreign investors have made some progress, but hardly enough to satisfy the country's highly politicized citizenry. At the same time South Africa has become an increasingly influential economic and political power, both on the African continent and beyond it.

Africa

South Africa (Ready Reference)

Official Name: The Republic of South Africa

Area: 1,223,201 sq km (about 472,281 sq mi.)

Location: Southern Africa, at the southern tip of the continent of Africa. Includes the Prince Edward Islands (Marion Island and Prince Edward

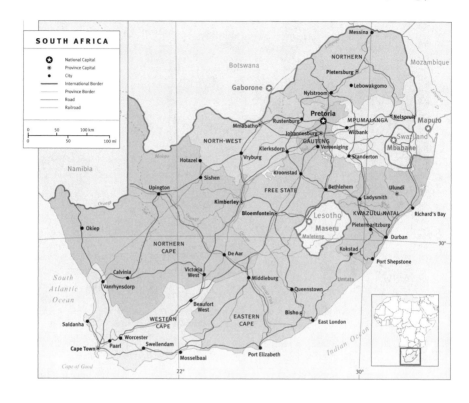

Island). South Africa borders Botswana, Namibia, Zimbabwe, and Mozambique; Lesotho and Swaziland lie within its borders.

Capitals: Pretoria (population 525,583 [administrative]); Cape Town (population 854,616 [legislative]); and Bloemfontein (population 126,867 [judicial]) (1991 estimates)

Other Major Cities: Johannesburg (712,507), Port Elizabeth (303,353), Germiston (134,005), Soweto (596,632; some estimate the number is closer to 2 million), and Durban (715,669)

Population: 42,834,520 (1998 estimate)

Population Density: 35 persons per sq km (about 90 persons per sq mi.)

Population Below Age 15: Total population: 35 percent (male 7,502,396; female 7,366,144 [1998 estimate])

Population Growth Rate: 1.42 percent (1998 estimate)

Total Fertility Rate: 3.16 children born per woman (1998 estimate)

Life Expectancy at Birth: Total population: 55.65 years (male 53.56 years; female 57.8 years [1998 estimate])

Infant Mortality Rate: 52.04 deaths per 1,000 live births (1998 estimate)

Literacy Rate (age 15 and over who can read and write): Total population: 81.8 percent (male 81.9 percent; female 81.7 percent [1995 estimate])

Education: The legacy of apartheid in South Africa manifests itself most clearly in education. Although government spending on black education has

Black residents of Katishong, a township east of Johannesburg, line up to vote in the first all-race elections in South African history in April 1994. *Reuters NewMedia Inc/Corbis*

increased significantly since the mid-1980s, at the end of the apartheid era expenditures for white pupils were about four times higher than those for black pupils. The teacher-to-student ratio for blacks was 1 to 60 in urban areas and 1 to 90 in rural areas. By comparison, the teacher-to-student ratio for whites averaged 1 to 30 or even lower. In the early 1990s South Africa's primary, secondary, and special schools annually enrolled about 5,794,100 blacks, 1,021,400 whites, 874,300 Coloureds, and 255,500 Asians. South Africa has numerous universities, with the following enrollment levels: 281,800 whites, 184,600 blacks, 42,100 Coloureds, and 34,800 Asians.

Languages: South Africa has 11 official languages: Afrikaans, English, Ndebele, Sesotho sa Leboa, Sesotho, siSwati, Tsonga, Tswana, Venda, Xhosa, and Zulu. Afrikaans, a variant of the Dutch language, is the first language of almost all Afrikaners and many Coloured people. English is used as the primary language by many whites and is also spoken by some Asians and blacks. Most blacks, however, primarily use one of the Bantu languages such as Xhosa, Sesotho, or Zulu.

Ethnic Groups: South Africa has a multiracial and multiethnic population. Blacks constitute 75.2 percent of the population, whites make up 13.6 percent of the population while Coloreds and Asians compose 8.6 and 2.6 percent of the population respectively. Blacks belong to nine ethnic groups: Zulu, Xhosa, Pedi, Sotho, Tswana, Tsonga, Swazi, Ndebele, and Venda. The Zulu are the largest of these groups, making up about 22 percent of the total black population. Whites are descended primarily from British, Dutch,

German, and French Huguenot (Protestant) settlers. South Africans of Dutch ancestry, who often have German and French heritage as well, are known as Afrikaners or Boers and form about three-fifths of the white population. Those of mixed racial origin, mainly black and Afrikaner and known as Coloured in South Africa, live chiefly in the Cape provinces. The Asians are mainly of Indian ancestry and are most numerous in the province of KwaZulu-Natal. A small number of people of Malay origin are also included in the Asian population. They reside mostly in the Cape provinces.

Religions: Christianity (followed by most whites and Coloureds and about 60 percent of blacks), Hindu (embraced by 60 percent of Indians), and Muslim (2 percent)

Climate: Nearly all of South Africa enjoys a mild, temperate climate. The High Veld receives about 380 to 760 mm (15 to 30 in.) of precipitation annually, the amount diminishing rapidly toward the west, where rainfall is often as low as 50 mm (2 in.) annually. Rainfall is deposited by the trade winds mainly between October and April. In the drier regions of the plateaus the amount of rainfall and the beginning of the rainy season vary greatly from year to year. The extreme southwest receives about 560 mm (22 in.) of rainfall, mostly between June and September.

The average January temperature range in Durban is 21° to 27° C (69° to 81° F). The corresponding temperature range in Johannesburg is 14° to 26° C (58° to 78° F); in Cape Town it is 16° to 26° C (60° to 78° F); the

Cape Town is one of South Africa's most popular tourist destinations and the country's legislative capital. Its location has made it an important port city since the seventeenth century. *CORBIS/Amos Nachoum*

winter temperature ranges follow the same regional pattern. The average July temperature range is 11° to 22° C (52° to 72° F) in Durban, 4° to 17° C (39° to 63° F) in Johannesburg, and 7° to 17° C (45° to 63° F) in Cape Town. Snow is rare in South Africa, although winter frosts occur in the higher areas of the plateau.

Land, Plants, and Animals: The topography of South Africa consists primarily of a great plateau region, which occupies about two-thirds of the country, bordered by the Drakensberg Mountains. The chief rivers of South Africa are the Orange, Limpopo, and Vaal. Numerous large mammals, including lions, elephants, zebras, leopards, monkeys, baboons, hippopotamuses, and antelope, are indigenous to South Africa. For the most part such animals are found only on game reserves. One of the most notable national game reserves is Kruger National Park in the northeast along the border with Mozambique.

Natural Resources: Gold, chromium, antimony, coal, iron ore, manganese, nickel, phosphates, tin, uranium, gem diamonds, platinum, copper, vanadium, salt, and natural gas

Currency: The rand

Gross Domestic Product (GDP): $270 billion (1997 estimate)

GDP per Capita: $6,200 (1997 estimate)

GDP Real Growth Rate: 3 percent (1997 estimate)

Primary Economic Activities: Gold, platinum, chromium, diamonds, agriculture, timber, and fishing

Primary Crops: Corn, wheat, sugar cane, fruits, and vegetables; dairy and beef cattle, poultry, and sheep

Industries: Mining, automobile assembly, metalworking, machinery, textile, iron, steel, chemical, fertilizer, and foodstuffs

Primary Exports: Gold, other minerals and metals, foodstuffs, and chemicals

Primary Imports: Machinery, transport equipment, chemicals, oil, textiles, and scientific instruments

Primary Trade Partners: European Union, the United States, Japan, and Switzerland

Government: South Africa is a republic. It is divided into nine provinces or administrative divisions: Eastern Cape, Free State, Gauteng, KwaZulu-Natal, Mpumalanga, North-West, Northern Cape, Northern Province, and Western Cape. President Thabo Mbeki presides over a bicameral legislature that comprises the National Assembly (400 seats) and the Senate (90 seats). Currently, any political party that wins 20 percent or more of the National Assembly votes in a general election is entitled to name a deputy executive president, and to become a member of the governing coalition, made up of the African National Congress, the Inkatha Freedom Party, and the National Party. Together they constitute a Government of National Unity.

The legislature adopted a constitution on April 27, 1994 (this interim constitution replaced the constitution of September 3, 1984). On May 8, 1996, the Constitutional Assembly voted 421 to 2 to pass a new constitution that, after certification by the Constitutional Court, gradually went into effect over a three-year period and came into full force with the national elections in May 1999. South Africa has universal suffrage for those age 18 and over.

North America

Southern Christian Leadership Conference,

civil rights organization led by Martin Luther King Jr. and a coalition of other southern black ministers that organized protests in the 1950s and 1960s against segregation and barriers to voting.

The civil rights activist Bayard Rustin once described the Southern Christian Leadership Conference (SCLC) as the "dynamic center" of the cluster of organizations that made up the Civil Rights Movement. It differed from such organizations as the Student Non-violent Coordinating Committee (SNCC) and the National Association for the Advancement of Colored People (NAACP), which functioned nationwide and sought to recruit individual members. SCLC served as an umbrella group for affiliates and initially concentrated its energies on America's segregated South. With prominent black ministers on its executive board and Rev. Martin Luther King Jr. at its helm, SCLC proved to be a guiding force and inspiration to the organizations and protesters engaged in the struggle for civil rights. In the words of one activist, "Southern Christian Leadership Conference is not an organization—it's a church."

In January 1957, 60 activists responded to a call for an Atlanta conference on nonviolent integration. Among the leaders were northern activists Rustin, Ella J. Baker, and Stanley Levison, and southern civil rights veterans King, Fred L. Shuttlesworth, Ralph Abernathy, C. K. Steele, Joseph Lowery, and William Holmes Borders. Shortly after this meeting the group established a permanent organization, the Southern Christian Leadership Conference, and elected King as president. The goal was to "to redeem the soul of America" through nonviolent resistance based on the teachings of Mohandas Gandhi. The group drew its strength from the black churches of the South, whose ministers were said to mirror the spirit of the community.

John Tilley and, later, Baker took the job of running the Atlanta headquarters. Despite the increasingly contentious climate in the South, where black students led sit-ins and Freedom Rides to protest segregation, SCLC's early activities were fairly mild, focusing on education programs and on bringing rural blacks to the voting booth.

A SNCC-led protest against segregation in Albany, Georgia, was already under way in late November 1961, when King and executive director Wyatt T. Walker brought the SCLC into its first major nonviolent campaign. In some ways it was unsuccessful; demonstrations and arrests provoked few changes and garnered little national attention. The federal courts, which had acted in support of earlier desegregation disputes, refused to back up the protesters. After a failed attempt to raise national support by calling attention to the imprisonment of King and Abernathy, SCLC retreated from Albany.

The SCLC's 1963 campaign in Birmingham, Alabama, succeeded in every way the Albany campaign had not. In a city where white supremacist Eugene "Bull" Connor controlled the police, SCLC launched Project C ("C" for confrontation). The movement drew criticism from white liberals like Robert Kennedy, as well as some blacks, who suggested that the protesters await the reforms promised by the recently elected mayor. But as King pointed out: "Justice too long delayed is justice denied." Without its usual supporters, the demonstration limped on, and black protesters who sat-in at white-only counters soon crowded the city jails.

A brilliant strategic move turned the tide of the faltering demonstration. On May 2, 1963, 700 black children marched from the 16th Street Baptist Church in through town. After police wagons were filled, the children were carted to jail in school buses. When 2,500 more young protesters marched the next day, the police turned fire hoses on them, and the international press turned its lenses on Birmingham's police. The world saw pictures of black children knocked down by a force of water so powerful that it tore the bark off nearby trees. Now under international pressure and the growing threat of a riot, Birmingham's officials returned to the bargaining table more willing to deal with SCLC.

As a result of the Birmingham protest, SCLC won a desegregation settlement. More important, the protest laid the groundwork for the nation's 1964 Civil Rights Act. After its Birmingham triumph, SCLC organized other desegregation campaigns in Savannah, Georgia, and St. Augustine, Florida, and played a pivotal role in the 1963 March on Washington. During Freedom Summer of 1964, it joined the Congress of Racial Equality (CORE) for a massive voter registration campaign.

The assassination of King on April 4, 1968, interrupted plans for the Poor People's Campaign. The SCLC resumed planning the Washington demonstration. Under its newly elected leader, Ralph Abernathy, the SCLC brought between 50,000 and 100,000 people to Washington to rally support for economic justice for African Americans.

After King's death the organization went into a tailspin, beset by a decline in contributions and internal dissension over Abernathy's leadership. Lowery revived the SCLC in the late 1970s by expanding the organization's operations beyond traditional civil rights programs, but the organization never regained its original stature.

Soweto,

South Africa, South African township near Johannesburg.

Situated 24 km (about 15 mi.) to the southwest of Johannesburg in the Gauteng Province, Soweto is one of the largest urban areas in southern Africa, with an estimated population of at least 2 million people. It has also become one of South Africa's most famous townships, mostly due to a massive uprising there in 1976, in which police killed hundreds of protesters. Once a squatters' camp, Soweto became not only a center of the fight against apartheid, but also one of the most visible symbols of its brutality.

Between World War I and World War II rapid industrialization in South Africa sparked a massive migration of rural Africans to Johannesburg, which was the center of the country's mining industry. Many of the migrant workers lived in camps outside town. In part due to white fears of black self-rule in the squatters' camps, the South African government in 1948 set aside 65 sq km (25 sq mi.) of land to accommodate the workers. They built thousands of two-room houses and named the new township Soweto, an abbreviation for "South-Western Townships." Soweto's population grew quickly as the result of continued voluntary migration and the new policies of the Afrikaner-dominated National Party government, which forcibly resettled blacks into townships.

Poverty, overcrowding, and oppression characterized life in Soweto under apartheid. The former archbishop Desmond Tutu, who lived in Soweto in the mid-1970s, recalled that at the time more than a million residents shared a single swimming pool. The schools were ill-equipped and underfunded—and increasingly staffed by teachers who had not completed university degrees. The typical house, which served as home for 12 to 15 people, lacked both internal plumbing and, until the 1980s, electricity.

Since the end of apartheid and Mandela's election as South Africa's president in 1994, conditions in Soweto have improved somewhat, although poverty and crime are still pressing problems. One of the most dramatic signs of change is that Soweto is now a popular tourist destination, with local entrepreneurs guiding visitors through a postapartheid Soweto.

Spain,

a country in southwestern Europe in which blacks have had a presence for centuries.

Black Africans have inhabited the Iberian Peninsula since the beginnings of recorded history. Blacks accompanied the Carthaginians when they colonized the Iberian Peninsula in the fifth century B.C.E. and blacks, both free and enslaved, were present in the social life of the Roman province of Spain.

A prime example of Moorish architecture is the Court of Lions at the Alhambra, once the palace of the Moorish monarchy in Granada, Spain. Built in the thirteenth and fourteenth centuries, the Alhambra was partially destroyed by Spain's King Charles I in the sixteenth century.
CORBIS/Adam Woolfitt

Throughout the Middle Ages both Christian and Muslim states on the peninsula enslaved black Africans. Moors, a people from northern Africa, provided most of the troops for the Muslim conquest of the Iberian Peninsula (711–718). Although the Arab ruling minority claimed political power under the caliphate of Cordoba (850–1033), the Moorish majority pushed for most of the changes in the emerging new society. The cultural life of al-Andalus, as Muslim Spain was known, helped shape modern Spanish society. Black African slaves, as well as gold transported across the Sahara, contributed to the wealth of Muslim Spain.

In Seville, the city with the largest black population in Spain during the Renaissance, blacks were frequently denied proper burial. Recent archaeological excavations have unearthed literal dumping grounds outside the old city walls for people who were of African descent. Life for black Africans was harder than for any other group in Spanish society. Malnutrition, physical exhaustion, and punishment constituted their common lot. In larger cities special quarters existed for blacks, both free and in bondage, since some masters did not allow slaves to live with them, and officials sought to keep blacks separate from the white population. Escape was very difficult in a hostile society, and punishment for it very harsh, in the form of lashes, branding, and amputations.

Free blacks had little opportunity to advance in society because they were excluded from almost every trade and profession. Laws and local ordinances limited the access of blacks to professional ranks, the church hierarchy, convents for women, universities, and practically all legitimate trade guilds. Various cities enacted laws limiting the movement of blacks, both free and enslaved. Laws prohibited blacks in most cases from carrying weapons either in cities or in the countryside at a time when violent crime was rampant, especially in cities like Madrid or Seville. Laws of limpieza de sangre, or "purity of blood" permitted legal discrimination against anyone of black African descent. Intermarriage after manumission and merger within a few generations with the non-black population led to the disappearance of a significant black population in Spain by the mid-eighteenth century.

Spain never officially abolished slavery. Although the government signed treaties with Great Britain to abolish the slave trade, Spain did not free slaves when they entered the European part of the empire, a practice followed in other European countries. Thus slave owners from Cuba and Puerto Rico who traveled back to Spain with black slaves did not lose them when they touched Spanish soil. The 1870 Moret Law, which proclaimed the gradual abolition of slavery in the Caribbean colonies, was the first document to suppress the institution legally. Restrictions imposed by the Spanish government successfully blocked any massive immigration of black colonial subjects to Spain. After the loss of Cuba and Puerto Rico in 1898, this possibility became even more remote.

Spanish society underwent a remarkable transformation during the 1970s. After General Franco's death in 1975 and the installation of a democratic regime in 1977, the Spanish economy, once so weak that its surplus work force had to emigrate to northern Europe, now required immigrants to fill low-wage jobs.

In addition to African immigrants, Dominican citizens of African descent, mostly women, have traveled to Spain seeking domestic employment in the houses of the Spanish urban middle class. They form a growing group of workers, together with Equatorial Guinean women, who are employed in domestic work because of their Spanish-language ability. The substantial presence of black African and Maghrebi citizens in Spain has challenged certain monolithic cultural and religious traditions. There are more practicing Muslims in Spain today than at any other point in its history since 1492. With Spain's integration into the European Union in 1986 the government adopted measures to stop the arrival of mostly undocumented immigrants, and bouts of xenophobic attacks against Africans and people of African descent have taken place on different occasions. Nongovernmental organizations and immigrant associations continually challenge discriminatory practices and forced repatriations of so-called illegal workers, mostly African. A new generation of Afro-Spaniards is growing in numbers: the Spanish Constitution of 1978 confers automatic citizenship to all born on Spanish soil. The present population of African descent in Spain was estimated in 1998 at more than 500,000—as a proportion of the Spanish population, it is the highest since the Middle Ages.

Latin America and the Caribbean

St. Kitts and Nevis,

a country in the Lesser Antilles, 113 km (70 mi.) south of Anguilla and 300 km (186 mi.) southeast of Puerto Rico in the Caribbean Sea.

As with most of the Caribbean, St. Kitts and Nevis's original inhabitants were Arawak and later Carib Indians, who migrated from South America

A woman stands behind the counter of her shop on Nevis. *CORBIS/Kit Kittle*

to settle in the islands between 5,000 and 7,000 years ago. The Caribs named St. Kitts Liamuiga, or "fertile land," because its volcanic soil was so fruitful for agriculture. On November 12, 1493, Christopher Columbus "discovered" the islands during his second exploratory trip to the Caribbean.

Both the English and French initially used St. Kitts as a strategic base for colonizing nearby islands—for the English, Antigua, Barbuda, Tortola, and Montserrat; for the French, Martinique, Guadeloupe, St. Martin, St. Barts, La Désirade, and Les Saintes. It was from this colonization that St. Kitts became known as the "mother colony of the West Indies." Nevis, on the other hand, was used primarily for agriculture. In 1834 slavery was finally abolished in all English colonies. At the end of the four-year "apprentice-ship" program, during which former slaves had to work for their former masters in exchange for a small salary, the blacks of St. Kitts and Nevis were finally free. But for all practical purposes, freedom brought the same economic and employment constraints that slavery had.

Universal suffrage was finally granted to all citizens in 1952, along with a legislature with a majority of elected members. The Labour Party easily won all of the available seats in the next elections, and for the first time in its 330-year history as a British Crown Colony, St. Kitts and Nevis was ruled by the majority of its people. In 1967 the country took an important step toward full independence when St. Kitts, Nevis, and the island of Anguilla became a single British state instead of a colony. Anguilla, which had been administered jointly with St. Kitts and Nevis, opposed the new arrangement, and in 1971 it returned to being a Crown Colony. Some Nevisians considered following Anguilla's lead, because they were also

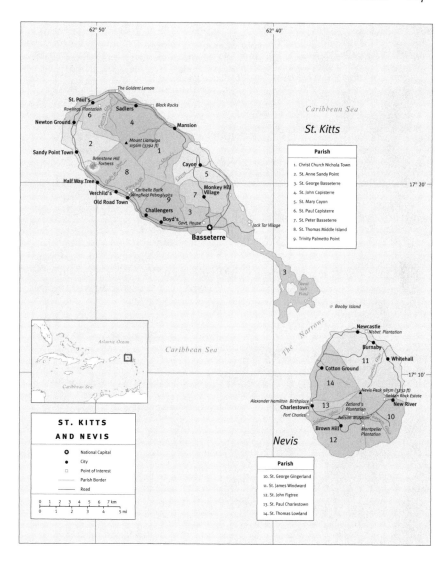

apprehensive that permanent affiliation with St. Kitts would threaten Nevis's autonomy. But the British government strongly encouraged St. Kitts and Nevis to remain together. Despite Nevisian dissent, on September 19, 1983, St. Kitts and Nevis became independent as a single nation.

Latin America and the Caribbean

St. Lucia,

country in the Caribbean Sea, approximately 42 km (25 mi.) south of Martinique and 33 km (20 mi.) north of St. Vincent.

The intense concentration of a soccer match shows in the play of these two men on St. Lucia. *CORBIS/Tony Arruza*

St. Lucia was inhabited first by the Arawak Indians, who migrated to the island around 200 C.E., and then by the Carib Indians, who replaced the Arawaks by about 800 C.E. The original Amerindian name for the island was Iouanalao, or "the place where the iguana is found." There has been some debate over when Europeans first sighted St. Lucia, though tradition holds that Christopher Columbus himself discovered the island on St. Lucy's feast day, December 13, 1502. What is certain, however, is that Carib resistance to European settlement on the island was fierce, and St. Lucian Caribs were able to resist European colonization until the mid-seventeenth century.

The sun sets behind the drying sails of boats in the harbor of Soufrière, on the west coast of St. Lucia. *CORBIS/Tony Arruza*

The first African slaves arrived in St. Lucia around 1763, brought by French planters who had purchased them from the slave traders who abducted them from their West African homes. It was during slavery that the patois still spoken today developed, a combination of French and several African languages. The fact that most St. Lucian blacks spoke French patois put them at a disadvantage when the country permanently became a British territory in 1814.

Since independence the country has been relatively prosperous, particularly as tourism has experienced strong growth in the 1990s. However, droughts and changes in the European market, which have threatened the banana industry in the last several years, serve as reminders of the country's need to continue diversifying its economic base. The need for improvements in education also remains a national priority, especially changes that will help the

Men play dominoes outside a house on St. Lucia. *CORBIS/Tony Arruza*

patois-speaking population prosper in the official English society. St. Lucia is already celebrated as the home of the Caribbean's two Nobel laureates, economist Sir Arthur Lewis and poet and playwright Derek Walcott. Prominent novelists such as Garth St. Omer also add to the island's reputation. Finally, tourist literature about St. Lucia is quick to celebrate the island's multicultural African, French, and British heritage as one of its greatest assets. St. Lucia is already a favorite site for visitors from around the world, and St. Lucians remain optimistic that their country will continue prospering into the next century.

North America

Student Non-violent Coordinating Committee (SNCC) (pronounced "snick"),

civil rights group that played a major role in the 1960s campaign to end segregation in the southern United States.

On February 1, 1960, four black college students attracted widespread attention when they refused to leave a whites-only lunch counter in an F. W. Woolworth store in Greensboro, North Carolina. The sit-in continued for several weeks and inspired dozens of similar sit-ins across the South. Although not the first time students had taken part in civil rights protests, the sit-in movement was among the largest and most spontaneous. Reacting to the protests, Ella J. Baker, executive director of the Southern Christian Leadership Conference (SCLC), held a conference for student activists in April at Shaw University in Raleigh, North Carolina. Baker believed that larger, more cautious civil rights groups such as the SCLC might have failed to serve students who were impatient for racial equality. She urged the 200 attendees to establish a new student group that would harness its energy and frustration to challenge white racism as well as the larger and more conventional civil rights groups.

Other civil rights leaders, such as SCLC's Martin Luther King Jr., argued that a united movement would be stronger than a divided one and invited the students to create a wing within SCLC. Representatives of the National Association for the Advancement of Colored People (NAACP) and the National Urban League made similar invitations. The students created a Temporary Coordinating Committee to debate the issue; in May the committee embraced the mainstream's practice of nonviolence but created an independent group, the Temporary Student Non-violent Coordinating Committee. ("Temporary" was dropped from the name in October.) Made up of both black and white members, the group elected Marion Barry, a student at Nashville's Fisk University who would later become mayor of Washington, D.C., SNCC's first chairman and set up its headquarters in Atlanta, Georgia. When Barry returned to graduate studies a few months later, he was replaced by Charles McDew, a student at South Carolina State College.

In its first months SNCC served mostly as a channel for student groups to communicate and coordinate the sit-in campaign. The images on national television of well-groomed, peaceful protesters being refused a cup of coffee and, in some instances, being hauled off to jail, generated sympathy among many whites across the country. Several SNCC and other protesters capitalized on the publicity with a "jail-no-bail" campaign. Refusing to pay fines or bail, the students served jail sentences, thereby filling southern jails and continuing media coverage. By the end of 1960 several chain stores in the Upper South and Texas responded to the movement by ending segregation at their lunch counters. Several cities also agreed to desegregate public restaurants.

Following the sit-in and Freedom Ride victories, SNCC joined with CORE, the NAACP, SCLC, and the Urban League in the Voter Education Project (VEP). Funded by large private grants, VEP sought to increase the number of southern blacks registered to vote. SNCC had failed at a similar voter-registration effort in rural Georgia in 1961 and 1962. When VEP funds became available in 1962, SNCC shifted its focus to Mississippi and Louisiana, where it also met stern resistance and succeeded in registering only a few blacks.

In 1963, however, several highly publicized conflicts changed the course of the movement. In May police in Birmingham brutally beat black and white protesters, prompting another wave of public sympathy. The next month Kennedy introduced a strong civil rights bill to Congress, which was passed during the administration of Lyndon Johnson as the Civil Rights Act of 1964. (The act prohibited segregation in several types of public facilities.) Liberal contributors responded to the violence by pouring large donations into virtually all of the civil rights groups, whose staffs and programs grew accordingly. In late 1963, when VEP decided to abandon Mississippi for lack of progress, SNCC, now led by John Lewis, could afford to stay.

Many SNCC activists were critical of the way larger civil rights groups "invaded" towns for a protest, then left after the protest ended. SNCC's field-workers in Mississippi believed they could best help blacks by living in their communities and working with them over the long term. In late 1963, with help from CORE and, nominally, other civil rights groups, SNCC revitalized the Council of Federated Organizations (COFO); COFO had been created in 1961 to help free jailed Freedom Riders. It would now oversee voter registration in Mississippi. Bob Moses, a Harvard graduate student, veteran SNCC field-worker, and leading advocate of commitment to communities, was placed in charge of COFO. COFO functioned largely as an arm of SNCC.

Amid the success many of COFO's black workers were angered by the role whites were playing in the organization. White students often came to the South for a few months (typically a summer), assumed high-profile leadership positions while there, then returned to safe campuses in the North while blacks continued the hard work. Many black activists were also tired of accepting beatings and jail sentences in order to win sympathy from white federal officials, white liberal donors, and the white public. They were weary as well of having to tone down their militancy and rhetoric at the request of whites in power. SNCC's Lewis voiced many of these frustrations during a speech in the March on Washington of August 1963; that Lewis was made to tone down his remarks by mainstream civil rights groups and white officials only further angered blacks in SNCC. For these reasons many COFO activists argued it was important for blacks to succeed on their own, without the help of white volunteers. Some even wondered if it would be possible to continue working with mainstream civil rights groups.

Moses was forced to address this debate when he proposed the Freedom Summer of 1964, a registration and education project that would build on the Freedom Vote. Moses argued forcefully that if COFO excluded whites, blacks had no moral standing to demand integration. Moreover, the movement would not receive as much publicity since national news groups would pay more attention to violence against whites than blacks. Moses's words were borne out when COFO's Michael Schwerner, James Chaney, and Andrew Goodman were murdered in June (Schwerner and Goodman were white) and the press and public responded with shock and outrage.

For years murders of blacks by whites in the South had gone unnoticed in the national media. President Johnson ordered a large FBI presence in Mississippi, and many whites became aware of the obstacles blacks faced when trying to vote in the Deep South. Still, COFO's 1000 volunteers managed to register only 1200 blacks statewide. Within COFO many student workers were convinced after the Schwerner, Chaney, and Goodman murders that nonviolence would not win blacks the vote. By the end of the summer SNCC officially defended the right of its Mississippi field secretaries to carry weapons.

Moses was able to exploit COFO's failure to register voters by creating a new party, the Mississippi Freedom Democratic Party (MFDP). Some 60,000 blacks joined the MFDP, which served as an alternative to Mississippi's all-white Democratic Party. With the presidential election of 1964 approaching, the MFDP sent 44 delegates to the national Democratic convention in Atlantic City, New Jersey. The delegation demanded to be seated at the convention in place of the regular Mississippi delegation. They were pledged to Johnson, while the white Democratic delegates were not. Although several northern states supported seating the MFDP, southern states threatened to walk out of the convention if the MFDP delegates were seated. Johnson, wary of losing the conservative South in the general election that fall, offered the MFDP a compromise: two of its black delegates would be seated along with the white delegates. The MFDP rejected the offer and, in a move largely coordinated by SNCC, walked out of the convention. In the aftermath, many whites across the country saw SNCC as an extremist group unwilling to bend, while many blacks became even more convinced that they could not work with whites.

In May 1966 SNCC formalized its shift in this direction by electing Stokely Carmichael (later Kwame Turé), a recent graduate of Howard University, to the chairmanship over John Lewis. Rejecting nonviolence, Carmichael argued at first that violence should be used in self-defense; later he called for offensive violence to overthrow oppression. Carmichael also denounced Johnson's civil rights bills, which were supported by the SCLC and the NAACP.

In June 1966, in Greenwood, Mississippi, Carmichael advocated Black Power in a well-publicized speech. Although "Black Power" had been used before as a shorthand for black pride and political equality, Carmichael popularized the term through repeated speeches. Many whites were offended by Carmichael's views, which they saw as racist or separatist, and most of the mainstream civil rights groups severed their few remaining ties with SNCC. SNCC's white staff and volunteers, who had already begun to drift away from the group, soon left. Eventually Carmichael expelled the remaining white staff and denounced SNCC's white donors. By early 1967 SNCC was near bankruptcy, and both its staff and membership had dwindled.

In June 1967, when Carmichael left SNCC to help lead the Black Panther Party, he was replaced by 23-year-old H. Rap Brown. In his first months Brown removed the word "Non-violent" from SNCC (renaming the group the Student National Coordinating Committee) and made urgent calls for violence. When Detroit rioted in the summer of 1967, Brown urged an audience in Cambridge, Massachusetts, to do the same. When a Cambridge school was set aflame hours later, Brown was charged with inciting a riot, one of several charges he would face in the following years. In May 1968 his legal problems forced him to resign SNCC's chairmanship. SNCC continued to operate into the early 1970s, but its impact on politics was minimal.

St. Vincent and the Grenadines,

country consisting of a chain of islands in the Caribbean Sea, with Grenada to the south and St. Lucia to the north (the southern end of the Grenadine Islands chain is administered with Grenada).

The Carib Indians who inhabited St. Vincent at the time of Christopher Columbus's 1498 arrival called their island Youlou or Hairoun, meaning "home of the blessed." Indeed, for centuries before the European invasion of the Caribbean, the hilly, dramatic islands now known as St. Vincent and the Grenadines were home to several indigenous groups, who fought to pre-

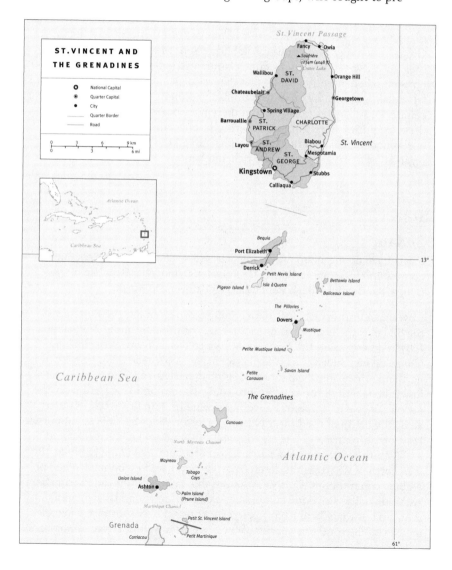

serve their islands after the colonists arrived. The first inhabitants of these islands were probably Ciboney Indians who arrived around 4300 B.C.E., followed by the Arawaks and then the Caribs.

The first outsiders that the Caribs allowed to settle in St. Vincent were not Europeans but Africans. In 1675 a Dutch slave ship sank off the coast of Bequia, one of the nearby Grenadine Islands. None of the whites on board survived, but a group of Africans made it to shore. They subsequently migrated to St. Vincent, where they were assimilated into the Carib community. These Africans and their descendants were called Black Caribs, distinguishing them from the indigenous Yellow Caribs. St. Vincent's reputation as a Carib stronghold quickly spread; escaped slaves from nearby St. Lucia and Barbados soon joined St. Vincent's black community.

Aside from a brief 1980 uprising in which student leaders from Union Island tried to secede from the rest of the state, St. Vincent and the Grenadines has enjoyed political stability. "Son" Mitchell, the prime minister since 1984, followed his father James Mitchell into politics. The 1980 uprising called attention to the fact that residents of the Grenadines often felt unfairly treated by St. Vincent, which accounts for 90 percent of the country's land and population, and there have been attempts to address these inequities. In recent years tourism has become an important source of revenue for the country, and St. Vincent and the Grenadines is often regarded as a playground for the rich and famous.

Africa

Sudan,

a country in northeastern Africa; with a coastline along the Red Sea, Sudan borders Eritrea, Ethiopia, Kenya, Uganda, the Democratic Republic of the Congo, the Central African Republic, Chad, Libya, and Egypt.

Covering a territory of close to one million square miles, the Republic of the Sudan is the largest nation in Africa. Stretching from the Nubian and Libyan deserts along the Egyptian border to the rain forests of the Nile-Congo divide, Sudan is a bridge between the Arabic-speaking peoples of northern Africa and the peoples of sub-Saharan Africa. The Nile River flows the length of the country, providing a common focus for the diverse peoples of Sudan. Its waters have transformed a narrow stretch of desert along the banks of the Lower Nile into a fertile valley capable of supporting large urban centers.

With the exception of a narrow strip of arable land along the Nile, the area north of Khartoum is desert, sparsely populated by nomadic Arab or Nubian communities. Cultivation is possible only with the aid of irrigation. At Wadi Halfa, a riverine community along the Egyptian border, rainfall averages less than 7 cm (3 in.) per year. As one moves southward rainfall increases. The southern quarter of the country is well watered, averaging 90

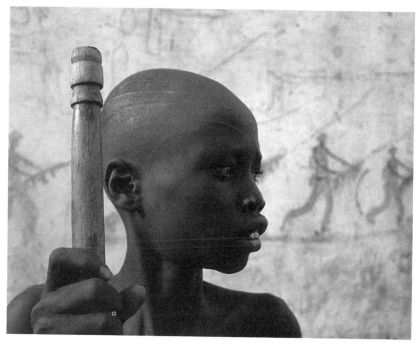

A Dinka boy stands in front of a wall painted with pictures of the civil war that displaced him from his home in southern Sudan. *CORBIS/Adrian Arbib*

cm (35 in.) per annum at Malakal and more than 127 cm (50 in.) along the Congo border. With the exception of the western portion, southern Sudan has been isolated from the north by a variety of natural obstacles. A 800-km (500-mi.) stretch of floating masses of vegetation, known as the Sudd (Arabic for "barrier"), clogged the White Nile and its tributaries over an area of roughly 100,000 sq km (40,000 sq mi.), thereby preventing all significant water transportation until the 1840s.

Africa

Sudan (Ready Reference)

Official Name: The Republic of the Sudan

Former Name: Anglo-Egyptian Sudan

Area: 2,505,813 sq km (about 967,495 sq mi.)

Location: North Africa, on the Red Sea, bordered by Ethiopia, Kenya, Uganda, Democratic Republic of the Congo, Central African Republic, Chad, Libya, and Egypt

Capital: Khartoum (population 473,597 [1983 estimate])

Other Major Cities: Omdurman, Khartoum North, and Port Sudan

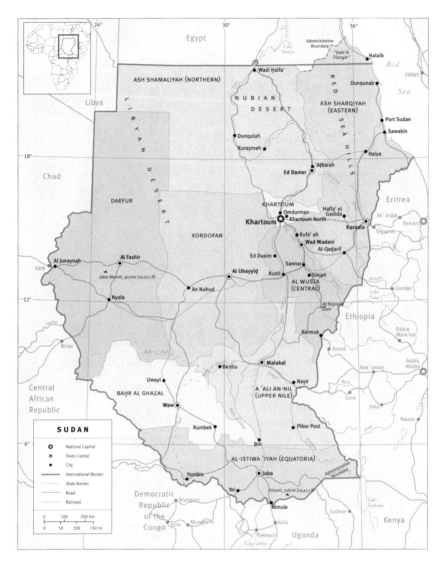

(data on population unavailable)

Population: 33,550,552 (1998 estimate)

Population Density: 8 persons per sq km (about 21 persons per sq mi.)

Population Below Age 15: 45 percent (male 7,769,266; female 7,499,510 [1998 estimate])

Population Growth Rate: 2.73 percent (1998 estimate)

Total Fertility Rate: 5.68 children born per woman (1998 estimate)

Life Expectancy at Birth: Total population: 55.97 years (male 55 years; female 56.98 years [1998 estimate])

Infant Mortality: 72.64 deaths per 1,000 live births (1998 estimate)

Literacy Rate (age 15 and over who can read and write): Total population: 46.1 percent (male 57.7 percent; female 34.6 percent [1995 estimate])

Education: Some 2.3 million elementary school students in the early 1990s, and about 696,000 students in secondary schools. Some 3,600 students attended vocational and teacher-training institutions, and more than 60,000 attended institutions of higher education, including the University of Khartoum, Omdurman Islamic University, the University of Juba, and the College of Fine and Applied Art.

Languages: Arabic is the official language. English is widely spoken, and African languages, used mainly in the south, include Nubian, Ta Bedawie, numerous dialects of Nilotic, Nilo-Hamitic, and Sudanic languages, and English.

A Dinka woman pounds millet with a wooden pole in southern Sudan, which has been devastated by civil war and famine since the 1960s. *CORBIS/Adrian Arbib*

Ethnic Groups: 39 percent of the Sudanese population is Arab, inhabiting the north of the country. Also in the north are the Beja, Jamala, and Nubian peoples. The Azande, Dinka, Nuer, and Shilluk inhabit the south.

Religions: The majority (70 percent) of Sudan's citizens are Sunni Muslim; indigenous beliefs account for about 20 percent of the population, and 5 percent of the Sudanese are Christian.

Climate: Arid desert in the north, tropical in the south. In the desert temperatures vary from 4.4° C (about 40° F) in the winter to 43.3° C (about 110° F) in the summer. Around Khartoum the average annual temperature is about 26.7° C (80° F); and annual rainfall, most of which occurs between mid-June and September, is about 254 mm (10 in.). In southern Sudan the average annual temperature is about 29.4° C (85° F), and annual rainfall is more than 1,015 mm (40 in.).

Land, Plants, and Animals: The northern third of Sudan is desert; central Sudan is characterized by steppes and low mountains; and the south has vast swamps and rain forests. Numerous species of acacia tree can be found along the Nile Valley in the north, and central Sudan has forests that include hashab, talh, heglig, and acacia. Ebony, silag, and baobab trees are common in the Blue Nile Valley, and ebony and mahogany trees grow in the White Nile Basin. Other species of indigenous vegetation include cotton, papyrus, castor-oil plants, and rubber plants. Animal life includes elephants, crocodiles, hippopotamuses, giraffes, leopards, lions, monkeys, tropical birds, and snakes.

Natural Resources: Petroleum, iron ore, copper, chromium ore, zinc, tungsten, mica, silver, and gold

Currency: The Sudanese pound

Gross Domestic Product (GDP): $26.6 billion (1997 estimate)

GDP per Capita: $875 (1997 estimate)

GDP Real Growth Rate: 5 percent (1997 estimate)

Primary Economic Activities: Agriculture, industry, and services

Primary Crops: Cotton, oilseed, sorghum, millet, wheat, gum arabic, and sheep

Industries: Cotton ginning, textiles, cement, edible oils, sugar, soap distilling, shoes, and petroleum refining

Primary Exports: Cotton, livestock, and gum arabic

Primary Imports: Foodstuffs, petroleum products, manufactured goods, machinery and equipment, medicines, chemicals, and textiles

Primary Trade Partners: European Union, Libya, Egypt, Saudi Arabia, Japan, and United States

Government: The Sudan, previously ruled by a military junta, currently has a transitional government, following presidential and National Assembly elections held in 1996, when Lt. Gen. Umar Hasan Ahmad al-Bashir and his supporters swept presidential and legislative elections, and won a five-year term. Hassan al Turabi was elected president of the National Assembly. The cabinet, consisting of 20 federal ministers, is appointed by the president.

Latin America and the Caribbean

Suriname,

a country located on the northeastern coast of South America; Suriname is bordered on the west by Guyana, on the east by French Guiana, and on the south by Brazil.

Suriname is a former Dutch colony located on the northeast corner of South America. Although Dutch is the official language, English, Hindi, Javanese, Sranana and Papiamento (both Creole languages), and numerous Amerindian languages are spoken widely. Suriname's 437,000 inhabitants

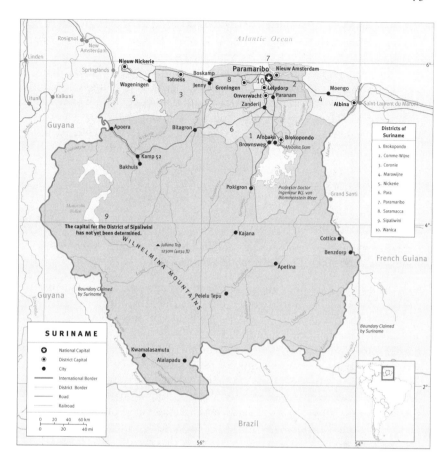

Districts of Suriname
1. Brokopondo
2. Comme-Wijne
3. Coronie
4. Marowijne
5. Nickerie
6. Para
7. Paramaribo
8. Saramacca
9. Sipaliwini
10. Wanica

come from diverse backgrounds, giving the country a unique mix of ethnicities: its population includes people of Javanese, so-called Hindustani (or East Indian), and Chinese origin, in addition to the region's original indigenous inhabitants. But Suriname is perhaps best known for its Creole and maroon (sometimes also called *bosnegers*, or "Bush Negroes" by outsiders) communities. Creoles are Afro-Surinames, the descendants of former slaves, freed blacks, and people of mixed African and

This Ndjuka man, pictured painting his canoe paddle in a traditional style, descends from the founders of one of Suriname's largest communities of maroons, or escaped slaves. *CORBIS/Adam Woolfitt*

European ancestry. Maroons are descendants of runaway slaves who are now organized into six distinct groups and live in semiautonomous villages. The maroon population in Suriname was the largest community of escaped slaves in South America, and (with the notable exception of Haiti) long constituted one of the most highly developed and autonomous communities of African descendants in the Americas. Both the maroon and Creole communities retain elements of African culture, including traditional African languages, oral histories, and religious ceremonies. In 1998 Creoles and maroons composed nearly 41 percent of Suriname's total population.

Africa

Swaziland,

a small landlocked southern African kingdom bordering South Africa to the north, west, and south, and Mozambique to the east.

Swaziland's beautiful, mountainous topography and unusually peaceful transition from colonialism to independence have earned it the nickname "the Switzerland of Africa." Swaziland is a kingdom, ruled jointly by a king and a queen mother, who trace their royal lineage back to the fifteenth century, making Swaziland one of only a handful of African nations to have survived the colonial period with most of its precolonial political system intact. This is due largely to the efforts of one man, King Sobhuza II, who managed to maintain his position and popularity during nearly half a century of British control. However, since Swaziland became independent in 1968, and particularly since Sobhuza's death in 1983, the nation's urban intellectuals and businesspeople have become increasingly dissatisfied with the old system of hereditary, autocratic rule. As mounting foreign debt and natural resource depletion have weakened Swaziland's once relatively prosperous economy, general strikes and civil unrest have jeopardized the fragile political stability that the current ruler, Mswati III, inherited from his revered predecessor. Bowing to domestic and international pressure, Mswati declared his support for democratic reforms and a new constitution in 1996, but so far he has failed to deliver on his promises.

Africa

Swaziland (Ready Reference)

Official Name: Kingdom of Swaziland

Area: 17,360 sq km (6,704 sq mi.)

Location: Southern Africa, between Mozambique and South Africa (landlocked; almost completely surrounded by South Africa)

Capital: Mbabane (administrative; population 46,000 [1990 estimate]); Lobamba (royal and legislative; [data on population unavailable])

King Sobhuza II, shown here in 1964 opening the railway between Swaziland and Mozambique, ruled the tiny nation from 1921 to 1982. *CORBIS/Hulton-Deutsch Collection*

Population: 966,462 (1998 estimate)

Population Below Age 15: 46 percent (male 223,648; female 224,782 [1998 estimate])

Population Growth Rate: 1.96 percent (1998 estimate)

Total Fertility Rate: 6 children born per woman (1998 estimate)

Life Expectancy at Birth: Total population: 38.53 years (male 37.31 years; female 39.79 years [1998 estimate])

Infant Mortality Rate: 103.37 deaths per 1,000 live births (1998 estimate)

Literacy Rate (age 15 and over who can read and write): Total population: 76.7 percent (male 78 percent; female 75.6 percent [1995 estimate])

Education: In the early 1990s about 180,300 children attended primary schools annually, and some 51,500 were enrolled in secondary schools. There is one major university, the University of Swaziland, located in Kwaluseni.

Languages: English and siSwati are the official languages; government business is conducted in English.

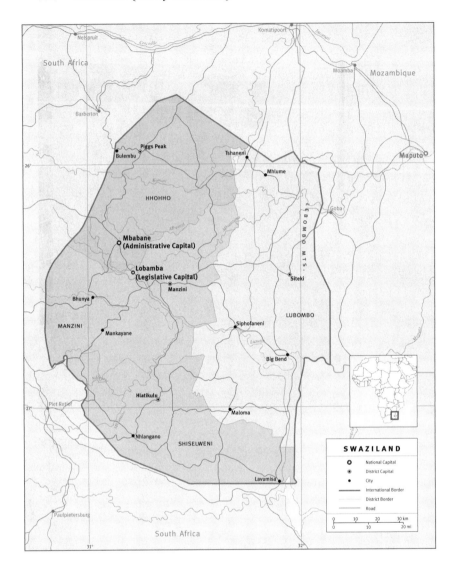

Ethnic Groups: Roughly 97 percent of the people in Swaziland are ethnic Swazi, although there are small populations of Zulu, Tsonga, Asians, and Europeans. Europeans constitute 3 percent of the population.

Religions: Christianity is the professed religion of 60 percent of the population: 40 percent practice indigenous beliefs.

Climate: The climate is mostly temperate, with cool temperatures at higher elevations and more tropical weather in the low veld. Precipitation, which is heavier toward the west, is concentrated in the warmer months of October through April; the rest of the year is characterized by sunny, clear weather. The temperature in Mbabane, located in the western highlands,

Swaziland's team enters the Olympic stadium in Atlanta, Georgia, in 1996. *CORBIS/Frank Seguin; TempSport*

ranges from 15° to 25° C (59° to 77° F) in January and 6° to 19° C (42° to 67° F) in July.

Land, Plants, and Animals: Swaziland has mostly mountains and hills, as well as some moderately sloping plains. Some 62 percent of the land comprises meadows and pastures. About 57 percent of the country's land has been set aside by the monarchy for exclusive use by the Swazi people. The principal rivers are the Komati, Lusutfu, and Umbuluzi. The steady flow of the rivers, fed by abundant rain in the mountains, supports irrigation and hydroelectric power projects in the lowlands.

Natural Resources: Asbestos, coal, clay, cassiterite, hydropower, forests, small gold and diamond deposits, quarry stone, and talc

Currency: The lilangeni

Gross Domestic Product (GDP): $3.9 billion (1997 estimate)

GDP per Capita: $3,800 (1997 estimate)

GDP Real Growth Rate: 3 percent (1997 estimate)

Primary Economic Activities: Subsistence agriculture, and mining

Primary Crops: Sugar cane, cotton, maize, tobacco, rice, citrus, pineapples, corn, sorghum, and peanuts; cattle, goats, and sheep

Industries: Mining (coal and asbestos), wood pulp, and sugar

Primary Exports: Sugar, wood pulp, cotton yarn, asbestos, and fresh and canned fruit

Surrounded by completed works, this Swaziland artist sculpts in soapstone. *CORBIS/Nik Wheeler*

Primary Imports: Motor vehicles, machinery, transport equipment, petroleum products, foodstuffs, and chemicals

Primary Trade Partners: South Africa, European Union (EU) countries, and Canada

Government: Swaziland is a monarchy and an independent member of the Commonwealth. National executive power in Swaziland is vested in a king, Mswati III, who appoints a prime minister and council of ministers. One house of parliament is the National Assembly, which has 65 members, 55 of whom are elected from a list of candidates nominated by traditional local councils or directly elected, and 10 of whom are appointed by the king. The 30-member Senate includes 10 members who are elected by the National Assembly and 20 who are appointed by the king. Judicial authority is vested in a high court and subordinate courts. Civil matters among Swazi are handled by traditional leaders, subject to appeals to the High Court.

T

Tango,

Argentine dance and musical genre, rooted in a combination of African, European, and native Argentine music and dance traditions.

Often referred to by Argentines as "a sad feeling that can be danced," the tango has become one of the most popular dance and musical forms worldwide. As a dance, the tango requires a couple to be chest-to-chest, in a tight embrace. "As the couple sways and pauses, bodies locked, feet twining in intricate *ochos* (figure eights) and *cortes* (short, rapid steps), it's as if they're carrying on an intensely intimate exchange," writes Chiori Santiago in *Smithsonian* magazine. As a musical form, tango has evolved from improvised dance pieces of the mid- to late nineteenth century—often performed by black and mulatto instrumentalis—to the modern *nuevo tango* compositions of the late Argentine musician Astor Piazzolla.

The black community of Buenos Aires played an indirect but significant role in the creation of the tango. By the mid-nineteenth century nearly a quarter of Buenos Aires's inhabitants were black, owing to the city's role as a port of entry for the slave trade in the previous century. Argentine blacks, who resided in poor neighborhoods, succeeded in preserving their culture through community events such as dance and music festivals. The most popular Afro-Argentine dance was the *candombe*, which fused syncopated rhythms and improvised steps from various African traditions. According to the early Argentine scholar of tango, José Gobello, the candombe was the precursor of the tango.

The Argentine historian Ricardo Rodríguez Molas contends that the word "tango," which in certain African languages means "closed place" or "reserved ground," is likely to be of African origin. Other scholars have traced the word back to the Latin verb *tangere*, meaning to touch; they believe that African slaves might have picked up the word "tango" from their European captors. In many parts of Latin America "tango" came to connote a place where blacks, both free and enslaved, gathered together to dance; while in Argentina, "tango" came to be associated with black dances in general. "It was in this sense," notes Collier, "that the word eventually reached Spain, as a name for African-American or African-influenced dances of transatlantic provenance."

Before World War II the tango was developed in dance halls, cafés, and brothels in the working-class *barrios* (districts) of Argentina's major cities. By 1913 the tango had become popular among the Argentine middle classes, who contributed to the development of a tango craze in Europe and Russia. By the 1920s Argentina had become one of the world's wealthiest nations. As the focal point of economic and demographic growth, Buenos Aires attracted a massive influx of predominantly Italian and Spanish immigrants. These immigrants introduced new instruments, such as the accordion and mandolin, and contributed to the development of *tango liso*, a style of tango that toned down some of the rougher movements. As Collier affirms, "This early division of dancing styles was fraught with significance for the future: the 'smooth' tango was undoubtedly the forerunner of the ballroom tango of the twentieth century, while the fierce, lubricious aggressiveness favoured in the outer barrios eventually faded away." Since the golden age of tango in the 1920s, tango music and dance have continued to gain popularity worldwide.

North America

Tanner, Henry Ossawa

(b. June 21, 1859, Pittsburgh, Pa; d. May 25, 1937, Paris, France), African American painter who was called "the first genius among Negro artists" by art historian James A. Porter.

The son of a bishop of the African Methodist Episcopal Church, Henry Ossawa Tanner was named after Osawatomie, the site of John Brown's antislavery raid in Kansas. Tanner began painting at age 13, and beginning in 1880 was a student at the Philadelphia Academy of Fine Arts, where he studied with Thomas Eakins. Tanner taught at Clark College in Atlanta, Georgia, from 1889 to 1891, when he relocated to Paris, largely to escape racial prejudice in America. In Paris, Tanner took courses at the Académie Julien and, with the exception of two brief visits home in 1893 and 1896, continued to live and paint there until his death in 1937.

While at the Pennsylvania Academy of Design and through 1890, Tanner painted traditional European subjects such as landscapes and animals. In the 1890s, however, Tanner began painting genre scenes of African American life, including his well-known works *The Banjo Lesson* (1893) and *The Thankful Poor* (1894). He is best known, though, for his paintings of biblical subjects, a theme Tanner began exploring in the mid-1890s, most famously in his 1896 painting *The Raising of Lazarus*. From 1894 to 1914

Tanner regularly exhibited his work at the Salon de la Société des Artistes Français in Paris, and after 1900 he also exhibited widely in the United States as well. In 1923 the French government named Tanner a chevalier of the French Legion of Honor.

Africa

Tanzania,

a country in southeastern Africa comprising former Tanganyika and the island of Zanzibar; bordered by eight countries and the Indian Ocean.

Tanzania defies most perceptions of poor, nonindustrialized nations. The first East African country to achieve independence, Tanzania immediately developed a stable, popularly supported, and democratically elected government that has successfully weathered both its political unification with the

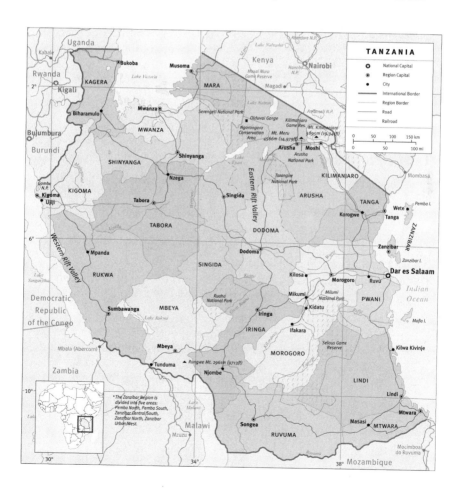

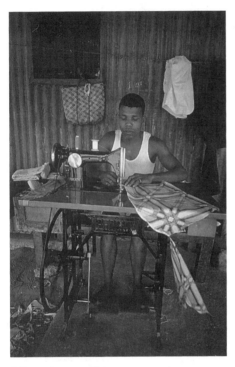

A Tanzanian man stitches up garments on a treadle-powered sewing machine.
CORBIS/Jack Fields

historically separate island of Zanzibar and the turmoil of neighbors afflicted with civil conflict, ethnic stratification, and autocratic regimes. Tanzania's economic path has also been different from most. Under the guidance of the country's first president, Julius K. Nyerere, Tanzania attempted to avoid the traps of neocolonialism and foreign dependency, instead embarking on a socialist experiment that sought to achieve local as well as national self-sufficiency. Although the experiment proved an economic disaster—not helped by the fact that much of rural Tanzania is resource-poor—it did raise Tanzania's standards of social welfare above those of most of its wealthier neighbors. Today Tanzania continues to struggle with widespread poverty, but progressive leaders have enabled the nation to seize new economic opportunities, and some observers note promising signs of recovery.

Africa

Tanzania (Ready Reference)

Official Name: United Republic of Tanzania

Former Names: United Republic of Tanganyika and Zanzibar

Area: 945,087 sq km (364,898 sq mi.)

Location: Eastern Africa, on the Indian Ocean, bordered by Burundi, Kenya, Malawi, Mozambique, Rwanda, Uganda, the Democratic Republic of the Congo, Zambia

Capital: Dar es Salaam (population 1,651,534 [1995 estimate])

Other Major Cities: Mwanza (population 2,280,206); Tanga (population 1,590,381); Zanzibar (population 456,934); Dodoma (population 1,502,344) (1995 estimates)

Population: 30,608,769 (1998 estimate)

Population Density: 55 persons per sq km (about 88 persons per sq mi. [1998 estimate])

Population Below Age 15: 45 percent (male 6,804,194; female 6,844,815 [1998 estimate])

Population Growth Rate: 2.14 percent (1998 estimate)

Total Fertility Rate: 5.5 children born per woman (1998 estimate)

Life Expectancy at Birth: Total population: 46.37 years (male 44.22 years; female 48.59 years [1998 estimate])

Infant Mortality Rate: 96.94 deaths per 1,000 live births (1998 estimate)

Literacy Rate (age 15 and over who can read and write): Total population: 67.8 percent (male 79.4 percent; female 56.8 percent [1995 estimate])

Education: Primary education in Tanzania is compulsory, but only 50 percent of eligible children are enrolled because not enough schools are available. Adult education campaigns have contributed to relatively high literacy rates. In the early 1990s government schools were attended annually by some 3.5 million elementary pupils and about 167,000 secondary students. In addition, many children attended private schools, which were mostly run by religious groups.

Languages: Tanzania's official languages are English and Swahili, and the latter is almost universally understood. Many people, however, continue to use the language of their ethnic group.

Ethnic groups: The Sukuma and the Nyamwezi represent about one-fifth of the population. Other significant groups include the Haya, Ngonde, Chagga, Gogo, Ha, Hehe, Nyakyusa, Nyika, Ngoni, Yao, and Maasai. The population also includes people of Indian, Pakistani, and Goan origin, and small Arab and European communities.

Religions: About one-third of the population follow traditional religions. About one-third practice the Islamic faith. Catholicism is the largest Christian denomination of Tanzania, with some 6 million adherents.

Climate: On the mainland coastal strip along the Indian Ocean the climate is warm and tropical, with temperatures averaging 27° C (80° F) and annual rainfall varying from 750 to 1,400 mm (30 to 55 in.). The inland plateau is hot and dry, with annual rainfall averaging as little as 500 mm (20 in.). The climate on the islands is generally tropical, but the heat is tempered by a sea breeze throughout the year. The annual mean temperature for the city of Zanzibar is 29° C (85° F) maximum, and 25° C (77° F) minimum; for Wete in Pemba, 30° C (86° F) maximum and 24° C (76° F) minimum.

Land, Plants, and Animals: Mainland Tanzania is generally flat and low along the coast, but a plateau at an average altitude of about 1,200 m (about 4,000 ft.) constitutes the greater part of the country. Isolated mountain groups rise in the northeast and southwest. The volcanic Kilimanjaro (5,895 m/19,340 ft.), the highest mountain in Africa, is located near the northeastern border. Three of the great lakes of Africa lie on the borders of the country and partially within it. Lake Tanganyika is located on the western border, Lake Victoria on the northwest, and Lake Malawi (Nyasa) on the southwest. Lakes Nyasa and Tanganyika lie in the Great Rift Valley, a tremendous geological fault system extending from the Middle East to Mozambique. Zanzibar, separated from the mainland by a 40-km (25-mi.) channel, is about 90 km (55 mi.) long and covers an area of 1,658 sq km (640 sq mi.). It is the largest coral island off the coast of Africa. Pemba, some 40 km (25 mi.) northwest of Zanzibar, is about 68 km (42 mi.) long and has an area of approximately 984 sq km (380 sq mi.). Wildlife includes antelope, zebra, elephant, hippopotamus, rhinoceros, giraffe, lion, leopard, cheetah, and monkey. Tanzania's national parks, among them Serengeti National Park, are home to many of these species.

Natural Resources: Diamonds, coal and iron ore, and hardwood forests

Currency: The Tanzanian shilling

Gross National Product (GDP): $21.1 billion (1997 estimate)

GDP per Capita: $700 (1997 estimate)

GDP Real Growth Rate: 4.3 percent (1997 estimate)

Primary Economic Activities: Agriculture, industry, services, and mining

Primary Crops: Coffee, sisal, tea, cotton, pyrethrum (insecticide made from chrysanthemums), cashews, tobacco, cloves (Zanzibar), corn, wheat, cassava (tapioca), bananas, fruits, and vegetables; cattle, sheep, and goats

Industries: Agricultural processing (sugar, beer, cigarettes, sisal twine), diamond and gold mining, oil refining, shoes, cement, textiles, wood products, and fertilizer

Primary Exports: Coffee, cotton, tobacco, tea, cashew nuts, and sisal

Primary Imports: Manufactured goods, machinery and transportation equipment, cotton piece goods, crude oil, and foodstuffs

Primary Trade Partners: Germany, United Kingdom, United States, Japan, Italy, Denmark, Netherlands, Kenya, and China

Government: Tanzania is governed under a constitution of 1977, as amended. The internal affairs of Zanzibar are administered under a constitution of 1985. Tanzania's chief executive is a popularly elected president, who serves a five-year term. The president (Benjamin Mkapa since November 22, 1995) appoints a vice president, prime minister (Fredrick Sumaye since November 27, 1995), and cabinet. Tanzania's legislature is the multiparty unicameral National Assembly. Of its 244 members, 169 (119 from the mainland and 50 from Zanzibar) are popularly elected to terms of up to five years. Most of the rest of the members are either elected by the National Assembly, appointed by the president, or sit by virtue of being commissioners of the country's regions.

North America

Tap Dance,

art form indigenous to the United States that combines African and European dance with a complicated jazz-based percussive sensibility created by elaborate footwork.

Tap dance originated in the cross-fertilization of African and Anglo-European cultures in the New World. During the 1600s the social dances of Irish and Scottish indentured laborers were fused with African Juba and ring dances. Slaves in the southern United States imitated the rapid toe and heel action of the Irish jig and the percussive sensibility of the Lancashire clog, danced in wooden shoes. Combined with West African body movements and rhythms, these new dances were the forerunners of the buck-and-wing dancing and clogging of the southern United States and of modern-day tap dancing.

The names of the innovators from the early slave community went unrecorded. When the slave dances were adapted theatrically for minstrel shows in the late 1820s, individual artists began to be recognized, though the first of these performers were black-faced white minstrels. William Henry Lane was the first African American to rise to prominence on the minstrel stage. When the ban on black performers on the minstrel stage was lifted after the Civil War, these venues became the site of numerous innovations in steps and choreography. Alongside the increasingly popular vaudeville performance of the late 1800s, the exposure that the minstrel stage offered helped launch the Broadway careers of performers such as Williams and Walker (Bert Williams and George Walker), Ulysses "Slow Kid" Thompson, and Bill Bailey while also forging the aesthetics of Broadway jazz dance and the Broadway musical. Behind them were many master tap dancers, including King Rastus Brown, who were born too soon to be accepted on the white stages.

Broadway ushered in a golden age for tap. The combination of sharply choreographed chorus lines performing to ragtime and early jazz with tap and other vernacular dances proved a hit with audiences and critics. During this period the marquee performers popularly associated with the genre—such as Bill "Bojangles" Robinson—rose to prominence.

If Broadway and, later, Hollywood cinema, gave tap its greatest exposure, the Hoofer's Club provided its unofficial academy. By the 1930s tap had become an integral part of Hollywood musicals. Prominent African American dancers, including Robinson, Sublett, the Nicholas Brothers, and the Berry Brothers, were often featured, but Hollywood best served the careers of whites such as Shirley Temple and Fred Astaire. Their success further popularized tap, making it the premier form of theatrical dance in the United States.

Tayyib, Salih al-

(b. 1929, al-Dabba, Sudan), contemporary Sudanese writer.

Al-Tayyib Salih was born in a large village in the northern province of
Sudan, where as a young man he received an Islamic schooling and worked
on the family's farm. Salih continued his education at Khartoum University
and then left Sudan to study in England. After completing degrees at the
University of London and the University of Exeter, he returned to his home
country to teach. Salih joined the British Broadcasting Corporation, working
his way up from scriptwriter to head of the Arabic language service. He has
since continued working in the fields of broadcast and print journalism.
Salih, who considers himself a socialist, has also occupied various advisory
government positions.

Salih started writing stories in the 1950s, but did not publish until
1964, when his friend the poet Tawfiq Sayigh began printing Salih's work
in the Beirut journal *Hiwar*. His stories, based on his childhood village life,
were infused with the mystical vision of Sufi Islam. In these stories his
writing style, often compared to magical realism, shows the influence of
traditional Arabic storytelling. He depicts a troubled marriage between a
European woman and a Sudanese man. (Salih himself had married a
British woman.) Many critics interpret his portrayal of personal relations as
representing the fraught relations between the First and Third World. In
1966 he published the stories as *Urs al-Zayn: Riwaya wa-sab qusas* (The
Wedding of Zein and Other Stories). The title novella *Urs al-Zayn* was
made into a play in Libya, and in 1976 it was made into an award-winning
Kuwaiti film.

Mawsim al-hijrah ila al-shamal (Season of Migration to the North) is
Salih's best-known novel; it is credited with transforming modern Arabic
writing. Taking up what would become a common theme in postcolonial
writing, the novel represented the alienation of an Islamic African man
returning from the West. It went beyond the issue of exile to consider what
it means to belong to a community, and traversed conventional norms in its
use of graphic sex and violence as metaphors for the penetrating, often
brutal, ways that cultures intersect. According to critic Kamal Abu-Deeb,
the novel also breaks with regional traditions of writing, "[focusing on]
African rather than Arab identity, social, cultural, and artistic issues rather
than political and ideological ones, the community rather than the State,
ordinary people rather than intellectuals, popular culture rather than official
culture, religious and mystical belief rather than secularism, the Sudanese
dialect rather than Standard Arabic, and the small village rather than the
great metropolis."

In 1971 Salih published *Bandar Shah, Daw al-bayt*, which explores the
nature of leadership in a contemporary village. He continued the story in
Bandar Shah, Maryud (1977). In 1976 he published "*Al-Rajul al-qubrusi*"
(translated as "The Cypriot Man"; 1980). In this story Salih took on one of

the most difficult subjects: the meaning of death. It was his last story before a 20-year literary silence, which continues to the present.

Theater, African overview of theatrical traditions in Africa.

Africa is home to several traditions of theater. Some of these traditions are of ancient origin, while others emerged with formal European colonization of the continent in the nineteenth century and the subsequent imposition of Western education, religion, and culture.

The older traditions are mostly nonscripted, improvisatory, and performed in indigenous African languages. Their conceptions of theater space and stage-audience relations are fluid and informal: any space can be turned into a performance stage, and the audience is free to interact with the performance in a variety of ways and even move in and out of the theater space during the performance. This type of performance is often public and the audience does not pay a fee, although performers could be rewarded in cash or kind for their artistry.

Many of the newer theater traditions are text based, written in European languages or indigenous African languages with Latin script. The plays are designed to be performed in more or less formal theater buildings with fixed relations between performers and audience. The audience usually pays a fee, although the theater may not be expressly commercial.

In all cases, as indeed in all societies, the functions of the theater traditions are broadly similar in their mixing of the pleasing and the pedagogical: their representations provide the audience with pleasurable entertainment while simultaneously channeling passions and sentiments in certain directions.

Theater in Africa could be categorized into four distinct traditions: festival theater, popular theater, development theater, and art theater.

Theater in the Caribbean,

the history of theater in the Spanish-, French-, and English-speaking Caribbean, particularly as it pertains to people of African descent.

Contemporary theater in the Caribbean has been shaped by the different cultures—Native American, European, African, East Indian, Madeiran, and Chinese—that have brought forms of performance from around the world to the Caribbean basin. Throughout the nineteenth and twentieth centuries in the Caribbean, the elements of stage and street performance, including written plays, storytelling, festivals, music and dance, combined to create new types of theater. During colonial times stage performance was often sponsored by the wealthy and evolved separately from African culture. More recently, however, performers and directors have begun to explore the African roots of a Caribbean theater through the incorporation of Afro-Caribbean religious practices and social rituals (such as dance, storytelling, and singing), which date to the period of slavery or earlier.

Third Cinema,

also called Third World cinema; a type of film and film theory prevalent in Africa, Latin America, and Asia that aims to transform society by educating and radicalizing the film audience through "subversive" cinema.

In the early 1960s a series of events paved the way for a new and distinctive type of Third World film. In Africa decolonization freed film directors such as Ousmane Sembène, Med Hondo, and Haile Gerima to make films for and about Africans. In Latin America and Asia revolutionary movements, combined with the development of Marxist film theory and Italian neorealism, inspired film directors such as Bolivian Jorge Sanjines and Indian Satyajit Ray to make politically charged films. Guided by the assumption that all film is ideological, they experimented with film as a weapon against the cultural imperialism of Hollywood.

During the next decade film directors from Africa, Asia, and Latin America met and discussed their work at meetings and international film festivals. They called their cinema "Third Cinema" to identify it with the Third World and to differentiate it from the "first," or traditional, cinema (characterized by commercial films produced by Hollywood) and the "second," or counter, cinema (characterized by art film movements such as French New Wave). By the late 1960s Third Cinema had established itself as an influential theory, especially in Africa.

Inspired by Marxist film criticism and the writings of Frantz Fanon, Third Cinema theory radically reinterprets the relationship between film, audience, and film director. It characterizes traditional film directors as agents of capitalism who "sell" to their passive audiences movies that promote colonial stereotypes and consumer society values. According to African American filmmaker Charles Taylor, traditional Hollywood cinema "concocts an artificial mental landscape harmonious with [capitalism's] need to depersonalize its audiences into zombies of its economy and addicts of its industrial culture, and to trash, trivialize, and erase the human culture that supply its victims."

By contrast Third Cinema must, in the words of Latin American directors Fernando Solanas and Octavio Gettino, produce "films that directly and explicitly set out to fight the System." Said director Jorges Sanjines, "the work of revolutionary cinema must not limit itself to denouncing, or to the appeal for reflection; it must be a summons for action." In fact, films such as *La hora de los hornos* (1968) and *Me gustan los estudiantes* (1969) provoked student riots in Uruguay and Venezuela during the late 1960s. Since the mid-1970s, however, the goal of most Third Cinema directors has been to inspire political and social change rather than complete revolution.

In sub-Saharan Africa most filmmakers subscribe to the ideas of Third Cinema and make films that are often quite critical of the postcolonial bourgeoisie. The films of Ousmane Sembène, Med Hondo, and Souleymane Cissé fuse documentary and fiction, and use ambiguous and unresolved endings to invite discussion from the audience. In Latin America and Asia, Third Cinema filmmakers now constitute only a small minority, but they continue to denounce capitalism and cultural imperialism as well as the persistent problem of racism.

North America

Thirteenth Amendment of the United States Constitution and the Emancipation Proclamation,

document that signaled the government's commitment to ending slavery, which was followed by the constitutional amendment that officially abolished slavery in the United States.

The Thirteenth Amendment is best understood against the background of the American Civil War. Although President Abraham Lincoln personally opposed slavery, ending slavery was not one of his administration's initial war aims. Instead he sought to "save the Union, and not either to save or destroy slavery." As president, Lincoln had sworn to uphold the Constitution; the Supreme Court had affirmed the constitutionality of slavery in its 1857 Dred Scott decision. As Southern states seceded, Lincoln had serious concerns about keeping the four border states—Delaware, Maryland, Kentucky, and Missouri—in the Union and about the loyalty of Northern Democrats. Also, he had promised slaveholders who were loyal to the federal government that they would be able to keep their slaves. Lincoln had first attempted to convince slaveholders in the border states gradually to eliminate slavery in return for compensation, but the slaveholders refused.

Lincoln's commitment to winning the war led him by 1862 to see emancipation as a necessity because he realized that slaves were a vital component of the Southern economy and that freeing slaves would destabilize the South. Thus in July 1862 Congress passed two laws regarding slaves. The first was a confiscation act that freed slaves from owners who had rebelled against the United States. The second was a militia act that enabled the president to use freed slaves in the army. In this context Lincoln was prepared to use presidential war powers to emancipate slaves in the rebel states.

Lincoln issued the Emancipation Proclamation on January 1, 1863,

In 1867 Louis Prang & Co., lithographers in Boston, issued *The American Declaration of Independence Illustrated*, in which the American Eagle lifts a recently freed black man and a white to freedom. Above their heads is the line: "Break every yoke; let the oppressed go free." *CORBIS/Bettmann*

declaring that slaves in all states still at war with the federal government were free and would remain so. While taking care to exempt border slave states and the three Confederate states that the Union controlled, Lincoln nevertheless endorsed the idea of recruiting freed slaves and free blacks for service in the armed forces. The Emancipation Proclamation, however, technically freed no one, because Lincoln's authority was not recognized in the Confederacy.

Many Republican Party members recognized that the proclamation was only a war measure that might have no lasting impact on the institution of slavery. Still, its effect was to signal the federal government's opposition to slavery and to bolster the abolitionist cause. The war ceased to be one aimed only at saving the Union and became a war to end slavery as well. An initial stream of escaping slaves slowly expanded to become a flood of runaways. In response to the proclamation's endorsement of black military enlistment, more than 180,000 blacks enrolled in the army and 10,000 in the navy by the end of the war.

A variety of forces began to press for a constitutional amendment to abolish slavery permanently. Women's groups were in the forefront in this battle, particularly the National Women's Loyal League, a predominantly white organization led by suffragists Susan B. Anthony and Elizabeth Cady Stanton. They believed that chattel slavery as practiced in the United States was closely linked to women's inferior place in society, and that progress in one area could result in progress in another. The Republican Party outlined support for such an amendment in its 1864 platform. Lincoln, after winning the 1864 presidential election, began pushing Congress to pass an amendment, using both his electoral mandate and his political skills to overcome Democratic opposition.

Early in 1865, shortly before the end of the Civil War and Lincoln's assassination, Congress approved the amendment. Its simplicity and brevity belies the fundamental changes it made to American society. Section 1 states that, "Neither slavery nor involuntary servitude, except as a punishment for crime whereof the party shall have been duly convicted, shall exist within the United States, or any place subject to their jurisdiction." Section 2 gives Congress the "power to enforce this article by appropriate legislation."

Although it was approved by Congress, the amendment had to be ratified by three-fourths of the states before becoming part of the Constitution. Most Northern states had ratified it, but it was up to President Andrew Johnson, who assumed the presidency after Lincoln's assassination in April 1865, to secure the necessary approval from Southern states. Johnson set very lenient terms for Southern reentry into American political society, but he required that Southern states ratify the amendment as a condition of readmission. Many state constitutional conventions, including those of Delaware and Kentucky, which had never outlawed slavery, opposed this requirement. Southern states especially disliked the second section, which provided for federal intervention if slavery were practiced. Johnson's tactics gained cooperation of enough states, and the amendment was ratified on December 18, 1865, finally abolishing legalized slavery throughout the United States.

North America

Thomas, Piri

(b. September 20, 1928, New York, N.Y.), Afro-Puerto Rican writer known for his innovative autobiographical works.

Piri Thomas was raised in the *barrios* (ghettos) of Spanish Harlem in New York City. His parents had immigrated to the United States from Puerto Rico. He attended public schools, where he was first introduced to institutionalized assimilation and racism. In 1952 he was incarcerated on charges of attempted armed robbery, and in prison he began writing his first book, the autobiography *Down These Mean Streets* (1967).

Down These Mean Streets gained critical acclaim for its portrayal of Spanish Harlem and its bold new literary style, which mixed Spanish Harlem dialect with slang Thomas had learned in prison. Thomas is known for his use of authentic Afro-Puerto Rican settings and dialect. Thomas went on to publish two more autobiographical works, *Saviour, Saviour, Hold My Hand* (1972) and *Seven Long Times* (1974). He also established himself as a playwright, authoring *Las calles de oro* (1970, The Golden Streets), and published a young adult book, *Stories of El Barrio* (1978). Thomas's works are included in the anthology *Boricuas: Influential Puerto Rican Work* (1995).

In addition to his writing, Thomas has been a community activist since his release from prison. He has volunteered in prison and drug rehabilitation programs in New York City since 1956, and received the Louis M. Rabinowitz Foundation Grant in 1962. In 1964 Time-Life Associates produced a documentary, *Petey and Johnny*, on his work with youth in street gangs. He was awarded a Lever Brothers Community Service Award in 1967, and since that year has been a staff associate for the Center for Urban Education in New York City.

Thomas moved to San Francisco in 1983, where he has expanded his work to explore musical mediums of expression, continuing to channel a voice from marginalized populations in the United States into the larger public consciousness.

Thurman, Wallace

(b. August 16, 1902, Salt Lake City, Utah; d. December 22, 1934, New York, N.Y.), African American writer of the Harlem Renaissance who espoused a frank and sometimes stark assessment of African American life in America.

In 1925 Wallace Thurman began his writing career at the University of Southern California, where he started and edited the short-lived *Outlet*, a literary magazine that discussed many ideas of the Harlem Renaissance. Leaving school for Harlem that same year, Thurman became a part of the cultural outpouring that he had been observing. He began working in New York City as an editorial assistant at a small magazine called *Looking Glass*, followed by positions at other publications, such as the white magazine *The World Tomorrow*. At the left-wing *Messenger*, where he was temporary editor, Thurman became associated with other writers in Harlem, including Langston Hughes and Zora Neale Hurston.

In 1926 Thurman helped found *Fire!!*, a journal intended to expose the new thinking of the Harlem Renaissance and publish writing about African Americans who broke free from mainstream American culture. Unfortunately, the journal, which Thurman edited, was plagued with financial problems, and an actual fire in a basement where many issues of *Fire!!* were stored secured the downfall of the publication after only one issue. Thurman started a similar magazine in 1928, *Harlem, a Forum of Negro Life*, which failed after one issue.

Despite his failures as a publisher, Thurman wrote three books, a play, and several articles and editorials for numerous magazines. His writing often satirized African American life and the Harlem Renaissance, depicting the contradictions within black thought of the time, especially in his novels *The Blacker the Berry* (1929) and *Infants of the Spring* (1932). His play *Harlem* was originally produced at the Apollo Theater in 1929 and may have been his largest success. His final novel, *The Interne* (1932), exposed the injustices at City Hospital on Welfare Island (now Roosevelt Island). He died at that hospital in 1934, of tuberculosis and consumption, related to chronic alcoholism.

Till, Emmett Louis

(b. July 25, 1941, Chicago, Ill.; d. August 28, 1955, LeFlore County, Miss.), African American teenager who was an early victim of civil rights-era violence.

Emmett Till was born and raised in Chicago, Illinois. When he was 14 years of age, he was sent to Mississippi to spend the summer with his uncle. Because of his northern upbringing, Till was not accustomed to the racial taboos of the segregated South; he bragged to his southern black friends that in Chicago he even had a white girlfriend. These unbelieving friends dared him to enter a store and ask a white woman for a date. Inside, Till hugged Carol Bryant's waist and squeezed her hand, then whistled at her as his friends rushed him away.

On August 28, 1955, Carol Bryant's husband, Roy, and his half-brother, J.W. Milam, abducted Till from his uncle's home. Three days later his naked, beaten, decomposed body was found in the Tallahatchie River; he had been shot in the head. The two white men were tried one month later by an all-white jury, and despite the fact that they admitted abducting Till, they were acquitted because the body was too mangled to be positively identified.

Till's murder became a rallying point for the Civil Rights Movement. Photographs of his open casket were reprinted across the country, and protests were organized by the National Association for the Advancement of Colored People (NAACP), the Brotherhood of Sleeping Car Porters, and such leaders as W. E. B. Du Bois. The public outrage over the injustice of the trial helped ensure that Congress included a provision for federal investigations of civil rights violations in the Civil Rights Act of 1957.

Togo,

a small coastal West African country located between Benin, Ghana, and Burkina Faso.

Despite its small size, Togo encompasses considerable geographic, ethnic, and economic diversity, which has haunted the country's political development. The German and French colonial administrations concentrated economic development in the mostly Ewe coastal region south of the Togo Mountains, while the more ethnically diverse north remained impoverished. Since independence Ewe prosperity and separatism have aroused northern resentment and fear. Togo has been called "the Jurassic Park of Africa," because of the persistence of its military dictatorship, led by a northerner, Gen. Gnassingbé Eyadéma, since 1967. Eyadéma's patronage has solidified his base of support in the north and among the powerful

Children raise their hands in a classroom in Togo, where about 76 percent of school-age children attend school. *CORBIS/Brian Vikander*

market women of the capital but alienated many in the more urbanized, mostly Ewe south. Although Eyadéma since 1989 has been promising a transition to more democratic rule, his government and military have repeatedly harassed opposition figures, disrupted elections, and blocked the formation of an independent electoral commission. After a long decline from the late 1970s through the early 1990s, the country's economy has showed signs of renewed strength. Harassment of opposition leaders and other irregularities tarnished Eyadéma's reelection in 1998, and Eyadéma's military regime seems determined to deflect the winds of democratic change.

Africa
Togo (Ready Reference)

Official Name: Togolese Republic
Former Name: French Togo
Area: 56,790 sq km (21,925 sq mi.)
Location: Western Africa, bordered by Burkina Faso, Benin, Ghana, and the Atlantic Ocean
Capital: Lomé (population 600,000 [1994 estimate])

Other Major Cities: Sokodé (population 55,000 [1987 estimate]) and Kpalimé (population 31,000 [1987 estimate])

Population: 4,905,827 (1998 estimate)

Population Density: 128 persons per sq km (about 207 persons per sq mi. [1998 estimate])

Population Below Age 15: 48 percent (male 1,190,812; female 1,180,739 [1998 estimate])

Population Growth Rate: 3.52 percent (1998 estimate)

Total Fertility Rate: 6.6 children born per woman (1998 estimate)

Life Expectancy at Birth: Total population: 58.7 years (male 56.5 years; female 61.1 years [1998 estimate])

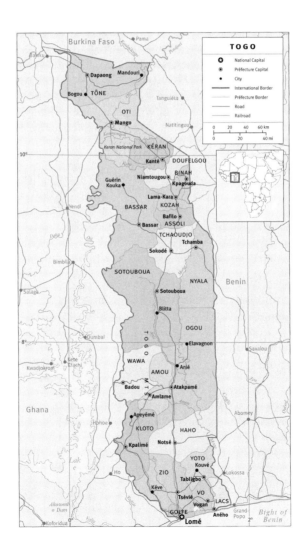

Infant Mortality Rate: 79.8 deaths per 1,000 live births (1998 estimate)

Literacy Rate (age 15 and over who can read and write): Total population: 51.7 percent (male 67 percent; female 37 percent [1995 estimate])

Education: In the early 1970s the Togolese government undertook a campaign to provide free education to all children between ages 2 and 15. By the early 1990s nearly 76 percent of all school-age children attended school. Missionary schools are also important and educate roughly half of all students.

Languages: French is the official language; it is used for administration, commerce, and in schools. Ewe, Mina, Dagomba, and Kabye (sometimes spelled Kabiye) are the four major African languages spoken in Togo.

Ethnic Groups: There are 37 different ethnic groups in Togo. The largest of these are the Ewe in the south, the Mina and the Kabré in the north.

Religions: About 70 percent of the population adhere to indigenous beliefs. About 20 percent are Christian; 10 percent are Muslim.

Climate: Tropical in the south and semi-arid in the north. Average annual temperatures range from 27° C (about 80° F) at the coast to 30° C (86° F) in the north. The south has two rainy seasons, from March to July and October to November. The annual rainfall in the south averages 875 mm (35 in.) and doubles in the mountains, a few kilometers in from the coast. In the north the average rainfall is 1145 mm (45 in.).

Land, Plants, and Animals: Togo's geography varies from tropical forest at the coast to savanna in the rest of the country. There are buffalo, antelopes, lions, and deer in the northern regions. In the forests there are snakes and monkeys. Hippopotamuses and crocodiles live in the rivers.

Natural Resources: Phosphates, limestone, and marble

Currency: The CFA franc

Gross Domestic Product (GDP): $6.2 billion (1997 estimate)

GDP per Capita: $1,300 (1997 estimate)

GDP Real Growth Rate: 4.8 percent (1997 estimate)

Primary Economic Activities: Agriculture, industry, and services

Primary Crops: Coffee, cocoa, cotton, yams, cassava (tapioca), corn, beans, rice, millet, sorghum, meat, and fish

Industries: Phosphate mining, agricultural processing, cement, handicrafts, textiles, and beverages

Primary Exports: Phosphates, cotton, cocoa, and coffee

Primary Imports: Machinery and equipment, consumer goods, food, and chemical products

Primary Trade Partners: European Union, Africa, United States, and Japan

Government: Togo is a republic under transition to multiparty democratic rule. The executive branch is led by President Gen. Gnassingbé Eyadéma and Prime Minister Edem Kodjo. The legislative branch is the elected 81-member National Assembly.

Tonton Macoutes

(also known as Tonton Makout), a fearsome paramilitary group established in Haiti under the dictatorship of François Duvalier.

The name Tonton Macoute was originally attached to a haunting character in Haitian folk literature. Translating roughly as "bogeyman with a basket," the name referred to an old bearded man who carried a bag of woven straw (a *macoute* in Creole) and appeared at night to carry away naughty children. Haitian mothers invoked the image of Tonton Macoute to encourage obedience among their children, saying: "If you do not behave, I'll call Tonton Macoute and he will drag you away."

When François Duvalier took power in Haiti on October 22, 1957, he soon inaugurated a regime of terror against his opponents. He desired a source of power parallel to, but independent from, the armed forces; in order to serve Duvalier's needs the new group would have to attach its loyalty exclusively to the Haitian leader. By July 1958 Duvalier had established his personal militia, the Tonton Macoutes. Duvalier's henchmen attacked, beat, raped, and harassed the opponents of his regime, initially wearing hoods to mask their features. (As a hood is called a *cagoule* in French, these forces were initially called *Cagoulards*; eventually the more popular Tonton Macoutes took hold.) Early in Duvalier's rule this force targeted academics and other intellectuals who might oppose Duvalier, provoking one of many waves of migration from Haiti to the United States and elsewhere. Though there are no solid estimates, it is believed that during the early Duvalier years the Tonton Macoutes killed tens of thousands of people. The militia's abuses were generally documented in urban Haiti, but less is known about the actions of the Tonton Macoutes in rural areas, where their presence was stronger and where the vast majority of the Haitian population resides.

The Tonton Macoutes, who were not officially acknowledged by the Haitian government, soon evolved into a pervasive secret police force in Haiti. In 1962 the Duvalier regime created a militia called the Volontaires de la Sécurité Nationale (VSN), whose connection to the Tonton Macoutes was suspected if not explicit.

When François Duvalier's rule passed on to his son, Jean-Claude Duvalier, the links between the police, the army, and the VSN/Tonton Macoutes became stronger, and many feel that the head of the Macoutes, Minister of the Interior Roger Lafontant, became the real power behind Jean-Claude Duvalier's rule. But some observers also argue that the Tonton Macoutes came to be increasingly critical of "Baby Doc" Duvalier, whom they saw as betraying the "ideals" of his father. These divisions within the VSN/Tonton Macoutes were partially responsible for the collapse of Jean-Claude Duvalier's spectacularly corrupt regime, which finally fell on February 7, 1986. Nevertheless, at the end of his rule, "Baby Doc" Duvalier declared a state of siege and called the Tonton Macoutes and the army into the streets, where they killed hundreds. The end of the Duvaliers' sovereignty thus provoked Carnivals and street celebrations. It also incited the *dechoukaj*, or "uprooting," a strong backlash against the Tonton Macoutes in which citizens killed scores of the organization's more visible members.

Though the Tonton Macoutes was not the first or the last paramilitary organization in Haiti, its use by Duvalier established a legacy of fear and violence that poses powerful dilemmas. Particularly urgent in a post-Duvalier and incipiently democratic Haiti is the issue of how to deal with past abuses, whether or not to bring past abusers to justice while seeking to create a unified, just, and democratic Haiti.

North America

Toomer, Jean

(b. December 26, 1894, Washington, D.C.; d. March 30, 1967), African American writer whose experimental novel of southern life, *Cane*, profoundly influenced twentieth-century black writers.

Jean Toomer's position in the canon of African American literature rests on his haunting narrative of southern life, *Cane*. Since its original publication in 1923, the novel has been rediscovered by successive generations of black writers, despite Toomer's later ambivalence toward his racial identity. Toomer, racially mixed but able to pass for white, sought a unifying thesis that would resolve the conflicts of his identity. He spent his life trying to evade the categories of American racial and ethnic identification, which he felt constricted the complexity of a lineage like his.

As a writer Toomer was nurtured in the 1910s and 1920s by Greenwich Village progressive aesthetes like Waldo Frank and Hart Crane, but *Cane* was inspired by his two-month stint as a substitute principal at the black Sparta Agricultural and Industrial Institute in Georgia in 1921. Entranced by Georgia's rural geography and its black folk traditions, he saw in southern life the harmony that escaped him, although he believed the culture to be disappearing through migration to the North and its encounter with modernity.

Author Jean Toomer's 1923 novel, *Cane*, influenced generations of African American writers. The author is shown here in 1934. *CORBIS/Bettmann*

Cane is a series of vignettes whose narrative structure moves from the South to the North and back to the South, forming a troubled synthesis of the two regions. The book was a commercial failure on its first publication, but critics initiated a chorus of praise that has spanned the generations. Members of the Harlem Renaissance and the Black Arts Movement, as well as later African American women writers like Toni Morrison and Alice Walker, have cited its influence and acclaimed the author's sensitive treatment of black folk life, his formal elegance, and his progressive, uninhibited approach to sexuality and gender.

Cane was Toomer's only work that explicitly treated the lives of African Americans; after its publication he disappeared from literary circles. In 1924 the restless author made the first of several pilgrimages to Fontainebleau, France, to study with the mystic and psychologist Georges Ivanovich Gurdjieff at the Institute for the Harmonious Development of Man. Gurdjieff believed that a transcendent "essence," obscured by a socially determined "personality," could be recovered through his teachings. Through Gurdjieff, Toomer found a way to express his attempts at defining a holistic identity. He taught Gurdjieff's philosophy in Harlem and Chicago until his break with the mystic in the mid-1930s.

Toomer wrote voluminously until his death, and although much of his writing received occasional praise for its experimentation, it was largely dismissed by African American critics, who saw it not only as propaganda for Gurdjieff's teachings, but as being white-identified. Indeed, in 1930 Toomer declined to be included in James Weldon Johnson's *Book of American Negro Poetry*, on the grounds that he was not a Negro. Toomer continued to strive for a sense of wholeness, however, and for a definition of what Henry Louis Gates Jr. has described as a "remarkably fluid notion of race." He found this in the potential of an "American" race, described in the 1936 long poem *Blue Meridian*—the last work published while he was alive—as a hybrid, "blue," comprising the black, the white, and the red races.

Africa

Touré, Ali Farka

(b. 1939, Kanau, Mali), African blues musician.

With a Grammy Award to his name and years of worldwide touring, Ali Farka Touré is one of the best-known African musicians outside Africa. As Touré, who is particularly popular in America, told the *New York Times*, "Where you are, you may call it the blues." But he says that his guitar style, which reminds listeners of John Lee Hooker, Lightnin' Hopkins, and other blues legends, is really in the "African tradition."

Growing up amid poverty in Mali, Touré was his parents' tenth child, but the first to reach adolescence. Nicknamed "the donkey" (Farka) by his family because of his stubbornness, Touré made music despite his parents' objections. By age 17 he had learned the traditional Malian instruments, including the single-stringed *njarka* and the harplike *ngoni*. During the 1960s he directed a group specializing in traditional music. They toured Europe, where he acquired his first guitar and began to learn about Western music.

In 1970 Touré joined the house band of Mali's national radio station as its guitarist, and spent the next ten years recording six albums, which were released in France and West Africa. By the 1980s Touré had begun to build a reputation outside Mali, which culminated in worldwide fame after the 1988 release of his self-titled album, *Ali Farka Touré*. Collaborations with Western artists such as Ry Cooder, Clarence "Gatemouth" Brown, the Chieftains, and Taj Mahal have expanded Touré's popularity as a guitarist and singer. His 1994 album *Talking Timbuktu* won a Grammy for best world music album. Despite that record's success, Touré had to cancel concert plans, in part to help defend his family's farming community during Mali's war with the Tuaregs.

Latin America and the Caribbean

Toussaint L'Ouverture, François Dominique
(b. May 1743?, Haut du Cap, Haiti; d. April 6, 1803, Fort de Joux [Jura], France), leader of the slave revolution that brought Haiti independence from France in 1804; a man who, in the words of Aimé Césaire, took "a population and turned it into a people."

There is little documentation regarding the life of François Dominique Toussaint L'Ouverture before the first slave uprising in 1791 in Saint-Domingue (as Haiti was known before independence). According to contemporary oral accounts, his parents were from Dahomey (present-day Benin) and his father was a powerful chief in that country before his enslavement. Toussaint was the first of eight children born on the Bréda plantation near the northern coast of Saint-Domingue. Born in the French colony and familiar with its culture, Toussaint was considered a Creole rather than an African, which—according to the logic of European colonialism—guaranteed him a more elevated social status. This status, and the plantation owner's affection for him, freed Toussaint from ever having to toil in the sugar cane fields. Instead he worked as a domestic servant in the plantation house. Toussaint was emancipated in 1776 at the young age of 33. In 1779 he rented a plot of land with 13 slaves attached to it and enjoyed the prerogatives of a colonizer, which included the amassing of a small fortune. From 1791, when he became politically active, until his death in 1803, he never publicly referred to this part of his life, choosing for political reasons to focus on his once having been a slave. Yet, in keeping with his complex history, his status as slave owner allowed him to gain the confidence of the French after the first slave revolts, even though he had actively participated in them. This confidence would prove decisive in his drive to bring independence to Saint-Domingue.

On the evening of August 22, 1791, the first slave revolt began under the leadership of the Jamaican Boukman. Toussaint, the only literate officer in the revolt, was named secretary of the movement. As Toussaint and others noted, those who rose up were reacting to a chasm between the ideals, on the one hand, of liberty, equality, and fraternity for all—which French political and intellectual leaders had been spreading throughout the world during and after the French Revolution of 1789—and, on the other hand, their lived experience as blacks, mulattos, and free men of color on Saint-Domingue. If all men were created equal, asked Saint-Domingues's people of color, how could slavery exist? The French responded to these questions and to the revolts they inspired by abolishing slavery in all the colonies on September 4, 1793. The first slave revolt had been successful. (Slavery, however, would be reinstated a few years later in all the French colonies and would remain in place until 1848.)

With the (temporary) abolition of slavery by the French and with the western part of the island under siege by the British and the Spanish in 1794, Toussaint offered his services to the French army. His valor and shrewdness in repelling the invaders allowed him to rise quickly through the ranks and become lieutenant governor of Saint-Domingue. But Toussaint was not satisfied with being second in command of the colony. As commander in chief of the military he did not hide his ambition to become the sole leader of Saint-Domingue. His considerable influence over the black population worried the French so much that in 1798 the French general Hédouville was sent to the colony with the secret mission of undermining Toussaint's authority. But Toussaint outmaneuvered Hédouville and others sent to unseat him diplomatically. Having gained control of the entire island of Hispaniola (present-day Haiti and the Dominican Republic), Toussaint formed a commission of ten called the Central Assembly, which drafted a constitution in 1801. While affirming that Saint-Domingue was still a French colony, the constitution rendered it administratively independent and named Toussaint L'Ouverture governor general of Saint-Domingue for life. Thereafter relations with France disintegrated completely. Napoleon Bonaparte, now first consul of France, sent forces led by his brother-in-law, General Charles Leclerc, to reclaim control of the colony. Leclerc and his 22,000 troops surrounded Toussaint in his stronghold in Crête-à-Pierrot, and on May 5, 1802, forced him to surrender. Toussaint was shipped to the Fort de Joux prison in France, where he died on April 6, 1803, from malnutrition and tuberculosis. Though the Haitian Revolution had lost its mastermind and leader, those who had served under him continued to fight for what he had envisioned and nearly achieved. On January 1, 1804, Jean-Jacques Dessalines, a protégé of Toussaint, was able to declare that the French colony of Saint-Domingue was now the independent republic of Haiti.

Toussaint's heroism and martyrdom have been memorialized by some of the Caribbean's most significant writers, including Martinican authors Edouard Glissant (*Monsieur Toussaint*, 1961) and Aimé Césaire (*Toussaint L'Ouverture*, 1961), and C. L. R. James (*The Black Jacobins*, 1938) of

Trinidad and Tobago. While not discounting the complexities and paradoxes that shaped his character, these writers and others have pointed to Toussaint's singular importance in the formation of modern Caribbean identity and to the inspiration he continues to provide in the struggles of Caribbean people for cultural and political independence.

Cross Cultural

Transatlantic Slave Trade

From the 1520s to the 1860s an estimated 11 to 12 million African men, women, and children were forcibly embarked on European vessels for a life of slavery in the Western Hemisphere. Many more Africans were captured or purchased in the interior of the continent, but a large number died before reaching the coast. About 9 to 10 million Africans survived the Atlantic crossing to be purchased by planters and traders in the New World, where they worked principally as slave laborers in plantation economies requiring a large work force. African peoples were transported from numerous coastal outlets from the Senegal River in West Africa and hundreds of trading sites along the coast as far south as Benguela (Angola), and from ports in Mozambique in southeast Africa. In the New World slaves were sold in markets as far north as New England and as far south as present-day Argentina.

The Early History of European Trade with Africa

The marketing of people in the interior of Africa predates European contact with West Africa. A trans-Saharan slave trade developed from the tenth to fourteenth century that featured the buying and selling of African captives in Islamic markets such as the area around present-day Sudan. A majority of those enslaved were females, who were purchased to work as servants, agricultural laborers, or concubines. Some captives were also shipped north across the deserts of northwest Africa to the Mediterranean coast. There, in slave markets such as Ceuta (Morocco), Africans were purchased to work as servants or laborers in Spain, Portugal, and other countries.

By the mid-1400s Portuguese ship captains had learned how to navigate the waters along the west coast of Africa and had begun to trade directly with slave suppliers who built small trading posts, or "factories," on the coast. European shippers were thus able to circumvent the trans-Saharan caravan slave trade. The slave trade to Europe began to decrease in the late 1400s with the development of sugar plantations in the Atlantic islands of Madeira and São Tomé. These two islands, located off West Africa and in the Gulf of Guinea, became leading centers of world sugar production and plantation slavery from the mid-1400s to the mid-1500s. Portuguese merchants dominated this early trade.

Much of the earliest European trade with West Africa, however, was in gold, not people. Europeans did not have the power to overcome African states before the late nineteenth century, and gold production, centered in Akan goldfields in the backcountry of present-day Ghana, remained in African hands. Europeans called this region the Gold Coast. Agreements between African and European elites and rivalries for the African gold trade resulted in the construction of dozens of trading forts, or stone castles, along a 161 km (100 mi.) coastal stretch of Ghana. (Several of these forts survive, have been repaired by the government of Ghana, and are tourist attractions today.) It was not until the late seventeenth century that the value of European goods traded for African people surpassed the value of goods exchanged for gold. Over time these gold forts became slave forts, where hundreds of Africans were confined in prisons awaiting sale and shipment.

The Slave Trade and Development of Plantations in the Americas

Christopher Columbus's "discovery" of the New World in 1492 marked the beginning of a transatlantic trading system. Via the slave trade, Africans played a leading role in the creation and evolution of this large and long-lasting "Atlantic system." Spanish adventurers arrived in the Americas hoping to trade for riches but soon enslaved the Native American peoples in their search for gold and silver. Disease, malnutrition, and Spanish atrocities led to the deaths of millions of the Indians of the Americas. By the 1520s the depopulation of the region prompted the Spanish government to look for alternative sources of labor. Officials contracted with Portuguese merchants to deliver Africans to Spanish territories in the New World. The first transatlantic slave voyages from Africa to the Americas occurred in the early 1520s on Portuguese vessels sailing from West Africa to the large Caribbean island of Hispaniola, the earliest European name for present-day Haiti and the Dominican Republic.

The transatlantic slave trade increased in the mid-1500s when the Spanish began to use African slave labor alongside Native Americans to mine silver in Peru. Slave ships sailed from Africa to Colombia and Panama, and African captives then were transported overland to the Pacific coast of South America. Until the early 1600s most Africans enslaved in the Americas worked in Peruvian or Mexican mines. The 1570s marked the development of sugar plantations in Brazil, a Portuguese colony, where merchants adopted production techniques pioneered in Madeira and São Tomé. By the 1620s African labor had replaced Indian labor on sugar plantations.

The development of an export-based plantation complex in North America and the Caribbean, areas neglected by the Spanish and Portuguese, awaited the arrival of the British, French, and Dutch in the early 1600s. In the initial development of the British colonies Virginia and Barbados (1630s–1640s), Jamaica (1660s), and South Carolina (1690s) and the French colonies Saint-Domingue (present-day Haiti), Martinique, and Guadeloupe (1660s–1680s), most laborers on the plantations were young European males who agreed to work for three to five years in return for free oceanic passage and food and housing in the Americas. These workers were

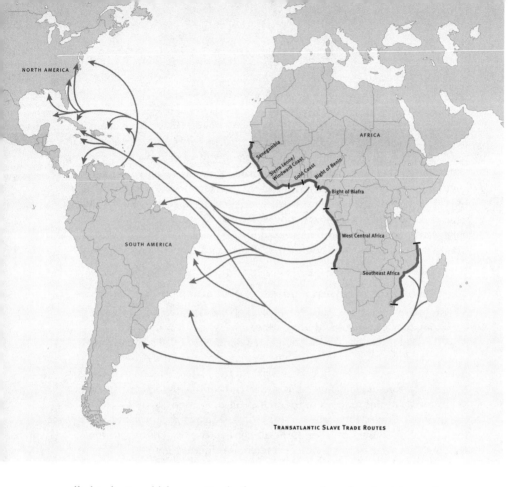

NORTH AMERICA

AFRICA

Senegambia
Sierra Leone/
Windward Coast
Gold Coast
Bight of Benin
Bight of Biafra
West Central Africa
Southeast Africa

SOUTH AMERICA

TRANSATLANTIC SLAVE TRADE ROUTES

called indentured laborers. By the late seventeenth and early eighteenth centuries tobacco, sugar, indigo (used to make blue dye), and rice plantations switched from European indentured labor to African slave labor. By the mid-1700s Brazil, Saint-Domingue, and Jamaica were the three largest slave colonies in the Americas. By the 1830s Cuba emerged as the principal Caribbean plantation colony. Throughout the history of the transatlantic slave trade, however, more Africans arrived as slaves in Brazil than in any other colony.

Dutch merchants did not develop extensive plantation colonies in the New World but they became large slave traders in the mid-seventeenth century. The small Dutch Republic was among the first European nations to develop modern commerce, and merchants there had access to shipping, port facilities, and banking credit. Dutch traders occupied several trading castles on the African coast, the most important of which was Elmina (in Ghana), a fort they captured from the Portuguese and rebuilt. The Dutch wrested control of the transatlantic slave trade from the Portuguese in the 1630s, but by the 1640s they faced increasing competition from French and British traders. By the 1680s a variety of nations, private trading companies, and merchant-adventurers sent slave ships to Africa: merchants from Denmark, Sweden, and the German states also organized slave voyages.

(continued on page 913)

1519 - 1867

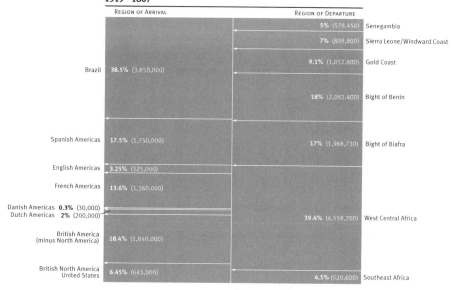

REGION OF ARRIVAL	REGION OF DEPARTURE

Brazil **38.5%** (3,850,000)

Spanish Americas **17.5%** (1,750,000)

English Americas **3.25%** (325,000)

French Americas **13.6%** (1,360,000)

Danish Americas **0.3%** (30,000)
Dutch Americas **2%** (200,000)

British America (minus North America) **18.4%** (1,840,000)

British North America United States **6.45%** (645,000)

5% (578,450) Senegambia

7% (809,800) Sierra Leone/Windward Coast

9.1% (1,052,800) Gold Coast

18% (2,082,400) Bight of Benin

17% (1,966,730) Bight of Biafra

39.4% (4,558,200) West Central Africa

4.5% (520,600) Southeast Africa

The data presented in the transatlantic slave trade diagrams were prepared by Stephen D. Behrendt, David Richardson, and David Eltis and drawn from the database they created at the W. E. B. Du Bois Institute for Afro-American Research, Harvard University. This database contains records of 27,233 voyages that set out to obtain slaves for the Americas. Based on these records, the estimated total number of Africans transported to the Americas during the transatlantic slave trade is 11,569,000.

1519 - 1600

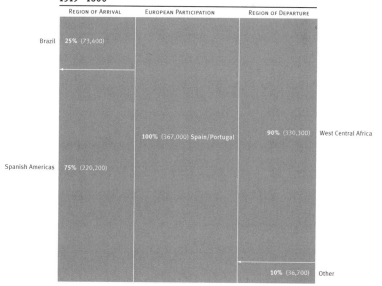

REGION OF ARRIVAL	EUROPEAN PARTICIPATION	REGION OF DEPARTURE

Brazil **25%** (73,400)

Spanish Americas **75%** (220,200)

100% (367,000) Spain/Portugal

90% (330,300) West Central Africa

10% (36,700) Other

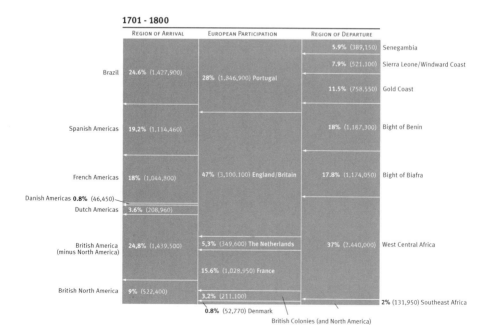

1601 - 1700

| REGION OF ARRIVAL | EUROPEAN PARTICIPATION | REGION OF DEPARTURE |

- Brazil **36.2%** (540,970)
- Spanish Americas **35.4%** (529,000)
- English Americas **21.9%** (327,000)
- French Americas **4.9%** (73,200)
- Danish Americas **0.9%** (13,450)
- Dutch Americas **0.8%** (11,960)

- **57.8%** (1,079,700) Portugal
- **26.9%** (502,500) England/Britain
- **11.6%** (216,680) The Netherlands
- **2.7%** (50,430) France
- **0.9%** (16,810) Denmark

- **5.3%** (99,000) Senegambia
- **0.5%** (9,300) Sierra Leone/Windward Coast
- **10.6%** (198,000) Gold Coast
- **22.3%** (416,560) Bight of Benin
- **6.1%** (114,000) Bight of Biafra
- **54.2%** (1,012,450) West Central Africa
- **1%** (18,680) Southeast Africa

1701 - 1800

| REGION OF ARRIVAL | EUROPEAN PARTICIPATION | REGION OF DEPARTURE |

- Brazil **24.6%** (1,427,900)
- Spanish Americas **19.2%** (1,114,460)
- French Americas **18%** (1,044,800)
- Danish Americas **0.8%** (46,450)
- Dutch Americas **3.6%** (208,960)
- British America (minus North America) **24.8%** (1,439,500)
- British North America **9%** (522,400)

- **28%** (1,846,900) Portugal
- **47%** (3,100,100) England/Britain
- **5.3%** (349,600) The Netherlands
- **15.6%** (1,028,950) France
- **3.2%** (211,100)
- **0.8%** (52,770) Denmark
- British Colonies (and North America)

- **5.9%** (389,150) Senegambia
- **7.9%** (521,100) Sierra Leone/Windward Coast
- **11.5%** (758,550) Gold Coast
- **18%** (1,187,300) Bight of Benin
- **17.8%** (1,174,050) Bight of Biafra
- **37%** (2,440,000) West Central Africa
- **2%** (131,950) Southeast Africa

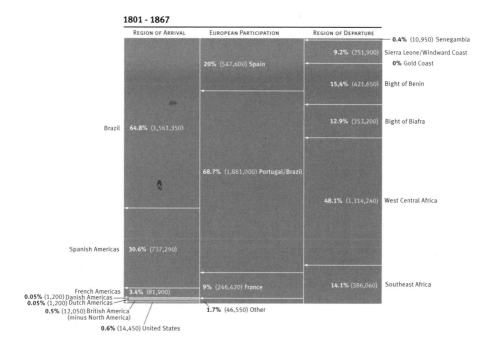

1801 - 1867

REGION OF ARRIVAL	EUROPEAN PARTICIPATION	REGION OF DEPARTURE

0.4% (10,950) Senegambia

9.2% (251,900) Sierra Leone/Windward Coast

0% Gold Coast

20% (547,600) Spain

15.4% (421,650) Bight of Benin

12.9% (353,200) Bight of Biafra

Brazil 64.8% (1,561,350)

68.7% (1,881,000) Portugal/Brazil

48.1% (1,314,240) West Central Africa

Spanish Americas 30.6% (737,290)

14.1% (386,060) Southeast Africa

French Americas 3.4% (81,900)

9% (246,420) France

0.05% (1,200) Danish Americas
0.05% (1,200) Dutch Americas
0.5% (12,050) British America (minus North America)

1.7% (46,550) Other

0.6% (14,450) United States

Throughout the eighteenth century—the height of the transatlantic slave trade—the largest traders were the British, Portuguese, and French.

The Middle Passage

From a European geographic perspective, the Middle Passage was the second, or middle, leg of the triangular voyage between Europe, Africa, and the Americas. This was the notorious cross-Atlantic journey during which hundreds of slaves were confined in irons below deck in crowded, hot, unsanitary, and inhumane conditions. The chance of insurrection was greatest during the first few weeks of the Middle Passage. During this time most slaves were kept below deck, naked or only partially clothed with a loincloth, shackled in pairs, right leg to left leg. Nonetheless, slaves sometimes broke free of their chains and attacked the crew with a variety of tools and small weapons. Slave vessels were equipped with guns and cannons which were placed on the raised quarterdeck to fire down upon slaves escaping through the hatches. Occasionally, Africans in war canoes attacked slave vessels from shore. Researchers have documented more than 450 slave insurrections or shore-based attacks, and there were undoubtedly many more that went unrecorded. Occasionally, some captives would regain the shores of Africa. More often the crew regained control of the ship or Africans were reenslaved upon reaching shore. Uprisings were extremely violent, and sometimes many slaves and most crew were killed. When African captives gained control of the ship, they kept a few crew alive to navigate the vessel.

Ships' officers confined the men, women, boys, and girls in separate compartments. Slave vessels were fitted with numerous wooden platforms between decks to allow captains to pack in greater numbers of captives. As the between-deck space was generally from 1.2 m (4 ft.) to 1.8 m (6 ft.), platforms reduced the headroom for captives to only a few feet. All slaves suffered from numerous scrapes and bruises from lying on these bare planks. Captains claimed that when safely away from shore, slaves were given greater freedom of movement. Women and children, some claimed, were never shackled and were allowed to roam above deck with minimal supervision. Recently, however, archaeologists discovered many small-sized leg irons from the wreck of the slave ship *Henrietta Marie* (c. 1700) off Florida. Women may have been separated from male slaves and given greater freedom of movement to increase the crews' sexual exploitation of them.

Cooks prepared meals of fish, beans, or yams in large copper vats below deck. Surgeons sometimes assisted in the preparation and distribution of food. Slaves were given food at mid-morning and late afternoon in small bowls (or "pannikins"). Weather permitting, groups of African captives were exercised above deck (in their leg irons) in an attempt to offset the debilitating effects of the Middle Passage. Officers, usually boatswains, mates, and surgeons, were armed with whips such as the cat-o'-nine-tails and forced the African captives to dance. The crew's power was enforced through such torture devices as thumbscrews and iron collars. There were several tubs in each compartment below deck in which slaves could relieve themselves, though hindered by being shackled in pairs. Mates generally had the job of cleaning the slave compartments below deck, which each day would be covered with excrement, blood, and filth. Some captains frequently ordered the rooms washed and dried with fire pans, though sometimes the filth was simply scraped off the decks. To counteract the stench, which was thought to promote sickness, slave vessels were fumigated with vinegars, berries, limes, tars, and turpentines.

By any measurement, mortality rates of both slaves and crew were extraordinarily high on the Atlantic crossing. The crowded, unsanitary conditions below deck were an ideal disease environment for outbreaks of dysentery, the disease from which many slaves died. In addition to gastrointestinal diseases, Africans also died from dehydration, smallpox, or measles. Slaves who resisted captivity sometimes died from flogging or other forms of punishment. Some slaves committed suicide by jumping overboard or by starving or hanging themselves. The resistance to eating was so common that vessels carried metal devices to force-feed slaves. Sailors died mostly from malarial and yellow fevers, to which African-born peoples had some acquired immunities. Early in transatlantic slave trade about 15 to 20 percent of African captives died on the Passage. By the later eighteenth century about 5 to 10 percent died, a reduction perhaps caused by improvements in hygiene and sanitation. Slave mortality rose in the nineteenth century during years when the British navy tried to enforce an international ban on the slave trade. About 15 to 20 percent of the crew died on the triangular voyage and sailors died at rates often greater than for all other overseas trades combined. Slave mortality usually increased during the last stages of a particularly long passage when there were shortages of food and water.

The Atlantic crossing lasted three to five weeks from West African trading sites such as the Gambia, Senegal, and Sierra Leone rivers. Near the equator, in regions such as the Bight of Benin and the Bight of Biafra (near present-day Nigeria), the voyage to the Americas took several months. A few French ships transported slaves from Mozambique or Madagascar to the Mascarene Islands in the Indian Ocean and then returned to France via Saint-Domingue in the West Indies, where additional cargoes of captives from southeast Africa were disembarked. These voyages—via the Indian Ocean—were the most complex in the transatlantic slave trade and took several years to complete. In the nineteenth century passage time in the trade fell dramatically due to advances in shipbuilding and speed.

The Marketing of Enslaved Africans in the Americas

Upon arriving in the Americas, African captives who survived the Atlantic crossing were "refreshed" with water and colonial provisions (such as citrus fruit) and were shaved and cleaned. Ointments (to hide scars from diseases such as yaws) and oils were applied on their skin in preparation for sale. Agents placed advertisements in colonial gazettes and in taverns for the sale of African labor, which usually occurred a few weeks after arrival. Many sales occurred on ship deck; other sales took place on wharves or in agents' houses or slave pens. Some planters contracted with merchants to purchase a preset number of slaves. Many slaves were sold by "scramble" or by auction. During the scramble planters or their representatives placed ropes or handkerchiefs around groups of slaves whom they wanted to purchase. During auctions the highest-valued slaves, often adult men, were sold first; then, over several weeks or even months, less-valued slaves were sold. The last slaves sold were often old, sick, or debilitated Africans. Termed "refuse slaves," they usually were purchased by doctors or poor colonists. In some sales "prime" slaves were sold by scramble and "refuse" slaves were sold at public auction. Occasionally slave cargoes included family members or relatives, but separation during sale was almost inevitable. Cargoes also usually comprised Africans from different ethnic groups, as can be noted through ethnic scarification. Some planters purchased slaves from a variety of ethnic backgrounds as part of labor control; other planters purchased Africans from the same areas of Africa to maintain work force unity.

Ship captains and colonial agents sold slave cargoes to planters for bills of exchange, which often were resold for return cargoes of plantation produce. Slave vessels were not specialist "West Indiamen" (large produce vessels built for storage capacity), however, and transported only a fraction of the produce of the Americas back to Europe. By the mid-eighteenth century many slave vessels began returning to Europe with the planters' bills of exchange and only small cargoes of plantation produce. Thus though many slave vessels sailed on triangular voyages over the course of about a year, some did not carry on a triangular trade. An important exception to the concept of a triangular trade was the large Brazil-to-Angola shuttle trade, which dates from the 1680s. By the nineteenth century small Brazilian vessels, built for speed, sometimes made three or four slave voyages per year in this direct trade.

Abolition of the Transatlantic Slave Trade

After centuries of broad acceptance, in the mid-eighteenth century some religious leaders began to question the morality of enslaving and owning humans. They began a campaign, termed the abolition movement, to end slavery. Faced with overwhelming opposition of colonial and business groups, the "abolitionists" realized that the first step toward ending slavery would be to end the transatlantic slave trade. Attacking the British slave trade was vital: the British were the largest slave traders by the mid-1700s. The abolition of the British trade was a 20-year process: Parliament first regulated the trade, limiting the number of slaves British vessels could carry from Africa, then closed a number of colonies to slave imports, and then in 1807 passed legislation to abolish the trade itself in 1808. The size of the British trade highlights the important abolitionist triumph: during the previous decade 150 British slave vessels had sailed per year for the African coast to purchase more than 40,000 African men, women, and children.

Five years earlier, in 1802 the small Danish slave trade ended by a government order enacted in 1792. The U.S. slave trade—centered in Rhode Island—was outlawed in 1807, the first year Congress could address the question of abolition, as agreed to by the compromise between northern and southern states writing the Constitution in 1787. (Abolition of the U.S. slave trade went into effect in 1808.) The French slave trade ended temporarily in the early 1790s after the slave revolution in the largest French colony, Saint-Domingue, removed the principal French slave market, and then the French government abolished slavery throughout French colonies in 1793–1794. With the ending of the Napoleonic Wars in 1814–1815, British diplomats attempted to end the international slave trade. The Dutch trade, which largely ended during the late eighteenth-century warfare with France, was abolished by decree in 1814. The restored, conservative French monarchy, however, did not agree to end French participation in the slave trade. French vessels continued to ship slaves to Martinique, Guadeloupe, and Cayenne (in present-day French Guiana), and the French government did not abolish slavery in French colonies until 1848. The French trade, however, had effectively ended by 1831 after a political revolution in the country.

After 1815 the transatlantic slave trade centered on the expanding sugar and coffee colonies of Brazil and Cuba. British diplomats continued to negotiate for a total ban on the slave trade, and British naval ships cruised the African coast to capture illegal slave ships. By the 1820s most slave voyages originated in the West Indies or Brazil. To avoid British confiscation, "flags of convenience" were carried on board. Many European- or American-owned slave vessels sailed under Spanish-Cuban registration. British naval pressure and changing Brazilian attitudes about the slave trade led to government measures that effectively ended the trade by the early 1850s. The remaining market of Cuba experienced a short-term increase in slave imports from 1853 to 1860 as slave and sugar prices rose. Prices fell in the 1860s, and by 1867 British, Spanish, and U.S. authorities were able to end the direct slave trade from Africa to Cuba.

Long-term Trends and Impacts of the Transatlantic Slave Trade

The slave trade undoubtedly increased the incidence of warfare and slave raiding among many African societies. Moreover, as about two-thirds of the captive Africans were men between ages 18 and 30, the slave trade likely removed essential workers and soldiers. In response to renewed external threats, villages may have been abandoned as they consolidated with other communities for protection. In certain areas the slave trade altered the ratio of men to women and adults to children, thus prompting further social changes, particularly in kinship structure and marriage patterns. The incidence of slavery increased in Africa during the slave trade era and increased again in the immediate aftermath of abolition, when external demand for slaves ended rather suddenly.

In the Americas the slave trade ensured that, for three centuries, the subtropical areas remained the focal point of New World economic activity. It also ensured a much more complex social milieu and cultural environment than would have been possible without contacts with Africa. With all of its horrors and inhumanity, the transatlantic slave trade was critical in the formation of the modern world.

Cross Cultural

Trans-Saharan and Red Sea Slave Trade,

traffic in African slaves across the Sahara and the Red Sea for export, mainly to Arabia and South Asia.

The trans-Saharan and Red Sea slave trades both date back several millennia. Ancient Egyptians, as well as Romans, Arabs, Turks, and Europeans, all drew slaves from the Nile Valley, particularly Nubia. But little is known about slave trades in and from Africa prior to the spread of Islam across North Africa beginning in the seventh century C.E.

Because many of the Arab, and later Berber, slave traffickers in North Africa were Muslim, and because they were supplying slaves primarily to Islamic societies in Arabia and South Asia, scholars often refer to the trans-Saharan and Red Sea commerce as the "Islamic Slave Trade." This is a misnomer, however, because the demand for slave labor and the role of slaves in the host societies predate the rise of Islam.

Compared to the transatlantic slave trade, slaving in the Sahara and

North Africa was always far less institutionalized, and most of the traders operated on a relatively small scale. The lack of written records combined with the huge time span of the commerce make it extremely difficult to estimate how many slaves were exported from the continent via these trade networks or how many died en route. Some scholars suggest that since about 1500 C.E., approximately 4 million slaves traveled along trans-Saharan routes while another 2 million people were sold into slavery by way of the Red Sea.

The trans-Saharan and Red Sea slave trades were also distinctive because approximately two-thirds of the slaves exported on these routes were female, destined to serve as concubines and domestic servants in Arabia and South Asia. In contrast, demand for cheap plantation labor in the Americas created the need for the high proportion of male slaves who were shipped across the Atlantic.

Along with items such as salt, gold, and ivory, slaves were among the few commodities considered valuable enough to merit risky, long-distance journeys by camel caravan across the Sahara, or on foot in the Horn of Africa. Trans-Saharan traders procured slaves taken primarily from the savanna and forest zones of West Africa, while slaves bound for the Red Sea came mostly from the Nile Valley, the Horn of Africa, and, to a lesser extent, the East African coast. Traders exchanged luxury items such as Indian cotton, perfumes, spices, and horses for slaves sold either by other merchants, based in market towns such as Tombouctou (Timbuktu) (in present-day Mali) or Darfur (in present-day Sudan), or by local rulers, who acquired slaves through raids, warfare, or tributes.

Once purchased, slaves typically traveled on foot, and many had to assist with daily chores en route. The routes they took shifted over time, partly due to the rise and fall of medieval savanna empires such as ancient Mali and Songhai. From Darfur one of the main routes was the Darb al-Arbain (Forty Day Road) to Asyut in Egypt. Mortality rates, not surprisingly, were high.

Upon their arrival in Mediterranean port cities such as Tunis and Tripoli, or Red Sea towns such as Sawakan, slaves were sold in marketplaces where overseers monitored exchanges between brokers and buyers. After the eighth century Islamic principles defined many of the rules of commerce: children under the age of seven could not be separated from their mothers, for example, and Muslim slaves could not be sold to non-Muslims. Buyers were also allowed a three-day trial period to inspect the constitution and health of the slave they had purchased. Women sold as concubines or into harems were often held in escrow by a third party until menstruation proved that they were not pregnant.

Although many slaves stayed on the African continent—especially men used in the armies of North Africa and Egypt—most boarded ships bound for the eastern Mediterranean, the Arabian Peninsula, the Persian Gulf, or India. Africa became an increasingly important source for slaves in Arabia and South Asia as more traditional sources from northern and central Europe were depleted during the twelfth century. Beginning in about the fourteenth century, slaves were also shipped to Italy and other European destinations. In addition to using female slaves for concubinage or domestic service, these buyers used male slaves as low-ranking soldiers or manual laborers on plantations or in cities. A relatively small number of male slaves were castrated; they served as eunuchs, often rising to positions of wealth and power because they were entrusted with important financial and political transactions.

Many scholars have noted the absence of a distinct African population in contemporary southwest Asia, suggesting that the majority of slaves, particularly women who served as concubines, became integrated into the host societies, most often under Muslim law. Male slaves were also circumcised and given Muslim names. Upon bearing a son to their owner, concubines could not be sold or given away. Furthermore, concubines were liberated upon their owner's death, and the child was considered a free individual. Many other slaves were probably manumitted after working a nine-year period, after which many pious Muslims felt that the slaves had worked sufficiently to have earned their freedom.

The trans-Saharan and Red Sea slave trades began to taper off as the abolitionist movement, particularly in England, gained momentum. The abolitionists imposed their political will on slavers through the administrations of newly established European colonies in North and West Africa, beginning with French-controlled Algeria in 1830. As late as 1910, however, slaves were secretly being moved from Tibesti (northern Chad) to the Libyan port city of Benghazi. Demand for African slaves in the Middle East has still not disappeared, particularly as the region has grown wealthy from its oil resources. Although Middle Eastern countries abolished slavery when they entered the League of Nations in the 1920s, a minor underground trade in slaves probably still exists.

Latin America and the Caribbean

Trinidad and Tobago,

a country consisting of two islands roughly 35 km (22 mi.) apart; the southernmost of the Windward Caribbean islands, Trinidad and Tobago lie just northeast of Venezuela.

Trinidad and Tobago is often celebrated as the birthplace of calypso, the famous Caribbean musical form that has spread across the world. The words to one popular calypso song praise another of the country's distinctive legacies: its ethnic diversity.

While these lyrics may idealize the country's racial harmony, the fact remains that Trinidad and Tobago is one of the most diverse Caribbean nations. Some of this diversity can be traced to the country's colonial origins. Tobago changed hands 22 times between 1626 and 1814. Trinidad place names in English, Spanish, French, Hindi, and native Carib Indian reflect the

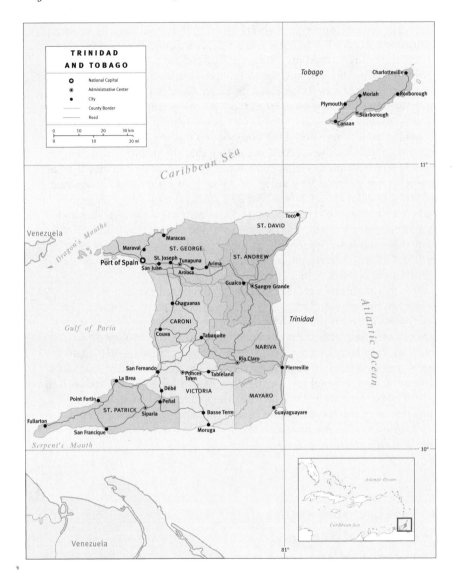

shifts in the island's population. Today more than 80 percent of Trinidadians and Tobagians are the descendants of either African slaves or East Indian indentured servants; this large segment of the population comprises nearly equal numbers of blacks and East Indians. The country's greatest challenge for the next century is uniting them in a common vision for a shared future.

Trinidad and Tobago are the southernmost islands in the Lesser Antilles chain and are only 16 km (10 mi.) off the northern coast of South America. Trinidad lies within sight of the Venezuelan coast. Because the island was originally part of the South American subcontinent, its flora, fauna, and natural resources resemble those of South America much more than they do those of other Caribbean islands. As a result of the country's affinity to South America, settlement patterns, agriculture, and industry all developed differently in Trinidad and Tobago than they did in many other Caribbean countries. Like those of most other Caribbean islands, however, Trinidad and Tobago's earliest populations were South American indigenous groups gradually migrating north from the South American continent.

Trinidad and Tobago's first inhabitants were Ienian Arawaks. Like the Taínan Arawaks who flourished on other Caribbean islands, the Ienian Arawaks were primarily fishers and farmers. They named Trinidad Lere, or "land of the hummingbirds." The next arrivals on Trinidad and Tobago were the Carib, who quickly outnumbered the Arawaks on Tobago. On Trinidad the Arawaks and the Caribs were able to coexist for a longer period of time. These groups occupied the islands when they were invaded by Christopher Columbus's crew in 1498.

Trinidadians and Tobagians are fortunate in that the oil industry has afforded them the highest standard of living in the Caribbean, and while that industry is not immune to recessions and downswings, it still promises to be a reliable backbone for the country for years to come. Like many Commonwealth Caribbean nations, Trinidad and Tobago has a national passion for cricket, and Trinidad and Tobago's contributions to literature, drama, and music are a crucial part of the country's cultural heritage. Many of the Caribbean's most celebrated writers, such as C. L. R. James, V. S. Naipaul, and Samuel Selvon, are from Trinidad. Nobel Laureate Derek Walcott lived in Trinidad for years, and while there he founded the Trinidad Theatre Workshop. The country is also well known for its popular music and cultural celebrations. Calypso and steelpan both originated in Trinidad, and the annual Carnival festival is one of the largest such celebrations in the world and attracts thousands of visitors from outside the country each year. These cultural resources help unify all Trinidadians and Tobagians; common celebrations and traditions in the "land of steelpan" strengthen the cherished brotherhood and sisterhood that are idealized in the calypso song.

North America

Truth, Sojourner

(b. 1797?, Ulster County, N.Y.; d. November 26, 1883, Battle Creek, Mich.), African American abolitionist, women's rights advocate, and religious visionary.

Sojourner Truth was one of the best-known black women of her time, rivaled only by Harriet Tubman, yet her life remains surrounded by mystery. Truth, who was illiterate, left no written record apart from her autobiographical *Narrative of Sojourner Truth*, dictated to Olive Gilbert in the late 1840s. Much of what we know about her was reported or perhaps invented by others. More so than Frederick Douglass, her prolifically autobiographical contemporary, Truth has been transformed into myth. Feminists emphasize her challenge to restrictive Victorian codes of femininity; Marxist historians proclaim her solidarity with the working class. Her spirit has been invoked on American college campuses in struggles to create African American and women's studies programs.

In their writings both Harriet Beecher Stowe and Douglass recount a central illustration of Truth's faith, which occurred at a protest gathering in Boston's Faneuil Hall after the passage of the Fugitive Slave Act of 1850. Truth sat in the front row, listening to Douglass speak. Events had led him to abandon the nonviolent approach of moral suasion, and he exhorted Southern slaves to take up arms and free themselves. Truth accepted his frustration, but not his loss of faith in God's justice. In a voice that carried throughout the hall, she asked a single question: "Frederick, is God dead?"

By Truth's own account this empowering faith came to her in a moment of divine inspiration after long and traumatic experiences under slavery, which included beatings by her master, John Dumont, and, according to Truth's biographer, Nell Irvin Painter, sexual abuse by his wife. Religion lay at the heart of Truth's transformation from victimized slave to powerful and charismatic leader. Her decision to take the name Sojourner Truth was, in fact, the culmination of a long process of self-remaking.

Born around 1797 in Ulster County, New York, 133 km (80 mi.) north of New York City, she was the next to youngest of 10 or 12 children, and her parents, James and Elizabeth Baumfree, named her Isabella. Her slave parents were Dutch speaking, and Isabella first spoke Dutch. Isabella belonged to a series of slave owners, including, from 1810 to 1827, Dumont. When Isabella was about 14, she married Thomas, an older slave owned by Dumont. Between about 1815 and 1826 they had four children, Diana, Peter, Elizabeth, and Sophia, and perhaps a fifth who died.

During 1826 and 1827 Isabella had a series of life-changing experiences. After her son, Peter, was illegally sold and taken to Alabama, she successfully sued for his return with the help of local Quakers.

When New York abolished slavery in 1827, Isabella gained her freedom and traveled to New York City, taking Peter and leaving her daughters with their father. In the city Isabella did housework for a living and attended both the African Methodist Episcopal Zion Church and a white Methodist church. She also began preaching at camp meetings, honing her oratorical skills and learning how to hold an audience. She became a follower of the self-proclaimed white prophet Matthias (Robert Matthews), joining his messianic commune from 1832 until its dissolution in scandal three years later. Little is known of the next several years of her life, although she evidently came under the influence of the Millerites, followers of William Miller, who calculated from biblical prophecies that the world would end in 1843.

In that year Isabella made a complete break with her past, took the name she believed that God had given her—Sojourner Truth—and preached at Millerite gatherings in New York, Connecticut, and Massachusetts. By December, however, with the Millerite prophecy unfulfilled, she joined the Northampton Association, a white utopian community in Florence, Massachusetts. This community, embracing the most advanced ideas of social reform, opened new vistas for Truth. It was there that she first met Douglass and William Lloyd Garrison, and began speaking on social reform as well as religious salvation. Although the Northampton Association broke up in 1846, Truth remained in Florence until she moved ten years later to live among spiritualist Progressive Friends in Battle Creek, Michigan, a Seventh-day Adventist community.

Truth insisted on the need to include black and working women in any vision of social reform, grounding her speeches in her own experience as a black woman and former slave. She earned a reputation for oratorical power and a ready wit, as seen in the best-known speech of her career, delivered at an 1851 women's rights convention in Akron, Ohio.

In Gage's memorable retelling, Truth punctuated her speech again and again with the emphatic question, "And ain't I a woman?" Scholars have come to doubt the accuracy of Gage's account, which was published 12 years after the event in question. Gage portrayed Truth facing down a hostile crowd dominated by male skeptics of women's rights and female advocates of sharply distinct gender roles. American scholar Nell Painter argues that this verbal confrontation was Gage's own dramatic invention. In rendering Truth's words, Gage employed a nearly unreadable dialect that reflected contemporary literary conventions about black speech far more than it did Truth's own voice. And Painter believes that Truth probably never uttered the line that has become central to her historical image.

Although her subsequent career is less widely known, Truth continued her reform activism. During the Civil War she journeyed to Washington, D.C., and met President Abraham Lincoln. From 1864 to 1868 she worked with the private National Freedmen's Relief Association and the federal Freedmen's Bureau, assisting freed slaves. In the 1870s Truth participated in the American Woman Suffrage Association. She also championed a proposal to allot Kansas lands to destitute former slaves, making her last major speaking tour in a fruitless effort to rally support. When thousands of southern blacks, known as the Exodusters, actually moved to Kansas in 1879, Truth applauded them and offered her assistance. She returned from Kansas in 1880 and lived with her daughters in Battle Creek until her death.

North America

Tubman, Harriet Ross

(b. 1820?, Dorchester County, Md.; d. March 10, 1913, Auburn, N.Y.), African American abolitionist who escaped from slavery and returned repeatedly to the South to lead other slaves to freedom.

Slave Life

Harriet Tubman was born on Maryland's eastern shore, one of 11 children of Harriet Greene and Benjamin Ross, both slaves. As a child she was called Araminta but later defiantly took her mother's first name. (Slaves were often forbidden to form such public attachments.) At a young age Tubman worked in her owner's house as well as in other households to which she was rented. As a teenager she worked in the fields, gaining strength and endurance. Still in her teens, she shielded a slave who was fleeing his owner. The owner hurled a two-pound weight at the runaway that missed and struck Tubman on the head, nearly killing her. For the rest of her life she was prone to sudden sleeping spells, dizziness, and headaches, and bore a deep gash.

In 1844 she married John Tubman, a free black man. Shortly after their marriage, she hired a lawyer to trace her mother's history as a slave. The lawyer discovered records showing that her mother had been briefly free because an earlier owner had died without making provision for her. Apparently, nobody told Harriet Greene that she was free, and a short while later she was returned to slavery. This discovery haunted Tubman. When Tubman's owner died in 1849, she feared that she and members of her family would be sold to the horrible conditions of the Deep South. Resolved to escape, she tried to convince her husband to join her, but he refused. She fled without him, traveling at night and hiding by day until she came to Pennsylvania, a free state.

The Underground Railroad

Tubman went to Philadelphia, where she cleaned and cooked for a living, saving her earnings for a return trip south to bring out other members of her family. In 1850 she made her first covert trip to Baltimore, where she rescued her enslaved sister and two children. Tubman soon became allied with black leader William Still of Philadelphia, white Quaker Thomas Garrett of Wilmington, Delaware, and other activists of the Underground Railroad. The Railroad was a loose network of abolitionists who arranged for the safe travel from South to North of fugitive slaves, and Tubman became its most successful conductor. In at least 15 trips to the South between 1850 and 1860, she guided more than 200 men, women, and children to freedom, including her own entire family. In 1857 she made perhaps her most remarkable journey, returning to the North with her aging parents.

After Congress passed the Fugitive Slave Act of 1850, which required Northern states to return escaped slaves, Tubman settled runaways in Canada, in what is now Ontario. She lived intermittently in Canada, settling with her parents in Auburn, New York, in the late 1850s.

After the Railroad

As Tubman's reputation grew (she was known among blacks and Northern whites as "Moses"), she gained the support and friendship of the day's leading progressives, including Ralph Waldo Emerson, Sojourner Truth, and Susan B. Anthony. Another supporter, William Seward, the New York senator and U.S. secretary of state, sold Tubman the land for her Auburn home on generous terms.

During the Civil War, Northern officials asked Tubman to help the Union Army. She traveled to South Carolina, where she served as liaison between the army and newly freed blacks, whom she schooled in self-suffi-ciency. Tubman also nursed wounded soldiers, organized and trained scouts, and helped lead a raid against Confederate troops. Although she received commendation from officers, she received no pay. After the war Tubman returned to Auburn to care for her parents. Prominent friends tried for two decades to convince the government to give Tubman a pension for her wartime services; failing this, they succeeded in 1890 in gaining her a small veteran's pension as Davis's widow. Tubman spent many of her later years working on behalf of woman suffrage.

Africa

Tunisia,
country in the northwest of Africa.

Tunisia has often been described as an oasis in the desert. The metaphor refers both to the country's natural beauty, which attracts thousands of tourists, and to its political and social climate. Tunisia has promoted itself as a secular, progressive oasis in North Africa, a haven from the troubles of the rest of the Arab world. Indeed, the country has been on the vanguard of Western-inspired reform since the nineteenth century. Yet with growing populist support within the nation for an Islamic party, it is worth noting that Tunisia has never really been isolated from its North African neigh-bors—neighbors with whom it shares the religion of Islam, and the legacy of Phoenician, Roman, Arab, and European conquest.

Africa

Tunisia (Ready Reference)
Official Name: Republic of Tunisia
Area: 163,610 sq km (63,170 sq mi.)
Location: Northern Africa, bordering the Mediterranean Sea, Algeria, and Libya
Capital: Tunis (population 674,100 [1994 estimate])
Other Major Cities: Safaqis (Sfax) (population 230,900), Susah (Sousse) (125,000), Bizerte (Bizerta) (98,900) (1994 estimates)
Population: 9,378,000 (1998 estimate)
Population Density: 92 persons per sq km (about 148 persons per sq mi.); about 75 percent of the population live in the coastal region
Population Below Age 15: 32 percent (male 1,541,853; female 1,451,035 [1997 estimate])
Population Growth Rate: 1.4 percent (1998 estimate)
Life Expectancy at Birth: Total population: 73.1 years (male 71.72 years; female 74.58 years [1998 estimate])

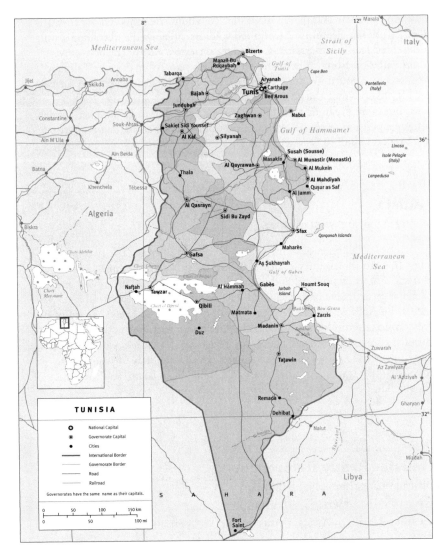

Infant Mortality Rate: 32.64 deaths per 1,000 live births (1998 estimate)

Literacy Rate (age 15 and over who can read and write): Total population: 66.7 percent (male 78.6 percent; female 54.6 percent [1995 estimate])

Education: Education in Tunisia is free, and virtually all eligible children attend primary school. In the early 1990s primary schools had a total enrollment of about 1.4 million pupils, and secondary, technical, and vocational schools, about 567,000.

Languages: Arabic is the official language of Tunisia, but French is used widely, particularly by the educated.

Ethnic groups: Arab-Berber 98 percent, European 1 percent, Jewish 1 percent

Religions: Muslim 98 percent, Christian 1 percent, Jewish 1 percent

Climate: A mild Mediterranean climate prevails in the north of Tunisia, with temperatures averaging 8.9° C (48° F) in January and 25.6° C (78° F) in July; the northern regions have a rainy season that lasts from October to May, with an average annual rainfall of 610 mm (about 24 in.). Toward the south the climate becomes progressively hotter and drier, with an annual rainfall of about 200 mm (about 8 in.) in the Sahara.

Land, Plants, and Animals: In the north low-lying spurs of the Maritime Atlas Mountains traverse the country, interspersed with fertile valleys and plains. The country's only major river, the Majardah, crosses the region from west to east, emptying into the Gulf of Tunis. To the south a plateau descends gradually to a chain of low-lying salt lakes, known as shatts, or chotts. On the south the shatts adjoin the Sahara, which constitutes about 40 percent of Tunisia's land area. The regions of the north are characterized by flourishing vineyards and by dense forests of cork oak, pine, and juniper trees. In the extreme south date palms flourish in oases. Among the wildlife are hyena, wild boar, jackal, gazelle, and hare, as well as several varieties of poisonous snakes, including cobras and horned vipers.

Natural Resources: Petroleum, phosphates, iron ore, lead, zinc, and salt

Currency: The Tunisian dinar

Gross Domestic Product (GDP): $56.5 billion (1997 estimate)

GDP per Capita: $6,100 (1997 estimate)

GDP Real Growth Rate: 5.6 percent (1997 estimate)

Primary Economic Activities: The Tunisian economy is dominated by agriculture and mining. Tourism is also important, and manufacturing is expanding.

Primary Crops: Wheat, barley, tomatoes, vegetables, melons, grapes, oranges, olives, and dates; sheep, goats, cattle, camels, horses, and poultry; sardines, pilchards, tuna, and whitefish

Industries: Petroleum, mining, tourism, textiles, footwear, food, and beverages

Primary Exports: Hydrocarbons, agricultural products, phosphates, and chemicals

Primary Imports: Industrial goods and equipment, hydrocarbons, food, and consumer goods

Primary Trade Partners: European Union countries, Middle East, Algeria, India, United States, Japan, and Switzerland

Government: According to the constitution of 1959 Tunisia is a free, inde-pendent, and sovereign republic. National executive power in Tunisia is exer-cised by the president, currently Zine El Abidine Ben Ali, who appoints a council of ministers headed by a prime minister, currently Hamed Karoui. Legislative power in Tunisia is vested in the unicameral National Assembly, with 163 members popularly elected to five-year terms. The National Assembly is currently dominated by the Constitutional Democratic Rally

Party (RCD; formerly the Destour Socialist Party). Tunisia is divided into 23 governorates, each headed by a governor who is appointed by the president.

Turks and Caicos Islands,
two groups of islands in the North Atlantic Ocean, southeast of the Bahamas.

There is still discussion over who first sighted the islands; some scholars believe it was Ponce de Leon in 1512, while others claim the Turks were actually the site of Christopher Columbus's first landing in the New World in 1492. It is clear, however, that during the next 150 years the Spanish returned to the islands just long enough to capture the Lucayans who lived there and sell them into slavery in other Spanish holdings in the Caribbean. The name "Caicos" is one of the Lucayans' lasting legacies, since it comes from their word *caya hico*, or "string of islands." The name "Turks" refers to an indigenous cactus that the colonists thought resembled a Turkish fez.

In 1678 English settlers from Bermuda began mining the salt flats in the Turks and Caicos Islands, bringing African slaves with them to do the miserable work. Salt immediately proved extremely profitable, and soon the British, Spanish, and French were fighting over the right to control the islands. Each group primarily used black slaves to carry out the mining. Cotton and sisal plantations were also established in the islands, but when

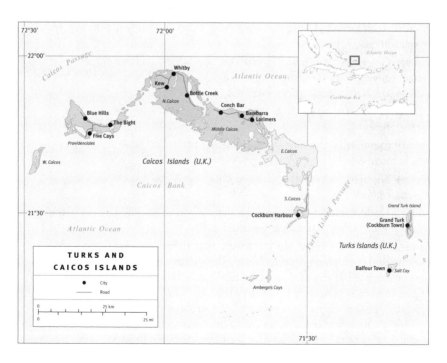

the soil proved too thin to support them for very long, the focus returned to the salt flats. By 1776 the Turks and Caicos Islands were officially declared part of the British Bahamian colony.

For much of the twentieth century there was a serious push by many islanders to have their country annexed to Canada; in the mid-1970s the question was considered in the Canadian Parliament. Canada ultimately declined because of fears of racial tensions between black islanders and the white Canadian majority, but in the mid-1980s 90 percent of Turks and Caicos residents continued to support association with Canada. In 1985 a major corruption scandal hit the islands when the chief minister, the minister of commerce and development, and another member of the Legislative Council were all arrested in the United States for drug trafficking. This did little to instill confidence in the Turks and Caicos Islands' own government.

But in the 1990s economic conditions were slowly improving, and were helping to stabilize the country. It was not until the 1960s that the salt industry, formerly the mainstay of the economy, finally collapsed, after international competition proved too much for the islands' unprofitable production techniques. Like many other Caribbean countries, the Turks and Caicos Islands then turned to tourism. Many Turks and Caicos Islanders have left the island seeking higher education or employment. But as tourism develops, poor immigrants from neighboring islands have begun coming to the Turks and Caicos Islands in search of jobs. Offshore banking has also brought new jobs to the islands. As a result of these developments the population has fluctuated several times over the last few decades as the ratio of immigrants to emigrants continues to shift. These changes are still in progress, and they will shape the course of the Turks and Caicos Islands for the next century.

North America

Turner, Nat

(b. October 2, 1800 Southampton, Va.; d. November 11, 1831 Southampton, Va.), African American slave who led the largest and most significant slave revolt in U.S. history.

Nat Turner was born on Benjamin Turner's plantation in Southampton County five days before the execution of the African American revolutionary Gabriel Prosser in Richmond, Virginia. Turner's father, whose name is unknown but who was also a Benjamin Turner slave, successfully escaped and is believed to have spent his life in the Great Dismal Swamp, which lies in southern Virginia and in North Carolina, with other escaped African Americans, as maroons.

Turner's mother, a slave named Nancy who was kidnapped from Africa in 1793, believed that he was destined for great things in his life, and she instilled this sense in him. That he acquired literacy in his boyhood added weight to his mother's convictions. Turner also accepted Christianity in his youth, became a preacher, and identified religion with freedom. He claimed to receive religious visions throughout his life.

Turner sought his own freedom, running away in 1821 after he had become the property of Benjamin Turner's son, Samuel. When Samuel Turner hired a harsh overseer, Nat Turner escaped, remaining free for approximately a month. During that time he experienced a vision indicating that he would lead a slave rebellion, and he returned to the plantation to await his signal to begin.

In February 1831, Turner, who was now at the home of Joseph Travis, believed that an eclipse of the sun signaled that the time had come for him to launch his rebellion.

Turner's rebellion lasted almost three days, killed 57 people, and resulted in the executions of more than 100 African American rebels. Some call this rebellion the First War, the Civil War being the second. Turner's rebellion was significant in that it was more violent than any other slave uprising and reshaped the debate over slavery in ways that led to the Civil War a generation later. The uprising intensified both the antislavery movement and the corresponding proslavery forces. It reinforced the notion held by some abolitionists that slaves would be willing to fight if outside forces organized and armed them. Proslavery forces began to endorse reducing the number of free blacks through colonization. Turner's rebellion also disproved the myth of the contented slave, and proved that African Americans would die to end slavery.

North America

Tuskegee University,

a historically black college in Tuskegee, Alabama, that was organized by Booker T. Washington to emphasize industrial education.

Although Tuskegee University was technically chartered by the Alabama state legislature to repay black voters for their support, its early history is almost synonymous with the name of its first administrator, nineteenth-century African American leader Booker T. Washington. Tuskegee's roots were in the post-Reconstruction era in the South, when higher educational opportunities for African Americans were still severely limited.

In February 1881 the Alabama legislature voted to set aside $2,000 a year to fund a state and normal school for blacks in Tuskegee. The trustees asked officials at several other black institutions to recommend someone to head the new school, and although they were implicitly asking for white candidates, Hampton Institute's president Samuel Chapman Armstrong suggested his black protégé, Washington. The trustees agreed to hire Washington as principal. He arrived in Tuskegee on June 24, 1881, and opened

Students at Tuskegee Institute in Tuskegee, Alabama, listen to a history lecture in 1902. In 1986, five years after its centennial, the school renamed itself Tuskegee University. *Corbis*

the Tuskegee Normal School in a shack adjacent to the black Methodist church on July 4. The first 30 students ranged in age from 16 to 40, and most were teachers hoping to further their own education.

Washington's most significant contribution was his strong belief in industrial education and training as the key to success for African Americans. Students were required to learn a trade and perform manual labor at the school, including making and laying the bricks for the buildings that became the first campus. Tuskegee's charter had mandated that tuition would be free for students who committed to teaching in Alabama public schools. The students' labor helped with financial costs, and Washington solicited much of the remaining funding from northern white philanthropists.

Tuskegee was incorporated as a private institution in 1892. Because social conventions would have prohibited white instructors from serving under a black principal, Tuskegee became the first black institution of higher learning with a black faculty. In 1896 the school hired a young teacher who would become famous—George Washington Carver, whose groundbreaking agricultural research received international recognition. Washington also became nationally accepted as a black leader during the 1890s, because many whites appreciated his accomodationist approach to race relations, and Tuskegee gained wide recognition and substantial funding.

Changes to the original industrial-training approach came gradually after Washington's death in 1915. Tuskegee awarded its first baccalaureate degree in 1925 and began its first college curriculum in 1927, with departments for business and teachers' and nurses' training. During World War II the U.S. Air Force established a flying school at Tuskegee that trained more than 900 black pilots known as the Tuskegee Airmen. Graduate programs in veterinary medicine, nursing, business, architecture, agriculture and home economics, education, and arts and sciences were eventually added. In the 1960s and 1970s Tuskegee became the first black college to be designated a Registered National Historic Landmark and a National Historic Site.

By the school's centennial in 1981, Tuskegee's campus included 150 buildings on 20.2 sq km (5,000 acres), and its endowment was approximately $22 million. Five years later the school changed its name to Tuskegee University. Today there are approximately 3,200 undergraduates enrolled at Tuskegee, and an additional 200 graduate students; the school offers 70 different degrees and has an especially strong engineering program.

Notable Tuskegee graduates include writer Ralph Ellison, who portrays a fictionalized version of the school and its "Founder" in his novel *Invisible Man*; Arthur W. Mitchell, the first black Democratic congressman; and actor/comedian Keenen Ivory Wayans. Tuskegee's 30,000 living alumni are professionals in communities across the country and across the world.

Africa

Tutu, Desmond Mpilo

(b. October 7, 1931, Klerksdorp, South Africa), former archbishop of the Anglican Church in South Africa, winner of the 1984 Nobel Peace Prize, and head of the Truth and Reconciliation Commission.

An outspoken critic of South Africa's apartheid system, Desmond Tutu became one of his country's most prominent symbols of resistance and hope, along with Nelson Mandela.

Tutu was raised in the Transvaal region. The son of a schoolteacher father, he walked miles each day to overcrowded and underequipped schools. The family was better off than most, however, and Tutu has described his childhood as happy. An attack of tuberculosis at age 14 kept Tutu out of school for nearly two years. While recuperating, he met Father Trevor Huddleston, a white Anglican priest known for his opposition to apartheid. Under Huddleston's influence, Tutu first became interested in the church, an interest that coexisted with his plans to become a teacher.

In 1954 he graduated from Bantu Normal College outside Pretoria and was certified as a teacher.

Tutu cut short his teaching career after the apartheid government passed the 1955 Bantu Education Act. The act effectively imposed a segregated and inferior educational system on black children. Tutu stayed at his position at Munsieville High School until his last class had graduated; then he resigned in 1958.

Now a family man—Tutu had married Leah Nomalizo Shenxane in 1955—he entered the seminary at Saint Peter's College in Rosettenville. In 1960 he graduated summa cum laude. He credited the Community of the Resurrection, the order that ran Saint Peter's, with his view that religious study "is authenticated and expressed in our dealings with our neighbor." It was a lesson he would take to his first posts as parish priest in two government-created townships. Tutu became known as a man of the people, treating his flock with warmth, humor, and love; he later wrote that "a good shepherd knows his sheep by name."

Advanced theological study at the University of London took Tutu away from South Africa in 1962, a time of increasing antiapartheid activism. While Tutu was then still relatively apolitical, it is clear that his time in England impressed upon him the depth of the injustices he and his countrymen faced at home. Along with his wife and the couple's four children, Tutu returned to South Africa in 1968 and became a lecturer at his alma mater, Saint Peter's College, which had recently become part of the Federal Theological Seminary. He witnessed the violent reprisals against black student protesters at nearby Fort Hare University, which at the time was the center of the Black Consciousness Movement led by Steve Biko.

Tutu spent another two years as a university lecturer in Lesotho, then returned with his family to England, where he became associate director of the Theological Educational Fund in London. His role as a leader in the antiapartheid struggle began in 1975, when he was elected to the position of dean of Johannesburg. Refusing to occupy the dean's residence, Tutu instead settled in the sprawling black township of Soweto, where a year later police massacred black schoolchildren who were protesting peacefully.

From 1976 to 1978 Tutu served as bishop of Lesotho. During this time Biko died in police custody, and Tutu gave the eulogy. He compared the martyred leader to Jesus Christ and prayed for black South Africans to find "a place in the sun in our own beloved country." In 1978 he returned to his own country to stay. For seven years he served as the general secretary of the South African Council of Churches, an organization known for its outspoken opposition to apartheid. The whole country was now Tutu's parish. At home, he worked tirelessly to free the country's many political prisoners; abroad, he called on the international community to use diplomatic and economic sanctions to pressure the apartheid regime.

In 1984 Tutu won the Nobel Peace Prize, and shortly thereafter he was named bishop of Johannesburg. Two years later Tutu became archbishop of Cape Town, where he continued to speak out against apartheid from a

Christian perspective. He once said, "If Christ returned to South Africa today he would almost certainly be detained under the present security laws, because of his concern for the poor, the hungry and the oppressed." In the decade after Tutu's appointment he saw most of his goals achieved; Mandela was released from prison in 1990 and in 1994 won the presidency in the country's first-ever democratic vote. In 1996 Tutu became chairman of the Truth and Reconciliation Commission (TRC), the body charged with investigating crimes committed during the apartheid era. During his three years as the TRC's chair, Tutu heard testmony from hundreds of perpetrators and victims—a duty that at times severely tested his skills as a peacemaker.

Uganda,

landlocked, equatorial East African country bordered by the Democratic Republic of the Congo, Rwanda, Tanzania, Kenya, and Sudan.

Uganda is a country of varied landscapes and extraordinary ethnic and linguistic diversity. Nilotic and central Sudanic speakers originally made their homes in the savannas of the north, while Bantu speakers settled the fertile lands in the south. While the British colonial administration used ethnic antagonisms to keep the population divided, the animosities between kingdoms and regions existed well before European intervention. The political, economic, and social significance of ethnic identities has changed over time, but ethnic antagonisms remain a formidable obstacle to the development of a national identity and a nonethnic political culture in independent Uganda.

The country has also played host to large numbers of immigrants and refugees. In addition to the colonial-era arrival of Asians, initially brought to build the railroads and later expelled by Idi Amin in 1972, large numbers of Kenyan Luo moved to Uganda in the last century, many of whom were also expelled by another Ugandan dictator, Milton Obote. Long torn by state-sponsored violence, Uganda enjoyed relative peace during the term of President Yoweri Museveni although it did receive thousands of Rwandan, Congolese, and Sudanese refugees fleeing violent conflicts in their own countries. Uganda's recent economic growth has drawn praise from the international community, though the future of this growth will depend at least partly on political events in what remains a highly unstable region.

This family lives in a displaced person's camp in northern Uganda. *CORBIS/Liba Taylor*

Africa

Uganda (Ready Reference)

Official Name: Republic of Uganda

Area: 241,139 sq km (93,104 sq mi)

Location: Eastern Africa, borders Kenya, Rwanda, Sudan, Tanzania, Democratic Republic of the Congo

Capital: Kampala (population 773, 463 [1991 estimates])

Other Major Cities: Jinja (population 60,979), Mbale (53,634), Gulu (42,841), Entebbe (41,638), Soroti (40,602), Mbarara (40,383) (1991 estimates)

Population: 22,167,195 (1998 estimate)

Population Density: 155 persons per sq km (about 250 persons per sq mi.)

Population Below Age 15: 51 percent (male 5,157,818; female 5,199,080 [1998 estimate])

Population Growth Rate: 2.85 percent (1998 estimate)

Total Fertility Rate: 7.09 children born per woman (1998 estimate)

Life Expectancy at Birth: Total population: 42.6 years (male 41.81 years; female 43.41 years [1998 estimate])

Infant Mortality Rate: 92.86 deaths per 1000 live births (1998 estimate)

Literacy Rate (age 15 and over who can read and write): Total population: 61.8 percent (male 73.7 percent; female 50.2 percent [1995 estimate])

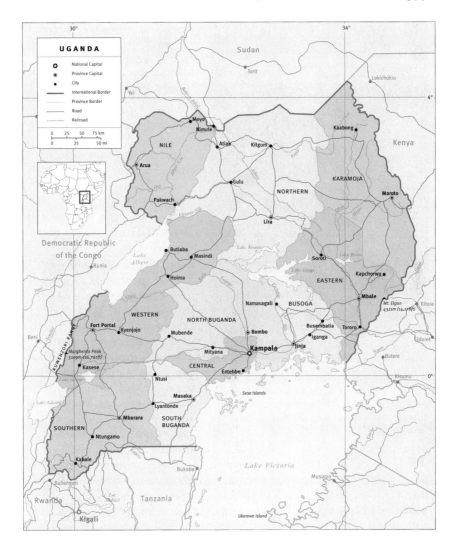

Education: The British educational system has been influential in Uganda, and missionary schools have played an important role in educating the people. In the late 1980s about 2.6 million pupils attended some 7900 primary schools in Uganda, and some 240,000 students were enrolled in more than 900 secondary, technical, and teacher-training schools. Makerere University in Kampala has historically been one of the top universities.

Languages: English, the official language, and Swahili, the language of commerce, are both widely spoken. About two-thirds of the people also speak one of several Bantu or Nilotic languages.

Ethnic Groups: About two-thirds of the people are included in the Ganda, Soga, Nyoro, Nkole, and Toro ethnic groups. The Acholi, Lango, and Karimojon ethnic groups predominate in the north.

A Ugandan copper miner rests. Rich in copper and other minerals, Uganda's natural resources were part of its appeal for such colonizers as Great Britain and Germany. *CORBIS/Hulton-Deutsch Collection*

Religions: About 60 percent of Uganda's inhabitants are Christian; approximately 5 percent are Muslim; others follow traditional religions.

Climate: Uganda's climate is mild and equable, mainly because of relatively high altitude. Temperature ranges from about 16° to 29° C (60° to 85° F). The average annual rainfall varies from some 760 mm (30 in.) in the northeast to about 1520 mm (60 in.) near Lake Victoria.

Land, Plants, and Animals: The area of Uganda includes Lake George and Lake Kyoga; parts of Lake Victoria, Lake Edward, and Lake Albert; and the Nile River from its outlet at Lake Victoria to Nimule on the Sudan frontier. The landscape is varied, with elevated plains, vast forests, low swamps, arid depressions, and snow-capped peaks, the highest of which is Margherita Peak (5,109 m/ 16,762 ft) in the Ruwenzori Range. Much of the south is forested, and most of the north is covered with savanna. Plant life includes mvuli tree and elephant grass of the Uganda plateau to the dry thorn scrub, acacia, and euphorbia of the southwest. Animals include chimpanzees, antelope (including the eland and hartebeest), elephants, rhinoceroses, lions, and leopard.

Natural Resources: Soil, gold, copper, tin, tungsten, and hydro-electricity potential

Currency: Ugandan shilling (USh)

Gross Domestic Product (GDP): $34.6 billion (1997 estimate)

GDP per Capita: $1,700 (1997 estimate)

GDP Real Growth Rate: 5 percent (1997 estimate)

Primary Economic Activities: Agriculture, industry, and services

Primary Exports: Coffee, cotton, and tea

Primary Imports: Petroleum products, machinery, textiles, metals, transportation equipment, and food

Primary Trading Partners: United States, European Union, and Kenya

Government: Uganda is a republic with a modified parliamentary system.

The 1995 constitution officially prohibited political parties until the year 2000, but allowed for nonparty presidential and legislative elections in 1996. Lieut. Gen. Yoweri Museveni, in power since a coup in 1985, won that presidential election by a wide margin; his appointed prime minister is Kintu Musoke.

Latin America and the Caribbean

Umbanda,

a religion practiced by millions of Brazilians that combines elements of African religious traditions with Roman Catholicism and European Spiritism.

Brazil is known for the vitality and diversity of its African-based religions, and of these Umbanda is the most widely practiced, with an estimated 20 million followers. Unlike Candomblé, whose fame is linked to the efforts of its leaders to reproduce faithfully the rituals and practices of its West African forbears, Umbanda represents a tendency toward eclecticism: diverse African traditions have blended with one another, with Roman Catholicism, and with Spiritism, a form of Spiritualism known in Brazil as *Espiritismo* or *Kardecismo*.

Like its rituals, whose roots lie in religions practiced by African slaves and overlain with other religious influences encountered in its Brazilian environment, Umbanda's popularity has moved far beyond the Afro-Brazilian population from which it derives. Its followers today are racially and ethnically diverse, ranging from Afro-Brazilian to Portuguese, Spanish, Italian, German, Lebanese, and Japanese, and are drawn from every economic level, from the wealthy elite to the poorest residents of shanty towns. Umbanda's membership has come to reflect the diversity of Brazil's population, and the faith is often viewed as a "Brazilian" rather than an "African" religion. Characteristically, many (though not all) practitioners also consider themselves Catholics. While some emphasize Umbanda's Spiritist dimensions, others defend its African identity and practices.

Umbanda shares with other Afro-Brazilian religions and Spiritism the understanding that a wide variety of deities and spirits may intervene in the daily lives of humans to help or to harm them. Through Umbanda rituals, followers pay homage to these entities, seek their protection, and solicit their help in resolving individual illnesses and personal problems. Umbanda is understood as a pragmatic and instrumental problem-solving religion.

At public ceremonies held each week in thousands of Umbanda churches (known as *centros* or *terreiros*), initiates and members of the congregation gather to celebrate Umbanda deities and spirits. They praise them with hymns, dancing, drumming, and hand clapping and call them to descend from the spirit world, take over or "possess" the bodies of trained initiates and, acting through them, conduct healing rituals and give advice. Members of the congregation then have individual consultations with the spirit counselors, receive ritual cleansings, and may discuss their problems. People confide in the spirits about their health, employment, finances, and family and romantic problems; the spirits may recommend further ritual treatments, give practical advice, or inform clients that they can recover only by undergoing initiation into Umbanda. This is a particularly common diagnosis when clients experience spontaneous spirit possession while watching the ceremony or during their consultation, and it is the most common route through which clients become initiated into ritual roles. New initiates undergo stages of initiation as well as training sessions in mastering spirit possession. But this process is less time consuming and less costly than in Candomblé, and new initiates may rise rapidly within the ritual hierarchy. Within a few years they may gain sufficient knowledge, prestige, and authority to found their own centro.

The most powerful spiritual personages of Umbanda are African deities known by the Yoruban term *orixá* (the same deities found in Candomblé). Each orixá is syncretized, or strongly identified with, a particular Roman Catholic saint or member of the Holy Family, and is often represented in its Roman Catholic form on Umbanda altars. Thus Ogun, Yoruban god of iron-working and of war, is identified with Saint George, and his representation on Umbanda altars is often in the form of a Roman Catholic statue of Saint George slaying the dragon. The orixás' histories are recounted in the Yoruba origin myth and each orixá has a distinctive personality and is identified with certain colors, foods, and healing herbs.

While the orixás are often petitioned for aid, the major spiritual entities in Umbanda are the *caboclos* (spirits of Brazilian Indians) and *pretos velhos* ("old blacks," or spirits of Africans enslaved in Brazil). Discarnate spirits of women and men who once lived on earth, they are less powerful than the orixás but more central because they conduct the healing activities in Umbanda ceremonies. Caboclo spirits are proud forest dwellers and warriors; they can be male or female. The caboclo spirits have individual names and hymns that detail their exploits, and they can often be identified in the ceremonies by their feather headdresses and large cigars. Pretos velhos are elderly, humble, and wise; they bear tales of enslavement. They are addressed familiarly as Father (*Pai*) or Aunt (*Tia*) and hobble about on canes puffing on their pipes.

North America
──

Underground Railroad,

beginning in the early nineteenth century and continuing well up to the Civil War, the so-called freedom train was a secret and extensive network of people, places, and modes of transportation that led runaway slaves from the southern United States to freedom in the North and Canada.

Freedom was never a luxury for African American slaves; it was a destiny that became epitomized in many Negro spirituals. The "freedom train" came infrequently and was often not on time. But when it did arrive, it was big enough and strong enough to carry the souls of the weary and to lighten

American artist C. T. Webber's 1893 painting shows fugitives arriving at Levi Coffin's farm in Wayne County, Indiana, a busy station on the Underground Railroad. *CORBIS*

the burdens of the downtrodden. The freedom train even brought hope and inspiration to those who could not physically make it on board. For years slaveholders mistakenly attributed the imagery of the freedom train in Negro spirituals to fanciful illusions in the minds of slaves about dying and going to heaven.

Known officially as the Underground Railroad, the freedom train was an extensive network of people, places, and modes of transportation—all working in the deepest secrecy to help transport slaves to freedom in the North and Canada. Many slaves made the journey with the help of guides, who were often free blacks committed to the cause of abolition. White abolitionists also made significant contributions, but the freedom train was a powerful political statement made by African Americans who chose to "vote for freedom with their feet."

Historians have traditionally underestimated and understated the role of blacks, and overestimated the role of sympathetic whites in the Underground Railroad. White abolitionists did provide safe houses, money, boats, and other material resources that were sometimes vital to successful escapes. But free blacks often risked much more—their own freedom and lives—in order to travel South, to help lead others to safety. Among the more prominent "conductors" of the freedom train was Harriet Tubman. A former slave who had escaped to the North, Tubman traveled to the South at least 15 times and guided more than 200 slaves to freedom. She epitomized the success and daring of the freedom train. Through her stories and those of others, there exists a rich legacy detailing the network that is said to have helped more than 1000 slaves each year to free themselves from bondage.

Few details of the Underground Railroad are known because of the extreme secrecy required in its operation, but there are reports of its existence as early as 1837. The exact number of slaves who were freed by the railroad is also not known because, in the interests of security, the conductors of the railroad could not keep records. Although this number was never high enough to threaten the institution of slavery itself, the legends and metaphor of the freedom train worried slaveholders. Tales that were often repeated throughout the nation included, for example, the story of Henry "Box" Brown, a black man who packed himself in a wooden crate and shipped himself to freedom in Philadelphia, and the story of William and Ellen Craft, a married couple whose escape was based on their disguise—she as a "Spanish gentleman" and he as her black slave. The accounts of runaway slaves instilled fear in the hearts of Southern slave owners, and inspired Northern abolitionists to form larger and stronger antislavery organizations.

As the Underground Railroad gained notoriety, its operations became even more secret. A virtually undetected escape route ran from Texas to Mexico, but almost no information exists about how it functioned or how many African Americans quietly blended into the Mexican populace. It became difficult to distinguish between fact and fiction in accounts of the escapes. But researchers have been able to uncover many details, especially from the accounts of free blacks who wrote memoirs or autobiographies. Free blacks such as William Still, David Ruggles, William Wells Brown, Frederick Douglass, and Henry Highland Garnet joined Tubman in the struggle for self-emancipation. Most worked in silence and sometimes even in disguise.

Runaway slaves waded through swamps, concealed themselves in the hulls of ships, hid on the backs of carriages, and navigated circuitous routes by using the North Star at night—always with the understanding that they might be caught or betrayed at any time. Many were pursued by professional slave catchers (some with dogs), who had the authority to detain and hold itinerant African Americans south of the Mason-Dixon Line. The Southern press was full of advertisements for escaped slaves. These descriptions constitute one of the few sources of accurate personal details about individuals in the slave community. The advertisements, in the slaveholders' own words, often mentioned maimed limbs and scars from whipping—vivid descriptions that Northern abolitionists used verbatim in their condemnation of slavery.

On the way to freedom slaves and their guides often found it difficult to obtain food, clothing, and shelter. Free blacks in cities such as Philadelphia and Boston formed "vigilance committees" to meet these and other needs. The committees cared for runaways after they arrived on free soil, hid them to prevent their recapture, and aided them on their way to Canada. The Philadelphia Association for the Moral and Mental Improvement of the People of Color was one of the most prominent black vigilance committees.

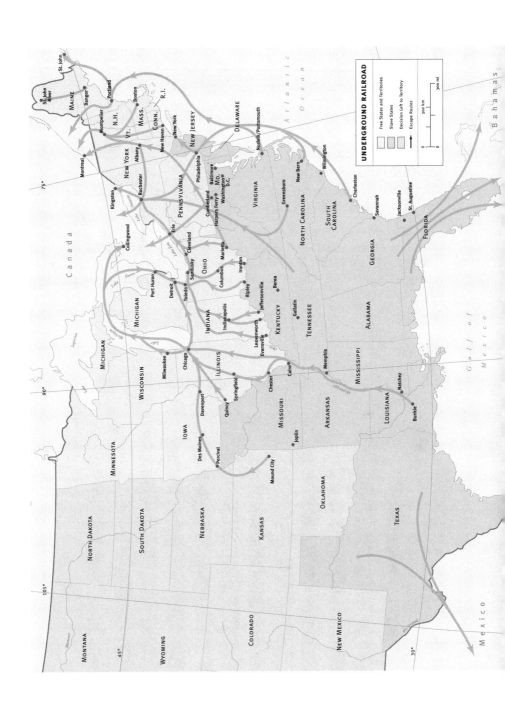

With the aid of black vigilance committees the Underground Railroad continued to guide slaves to freedom up until the time of the Civil War itself, when thousands of slaves freed themselves by leaving the plantations and escaping behind Union Army lines. For those who still labored as slaves at the beginning of the Civil War, the legend of the Underground Railroad held out hope.

North America

United Negro College Fund,

an American organization founded on April 25, 1944, to provide financial support to students at historically black colleges and universities.

At its inception the United Negro College Fund (UNCF) was a consortium of 27 institutions with 14,000 students. Today there are 39 member colleges, and the UNCF has financially helped more than 300,000 African Americans to graduate. The UNCF headquarters is in Fairfax, Virginia, and there are 20 regional offices.

With the motto "A mind is a terrible thing to waste," the UNCF's programs help provide low-cost, quality education for deserving students and

**ADMISSIONS TO 4-YEAR COLLEGES AND UNIVERSITIES
1972–1991 (in thousands)**

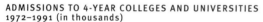

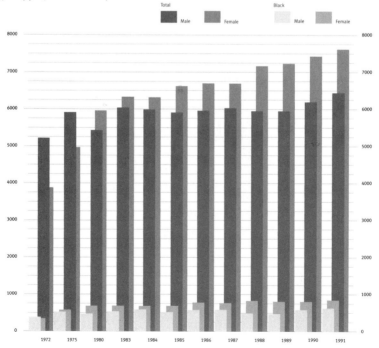

Source: *Encyclopedia of African-American Culture and History* (1996): "College Enrollment, 1972-1991" (Table 6.12); *Statistical Abstracts*, 1993.

HISTORICALLY BLACK COLLEGES AND UNIVERSITIES			
State	City	Institution	Founding Date
Alabama	Birmingham	Miles College	1905
	Huntsville	Oakwood College	1896
	Montgomery	Alabama State University	1866
	Normal	Alabama A&M University	1875
	Talladega	Talladega College	1867
	Tuscaloosa	Stillman College	1876
	Tuskegee	Tuskegee University	1881
Arkansas	Little Rock	Arkansas Baptist College	1884
	Little Rock	Philander-Smith College	1877
	Pine Bluff	University of Arkansas at Pine Bluff	1873
Delaware	Dover	Delaware State University	1891
District of Columbia	Washington	Howard University	1867
	Washington	University of the District of Columbia	1851
Florida	Daytona Beach	Bethune-Cookman College	1904
	Jacksonville	Edward Waters College	1866
	Miami	Florida Memorial College	1879
	Tallahassee	Florida A&M University	1887
Georgia	Albany	Albany State College	1903
	Atlanta	Atlanta University	1865
	Atlanta	Charles H. Mason Theological Seminary	1970
	Atlanta	Clark College	1869
	Atlanta	Gammon Theological Seminary	1883
	Atlanta	Johnson C. Smith Theological Seminary	1867
	Atlanta	Morehouse College	1867
	Atlanta	Morehouse School of Medicine	1974
	Atlanta	Morehouse School of Religion	1867
	Atlanta	Morris Brown College	1881
	Atlanta	Phillips School of Theology	1945
	Atlanta	Spelman College	1881
	Atlanta	Turner Theological Seminary	1894
	Augusta	Paine College	1882
	Fort Valley	Fort Valley State College	1895
	Savannah	Savannah State College	1890
Kentucky	Berea	Berea College	1855
	Frankfort	Kentucky State University	1886
Louisiana	Baton Rouge	Southern University and A&M College, Baton Rouge	1880
	Grambling	Grambling State University	1901
	New Orleans	Dillard University	1869
	New Orleans	Southern University at New Orleans	1956
	New Orleans	Xavier University of Louisiana	1915
	Shreveport	Southern University at Shreveport	1964
Maryland	Baltimore	Coppin State College	1900
	Baltimore	Morgan State University	1867
	Bowie	Bowie State College	1865
	Princess Anne	University of Maryland, Eastern Shore	1886
Mississippi	Holly Springs	Rust College	1866
	Itta Bena	Itta Bena	1946
	Jackson	Jackson	1877
	Lorman	Lorman	1871
	Tougaloo	Tougaloo	1869

(continued on next page)

State	City	Institution	Founding Date
Missouri	Jefferson City	Lincoln University	1866
	St. Louis	Harris-Stowe State University	1857
North Carolina	Charlotte	Johnson C. Smith University	1867
	Concord	Barber-Scotia College	1867
	Durham	North Carolina Central University	1909
	Elizabeth City	Elizabeth City State University	1891
	Fayetteville	Fayetteville State University	1867
	Greensboro	Bennett College	1873
	Greensboro	North Carolina A&T State University	1891
	Raleigh	Shaw University	1865
	Raleigh	Saint Augustine's College	1867
	Salisbury	Livingstone College	1879
	Winston-Salem	Winston-Salem State University	1892
Ohio	Wilberforce	Central State University	1887
	Wilberforce	Wilberforce University	1856
Oklahoma	Langston	Langston University	1897
Pennsylvania	Cheyney	Cheyney University	1837
	Lincoln	Lincoln University	1853
South Carolina	Columbia	Allen University	1870
	Columbia	Benedict College	1870
	Denmark	Vorhees College	1897
	Orangeburg	Claflin College	1869
	Orangeburg	South Carolina State University	1872
	Sumter	Morris College	1908
Tennessee	Jackson	Lane College	1882
	Knoxville	Knoxville College	1863
	Memphis	LeMoyne-Owen College	1862
	Nashville	Fisk University	1866
	Nashville	Meharry Medical College	1876
	Nashville	Tennessee State University	1912
Texas	Austin	Huston-Tillotson College	1875
	Hawkins	Jarvis Christian College	1912
	Houston	Texas Southern University	1927
	Marshall	Wiley College	1873
	Prairie View	Prairie View A&M University	1876
	Tyler	Texas College	1894
	Wac	Paul Quinn College	1872
Virginia	Hampton	Hampton University	1868
	Lawrenceville	Saint Paul's College	1883
	Norfolk	Norfolk State University	1935
	Petersburg	Virginia State University	1882
	Richmond	Virginia Union University	1865
West Virginia	Bluefield	Bluefield State College	1895
	Institute	West Virginia State College	1891

Source: *Encyclopedia of African-American Culture and History* (1996): "Historically Black Colleges and Universities" (Table 6.13).

include premedical summer enrichment seminars, international exchange, and technical assistance to faculty and administration at historically black colleges and universities. Many alumni of historically black schools who received UNCF support have gone on to become leaders in the legal and medical fields, academia, politics, and government.

The UNCF's largest gift was a $42 million grant from the Lilly Endowment, the country's biggest foundation, in 1998. According to the UNCF, the grant will contribute to the fund's capital projects by providing money for new construction, building renovation, laboratory equipment, and information technology upgrades. This is in addition to need—based as well as merit scholarships, and faculty support via endowed chairs and curriculum development.

Cross Cultural

Universal Negro Improvement Association,

an influential international organization advocating African repatriation, self-government, and economic autonomy that thrived during the 1920s under the leadership of founder Marcus Garvey.

Founded in Kingston, Jamaica, in 1914 by black nationalist Marcus Garvey, the Universal Negro Improvement Association (UNIA) is widely recognized as the largest international organization in history of people of African descent. Its full name, the Universal Negro Improvement Association and Conservation and African Communities (Imperial) League, reflects its dual purpose: to promote black social mobility through racial uplift and economic prosperity, and to aid black repatriation and the creation of an autonomous black state in Africa.

It was as a charitable organization that the UNIA first emerged. Garvey envisioned an organization modeled after Masonic and Greek—letter societies that would provide Jamaican blacks with the kind of industrial education offered in the United States by Booker T. Washington's Tuskegee Institute. Yet Garvey was unable to find sufficient support for the UNIA in Jamaica. Attributing this disinterest to a lack of a racial consciousness among black Jamaicans, Garvey moved the UNIA to Harlem, New York, in 1918.

Adopting a strident black nationalist posture in response to the antiblack violence of the Red Summer of 1919, the UNIA provided a vehicle for the political aspirations of the "New Negro". The organization flourished, aided by the brisk sale of shares in the Black Star Line, Inc., a shipping company intended to forge economic ties between the United States and Africa and to support repatriation.

The UNIA saw itself as Africa's government in exile—replete with a national flag and uniformed officers spectacularly displayed at its conventions and parades—with Garvey as its provisional president. Its journal, the *Negro World*, was cited as an instrument of anticolonial insurrection and banned in several African countries. By the early 1920s the UNIA's slogan, "One God, One Aim, One Destiny," had become the rallying cry for an estimated 1 million members distributed among thousands of local branches throughout the African diaspora.

The decline of the UNIA was as quick as its ascent. In 1923, in the wake of the collapse of the Black Star Line, the organization was thrown into disarray when Garvey was imprisoned on charges of mail fraud—charges that were in fact orchestrated by integrationist African Americans. After Garvey's release and deportation to Jamaica, the UNIA was splintered by competing claims to its leadership. Garvey tried to resurrect the UNIA in Jamaica in 1929, but the stock market crash of that year depleted the organization's resources. In 1935 Garvey tried again to launch the organization, this time in London, England, but lost support when he was openly critical of the Ethiopian emperor Haile Selassie I's policies during the Italo-Ethiopian War.

Although membership had dwindled by the time of Garvey's death in London in 1940, a number of UNIA branches have tenaciously survived until the present day, preserving the legacy of the most powerful movement of black self-determination in the twentieth century.

Uruguay,

republic of southeastern South America bordered on the northeast and north by Brazil, on the west by Argentina, and on the east by the Atlantic Ocean. With an area of 176,215 sq km (68,037 sq mi.), it is the second-smallest country in South America after Suriname. Its capital is Montevideo.

Uruguay has long enjoyed a reputation as the Switzerland of the Americas, due in part to its small size, its dominant population of European descent, and a perception that it is a country free of racial tensions or other conflicts. The true racial history of Uruguay is much more complicated than this image suggests. Blacks constitute a tiny minority of present-day Uruguayans (about 6 percent of the population), but this was not always the case. In fact, throughout Uruguay's history blacks played an integral role in the nation's development. Afro-Uruguayans today are the inheritors of this legacy, though in standard histories they are sometimes reviled and more often than not forgotten.

The Official History

Before Spaniards arrived in the area now known as Uruguay, a number of seminomadic indigenous groups inhabited the region. The largest of these groups were the Charrúa and the Chaná, who survived principally by hunting and fishing. In 1516 the Spanish explorer Juan Díaz de Solís sailed into the Río de la Plata (the estuary that separates western Uruguay from eastern Argentina) and established a small, short-lived settlement on the riverbank. Before the year was out, the Charrúa killed Díaz and his party. The region was of little interest to Spanish colonizers, as it seemed of minimal economic value. The first permanent Spanish settlement would not be established in Uruguay until 1624, when a small party encamped at the Río Negro at Soriano.

This area came to be known as the Banda Oriental (Eastern Bank), and from the late seventeenth through much of the eighteenth century, it was a zone of contention between Spanish colonists and Portuguese colonists from Brazil. In 1680 the Portuguese founded Colônia do Sacramento on the bank of the Río de la Plata, opposite Buenos Aires. The Spanish made little effort to displace this settlement until the 1720s, when they constructed the fortified city of San Felipe de Montevideo, from which they launched attacks on the Portuguese. The Portuguese finally ceded in 1777, and the region came under the administrative control of the viceroyalty of La Plata.

In the second decade of the nineteenth century Uruguayans fought successfully for their independence, but the country was occupied by and finally annexed to Brazil in 1821. An insurgent group known as the Immortal 33, led by Juan Antonio Lavalleja and aided by Argentina, fought the occupation. A treaty signed in 1828, with British mediation, established Uruguay as an independent buffer zone between Argentina and the Brazilian Empire, and a provisional assembly was established. On July 18, 1830, the assembly ratified a constitution that officially founded the República Oriental del Uruguay (Eastern Republic of Uruguay).

During most of the nineteenth century, the new republic was plagued by fighting between two contending political factions comprising supporters of the nation's first two presidents: Fructuoso Rivera (1830–1834; 1838–1842) and Manuel Oribe (1835–1838). The factions were named for the colors adopted by each: the Colorado Party (red), supporting Rivera, and the Blanco Party (white), for Oribe. Both survive today as the dominant political parties. Between 1865 and 1868 Uruguay allied itself with Brazil and Argentina against Paraguay in the War of the Triple Alliance. The Colorado Party became dominant during the course of the century; after 1865 the Blanco Party would remain out of power until 1958.

Uruguay in the twentieth century gained its reputation as a progressive, democratic republic. President José Batlle y Ordóñez (1903–1907; 1911–1915) initiated a period of social reforms that included concessions to labor as well as provisions for social security. Democratic rule was disrupted by a period of authoritarian rule in the 1930s and by a repressive military government between 1973 and 1984. Uruguay's transition to democracy since 1984 has been regarded as one of the most successful in Latin America, as the traditional Blanco and Colorado parties reemerged in what appears to be a remarkably stable regime.

Africans in Colonial Uruguay

Spaniards brought Africans to the region as early as 1534. These *ladinos* (slaves who had been Hispanicized in Spain rather than being brought directly from Africa) took part in early explorations of the Río de la Plata, although nearly all of them settled with their masters in what is now Argentina.

The Uruguayan slave trade was born from a quirk of conquest and geography. By the end of the sixteenth century Spain had extended its slave-capture and trading operations to the Angola region of southern Africa. As they were in the slave trade in northern Africa, captives were shipped by sea to bustling colonies such as Mexico and the Audiencia de Cartagena (in present-day Colombia), all in the northern half of the Americas. The sea voyage from Angola, however, was even more brutal than that from northern Africa, and many more slaves died en route. Spanish slave traders realized by the end of the sixteenth century that if slaves were transported across a shorter sea route—say, to the Río de la Plata—and then transferred overland to distant points, fewer of them would die. As a result Buenos Aires (in what would later become Argentina) soon became a major point of disembarkation for slaves from southern Africa. By the end of the seventeenth century the Spaniards had discovered that Montevideo, 200 km (120 mi.) east of Buenos Aires on the Río de la Plata, had a remarkable natural harbor, and in 1724 they began a settlement there. In no time the bulk of the slave trade had moved from Buenos Aires to Montevideo, the future capital of Uruguay.

From the earliest days the Spanish government tried to exercise strict control over the arrival of slaves in the Río de la Plata region, mostly in order to tax the lucrative trade. Only a few authorized traders were allowed to bring slaves to a region. However, as in other parts of Spanish America, slave traders in the Río de la Plata often succeeded in smuggling contraband slaves past officials. In La trata de negroa en Río de la Plata durante el siglo XVIII (1958), historian Elena Fanny Scheüss de Studer calculates that only 288 of nearly 13,000 slaves who came to the Río de la Plata region between 1606 and 1655 arrived legally. She estimates that between 1680 and 1806—an era of mostly tighter Spanish control—perhaps 50 percent of all arrivals from Africa were still smuggled into Río de la Plata. In addition to these contrabands, it appears likely that many slaves were shipped to Montevideo from Rio de Janeiro in Portuguese Brazil—in violation of both Spanish and Portuguese law.

Beginning in 1740 Spain bowed to the reality of its ineffectual control of the slave trade and allowed any colonist with the means to buy a *licencia* (license) to purchase as many Africans as he wanted from any slave trader of any nation not warring against Spain. The licencias were costly, so only a few could afford them; nonetheless, the introduction of licencias opened the door to a much larger legal slave trade. Colonial records show that in one brief period—from 1780 to 1783–17 licencias were granted in the Río de la Plata region, allowing the importation of 3400 blacks to Montevideo and Buenos Aires. From 1783 to 1792, 10 more licencias allowed the importation of 4600 more slaves. Most of these slaves were presumably shipped to distant points, like Peru and New Granada (present-day Colombia, Ecuador, Venezuela, and Panama), since by 1803 Montevideo had only 899 slaves.

During roughly the same era, in 1776, Spain recognized the increasing importance of the Río de la Plata region by establishing the viceroyalty of La Plata, which included what is today Uruguay, Argentina, Bolivia, and Paraguay. The viceregal seat of La Plata was in Buenos Aires. Two decades later Spain acknowledged that even its efforts under the licencia system to control the slave trade were futile; in 1795 the viceroyalty of La Plata abandoned the system altogether. Any Spanish citizen was allowed to buy slaves from any source not at war with Spain.

Slave Labor, Life, and Rebellion

The conditions under which slaves labored in Uruguay are "difficult to analyze," according to historian Leslie Rout in The African Experience in Spanish America. Aside, perhaps, from domestic service, slaves did not dominate any industry or occupation in Uruguay; moreover, the plantations or mines that were the province of slaves in much of the rest of Spanish America were virtually nonexistent in Uruguay. Montevideo, a commercial port and practically the only settlement of importance in Uruguay, was indisputably the home of most Uruguayan slaves. Female slaves dominated the domestic industries of cooking, cleaning, laundering, and child rearing, while male slaves worked as manual laborers on docks and in the ranching operations around Montevideo.

The burden of Africans in Uruguay was worsened by the sharp distinctions that Spanish colonists drew between dark-skinned and light-skinned blacks. The latter were in all things favored (if only slightly), and the former disparaged. In May 1760 the *cabildo* (council) of Montevideo passed a series of acts governing *pardos* (mulattos, usually lighter skinned) and *morenos* ("full-blood" blacks, usually darker skinned). Under the acts pardos were allowed to become certain types of tradesmen, including tailors and cobblers, while morenos were forbidden to do anything but physical and domestic labor.

Such racial distinctions persisted despite a few efforts by the Spanish government to diminish them. In 1795, for example, the Spanish Crown allowed blacks to buy writs of gracias al sacar, meaning literally "thanks for the exclusion." The writs were a royal dispensation that freed a person from certain caste restrictions. However, in the viceroyalty of La Plata writs were rarely issued, and only those issued to very light-skinned blacks were honored. Darker-skinned blacks who bought them often found them unredeemable. Because of these and similar caste barriers, intermarriage of blacks and whites in La Plata was quite rare; however, as in the rest of Spanish America, the prohibition against white men taking female slaves as concubines was less strict.

Avenues to freedom that were open to slaves in other parts of the Spanish Empire were relatively less accessible to Afro-Uruguayans. In *Negro uruguayo hasta abolición* (1965, The Uruguayan Black Until Abolition), historian Paulo de Carvalho Neto holds that, with the exception of some illegitimate mulatto children with white fathers, the only way for blacks to escape slavery was through death. Historian Carlos Rama agrees, for the most part, adding that a very few slaves were freed as a result of being treated with extreme cruelty, and a few more were allowed to buy their freedom.

Rebellion, then, was one of the very small number of paths to freedom, but even this method was less successful in Uruguay than elsewhere. In 1803, 20 black men, most but not all slaves, gathered in secret to devise a plot for fleeing Montevideo and soon thereafter fled with their wives and children. After several days of travel they established a settlement on a small island in the River Yi, some 200 km (120 mi.) north of Montevideo. Their freedom, however, was short-lived; a militia from the town of Villa de la Concepción de Minas attacked them soon after they had settled. In the skirmish that followed, all of the blacks were either captured and re-enslaved or killed in the fighting.

War Against Spain and Emancipation

The first hint of change in the life of the Uruguayan slave came during the wars of liberation against Spain in the second decade of the nineteenth century. Afro-Uruguayans quickly learned that they could better their social standing by serving in the rebel armies. The rebels, for their part, were not typically possessed of a liberal attitude toward blacks; they were simply desperate enough for troops to enlist anyone who could fight. At first this meant allowing free blacks to fight; later it meant giving guns to slaves.

José Artigas, who would later be considered the father of Uruguay, put together the most formidable army of blacks and mulattos, most of them freedpeople but many of them slaves, to serve alongside white rebels. In 1812 the Sixth Regiment, composed almost entirely of blacks, gained enduring fame through its part in a daring bayonet charge at El Cerrito. Another battalion, *Los Libertos Orientales* (The Freedmen of the East), fought almost continuously between 1816 and 1820.

Although their fighting earned blacks a meas ure of respect, the limitations of caste did not fall away. Indeed, black soldiers were usually assigned to the most dangerous fighting yet received the worst food and equipment. Their lot had changed little enough that when a Brazilian force took advantage of the wars against Spain and invaded Uruguay in 1817, more than a hundred of Artigas's black troops switched sides for the flimsy promise that "someday" Brazil would make them free. Many blacks nonetheless remained loyal to the rebel forces, and as the target of rebel attacks shifted from Spanish to Brazilian troops, blacks continued to play a crucial role.

Brazil completed its conquest and annexation of Uruguay by 1821, under the name Cisplantine Province. A small group of insurgents, known as the Immortal 33, reasserted the independence of Uruguay in 1825. Little acknowledged among modern Uruguayans is that a handful of the Immortal 33 were black. Black rebels are not completely forgotten, however. Col. Lorenzo Barcala, an Argentinian known as "the black caballero," played a major role from 1825 to 1828 in the eviction of the Brazilians from Uruguay. Manuel Antonio Ledesma ("Ansina") is known as the aide who faithfully accompanied Artigas to his death in Paraguay. Barcala and Ansina were among the few blacks, however, to attain high-ranking positions.

On September 7, 1825, the rebel forces established a congress at which they passed a free-womb law: anyone born to a slave from that date forward was born free. They then opened the ranks of their army to blacks and mulattos—both free and slave. In May 1829 another provisional legislature, established after the 1828 peace agreement recognizing Uruguayan independence, freed all slaves who fought in the struggle for liberation, and in 1830 it ratified the republic's first constitution.

The constitution of the new country included several positive changes for slaves. It reaffirmed the acts of the earlier congresses, asserting that all newborn children of slaves were born free. The overseas slave trade was banned, and any slave whose master had fled to Brazil during or after the fighting was declared free. Still, the old caste distinctions remained. Former slaves found it extremely difficult to find work or decent housing, and many slaves who had fought in the war were denied their freedom because they had no proof of their enlistment.

In 1832 a group of slaves and freedpeople prepared for revolt behind an Afro-Uruguayan named Santa Colombo, who had been a military aide to President Fructuoso Rivera. The government uncovered the plot in May 1832, sentenced the freedpeople to death or long jail terms, and sentenced slaves to 200 lashes. Because several of the plotters had fought against Spain and Brazil in the liberation, many Uruguayans pleaded for leniency on behalf of the prisoners. Eventually the death sentences were commuted.

The constitution's promises to end the slave trade notwithstanding, between 1829 and 1841 some 4000 slaves were brought illegally from Brazil to Uruguay. President Rivera apparently abetted much of the illegal trade. In 1837 a law was passed declaring that all blacks thenceforth brought into the country would be free (with some exceptions, such as runaway slaves from other countries, who were to be returned). The law also established a system of patronato, which effectively extended the period of servitude by placing blacks under the "tutelage" of their masters for a determined period of time. Abolition in Uruguay was given impetus by the conflicts in the country and the need for soldiers. Fighting between Blanco and Colorado factions flared following Rivera's 1838 coup against Presi dent Manuel Oribe. In 1841, when Blanco rebels, supported by Argentina, threatened Rivera, he freed his many slaves and drafted them into the army. In December 1842 his successor, Joaquín Suárez, abolished slavery throughout the country and drafted all former male slaves into the army. In the hope of winning compliance from slave owners, he promised compensation for the freed slaves. But most slave owners flouted the law, and many sold their slaves in neighboring Brazil.

In 1843 Suárez's troops were backed into Montevideo. The rebels, led by deposed president Oribe, laid siege to the city until 1851, when a signed truce declared that there were no victors or vanquished. Like the besieged, the attacking army also relied heavily on black forces. In October 1846, the third year of the siege, Oribe too declared slavery in Uruguay abolished. Following the truce, a law passed in 1853 abolished the patronato system, freeing all blacks in the country.

In addition to prompting some Uruguayan slave owners to sell their slaves in Brazil, abolition produced a substantial immigration of escaped Brazilian slaves to Uruguay. Given the extent of this migration, the 1851 peace agreement, in which Brazilian intervention was decisive, included an agreement to return escaped slaves to Brazil, but this provision was largely ignored.

Beyond Emancipation

Despite abolition many former slaves had no choice but to continue working for their former masters, and slavelike conditions and racial discrimination persisted. In 1860, for example, the Montevideo police force prohibited blacks from being hired as night watchmen. In 1878 a furor erupted when supporters of civil rights tried to gain admittance for blacks to public schools alongside whites.

Afro-Uruguayans, however, were also confronted with a flood of white immigrant labor, which reduced their economic opportunities. In 1842 nearly 20 percent of Montevideo's residents were black. After emancipation Uruguay faced two problems that could be addressed with one solution: it needed a larger labor base to fuel its economic growth, and it "needed" to preserve its white character. Hence between 1850 and 1930 more than a million Europeans, almost all of them white, immigrated to Uruguay. A few blacks also found their way to Uruguay during the early part of this period, but in 1886 the Uruguayan government made clear its preference for white immigrants: people of African origin were barred from settling in Uruguay. A study conducted by Uruguay's National Statistics Institute in 1996–1997 found that approximately 6 percent of Uruguayans identify themselves as black.

In the context of the new European competition for jobs in Uruguay, the stigma of being black persisted. Afro-Uruguayans were clustered in low-paying positions and typically lived in the slums of Montevideo well into the twentieth century. In May 1956 the magazine *Marcha* studied nearly 15,000 barbers, hotel porters, bus drivers, conductors, guards, and store clerks; only 11 of them were black or mulatto, indicating that Afro-Uruguayans had not achieved even the faintest hold on the middle class. Marcha also reported that from 1900 to 1956 the National University of Uruguay graduated just two lawyers and one doctor of African heritage. In a separate study in the same year, 700 white Uruguayan students were asked whether they would marry a black; 77 percent said no. When asked whether they would invite a black person to a birthday party, 62 percent said no.

Under such conditions, Afro-Uruguayans created political and cultural organizations of their own. In the early twentieth century they formed groups for socializing and other kinds of support, such as the Black Race Cultural Association and the Colonia Sport and Social Club, both head-quartered in Montevideo. In 1917 the magazine *Nuestra Raza* (Our Race) began reporting on issues of concern among the black community. Before going out of business in 1948, Nuestra Raza helped introduce Afro-Uruguayans to the music of Julián García Rondeau, the art of Ramón Preya, and the poetry of its editor, Pilar Barrios. Barrios was also the secretary of the Black Autochthonous Party. Organized in 1937 and comprising mainly black intellectuals, many of whom were connected with Nuestra Raza, the Black Autochthonous Party took a stand for social justice while seeking to appeal broadly to all Afro-Uruguayans. Nonetheless, after the party's poor showing in the 1938 elections, its activities declined, and it finally disbanded in 1944.

After World War II the Uruguayan government extended free education to all classes, allowing all blacks for the first time to enter school with whites. Black culture, however, was not studied, a fact that recent historians have attributed to the broader ideal of "whitening" the country, which emphasizes its European influences while erasing its African ones. Most Afro-Uruguayan ethnic societies disappeared; the few that existed in the 1990s were generally weak and often dependent on overseas donations. In its 1996–1997 study the National Statistics Institute found that the average income of blacks was about 65 percent that of whites. Historian Alejandrina da Luz wrote in 1995, "Thus 'invisibility' became official policy. As they grow up, young Afro-Uruguayans today will find that their nation's history records only one black person: the loyal soldier Ansina. There are no black writers in Uruguayan literature; only in the United States are there black musicians; and in painting, black people appear only on canvas. Dozens of Afro-Uruguayan writers, dramatists, painters, musicians, and so on, seem to have faded away."

Africa

Usman dan Fodio

(b. 1750?; d. 1817?), Muslim religious leader and founder of the Sokoto Caliphate in what is now northern Nigeria.

A Fulani born in the Hausa state of Gobir, Usman dan Fodio studied the Koran with his father, an eminent scholar, then moved from place to place to study with other religious scholars. When he was 25 years old, he began teaching and preaching, and from this time his reputation as a holy man grew. He taught Islam in Gobir, and he was probably engaged as tutor to the future sultan Yunfa because of his learned reputation.

Usman criticized the Hausa ruling elite for their heavy taxation and other practices that he claimed violated Islamic law. His call for Islamic reform (and tax reduction) earned him a wide following in the 1780s and 1790s, when he became a political threat to Gobir sultan Nafata. When Yunfa assumed power as sultan in 1802, he ordered the repression of Usman's followers. Following the example of the prophet Muhammad, Usman went on a *hijrah* (spiritual migration), was elected *imam* (leader) of the reformist Muslims, and launched the *jihad* (holy war) that would bring down the Hausa royalty. In the conquered areas Usman set up emirates whose leaders acknowledged his religious sovereignty, and in October 1808 the Gobir capital, Alkalawa, fell. In former Gobir, Usman established a new capital, Sokoto, from which he ruled virtually all of Hausaland. After 1812 Usman withdrew into private life, writing many works on the proper conduct of the pious Islamic community. After his death in 1817, his son Muhammad Bello succeeded him as the ruler of the Sokoto Caliphate, then the largest state in Africa south of the Sahara.

Valdés, Gabriel de la Concepción ("Plácido")

(b. March 18, 1809, Matanzas, Cuba; d. June 26, 1844, Matanzas, Cuba),
Cuban poet, journalist, patriot, and martyr best known for his protest poems
and his alleged involvement in the Conspiración de la Escalera.

Gabriel de la Concepción Valdés, more generally known by his pseudonym
"Plácido," was born in Matanzas to a white mother, the Spanish dancer Concepción Vásquez, and a black father, Diego Ferrer Matoso, who was prohibited, like all Cuban blacks, from placing "Don" before his name. Plácido was
abandoned as an infant, left at an orphanage on April 6, 1809; a note found
with him was inscribed with the name "Gabriel de la Concepción." He was
given a last name, Valdés, and the phrase "al parecer, blanco" (appears
white) was inscribed on his baptism certificate. In his *Biografías Americanas*
(1906), Enrique Piñeyro laments the fact that Plácido's remorseful father
retrieved him soon after abandoning him; if he had not reclaimed his son,
Plácido would have "lost any trace of his previous servile condition." As it
was, Piñeyro says, his father's retrieval of him "condemned the poor thing
to a perpetual inferior situation, to an irredeemable fortune." Even free
blacks in 1840s Cuba enjoyed little economic and social mobility; however,
Plácido's paternal grandmother taught him to read and write.

At age 14 Plácido began working as a cashier in a publishing house. The
pay was meager, and the few books and periodicals the business managed to
publish were strictly regulated by colonial censorship. Plácido abandoned
the press to become a *peinetero* apprentice, crafting women's hair combs
from tortoiseshell. Known for his improvisational skills as a poet, in 1837 he
started contributing a daily poem to the newspaper *La aurora de Matanzas*.
His "poetry of occasion"—laudatory poems commissioned for distinguished
members of society—supplemented his income.

In 1838 Plácido published *Poesías*, followed in 1842 by a collection of
letrillas and *epigramas* titled *El veguero*. In that same year a promotion at *La*

aurora enabled him to dedicate his professional efforts to literary pursuits and his personal ones to married life with a new wife. The "nearly white" poet clearly established his political and ethnic affiliations when he married a woman "de pura sangre africana" (of pure African blood). Many Spanish epic poems compared Spain's empire to that of Rome. In this vein, poems like "Death of Caesar," or "*Juramento*"—which challenged imperial rule and which many Cubans knew by heart—set the stage for Plácido's impending demise.

In 1844 Plácido was executed by colonial troops, accused of participating in a plot to organize a slave revolt in the state of Matanzas and ultimately to win independence for Cuba. Many blacks, slaves and free alike, were brought in for questioning, tortured, and executed. The purge nearly wiped out the leaders of Cuba's free black population, and in the aftermath of the Conspiración de la Escalera prominent mulattos like journalists Rafael Serra y Montalvo ("the Cuban Booker T. Washington"), politician and activist Juan Gualberto Gómez, and Antonio Maceo, a general in the independence forces, would continue to be the focus of white fears of blacks. Plácido himself was tried partly on the basis of his verse. Three of his most famous poems, "*Adiós a mi lira*" (Goodbye to My Lyre), "*Despedida a mi madre*" (Farewell to My Mother), and "*Plegaria a Dios*" (Prayer to God), are said to have been written in prison only a few days before his death.

Though Plácido's fame increased after his death, he was renowned during his lifetime. His work has received a varied reception. One Spanish critic compared him to Luis de Góngora y Argote, a pillar of seventeenth-century baroque poetry. Some honor Plácido simply for the heroic circumstances of his death; others deem his verse "inferior," citing the poet's lack of education. Most critics remark on his versatility both in style and form. His themes ranged from love to religion to liberty, and his styles included the didactic, elegiac, patriotic, improvised, and satiric. Nor did he limit his choice of form; he composed ballads, letrillas, *redondillas*, *octavas*, and *décimas* in the "popular" styles and "learned" verse in odes and sonnets. Some critics, like Richard Jackson, argue that Plácido should be celebrated both as a poet and a national hero.

Valdés, Jesús (Chucho)

(b. October 9, 1941, Quivican, Cuba), an Afro-Latin jazz pianist and one of the foremost jazz musicians in Cuba; the founder in 1973 of Irakere, Cuba's most significant jazz orchestra.

The jazz pianist Jesús "Chucho" Valdés is one of Cuba's most prominent musicians. He is the son of the Cuban pianist and bandleader Bebo Valdés, who was for many years musical director at Havana's famed Tropicana night club. In 1960, when his father defected from Cuba following Fidel Castro's revolution, Chucho Valdés remained behind. Because of the U.S. commercial and political embargo on Cuba, decreed on October 20, 1960, Valdés remained virtually unknown to the American jazz public for many years. But during the 1990s he has found greater opportunities to perform and record in the United States, and has begun to reach a wider American audience despite the continued political intransigence between the United States and Cuba.

Valdés began playing piano at age 3, and by the time he was 16 was leading his own group. He was particularly inspired by American jazz trumpeter John Birks "Dizzy" Gillespie, the co-creator—along with alto saxophonist Charlie "Bird" Parker—of bop or modern jazz. During the 1940s and 1950s Gillespie also participated in some of the formative experiments in Afro-Cuban jazz, including a recording of Chico O'Farrill's arrangement of *Manteca* (1948). Following the U.S. embargo on Cuba, Valdés and other Cuban jazz players were effectively cut off from the musical developments taking place in the United States, except via Willis Conover's Music U.S.A. program on the Voice of America. Valdés went on to study at the Havana Conservatory, and in 1967 founded the Orquestra Cubana de Música Moderna (OCMM).

Around 1972 Valdés and several other prominent Cuban jazz musicians left the OCMM and formed a new group that ultimately took the name Irakere, the Yoruba word for forest or woods. Valdés served both as the group's leader and as its principal composer and arranger. Irakere played an infectious Afro-Cuban jazz-rock that, in part, reflected the musical influence of trumpeter Miles Davis, who was instrumental in popularizing the use of rock-style rhythms and electric instruments in jazz. Irakere gained a wide following in Cuba and in the many other parts of the world where the band toured. Because of lingering cold war hostilities, however, it has had few opportunities to play in the United States.

During the 1970s word of Valdés and his superb ensemble gradually reached the United States, particularly through the reports of the few American jazz musicians who performed in Cuba. When Gillespie and his quintet first appeared in Cuba in 1977, they played a memorable concert with Irakere, and Gillespie befriended two of Irakere's founding members: trumpeter Arturo Sandoval and saxophonist Paquito D'Rivera. Sandoval and D'Rivera subsequently left Cuba and commenced successful jazz careers in the United States, including stints during the 1980s with Gillespie's United Nation Orchestra.

In the 1990s, however, Valdés found new opportunities to bring together the two nations as well as the African American and Cuban musical heritages. In 1992 he became president of the Havana Jazz Festival, at which he has presented a number of prominent jazz musicians, including trumpeter Roy Hargrove and saxophonist David Sanchez. In 1996 Valdés joined Crisol, a Cuban American big band under the leadership of Hargrove, which on a number of occasions brought him to New York City. On one of those visits he played for several nights at Bradley's, the New York nightclub. More recently Valdés signed a recording contract with EMI Canada—as *New York Times* music critic Ben Ratliff observed, to do so "with the company's American office would constitute trading with the enemy."

Early in 1998 Valdés played two well-received solo concerts at New York City's Lincoln Center for the Performing Arts, as part of an extended program celebrating Cuban music. Ratliff vividly depicted Valdés's playing in one of those concerts, particularly emphasizing his rhythmic artistry: "[H]e opened with big, sonorous chords, then attenuated his playing into a waltz rhythm, then dived into swirling atonality. In serpentine legato runs, he never missed a note; dozens of tiny dots whizzed by each second, steely and well-defined. . . . One of Mr. Valdés's best conceits was to bring wild abstractions into montuno sections: as the right hand pumped out a two-three clavé, the left hand sketched a torrid storm that hewed to no rhythmic cycle."

In his Lincoln Center debut Valdés not only performed such jazz standards as *Yesterdays* and *Autumn Leaves*, but also *La Comparsa*, composed by Cuban classical music composer Ernesto Lecuona.

During his years as director of Irakere, Valdés often found himself playing electric keyboards rather than the piano. But recently he has cut back his involvement in that group—turning over its leadership to his son Chuchito—in order to concentrate on his piano playing.

Latin America and the Caribbean

Valdés, José Manuel

(b. July 29, 1767, Lima, Peru; d. 1843?, Lima, Peru), Peruvian of African and indigenous descent; a famed doctor, poet, professor, philosopher, and a member of parliament.

The natural child of a washerwoman and a musician, José Manuel Valdés was born in Lima, Peru's capital city, when nearly half its population was black. Though his parents could not afford to educate him, his godparents and mother's employers stepped in, seeing to his early education at a prominent religious school. He would later become the first black writer to publish in Peru, both as a doctor and as a poet, as early as 1791.

After completing school Valdés yearned to become a priest, but during the colonial period blacks were denied access to the priesthood by the Roman Catholic Church, and he turned instead to medicine. He could have prospered as a *romancista*, a type of medical practitioner whose training was limited and whose practice was restricted to "external remedies." Rather, in 1788 he took the more challenging route and pursued the title of *latinista* surgeon, for which he studied anatomy and surgical techniques. As a *latinista* surgeon he was allowed to perform emergency surgeries and administer purgatives.

As his finances continued to improve, he threw himself whole-heartedly into his work, importing the latest surgical instruments and books on surgery from Europe while learning French, English, and Italian. The fruits of his labor appeared in a published dissertation on methods for curing dysentery. During these years another hypothesis of his, namely that uterine cancer was not contagious, was sharply criticized by some of his contemporaries, but was proven correct not long after by European researchers.

The 1790s witnessed the heyday of French philosophers and encyclopedists, spreading liberalism and expounding on the universality of political rights. Yet Valdés, a free black, was denied access to the priesthood, the military, and the university. It took a dispensa, an official dispensation from King Carlos VI, to "pardon" his color and allow him to attend the University of Lima in 1807. Later on he was issued a similar document from the pope granting him access to the priesthood, but the Cabildo Metropolitano, upset by his petition, discouraged him from following through. As a practicing physician he became well known in Europe for his medical theories, and as a university professor in Lima he continued to publish medical papers. In 1815, before Peru achieved independence from Spain, he was welcomed into the Royal Academy of Medicine in Madrid.

His literary career developed later in life. Valdés is one of a handful of well-known early republican writers of African descent, such as Candelario Obeso (1849–1884) in Colombia. Valdés wrote mainly mystical poetry, in addition to a biography of Fray Martín de Porres (1579–1639), the black Peruvian saint canonized by the Roman Catholic Church. Valdés also wrote Poesías espirituales (1818, Spiritual Poetry) and Salterio Peruano (1833), a poetic translation of the Psalms. Not all of his work was strictly religious in nature. He contributed articles to El Mercurio Peruano, a progressive and republican newspaper, and composed odes to independence-era generals José de San Martín (Oda a San Martín) and Simón Bolívar (Lima libre y pacificada), well known for their pro-abolition stance.

With the advent of the Peruvian Republic, Valdés was elected to Congress to represent Lima in 1831. He became a member of the illustrious Patriotic Society and was appointed Médico de Cámara del Gobierno, a position similar to United States surgeon general. He received an important Peruvian award, the Order of the Sun of Peru, before attaining a succession of important medical and university titles.

Latin America and the Caribbean

Valdés, Merceditas

(b. October 14, 1928, Havana, Cuba; d. June 13, 1996, Havana, Cuba), Afro-Cuban singer, interpreter, and arranger of religious and secular Afro-Caribbean music; a well-known *santera* (a practitioner of Santería, the traditional Yoruba religion, as practiced throughout Cuba).

Mercedes Valdés, or Merceditas, as she was widely known, began her distinguished artistic career in the 1940s, studying at Havana's Supreme Art Institute under José Alonso. As a student, she received awards for several works, including Babalú, La Negra merece, and El chureo.

During the late 1940s Valdés began to display her interpretive talents over the airwaves on Radio Cadena Suaritas. These appearances established the young artist's position as one of Cuba's most prominent interpreters of traditional Yoruban religious music. In the late 1950s Valdés's Santería recordings for the Panart label helped to secure her importance in the Afro-Cuban movement.

Throughout her career Valdés gained the recognition of Cuba's most acclaimed musicologists and critics, including the anthropologist Fernando Ortiz and the musicologist Argeliers León. In addition, she performed with many notable Cuban artists such as the composer Ernesto Lecuona, the tres player and maestro Arsenio Rodríguez, the great sonero singer Benny Moré, Zún-Zún Babaé, the percussionist Mongo Santamaría, and the jazz pianist Charlie Palmieri. In 1995 Valdés performed as a member of the Cuban All Stars, and her recordings have been featured on several Cuban compilations, including *Messidor's Finest* and *Cuba: I Am Time* (1997).

By the time of her death in 1996 Valdés had succeeded in bringing Afro-Cuban culture to the world through her acclaimed live appearances and recordings. She also proved her versatility, performing dancehall boleros, rumbas, and sones alongside traditional Santería music.

Valdés consistently received the highest recognition for her work, including a national recognition medal from the Cuban Cultural Ministry. Musicologist Angeliers León aptly characterized Valdés's importance to Cuban culture, and the preservation of Yoruban tradition: "Merceditas Valdés is one of the best exponents of the Yoruban language and its rites, transmitting them through their ancestors and contributing towards a greater knowledge of this African heritage."

Latin America and the Caribbean

Valiente, Juan

(b. ?; d. 1553), slave who fought with Spanish colonial armies first in Central America and then in the Southern Cone. He received an encomienda, a land grant, from the Spanish Crown in 1550, and he is thought to be the first black to have received one. He died in battle in 1553.

Africa

Valley of the Kings,

an ancient Egyptian Pharaonic cemetery.

During the Old and Middle Kingdoms of ancient Egypt (2980–1580 B.C.E.), the pharaohs commissioned pyramid tombs and temples in anticipation of their journeys to the afterlife. They filled these tombs with the goods considered necessary for the next life, including jewels, precious metals, food, tools, furniture, and even royal servants and pets. These riches lured grave robbers, who stripped most of the known tombs virtually bare. Beginning with Amenhotep I (r. 1514–1493 B.C.E.), however, the pharaohs located their burial complexes on the west bank of the Nile, across the river from

Thebes, in a valley hidden by cliffs and a narrow entrance. Amenhotep I had his temple and tomb built into the side of the limestone cliffs in the valley, with deep corridors stretching as far as 100 m (328 ft.) below the earth. Traditionally, work on a pharaoh's tomb began the day he ascended the throne and ended the day he died.

More than 60 such tombs have been rediscovered since the eighteenth century. Over time desert sand had covered the entrances to most of the tombs, and their locations had been forgotten. In 1799, however, army engineers accompanying France's Napoleon I rediscovered several of them, and Europeans proceeded to excavate the tombs and remove their precious contents to museums in their home countries. Perhaps the most extraordinary discovery was of the tomb of the boy king Tutankhamen in 1922. Located on the valley floor, it was robbed twice but escaped large-scale looting because the construction of a later tomb covered its entrance with sand and rubble. Although it is by far the smallest tomb in the valley, it yielded archaeologists more than 5,000 artifacts, many of which now reside in the Cairo Museum. During the 1980s archaeologists discovered a tomb that they believe contains 52 sons of Ramses II (r. 1279?–1212? B.C.E.). Scientists have been excavating this tomb ever since. In late 1997 they commissioned the DNA testing of four mummies to determine if they were in fact Ramses' offspring. The Valley of the Kings is also the final resting place for Hatshepsut (r. 1503–1482 B.C.E.), one of the few women who ever ruled Egypt.

Archaeologists worry that these ancient monuments, which have faced centuries of humidity, pollution, and flash floods, are deteriorating. Some say that it is only a matter of time before they are lost forever. In addition, thieves and vandals have been plundering the monuments for thousands of years. Yet the walls of these tombs still contain elaborate bas-relief artwork that provides information and insight into the beliefs and practices of one of the world's oldest and greatest civilizations. As a result Egyptologists have declared the valley the richest archaeological site in the world. Archaeologists are currently developing preservation plans, creating detailed topographic maps of the tombs they have already discovered, and outlining possibilities for further excavations.

North America

VanDerZee, James Augustus

(b. June 29, 1886, Lenox, Mass.; d. May 15, 1983, Washington, D.C.), African American photographer whose work recorded and contributed to the Harlem Renaissance.

James VanDerZee was born in Lenox, Massachussetts, and made his earliest photographs there in 1900, after he won a camera for peddling large amounts of sachet powder. He immediately embraced photography and by the time he moved to New York City in 1906 had mastered the rudiments of the craft. After a job as a waiter, a short stay in Virginia, and a job snapping portraits in a New Jersey department store, VanDerZee opened his own studio in Harlem. From 1916 to 1931 he kept shop at 135th Street and Lenox Avenue, serving as the neighborhood's preeminent photographer.

VanDerZee documented faces and facets of the Harlem Renaissance, as well as numerous weddings, funerals, business clubs, and sports teams. In 1924 Marcus Garvey contracted with him to be the official photographer of the Universal Negro Improvement Association (UNIA). In addition to making documentary photographs that were realistic in style, VanDerZee experimented with photographic techniques—such as doctoring negatives and creating double exposures—demonstrating his artistic as well as technical ability.

Although VanDerZee's business survived the Great Depression and World War II, it began to wane during the early 1950s. For a time he supported himself by running a mail-order restoration service, but in 1969 he was evicted from his studio. At the same time, however, he caught the public eye through his contributions to *Harlem on My Mind*, an exhibition at New York City's Metropolitan Museum of Art. Soon afterward a group of young photographers, including Harlem curator Reginald McGhee, founded the James VanDerZee Institute (now defunct), which organized exhibitions of his work.

As public recognition of VanDerZee's work grew, the photographer regained the prosperity of his early career. The return to success was strengthened by his marriage to Donna Mussenden in 1978. Mussenden, 60 years his junior, took charge of him and his estate, helped win back copyrights, and transformed the VanDerZee legacy into a business. She also helped VanDerZee with his final project, a series of celebrity portraits shot in the early 1980s.

James VanDerZee died on May 15, 1983, at age 96. Over the course of his long career he photographed numerous African American celebrities, including Muhammad Ali, Bill Cosby, Miles Davis, Eubie Blake, Romare Bearden, Cicely Tyson, Jean-Michel Basquiat, Ossie Davis,and Ruby Dee. He received awards from many institutions, including an honorary doctorate from Howard University.

North America

Van Peebles, Melvin

(b. August 21, 1932, Chicago, Ill.), author, filmmaker, and playwright, perhaps best known for his groundbreaking 1971 independent film, *Sweet Sweetback's Baadasssss Song.*

Melvin Van Peebles has traded stocks on the floor of the American Stock Exchange, published numerous novels, and directed, produced, composed, and starred in American films and plays. He is an innovative and successful entrepreneur who has worked for more than four decades to offer new, and sometimes controversial, images of African Americans.

Van Peebles was born in 1932 on the South Side of Chicago, but spent most of his adolescent years with his father, a tailor in Phoenix, Illinois. After graduating from high school in 1949 and from Ohio Wesleyan University in 1953, Van Peebles served as a flight navigator for three and a half years in the United States Air Force. After leaving the military he spent brief periods in Mexico and San Francisco—where he was married—before moving to Europe. He studied at the Dutch National Theatre in the Netherlands, then moved to France in the early 1960s. During nearly a decade in Paris, Van Peebles wrote and published several novels in French, including *La permission*, which he filmed under the title of *The Story of the Three-Day Pass* and which concerns a black U.S. serviceman. The film won critical acclaim and helped Van Peebles earn a studio contract with Columbia Pictures.

Van Peebles returned to the United States and in 1969 directed *Watermelon Man*, a comedy about a racist white insurance salesman who wakes up one day to find that he has become black. Van Peebles took the proceeds from the film and made *Sweet Sweetback's Baadasssss Song* (1971), one of the most successful and controversial independent films of the era. *Sweetback* pushed the limits of cinematic decorum, combining sex and violence in its depiction of a black sex worker who witnesses the murder of a young black revolutionary by two white police officers. It was one of the first "blaxpoitation" films of the 1970s and its success opened doors for African American directors, camera operators, designers, and editors.

In the early 1970s Van Peebles staged two plays on Broadway: the musical *Ain't Supposed to Die a Natural Death*, and *Don't Play Us Cheap*, based on his novel *Don't Play Us Cheap: A Harlem Party*. Later in the decade he wrote scripts for two television productions, *Just an Old Sweet Song* and *Sophisticated Gents*. Van Peebles turned his attention to business in the early 1980s and became an options trader on the floor of the American Stock Exchange. Drawing on his success, he published two books on the options market. Since then he has written a novel and appeared in the 1993 movie *Posse*, an all-black Western by his son, Mario Van Peebles.

North America

Varick, James

(b. 1750, Orange County, New York; d. July 22, 1827, New York, New York), founder of the African Methodist Episcopal Zion Church.

James Varick was a widely influential free black in New York City at the turn of the nineteenth century. Although both of his parents had Dutch Reformed Church connections, he joined the white John Street Methodist Church. Later he and other blacks withdrew to create the first African

American congregation in New York. A shoemaker by trade, he also taught school; participated in black Masonic, mutual aid, and anticolonization societies; petitioned for the right to vote; and was one of the founders of *Freedom's Journal*, the first black American newspaper.

The congregation Varick established grew into a denomination, the African Methodist Episcopal Zion Church (AME Zion), and on July 30, 1822, Varick was elected its first bishop. The denomination, like the African Methodist Episcopal Church founded by Richard Allen, kept Methodist theology, polity, and worship, but practiced its faith in a black organization under black control. Largely middle class in makeup, the AME Zion Church has been a major institution in African American history. Varick's ashes are preserved in Mother Zion AMEZ Church on 137th Street in Harlem.

Latin America and the Caribbean

Vasconcelos, José

(1722?–1760?), Afro-Mexican poet famous for his wit and humor about whom very little information is known. His improvised verses were published by Nicolás León in 1912 under the title *El negrito poeta mexicano y sus populares versos* (The Little Black Mexican Poet and His Popular Verses).

Latin America and the Caribbean

Vasconcelos, Naná (Juvenal de Hollanda Vasconcelos)

(b. August 2, 1944, Recife, Brazil), Afro-Brazilian percussionist and master of the traditional Brazilian *berimbau*.

Naná Vasconcelos is one of the most significant and influential percussionists of the last 30 years. At age 12 he began playing percussion—bongos and maracas—in the band led by his guitarist father. Later he took up drums and played in a bossa nova band. He is a master of the odd-numbered rhythms, such as 5/4 and 7/4, that are common in northeastern Brazil. In the mid-1960s Vasconcelos joined the band of Afro-Brazilian singer Milton Nascimento and moved to Rio de Janeiro. There he learned to play the berimbau, a traditional Afro-Brazilian percussion instrument shaped like an archer's bow with an attached gourd resonator. The berimbau produces a distinctive buzzing tone when the instrument's single wire string is struck with a thin wooden stick. Its tonal quality can be altered depending on the position of the gourd resonator, and its pitch depends on whether the musician places a coin against the wire.

In 1971 Vasconcelos joined the band of Argentinian tenor saxophonist Gato Barbieri and toured Argentina, the United States, and Europe. After the end of the tour he stayed in Paris for two years, performing and working with handicapped children. In Europe he played with American avant-garde jazz trumpeter Don Cherry and with Brazilian jazz musician Egberto Gismonti. Together with Cherry and Collin Walcott, Vasconcelos formed Codona, an influential trio that combined the musical traditions of several continents. In 1976 Vasconcelos moved to New York City, where, as a mul-titalented percussionist, he was soon in demand.

Vasconcelos has recorded with such diverse musicians as blues legend B. B. King, jazz pianist Keith Jarrett, fusion guitarist Pat Metheny, and the rock group Talking Heads. He has played with a wide variety of Brazilian musicians, including guitarist and political activist Caetano Veloso, pianist and singer Ivan Lins, and vocalist Marisa Monte. In addition, Vasconcelos has released several albums under his own name, among them *Bush Dance* (1986) and *Storytelling* (1995), both featuring his unique and complex multi-instrumental sound.

North America
___

Vaughan, Sarah

(b. March 27, 1924, Newark, N.J.; d. April 3, 1990, Hidden Hills, Calif.), African American jazz singer and pianist lauded for her ability to command pitch and dynamics across three vocal octaves, Vaughan's singing style was informed by the harmony and improvisation of jazz horn sections.

Sarah Vaughan's parents, both of whom were musicians, cultivated and nurtured her early interest in music. She began taking piano lessons at age 7 and organ lessons at 8. By age 12 she was playing the organ for the Mount Zion Baptist Church and singing in its choir. She later attended Arts High School in Newark, New Jersey.

In 1942 Vaughan entered and won an amateur-night contest in which she sang "Body and Soul." Her award was $10 and a week of performances at the Apollo Theater, an engagement that led to her being hired as a vo-calist and second pianist in Earl "Fatha" Hines's big band. In 1944 she joined singer Billy Eckstine's band. She recorded the hit "Lover Man" (1945) with Charlie Parker and Dizzy Gillespie, also members of Eckstine's ensemble, before launching her solo career in 1946 at the New York Cafe Society. In 1949 she landed a five-year recording contract with Columbia Records. Vaughan sustained her success as a singer through the early 1980s, recording on numerous labels, performing with a variety of jazz artists, and touring several countries.

Nicknamed "Sassy" and the "Divine One," Vaughan repeatedly was voted the top female vocalist by *Down Beat* and *Metronome* jazz magazines between 1947 and 1952. Her 1982 album *Gershwin Live!* won a Grammy Award, and in 1989 she received the Grammy Lifetime Achievement Award. Vaughan was inducted into the Jazz Hall of Fame in 1990.

Vee Jay Records,

the most influential and successful African American-owned record company before the appearance of Motown Records.

Vee Jay Records was founded in Chicago in 1952–1953, and it quickly emerged as America's most successful black-owned record company. Vee Jay recorded gospel music, jazz, blues, rhythm and blues, and early soul, but it was unique in concentrating on vocal harmony groups. Like many small record companies, Vee Jay was a family affair, involving Vivian Carter Bracken, her husband James Bracken, and her brother Calvin Carter. Vivian was a disc jockey in Gary, Indiana, where she and James owned a record store. Carter suggested the name Vee Jay, based on the first initials of his sister's and his brother-in-law's first names.

Vee Jay's first vocal group was the Spaniels, which featured the cool lead of James "Pookie" Hudson and which had a major hit with "Goodnight Sweetheart Goodnight" (1954). Other important Vee Jay vocal group hits included the El Dorados's "At My Front" (1955); the Dells's "Oh What a Nite" (1957); a memorable "For Your Precious Love" (1958) by the original Impressions, featuring Jerry Butler and Curtis Mayfield; and "Duke of Earl" by the Dukays, credited solely to the group's lead singer, Gene Chandler.

Within two years of releasing its first Spaniels' single, Vee Jay owned a building on Chicago's Michigan Avenue directly across from the offices of Chess Records, which was a major producer of music for the African American market, featuring such best-selling artists as Muddy Waters, Chuck Berry, and the Moonglows. Besides vocal groups, Vee Jay recorded a number of other significant talents in the late 1950s and early 1960s, including bluesmen John Lee Hooker and Jimmy Reed, solo vocalists Jerry Butler, Dee Clark, and Betty Everett, and gospel singers such as the Staple Singers and Alex Bradford. The company also recorded jazz, including tenor saxophonist Wardell Gray's last recording session, in 1955.

During the early 1960s Vee Jay stood on a par not only with Berry Gordy's fast-growing Motown Records, but also with the independents that focused on the audience for African American R&B and soul music: Chess, Atlantic, and Stax Records. But rapid expansion, sloppy finances, and internal bickering forced the company to declare bankruptcy in 1965.

Vega, Ana Lydia

(b. December 6, 1946, Santurce, Puerto Rico), writer, feminist critic, and professor of French and Caribbean literature at the University of Puerto Rico at Rio Piedras who regards Afro-Puerto Rican themes and popular language as central to her intellectual production.

Notable among the works of Ana Lydia Vega are *Vírgenes y mártires* (1981), the author's first book, which was coauthored with Carmen Lugo Filipp; *Encancaranublado y otros cuentos de naufragio* (1982), which won Vega the 1982 Casa de Las Americas Prize; *La gran fiesta* (1986), a screenplay that was made into a movie; *Pasión de historia y otras historias de pasión* (1987); and *Falsas crónicas del sur* (1991). Various Vega stories and a novella were translated into English by Andrew Hurley and appeared under the title *True and False Romances* (1994).Vega has received numerous awards for her work, including the PEN (International Association of Poets, Playwrights, Editors, Essayists, and Novelists) Club of Puerto Rico National Literature Prize on several occasions, the prestigious Casa de Las Americas Prize of Cuba (1982), the Juan Rulfo International Short Story Prize (1984), the Premio Casa del Autor Puertorriqueño (1985), and the Guggenheim Fellowship for Literary Creation (1989).

Vega's profound knowledge of Spanish and African oral tradition has been an important influence on her writing. The author wrote her 1978 doctoral thesis on Haiti's King Cristophe in Antillean theater and in black theater in the United States, and her narratives often include tales and thematic elements from African folklore. Vega received early exposure to oral tradition through her father, who was an expert in décimas, an oral form of poetic improvisation typical of black troubadours. She has a superb ear for popular language that informs her skillful use of various types of verbal play such as jokes, puns, and riddles to underscore her biting humor. Vega's writing is also characterized by an alternation between formal and vernacular speech, an incisive examination of machismo in Caribbean societies, and vivid depictions of socially motivated violence. All of this serves her well and contributes to the powerful, distinctive quality of her writing. Vega has gained a wide following, and her works engender much discussion in a variety of publications.

Latin America and the Caribbean

Venezuela,

country of South America bordered on the east by Guyana, on the south by Brazil, on the west and southwest by Colombia, and bounded on the north by the Caribbean Sea and Atlantic Ocean.

Venezuela is often described as the country of *café con leche* (coffee and milk), a "racial democracy" with little or no racism where blacks, whites, and Native Americans intermingle freely, both physically and culturally. As in other Latin American countries that also make this claim, in Venezuela the reputation is sustained by the country's history of miscegenation and the "celebration" (read, "folklorization") of Afro-Venezuelan cultural manifestations. Much is hidden behind the label racial democracy. For although

there may be few formal barriers to social mobility for Afro-Venezuelans, they nonetheless face discrimination and racism that place them at the bottom of the economic and political hierarchy.

The Official History

Christopher Columbus sighted the coast of present-day Venezuela in 1498 during his third voyage to the New World, but the first Spanish settlements were not established until the 1520s. The city of Caracas was established in 1567.

Accompanying the first of the Spanish conquistadors were ladinos. Ladinos were black slaves who had been Hispanicized in Spain before coming to America, as opposed to bozales, slaves who later came directly from Africa. On occasion ladinos fought against the native populations; more often they cleared land for the roads, small settlements, and farm plots of the Spaniards. For their role in the conquest, some ladinos were given their freedom and exempted from taxes.

The area of Venezuela did not immediately yield the riches that were found elsewhere in Spanish America. Its economic life consisted largely of subsistence farming, performed by slaves. There was also some mining of pearls near the eastern islands of Cubagua and Margarita. The earliest divers were probably ladinos, but they were soon replaced by bozales, brought directly to Venezuela from Guinea and Cape Verde. Between 1500 and

1550 at least 5000 such slaves arrived in Venezuela. Only a few of them—those who distinguished themselves by bringing up the largest pearls—were able to buy their freedom.

As Spanish colonists grew rich from the pearl beds, a few of them established larger farms and ranches and began exploring for mineral deposits. After the founding in 1567 of Caracas, which would become the capital of Venezuela, masters and slaves fanned gradually south across the country, pressing inland among the surviving Indians. Late in the sixteenth century gold was discovered in several locations, and slaves were sent to the dank, subterranean mines to dig the gold. They were worked routinely to the point of exhaustion and, not infrequently, death—thus requiring the importation of more slaves. By 1600 Venezuela had a black slave population of about 13,000.

The mines of Venezuela, however, were never to become the primary basis of the colonial economy, and in the seventeenth century mining gave way to plantation farming. Wheat, tobacco, and cotton were grown, but the largest crops were cacao, the tropical evergreen tree prized for its cocoa (and thus chocolate), and the dye indigo. Slaves were, of course, the primary laborers. Early in the seventeenth century the Roman Catholic Church, which the Spanish Crown had entrusted with governing Venezuela, held most of Venezuela's land. During this period much of a slave's life on a plantation was typical of slave-plantation life elsewhere in the New World: work began under the supervision of a master at 5:00 A.M. and ended at about 9:00 P.M. During harvest season work often continued until midnight.

However throughout the seventeenth century more and more private landholders gained access to the fertile cacao valleys of central Venezuela. With this expansion the influence of the Church eroded, with important implications for slaves. First, because the private landholders were so few, slaves so numerous, and central Venezuela bereft of white settlements, the slave owners relied heavily upon slave foremen to oversee the farming. Eventually both the need for labor and the expanse of cultivated land were great enough that most slave owners allowed slaves to establish conucos, or small homesteads where slaves built houses, grew their own food, and could intermingle more or less freely with other slaves.

The conucos were beneficial to both slave and slaveholder. Because the slaves grew their own food and made their own goods, slaveholders did not have to provide these items. The slaves, meanwhile, were spared the rigorous and often harsh enforcement of white masters, as well as the cultural and religious imperialism of living among whites. Moreover, black field bosses and crew chiefs gained rudimentary experience in management and accounting.

Another important effect of the shift from Church control to private control was that by the end of the seventeenth century the Church had lost so much of its land base that it was desperate for tax money. As a result it offered Venezuela's many slaves the right to establish their own religious brotherhoods. The Church stood to benefit from granting this right since it had the power to tax assemblies.

By the turn of the nineteenth century most slaves were no longer of strictly African descent. Due to the remote nature of many of the cacao haciendas, Africans often married and bore children with Indians, creating a mixed race known as zambos. Moreover, in part because early colonial Venezuela had few white women, Spanish colonists often had sexual relations with black women, producing another racial category, called mulattos or pardos ("browns," referring to people of mixed blood). By the time of the wars of independence in the second decade of the nineteenth century, a large portion of Venezuelans could not be certain of their racial ancestry, and a significant portion of "white" Venezuelans had at least a trace of African or native blood, or both.

Venezuela asserted its independence from Colombia in January 1830 and later that year reaffirmed its commitment to freeing slaves. In 1845 Gen. José Tadeo Monagas was elected president with the Conservative Party, but three years later he switched to the Liberal Party and expelled many Conservatives from Congress. To shore up his power and head off a possible revolt, he declared all manumisos free at age 21. Monagas later ceded power to his brother, José Gregorio Monagas, who conscripted blacks into the army when a revolt broke out against him in May 1853. The rebel troops, which were quickly put down, also used black soldiers.

In order to shore up his support and stave off further revolt, Monagas declared all slaves free in March 1854. He promised slaveholders that they would receive payments in compensation for their lost property, but his regime collapsed shortly thereafter and no payments were made. The emancipation, however, survived the regime. Some 30,000 remaining slaves were at last finally freed.

Many Afro-Venezuelans gained political offices in rural areas and in the central government. In July 1966 the ban on black immigration was officially dropped.

In 1968 the government provided a host of subsidies and scholarships promoting the study and practice of Afro-Venezuelan arts, especially music, dance, and theater. During the 1970s and 1980s most of Venezuela's universities received funding for curricula in Afro-Venezuelan arts and culture. As elsewhere in Latin America, African culture and beliefs in Venezuela have become inextricably intertwined with the fabric of the larger society. In religion, for example, African spiritual beliefs melded with Roman Catholicism to form a Creole religion in which Roman Catholic saints are worshiped alongside black and native deities. Mass in the Creole religion is held to the beat of African drums, and the roles of traditional healer and priest often merge. On the day of Corpus Christi, a traditional Roman Catholic holiday, religious brotherhoods in Afro-Venezuelan towns typically perform dances with masks and movements that have been traced to the Congo.

In the 1990s most blacks in Venezuela still lived in poverty and held little political power. In 1993, however, Acción Democrática placed its first black presidential candidate on the ballot. Also, Afro-Venezuelan Aristúbolo Isturiz, a member of Causa R, a recently created party with roots in the labor movement, was elected mayor of Caracas.

Latin America and the Caribbean

Venezuelan Religion, African Elements in

Because slaves first arrived in Venezuela before 1800 and were immediately converted, at least superficially, to Roman Catholicism, African religious elements in Venezuela have survived only in fragmentary form in popular rituals for saints and in a few beliefs and practices.

African elements in Venezuelan folk-Catholic practices are found in rural regions with a predominantly black population, such as the Barlovento, the central coast, the southern coast of Lake Maracaibo, and some areas of Yaracuy, Lara, and Carabobo. African elements in the folk Catholicism of these areas are incorporated into the festivals held for particular saints by local brotherhoods. In Carabobo, Yaracuy, Miranda, and Aragua, for example, Saint John is the patron of black peasants and fishermen. On the eve of his feast, *erum* dances are held, while old women sing *sirenas* for the saint, similar to African praise songs. Early the next morning Saint John's icon is bathed in the river and then carried from house to house by drummers, singers, and dancers who are offered food and drinks. The participants use special homemade drums, which are used only during rituals. The faithful thank the saint for having answered their prayers. A similar ceremony is held in Lara in honor of Saint Anthony: celebrants engage in ritual stick fights during a procession with his statue—a custom also widely seen in West Africa.

In the region of Zulia, San Benito of Palermo is the patron of black peasants. His feast is celebrated with drum dances and processions held between Christmas and January 6 in different black villages. The rhythms and drumbeats used in this ceremony have kept their original African flavor. In recent years many traditional customs have disappeared, and the dances for the patron saints, once considered a solemn obligation, are now becoming tourist attractions.

"Devil Dances" are another type of Venezuelan festival that exhibits African elements. These dances are held annually on the Catholic festival of Corpus Christi Day in eight or nine different villages with predominantly black inhabitants. The most traditional dances take place in the isolated village of Chuao, in Aragua, where the male-only fraternity of Diablos (or devils) is responsible for the celebration, while the dances in honor of Saint John are organized by a female-dominated group. The "devils" wear colorful gowns and masks made of papier-mâché that are reminiscent of masks used in similar rituals in the Bapende, in the Congo area of Africa; their dances are similar to masked dances held in Central Africa. During these dances, which are considered a solemn obligation, the gender dichotomy also exists: one man wears a female mask, representing the "wife of the devil." It is important to note that the "devils" are not evil. On the contrary, the dancers dressed as devils visit the homes of the fraternity members in order to chase evil away. The dancers can also be compared to the *egunguns* in Benin and Nigeria, who represent the departed ancestors, visiting their living kin in order to bring good luck and chase evil away. Although in San Francisco de Yare the annual devil dances are watched by thousands of tourists, the members of the fraternity have preserved their original solemn ritual.

Some African elements are also found in the funeral rites in the Yaracuy and Barlovento regions. During the nightly wake held in the home of the departed, the women wail for the deceased while the men play cards. Mourners place a glass of water next to the coffin, as it is believed that the soul of the dead is still present and may be thirsty. They also place some personal objects, such as a comb, a toothbrush, and a cap, into the coffin for the spirit's journey to the other world; then they take the coffin out of the house through a hole made in the wall, which is carefully covered up again, so that the spirit cannot find its way back. After praying for nine nights in front of an improvised altar in the house of the departed, the people smash a table upon which flowers, candles, and photos of the dead have been placed. They make noise to indicate to the dead soul that the ritual is over and that it may now depart in peace and not disturb the living. On the night before All Souls' Day, celebrated annually on November 2, black peasants visit the graves of their departed relatives and sometimes spend the whole night in the cemetery. They leave food and libations there for the dead.

In addition to rituals and festivals that historically developed in Venezuela, other Afro-Latin religions are increasingly popular. During the past 40 years, for example, Santería has been introduced to Venezuela by Cubans and Venezuelans who have traveled to Miami and Puerto Rico. The majority of converts to this religion belong to the middle class, because initiation ceremonies are expensive. However, Venezuelans of all classes consult *babalawos*, or priests of the Santería religion, to help solve personal problems. Santería beliefs and practices have also been introduced into the native cult of Maria Lionza, which has its roots in both Amerindian beliefs and the teachings of Allan Kardec, a European spiritist. In this cult spirits of different origins are summoned to take possession of mediums in trance, and the spirits can then be consulted by the faithful. This cult is utilitarian in nature: the spirits prescribe cleansing rituals to get rid of evil influences and give advice on how to heal illnesses.

Until about 30 years ago most spiritual entities consulted in the cult of Maria Lionza were spirits of nature or of departed persons of importance, such as Amerindian chiefs who fought the Spanish conquerors or Simón Bolívar, the hero of Latin American independence. In recent years the *siete potencias africanas*—the seven most important orishas of the Cuban-Yoruba pantheon—have been consulted through the mediums. Animal sacrifices are offered to them, drums are used to call the spirits, and colors have a symbolic value, just as in Santería.

Venezuelan cultists often ignore the true African origin of these entities, although today they speak about the "African court," to which, incidentally, the Viking spirits also belong, although they are depicted as bearded white savages. Recently Venezuelan folk healers have begun to mention specific countries in their divination practices, and they may invoke the African spirits to help them in their spiritual work.

In addition to Santería, the Brazilian religion of Umbanda was introduced to Venezuela about 15 years ago by a white Uruguayan *pai de santo*, or priest. He presides over a center, frequented by members of the middle class, where Afro-Brazilian *caboclo* and *preto velho* spirits manifest themselves in initiated mediums who are consulted by adherents.

Overall, the globalization of Afro-American religion and the influence of religions such as Santería and Umbanda in Venezuela stem from media coverage, the expansion of esoteric literature, and frequent reunions of cultists and esoterics. The prospects for historically Venezuelan religions, though, are quite different. While the cult of Maria Lionza is subject to a re-Africanization process, in which spirits are increasingly identified as being of African origin, traditional folk religiosity is vanishing as the population of Venezuela is becoming more urbanized.

Latin America and the Caribbean

Virgin Islands (United States and British),

a group of more than 100 Caribbean islands (of which approximately 20 are inhabited) located between the Caribbean Sea and the North Atlantic Ocean, east of Puerto Rico. The group is divided politically into two dependent territories: the British Virgin Islands and the United States Virgin Islands. The main inhabited islands are St. Croix, St. Thomas, and St. John (all U.S. territories), and Tortola, Anegada, Virgin Gorda, and Jost Van Dyke (all British possessions).

When Christopher Columbus first sighted this archipelago of islands in November 1493, he named them Las Once Mil Virgenes (The Eleven Thousand Virgins) both to commemorate the legend of Saint Ursula and her 11,000 martyred virgins and to exaggerate the magnitude of his find to his patron, Queen Isabella of Spain. In reality the total number of Virgin Islands is much closer to 110 than to 11,000. Many of the islands are small and uninhabited, and to outsiders the Virgin Islands are often synonymous with the five large islands that have become immensely popular tourist destinations: St. Croix, St. John, and St. Thomas in the United States group, and Tortola and Virgin Gorda in the British group. The fact that the islands are split into United States and British territories is the end result of the region's complex history of slavery, colonization, and resistance—the story that lies behind today's resorts and restaurants.

The first inhabitants of the Virgin Islands were probably the Ciboney Amerindians, who appear to have migrated from South America to what is now St. Thomas in approximately 300 B.C.E. Within 500 years they were replaced by the Arawaks, who were mainly farmers and who eventually spread out to Tortola and several other Virgin Islands. Beginning at the end of the fourteenth century the Arawaks were overtaken by the more aggressive Caribs, who named St. Croix "Ay Ay" and established themselves on many other islands as well. But it was Columbus's intrusion that would have the most lasting effects.

Columbus and his crew were the first Europeans to "discover" the Caribbean Islands, and in their journeys they nominally claimed each island they saw for the Spanish flag. But because the Virgin Islands were smaller than many of the other Caribbean Islands and were not as rich in minerals and other natural resources, the Spanish chose not to settle them, and the islands were largely ignored during the first century of Caribbean colonization. By the 1600s, however, Europeans were pursuing expansion in the region in earnest.

The struggle for domination inevitably resulted in some conflicts. St. Croix was first shared by the English and Dutch, then held solely by the English, overtaken by the Spanish, then the French, then given to the Knights of Malta and returned to the French before it was sold to the Danish West India and Guinea Company in 1733. St. Thomas was occupied by the Danish, attacked by the Dutch, and captured and then abandoned by the English before being reclaimed by Denmark in 1671. Tortola was settled by Dutch buccaneers before being attacked and captured by the English in 1665. It was not until the beginning of the eighteenth century that the Virgin Islands had reached a more or less stable political configuration, with the islands grouped into Danish and English holdings. By then it was clear just what was at stake for each of these colonial powers: the Virgin Islands were developing into flourishing slave economies.

Once it was discovered that the islands' soil would support both cotton and sugar, settlers were eager to cultivate these crops. The white population at the time was an unpredictable assortment that included Quaker religious dissenters, then-infamous buccaneers, and ex-convicts who were sent to the West Indies as part of their jail sentences. It was clear that these white settlers would not provide all of the labor the new plantations would require. In 1673 the first consignment of 103 African slaves, probably taken from homes in Guinea, landed in St. Thomas. By 1715 the island had 160 plantations and 3,042 slaves.

Similarly drastic gains were made across the region by the mid-1700s, and in response to the new demand, Charlotte Amalie in St. Thomas became one of the world's largest slave markets in the eighteenth century. On both sets of islands the working conditions were arduous, the clothing and food given in compensation were minimal, and punishments were

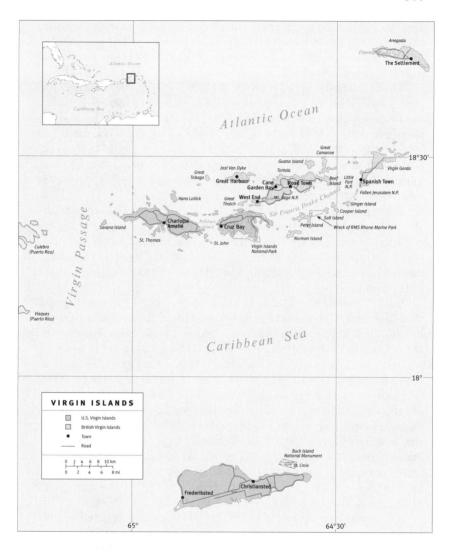

harsh. As one historian said, "It is difficult to characterize any slave system as more repressive than that of the Virgin Islands."

One drought in 1725–1726 resulted in a scarcity of food, and many planters chose simply to let their slaves starve to death. In all cases slaves were left with virtually no avenues of formal redress. On the British islands a slave who resisted a white owner could have his nose split, any member amputated, or "as many number of stripes" as the master chose to inflict. On the Danish islands a slave who struck a white person or even threatened to strike one "should be pinched and hung"—or, if the person chose to pardon him, "should lose his right hand." Death by various means of torture was permitted for a wide range of crimes, and especially for being suspected of making any plans to run away. But it was little surprise that many slaves still took the opportunity to escape when they could, and also little surprise that slaves in the Virgin Islands led two of the most dramatic revolts in the Caribbean.

The first was the St. John revolt in 1733. In the months leading up to the uprising, a drought, two hurricanes, and an insect plague had made the slaves' already desperate situation intolerable. The passage of a new, brutally restrictive slave code in September 1733 proved to be the last straw. The leaders of the revolt—allegedly African-born slaves of royal, West African origin—captured St. John's only fort and gave the signal for an islandwide uprising. At that time St. John had 1,087 slaves and only 208 whites; the slaves were able to control the island for six months.

It was not until August 1734 that the last rebels finally surrendered; although they had been promised a free pardon, they were instead publicly executed by torture. Many other rebels had committed suicide rather than be recaptured. While their daring effort ultimately ended in tragedy, it provided a powerful signal of the Africans' uncompromising commitment to freedom.

In 1790 British slaves led an uprising on Tortola after a rumor spread that England had granted them their freedom and their masters were holding it back. The rumors had some basis in reality, because by the end of the eighteenth century Britain was already calling for abolition. Several planters on the British islands had already begun manumitting groups of slaves, leading to a growing class of free blacks whose numbers grew even larger after Britain abolished the slave trade in 1808. From that time on illegal cargoes of slaves found on British ships were seized and "liberated"; but instead of being returned to their African homes, they were brought to the West Indies and set free there. Not surprisingly, as the number of free blacks in the islands increased, blacks who remained enslaved grew even more convinced of their own right to be free. British Virgin Islands slave insurrections flared up in 1823, 1827, 1830, and 1831. Full emancipation of all English slaves was finally established on August 1, 1834.

The apprenticeship period that followed emancipation mandated that all slaves remain with their former owners for another four years, and so essentially extended slavery until 1838. But black British Virgin Islanders were still relieved, above all, to be finally free.

In the Danish West Indies, although the slave trade had been abolished in 1792, slavery itself remained legal until 1848. That year, on July 3, Moses Gottlieb, also known as Buddhoe, led fellow St. Croix slaves in another dramatic uprising—arguably among the most successful in history. In this action slaves sacked the houses of the police assistant, the town bailiff, and a wealthy merchant and then took over the fort, threatening to burn the entire town if they were not emancipated within the hour. Most of the whites had already taken refuge on ships docked in the harbor. Sensing just how serious the threat was, within the hour the governor general read the Proclamation of Emancipation, which declared that "all unfree in the Danish West India

Islands are from today free." Thus these St. Croix slaves became one of the few groups of enslaved people to succeed in liberating themselves.

Across the Caribbean, however, true economic and social freedom came slowly for black Virgin Islanders. In the Danish West Indies the 1849 Labor Act made working conditions for newly emancipated blacks nearly as restrictive as they had been under slavery. In the British West Indies the 1867 reversion to an appointed governing council—and the abolition of free elections—ensured that the colonies would be governed by their white minorities. In both sets of colonies prevailing social traditions continued to enforce racism and racial separation, on the theory that free blacks were still different from and inferior to free whites. In the Virgin Islands and across the Caribbean, the abolition of slavery also led to a decline in economic productivity. In a tight economy it was the black workers who suffered most.

It was this economic decline that first led Denmark to contemplate selling its colonies to the United States in 1866. After talks that extended over the next 50 years, the transfer became a reality on March 31, 1917. The twentieth century had already brought some small improvements to the Virgin Islands, as both the Danish and British governments had begun establishing schools and banks. Events in 1915 in St. Croix marked the beginning of changes that eventually spread throughout the Caribbean. That year D. Hamilton Jackson formed the first labor union in the West Indies. Within decades the labor movement became the basis not only for a dramatic improvement in working conditions across the region but also for the push for increased self-government. In islands across the Caribbean the black workers who joined labor unions eventually became the black politicians and voters who won independence from their colonial powers.

Virgin Islanders were no different in their desire for greater political authority, and over time legislative changes ensured that the majorities would indeed rule in the islands. Full electoral government came to the British islands in 1967, and the U.S. islands in 1970. But both groups of islands chose not to push for full independence, undoubtedly because of the strong economic benefits that the islands received from the United States and Britain. This was especially true in the case of the U.S. islands, and in 1958 the British islands had even declined to join the West Indies Federation established by the rest of the British Caribbean because of their own wish to keep their strong economic ties to the U.S. islands.

The economies of each of the Virgin Islands also changed dramatically with the advent of the tourist industry. Today the Virgin Islands have some of the highest standards of living in the Caribbean, and the U.S. islands in particular have become a haven for other West Indian immigrants. This prosperity comes largely from the islands' continuing status as dependent territories. But much of it is also directly linked to their popularity as tourist destinations, particularly among American and British tourists. For the islands' black majorities, this has meant jobs in every sector of the tourist industry, from service to construction.

Virgin Islanders today enjoy citizenship status in their respective countries but retain the Afro-Caribbean cultural heritage of their island homes. A 1995 hurricane caused significant damage in the islands, but by 1998 the tourist industry had already begun its comeback. The Virgin Islands are entering the twenty-first century as one of the Caribbean's most successful regions, and this new period of relative prosperity is a welcome change and reward for Virgin Islanders.

Vodou,

a religion originally developed and practiced by slaves and freed blacks in Haiti; since the 1987 constitution it has been recognized as the country's national religion.

The slave trade displaced millions of Africans from their native lands. Uprooted from their societies, the Africans brought with them their family values, beliefs, traditions, and religious practices. Although Haiti's culture derives from three sources—African, Amerindian, and European—Haiti emerged as a nation whose African contributions form its principal cultural traits. The Vodou religion must be interpreted within this framework.

Origins of the Religion

The slaves from more than a hundred different ethnic groups who came to Haiti lacked a common language. They were able to unite only through their recreated African religion, Vodou. The colonial powers systematically intermixed Africans so that any recollection of language, lineage, or ties to the motherland, known as *Ginen*, the term for the mythical African homeland, would be permanently lost. Colonialists imposed European values and Roman Catholicism upon the slave population. In an attempt to stop the practice of Vodou, slave gatherings were forbidden. Thus slaves were forced to worship their African deities secretly and to hide their allegiance to their ancestral religion. These interdictions, repressive measures, and the clandestine nature of Vodou ceremonies led to the revalorization of the very African cultural values that Europeans tried to suppress.

This regrouping around a common past and ideal has consistently played a role in Haitian political life and has fueled a number of mass movements, culminating in the war for independence and, much later, in the 1986 overthrow of the Duvalier dictatorship. A turning point in this saga was the 1791 Bois Caiman Vodou ritual and political congress, orchestrated by Boukman, which led to a general slave uprising that became a war of national liberation. Vodou's close ties to its African origins are also a result of Haiti's isolation from the rest of the world following its 1804 successful slave revolution.

The history of persecution of Vodou practitioners continued with the 1896, 1913, and 1941 antisuperstition campaigns, which destroyed shrines and led to the massacre of hundreds of people who admitted their adherence to Vodou. The period of the American occupation (1915–1934) as well as the post-Duvalier era were also times of severe persecution of Vodouists. Roman Catholicism, headed exclusively by Westerners until the 1960s, had the political and financial support of the state and remained the country's sole official religion until the constitution of 1987 recognized freedom of religion.

Meaning and Significance

Popular labeling of Vodou as "witchcraft" and "magic" has been a historical tradition perpetuated in Hollywood films and supermarket tabloids, which sustain these same popular myths. Vodou, the preferred term used to designate the Haitian religion, is of Dahomean origin and derives from the Fon word for "God" or "Spirit." Other accurate spellings include *Vodun*, *Vodoun*, or the French Vaudou, but never *voodoo*, the sensationalist and derogatory Western creation. Vodou is a comprehensive system of knowledge that has nothing to do with simplistic and erroneous images of sticking pins into dolls, putting a hex on an adversary, or turning innocents into zombies. It is an organized form of communal support that provides meaning to the human experience in relation to the natural and supernatural forces of the universe.

Despite media portrayals, Vodou shares many elements with other religions. Like members of other persuasions, Vodouists believe in creating harmony, in keeping a balance, and in cultivating virtues and positive values. With its reverence for the ancestors, Vodou is the cement that binds family and community life in Haiti.

Vodou is essentially a monotheistic religion that recognizes a single and supreme spiritual entity or God, known as Mawu-Lisa among the Fon, Olorun among the Yoruba, and Bondye or Gran Met in Haiti. The Haitian religion originated from the fusion of rituals of a range of African ethnic groups—in particular, the Fon, Yoruba, Igbo, Hausa, Ewe, and Kongo. Scholars have called African culture "additive," in the sense that it often adapted foreign elements into its structure. Following the same pattern, Vodou absorbed many aspects of Roman Catholicism into its ritual. Vodouists use Roman Catholic prayers and hymns at the beginning of ceremonies and use the Gregorian calendar to mark the celebrations of the *lwas*, the spirit intermediaries between humans and God who have been linked to the iconography and stories about Roman Catholic saints. For the *servitors* of the spirits, as Vodouists typically refer to themselves, there is no conflict between Vodou and Roman Catholicism. This syncretism is the subject of debates among scholars: some hold that Roman Catholic practices were actually absorbed into Vodou; others contend that the Haitians never accepted the European elements and instead simply used the saints and Christian rituals as a cover to continue their own practices. Whichever interpretation one accepts, syncretism remains a basic part of Haitian Vodou.

In addition to its visible cultural and ritual dimensions, expressed through the arts, especially in Haitian music and dance, Vodou's teaching and belief system include social, economic, political, and practical components. Today, for example, Vodou's teachings are concerned with what can be done to overcome the limiting social conditions in Haiti, a country that has been strenuously challenged from within and outside its borders. Vodou addresses such questions as what to do in case of illness in a country that counts only one physician for 23,000 people, and what to do before embarking upon major undertakings, such as marriage, business transactions, or traveling abroad. Vodou gives its adherents positive means to address these issues and provides support in times of challenging economic moments and difficult political transitions.

Most Vodou ceremonies conform to one of two major rites. The Rada rite retained from the Old Kingdom of Dahomey (present-day Nigeria, Benin, and Togo) is generally agreed to be most faithful to West African tradition. The Petwo rite is a newer development that arose out of the crucible of the New World plantation system and encompasses elements of the Kongo culture as well as the practices of many other groups from Central Africa to Angola in the southwest. The Rada rite is Vodou's most elaborate rite and includes the great communal spirits, or lwa, such as Atibon Legba, Marasa Dosou Dosa, Danbala and Ayida Wedo, Azaka Mede, Ogou Feray, Agwe Tawoyo, Ezili Freda Daome, Lasirenn and Labalenn, and Gede Nimbo. It is generally assumed by Vodou practitioners and researchers alike that the Rada lwa are *dous* or "sweet." These *fle Ginen*, or true spirits of Africa, are the first lwas to be saluted in ceremonies. Many maintain that the Petwo lwa are *anme*, or "bitter." Associated with fire, they are said to be *lwa cho*, or "hot lwa," engaging in forceful behavior. The Petwo rite includes major lwa such as Met Kalfou, Simbi Andezo, Ezili Danto, and Bawon Samdi. Some of the lwa exist *andezo*, or in two cosmic substances, and are served in both Rada and Petwo rituals. Contrary to popular conception, the line between Rada and Petwo is not as rigid as it appears: much of what is described as Rada goes for Petwo.

Possession, an important dimension of Vodou worship, is among the least understood aspects of the religion. Through possession both the lwa and the community are affirmed. The participants (in particular, the priests and priestesses, the *houngans* and *manbos*, and the other initiates, the *ounsis*) transcend their materiality by becoming spirits, and the spirits renew their vigor by dancing and feasting with the *chwal*, or horses, for it is said that during possession the lwa rides a person like a cavalier rides a horse. Equally important, possession is a time when the lwa communicate in a tangible way with the people, who during such times receive answers to pressing questions.

The Future of Vodou

Though Vodou continues to be viewed with ambivalence, increasingly people have been practicing it more openly in Haiti and abroad. Today scholars, patriots, and grassroots organizers continue a crusade for greater respect for Haiti's ancestral religion. Reputable artists, scholars, and writers are affirming their involvement with Vodou. In the past ten years, with the advent of the "root culture" movement driven by the progressive wing of culturalists, Vodou-inspired musical groups such as Boukman Eksperyans, Boukan Ginen, RAM, and the Fugees, and organizations such as Zantray, Bode Nasyonal, and New Rada Community have emerged. The touring *Sacred Arts of Haitian Vodou* exhibition constituted one more effort in a series of activities aimed at fostering a better understanding of Vodou. Finally, a 1997 conference held at the University of California, Santa Barbara, in which Haitian scholars and Vodou practitioners met to discuss the role of Vodou in the development of Haiti, led to the creation of the Congress of Santa Barbara, an international scholarly association for the study of Haitian Vodou. However, no single person or organization has the final word on Vodou, which remains a complex but decentralized system of univer sal knowledge, cultural practices, and communal support.

North America

Voting Rights Act of 1965,

legislation that charged the federal government of the United States with helping disfranchised African Americans regain the right to vote in the South.

In the century following Reconstruction, African Americans in the South faced overwhelming obstacles to voting. Despite the Fifteenth and Nineteenth Amendments to the U.S. Constitution, which had enfranchised black men and all women respectively, southern voter registration boards used poll taxes, literacy tests, and other bureaucratic impediments to deny African Americans their legal rights. Southern blacks also risked harassment, intimidation, economic reprisals, and physical violence when they tried to register or vote. As a result African Americans had little if any political power, either locally or nationally. In Mississippi, for instance, only 5 percent of eligible blacks were registered to vote in 1960.

The Voting Rights Act of 1965, meant to reverse this disfranchisement, grew out of both public protest and private political negotiation. Starting in 1961, the Southern Christian Leadership Conference (SCLC), led by Rev. Martin Luther King Jr., staged nonviolent demonstrations in Albany, Georgia, and Birmingham, Alabama. King and the SCLC hoped to attract national media attention and pressure the U.S. government to protect African Americans' constitutional rights. The strategy worked. Newspaper photos and television broadcasts of Birmingham's notoriously racist police commissioner, Eugene "Bull" Connor, and his men violently attacking the SCLC's peaceful protesters with water hoses, police dogs, and nightsticks awakened the consciences of white Americans.

Selma, Alabama, was the site of the next campaign. In the first three months of 1965 the SCLC led local residents and visiting volunteers in a

BLACK VOTER REGISTRATION IN THE SOUTH 1940–1984
Estimated percentage of voting-age blacks registered

State	1940	1947	1952	1960	1962	1964	1968	1976	1980	1982	1984
Alabama	0.4	1.2	5.0	13.7	13.4	23.0	56.7	58.4	55.8	69.7	74.0
Arkansas	1.5	17.3	27.0	37.3	34.0	49.3	67.5	94.0	57.2	63.9	67.2
Florida	5.7	15.4	33.0	38.9	36.8	63.8	62.1	61.1	58.3	59.7	63.4
Georgia	3.0	18.8	23.0	29.3	26.7	44.0	56.1	74.8	48.6	50.4	57.9
Louisiana	0.5	2.6	25.0	30.9	27.8	32.0	59.3	63.0	60.7	61.1	65.7
Mississippi	0.4	0.9	4.0	5.2	5.3	6.7	54.4	60.7	62.3	64.2	77.1
North Carolina	7.1	15.2	18.0	38.1	35.8	46.8	55.3	54.8	51.3	50.9	65.4
South Carolina	0.8	13.0	20.0	15.6	22.9	38.7	50.8	56.5	53.7	53.9	58.5
Tennessee	6.5	25.8	27.0	58.9	49.8	69.4	72.8	66.4	64.0	66.1	69.9
Texas	5.6	18.5	31.0	34.9	37.3	57.7	83.1	65.0	56.0	49.5	71.5
Virginia	4.1	13.2	16.0	22.8	24.0	45.7	58.4	54.7	53.2	49.5	62.3
Average	3.0	12.0	20.0	29.1	29.4	43.1	62.0	63.1	55.8	56.5	66.2

Sources: David Garrow, *Protest at Selma* (1978); U.S. Department of Commerce, Bureau of Census, *Statistical Abstract* (1976, 1981, 1982-1983, 1986).

SOUTHERN AFRICAN AMERICAN VOTERS, POTENTIAL AND ELIGIBLE, 1976–1990

Year	Population (in millions)		% Registered				% Voted			
			Presidential Election Years		Congressional Election Years		Presidential Election Years		Congressional Election Years	
	Total	Black	Total	Black	Total	Black	Total	Black	Total	Black
1976	146.5	14.9	66.7	58.5	–	–	59.2	48.7	–	–
1978	151.6	15.6	–	–	62.6	57.1	–	–	45.9	37.2
1980	157.1	16.4	66.9	60.0	–	–	59.2	50.5	–	–
1982	165.5	17.6	–	–	64.1	59.1	–	–	48.8	43.0
1984	170.0	18.4	68.3	66.3	–	–	59.9	55.8	–	–
1986	173.9	19.0	–	–	64.3	64.0	–	–	46.0	43.2
1988	178.1	19.7	66.6	64.5	–	–	57.4	51.5	–	–
1990	182.1	20.4	–	–	62.2	58.8	–	–	45.0	39.2

Sources: U.S. Bureau of the Census, *Current Population Reports*, Series P-20, no. 453, and earlier reports; *Encyclopedia of African-American Culture and History* (1996): "Voting-Age Population, Percentage Reporting Registered, 1976–1990" (Table 11.7).

series of marches demanding an equal right to vote. As they did in Birmingham, protesters met with violence and imprisonment in Selma. King himself wrote a letter from the Selma jail, published in the New York Times, in which he said, "There are more Negroes in jail with me than there are on the voting rolls" in Selma. In the worst attack yet, on Sunday, March 7, a group of Alabama state troopers, local sheriff's officers, and unofficial possemen used tear gas and clubs against 600 peaceful marchers. By now, as King had predicted, the nation was watching.

President Lyndon B. Johnson, who succeeded to the presidency after the 1963 assassination of John F. Kennedy, made civil rights one of his administration's top priorities, using his formidable political skills to pass the Twenty-fourth Amendment, which outlawed poll taxes, in 1964. Now, a week after "Bloody Sunday" in Selma, Johnson gave a televised speech before Congress in which he not only denounced the assault but called it "wrong-deadly wrong" that African Americans were being denied their constitutional rights. Johnson went on to dramatically quote the movement's motto, "we shall overcome."

Two days later the president sent the voting rights bill to Congress. The resolution, signed into law on August 6, 1965, empowered the federal government to oversee voter registration and elections in counties that had used tests to determine voter eligibility or where registration or turnout had been less than 50 percent in the 1964 presidential election. It also banned discriminatory literacy tests and expanded voting rights for non-English-speaking Americans.

The law's effects were wide and powerful. By 1968 nearly 60 percent of eligible African Americans were registered to vote in Mississippi, and other southern states showed similar improvement. Between 1965 and 1990 the number of black state legislators and members of Congress rose from 2 to 160. Despite finally reclaiming their constitutional voting rights, however, many African Americans in the South and elsewhere saw little progress on other fronts. They still faced illegal job discrimination, substandard schools, and unequal health care. Following its major victories—the Civil Rights Act of 1964 and the Voting Rights Act of 1965—the liberal, integrationist Civil Rights Movement began to be eclipsed by the more radical Black Power Movement.

The Voting Rights Act was extended in 1970, 1975, and 1982—the last time despite vigorous resistance from the Reagan administration. Fearing a largely Democratic black vote, the Republican Party adopted various means to minimize it, including at-large elections and redistricting to dilute black representation. The party also attacked as racial gerrymandering the new "majority-minority" congressional districts drawn by the U.S. Justice Department. In 1996 the Supreme Court agreed, outlawing the use of racial factors in deciding district lines. Some prominent African Americans, like Harvard University law professor Lani Guinier, argued that minority votes would be more effective in a system of proportional representation.

Despite these setbacks and debates, the Voting Rights Act had an enormous impact. It re-enfranchised black southerners and helped elect African Americans at the local, state, and national levels. By 1989 there were an estimated 7200 black officeholders, of whom 67 percent were in the South.

Walcott, Derek Alton

(b. January 23, 1930, Castries, St. Lucia), poet, playwright, and Nobel laureate who developed a distinctly Caribbean literary style rooted in a mastery of the classical European tradition.

Derek Alton Walcott, winner of the 1992 Nobel Prize in literature, is widely regarded as one of the most important writers ever to emerge from the English-speaking Caribbean. "In the manner of Joyce and Yeats," wrote critic Stephen Breslow soon after Walcott was awarded the Nobel Prize, "Walcott has merged a profound, rhapsodic reverie upon his remote birthplace—its people, its landscape, and its history—with the central, classical tradition of Western civilization."

Many postcolonial critics have charged, however, that Walcott is out of touch with the very West Indians who are his subject matter. His embrace of Europe, combined with his disavowal of the Africanist aesthetic advocated by black nationalists of the 1960s and 1970s, have led to accusations of elitism. Walcott's writing is often unfavorably compared with that of fellow West Indian author Edward Kamau Brathwaite, whose work is deemed more populist. Walcott, in turn, dismisses this criticism as reactionary and bristles at the suggestion that art should be subservient to politics.

Walcott's belief in the universal potential of art and its ability to transcend the particularities of local political issues is manifest in a cosmopolitanism that moves beyond a simple valorization of the European canon. He admires the work of German dramatist and composer Bertolt Brecht, whose interest in Oriental theater introduced Walcott to Asian cultural traditions. Japanese film director Akira Kurosawa's *Rashomon* (1950) helped inspire the development of Walcott's Obie Award-winning masterpiece, *Dream on Monkey Mountain* (1967).

Nonetheless, Walcott makes extensive use of Caribbean vernaculars.

The dialogue in *The Sea at Daughin* (1954), for example, utilizes the Creole spoken by St. Lucia's fishermen. These fishermen are also the subject of his celebrated epic poem, *Omeros* (1990). *Drums and Colour* (1958), the retelling of Caribbean history that was commissioned for the opening of the inaugural Federal Parliament of the West Indies, has the energy and flavor of Carnival. Masquerade, mime, and calypso were incorporated into the play, and revelers danced and sang during intermissions, creating the atmosphere of West Indian bacchanal. Additionally, during his 17-year relationship with the Trinidad Theatre Workshop, Walcott combined regional art, music, language, and dance to create almost ritualistic performances.

North America

Walker, Alice

(b. February 9, 1944, Eatonton, Ga.), African American writer, essayist, and poet, and Pulitzer Prize-winning author of *The Color Purple*.

In a passage from her 1983 essay collection *In Search of Our Mothers' Gardens: Womanist Prose*, Alice Walker reflects that "one thing I try to have in my life and in my fiction is an awareness of and openness to mystery, which, to me, is deeper than any politics, race, or geographical location." Walker was the youngest of eight children of sharecropping parents Willie Lee Walker and Minnie Tallulah (Grant) Walker. Her childhood was colored by an accident at age eight: she lost sight in one eye when an older brother shot her with a BB gun. Socially outcast as a result of her disfigured appearance, Walker became absorbed in books and began to write poetry while young.

Walker has said that while she was in high school, her mother gave her three important gifts: a sewing machine, which gave her the independence to make her own clothes; a suitcase, which gave her permission to leave home and travel; and a typewriter, which gave her permission to write. Walker graduated from high school as class valedictorian, and from 1961 to 1963 attended Spelman College in Atlanta on a scholarship. But when the "puritanical atmosphere" at Spelman became oppressive, Walker transferred to Sarah Lawrence College, where she completed a B.A. in 1965.

Walker then spent time in Georgia and Mississippi, where she registered voters, and in New York City, where she worked at the welfare department. She also married white human rights lawyer and activist Mel Leventhal in 1967, and in 1969 she gave birth to their daughter, Rebecca. She was divorced in 1977. Through all this activity Walker continued to write.

Walker published her first novel, *The Third Life of Grange Copeland*, in 1970 at age 26. Two years later she published *In Love and Trouble*, a short story collection, and the poetry collection *Revolutionary Petunias and Other Poems*. In 1976 she published her second novel, *Meridian*. By this point Walker was well established among the rising generation of black women writers. Her work is often praised for its portrayals of individuals and individual relationships, but it is also known for its depictions of the ways in which individuals can rely on their collective culture and cultural heritage to sustain them.

As Walker continued publishing her essays and poetry, she developed a second career as an educator. She has taught black studies and creative writing at Jackson State College, Tougaloo College, Wellesley College, and the University of Massachusetts at Boston; has served as a distinguished writer in African American studies at the University of California at Berkeley; and was named the Fannie Hurst Professor of Literature at Brandeis University. In 1983, however, she became internationally known with the publication of her third novel, *The Color Purple*.

The Color Purple portrays Celie, a rural black woman in an abusive marriage, as she struggles to find her self-worth. Told entirely in the form of letters—Celie's simple letters to God, her letters to her lost sister Nettie, and Nettie's letters to Celie—the powerful narrative won the 1983 Pulitzer Prize and established Walker as a major American novelist. In 1985 *The Color Purple* was made into a popular movie that was both praised for its portrayal of African American heroines and condemned for its portrayal of black men. Walker reflected on the complicated issues surrounding the film's production in her essay collection *The Same River Twice: Honoring the Difficult* (1996).

One year after *The Color Purple*, Walker published *In Search of Our Mothers' Gardens*, an influential essay collection that introduced the new term womanism as a way of defining black women's feminism. In 1984 she cofounded *Wild Tree Press* in Novarro, California. Since then Walker's publications have included the novels *The Temple of My Familiar* (1989) and *Possessing the Secret of Joy* (1992), another essay collection, several volumes of poetry, and a children's book.

Walker's numerous honors and awards include a National Endowment for the Arts grant and fellowship, a Radcliffe Institute fellowship, an honorary Ph.D. from Russell Sage College, a National Book Award nomination, a Guggenheim Award, and an O'Henry Award. An outspoken liberal political activist. Walker's *Anything We Love Can Be Saved: A Writer's Activism* was published in 1997.

North America

Walker, David

(b. 1785?, Wilmington, N.C.; d. June 28, 1830, Boston, Mass.), African American abolitionist, civil rights activist, and advocate of African independence best known for his fiery pamphlet *Walker's Appeal . . . to the Colored Citizens of the World* (1829).

During the antebellum years David Walker was prominent among a generation of politically outspoken free blacks that included Frederick Douglass,

Martin Robison Delany, and the Reverend Henry Highland Garnet. Walker, according to historian Sterling Stuckey, deserves recognition as "the father of black nationalist theory in America." His most lasting achievement was his essay, *Walker's Appeal . . . to the Colored Citizens of the World*, which in part called on African American slaves to revolt against their masters to gain their freedom.

The son of a white mother and a slave father, Walker was born free, taking the status of his mother as stipulated by North Carolina law. Little is known of his life before he moved to Boston in the late 1820s. In particular, it is not known how he learned to read and write. The antebellum South made scant provision for educating African Americans, whether slave or free. Yet before moving to the North, Walker had acquired an education that included a familiarity with Thomas Jefferson's *Notes on the State of Virginia* (1785). He also had ample opportunity to observe the evils of slavery firsthand.

In Boston Walker commenced a used clothes business and quickly gained recognition in the local black community. Walker was evidently a natural leader. He was physically impressive: his wife Eliza described him as "prepossessing, being six feet in height, slender and well-proportioned. His hair was loose, and his complexion was dark." Walker played an active role in the Massachusetts General Colored Association, established in 1826, and was an agent for the first African American newspaper, *Freedom's Journal* (1827–1829).

In an 1828 address to the Massachusetts General Colored Association, Walker exhorted free blacks to improve their lot through mutual aid and self-help organizations. He roundly condemned the passivity of those who acquiesced in racial injustice. In September of the following year Walker published his *Appeal*, which further extended his argument for black activism and solidarity. Rejecting Jefferson's contention in *Notes on the State of Virginia* that blacks were inherently inferior, Walker called on African Americans to acquire copies of the book, in order to study and refute it. "[L]et no one of us suppose," he wrote, "that the refutations which have been written by our white friends are enough—they are whites—we are blacks."

Besides advocating the violent overthrow of slavery and the formation of black civil rights and self-help organizations, the *Appeal* called for racial equality in the United States and independence for the peoples of Africa. As Stuckey observed, Walker was "the precursor of a long line of advocates of African freedom, extending all the way to Paul Robeson and Malcolm X in our time."

To distribute his pamphlet, Walker relied on the mails and on seamen traveling to Southern ports. Alarmed Southern leaders responded by passing stricter laws against such "seditious" literature and against teaching free blacks to read or write. The Georgia state legislature went so far as to place a price on Walker's head: $10,000, if he were delivered alive, or $1,000, if dead. Walker encountered sharp criticism in the North as well, even from such white abolitionists as William Lloyd Garrison and Benjamin Lundy.

In 1830, nine months after publishing his *Appeal*, Walker died under mysterious circumstances. Rumor held that he had been poisoned, but the charge was never verified.

North America

Walker, Margaret

(b. July 7, 1915, Birmingham, Ala.; d. September 15, 1998, Jackson, Miss.), poet, novelist, and university teacher; the first African American woman to win a prestigious literary prize.

Margaret Walker began writing poems at age 11. Langston Hughes read her poetry when she was 16 and persuaded her parents to take her out of the South so she could "develop into a writer." She matriculated at Northwestern University, where she was influenced by W. E. B. Du Bois, and graduated in 1935. She left Chicago in 1939 to enter the creative writing M.A. program at the University of Iowa. There she published in 1942 a collection of poems, *For My People*, which won the prestigious Yale Young Poets Award. The book's poems, like her work as a whole, display a pride in her African American heritage and interweave autobiographical elements with larger themes of black history. She also wrote a historical novel, *Jubilee*, not completed until 1966, which was based on the life of her grandmother, who lived during the Civil War. It is one of the first modern novels about slavery told from an African American perspective.

Walker published more than ten books, including poems, essays, and short stories. Among these are her *Ballad of the Free* (1966), *Prophets for a New Day* (1970), and *October Journey* (1973). In the 1960s she received her Ph.D. from the University of Iowa and began teaching creative writing at Jackson State College in Mississippi, where she retired in 1979. The books she published since then include a biography of Richard Wright, a volume of poetry that includes old and new works, and a collection of essays.

North America

Walker, Sarah ("Madam C. J.")

(b. December 23, 1867, Delta, La.; d. May 25, 1919, New York, N.Y.), African American entrepreneur who developed special hair care products and styling techniques for black women.

Born to indigent former slaves Owen and Minerva Breedlove, Sarah Walker grew up in poverty on the Burney plantation in Delta, Louisiana, working in the cotton fields from sunrise to sunset. Uneducated in her youth, she learned as an adult to read and write. At age 14 she married Moses McWilliams, who was reportedly killed by a white lynch mob two years after their daughter A'Lelia's birth in 1885.

Walker worked as a domestic until she took several risks as an entrepreneur in black women's hair care products. To meet the needs of women who did not have running water, supplies, or equipment, Walker created a hot comb with specially spaced teeth to soften or straighten black hair. She also created the Wonderful Hair Grower for women who had experienced hair loss through improper care. Business differences ended her marriage to C. J. Walker, a newspaperman whose advertising and mail order knowledge contributed to the business.

Walker was the first woman to sell products via mail order, to organize a nationwide membership of door-to-door agents, the Madam C. J. Walker Hair Culturists Union of America, and to open her own beauty school, t he Walker College of Hair Culture. Walker and her daughter A'Lelia established a chain of beauty parlors throughout the United States, the Caribbean, and South America.

By 1914 company earnings grossed more than a million dollars. In addition to making substantial contributions to black women's education, Walker owned a house in Harlem, dubbed the "Dark Tower," and Villa Lewaro, a neo-Palladian-style, 34-room mansion designed by Vetner Woodson Tandy, the first registered black architect. Walker's homes were frequented by Harlem Renaissance notables after her death in 1919 when her daughter took over the helm. Walker's empire, in keeping with her wishes, has since been exclusively managed by her female descendants. In 1976 Villa Lewaro was listed on the National Register of Historic Places.

North America

Waller, Thomas Wright ("Fats")

(b. May 21, 1904, New York, N.Y.; d. December 15, 1943, Kansas City, Mo.), African American jazz pianist, vocalist, organist, and composer whose combination of musical sophistication and lyrical humor made him one of the most popular entertainers of his day.

Fats Waller, born Thomas Wright Waller, was born and raised in New York City, where his father was a Baptist minister. As a boy he charmed his classmates with animated facial gestures while playing piano at school talent shows. During his teenage years he played the organ at various Harlem theaters to accompany silent films. In 1920, the year he left home, he married Edith Hatchett. They divorced three years later, and in 1926 Waller married Anita Rutherford.

Having learned the fundamentals of piano in his childhood, Waller later studied stride piano under Russell Brooks and James P. Johnson. In the 1920s Waller played at Harlem rent parties and nightclubs and composed music for shows and revues. He collaborated with songwriter Andy Razaf to produce some of his best-known numbers: "Honeysuckle Rose" (1928), "(What Did I Do to Be So) Black and Blue?" (1929), and "Ain't Misbehavin'" (1929).

During the 1930s Waller toured the United States and Europe with his own band, appeared on radio broadcasts and in Hollywood films, and recorded hundreds of songs on the Victor label.

On April 27, 1928, Waller became the first jazz soloist to perform at Carnegie Hall. He is also credited with being the first musician to record jazz music on a pipe organ. *Ain't Misbehavin'*, a tribute to Waller, won the Tony Award for best Broadway musical in 1978.

North America

Wall of Respect, The,

a street mural on the South Side of Chicago, Illinois, depicting numerous black heroes; considered the founding work of the black mural movement.

In 1967, at the beginning of the Black Power Movement, painter William Walker assembled a group of some 20 African American artists to execute a mural celebrating prominent figures in black history. Most of these artists were members of a Chicago-based organization called the Visual Arts Workshop of OBAC (Organization of Black American Culture). Together these artists planned the mural's design and raised the money needed to finance the project. They decided to paint the mural on the side of a two-story, boarded-up tenement building at the intersection of 43rd Street and Langley Avenue. Once a thriving part of the city, this predominantly black area of Chicago had deteriorated into a slum. The mural is a patchwork of famous African Americans, including Charlie "Bird" Parker, Muhammad Ali, and Gwendolyn Brooks.

The artists' objective in painting the *Wall of Respect* was to lift the local black community's morale through highly visible, dignified images of famous black Americans. The response was overwhelmingly positive. People arrived from miles around to view the mural, and the publicity it generated led to the construction of a human resources center in the impoverished neighborhood. Furthermore, the *Wall of Respect* sparked a national black mural movement in which inner-city African American artists began to embellish their neighborhoods with positive black imagery. This movement was ideologically linked to the contemporary Black Power Movement in that it sought to challenge the white-supremacist social order, and aesthetically linked to the mural traditions of postrevolutionary Mexico and Depression-era America in that its artists portrayed historical figures in a social realist vein.

Shortly after the *Wall of Respect* was finished, the Visual Arts Workshop of OBAC broke up. Many of the artists went on to found AfriCOBRA (African Commune of Bad Relevant Artists) in 1968. Although a fire destroyed the *Wall of Respect* in 1971, AfriCOBRA has continued to produce public works of art meant to liberate and uplift the African American community.

Washington, Booker Taliaferro

(b. April 5, 1856, Franklin County, Va.; d. November 14, 1915, Tuskegee, Ala.), African American founder of the Tuskegee Institute, who urged blacks to accommodate themselves to the white South and concentrate on economic self-advancement; supported by influential whites, he became the most prominent black American of the late nineteenth and early twentieth century.

Booker T. Washington was born Booker Taliaferro, a slave, in rural Virginia. His mother, Jane, was the plantation's cook; his father was a white man whose identity he never knew. Washington worked as a servant in the plantation house until he was liberated by Union troops near the end of the Civil War. After the war his family moved to Malden, West Virginia, where they joined Washington Ferguson, also a former slave, whom Jane had married during the war. At school he gave himself the last name Washington for reasons still debated by historians.

In 1872 Washington left Malden, traveling on foot to Virginia's Hampton Institute, which had opened only a few years earlier as a school for blacks. Its white principal, General Samuel Chapman Armstrong, believed the South's blacks needed a practical, work-based education that would also teach character and morality. Hampton offered not only agricultural and mechanical classes but training in cleanliness, efficiency, discipline, and the dignity of manual labor as well.

Washington was a diligent student, adopting Armstrong's credo so thoroughly that many historians have concluded that the rest of Washington's public life was a manifestation of Armstrong's philosophy. Graduating with honors in 1875, Washington returned to West Virginia to teach. In 1878 he attended Wayland Seminary in Washington, D.C., a school offering a decidedly conventional training in the liberal arts. Washington's experience at Wayland—where the black students knew little of manual labor, and, moreover, seemed uninterested in returning South to help rural blacks—further convinced him of the rightness of Armstrong's methods. After a year at Wayland, Washington returned to Hampton, this time as a member of the faculty. He grew closer to Armstrong, and in 1881, when Armstrong was asked by the state of Alabama to name a white principal to head a new school for blacks, he instead suggested Washington.

Tuskegee

The Tuskegee Institute in Macon County, Alabama, had been apportioned $2,000 by the state legislature for salaries, but nothing for land or buildings. Washington began classes with a handful of students in a shanty owned by a black church. Intending Tuskegee to be a replica of Hampton, he established a vocational curriculum for both boys and girls that included such courses as carpentry, printing, tinsmithing, and shoemaking. Girls also took classes in cooking and sewing, and boys learned farming and dairying.

Manners, hygiene, and character also received heavy emphasis, and each day was framed by a rigid schedule that included daily chapel. The earliest students were set to work building a kiln, then making bricks, then erecting buildings. The school sold additional bricks to pay part of its expenses, and Washington secured the rest of the funds from philanthropists, mostly white and mostly Northern, to whom Armstrong had introduced him.

A good deal of Washington's work took place beyond the school's walls. He placated the hostile whites of Tuskegee with assurances that he was counseling his students to set aside political activism in favor of economic gains. He also assured skeptical legislators that his students would not flee the South after their education but instead would be productive contributors to the rural economy. These messages resonated with whites not just in the South but also in the North among Tuskegee's benefactors.

Steel magnate Andrew Carnegie, who became the most generous donor to Tuskegee during Washington's lifetime, said Washington was "one of the most wonderful men . . . who has ever lived." Blacks also praised the man who built a school from the dirt of the Deep South that had succeeded, by 1890, in training 500 African Americans a year on 500 acres of land.

These triumphs, however, were underscored by pockets of tragedy in Washington's personal life. His first wife, Fanny Smith Washington, a graduate of Hampton and Washington's girlfriend since Malden, died from a fall in 1884, just two years after their marriage. His second wife, Olivia Davidson Washington, also a graduate of Hampton and in chronically poor health, died in 1889. Washington's third wife, Margaret Murray Washington, was a graduate of Fisk University and, like Olivia Washington, held the title of lady principal of Tuskegee. Margaret Washington helped her husband for the rest of his life and also led regional and national federations of black women.

Although Tuskegee earned him a measure of popularity, Washington did not become a national leader until he spoke, in September 1895, at the Cotton States and International Exposition in Atlanta, Georgia. Over the previous several years relations between the races had steadily deteriorated. The South had codified its discriminatory Jim Crow laws, and violence, especially lynching, was common. Earlier in the year Frederick Douglass, the acknowledged leader of blacks North and South, died, and no clear successor had yet emerged. Washington was the only black speaker chosen to address the mixed-race crowd in Atlanta.

He urged southern blacks to "cast down your bucket where you are"— that is, to remain in the South—and to accept discrimination as unchangeable for the time being. "In all things that are purely social," he said, "we can be as separate as the fingers, yet one as the hand in all things essential to mutual progress." Blacks should first commit themselves to economic improvement, Washington stated; once they had achieved that, he assured his listeners, improvement in civil rights would follow.

The speech, which critics called the Atlanta Compromise, won nearly unanimous acclaim from both blacks and whites. Even the black intellectual W. E. B. Du Bois, who later broke sharply with Washington's accommodating position, praised Washington's message at the time. Donations from white Americans flowed in larger amounts to Tuskegee, and soon white journalists, politicians, and philanthropists sought Washington's word on all things racial.

In 1898 President William McKinley visited Tuskegee, offering praise that further elevated Washington's stature. Although in public Washington disdained politics, in private he assiduously cultivated his own power. He secretly owned stock in several black newspapers, which he influenced to provide favorable reports about him and Tuskegee. Other black newspapers he quietly cajoled, persuaded, and occasionally coerced into giving him positive coverage. At his heavily attended lectures around the country, he endeared himself to whites by telling stories about "darkies"—blacks who fit racist stereotypes—portraying them as lovable, gullible, and shiftless. These stories alienated black intellectuals.

In 1901 Washington published his ghost-written autobiography, *Up From Slavery*. Told simply but movingly, it is a classic American tale of success through hard work. Almost instantly it became a best-seller and was translated into several languages. Theodore Roosevelt, who had become president the same year, invited Washington to the White House for lunch, prompting a flurry of angry editorials in the white South but further increasing Washington's power and appeal elsewhere. Roosevelt (as did President William Howard Taft after him) sought Washington's advice on racial and southern issues.

In a short time Washington became a dispenser of Republican Party patronage throughout the South and parts of the North. Blacks soon learned that Washington's endorsement was essential for any political appointment or, for that matter, for funding by white philanthropic groups, who readily deferred to Washington's opinions. He, in turn, used his wealth and power secretly to finance some court cases and other activities challenging Jim Crow laws. He also provided the main impetus for founding the National Negro Business League, which served to advocate his Tuskegee philosophy throughout the country. Some observers referred to the powerful Washington as the Wizard of Tuskegee, and to his operation as the Tuskegee Machine.

In 1903 W. E. B. Du Bois published *The Souls of Black Folk*. In one of its essays, "Of Mr. Booker T. Washington and Others," he criticized Washington for failing to realize that economic power could not be had without political power, because political power was needed to protect economic gains. Moreover, Du Bois believed that Washington's disparagement of liberal arts education would rob the race of well-trained leaders.

Du Bois insisted that in a time of increasing segregation and discrimination, blacks must struggle for their civil rights rather than accommodate inequality. Washington, then at the peak of his power, was stung by Du Bois's criticisms, and "Of Mr. Booker T. Washington and Others" allowed critics to be more open over the next several years.

The greatest threat to Washington's conservatism and power came in 1909 with the founding of the National Association for the Advancement of Colored People (NAACP). The NAACP, which sought to address the neglected civil rights of blacks, was a direct challenge to Washington, as was its predecessor, Du Bois's Niagara Movement. Washington tried at first to stifle the group; failing that, he sought a rapprochement. As that, too, failed, increasing numbers of blacks gravitated to the NAACP, and Washington's base of power began to weaken.

The election in 1913 of Democrat Woodrow Wilson to the presidency dealt Washington another blow, as his duties as dispenser of Republican patronage came to an end. Washington nonetheless remained personally prominent until his death in 1915. At that time the Tuskegee Institute had a faculty of 200, an enrollment of 2,000, and an endowment of $2 million.

North America

Washington, Denzel

(b. December 28, 1954, Mount Vernon, N.Y.), Academy Award-winning African American actor.

Denzel Washington grew up in the middle-class family of a Pentecostal minister and a beauty shop owner. Washington won a small role in the 1977 television movie *Wilma*, a film about Olympic star Wilma Rudolph, before he graduated from Fordham University in 1977 with a B.A. in journalism. After graduating, he pursued acting professionally, studying drama at the American Conservatory in San Francisco, California.

Washington first achieved recognition for his stage performances. His portrayals of Malcolm X in *Chickens Coming Home to Roost* and *Private Peterson* in the Obie Award-winning *A Soldier's Play* won Washington critical acclaim for carefully chosen roles that resisted Hollywood's stereotypical options for blacks. Washington's stage performances led to a role in the popular television drama *St. Elsewhere* from 1982 to 1988, in which he played the dedicated Dr. Philip Chandler. In 1984 he began his successful transition from television to film when critics praised his reprise of the Private Peterson role in *A Soldier's Story*, the screen adaptation of *A Soldier's Play*.

By the end of the 1980s Washington had become one of Hollywood's most critically and commercially successful actors. He has received four Academy Award nominations, two for Best Supporting Actor (*Cry Freedom*, 1987, and *Glory*, 1989, which he won) and two for Best Actor (Malcolm X in Spike Lee's film of the same name, 1992, and *Training Day*, 2001, which he also won). In addition to collaborating with Lee (in *Malcolm X*, and 1990's *Mo' Better Blues*), Washington has worked with some of film's most respected directors, including Jonathan Demme (*Philadelphia*, 1993) and Kenneth Branagh (*Much Ado About Nothing*, 1993). He recently directed his first film as well as solidified his leading-man status with his role opposite Whitney Houston in *The Preacher's Wife*, a remake of a Cary Grant film.

North America

Washington, Harold

(b. April 15, 1922, Chicago, Ill.; d. November 25, 1987, Chicago, Ill.), African American politician, the first African American mayor of Chicago, Illinois (1983–1987).

Washington began his political career when he succeeded his deceased father in 1953 as a Democratic party precinct captain. After holding positions as a city attorney (1954–1958) and a state labor arbitrator (1960–1964), he served in the Illinois House of Representatives (1965–1976). He then advanced to seats in the Illinois State Senate (1976–1980) and the U.S. House of Representatives (1980–1983). He was active in the 1982 effort to extend the 1965 Voting Rights Act.

In 1977 Washington made an unsuccessful bid to become the mayor of Chicago. In 1983 he again entered the mayoral race and defeated Jane Byrne and Richard M. Daley in the primaries. He edged out Republican Bernard Epton in the general election on April 12, 1983, to become the city's first African American mayor.

Washington increased racial diversity in city administration, assuring equal opportunities for women and minorities seeking employment, and ended city patronage. He had difficulty implementing his initiatives since the majority of the 50 city council seats were held by his political opponents. In 1986, after a federal court called for new elections in certain wards that were deemed racially biased, however, Washington achieved more legislative success. He unexpectedly died of a heart attack shortly after his reelection in 1987, ending hope for a popular, progressive, multiracial city government.

North America

Waters, Ethel

(b. October 31, 1896?, Chester, Pa.; d. September 1, 1977, Chatsworth, Calif.), African American singer and actress who brought black urban blues into the mainstream.

Ethel Waters was born to a 12-year-old mother, Louise Anderson, who had been raped by a white man, John Waters. Although she was raised by her maternal grandmother, she took her father's surname. Reared in poverty, she left school at age 13 in order to support herself through domestic housework.

Waters performed for the first time at age five in a children's church program. She was called Baby Star and later, performing on the black vaudeville circuit, became known as Sweet Mama Stringbean. After moving to New York City in 1919, at the start of the Harlem Renaissance, Waters recorded songs for Black Swan Records and then Colombia Records while playing in revues and performing on the white vaudeville circuit during the 1920s. Two of her more popular songs were "Dinah" (1925) and "Stormy Weather" (1933). By refining the genre's lyrics and performance, Waters introduced urban blues to a white audience. Her stylistic alterations created a niche for the black nightclub singers who gained popularity from the 1930s through the 1950s.

In 1927 Waters's career as an actress began with the musical Africana. She played singing roles in other Broadway productions: *Blackbirds* (1930), *Rhapsody in Black* (1931), *As Thousands Cheer* (1933), *At Home Abroad* (1936), and *Cabin in the Sky* (1940). Waters played more dramatic roles in *Mamba's Daughters* (1939) and *The Member of the Wedding* (1950). Appearing in nine films between 1929 and 1959, she received an Academy Award nomination as Best Supporting Actress for *Pinky* (1949). Through these roles Waters transformed the image of the older black woman from that of the servile "Mammy" to the self-sufficient Earth Mother. She toured with evangelist Billy Graham from 1957 to 1976. Waters is the a uthor of two autobiographies: *His Eye Is on the Sparrow* (1951) and *To Me It's Wonderful* (1972).

North America

Watts, André

(b. June 20, 1946, Nuremberg, Germany), African American concert pianist, the first black American instrumental superstar.

Since his rise to prominence in 1963, André Watts has been one of the world's leading classical pianists. At age 16, he became the first black instrumental soloist in more than 60 years to perform with the New York Philharmonic Orchestra, under conductor Leonard Bernstein. Within a decade he was renowned worldwide for his poetic style, technical brilliance, and fiery temperament. According to music critic Elyse Mach, "Watts is to a concert stage as lightning is to thunder. Explosive. More than any other pianist, his performances are reminiscent of what a Liszt concert must have been like: mesmerizing, theatrical, charged with energy."

Watts ascribes his career success largely to luck and what he calls "a combination of those funny, indefinable qualities that are in a person at birth." He also cites his mother as a critical influence: "I wouldn't be a pianist today if my mother hadn't made me practice." He was born in a U.S. Army camp in Nuremberg, Germany, the only child of Herman Watts, an African American career soldier, and Maria Alexandra Gusmits, a Hungarian who had been displaced in Germany following World War II. When he was four he began playing a miniature violin and at age seven studied piano with his mother, an accomplished pianist. In 1954 his family moved to Philadelphia, Pennsylvania, where he received a private school education and studied at the Philadelphia Academy of Music.

Watts first performed publicly at age nine, playing the Haydn Concerto in D Major in a children's concert sponsored by the Philadelphia Orchestra. Several performances with other orchestras followed, and at age 16 he won an audition to perform in a nationally televised Young People's Concert with the New York Philharmonic, playing Liszt's Piano Concerto no. 1. His performance stunned audiences and music critics alike.

In late January 1963, a few weeks after the Liszt performance, Leonard Bernstein, who predicted "gianthood" for the young pianist, invited Watts to substitute as a soloist for ailing pianist Glenn Gould. Bernstein proved instrumental in Watts's success: the young artist's second New York Philharmonic performance won him a ten-minute standing ovation and invitations to perform with the world's major orchestras, which were usually closed to black instrumentalists without the backing of an eminent conductor or music manager. Spared the ordeals of competitive life, he focused on his artistry and academic education.

In 1969 Watts enrolled at Baltimore's Peabody Conservatory of Music, where he studied with pianist Leon Fleisher and, in 1972, obtained his Artist's Diploma. That same year he became the youngest person ever to receive an honorary doctorate from Yale University. Meanwhile, his international career flourished. In 1966 he made his European debut with the London Symphony Orchestra and also performed his first solo recital in New York City. He recorded extensively and continued to tour throughout Europe, Asia, and the United States. During the late 1960s and 1970s he was often chosen to perform at important political occasions: he became the first American pianist to play in the People's Republic of China, as a soloist with the Philadelphia Orchestra. In 1973 he toured Russia.

Africa

Weah, George

(b. October 1, 1966, Monrovia, Liberia), Liberian international soccer player.

In the 1990s George Weah emerged as one of the best soccer players in the world and the unofficial leader of the approximately 350 Africans who play soccer in Europe. After a difficult childhood in Monrovia, Weah became a devout Muslim and a talented athlete who, at the time, used his African name, Oppong. Weah began his career playing for teams in Monrovia and Yaoundé, Cameroon. In 1988 he moved to Europe, where he played for AS Monaco (1988–1992), Paris St. Germain (1992–1995), and Italian champion AC Milan (1995–). In 1995 soccer's international governing body, Fédération Internationale de Football Association (FIFA), named Weah the top player of the year, marking the first time the award had gone to an African. A striker, the 1.8-m (6-ft.) tall Weah is known for his ball control and ferocious shooting.

Weah is usually soft-spoken, but he criticized groups that were fighting in Liberia's civil war. Afterward, his relatives were attacked, and his house and property were destroyed. In 1996 Weah spent more than $50,000 of his own money to help finance Liberia's ultimately unsuccessful bid to play in the 1998 World Cup, an act that won him the FIFA Fair Play Award. Weah injured his back in 1997; this put his contract with Milan through the year 2000 into question. In interviews Weah has stated that he would like to end his soccer career in New York City, where he owns a restaurant and has many friends and family members. He routinely donates money to the SOS Children's Villages in Liberia; he says that he would like to work for the United Nations Children's Fund (UNICEF) after his retirement.

Weaver, Robert Clifton

(b. December 29, 1907, Washington, D.C.; d. July 17, 1997, New York, N.Y.), first African American United States cabinet member; secretary of housing and urban development (1966–1968).

The son of Mortimer and Florence Weaver, Robert Clifton Weaver grew up attending segregated schools in Washington, D.C. After graduating from high school, he attended Harvard University, where his older brother, Mortimer, was pursuing graduate studies in English. Weaver was refused dormitory accommodations because he was black, so he moved off campus to become his brother's roommate. He graduated cum laude with a degree in economics in 1929, the same year Mortimer died unexpectedly. Weaver remained at Harvard, taking an M.A. in 1931 and a Ph.D. in economics in 1934.

Weaver began his government career in 1933 when Secretary of the Interior Harold Ickes hired him as a race relations adviser in the housing division. By 1937 Weaver had become special assistant to the administrator of the U.S. Housing Authority, a post he held until 1940. As a high-ranking African American in President Franklin D. Roosevelt's administration, Weaver was a member of the "Black Cabinet," an informal network of African Americans who worked to end racial discrimination in the federal government and the programs it administered.

In 1944, after serving on the National Defense Advisory Committee, the Manpower Commission, and the War Production Board, Weaver was appointed the director of the Mayor's Committee on Race Relations in Chicago, Illinois, and then of the American Council on Race Relations. During this time he published two critical studies of discrimination in the United States, *Negro Labor: A National Problem* (1946) and *The Negro Ghetto* (1948).

In 1955 New York governor Averell Harriman made Weaver the first African American to hold a state cabinet-level position by naming him state rent commissioner. Weaver held this post until 1960, when President John

President Lyndon Johnson congratulates Robert C. Weaver at his swearing in as secretary of the Department of Housing and Urban Development in 1966. *CORBIS*

F. Kennedy named him director of the U.S. Housing and Home Finance Agency, making him the highest-ranking African American in government.

Kennedy intended to establish a cabinet-level agency to address urban affairs with Weaver as its head. However, southern members of Congress who opposed an African American cabinet member in general and Weaver's strong support of integrated housing in particular blocked Kennedy's plan. The agency, the Department of Housing and Urban Development (HUD), was not established until President Lyndon B. Johnson was elected in 1965. In 1966, with Johnson better able to exercise power in the Congress, Weaver became the first HUD secretary and the first African American cabinet member.

Weaver effectively administered HUD, but his more ambitious and imaginative plans, such as Demonstration Cities and the Metropolitan Development Act, were unsupported because of the precedence given by the federal government to the Vietnam War and because of conservative reaction to ghetto rioting from 1965 to 1968. In 1969 Weaver ended his career in government, becoming president of City College of New York's

(CCNY's) Baruch College. In 1971 he became distinguished professor of urban affairs at CCNY's Hunter College, and he became professor emeritus in 1978.

Weaver's public service extended beyond his careers in government and education. He chaired the board of directors of the National Association for the Advancement of Colored People (NAACP) in 1960, and was president of the National Committee against Discrimination in Housing from 1973 to 1987. In addition, Weaver received the Spingarn Medal in 1962, the New York City Urban League's Frederick Douglass Award in 1977, the Schomburg Collection Award in 1978, and the Equal Opportunity Day Award from the National Urban League in 1987.

Wells-Barnett, Ida Bell

(b. July 16, 1862, Holly Springs, Miss.; d. March 25, 1931, Chicago, Ill.), African American journalist, advocate of civil rights, women's rights, and economic rights, and antilynching crusader.

Ida B. Wells-Barnett, the first of Jim and Elizabeth Wells's eight children, was born six months before the Emancipation Proclamation went into effect. She attended Shaw University (now Rust College) in her hometown of Holly Springs, Mississippi, until she was forced to drop out when her parents died of yellow fever in 1878. Following their deaths, Wells-Barnett supported herself and her siblings by working as a schoolteacher in rural Mississippi and Tennessee. She took summer courses at Fisk University and continued to teach through 1891, when she was fired for writing an editorial that accused the Memphis school board of providing inadequate resources to black schools.

In May 1884 Wells-Barnett filed suit against a railroad company after she was forced off a train for refusing to sit in the Jim Crow car designated for blacks. She was awarded $500 by a circuit court, but the decision was overruled by the Tennessee Supreme Court in 1887, a rejection that only strengthened her resolve to devote her life to upholding justice.

Wells-Barnett embarked on a career in journalism when she was elected editor of *The Evening Star* and then *The Living Way*, weekly church newspapers in Memphis. She became the editor of *Free Speech*, also in Memphis, in 1889. Her articles, written under the alias "Iola," were direct and confrontational, and two editorials she wrote in 1892 in response to the persecution and eventual lynching of three black businessmen were particularly controversial. The first, published on March 9, encouraged blacks to leave Memphis for Oklahoma and to boycott segregated transportation. The second, which appeared on May 21, suggested that white women were often the willing initiators in interracial relationships. Whites who were angered by her work responded by wrecking the offices and press of *Free Speech*.

Wells-Barnett took refuge in the North, reporting in the black newspapers the *New York Age* and the *Chicago Conservator* on the violence and injustices being perpetrated against African Americans. Through a lecture tour of England, Scotland, and Wales in 1893 and 1894, Wells-Barnett inspired international organizations to apply pressure on America to end segregation and lynching. In 1895 she published an analysis of lynching, *A Red Record: Tabulated Statistics and Alleged Causes of Lynching in the United States*, which argued that the impetus behind lynching was economic.

During the last fifteen years of her life Wells-Barnett wrote extensively on the race riots in East St. Louis (1917), Chicago (1919), and Arkansas (1922), and continued to promote civil rights and justice for African Americans. A low-income housing project in Chicago was named in her honor in 1941, and in 1990 the U.S. Postal Service issued an Ida B. Wells-Barnett stamp.

North America

Wells, Willie

(b. October 10, 1908, Austin, Tex.; d. January 24, 1989, Austin, Tex.), star of the Negro Baseball Leagues who was posthumously elected to the Baseball Hall of Fame.

Willie Wells grew up playing baseball in the sandlots of San Antonio, Texas. In 1924, at age 16, he signed to play with the St. Louis Stars of the Negro National League (NNL). A gifted shortstop, Wells worked hard to develop his hitting and won batting titles in the 1929 and 1930 seasons. A fierce competitor (fans nicknamed him "El Diablo" when he played in Mexico), Wells led the Stars to NNL championships in 1928, 1930, and 1931.

The NNL folded after the 1931 season, and Wells signed with the Chicago American Giants. The Giants won the 1932 championship as part of the Negro Southern League, and the 1933 championship as part of revamped NNL. In 1936 Wells joined the Newark Eagles of the NNL, where he was part of what was called the "million-dollar infield." He spent the late 1930s starring in the Latin American leagues in Cuba and Mexico. In 1942 he became Newark's player-manager, batted .361, was chosen for Cum Posey's All-American Dream Team, and was considered one of the top five players in baseball.

Wells retired in 1949 with a career batting average of .334 in the Negro Leagues (.392 in exhibition games against major leaguers) and played in eight All-Star games. He later managed the Winnipeg Buffaloes in Canada and the Birmingham Black Barons in the United States. In 1997 he was posthumously voted into the Baseball Hall of Fame.

West, Cornel

(b. June 2, 1953, Tulsa, Okla.), African American philosopher, theologian, and activist.

Cornel West was born in Oklahoma—a place once envisioned as a homeland for Native Americans displaced by European colonization, and for African Americans acting on the idea of freedom promised by emancipation. The grandson of a Baptist minister, he was reared in the Baptist Church, and the church has remained a profound presence in his life. Even as a child, West was articulate, outspoken, and politically engaged—in elementary school he convinced a group of his classmates to stop saluting the flag to protest the second-class citizenship afforded to African Americans.

West encountered the activities of the Black Panther Party while growing up in Sacramento, California. The Panthers informed his early thinking about democratic socialism and acquainted him with an internationalist vision for black enfranchisement. He was also inspired by the teachings of Martin Luther King, Jr., and Malcolm X, as well as by the music of John Coltrane and James Brown. By the time he won a scholarship to Harvard University in 1970, West was already well on his way to becoming an activist-scholar. "Owing to my family, church, and the black social movements of the 1960s," he recalled, "I arrived at Harvard unashamed of my African, Christian, and militant decolonized outlooks." While in Cambridge he worked with the Black Panther Party, volunteering at their children's breakfast program.

After three years at Harvard, West graduated magna cum laude in 1973 and chose to pursue graduate studies in philosophy at Princeton. In 1977 he began teaching at Union Theological Seminary in New York City. His doctoral dissertation, completed in 1980, was later revised and republished as the *Ethical Dimensions of Marxist Thought* (1991).

A center of liberation theology and black theological education, Union was an ideal place for West's commitment to what he calls a prophetic criticism: "a self-critical and self-corrective enterprise of human 'sense-making' for the preserving and expanding of human empathy and compassion." It is through this philosophic and spiritual enterprise that West understands the experience of race in America, a point made clear by *Prophesy Deliverance! An Afro-American Revolutionary Christianity*, published in 1982.

In 1984 West left Union for Yale Divinity School, where he was granted a full professorship in religion and philosophy. He returned to Union in 1987, but shortly after was recruited to direct Princeton University's program in Afro-American studies. In 1988 West joined Princeton as professor of religion and, working with a community of scholars that included novelist Toni Morrison, he helped revitalize the Afro-American Studies Department. Excited by the possibilities of a group of scholars working across disciplines in the field of African American studies, West joined Harvard in

1993. In 1998 he was appointed the prestigious university professorship, becoming the first Alphonse Fletcher Jr. University Professor.

West's scholarly writing pursues philosophical inquiry into the realm of the political, exploring the existential dimension within the moral, spiritual, and political space. Moreover, he traces this relationship in the work of his philosophic forbears. In *The American Evasion of Philosophy* (1989) West explores the history of American pragmatism, reading the American philosophic tradition, from Ralph Waldo Emerson to Richard Rorty, as an ongoing cultural commentary that responds to American society itself. In *Keeping Faith: Philosophy and Race in America* (1993) he continues to engage with philosophy, spiritual tradition, and history.

A mesmerizing speaker, West draws upon an African American tradition of rhetoric and improvisational public speaking. He has collected some of his many talks and essays in a four-volume work, *Beyond Eurocentrism and Multiculturalism* (1993). After publishing several books and articles addressed primarily to an academic audience, West turned to a broader readership with *Race Matters* (1993). He and Gates copublished *The Future of the Race* in 1996; in 1998 he coauthored a book on parenting and family policy with Sylvia Ann Hewlett.

West, Dorothy

(b. June 2, 1907; d. August 16, 1998, Boston, Mass.), African American author and journalist, literary figure of the Harlem Renaissance who specialized in short stories.

The only child of Rachel Pease Benson and Isaac Christopher West, Dorothy West started her education at age two under the tutelage of Bessie Trotter, sister of the *Boston Guardian's* militant editor, William Monroe Trotter. After attending Farragut and Martin schools, she went to Girl's Latin High School, from which she graduated in 1923. West continued her education at Boston University and the Columbia University School of Journalism.

West's career as a writer began at age seven when the *Boston Globe* published her first short story, "Promise and Fulfillment." In 1926 West, then living in New York among the luminaries of the Harlem Renaissance, shared second-place honors with Zora Neale Hurston in a national writing competition organized by the National Urban League's Opportunity. Her interest in the arts was not only literary, and in 1927 she traveled to London as a cast member of the play *Porgy*. In the early 1930s she went to the Soviet Union to participate in the film *Black and White* and remained there for a year after the project was abandoned.

Returning to New York, West founded two short-lived literary journals:

Challenge in 1934 (six issues) and *New Challenge* in 1937 (one issue). After working as a welfare investigator for a year and a half, West found employment with the federal government's Works Progress Administration's Federal Writers' Project through the early 1940s. She moved to Martha's Vineyard in Massachusetts in 1945 and wrote regularly for the Martha's Vineyard *Gazette*. She published *The Living Is Easy* (1948) and *The Wedding* (1995), and more than 60 short stories. In 1997 television producer Oprah Winfrey made *The Wedding* into a popular television miniseries.

Africa

Western Sahara,

a former Spanish province bordering Morocco to the north, Mauritania to the south, the Atlantic Ocean to the west, and Algeria to the east.

Western Sahara is a former Spanish colony. Today it is the site of a conflict between the Polisario Front (a political and military organization of the Sahrawi people) and the kingdom of Morocco. The Polisario Front wants independence for Western Sahara while Morocco wants to annex the province, which it claims on the basis of historical events. Although the area's environment is largely desert, vast phosphate deposits make it economically attractive.

Africa

Western Sahara (Ready Reference)

Official Name: Western Sahara
Former Name: Spanish Sahara
Area: 267,000 sq km (about 103,000 sq mi.)
Location: North Africa, on the North Atlantic Ocean; borders Morocco, Algeria, and Mauritania
Capital: None (under de facto control of Morocco)
Other Major Cities: El Aaiún and Ad Dakhla (Villa Cisneros) (population data unavailable)
Population: 233,730 (1998 estimate)
Population Density: Data unavailable
Population Below Age 15: Data unavailable
Population Growth Rate: 2.4 percent (1998 estimate)
Total Fertility Rate: 6.75 children born per woman (1998 estimate)
Life Expectancy at Birth: Total population: 48.41 years (male 47.32 years; female 49.83 years [1998 estimate])

Infant Mortality Rate: 139.74 deaths per 1,000 live births (1998 estimate)

Literacy Rate (age 15 and over who can read and write): Data unavailable

Education: Data unavailable

Languages: Hassaniya Arabic and Moroccan Arabic

Ethnic Groups: Arab and Berber

Religion: Muslim

Climate: Hot, minimal rainfall inland, moist winds offshore; harmattan haze predominates inland, fog along the shore

Land, Plants, and Animals: Almost entirely desert, interrupted by occasional rocky or sandy areas, with low mountains in the south and northeast. Vegetation is sparse, but occasional rainfall permits some nomadic animal husbandry (of sheep, goats, and camels).

Natural Resources: Phosphates and iron ore

Currency: The Moroccan dirham

Gross Domestic Product (GDP): Data unavailable

GDP per Capita: Data unavailable

GDP Real Growth Rate: Data unavailable

Primary Economic Activities: Pastoral nomadism, fishing, oasis gardening, and phosphate mining

Primary Crops: Various fruits and vegetables; camels, sheep, and goats

Industries: Animal husbandry and subsistence farming are practiced by half the labor force.

Primary Export: Phosphates

Primary Imports: Fuel for fishing fleets, and foodstuffs

Primary Trade Partners: Morocco claims and administers Western Sahara, so trade partners are included in overall Moroccan accounts.

Government: Territory administratively controlled by Morocco. The territory's legal status and sovereignty have not been resolved. Both Morocco and the Polisario Front (Popular Front for the Liberation of the Saguia el-Hamra and Rio de Oro) have contested the territory. In February 1976 the Polisario declared a government-in-exile of the Sahrawi Arab Democratic Republic (SADR), and thousands of Sahrawis were displaced by political turmoil and relocated to a settlement in southwest Algeria. In April 1976 Morocco and Mauritania divided the territory between the two countries. Polisario guerrillas forced Mauritania to surrender its claims in 1979; Morocco has had administrative control since then. The Polisario's government-in-exile became a member of the Organization of African Unity in 1984. United Nations forces have been monitoring the territory since a 1991 cease-fire on guerrilla activities. In late 1997 Polisario and Moroccan representatives had tentatively agreed to allow a referendum on Western Sahara self-determination to be held sometime in 1998. The referendum was postponed repeatedly due to disagreements over voter eligibility.

West Indies,

archipelago in the northern part of the Western Hemisphere that separates the Caribbean Sea from the Atlantic Ocean. Visited and called the Indies by Christopher Columbus, it was subsequently designated the West Indies to distinguish it from the East Indies archipelago.

The West Indies comprises three main island chains that extend in a roughly crescent shape from the eastern tip of the Yucatán Peninsula in Mexico and southeastern Florida in the United States to the Venezuelan coast of South America. The Bahamas, in the north, form a southeasterly line. The Greater Antilles, comprising the islands of Cuba, Hispaniola, Jamaica, and Puerto Rico, lie in the center. To the southeast, arching southward from Puerto Rico and then westward along the Venezuelan coast, are the Lesser Antilles, comprising the Leeward Islands and Windward Islands. Barbados, Trinidad and Tobago, and the Netherlands Antilles are often considered part of this third chain. The land area of the West Indies totals about 235,700 sq km (91,000 sq mi.), and the total population (according to a 1990 estimate) is about 34 million.

Most of the noncoral islands of the West Indies are mountainous, projecting remnants of submerged ranges related to Central and South American mountain systems. Elevations of about 2,130 to 2,440 m (7,000 to 8,000 ft.) are common in the Greater Antilles; the highest point (3,175 meters/10,417 feet) is Pico Duarte in the Cordillera Central of the Dominican Republic. The inner chain of the Lesser Antilles, part of a submerged volcanic ridge, consists mainly of volcanic cones, a number of which are still active. The outer chain is composed largely of coral and uplifted limestone. Elevations in the Lesser Antilles rarely exceed 1,524 m (5,000 ft.). The southernmost part of the archipelago, from Trinidad to Aruba, is geologically related to South American rock and mountain formations. The Bahamas and northern central Cuba, relatively flat limestone and coral formations, are geologically related to formations in Florida and the Yucatán Peninsula. Several deep ocean trenches lie close offshore and parallel to the islands of the Greater and Lesser Antilles, marking unstable crustal zones in which earthquakes may occur.

Politically, the West Indies comprises 13 independent nations and a number of colonial dependencies, territories, and possessions. The Republic of Cuba, consisting of the island of Cuba and several off-lying islands, is the largest West Indies nation. Haiti and the Dominican Republic, two other independent nations, occupy Hispaniola, the second-largest island of the archipelago. Jamaica, Barbados, the Bahamas, Trinidad and Tobago, Dominica, Grenada, St. Kitts and Nevis, St. Lucia, St. Vincent and the Grenadines, and Antigua and Barbuda are the other sovereign nations.

Sovereignty over nearly all the other West Indies islands is distributed among the United States, France, the Netherlands, and Great Britain. Puerto Rico, the fourth-largest island of the archipelago, is a commonwealth of the United States, and several of the Virgin Islands are United States territories. The French West Indies includes Martinique, Guadeloupe, and a number of small island dependencies of Guadeloupe. The Dutch possessions consist of Curaçao, Bonaire, Aruba, and smaller Lesser Antilles islands. Venezuela holds about 70 Lesser Antilles islands. Dependencies of Great Britain are the Cayman Islands, Turks and Caicos Islands, and some of the Virgin Islands.

North America

Wharton, Clifton Reginald, Sr.

(b. May 11, 1899, Baltimore, Md.; d. April 28, 1990, Phoenix, Ariz.), American lawyer and ambassador who was the first African American to enter the Foreign Service and the first African American diplomat to head a U.S. delegation to a European country.

Clifton Reginald Wharton Sr. was raised in Boston, Massachusetts, where he graduated from English High School and in 1920 received a law degree from Boston University. He received an advanced law degree from the same institution after practicing law in Boston from 1920 to 1923. He then left Boston and worked in Washington, D.C., as an examiner in the Veteran's Bureau and as a law clerk in the State Department. In Washington Wharton embarked on his career in international diplomacy. From 1925 to 1945 he served as a diplomat in Liberia (1925–1929), Spain (1930–1941), and Madagascar (1942–1945). Following these assignments, he was consul general at the U.S. embassy in Portugal from 1949 to 1950.

Wharton practiced diplomacy under both Democratic and Republican administrations. In 1953 he became the consul general to France. Five years later President Dwight D. Eisenhower re-appointed him as U.S. minister t o Romania, and in 1961 President John F. Kennedy appointed him U.S. ambassador to Norway. Wharton retired from the Foreign Service in 1964, one year after having received an honorary doctorate of law degree from Boston University.

North America

Wheatley, Phillis

(b.1753?, the Gambia, West Africa; d. December 5, 1784, Boston, Mass.), poet, the first African American to publish a book; considered the founder of the African American literary tradition.

> *Some view our sable race with scornful eye,*
> *"Their colour is a diabolic dye."*
> *Remember, Christians, Negroes, black as Cain,*
> *May be refined, and join the angelic train.*

So ends Phillis Wheatley's 1773 poem, "On Being Brought from Africa to America." The poem is remarkable not only for the honest way it speaks about color prejudice among white Christians—never a polite subject, and certainly not one in 1773—but for the singular achievements of the author. Wheatley wrote the original version of this poem in 1768, seven years after she had come to America as a seven-year-old child and as an African slave. At the time of its publication in 1773, she was just 19 years old, yet already an internationally celebrated poet whose admirers included Benjamin Franklin and George Washington. She had also become the first African American—and the second American woman—to publish a book.

Just 19 when her first collection of poetry was published in 1773, Phillis Wheatley is pictured here in the frontispiece of that volume. This portrait of the poet is attributed to African American artist Scipio Moorhead.
CORBIS/Bettmann

Wheatley was born, probably in 1753, in The Gambia, West Africa, but in 1761 she was stolen from her parents and transported on a slave ship to Boston, Massachusetts. There she was sold to John and Susanna Wheatley. When Susanna realized that Phillis had a talent for learning, she allowed her daughter Mary to tutor Phillis in Latin, English, and the Bible. Wheatley soon began composing her own poetry, and her first published poem appeared in the *Newport Mercury* newspaper on December 21, 1767.

Over the next five years several more of Wheatley's poems were published in local papers. In October 1770 she wrote an elegy for the English evangelical minister George Whitefield that was so popular that it was also reprinted in England, bringing her international recognition. But when Wheatley tried in 1772 to publish her first volume of poetry, publishers still felt they needed to guarantee to skeptical readers that a black slave could have written the poems she said were hers. She underwent an oral examination by 18 of "the most respectable Characters in Boston," including the governor of Massachusetts, to prove that she was indeed literate and articulate enough to have composed the poems. Wheatley passed the exam but still could not secure a Boston publisher.

Wheatley found an ally across the Atlantic in Selina, countess of Huntingdon, an evangelical Englishwoman with ties to Whitefield who had read her poetry and who arranged for her book to be published in London. In 1773 *Poems on Various Subjects, Religious and Moral* appeared. The frontispiece of the original edition, requested by the countess, makes the author's identity—and ability—very clear: under the caption "Phillis Wheatley, Negro Servant to Mr. John Wheatley of Boston," there is an engraving of the young black woman at her desk, with a piece of paper in front of her, a book at one hand, and a pen in the other. The image is thought to be the work of Scipio Moorhead, a young African American slave artist.

Wheatley traveled to England to oversee the book's publication, but the trip served other purposes as well. She met many British dignitaries and intellectuals, all of whom celebrated her literary ability, and American diplomat Benjamin Franklin came to call on her in London. Shortly after her trip her owners decided to free her—according to Wheatley, "at the desire of my friends in England."

Wheatley's poetic subjects were often the people and places that made news around her. She wrote numerous elegies for friends and acquaintances and also several popular poems supporting the colonists in the Revolutionary War, even though the white Wheatleys were Tories. A poem she wrote in October 1775 in honor of George Washington so impressed him that he invited her to a private visit with him in his Cambridge, Massachusetts, military headquarters. Washington was himself a slaveholder, but some scholars have speculated that his conversation with Wheatley may have influenced his later discomfort with slavery.

Some readers have criticized Wheatley because her subject matter is not more distinctly African American, and especially because some of her poetry even appears to condone slavery. However Wheatley's letters, recently recovered, show clearly that she was aware of racial prejudice and injustice, and that she identified with other people of African descent. Recent scholars agree with Wheatley's implication that her poems supporting the American colonists are part of a larger discourse on freedom from tyranny, a discourse that was inextricably linked to the question of slavery—but that she chose to couch in terms her immediate audience would receive best.

In 1778 Wheatley married a free black Bostonian, John Peters. The next year she circulated a proposal for a new collection of poetry, indicating she had written dozens of new poems since 1773. But in a country now at war, the interest that had attended the publication of her first book had waned. Wheatley could not find a publisher and retreated from the public eye. Her short marriage was unhappy, marred by the deaths in infancy of her first two children. On December 5, 1784, Wheatley died in childbirth along with her third child.

At the time of her death Wheatley was living in poverty and obscurity on the outskirts of Boston, but the memory of the famed "Ethiopian muse" was strong enough that her obituary was printed in the Boston papers. Since the early nineteenth century other African American writers have continually acknowledged their debt to her accomplishments. Wheatley is celebrated as the founder of the African American literary tradition, and contemporary readers continue to learn more about the complexities she brought to that role.

White, Charles

(b. April 2, 1918, Chicago, Ill.; d. October 3, 1979, Los Angeles, Calif.), African American artist specializing in black-and-white graphic work whose oeuvre celebrates the courage and dignity of historic black leaders and common African Americans.

Charles White was born to unmarried parents, Ethel Gary and Charles White Sr., who separated when White was three years old. He was raised by his mother in Chicago. After winning a national pencil sketch contest in 1937, White attended the Art Institute of Chicago for a year, then worked as an artist in the Works Progress Administration during the late 1930s. In 1941 White traveled through the South on a Rosenwald Fellowship. He moved to New York City in 1942 and studied at the Art Students League.

In 1944, while serving in the army, White was diagnosed with tuberculosis and was hospitalized for three years. In 1947 he had his first one-man show at the ACA Gallery in New York City, after which he went to Mexico, where he worked for nearly a year at the printmaking workshop Taller de Graphica. During this time White divorced his wife, the sculptor Elizabeth Catlett, whom he had married in 1941, and married Frances Barrett in 1950. The couple moved in the mid-1950s to Los Angeles, where White became a teacher at the Otis Art Institute in 1965. White also served as a distinguished professor at Howard University's School of Art before his death in 1979.

Among White's better-known works are the mural *Contribution of the Negro to American Democracy* (1943), executed at Hampton Institute in Virginia, and his series of works based on Civil War posters announcing slave auctions or awards for runaway slaves. One of White's most prestigious honors came in 1972 when he became the second African American to be elected a member of the National Academy of Design since the 1927 election of Henry Ossawa Tanner. President Jimmy Carter honored White posthumously at the 22nd annual meeting of the National Conference of Artists.

White, José

(b. January 1, 1836, Matanzas, Cuba; d. March 12, 1918, Paris, France), Afro-Cuban violinist and professor of classical music, author of the famous "La bella Cubana" (The Beautiful Cuban Maid), a nationalistic composition popular during the nineteenth-century Cuban struggles for independence.

José White grew up in Matanzas, an important city east of Havana and a major center of African culture, where he began studying violin, first with his father and later with another Afro-Cuban violinist, J. M. Roman. During this period White developed a reputation as a virtuoso performer and made the acquaintance of North American romantic composer Louis Gottschalk. Gottschalk was so impressed by White's talent that he offered to accompany him in a concert, which took place in Matanzas on March 21, 1855.

A year later, at age 19, White moved to Paris, where he studied classical composition with the famous French violinist Jean Delphin Alard at the Paris Conservatory. By this time he could play 18 other instruments in addition to the violin. While studying at the conservatory, White met Italian opera composer Rossini, whose salon attracted such names as Frédéric Chopin and Franz Liszt. Soon after, Rossini organized several private concerts featuring the Cuban violinist. French composers Charles Gounod, Daniel Auber, and Charles Ambroise began writing music for White.

In 1864, after the death of Alard, White was offered his mentor's teaching position at the Paris Conservatory. He later served briefly as the director of the Rio Conservatory in Brazil. Mounting political tensions, however, soon prompted him to leave his post and return to France.

Though he was principally known as a performer, White also made a name for himself as a composer. Many of his works still survive, including a concerto, a string quartet, a collection of studies for violin, several nationalistic pieces, such as "Marcha cubana," and perhaps his most famous composition, the *habanera* (a Cuban dance in slow duple time) "La bella Cubana". Indeed, because of such overtly patriotic pieces he was forced to flee the wrath of Spanish authorities, as Cuba would not gain its independence until 1898.

By the time of his death in 1918 José White had given concerts throughout Europe and Latin America. In addition, he had performed with orchestras in the United States during a time when few North American blacks were afforded such an opportunity.

North America

White, Walter Francis

(b. July 1, 1893, Atlanta, Ga.; d. March 21, 1955, New York, N.Y.), African American civil rights leader who built the foundations of the Civil Rights Movement as an official of the National Association for the Advancement of Colored People (NAACP), and influential author of the Harlem Renaissance.

Walter White grew up in a racially mixed neighborhood and, as a light-skinned, blue-eyed man, was able to pass for white. He credited a 1906 race riot in Atlanta, during which he defended his family's home from fire, as the incident that ignited his race consciousness as a black man. From that point on, he chose to live as an African American fighting for political and social justice.

After graduating from Atlanta University in 1916, White's activism with the Atlanta branch of the National Association for the Advancement of

Colored People (NAACP) became his career. In 1918 he moved to New York to serve as assistant to NAACP executive secretary James Weldon Johnson. He was an invaluable researcher for the NAACP's antilynching efforts; passing for white, he investigated lynchings and other racially motivated crimes without hindrance. White's reports for the NAACP were fodder for his fiction; his two novels, *The Fire in the Flint* (1924) and *Flight* (1926), both concern the responses of educated blacks, or "New Negroes," to racial injustice. Although the novels sometimes sacrifice plot and characterization to political message, they earned White a Guggenheim Fellowship in 1926. White used money from the fellowship for support while writing a seminal investigation of lynching, *Rope and Faggot: A Biography of Judge Lynch* (1929).

As executive secretary of the NAACP from 1931 to 1955, White worked with A. Philip Randolph to secure the establishment of the Fair Employment Practices Committee in 1941; his efforts also helped produce the executive orders banning discrimination in war-related industries that same year and in the entire United States military in 1948. A delegate with W. E. B. Du Bois and Mary McLeod Bethune to the founding of the United Nations in 1945, White also became involved with seeking justice for the African diaspora. One of White's most lasting achievements as NAACP executive secretary was the recruitment of Charles Hamilton Houston to serve as the NAACP's first full-time chief counsel. Under Houston's leadership and fueled by White's tireless fundraising efforts, the NAACP undertook a series of legal challenges to segregation, culminating in the 1954 United States Supreme Court's historic *Brown v. Board of Education* decision, which finally toppled segregated education in the United States.

North America

Wilder, Lawrence Douglas

(b. January 17, 1931, Richmond, Va.), American politician and the first African American to be elected governor in the United States.

L. Douglas Wilder has served his home state of Virginia as state senator, lieutenant governor, and governor. A native of Richmond, the son of an insurance agent and a domestic worker, Wilder has made a career of conciliating tensions between the races.

Educated at the historically black Virginia Union University (1947–1951) and a graduate of Howard University Law School in Washington, D.C., in 1959, Wilder was always aware of the political possibilities of his own success. A recipient of the Bronze Star for bravery in the Korean War, he used his recognition as a platform to fight successfully for the promotion of passed-over African American military commanders. A self-made millionaire in his law practice, he parlayed his money and influence into a campaign for state senator in 1969. Wilder's success as a Democrat in a largely white, Republican state flows from his position as a "healer" of racial strife, his moderate views on social policy, his fiscal conservatism, and his ability to remake himself to suit the national political climate.

In the Virginia state legislature from 1969 to 1985, Wilder worked continually to end discrimination in the areas of employment and housing opportunities. In 1985 he ran successfully for lieutenant governor, and four years later he became governor of Virginia. Wilder was the first African American to be elected governor in the United States. (Prior to Wilder only one other black person had served as governor. P. B. S. Pinchback briefly became governor of Louisiana in 1872 after the sitting governor was impeached.)

Wilder's record as governor was mixed. Some claim that too much of Virginia's economic success came at the expense of social programs; others cite Wilder's flip-flopping on issues like capital punishment as evidence of his pandering to white, conservative voters. Nevertheless, Wilder's political ticket was still hot in 1991, when he made an unsuccessful bid for the Democratic nomination for president. Although he withdrew, he emerged as a major spokesperson for the Democratic Party nationally when he delivered the nominating speech for Vice President Al Gore at the Democratic National Convention. Wilder's gubernatorial term ended in 1994. He currently teaches politics at Virginia Commonwealth University and is actively pursuing the establishment of a slavery museum.

North America

Wilkins, Roy Ottoway

(b. August 30, 1901, St. Louis, Mo.; d. September 8, 1981, New York, N.Y.), African American journalist, civil rights leader, and director of the National Association for the Advancement of Colored People (NAACP).

Before Roy Wilkins was born, his father had been forced to flee St. Louis to avoid being lynched for refusing to follow a white man's order to get out of the road. Wilkins grew up in St. Paul, Minnesota, where he attended racially integrated schools. He became urgently aware of racial matters at age 18, when three Minnesotan black men were lynched by a mob of 5,000 whites. Upon enrolling in the University of Minnesota, Wilkins became active in the National Association for the Advancement of Colored People (NAACP), as well as on the campus newspaper. He would pursue both interests in Kansas City following graduation. Wilkins worked for the *Kansas City Call*, an African American newspaper, until 1931. He then became assistant executive secretary for the NAACP, a position he held while editing the organization's newspaper, the *Crisis*, until 1949.

In 1955 Wilkins was appointed to serve as the NAACP's executive director, the organization's highest administrative post. He steered the NAACP through the Civil Rights Movement's most turbulent era, and with Martin Luther King, Jr., helped to organize the March on Washington in

1963. Throughout his career Wilkins upheld the principle of nonviolent, legal forms of redress, which tended to alienate him from more radical black groups. Wilkins's struggles for equality and civil rights brought him many awards and earned him the nickname "Mr. Civil Rights."

North America

Williams, Mary Lou

(b. May 8, 1910, Atlanta, Ga.; d. May 28, 1981, Durham, N.C.), African American pianist, composer, arranger, and educator known as the "First Lady of Jazz" and considered the most significant female instrumentalist in jazz history for contributing to the development of both the Kansas City swing style of the 1930s and the bebop style of the early 1940s.

Born Mary Elfrieda Scruggs, Mary Lou Williams began playing piano professionally at age six in Pittsburgh, Pennsylvania. Her early influences included Earl Hines, Jelly Roll Morton, and Lovie Austin. As an adolescent, Williams performed in the Theater Owners' Booking Association (TOBA) black vaudeville circuit alongside such figures as Fats Waller, Duke Ellington, and Willie "The Lion" Smith. In 1926 she married John Williams, a saxophonist and bandleader.

Williams began arranging in 1929 after she joined the Andy Kirk Band, first based in Oklahoma City and later in Kansas City, composing blues-based works that influenced the development of 1930s swing. During the 1930s she performed and arranged for Louis Armstrong, Cab Calloway, Ellington, and others. Williams moved to New York City in 1942 and joined Ellington's band as principal arranger and pianist, composing such notable works as "Trumpet No End" (1942). In the 1940s she mentored and jammed with many of the young beboppers, including Charlie Parker, Thelonious Monk, Bud Powell, and Dizzy Gillespie. Her famous *Zodiac Suite*, written in 1945, was adapted and performed by the New York Philharmonic in Carnegie Hall the following year.

In the 1950s Williams converted to Roman Catholicism and began concentrating on charitable activities and composing religious pieces. In 1957 she resumed per-

Pianist and arranger Mary Lou Williams was the most influential woman instrumentalist in the history of jazz, influencing both Kansas City swing and bebop. *CORBIS/Bettmann*

forming and also formed Mary Records, the first record company established by a woman. Her major religious work, *Mary Lou's Mass* (1969), was commissioned by the Vatican and adapted for ballet by Alvin Ailey two years later. Williams went on to receive numerous honorary doctorates and two Guggenheim Fellowships. She taught courses on jazz at a number of colleges and universities, including Duke University in Durham, North Carolina, where she died in 1981.

North America

Wilson, August

(b. April 27, 1945, Pittsburgh, Pa.), playwright and poet; two-time winner of the Pulitzer Prize in drama.

August Wilson was born Frederick August Kittel in a poor, mixed-race neighborhood of Pittsburgh, Pennsylvania, known as the Hill. His father, a white German baker, was rarely around; his mother held cleaning jobs and received welfare payments to support her six children. When Wilson was a young teenager, his mother remarried and the family moved to a mostly white neighborhood. Wilson's encounters with racism in his new home were more direct, including a pivotal incident in which a teacher wrongly accused him of plagiarizing a paper.

In 1960 Wilson dropped out of school but continued his education in the libraries of Pittsburgh, where he read black writers such as Richard Wright and Ralph Ellison. He received another sort of education in the barbershops, cafés, and street corners that were frequented by a wide range of blacks. In 1965 Wilson began to write poetry. He was heavily influenced by the lyricism of Welsh poet Dylan Thomas and, later, by the Black Nationalism of African American poet and playwright Amiri Baraka. Baraka and other activists of the late 1960s argued that blacks, especially black artists, needed to be more race-conscious. Wilson agreed and spent many of the following years bringing life to black history and culture. In 1968, with little previous experience in the theater, he and a friend founded the Black Horizon Theater in his old neighborhood, the Hill. The company featured minor plays by and about blacks. Around this time he also discovered and immersed himself in the blues—the genre's pained, harmonic realism gave him the inspiration for many of his later plays. In a culminating act of symbolism, he rejected his last name, the name of his white father, and took his mother's maiden name, Wilson, in recognition of her black heritage.

Wilson still believed himself to be a poet, but in the early 1970s he began writing plays. In 1977 he wrote *Black Bart and the Sacred Hills*, a musical satire about an outlaw of the Old West that was produced four years later in St. Paul, Minnesota. He finished two more plays (one of which, *Jitney*, about jitney drivers in Pittsburgh, was produced regionally) before Lloyd Richards, dean of the Yale Drama School, noticed his play *Ma Rainey's Black Bottom* in 1982.

Set in Chicago in the 1920s, *Ma Rainey* presents a fictional day in the real life of blues legend Gertrude "Ma" Rainey. Using realistic dialogue, the play depicts black musicians being exploited by white record companies and directing their rage at other blacks instead of their white oppressors. Richards produced the play first at the Yale Repertory Theatre, then on Broadway, establishing a pattern that he and Wilson, working collaboratively, used in Wilson's future plays. Although a few reviewers criticized *Ma Rainey* for overemphasizing politics, others praised it for presenting a poignant account of the effect of racism.

Shortly after writing *Ma Rainey*, Wilson wrote *Fences*, which focuses on the frustrations and responsibilities of a former Negro League baseball player, now a garbage man, barred from playing in the major leagues. *Fences*, winner of the 1987 Pulitzer Prize in drama, strengthened the playwright's reputation for deft presentation of the consequences of racism. His next play, *Joe Turner's Come and Gone* (1986), further distinguished Wilson by debuting on Broadway while *Fences* was still running there. Set in a Pittsburgh boardinghouse in 1911, *Joe Turner* chronicles the life of a black freedman who comes North to find his wife, who fled while he was enslaved. Mystical and metaphorical, the play explores assimilation by African Americans into American society and is at once bitter and optimistic.

The Piano Lesson, immensely popular with both critics and audiences, followed in 1987. Set in 1936, its main characters are descendants of a slave family whose father and grandmother were traded for a piano. The grieving grandfather carved likenesses of his wife and son in the piano, which is now in the family's possession. The family is divided between those who want to sell the piano to buy the land where their ancestors were slaves and those who want to preserve the piano as an heirloom. *The Piano Lesson* won both a Pulitzer Prize and a Tony Award for best play.

In 1990 Wilson wrote *Two Trains Running*, a portrayal of friendships and conflicts during the late 1960s; in 1995 he wrote *Seven Guitars*, a portrayal of relationships among a group of musicians set in Pittsburgh in 1948. Wilson has declared that he will write a drama about black American life in each decade of the twentieth century.

North America

Wilson, Fred

(b. 1954, New York, N.Y.), African American sculptor, mixed media and installation artist.

The son of parents of mixed descent, Fred Wilson received a bachelor of fine arts degree from the State University of New York at Purchase in 1976. After completing his degree, Wilson worked as an administrator in various New York museums, including the Museum of Natural History and the

Metropolitan Museum of Art. Between 1978 and 1980 he worked as an artist in East Harlem and was funded by the Comprehensive Employment Training Act (CETA).

Wilson began an association with the Just Above MidTown Gallery in 1981, a space known for its congeniality to African American artists. In 1987 Wilson was the director of the Longwood Art Gallery of the Bronx Council of the Arts, for which he curated the show *Rooms with a View: The Struggle Between Culture and Content and the Context of Art*. The show employed three spaces in the gallery. One was appointed like a "turn of the century salon" museum space, another like a contemporary gallery, and a third like an ethnographic museum. The exhibition questioned issues of insitutional space and history, challenging viewers to radical interrogation of their conception of a museum and museums' relationship to African Americans.

In 1992 Wilson created the award-winning installation *Mining the Museum*, sponsored by the Museum for the Contemporary Arts in Baltimore. The installation used artifacts found at the Maryland Historical Society to explore the ways in which the historical society defined itself and Maryland's history by excluding the experience of African Americans in the state. Wilson juxtaposed seemingly unrelated objects to reinforce his point. For example, in a vitrine displaying nineteenth-century silver work from the state of Maryland, he included a set of slave shackles crafted at the same time.

Wilson's most recent work has involved installations featuring racially stereotypical bric-a-brac, such as Aunt Jemima dolls, that raise questions about stereotypes and racial prejudice. He has had solo exhibitions at the Indianapolis Museum of Art, the Seattle Art Museum, the Museum for Contemporary Art in Baltimore, and the Museum of Contemporary Art in Chicago. In 1994 Wilson represented the United States in the Fourth International Cairo Biennial in Egypt. He has also participated in numerous group shows across the country and around the world, including the 1996 *New Histories* exhibition at the Insititute for Contemporary Art in Boston. In addition to receiving numerous awards and grants in recognition of his work, Wilson has lectured at universities and art colleges across the United States.

North America

Wilson, Harriet E. Adams

(b. 1828?, Milford, N.H.; d. 1870?), American writer whose book, *Our Nig*, published in 1859, is considered the first novel published by an African American woman and the first novel published by an African American in the United States.

Little is known about the life of Harriet E. Adams Wilson. The 1850 federal census lists a 22-year-old "Black" woman named Harriet Adams living with the Samuel Boyles family in the town of Milford, N.H., which suggests that she was born around 1828. In 1851 she married Thomas Wilson, a free man who pretended to be a fugitive slave from Virginia so he could lecture on the horrors of slavery. Shortly after the birth of the couple's son, George

Mason Wilson, in May or June 1852, Thomas Wilson abandoned the family. Wilson, who was unable to work because of the physical and emotional abuse inflicted by her employers, lost custody of her son. She began writing to earn enough money to reclaim him. He died five and one-half months after her book's Boston publication in 1859.

Our Nig; or, Sketches from the Life of a Free Black, in a Two-Story White House, North. Showing That Slavery's Shadows Fall Even There, is a largely autobiographical novel that explicitly compares the racist conditions suffered by a black indentured servant to slavery in the South. Using the slave narrative as a model, Wilson indicts Northern treatment of blacks. Possibly because of its controversial stand, the book was published at the author's own expense and sold poorly.

The story is told mostly through the eyes of a young girl, the novel's protagonist, Alfrado, a mulatto who is abandoned by her white mother after her black father dies. Left with a white family, she is severely mistreated by the mother and one of the daughters. Although the men of the family are absentmindedly fond of her, they are unable to protect her from the hunger, beatings, and scolding that she constantly endures. Misfortune continues into Alfrado's adulthood when the husband, who she thought would save her, leaves her and her young child. The novel ends with Alfrado, broken in body but not in spirit, expressing her contempt for a society that allowed her virtual slavery.

North America

Winfrey, Oprah Gail

(b. January 29, 1954, Kosciusko, Miss.), African American talk show host, Academy Award-nominated actress, and producer whose syndicated television show, *The Oprah Winfrey Show*, is the most popular talk show ever.

Oprah Winfrey was born on a Mississippi farm and raised by her paternal grandmother until she was six years old, when she moved to Milwaukee to live with her mother, Vernita Lee. Though Winfrey did well in school, she was allegedly sexually abused by male relatives and became increasingly troubled as a teenager. Her mother, a maid who was busy raising two other children, eventually sent Winfrey to live with her disciplinarian father, a barber and businessman in Nashville, Tennessee. Winfrey flowered under Vernon Winfrey's strict supervision, excelling academically and as a public speaker. At age 16 she won a partial scholarship to the Tennessee State University in a public speaking contest sponsored by the Elks Club.

As a freshman at Tennessee State University, Winfrey worked briefly as a radio newscaster before victories in two local beauty pageants helped land her a news anchor position at WTVF-TV in Nashville. In 1976, only a few months shy of her bachelor's degree at Tennessee State University, Winfrey landed a job as a reporter and evening news co-anchor at WJZ-TV in Balti-

more. Although she did not succeed in that position, the station management realized that Winfrey, who had no formal journalistic training, was
better suited to cohosting WJZ's morning talk show, *People Are Talking*.
Winfrey helped turn the show into a ratings success with her personable
interviewing style and charismatic presence.

After eight years as the cohost of *People Are Talking*, Winfrey was offered
a job as the host of *A.M. Chicago*, a Chicago talk show that aired opposite
Phil Donahue's popular morning show and lagged behind it in the ratings.
In one month Winfrey's ratings equaled Donahue's, and in three, surpassed
them. Donahue acknowledged Winfrey's ratings supremacy by moving his
show to New York City in 1985. In 1985 *A.M. Chicago* was renamed *The
Oprah Winfrey Show*, and it was syndicated in 1986. It eventually became
the highest-rated talk show in television history. By 1997, 15 to 20 million
viewers watched it daily in the United States, and it was seen in more than
132 countries. The show has received 25 Emmy Awards, 6 of them for best
host. In 1996 *Time* magazine named Winfrey one of the 25 most influential
people in the world.

Also a talented actress, in 1985 Winfrey earned Golden Globe and
Academy Award nominations for her portrayal of Sofia in the film *The
Color Purple*, based on Alice Walker's book of the same name. In 1986 Winfrey founded HARPO Productions, becoming only the third woman to own
her own television and film studios. Based in Chicago, HARPO (Oprah
spelled backwards) owns and produces *The Oprah Winfrey Show* as well as
such dramatic miniseries as *The Women of Brewster Place* (1988), based on
the book by Gloria Naylor, and *The Wedding* (1998), based on the book by
Dorothy West. In addition to supporting African American literature
through her television movies, Winfrey presents an on-air book club that
has brought new readers to such writers as Toni Morrison.

A political activist as well as an entertainer, Winfrey testified before the
U.S. Senate Judiciary Committee, describing the sexual abuse she suffered
as a child, and worked for the passage of the National Child Protection Act
in 1991, which provides for the establishment of a nationwide database of
convicted child abusers. In December 1993 President Bill Clinton signed
"Oprah's Bill" into law. Her many philanthropic ventures include donations
of time and money to efforts aimed at protecting children and to the establishment of educational scholarships.

North America

Womanism,

**a term to encompass the variety of ways that African American women support
each other and relate to the world.**

The term "womanism" was coined by the African American writer Alice
Walker in her 1983 book *In Search of Our Mothers' Gardens*. Walker defined
a womanist as a black feminist who continues the legacy of "outrageous,

audacious, courageous, and willful, responsible, in charge, serious" African American women—women who are agents for social change for the whole-ness and liberation of black people, and, by extension, the rest of humanity. A womanist can be a lesbian, a heterosexual, or a bisexual woman. She celebrates and affirms African American women's culture and beauty. She loves herself.

Although the words "Christianity" and "religion" do not appear in Walker's definition, the word "womanism" has religious as well as secular usage. Because Walker emphasizes African American women's love for the spiritual, black Christian women have used the womanist concept to articulate their participation in, and witness to, divine power and presence in the world. Womanist Christian thought and practices began to flourish in the mid-1980s as a way to challenge racist, sexist, and white feminists' religious discourse and practice, all of which ignored the black experience in church and society.

The secular use of the word "womanist" identifies a culturally specific form of women-centered politics and theory. It finds the term "feminist" inappropriate because of its identification with a predominantly white movement, and because "feminist" has often been used to label a woman as a lesbian, regardless of her actual sexual orientation. Because of this, some women have challenged the term "womanist" as homophobic.

North America

Woodruff, Hale Aspacio

(b. August 26, 1900, Cairo, Ill.; d. September 6, 1980, New York, N.Y.), African American painter and teacher who is best known for his *Amistad Murals*.

Hale Woodruff attended public schools in Nashville, Tennessee, where he was raised by his mother. In 1920 he moved to Indianapolis to study art at the John Herron Art Institute, supporting himself with part-time work as a political cartoonist. During this period he developed an interest in African art, which influenced his later work. In 1926 Woodruff won a Harmon Foundation Award to study at the Académie Moderne de la Grande Chaumière in Paris from 1927 to 1931.

Woodruff returned to the United States in 1931 and founded the art department at Atlanta University, where he helped to develop a cohesive national African American arts community. In addition to teaching, Woodruff brought exhibitions to Atlanta University that featured a wide range of African American artists who were often excluded from mainstream art exhibitions. To promote African American art and artists further, Woodruff organized the Atlanta University Annuals in 1942, a national juried exhibition that continued until 1970. Woodruff used the Annuals to promote the interests of his students, including Frederick Flemister, Eugene Grigsby, Wilmer Jennings, and Hayward Oubré, and independent artists such as Charles Alston, Elizabeth Catlett, Lois Mailou Jones, and William H. Johnson.

A gifted artist as well as teacher, Woodruff achieved his greatest fame with the *Amistad Murals*, painted for Talladega College's Savery Library. The work reflects the influence of Mexican muralist Diego Rivera, with whom Woodruff studied briefly in 1934, and depicts moments of "the Amistad Incident," the 1839 mutiny by kidnapped Africans aboard a slave ship against their captors. The first panel, *The Mutiny Aboard the Amistad, 1839*, shows the violent struggle that occurred when the enslaved Africans sought to capture the ship. The second panel, *The Amistad Slaves on Trial at New Haven, Connecticut, 1840*, depicts a scene from the trial, as a white sailor who survived the attack accuses the African Cinque of leading the mutiny. The third panel, *The Return to Africa, 1842*, portrays the mutineers after winning their court case and returning home.

Woodruff moved to New York in 1946 and began teaching at New York University (NYU). During this period he abandoned figurative painting and shifted to an abstract expressionist style. He adopted abstract expressionism's spontaneity but also included design components of the African art he became interested in as a student, including Asante gold weights, Dogon masks, and Yoruba Shango implements. Woodruff also continued to support other African American artists. In 1963 Woodruff cofounded Spiral, a group whose members sought to represent the Civil Rights Movement in the visual arts. Woodruff was awarded a Great Teacher Award by NYU in 1966, and in 1968 he became professor emeritus at NYU. In April 1980, shortly before his death, he was one of ten African American artists honored by President Jimmy Carter at a White House reception for the National Conference of Artists.

North America

Woodson, Carter Godwin

(b. December 19, 1875, New Canton, Va.; d. April 3, 1950, Washington, D.C.), African American historian and educator who pioneered the research and dissemination of African American history.

One of nine children, Carter G. Woodson grew up on his family's farm in rural Virginia. His mother, a former slave who had secretly learned to read and write as a child, and two of his uncles, who received training at Freedmen's Bureau schools, tutored him and cultivated his interest in learning. In 1892 Woodson moved to Huntington, West Virginia, where he worked in coal mines.

At age 20 Woodson enrolled at Frederick Douglass High School, the only all-black school in the area. He completed the four-year curriculum in two years even though he was working to pay his tuition. Following his graduation he obtained a teaching position in Winona, West Virginia. But in 1901 Woodson returned to his former high school to teach and later to serve as principal. Meanwhile, he intermittently attended Berea College in

Kentucky, an integrated school established by abolitionists, from which he graduated in 1903.

Woodson was then hired by the U.S. War Department to teach English to Spanish-speaking students in the Philippines. While abroad he studied Spanish and other Romance languages through University of Chicago correspondence courses. Returning to the United States following travel in Europe, he matriculated at the University of Chicago in 1907 and received both bachelor's and master's degrees in European history in 1908. Woodson then entered the doctoral program in history at Harvard University and the next year initiated a ten-year teaching career at Dunbar High School in Washington, D.C. He received the Ph.D. in 1912, making him only the second African American to earn a Harvard doctorate degree.

In 1915 Woodson established the Association for the Study of Negro Life and History (ASNLH, later the Association for the Study of Afro-American Life and History). The organization's aim was to encourage research and writing about the black experience, to publish this writing, and to raise funds to support researchers and writers. As extensions of the ASNLH, Woodson founded the *Journal of Negro History* (1916), the *Associated Publishers* (1921), and the *Negro History Bulletin* (1937). The *Journal of Negro History* was for the general reader. The Associated Publishers generated revenue to "make possible the publication and circulation of valuable books on colored people not acceptable to most publishers." The *Negro History Bulletin* provided elementary and secondary teachers lessons in African American history.

Woodson always had difficulty securing funds for the ASNLH. He solicited numerous foundations without much success. Although he could have alleviated the ASNLH's financial problems by affiliating it with a university, he rejected this solution in order to maintain his own independence and control over the organization. Money came from Woodson's own meager teaching salary, the income generated by his numerous publications, and the contributions of the African American community.

One of Woodson's enduring achievements is his initiation of Black History Month. In 1926 he launched Negro History Week, a commemoration of black achievement held the second week of February, which marked the birthdays of Frederick Douglass and Abraham Lincoln. To encourage African Americans to celebrate Negro History Week, Woodson distributed kits containing pictures of and stories about notable African Americans. Negro History Week was changed to Black History Month in the 1960s.

Woodson was a prodigious writer, authoring or coauthoring 19 books on various aspects of African American history. He was one of the first scholars to consider slavery from the slaves' perspective, to compare slavery in the United States to slavery in Latin America, and to note the African cultural influences in New World slave culture.

Woodson's mission was to dispel the racist myths about African Americans and their past that the historical writings of white scholars promulgated. He asserted, "If a race has no history, if it has no worthwhile tradition, it becomes a negligible factor in the thought of the world, and it stands in danger of being exterminated."

Perhaps more than any other person, Woodson helped African American history develop into a widely recognized and respected academic discipline. He believed that "the achievements of the Negro properly set forth will crown him as a factor in early human progress and a maker of modern civilization."

Woods, Tiger

(b. December 30, 1975, Cypress, Calif.), the first African American and Asian American, and the youngest golfer, to win a major golf tournament.

When Eldrick "Tiger" Woods decided to leave Stanford University in August 1996 to play professional golf, the expectations placed on him were high. A golf prodigy whose father, Earl Woods, taught his son to play golf before the boy could even read, Woods had recorded two holes-in-one by age six. By 1996 he possessed a complete and polished game with the power to hit 300-yard drives routinely, and the touch necessary for a solid "short game" (shots from within 60 yards of the hole, including putting).

Experts lauded Woods's great physical skills, as well as his competitive desire and mental composure, for which Woods credited his father, a former Green Beret in the Vietnam War. Woods had also amassed many amateur titles, including six United States Golf Association national championships, a record-setting three consecutive U.S. Amateur championships, a National College Athletic Association championship.

Woods successfully joined the professional ranks by winning two of the first seven tournaments he entered. In April 1997 Woods won the Masters Tournament, golf's most prestigious tournament, shooting a record-setting 270 and winning by the largest margin in Masters history, 12 strokes. He also set a handful of unofficial records, including the first African American and Asian American (his mother, Kutilda [Punsawad] Woods, comes from Thailand) to win a major golf tournament, as well as being the youngest Masters winner. Woods ended 1997 with four tournament wins and nine top-ten finishes.

Woods has had a great impact on the social aspects of golf. When Woods won the Masters, many credited him with breaking racial stereotypes that had labeled athletes of color as poor golfers. Woods himself cited black golfers who paved the way for him, such as Lee Elder, the first African American to play in the Masters, and Ted Rhodes, the first African American to play in the U.S. Open. In addition to winning the respect and admiration of his colleagues on the tour, Woods has increased golf's popularity among African Americans and other minorities.

Wright, Richard

(b. September 4, 1908, Roxie, Miss.; d. November 28, 1960, Paris, France), African American novelist, among the first to show the destructive effects of white racism on both blacks and whites.

Richard Wright was born in rural Mississippi near Natchez, where white hostility was all-pervasive. His mother was a former schoolteacher; his father was a farmer who drank heavily and abandoned the family in 1914. In the absence of her husband Wright's mother took a series of low-wage, unskilled jobs to support her two boys. Moving from town to town, the family settled in Memphis, then in rural Arkansas, often going hungry. After his mother suffered a debilitating stroke, Wright returned to Mississippi in the care of his stern religious grandmother, who disapproved of his literary inclinations. The experience left Wright eager to leave the area and disdainful of religion.

Upon completing the ninth grade, Wright went North, first to Memphis, then to Chicago. He discovered and read H. L. Mencken, whose journalism inspired Wright's later writing, as well as Fyodor Dostoyevsky, Sinclair Lewis, Sherwood Anderson, and Theodore Dreiser. In Chicago in the late 1920s and early 1930s he held odd jobs, eventually settling in the U.S. Post Office, which was nicknamed "the University" for its high density of radical intellectuals.

Wright attended meetings of the John Reed Club, an organization of leftist writers, and soon became active in the Communist Party. Encouraged by party members, Wright published poetry, short stories, and articles in Communist newspapers and other left-wing journals. He later said that he had hoped his writings would bridge the gap between party leaders and common people. Beginning in 1935, for several years he wrote travel guides for the depression-era Federal Writers' Project, first in Chicago, then in Harlem. He also produced fiction—a collection of forceful short stories about racial oppression and a humorous novel about working-class blacks in Chicago. Some of these stories were published in leftist periodicals; the novel was published in 1963, after his death, as *Lawd Today*.

Wright's debut in mainstream publishing came in 1938 with the publication of *Uncle Tom's Children*, a collection of cruel novellas based on his southern childhood. The book was widely read, and its accounts of the pernicious effects of racism moved and impressed reviewers. Still, Wright was disappointed. He had intended readers to see and feel the devastation of racism on all of society, not just on African Americans.

His next novel, *Native Son* (1940), was merciless. In the story, Bigger Thomas, a young black man hardened by racism and ignorance, accidentally kills a white woman and is condemned to death. Although Bigger's Communist lawyer argues that guilt belongs to the society that would not accept him and drove him to brutality, Bigger, in fact, has tasted his first freedom in the act of murder: for once in his alienated life he has brought about an event to which others must respond. Editors toned down the original manuscript (the restored original version was published only in 1992), but *Native Son* was still the most militant protest novel about American race relations of its time. It became a huge best-seller, a Book-of-the-Month Club selection, and was dramatized on Broadway in a production by Orson Welles. Many reviewers marveled that Wright could make Bigger Thomas an unsympathetic character yet nonetheless force white readers to see their own guilt in Bigger's crime. Other reviewers, while appreciative of the novel's power, criticized Wright for presenting a stereotype and a victim in Bigger Thomas.

In 1944 Wright wrote an essay for the *Atlantic Monthly* titled "I Tried to Be a Communist" in which he expressed his long disenchantment with the dogma of the Communist Party as well as its refusal to speak and act on black civil rights. Shortly thereafter he published *Black Boy* (1945), the autobiography of his youth in the South. Like his previous works, *Black Boy* was unrelenting in its depiction of the scarring effects of racism and poverty. A few critics complained that it gave a one-sided picture of the South, but most heralded it as searing and precise, even a masterpiece.

In the late 1940s Wright traveled to France at the invitation of American expatriate writer Gertrude Stein. He was warmly received in Paris, where he met many of the country's leading intellectuals, including Jean-Paul Sartre and Simone de Beauvoir. Feeling the tensions of racism on his return to New York City and annoyed at being acclaimed only as a great black writer, he emigrated to France with his second wife—he had been briefly married at the beginning of the 1940s—and young daughter.

In France, Wright was deeply influenced by existentialism, a philosophy emphasizing the isolation of the individual in a hostile or indifferent universe. He wrote three more novels, none of which was well received in America, partly because they overintellectualized the question of race, partly because they were perceived as out of touch with recent developments in American race relations, and partly because many critics were upset with him for leaving the United States. Wright also wrote extensively about colonialism in Africa; in his last years he became an international spokesman for Pan-Africanism. He died in Paris.

Among Wright's other works are the novels *The Outsider* (1953), *Savage Holiday* (1954), and *The Long Dream* (1958); the collection of stories *Eight Men* (1961); the nonfiction works *Black Power* (1954), *The Color Curtain* (1956), *Pagan Spain* (1957), and *White Man, Listen!* (1957); and the expanded autobiography, *American Hunger* (1977).

X Y

Yoruba,

a group of peoples sharing the Yoruba language and a range of cultural traditions, concentrated in Nigeria but forming smaller communities in Benin and Togo.

Today more than 20 million people speak some dialect of Yoruba, which belongs to the Kwa group of the Niger-Congo languages. Most Yoruba speakers live in southwestern Nigeria. They form a majority in Lagos, Africa's second most populous city.

Yoruba speakers are traditionally among the most urbanized African people. For centuries before British colonization, most Yoruba speakers inhabited a complex, urbanized society organized around powerful city-states. These densely populated cities centered on the residence of the king, or *oba*. The basic social units were patrilineages in which inheritance, descent, and political position passed through the male line. Though they lived in cities, traditionally most Yoruba men farmed crops such as yams, maize, plantains, peanuts, millet, and beans in the surrounding countryside. Many men also engaged in crafts such as blacksmithing, manufacturing textiles, and woodworking. Traditionally, Yoruba women specialized in marketing and trade, and could gain considerable independence, status, and wealth through their commercial activity. While many Yoruba speakers continue to farm and trade today, they generally also grow and sell cash crops such as cocoa. Meanwhile, the millions of Yoruba in modern cities such as Lagos pursue a diverse array of manufacturing and service occupations.

Originally Hausa speakers used the name Yoruba for the people of the Oyo Kingdom. Europeans appropriated the term to refer to all speakers of the Yoruba language. Yoruba speakers identify themselves as members of several different groups, including the Ife, Isa, and Ketu. Some of these Yoruba-speaking groups identify with the larger community of Yoruba speakers. Others, such as the Sabe, Idaisa, and Ketu, consider themselves separate ethnic groups and do not feel a sense of community with other Yoruba speakers, though they share Yoruba origin myths. All of these groups, however, share a similar material culture, mythology, and artistic tradition.

Art historians consider thirteenth- and fourteenth-century Yoruba bronzes and terra cotta sculptures to be among Africa's greatest artistic achievements. Yoruba oral histories, folklore, and proverbs have also won international acclaim. Traditional Yoruba religious beliefs recognize a supreme god presiding over a complex pantheon of hundreds of lesser gods. Over the past several centuries Islam and Christianity have spread to Yorubaland. Many Yoruba take a pluralistic approach to religion that integrates traditional religious elements with Christian and Muslim beliefs, as in the Aladura spiritualist movement.

According to folklore, the Yoruba originated from the mythical Olorun, god of the sky, whose son, Oduduwa, founded the ancient holy city of Ile-Ife around the eighth century C.E. Linguistic and archaeological evidence suggest that, in fact, speakers of a distinct Yoruba language emerged near the Niger-Benue confluence some 3,000 to 4,000 years ago. From there they migrated west to Yorubaland between the eighth and eleventh century. Strategically located on the fertile borderland between the savanna and the forest zones, Ile-Ife was the center of a powerful kingdom by the eleventh century, one of the earliest in Africa south of the Sahel. Its rulers taxed both food surpluses and trade. While the institution of kingship probably predates the emergence of Ile-Ife, the holy city became the preeminent Yoruba spiritual and cultural center.

In time other Yoruba cities rose to prominence. Oyo probably originated in the eleventh century and became a substantial city by the fourteenth century. Other Yoruba city-states emerged around the same time. During the fifteenth and sixteenth centuries the nearby non-Yoruba kingdom of Benin conquered parts of eastern and southern Yorubaland.

Oyo, however, became a powerful military state by the seventeenth century. The rulers of Oyo acquired horses by selling slaves to Europeans and reselling European manufactured goods to Hausa traders. The Oyo cavalry invaded neighboring Yoruba and non-Yoruba kingdoms alike, including Dahomey. By the late eighteenth century, however, Oyo, suffering from internal rivalries, began to disintegrate. During the early nineteenth century Dahomey won its independence in a war that further weakened Oyo. During the 1830s Muslim Fulani from the Sokoto caliphate conquered northern regions of Oyo and cut off its access to trade with the Hausa. By 1840 the Oyo Kingdom had completely collapsed.

Wars among Yoruba groups and city-states raged for much of the rest of the nineteenth century. The protracted warfare left many Yoruba vulnerable to enslavement. Large numbers were sold to traders who transported them to Latin America. To this day Yoruba culture remains influential in Brazil and Cuba, where Santería religious practice carries on Yoruba traditions.

Aiming to repress the slave trade, encourage the production of raw materials, and open markets for British manufactures, Great Britain sought a foothold in the region. In 1851 the British navy seized Lagos, allegedly to shut down the slave market there. In 1888 most of Yorubaland became a protectorate of Great Britain. The colonial administration imposed peace among warring groups after 1892 in an effort to promote its commercial interests. Under the British policy known as indirect rule, Yoruba kings lost their sovereignty but retained a role in local government.

As the capital of British Nigeria, Lagos, dominated by Yoruba, became the center of Nigerian political and economic life. Colonial authorities introduced cocoa as a cash crop in Yorubaland and developed a modern infrastructure of railroads, highways, and schools in the region. As a result large numbers of Yoruba earned substantial cash incomes, became literate in English, and gained positions in the colonial civil service. By the time of independence Yoruba speakers occupied a dominant position in Nigeria's economy and government. Since independence, however, the more numerous northern Hausa have dominated the elected and military governments that have ruled Nigeria, and the relatively prosperous Yoruba have tended to remain political outsiders, often subject to repression.

North America

Young, Andrew

(b. October 23, 1932, New Orleans, La.), African American civil rights activist and politician who was the first black U.S. ambassador to the United Nations.

Raised in an affluent African American family in New Orleans, Andrew Young as a child had opportunities available to few blacks in the American South. Among these was an exceptional education: he attended Howard University and Hartford Theological Seminary. He was ordained a Congregational minister in 1955 and soon after accepted a position in a diocese in rural Georgia and Alabama. This experience made him keenly aware of the poverty African Americans suffered in the rural South and inspired his work as a civil rights activist.

In 1959 Young moved to New York City to be the assistant director of the National Council of Churches and to raise financial support for civil rights activities in the South. He returned to Georgia two years later and joined the Southern Christian Leadership Conference (SCLC). His energetic work as funding coordinator and administrator of the SCLC's Citizenship Education Programs soon won him the admiration of Martin Luther King, Jr. The two men became close associates, and Young helped King organize SCLC marches in the South.

Young became executive director of the SCLC in 1964 and executive vice president in 1967. After King's death Young helped to guide the SCLC toward activities promoting social and economic improvements for African Americans. He retired from these positions in 1970, but remained on the board of directors until 1972.

In 1972 Young became the first African American to be elected to the U.S. House of Representatives from Georgia since Reconstruction. While a representative, Young played an instrumental role in winning for the presidential candidate Jimmy Carter the vital backing of those members of the African American community who questioned Carter's commitment to civil rights.

Young resigned from the House of Representatives in 1977 when Carter appointed him U.S. ambassador to the United Nations. As ambassador Young improved communications between the United States and African nations. He was instrumental in focusing American foreign policy on sub-Saharan Africa and bringing American attention to the conditions of apartheid in South Africa. Young resigned from the position in 1979 after he was criticized for his contacts with the Palestine Liberation Organization.

In 1982 Young was elected mayor of Atlanta, an office which he held until 1989. In 1990 he made an unsuccessful bid in the Georgia gubernatorial race and retired from politics. In 1994 he published his memoir, *A Way Out of No Way*, and returned to public life to cochair the Atlanta Committee for the 1996 Summer Olympic Games.

North America

Young, Coleman Alexander

(b. May 18, 1919, Tuscaloosa, Ala.; d. November 29, 1997, Detroit, Mich.), five-term mayor of Detroit, Michigan, former autoworker, member of the Tuskegee Airmen, and founder of the National Negro Labor Council.

Coleman Young, Detroit's first black mayor, presided for nearly twenty years over America's eighth-largest city—and one of its most troubled. By 1973, when Young first ran for mayor, the auto industry that had been Detroit's economic base was in serious decline. Most whites had fled to the nearby suburbs, leaving the city with a population that was approximately 70 percent African American. Poverty sent the crime rate soaring, and the city's infrastructure fell into a state of decay. Young, a state senator at the time, received 92 percent of the black vote when he defeated police chief John Nicholls in the mayoral election.

Over his 20 years in office Young launched a series of revitalization projects, including a new rail system and a General Motors automobile plant as well as construction of the Joe Louis Arena and the multi-use Renaissance Center on Detroit's waterfront. He worked to integrate the police department, which he had dubbed "an army of occupation" during his first campaign. In addition, Young dramatically increased city contracts with minority-owned businesses, winning lasting popularity among the city's working-class African Americans. Despite his often abrasive style, which drew criticism from many white suburbanites and the local media, he was elected to an unprecedented five terms, stepping down in 1993 at age 75. Young died of respiratory failure in Detroit four years later.

Young, Lester Willis ("Prez")

(b. August 27, 1909, Woodville, Miss.; d. March 15, 1959, New York, N.Y.), African American tenor saxophonist whose distinctive approach and tone inspired many musicians during the 1940s and 1950s.

Singer Billie Holiday gave Lester Young his nickname "Prez" (short for "president") during the 1930s: it was an era of dukes, counts, and kings of swing, and she insisted that Young should hold the highest office in the land. Today he is most widely heard through his musical collaborations with Holiday. During and after the swing era he and Coleman Hawkins offered the major alternative approaches to the tenor saxophone in jazz.

As an improviser Hawkins relied upon arpeggios built over the harmonies of each chord in a song. Young's improvisations were linear-melodies stretched across the chord sequence. Hawkins aggressively pushed the beat; Young's playing was gentle, and consistently behind the beat. Hawkins's tone was full, even harsh; Young's was light.

Young came from a musical family that moved during his childhood from Mississippi to New Orleans to Minneapolis. He learned several instruments and played in the successful Young family band. In 1927, while playing with another group, he took up the tenor saxophone. Eventually he settled in Kansas City, then a booming jazz center. He joined Bennie Moten's band in 1933, then left for New York City to fill the saxophone chair recently vacated by Hawkins in Fletcher Henderson's band. The Henderson band, accustomed to Hawkins's style, ridiculed Young, and he soon returned to Kansas City. But while he was in New York City, a chance encounter in a Harlem jam session introduced him to Billie Holiday, with whom he would collaborate in a classic series of recordings in the late 1930s and early 1940s.

Young influenced few saxophonists during the 1930s. However, the musician upon whom he had the greatest impact—alto saxophonist Charlie Parker—became the key jazz soloist to arise between Louis Armstrong in the 1920s and John Coltrane in the 1960s. Parker, a creator of bop during the 1940s, extended Young's style and made it his own. Parker's early recordings reveal his deep debt to Young.

Young rejoined the Count Basie band in 1935, and in 1936 he made his recording debut with a quintet drawn from that band. Producer John Hammond later recalled it as "one of the only perfect sessions I ever had." Musicologist Gunther Schuller described Young's solo on "Lady Be Good" as "quintessential Lester Young: economical and lean . . . and masterful in its control of form." Young remained with Basie between 1935 and 1940, and returned in 1943 for a stint that ended when he was drafted. During the late 1930s he also recorded regularly with Holiday. His improvised fills and counter melodies behind her vocals define the interplay that is the essence of jazz.

After World War II, Young did not fare well, although his musical star was clearly ascendant. A large number of saxophonists—including Wardell Gray, Paul Quinichette (nicknamed the Vice President), and numerous white saxophonists such as Stan Getz and Zoot Sims—modeled their playing on Young's. On the other hand, his recordings suggest his unhappiness, which some attributed to his traumatic military experience, and others to his heavy drinking.

Even in the 1950s Young occasionally recaptured the fragile beauty of his early playing. In a 1956 series of recordings—including *The Jazz Giants* and three albums recorded at a nightclub in Washington, D.C.—Young was in prime form. But when he performed with Holiday in the 1957 television special "The Sound of Jazz," their performance had an aura of tragic finality. Young and Holiday died in 1959 within four months of each other.

North America

Young, Whitney Moore, Jr.

(b. July 31, 1921, Lincoln Ridge, Ky.; d. March 11, 1971, Lagos, Nigeria), former executive director of the National Urban League (NUL) who shaped the organization's policy and lobbied industry to provide employment opportunities for African Americans.

When he was named executive director of the National Urban League (NUL) in October 1961, many observers believed that Whitney Young Jr. was not qualified to hold the position. He had served as industrial relations secretary for the St. Paul, Minnesota, branch of the NUL from 1947 to 1949; as executive secretary of the Omaha, Nebraska, branch from 1949 to 1954; and as dean of the Atlanta University School of Social Work from 1954 to 1961. Still, by traditional NUL standards he was young and inexperienced. As executive director during the 1960s, however, Young guided the organization through one of the most socially and politically tumultuous decades in U.S. history.

The NUL was much less militant than many other organizations involved in the Civil Rights Movement. Since its inception in 1910 it had sought to promote African American participation in the U.S. political system, rather than to change the system itself. In the 1960s though the NUL did not embrace the direct action of other civil rights organizations— it did not sponsor sit-ins, protest marches, bus boycotts, or voter registration drives—under Young's leadership it took a more active stance that better aligned it with black political and social thought of the day. The NUL provided support for civil rights activists, including co-sponsorship of the March on Washington for Jobs and Freedom in 1963.

Young, who had grown up on the campus of the Lincoln Institute, a vocational high school for blacks at which his father was the principal and the faculty was integrated, was accustomed to interracial cooperation. He used his considerable social and political skills to become an unofficial adviser to presidents John F. Kennedy, Lyndon B. Johnson, and Richard Nixon. Johnson drew on some of Young's ideas for his War on Poverty. Young's relationships with white business leaders brought increased employment to blacks and increased funding to the NUL.

Young, who held a master's degree in social work from the University of Minnesota, also called for a "Domestic Marshall Plan" for blacks. In 1968 he introduced the NUL's New Thrust, a program designed to help eliminate ghettos and to increase affordable housing, health care, and educational opportunities for the poor. In addition, Young wrote a weekly column, "To Be Equal," for the *New York Amsterdam News*. In 1964 a collection of those columns was published as *To Be Equal*. Young died in 1971 while swimming during a visit to Nigeria.

Africa

Youssou N'Dour

(b. 1959?, Dakar, Senegal), Senegalese singer of world beat music; best known for blending traditional Senegalese musical techniques with Cuban and jazz inflections.

Youssou N'Dour was born in Dakar. His mother was a *griot* (a traditional Senegalese musician), and she taught him the basics of local music, including *tasso* (a kind of rap) and *bakou* (a traditional chant).

Youssou N'Dour began singing with local music and theater groups at age 12. At age 15 he joined the Senegalese band Super Diamono, and toured West Africa in 1975. The following year he began his singing career with the Star Band No. 1, and in 1977 he formed his own band, the Etoile de Dakar, renaming it Super Etoile de Dakar in 1981. Super Etoile de Dakar toured Europe in 1984, playing a modern version of mbalax (a traditional rhythm throughout Wolof-speaking Senegal). The band made its North American debut in 1985.

After recording the songs "Immigrés" and "Nelson Mandela", Youssou N'Dour gained the attention of British rock singer and songwriter Peter Gabriel. The Senegalese musician played on Gabriel's best-selling album *So* (1986), and in 1987 he went on tour with Gabriel in the United States, Japan, and Europe. Youssou N'Dour also sang on *Graceland* (1986), the highly successful album by American singer and songwriter Paul Simon, and in 1988 he played at the London birthday concert held for South African activist (and future president) Mandela. In 1989 Youssou N'Dour toured in support of Amnesty International, a human rights organization.

By the time Youssou N'Dour recorded *The Lion* (1989), which was sung partly in English and partly in Wolof, his music had become an intricate blend of Western pop instrumentation (distorted guitars and synthesizers) and traditional Senegalese instruments such as the *tama* (talking drum). Youssou N'Dour's 1994 album *Wommat* (Wolof for "the guide") included "Seven Seconds," his hit duet with Swedish-born pop singer Neneh Cherry.

Z

Zambia,

a landlocked country in Central Africa that borders Angola, the Democratic Republic of the Congo, Tanzania, Malawi, Mozambique, Zimbabwe, Botswana, and Namibia.

An unbalanced economy, the legacy of colonialism, has stunted Zambia's economic and political development. For years foreign firms shipped mineral wealth from the region that is today Zambia. In an era of declining world-market prices, however, Zambia's continued reliance on mining, particularly of copper, has thwarted the ambitions of nationalist leaders to harness the country's mineral wealth for the good of its people. Poor soils have aggravated Zambia's economic stagnation by impeding successful cash crop production and agricultural self-sufficiency. Rural villagers fleeing the impoverished countryside have contributed to an unusually high rate of urbanization. However, as earnings from copper exports have declined since the 1970s, and as international donors have forced Zambia's government to introduce painful austerity measures, the nation's city dwellers have experienced hardship as well. Popular unrest and urban rioting compelled Zambia's nationalist leader, Kenneth Kaunda, to abandon authoritarian rule in 1991 and to accept multiparty elections that resulted in his defeat. Ironically, the freely elected government, led by Frederick Chiluba, has faced allegations of corruption and has taken questionable steps to exclude opponents, including Kaunda, from power. Zambia's people have had to defer hopes for economic and political renewal.

Traces of human occupation date back over a million years in Zambia, as in other parts of East and Central Africa. Human remains dating from 30,000 to 100,000 years ago have been uncovered at Kabwe. Early rock art in Zambia shows animals, people, and objects dwarfed by abstract designs. Difficult to date, this art may be as much as 6,000 years old. Anthropolo-

Water pours over Rainbow Falls and Knife Edge at the eastern cataract of Victoria Falls, on the border between Zimbabwe and Zambia. The local name for the falls is *Mosi-oa-Tunya*, which means "the smoke that thunders." *CORBIS/Charles & Josette Lenars*

gists believe that the region's earliest inhabitants—hunters and gatherers—may have been the ancestors of present-day Khoisan speakers or pygmy populations.

Africa

Zambia (Ready Reference)

Official Name: Republic of Zambia

Former Name: Northern Rhodesia

Area: 752,610 sq km (290,586 sq mi.)

Location: Southern Africa; borders Angola, Democratic Republic of the Congo (formerly Zaire), Tanzania, Malawi, Mozambique, Zimbabwe, and Namibia

Capital: Lusaka (population 952,000 [1993 estimate])

Other Major Cities: Ndola (population 589,000), Kitwe (605,000) (1993 estimate); Kabwe (population 381,000), Chingola (161,000), Mufulira (146,999) (1992 estimate)

Population: 9,460,736 (1998 estimate)

Population Density: Data unavailable

Population Below Age 15: 49 percent (male 2,342,043; female 2,316,357 [1998 estimate])

Population Growth Rate: 2.1 percent (1998 estimate)

Total Fertility Rate: 6.41 children born per woman (1998 estimate)

Life Expectancy at Birth: Total population: 37.07 years (male 36.81 years; female 37.33 years [1998 estimate])

Infant Mortality Rate: 92.57 deaths per 1,000 live births (1998 estimate)

Literacy Rate (age 15 and over who can read and write in English): Total population: 78.2 percent (male 85.6 percent; female 71.3 percent [1995 estimate])

Education: School attendance has increased substantially since Zambia's independence in 1964. In the early 1990s about 1.5 million pupils were enrolled in primary schools. In the late 1980s about 161,300 pupils were enrolled in secondary schools; vocational and teacher-training schools had

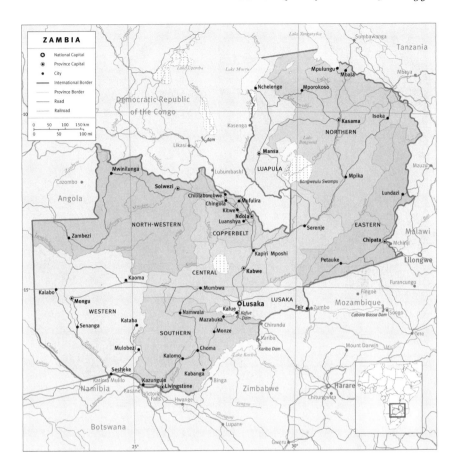

8,000 pupils; and the University of Zambia (founded in 1965), at Lusaka, had about 7,400 students.

Languages: The official language is English. More than 70 African languages are spoken, including Bemba, Lozi, Luvale, Tonga, and Nyanja.

Ethnic Groups: 98.7 percent of the population belong to 1 of 70 Bantu-speaking ethnic groups, including the Bemba, the Nyanja, and the Tonga. Europeans make up less than 2 percent of the population.

Religions: Christian (50 percent to 75 percent), Muslim and Hindu (24 percent to 49 percent), indigenous beliefs (1 percent)

Climate: Zambia enjoys a pleasant subtropical climate because of its high altitude. The average temperature in Lusaka during July, the coldest month of the year, is 16° C (61° F); the hottest month, January, has an average temperature of 21° C (70° F). Annual rainfall ranges from 750 mm (30 in.) in the south to 1,300 mm (51 in.) in the north. Nearly all of the rain falls between November and April.

Land, Plants, and Animals: Most of Zambia is high plateau with a flat or

A tailor sews in his stall at Bamba Market in Lusaka, capital of Zambia. *CORBIS/Caroline Penn*

gently undulating terrain. Elevations average between about 1,100 and 1,400 m (3,500 and 4,500 ft.). Mountains in the northeast reach 2,164 m (7,100 ft.). Major rivers are the Zambezi in the west and south and its tributaries, the Kafue in the west and the Luangwa in the east; and the Luapula and Chambeshi in the north. Lake Bangweulu, in the north, is surrounded by a vast swampy region. Lake Kariba is a large reservoir formed by Kariba Dam on the Zambezi River. Animals include elephants, lions, rhinoceroses, and several varieties of antelope.

Natural Resources: Copper, cobalt, zinc, lead, coal, emeralds, gold, silver, uranium, and hydropower potential

Currency: The Zambian kwacha

Gross Domestic Product (GDP): $8.8 billion (1997 estimate)

GDP per Capita: $950 (1997 estimate)

GDP Real Annual Growth Rate: 3.5 percent (1997 estimate)

Primary Economic Activities: Zambia's copper-mining sector accounts for more than 80 percent of the nation's foreign currency intake. More than 85 percent of Zambia's population are employed in agriculture.

Primary Crops: Corn, sorghum, rice, peanuts, sunflower seeds, tobacco, cotton, sugar cane, cassava (tapioca), livestock, and poultry

Industries: Copper mining and processing, construction, foodstuffs, beverages, textiles, chemicals, and fertilizer

Primary Exports: Copper, zinc, cobalt, lead, and tobacco

Primary Imports: Machinery, transportation equipment, foodstuffs, fuels, and manufactures

Primary Trade Partners: Japan, South Africa, the United States, India, Thailand, and Malaysia

Government: Zambia won independence from the United Kingdom on October 24, 1964. It is a constitutional republic and a multiparty democracy with a president elected to a five-year term by direct universal suffrage. The president appoints a cabinet from among the members of the unicameral legislative body, the National Assembly. The 150 members of this body are likewise directly elected for five-year terms. The dominant political party is the Movement for Multiparty Democracy; others include the National Party and the Zambian Democratic Congress.

Africa

Zanzibar,

island off the east coast of Africa; it is part of the United Republic of Tanzania.

An island often overshadowed by its larger partner in the United Republic of Tanzania, Zanzibar nevertheless maintains a history and culture different and separate from that of the mainland. Once a key port on the thriving Indian Ocean trade routes, Zanzibar's history has been shaped by the people who sought to participate in and control these trades. Consequently, Zanzibar's population and culture reflect not only its proximity to the East Africa coast, but the influences of Asians, Arabs, and Europeans. During the colonial era European powers took advantage of Arab hegemony to assume economic control of this thriving city-state and, in an effort to increase its prosperity, turned Zanzibar into a mono-crop export economy. Since independence Zanzibar, with the aid of its mainland Tanzania, has tried to overcome this colonial legacy and prepare to compete in a global market in which one-crop economies are becoming obsolete.

Latin America and the Caribbean

Zapata Olivella, Manuel

(b. March 17, 1920, Lorica, Colombia), Afro-Colombian writer, essayist, physician, anthropologist, diplomat, and leading intellectual and artist of twentieth-century Latin America. Zapata Olivella is one of the most intriguing voices to emanate from the diaspora and, together with Nancy Morejón and Quince Duncan, among its most admired Afro-Hispanic writers.

Manuel Zapata Olivella's frequent use of the word "mulatto" (a person of both African and European descent) to describe his background suggests a biological union as much as a cultural mixture. Focusing less on phenotype and more on what the Afro-Cuban poet Nicolás Guillén would term "cultural mulatez," or the mixing of cultures that characterizes the Caribbean,

Zapata Olivella has sought to uncover what unites peoples rather than what separates them. Both his parents are of African descent, and he frequently reflects on the constant racial and cultural dynamics that define Latin America. However, from the naming of one of his daughters Harlem to the writing of one of the most artistically accomplished novels about the diaspora, the 1983 *Changó, el gran putas* (Shango: The Greatest S.O.B.), Zapata Olivella is a strong voice in the dialogue on the contribution of African culture to the world. He provides a telling case study for a cultivated sense of an African connection in Latin America.

Born in the small town of Lorica on the western Caribbean coast of Colombia, Zapata Olivella used the area's rich folklore in his first novel, *Tierra mojada* (1947, Wetlands), to explore the conflicting social relations of the region. The novel recounts in accessible language and a straightforward narrative the struggles between a soon-to-be landless, rice-growing community and a large landowner and political boss. Other central characters are the parish priest, with whom the boss works in cahoots, and the local schoolteacher, a communist sympathizer and a civil rights leader who tries to defend the peasant community. Though simplistic in its approach to issues of good and evil and social disparity, *Tierra mojada* contains many of the thematic characteristics that Zapata Olivella's works would share over the decades: concern for the downtrodden, a sense of history from the viewpoint of the dispossessed, and issues of racial and cultural identity.

Zapata Olivella worked on *Tierra mojada* while traveling from Colombia up through Central America to Mexico and then to the United States. His adventures throughout the Americas are delightfully retold in a series of travel narratives. Most noteworthy is *He visto la noche: Las raíces de la furia negra* (1949, I Have Seen the Night: The Roots of Black Fury), in which the impressionable young man seeks out his African American brothers in the United States in the aftermath of the Harlem Riots of 1943. It was at this time that Zapata Olivella developed a friendship with Langston Hughes.

Clearly, Olivella's experiences in the United States helped shape a black worldview that grew sharper with each decade. While several of his later works militantly pursue the theme of blackness, three works in particular stand out: the novel *Chambacú: Corral de negros* (1963; translated as Chambacú: Black Slum, 1989); the short story "Un extraño bajo mi piel" (1967, A Stranger under My Skin); and the critically acclaimed *Changó, el gran putas*.

Chambacú: Corral de negros, awarded the prestigious Cuban Casa de las Américas literary prize in 1963, highlights the mistreatment of Afro-Colombians in the coastal city of Cartagena, Colombia. Set against the backdrop of the Korean War (1950–1953), a war many felt Colombians fought because of U.S. pressure, the action of the novel charts out the path of a black community in the small black town of Chambacú. As the war breaks out, the town is surrounded and occupied by the local military forces who try forcefully to recruit soldiers to man the battle lines. The move is resisted by the population, led by Máximo, a local political activist who is captured and tortured by the army. Translated by Jonathan Tittler in 1989, Chambacú has been cited as exemplary of Zapata

Olivella's aesthetic of protest against the degradation and oppression of Afro-Colombians.

The story "A Stranger under My Skin," published in the collection of short stories *¿Quién dió el fusil a Oswaldo?* (1967, Who Passed the Gun to Oswald?), is a humorous probe of one black man's self-loathing. A half-black, half-white mulatto, Leroy Elder, the main character in the story, regrets his black side so much that his life is forever altered. Translated by Brenda Frazier and published in the *Afro-Hispanic Review* in 1983, the story takes its cue from the Martinican political philosopher and revolutionary Frantz Fanon's *White Mask, Black Skin* (1952), and is one of the most powerful psychological explorations of pain and suffering available in fiction.

When *Changó* was first published in 1983, it constituted a significant breakthrough in Spanish American literature. For the first time the African cultural component was successfully integrated on its own terms as Spanish American and black history in the Americas was told by black narrators and viewed from an Afrocentric perspective. Further, *Changó* manages to accomplish what no other fictive work has: it provides a sense of the whole of the African diaspora in the Americas. The novel opens with an epic poem that recounts the fall from grace and exile of the orisha Changó, a deity in the Yoruba religion of Nigeria and in Yoruba-derived religious traditions in the African diaspora. As a consequence of his own exile, Changó expels the human race from Africa and condemns them to the Middle Passage and slavery. Similarly, the novel recounts the struggles for freedom during colonial times, the Haitian Revolution, the postcolonial fight for equality, and the civil rights struggles in the United States. Some of the best-known historical figures in black history appear as narrators or literary personae, among them Benkos Biohó, the sixteenth-century leader of a Colombian maroon community; Toussaint L'Ouverture, the Haitian Revolution's military leader; Aleijadinho, the eighteenth-century Brazilian sculptor; and the twentieth-century political thinker Malcolm X.

In addition to writing fiction, Zapata Olivella has been a leading interpreter of racial and cultural *mestizaje* (cultural mixing in Latin America). However, unlike the proponents of "racial democracy" (the belief that racial mixture dilutes social tension in Latin America), Zapata Olivella views *mestizaje* as the form that oppressed groups have used to resist assimilation and genocide. In his 1990 biography, *¡Levántate mulato!* (Rise Up, Mulatto!, originally in French in 1987), Zapata Olivella writes: "America was blackened by the importation of Africans, not because of their black skin, but because of their resistance, their struggles against slavery, their joining forces with Native Americans to fight against the oppressors."

Zapata Olivella also coordinated the first Congress of Black Culture of the Americas, which took place in 1977 in Cali, Colombia. His *La rebelión de los genes: El mestizaje americano en la sociedad futura* (1997, The Revolt of the Genes: Mestizaje in the Future of American Societies), is an extensive essay that presents a historical and political analysis of *mestizaje* and its consequences for an increasingly globalized world.

Zeferina,

black female leader of an 1826 slave revolt outside of Salvador, Bahia, Brazil.

In the first half of the nineteenth century the northeastern part of Brazil witnessed a large number of slave revolts. Historians attribute the high incidence of slave rebellions at this time to the growth of the sugar industry, the intensified importation of African slaves, the fact that many of these slaves shared a common language and culture, and the increasing demands made of slave labor, among other factors. These conditions encouraged many slaves to run away and form isolated communities known as *quilombos*. Alone or in cooperation with the free black or enslaved populations, quilombo members planned and carried out rebellions against the slave-holding society. The insurrection led by Zeferina in December 1826 was just 1 of some 20 revolts that occurred in the northeastern state of Bahia between 1807 and 1835.

Zeferina was a member of the Urubu (Vulture) quilombo located just outside of Bahia's capital, Salvador. With the assistance of other slaves, Zeferina and the Urubu quilombo made plans to invade the city and kill all of its white inhabitants on Christmas Day 1826. On December 16, however, a violent encounter between escaped slaves who were transporting food to the quilombo and a white farming family set the revolt into motion prematurely. In the following days slave hunters made several unsuccessful attempts to overthrow Urubu; after suffering some casualties, they joined forces with a small group of soldiers from Salvador and the Pirajá district, and attacked Urubu again. While many of the slave rebels carried knives and guns, Zeferina armed herself with a bow and arrows. She led a fierce counterattack in which some 50 blacks exchanged gunfire with the soldiers and assaulted them while intermittently yelling, "Death to whites! Long live blacks!" The colonial forces ultimately vanquished the quilombo, killing four blacks and taking ten others as prisoners, including Zeferina. Soldiers extolled her courage and prowess in battle. Upon seeing her, the provincial president Manoel Ignácio da Cunha Menezes called her a "queen." In the end nearly all of the other captives were returned to their masters, but Zeferina was sentenced to prison and hard labor.

The known personal history of Zeferina begins with the 1826 rebellion she spearheaded and ends with her interrogation and sentencing. As in the case of many slaves, her individual identity is shrouded in ambiguity. Historical documents indicate that after the incident Zeferina stated that the majority of the Urubu quilombo members were Nagôs, that is, members of the Yoruba ethnic group originating in the southwest parts of Nigeria and Benin. Religious artifacts found in the quilombo living quarters also testify to the Yoruban character of the Urubu quilombo. In particular, the color red found on much of the religious paraphernalia is associated with the African god of thunder and lightning, Shangó, who is also the ancestral king of the Yoruban kingdom of Oyo.

Though women have long occupied an important leadership position as *mães de santos* (priestesses) in the Brazilian religion Candomblé, their role as quilombo community leaders during Brazil's long era of slavery has been discussed less often. As members of escaped slave communities, black women were occasionally required to take up arms against colonial forces in defense of their autonomy. In the struggle for freedom some women died anonymously and others escaped, their valiant efforts unrecorded. Zeferina is a symbol of the spirit with which so many slaves, both men and women, fought to achieve freedom in Brazil.

Latin America and the Caribbean

Zenón Cruz, Isabelo

(b. 1939, Humacao, Puerto Rico), Afro-Puerto Rican writer, scholar, and professor of literature at the University of Puerto Rico, best known for his two-volume study *Narciso descubre su trasero: El negro en la cultura puertor-riqueña*, published in 1974–1975. This study represents one of the first and more important attempts to analyze and discuss the complexities of race relations, racism, and prejudice in Puerto Rico.

Guided and inspired by the writings of Martinican political philosopher Frantz Fanon and American political activist Eldridge Cleaver, Isabelo Zenón Cruz defends the importance of African heritage in the formation of a Puerto Rican identity. *Narciso descubre su trasero* (Narcissus Discovers His Backside) questions the often accepted myth of racial harmony in the definition of a Puerto Rican identity, and presents extensive evidence of how racism and prejudice have always been part of Afro-Puerto Ricans' reality. It examines the historical, social, and cultural circumstances that have marginalized Afro-Puerto Ricans.

According to Zenón Cruz, the importance of Afro-Puerto Ricans has always been underestimated. To prove this he includes in his study a wide range of topics that he approaches with criticism and irony, using historical facts and anecdotes. In his extensive and comprehensive discussion of education, politics, language, the arts, religion, sports, and Puerto Rican folklore—to name a few topics—Zenón Cruz examines commonly accepted ideals. Another important contribution of Zenón Cruz's study is his inclusion and discussion of outstanding Afro-Puerto Rican figures in each one of these areas. The analysis of these examples serves as evidence of how prejudice is completely embedded in the way the black race is perceived in Puerto Rico. He also examines how racism is perpetuated in every aspect of the island's social and cultural life, and why it is even perpetuated by Afro-Puerto Ricans.

Zenón Cruz's study also denounces the blind spots of previous scholars, critics, poets, and writers who have ignored Afro-Puerto Rican contributions. His harsh critique addresses the apparent general indifference of the Puerto Rican left to questions of "race," especially that of the independence movement. For this reason his study was received with enthusiasm by some, but it was also dismissed and ignored by others. Nevertheless, in several of the island's newspapers it provoked a debate that had been almost nonexistent before the study's publication. Zenón Cruz exposed and addressed the taboos and complexities that permeate notions of race on the island.

In Zenón Cruz's version of the Greek myth, Narcissus discovers his behind rather than his face. This serves as a meaningful image of the ideology and politics concerning race relations in Puerto Rico. It brings to the surface many underlying truths, unveils the underestimation of African heritage and importance in Puerto Rico, confronts and questions official discourses, and plays a key role in the discussions about Afro-Puerto Rican identity.

Zenón Cruz also authored the book *El anhelo de la inmortalidad del alma en Unamuno*, and his works have been published in newspapers and magazines, including *Guajana*, *Educación*, *Llama*, *Humacao*, and *Ecos Grises*.

Zimbabwe,

country in southern Africa that borders Zambia, Mozambique, South Africa, and Botswana.

The Zimbabwean plateau, bounded in the south by the Limpopo River, in the north by the Zambezi, and in the east by the eastern highlands and Chimanimani mountains, includes such natural wonders as Victoria Falls and the historic Matopos hills. It is also an area that has experienced three

A woman sifts groundnuts at a village in Zimbabwe. An important ingredient in many African diets, groundnuts are primarily raised for sustenance, not export. *CORBIS/Hulton-Deutsch Collection*

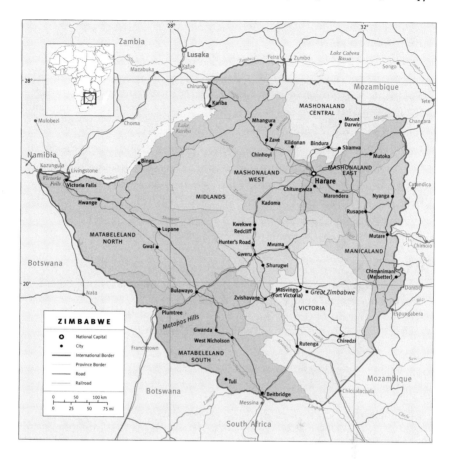

great waves of violence: the first as a result of the Zulu *mfecane* from South Africa; the second from colonial conquest; and the third during the war for independence. Land has been the issue that has most dramatically defined the country's history and politics.

Africa

Zimbabwe (Ready Reference)

Official Name: Republic of Zimbabwe

Former Name: Rhodesia

Area: 390,759 sq km (about 150,873 sq mi.)

Location: Southern Africa; borders South Africa, Botswana, Mozambique, and Zambia

Capital: Harare (population 1,184,169 [1992 estimate])

Other Major Cities: Bulawayo (population 621,000), Chitungwiza

(274,000), Gweru (124,700), Kwekwe (75,000), and Mutare (68,700) (1992 estimates)

Population: 11,044,147 (1998 estimate)

Population Density: 30 persons per sq km (about 76 persons per sq mi.)

Population Below Age 15: 44 percent (male 2,439,907; female 2,397,761 [1998 estimate])

Population Growth Rate: 1.12 percent (1998 estimate)

Total Fertility Rate: 3.86 children born per woman (1998 estimate)

Life Expectancy at Birth: Total population: 39.16 years (male 39.12 years; female 39.19 years [1998 estimate])

Infant Mortality Rate: 61.75 deaths per 1,000 live births (1998 estimate)

Literacy Rate (age 15 and over who can read and write in English): Total population: 85 percent (male 90 percent; female 80 percent [1995 estimate])

Education: Primary education in Zimbabwe is free and compulsory between ages 7 and 15. In the early 1990s approximately 2.4 million students were enrolled annually in primary schools and 657,000 in secondary schools. About 61,600 were enrolled in institutions of higher education, including a number of teachers' colleges and several agricultural and technical schools.

Languages: English is the official language. The most prevalent Bantu languages are Shona and Sindebele (the language of the Ndebele, sometimes called Ndebele).

Ethnic Groups: The bulk of Zimbabwe's population is formed by two major Bantu-speaking ethnic groups: the Shona, who constitute 80 percent of the total population, and the Ndebele (Matabele), who constitute about 19 percent of the total and are concentrated in the southwestern regions. The country also has small minorities of Europeans, Asians, and persons of mixed race.

Religions: Half of the population practices various syncretic religions, fusions of traditional African religions and Christianity. Approximately 25 percent are Christian, principally Roman Catholic or Anglican Communion; this number also includes many Protestant sects. About 24 percent practice traditional religions, and about 1 percent are Hindu or Muslim.

Climate: Although Zimbabwe lies in a tropical zone, its climate is moderated by high elevation. The average temperature is 16° C (60° F) in July, and 21° C (70° F) in January. Average rainfall is about 890 mm (35 in.) in the High Veld and less than 610 mm (24 in.) in most parts of the Middle Veld. The rainy season is from November to March.

Land, Plants, and Animals: Zimbabwe occupies part of the great plateau of southern Africa. Its most prominent feature is a broad ridge that runs southwest to northeast across the country at elevations of 1,200 to 1,500 m (4,000 to 5,000 ft.), the High Veld. On either side of the ridge the land slopes downward, in the north to the Zambezi River and in the south to the

Limpopo River. These areas are known as the Middle Veld. Along the eastern border is a mountain range. The land of Zimbabwe is primarily covered with savanna; a particularly lush grass grows during the moist summers. Animals include elephants, hippopotamuses, lions, hyenas, crocodiles, antelope, impalas, giraffes, and baboons.

Natural Resources: Mineral resources include coal, chromium ore, asbestos, gold, nickel, copper, iron ore, vanadium, lithium, tin, and platinum group metals.

Currency: The Zimbabwe dollar

Gross Domestic Product (GDP): $24.9 billion (1996 estimate)

GDP per Capita: $2,200 (1996 estimate)

GDP Real Growth Rate: 8.1 percent (1996 estimate)

Primary Economic Activities: Agriculture (70 percent of the labor force, 40 percent of exports), mining (only 5 percent of employment and GDP, but 40 percent of exports), and manufacturing

Primary Crops: Tobacco, corn, cotton, wheat, coffee, sugar cane, and peanuts; cattle, sheep, goats, and pigs

Industries: Mining, steel, clothing and footwear, chemicals, food processing, fertilizer, beverage, transportation equipment, and wood products

Primary Exports: Agricultural products (especially tobacco), nickel metal, cotton, manufactures, gold, ferrochrome, and textiles

Primary Imports: Machinery and transportation equipment, other manufactures, chemicals, and fuels

Primary Trade Partners: European Union (especially United Kingdom, Germany, Italy), South Africa, Japan, United States, and Botswana

Government: Zimbabwe won independence from the United Kingdom on April 18, 1980. It is a parliamentary democracy. The executive branch is led by President Robert Gabriel Mugabe. He appoints a cabinet, which is in turn responsible to the legislative branch, the 150-member House of Assembly. Of these members, 120 are directly elected by popular vote to serve six-year terms; 12 are chosen by the president; 10 are traditional chiefs chosen by their colleagues; and 8 are chosen by provincial governors. The dominant political party, that of President Mugabe, is called the Zimbabwe African National Union-Patriotic Front (ZANU-PF).

Latin America and the Caribbean

Zobel, Joseph

(b. 1915, Petit-Bourg, Martinique), Martinican writer and critic who portrays the life of the black underclass of Martinique, from whose ranks he comes.

After his schooling in Fort-de-France, Joseph Zobel moved to the poverty-stricken southern part of the island of Martinique. The result of Zobel's time among the peasants of Le Diamant is his first published novel, *Diab'la* (1946), a work that underscored the need for land reform by suggesting, not without some temerity, that those who work the land should own it. Although completed in 1942, the book was censured by the Vichy government, which occupied Martinique during World War II. A collection of Zobel's stories published just after the war, *Laghia de la mort* (1946), exemplified what could be called Martinican social realism, exposing the brutal existence of plantation workers.

Zobel's best-known work, the semiautobiographical, coming-of-age story *La rue cases-nègres* (1950; winner of the Prix des Lecteurs), explores different territory, recounting a young man's transition from the village to the city, from the peasantry to the intellectual class. Zobel's innovative use of Creole dialogue in this novel helped spark the Créolité literary movement that includes Patrick Chamoiseau and Raphaël Confiant. Like many writers of his generation, Zobel flirted with a return to Africa.

In 1957 Zobel left France for Dakar, Senegal, and in 1962—in a newly independent Senegal under President Léopold Sédar Senghor—served as cultural adviser to the nascent Radio Senegal and helped establish and run the Sengalese Cultural Services. But Zobel grew disenchanted with Senghor's Négritude-inspired ethnic nationalism. He returned to France, settling in the south, and published a collection of short stories, *Le soleil partagé* (1964), which promotes a model of racial reconciliation based on the values of the peasant class. With the advent of magical realism in the Caribbean, Zobel's brand of Balzacian social commentary fell decidedly out of fashion. The success of the film version of *La rue cases-nègres* (1983), directed by Euzhan Palcy, has led, however, to a positive reappraisal of his work in recent years.

Latin America and the Caribbean

Zouk,

contemporary popular music of the French-and Creole-speaking Caribbean.

Like American rap music and Jamaican reggae, zouk is the music of the descendants of African slaves in societies previously dominated by whites. The comparison between the genres, though, ends there. Sung in Creole and carried by an up-tempo dance rhythm, zouk is neither didactic nor explicitly political; it is in no way protest music. Rather, as its name implies ("zouk" is a Creole word first employed in Martinique that means "a party" or "to party"), zouk is a Carnivalesque music that celebrates Caribbean Creole culture, principally by drawing its lyrical themes from Creole folklore. Thanks to the sense of cultural pride (and, it should be noted, the urge to dance) that zouk fosters in its Creole-speaking audience, this festive music has become the most popular genre in the French overseas departments of Martinique and Guadeloupe as well as in the neighboring islands of Dominica, St. Lucia, and Haiti. But zouk's popularity is not confined to the Caribbean sphere. In recent years zouk performers such as Kassav, Zouk Machine (led by three female vocalists), and Malavoi have developed substantial followings in Europe—and, in particular, in France—as well as in Africa.

Although zouk musicians generally steer clear of questions of racial and ethnic origins in their lyrics, they do evoke their African roots in the music. Zouk's rhythm, produced by traditional drums and, more recently, drum machines, has its source in the rhythm of the traditional West African drum or *tam-tam*. This influence can also be felt in zouk's musical predecessors: *gwo ka* (Creole for "large drum"), a traditional Guadeloupean drum music, and *biguine*, the Martinican music of the 1940s and 1950s that is zouk's clearest musical forebear, both of which integrate elements of African drumming. Kassav, the most successful and influential of zouk bands, used the *gwo ka* in its earliest recordings, and the traditional rhythms of *gwo ka* can still be detected in most zouk songs.

But zouk's success can also be attributed to its integration of many contemporary musical styles, including jazz, funk, salsa, calypso, *cadence-lypso* (from Dominica), and compas direct (from Haiti). If there is a controversy surrounding zouk, it centers on this very point. According to zouk's detractors, the music has drifted too far from its roots and is no longer representative of Creole culture. This multiplicity of influences is seen by its fans as zouk's strongest point and, paradoxically, that which makes the music distinctly Caribbean. Zouk, like Caribbean culture, is nothing if not the creolization or mixture of American, European, and African cultural practices.

Africa

Zulu,

the largest ethnic group in South Africa, with a population of approximately 6 million.

The Zulu are one of many southern African peoples belonging to the broader Nguni linguistic group. Like other Nguni groups such as the Xhosa, the Zulu speak a Bantu language, and their ancestors are believed to have migrated into southern Africa sometime after the second century C.E. They settled in village communities, cultivated grains such as millet, and kept cattle, which became an important symbol of wealth. Also like other Nguni groups, the Zulu developed a distinct language well before they forged a collective identity or a centralized political structure. These did not emerge until the late eighteenth century, when competition for grazing lands and access to sources of ivory, an important trade commodity, fostered conflict among Nguni clans.

At that time only members of one Nguni clan identified themselves as Zulu, which was the name of one of the clan's founding ancestors. But not long after Shaka became the clan chief in 1815, the Zulu began a campaign of conquest and expansion known as the *mfecane*, which led to the incorporation of many other peoples. A brilliant military leader, Shaka soon built an army of more than 40,000 rigorously trained soldiers. Shaka also introduced several important military innovations, such as the short stabbing spear, which gave Zulu troops a distinct advantage over their adversaries. In a period of only ten years Shaka had built a kingdom—Zululand—that encompassed most of the area now known as Natal Province.

Shaka claimed absolute authority over his kingdom. His hierarchical leadership style was retained by subsequent Zulu rulers and later adopted by Inkatha, a twentieth-century Zulu political organization. In conquered territories Shaka appointed his own officials; any subjects who refused Shaka's overrule could be killed immediately. In addition, conquered peoples were expected to serve in the Zulu army, herd the king's cattle, and hunt elephants for ivory. Shaka consolidated his authority by conducting frequent cattle raids on neighboring groups, such as the Mpondo. A portion of the cattle was distributed to Shaka's chiefs and army officers to encourage their loyalty.

Despite these tactics, however, Shaka faced internal opposition, and in 1828 he was assassinated by his half brother Dingane. But Dingane lacked Shaka's military acumen and fared poorly in battles against the expansionist Afrikaners (also known as Boers). Although the Zulu lost land to the Afrikaners during the mid-nineteenth century, they did not fall under European colonial rule until 1883, when Zululand was invaded by British troops.

As part of Great Britain's Natal Colony, Zululand was divided into 13 chiefdoms, and the Zulu king Dinuzulu was exiled. Missionaries encouraged the Zulu to forsake practices of ancestor worship in favor of Christianity. Zulu farmers initially profited from strong markets for maize in Durban and other rapidly growing cities, but government policies eventually alienated most Zulu farmland. Zulu men were consequently forced to migrate in search of wage labor, typically either in the gold mines or on sugar plantations. After the National Party came to power in South Africa in 1948, its system of apartheid assigned all the country's Africans to one of ten "tribal" homelands (also known as Bantustans). The Zulu homeland was called KwaZulu and ruled by nominally independent "tribal" authorities.

In 1976 Mangosutho Gatsha Buthelezi became the chief minister of KwaZulu. He began encouraging Zulu nationalism through the revived Inkatha Ya Ka Zulu, a Zulu cultural organization founded in 1928. A descendant of the nineteenth-century Zulu king Cetshwayo, Buthelezi spoke out against apartheid, but his ethnic separatism and willingness to collaborate with the white-ruled South African government soon put him—and Inkatha's Zulu membership—at odds with antiapartheid groups such as the African National Congress (ANC). During the 1980s and early 1990s the rivalry between the two groups often turned violent.

After Inkatha became an official political party in 1990 (the Inkatha Freedom Party, or IFP), it joined with far-right Afrikaner organizations to oppose democratic negotiations led by the ANC and the National Party, and Buthelezi pressed for a separate Zulu state. After the election of Nelson Mandela as president of postapartheid South Africa in 1994, the IFP pulled out of the South African Constitutional Assembly to protest the ANC government. Relations between the two parties remain contentious. In the former Zulu homeland, however, organizations such as the KwaZulu-Natal Arts and Culture Council are encouraging "nonpartisan" forms of Zulu nationalism.

Latin America and the Caribbean

Zumbi

(b. 1655?; d. November 20, 1695), legendary leader of the seventeenth-century quilombo (escaped slave colony) of Palmares in northeastern Brazil.

Zumbi, the most vehement opponent of slavery in colonial Brazil, is closely linked with the settlement of Palmares, established by escaped slaves in Brazil's northeastern state of Alagoas. Escaped slaves first settled in this mountainous, forested region sometime between the end of the sixteenth century and the early years of the seventeenth century. Because of the abundance of palms, the settlement became known as Palmares. During the Dutch occupation of northeastern Brazil (1630–1654), Palmares received a large number of fugitive slaves and grew into a formidable, populous federation of villages covering a vast area of land from northern Alagoas to southern Pernambuco. Palmares's sophisticated fortifications and well-equipped defense force enabled it to resist repeated military incursions following the expulsion of the Dutch until it was finally conquered in 1694. The story of Zumbi is closely tied to Palmares, the largest and longest lasting quilombo in the history of the colonial Americas.

What little is known about Zumbi's early life is based on the personal records of a seventeenth-century priest named Antônio Melo, which have not been reliably documented. According to these sources, Zumbi was born in Palmares in 1655 and was captured that same year during a Portuguese attack on the quilombo. Zumbi was later placed under the care of Melo, who baptized him Francisco and taught him Portuguese, Latin, and other subjects. Research on Melo's written records indicates that in 1670, Zumbi ran away to Palmares.

Zumbi then began to appear in firsthand accounts of military missions sent by the Portuguese to destroy Palmares. Reports from a 1675–1676 campaign relate that Zumbi suffered a leg wound and describe him as "a black man of singular bravery, great spirit, and rare constancy." At this time Zumbi served as the war commander under Ganga Zumba, Zumbi's uncle and the leader of Palmares during the second half of the seventeenth century.

After being wounded in a 1677 attack, Ganga Zumba agreed to a peace treaty with the governor of Pernambuco the following year and, under its terms, relocated part of Palmares to the Cucaú Valley. According to official state documents, at this time Zumbi was part of the rebel faction that opposed the concession to colonial authorities. In 1680 he allegedly poisoned Ganga Zumba and became the new king of Palmares. Zumbi successfully spearheaded the defense of Palmares through 1694, when military units from São Paulo and the northeast vanquished the quilombo following a series of campaigns that lasted some two years.

Zumbi and a small band of his followers escaped during the final, 22-day-long battle. He avoided capture for more than a year until a member of his group disclosed his whereabouts to colonial forces, which ambushed and killed him on November 20, 1695. After Zumbi's death, colonial authorities publicly displayed his head in Pernambuco's capital, Recife. An alternate version of his death recounts that he and some 200 other residents of Palmares jumped off a cliff rather than be re-enslaved.

Until recently the memory of Zumbi survived only in the oral histories of Afro-Brazilians. There are records of Zumbi being publicly celebrated by Bahian afoxés around the turn of the twentieth century and in an Afro-Brazilian festival in Alagoas in the 1930s. But during the 1970s this black hero began to gain much more recognition. Civil rights activism in the United States prompted a surge of black consciousness throughout Brazil and renewed interest in Afro-Brazilian history. In 1978 the Movimento Negro Unificado (United Black Movement) declared November 20 National Black Consciousness Day. On May 13, 1988, the centenary of the abolition of slavery in Brazil, Afro-Brazilians invoked Zumbi during their protests of enduring discrimination and inequalities. In 1995 there were widespread observances of the tercentenary of Zumbi's death, including the first continental congress of blacks in São Paulo (Congreso Continental dos Povos Negros das Américas) and a march in the capital city, Brasília, led by the Movimento Negro Unificado.

Such actions have helped make Zumbi a national hero, and Palmares a registered historical landmark. To many black Brazilians Zumbi symbolizes the ongoing Afro-Brazilian struggle for economic and political equality. In the words of Joel Rufino, president of the Palmares Foundation, a commission that organizes the annual celebration of Zumbi, "For us blacks, the example of Zumbi inspires our fight for justice and the right to be full-fledged citizens without fear and shame of our blackness."

North America

Zydeco,

the music of black Creoles in southwest Louisiana whose principal instruments are the accordion and the washboard.

Zydeco music, like the Louisiana cuisine gumbo, is an amalgamation of several cultural influences. It is rooted most strongly in French and African musical traditions, but Native American, German, and Spanish cultures have also informed its development. The history of settlement in Louisiana reveals how these various groups of people came together to forge the hybrid culture that spawned zydeco music.

Around 1700 several thousand Acadians who had been exiled from Nova Scotia by the British formed a French-speaking colony in Louisiana. They became known as Cajuns, a colloquialism for Acadians, and worked primarily as tenant farmers. Very few owned slaves, and they had a mutually influential relationship with the people of African descent, known as Creoles, who had been brought to Louisiana from other North American colonies or from the French-and Spanish-speaking Caribbean. These two ethnic groups, in turn, interacted with Native Americans and European immigrants. The sociocultural exchanges among these different ethnic groups during the late nineteenth century resulted in the emergence of two musical forms in the early twentieth century: zydeco and cajun.

Zydeco and cajun are closely related yet distinct musical forms. They have a similar instrumentation, including at least one fiddle, a guitar, and a button accordion backed by a bass and drums. Both zydeco and cajun are played in such contexts as nightclubs, picnics, and house parties, where people often dance as couples. Historian Barry Jean Ancelet explains that although both zydeco and cajun are bluesy, improvisational dance musics that speak of lost love and hard times, cajun music is smoother and emphasizes melody, while zydeco tends to be faster and more syncopated. Part of this rhythmic difference stems from the use in zydeco music ensembles of a corrugated sheet of metal worn over the shoulders like a vest that, when played with eating utensils, makes a raspy sound. In addition, even though zydeco and cajun musicians sing in both French Creole and English, there seems to be a greater prevalence of English lyrics in zydeco music.

The first commercial recordings of zydeco and cajun music were made during the late 1920s and early 1930s. In 1928 accordion player Joseph Falcon accompanied his wife, Cleoma, who sang lead vocals and played the guitar, on the earliest cajun music recording. The first black Creole to make a record was accordion player Amédé Ardoin, who, after performing with cajun fiddler Dennis McGee on a 1929 record, recorded his own songs in the early 1930s. In the late 1930s folklorists John and Alan Lomax made numerous recordings of early zydeco music for the Library of Congress, including the famed "Les haricots sont pas salés." The term "zydeco" is in fact a creolized pronunciation of the first two words of this song's title, which literally translates to "the snap beans ain't salty," but is used colloquially to convey the idea that "times are hard."

Many historians agree that Creoles were the first to pick up and master the button accordion, which became a staple of zydeco music. The accordion player widely recognized as the king of zydeco, Clifton Chenier, continued the legacy of Ardoin. Chenier emerged as a musician in the 1950s and pioneered the use of the piano accordion and brass horns, which replaced the fiddle, in zydeco music. His compositions were influenced by the sounds of rhythm and blues, soul, and blues music popular during the post-World War II period. Some of his better-known songs are "Black Gal" (1965), "Jambalaya" (1975), and "Country Boy Now" (1984), from his Grammy Award-winning album *I'm Here!* Two other major zydeco artists are accordionist Boozoo Chavis and singer Queen Ida. Though the bayou region of Louisiana continues to be the cradle of zydeco music, the genre is played along the Gulf Coast from Louisiana to Texas and is gaining national and international recognition.

Select Bibliography

ABAJIAN, JAMES DE T. *Blacks and their Contributions to the American West* (1974).

ABBOTT, D. "Revolution by Other Means," interview with Angela Davis, *New Statesman* 114 (14 August 1987): 16–17.

ABBOTT, ELIZABETH. *Haiti: The Duvaliers and their Legacy* (1988).

ABDUL-JABBAR, KAREEM, WITH MIGNON McCARTHY. *Kareem* (1990).

ABENON, LUCIEN. *Petite histoire de la Guadeloupe* (1992).

ABERNATHY, RALPH DAVID. *And the Walls Came Tumbling Down: An Autobiography* (1989).

ABRAHAMS, R. G. *The Nyamwezi Today: A Tanzanian People in the 1970s* (1981).

ABRAHAMS, ROGER D. *Deep Down in the Jungle: Negro Narrative Folklore from the Streets of Philadelphia* (1964).

——. *Singing the Master: The Emergence of African American Culture in the Plantation South* (1992).

——. *Talking Black* (1976).

ABRAHAMS, ROGER, AND JOHN SZWED. *After Africa: Extracts from British Travel Accounts and Journals of the Seventeenth, Eighteenth and Nineteenth Centuries Concerning the Slaves, their Manners, and Customs in the British West Indies* (1983).

ABREU, MAURICIO DE. *Evoluçáo urbana do Rio de Janeiro* (1987).

ABU-LUGHOD, JANET L. *Rabat: Urban Apartheid in Morocco* (1980).

ABU-JAMAL, MUMIA. *Live from Death Row* (1996).

ACHEBE, CHINUA. *Hopes and Impediments: Selected Essays* (1988).

ADAIR, GENE. *George Washington Carver* (1989).

ADAMS, BARBARA ELEANOR. *John Henrik Clarke: The Early Years* (1992).

ADAMS, W. M., A. S. GOUDIE, AND A. R. ORME. *The Physical Geography of Africa* (1996).

ADÉLAÍDE-MERLANDE, JACQUES. *Delgrés, ou, la Guadeloupe en 1802* (1986).

ADENAIKE, CAROLYN KEYES, AND JAN VANSINA, EDS. *In Pursuit of History: Fieldwork in Africa* (1996).

ADJAYE, JOSEPH K., AND ADRIANNE R. ANDREWS, EDS. *Language, Rhythm, and Sound: Black Popular Cultures into the Twenty-First Century* (1997).

"African-American Quilts: Tracing the Aesthetic Principles." *Clarion* 14, no. 2 (Spring 1989): 44–54.

"African Symbolism in Afro-American Quilts." *African Arts* 20, no. 1 (1986).

"Afro-Brazilian Religion." Special issue of *Callaloo* 18, no. 4 (1995).

AGRONSKY, JONATHAN. *Marion Barry: The Politics of Race* (1991).

AGORSAH, E. KOFI, ED. *Maroon Heritage: Archaeological, Ethnographic, and Historical Perspectives* (1994).

AGUIRRE BELTRÁN, GONZALO. *El negro esclavo en Nuevo España: La formación colonial, la medicina popular y otros ensayos* (1994).

ALAGOA, E. J., F. N. ANOZIE, AND NWANNA NZEWUNWA, EDS. *The Early History of the Niger Delta* (1988).

ALBERTSON, CHRIS. *Bessie* (1972).

ALGOO-BAKSH, STELLA. *Austin C. Clarke: A Biography* (1994).

ALIE, JOE A. D. *A New History of Sierra Leone* (1990).

ALLAN D. AUSTIN, ED. *African Muslims in Antebellum America: A Source Book* (1984).

ALLEN, PHILIP M. *Madagascar: Conflicts of Authority in the Great Island* (1995).

ALPERT, HOLLIS. *The Life and Times of Porgy and Bess* (1990).

ALVAREZ NAZARIO, MANUEL. *El elemento afronegroide en el español de Puerto Rico: Contribución al estudio del negro en América* (1974).

AL-AMIN, JAMIL. *See* Brown, H. Rap.

The Amistad Case: The Most Celebrated Slave Mutiny of the Nineteenth Century, 2 vols. (1968).

AMMONS, KEVIN. *Good Girl, Bad Girl: An Insider's Biography of Whitney Houston* (1996).

ANDERSON, JEAN BRADLEY. *Durham County: A History of Durham County, North Carolina* (1990).

ANDERSON, JERVIS. *A. Philip Randolph: A Biographical Portrait* (1973).

——. *Bayard Rustin: Troubles I've Seen: A Biography* (1997).

ANDERSON, MARIAN. *My Lord, What a Morning: An Autobiography* (1956).

ANDREWS, BENNY. *Between the Lines: 70 Drawings and 7 Essays* (1978).

ANDREWS, GEORGE REID. *Blacks and Whites in São Paulo, Brazil, 1888–1988* (1991).

ANDREWS, WILLIAM L. *The Literary Career of Charles W. Chesnutt* (1980).

——. *Sisters of the Spirit: Three Black Women's Autobiographies of the Nineteenth Century* (1986).

——. *To Tell a Free Story: The First Century of Afro-American Autobiography, 1760–1865* (1986).

ANDREWS, WILLIAM L., AND HENRY LOUIS GATES, JR., EDS. *The Civitas Anthology of African American Slave Narratives* (1999).

ANGELL, ROGER. *The Summer Game* (1972).

ANJOS, JOANA DOS. *Ouvindo historias na senzala* (1987).

ANTOINE, JACQUES CARMELEAU. *Jean Price-Mars and Haiti* (1981).

ANTOINE, RÉGIS. *La littérature franco-antillaise* (1992).

APARICIO, RAÚL. *Sondeos* (1983).

APPIAH, KWAME ANTHONY. *In My Father's House: Africa in the Philosophy of Culture* (1992).

APTHEKER, HERBERT. *American Negro Slave Revolts.* 6th ed. (1993).

——. *Nat Turner's Slave Rebellion* (1966).

——. *"One Continual Cry": David Walker's Appeal to the Colored Citizens of the World 1829–30: Its Setting and its Meaning, Together with the Full Text of the Third, and Last, Edition of the Appeal* (1965).

ARAUJO, EMANOEL, ED. *The Afro-Brazilian Touch: The Meaning of its Artistic and Historic Contribution.* Translated by Eric Drysdale (1988).

ARMAS, JOSÉ R. DE, AND CHARLES W. STEELE. *Cuban Consciousness in Literature: 1923–1974* (1978).

ARNOLD, A. JAMES. *Modernism and Negritude: The Poetry and Poetics of Aimé Césaire* (1981).

ASANTE, MOLEFI KETE. *The Afrocentric Idea* (1987).

——. *Afrocentricity* (1988).

——. *Kemet, Afrocentricity, and Knowledge* (1990).

ASCHENBRENNER, JOYCE. *Katherine Dunham: Reflections on the Social and Political Aspects of Afro-American Dance* (1981).

ASCHERSON, NEAL. *The King Incorporated: Leopold II in the Age of Trusts* (1963).

ASHBAUGH, CAROLYN. *Lucy Parsons: American Revolutionary* (1976).

ASHE, ARTHUR. *Days of Grace: A Memoir* (1993).

——. *A Hard Road to Glory: A History of the African-American Athlete* (1988).

AUSTERLITZ, PAUL. *Merengue: Dominican Music and Dominican Identity* (1997).

AUSTIN-BROOS, DIANE. *Jamaica Genesis: Religion and the Politics of Moral Orders* (1997).

AVERILL, GAGE. *A Day for the Hunter, A Day for the Prey* (1997).

AXELSON, ERIC. *Portuguese in South-East Africa, 1488–1600* (1973).

AYISI, RUTH A. "The Urban Influx." *Africa Report* (November-December 1989).

AYOT, H. OKELLO. *Historical Texts of the Lake Region of East Africa* (1977).

AZEVEDO, CELLA MARIA MARINHO DE. *Onda negra, medo branco: O negro no imaginario das elites, seculo XIX* (1987).

AZEVEDO, MARIO. *Historical Dictionary of Mozambique* (1991).

AZEVEDO, THALES *Les élites de couleur dans une ville brésilienne* (1953).

BABB, VALERIE MELISSA *Ernest Gaines* (1991).

BACELAR, JEFFERSON ALFONSO. *Etnicidade: Ser negro em Salvador* (1989).

BAER, HANS A., AND MERRIL SINGER. *African-American Religion in the Twentieth Century: Varieties of Protest and Accommodation* (1992).

BAILEY, PEARL. *Between You and Me: A Heartfelt Memoir of Learning, Loving, and Living* (1989).

——. *The Raw Pearl* (1968).

BAKER, DAVID. *The Jazz Style of Cannonball Adderley* (1980).

BAKER, HOUSTON A., JR. *Blues, Ideology, and Afro-American Literature: A Vernacular Theory* (1980).

BALANDIER, GEORGES. *Daily Life in the Kingdom of the Kongo: From the Sixteenth to the Eighteenth Century* (1968).

BALL, WENDY, AND TONY MARTIN. *Rare Afro-Americana: A Reconstruction of the Adger Library* (1981).

BALUTANSKY, KATHLEEN M., AND MARIE-AGNÈS SOURIEAU, EDS. *Caribbean Creolization: Reflections on the Cultural Dynamics of Language, Literature, and Identity* (1998).

BANDEIRA, MARIA DE LOURDES. *Territorio negro em espaço branco: Estudo antropologico de Vila Bela* (1988).

BAQUERO, GASTON. *Indios, blancos y negros en el caldero de America* (1991).

BARAKA, AMIRI. *The Autobiography of LeRoi Jones* (1984).

BARBOSA DEL ROSARIO, PILAR. *La obra de José Celso Barbosa.* 4 vols. (1937).

BARBOUR, DOUGLAS. *Worlds Out of Words: The SF Novels of Samuel R. Delaney* (1979).

BARFIELD, THOMAS J. *The Nomadic Alternative* (1993).

BARKER, DANNY. *A Life in Jazz* (1986).

BARNES, STEVE. "The Crusade of Dr. Elders." *New York Times Magazine* (October 15, 1989): 38–41.

BARNETT, ALAN W. *Community Murals: The People's Art* (1984).

BARNWELL, P. J., AND AUGUSTE TOUSSAINT. *A Short History of Mauritius* (1949).

BARRADAS, EFRAÍN. *Para leer en puertorriqueno: Acercamiento a la obra de Luis Rafael Sánchez* (1981).

BARREDA-TOMÁS, PEDRO M. *The Black Protagonist in the Cuban Novel* (1979).

BARROW, STEVE, AND PETER DALTON. *Reggae: The Rough Guide* (1997).

BASH, BARBARA. *Tree of Life: The World of the African Baobab* (1994).

BASIE, WILLIAM JAMES ("COUNT"), AS TOLD TO ALBERT MURRAY. *Good Morning Blues: The Autobiography of Count Basie* (1985).

"A Basis for Interracial Cooperation and Development in the South: A Statement by Southern Negroes." In *Southern Conference on Race Relations* (1942).

BASS, CHARLOTTA SPEARS. *Forty Years: Memoirs from the Pages of a Newspaper* (1960).

BASTIDE, ROGER, AND FLORESTAN FERNANDES. *Relacoes raciais entre negros e brancos em Sao Paulo (1955).*

BAUM, ROBERT M. *Shrines of the Slave Trade: Diola Religion and Society in Precolonial Senegambia* (1999).

BEACH, DAVID. *The Shona and their Neighbours* (1994).

BEARDEN, JIM, AND LINDA BUTLER. *Shadd: The Life and Times of Mary Shadd Cary* (1977).

BEARDEN, ROMARE, AND HARRY HENDERSON. *A History of African-American Artists from 1792 to the Present* (1993).

BEAUFORD DELANEY. *A Retrospective* (1978).

BECHKEY, ALLEN. *Adventuring in East Africa* (1990).

BECKFORD, RUTH. *Katherine Dunham: A Biography* (1979).

BECKLES, HILARY. *Afro-Caribbean Women and Resistance to Slavery in Barbados* (1988).

———. *Black Masculinity in Caribbean Slavery* (1996).

——. *Black Rebellion in Barbados: The Struggle against Slavery,* 1627–1838 (1984).

——. *A History of Barbados: Amerindian Settlement to Nation-State* (1990).

——. *Natural Rebels: A Social History of Enslaved Black Women in Barbados* (1989).

——. *White Servitude and Black Slavery in Barbados,* 1627–1715 (1989).

——, ED. *Inside Slavery: Process and Legacy in the Caribbean Experience* (1996).

BECKWOURTH, JAMES P. *The Life and Adventures of James P. Beckwourth, Mountaineer, Scout and Pioneer and Chief of the Crow Nation of Indians.* Edited by T. D. Bonner (1965).

BEDINI, SILVIO. *The Life of Benjamin Banneker* (1971–1972).

BEETH, HOWARD, AND CARY WINTZ. *Black Dixie: Afro-Texan History and Culture in Houston* (1992).

BEGO, MARK. *Aretha Franklin* (1989).

BEHAGUE, GERARD H., ED. *Music and Black Ethnicity: The Caribbean and South America* (1994).

BELL, BERNARD. *The Afro-American Novel and its Tradition* (1987).

BELLEGARDE-SMITH, PATRICK. *In the Shadow of Powers: Dantès Bellegarde in Haitian Social Thought* (1985).

——. Race, Class and Ideology: Haitian Ideologies for Underdevelopment 1806–1934 (1985).

BELL, HOWARD H. *Search for a Place: Black Separatism and Africa,* 1860 (1969).

BELL, MALCOM. *The Turkey Shoot: Tracking the Attica Cover-Up* (1985).

BENBERRY, CUESTA. *Always There: The African-American Presence in American Quilts* (1992).

BENNETT, LERONE, JR. *Before the Mayflower* (1962; revised ed., 1987).

BENNETT, NORMAN. *Arab versus European: Diplomacy and War in Nineteenth-Century East Central Africa* (1986).

BENNETT, ROBERT. "Black Episcopalians: A History from the Colonial Period to the Present." *Historical Magazine of the Protestant Episcopal Church* 43, no. 3 (September 1974): 231–45.

BENOIT, EDOUARD. "Biguine: Popular Music of Guadeloupe, 1940–1960." In *Zouk: World Music in the West Indies,* ed. Jocelyne Guilbault (1993).

BENSTON, KIMBERLY, ED. *Speaking for You: The Vision of Ralph Ellison* (1995).

BENTLY, GEORGE R. *A History of the Freedmen's Bureau* (1955).

BERENDT, JOACHIM. *The Jazz Book: From Rag-time to Fusion and Beyond.* 6th ed. (1992).

BERGER, PHIL. *Blood Season: Tyson and the World of Boxing* (1989).

BERLIN, IRA. *Slaves without Masters: The Free Negro in the Antebellum South* (1974).

BERNABÉ, JEAN, PATRICK CHAMOISEAU, AND RAPHAËL CONFIANT. *Eloge de la créolite / In Praise of Creoleness.* Translated by M. B. Taleb-Khyar (1993).

BERND, ZILA. *Introdução à literatura negra* (1988).

BERNSEN, CHARLES. "The Fords of Memphis: A Family Saga." *Memphis Commercial Appeal* (July 1–4, 1990).

BERNSTEIN, IVER. *The New York City Draft Riots: Their Significance for American Society and Politics in the Age of the Civil War* (1990).

BERROU, RAPHAEL. *Histoire de la littérature haïtienne illustrée par les textes.* 3 vols. (1975–1977).

BERRY, CHUCK. *Chuck Berry: The Autobiography* (1987).

BERRY, JAMES. *Chain of Days* (1985).

BERRY, JASON. *Amazing Grace: With Charles Evers in Mississippi* (1973).

BERTLEY, LEO W. *Canada and its People of African Descent* (1977).

BEYAN, AMOS J. *The American Colonization Society and the Creation of the Liberian State: A Historical Perspective, 1822–1900* (1991).

BIANCO, DAVID. *Heat Wave: The Motown Fact Book* (1988).

BIBB, HENRY WALTON. *Narrative of the Life and Adventures of Henry Bibb, an American Slave* (1849).

BICKERTON, DEREK. "The Language Bioprogram Hypothesis." *Behavioral and Brain Sciences* 7 (1984): 173–221.

BIEBUYCK, DANIEL P., SUSAN KELLIHER, AND LINDA McRAE. AFRICAN ETHNONYMS: INDEX TO ART-PRODUCING PEOPLES OF AFRICA (1996).

BIRMINGHAM, DAVID, AND RICHARD GRAY. *Pre-Colonial African Trade: Essays on Trade in Central and Eastern Africa before 1900* (1966).

BISHOP, JACK. *Ralph Ellison* (1988).

"Black Clout in Clinton Administration." *Ebony* 48, no. 7 (May 1993): 60.

BLACK, PATTI CARR, ED. *Something to Keep You Warm* (1981).

"Blacks in U.S. Foreign Policy: A Retrospective." *TransAfrica Forum* (1987).

"Black Women: Sisters Without Leaders." *Economist* (November 1, 1997): 31.

BLAKELY, ALLISON. *Blacks in the Dutch World: The Evolution of Racial Imagery in a Modern Society* (1993).

——. *Russia and the Negro: Blacks in Russian History and Thought* (1986).

BLANCHARD, PETER. *Slavery and Abolition in Early Republican Peru* (1992).

BLAND, RANDALL W. *Private Pressure on Public Law: The Legal Career of Justice Thurgood Marshall* (1973).

BLANCQ, C. C. *Sonny Rollins: The Journey of a Jazzman* (1983).

BLASSINGAME, JOHN W., ED. *The Frederick Douglass Papers*. 4 vols. (1979–1991).

——. *The Slave Community: Plantation Life in the Antebellum South*. Rev. ed. (1979).

BLASSINGAME, JOHN W., AND MAE G. HENDERSON, EDS. *Antislavery Newspapers and Periodicals*. 5 vols. (1980).

BLESH, RUDI, AND HARRIET JANIS. *They All Played Ragtime*. 4th ed. (1971).

BLIER, SUZANNE PRESTON. *African Vodun: Art, Psychology, and Power* (1995).

——. *The Royal Arts of Africa: The Majesty of Form* (1998).

BLIGHT, DAVID W. *Frederick Douglass' Civil War: Keeping Faith in Jubilee* (1989).

BLOCH, HERMAN D. *The Circle of Discrimination: An Economic and Social Study of the Black Man in New York* (1969).

BLOCH, M. *Placing the Dead: Tombs, Ancestral Villages, and Kinship Organization in Madagascar* (1971).

BLY, NELLIE. *Oprah! Up Close and Down Home* (1993).

BOFF, C., AND L. BOFF. *Introducing Liberation Theology* (1987).

BOGGS, VICTOR. *Salsiology: Afro-Cuban Music and the Evolution of Salsa in New York City* (1992).

BOGLE, DONALD. *Blacks in American Films and Television: An Illustrated Encyclopedia* (1988).

——. *Dorothy Dandridge: A Biography* (1997).

——. *Toms, Coons, Mulattoes, Mammies, and Bucks : An Interpretive History of Blacks in American Films*. 3d ed. (1994).

BOLCOM, WILLIAM, AND ROBERT KIMBALL. *Reminiscing with Sissle and Blake* (1973).

BOLLAND, O. NIGEL. *A History of Belize: Nation in the Making* (1997).

BOLOUVI, LEBENE PHILIPPE. *Nouveau dictionnaire étymologique afro-brésilien: Afro-brasilérismes d'origine Ewe-Fon et Yoruba* (1994).

BONGIE, CHRIS. "The (Un)Exploded Volcano: Creolization and Intertextuality in the Novels of Daniel Maximin." *Callaloo* 17, no. 2 (Summer 1994): 627–42.

BONILLA, ADRIAN. "Conversación con Adalberto Ortiz." *Cultura: Revista del Banco Central del Ecuador* 6, no. 16 (1983): 189–96.

BOODOO, KEN I., ED. *Eric Williams: The Man and the Leader* (1986).

BOONE, GRAEME M., AND JAMES CLYDE SELLMAN, "The Jook Joint: An Historical Note." Liner essay to *Quincy Jones, Q's Jook Joint* (1995).

BORDERS, WILLIAM H. *Seven Minutes at the Mike in the Deep South* (1943).

BOSKIN, JOSEPH. *Sambo: The Rise and Demise of an American Jester* (1986).

BOURDILLON, M. F. C. *The Shona Peoples: An Ethnography of the Contemporary Shona, with Special Reference to their Religion* (1987).

BOURNE, M. "Bob, Baroque, the Blues: Modern Jazz Quartet." *Down Beat* 59, no.1 (January 1992): 24.

BOVILL, E. W. *The Niger Explored* (1968).

BOWMAN, J. WILSON. *America's Black Colleges: The Comprehensive Guide to Historically and Predominantly Black 4-Year Colleges and Universities* (1992).

BOWMAN, LARRY W. *Mauritius: Democracy and Development in the Indian Ocean* (1991).

BOWSER, FREDERICK P. *The African Slave in Colonial Peru 1524–1650* (1974).

BOXER, C.R. *The Dutch in Brazil, 1624–1654* (1957).

——. *The Portuguese Seaborne Empire, 1415–1825* (1969).

BOYER, JAY. *Ishmael Reed* (1993).

BOYKIN, KEITH. *One More River to Cross: Black & Gay in America* (1996).

BOZONGWANA, WALLACE. *Ndebele Religion and Customs* (1983).

BRACEY, JOHN H., JR., ET AL, EDS. *Black Nationalism in America* (1970).

BRAGG, GEORGE FREEMAN. *The History of the Afro-American Group of the Episcopal Church* (1968).

——. *The Story of the First Blacks: Absalom Jones* (1929).

BRANCH, TAYLOR. *Parting the Waters: America in the King Years: 1954–63* (1988).

BRANDSTRÖM, PER. "Who is Sukuma and Who is a Nyamwezi?: Ethnic Identity in West-Central Tanzania." In *Working Papers in African Studies* no. 27 (1986).

BRAND-WILLIAMS, ORALANDAR. "Million Woman March: Black Women Vow to 'Act on Power,'" *Detroit News* (October 26, 1997).

BRATHWAITE, EDWARD KAMAU. *Roots* (1993).

BRAUSCH, GEORGES. *Belgian Administration in the Congo* (1961).

BRIGHAM, DAVID R. "Bridging Identities (The Works of Dox Thrash, Afro-American Artist)." *Smithsonian Studies in American Art* (Spring 1990).

BRISBANE, ROBERT. *Black Activism: Racial Revolution in the U.S., 1954–70* (1974).

BRISTOW, PEGGY, ET AL. *We're Rooted Here and They Can't Pull Us Up: Essays in African Canadian Women's History* (1994)

BRITT, STAN. *Dexter Gordon: A Musical Biography* (1989).

BRODE, DOUGLAS. *Denzel Washington: His Films and Career* (1996).

BRODERICK, FRANCIS L., AUGUST MEIER, AND ELLIOTT M. RUDWICK. *Black Protest Thought in the Twentieth Century.* 2d ed. (1971).

BROOKSHAW, DAVID. *Race and Color in Brazilian Literature* (1986).

BROUGHTON, SIMON, MARK ELLINGHAM, DAVID MUDDYMAN, AND RICHARD TRILLO. *World Music: The Rough Guide* (1994).

BROUSSARD, ALBERT S. *Black San Francisco: The Struggle for Racial Equality in the West, 1900–1954* (1993).

BROWN, A. THEODORE, AND LYLE W. DORSETT. *K.C.: A History of Kansas City, Missouri* (1978).

BROWN, CLAUDE. *Manchild in the Promised Land* (1965).

BROWN, DIANA DEGROAT. *Umbanda: Religion and Politics in Urban Brazil* (1994).

BROWN, GEOFF, AND CHRIS CHARLESWORTH. *A Complete Guide to the Music of Prince* (1995).

BROWN-GUILLORY, ELIZABETH. "Alice Childress: A Pioneering Spirit," *Sage: A Scholarly Journal on Black Women* (Spring 1987): 104–9.

BROWN, HENRY. *Narrative of Henry Box Brown Who Escaped from Slavery Enclosed in a Box Three Feet Long and Two Wide, with Remarks upon the Remedy for Slavery* (1849).

BROWN, H. RAP. *Die, Nigger, Die!* (1969).

BROWNING, BARBARA. *Samba: Resistance in Motion* (1995).

BROWN, MERVYN. *A History of Madagascar* (1995).

——. *Madagascar Rediscovered: A History from Early Times to Independence* (1978).

BROWN, RUTH, WITH ANDREW YULE. *Miss Rhythm: The Autobiography of Ruth Brown, Rhythm & Blues Legend* (1996).

BROWN, SCOTT E. *James P. Johnson: A Case of Mistaken Identity* (1986).

BROWN, STERLING A. "A Century of Negro Portraiture in American Literature." In *Black Insights: Significant Literature by Black Americans—1760 to the Present*, ed. Nick Aaron Ford (1971): 66–78.

BROWN, TONY. *Black Lies, White Lies: The Truth According to Tony Brown* (1995).

BRUCE, DICKSON D., JR. *Black American Writing from the Nadir: The Evolution of a Literary Tradition, 1877–1915* (1989).

BRUNDAGE, W. FITZHUGH, ED. *Under Sentence of Death: Lynching in the South* (1997).

BRYAN, T. J. "The Published Poems of Helene Johnson," *Langston Hughes Review* 6 (Fall 1987): 11–21.

BRYANT-JACKSON, PAUL, AND LOIS MORE OVERBECK, EDS. *Intersecting Boundaries: The Theater of Adrienne Kennedy* (1992).

BUCKLER, HELEN. *Daniel Hale Williams: Negro Surgeon* (1968)

BUCKLEY, GAIL LUMET. *The Hornes: An American Family* (1986).

BUENO, EVA PAULINO. *Resisting Boundaries: The Subject of Naturalism in Brazil* (1995).

BUGNER, LADISLAS, ED. *The Image of the Black in Western Art* (1976–).

BUHLE, PAUL. *C. L. R. James: The Artist as Revolutionary* (1988).

BULHAN, HUSSEIN ABDILAHI. *Frantz Fanon and the Psychology of Oppression* (1985).

BULLOCK, PENELOPE L. *The Afro-American Periodical Press, 1838–1909* (1981).

BUNI, ANDREW. *The Negro in Virginia Politics, 1902–1965* (1967).

BUNWAREE, SHEILA S. *Mauritian Education in a Global Economy* (1994).

BURCKHARDT, TITUS. *Fez, City of Islam* (1992).

BURDICK, JOHN. *Blessed Anastacia: Women, Race and Popular Christianity in Brazil* (1998).

——. "The Spirit of Rebel and Docile Slaves: The Black Verson of Brazilian Umbanda." *Journal of Latin American Lore* 18 (1992): 163–87.

BURNS, KHEPHRA. "A Love Supreme: Ruby Dee & Ossie Davis." *Essence* (December 1994).

BUSBY, MARK. *Ralph Ellison* (1991).

BUSH, MARTIN. *The Photographs of Gordon Parks* (1983).

BUSTIN, EDOUARD. *Lunda under Belgian Rule: The Politics of Ethnicity* (1975).

BUTLER, ADDIE LOUISE JOYNER. *The Distinctive Black College: Talladega, Tuskegee and Morehouse* (1977).

CAAMAÑO DE FERNÀNDEZ, VICENTA. *El negro en la poesìa dominicana* (1989).

CABRERA GOMEZ, JORGE. *El Baobab* (1996).

CABRERA, LYDIA. *Anaforuana: Ritual y simbolos de la iniciacion en la sociedad secreta* (1975).

———. Anago: *Vocabulario lucumi (el yoruba que se habla in Cuba)* (1957).

———. *Los animales en el folklore y la magia de Cuba* (1988).

———. *Cuentos negros de Cuba* (1972).

———. *Francisco y Francisca: Chascarrillos de negros viejos* (1976).

———. *La lengua sagrada de los nanigos* (1988).

———. *El monte, Igbo, Finda, Ewe orisha, vitti nfinda: (Notas sobre las religiones, la magia, las supersticiones y el folklore de los negros criollos y del pueblo de Cuba)* (1968).

———. *La Regla Kimbisa del Santo Cristo del Buen Viaje* (1977).

———. *Reglas de Congo: Palo Monte Mayombe* (1979).

———. *La sociedad secreta Abakua, narrada por viejos adeptos* (1959).

———. *Yemaya y Ochun* (1974).

CAGIN, SETH, AND PHILIP DRAY. *We Are Not Afraid: The Story of Goodman, Schwerner, and Chaney and the Civil Rights Campaign for Mississippi* (1988).

CALCAGNO, FRANCISCO. *Poetas de color* (1878).

CALLAGHAN, BARRY, ED. *The Austin Clarke Reader* (1996).

CALVO OSPINA, HERNANDO. *Salsa! Havana Heat, Bronx Beat.* (1992).

CAMARGO, OSWALDO. *A razão da chama: Antologia de poetas negros brasileiros* (1986).

CAMINHA, ADOLFO. *The Black Man and the Cabin Boy.* Translated by E. Lacey (1982).

CAMPBELL, ELAINE, AND PIERRETTE FRICKEY, EDS. *The Whistling Bird: Women Writers of the Caribbean* (1998).

CAMPBELL, JAMES T. *Songs of Zion: The African Methodist Episcopal Church in the United States and South Africa* (1995).

CAMPBELL, STANLEY W. *The Slave Catchers: Enforcement of the Fugitive Slave Law, 1850–1860* (1968).

CANNON, STEVE, TOM FINKELPEARL, AND KELLIE JONES. *David Hammons: Rousing the Rubble* (1991).

CANTAROW, ELLEN, AND SUSAN GUSHEE O'MALLEY. "Ella Baker: Organizing for Civil Rights." In *Moving the Mountain: Women Working for Social Change* (1980).

CAPECI, DOMINIC J., JR. *The Harlem Riot of 1943* (1977).

CARBY, HAZEL V. *Reconstructing Womanhood: The Emergence of the Afro-American Woman Novelist* (1987).

CAREW, JAN. *Fulcrums of Change: Origins of Racism in the Americas* (1988).

CARMICHAEL, STOKELY, AND CHARLES V. Hamilton. *Black Power: The Politics of Liberation in America* (1992).

CARMICHAEL, TREVOR, ED. *Barbados: 30 Years of Independence* (1996).

CARNER, GARY, ED. *The Miles Davis Companion: Four Decades of Commentary* (1996).

CARO, TIMOTHY M. *Cheetahs of the Serengeti Plains: Group Living in an Asocial Species* (1994).

CARPENTER, BILL. "Big Mama Thornton: 200 Pounds of Bugaloo." *Living Bluesletter* no. 106 (November 1992).

CARPENTIER, ALEJO. *La música en Cuba* (1946).

——. *Obras Completas* (1983–).

CARR, IAN. *Miles Davis: A Biography* (1982).

CARROLL, PATRICK JAMES. *Blacks in Colonial Veracruz: Race, Ethnicity, and Regional Development* (1991).

CARSON, CLAYBORNE. *In Struggle: SNCC and the Black Awakening of the 1960s* (1981).

CARVALHO, JOSÉ JORGE DE, AND RITA LAURA SEGATO. *Shango Cult in Recife, Brazil* (1992).

CASH, EARL A. *John A. Williams: The Evolution of a Black Writer* (1975).

CASSIDY, FREDERIC G. *Jamaica Talk: Three Hundred Years of the English Language in Jamaica* (1961).

CASTELLANOS, JORGE, AND ISABEL CASTELLANOS. *Cultura afrocubana: Las religiones y las lenguas. 3 vols.* (1992).

CASTLEMAN, CRAIG. *Getting Up: Subway Graffiti in New York* (1984).

CASTOR, ELIE, AND RAYMOND TARCY. *Félix Eboué: Gouverneur et philosophe* (1984).

CASTRO, RUY. *Chega de saudade: A história e as histórias da bossa nova* (1990).

CAYETANO, SEBASTIAN. *Garifuna History: Language and Culture of Belize, Central America and the Caribbean.* Rev. ed. (1997).

CENTRO DE ARTICULAÇÃO DE POPULAÇÕES MARGINALIZADAS. *The Killing of Children and Adolescents in Brazil.* Translated by Joscelyne Vera Mello (1991).

CHAFETS, ZE'EV. *Devil's Night and Other True Tales of Detroit* (1990).

CHALLENOR, HERCHELLE SULLIVAN. "The Influence of Black Americans on U.S. Foreign Policy Toward Africa." *Ethnicity and U. S. Foreign Policy* (1981).

CHAMBERLAIN, HOPE. "Against the System: Shirley Chisholm." In *A Minority of Members: Women in the U. S. Congress* (1973).

CHAMBERLAIN, WILT. *The View From Above* (1991).

CHAMBERS, JACK. *Milestones.* 2 vols. (1983–1985).

CHAMBERS, VERONICA. "The Essence of Essence." *New York Times Magazine* (June 18, 1995).

CHANAN, MICHAEL. *The Cuban Image: Cinema and the Cultural Politics in Cuba* (1985).

CHANOCK, MARTIN. *Law, Custom and Social Order: The Colonial Experience in Malawi and Zambia* (1985).

CHAPELLE, TONY. "Vanessa's Comeback." *The Black Collegian* (February 1995).

CHAPPELL, KEVIN. "The 3 Mayors Who Made it Happen." *Ebony* (July 1996): 66.

Charte de la révolution socialiste Malagasy Tous Azimuts (1975).

CHARTERS, SAMUEL B. *The Bluesmen.* 2 vols. (1967–1977).

CHENEY, ANNE. *Lorraine Hansberry* (1984).

CHIGWEDERE, AENEAS S. *Birth of Bantu Africa* (1982).

CHILTON, JOHN. *The Song of the Hawk: The Life and Recordings of Coleman Hawkins* (1990).

CHISHOLM, SHIRLEY. *Unbought and Unbossed* (1970).

CHRISMAN, ROBERT, AND ROBERT L. ALLEN, EDS. *Court of Appeal: The Black Community Speaks Out on the Racial and Sexual Politics of Clarence Thomas vs. Anita Hill* (1992).

CHRISTIAN, BARBARA. *Black Feminist Criticism: Perspectives on Black Women Writers* (1985).

——. *Black Women Novelists: The Development of a Tradition, 1892–1976* (1980).

CHRISTIE, IAIN. *Samora Machel: A Biography* (1989).

CHRISTOPHER, A. J. *The Atlas of Apartheid* (1994).

CHUCHO GARCIA, JESUS. *La diaspora de los Kongos en las Americas y los Caribes* (1995).

CHURCH, ANNETTE, AND ROBERTA CHURCH. *The Robert Churches of Memphis* (1975).

CLANCY-SMITH, JULIA A. *Rebel and Saint: Muslim Notables, Populist Protest, Colonial Encounters: Algeria and Tunisia, 1800–1904* (1994).

CLAIRMONT, DONALD, AND DENNIS MAGILL. *Africville: The Life and Death of a Canadian Black Community.* Rev. ed. (1987).

CLARKE, A.M. *Sir Constantine and Sir Hugh Wooding* (1982).

CLARKE, DUNCAN. *The Art of African Textiles* (1997).

CLARKE, GEORGE ELLIOTT, ED. *Fire on the Water: An Anthology of Black Nova Scotian Writing.* 2 vols. (1991–1992).

CLARK, SEBASTIAN. *Jah Music* (1980).

CLARK, SEPTIMA. *Echo in My Soul* (1962).

CLARK, SEPTIMA, WITH CYNTHIA STOKES BROWN. *Ready from Within: Septima Clark and the Civil Rights Movement* (1986).

CLASH, M.G. *Benjamin Banneker, Astronomer and Scientist* (1971).

"Claude Albert Barnett." *New York Times* (August 3, 1967).

CLAYTON, ANTHONY. *The Zanzibar Revolution and its Aftermath* (1981).

CLAY, WILLIAM L. *Just Permanent Interests: Black Americans in Congress, 1870–1991* (1992).

COBB, W. MONTAGUE. *The First Negro Medical Society: A History of the Medico-Chirurgical Society of the District of Columbia* (1939).

COHEN, DAVID W., AND JACK P. GREENE. *Neither Slave nor Free: The Freedman of African Descent in the Slaves Societies of the New World Baltimore* (1972).

COHEN, RONALD, GORAN HYDEN, AND WINSTON P. NAGAN, EDS. *Human Rights and Governance in Africa* (1993).

COLE, HERBERT. *Christophe: King of Haiti* (1967).

COLEMAN, JAMES W. *Blackness and Modernism: The Literary Career of John Edgar Wideman* (1989).

COLEMAN, LUCRETIA NEWMAN. *Poor Ben: A Story of Real Life* (1890).

COLI, SUZANNE M. *George Washington Carver* (1990).

COLLIER, ALDORE. "Maxine Waters: Telling It Like It Is in L.A." *Ebony* (October 1992).

——. "Pointer Sisters Shed Old Look, Old Clothes to Reach New Heights." *Jet* (April 15, 1985): 58.

——. "Whatever Happened to the Nicholas Brothers?" *Ebony* (May 1985).

COLLIER, JAMES LINCOLN. *The Making of Jazz: A Comprehensive History* (1978).

COLLINS, L. M. *One Hundred Years of Fisk University Presidents* (1989).

COLLINS, R. *New Orleans Jazz: A Revised History: The Development of American Jazz from the Origin to the Big Bands* (1996).

COLLINS, ROBERT O. *The Waters of the Nile: Hydropolitics and the Jonglei Canal, 1900–1988* (1990).

CONDÉ, MARYSE, AND MADELAINE COTTENET-HAGE, EDS. *Penser la Créolité* (1995).

CONE, JAMES H. *Martin and Malcolm and America: A Dream or a Nightmare* (1991).

CONGRESS, RICK. *The Afro-Nicaraguans: The Revolution and Autonomy* (1987).

CONNIFF, MICHAEL L. *Black Labor on a White Canal: Panama 1904–1981* (1985).

CONNIFF, MICHAEL L., AND THOMAS J. DAVIS. *Africans in the Americas: The History of the Black Diaspora* (1994).

CONNOLLY, HAROLD X. *A Ghetto Grows in Brooklyn* (1977).

CONRAD, ROBERT EDGAR, ED. *Children of God's Fire: A Documentary of Black Slavery.* (1983).

——. *The Destruction of Brazilian Slavery, 1850–1888* (1993).

CONSENTINO, DONALD J., ED. *Sacred Arts of Haitian Vodou* (1995).

COOK, DAVID, AND MICHAEL OKENIMPKE. *Ngugi wa Thiong'o: An Exploration of His Writing,* 2d ed. (1997).

COOLIDGE, CHRISTOPHER R. "Reply: Tolerance of Racial, Ethnic Jokes." In *ADS-L Digest 22* (February 22, 1997).

COOPER, GARY. "Stage Coach Mary: Gun Toting Montanan Delivered U.S. Mail," as told to Marc Crawford in *Ebony* 14 (October 1959): 97–100.

COOPER, RALPH, WITH STEVE DOUGHERTY. *Amateur Night at the Apollo: Ralph Cooper Presents Five Decades of Great Entertainment* (1990).

COOPER, WAYNE F. *Claude McKay: A Rebel Sojourner in the Harlem Renaissance: A Biography* (1987).

COPPIN, FANNY JACKSON. *Reminiscences of School Life, and Hints on Teaching* (1913).

CORDOBA, AMIR SMITH, ED. *Vision sociocultural del negro en Colombia* (1986).

CORNELIUS, WAYNE A. "Spain: The Uneasy Transition from Labor Exporter to Labor Importer." In *Controlling Immigration: A Global Perspective,* ed. Wayne A. Cornelius, Philip L. Martin, and James F. Hollifield (1994).

CORNISH, DUDLEY T. *The Sable Arm: Negro Troops in the Union Army, 1861–1865* (1956).

CORTÉS LÓPEZ, JOSÉ LUIS. *La esclavitud negra en la España peninsular del siglo XVI* (1989).

Cortner, Richard C. *A Mob Intent on Death: The NAACP and the Arkansas Riot Cases* (1988).

CORY, HANS H. *Sukuma Law and Custom* (1953).

COUFFON, CLAUDE. *René Depestre* (1986).

COUNTER, S. ALLEN. *North Pole Legacy: Black, White and Eskimo* (1991).

COURTNEY-CLARKE, MARGARET. *Ndebele: The Art of an African Tribe* (1986).

COVELL, MAUREEN. *Historical Dictionary of Madagascar* (1995).

——. *Madagascar: Politics, Economics, and Society* (1987).

COX, HARVEY. *Fire From Heaven: The Rise of Pentecostal Spirituality and the Reshaping of Religion in the Twenty-First Century* (1995).

CRAFT, WILLIAM, AND ELLEN CRAFT. *Running a Thousand Miles for Freedom; or, The Escape of William and Ellen Craft from Slavery* (1860; reprint ed., 1991.).

CREEL, MARGARET WASHINGTON. *A Peculiar People: Slave Religion and Community-Culture Among the Gullahs* (1988).

CRESPO R., ALBERTO. *Esclavos negros en Bolivia* (1977).

CRIPPS, THOMAS. *Making Movies Black: The Hollywood Message Movie from World War II to the Civil Rights Era* (1993).

——. *Slow Fade to Black: The Negro in American Film 1900–1942* (1977).

CROUCHETT, LORRAINE J. *Delilah Leontium Beasley: Oakland's Crusading Journalist* (1990).

CRUISE O'BRIEN, DONALD. *The Mourides of Senegal: The Political and Economic Organization of an Islamic Brotherhood* (1971).

CUDJOE, SELWYN, ED. *Caribbean Women Writers: Essays from the First International Conference.* (1990).

——. *Resistance and Caribbean Literature* (1980).

CULLEN, COUNTEE. *My Soul's High Song: The Collected Writings of Countee Cullen, Voice of the Harlem Renaissance.* Edited by Gerald Early (1991).

CULLMAN, BRIAN. "Cheb Khaled and the Politics of Pleasure." *Antaeus* (Fall 1993).

CUNEY-HARE, MAUD. *Norris Wright Cuney: A Tribune of the Black People* (1995).

CUNNINGHAM, CAROL, AND JOEL BERGER. *Horn of Darkness: Rhinos on the Edge* (1997).

CURRY, LEONARD P. *The Free Black in Urban America, 1800–1850: The Shadow of the Dream* (1981).

CURTIN, PHILIP D. *The Atlantic Slave Trade: A Census* (1969).

CUTLER, JOHN HENRY. *Ed Brooke: Biography of a Senator* (1972).

DABNEY, VIRGINIUS. *Richmond: The Story of a City* (1976).

DABNEY, WENDELL P. *Cincinnati's Colored Citizens: Historical, Sociological, and Biographical* (1926).

DABYDEEN, DAVID. "On Not Being Milton: Nigger Talk in England Today." In *The Routledge Reader in Caribbean Literature,* ed. Alison Donnell and Sarah Lawson Welsh (1996).

DAHL, OTTO C. *Malgache et Maanjan: Une comparaison linguistigue* (1951).

DALFIUME, RICHARD M. *Desegregation of the U. S. Armed Forces: Fighting on Two Fronts, 1939–1953* (1969).

DALTON, NARINE. "The Maestros: Black Symphony Conductors are Making a Name for Themselves." *Ebony* (February 1989): 54–57.

DALY, VERE T. *A Short History of the Guyanese People* (1975).

DANCE, DARYL C. *Shuckin' and Jivin': Folklore from Contemporary Black Americans* (1978).

DANIELS, DOUGLAS HENRY. "Lester Young: Master of Jive." *American Music* 3 (Fall 1985): 313–28.

———. *Pioneer Urbanites: A Social and Cultural History of Black San Francisco* (1980).

DANIEL, WALTER C. *Afro-American Journals, 1827–1980: A Reference Book* (1982).

DASH, J. MICHAEL. *Edouard Glissant* (1995).

DASH, JULIE. *Daughters of the Dust: The Making of an African American Woman's Film* (1992).

DATES, JANNETTE L., AND WILLIAM BARLOW, EDS. *Split Image: African Americans in the Mass Media* (1990).

DATT, NORMAN. Cheddi B. Jagan: *The Legend* (1997).

DAVENPORT, M. MARGUERITE. *Azalia: The Life of Madame E. Azalia Hackley* (1947).

DAVIES, CAROL BOYCE, AND ELAINE SAVORY FIDO, EDS. *Out of the Kumbla: Caribbean Women and Literature* (1990).

DAVIS, ARTHUR P. *From the Dark Tower: Afro-American Writers, 1900–1960* (1974).

DAVIS, BENJAMIN O., JR. *Benjamin O. Davis, Jr., American: An Autobiography* (1991).

DAVIS, CHARLES T., AND HENRY LOUIS GATES, JR., EDS. *The Slave's Narrative* (1985).

DAVIS, CYPRIAN. *The History of Black Catholics in the United States* (1990).

DAVIS, DARIÉN J., ED. *Slavery and Beyond: The African Impact on Latin America and the Caribbean.*

DAVIS, DAVID BRION. *The Problem of Slavery in the Age of Revolution, 1770–1823.* 2d ed. (1998).

———. *The Problem of Slavery in Western Culture* (1966).

———. *Slavery and Human Progress* (1984).

DAVIS, H. P. *Black Democracy: The Story of Haiti* (1967).

DAVIS, JAMES J. "Entrevista con el dominicano Norberto James Rawlings." *Afro-Hispanic Review* (May 1987):16–18.

DAVIS, MICHAEL D. *Black American Women in Olympic Track and Field: A Complete Illustrated Reference* (1992).

DAVIS, RUSSELL. *Black Americans in Cleveland from George Peake to Carl B. Stokes, 1796–1969* (1972).

DAVIS, STEPHEN, AND PETER SIMON. *Reggae International* (1983).

DAVIS, THOMAS J. *A Rumor of Revolt: The "Great Negro Plot" in Colonial New York* (1985).

DAWKINS, WAYNE. *Black Journalists: The NABJ Story* (1993).

DAYAN, JOAN. "France Reads Haiti: An Interview with René Depestre." *Yale French Studies* 83: 136–153.

DEERR, NOEL. *The History of Sugar.* 2 vols. (1949–1950).

DELERIS, FERDINAND. *Ratsiraka: Socialisme et misère à Madagascar* (1986).

DELIUS, PETER. *A Lion Amongst the Cattle: Reconstruction and Resistance in the Northern Transvaal* (1996).

DEREN, MAYA. Divine Horsemen: *The Living Gods of Haiti* (1953).

DERRICOTTE, TOI. *The Black Notebooks: An Interior Journey* (1997).

DESMANGLES, LESLIE G. *The Faces of the Gods: Vodou and Roman Catholicism in Haiti* (1992).

DE WILDE, LAURENT. *Monk* (1997).

DIAWARA, MANTHIA: *Politics and Culture* (1992).

——, ED. *Black American Cinema* (1993).

DÍAZ AYALA, CRISTOBAL. *Música cubana del areyto a la nueva trova* (1981).

DIEDHIOUS, DJIB. "Paulin S. Vieyra a rencontré le cinéma africain." *Le Soleil* (December 27, 1982).

DILLON, MERTON L. *Benjamin Lundy and the Struggle for Negro Freedom* (1966).

DIOP, CHEIKH ANTA. *Nations nègres et culture: De l'antiquité Nègre-Egyptienne aux problèmes culturels de l'Afrique noire d'aujourd'hui.* 2d ed. (1965).

DITTMER, JOHN. *Black Georgia in the Progressive Era, 1900–1920* (1977).

——. *Local People: The Struggle for Civil Rights in Mississippi* (1995).

DIXON, WILLIE. *I Am the Blues: The Willie Dixon Story* (1989).

DOMÍNGUEZ ORTIZ, ANTONIO. "La esclavitud en Castilla durante la Edad Moderna." In *Estudios de historia social de España*, ed. Carmelo Viñas y Mey. 2 vols. (1952). Vol. II, pp. 369–427.

DONOVAN, NANCY, AND LAST, JILL. *Ethiopian Costumes* (1980).

DORSEY, CAROLYN. "Despite Poor Health: Olivia Davidson Washington's Story." *Sage: A Scholarly Journal on Black Women* (Fall 1985).

DORSEY, DAVID. "The Art of Mari Evans." In *Black Women Writers* (1984): 170–89.

DORSEY, THOMAS ANDREW. *Say Amen, Somebody* (1983).

DORSINVILLE, ROGER. *Jacques Roumain* (1981).

D'ORSO, MICHAEL. *Like Judgement Day: The Ruin and Redemption of a Town Called Rosewood* (1996).

DOUGLASS, WILLIAM. *Annals of the First African Church in the United States of America, Now Styled the African Episcopal Church of St. Thomas, Philadelphia* (1862).

DRAGO, EDMUND L. *Initiative, Paternalism, and Race Relations: Charleston's Avery Normal Institute* (1990).

DRAKE, SANDRA E. *Wilson Harris and the Modern Tradition: A New Architecture of the World* (1986).

DRAKE, ST. CLAIR. *Black Folk Here and There: An Essay in History and Anthropology.* 2 vols. (1987–1990).

DRAKE, ST. CLAIR, AND HORACE R. CAYTON. *Black Metropolis: A Study of Negro Life in a Northern City* (1945).

DRESCHER, SEYMOUR, AND STANLEY L. ENGERMAN, EDS. *A Historical Guide to World Slavery* (1998).

DRISKELL, DAVID. *Hidden Heritage: Afro-American Art, 1800–1950* (1985).

"Dr. Lillie M. Jackson: Lifelong Freedom Fighter." *Crisis* 82 (1975).

DROT, JEAN-MARIE. *Peintures et dessins, vaudou d'Haïti* (1986).

DUANY, JORGE, AND PETER MANUEL. "Popular Music in Puerto Rico: Toward an Anthropology of Salsa." *Latin American Music Review* 5 (1984): 186–216.

DUBOFSKY, MELVYN, AND STEPHEN BURWOOD, EDS. *Women and Minorities During the Great Depression* (1990).

DU BOIS, SHIRLEY GRAHAM. *His Day is Marching On: A Memoir of W. E. B. Du Bois.* (1971).

DU BOIS, W. E. B. *Black Reconstruction in America* (1935).

——. *The Souls of Black Folk: Essays and Sketches* (1903).

DUFFY, SUSAN. "Shirley Chisholm." *American Orators of the Twentieth Century,* ed. Barnard K. Duffy and Halford R. Ryan (1987).

DUGGAN, WILLIAM, AND JOHN CIVILLE. *Tanzania and Nyerere: A Study of Ujamaa and Nationhood* (1976).

DUGGY, JOHN. PRINCE: *An Illustrated Biography* (1995).

DUMMETT, CLIFTON O., AND LOIS DOYLE DUMMETT. *Afro-Americans in Dentistry: Sequence and Consequence of Events* (1978).

DUNBAR-NELSON, ALICE. *Give Us This Day: The Diary of Alice Dunbar-Nelson,* ed. Gloria T. Hull (1984).

DUNCAN, JOHN. "Negro Composers of Opera." *Negro History Bulletin* (January 1966): 79–80, 93.

DUNCAN, QUINCE. *Cultura negra y teologia* (1986).

——. *Dos estudios sobre diaspora negra y racismo* (1987).

DUNDES, ALAN, ED. *Mother Wit From the Laughing Barrel: Readings in the Interpretation of Afro-American Folklore* (1990).

DUNN, RICHARD S. *Sugar and Slaves: The Rise of the Planter Class in the English West Indies, 1624–1713* (1972).

DUNNING, JAMES MORSE. *The Harvard School of Dental Medicine: Phase Two in the Development of a University Dental School* (1981).

DURHAM, PHILIP, AND EVERETT L. JONES. *The Negro Cowboys* (1965).

DURIX, JEAN-PIERRE. *Dictionary of Literary Biography* (1992).

DUSTER, ALFREDA, ED. *Crusade for Justice: The Autobiography of Ida B. Wells* (1970).

DUSTER, TROY. *Backdoor to Eugenics* (1990).

DYNES, WAYNE R., ED. *Encyclopedia of Homosexuality* (1990).

EDELMAN, MARIAN WRIGHT. *The Measure of Our Success: A Letter to My Children and Yours* (1992).

EDRERIA DE CABALLERO, ANGELINA. *Antonio Medina, el don Pepe de la raza de color* (1938).

EGERTON, DOUGLAS R. *Gabriel's Rebellion: The Virginia Slave Conspiracies of 1800 and 1802* (1993).

EHRET, CHRISTOPHER, AND M. POSNANSKY. *The Archaeological and Linguistic Reconstruction of African History* (1982).

EHRLICH, WALTER. *They Have No Rights: Dred Scott's Struggle for Freedom* (1979).

ELDERS, JOYCELYN. *Joycelyn Elders, M.D.: From Sharecropper's Daughter to Surgeon General of the United States of America* (1997).

ELIAS, JOÃO. *A impotencia da raca negra não tira da fraqueza dos brancos.* 2d ed. (1994).

ELLISON, RALPH. *Romare Bearden: Paintings and Projections* (1968).

——. *Shadow and Act* (1964).

ELLSWORTH, SCOTT. *Death in A Promised Land: The Tulsa Race Riot of 1921* (1982).

ELY, MELVIN PATRICK. *The Adventures of Amos 'n' Andy: A Social History of an American Phenomenon* (1991).

EMECHETA, BUCHI. *Head Above Water* (1986).

EMERY, LYNNE FAULEY. *Black Dance in the United States from 1619 to 1970* (1980).

Enciclopédia da música Brasileira: Erudita, folclórica, popular (1977).

EQUIANO, OLAUDAH. *Equiano's Travels: His Autobiography: The Interesting Narrative of the Life of Olaudah Equiano or Gustavus Vassa, the African.* Edited by Paul Edwards (1967).

ERLEWINE, MICHAEL, ET AL, EDS. *All Music Guide to Jazz: The Experts' Guide to the Best Jazz Recordings* (1996).

ERLMANN, VEIT, AND DEBORAH PACINI HERNANDEZ, EDS. "The Politics and Aesthetics of Transnational Musics." Special issue of *World of Music* 35, no. 2 (1993).

ERSTEIN, HAP. "Richards, Wilson Team Up on Prize Dramas." *Washington Times* (November 8, 1991): E1.

ESTES, J. WORTH. *The Medical Skills of Ancient Egypt* (1993).

ESTUPIÑAN TELLO, JULIO. *Historia de Esmeraldas* (1977).

EVANS, MARI. *Black Women Writers (1950–1980): A Critical Evaluation* (1984).

EVERS, CHARLES, AND GRACE HASKELL, EDS. *Evers* (1971).

EWERS, TRAUTE. *The Origin of American Black English: Be-Forms in the HOODOO Texts* (1996).

FABRE, MICHEL. "The Last Quest of Horace Cayton." *Black World* 19 (May 1970): 41–45.

——. *The Unfinished Quest of Richard Wright*. Translated by Isabel Barzun (1973).

FAIRCLOUGH, ADAM. *To Redeem the Soul of America: The Southern Christian Leadership Conference and Martin Luther King, Jr* (1987).

FAIR, LAURA. "Dressing Up: Clothing, Class and Gender in Post-Abolition Zanzibar." *Journal of African History* 39 (1998): 63–94.

FANON, FRANTZ. *Black Skin, White Masks*. Translation of *Peau noire, masques blancs* by Charles Lam Markmann (1967).

FARMER, JAMES. *Lay Bare the Heart: An Autobiography of the Civil Rights Movement* (1985).

FARNSWORTH, ROBERT M. *Melvin B. Tolson, 1898–1966: Plain Talk and Poetic Prophecy* (1984).

FARRISON, WILLIAM EDWARD. *William Wells Brown: Author and Reformer* (1969).

FEHRENBACHER, DON E. *The Dred Scott Case: Its Significance in American Law and Politics* (1978).

FELDMAN, LINDA. "Norton Biography." *Christian Science Monitor* (March 31, 1992): 14:1

FERGUSON, JAMES. *Papa Doc, Baby Doc: Haiti and the Duvaliers* (1987).

FERGUSON, MOIRA. *Jamaica Kincaid: Where the Land Meets the Body* (1994).

FERGUSON, SHEILA. *Soul Food: Classic Cuisine from the Deep South* (1989).

FERRIS, WILLIAM, ED. *Afro-American Folk Arts and Crafts* (1983).

FERRIS, WILLIAM, AND BRENDA MCCALLUM, EDS. *Local Color: A Sense of Place in Folk Art* (1982).

FIELDS, BARBARA JEANNE. *Slavery and Freedom on the Middle Ground: Maryland During the Nineteenth Century* (1985).

FILHO, LUÍS VIANA. *O Negro na Bahia* (1988).

FITZGERALD, MARY ANN, HENRY J. DREWAL, AND MAYO OKEDIJI. "Transformation through Cloth: An Egungun Costume of the Yoruba." *African Arts* 28 (1995).

FLASCH, JOY. *Melvin B. Tolson* (1972).

FLEISCHER, NAT. *Black Dynamite: The Story of the Negro in the Prize Ring from 1782 to 1838* (1938).

FLETCHER, MARVIN E. *America's First Black General: Benjamin O. Davis, Sr.* (1989).

———. *The Black Soldier and Officer in the United States Army, 1891–1917* (1974).

FLETCHER, TOM. *One-Hundred Years of the Negro in Show Business* (1984).

FLINT, J. E. "Zanzibar 1890–1950." *In History of East Africa*, ed. Vincent Harlow and E. M. Chilver (1965).

FLOMENHAFT, ELEANOR, ED. Faith Ringgold: *A 25-Year Survey* (1990).

FLOYD, SAMUEL, ED. *Black Music in the Harlem Renaissance* (1990).

FLYNN, JOYCE, AND JOYCE OCCOMY STRICKLIN, EDS. *Frye Street and Environs: The Collected Works of Marita Bonner Occomy* (1987).

FOGEL, ROBERT W. *Without Consent or Contract: The Rise and Fall of American Slavery* (1989).

FOLEY, ALBERT S. *Bishop Healy: Beloved Outcaste* (1954).

FONER, ERIC. *Reconstruction: America's Unfinished Revolution, 1863–1877* (1988).

FONER, PHILIP. *Antonio Maceo* (1977).

———. *Black Panthers Speak* (1995).

———. *Blacks in the American Revolution* (1976).

———. *Organized Labor & the Black Worker 1619–1973* (1974).

———. *The Spanish-Cuban-American War and the Birth of U.S. Imperialism. Vol. I* (1962).

FONER, PHILIP, ED. *Black Socialist Preacher: The Teachings of Reverend George Washington Woodbey and his Disciple Reverend George W. Slater, Jr.* (1983).

FONER, PHILIP, AND RONALD LEWIS. *Black Workers: A Documentary History from Colonial Times to the Present* (1989).

FOOTE, JULIA. *A Brand Plucked From the Fire*. In *Spiritual Narratives*, ed. Henry Louis Gates Jr. (1988).

FORBES, JACK D. *Africans and Native Americans: The Language of Race and the Evolution of Red-Black Peoples* (1988).

FORBES, STEVEN. *The Baymen of Belize and How They Wrested British Honduras from the Spaniards* (1997).

FORMAN, JAMES. *The Making of Black Revolutionaries* (1985).

FOSTER, FRANCES SMITH. "Adding Color and Contour to Early American Self-Portraitures: Autobiographical Writings of Afro-American Women." In *Conjuring: Black Women, Fiction and Literary Tradition*, ed. Marjorie Pryse and Hortense J. Spillers (1985).

——. *Written By Herself: Literary Production by African American Women, 1746–1892* (1993).

FOUCHET, MAX POL. *Wifredo Lam*. (1976).

FOWLER, VIRGINIA. *Nikki Giovanni* (1992).

FRADY, MARSHALL. *Jesse: The Life and Pilgrimage of Jesse Jackson* (1996).

FRANCO, JOSÉ LUCIANO. *Apuntes para una historia de su vida*. 3 vols. (1951–1957).

Franco Silva, Alfonso. *La esclavitud en Sevilla y su tierra a fines de la edad media* (1979).

FRANKLIN, CHARLES LIONEL. *The Negro Labor Unionist of New York: Problems and Conditions among Negroes in the Labor Unions in Manhattan with Special Reference to the N.R.A. and Post-N.R.A. Situations* (1936).

FRANKLIN, JOHN HOPE. *The Free Negro in North Carolina, 1790–1863* (1943).

——. *From Slavery to Freedom: A History of Negro Americans* (1988).

——. *Race and History: Selected Essays, 1938–1988* (1989).

FRANKLIN, JOHN HOPE, AND AUGUST MEIER, EDS. *Black Leaders of the Twentieth Century* (1982).

FRANKLIN, VINCENT P. *The Education of Black Philadelphia: The Social and Educational History of a Minority Community, 1900–1950* (1979).

FRANK, RUSTY E. *Tap! The Greatest Tap Dance Stars and Their Stories, 1900–1955* (1990).

FRAZIER, E. FRANKLIN. "Durham: Capital of the Black Middle Class." In Alain Locke, ed. *The New Negro* (1925).

——. *On Race Relations: Selected Writings*, ed. Gilbert Edwards (1968).

FRAZIER, JOE, AND PHIL BERGER. *Smokin' Joe: The Autobiography of a Heavyweight Champion of the World, Smokin' Joe Frazier* (1996).

FREEDBERG, SYDNEY P. *Brother Love: Money, Murder, and a Messiah* (1994).

FRENCH, WILLIAM P. "Black Studies: Getting Started in a Specialty." *AB: Bookmans Weekly* (February 22, 1988): 737–41.

FREYRE, GILBERTO. *O Brasil em face das Africas negras e mesticas* (1963).

——. *The Masters and the Slaves: A Study in the Development of Brazilian Civilization*. Translation of *Casa grande e senzala* by Samuel Putnam (1986).

FREY, SYLVIA. *Water From the Rock: Black Resistance in a Revolutionary Age* (1991).

FRIEDEMANN, NINA S. DE. *Lengua y sociedad en el palenque de San Basilio* (1983).

——. *Ma ngombe: Guerreros y ganaderos en Palenque*. 2d ed. (1987).

——. *La saga del Negro: Presencia africana en Colombia* (1993).

FRIEDEMANN, NINA S. DE., AND ALFREDO VANIN, COMP. *Entre la tierra y el cielo: Magia y leyendas del Chocó* (1995).

FRIEDMAN, LAWRENCE J. *Gregarious Saints: Self and Community in American Abolitionism, 1830–1870* (1982).

FINLAYSON, IAIN. *Tangier: City of the Dream* (1992).

FOX, STEPHEN R. *The Guardian of Boston: William Monroe Trotter* (1970).

FOX, TED. *Showtime at the Apollo* (1983).

FRY, GLADYS-MARIE. *Stitched from the Soul: Slave Quilts from the Ante-Bellum South* (1990).

FREDERICKS, MARCEL, JOHN LENNON ET AL. *Society and Health in Guyana* (1986).

FUNARI, PEDRO PAUL A., MARTIN HALL, AND SIAN JONES, EDS. *Historical Archaeology: Back from the Edge* (1999).

FUNDAÇÃO CASA DE RUI BARBOSA. *O Abolicionista Rui Barbosa* (1988).

FUNKE, LEWIS. *The Curtain Rises: The Story of Ossie Davis* (1971).

FYFE, CHRISTOPHER. *Sierra Leone Inheritance* (1964).

GABBARD, KRIN, ED. *Representing Jazz* (1995).

GABRIEL, TESHOME. *Third Cinema in the Third World: The Aestheties of Liberation* (1982).

GADELII, KARL ERLAND. *Lesser Antillean French Creole and Universal Grammar* (1997).

GAINES, ERNEST. *Porch Talk with Ernest Gaines: Conversations on the Writer's Craft*, ed. Marcia Gaudet and Carl Wooton (1990).

GALEANO, EDUARDO. *Football in Sun and Shadow* (1998).

GAMBINO, FERRUCCIO. "The Transgression of a Laborer: Malcolm X in the Wilderness of America." *Radical History Review* 55 (Winter 1993): 7–31.

GAMBLE, DAVID. *The Wolof of Senegambia, Together with Notes on the Lebu and the Serer* (1967).

GANDY, SAMUEL LUCIUS. *Human Possibilities: A Vernon Johns Reader* (1977).

GANGITANO, LIA AND STEVEN NELSON, EDS. *New Histories* (1996).

GARCÍA, HORACIO, ED. *Pensamiento revolucionario cubano*. Vol. I (1971).

GARCÍA, JUAN. *Cuentos y décimas afro-esmeraldeñas* (1988).

GARCÍA, JUAN MANUEL. *La Masacre de Palma Sola (Partidos, lucha política y el asesino del general): 1961–1963* (1986).

GARFINKEL, HERBERT. *When Negroes March: The March on Washington Movement in the Organizational Politics for FEPC* (1959).

GARROW, DAVID J. *Bearing the Cross: Martin Luther King, Jr., and the Southern Christian Leadership Conference* (1986).

——. *Protest at Selma: Martin Luther King, Jr., and the Voting Rights Act of 1965* (1978).

GASPAR, DAVID BARRY. *Bondmen and Rebels: A Study of Master-Slave Relations in Antigua* (1985).

GATES, HENRY LOUIS, JR. *Black Literature and Literary Theory* (1984).

——. *Colored People: A Memoir* (1994).

——. *Figures in Black: Words, Signs, and the Racial Self* (1992).

——. *Loose Canons: Notes on the Culture Wars* (1992).

——. *The Signifying Monkey: Towards A Theory of Afro-American Literary Criticism* (1988).

——. *Thirteen Ways of Looking at a Black Man* (1997): 155–79.

GATES, HENRY LOUIS, JR., ED. *Bearing Witness: Selections from African-American Autobiography in the Twentieth Century* (1991).

——, ED. *The Classic Slave Narratives* (1987).

——, ED. *Collected Black Women's Narratives: The Schomburg Library of Nineteenth-Century Black Women Writers* (1988).

GATES, HENRY LOUIS, JR., AND KWAME ANTHONY APPIAH, EDS. *Richard Wright: Critical Perspectives Past and Present* (1993).

——. Gloria Naylor: *Critical Perspectives Past and Present* (1993).

GATES, HENRY LOUIS, JR., AND NELLIE Y. MCKAY. *The Norton Anthology of African American Literature* (1997).

GATES, HENRY LOUIS, JR., AND CORNEL WEST. *The Future of the Race* (1996).

GATEWOOD, WILLARD B. *Aristocrats of Color: The Black Elite, 1880–1920* (1990).

GAVINS, RAYMOND. *The Perils and Prospects of Southern Black Leadership: Gordon Blaine Hancock, 1884–1970* (1977).

GAYLE, ADDISON, JR., ED. *The Black Aesthetic* (1971).

GAY, ROBERT. *Popular Organization and Democracy in Rio de Janeiro: A Tale of Two Favelas* (1994).

GEARY, LYNETTE G. "Jules Bledsoe: The Original 'Ol' Man River'." *Black Perspective in Music* 17, nos. 1, 2 (1989): 27–54.

GEIS, IMMANUEL. *The Pan-African Movement: A History of Pan-Africanism in America, Europe and Africa* (1974).

GELPÍ, JUAN. *Literatura y paternalismo en Puerto Rico* (1993).

GENOVESE, EUGENE D. *Roll, Jordan, Roll: The World the Slaves Made* (1974).

GEORGE, CAROL V. R. *Segregated Sabbaths: Richard Allen and the Emergence of Independent Black Churches 1760–1840* (1972).

GEORGE, NELSON. *Elevating the Game: Black Men and Basketball* (1992).

——. *Where Did Our Love Go?: The Rise and Fall of the Motown Sound* (1985).

GEORGE, NELSON, ET AL., EDS. *Fresh: Hip Hop Don't Stop* (1985).

GERBER, JANE S. *Jewish Society in Fez, 1450–1700: Studies in Communal and Economic Life* (1980).

GIBB, H.A.R. Ibn Battuta: *Travels in Asia and Africa 1325–1354* (1929).

GIBSON, BOB. *From Ghetto to Glory: The Story of Bob Gibson* (1968).

GIDE, ANDRÉ. *Travels in the Congo* (1962).

GILARD, JACQUES. "Crescencio ou don Toba? Fausses questions et vraies réponses sur le 'vallenato'." *Cahiers du monde hispanique et luso-brésilien, Caravelle* 48 (1987): 69–80.

GILL, GERALD R. "Win or Lose—We Win." In *The Afro-American Woman: Struggles and Images* (1978).

GILLESPIE, JOHN BIRKS ("DIZZY"), WITH AL FRASER. *Dizzy To BE, or Not . . . to BOP: The Autobiography of Dizzy Gillespie* (1979).

GILROY, PAUL. *There Ain't No Black in the Union Jack: The Cultural Politics of Race and Nation* (1991).

GIRAL, SERGIO. "Cuban Cinema and the Afro-Cuban Heritage." Interview by Julianne Burton and Gary Crowdus. In *Film and Politics in the Third World*, ed. John D. H. Downing (1987).

——. "Sergio Giral on Filmmaking in Cuba." Interview by Ana M. López and Nicholas Peter Humy. In *Cinemas of the Black Diaspora: Diversity, Dependence, and Oppositionality*, ed. Michael T. Martin (1995).

GIRVAN, NORMAN. *Poverty, Empowerment and Social Development in the Caribbean* (1997).

GLAZIER, STEPHEN D. *Marchin' the Pilgrims Home* (1983).

———, ED. *Perspectives on Pentecostalism: Case Studies from the Caribbean and Latin America* (1980).

GLEN, JOHN M. *Highlander: No Ordinary School, 1932–1962* (1988).

GLISSANT, EDOUARD. *Caribbean Discourse: Selected Essays.* Translated by J. Michael Dash (1989).

GOGGIN, JACQUELINE ANNE. *Carter G. Woodson: A Life in Black History* (1993).

GOINGS, KENNETH W. *Mammy and Uncle Mose: Black Collectibles and American Stereotyping* (1994).

GOLDBERG, JANE. "A Hoofer's Homage: John Bubbles." *Village Voice* (December 4, 1978).

GONZÁLEZ BUENO, GLADYS. "An Initiation Ceremony in Regla de Palo." In *AfroCuba: An Anthology of Cuban Writing on Race, Politics and Culture,* ed. Pedro Pèrez Sarduy and Jean Stubbs (1993).

GONZÁLEZ DÍAZ, ANTONIO MANUEL. *La esclavitud en Ayamonte durante el Antiguo Régimen (siglos XVI, XVII y XVIII)* (1997).

GONZÁLEZ ECHEVARRIA, ROBERTO. *Myth and Archive: A Theory of Latin American Narrative* (1998).

———. *The Pride of Havana: The History of Cuban Baseball* (1999).

GONZALEZ-PEREZ, ARMANDO. *Acercamiento a la literatura afrocubana: Ensayos de interpretación* (1994).

GONZALEZ-WHIPPLER, MIGENE. *The Santeria Experience: A Journey into the Miraculous.* Rev. and exp. ed. (1992).

GOODHEART, LAWRENCE B., ET AL., EDS. *Slavery in American Society.* 3d ed. (1993).

GOODWIN, ANDREW, AND JOE GORE. "World Beat and the Cultural Imperialism Debate." *Socialist Review* 20, no. 3 (1990): 63–80.

GORDON, ALLAN M. *Echoes of Our Past: The Narrative Artistry of Palmer C. Hayden* (1988).

GORDON, P. "The New Right, Race, and Education." *Race and Class* 29, no. 3 (Winter 1987).

GOSNELL, HAROLD F. *Negro Politicians: The Rise of Negro Politics in Chicago* (1967).

GOURAIGE, GHISLAIN. *Histoire de la littérature haïtienne (de l'indépendance à nos jours)* (1982).

GOUREVITCH, PHILIP. *We Wish to Inform You that Tomorrow We Will Be Killed with Our Families: Stories from Rwanda* (1998).

GOURSE, LESLIE. *Unforgettable: The Life and Mystique of Nat King Cole* (1991).

GRANDA GUTIERREZ, GERMAN DE. *Estudios sobre un area dialectal hispanoamericana de poblacion negra: Las tierras bajas occidentales de Colombia* (1977)

GRANT, JOANNE. *Fundi: The Story of Ella Baker* (1981).

GRATIANT, GILBERT. *Fables créoles et autres récits* (1995).

GRAY, JOHN MILNER. *History of Zanzibar from the Middle Ages to 1856* (1962).

GRAY, RICHARD. *Black Christians and White Missionaries* (1990).

GREENBAUM, SUSAN. "A Comparison Between African-American and Euro-American Mutual Aid Societies in 19th-Century America." *Journal of Ethnic Studies* 19 (Fall 1991): 95–119.

GREENBERG, CHERYL LYNN. *"Or Does It Explode?": Black Harlem in the Great Depression* (1991).

GREENBERG, JACK. *Crusaders in the Courts: How a Dedicated Band of Lawyers Fought for the Civil Rights Revolution* (1994).

GREENE, LORENZO JOHNSTON. *Selling Black History for Carter G. Woodson* (1996).

GREENE, LORENZO JOHNSTON, GARY R. KREMER, AND ANTONIO F. HOLLAND. *Missouri's Black Heritage* (1993).

GREEN, TIM. *The Dark Side of the Game: The Unauthorized NFL Playbook* (1996).

GREGORY, DICK, WITH MARK LANE. *Up From Nigger* (1976).

GREGORY, DICK, WITH MARTIN LIPSYTE. *Nigger: An Autobiography* (1964).

GREGORY, PAYNE J., AND SCOTT C. RATZAN. *Tom Bradley: The Impossible Dream: A Biography* (1986).

GRENARD, STEVE. *Handbook of Alligators and Crocodiles* (1991).

GRIAULE, MARCEL. *Conversations with Ogotemmeli: An Introduction to Dogon Religious Ideas* (1965).

GROIA, PHILIP. *They All Sang on the Corner: A Second Look at New York City's Rhythm and Blues Vocal Groups* (1983).

GROSSMAN, JAMES R. *Land of Hope: Chicago, Black Southerners and the Great Migration* (1989).

GRUDIN, EVA UNGAR. *Stitching Memories: African-American Story Quilts* (1990).

GUERRERO, EDWARD. *Framing Blackness: The African American Image in Film* (1993).

GUILBAULT, JOCELYNE, WITH GAGE AVERILL, EDOUARD BENOÎT, AND GREGORY RABESS. *Zouk: World Music in the West Indies* (1993).

GUILLÉN, NICOLAS. *Martín Morúa Delgado: ¿Quién fue?* (1984).

GURALNICK, PETER. *Searching for Robert Johnson* (1989).

——. *Sweet Soul Music: Rhythm and Blues and the Southern Dream of Freedom* (1986).

GUTMAN, BILL. *The Harlem Globetrotters* (1977).

GUTMAN, HERBERT G. *The Black Family in Slavery and Freedom, 1750–1925* (1976).

GUY-SHEFTALL, BEVERLY, AND JO MOORE STEWART. *Spelman: A Centennial Celebration* (1981).

GUZMAN, JESSIE P. *Crusade for Civic Democracy: The Story of the Tuskegee Civic Association, 1941–1970* (1985).

HABEKOST, CHRISTIAN. *Verbal Riddim: The Politics and Aesthetics of African-Caribbean Dub Poetry* (1993).

HACKETT, ROSALIND. *Art and Religion in Africa* (1996).

HAIR, WILLIAM IVY. *Carnival of Fury: Robert Charles and the New Orleans Race Riot of 1900* (1976).

HALE, LINDSAY, "Preto Velho: Resistance, Redemption and Engendered Representations of Slavery in a Brazilian Possession-Trance Religion." *American Ethnologist* 24, no. 2 (1997): 392–414.

HALL, JACQUELYN DOWD. *Revolt Against Chivalry: Jessie Daniel Ames and the Women's Campaign Against Lynching* (1979).

HALL, MARGARET, AND TOM YOUNG. *Confronting Leviathan: Mozambique Since Independence* (1997).

HALL, RICHARD. *Stanley: An Adventurer Explored* (1974).

HALL, STUART. "Racism and Reaction." *In Five Views on Multi-Racial Britain* (1978).

HALL, STUART, AND BRAM GIEBEN, EDS. *Formations of Modernity* (1992).

HALL, STUART, AND MARTIN JACQUES, EDS. *New Times: The Changing Face of Politics in the 1990s* (1990).

HAMER, MARY. *Signs of Cleopatra: History, Politics, Representation* (1993).

HAMILTON, CHARLES V. *Adam Clayton Powell, Jr.: The Political Biography of an American Dilemma* (1991).

HAMILTON, HOLMAN. *Prologue to Conflict: The Crisis and Compromise of 1850* (1964).

HAMILTON, KENNETH MARVIN. *Black Towns and Profit: Promotion and Development in the Trans-Applachian West, 1877–1915* (1991).

HAMNER, ROBERT D, ED. *Critical Perspectives on Derek Walcott* (1993).

HANCHARD, MICHAEL GEORGE. *Orpheus and Power: The Movimento Negro of Rio de Janeiro and São Paulo, Brazil, 1945–1988* (1994).

HANDY, D. ANTOINETTE. "Conversations with Mary Lou Williams: First Lady of the Jazz Keyboard." *Black Perspectives on Music* 8 (Fall 1980): 195–214.

HANDY, WILLIAM C. *Father of the Blues: An Autobiography.* Edited by Arna Bontemps (1941).

HANSEN, EMMANUEL. *Frantz Fanon: Social and Political Thought* (1977).

HARDESTY, VON, AND DOMINICK PISANO. *Black Wings: The American Black in Aviation* (1983).

HARDY, CHARLES, AND GAIL F. STERN, EDS. *Ethnic Images in the Comics* (1986).

HARDY, GAYLE J. *American Women Civil Rights Activists: Biobibliographies of 68 Leaders, 1825–1992* (1993).

HARLAN, LOUIS R. *Booker T. Washington: The Making of a Black Leader, 1856–1901* (1972).

HARPER, MICHAEL S., ET. AL., EDS. *Chant of Saints: A Gathering of Afro-American Literature, Art, and Scholarship* (1979).

HARRINGTON, OLIVER. *Why I Left America and Other Essays* (1993).

HARRIS, FRED R., AND ROGER WILKINS, EDS. *Quiet Riots: Race and Poverty in the United States* (1988).

HARRIS, JESSICA B. *Iron Pots and Wooden Spoons: Africa's Gifts to New World Cooking* (1989).

HARRIS, MICHAEL. *The Rise of the Gospel Blues: The Music of Thomas Andrew Dorsey in the Urban Church* (1992).

HARRISON, ALFERDTEEN, ED. *Black Exodus: The Great Migration from the American South* (1991).

HARRISON, EARL. *The Dream and the Dreamer* (1956).

HARRIS, ROBERT. "Early Black Benevolent Societies, 1780–1830." *Massachusetts Review* 20 (Autumn 1979): 603–28.

HARRIS, WILLIAM HAMILTON. *Keeping the Faith: A. Philip Randolph, Milton P. Webster, and the Brotherhood of Sleeping Car Porters, 1925–37* (1977).

HARRIS, WILLIAM J. *The Poetry and Poetics of Amiri Baraka: The Jazz Aesthetic* (1985).

HARRIS, WILSON. *History, Fable, and Myth in the Caribbean and the Guianas* (1970).

HART, DAVID. *The Volta River Project: A Case Study in Politics and Technology* (1980).

HASKINS, JAMES. *Black Dance in America: A History through its People* (1990).

——. *Bricktop* (1983).

——. *Mabel Mercer: A Life* (1987).

——. *Pinckney Benton Stewart Pinchback* (1973).

HASKINS, JAMES, AND N. R. MITGANG. *Mr. Bojangles: The Biography of Bill Robinson* (1988).

HAYDEN, DOLORES. "Biddy Mason's Los Angeles, 1856–1891." *California History* 68 (Fall 1989): 86–99.

HAYDEN, TOM. *Rebellion in Newark: Official Violence and Ghetto Response* (1967).

HAYES, DIANA L. *And Still We Rise: An Introduction to Black Liberation Theology* (1996).

HAYGOOD, WIL. *King of the Cats: The Life and Times of Adam Clayton Powell, Jr.* (1993).

HAYNES, KARIMA A. "Mae Jemison: Coming in from Outer Space." *Ebony* 48, no. 2 (Dec. 1992):118.

HAYWOOD, HARRY. *Black Bolshevik: Autobiography of an Afro-American Communist* (1978).

HAZAEL-MASSIEUX, MARIE-CHRISTINE. "Le Criole aux Antilles: Evolutions et Perspectives." In Yacou Alain, ed., *Créoles de la Caraïbe: Actes du Colloque universitaire en hommage à Guy Hazael-Massieux, Pointe-à-Pitre, le 27 mars 1995* (1996): 179–200.

HEDGEMAN, ANNA ARNOLD. *The Trumpet Sounds: A Memoir of Negro Leadership* (1964).

HEDRICK, JOAN. *Harriet Beecher Stowe: A Life* (1994).

HEILBUT, ANTHONY. *The Gospel Sound: Good News and Bad Times* (1971).

HELDMAN, MARILYN E., STUART MUNRO-HAY, AND RODERICK GRIERSON. *African Zion: The Sacred Art of Ethiopia* (1993).

HELG, ALINE. *Our Rightful Share: The Afro-Cuban Struggle for Equality, 1886–1912* (1995).

HELLER, PETER. *Bad Intentions: The Mike Tyson Story* (1989).

HELM, MCKINLEY. *Angel Mo' and Her Son, Roland Hayes* (1942).

HEMENWAY, ROBERT. *Zora Neale Hurston: A Literary Biography* (1980).

HEMPHILL, ESSEX, ED. *Brother to Brother: New Writings by Black Gay Men* (1991).

HENDERSON, ALEXA BENSON. *Atlanta Life Insurance Company: Guardian of Black Economic Dignity* (1990).

HENDERSON, HARRY, AND GYLBERT GARVIN COKER. *Charles Alston: Artist and Teacher* (1990).

HENSON, MATTHEW A. *A Black Explorer at the North Pole 1866–1955* (1989).

HENZE, PAUL B. *The Defeat of the Derg and the Establishment of New Governments in Ethiopia and Eritrea* (1992).

HEUMAN, GAD, ED. *Out of the House of Bondage: Runaways, Resistance, and Marronage in Africa and the New World* (1986).

HEYMOUNT, GEORGE. "Blacks in Opera." *Ebony* (November 1981): 32–36.

HIDALGO ALZAMORA, LAURA. "Del ritmo al concepto en la poesía de Preciado." *Cultura, Revista del Banco Central del Ecuador 3*, no.7 (May-August 1980): 102–19.

HIGGINBOTHAM, A. LEON. *In the Matter of Color: The Colonial Period* (1978).

——. *Shades of Freedom: Racial Politics and Presumptions of the American Legal Process* (1996).

HIGGINBOTHAM, EVELYN BROOKS. *Righteous Discontent: The Women's Movement in the Black Baptist Church, 1880–1920* (1993).

HILL, DANIEL G. *The Freedom Seekers: Blacks in Early Canada* (1981).

HILL, DONALD. *Calypso Calaloo: Early Carnival Music in Trinidad* (1993).

HILL, ROBERT A., ED. *The Crusader*. 3 vols. (1987).

——. *The Marcus Garvey and Universal Negro Improvement Association Papers* (1983–1991).

HINE, DARLENE CLARK, ED. *Black Women in America: An Historical Encylopedia*. 2 vols. (1993).

HIRO, DILIP. *Desert Shield to Desert Storm: The Second Gulf War* (1992).

HIRSH, ARNOLD R., AND JOSEPH LOGSDON. *Creole New Orleans: Race and Americanization* (1992).

HIRSCHORN, H. H. "Botanical remedies of South and Central America and the Caribbean: An Archival Analysis." *Journal of Ethnopharmacology 4*, no. 2 (1981).

HOCHSCHILD, ADAM. *King Leopold's Ghost: A Story of Greed, Terror, and Heroism in Colonial Africa* (1998).

HODGES, LEROY. *Portrait of an Expatriate: William Gardner Smith, Writer* (1985).

HOFFMAN, FREDERICK J., CHARLES ALLEN, AND CAROLYN R. ULRICH. *The Little Magazine: A History and a Bibliography* (1946).

HOFFMAN, LARRY G. *Haitian Art: The Legend and Legacy of the Naïve Tradition* (1985).

HOFFMANN, LÉON-FRANÇOIS. *Littérature d'Haïti* (1995).

HOFLER, ROBERT. "Minority View: Seeing White, Being Black: Interview with Lou Gossett Jr." *Life* (March 1989).

HOLANDA, AURÉLIO BUARQUE DE. "Teixeira e Souza." *In O Romance Brasileiro*, ed. Olivio Montenegro (1952).

HOLDREDGE, HELEN. *Mammy Pleasant* (1953).

HOLLOWAY, JOSEPH E., ED. *Africanisms in American Culture* (1990).

HOLM, JOHN. *Pidgins and Creoles*. 2 vols. (1988–1989).

HOLT, RACKMAN. *Mary McLeod Bethune: A Biography* (1964).

HOLWAY, JOHN B. *Josh and Satch: The Life and Times of Josh Gibson and Satchel Paige* (1991).

HOLYFIELD, EVANDER, AND BERNARD HOLYFIELD. *Holyfield: The Humble Warrior* (1996).

HOOKS, BELL, "Black is a Woman's Color." In *Bearing Witness: Selections from African-American Autobiography in the Twentieth Century*, ed. Henry Louis Gates Jr. (1991).

HOOKS, BELL, AND CORNEL WEST. *Breaking Bread: Insurgent Black Intellectual Life* (1991).

HOPE KING, RUBY. *Education in the Caribbean: Historical Perspectives* (1987).

HORACE, LILLIAN B. *"Crowned with Glory and Honor": The Life of Rev. Lacey Kirk Williams* (1978).

HORNE, GERALD. *Communist Front? The Civil Rights Congress, 1946–56* (1988).

HORTON, AIMEE ISGRIG. *The Highlander Folk School: A History of its Major Programs, 1932–1961* (1989).

HOSHER, JOHN. *God in a Rolls Royce: The Rise of Father Divine: Madman, Menace, or Messiah* (1936).

HOSIASSON, JOSE. "Kid Ory." *New Grove Dictionary of Jazz* (1988).

HOUSE, ERNEST R. *Jesse Jackson and the Politics of Charisma: The Rise and Fall of the PUSH/Excel Program* (1988).

HOWAT, GERALD. *Learie Constantine* (1975).

HOWES, R. "The Literature of Outsiders: The Literature of the Gay Community in Latin America." In *Latin American Masses and Minorities: Their Images and Realities* (1987).

HOWE, STEPHEN. *Afrocentrism: Mythical Pasts and Imagined Homes* (1998).

HOYOS, F. A. *A History from the Amerindians to Independence* (1978).

HUCKABY, ELIZABETH. *Crisis at Central High School: Little Rock, 1957–58* (1980).

HUGGINS, NATHAN IRVIN. *Harlem Renaissance* (1971).

HUGHES, C. ALVIN. "We Demand Our Rights: The Southern Negro Youth Congress, 1937–1949." *Phylon* 48, no. 1 (Spring 1987): 38–50.

HULL, GLORIA T. *Color, Sex, and Poetry: Three Women Writers of the Harlem Renaissance* (1987).

HUNTER-GAULT, CHARLAYNE. *In My Place* (1992).

HUNTINGTON, RICHARD. *Gender and Social Structure in Madagascar* (1988).

HURD, MICHAEL. *Black College Football, 1892–1992: One Hundred Years of History, Education, and Pride* (1993).

HURLEY, DANIEL. *Cincinnati, The Queen City* (1982).

HURSTON, ZORA NEALE. "Hoodoo in America." *Journal of American Folklore* 44 (1931): 414.

———. *I Love Myself When I am Laughing . . . and Then Again When I am Looking Mean and Impressive: A Zora Neale Hurston Reader,* ed. Alice Walker (1979).

———. *Mules and Men* (1935).

HUTCHINSON, EARL OFARI. *Betrayed: A History of Presidential Failure to Protect Black Lives* (1996).

———. *Blacks and Reds: Race and Class in Conflict, 1919–1990* (1995).

IANNI, OCTÁVIO. *Escravidão e racismo.* 2d ed. (1988).

IHONVBERE, JULIUS O. *Economic Crisis, Civil Society, and Democratization: The Case of Zambia* (1996).

ILLINOIS STATE MUSEUM. *Healing Walls: Murals and Community, A Chicago History* (1996).

"Interview: Queen Mother Moore." *Black Scholar* 4 (March-April 1973): 47–55.

IOAKIMIDIS, DEMETRE. "Chu Berry." *Jazz Monthly* (March 1964).

IRVINE, CECILIA. "The Birth of the Kimbanguist Movement in Bas-Zaire, 1921." *Journal of Religion in Africa* 6, no. 1 (1974): 23–76.

ISICHEI, ELIZABETH. *A History of African Societies to 1870* (1997).

JACKSON, CARLTON. *Hattie: The Life of Hattie McDaniel* (1990).

JACKSON, KENNETH T., AND BARBARA B. JACKSON. "The Black Experience in Newark: The Growth of the Ghetto, 1870–1970." *In New Jersey*

Since 1860: New Findings and Interpretations, ed. William C. Wright (1972).

JACKSON, LUTHER P. *Free Negro Labor and Property Holding in Virginia, 1830–1860* (1942).

JACKSON, REGINALD, WITH MIKE LUPICA. *Reggie* (1984).

JACKSON, RICHARD L. *Black Writers in Latin America* (1979).

JACOBS, DONALD M. *Antebellum Black Newspapers* (1976).

——. "David Walker: Boston Race Leader, 1825–1830." *Essex Institute Historical Collections* 107 (Jan. 1971): 94–107.

JACOBS, HARRIET. *Incidents in the Life of a Slave Girl, Written by Herself,* ed. Jean Fagan Yellin (1987).

JACOBSON, MARK. "When He Was King: Former Heavyweight Boxing Champ Larry Holmes." *New York* 30, no. 28 (July 28, 1997): 32–35.

JACQUES-GARVEY, AMY, ED. *Philosophy and Opinions of Marcus Garvey* (1923–1925).

JADIN, LOUIS. *Le Congo et la secte des Antoniens* (1961).

JAGAN, CHEDDI. *The West on Trial: My Fight for Guyana's Freedom* (1967).

JAMES, ADEOLA. *In Their Own Voices: African Women Writers Talk* (1990).

JAMES, C.L.R. *The Black Jacobins: Toussaint L' Ouverture and the San Domingo Revolution* (1963).

——. *A History of Pan-African Revolt* (1969).

JAMES, M. *Ten Modern Jazzmen: An Appraisal of the Recorded Work of Ten Modern Jazzmen* (1960).

"J. A. Rogers: Portrait of an Afro-American Historian." *Black Scholar* 6, no. 5 (January-February 1975): 32–39.

JASEN, DAVID A., AND TREBOR TICHENOR. *Rags and Ragtime: A Musical History* (1989).

JEFFREY, HENRY B., AND COLIN BABER. *Guyana: Politics, Economics, and Society: Beyond the Burnham Era* (1986).

JENKINS, MARK. *To Timbuktu* (1997).

JIMÉNEZ-ROMAN, MIRIAM. "Un hombre (negro) del pueblo: José Celso Barbosa and the Puerto Rican 'Race' towards Whiteness." *Centro de Estudios Puertorriqueños* (Spring 1996).

JIMENO, MYRIAM, AND MARÍA LUCIA SOTOMAYOR, LUZ MARÍA VALDERRAMA. *Chocó: Diversidad cultural y medio ambiente* (1995).

JOHNS, CHRIS. *Valley of Life: Africa's Great Rift* (1991).

JOHNSON, ABBY ARTHUR, AND RONALD MABERRY JOHNSON. "Charting a New Course: African American Literary Politics since 1976." In *The Black Columbiad: Defining Moments in African American Literature and Culture,* ed. Werner Sollors and Maria Diedrich (1994), pp. 369–81.

——. *Propaganda and Aesthetics: The Literary Politics of African-American Magazines in the Twentieth Century* (1991).

JOHNSON, CECIL *Guts: Legendary Black Rodeo Cowboy Bill Pickett* (1994).

JOHNSON, DIANE. *Telling Tales: The Pedagogy and Promise of African American Literature for Youth* (1990).

JOHNSON, JOHN H., AND LERONE BENNETT, JR. *Succeeding Against the Odds* (1989).

JOHNSON, JAMES WELDON. *Black Manhattan* (1930).

——. Preface to *The Book of American Negro Poetry* (1922).

JOHNSON, RANDAL. *Cinema Novo x 5: Masters of Contemporary Brazilian Film* (1984).

JOHNSTON, J. H. "Luther Porter Jackson." *Journal of Negro History* (October 1950): 352–55.

JONAS, JOYCE. *Anancy in the Great House: Ways of Reading West Indian Fiction* (1991).

JONES, HOWARD. *Mutiny on the Amistad: The Saga of a Slave Revolt and its Impact on American Abolition, Law and Diplomacy* (1987).

——. "The Peculiar Institution and National Honor: The Case of the Creole Slave Revolt." *Civil War History* 21 (1975): 28–50.

JONES, JAMES H. *Bad Blood: The Tuskegee Syphilis Experiment* (1993).

JONES, JOYCE. "The Best Commerce Secretary Ever." *Black Enterprise* 26, no. 11 (1990).

JONES, RALPH H. *Charles Albert Tindley: Prince of Preachers* (1982).

JONES, TAD. "Professor Longhair." *Living Blues* 26 (March-April 1976): 16–29.

JORDAN, BARBARA, AND SHELBY HEARON. *Barbara Jordan: A Self-Portrait* (1979).

JOSEPH, CLIFTON. "Jump Up and Beg." *Toronto Life* (August 1996).

JOYCE, DONALD FRANKLIN. *Black Book Publishers in the United States: A Historical Dictionary of the Presses, 1817–1990* (1991).

——. *Gatekeepers of Black Culture: Black-Owned Book Publishing in the United States, 1817–1981* (1983).

JOYCE, PETER. *Anatomy of a Rebel: Smith of Rhodesia: A Biography* (1974).

JOYNER, CHARLES. *Down by the Riverside: A South Carolina Slave Community* (1989).

JULIEN, ISAAC. *Looking for Langston: A Meditation on Langston Hughes (1902–1967) and the Harlem Renaissance, with the Poetry of Essex Hemphill and Bruce Nugent (1906–1987)* (1992).

KAHAN, MITCHELL D. *Heavenly Visions: The Art of Minnie Evans* (1986).

KAPLAN, SIDNEY. "The Miscegenation Issue in the Election of 1864." In *American Studies in Black and White: Selected Essays, 1949–1989,* ed. Allan D. Austin (1991): 47–100.

KAPLAN, SIDNEY, AND EMMA NOGRADY KAPLAN. *The Black Presence in the Era of the American Revolution.* 2d ed. (1989).

KAPLAN, STEVEN. *The Beta Israel (Falasha) in Ethiopia: From Earliest Times to the Twentieth Century* (1992).

KARENGA, MAULANA. *The African American Holiday of Kwanzaa: A Celebration of Family, Community, and Culture* (1988).

——. *Introduction to Black Studies.* 2d ed. (1993).

KATZ, JONATHAN. *Resistance at Christiana: The Fugitive Slave Rebellion, Christiana, Pennsylvania, September 11, 1851: A Documentary Account* (1974).

KATZMAN, DAVID. *Before the Ghetto: Black Detroit in the Nineteenth Century* (1973).

KATZ, WILLIAM L. *Black People Who Made the Old West* (1992).

——. *The Black West* (1987).

KECKLEY, ELIZABETH. *Behind the Scenes; or, Thirty Years a Slave and Four Years in the White House* (1868).

KELLEY, ROBIN D. G. *Hammer and Hoe: Alabama Communists During the Great Depression* (1990).

KENNEDY, ADRIENNE. *People Who Led to My Plays* (1987).

KENNEDY, RANDALL. *Dred Scott and African American Citizenship* (1996).

——. *Race, Crime, and the Law* (1997).

KENNEY, WILLIAM HOWLAND. *Chicago Jazz: A Cultural History, 1904–1930* (1993).

——. "Jimmie Noone, Chicago's Classical Jazz Clarinetist." *American Music* 4 (1986): 145–58.

KENYATTA, JOMO. *Facing Mount Kenya: The Tribal Life of the Gikuyu* (1938).

KEPPEL, BEN. *The Work of Democracy: Ralph Bunche, Kenneth B. Clark, Lorraine Hansberry, and the Cultural Politics of Race* (1995).

KESSELMAN, LOUIS. *The Social Politics of FEPC: A Study in Reform Pressure Movements* (1948).

KESSLER, JAMES H. *Distinguished African American Scientists of the Twentieth Century* (1996).

KESTELOOT, LILYAN. *Black Writers in French: A Literary History of Negritude*. Translated by Ellen Conroy Kennedy (1991).

KEVLES, DANIEL. *In the Name of Eugenics: Genetics and the Uses of Human Heredity* (1985).

KHAZANOV, A. *Agostinho Neto* (1986).

KIM, AEHYUNG, AND BRUCE BENTON. *Cost-benefit Analysis of the Onchocerca Control Program (OCP)* (1995).

KINCAID, JAMAICA. *A Small Place* (1988).

KING, B. B., WITH DAVID RITZ. *Blues All Around Me: The Autobiography of B. B. King* (1996).

KING, BRUCE, ED. *West Indian Literature* (1979).

KING, CORETTA SCOTT. *My Life with Martin Luther King, Jr.* (1969).

KINGDON, ZACHARY, "Chanuo Maundu: Master of Makonde Blackwood Art." *African Arts* (Autumn 1996).

KIPLE, KENNETH F. *The Caribbean Slave: A Biological History* (1984).

KIRSH, ANDREA, AND SUSAN FISHER STERLING. *Carrie Mae Weems* (1992).

KIRWAN, ALBERT DENNIS. *John J. Crittenden: The Struggle for the Union* (1962).

KISKA, TIM. "CBS' Ed Bradley Recalls Childhood Days in Detroit." *Detroit News* (March 21, 1997) A, 2:2.

KITT, EARTHA. *Alone with Me* (1976).

——. *Thursday's Child* (1956).

KITWANA, BAKARI. *The Rap on Gangsta Rap: Who Run It? Gangsta Rap and Visions of Black Violence* (1994).

KLAPISCH, BOB. *High and Tight: The Rise and Fall of Dwight Gooden and Darryl Strawberry* (1996).

KLEHR, HARVEY. *The Heyday of American Communism: The Depression Decade* (1984).

KLEIN, HERBERT S. *African Slavery in Latin America and the Caribbean* (1986).

——. *The Middle Passage: Comparative Studies in the Atlantic Slave Trade* (1978).

——. *Slavery in the Americas: A Comparative Study of Virginia and Cuba* (1967).

KLEMENT, FRANK L. *The Copperheads of the Middle West* (1972).

KLEPPNER, PAUL. Chicago *Divided: The Making of a Black Mayor* (1985).

KLOTMAN, PHYLLIS RAUCH, ED. *Screenplays of the African American Experience* (1991).

KLOTS, STEVE. *Richard Allen* (1991).

KLUGER, RICHARD. *Simple Justice: The History of Brown v. Board of Education and Black America's Struggle for Equality* (1975).

KNAACK, TWILA. *Ethel Waters: I Touched a Sparrow* (1978).

KNIGHT, FRANKLIN. *The African Dimension in Latin American Societies* (1974).

——. *Slavery and the Transformation of Society in Cuba, 1511–1760: From Settler Society to Slave Society* (1988).

KNIGHT, GLADYS. *Between Each Line of Pain and Glory: My Life Story* (1997).

KOLCHIN, PETER. *American Slavery, 1619–1877* (1993).

KONCZACKI, Z. A. *The Economics of Pastoralism: A Case Study of Sub-Saharan Africa* (1978).

KOOK, HETTY, AND GORETTI NARAIN. "Papiamento." In *Community Languages in the Netherlands*, ed. Guus Extra and Ludo Verhoeven (1993): 69–91.

KORNWEIBEL, THEODORE, JR. *No Crystal Stair: Black Life and the Messenger, 1917–1928* (1975).

KOSTARAS, JAMES GEORGE. *Fez: Transformation of the Traditional Urban Environment* (1986).

KOSTARELOS, FRANCES. *Feeling the Spirit: Faith and Hope in an Evangelical Black Storefront Church* (1995).

KOTLOWITZ, ALEX. "A Bridge Too Far? Benjamin Chavis." *New York Times Magazine* (June 12, 1994).

KOTTAK, CONRAD P. *The Past and the Present: History, Ecology, and Cultural Variation in Highland Madagascar* (1980).

KOUSSER, J. MORGAN. *The Shaping of Southern Politics: Suffrage Restriction and the Establishment of the One-Party South, 1880–1910* (1974).

KRADITOR, AILEEN S. *Means and Ends in American Abolitionism: Garrison and his Critics on Strategy and Tactics, 1834–1850* (1989).

KREAMER, CHRISTINE M. *A Life Well Lived: Fantasy Coffins of Kane Quaye* (1994).

KREMER, GARY R., ED. *George Washington Carver in His Own Words* (1987).

KUREISHI, H. "Dirty Washing." *Time Out* (London) (November 14–20, 1985).

KUSMER, KENNETH. *A Ghetto Takes Shape: Black Cleveland, 1870–1930* (1976).

KUTZINKSI, VERA. *Sugar's Secrets: Race and the Erotics of Cuban Nationalism* (1993).

KWAMENAH-POH, M., J.TOSH, R. WALLER, AND M. TIDY. *African History in Maps* (1982).

LABELLE, MICHELINE. *Idéologie de couleur et classes sociales en Haïti*. 2d ed. (1987).

LABOV, WILLIAM. *Language in the Inner City: Studies in the Black English Vernacular* (1972).

LA GUERRE, JOHN GAFFAR. *Enemies of Empire* (1984).

LAMBERT, BRUCE. "Doxey Wilkerson is Dead at 88: Educator and Advocate for Rights." *New York Times* (June 18, 1993): D 16.

LANE, ANN J. *The Brownsville Affair: National Crisis and Black Reaction* (1971).

LANE, ROGER. *Roots of Violence in Black Philadelphia, 1860–1900* (1986).

LANNING, MICHAEL LEE, LT. COL. (RET.). *The African-American Soldier: From Crispus Attucks to Colin Powell* (1997).

LAPP, RUDOLPH M. *Blacks in Gold Rush California* (1977).

LAURINO, MARIA. "Sensitivity Comes From 'The Soles of the Feet.'" Interview with Anna Deveare Smith, *New York Newsday* (Feb. 23, 1994).

LAWLAH, JOHN W. "The President-Elect." *Journal of the National Medical Association* 55 (November 1963): 551–554.

LAWRENCE, ELIZABETH A. *Rodeo: An Anthropologist Looks at the Wild and the Tame* (1982).

LEAMAN, OLIVER. *Averroes and His Philosophy* (1988).

LEAVY, WALTER. "Howard University: A Unique Center of Excellence." *Ebony* (September 1985): 140–142.

——. "Is Tony Gwynn the Greatest Hitter in Baseball History?" *Ebony* (August 1997): 132.

LECKIE, WILLIAM. *The Buffalo Soldiers: A Narrative of the Negro Cavalry in the West* (1967).

LEEDS, ANTHONY, AND ELIZABETH LEEDS. *A Sociologia do Brasil Urbano (The Sociology of Urban Brazil)*. Translated by Maria Laura Viveiros de Castro (1977).

LEE, JARENA. *The Life and Religious Experience of Jarena Lee* (1849). Reprinted *in Sisters of the Spirit: Three Black Women's Autobiographies of the Nineteenth Century*. Edited by William L. Andrews (1986).

LEEMING, DAVID. *James Baldwin: A Biography* (1994).

LEES, GENE. *Oscar Peterson: The Will to Swing* (1988).

LEFEVER, ERNEST W. *Crisis in the Congo: A United Nations Force in Action* (1965).

LEGUM, COLIN, AND GEOFFREY MMARI. *Mwalimu: The Influence of Nyerere* (1995).

LEMANN, NICHOLAS. *The Promised Land: The Great Black Migration and How It Changed America* (1991).

LEMARCHAND, RENÉ. *Political Awakening in the Belgian Congo* (1964).

LEÓN, ARGELIERS. *Del canto y el tiempo* (1984).

LEON, ELI. *Who'd a Thought It: Improvisation in African-American Quiltmaking* (1987).

LEONS, WILLIAM, AND ALLYN MACLEON STEARMAN. *Anthropological Investigations in Bolivia* (1984).

LEREBOURS, MICHEL PHILIPPE. *Haïti et ses peintres.* 2 vols. (1989).

LERNER, GERDA, ED. *Black Women in White America: A Documentary History* (1972).

LERNER, MICHAEL, AND CORNEL WEST. *Jews and Blacks: Let the Healing Begin* (1995).

LESLAU, WOLF, TRANS. *Falasha Anthology* (1954).

LESLIE, WINESOME J. *Zaire: Continuity and Political Change in an Oppressive State* (1993).

LEVINE, DONALD N. *Greater Ethiopia: The Evolution of a Multi-Ethnic Society* (1974).

LEVINE, LAWRENCE W. *Black Culture and Black Consciousness* (1977).

LEVINE, ROBERT M., AND JOSÉ CARLOS SEBE BOM MEIHY. *The Life and Death of Carolina Maria de Jesus* (1995).

LEWIS, DAVID LEVERING. *W. E. B. Du Bois: Biography of a Race* (1993).

——. *When Harlem Was in Vogue* (1981).

LEWIS, GORDON K. *Main Currents in Caribbean Thought: The Historical Experience of Caribbean Society and its Ideological Aspects, 1492–1900* (1983).

LEWIS, LANCELOT S. *The West Indian in Panama: Black Labor in Panama, 1850–1914* (1980).

LEWIS, MARVÍN A. *Ethnicity and Identity in Contemporary Afro-Venezuelan Literature: A Culturalist Approach* (1992).

LEWIS, MARY L. "The White Rose Industrial Association: The Friend of the Strange Girl in New York." *Messenger* 7 (April 1925): 158.

LEWIS, SAMELLA. *African American Art and Artists* (1990).

——. *The Art of Elizabeth Catlett* (1984).

LEWIS, SAMELLA, AND RICHARD POWELL. *Elizabeth Catlett: Works on Paper, 1944–1992* (1993).

LHAYA, PEDRO. *Juan Pablo Sojo, pasión y acento de su tierra* (1968).

LIBBY, BILL. *Goliath: The Wilt Chamberlain Story* (1977).

LICHTENSTEIN, GRACE, AND LAURA DANKNER. *Musical Gumbo: The Music of New Orleans* (1993).

LIEBENOW, J. GUS. *Colonial Rule and Political Development in Tanzania: The Case of the Makonde* (1971).

LIEB, SANDRA. *Mother of the Blues: A Study of Ma Rainey* (1981).

LIGHT, ALAN. "Curtis Mayfield: An Interview." *Rolling Stone* (October 28, 1993).

LINARES, OLGA. *Power, Prayer, and Production: The Jola of Casamance, Senegal* (1992).

LINCOLN, C. ERIC, AND LAWRENCE MAMIYA. *The Black Church in the African American Experience* (1990).

LINSLEY, ROBERT. "Wifredo Lam: Painter of Negritude." *Art History* 2, no. 4 (1988): 527–544.

LIPSKI, JOHN M. *The Speech of the Negros Congos of Panama* (1989).

LIPZITZ, GEORGE. *A Life in the Struggle: Ivory Perry and the Culture of Opposition* (1988).

LITVIN, MARTIN. *Hiram Revels in Illinois: A Biographical Novel about a Lost Chapter in the Life of America's First Black U.S. Senator* (1974).

LITWACK, LEON F. *Been in the Storm So Long: The Aftermath of Slavery* (1979).

——. *Trouble in Mind: Black Southerners in the Age of Jim Crow* (1998).

LITWACK, LEON F., AND AUGUST MEIER, EDS. *Black Leaders of the Nineteenth Century* (1988).

LIVINGSTON, JANE, JOHN BEARDSLEY, AND REGINIA PERRY. *Black Folk Art in America, 1930–1980* (1982).

LLERENA VILLALOBOS, RITO. *Memoria cultural en el vallenato* (1985).

LLEWELYN-DAVIES, MELISSA. *Some Women of Marrakech*. Videotape, Granada Television (1981).

LOCKE, ALAIN. *The New Negro* (1925).

LOCKE, MARY. *Anti-Slavery in America from the Introduction of African Slaves to the Prohibition of the Slave Trade (1619–1808)* (1901).

LOCKE, THERESA A. "Willa Brown-Chappell, Mother of Black Aviation." *Negro History Bulletin* 50 (January-June 1987): 5–6.

LOCKHART, JAMES. *Spanish Peru, 1532–1560: A Social History* (1994).

LODER, KURT. "Bo Diddley Interview." *Rolling Stone* (February 12, 1987).

LOFTON, JOHN. *Denmark Vesey's Revolt: The Slave Plot that Lit a Fuse to Fort Sumter* (1983).

LOGAN, RAYFORD. *Howard University: The First Hundred Years, 1867–1967* (1969).

LOGAN, RAYFORD, AND MICHAEL R. WINSTON. *Dictionary of American Negro Biography* (1982).

LOMAX, ALAN. *Mister Jelly Roll: The Fortunes of Jelly Roll Morton, New Orleans Creole and Inventor of Jazz* (1973).

———. *The Land Where the Blues Began* (1993).

LONG, RICHARD. *The Black Tradition in American Dance* (1989).

LOOS, DOROTHY SCOTT. *The Naturalistic Novel of Brazil* (1963).

LOPES, HELENA T. *Negro e cultura no Brasil* (1987).

LOPES, JOSÉ SERGIO LEITE. "Successes and Contradictions in 'Multiracial' Brazilian Football." In *Entering the Field: New Perspectives on World Football*, ed. Gary Armstrong and Richard Giulianotti (1997).

LOTZ, RAINER, AND IAN PEGG, EDS. *Under the Imperial Carpet: Essays in Black History, 1780–1950* (1990).

LOVE, NAT. *The Life and Adventures of Nat Love, Better Known in the Cattle Country as "Deadwood Dick"* (1907; reprint ed., 1995).

LOVE, SPENCIE. *One Blood: The Death and Resurrection of Charles Drew* (1996).

LOVETT, CHARLES C. *Olympic Marathon: A Centennial History of the Games' Most Storied Race* (1997).

LOZANO, WILFREDO, ED. *La cuestión haitiana en Santo Domingo* (1992).

LUIS, WILLIAM. *Literary Bondage: Slavery in Cuban Narrative* (1990).

———, ED. *Voices from Under: Black Narrative in Latin America and the Caribbean* (1984).

LUMDSEN, I. *Society and the State in Mexico* (1991).

LUNDY, ANNE. "Conversations with Three Symphonic Conductors: Dennis De Couteau, Tania Leon, Jon Robinson." *Black Perspective in Music*, no. 2 (Fall 1988): 213–25.

LYNCH, HOLLIS R. *Black American Radicals and the Liberation of Africa: The Council on African Affairs, 1937–1955* (1978).

LYNCH, JOHN ROY. *Reminiscences of an Active Life: The Autobiography of John Roy Lynch.* Edited by John Hope Franklin (1970).

LYONS, LEONARD. *The Great Jazz Pianists: Speaking of Their Lives and Music* (1983).

MACDONALD, J. FRED. *Blacks and White TV: African Americans in Television Since 1948.* Rev. ed. (1992).

MACEO, ANTONIO. *El pensamiento vivo de Maceo: Cartas, proclamas, artículos y documentas.* Edited by José Antonio Portuondo (1960).

MACGAFFEY, WYATT. *Religion and Society in Central Africa: The BaKongo of Lower Zaire* (1986).

MACHARIA, KINUTHIA. *Social and Political Dynamics of the Informal Economy in African Cities: Nairobi and Harare* (1997).

MACKEY, NATHANIEL, ED. "Wilson Harris Special Issue." *Callaloo* (1995).

MACROBERT, IAIN. *The Black Roots and White Racism of Early Pentecostalism in the U.S.A.* (1988).

MAES-JELINEK, HENA, ED. *Commonwealth Literature and the Modern World* (1975).

MAGALHÃES, R., JR. *A Vida Turbulenta de José do Patrocínio* (1972).

MAGUBANE, VUKANI. "Graca Machel." *Ebony* (May 1997).

MAIN, MICHAEL. *Kalahari: Life's Variety in Dune and Delta* (1987).

MAIO, MARCOS CHOR. *A História do Projeto UNESCO: Estudos raciais e ciências sociais no Brasil* (1997).

MAIR, GEORGE. *Oprah Winfrey: The Real Story* (1994).

MAKEBA, MIRIAM, WITH JAMES HALL. *Makeba: My Story* (1988).

MALCOLM X, WITH ALEX HALEY. *The Autobiography of Malcolm X* (1964).

MALONE, JACQUI. *Steppin' on the Blues: The Visible Rhythms of African-American Dance* (1996).

MALTBY, MARC S. *The Origins and Early Development of Professional Football* (1997).

MANDELA, NELSON. *Long Walk to Freedom: The Autobiography of Nelson Mandela* (1994).

——. *The Struggle Is My Life: His Speeches and Writings Brought Together to Mark His 60th Birthday* (1978).

MANESS, LONNIE E. "The Fort Pillow Massacre: Fact or Fiction." *Tennessee Historical Quarterly* 48 (Winter 1986): 287–315.

MANGIONE, JERRE. *The Dream and the Deal: The Federal Writers' Project, 1935–1945* (1972).

MANLEY, ALBERT E. *A Legacy Continues: The Manley Years at Spelman College, 1953–1976* (1995).

MANNICK, A. R. *Mauritius: The Politics of Change* (1989).

MANUEL, PETER, ED. *Essays on Cuban Music: North American and Cuban Perspectives* (1991).

MANUEL, PETER, WITH KENNETH BILBY AND MICHAEL LARGEY. *Caribbean Currents: Caribbean Music from Rumba to Reggae* (1995).

MANUH, TAKYIWAA. "Diasporas, Unities, and the Marketplace: Tracing Changes in Ghanaian Fashion." *Journal of African Studies* 16, no.1 (Winter 1998).

MAPP, EDWARD. *Directory of Blacks in the Performing Arts* (1990).

MARCUS, HAROLD G. *A History of Ethiopia* (1994).

MARKMANN, CHARLES LAM. *The Noblest Cry: A History of the American Civil Liberties Union* (1965).

MARKOWITZ, GERALD E., AND DAVID ROSNER. *Children, Race, and Power: Kenneth and Mamie Clark's Northside Center* (1996).

MARQUIS, DONALD M. *In Search of Buddy Bolden: First Man of Jazz* (1978).

MARSHALL, RICHARD, ET. AL. *Jean-Michel Basquiat* (1992).

MARSH, J. B. T. *The Story of the Jubilee Singers with Their Songs* (1880; reprint ed., 1971).

MARTEENA, CONSTANCE HILL. *The Lengthening Shadow of a Woman: A Biography of Charlotte Hawkins Brown* (1977).

MARTÍ, JOSÉ. *Cuba, Nuestra América, los Estados Unidos* (1973).

——. *En los Estados Unidos* (1968).

MARTIN, ESMOND BRADLEY. *Zanzibar: Tradition and Revolution* (1978).

MARTIN, JAY, ED. *A Singer in the Dawn: Reinterpretations of Paul Laurence Dunbar* (1975).

MARTIN, MARIE-LOUISE. *Kimbangu: An African Prophet and His Church* (1975).

MARTIN, MICHAEL T., ED. *Cinemas of the Black Diaspora: Diversity, Dependence, and Oppositionality* (1995).

MARTIN, REGINALD. *Ishmael Reed and the New Black Aesthetic Critics* (1988).

——. "Total Life Is What We Want: The Progressive Stages of the New Black Aesthetic in Literature." *South Atlantic Review* (November 1986): 46–47.

MARTINS, LEDA MARIA. *A cena em sombras* (1995).

MARTIN, TONY. *Race First: The Ideological and Organizational Struggles of Marcus Garvey and the Universal Negro Improvement Association* (1986).

MASON, TONY. *Passion of the People? Football in South America* (1995).

MATORY, J. LORAND. *Sex and the Empire That Is No More: Gender and the Politics of Metaphor in Oyo Yoruba Religion* (1994).

MATTA, ROBERTO DA. Carnivals, *Rogues, and Heroes: An Interpretation of the Brazilian Dilemma*. Translated by John Drury (1991).

MATTHEWS, MARCIA M. *Henry Ossawa Tanner, American Artist* (1969).

MATTOSO, KATIA M. DE QUEIRÓS. *To Be a Slave in Brazil, 1550–1888*. Translated by Arthur Goldhammer (1994).

MAYNARD, OLGA. *Judith Jamison: Aspects of a Dancer* (1982).

MAZRUI, ALI A. *The Africans: A Triple Heritage* (1986).

MCADAM, DOUG. *Freedom Summer* (1988).

MCBROOME, DELORES NASON. *Parallel Communities: African Americans in California's East Bay, 1850–1963* (1993).

MCCABE, BRUCE. "Bringing the Streets to the Stage." *Boston Globe* (April 18, 1997): F 3.

MCCORMICK, RICHARD P. "William Whipper: Moral Reformer." *Pennsylvania History* 43 (January 1976): 22–46.

MCDONNELL, PATRICK, KAREN O'CONNELL, AND GEORGIA RILEY DE HAVENON. *Krazy Kat: The Comic Art of George Herriman* (1986).

MCDOWELL, ROBERT. "The Assembling Vision of Rita Dove." *Callaloo* 9 (Winter 1986): 61–70.

MCELVAINE, ROBERT S. *The Great Depression: America, 1929–1941* (1984).

MCFEELY, WILLIAM S. *Frederick Douglass* (1991).

MCGOWAN, CHRIS, AND RICARDO PESSANHA. *The Brazilian Sound: Samba, Bossa Nova, and the Popular Music of Brazil* (1991).

MCKIBLE, ADAM. "'These Are the Facts of the Darky's History': Thinking History and Reading Names in Four African American Tests." *African American Review* 28 (1994): 223–35.

MCKIVIGAN, JOHN R. *The War against Proslavery Religion: Abolitionism and the Northern Churches, 1830–1865* (1984).

MCLARIN, KIMBERLY J. *Native Daughter* (1994).

MCLENDON, JACQUELYN Y. *The Politics of Color in the Fiction of Jessie Fauset and Nella Larsen* (1995).

McMILLAN, DELLA E. *Sahel Visions: Planned Settlement and River Blindness Control in Burkina Faso* (1995).

McMURRY, LINDA O. *Recorder of the Black Experience: A Biography of Monroe Nathan Work* (1985).

McNEIL, GENNA RAE. *Groundwork: Charles Hamilton Houston and the Struggle for Civil Rights* (1983).

McPHERSON, JAMES M. *The Negro's Civil War: How American Negroes Felt and Acted During the War for the Union* (1965).

MEIER, AUGUST. "Introduction: Benjamin Quarles and the Historiography of Black America." In *Benjamin Quarles, Black Mosaic: Essays in Afro-American History and Historiography* (1989): 3–21.

——. *Negro Thought in America, 1880–1915: Racial Ideologies in the Age of Booker T. Washington* (1963).

MEIER, AUGUST, AND JOHN H. BRACEY, JR. "The NAACP as a Reform Movement: 1909–1965." *Journal of Southern History* 49, no. 1 (February 1993).

MEIER, AUGUST, AND ELLIOTT RUDWICK. *Black History and the Historical Profession* (1986).

——. *CORE: A Study in the Civil Rights Movement, 1942–1968* (1973).

MELHEM, D.H. "Dudley Randall: A Humanist View." *Black American Literature Forum* 17 (1983).

MELLAFE R., ROLANDO. *La introducción de la esclavitud negra en Chile: Tráfico y rutas* (1984).

MENTON, SEYMOUR. *Prose Fiction of the Cuban Revolution* (1975).

MERCER, K. "Imagining the Black Man's Sex." In *Photography/Politics: Two*, ed. P. Holland et. al. (1987).

MÉRIAN, JEAN-YVES. *Aluísio Azevedo, Vida e Obra (1857–1913): O Verdadeiro Brasil do Século XIX* (1988).

METCALF, GEORGE R. *Black Profiles* (1968).

MÉTRAUX, ALFRED. "UNESCO and the Racial Problem." *International Social Science Bulletin* 2, no. 3 (1950): 384–90.

——. *Voodoo in Haiti* (1959).

MIDDLETON, JOHN, ED. *Encyclopedia of Africa South of the Sahara*. 4 vols. (1997).

MILES, ALEXANDER. *Devil's Island: Colony of the Damned* (1988).

MILLER, ERROL. *Education for All: Caribbean Perspectives and Imperatives* (1992).

MILLER, FLOYD J. *The Search for a Black Nationality: Black Colonization and Emigration, 1787–1863* (1975).

MILLER, RANDALL M., AND JOHN DAVID SMITH, EDS. *Dictionary of Afro-American Slavery.* 2d ed. (1997).

MILLS, KAY. "Maxine Waters: 'I Don't Pretend to Be Nice No Matter What . . .'." *The Progressive* (December 1993).

MINER, HORACE. *The Primitive City of Timbuctoo* (1954).

MINNICK-TAYLOR, KATHLEEN, AND CHARLES TAYLOR II. *Kwanzaa: How to Celebrate It in Your Own Home* (1994).

MINORITY RIGHTS GROUP, ED. *No Longer Invisible: Afro-Latin Americans Today* (1995).

MINTER, WILLIAM. *Apartheid's Contras: An Inquiry into the Roots of War in Angola and Mozambique* (1994).

MINTZ, SIDNEY. *Sweetness and Power* (1985).

MINTZ, SIDNEY, AND SALLY PRICE, EDS. *Caribbean Contours* (1985).

MIMANYARA, ALFRED M. *The Restatement of Bantu Origin and Meru History* (1992).

MOBERG, MARK. *Myths of Ethnicity and Nation: Immigration, Work, and Identity in the Belize Banana Industry* (1997).

Models in the Mind: African Prototypes in American Patchwork (1992).

MOISE, CLAUDE. *Constitutions et luttes de pouvoir en Haiti (1804–1987)* (1988–1990).

MOISÉS, MASSAUD. *História da literatura Brasileira. Vol. II* (1989).

MOON, ELAINE LATZMAN, ED. *Untold Tales, Unsung Heroes: An Oral History of Detroit's African American Community, 1918–1967* (1994).

MOOREHEAD, ALAN. *The White Nile* (1971).

MOORE, JESSE THOMAS. *A Search for Equality: The National Urban League, 1910–1961* (1981).

MOORE, JOSEPH THOMAS. *Pride Against Prejudice: The Biography of Larry Doby* (1988).

MOORE, ROBIN. *Nationalizing Blackness: Afrocubanismo and Artistic Revolution in Havana, 1920–40* (1997).

MOORE, ZELBERT L. "Solano Trindade Remembered, 1908–1974." *Luso-Brazilian Review* 16 (1979): 233–38.

MORALES, FLORENTINO. "El poeta esclavo." *Conceptos* 2, no. 27 (December 1989): 2–3.

MORAN, CHARLES. *Black Triumvirate: A Study of L'Ouverture, Dessalines, Christophe: The Men Who Made Haiti* (1957).

MORDECAI, PAMELA, AND BETTY WILSON, EDS. *Her True-True Name* (1989).

MORELL, VIRGINIA. *Ancestral Passions: The Leakey Family and the Quest for Humankind's Beginnings* (1995).

MORENO NAVARRO, ISIDORO. *Los cuadros del mestizaje americano: Estudio antropológico del mestizaje* (1973).

MORGAN, PHILIP D. *Slave Counterpoint: Black Culture in the Eighteenth-Century Chesapeake and Lowcountry* (1998).

MORGAN, THOMAS L., AND WILLIAM BARLOW. *From Cakewalks to Concert Halls: An Illustrated History of African American Popular Music from 1895–1930* (1992).

MORNA, COLLEEN. "Graca Machel: Interview." *Africa Report* (July-August 1988).

MORRIS, MERVYN. "Louise Bennett." In *Encyclopedia of Post-Colonial Literatures in English*. Vol. I, ed. Eugene Benson and L. W. Conolly (1994).

MORRIS, THOMAS D. *Free Men All: The Personal Liberty Laws of the North, 1780–1861* (1974).

MORRISON, TONI. *Playing in the Dark: Whiteness and the Literary Imagination* (1992).

——, ED. *Race-ing Justice, En-gendering Power: Essays on Anita Hill, Clarence Thomas, and the Construction of Social Reality* (1992).

MORROW, CURTIS. *What's A Commie Ever Done to Black People?: A Korean War Memoir of Fighting in the U.S. Army's Last All Negro Unit* (1997).

MORSE, STEPHEN S. *Emerging Viruses* (1993).

MORSHA, A. C. "Urban Planning in Tanzania at the Crossroads." *Review of Rural and Urban Planning in Southern and Eastern Africa* (1989): 79–91.

MOSBY, DEWEY F., DARRELL SEWELL, AND RAE ALEXANDER-MINTER. *Henry Ossawa Tanner* (1991).

MOSELEY, THOMAS ROBERT. "A History of the New York Manumission Society." Ph.D. Diss. University of Michigan, 1963.

MOSES, WILSON JEREMIAH. *Black Messiahs and Uncle Toms: Social and Literary Manipulation of a Religious Myth* (1982).

——. *The Golden Age of Black Nationalism: 1850–1925* (1978).

MOSQUERA, GERARDO. "Modernism from Afro-America: Wifredo Lam." In *Beyond the Fantastic: Contemporary Art Criticism from Latin America*, ed. Gerardo Mosquera (1996).

MOSS, ALFRED A., JR. *The American Negro Academy: Voice of the Talented Tenth* (1981).

MOTA, ANA MARITZA DE LA. "Palma Sola: 1962," *Boletín: Museo de hombre dominicano* 14 (1980): 197–223.

MOTT, LUIZ. Escravidão, *Homossexualidade e Demonologia* (1988).

MOUNTOUSSAMY-ASHE, JEANNE. *View-finders: Black Women Photographers* (1986).

MUDIMBE-BOYI, ELISABETH. *L'oeuvre romanesque de Jacques-Stéphen Alexis : Une écriture poétique, un engagement politique* (1992).

MUDIMBE, VALENTIN. *The Invention of Africa: Gnosis, Philosophy, and the Order of Knowledge* (1988).

MUNFORD, CLARENCE. *Race and Reparations: A Black Perspective for the Twenty-First Century* (1996).

MUNRO-HAY, STUART. *Aksum: An African Civilization of Late Antiquity* (1991).

MUNRO-HAY, STUART, AND RICHARD PANKHURST. *Ethiopia* (1995).

MUNSLOW, BARRY, ED. *Samora Machel, An African Revolutionary: Selected Speeches and Writings* (1985).

MURPHY, JOSEPH M. *Working the Spirit: Ceremonies of the African Diaspora* (1994).

MURRAY, PAULI. *Dark Testament and Other Poems* (1970).

———. *Proud Shoes: The Story of an American Family* (1956).

———. *Song in a Weary Throat: An American Pilgrimage* (1987).

MUSICK, PHIL. *Reflections on Roberto* (1994).

MYRDAL, GUNNAR. *An American Dilemma: The Negro Problem and Modern Democracy* (1944).

NADEL, ALAN, ED. *May All of Your Fences Have Gates: Essays on the Drama of August Wilson* (1994).

NAISON, MARK. *Communists in Harlem During the Depression* (1983).

NALTY, BERNARD C. *Strength for the Fight: A History of Black Americans in the Military* (1986).

NASCIMENTO, ABDIAS DO. *Africans in Brazil: A Pan-African Perspective* (1992).

———. *Dramas para negros e prologo para brancos: Antologia de teatro negro-brasileiro.* (1961).

———. *Orixas: Os deuses vivos da Africa* (1995).

———. *O quilombismo: Documentos de uma militancia pan-africanista* (1980).

——. *Racial Democracy in Brazil, Myth or Reality?: A Dossier of Brazilian Racism.* Translated by Elisa Larkin do Nascimento; foreword by Wole Soyinka (1977).

——, ED. *O Negro revoltado* (1968).

NASH, GARY B. *Forging Freedom: The Formation of Philadelphia's Black Community, 1720–1840* (1988).

——. *Race and Revolution* (1990).

NAVARRETE, MARÍA CRISTINA. *Historia social del negro en la colonia: Cartagena, siglo XVII* (1995).

NAVARRO, DESIDERIO. *Ejercicios del criterio* (1988).

NEFT, DAVID S. *The Football Encyclopedia: The Complete History of Professional NFL Football, from 1892 to the Present* (1991).

NEWBY, I. A. *Black Carolinians: A History of Blacks in South Carolina from 1895 to 1968* (1973).

NEWFIELD, JACK. *Only in America: The Life and Crimes of Don King* (1995).

NEWMAN, RICHARD. *Words Like Freedom: Essays on African-American Culture and History* (1996).

——. Lemuel Haynes: *A Bio-bibliography* (1984).

——, COMP. *Black Access: A Bibliography of Afro-American Bibliographies* (1984).

NEWTON, HUEY P. *To Die for the People: The Writings of Huey Newton* (1972).

——. *War Against the Panthers: A Study of Repression in America* (1997).

"New Voice of the NAACP." Interview in *Newsweek* 46 (November 22, 1976).

NGUGI WA THIONG'O. *Decolonising the Mind: The Politics of Language in African Literature* (1986).

——. *Moving the Centre: The Struggle for Cultural Freedoms* (1993).

NICOLAS, ARMAND. *Histoire de la Martinique.* 2 vols. (1996).

——. *La Révolution antiesclavagiste de mai 1848 à la Martinique* (1967).

NINA RODRIGUES, RAIMUNDO. *Os Africanos no Brasil* (1977).

NKOMO, JOSHUA. *Nkomo: The Story of My Life* (1984).

——. *Zimbabwe Must and Shall be Totally Free* (1977).

NOBLE, PETER. *The Negro in Films* (1948).

NOBRE, CARLOS. *Mães de Acari: Uma história de luta contra a impunidade* (1994).

NOONAN, JOHN T. *The Antelope: The Ordeal of the Recaptured Africans in the Administrations of James Monroe and John Quincy Adams* (1977).

NORMENT, LYNN. "Vanessa L. Williams: On her Painful Divorce, the Pressures of Superstardom and her New Life as a Single Mom." *Ebony* (October 1997).

NORRIS, H. T. *The Berbers in Arabic Literature* (1982).

NORRIS, JERRIE. *Presenting Rosa Guy* (1988).

NORTHRUP, SOLOMON. *Twelve Years a Slave: Narrative of Solomon Northrup, a Citizen of New York, Kidnapped in Washington City in 1841, and Rescued in 1853, from a Cotton Plantation near the Red River, in Louisiana* (1853).

NOTCUTT, LESLIE A., AND GEORGE C. Lantham. *The African and the Cinema: An Account of the Bantu Educational Cinema Experiment During the Period March 1935 to May 1937* (1937).

NOTTEN, ELEONORE VAN. *Wallace Thurman's Harlem Renaissance* (1994).

NUGENT, JOHN PEER. *Black Eagle* (1971).

NUNN, JOHN F. *Ancient Egyptian Medicine* (1996).

NYERERE, JULIUS K. *The Arusha Declaration: Ten Years After* (1977).

——. *Freedom and Socialism: Uhuru na Ujamaa: A Selection from Writings and Speeches, 1965–1967* (1968).

——. *Ujamaa: Essays on Socialism* (1971).

OATES, STEPHEN B. *The Fires of Jubilee: Nat Turner's Fierce Rebellion* (1975).

——. *To Purge This Land with Blood: A Biography of John Brown.* 2d ed. (1984).

OBADELE, IMARI. *America the Nation State: The Politics of the United States from a State-Building Perspective* (1988).

OCHS, STEPHEN J. *Desegregating the Altar: The Josephites and the Struggle for Black Priests, 1871–1960* (1970).

OFCANSKY, THOMAS, AND RODGER YEAGER. *Historical Dictionary of Tanzania* (1997).

OGOT, BETHWELL A. *Africa and the Caribbean* (1997).

OÍLIAM, JOSÉ. *O Negro na Economia Mineira* (1993).

OLANIYAN, TEJUMOLA. *Scars of Conquest/Masks of Resistance: The Invention of Cultural Identities in African, African-American, and Caribbean Drama* (1995).

OLIVER, PAUL. *Songsters and Saints: Vocal Traditions on Race Records* (1984).

——, ED. *Black Music in Britain: Essays on the Afro-Asian Contribution to Popular Music* (1990).

OLSON, JAMES STUART. *The Peoples of Africa: An Ethnohistorical Dictionary* (1996).

OLSON, SHERRY. *Baltimore: The Building of an American City*. Rev. and exp. ed. (1997).

OLWIG, KAREN FOG. *Cultural Adaptation and Resistance on St. John: Three Centuries of Afro-Caribbean Life*.

O'MEALLY, ROBERT G. *The Craft of Ralph Ellison* (1980).

OODIAH, MALENN. *Mouvement militant mauritien: 20 ans d'histoire (1969–1989)* (1989).

O'REILLY, KENNETH. *Nixon's Piano: Presidents and Racial Politics from Washington to Clinton* (1995).

ORIARD, MICHAEL. *Reading Football: How the Popular Press Created an American Spectacle* (1993).

ORMOND, ROGER. *The Apartheid Handbook: A Guide to South Africa's Everyday Racial Policies* (1985).

OROVIO, HELIO. *Diccionario de la música cubana: Biográfico y técnico* (1992).

ORTIZ, FERNANDO. *Los bailes y le teatro de los negros en el folklore de cuba* (1951).

———. *Los instrumentos de la musica afrocubana*. 5 vols. (1952–1955).

———. *La música afrocubana* (1974).

———. *Los negros brujos* (1995).

———. *Wifredo Lam y su obra vista a traves de significados criticos* (1950).

ORTIZ, RENATO, "Ogum and the Umbandista Religion." *In Africa's Ogun: Old World and New*, ed. Santra Barnes (1989): 90–102.

OSOFSKY, GILBERT. *Harlem: The Making of a Ghetto: Negro New York, 1890–1930* (1971; revised ed., 1996).

OSPINA, HERNANDO CALVO. *Salsa: Havana Beat, Bronx Beat* (1985).

OSSMAN, SUSAN. *Picturing Casablanca: Portraits of Power in a Modern City* (1994).

OTHAM, HAROUB. *Zanzibar's Political History: The Past Haunting the Present?* (1993).

OTIS, JOHNNY. *Upside Your Head!: Rhythm and Blues on Central Avenue* (1993).

OTTLEY, ROI. *The Lonely Warrior: The Life and Time of Robert S. Abbott* (1955).

OTTLEY, ROI AND WILLIAM WEATHERBY, EDS. *The Negro in New York: An Informal Social History* (1967).

OWENS, THOMAS. *Bebop: The Music and its Players* (1995).

PACINI HERNÁNDEZ, DEBORAH. "The Picó Phenomenon in Cartagena, Colombia." *América Negra* 6 (December 1993): 69–115.

PAINTER, NELL IRVIN. *Exodusters: Black Migration to Kansas after Reconstruction* (1986).

———. "Martin R. Delany: Elitism and Black Nationalism." In *Black Leaders of the Nineteenth Century*, ed. Leon Litwack and August Meier (1988): 148–171.

———. *Sojourner Truth: A Life, A Symbol* (1996).

PAIVA, EDUARDO FRANCA. *Escravos e libertos nas Minas Gerais do século XVIII: Estratégias de resisténcia através dos testamentos* (1995).

PALMER, COLIN. *Slaves of the White God: Blacks in Mexico, 1570–1650* (1976).

PALMER, RICHARD. *Oscar Peterson* (1984).

PALMER, ROBERT. *Deep Blues* (1981).

PAQUET, SANDRA POUCHET. *The Novels of George Lamming* (1982).

PARIS, PETER. *Black Religious Leaders: Conflict in Unity* (1991).

PARK, THOMAS K. *Historical Dictionary of Morocco* (1996).

PATTERSON, JAMES T. *America's Struggle Against Poverty, 1900–1994* (1994).

PATTERSON, ORLANDO. *Freedom in the Making of Western Culture* (1991).

———. *The Ordeal of Integration: Progress and Resentment in America's "Racial" Crisis* (1997).

———. *Rituals of Blood: Consequences of Slavery in Two American Centuries* (1998).

PATTERSON, WILLIAM. *The Man Who Cried Genocide: An Autobiography* (1971).

PAUL, JOAN, RICHARD V. McGhee, and Helen Fant. "The Arrival and Ascendance of Black Athletes in the Southeastern Conference, 1966–1980." *Phylon* 45, no. 4 (1984): 284–97.

PAYNE, DANIEL A. *History of the African Methodist Episcopal Church*. Vol. I (1891; reprint ed., 1968).

PEASE, JANE H., AND WILLIAM H. PEASE. *They Who Would Be Free: Blacks' Search for Freedom, 1830–1861* (1974).

PENKOWER, MONTY NOAM. *The Federal Writers' Project: A Study in Government Patronage of the Arts* (1983).

PENVENNE, JEANNE. *African Workers and Colonial Racism: Mozambican Struggles in Lourenço Marques, 1877–1962* (1997).

PÉREZ SANJURJO, ELENA. *Historia de la música cubana* (1986).

PERKINS, KENNETH J. *Historical Dictionary of Tunisia* (1997).

PERKINS, LINDA M. *Fanny Jackson Coppin and the Institute for Colored Youth: A Model of Nineteenth-Century Black Female Educational and Community Leadership, 1865–1902* (1978).

PERLMAN, JANICE. *The Myth of Marginality: Urban Poverty and Politics in Rio de Janeiro* (1973).

PERN, STEPHEN. *Another Land, Another Sea: Walking Round Lake Rudolph* (1979).

PERRY, BRUCE. *Malcolm: The Life of a Man Who Changed Black America* (1991).

PERRY, REGINA A. *Free Within Ourselves: African-American Artists in the Collection of the National Museum of American Art* (1992).

PETERSON, CARLA. *Doers of the Word: African-American Women Speakers and Writers in the North (1830–1880)* (1995).

PETERSON, KIRSTEN HOLST, AND ANNA RUTHERFORD. *Chinua Achebe: A Celebration* (1991).

PETERSON, ROBERT. *Only the Ball Was White: A History of Legendary Black Players and All-black Professional Teams* (1992).

PETERS, WALLACE, AND HERBERT M. GILLES. *Color Atlas of Tropical Medicine and Parasitology* (1995).

PFAFF, FRANÇOISE. *Conversations with Maryse Condé* (1996).

PHELPS, J. ALFRED. *Chappie: America's First Black Four-Star General: The Life and Times of Daniel James, Jr.* (1991).

PHELPS, TIMOTHY M., AND HELEN WINTERNITZ. *Capitol Games: The Inside Story of Clarence Thomas and Anita Hill, and a Supreme Court Nomination* (1993).

PHILLIPS, CHRISTOPHER. *Freedom's Port: The African American Community of Baltimore, 1790–1860* (1997).

PICTON, JOHN, AND JOHN MACK. *African Textiles* (1989).

PIMPÃO, ÁLVARO JÚLIO DA COSTA. "José Basilio da Gama. Edição Comemorativa do Segundo Centenário." *Brasília* 2 (1942): 777–80.

PINO, JULIO CESAR. *Family and Favela: The Reproduction of Poverty in Rio de Janeiro* (1997).

PINTO, LUIZ DE AGUIAR COSTA. *O Negro no Rio de Janeiro: Relações de raças numa sociedade em mudança* (1953).

PIVEN, FRANCES FOX, AND RICHARD A. Cloward. *Poor People's Movements: Why They Succeed, How They Fail* (1977).

PLACKSIN, SALLY. *American Women in Jazz: 1900 to the Present: Their Words, Lives, and Music* (1982).

PLACOLY, VINCENT. *Dessalines, ou, la passion de l'indépendance* (1983).

PLASTOW, JANE. *Ethiopia: The Creation of a Theater Culture* (1989).

PLATO, ANN. *Essays: Including Biographies and Miscellaneous Pieces, in Prose and Poetry* (1841).

PLATT, ANTHONY M. *E. Franklin Frazier Reconsidered* (1991).

PLOWDEN, MARTHA WARD. *Olympic Black Women* (1996).

PLUCHON, PIERRE, AND LOUIS ABENON, EDS. *Histoire des Antilles et de la Guyane* (1982).

POITIER, SIDNEY. *This Life* (1980).

POLAKOFF, CLAIRE. *Into Indigo: African Textiles and Dyeing Techniques* (1980).

POLLAK-ELTZ, ANGELINA. *Black Culture and Society in Venezuela (La Negritud en Venezuela)* (1994).

——. *La medicina popular en Venezuela* (1987).

——. *La religiosidad popular en Venezuela* (1994).

PORTER, DAVID L., ED. *Biographical Dictionary of American Sports: Basketball and Other Indoor Sports* (1989).

PORTER, DOROTHY B. "Maria Baldwin." *Journal of Negro History* (Winter 1952): 94–96.

PORTER, JAMES AMOS. *Modern Negro Art* (1943).

POSADA, CONSUELO. *Canción vallenata y tradición oral* (1986).

POTASH, CHRIS, ED. *Reggae, Rasta, Revolution: Jamaican Music from Ska to Dub* (1997).

POTTER, DAVID M. *The Impending Crisis, 1848–1861* (1976).

POUPEYE, VEERLE. *Modern Jamaican Art* (1998).

POVOAS, RUY DO CARMO. *A linguagem do candomble: Niveis sociolinguisticos de integração afro-portuguesa* (1989).

POWELL, COLIN L. *My American Journey* (1995).

POWELL, IVOR. *Ndebele: A People and Their Art* (1995).

POWELL, RICHARD J. *Black Art and Culture in the Twentieth Century* (1997).

——. *Homecoming: The Art and Life of William H. Johnson* (1991).

POWLEDGE, FRED. *Free at Last? The Civil Rights Movement and the People Who Made It* (1991).

PRANDI, J. REGINALDO. *Herdeiras do axé: Sociologia das religiões afro-brasileiras* (1996).

PRATHER, H. LEON. *We Have Taken A City: Wilmington Racial Massacre and Coup of 1898* (1984).

PRESCOTT, LAURENCE E. *Candelario Obeso y la iniciación de la poesía negra en Colombia* (1985).

PRICE, JOE X. *Redd Foxx, B.S. (Before Sanford)* (1979).

PRICE-MARS, JEAN. *La República de Haití y la República Dominicana* (1958).

PRICE, RICHARD, ED. *Maroon Societies: Rebel Slave Communities in the Americas.* 3d ed. (1996).

PRICE, SALLY, AND RICHARD PRICE. *Maroon Arts: Cultural Vitality in the African Diaspora* (1999).

PRIDE, CHARLEY. *Pride: The Charley Pride Story* (1994).

PRIMM, JAMES NEAL. *Lion of the Valley, St. Louis, Missouri* (1981).

PRUTER, ROBERT. *Doowop: The Chicago Scene* (1996).

PRYSE, MARJORIE. "'Patterns Against the Sky': Deism and the Motherhood in Ann Petry's *The Street*." In *Conjuring: Black Women, Fiction and Literary Traditions*, ed. Marjorie Pryse and Hortense Spillers (1985).

QUARLES, BENJAMIN. *Black Abolitionists* (1969).

——. *The Negro in the American Revolution* (1961).

——. *The Negro in the Civil War* (1953).

QUERINO, MANUEL. *The African Contribution to Brazilian Civilization.* Translated by E. Bradford Burns (1978).

——. *A Bahia de Outoura* (1955).

——. *Costumes africanos no Brasil* (1938).

——. *A raça africana e os seus costumes* (1955).

QUILLEN, FRANK U. *The Color Line in Ohio* (1913).

QUILOMBHOJE. *Criação crioula, nu elefante branco* (1987).

QUINN, CHARLOTTE. *Mandingo Kingdoms of the Senegambia: Traditionalism, Islam, and European Expansion* (1972).

QUIROZ OTERO, CIRO. *Vallenato: Hombre y canto* (1982).

RABINOWITZ, HOWARD N. *Race Relations in the Urban South, 1865–1890* (1996).

RAGAN, SANDRA L. ET AL, ED. *The Lynching of Language: Gender, Politics, and Power in the Hill-Thomas Hearings* (1996).

RAHIER, JEAN. *La décima: Poesía oral negra del Ecuador* (1987).

RAINWATER, LEE. *Behind Ghetto Walls: Black Families in a Federal Slum* (1970).

RAJOELINA, PATRICK. *Quarante années de la vie politique de Madagascar, 1947–1987* (1988).

RAKE, ALAN. *Who's Who in Africa: Leaders for the 1990s* (1992).

RAKODI, CAROLE. *Harare: Inheriting a Settler-Colonial City: Change or Continuity* (1995).

RAMOS, ARTHUR. *The Negro in Brazil* (1951).

RAMOS GUEDEZ, JOSÉ MARCIAL. *El negro en Venezuela: Aporte bibliografico* (1985).

RAMPERSAD, ARNOLD. *The Art and Imagination of W. E. B. Du Bois* (1990).

——. *Jackie Robinson: A Biography* (1997).

——. *The Life of Langston Hughes.* 2 vols. (1986–1988).

RANVAUD, DON. "Interview with Med Hondo." *Framework* (Spring 1978): 28–30.

Rap on Rap: Straight Up Talk on Hip Hop Culture. Compiled by Adam Sexton (1995).

RASKY, FRANK. "Harlem's Religious Zealots." *Tomorrow* (Nov. 1949): 11–17.

RAPER, ARTHUR F. *The Tragedy of Lynching* (1933).

RAWLEY, JAMES A. *The Transatlantic Slave Trade: A History* (1981).

RAY, BENJAMIN. *African Religions: Symbol, Ritual, and Community* (1976).

READER, JOHN. *Africa: A Biography of the Continent* (1998).

READ, FLORENCE. *The Story of Spelman College* (1961).

REDD, LAWRENCE N. *Rock Is Rhythm and Blues: The Impact of Mass Media* (1974).

REDKEY, EDWIN S. *Black Exodus: Black Nationalist and Back-to-Africa Movements, 1890–1910* (1969).

REDMON, COATES. *Come As You Are: The Peace Corps Story* (1986).

REGO, WALDELOIR. *Capoeira Angola: Ensaio socio-etnografico* (1968).

REID, CALVIN. "Caught in the Flux." *Transition* (Spring 1995).

REID, IRA DE AUGUSTINE. *The Negro Immigrant: His Background, Characteristics, and Social Adjustment, 1899–1937* (1939).

REIS, JOÃO JOSÉ. *Slave Rebellion in Brazil: The Muslim Uprising of 1835 in Bahia.* Translated by Arthur Brakel (1993).

"Religious Symbolism in African-American Quilts." *Clarion* 14, no. 3, (Summer 1989): 36–43.

Report of the National Advisory Commission on Civil Disorders (1968).

RENDER, SYLVIA LYONS. *Charles W. Chesnutt* (1980).

RESWICK, IRMTRAUD. *Traditional Textiles of Tunisia and Related North African Weavings* (1985).

REYNOLDS, MOIRA DAVIDSON. *"Uncle Tom's Cabin" and Mid-Nineteenth Century United States: Pen and Conscience* (1985).

RIBEIRO, RENÉ. *Religião e relações raciais* (1956).

RIBOWSKY, MARK. *Don't Look Back: Satchel Paige and the Shadows of Baseball* (1994).

RICHARDS, LEONARD L. *Gentleman of Property and Standing: Anti-Abolition Mobs in Jacksonian America* (1970).

RICHARDSON, JOE M. *A History of Fisk University, 1865–1946* (1980).

RICHARDSON, MICHAEL, ED. *Refusal of the Shadow: Surrealism and the Caribbean.* Translated by Krzysztof Fijalkowski and Michael Richardson (1996).

RICHMOND, MERLE. *Bid the Vassal Soar: Interpretative Essays on the Life and Poetry of Phillis Wheatley* (ca. 1753–1784) and George Moses Horton (ca. 1797–1883) (1974).

RICH, WILBUR C. *Black Mayors and School Politics: The Failure of Reform in Detroit, Gary, and Newark* (1996).

——. *The New Black Power* (1987).

RILEY, JAMES A. *The Biographical Encyclopedia of the Negro Baseball Leagues* (1994).

——. *Dandy, Day and the Devil* (1987).

RINGGOLD, FAITH. *We Flew Over the Bridge: The Memoirs of Faith Ringgold* (1995).

RISHELL, LYLE. *With A Black Platoon in Combat: A Year in Korea* (1993).

RITCHIE, CARSON. *Rock Art of Africa* (1979).

RITZ, DAVID. *Divided Soul: The Life of Marvin Gaye* (1985).

RIVLIN, BENJAMIN, ED. *Ralph Bunche: The Man and His Times* (1990).

RIVLIN, GARY. *Fire on the Prairie: Chicago's Harold Washington and the Politics of Race* (1993).

ROBERTS, JOHN STORM. *The Latin Tinge: The Impact of Latin American Music on the United States* (1979).

ROBERTS, A. D. "Tippu Tip, Livingstone, and the Chronology of Kazembe." *Azamoa* 2 (1967).

ROBERTS, ANDREW. *A History of Zambia* (1976).

ROBERTS, A. "Nyamwezi Trade." In *Pre-colonial African Trade,* ed. R. Gray and D. Birmingham (1970).

ROBERTS, MARTIN. "'World Music' and the Global Cultural Economy." *Diaspora* 2, no. 2 (1992): 229–41.

ROBERTS, RANDY. *Papa Jack: Jack Johnson and the Era of White Hopes* (1983).

ROBESON, PAUL. *Here I Stand* (1958).

ROBESON, SUSAN. *The Whole World in His Hands: A Pictorial Biography of Paul Robeson* (1981).

ROBINSON, DONALD. *Slavery in the Structure of American Politics, 1765–1820* (1971).

ROBINSON, JACKIE, WITH ALFRED DUCKETT. *I Never Had It Made* (1972).

ROBINSON, JO ANN GIBSON. *The Montgomery Bus Boycott and the Women Who Started It: The Memoir of Jo Ann Robinson* (1987).

ROBINSON, JONTYLE THERESA, AND WENDY GREENHOUSE. *The Art of Archibald J. Motley, Jr.* (1991).

ROBINSON, RAY, AND DAVE ANDERSON. *Sugar Ray* (1969).

ROBINSON, WILLIAM H. *Phillis Wheatley and Her Writings* (1984).

RODMAN, SELDEN. *Renaissance in Haiti: Popular Painters in the Black Republic* (1948).

——. *Where Art is Joy: Haitian Art: The First Forty Years* (1988).

RODNEY, WALTER. *A History of the Guyanese Working People, 1881–1905.* (1981).

ROGERS, KIM LACY. *Righteous Lives: Narratives of the New Orleans Civil Rights Movement* (1993).

ROLLIN, FRANK A. *Life and Public Services of Martin R. Delany, Sub-assistant Commissioner, Bureau Relief of Refugees, Freedmen, and of Abandoned Lands, and Late Major 104th U.S. Colored Troops* (1868).

ROLLOCK, BARBARA. *Black Authors and Illustrators of Children's Books* (1988).

ROMAINE, SUZANNE. *Bilingualism* (1989).

RONDÓN, CÉSAR MIGUEL. *El libro de la salsa: Cronica de la música del Caribe urbano* (1980).

RO, RONIN. *Gangsta: Merchandizing the Rhymes of Violence* (1996).

ROSE, AL. *Eubie Blake* (1979).

ROSELLO, MIREILLE. *Littérature et identité créole aux Antilles* (1992).

ROSE, TRICIA. *Black Noise: Rap Music and Black Culture in Contemporary America* (1994).

ROSE, WILLIE LEE, ED. *A Documentary History of Slavery in North America* (1976).

Ross, B. Joyce. *J. E. Spingarn and the Rise of the NAACP, 1911–1939* (1972).

Roth, David. *Sacred Honor: A Biography of Colin Powell* (1993).

Roulhe, Nellie C. *Work, Play, and Commitment: A History of the First Fifty Years, Jack and Jill of America, Incorporated* (1989).

Rout, Leslie B. *The African Experience in Spanish America, 1502 to the Present Day* (1976).

Rovine, Victoria. "Bogolanfini in Bamako: The Biography of a Malian Textile." *African Arts* 30 (1997).

Rowell, Charles H., and Bruce Willis. "Interview with Afro-Brazilian playwright and poet Luiz Silva Cuti." *Callaloo* 18, no. 4 (Fall 1996): 729–33.

Rueda Novoa, Rocío. *Zambaje y autonomìa: La historia de Esmeraldas siglos XVI-XIX* (1990).

Ruedy, John. *Modern Algeria: The Origins and Development of a Nation* (1992).

Rudwick, Elliott M. *Race Riot at East St. Louis, July 2, 1917* (1964).

Ruff, Shawn Stewart. *Go the Way Your Blood Beats: An Anthology of Lesbian and Gay Fiction by African-American Writers* (1996).

Rule, Sheila. "Fredi Washington, 90, Actress; Broke Ground for Black Artists." *New York Times* (June 30, 1994): D21.

Russell, Ross. *Bird Lives: The High Life and Hard Times of Charlie (Yardbird) Parker* (1973).

——. *Jazz Style in Kansas City and the Southwest* (1971).

Russell-Wood, A. J. R. *The Black Man in Slavery and Freedom in Colonial Brazil* (1982).

Sack, Kevin. "A Dynamic Farewell from a Longtime Rights Leader." *New York Times* (July 29, 1997).

——. "Ex-Charlotte Mayor Earns Helms Rematch." *New York Times* (May 8, 1996): B10.

Sagini, Mashak M. *The African and the African American University: A Historical and Sociological Analysis* (1996).

Salem, Norma. Habib *Bourguiba, Islam and the Creation of Tunisia* (1984).

Salzman, Jack, David Lionel Smith, and Cornel West, eds. *Encyclopedia of African-American Culture and History.* 5 vols. (1996).

Samkange, Stanlake. *What Rhodes Really Said About Africans* (1982).

Sammons, Jeffrey T. *Beyond the Ring: The Role of Boxing in American Society* (1988).

SAMMONS, VIVIAN O. *Blacks in Science and Medicine* (1990).

SÁNCHEZ-BOUDY, JOSÉ. *Diccionario de cubanismos más usuales (Como habla el cubano)*. 6 vols. (1978–1992).

SANDERSON, PETER. *Marvel Universe* (1995).

SANDOVAL, ALONSO DE. *De instauranda aethiopum salute - Un tratado sobre la esclavitud.* Translated by Enriqueta Vila Vilar (1987).

SAN MIGUEL, PEDRO. "The Dominican Peasantry and the Market Economy: The Peasants of the Cibao: 1880–1960." Ph.D. diss. Columbia University, 1987.

———. "The Making of a Peasantry: Dominican Agrarian History from the Sixteenth to the Twentieth Century." *Punto y Coma* 2, nos.1 and 2 (1990): 143–62.

SANTINO, JACK. *Miles of Smiles, Years of Struggle: Stories of Black Pullman Porters* (1989).

SANTOS, SYDNEY M. G. DOS. *André Rebouças e seu tempo* (1985).

SARTRE, JEAN-PAUL. "Orphée Noire." *Situations* 3 (1949): 227–86.

SATCHEL, LEROY. *Pitchin' Man: Satchel Paige's Own Story* (1992).

SATER, WILLIAM F. "The Black Experience in Chile." *In Slavery and Race Relations in Latin America*, ed. Robert Brent Toplin (1974).

SAUNDERS, A. C. *A Social History of Black Slaves and Freedmen in Portugal (1441–1555)* (1982).

SAVIANI, DERMEVAL, GERMAN RAMA, NORBERTO LAMARRA, INÉS AGUERRONDO, AND GREGÓRIO WEINBERG. *Desenvolvimento e educação na América Latina* (1987).

SAVOIA, RAFAEL. *Actas del Primer Congreso de Historia del Negro en el Ecuador y Sur de Colombia, Esmeraldas, 14–16 de octubre* (1988).

———, ED. *El Negro en la historia: Raices africanas en la nacionalidad ecuatorana* (1992).

SCARANO, JULITA. *Cotidiano e solidariedade: Vida diária da gente de cor nas Minas Gerais, século XVIII* (1994).

SCHAFFER, MATT, AND CHRISTINE COOPER. *Mandinko: The Ethnography of a West African Holy Land* (1980).

SCHARFMAN, RONNIE L. *"Engagement" and the Language of the Subject in the Poetry of Aimé Césaire* (1987).

SCHATZBERG, MICHAEL. *The Dialectics of Oppression in Zaire* (1988).

SCHEADER, CATHERINE. *Shirley Chisholm: Teacher and Congresswoman* (1990).

SCHIEFFELIN, BAMBI, AND RACHELLE DOUCET. "The 'Real' Haitian Creole: Ideology, Metalinguistics, and Orthographic Choices." *American Ethnologist* 21, no. 1 (1994): 176–200.

SCHNEIDER, JOHN J., AND D. STANLEY EITZEN. "Racial Segregation by Professional Football Positions, 1960–1985." *Sociology and Social Research* 70, no. 4 (1986): 259–61.

SCHNEIDER, JOHN T. *Dictionary of African Borrowings in Brazilian Portuguese* (1991).

SCHREINER, CLAUS. *Música brasileira: A History of Popular Music and the People of Brazil.* Translated by Mark Weinstein (1993).

SCHUBERT, FRANK. *Black Valor: Buffalo Soldiers and the Medal of Honor, 1870–1898* (1997).

SCHULLER, GUNTHER. *Early Jazz: Its Roots and Musical Development* (1968).

——. *The Swing Era: The Development of Jazz, 1930–1945* (1989).

SCHWARTZMAN, MYRON. *Romare Bearden: His Life and Art* (1990).

SCHWARTZ-BART, SIMONE. *The Bridge of Beyond.* Translated by Barbara Bray. Introduction by Bridget Jones (1982).

SCHWARZ, ROBERTO. *Misplaced Ideas: Essays on Brazilian Culture* (1992).

SCOTT, KENNETH. "The Slave Insurrection in New York in 1712." *New York Historical Society Quarterly* 45 (January 1961).

SECRETAN, THIERRY. *Going into Darkness: Fantastic Coffins from Africa* (1995).

SENGHOR, LÉOPOLD SEDAR. *Liberté.* 5 vols. (1964–1993).

SERAILE, WILLIAM. *Voice of Dissent: Theophilus Gould Steward (1843–1924) and Black America* (1991).

SERELS, M. MITCHELL. *A History of the Jews of Tangier in the Nineteenth and Twentieth Centuries* (1991).

SHARP, WILLIAM FREDERICK. *Slavery on the Spanish Frontier: The Colombian Chocó, 1680–1810* (1976).

SHANNON, SANDRA G. *The Dramatic Vision of August Wilson* (1995).

SHAW, ARNOLD. *Honkers and Shouters: The Golden Years of Rhythm and Blues* (1978).

SHAW, DONALD L. *Alejo Carpentier* (1985).

SHERMAN, JOAN. *Invisible Poets: Afro-Americans of the Nineteenth Century.* 2d ed. (1989).

SHERMAN, RICHARD B. *The Case of Odell Waller and Virginia Justice, 1940–1942* (1992).

SHIELDS, JOHN C. "Phillis Wheatley." In *African American Writers*, ed. Valerie Smith (1991).

SHOCKLEY, ANN ALLEN. *Afro-American Women Writers, 1746–1933: An Anthology and Critical Guide* (1988).

SHOGAN, ROBERT, AND TOM CRAIG. *The Detroit Race Riot: A Study in Violence* (1964).

SHOMAN, ASSAD. *13 Chapters of a History of Belize* (1994).

SHUCARD, ALAN R. *Countee Cullen* (1984).

Sierra Leone: Twelve Years of Economic Achievement and Political Consolidation under the APC and Dr. Siaka Stevens, 1968–1980 (1980).

SILL, ROBERT. *David Hammons in the Hood* (1994).

SILVA, J. ROMÃO DA. *Luís Gama e suas poesias satíricas* (1981).

SILVERA, MAKEDA, ED. *The Other Woman: Women of Colour in Contemporary Canadian Literature* (1994).

SILVESTER, PETER. *A Left Hand like God: A History of Boogie-Woogie Piano* (1988).

SIMKINS, CUTHBERT O. *Coltrane: A Musical Biography* (1975).

SIMMONS, DIANE. *Jamaica Kincaid* (1994).

SIMO, ANA MARÍA. *Lydia Cabrera: An Intimate Portrait* (1984).

SIMMS, PETER. *Trouble in Guyana: An Account of People, Personalities, and Politics as They Were in British Guiana* (1966).

SIMPSON, DAVID IAN H. *Marburg and Ebola Virus Infections: A Guide for Their Diagnosis, Management, and Control* (1977).

SIMPSON, GEORGE EATON. *Black Religions in the New World.* (1978).

——. *The Shango Cult in Trinidad* (1965).

SIMS, JANET L. *Marian Anderson: An Annotated Bibliography and Discography* (1981).

SIMS, LOWERY STOKES. *Robert Colescott, A Retrospective 1975–1986* (1987).

SIMS, RUDINE. *Shadow and Substance: Afro-American Experience in Contemporary Children's Fiction* (1982).

SINGER, BARRY. *Black and Blue: The Life and Lyrics of Andy Razaf* (1992).

SINNETTE, ELINOR DES VERNEY. *Arthur Alfonso Schomburg, Black Bibliophile & Collector: A Biography* (1989).

SINNETTE, ELINOR DES VERNEY, W. PAUL COATES, AND THOMAS C. BATTLE, EDS. *Black Bibliophiles and Collectors: Preservers of Black History* (1990).

SITKOFF, HARVARD. *A New Deal for Blacks: The Emergence of Civil Rights as a National Issue.* Vol. I, *The Depression Decade* (1978).

SKIDMORE, THOMAS E. *Black Into White: Race and Nationality in Brazilian Thought* (1974; revised ed., 1993).

SLATER, LES. "What is Mas? What is Carnival? Profiling Carnival and its Origins." *Black Diaspora: A Global Black Magazine* (August 1997).

SLAUGHTER, THOMAS PAUL. *Bloody Dawn: The Christiana Riot and Racial Violence in the Antebellum North* (1991).

SMITH, ANNA DEVEARE. *Fires in the Mirror: Crown Heights, Brooklyn and Other Identities* (1993).

SMITH, BARBARA, ED. *Home Girls: A Black Feminist Anthology* (1983).

SMITH, CHARLES MICHAEL. "Bruce Nugent: Bohemian of the Harlem Renaissance." In *In the Life: A Black Gay Anthology*, ed. Joseph Beam (1986).

SMITH CÓRDOBA, AMIR. *Vida y obra de Candelario Obeso* (1984).

SMITH, IAN DOUGLAS. *The Great Betrayal: The Memoirs of Ian Douglas Smith* (1997).

SMITH-IRVIN, JEANNETTE. *Footsoldiers of the Universal Negro Improvement Association: Their Own Words* (1988).

SMITH, JESSIE CARNEY. *Black Academic Libraries and Research Collections: An Historical Survey* (1977).

——, ED. *Notable Black American Women.* 2 vols. (1992–1996).

SMITH, KEITHLYN B. *No Easy Pushover: A History of the Working People of Antigua and Barbuda, 1836–1994* (1994).

SMITH, KEITHLYN B., AND FERNANDO C. *To Shoot Hard Labour: The Life and Times of Samuel Smith, an Antiguan Workingman, 1877–1982* (1986).

SMITH, ROBERTA. "A Forgotten Black Painter Is Saved from Obscurity." *New York Times* (June 12, 1992): C18.

SMITH, RONNA. "Vida de Adalberto Ortiz." *Cultura: Revista del Banco Central del Ecuador* 6, no. 16 (1983): 99–118.

SMITH, S. CLAY, JR. "Patricia Roberts Harris: A Champion in Pursuit of Excellence." *Howard Law Journal* 29, no. 3 (1986): 437–55.

SMITH, WILLIAM E. "Commandments Without Moses: Abandoning His Principles, Sullivan Wants U. S. Firms to Pull Out." *Time* (June 15, 1987).

SNOWDEN, FRANK M., JR. *Before Color Prejudice: The Ancient View of Blacks* (1983).

——. *Blacks in Antiquity; Ethiopians in the Greco-Roman Experience* (1970).

SOLLORS, WERNER. *Amiri Baraka/LeRoi Jones: The Quest for a "Populist Modernism"* (1978).

——. *Neither Black nor White, Yet Both: Thematic Explorations of Interracial Literature* (1997).

——, ED. *Multilingual America: Transnationalism, Ethnicity, and the Languages of American Literature* (1998).

SOLOW, BARBARA L., ED. *Slavery and the Rise of the Atlantic System* (1991).

SOMJEE, SULTAN. *Material Culture of Kenya* (1993).

SOMMER, DORIS, *Foundational Fictions : The National Romances of Latin America* (1991).

SOTO, SARA. *Magia e historia en los "Cuentos negros": "Por que" y "Ayapa" de Lydia Cabrera* (1988).

SOUTHERN, EILEEN. *The Music of Black Americans: A History* (1983).

SOYINKA, WOLE. *The Burden of Memory, the Muse of Forgiveness* (1999).

——. *Myth, Literature, and the African World* (1976).

——. *The Open Sore of a Continent: A Personal Narrative of the Nigerian Crisis* (1996).

SPELLMAN, A. B. *Black Music: Four Lives* (1970).

SPINNER, THOMAS J., JR. *A Political and Social History of Guyana, 1945–1983* (1984).

SPIVAK, GAYATRI CHAKTAVORTY. *In Other Worlds: Essays in Cultural Politics* (1987).

SPOFFORD, TIM. *Lynch Street: The May 1970 Slayings at Jackson State College* (1988).

STAMPP, KENNETH M. *The Peculiar Institution: Slavery in the Ante-Bellum South* (1956).

STAM, ROBERT. *Tropical Multiculturalism: A Comparative History of Race in Brazilian Cinema and Culture* (1997).

STAM, ROBERT, AND RANDAL JOHNSON. *Brazilian Cinema*. Rev. and exp. ed. (1995).

STANLEY, HENRY MORTON. *In Darkest Africa; or, The Quest, Rescue and Retreat of Emin, Governor of Equatoria* (1890).

——. *Through the Dark Continent; or The Sources of the Nile around the Great Lakes of Equatorial Africa and Down the Livingstone River to the Atlantic Ocean* (1878).

ST. BOURNE, CLAIR. "The African-American Image in American Cinema." *Black Scholar* 21, no.2 (March-May 1990): 12 (8).

STEARNS, MARSHALL, AND JEAN STEARNS. *Jazz Dance: The Story of American Vernacular Dance*. Rev. ed. (1979).

STEIN, JUDITH E., ET AL. *I Tell My Heart: The Art of Horace Pippin* (1993).

STEIN, STEVE J. "Visual Images of the Lower Classes in Early Twentieth-Century Peru: Soccer as a Window to Social Reality." In *Windows on Latin America: Understanding Society through Photographs*, ed. Robert M. Levine (1987).

STEPAN, NANCY. *The Idea of Race in Science* (1982).

STEPHENS, THOMAS M. *Dictionary of Latin American Racial and Ethnic Terminology* (1989).

STEPTO, ROBERT B. "After Modernism, After Hibernation: Michael Harper, Robert Hayden, and Jay Wright." In *Chant of Saints: A Gathering of Afro-American Literature, Art, and Scholarship* (1979).

———. *From Behind the Veil: A Study of Afro-American Narrative* (1979)

STERLING, DOROTHY. *Black Foremothers: Three Lives* (1988).

———. *The Making of an Afro-American: Martin Robison Delany 1812–1885* (1971).

———. *We Are Your Sisters: Black Women in the Nineteenth Century* (1984).

STERN, YVAN. "Interview: Souleymane Cissé." *Unir Cinema* 23–24 (March-June 1986): 44–45.

STEVENSON, BRENDA, ED. *The Journals of Charlotte Forten Grimké* (1988).

STEVENS, PHILLIPS, JR. "Magic" and "Sorcery and Witchcraft." In *Encyclopedia of Cultural Anthropology*, ed. Melvin Ember and David Levinson (1996).

STEVENS, SIAKA. *What Life Has Taught Me* (1984).

STEWART-BAXTER, DERRICK. *Ma Rainey and the Classic Blues Singers* (1970).

STILL, JUDITH ANNE. *William Grant Still: A Bio-bibliography* (1996).

STILL, WILLIAM. *The Underground Railroad: A Record of Facts, Authentic Narratives, Letters, &c., Narrating the Hardships, Hair-breadth Escapes, and Death Struggles of the Slaves in Their Efforts for Freedom, as Related by Themselves and Others or Witnessed By the Author: Together with Sketches of Some of the Largest Stockholders and Most Liberal Aiders and Advisers of the Road* (1872).

STINSON, SULEE JEAN. *The Dawn of Blaxploitation: Sweet Sweetback's Baadasssss Song and its Audience* (1992).

STORY, ROSALYN M. *And So I Sing: African American Divas of Opera and Concert* (1990).

STRAUSS, NEIL. "Curtis Mayfield" (interview). *New York Times* (February 28, 1996).

STRAUS, NOEL. "Dorthy Maynor Berkshire Soloist." *New York Times* (August 10, 1939).

STOWE, HARRIET BEECHER. *Uncle Tom's Cabin: Authoritative Text. Backgrounds and Contexts* (Norton Critical Edition) (1994).

STREICKER, JOEL. "Policing the Boundaries: Race, Class and Gender in Cartagena, Colombia." *American Ethnologist* 22, no. 1 (1995), 54–74.

STUART, CHRIS, AND TILDE STUART. *Africa's Vanishing Wildlife* (1996).

——. *Chris and Tilde Stuart's Field Guide to the Mammals of Southern Africa* (1994).

STUCKEY, STERLING. *Slave Culture: Nationalist Theory and the Foundations of Black America* (1987).

SUGGS, HENRY LEWIS. *P. B. Young, Newspaperman: Race, Politics, and Journalism in the New South, 1910–1962* (1988).

SULLIVAN, PATRICIA. *Days of Hope: Race and Democracy in the New Deal Era* (1996).

SUMMERVILLE, JAMES. *Educating Black Doctors: A History of Meharry Medical College* (1983).

SUPER, GEORGE LEE, MICHAEL GARDEN, AND NANCY MARSHALL, EDS. *P. H. Polk: Photographs* (1980).

SUTTON, JOHN E. G. *Dar es Salaam: City, Port, and Region* (1970).

SUZIGAN, GERALDO. *Bossa nova: música, política, educação no Brasil* (1990).

SWEETMAN, DAVID. *Women Leaders in African History* (1984).

SWENSON, JOHN. *Stevie Wonder* (1986).

SYLVANDER, CAROLYN WEDIN. *Jessie Redmon Fauset, Black American Writer* (1981).

TARRY, ELLEN. *The Other Toussaint: A Modern Biography of Pierre Toussaint, a Post-Revolutionary Black* (1981).

TATE, CLAUDIA. *Domestic Allegories of Political Desire: The Black Heroine's Text at the Turn of the Century* (1992).

TAYLOR, FRANK. *Alberta Hunter: A Celebration in Blues* (1987).

TAYLOR, PATRICK. *The Narrative of Liberation: Perspectives on Afro-Caribbean Literature, Popular Culture, and Politics* (1989).

TAYLOR, QUINTARD. *The Forging of a Black Community: Seattle's Central District from 1870 through the Civil Rights Era* (1994).

TEIXEIRA, IVAN. *Obras poéticas de Basílio da Gama* (1996).

TENENBAUM, BARBARA A., ED. *Encyclopedia of Latin American History and Culture.* 5 vols. (1996).

"The Ten Most Beautiful Black Women in America (A Wide Range of External and Internal Beauty)." *Ebony* (July 1987).

TERRY, DON. "Hatcher Begins Battle to Regain Spotlight in Gary." *New York Times.* (May 6, 1991): A12.

TERRY, WALLACE, ED. *Bloods: An Oral History of the Vietnam War, by Black Veterans* (1984).

THOBY-MARCELIN, PHILIPPE. *Panorama de l'art Haïtien* (1956).

THOMAS, ANTONY. *Rhodes* (1996).

THOMAS, BETTYE COLLIER. "Harvey Johnson and the Baltimore Mutual United Brotherhood of Liberty, 1885–1910." In *Black Communities and Urban Development in America, 1720–1990: From Reconstruction to the Great Migration, 1877–1917,* ed. Kenneth L. Kusmer. Vol. IV, part 1 (1991).

THOMAS, BROOK. *Plessy v. Ferguson: A Brief History with Documents* (1997).

THOMAS, DAVID S. G. *The Kalahari Environment* (1991).

THOMAS, HUGH. *Cuba: The Pursuit of Freedom* (1971).

THOMPSON, FRANCESCA. "Final Curtain for Anita Bush." *Black World* 23 (July 1974): 60–61.

THOMPSON, LESLIE. *An Autobiography* (1985).

THOMPSON, ROBERT FERRIS. *Flash of the Spirit: African and Afro-American Art and Philosophy* (1983).

——. *Jean-Michel Basquiat* (1985).

THORNTON, J. MILLS III. "Challenge and Response in the Montgomery Bus Boycott of 1955–1956." *Alabama Review* 33 (1980): 163–235.

THORNTON, JOHN. *Africa and Africans in the Making of the Atlantic World: 1400–1800* (1998).

THORPE, EDWARD. *Black Dance* (1990).

THURMAN, HOWARD. *With Head and Heart: The Autobiography of Howard Thurman* (1979).

TIBBLES, ANTHONY, ED. *Transatlantic Slavery: Against Human Dignity* (1994).

TILLERY, TYRONE. *Claude McKay: A Black Poet's Struggle for Identity* (1992).

TIMBERLAKE, LLOYD. *Africa in Crisis: The Causes, the Cures of Environmental Bankruptcy* (1985).

TINGAY, PAUL, AND DOUG SCOTT. *Handy Guide: Victoria Falls* (1996).

TINHORAO, RAMOS JOSÉ. *Os Negros em Portugal: Uma presença silenciosa* (1988).

TIPPU TIP. *Maisha ya Hamed bin Muhammed el Murjebi, Yaani Tippu Tip, kwa Maneno Yake Mwenyewe.* Translated by W. H. Whitely (1966).

TOBIAS, CHANNING. "Autobiography." In *Thirteen Americans: Their Spiritual Biographies* (1953).

TOMKINS, CALVIN, "A Sense of Urgency." *New Yorker* (March 1989): 48–74.

TOOBIN, JEFFREY. *The Run of His Life: The People v. O. J. Simpson* (1996).

TOOP, DAVID. *Ocean of Sound: Aether Talk, Ambient Sound, and Imaginary Worlds* (1995).

TOPLIN, ROBERT BRENT. *The Abolition of Slavery in Brazil* (1972).

TORRENCE, RIDGELY. *The Story of John Hope* (1948).

TOUREH, FANTA. *L'imaginaire dans l'úuvre de Simone Schwartz-Bart: Approche d'une mythologie antillaise* (1986).

TOUSSAINT, AUGUSTE. *History of Mauritius* (1977).

TREXLER, HARRISON. *Slavery in Missouri, 1804–1865* (1914).

TREVISAN, JOÃO SILVERIO. *Perverts in Paradise.* Translated by Martin Foreman (1986).

TRUTH, SOJOURNER, AND OLIVE GILBERT, *Narrative of Sojourner Truth, a Northern Slave, Emancipated from Bodily Servitude by the State of New York, in 1828 (1850).*

TURNBULL, COLIN M. *The Forest People* (1961).

TURNER, FREDERICK W. *Remembering Song: Encounters with the New Orleans Jazz Tradition.* Exp. ed. (1994).

TURNER, LORENZO DOW. *Africanisms in the Gullah Dialect* (1949).

TURNER, MARY. *From Chattel Slaves to Wage Slaves: The Dynamics of Labour Bargaining in the Americas* (1995).

——. *Slaves and Missionaries: The Disintegration of Jamaican Slave Society* (1982).

TUSHNET, MARK V. *The NAACP's Strategy Against Segregated Education, 1925–1950* (1987).

TUTTLE, WILLIAM M., JR. *Race Riot: Chicago in the Red Summer of 1919* (1970).

——, ED.W. E. B. Du Bois (1973).

TYGIEL, JULES. *Baseball's Great Experiment: Jackie Robinson and His Legacy* (1983).

UCHE, NENA. "Textiles in Nigeria." *African Technology Forum* 7, no. 2 (1994).

ULLMAN, MICHAEL. *Jazz Lives: Portraits in Words and Pictures* (1980).

ULLMAN, VICTOR. *Martin R. Delany: The Beginnings of Black Nationalism* (1971).

Unesco General History of Africa. 8 vols. (1981–1993).

URBAN, W. J. *Black* Scholar: Horace Mann Bond 1904–1972 (1992).

URQUHART, BRIAN. *Ralph Bunche: An American Life* (1993).

VALDEZ AGUILAR, RAFAEL. *Sinaloa: Negritud y olvido* (1993).

VAN DEBURG, WILLIAM L. *New Day in Babylon: The Black Power Movement and American Culture, 1965–1975* (1992).

VANDERCOOK, JOHN W. *Black Majesty: The Life of Christophe, King of Haiti* (1934).

VAN SERTIMA, IVAN. *Blacks in Science: Ancient and Modern* (1991).

——, ED. *African Presence in Early America* (1987).

——, ED. *African Presence in Early Europe* (1985).

——, ED. *Black Women in Antiquity* (1984).

VAN SERTIMA, IVAN, AND RUNOKO RASHIDI, EDS. *African Presence in Early Asia* (1988).

VANSINA, JAN. *Les anciens royaumes de la savane: Les états des savanes méridionales de l'Afrique centrale des origines à l'occupation coloniale* (1965).

——. *Art History in Africa: An Introduction to Method* (1984).

——. *The Children of Woot: A History of the Kuba Peoples* (1978).

——. *Kingdoms of the Savanna* (1966).

——. *Oral Tradition as History* (1985).

——. *Paths in the Rainforests: Toward a History of Political Tradition in Equatorial Africa* (1990).

VAN TASSEL, DAVID D., AND JOHN J. Grabowski. *Cleveland: A Tradition of Reform* (1986).

——. *The Encyclopedia of Cleveland History* (1987).

VARELA, BEATRIZ. *El español cubano-americano* (1992).

VASQUEZ DE URRUTIA, PATRICIA, ED. *La democracia en blanco y negro: Colombia en los anos ochenta* (1989).

VEDANA, HARDY. *Jazz em Porto Alegre* (1987).

VENET, WENDY HAMMOND. *Neither Ballots Nor Bullets: Women Abolitionists and the Civil War* (1991).

VERBEKEN, AUGUSTE. *Msiri, roi du Garenganze: L' homme rouge du Katanga* (1956).

VERGER, PIERRE. *Bahia Africa Bahia: Fotografias* (1996).

——. *Bahia and the West African Trade, 1549–1851* (1964).

——. *Dieux d'Afrique; Culte des Orishas et Vodouns à l' ancienne côte des esclaves en Afrique et à Bahia, la baie de tous les saints au Brésil.*

——. *Ewe: Le verbe et le pouvoir des plantes chez les Yoruba* (1997).

——. *Flux et reflux de la traite des nègres entre le Golfe de Bénin et Bahia de todos os Santos, du XVIIè au XIXè siècle* (1968).

——. *Orixas: Deuses iorubas na Africa e no Novo Mundo* (1981).

——. *Retratos da Bahia, 1946 a 1952* (1980).

VERGER, PIERRE, AND JORGE AMADO. *Iconografia dos deuses africanos no candomblé da Bahia* (1980).

VÉRIN, PIERRE. *The History of Civilization in North Madagascar.* Translated by David Smith (1986).

VÉRIN, PIERRE, C. P. KOTTACK, AND P. GORLIN. "The glottochronology of Malagasy speech communities." *Oceanic Linguistics* 8 (1970): 26–83.

VERÍSSIMO, INÁCIO JOSÉ. *André Rebouças através de sua auto-biografia* (1939).

VESTAL, STANLEY. *Mountain Men* (1937).

VICKERY, WALTER N. *Alexander Pushkin* (1970).

VINES, ALEX. *Renamo: Terrorism in Mozambique* (1991).

VITIER, CINTIO, AND FINA GARCÍA MARRUZ, EDS. *Flor oculta de poesía cubana* (1978).

——. Temas martianos (1981).

VLACH, JOHN MICHAEL. *The Afro-American Tradition in the Decorative Arts* (1978).

VOGEL, ARNO. *A galinha-d'Angola: Iniciacão e identidade na cultura afro-brasileira* (1993).

WADE, PETER. *Blackness and Race Mixture: The Dynamics of Racial Identity in Colombia* (1993).

——. *Race and Ethnicity in Latin America* (1997).

WAGLEY, CHARLES., ED. *Race and Class in Rural Brazil.* 2d ed. (1963).

WAHLMAN, MAUDE SOUTHWELL. *Contemporary African Arts* (1974).

——. *Signs and Symbols: African Images in African-American Quilts* (1993).

WAKHIST, TSI TSI. "Taking the Helm of the NAACP: The Ever-Ready Evers-Williams." *Crisis* 102 (May/June 1995): 14–19.

WALDMAN, GLORIA F. *Luis Rafael Sánchez: Pasión teatral.* (1988).

WALKER, ETHEL PITTS. "The American Negro Theater." In *The Theater of Black Americans,* ed. Errol Hill (1987).

WALKER, GEORGE E. *The Afro-American in New York City, 1827–1860* (1993).

WALKER, JAMES W. ST. G. *The Black Loyalists: The Search for a Promised Land in Nova Scotia and Sierra Leone, 1783–1870* (1992).

WALKER, MELISSA. *Down from the Mountaintop: Black Women's Novels in the Wake of the Civil Rights Movement, 1966–1989* (1991).

WALLS, WILLIAM J. *The African Methodist Episcopal Zion Church: Reality of the Black Church* (1974).

WARD, WILLIAM EDWARD. "Charles Lenox Remond: Black Abolitionist, 1838–1873." Ph.D. diss., Clark University, 1977.

WARE, GILBERT. *William Hastie: Grace Under Pressure* (1984).

WASHINGTON, BOOKER T. *Up From Slavery* (1901).

WASHINGTON, JAMES M. *Conversations with God* (1994).

WATKINS, MEL. *On The Real Side: Laughing, Lying, and Signifying. The Underground Tradition of African-American Humor* (1994).

WATSON, ALAN. *Slave Law in the Americas* (1989).

WATSON, DENTON L. *Lion in the Lobby: Clarence Mitchell, Jr.'s Struggle for the Passage of Civil Rights Laws* (1990).

WATTS, JILL. *God, Harlem U.S.A.: The Father Divine Story* (1992).

WEARE, WALTER B. *Black Business in the New South: A Social History of the North Carolina Mutual Life Insurance Company* (1973).

WEAVER, JOHN DOWNING. *The Brownsville Raid* (1970).

——. *The Senator and the Sharecropper's Son: Exoneration of the Brownsville Soldiers* (1997).

WEAVER, ROBERT C. "The Health Care of Our Cities." *National Medical Association Journal* (January 1968): 42–48.

WEBB, BARBARA J. *Myth and History in Caribbean Fiction: Alejo Carpentier, Wilson Harris, and Edouard Glissant* (1992).

WEBB, LILLIAN ASHCROFT. *About My Father's Business: The Life of Elder Michaux* (1981).

WEINBERG, KENNETH G. *Black Victory: Carl Stokes and the Winning of Cleveland* (1968).

WEINSTEIN, BRIAN. *Eboué* (1972).

WEINSTEIN, NORMAN. *A Night in Tunisia: Imaginings of Africa in Jazz* (1993).

WEISS, NANCY J. *Farewell to the Party of Lincoln: Black Politics in the Age of FDR* (1983).

——. *Whitney M. Young, Jr., and the Struggle for Civil Rights* (1989).

WELLS-BARNETT, IDA B. *On Lynchings: Southern Horrors; A Red Record; Mob Rule in New Orleans* (1969).

WESLEY, CHARLES H. *Charles H. Wesley: The Intellectual Tradition of a Black; Historian,* ed. James L. Conyers, Jr. (1997).

WESLEY, DOROTHY PORTER. "Integration Versus Separatism: William Cooper Nell's Role in the Struggle for Equality." *In Courage and Conscience: Black and White Abolitionists in Boston,* ed. Donald M. Jacobs (1993): 207–24.

WEST, CORNEL. *Beyond Eurocentrism and Multiculturalism* (1993).

——. *Black Theology and Marxist Thought* (1979).

——. *Keeping Faith: Philosophy and Race in America* (1993).

——. *Prophetic Reflections: Notes on Race and Power in America* (1993).

——. *Race Matters* (1993).

WEST, GUIDA. *The National Welfare Rights Movement: The Social Protest of Poor Women* (1981).

"What Martin Luther King Would Do Now about Drugs, Poverty and Black-Jewish Relations: Widow and Associates Tell How He Would Respond to Today's Burning Issues." *Ebony* (January 1991).

WHEAT, ELLEN HARKINS. *Jacob Lawrence, American Painter* (1986).

WHEELER, B. GORDON. *Black California: The History of African-Americans in the Golden State* (1993).

WHITE, ALVIN, "Let Me Tell You about My Love Affair with Florence Mills." *Sepia* 26, no. 11 (November 1977).

WHITE, TIMOTHY. *Catch a Fire: The Life of Bob Marley.* Rev. and enl. ed. (1998).

WHITE, WALTER F. *A Man Called White: The Autobiography of Walter White* (1948; reprint ed., 1995).

——. *Rope and Faggot: A Biography of Judge Lynch* (1929).

WHITFIELD, STEPHEN J. *A Death in the Delta: The Story of Emmett Till* (1988).

WHITING, ALBERT N. *Guardians of the Flame: Historically Black Colleges Yesterday, Today, and Tomorrow* (1991).

WHITMAN, MARK, ED. *Removing a Badge of Slavery: The Record of Brown v. Board of Education* (1993).

WHITTEN, NORMAN. *Black Frontiersmen: A South American Case* (1974).

——, ED.*Cultural Transformations and Ethnicity in Modern Ecuador* (1981).

WICKER, TOM. *A Time to Die* (1975).

WIENER, LEO. *Africa and the Discovery of America.* Vol. I (1920).

WIGG, DAVID. *And Then Forgot to Tell Us Why: A Look at the Campaign Against River Blindness in West Africa* (1993).

WIKRAMANAYAKE, MARINA. *A World in Shadow: The Free Black in Antebellum South Carolina* (1973).

WILKINS, ROY. *Standing Fast: The Autobiography of Roy Wilkins* (1982).

WILLIAMS, ELSIE A. *The Humor of Jackie Moms Mabley: An African American Comedic Tradition* (1995).

WILLIAMS, ERIC. *Capitalism and Slavery* (1944; reprinted, 1994).

———. *Inward Hunger: The Education of a Prime Minister* (1969).

WILLIAMS, LORNA V. "Morúa Delgado and the Cuban Slave Narrative." *Modern Language Notes* 108, no. 2 (March 1993): 302–13.

———. *The Representation of Slavery in Cuban Fiction.* (1994).

WILLIAMS, MICHAEL W. *Pan-Africanism: An Annotated Bibliography* (1992).

WILLIAMSON, JANICE. *Sounding Differences: Conversations with Seventeen Canadian Women Writers* (1993).

WILLIAMSON, JOEL. *After Slavery: The Negro in South Carolina During Reconstruction, 1861–1877* (1965; reprint ed., 1990).

———. *The Crucible of Race: Black-White Relations in the American South Since Emancipation* (1984).

———. *New People: Miscegenation and Mulattoes in the United States* (1980).

WILLIAMS, PONTHEOLLA T. *Robert Hayden: A Critical Analysis of His Poetry* (1987).

WILLIAMS, ROGER. *The Bonds: An American Family* (1971).

WILLIS, SUSAN. "Crushed Geraniums: Juan Francisco Manzano and the Language of Slavery." In *The Slave's Narrative*, ed. Charles T. Davis and Henry Louis Gates, Jr. (1985).

———. *Specifying: Black Women Writing the American Experience* (1987).

WILLIS-THOMAS, DEBORAH. *Black Photographers, 1840–1940: An Illustrated Bio-Bibliography* (1985).

———. *An Illustrated Bio-Bibliography of Black Photographers, 1940–1988* (1989).

WILMER, VALERIE. "'Blackamoors' and the British Beat." In *Views on Black American Music*, no. 3 (1985–1988): 60–64.

WILSON, CHARLES REAGAN, AND WILLIAM FERRIS, EDS. *Encyclopedia of Southern Culture* (1989).

WILSON, MARY, WITH PATRICIA ROMANOWSKI AND AHRGUS JULLIARD. *Dreamgirl: My Life as a Supreme* (1986).

WILSON, WILLIAM JULIUS. *The Bridge over the Racial Divide: Rising Inequality and Coalition Politics* (1999).

———. *When Work Disappears: The World of the New Urban Poor* (1996).

WINANT, HOWARD. "Rethinking Race in Brazil." *Journal of Latin American Studies* 24 (1992): 173–92.

WINCH, JULIE. *Philadelphia's Black Elite: Activism, Accommodation, and the Struggle for Autonomy, 1787–1848* (1988).

WINKS, ROBIN W. *The Blacks in Canada: A History* (1997).

WIPPLER, MIGENE GONZÁLEZ. *Santería: The Religion* (1982).

WOIDEK, CARL. *Charlie Parker: His Music and Life* (1996).

WOLFENSTEIN, EUGENE VICTOR. *The Victims of Democracy: Malcolm X and the Black Revolution* (1981).

WOLSELEY, ROLAND E. *The Black Press, U.S.A.* (1990).

WOODBRIDGE, HENSLEY C. "Glossary of Names Found in Colonial Latin America for Crosses Among Indians, Negroes, and Whites." *Journal of the Washington Academy of Sciences* 38 (1948): 353–62.

WOOD, JOE, ED. *Malcolm X: In Our Own Image* (1992).

WOOD, PETER H. *Black Majority: Negroes in Colonial South Carolina from 1670 through the Stono Rebellion* (1974).

WOOD, PETER H., AND KAREN C. C. DALTON. *Winslow Homer's Images of Blacks: The Civil War and Reconstruction Years* (1988).

WOODSON, CARTER G. "The Negroes of Cincinnati Prior to the Civil War." In *Free Blacks in America, 1800–1860*, ed. John Bracey, Jr. August Meier, and Elliot Rudwick (1971).

WOODS, SYLVIA. *Sylvia's Soul Food: Recipes from Harlem's World Famous Restaurant* (1992).

WOODWARD, C. VANN. *Origins of the New South: 1877–1913* (1951).

——. *Reunion and Reaction: The Compromise of 1877 and the End of Reconstruction* (1951; reprint ed. 1991).

——. *The Strange Career of Jim Crow* (1955).

Woolman, David S. *Stars in the Firmament: Tangier Characters, 1660–1960s* (1997).

WORCESTER, KENT. *C. L. R. James and the American Century, 1938–1953* (1980).

WORLD BANK. *Mauritius Country Report* 4 (1988).

WRIGHT, GILES R. *Afro-Americans in New Jersey: A Short History* (1988).

WRIGHT, LEE ALFRED. *Identity, Family, and Folklore in African American Literature* (1995).

WRIGHT, RICHARD R., JR. *The Negro in Pennsylvania, A Study in Economic History* (1969).

WUBBEN, HUBERT H. *Civil War Iowa and the Copperhead Movement* (1980).

WYNES, CHARLES E. *Charles Richard Drew: The Man and the Myth* (1988).

XAVIER, ISMAIL. *Allegories of Underdevelopment: Aesthetics and Politics in Modern Brazilian Cinema* (1997).

YANCEY, DWAYNE. *When Hell Froze Over: The Untold Story of Doug Wilder: A Black Politician's Rise to Power in the South* (1988).

YAU, JOHN. "Please, Wait by the Coatroom: Wifredo Lam in the Museum of Modern Art." *Arts Magazine* 4 (1988): 56–59.

YELLIN, JEAN FAGAN, AND JOHN C. VAN HORNE, EDS. *The Abolitionist Sisterhood: Women's Political Culture in Antebellum America* (1994).

YOHE, KRISTINE A. "Gloria Naylor." In *The Oxford Companion to African American Literature,* ed. James David Hart and Phillip W. Leininger. 6th ed. (1995).

YOUNG, ANDREW. *An Easy Burden: The Civil Rights Movement and the Transformation of America* (1996).

——. *A Way Out of No Way: The Spiritual Memoirs of Andrew Young* (1994).

YOUNG, CRAWFORD. *Politics in the Congo: Decolonization and Independence* (1965).

ZANGRANDO, ROBERT. *The NAACP Crusade Against Lynching, 1909–1950* (1980).

ZENÓN CRUZ, ISABELO. *Narciso descubre su trasero: El negro en la cultura puertorriqueña.* 2d ed. (1975).

ZIELINA, MARIA CARMEN. *La africania en el cuento cubano y puertorriqueño* (1992).

ZINN, HOWARD. *SNCC: The New Abolitionists* (1965).